Memory Management for All of Us, Deluxe Edition

Memory Management for All of Us

Deluxe Edition

John M. Goodman, Ph.D.

John C. Lunsford, research engineer
Michele Miller, research assistant

SAMS
PUBLISHING

A Division of Prentice Hall Computer Publishing
11711 North College, Carmel, Indiana 46032 USA

This book is dedicated to the many PC users who are not content merely to have their PCs work as they did when they came from the store or factory. These brave people have decided to become masters of their machines, pushing their PCs to the pinnacle of performance. I admire them. I hope that this book helps them reach their goals more quickly and easily and with a greater understanding of what they did to get there.

International Standard Book Number: 0-672-30306-x

Library of Congress Catalog Card Number: 92-82082

96 95 94 93   4 3 2 1

Interpretation of the printing code: the rightmost double-digit number is the year of the book's printing; the rightmost single-digit, the number of the book's printing. For example, a printing code of 93-1 shows that the first printing of the book occurred in 1993.

Composed in MCPdigital by Prentice Hall Computer Publishing.

Printed in the United States of America

Publisher
Richard K. Swadley

Associate Publisher
Jordan Gold

Acquisitions Manager
Stacy Hiquet

Acquisitions Editor
Gregg Bushyeager

Senior Editor
Grant Fairchild

Editorial Coordinators
Bill Whitmer
James R. Welter II

Editorial Assistants
Sharon Cox
Molly Carmody

Marketing Manager
Greg Wiegand

**Director of Production
and Manufacturing**
Jeff Valler

Production Manager
Corinne Walls

Imprint Manager
Kelli Widdifield

Book Designer
Michele Laseau

Production Analyst
Mary Beth Wakefield

Proofreading/Indexing Coordinator
Joelynn Gifford

Graphics Image Specialists
Tim Montgomery
Dennis Sheehan
Sue VandeWalle

Production
Lisa Daugherty
Mitzi Foster Gianakos
Dennis Clay Hager
Howard Jones
Sean Medlock
Mike Mucha
Juli Pavey
Angela M. Pozdol
Linda Quigley
Michelle Self
Barbara Webster
Dennis Wesner
Donna Winter

Indexers
Jeanne Clark
John Sleeva

*Special thanks to Hilary Adams,
Scott Daniel, C. Herbert Feltner,
John Gose, John Kaczala,
David Knispel, Richard Leach,
James P. McCarter, Marcia Ross,
and Robert E. Waring for
helping to ensure the technical
accuracy of this book.*

OVERVIEW

CONTENTS

5 Some Important Warnings, *83*

Part II How It All Works

This part of the book gives an easy-to-understand introduction to the field of memory management. To do that, it starts at the beginning with the most basic concepts, and it continues through all the latest tricks of the trade. Read this for a good grounding or a quick refresher; doing so will make reading installation manuals for both software and hardware much more understandable.

6 Memory Fundamentals, *113*

7   How PCs Work, *175*

10 How Memory in a PC Gets Used, *329*

11 Fancier Memory Maps (Protected-Mode Complexities), *407*

12 The Infamous DOS 640KB Barrier, *457*

13 Brief History Of Some Chips, *487*

19 Memory Management—the Task, *643*

20 Memory Management— Strategies and Tactics, *659*

21 Memory Management— Automatic Solutions, *721*

22 A Review of Memory-Management Principles, *827*

Part III An Overview Of Your Options

Many readers will want to start here, to check out what they can do for their PC. If the advice in this section is hard for you to understand, you will need to read Part I or Part II first. In any case, you'll need to know which class of PC you have; see Chapter 3 for help with this.

Part IV Specific Products

The fundamentals apply in all cases. The specific suggestions in Part III are meant to help guide you toward those products you can use in your PC. This section lists more comprehensively many popular products now on the market. It covers hardware and software, including that sold in stores and that available as shareware.

30 Software-Based Products—Other Good Uses for RAM, *917*

Part V Dealing With Difficulties

Life is not always what you want it to be. If you find the recommendations in the earlier chapters difficult to follow, this part may be your salvation. Here you will find out some things to watch out for, how to go about solving PC memory problems, and how to get additional help if you need it.

31 A Bestiary of Memory-Management "Gremlins", *925*

Part VI Examples And Tips For Optimizing Your PC

Are you impatient with explanations? Do you want to be shown what you need to do, instead of having to learn all the principles, and then figure out for yourself what will work for you? Then this section is where you'll want to begin. Here you'll find a lot of examples and specific suggestions. If, however, you find that these examples are too briefly explained, you'll find many more details in earlier Parts of the book.

Foreword

The joke goes like this:

> "What do you get when several thousand competitive enemies take a pathetically tired and slow 4.77 megahertz 8088-based PC with 64 kilobytes of memory and cassette-tape mass storage, then spend more than a decade fighting with each other as they slowly upgrade it to an ultra-powerful 50 megahertz 486-based workstation with 16 megabytes of RAM and several hundred megabytes of hard disk storage?

The sad answer is no joke at all: "You get the IBM-compatible PC."

The PC "standard" of the 1990s is, without any doubt, the single most messed-up nightmare crock of kludgery, miscommunication, competition, and compromise that modern man has ever assembled. Ever since its birth, the poor PC has been saddled with a never-ending profusion of incompatible buses, inconsistent keyboards, conflicting display technologies, competing operating environments, new-and-improved disk formats, and what have you. If PCs weren't so amazingly useful, we would probably have given up on them long ago. But these confusing piles of plastic and circuitry can be so effective that we have no choice except to struggle to understand them and force them to work for us. When you stop to think about it, it's really quite phenomenal that PC users are willing to tolerate so much confusion.

Nowhere in the PC realm are things more confusing than in the area of memory management. So many ill-conceived, half-baked, short-lived, and abandoned memory-management "standards" have been designed, implemented, and obsoleted throughout the years that an all-inclusive guide to the past and present of PC memory management has been a virtual necessity. This incredible work by John Goodman is just such a guide.

The topic of memory management is so important that many other attempts have been made to explain it. This book stands apart from all the others by successfully pulling every possible aspect of the memory-management problem together in one place, and then organizing it and carefully explaining it. Referring to this achievement as "comprehensive" would be a little like referring to an atom bomb as "noisy," but anything less would have been incomplete.

The book you're holding in your hands right now has forever obsoleted all others on the subject. Whether you're an upstart beginner wondering what a PC is all about, a casual user wanting to get the most from your PC, or a super-power user determined to wring every last drop of real-time performance from the machine, this clearly written and thorough masterpiece explains *everything* there is to know. Whether you read it from cover to cover, browse it from chapter to chapter, or use it as a well-indexed quick reference guide, every page will reveal fresh insights and clear, clean explanations. You will be as glad that you've found this book as I am that John wrote it.

Steve Gibson
President, Gibson Research Corporation
Author of *SpinRite* and columnist
for *InfoWorld*

INTRODUCTION

This is a book about PCs, memory, and managing that memory. No matter what kind of IBM *PC*, *PS/1*, *PS/2* or compatible personal computer you have, this book can help you make it work for you better, harder, and faster. It also may help you understand how it is able to do those things.

Why is memory such a big deal? What is memory management? Do you need to know how to manage your PC's memory? There are two reasons you might need to know these things: (1) If you want your PC to do only more complicated things than it now can, or (2) if you want it to do what it now does but quicker, and with less effort on your part.

That seems to me to be about the same as a dentist telling you to brush only those teeth that you want to keep. Of course you want your PC to help you get your work accomplished more quickly and easily. And if it could do more than it now does, that would be wonderful, too.

I suppose you might argue that it is too hard to learn all this—and besides, it will cost you an arm and a leg to put what you learn into practice. Not so. Anyone willing to devote even a modest amount of effort can learn at least the basics of memory management.

Becoming a wizard-level master takes a bit more time. Fortunately, that's not necessary to get great benefit from this topic. On the other hand, if you do aspire to the highest levels of memory-management knowledge, this book will also help you get there.

Why is memory such a big deal? Your PC has more memory circuits in it than any other kind. That's true even though you may wish it had a lot more. Every time your PC does anything, it uses memory. If you give it more memory—and if you also do some special extra things to enable your PC to take advantage of that added memory—it will be able to do more and do it faster.

It is not enough just to add the memory. You must do those other special things, or all that added memory (and the effort and money you spent putting it in your PC) will be wasted. This book explains why that is so. It also sets out the ways you can make the memory you already have do more for you, and tells how to add yet more memory and put it to good use.

Here you will find the key insights and valuable tricks that I have learned about memory and memory management in ten years of working and playing with IBM PCs and their close kin. Further, you'll learn much of what I have gleaned from reading the trade press and talking with many people at all levels of this industry. Some of these sources are my friends. Others are my clients. Still others are the founders, presidents, and other key personnel at many of the most important companies making PC-related products.

I have worked hard to make sure this book will not overwhelm you. Some clear guideposts will help distinguish the essential material from the technical digressions and merely interesting background information. You can find just the parts you want and skip the rest.

Before you plunge into any of the five main parts to this book, you might like a quick overview of what you will and won't learn, and discover some tips on how you can use this book to best advantage. But even before that, there are some things you must understand.

An Important Notice

This is a big book, filled with information. Several special conventions have been followed to help you find what you need. Here are the typographic conventions that you must understand in order to use this book most effectively.

Warnings

Some things you might do could be dangerous to the health of you, your PC, or your data. When these things are discussed, you will see a warning message set off like this:

> **Warning** The boldface word or phrase tells you the kind of warning or caution that follows. The paragraphs that follow will tell you what to do or what not to do, or they will direct you to another place in the book where suitable precautions are more fully discussed.

> This book comes with a diskette. On it you will find a hypertext database called the Memory Management for All of Us, Deluxe Edition, Memory Information System or the MEMINFO database, for short. It contains information on concepts, products, and manufacturers that

otherwise would be in an appendix. The advantage of the hypertext database is that you can look up information in it more efficiently, and jump from one item to related ones very easily.

Most things you will want to look up there are indexed for the easiest access. You also can do a full text search for any word or phrase that interests you.

In addition to the hypertext database, the diskette also contains a number of useful programs. See Appendix C for details on what the diskette contains.

Jargon

Every technical field has jargon. These are words and phrases that have special meanings for the field. You may know the normal English meaning of the words yet not understand their jargon meaning. This makes it important that you know which terms are jargon and that you be able to find out just what each one means. This book uses three strategies to help you in this regard:

- Most but not all jargon is defined or described near where it first appears in the text. Every time a new term is introduced, it will appear in *italics*.

Every jargon word or phrase can be found in the hypertext database on the diskette. Run MEMINFO and select "Concepts." That glossary is a handy place to get a quick definition of those terms.

- Every jargon word or phrase is also listed in the Index. The Index directs you to the page or pages where that term is defined or described in detail.

Product Names

Many products are mentioned in this book. Each of them is set in italics. For example, Microsoft *Windows* is a product.

You can look up all the products mentioned in this book and their manufacturers in the hypertext database on the diskette. Run MEMINFO and select "Products by Type" if you want to find a product by its category; select "Products by Name" to look up the products by name. Select "Manufacturers" to look up a manufacturer by name. (You will be able to jump directly from a product name to the screen showing information on it manufacturer, or from a manufacturer to a screen describing the memory products it makes.)

Most of these products are copyrighted by, or their names are trademarks or registered trademarks of, their producers. We hereby acknowledge those copyrights and trademarks.

Was This Book Written for You?

I had in mind four types of reader while writing this book. If you fit into any of these groups, you will find this book helpful.

Those Who Need Help, Fast

You will especially appreciate the short guide in Part III and the suggestions in Part VI. Once you know what sort of system you have, Part III will let you know right away just what your memory management options are. (If you are unsure what kind of PC system you have, first check the table on the inside of the front cover, or go to Chapter 3 in Part I.) Part VI shows many practical examples.

If you are in a hurry because your PC is not working, turn to Part V for some practical tips. Once you have your PC back to normal, you can return to the earlier parts of the book.

Please remember that sometimes going more slowly gets you where you want to go sooner than rushing in. You'll be better able to take advantage of the products mentioned in Parts III, IV, and V if you first master the material in Parts I and II. There you will learn all the principles as well as the meaning of all the jargon that so clutters this field.

Beginners

This refers not only to people who only recently began using PCs; it also refers to people who may have been using PCs for a very long time, but who have not studied memory-management principles or the design of PCs before.

The main text has been written for you. If you read the book from the beginning through Parts I and II, only skipping the asides and technical notes, you will be able to learn all the fundamentals of this field.

Those with Inquiring Minds

I hope everyone finds this book interesting—perhaps even fascinating. If you want to understand as fully as possible how PCs use memory, what memory management is, and how it can be accomplished, this book is full of what you want to know. Feel free to skip around, reading whatever interests you.

Some of the paragraphs are not really a necessary part of the main story. These paragraphs come in three types: the first are asides—additional information that I have included because it may interest you; the second type contains more in-depth technical discussions and requires more background knowledge on the part of the reader; and a third type contains important definitions.

These special paragraphs are boxed so that you can easily see where they end and the main story picks up again. Additionally, all these paragraphs have an icon beside the first paragraph in each group, showing you which kind of special paragraph you are reading. The technical notes are shaded to make them more distinct.

This is what a paragraph of the first type, the asides with additional but nonessential information, will look like. Sometimes this is historical background. Other times it will contain material that is only tangentially related to the main story.

Paragraphs of the second kind, technical notes, look like this. These are more jargon-laden than the rest of the text and presume a higher-level background in the field.

This is the third type of special paragraph. It will contain an important definition.

Notice especially any paragraphs labeled with this icon. These are tips that will help you achieve your memory management goals more easily and more surely. Every reader will want to look at these paragraphs.

You can skip all of these specially marked paragraphs except the Warnings and Tips without missing any essential ideas. Or you can dip into them to see if you understand and enjoy the material presented there.

Technicians and Gurus Seeking the Deepest Possible Explanations

I hope you enjoy reading all of the book, but if you want to seek out the most technical aspects, you can skip ahead looking for the technical notes. These paragraphs amplify the material in the main portion of the text using a higher level of technical detail and more jargon.

Are You in a Hurry?

This is a rather long introduction. You say you are in a hurry to get on with things? Okay, but before you leap ahead, here is a quick way to find out where you might best turn next.

Take the following short test. You will grade yourself, so be honest. (You don't even have to write out your answers, but do take a moment to see how you would formulate them.) If you can confidently and clearly answer a question, give yourself 10 points.

Warning   When you see the questions, you may think some of them are quite out of place here. You may feel *sure* you don't need to know all of these things in order to understand PC memory management. On the contrary, these are all vital terms. You will run into them and you must know, at least moderately well, what each one means.

In this test, all jargon is displayed in **boldface type**. Be sure you can explain what each term means. Imagine trying to teach this material to a class of people new to computers. After you have decided how you would explain a term, compare your definition with that in the Glossary (Appendix C).

If you are unsure how to explain a term or concept to someone else, don't give yourself any points for that question. (I leave it up to you to figure out when your answers deserve something between 0 and 10 points.) The maximum score is 200 points.

A high score means you are ready to start with Part III or Part IV. A low score means that reading Parts I and II first will enable you to get more from the later sections. If your score is somewhere in the middle, skim the first two parts. If you find yourself learning something that seems valuable, slow down and read more carefully.

If you just can't stand turning all those pages, and you need to learn the answers to only a few questions, you can jump to the chapter or chapters indicated after each question that stumped you. There you will find a discussion of that topic. (Use the Index if you want to find the exact page or pages to check.)

Do you know…

1. …the difference between **RAM** and **ROM** (two kinds of **memory**) and between both of them and disk **storage**? (Chapters 2 and 6)

2. …how to read **hexadecimal** numbers? (Chapter 6)

3. …the difference between **I/O ports** and **memory locations**? (Chapter 6)

4. …what a **virtual disk** (also known as a **RAM disk**) is? (Chapter 6)

5. …the relationship between **interrupts**, **IRQ numbers**, and **Interrupt Service Routines**? (Chapters 7 and 10)

6. …the difference between **memory** and **memory address space**? (Chapters 8 and 14)

7. …the difference between **Expanded** and **Extended memory**? (Chapter 8)

8. …the difference between **Upper** and **High memory**? (Chapter 8)

9. …what a **TSR** is? (Chapter 10)

10. ...what a **device driver** is? (Chapter 10)

11. ...what the infamous **"DOS 640KB barrier"** is and why we are still struggling with it? (Chapter 12)

12. ...how **memory caching** and **disk caching** are the same, and how they are different? (Chapter 14)

13. ...the difference between **video RAM** and regular **DRAM**? (Chapters 2 and 16)

14. ...what **parity** means? (Chapter 16)

15. ...when **parity checking** is done and when it is not? (Chapter 16)

16. ...what a **wait state** is? (Chapter 17)

17. ...why **memory** must be **allocated** and what that entails? (Chapter 19)

18. ...what **Shadow RAM** is? (Chapter 20)

19. ...how to **configure** your **PC** using its **DIP switches** and **jumpers**? (Chapters 9, 15, 20, and 21)

20. ...how to configure it through its **CMOS setup**, the **CONFIG.SYS** file, and the **AUTOEXEC.BAT** file? (Chapter 20)

How did you do? I hope you found this little test enlightening. People often find some things difficult to express once they are pressed to explain them to others. If you found this happening to you as you took this test, don't worry. You can change that by reading on.

I hope you know now whether you are ready to jump directly into Parts III and IV, or whether you might better take your time and start nearer the beginning. But before you go, please study carefully the material in Chapter 5, "Some Important Warnings." You may already know these things, but it never hurts to be reminded.

How to Use This Book

By now, if you have checked out the Table of Contents and read this far in the Introduction, you have a pretty good idea of what to expect in the rest of this book. Here are some brief recommendations, according to what you are looking for:

- **If you want to learn it all,** start at the beginning and read it straight through.

- **If you want to optimize your PC and you want to do it now,** start with Part III. You may have to go back to Part II or even Part I if you find you don't know some of the jargon or some of the fundamental principles, though.

- **If you are not very technically proficient,** skip all the technical notes (unless you find yourself enjoying them anyway).

- **If you are already an expert,** but you want to know more, pay special attention to the technical notes.

- **If you want help with a particular product,** look in Part IV. Please read the discussion in Chapter 26 before you look for the specific product description.

- **If you are having a problem with your PC's memory right now,** go to Part V. Don't try to improve your PC until you get the immediate problem solved, or at least until you understand what is going on inside it.

Don't forget to check out the appendixes and the MEMINFO hypertext database on the enclosed diskette. You'll find quick definitions of all the jargon in this book and an explanation of the customary ways this industry describes very small or very large quantities. Other appendixes tell you where and how to get what you need, and how to do that safely.

What You Will Learn

If you are in a hurry you can leave the Introduction now and go to whatever chapter most appeals to you. Of course, you can return later on, if you want to see what else this Introduction contains.

Now that the folks in a hurry have gone on ahead, let's slow down a bit and cover some interesting points in more depth. We'll start with an overview of what this book can do for you.

A reasonable question to ask about any book is "What am I going to learn?" To answer this question, here is a brief description of *what* is *where* in this book.

In Part I: Orientation

This part covers the definitions and background information you need to understand the rest of the book. It also helps you learn what sort of PC you now have and how to assess your PC memory needs. This section introduces the idea of the six main classes of PC for the purposes of memory management. Be sure to read "How to Find Out What You Have Now," in Chapter 3, as well as Chapter 5. Both are important for the later material.

In Part II: How It All Works

Here is the core of the book, explaining memory and memory management. Although not every possible memory-management product or trick is described in this book, you will learn all the principles you need to evaluate any that are not covered.

In Part III: An Overview of Your Options

What you can do depends on what you have to work with. Check here to learn quickly what your options are for memory management and upgrades. If you are not sure which class of PC you have, go back to Chapter 3 in Part I.

In Part IV: Specific Products

This part contains detailed information on a wide variety of products. All the most popular (and some of the less popular) ones are included. These include a wide range of solutions, from simple software tools to full motherboard replacements.

In Part V: Dealing with Difficulties

Someone once said, "Murphy was an optimist." Here you will find help when things don't go as you had hoped. If that describes your experiences with PC memory, this part may be where you need to turn first.

In Part VI: Examples and Tips

Many people learn best by seeing how someone else does things. This section contains many examples of the specific steps you need to take to do effective memory management in your PC. You'll also find here some tips that will help you achieve your goals more easily.

In the Appendixes and on the Included Diskette

In addition to a glossary and a list of products and manufacturers, you will also find some advice about where and how to buy whatever you need. This could be the most important part of the book—especially if, as could easily happen, it is the part that saves you the most money and the most grief.

What You Won't Learn

It is impossible to list all of the things that this book does *not* contain. The next few paragraphs explain some things you might have expected, but will have to seek elsewhere. (Some of the possible "elsewheres" are also mentioned.)

Basic DOS Commands

The discussions in this book assume that you already know how to operate your PC. That includes knowing what the basic DOS commands are and how to execute them.

Many good books have been written on this subject. First look at the reference manual that came with your copy of DOS. If that seems too cryptic, you may want to try a more tutorial book.

Here are a few good ones:

DOS Secrets Unleashed by Alan Simpson (Sams, 1993)

DOS 6 for the Guru Wanna-Be by Paul McFedries (Sams, 1993)

The Absolute Beginner's Guide to Memory Management by Mike Miller (Sams, 1993)

DOS 6.0 Power Tools by John M. Goodman and John Socha (Bantam, 1993)

Easy DOS, by Shelly O'Hara (Que, 1991)

The First Book of MS-DOS 6 by Joe Kraynak (Alpha Books, 1993)

10 Minute Guide to MS-DOS 6 by Jennifer Flynn (Alpha Books, 1991)

A shareware tutorial program, *DOS Practice,* can be found on many bulletin boards under the name DOSPRACT.ZIP. It is a bit dated, but it covers the fundamentals quite nicely.

How to Manage Your Hard Disk

Information in PCs is often stored on hard disks. Managing them is important, but is not the focus of this book. Many authors have written books devoted solely or primarily to this topic.

You might wish to look at the following:

Hard Disk Power with the Jamsa Disk Utilities by Kris Jamsa (Sams, 1990)

Hard Disk Quick Reference 1992 Edition by Edmund X. deJesus (Que, 1992)

Introduction to Hard Disk Management by Que Development Group (Que, 1992)

Using Your Hard Disk by Robert Ainsbury (Que, 1991)

If you want to understand how your hard disk works, the ways it might fail you, and how to postpone those failures or recover from them, a book I recommend (since I wrote it!) is *Hard Disk Secrets* (IDG Books Worldwide, 1993). Don't let the title mislead you. Although it does tell some of the really arcane secrets about hard disks, this book is for anyone interested in learning about how their hard disk works, in as much or as little depth as he or she may wish. It does not, however, contain much about managing your hard disk's contents.

Every Last Product or Trick You May Wish to Use Someday

Large though it is, this book cannot possibly cover every single memory-management software or hardware product nor, of course, every obscure memory-management trick. There is a nearly unlimited number of them out there, and more are being invented daily.

So, although this book discusses many popular products in detail, it will be even more valuable if you use it to gain the basic understanding that lets you choose intelligently even among the products or tips not covered here.

A Request

I have a request of you: Tell me about your favorite memory-management tricks and products. Let me know what you have found to be effective for your PC. Tell me your horror stories, too. Perhaps in a later edition I can give you credit for bringing these things to my attention. (Be sure to tell me clearly whether you are willing to be credited or quoted. If you wish only to alert me to something, but don't want your name used in connection with it, tell me and I will do that.) Mail your accolades and sad tales to:

John M. Goodman, Ph.D.
P.O. Box 746
Westminster, CA 92684-0746

Versions of Software Covered

I hope this book continues to be useful for many years. In that time, I am sure many of the programs mentioned here will be improved. What, you may wonder, are the versions of various programs discussed here?

DOS

This book focuses on the currently supported versions of DOS. These are, for MS-DOS, versions 3.30, 3.31, 4.01, 5.0, and 6.0. For *PC DOS*, the current versions are 3.3, 4.0, and 5.0. The current version of *DR DOS* is 6.0. Many people still use a version released before any of these. If what you are using does what you want, that's fine. Still, you may want to know how changing to a later version can help you—or hurt you!

In terms of memory management, DOS 5 is a whole new game. (That was true when *DR DOS* 5 first came out. The release of *MS-DOS* 5 and *PC DOS* 5, then *DR DOS* 6, and now *MS-DOS* 6 and *PC DOS* 6 have only modestly furthered that revolution.) There are important differences among the various earlier versions, but none that were nearly as significant as those between any earlier version and DOS 5 or 6. For this reason I'll cover DOS-related issues twice—once for DOS 5 or 6, and once for the earlier versions.

Not many people upgraded from DOS 3.x to DOS 4. That's understandable. DOS 4 attempted some wonderful things. It also contained some major mistakes. DOS 5 was in part a recognition and correction of those mistakes.

By DOS 3.x I mean all variations of DOS 3, namely versions 3.0, 3.1, 3.2, 3.21, 3.3, and 3.31. Anytime you see version *N.x*, here or in most any other writing on computers, the meaning will be similar to this.

If you are now using DOS 4, I urge you to upgrade to DOS 5 or 6. If you are using DOS 3.3 or some earlier version, you can stay with it, or you can upgrade. This book may help you decide whether or not to upgrade.

Microsoft Windows

Next to DOS, *Windows* is the most popular software product of all time. So it gets a lot of attention from everyone. This book is no exception. In many places I mention *Windows* (and I also discuss some important alternatives to *Windows*).

The current version of *Windows* is 3.1. Many people using *Windows* are still at version 3.0 The differences between *Windows 3.x* and all earlier versions is even more pronounced than the differences between DOS 5 and all prior versions of DOS. (By *Windows* 3.1 I include the current version of the ordinary, single-user *Windows*, and the networked version, *Windows for Workgroups*.)

In fact, if you use *Windows* and are serious about memory management, you surely will want to upgrade to *Windows* 3. For that reason, all the discussion of memory management under *Windows* in this book assumes you are using version 3.x. Most of what there is to say applies equally to versions 3.0 and 3.1. Where there are significant differences, they are pointed out.

Other Programs

Many other programs are described here. To keep the book to a manageable size, in most cases just the latest version of each is covered.

Memory management is at the heart of your PC. Anything that changes how your PC manages its memory ultimately affects how all the programs in that PC work. If you change how your PC manages its memory (by applying some of what you learn here), you may want to contact the manufacturers of all your major application programs and your principal utility programs to see if you must upgrade them in order to use them safely in your PC's new operating environment.

Some Reasons You Need the Information in This Book

This is "the best of times" and "the worst of times" to write a book about memory management in PCs. Never has the need for this book been more acute. Never have there been so many things to say about the subject and so much confusion in people's minds. When, a few months ago, I told one quite knowledgeable person what I was working on, she guffawed, "You want to write a book on PC memory management this year? Microsoft recently released *MS-DOS* 6, and they're about to release *Windows NT* 3.1. Novell is about to release *Novell DOS* (a.k.a. *DR DOS*), version 7. The way those products change things, you've got to be crazy to do this now!"

Actually, these hot news items, which nearly everyone has heard about and which almost no one fully understands, make it all the more important that this book be written now and that it be written well. It also makes that job quite challenging.

Several Key Facts and Trends

As I thought about this project, several key reasons that it is needed came to mind—reasons you need the information it contains.

- PC *users* need information about memory management because *they* are the ones who have to do the work.

- PCs are just too diverse for any one company to have all the answers in a ready-to-use package. Sure, you need the products those companies offer, but you also need to understand how to apply them to *your* PC.

- Doing effective memory management can be hard work. Some users just don't bother.

- Ineffective memory management means giving up the possibility of doing many useful things with your PC. Not only might it be impossible for you to run that latest, greatest whiz-bang program you read about, you may also be prevented from upgrading to the current version of the applications you depend on every day.

- Task switching and multitasking are getting ever more popular. These techniques have added greatly to the effectiveness with which many people are able to use their PCs, but making the techniques work well (or at all) requires some understanding of how your PC uses its memory.

- Application programs are getting bigger all the time.

- PCs are being connected to networks in ever larger numbers.

Each of these facts and trends makes memory management not only nice to understand and use; for many PC users it has become absolutely vital. That's a pretty compelling argument for learning about this subject.

In fact, you may be champing at the bit, eager to get on with that learning right now. If so, please feel free to leave the Introduction now and plunge into Chapter 1 or whatever place you wish to start.

The rest of this Introduction is a more leisurely discussion of the background behind the facts and trends I have just set out. Here you will find some history about the industry, and learn some of the reasons we must still struggle with the unfortunate side effects of certain key decisions that now seem very ancient (by PC standards).

The PC Industry Is Chaotic

The reason that PCs are so numerous is also the reason that they are so tricky and confusing. IBM decided, when it introduced the first PC, to make public how it built them. This open-architecture decision was a radical departure from IBM's earlier practices.

This was a very important decision on IBM's part; it has led directly to the present situation. Today there are over 70 million PCs in use, hundreds of different companies creating hardware to go into those PCs, and thousands of developers publishing software to run on them.

The original PC came with a very restricted set of options. That was all IBM could reasonably offer on a new machine for an unknown market. Because the design was published, *anyone* could—and sometimes it seemed as if *everyone* did—make add-on pieces enabling the PC do an almost unlimited number of new things.

This explains why PCs were adopted so enthusiastically by businesses. If IBM's *PC*, alone, didn't do what you wanted a small computer to do, somewhere you could find the additional software or hardware to enable it to do whatever you wanted.

This open architecture is also why IBM no longer makes any computers bearing the label IBM *Personal Computer*. Other manufacturers found they could make near copies of the IBM *PC* (actually, they were mostly copies of the IBM *PC/XT*, and later on the IBM *PC/AT*) and sell them for less than IBM charged. These compatibles and clones worked just as well as IBM's computers. In time, prices fell dramatically, and sales of PCs, counting all the different makers, rose spectacularly. The consumer was the big winner in this. IBM lost market share and eventually decided to stop making *Personal Computers* (ones bearing that name; they still make personal computers, but the names vary).

The newer personal computers from IBM, the *PS/2* and *PS/1* lines, also are open-architecture machines, but with some differences. IBM has held onto some of the design features a bit more tightly than they did with the original PC design.

Initially, IBM offered to license other manufacturers to create clones with the new **Micro Channel Architecture** (MCA) bus (introduced with the *PS/2*, models 50 and above). The catch was that the licensees would have to pay not only a 5 percent royalty on the sales of those machines, but also a 1 percent royalty on all their earlier sales of any other PC clone models. For major clone makers like Compaq, that was far too expensive. They and eight other firms, called the "Gang of Nine," banded together to make an alternative, now referred to as EISA machines. (In Chapter 14 you will learn all about the original design, now often called the **Industry Standard Architecture** (ISA) and the two newer designs, MCA and EISA.)

IBM's response to the EISA machines was to relent a bit on its MCA licensing policy. Time will tell if IBM can choose a path that is liberal enough to promote the sales of their *PS/2*s, yet not so free that wild cloning recurs.

This history is in marked contrast to what has happened (so far) with the Apple *Macintosh* computer line. Apple Computer, Inc. has kept close control over who can make what objects go into those computers. Until 1991 no clones were allowed. This has led to a much more orderly market. On the other hand, perhaps in part because of these tight controls, there are only about one-fifth as many Macs as PCs.

There is a down side to the wild way PCs have proliferated. No one is in control. Each PC maker creates machines that are subtly different from all the others. Each works hard to make its products sufficiently like a "real" PC, but their ideas of what constitutes "sufficiently alike" are not always clear, nor are they necessarily what you need.

In particular, each maker of a PC clone tries to ensure that its machines will run all the software and accept all the hardware add-ons that a true-blue IBM PC would. (This statement applies equally to AT clones and 386 clones.) Similarly, the makers of software or hardware add-ons for PCs try to make their products work well in the computing environment created in an IBM PC (or any sufficiently compatible clone).

Each supplier does extensive tests to be sure that its products will measure up. But normally it tests only for compatibility with IBM-brand PCs and perhaps a selected few of the other, most popular clones. No one can test against every maker's clone. And no one can have test PCs equipped with all possible PC programs and hardware add-ons.

Make no mistake: The other makers' clones generally *are different* from the IBM PCs. In the beginning they had to be different. Legally only IBM could make what IBM defined as its *Personal Computer*. Others could make very similar machines, but not exact copies.

As the industry matured two things happened. Some of the larger clone makers got licenses from IBM to make essentially identical copies of the IBM design. Others simply made accurate copies, without a formal license, and so far have gotten away with it (though they were, at least at first, inhibited from making copies of the MCA machines, as was mentioned above).

What really caused the worst problems in the early days, and still causes problems, were not inaccuracies in the copying of IBM's design, but the many, diverse ways in which the clone makers have attempted to *improve* on IBM's design. After all, they need to distinguish themselves from IBM. Some chose simple price competition. Others have sought to protect their profit margins, yet be attractive, by offering PCs with greater speed, more options, or other key differences.

The unfortunate result is that while every new clone computer will run the standard PC software and accept the standard PC hardware add-ons, and every new software product will run on a standard PC, there is no guarantee that each software product or hardware add-on will function in every PC clone. (Even the level of compatibility I have just described is not always achieved, but it is the minimum standard of compatibility that the manufacturers strive for.)

What is worse, once you add just one nonstandard piece to your PC, your PC becomes nonstandard. That means you now have a greater chance of finding that the next thing you wish to add will turn out to be not quite compatible with your system.

This book identifies some of the combinations of memory management software or hardware and major PC applications that are known to work well together and some that definitely do not. For some of those that work together, but only when you do something "just so," you will learn here just what you must do.

PC Programs Are Growing Ever Larger

In the dawn of the personal computer age (in the mid- to late-1970s) memory was an even more precious resource than it is now. It cost much more per kilobyte than it now does, and there were tight limits on how much you could install in one of the small computers of that day. If yours had 16KB of RAM you were among the fortunate few. Programs written for those machines were, naturally, quite small. The idea of having more than one program at a time in the machine was only a pipe dream.

By 1981 (when IBM introduced its original PC) memory prices had come down a bit. The first IBM *PC*s came with a minimum of 16KB of RAM. Further, these new computers offered unprecedented room for expansion. Instead of a maximum of 48KB (or maybe 64KB) that its predecessors could accommodate, the IBM *PC* could accept a whopping 640KB of RAM. At the time, that seemed like an almost unlimited amount.

That it was not unlimited soon became clear. People found that PCs could solve much more complex business problems, but to do so they needed all that extra RAM—if not more. A particularly big success was Lotus *1-2-3*, a big program that manipulated big spreadsheets for big companies. Very soon users of *1-2-3* and other programs with similarly large appetites for RAM found themselves once again running out of memory.

Since then users' expectations have risen. Users no longer accept as adequate what once seemed marvelous. Programs must be larger to meet heightened expectations, and the data they manipulate takes up much more room.

As if that weren't enough, now users want, and almost insist, that PCs do more things (at least apparently) all at once. A PC user is more efficient when blessed with enough memory to hold more than one task and with the ability to switch quickly between them. Even better is to have the PC working on more than one application at the same time.

People Are Using Ever More Resident Stuff

One way to achieve the illusion that your PC is doing more than one task at a time is to have multiple programs resident in its RAM and to jump between them at the touch of a key. Another way is to have the PC automatically jump from task to task, spending just fractions of a second on each one in turn (thus giving the illusion that it is working on all of them at once). The first of these techniques is called task switching; the other is multitasking. What they have in common is that to work well all the programs involved must be in the PC's RAM simultaneously.

So you load up your PC with resident software (mostly some utility programs that are always there, ready to work at the touch of a special *hot key*), or else load a multitasking operating environment and, within it, try to run several (possibly very large) application programs.

It also is increasingly the case that PCs are connected to other PCs over a network, or are used as terminals linked to a mainframe computer. For either use, yet another program must reside in the PC's memory to manage that network or mainframe link.

Does managing all this sound like a challenge? It gets even worse. All these different programs, network interface cards, and other goodies are made by a host of different companies. Getting them all to fit into the PC at the same time is only the first problem.

Getting It All to Coexist Peacefully Can Be a Nightmare

Getting the many programs you want to use to fit into your RAM merely enables you to find out whether or not they all can run without interference. Very often they cannot. You may make some of them work together smoothly by eliminating a few of the troublemakers. Or perhaps if you load them in a different order, they all can work together.

You may have several sets of programs that work: Program A will run with programs B and C, but not with program D; however, B will run with C and D just fine, if A is not around. That sort of thing.

Are you getting the idea that a lot of experimentation is called for? You're right. This book describes some of the things that can work together and how, but often you must experiment on your own. That's why the information in Parts I and II is so important. What you learn about how PCs work, and especially about how their memory is organized, can make your experiments more a matter of planned explorations and less a matter of trial and error. You need no longer rely on sheer, dumb luck to find a successful solution.

Getting It All to Coexist Peacefully
Can Be Wonderful—Once You Accomplish It

It's worth the effort. Truly, you are more effective when your PC does more for you, with less effort in less time. That's possible only if you are able to set it up to do task switching or multitasking, and if your network connections don't get in the way of your application programs.

Imagine you are working at your PC. It is doing all the following things at once:

- Receiving a file over a phone line.

- Printing a multi-page document.

- Recalculating a large spreadsheet file or sorting a large database.

- And meanwhile you are working on a letter in your word processor.

A colleague asks you a question, and without a thought, you touch a key and pop up your notes to find the answer. This is a PC that really is helping its user be more effective. It is working hard, so the user can work better. But this is only possible if someone has done the right things to help that PC manage its memory.

Some Tricks Don't Really Pay Off

Some people try too hard. They want every last possible byte of free RAM. They want all possible TSRs and device drivers loaded at once, plus the largest possible spreadsheets and databases, and more.

You can spend inordinate amounts of time trying to tweak the very last little bit out of your PC. In the process you may make a wonderful setup, or you may create the world's worst nightmare.

If you save RAM, but make your PC harder to operate and less fun to use, that's no bargain. Worse, if you make your system unstable (prone to crashing on you at any time), that is counterproductive. So while a part of my task is to show you the wonderful things you will want to try, another part is to show you some of the things you *could* do, but which you probably should *not* do.

A Final Word

It's time for you to get on to the main body of the book. I hope you enjoy reading it as much as I enjoyed writing it. And I hope you will learn as much as I found myself having to learn before I could complete it. (Along the way, I many times rediscovered a truth you may also encounter: that often you *think* you understand a concept fully—until you try to explain it clearly to someone else!)

ACKNOWLEDGMENTS

I have many people to thank for helping make this book a reality, and I am pleased to have this opportunity to do so publicly. I shall begin with Richard Swadley, publisher of Sams. This book was his idea in the first place. Next is my agent, Bill Gladstone, who thought of me as the person to write the book. Stephen Poland and Gregg Bushyeager, editors at Prentice Hall, were my champions as the project dragged on far longer than any of us had at first anticipated. Thanks to all of you for believing in me and in the worth of this project.

No one individual (at least no one I have spoken to) knew all the things I needed to learn in order to write this book. Many different people helped me most generously. I was given a lot of very technical information, often the sort that one might have thought would be withheld as "proprietary," by representatives of most of the companies listed in the MemInfo hypertext database on the diskette that accompanies this book. A few of these people stand out in my mind as having been extraordinarily generous with their time and knowledge, and I want to acknowledge them by name for this very special help.

Scott Daniel, president of Quadtel, was my technical reviewer and local guru. He spent far more hours than either he or I had anticipated would be needed when this project began, both in his careful reading of my manuscript and in tutoring me in some of the fine points of memory management and BIOS software design.

Bruce Schafer, president of Multisoft, spent hours on the phone helping me understand both his and his competitors' products. Doug Proctor, also from Multisoft, spent still more time tracking down obscure problems I was having and helping fill in more of the holes in my knowledge.

Frank Gilluwe, president of V Communications, shared his knowledge most generously as well. Often he was able to point me in helpful directions, giving me questions to ask others that would ultimately give me the insights I needed. Gary Clow and Bruce Beheimer at Stac Electronics helped me in a similar fashion.

Mike White at LaserTools and Dan Spear at Quarterdeck Office Systems fielded many questions with patience and good humor. Bob Smith and Paul Tarlow at Qualitas helped me understand both memory management and memory managers, and the very special considerations that apply to IBM's PS/2 line of computers.

Ken Woog and Dale Busciano at Quadtel corrected some significant mistaken impressions I had about the design of PCs and their BIOS code. Mike Dryfoos at Microsoft helped me understand the inner workings of MS-DOS.

Bob Gardyne at Video Seven gave me incredible detail on the design of PC video systems and taught me about the sources of some arcane but important memory-management problems that arise in that area, as well as how they can be handled effectively.

All these people and many more helped make me aware of the things I needed to say in the book. I only hope I remembered and was able to include all the points they felt were most important.

A large number of other people helped me make the book more readable. Some of them did so by sharing with me their ignorance of memory management. They read drafts of my manuscript and showed me where they got confused. Others were already experts in their own right. They pointed out limitations and errors in my explanations.

Here in alphabetical order, are the names of my manuscript readers: George Austin, Bob Basaraba, Marcel Charpentier, Jerry Corners, M.D., Steve Donegan, Stan Dvoskin, Linda Fox, Paul Fuller, Bill Gilliland, Kris Jamsa, Tom Kilpatrick, Dan Likins, Max Lockie, John Lunsford, Michele Miller, Bob Moore, Anne Perrah, Bill Phillips, Lowell Shatraw, and Michael Springer. Thank you all for your considerable assistance.

I had the great good fortune to have Michele Miller as a research assistant for much of this project. She created the first draft of the information now in the MemInfo hypertext database—and in the Appendices C, D, and E in the first edition of this book—(the Glossary and Guide to Products and Manufacturers). Even before that, she helped me get organized, and she helped out in many other ways as well. Thank you, Michele, for your generosity and your marvelous sense of organization.

Tuong Le spent several months helping me test software and capturing many of the screen images you will find here. Jeannine dePenne created the charming and witty cartoons. Sunny Lockie scanned Jeannine's images into digital form.

During the preparation of the Deluxe Edition I was fortunate to have John Lunsford helping me nearly full-time. His attention to detail and his knowledge of the industry have both helped make this work more up-to-date and more accurate than would otherwise have been the case.

Michael Muller has also been working with me on this edition. He did much of the work of converting the printed Appendices from the first edition into the hypertext form in which you will find them on the diskette included with this book. Michael helped me in other ways too numerous to list.

Once the manuscript got to the publisher, many more folks got involved. Their contributions are not minor. I don't even know the names of all the editors, artists, and production staff who collaborated to make sure this would be a fine book. Linda Hawkins, senior production editor, was my main contact with them. She also became one of my best cheerleaders. Thank you, Linda, for your able assistance and your enthusiasm.

Naturally, despite all the help I have mentioned, I alone am responsible for any errors that remain in the book. I can assure you, though, that because of all the help I received there are fewer of them than would otherwise have been the case.

I also wish to thank Christy Gersich at Microsoft for helping me get advance information on their products and samples of some of them.

I thank Amkly computers for loaning me one of the fine 486/EISA workstations. I could not have finished this project on time without it, and I also learned more about the EISA bus from my experiences with it.

The manuscript was prepared using Microsoft's Word for DOS, version 5.5. Screens were captured with Collage Plus or Hijaak. All other figures were created using CorelDRAW!, version 2.01, and many were later revised using version 3.0. This includes the line art, which is the bulk of the figures, and also converting the cartoons from scanned images to vector-art EPS files.

Trademarks

ORIENTATION

Part I is to help make sure your background knowledge is adequate for a full understanding of Part II, in which the fundamentals of PC memory management are covered. Some very basic terms, like *PC*, are defined. Terms that are not discussed here are covered later in the book, so even the experts (who may skip this part) will understand what we mean by those terms.

Remember, you can look up a quick definition of most terms in the hypertext Memory Information System on the *Memory Management for All of Us, Deluxe Edition* diskette.

Part I provides a clear, complete definition of what PCs are and what they are not, plus a description of the kinds of PC memory we will be discussing. You'll also find help in determining what sort of PC you have, and whether to increase its memory or better use the memory your PC already has.

Finally, there is a chapter with some important warnings. It is in this part because it covers things the experts should already know. (But even they are urged to read that chapter, just in case.)

1

WHAT IS A PC?

There are many things this term could mean. Here you'll learn what it means in this book, and the meanings of several other important terms.

This is a book about PCs. The simplest definition is that those letters stand for "personal computer." More specifically, for the purposes of this book, I mean a personal computer that is "compatible" with some model of IBM personal computer running some form of *PC DOS* or *MS-DOS*. I'll repeat that:

> In this book, *PC* means a personal computer that is compatible with some model of IBM personal computer running some form of *PC DOS* or *MS-DOS*.

Take a look at those pieces of jargon, one at a time. Along the way we will answer three questions: (1) What is "personal" about a personal computer? (2) What does it mean to be "compatible" with an IBM personal computer? And (3) why include only PCs running DOS?

What Makes a Computer "Personal"?

IBM makes many computers of many different kinds. Some are large, some medium, and now some are quite small. In what way can you measure the size of a computer, and how can you decide if it is a "personal" one or not?

For many reasons, the most useful size measurement is the purchase price of the computer. This is a much better defining characteristic than, say, the computer's ability to do certain kinds of math, its speed, or its capacity for storing information. The size of computers, by all those measures, has changed radically through the years. What has not changed nearly as much is the amount people can afford to spend on them.

A *personal computer*, therefore, is one that an individual can afford to buy, or that a company can afford to let only one person use. By this standard, IBM has made many different models of personal computer (although they are just a fraction of all the computer models IBM has made).

> When IBM introduced their first personal computer in 1981, the IBM *Personal Computer* (IBM *PC*), it was quite a departure for the company. Up to that time, IBM had made only large computers which cost huge amounts of money. No individual could afford to buy one, and a company that bought one couldn't afford to let only one person use

it. Instead, those computers typically ran 24 hours a day, tended by a full-time, trained staff. These large multiuser computers, often referred to as *mainframes,* are still an important part of the IBM product line.

It appears that IBM thought that, with the original IBM *PC*, it had designed a perfect small computer for use by home hobbyists and some other (not clearly defined) classes of individuals. Yet, to everyone's surprise, the IBM *PC* turned out to be just what smaller businesses needed and wanted. Soon, even large companies bought them in vast numbers.

In the years that followed, IBM made several other models of personal computer. In 1982 they brought out a significantly upgraded version of the IBM *PC* called the IBM *PC/XT*. It included a large (for the time) 10MB hard disk. The next big jump, in 1984, was the IBM *PC/AT*. The most significant new feature in this model was its 16-bit-wide data bus. (IBM never said why they used the letters XT and AT, though many have surmised those stand for Extended Technology and Advanced Technology, respectively.)

In 1986, IBM announced they were going to stop making *Personal Computers*; instead, they were introducing something completely new, the IBM *PS/2*. The letters *PS* stood for Personal System. No one was told just what the /2 meant, though many said it was simply IBM's second major attempt to make a personal-scale computer. Many models of *PS/2* were introduced (five of them right away and others from time to time since).

Many people confuse the *PS/2* line with the Micro Channel Architecture (MCA). Not all *PS/2*s use the MCA design. Some are simply the older design (now commonly referred to as Industry Standard Architecture, or ISA, machines) put in a new box. The only common element to all of the models of the *PS/2* line is the new logo design.

The latest twist on the IBM personal computer came with IBM's introduction, in 1989, of the *PS/1*. Not only is it a small computer designed for use by individuals, it is marketed in a totally new way for IBM: through Sears and other major retail chain stores.

The principal significance of IBM's various personal computers is that they are more alike than they are different. They all run the same operating system (DOS). They all are able to run many of the same programs. (Some programs do require one of the more powerful models.) Any program that runs on the original IBM *PC* will work perfectly on any of the later personal computers from IBM. This is often referred to as *downward compatibility* or *backward compatibility.*

Since these personal computers are very much alike, at least in terms of what programs they can run, collectively they are a single market for software developers. (Lately this market has become somewhat fragmented as some software developers target only the owners of higher-end PC models.)

IBM did not have the PC field to itself, at least not for long. Once it was clear that businesses and individuals in huge numbers were willing to pay for small computers, many other companies got into the act. They built computers that worked almost exactly like the IBM personal computers. In the process they defined a new term, *PC-compatible*, or, as it is often called more casually, *PC clone.* (We'll look at just what *compatible* means shortly.)

As more and more PC-like computers were made by companies other than IBM, a new, informal standard was born: the IBM standard of personal computing. It was first defined as how IBM made personal computers, but now the definition belongs to the whole industry. Whether or not IBM continues to make compatible computers, this standard will survive.

Some people use the term *Industry Standard Architecture,* abbreviated *ISA,* to stand for what I call the "IBM standard of personal computing." Others reserve that term for the design of the Input/Output bus used in the IBM *PC/AT.* (You will find the details of the ISA as a bus design in Chapter 14.)

One variation (and the practice followed in this book) uses *AT* to stand for any personal computer that generally follows the design of the IBM *PC/AT*. Others extend the term *AT* to include not only clones of that model, but also those PCs built using Intel's 386, 486, and Pentium processor chips or any substantially equivalent processor chip (including computers whose internal design differs in some important ways from the IBM *PC/AT*), as long as they use the ISA bus.

Some people use the term *compatible* to refer to any computer that is similar to any IBM personal computer, from the IBM *PC* to the latest *PS/2* model. Others restrict the term to just those PCs that use the ISA bus.

What Is Not a PC?

Other than computers that cost too much, many other computers are not PCs. They may be called personal computers in some other contexts, but they are not what is meant here by a PC.

Before the emergence of the personal computer, several companies (most notably DEC) introduced computers much smaller than the typical models made by IBM. They called these computers minicomputers. Smaller businesses adopted them in large numbers. These are quite expensive machines, typically costing $30,000 or more. Therefore, most companies that buy them use them in much the same manner as mainframes, running them 24 hours a day and letting many people use them simultaneously.

Now, as microcomputers (computers built using a microprocessor as the CPU chip) are developing more and more power, they are beginning to invade the minicomputer realm. The most powerful and costly of the 486-based computers may do as much and cost nearly as much as some of the smaller minicomputers. By our present definition that makes them not quite PCs.

For our purposes, a PC is not a computer that merely emulates the IBM standard of personal computing. Nor is it a computer running an

operating system other than DOS. It does include computers that run alternative operating environments on top of DOS.

Again, don't worry if you don't know what the terms *emulate* or *operating environment* mean. They will be explained later in this chapter. *DOS*
and *operating system* will be explained at length in Chapter 10.

What Does "Compatible with IBM's Personal Computers" Really Mean?

It is supposed to mean that any PC-compatible, or PC clone as they are
sometimes called, will have all the same functionality for any conceivable
program as a true-blue (IBM-brand) PC. Strictly speaking, by this definition almost no PC clone is fully compatible.

In the section "The PC Industry Is Chaotic" in the introduction to this
book, the history of the PC is recounted, including a discussion of the rise
of the clones and the ways in which clones sometimes are and sometimes
are not compatible.

The most important point to realize is that no matter what the PC
maker's claims may be, compatibility with the full "IBM standard of personal computing" has continued to be a somewhat elusive goal. Most clone
makers now do a very good job of hiding the incompatibilities of their
products—most of the time.

> The list of PC-compatible computers includes machines made by
> Acer, ALR, Amkly, AST, and AT&T, just to name some makers whose
> names start with A. That doesn't begin to cover the industry.
>
> A *short* list of some other major PC manufacturers (according to our
> present definition) might include Compaq, CompuAdd, Dataworld,
> Dell, Dolch, DTK, Ergo, Epson, Gateway 2000, Hewlett-Packard,
> Hyundai, Insight, IBM, Leading Edge, Memorex-Telex, NEC,
> Northgate, Packard-Bell, Panasonic, PC Brand, Sharp, Stan-
> dard Computer, Swan, Tandon, Tandy (Radio Shack)/GRID,
> Tangent, Texas Instruments, Toshiba, Unisys, USA Flex, Wang, Wyse,
> Zenith, and Zeos.

The true test of a compatible is whether or not it runs all the programs
you care to run. If it does, you have no reason to be concerned. If it fails
that test, though, for just one application that is important to you, it doesn't
matter how many others it can run.

In the early days of PC clone making, the usual tests people ran to check compatibility were Microsoft's *Flight Simulator* and Lotus *1-2-3*. Almost any PC that could run those two would run any important commercial software. This was an important test at the time (the early to mid-'80s), as many clones could not pass it.

Virtually any clone made today can run both *Flight Simulator* and *1-2-3* with ease. The remaining problems tend to be more subtle, mostly showing up if you mix different clone brands of hardware, or if you don't use the clone makers' customized versions of certain key software, most importantly their versions of DOS.

The compatibility question is by no means a dead one. Though fortunately problems are relatively rare, when they occur they can be very serious. If you use various parts from different clone makers in the same PC you could be inviting trouble. If you do take this risk, you had better be careful to test the complete PC thoroughly, especially whenever you add some new part or begin using it in some new way.

All these PC-compatible computers have something essential in common. They all use as their central processor one of the chips manufactured by the Intel corporation in what Intel calls their 80x86 family, or they use one of Intel's competitors' chips that is functionally equivalent to an Intel 80x86 chip. In Chapter 13, you will meet every member of that Intel family and most of the popular alternatives.

What Is an Emulator?

An *emulator* is something that acts just like something else, but is intrinsically different. It is possible to make a computer that is not a PC act very much like a PC. When you do this, what you get is an emulator and not really a PC. The nature of memory management makes this distinction absolutely crucial.

My definition of a PC excludes a number of popular small computers. For example, it does not include the Apple *Macintosh* family. Nor does it include the Commodore *Amiga*, or computers made by Atari. All of these are a lot like PCs, but they are not considered PCs in this book because they differ in some crucial ways from the PCs built by IBM and the many other manufacturers of IBM clones.

In this book the Intel microcomprocessors with the 80?86 designations (8086, 8088, 80286, 80386, 80486, and Pentium) are referred to collectively as the 80x86 chips.

These non-PC computers aren't PCs by our definition because they use a different central processor chip (made by Motorola). That means two things: These computers have a different internal architecture, and their processors "speak"—and thus can only understand programs written in—a different language.

Sometimes one of those non-PC small computers can be made to emulate a PC by using special add-in hardware or a special program. For example, by loading the program *SoftPC*, you can run PC programs on a *Macintosh*.

Any such hybrid is so different in its internal details that one cannot usefully lump it in with PCs for the purposes of this book. So, once again: When you see *PC* in this book it always means a personal computer built around some member of the Intel 80x86 family of central processor chips.

The memory upgrade hardware covered here needs to be plugged into a "real" PC (which is to say, a computer that is very nearly a clone of an IBM *PC*, *PS/1*, or *PS/2*). The software covered here, at least for the most part, depends so much on the details of the computer's hardware that it too will work only on a "real" PC.

There is one class of emulator that is more nearly a real PC. This is a non-PC into which one has plugged a slave processor board containing all the crucial pieces of what is recognized as a PC. An example is the *Bridgeboard* for some models of Commodore's *Amiga* computer. This board, plus a floppy disk drive, contains all the components of a PC clone computer except the keyboard and monitor. Those are supplied by the host *Amiga*. In some models of *Amiga* there are even special expansion slots controlled by the *Bridgeboard* into which one can plug regular PC option cards.

If you have this sort of PC (IBM-compatible) within a PC (IBM-incompatible), you may be able to use some of the software or hardware products discussed in this book on the internal PC. For those purposes you have either an XT or an AT clone (depending on which model of slave PC board you have installed).

Why Include Only Computers Running DOS?

This book focuses on PCs that use some version of the *MS-DOS* or *PC DOS* operating system software, or the very similar operating system software from Digital Research called *DR DOS*. (Now that Digital Research has been bought by Novell, future versions of their DOS will be called *Novell DOS*.) These operating systems come in many "flavors" (for example, Compaq, Tandy, and Wyse) and versions (for example, 2.11, 3.3, and 5.0). Figure 1.1 shows the IBM "flavor," *PC DOS*, version 3.3. The "flavor" differences are discussed in Chapter 10. While there are some important differences, they share so much in common that you can refer to them all simply as DOS most of the time.

Why impose this limitation on what will be called a PC? Most of the software I am going to discuss needs DOS to run. Since almost all the PC clones in the world run DOS most or all of the time, this is not much of a limitation.

A few places in this book mention some quite different operating systems that can be used on a PC. Mainly these references are either to *OS/2* or to *UNIX*. (There are several other operating systems that can be used on PCs, but none of them have become very popular. Two that are about to become available, and which offer some interesting possibilities, are Microsoft's *Windows NT* and NeXT's *NeXTSTEP 486*. Since these are, at the time of this writing, only still unreleased "vaporware," we don't yet know how good or how popular they ultimately will turn out to be.)

```
The IBM Personal Computer DOS
Version 3.30 (C)Copyright International Business Machines Corp 1981, 1987
           (C)Copyright Microsoft Corp 1981, 1986

A>
```

Figure 1.1 The famous DOS prompt (IBM's *PC DOS*, version 3.3).

Both OS/2 and UNIX have attracted a significant number of enthusiasts. Indeed, in some circumstances they can be a better choice than *MS-DOS.* But the vast majority of PC users still run DOS.

These operating systems only work well on the more advanced models of PC. Both *UNIX* and *OS/2,* version 2, can take full advantage of the 32-bit instructions available in the 386, 486, and Pentium processors. More importantly, they also can use the full memory-management capabilities built into those chips. Of all the DOS versions, only DOS 5 and 6 come close to using all the memory-management features, and no version of DOS uses 32-bit instructions.

A major purpose of this book is to teach you how to get many of the benefits offered by *OS/2* and *UNIX* without suffering the usually painful experience of converting to either of those operating systems. The good news is, you can get almost all those benefits without having to give up your favorite DOS programs and without having to learn a whole new way to use your PC. In time, as the makers of *OS/2* and *UNIX* learn more and improve their products further, changing from DOS may become easier; but for now, it is almost certainly more difficult than any of the options detailed here.

PCs Include Computers Running Microsoft Windows and Other GUIs or DOS Shell Programs

Our focus on DOS machines also includes PCs that run various operating environments on top of DOS. That includes Quarterdeck Office System's *DESQview*, Microsoft's *Windows* and *Windows for Workgroups*, and *GeoWorks Ensemble*; it also includes task-switching program managers such as SoftLogic's *Software Carousel*. Finally, we will include a number of DOS shell programs, such as Lotus *Magellan* and *Xtree Gold*, and the shell program shipped with DOS (starting with version 4), *DOSSHELL* (see Figure 1.2).

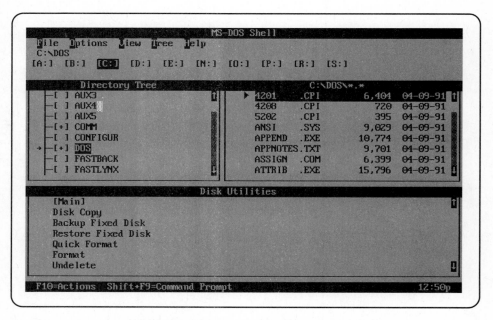

Figure 1.2 The *MS-DOS*, version 6.0, DOSSHELL.

What a lot of jargon! What is an operating environment? What is a DOS shell program, and how does it differ from a task-switching program manager or an operating environment? Explanations coming right up, and I'll throw in some for GUIs, CUIs, and WYSIWYG as well.

Operating Systems and Operating Environments

An *operating environment* is the way you and your computer communicate, the way it "looks and feels" to you. It also means how your computer appears to the application programs running under its control. The operating environment does not control what is going on at the deepest levels; that is determined by the *operating system* software.

While all the programs I'll be discussing run on top of DOS (that's the operating system), only *DESQview*, *Windows* (see Figure 1.3), and *GeoWorks Ensemble* (see Figure 1.4) are full operating environments. The rest do not modify how the computer looks to an application program, although they do alter its appearance to you.

Windows now means any of several products from Microsoft. All of them carry version number 3.1. They differ in their size and capability and in the target hardware for which they were developed.

The smallest of them is called *Modular Windows*. It is meant for use on machines that are less capable than the typical PC, possibly including home video games of the future, and maybe even copy machines, washing machines, and so on.

The next larger product is good, old *Windows*. This is the original Windows, version 3.1.

The next more capable product is *Windows for Workgroups*. Essentially a bundle of Windows, a peer-to-peer networking product more-or-less similar to *LANtastic*, and an electronic mail program, *Windows for Workgroups* is, for memory management purposes, no different from Windows (plus, of course, a network of some kind). In particular, the fact that the parent Windows part of *Windows for Workgroups* "understands" the network it is running on does nothing to reduce the amount of memory needed for the network drivers, nor does it change the amount of conventional or upper memory needed for Windows and Windows application programs.

The top-of-the-line version of *Windows*, just now coming to market, is *Windows NT*. This very powerful version is intended primarily for use in larger PCs, especially those that function as network servers. It is more like OS/2 than it is like Windows in terms of its internal structure and its use of memory—even though in appearance it is very close to ordinary *Windows*.

Since *Windows NT* is so different (and since, at the time of this writing, it is still unreleased "vaporware"), I shall say no more about it in this book.

GUIs, CUIs, and WYSIWYG

Both *Windows* and *GeoWorks Ensemble* provide, as a major aspect of their operating environments, what is now called a *GUI* (pronounced "gooey"). This is an acronym for *Graphical User Interface.* A user interface is simply the way you, the computer's user, communicate with your computer. For information coming to you, it mostly means what you see on your screen. For information going the other way, it means how you use your keyboard and any other input device (for example a mouse) to communicate with your computer.

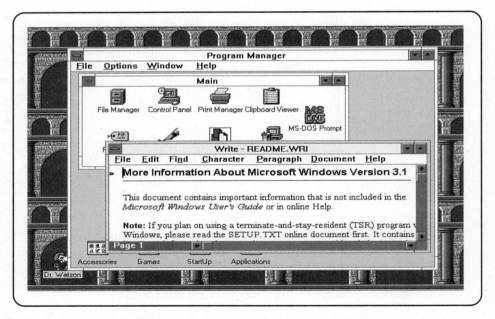

Figure 1.3 The best-selling GUI for DOS: Microsoft's *Windows* 3.1.

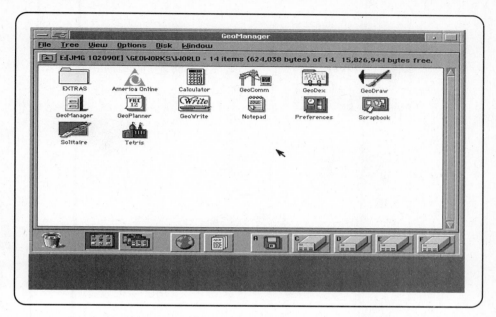

Figure 1.4 A powerful GUI that is effective even on PCs and XTs: *GeoWorks Ensemble*.

More specifically, a GUI means that information is presented on the screen in a graphical form, with icons and other images that are not merely text. It has also come to mean that you interact with your computer less by typing on the keyboard and more by pointing to objects or controls on the screen, usually by using a mouse, trackball, or graphic tablet. Notice I said *less* typing; you still must be facile with a computer keyboard to get full benefit from any PC.

The first of the programs mentioned at the start of this section, *DESQview*, does not provide a GUI. Instead it provides a *CUI*, or *Character-based User Interface* (see Figure 1.5). (CUI rhymes with GUI.) Unlike GUI, the term CUI is not commonly used, yet it seems a fairly obvious analog to GUI. In this respect, *DESQview* resembles the DOS shell programs to be discussed shortly. It differs from them, and is more like *Windows* and *GeoWorks Ensemble*, in that it presents a radically different appearance of the computer to application programs running under its control.

Another term you often hear is WYSIWYG. This is an acronym for *What You See Is What You Get.* This refers to a computer operating environment in which the appearance of text and other objects in a screen display of a document very closely resembles how they will appear on paper when that document is printed.

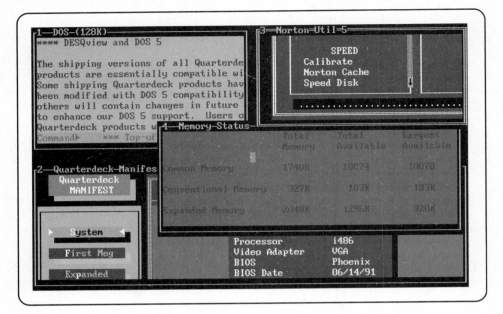

Figure 1.5 A popular text-based multitasking environment for DOS: *DESQview*, version 2.41.

A GUI can provide a WYSIWYG environment. A CUI cannot. That is because the CUI can only display letters and other symbols from a single character set (usually the character set built into the display card), while more and more modern documents include complex fonts and graphic images.

This is one of the limitations of CUIs. On the other hand, since a CUI need only send a modest amount of information to the screen for each of a limited set of character positions (most often just two bytes for each of 2,000 locations on the screen), it can redraw part or all of the screen image very quickly. A GUI, on the other hand, must send out a color and brightness value for a very large number of pixels on the screen. (Half a byte for each of 307,200 pixels is typical for VGA resolution [640×480] with 16 on-screen colors.) This means that to redraw the screen the GUI must send much more information than the CUI (more than 38 times as much in our example).

This is why *DESQview* is practical on even the slowest IBM *PC*, while *Windows* and, to a lesser extent, *GeoWorks Ensemble* need at least a moderately fast 286-based PC.

The other side of the coin is that a WYSIWYG environment can greatly heighten productivity in some situations. If you can preview documents on-screen and see accurately how they are going to look, it may be possible to avoid printing a large number of test copies before getting an acceptable document. This is a potent argument for using a GUI operating environment.

There is just one gap in this argument. Not all GUIs provide WYSIWYG. The potential is there, but the operating environment must be specially programmed to give this feature. *Windows,* for example, does not provide WYSIWYG unless you augment it with one of several third-party utility programs. (This is true for *Windows,* version 3.0. You must add *Adobe Type Manager* or a similar product to get WYSIWYG. With version 3.1, *Windows* offers WYSIWYG, but only for documents created exclusively with TrueType fonts.) *GeoWorks Ensemble,* on the other hand, has full WYSIWYG built into its basic operating environment.

The fundamentally different appearance of the computer to application programs running under *DESQview, Windows,* or *GeoWorks Ensemble* is very important. The details of the appearance they present differ somewhat, but these three programs have much in common at that level, enough so that they share a very special capability: multitasking. Just what this means and why it is so special will be explained in Chapter 21.

While these three operating environments are very different from plain DOS or DOS plus a DOS shell, all three require the presence of DOS to run. Each can still run DOS programs, though they can do more with software written to take advantage of their special qualities.

Task-Switching Program Managers

A *task-switching program manager* is a control program that manages several application programs. It allows you to jump from one application to another without shutting down the first one; later you can jump back to the first application without shutting down the second one. When you do jump back, you will find yourself exactly where you were before.

These capabilities come in many packages. SoftLogic's *Software Carousel* is one of the better-known ones. WordPerfect's *WordPerfect Office* is another (Figure 1.6), as is the shareware program *B&F* (for Back and Forth). Starting with version 4, DOS has included a task switcher in its shell program, *DOSSHELL.* Chapter 23 describes all of these programs and several others with the same abilities.

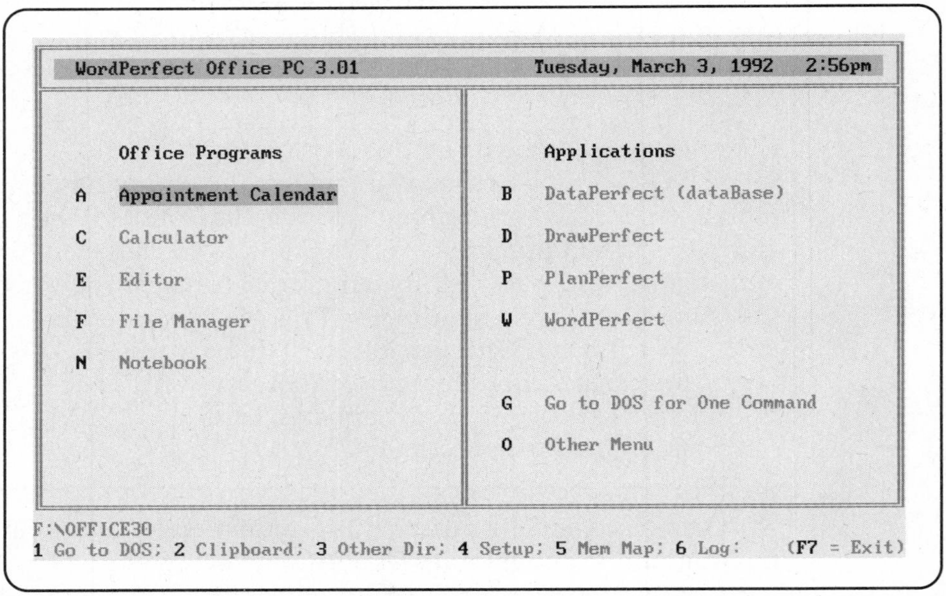

```
┌─────────────────────────────────────────────────────────────────────┐
│ WordPerfect Office PC 3.01              Tuesday, March 3, 1992  2:56pm│
│ ┌─────────────────────────────────┬─────────────────────────────────┐│
│ │                                 │                                 ││
│ │     Office Programs             │     Applications                ││
│ │                                 │                                 ││
│ │  A  Appointment Calendar        │  B   DataPerfect (dataBase)      ││
│ │                                 │                                 ││
│ │  C  Calculator                  │  D   DrawPerfect                 ││
│ │                                 │                                 ││
│ │  E  Editor                      │  P   PlanPerfect                 ││
│ │                                 │                                 ││
│ │  F  File Manager                │  W   WordPerfect                 ││
│ │                                 │                                 ││
│ │  N  Notebook                    │                                 ││
│ │                                 │  G   Go to DOS for One Command   ││
│ │                                 │                                 ││
│ │                                 │  O   Other Menu                  ││
│ │                                 │                                 ││
│ └─────────────────────────────────┴─────────────────────────────────┘│
│ F:\OFFICE30                                                           │
│ 1 Go to DOS; 2 Clipboard; 3 Other Dir; 4 Setup; 5 Mem Map; 6 Log:  (F7 = Exit)│
└─────────────────────────────────────────────────────────────────────┘
```

Figure 1.6 Task switching is easy using *WordPerfect Office*.

Some of these programs can be set to load several applications automatically and then drop out of view, letting you swap among those applications at the touch of a hot key. Others display a menu of applications whenever you want to switch. At their best, these programs not only let you jump among tasks; they also can keep you from having to see the DOS prompt—ever.

Some task-switching program managers offer only half this capability. They allow you to jump away from the first application to run a second one, but you must close the second application before you can return to the first one.

Perhaps the most popular program that offers this partial task-switching capability is the SHELL program included in *PC Tools* that is from Central Point Software. The *Swap Utilities* allow adding this capability to a number of application programs. See Chapter 23 for more details.

DOS Shell Programs

DOS shell programs are very popular. There are even more of them around than there are either task switchers or alternative operating environments for DOS. Among the most popular DOS shell programs are *Xtree Gold* (see Figure 1.7), *Magellan* from Lotus, and *Norton Commander* from Symantec's Peter Norton group. There are dozens more. (Chapter 23 describes these and some others.)

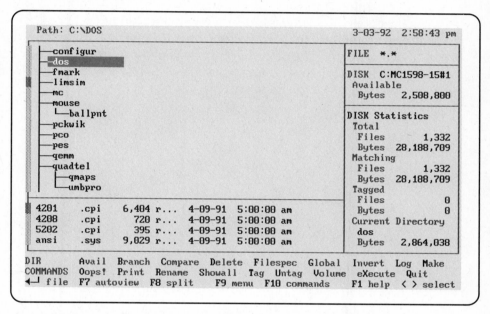

Figure 1.7 A very popular way to navigate disks and manage files is also a program launcher: *Xtree Gold*, version 2.5.

All these programs operate on top of DOS. Their purpose is to provide you with a more intuitive and easier way to find files, launch programs, and generally do what you need to do with your PC. None of these programs is capable of multitasking.

Before ending this discussion, it may be worth noting that there are even programs that provide the functionality of a DOS shell but do so with the appearance of a GUI. One such is *Titus DOS* from Titus Communications. While it looks like *Windows*, it works as only a simple program launcher.

A Recap

In this chapter you learned what a PC is, at least as the term is used in this book. You also learned some things a PC is not (and about some small computers that are, therefore, not PCs). You learned the terms *emulator, operating environment, task-switching program manager, DOS shell program, GUI, CUI,* and *WYSIWYG.* And you now know what it means for a computer to be compatible with the IBM standard of personal computing.

The term *PC* is one of three crucial terms you must understand before you can understand fully even the title of this book. You still must learn precisely what memory is in a PC, and what it means to "manage" that memory. The next chapter answers the question, "What is memory?" You will have to wait until Chapter 19 to learn what I mean by the phrase "managing a PC's memory."

2

WHAT KINDS OF MEMORY ARE WE TALKING ABOUT?

Perhaps the most common confusion about memory in PCs concerns the many different kinds you can have and what is special about each one. Here you'll begin to clear up that confusion (a process that continues in Chapter 8).

Computers must have some way to retain information. They must keep the data they process, and they must keep information about the processing they are to perform.

The places that hold information in a computer are called *memory* and *storage.* It has become traditional to give different meanings to these two words for information-holding places.

Local Versus Remote Information Retention (Memory Versus Storage)

There are several different kinds of what is loosely called memory in any PC. You may have heard many different terms referring to memory. In Part II, you can learn all about these terms, but for now I'll keep things simple. Your PC really has only two broad kinds of information-holding places.

The first kind of holding place is usually called RAM or ROM (these terms are defined later in this chapter). These places are directly connected to the central processing unit (CPU), and their contents are immediately accessible to it. This is the memory the PC uses to run programs and do calculations. (You keep programs and data files on a disk, but the only time the programs run or the data gets modified is when a copy of that program or data is in your PC's RAM.)

This is *electronic memory.* It resides on a set of integrated circuit chips (ICs) and, being fully electronic in nature, it works very quickly.

The other kind of holding place is more remote. (This means the CPU cannot directly move information into or out of it.) It is used for long-term data and program storage. Most often this is magnetic storage on some sort of disk, although it can be on magnetic tape, optical disks, or any of a variety of other media.

Magnetic media provide a great place for keeping information, but they do have one deficiency compared to electronic memory: While it takes very little time in human terms to save a chunk of information to magnetic storage or to retrieve it, in electronic terms the time it takes is almost interminable. The reason is that magnetic storage always involves moving mechanical parts. Moving them takes time, much more time than moving electrons. (Another name for this kind of holding place is electro-mechanical storage.)

Optical storage is steadily gaining in popularity. The attraction is a very large storage capacity in a small space, with a relatively low cost per megabyte. Two factors have slowed the development of these systems. One is that despite a low per-megabyte cost, the absolute cost of these systems has, until recently, been quite high. Second is their relatively slow speed. Their access times and data transfer rates are much slower than for hard disks.

There are three kinds of optical computer information storage systems: *CD-ROM, WORM,* and *read-write optical.* The first kind, and by far the least expensive, uses a compact disc, much like an audio compact disc. CD-ROM stands for **C**ompact **D**isc-**R**ead **O**nly **M**emory. As the name suggests, it can only be used for information prerecorded on the disks. The WORM drives are **W**rite **O**nce, **R**ead **M**ostly devices. These are similar to PROMs, in that you can record information at any one location only once. The third variety, read-write optical (sometimes they use magneto-optical technology, which is why that is another common name for this type of drive), is most like a normal hard drive. The salient differences are a generally larger capacity, slower speed, and much higher cost (so far).

Since this remote storage is generally much slower than RAM and ROM and, more to the point, much slower than the central processor chip, it is unsuitable for direct use in the instant-to-instant job of computing.

This difference in speed is the main reason magnetic storage is a bit removed from the computing process. Only electronic chips are fast enough to keep up in that arena. (In Chapters 14, 16, and 17 you will learn that sometimes electronic memory chips aren't fast enough to keep up with today's speedy processor chips, and you'll learn some ways to deal with that problem.)

There are such things as fully electronic storage devices. They are called *solid-state disks.* These devices work about as fast as the main system RAM, but since they are provided with a means to keep them powered at all times (a battery and charger, usually), they also have nearly the permanency of magnetic media. A phrase used to describe that feature is *nonvolatile memory.* One example of this technology is the line of *Silicon Disks* from Atto Technology.

Solid-state disks have only one disadvantage, but so far it has proven to be a big one: They cost between ten and one hundred times as much, per megabyte, as magnetic storage devices. Except for their cost, they are wonderful. Because of that, they are—so far—very rare.

To reiterate, we use the two words, *memory* and *storage,* in the following way and in this way only:

Memory   Immediately accessible information-holding places (normally electronic and very fast).

Storage   Remote information-holding places (normally magnetic/mechanical, and thus slower than memory).

This book is concerned mostly with the management of memory. Management of disk storage is a topic that has been covered by many authors quite competently and completely. This book fills the need for equally comprehensive information about RAM and ROM management.

The two topics sometimes overlap. It is possible and sometimes very useful to use some disk space to imitate RAM (called *virtual memory*) or some RAM to imitate a disk (a *virtual disk*). You need to know how and how well such imitations can be done. Only then can you understand why you would or would not want to use them.

Put another way, the focus of this book is on making your computer compute better. Hard disk management books focus on how to arrange information on your computer's hard disk in ways that will increase your efficiency, and to a lesser degree enhance the efficiency of your computer.

Meet Some of the Actors (and Learn Their Funny Names)

You will get to know all about the many different kinds of electronic memory and memory chips in Chapter 16. But since their names fill most discussions about PCs, it may be useful for you to get a brief introduction to them now. After you read Chapters 16 and 17, you also will know when to use which ones, and why.

Some Common Varieties of Electronic Memory

RAM stands for *Random-Access Memory*. This means memory you can access at random, as opposed to *sequential access*, which is the term used to describe magnetic tape as an information-holding medium. Anytime you want to read from or write to two separate locations on a tape, you must go past all the intervening locations on the way. Randomly accessible memory allows you to go directly to each location in any order you choose.

> A PC disk drive provides neither strictly random access nor fully sequential access. It is a hybrid of the two. The heads may be moved to any cylinder you like and the particular head you want can be activated at random. But then you must wait until the sector you are interested in comes around to the head.

While it is technically accurate to apply the term *random-access memory* to any memory with random accessibility, it has become customary to use it almost exclusively for those randomly accessible memory units that operate at electronic speeds and can easily change the information they are storing. Another name for this last feature, and now almost a synonym for RAM, is *read-write memory*.

RAM is where the PC stores working copies of programs and the data these programs process. An important property of most RAM is that these chips "forget" everything the instant the electric power is removed. That's why they can be used only to store temporary copies of your valuable information. Some varieties of RAM follow:

- *SRAM* stands for *Static Random-Access Memory*. The only common use for these in PCs is as the super-fast (and super-expensive) chips in the most demanding parts of the highest performance PCs.

- *DRAM* stands for *Dynamic Random-Access Memory*. These are the moderately fast, quite inexpensive memory chips used in most PCs.

- *VRAM* stands for *Video Random-Access Memory*. These chips are a special kind of DRAM (called dual-ported) used mostly in extra-fast video display cards.

ROM stands for *Read-Only Memory*. This is also randomly accessible, electronically fast memory. It is really a special kind of RAM, but there is one very important difference between RAM and ROM. As its name suggests, the information contained in ROM cannot change. This is a great way to store a few programs or some data that the CPU chip must always have immediately accessible. It is not useful for much else. A PC absolutely must have some of this (at least for a start-up program and some essential data tables). It usually has much more of the read-write kind of RAM.

> If you want to confound your friends, cultivate the habit of calling RAM by the longer and harder-to-pronounce name, *RWRAM*, standing for *Read-Write Random-Access Memory*. Then when you want to speak of ROM use the more complete term *RORAM*, standing for *Read-Only Random-Access Memory*. Of course, if this idea appeals to you, then you probably confound your friends already, and this will not add much to their confusion.

- *Mask-Programmable ROM* is the name given to memory chips whose information is manufactured into them at the factory. These are the only ROM chips that truly are forever. They cannot have their information content changed at all.

There are also several varieties of "almost-ROMs." These are chips that retain whatever information you put into them for years. What is special about them is that the information they hold can be altered, though not necessarily easily. It may be an oxymoron, but everyone calls them **P**rogrammable **R**ead-**O**nly **M**emory chips. Here are the most important varieties:

- *PROM* is an acronym for *Programmable Read-Only Memory*. If you read or hear the term *PROM*, it probably refers to *fuse-programmable ROM*. These chips will remember what you tell them just about forever. You can alter the information stored in each location within them, with some difficulty, just once. Another name for these chips is *One-time-programmable Read-Only Memory* (*OTP-ROM*).

> When these chips are manufactured, every single bit location has a solid piece of "wire" (a conductive trace on or in the surface of the silicon chip) that shorts out that location. This makes it report that it is storing a one-bit there.

By overloading that location in just the proper manner, that "wire" can be blown out just like an overloaded fuse. That makes the location report that it is storing a zero-bit. This change is irreversible. That is why one can only program these devices once at any given location, to change the one into a zero.

- *EPROM* stands for *Erasable Programmable Read-Only Memory*. These chips are like PROMs in that they will remember what you tell them (for several years at least). They are different in that you can erase them by shining a bright ultraviolet light through a window on top of the chip. They are also called *UV-EPROMs*.

  When you erase one of these, it "forgets" all of the information it contains. To erase it, you remove the memory chip from the computer, place it in a special UV eraser, and shine the UV light on it for at least several minutes. Loading the chip with new information is done in another special machine before the chip is put back into the computer. That operation also takes minutes.

- *EEPROM* stands for *Electrically Erasable Programmable Read-Only Memory*. The name says it. These chips remember what you tell them until, by using a special electrical signal, you erase that information and start over again.

  When you want to erase some of the information, typically you must erase it all. This takes a significant amount of time (a fraction of a second). Writing the new information usually takes several seconds.

- *Flash PROM* is the newest kind of PROM. Sometimes called *Flash RAM,* these chips are merely a special kind of EEPROM. They can have small parts of their stored information erased independently. Erasure takes about a second.

  Reading from these devices and writing new information to them takes about the same time. This characteristic makes Flash RAM chips especially suitable for use as electronic replacements for disk drives. They may also find popularity as easily reprogrammable BIOS ROM chips. This possibility is described in more detail in Chapter 16.

While there are exceptions, most ROMs cannot be read as quickly as the RAM chips commonly used in PCs. This is why shadow RAM is sometimes used. You can learn all about that subject in Chapter 20.

Once again, this is just an introduction to these characters with the odd-sounding names. Chapter 10 contains more details. My purpose here is just to familiarize you with the most common terms you will see in advertisements and hear mentioned in discussions about PC memory.

Some Ways Memory Chips Are Packaged

Modern radios, TV sets, and digital wristwatches—let alone the modern computer—would not be possible without *integrated circuits.* These are a means of putting many individual electronic circuits onto single, small pieces of highly refined material, usually silicon.

This invention is crucial, for the largest expense in making and using circuits is in handling them. By putting as many as a million circuits into one small package, it is possible to make and sell the entire collection for just a few dollars. Before integrated circuits, that same collection of around a million transistors, each in its own package, would have cost at least several hundred thousand dollars—and wiring them all together would have more than doubled that cost.

There are many ways that memory circuits can be packaged. The circuits are first crafted onto a single large wafer of silicon. After testing the individual circuits, this wafer is divided into many small chips. Each chip, perhaps along with other similar chips, must be mounted in a package that can both protect it and connect its leads with the larger overall computer circuit. Here are a few of the more popular package names:

- *DIP* stands for *Dual Inline Package*. These are the little many-legged "bugs" that are so ubiquitous on the circuit boards of most PCs (see Figure 2.1a). The legs are its connections to the outside world. The DIP is either inserted in a socket or its legs are pushed through holes in a circuit board and soldered in place.

- *SOJ* (*Small Outline J-lead*) and *Miniflat* are two surface-mount packages (see Figure 2.1b and c). These are soldered or welded to a circuit board. Their closer lead spacing, their small body size, and the fact that they only attach to one side of the circuit board all contribute to a much higher memory density than is possible with DIPs.

- *SIMM* stands for *Single Inline Memory Module*. This is a small circuit board sporting a number of memory chips. It connects to the larger circuit through gold-plated fingers on one edge of the board. See Figure 2.1c. (The individual chips on this SIMM are in SOJ packages.)

- *SIP* stands for *Single Inline Package*. Imagine cutting off all the legs on one side of a DIP and standing it on edge. That's a SIP. See Figure 2.1d.

- *SIPP* means *Single Inline Pin Package*. This is a SIMM with round pins instead of flat leads.

- *ZIP* means *Zigzag Inline Package*. Not surprisingly, this is another variation on the SIP, this time with the pins staggered along one edge of the package. See Figure 2.1e.

- *UV-EPROM* chips are packed in a special kind of DIP with a window on top. Shining bright ultraviolet light through the window erases the information stored in the circuits of the chip. See Figure 2.1f.

A Recap

Now you know what memory is (as opposed to storage), and you have been introduced to the funny names for all the most important types of memory chips and the packages in which they arrive.

This means that you now know the meaning of two of the three crucial terms that describe the subject of this book: *PC* and *memory*. Before going on to define the third term, *memory management*, we must cover some more background information. The next chapter leads you through an assessment procedure to see what the pieces of your PC system are. Chapter 4 helps you figure out just what you need. Part I then ends with a chapter with some important warnings.

Part II (Chapters 6 through 22) will finally answer the question "What is memory management in PCs?" and tell you the principles behind it.

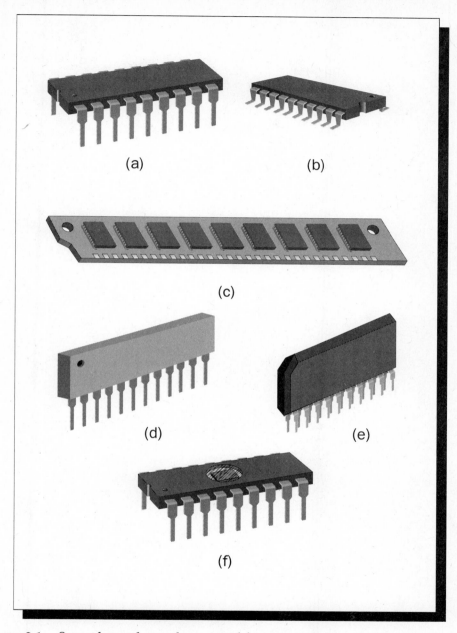

Figure 2.1. Several popular packages used for memory chips: (a) DIP, (b)Miniflat, (c) SIMM, (d) SIP, (e) ZIP, and (f) UV-EPROM.

3

ASSESSING YOUR PRESENT SYSTEM

What do you have in your present PC? You must know this to know what you can do with it and what you may need to add to it. This chapter helps you determine both the hardware and the essential software that make up your PC.

Before you can improve your PC, you need to know what you already have. This chapter will help you to find out and to see where your PC fits into a useful classification scheme.

Perhaps the clearest way to explain what you need to know is through a checklist. In the next section you will find a number of questions. If you don't know the answer to some of the questions (or even if you don't know what some of the words in the questions mean), don't worry; just skip over them for now. At least you'll have an idea of what facts you must discover about your PC.

If you can easily answer all the questions, you *could* skip the following section, "How To Find Out What You Have Now." Please don't. While the primary purpose of that section is to help you find answers to these assessment questions, its secondary purpose is to define six broad classes of PCs and help you find out which one yours fits in. Knowing which class your PC belongs to will tell you which of Chapters 23, 24, and 25 you will be most interested in reading. These classes are also referred to in many other places in this book.

If you have any doubts about how to answer one or more of the assessment questions, you definitely will want to read the section, "How to Find Out What You Have Now." It will give you a number of strategies for finding the answers to the assessment questions, even if you don't understand exactly what all the words in some of the questions mean!

Your Present System (an Assessment Checklist)

1. The central processing unit (CPU) in your PC is (check one of the following):

   ___ An Intel *8088, 8086* or equivalent (these include the Intel *80C88* and *80C86* as well as the *NEC V20* and *V30* and various other equivalent CPU chips).

   ___ An Intel *80286* or equivalent (including the *80C286* from Intel or either of these numbers from AMD, Harris or another maker).

   ___ An Intel *80386SX* or equivalent (AMD is an alternative source for this).

   ___ An Intel *80386DX* or equivalent (AMD is an alternative source for this).

___ An Intel *80486SX* or *80486DX* or equivalent (AMD is an alternative source for this).

___ An Intel *Pentium*.

2. How much random access memory (RAM) do you have in your PC and how is it configured? Complete the following (1,024KB [kilobytes] = 1MB [megabyte]):

   _____ KB or _____ MB of conventional memory

   _____ KB or _____ MB of extended memory

   _____ KB or _____ MB of expanded (EMS) memory

3. Does your PC have a plug-in card installed which includes EMS hardware? ___ yes, ___ no. If yes, complete the following:

   It is compatible with (check one) version ___ 3.2 or ___ 4.0 of the LIM specification and supplies _____ KB of the expanded memory listed in the previous question.

4. Record the manufacturer and model of your PC's motherboard system logic (chip set):

   Manufacturer: _____.

   Model: _____.

   (Some possible manufacturer names are Chips and Technology, Headland Technology, IBM, Intel, LSI, Opti, Texas Instruments, and Western Digital.)

   Is it capable of supplying shadow RAM? ___ yes, ___ no.

   Is it capable of supplying EMS memory using some of the installed motherboard RAM? ___ yes, ___ no. If yes, complete the following:

   That EMS memory is compatible with version ___ 3.2 or ___ 4.0 of the LIM specification.

   Does it include Flash Bios? ___ yes, ___ no.

5. Record the total hard disk storage space you have: (**Note:** This question is not, strictly speaking, a part of your memory-management assessment. But it does address an important aspect of what you have, so it is included here. To work on hard disk management, you'll need this information; it is also important

to know this if you add a large program for memory management or an alternative operating environment.)

_____ MB, of which _____ MB are now available for use.

6. What other memory do you have in your PC? Complete all that apply:

___ A monochrome video card with _____ KB of RAM

___ A CGA video card with _____ of RAM (usually 32KB)

___ An EGA video card with _____ KB of RAM (64KB up to 256KB)

___ A VGA video card with _____ KB of RAM (256KB up to 2 MB)

___ An XGA video card with _____ MB of RAM (typically 4MB)

___ A network card with _____ KB of RAM

___ A caching hard disk controller card with _____ KB of RAM

A solid-state disk with _____ KB of RAM

7. Which brand and version of DOS are you using?

___ *PC DOS* (IBM), version _____

___ *MS-DOS* (Microsoft), version _____

If you use *MS-DOS*, it may be the "vanilla" version or one customized by a PC hardware manufacturer. Enter here the manufacturer's name if your *MS-DOS* copy has been customized: _____

___ *DR DOS* (Digital Research) (or) *Novell DOS* (Novell) version _____

8. Do you use an expanded memory manager? If so, provide its name and version.

Name: _____, version: _____.

9. Do you use an XMS manager? If so, provide its name and version.

Name: _____, version: _____.

10. Are you using another memory-management program? (Some possible names include *386MAX*, *QEMM*, *Memory Commander*, *QMAPS*, *QRAM*, *Move'Em*, *LIMSIM*, *Above Disk*, *Turbo EMS*, and

UMBPro.) If so provide its name and version (you could be using more than one, though not likely at the same time, in which case list each of them here):

Name: _____, version: _____.

Name: _____, version: _____.

Name: _____, version: _____.

11. Are you presently loading anything into the HMA (**High Memory Area**)? (___ yes, ___ no) If yes, which program uses the HMA? (**Note:** Only one program **at a time** can use the HMA.)

Name: _____, version: _____.

Name: _____, version: _____.

Name: _____, version: _____.

12. Are you using an alternative operating environment on top of DOS? If so, indicate which one here:

___ Microsoft *Windows*, version _____.

___ Quarterdeck's *DESQview*, version _____.

___ *GeoWorks Ensemble*, version _____.

___ Other: _____, version: _____.

13. Are you using a task-switching program manager or a DOS shell program? If so indicate which one(s) here:

Name: _____, version: _____.

Name: _____, version: _____.

Name: _____, version: _____.

14. List all the device drivers you normally load through your CONFIG.SYS file:

Name: _____, version: _____.

Name: _____, version: _____.

Name: _____, version: _____.

Name: _____, version: _____.

Name: _____, version: _____.

Name: _____, version: _____.

15. List all the TSR programs you normally load in your PC:

    Name: _____, version: _____.

    Name: _____, version: _____.

    Name: _____, version: _____.

    Name: _____, version: _____.

    Name: _____, version: _____.

    Name: _____, version: _____.

16. Is your PC connected to a network? ___ yes, ___ no. If yes, provide the brand of network and the version of the software you are using here:

    Name: _____, version: _____.

17. If your PC is connected to a network, what is the nature of that connection? (Some possibilities are an *EtherNet*, *Token Ring*, or *ARCnet* card, or a serial port connection, also known as a "zero-slot LAN.")

    Type of network connection: _____.

18. Some options in a PC use a portion of the memory address space for option ROMs or for some RAM. If you have any such options you must determine which areas of memory they are using. As you do so, list each one here:

    Option name: _____ using addresses from _____ (hexadecimal) to _____ (hexadecimal) for (check one) ___ RAM or ___ ROM.

    Option name: _____ using addresses from _____ (hexadecimal) to _____ (hexadecimal) for (check one) ___ RAM or ___ ROM.

    Option name: _____ using addresses from _____ (hexadecimal) to _____ (hexadecimal) for (check one) ___ RAM or ___ ROM.

    Option name: _____ using addresses from _____ (hexadecimal) to _____ (hexadecimal) for (check one) ___ RAM or ___ ROM.

Option name: _____ using addresses from
_____ (hexadecimal) to _____ (hexadecimal) for (check
one) ___ RAM or ___ ROM.

Option name: _____ using addresses from
_____ (hexadecimal) to _____ (hexadecimal) for (check
one) ___ RAM or ___ ROM.

There, that ought to do it. These are not all the questions you might usefully ask about your PC, but the answers provide a good starting point for figuring out what memory you have and what strategies you are using to manage it.

Before you go on to the next chapter, read the following section at least enough to understand in which of the six classes of PC yours belongs. You'll need that information to answer some questions in Chapter 4.

How to Find Out What You Have Now

While some PC owners know just what they have in that big, beige box called the system unit, many more haven't a clue. If you don't know what sort of PC you have, you can't know what you could do to improve it.

Knowing what you have means more than just knowing what all the pieces of hardware are. You also need to know:

- Which major application programs you run.

- What operating system (both type and version) you are using.

- What (if any) operating environment, task-switching program manager, or DOS shell program you are using.

- What device drivers and utility programs are loaded in your system.

- How much memory each of your application programs needs.

This section offers you several strategies to find out that information about your PC. Along the way you should find your answers to the assessment checklist near the beginning of this chapter.

The Six Classes of PC Hardware

What you are about to read may confuse you if you don't know the meaning of some of the jargon. Don't let that concern you. For now, you don't need to know how to define all these terms. That knowledge will come as you read Part II. What matters is to determine into which class of PC yours fits. This section will give you all you need to determine that.

All PCs can be put into one of six classes. Which one your PC falls into determines some fundamental limits on what you can do in terms of memory upgrades and memory management. Which CPU chip is used in your PC is almost enough to determine which class of PC you have. In some cases, there are some extra facts you need to know to make the final discrimination.

The six classes of PCs are distinguished by the answers to these three questions: (1) How much total memory can this PC address? (2) Can this PC have any upper (RAM) memory? (3) Is this PC able to run the latest generation of memory-management software?

> The first distinction matters if you need to have huge amounts of RAM. The second one controls how much room you can open up for a conventional DOS program (by loading programs into upper memory).
>
> The third distinction is of more general applicability than might at first appear. It really is about separating those PCs that can run any program that includes 32-bit instructions from those that cannot.

Figure 3.1 shows a whimsical representation of three broad categories of PC, based just on how much memory each can have at most. Think of this capacity as the size of the information "bookshelves" in the PC. Just as having a lot of bookshelf space doesn't necessarily imply having a lot of books, so, too, having the potential for a lot of memory is not the same thing as having a lot of memory. But without bookshelf space, you have nowhere to keep books, and without a PC having the ability to accommodate large amounts of RAM, there is no way you can add that much RAM to it.

Figure 3.1.   Three broad categories of PC, based on the maximum total memory each can have.

Figure 3.2 shows the six classes of PC. It also shows you the answers to the three questions listed above for each class, namely how much total memory each can have (at most), and which ones can have upper memory or can run the latest, most advanced memory-management (and other 32-bit) software.

Category	I		II			III
Maximum Extended Memory	0 MB		15 MB			4 GB
Can have Upper Memory Blocks (UMBs)	NO	YES	NO	YES		
Can run programs that use 32-bit instructions	NO				YES	
Processor Type	8088 or 8086	8088 or 8086 with special hardware	80286	80286 with special hardware	386SX	386DX, 486SX, 486DX or Pentium
Class	1	2	3	4	5	6

Figure 3.2. The six classes of PC for the purposes of memory upgrades and memory management. (Also shown on the inside front cover for quick reference.)

If you already know the answers to assessment questions 1, 3, and 4, then you will immediately recognize your PC's class in the list below. If not, you'll be able to place it from the information you gather as you follow the suggestions provided. First, though, here is a list of those classes with a brief description of each.

- Class 1: The simple XTs.

  This group includes the original IBM *PC*, the IBM *PC/XT*, the IBM *PS/2*, models *25* and *30*, and all the clones of those machines.

  A subgroup of this class is those XTs which have an expanded memory plug-in board conforming to the **L**otus-**I**ntel-**M**icrosoft **E**xpanded **M**emory **S**pecification (LIM EMS), version 3.2 or earlier. (PCs whose EMS memory conforms to a later version of that specification are in class 2.)

  Some PCs that would otherwise be in this class have been lifted out of it by adding some other hardware. For example, an Orchid *Tiny Turbo* card will move an IBM *PC* or IBM *PC/XT* up to class 4, while an Intel *Inboard 386/PC* will move a PC all the way up to class 5, though in each of these cases the converted PC has some limitations not shared by other members of its new class.

- Class 2: Fancier XTs.

  These computers are XTs that have been upgraded with a special kind of expanded memory card conforming either to the LIM EMS, version 4.0, or to the EEMS (**E**nhanced **E**xpanded **M**emory **S**pecification). This is enough of a difference to make for some interesting new possibilities in memory management. (If you have an EEMS expanded memory card, you can get full LIM 4.0 EMS performance simply by upgrading to a new software driver program.)

  In some PCs that would otherwise be in class 1, this upgrade is not done by plugging in a special memory card. Instead, they have a special feature in their motherboard system logic (also known as their chip set) that enables it to create EMS memory out of motherboard memory. If that EMS memory conforms to version 4.0 of the LIM EMS standard, then those PCs are class 2 machines.

- Class 3: Simple ATs.

  This group of 80286-based PCs includes the original IBM *PC/AT*, the IBM *PC/XT 286*, and the IBM *PS/2*, model 30-286. And, of course, it includes all the clones of those machines.

- Class 4: ATs with LIM 4.0 EMS.

  These are 80286-based PCs. Some of them have an actual EMS plug-in card installed. Others emulate the effect of such a card through the use of a special feature in their motherboard system logic (also known as their chip set) that can convert some of what would otherwise be extended memory on the motherboard into EMS memory. The most famous maker of such chip sets is Chips and Technology. They use designations such as *NEAT* or *LEAP* for their chip sets. There are other makers of motherboard system logic, many of whose designs have similar features.

- Class 5: 386SX-based PCs.

    Any PC with an 80386SX CPU chip is in this class. The IBM *PS/2* models 55SX and 65SX are members. Many clone computers, including some very popular laptop computers, fall into this class.

    Some PCs with a lower-level processor have been moved into this class by the addition of a processor upgrade.

- Class 6: 386DX-, 486-, or Pentium-based PCs.

    The first computer in this class was the *Compaq DeskPro 386*. This group now includes all the models in the IBM *PS/2* line numbered 70 or above, plus a great many clones.

    A comment on the PC classes: Having a PC in a higher class allows you to do more with its memory. Nothing *requires* you to do so. Many people have class 5 or 6 PCs that they use as if they were class 3 machines. Since you are reading a book on memory management, you probably want at least to know what new memory tricks are possible if yours is one of the higher class PCs. Just remember that you can always opt not to use some of those tricks if you find you don't need them.

Classifying Your PC

How do you figure out which of these classes of PC you have? All it takes to place your PC are the answers to assessment questions 1, 3, and 4. If you don't already have those answers, read on. (It is a good idea to read on anyway, and to try out the various suggestions. You may learn other valuable things about your PC.)

There are many different ways to ferret out information about your PC. I'll start with the easiest. While your main goal is to determine your PC's class, an important secondary goal is to find answers for all the questions on the assessment checklist. This section tells you several ways to go about looking. The two later sections ("Counting All Your PC's Memory" and "Looking for Memory Management and Other Operating Environment Software") help you interpret what you find.

Some Especially Easy Clues

Sometimes a PC comes with a clear label that declares what it is. If it says IBM *Personal Computer*, it is a *PC* (which is in the XT class of PC); if it says it is an IBM *PC/AT*, that's what it is. Many XT clones have XT in their name. Similarly, AT and 386 get included in the names of many clone computers.

Naturally, this is only a hint as to what is inside the box. In particular, you will not know from this clue alone exactly which model of PC, XT, or AT you have, but it does give you a good starting point. Someone could have upgraded even a lowly PC to class 2, 3, 4, or 5 by adding one or more plug-in cards. I'll cover how to check for that possibility shortly.

Another easy way to get valuable information may be by looking at your sales slip. Whoever sold you the PC may have written down what kind it is and what options it contains.

Watch the Screen As Your PC Boots

When you turn on your PC, it starts itself automatically. This is something even mainframe computers were unable to do as recently as 30 years ago. Back then the computer operator had to enter a small program, called the *bootstrap loader*, by toggling some switches on the front panel. Once that program was running, the computer was able to load an operating system (usually from a magnetic tape or a deck of punched cards) and the computer was up and running. The name *bootstrap loader* comes from the expression, "pulling yourself up by the bootstraps."

All modern computers can boot themselves. They are built to run a permanently installed program as the very first thing when "waking up." That program usually is designed to load an operating system, but first it can do a number of useful tests.

The boot program in a PC is located in a ROM on the motherboard. That ROM also contains a number of miniprograms that can be used by application programs to operate the hardware. Collectively these programs are called the PC's *Basic Input-Output System,* or *BIOS.*

The first thing any PC does when you turn it on is check itself. This *Power On Self Test,* or *POST,* does more than determine which of the six classes of computer you have. It also tests the integrity of the RAM in your PC and looks to see what other parts it has. When the POST finishes, the bootstrap loader finds and loads the operating system which then initializes the computer, readying it for work. This whole process is called *booting* the computer.

By watching the messages that appear on your PC's screen during the POST and as the boot process finishes, you may be able to tell which class of PC you have. (These messages also provide information you will need to answer some of the questions in the assessment checklist, so copy them down even if they are not relevant to the simple task of classifying your PC.)

What the POST Tells You

You want to know all that the POST has to tell you. Its messages are valuable clues, and they are certainly easy to come by. However, there may be one difficulty. Some PCs work too fast: the messages come so rapidly that they scroll off the screen before you can read them.

Sometimes you can make the PC pause long enough to let you read those messages by pressing the Pause key (if your keyboard has that key) or by holding down the Ctrl key and pressing the NumLock key. Pressing any other key will start your PC going again. If that works, write down each of the messages, pausing and restarting the PC as necessary.

Alternatively, you might try pressing the PrintScreen key. On some PCs you must hold down the Shift key and then press the PrintScreen key. If you are lucky, this will send a copy of whatever is on-screen to your printer. (Naturally you must first be sure your printer is turned on, on-line, and has enough paper.) On some keyboards the PrintScreen label is printed on the front edge of the key cap, so look there as well as on the key tops.

These techniques may only work for messages that come during the processing of the AUTOEXEC.BAT file, not those that appear during CONFIG.SYS processing.

Finally, you may simply have to reboot your computer several times, watching very closely each time. Write down another part of the messages each time until you finally have them all recorded. (If your PC has a reset button, use that to do these reboots. If your PC does not, you can use Ctrl-Alt-Del to see all but the earliest messages. Either of these methods is a little kinder to your PC than turning the power off and back on.)

What should you look for? Many PCs first put up a message saying which video card they have and perhaps tell how much memory is installed on that card. After that, if yours is a clone PC, you will most likely get a message telling you the make and version of the motherboard BIOS. This is not always the same as the make of the motherboard system board logic (the chip set), but it often is. (IBM makes both the BIOS and the motherboard system logic for its PCs. Its BIOS does not normally put any identification messages on-screen; only a non-IBM BIOS does.)

Next you will see some numbers as the PC checks its RAM. If there is only one number, its maximum value will be the total amount of RAM you have, including both conventional memory and extended memory. If you have two numbers, the left-hand one is usually the conventional memory and the right-hand one is the extended memory. Rarely you will see three numbers at this time, with the third one identified as the amount of expanded memory you have.

One exception you may wish to note: If there are some bad RAM chips in your PC, the POST will stop testing memory when it comes to them. The maximum number reported on-screen is what it found without accessing the bad chip(s). If you are getting a smaller number than you expect, this is one possible cause.

Some POST programs will give an error message when they detect a bad location in RAM. Others will simply stop RAM testing, record how much good RAM they found, and go on to the next step in booting the PC.

If you have a PC in classes 3 through 6 and the information in its CMOS chip (the nonvolatile memory chip that holds configuration information about your PC) about how much RAM you have gets altered, the POST may stop checking when it reaches that altered value. Before you suspect you have bad RAM chips, it is worth checking the CMOS chip entries for conventional and extended memory. (You do that checking by running your PC's setup program, but read the upcoming warning note before you do this.)

If yours is a PC- or XT-class machine (one using an 8088 or 8086 CPU chip), you cannot have any extended memory, so all you will see here is your conventional memory. (Chapters 13 and 14 explain this limitation.) If yours is an AT, 386, 486, or Pentium machine (one using an 80286, 80386, 80486, or Pentium CPU chip), you could have both conventional and extended memory. If the POST does not show you the two numbers separately you will have to check further to see how your total RAM is apportioned between these two uses.

Device Driver Announcements

The next set of messages is likely to announce the loading of various device drivers. A device driver is a program that extends the BIOS or DOS to enable it to handle some new device. (These include both physical devices, such as a mouse, and logical fictions, such as a virtual disk created out of extended memory. Chapter 10 explains this idea in more detail and defines BIOS and DOS.)

If you have hardware EMS (that is, a plug-in EMS memory card), and you have included the appropriate driver line in your CONFIG.SYS file, you will see that program announce its presence. That driver program also may test the EMS memory and in the process tell you how much of it there is.

If you have a machine in classes 4 through 6, you may have an EMS device driver that is converting extended memory into expanded memory. Look for the name of the driver (which will be near the beginning of its announcement line) to help you know if this is the case.

If the device name is EMM386, *QEMM* (QEMM.SYS or QEMM386.SYS), *386MAX, QMAPS*, or *Memory Commander* (MC.SYS), you most likely have a 386, 486, or Pentium processor (a PC in class 5 or 6) and this device driver could be providing EMS memory by converting some of your extended memory. To know whether it is, you will have to look at the relevant lines of your CONFIG.SYS file or use a utility program provided with that device driver—unless, that is, you see a clear announcement on-screen about how much EMS memory it has created for you. (Device driver names in the CONFIG.SYS file include their extension—commonly EXE, SYS, COM, or BIN.)

If the device driver name is *QRAM, MOVE'EM*, or *UMBPRO*, you most likely have a PC in class 4. Again, this device driver could be providing EMS memory, but to be sure you will have to check a bit further (unless it tells you on-screen).

Other device driver announcements may tell you about loading a mouse driver, an interface to some network card, an optical disk interface, or the like. These are not *providers* of memory; they are *consumers* of it. Knowing which ones you have will be valuable as you try to figure out your PC's memory budget.

Looking for TSR Programs

Once the CONFIG.SYS file is fully processed and the command processor is loaded, your PC begins processing the AUTOEXEC.BAT file. (Don't worry if these terms are gobbledegook to you now. Chapters 10 and 20 explain them in great detail.)

Some lines in your AUTOEXEC.BAT file may direct the PC to do things that don't affect its use of memory; others may cause actions that do. In particular, you may be loading a number of **T**erminate and **S**tay **R**esident programs (TSRs for short). The DOS programs PRINT and AP-PEND are examples. *SideKick* and *Superkey* are two more. Spotting a TSR at this point is not easy unless you can identify it by name. You probably will have to wait until a later stage and use a utility program to be sure which TSR programs are loaded.

Look at Your PC's CMOS Data

If you have an AT or higher class of PC (one in classes 3 through 6), you have something called a CMOS chip, on which information about your PC's configuration is stored—information you are trying to discover.

CMOS stands for *Complementary Metal-Oxide Semiconductor*, and it refers to the process by which the chip was made. The significance of the CMOS process is that chips made this way require very little power to operate. The CMOS chip in your PC has a small amount of RAM, and it is kept operating by a small battery which will probably last several years. This means it can retain information about your PC's configuration between work sessions, even though you may turn off power to the PC.

This same CMOS chip also keeps track of the time and date. It does this by using an oscillator circuit, either on the chip or near it on the motherboard. Often the first symptom that the CMOS chip's battery is failing is that the PC will "wake up" with an erroneous idea of what time it is.

It's a bit of a misnomer to call this configuration storage chip your PC's CMOS chip. This suggests that there are no other chips in your PC that were manufactured using the CMOS process. Once that was true, but now it hardly ever is. Still, the name has stuck, so if you hear or read about a CMOS chip in a PC, you can be fairly sure that the reference is to the clock and configuration information storage chip.

If, during the boot process, you have ever seen a message such as Press DEL for setup or diagnostics or Press F2 for setup, you have one of these chips. (There are other wordings; these are typical.) You also have a CMOS chip if your installation manual included a floppy disk with a SETUP program. IBM brand PCs, including all models of the IBM *PS/2* line have this program on their *Diagnostic Diskette* (PCs) or *Reference Diskette* (*PS/2*s). In all cases those programs are activated by booting off that special floppy disk.

Warning   If your PC requires the use of a SETUP program run from floppy disk, it may be one of the few that will not display the configuration information. One of these (fortunately fairly rare) PCs only allows you to tell it what its configuration is. If you don't know the right answers and you guess wrong, you could render your PC unable to boot or otherwise impair its operation.

Some early IBM *PC/AT*s have this problem. If you do not know whether yours does, be sure to find out what the configuration is independently of the setup procedure before you run it for the first time.

In Chapter 5, in the section "When and How to Make Your Safety Boot Diskette," I describe a program that captures your CMOS chip's data to a disk file. A companion program can restore the data from that file if you should ever need to. Several of the programs discussed in Chapter 28 will either display the contents of the CMOS or print them on paper. If you can, run one of those programs before using an unknown SETUP program.

If yours is one of the PCs with a CMOS chip, find out what data it has stored in it. You can run the setup procedure specified by the PC's manufacturer, or you could use a third-party utility program. If you suspect yours is one of the PCs that doesn't easily give up its secrets when you run its own setup program, you may have to run a third-party utility program to get that information.

Don't change any of the values stored there (unless you are sure they were entered incorrectly before). Just write down the various values. This will go a long way toward answering the assessment questions.

To activate the setup program for IBM *PC/ATs*, boot from their *Diagnostic Diskette* or *Advanced Diagnostic Diskette*. You will be presented with a menu displaying SETUP as one of its options. Running this program may take several minutes, presenting the information very little at a time. This means you must go through many screens to learn or set all of it. The third-party utility programs often provide a much nicer way of reading or changing the CMOS chip information on these PCs.

Another Warning Be careful not to use third-party setup programs intended for use on any clone PC on a *Micro Channel* or EISA bus PC. These computers store more information in their CMOS chip's RAM. Third-party programs don't necessarily allow for that. They can damage the information in the CMOS chip on these more advanced PCs. Fortunately, all these advanced PCs come with a fine, easy-to-use setup program of their own.

One thing to watch out for: Some disk controllers and some disk partitioning (software) device drivers do not rely on the numbers stored in the CMOS chip to decide what size disk you have. If you have one of those, you won't get the true size of your hard disk from the entry in the CMOS table. Run the DOS program CHKDSK or some other utility program to find out the actual size as it appears to DOS.

There are several reasons why the disk size you find in the CMOS might not be the same as the size seen by DOS. One is that your disk may be partitioned for use by two or more operating systems. The size DOS sees will only be that of the region accessible to it. Another is that you may have a disk whose size is not among those listed in the BIOS table that is used to interpret the CMOS entry. In that case you can use a disk controller or a partitioning device driver to access all of the disk, but in this case the CMOS size may be wildly wrong. Finally, if you are using an on-the-fly data compression program, like *Stacker*, you may seem to have a larger disk drive than the real size, which in that case may well be the size listed in the CMOS table.

Most newer PCs use a setup program that is permanently installed in the motherboard BIOS ROMs. This is especially convenient, for it allows you to run the setup program anytime you want without having to locate some special floppy disk. These are the PCs that may give you the message Press DEL to run setup or diagnostics or something similar.

Some of these PCs show you such a message every time you boot them. Others will display that message only if the POST finds a problem. So you might have a ROM-based setup program even if you have never seen any indication of it on-screen.

The setup program in some of these PCs displays a single screen of information, somewhat like that shown in Figure 20.2 or 20.4. Others have a second screen, possibly something like Figure 20.5. If your PC has such a setup program, be sure to look for a message on the first screen mentioning the second screen. (For example, it might say Press PgUp for CS8230 options.)

PCs in class 3 or 4 that have a second screen to their ROM BIOS-based setup program usually have one of the special motherboard system logic chip sets that can provide shadow RAM and/or EMS memory out of extended memory. That second screen may make clear what those capabilities are, but only if the BIOS is capable of activating those features. These PCs also store more information in their CMOS chip than the generic setup programs accommodate. Use only the ROM-based setup program on these PCs.

Using a Utility Program

Often the easiest way to find out which class of PC you have (and much more) is to use a diagnostic utility program. There are many different ones; most are quite good. Chapter 28 describes more than a dozen of them.

Almost any of these programs will tell you which CPU chip your PC uses. They also will show you how much conventional, extended, and expanded memory you have. Most of them are able to display the device drivers and the TSR programs you have loaded. They won't show you the version numbers of those programs; for that you will have to watch the on-screen messages as those programs load, or you will have to check the documentation that came with each of them.

Look Inside

Often the best way to know what is inside your PC's system unit is to open it up and look. Of course, it helps to know what you are looking at. Even if you don't know what the various parts look like, it still may be instructive for you to open the case and peer inside. You may recognize more than you expect. You certainly won't do any harm—if you only look.

Opening up your PC is not as radical as you might imagine. IBM intended from the very first for mere mortals to open their PCs' cases. The IBM *Guide to Operation* for each of their PC models provides detailed instructions. Many clone makers have been similarly explicit and helpful. Unfortunately, some have not. If you did not receive a printed guide on how to open your PC and you feel insecure about doing so, you may wish to find a knowledgeable person to help you.

Before you open the case, be sure you won't void your dealer's warranty. Many dealers put a seal on the case and will warrant the PC only as long as that seal is not broken. If you have any doubt, call your dealer first for permission to open the case.

If you paid full price for your PC, you probably did so because you want some of the extra service a good dealer can provide. Give that dealer a chance to help you; it is the only way you ever will get your money's worth on the purchase.

Important Warning! Before you remove even the screws that secure the system unit's cover, please unplug the unit from the power line and from every other part of your computer system. That includes all the cables going from the system unit to your monitor and printer, perhaps a phone line connected to an internal modem, and so on. Once you have the cover off and before each time you reach inside the unit, please be sure to touch the frame first.

There are two things that you will accomplish by this precaution. One is to protect yourself against any possibility of electric shock (at least of a dangerous level), and the other is to prevent damage to your PC.

Some people have suggested leaving the power cord plugged in to be sure the PC frame will stay at ground potential. This is a bad idea. See the discussion in Chapter 17 for more details on this point.

Do not try to open the power supply (the large silver box in one corner or along one side of your system unit). There is nothing in there you need to see, and there can be hazardous voltages inside that box.

These simple precautions will go a long way toward preventing you from damaging yourself or your PC. (Chapter 17, in the section "How to Add Memory Safely," contains more safety recommendations; read them now if you are anxious about what to do or not do.)

What are you looking for? First, you want to know what kind of CPU chip your PC uses. Next, you want to know what memory is on its motherboard and something about the motherboard system logic (the chip set). Finally, you want to know about all the plug-in cards you have in your PC.

Locating the CPU Chip

The *CPU chip* is one of the rectangular, black or purple, ceramic or plastic objects mounted on the motherboard. The *motherboard* is the large printed circuit board containing most of the parts of your PC.

This is called the motherboard because it has special connectors on it into which various plug-in cards are fitted. They are called *option cards.* These special connectors collectively make up the PC's *bus.*

These names are a bit curious. The cards that plug into the motherboard ought, you would think, be its "children." Instead, the term *daughterboard* is normally used only for small cards that plug onto option cards. (Perhaps those should be called granddaughter cards?)

In a few PC designs the CPU is not mounted on the motherboard; in those cases, it is on one of the plug-in cards.

The CPU chip may be out in plain sight, or it may be tucked away under a disk drive. Usually it is mounted in some sort of socket. An exception is the 80386SX chip. It is a relatively small, square chip that is soldered onto the surface of the motherboard. You will have to look very carefully to see the CPU number, as it is often printed in tiny type in a color that barely contrasts with the chip's package. But persevere; it must be there somewhere! (A dental examining mirror and a flashlight are often very useful.)

Some PCs have chips mounted on both sides of some of their circuit boards; seeing both sides of the motherboard might require unscrewing it from the case. Do that with care, if at all; follow any directions your user manual has on this point.

Once you have found the CPU chip, the number on it tells which processor your PC uses. Sometimes that number is hard to read. If the manufacturer's name is Intel, this PC could be in any of the six classes. AMD is a manufacturer of CPU chips whose offerings span the classes 3 through 6. Harris means it is in class 3 or 4. If the CPU manufacturer's name is NEC, it is most likely a class 1 or 2 PC.

Also be aware that there may be several large, square chips on the motherboard all made by the same manufacturer. That is probably the system logic chip set. Don't confuse that manufacturer's name with the manufacturer of the CPU (or of the BIOS, for that matter).

Counting RAM

Now look for your motherboard memory chips or modules. There are often many of these. If so, they will be regularly arranged. The descriptions and figure in Chapter 2 may help you find them. You may also need to look at the information on chip numbering in Chapter 16 (see Figures 16.1) and on common chip layouts in Chapter 17 (see Figure 17.6 and the nearby text). You want to know how many RAM chips or modules you have and how much information each one can store.

Motherboard System Logic

Look for some big, square chips on the motherboard. Unless it is quite old, your PC may well have several of them, all made by the same company. Look for the company name (for example, Chips and Technology, Headland Technology, IBM, Intel, LSI, Opti, Texas Instruments, or Western Digital) and also note the chip part numbers. These chips contain the motherboard system logic.

Adapter Cards

Notice where the video cable attaches to your PC. If it connects directly to the motherboard, the video RAM will be located there also. If it connects to a plug-in card, then that is your video adapter, and the video RAM will be on that card.

Finally, look at all the other cards plugged into your PC. Try to identify the function of each one.

Other Cards and Upgrade Options

Not every PC has all, or even any, of the options discussed in this section. Skim it to see if you recognize something you see in your PC. If not, continue at "Ask Others for Help."

If your PC's CPU chip has been removed from its socket and you have a plug-in card connected to that socket with a short, wide ribbon cable, that may be a processor upgrade card. Look on it for a CPU chip, probably of a higher class than the basic PC into which this card is plugged.

Look very carefully at how much memory is on that card (and any daughterboard card plugged into it). For many memory-management purposes that amount is more important than what is on the motherboard or any other plug-in card.

Your network card is, of course, the one connected to the network cable. If you have a phone line connected to a plug-in card, it is probably either a fax or modem card (or it could provide both capabilities). If you have a second monitor and keyboard connected to a plug-in card, that is a slave processor unit. Look at that one carefully, as you want to include in your inventory any memory it has on it.

Another important card to look for is the hard disk controller card. Most PCs in classes 1 and 2 have one controller connected to the floppy disk drive(s) and, if that PC has a hard drive, a second controller connected to the hard disk. Most ATs, 386-, 486-, and *Pentium*-based PCs (those in classes 3 through 6) have only one disk controller; it is a combined floppy and hard disk controller and is connected to all disk drives.

When you locate your hard disk controller, see if it has a large amount of RAM on it. If so, it is probably a caching hard disk controller. If it is, you may be able to save a lot of your system RAM, since you won't get much added benefit from using a software disk cache in addition.

Telling which kind of video adapter you have is usually easy: examine its back panel connectors (see Figure 3.3). Seeing how much memory it holds is also pretty simple. If it uses individual chips, they will be in banks of eight, not nine as is usual on the motherboard and on most memory add-in cards. Similarly if it uses memory modules, they will be "by 8" modules instead of "by 9" ones.

Some monochrome adapters do not have a printer port, but a few CGA adapters do. Some CGA adapters have two RCA phono jacks; both carry composite video, one with color burst and one without. EGA and VGA adapters have a *feature* connector (card edge or post-and-header style) near the top edge of the card. Some VGA cards have a switch block similar to that on an EGA card. A few VGA cards have both the DB-9 and DB-15 connectors to accommodate both TTL and analog monitors.

Ask Others for Help

If you are unable to figure out with confidence what you have in your PC, don't hesitate to ask for help. It is important that you know what you have, and it may be that the easiest way to get that information is by asking someone knowledgeable to look at your PC for you. Chapter 33 gives some suggestions on how to find suitable people to ask.

Counting All Your PC's Memory

In the previous section, you learned how to find the contents of your PC. In this section, you will learn the significance of at least some of what you found. (The next section will help with the rest.)

Specifically, you are concerned with finding out for sure just how much conventional, extended, and expanded memory you have. This section ends with some suggestions about other places in your PC system, besides these categories, where you may have memory.

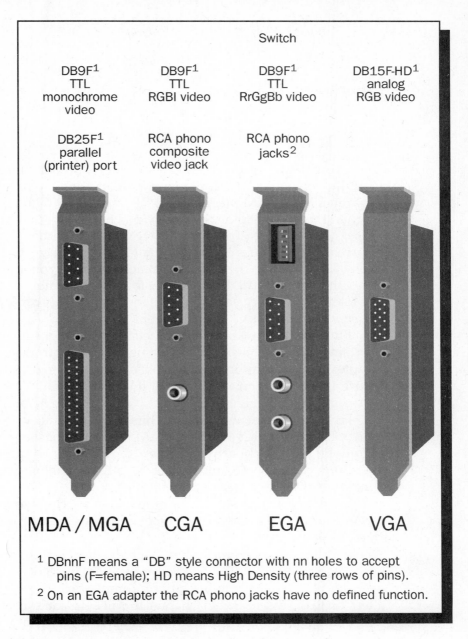

Figure 3.3.   How to tell what kind of video adapter you have.

Even with the best utility program, you may miss some or all of your expanded memory. The reason is that expanded memory is invisible to the PC until a special program, called an expanded memory manager, is loaded. That happens only if your CONFIG.SYS file has a suitable line in it directing the PC to load that software.

Main RAM

When you looked inside your PC, you noted how many memory chips or modules you could find, and of what kinds. Now you need to figure out how much total RAM they contain.

First, you need to discover how much memory one chip or module of each kind contains. Then you simply multiply that amount by the number of chips or modules of that kind that you found to get the total memory of that kind. Add up the memory of each kind that you found, and you'll get a total figure for all the RAM you found. (Remember not to include in this total any memory you may have found on a LAN card, video card, or slave processor card.)

But how do you know how much memory is in a chip or module of a certain kind? You have to be able to figure this out from its part number. Chapter 16 covers this in considerable detail. Refer to that discussion and Figure 16.1 if you don't know what the various kinds of memory chips you found contain. Figures 2.1 and 17.6 will also be helpful.

First determine the number of bits in each memory chip or module. Remember that in PCs the main RAM normally consists of bytes (8 bits each) with one bit of parity to protect the integrity of each byte. (Video RAM and, rarely, some other option card RAM will only have the 8-bits per byte, without the extra parity bit.)

There are several ways to arrange memory chips to make up the 9 bits including parity for some number of bytes. One way is nine bit-wide chips in a row to hold as many bytes with parity as there are bits held in each chip. Another common form is a memory module with some number of bytes plus parity. This is called a "by 9" or "by 18" or "by 36" memory module. You may have found a more complex arrangement, but careful attention to the discussion in Chapter 16 will help you sort it out. You may also want to refer to the discussion in Chapter 17, especially that near Figure 17.6.

Here is an example (typical of many XT clones and shown schematically in Figure 9.1 and also in Figure 15.1): Suppose you find four banks of nine chips each. The first two banks contain chips each of which is labelled as part number 41256. Chips in the next two banks carry the part number 4164. What have you found? The 4164 chips each hold 64K bits and the 41256 chips each hold 256K bits. A row of nine 4164 chips, therefore, holds 64K bytes of memory with parity. The rows of 41256 chips hold exactly four times that much, or 256KB. Adding up all of these amounts (256KB + 256KB + 64KB + 64KB) tells you this motherboard has 640KB of RAM on it.

If the number you come up with for your PC's total RAM is larger than the total of the numbers declared on-screen during the POST, you quite possibly have some (inactive) expanded memory. This happens most often with PCs in class 1 or 2, but it could happen for any class of PC.

Look at the CONFIG.SYS file in the root directory of your boot disk. (For most PC users with a hard disk, that is C:\.) Type it to your screen or look at its contents with a utility program. Is there a line that looks something like this: DEVICE = C:\DRIVERS\REMM.SYS (possibly with some more numbers, letters, and symbols at the end of the line)?

The part that is given here as = C:\DRIVERS\ could have been some other path to that program. The driver name might not be REMM.SYS. Instead it might be HPEMM.SYS, CEMM.SYS, EMM.SYS, or simply MM.SYS. Whatever it is, most likely it will have the letters MM somewhere in its name. If you do find such a line, it almost certainly indicates that you have expanded memory and that this memory should show up when you looked at the screen messages during boot and again when you checked your PC with a utility program.

If you don't find any such line, you may have inactive expanded memory and all you have to do to activate it is add the appropriate line to your CONFIG.SYS file.

If your PC is in class 4, you may have some EMS memory that has been converted from extended memory by your motherboard system logic. Just how much gets converted is determined by an entry in your CMOS. (See Chapter 20 for details.)

PCs in classes 5 and 6 can convert extended memory into expanded (and back again) once they get running. For those PCs, for the purposes of this assessment, you are interested mainly in the total extended and conventional memory you have, that is, all the RAM you can find on the motherboard and any plug-in memory add-on cards. (This does not include any video memory you might find on the motherboard or any memory on a plug-in slave processor, LAN adapter, or hard disk controller card.)

Other System Unit Memory

Now consider any memory you may have found that is not a part of your PC's conventional, extended, or expanded RAM. This category covers any memory you found on a video, slave processor, LAN, or hard disk controller card. It also would include the RAM in a solid-state disk, if you're fortunate enough to have one.

You will know the purpose of each of these groups of memory chips once you know what kind of card they are on. (The one exception is video RAM on the motherboard, in which case this RAM is usually located away from the main RAM area, nearer to the video output connector.) Just notice how much you found of each kind in the appropriate place on the assessment checklist.

Memory Outside the System Unit

Significant amounts of RAM in your PC system may be located outside the system unit. It won't show up on your assessment checklist, but knowing about it can help you make your system perform at its best.

One very significant place it could be is in your printer. Some printers have just a few kilobytes of RAM to serve as a *buffer*. That can be enough to make a dramatic difference. If you print a short, text-only document to such a printer, all of the document will fit into the printer's memory. That means your PC can quickly send the whole job there and then get back to doing other things. The printer will go on printing as long as it must, until the complete document is printed.

A short document, in these terms, simply means one that fits in its entirety into the printer's memory. A page of text might contain two to five thousand characters. So a buffer of 20KB would suffice for four to ten pages of text. A document with many complex graphics, on the other hand, might require several hundred kilobytes per page. For that kind of print job, a 20KB buffer is almost no use at all.

There are printers that have from half a megabyte up to several megabytes of RAM. These are mostly laser printers or other page printers. (A *page printer* composes an image of the entire page in its memory, then prints the whole page; a *line printer* prints pages a line at a time, and a *character printer* prints just one character at a time.)

Having all that memory in your page printer does two things: It allows you to print more complex pages, with more downloaded fonts and fancier, larger graphic images. That memory also can serve as a buffer able to store information for printing out several pages. The former capability may be essential to get your work done at all (if you must print that sort of complex page). The latter one will speed your work, for just as with the small buffer and the text-only documents mentioned a few paragraphs ago, this ample supply of RAM will serve to keep your printer supplied with work while letting you and your PC get back to the job of creating other pages.

Another printer-related place to look for RAM is in a printer switch or print spooler, if you have one. This is a box that is placed between the PC and the printer. Some very simple *printer switches* merely connect the printer to one PC at a time. They don't need (and usually don't have) any memory in them.

At the other extreme, some *print spoolers* are just boxes filled with memory and the minimal amount of intelligence (some logic circuits or a very simple fixed-purpose computer) needed to buffer print jobs in that memory and to parcel them out to the printer as it becomes ready for them.

Finally, there are some printer switches that include *print spool buffers*. They do both tasks. Specifically, they may be able to accept print jobs from several PCs, automatically and simultaneously, and to keep those jobs separate so they eventually get printed out properly. Some of the most complex can be commanded from the PC to allow you to manage the files in the print queue.

Whatever sort of printer switch and/or print spool buffer you may have, find out how much memory it contains. That memory, plus any buffer memory in your printer is able to do a task for which you might otherwise have to commit memory in your PC's system unit. Knowing about it can save you from inadvertently wasting some of your PC's valuable RAM on a software print spooler inside your PC.

Looking for Memory-Management and Other Operating Environment Software

In the section "Watch the Screen As Your PC Boots," earlier in this chapter, you learned some ways to spot memory-management software. In this section you will learn what you are doing now to manage your memory;

find out what, if any, operating environment, task-swapping program manager, or DOS shell program you are using; and determine which device drivers and TSR programs you have loaded into your PC's memory.

Finding out which of these programs you are using is important because they are often incompatible with the memory-management software you may choose to add. If you know about the incompatibility beforehand, you won't be surprised if the new software complains during its installation (or if your PC hangs when you try to run it after installation). It is easy enough to remove the offending programs if you know that they are in place.

EMS and XMS Managers

An earlier section covered most of the telltale signs that indicate that an expanded memory (EMS) manager is loaded. But that is only one kind of memory manager you may have. Another important kind is an XMS manager. This name stands for an e**X**tended **M**emory **S**pecification compliant memory-management program. It manages extended memory, as you might imagine from its name, but it does quite a bit more. The details on what it is and what it does are in Chapters 12 and 19.

The surest sign that you have an XMS manager loaded is a message saying that the High Memory Area (HMA) is available for use. Figure 3.4 shows the messages displayed by a couple of common memory managers, one for EMS and the other for XMS.

PCs in classes 5 and 6 (those whose CPU chip is a 386, 486, or a Pentium) can do some fancy memory-remapping tricks. But they can't do them without help from a suitable memory management program. Typically, these programs offer the functionality of both an EMS manager and an XMS manager. Some popular ones are *QEMM*, *386MAX*, *Memory Commander*, and *QMAPS*. Figure 3.5 shows the display produced by *386MAX*.

Operating Environments

The only popular DOS-based alternative operating environments for PCs at this time are Quarterdeck's *DESQview*, Microsoft's *Windows*, and *GeoWorks Ensemble*. You probably know if you are running one of these. Figures 1.3 through 1.5 are typical screen images from these programs.

```
Classic Bus Expanded Memory Manager            Version 4.0  Rev. D
Copyright 1985, 1987, 1988, 1989               Intel Corporation

   Testing DOS extended memory and expanded memory partitions.
   Total memory 1024  Kbytes

HIMEM: DOS XMS Driver, Version 2.60 - 04/05/90
XMS Specification Version 2.0
Copyright 1988-1990 Microsoft Corp.

Installed A20 handler number 1.
64K High Memory Area is available.
```

Figure 3.4.   Intel's EMM.SYS and Microsoft's HIMEM.SYS sign-on messages on an AT clone with an Intel Above Board.

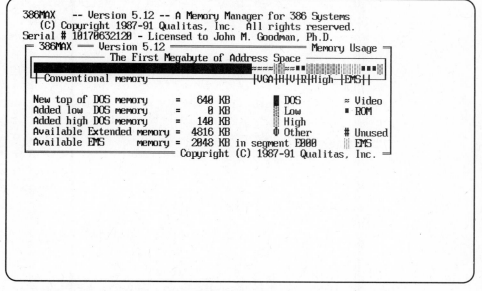

Figure 3.5.   Boot message from 386MAX, showing one particular PC's memory configuration and a summary of its current uses.

Task-Swapping Program Managers and DOS Shell Programs

Do you normally select your tasks from a menu, or do you enter program names at the DOS prompt? If you pick items from a menu, you may be using some sort of DOS shell program.

If you see a menu on your screen, but also see a DOS prompt, you could be using a popular batch file alternative to a DOS shell program. If this is the case, you will find that you can type any valid DOS command and have it execute; in a typical menu program, you can pick only from those items listed in the menu.

While menu programs limit what you can do, they also add new power not normally associated with the simple DOS prompt. For example, you may be in the middle of one program and, without closing that program, be able to return to the menu or jump to another program, then later jump back to the first one and find it right where you left it. If you can do this, you are using a task-swapping program manager (which is a DOS shell program and more).

Most menu programs identify themselves somewhere on the main menu. Likewise for task-swapping program managers. The only exception would be if your swapper is configured to stay invisible, moving you from program to program as you touch various hot keys.

In the latter case you will have to examine your AUTOEXEC.BAT file to see what program is named on its last line. That, most likely, is your swapper.

One limited-purpose task swapper is worth mentioning here. If you have *SideKick* loaded, you can pop up its menu or any one of its several miniapplication programs at the touch of a special key. You can make that miniapplication vanish just as easily. This is a limited form of task swapping. You can only go between those miniapplications and whatever else you were doing. The foreground program (the one you were running before you popped up *SideKick*) cannot be swapped away in favor of just any other application. Unless you were running some other DOS shell program, you will have had to type the name of that foreground application to start it.

SideKick is not the only TSR desktop utility program. A number of them are discussed in Chapter 28. All offer similar functionality, although with different pop-up miniapplications.

An opposite case, also discussed in Chapter 28, is a swap program that swaps away from a fixed program to any other DOS program. One collection of programs of this kind is the *Swap Utilities*. There is one of them for each of a limited set of applications. You can recognize them by their name, which always begins with "SWAP." *SWAPIS*, for example, will load the personal information manager *InfoSelect*, and then let you swap away from it.

Watch Out for VDISK

There is one device driver you might find loaded in your system that can give you a lot of grief when you try to add a memory management program: the IBM virtual disk program, VDISK. This program has been included with every copy of IBM's *PC DOS*, starting with version 3.0. Since many people use *PC DOS* on non-IBM hardware, you may be using it even though your PC is not the IBM brand.

VDISK was the first program that could use a PC's extended memory. It allowed the owners of early IBM *PC/AT*s to put that extended memory to use as a very fast simulation of a floppy disk drive. This was wonderful. Unfortunately, if you load both an XMS memory manager and an early version of VDISK (version 3.x), you will very likely lose some of your data.

This happens because of the unique way VDISK uses extended memory. The designers of VDISK apparently didn't consider the possibility that other DOS programs would ever use extended memory.

VDISK (in those early versions) just grabs what it wants and uses it. If you load more than one copy of VDISK, the later copies will notice the space taken by the earlier copies and will grab different portions of extended memory. What you may not do is load VDISK (version 3.x) and any XMS memory manager. This is because VDISK is blissfully unaware of any notion of extended memory management, and so can easily clobber an XMS memory manager and any programs it might have loaded into extended memory. (See Chapter 21 for details on how VDISK, version 3.x, works and why it is incompatible with XMS memory managers.)

You can detect VDISK by its sign-on message. It will identify itself and its version and tell how large a virtual disk it is creating. If you see that message when you boot your PC, and if the version of VDISK is 3.x, watch out!

The problem only occurs for VDISK versions 3.0 through 3.3. That might sound like it is only a small problem. Actually, though, a significant number of PC users are still using one of these versions of *PC DOS*. It took only three years from the introduction of the IBM *PC* and DOS, version 1.0, until the introduction of DOS, version 3.0. Four more years went by before the introduction of DOS, version 4.0. Even now, more than a year after PC DOS version 5 was introduced, version 3.3 is still an officially supported DOS version.

If you use *MS-DOS* or *PC DOS* version 5.02 or later, you more likely will find you are using *RAMDRIVE,* the Microsoft-created alternative to VDISK. Do not confuse VDISK with *RAMDRIVE. RAMDRIVE* has a similar sign-on message, except for its name. It also provides a very fast, simulated floppy disk drive created from extended memory. While, like VDISK, it can utilize extended memory without benefit of any memory manager, every version of *RAMDRIVE* will cooperate gracefully with an XMS memory manager if one is present, which is something that early versions of VDISK cannot do.

A Recap

This chapter began with an assessment checklist. If you have completed it, you have a pretty good picture of what is in your PC's system unit. If you know what peripheral devices are attached to that system unit, you have a fairly good picture of your total system.

The data in your completed assessment checklist is the information you need in order to know what improvements are possible for your system. It also tells you about some of the things that may stand in your way. (You may have found some device drivers or TSR programs loaded that will limit what you can do about memory management. You might end up having to replace them, or simply do without them, if you are to significantly improve what your PC can do.)

The next chapter guides you in taking a close look at your needs for improved memory management. Those needs define where you want to get in improving your PC. Knowing where you are now (from your assessment checklist) and where you want to be makes it possible to begin making plans that will get you there.

4

WHAT ARE YOUR NEEDS?

Once you know what you have, you must figure out what you need, so you can go about getting it.

You say you have an itch for more memory or better memory management? Well, to get relief, you'd better know precisely where to scratch.

In medicine there is a concept known as the *presenting problem*: what the patient complains about. Then there is the real problem: what the diagnostician discovers is wrong after some clarifying questions and perhaps some diagnostic tests.

This chapter poses some clarifying questions which may serve as your diagnostician's questions. You may be able to answer them by referring to the assessment checklist in the previous chapter or through some reflection, or you may have to do some diagnostic tests on your system to discover the correct answers. Eventually, with a bit of luck, you'll be able to locate your particular itch. Scratching it is up to you.

The suggestions given here for solving various problems are quite terse. They assume that you know (or will soon learn) some rather technical jargon. Just realize how lucky you are to be holding this book—Part II will teach you everything you need to know!

Is What You Have Now What You Need?

This may be the most important question of all. If you already have all you need, you don't have to do anything to get what you need. In particular, if you have the pieces you need (all the right hardware and the right software), you may need only to learn how to use them effectively to achieve your goals. This book will help you do that.

Do You Have a Problem?

You may be reading this book because you know you have a memory-management problem. If so, you can probably tell why you think you do. That is a *symptom* of what you need, but not your need itself. This section describes a number of presenting problems and in each case suggests possible real problems they could represent. This is followed with some suggestions for solving those real problems.

On the other hand, maybe you're happy with how your PC is working now; perhaps you don't have any urgent need to make changes. You then have the luxury of browsing through this book to learn about the field, unpressured by the need to solve a problem. The information you gather here may someday be just what you need when you do want to change how your PC works.

If You Don't Have Enough Memory to Run an Important Application Program

Suppose you know you need more memory, or at least you need to be able to use more of it. You may have gotten a message saying Insufficient memory to load program (or something like that). This usually means DOS found it could not load the program and give it as much memory as it was requesting. Or perhaps DOS loaded the program, but you then found out you couldn't do anything useful with it before you got an out of memory message. There are several cases to consider.

You May Have Too Little Conventional Memory

Do you have 640KB of conventional memory in your PC? (One way to see is by running the DOS programs CHKDSK or MEM. Among other numbers, you will see one labelled bytes total conventional memory or something like that. This number should be 655360 or close to it.) If it is substantially smaller than that, you must add more memory. When you do, you will have an opportunity to do more than just that. Memory is relatively cheap these days, so it seldom makes sense to add only what it would take to fill your PC to 640KB. If you have a PC in class 1 or 2, put in a board that will *backfill* your conventional memory and provide some expanded memory. (See the discussion of the classes of PC in the previous chapter, and refer to Figures 3.1 and 3.2.) Get a megabyte or two of RAM (at least). Another common feature for these memory cards is a battery-powered "real-time clock." That is very useful if your PC doesn't already have one. (Before you buy anything more for your PC, please read Appendix B.)

When you are ready to start shopping, consult the MemInfo hypertext database on the included diskette. It will help you compose your shopping list and help you contact the manufacturers of the products that most interest you.

The term *backfill* comes from the construction industry, where it means to refill a hole. In PCs, it means to add enough memory to fill to capacity the conventional memory space. (Ordinarily that means to add memory up to 640KB, though in some cases you can add even more. See Chapter 8 for details.)

The real-time clock is a feature introduced by IBM with its *PC/AT*, and is now standard on all PCs in classes 3 through 6. PCs in class 1 or 2 do not ordinarily include a real-time clock. Adding that feature on a plug-in card and activating it with a program in your AUTOEXEC.BAT file will allow DOS to know the correct time and date when it wakes up. Never again during the boot process will you have to answer questions about what date or time it is, nor will all your files be dated January 1, 1980 (which is what happens when you press the Enter key instead of answering those questions).

That same memory board also can give you some extra I/O ports or a floppy disk controller. Just be sure that you remove the ones you had before, disable those features on the new board, or otherwise prevent conflicts between the new and the old ones. If you don't, the board is very likely to cause you more problems than the new RAM is worth.

Early PCs in classes 1 and 2 often had a separate card for the floppy disk controller and the hard disk controller (if they even had a hard disk). Any I/O ports they had were located on other plug-in cards. Many modern PCs have one combination controller for both hard and floppy disk drives. Or they may have the floppy disk controller built into the motherboard. The I/O ports are often also built into the motherboard.

Some multifunction plug-in cards (which often include a real-time clock, additional memory, and perhaps some input/output ports) also have a floppy disk controller. Generally, you can disable the floppy disk controller portion and each of the I/O port sections of the plug-in card (by a DIP switch or jumper setting), and sometimes you can disable those on the motherboard as well (perhaps through a software setup program).

It is possible to have more than one floppy controller in a PC, but unless you are careful to make sure each is located at a different range of I/O port addresses, they will conflict with each other and neither will work. Similarly, you can have many I/O ports, but they must each have an address range that is not used by anything else in your PC. Also, supply each function with its own IRQ level or decide you won't need interrupt support for at least some of them. You will need to consult the manuals that come with the PC or its motherboard and those that come with each of the plug-in cards to find out what is possible.

If you discover that you have a PC in classes 3 through 6 with too little memory, put in as much additional memory as you can afford. There's no such thing as too much memory!

There is one other case to consider before you run out to buy RAM chips. Some of these PCs are able to split the first megabyte of their RAM in at least two ways. One is 512KB of conventional and 512KB of extended memory. The other is 640KB of conventional and 384KB of extended memory. Be sure you tell the setup program to supply 640KB of conventional memory if you have at least that much total RAM.

You May Have 640KB, but That Still May Not Be Enough

Some programs are real memory hogs. They require more than just conventional memory. Lotus *1-2-3*, Release 3.x, is an example. It demands a minimum of 384KB of extended memory or expanded memory in addition to your conventional memory just to load! Memory to hold large spreadsheets is over and above that.

Check the box or the documentation that came with the application that is giving you trouble. It should tell you what the program's RAM requirements are. Further, it should break that requirement down by conventional, extended, and/or expanded memory. Just be sure you have available at least as much of each kind as it needs.

If your PC is in class 1 or 2 and the programs you wish to run require extended memory, you have little choice. You will have to upgrade your PC at least to class 3. There is more than one way to do that. Chapters 23 and 27 cover several of them.

If you want to add expanded memory to a PC in class 1, you must add an expanded memory board. (You can't add extended memory to PCs in class 1 or 2.) If you have a PC in class 2, you may have to add more RAM chips to your present expanded memory board.

PCs in class 3 that need expanded memory can obtain it in several ways. One is an expanded memory card. Another is by adding extended memory and then converting it to expanded through software. Usually, the best choice will be the added card, especially if that provides full compatibility with the Lotus-Intel-Microsoft Expanded Memory Specification, version 4.0 (LIM 4.0 EMS). Again, see Chapter 9 for more details.

If your PC is in class 4, you can use either a plug-in memory board or a special memory manager to activate the motherboard system logic features that convert extended memory into expanded memory. Which way to go depends mostly on which makes it easier to change, later on, the amount of extended memory that is converted. Many PC users find they have varying needs for expanded memory, depending on what they are doing. So, make changing the amount you have as easy as you can. Of course, if you don't have enough extended memory to spare, you must also add more extended memory, either on the motherboard or on a plug-in card. (Chapter 15 covers the pros and cons of each of these alternatives.)

PCs in classes 5 and 6 can (and should) be set up to produce any needed expanded memory from extended memory. Again, if you haven't enough total RAM, add what you must (or more).

Warning   Watch out, there are some interesting "gotchas" lurking here. If you have hardware EMS (an expanded memory card or if you are converting shadow RAM to EMS) and if you have loaded the program which manages that EMS memory (the Expanded Memory Manager, or EMM for short), you won't be able to run *Windows* in enhanced mode. The reason is that *Windows* wants to provide its own expanded memory services for any program running under *Windows.* The solution to this problem is simply to reboot your PC without the call to the EMM program in your CONFIG.SYS file. *Windows* will then run happily in enhanced mode (provided its other requirements are met).

Here is another one: If you have plenty of extended memory and just a small amount of available expanded memory, Lotus *1-2-3*, Release 3.x, will refuse to load. This is because *1-2-3* looks first for expanded memory and uses that if it is available. If there is some, but not enough available expanded memory, Lotus *1-2-3* will fail to load no matter how much extended memory you have. Making sure you have *no* available expanded memory will solve this problem.

The opposite case has an added quirk. If you have a 386- or 486-based PC (one in class 5 or 6), you may have converted a lot (perhaps nearly all) of your extended memory into expanded memory. Lotus *1-2-3* can get what it needs for its program to load, but only if the expanded memory is what is termed *VCPI-compatible.* (See Chapter 12 for an explanation of what this means.) Not all the programs that make expanded out of extended memory have that compatibility. If yours doesn't, and you don't have at least 384KB of free extended (or XMS) memory, Lotus *1-2-3* will again refuse to load.

There are several ways to add extended memory to a PC in classes 3 through 6. Look at the discussion in Chapters 15, 24, and 25 before you choose which one to use.

What about programs that refuse to load even though they don't require any extended or expanded memory? That can mean only one thing: You have too many TSRs and/or device drivers loaded. (Occasionally, you may see this symptom when the program you are trying to load has become damaged, but this is rare. You can check for this rare difficulty by comparing the files that make up the program in question with their original counterparts on the master disks for that program.)

You Might Run Out of System Resources

Windows users face some special problems. Windows uses memory in some special ways. Mostly these ways let it get full use out of all the memory you have (both conventional and extended, but not expanded memory on a hardware expanded memory card). There is one way, however, in which Windows can run out of memory "prematurely."

Windows sets aside a small amount of memory for what it calls "System Resources." These are two or three 64KB regions (called "local heaps" by programmers) in which it keeps track of the graphical objects on the screen and the program objects in memory. As soon as it runs out of free space in either of these two regions, Windows is unable to continue, no matter how much unused RAM you may have elsewhere.

In version 3.1 of Windows, Microsoft made some changes that help matters a little. Most importantly, they expanded the total RAM allocated for System Resources from 128KB to 192KB. Still, many people run into the system resources limitation long before they run out of free RAM.

You Might Have Too Many TSRs or Device Drivers

Since all PC programs are written to run in somebody's PC, you can be sure you have enough conventional memory if you have 640KB. After all, almost no one has more than that.

If you do not have EGA or VGA or if you never use any graphics modes for those video cards, you could have more conventional memory, up to 736KB in some cases. Program authors never count on this, though, so having "merely" 640KB of conventional memory is always enough.

This is a case of not enough *available* conventional memory. Something is using up too much of it. The things that you must have in that memory (loaded prior to loading and running your application program) include DOS and maybe some device drivers or TSRs. If you haven't enough memory to run the application, you must have too many device drivers or TSRs, since you can't do without DOS.

Actually, that's not completely true: If you are running DOS version 4, you are committing a lot more of your conventional memory to DOS than with any other version. Just changing to DOS 5 or 6 may solve your problem. This is especially true for PCs in classes 3 through 6, for then much of DOS itself can be loaded into the High Memory Area. For those PCs, even changing from DOS 3.x (which takes much less conventional memory than DOS 4) to DOS 5 or 6 can produce significant conventional memory savings.

If you can't solve the problem by changing DOS versions, you will have to get rid of some of those pesky device drivers or TSRs, or move at least some of them out of the first 640KB of memory. Frequently, both are viable ways to go. The discussion in Chapters 19-21 will help you decide what to do.

"Dancing" TSRs—Now You See Them, Now You Don't

Another variation on the too-little-conventional-memory story goes this way: You can run each program you need to run, but some of them require you to unload everything else (all device drivers and TSRs) before they will load. But you *need* to be able to use at least some of those helper programs—even with that big application—and you'd like to be able to use all of them. You wonder if having more memory or better memory management might help.

The most likely answer is the same in each case, and it's good news: Yes, you probably can solve this problem. This time you need to look at the techniques of TSR management, task swapping, or maybe even multitasking. Chapter 21 is where to head next. (But maybe you should detour through many or all of the intervening chapters to be sure you pick up all the necessary background information.)

If You Can Run Every Program You Have Alone, but the Ones You Need to Run Together Won't

This is a tough one. It means one of two things:

- You have a problem of bad program interaction.
- You simply don't have room for all those programs in memory at once.

If you have the first problem, you may be out of luck. There are some programs that just won't work together. Sometimes you can solve things by replacing one of the offenders with another program that does the same job, but does it just a bit differently.

You know you have the second problem if you cannot even load all the programs you need into RAM at one time. You get that old Insufficient memory message. In this case there is hope. You may simply need to move some of the programs out of the first 640KB or expand that territory until it can accept all the programs you need to run together. Again, the information in Chapters 19-21 will help you.

Do You Have Some Significant Opportunities to Improve Your PC?

Even if your PC works satisfactorily, and you can run all the programs and program combinations you need right now, your PC probably could help you do your work even more quickly or more easily. Almost everyone would like that. So read on to see if you could gain some significant benefits from implementing one of the changes suggested here (even though you may not have to right now).

If you don't have at least some sort of task-switching setup in your PC, you may well be wasting some of your work time. If you have to close down your word processor and start your database program to look up somebody's phone number, then shut down the database program, reload the word processor, reload the letter you were working on, find your place again, and then copy in the phone number (which you'd better have written down on some scrap of paper since you won't be able to remember it all this time), you could derive a lot of benefit from task-switching software.

That may be all you need. The next step up from that, multitasking, may be more than you will ever require. Most task switchers also include some mechanism for copying information from one program to another, so you not only save time going from task to task, you also can stop using up all your *Post-it*s as scratch paper.

On the other hand, do you ever call up a mainframe, an electronic bulletin board, or an information service (such as *CompuServe*) and download large files? If so, a multitasking operating environment lets you to continue working with your PC while that download is going on. Equally, if you hate waiting for your PC to finish any task (printing, recalculating a spreadsheet, sorting a large database, and so on), and if you want to use your PC to do something else while you wait, multitasking can be a dream come true.

But remember one very important point: There's no such thing as a free lunch. When you multitask your PC, it performs each of the tasks at least a little bit slower (and maybe a whole lot slower) than when it is working on one task at a time. Your PC never really does more than one thing at a time—it just seems that way. A multitasking PC doles out fractions of its time to each task (plus some time for overhead—that is, keeping track of what to do next), and it does this so quickly that you usually don't notice the switches. With task switching, on the other hand, your PC is devoted fully to the particular task that has the focus. All other tasks are temporarily suspended.

Let me make this very clear: If your PC is waiting for you to decide which key to press next (as is often the case when using a word processor, for example), multitasking will actually enable your PC to do more work in a given interval of time. If, however, you can keep it busy on each of its processes when they are running alone, running them alone will get those jobs done more quickly than multitasking all of them together. Of course, the convenience of having them all going at once may outweigh the inefficiency.

You can set up most multitasking software to do simple task switching. But, if task switching is all you want, you may be better served by a program that can do only that.

Chapter 21 describes both task-switching program managers and multitasking operating environments in detail. Chapter 29 gives additional information on these topics.

A Concluding Comment

Now you know both what you have and what you need, and you are ready to start going from where you are to where you want to be. You may have an idea for a solution you want to try now. Or perhaps you don't fully understand the suggestions you just read. In that case, you must learn more about the principles of PC design, memory, and memory management. Fortunately for you, that's coming right up.

Actually, the next chapter is a digression on safety. It really wouldn't do to have you trying grand experiments on your PC only to lose all your data, would it? Or, to put this another way, before you begin the trip, you need to find the safety belt and buckle up.

5

SOME IMPORTANT WARNINGS

This chapter is meant to scare you. Even experts often forget this good advice. Check out these horrors before you make any changes to your system. You may save yourself a whole lot of grief.

This chapter is meant to scare you. It recounts some of the ways you can do yourself in, quite innocently. Of course, your innocence does not matter one whit; when you suffer a serious data loss or some other disaster with your PC, you have no one to plead your innocence to, nor can anyone help you recover what you have lost (usually).

Once you start experimenting with memory management, you are quite likely to get yourself into trouble. It need not be serious trouble, but it certainly could be. The precautions listed here may make the difference between an annoying intermission in your adventures and a full-fledged disaster.

Read these cautionary notes and remember them. Especially read the advice about the Safety Boot Diskette (and follow it) before you make any major changes to your PC system.

There is nothing particularly arcane about most of this advice. Nor, unfortunately, is there anything very unusual about the disasters it is meant to guard against. Even people who are only moderately expert in the use of PCs have probably heard much of this before. Still, it bears repeating; all too often even experts (perhaps especially experts) tend to ignore good practice. It really is true that haste makes waste.

Some Tricks Don't Really Pay Off

Most of the advice in this book is geared toward helping you get as much as you can out of the RAM in your PC. But be sensible about it—the real goal is to make your PC do more of what you want. Surely you aren't trying to keep yourself occupied figuring out why your PC won't do today what it would do yesterday. An unstable system is a troubleshooter's nightmare.

Remember this, please: If you manage to save a few bytes more of your RAM but make your PC harder or less fun to use in the process, that is no bargain.

Some Specific Things You Probably Should Not Do

Here are just a couple of examples of the things you could do, but that you probably should not do. These are put here just to alert you to this kind of information. There is more of it elsewhere in the book.

- Using FASTOPEN can speed access to files. Read Chapter 20 to learn why this can sometimes be horribly dangerous.

- Not using SHARE can save you several kilobytes of your most precious conventional RAM, but it also can lead to disaster. (Many people think that since their computer is not on a network and they have upgraded to DOS 5 they can forget this warning. They are wrong!) This is discussed more later in this chapter and in Chapter 20.

Learn to Use Common Sense

In addition to other tips to avert minor (or major) tragedies, you also will find elsewhere in this book some practical counsel. For example, when should you take some time and try to hand-optimize the loading of programs into upper memory, and when is it appropriate to accept some easier approach? Look for these tips.

The Importance of Having a Safety Boot Diskette

I call it a Safety Boot Diskette. One of my friends calls it the "save your fanny" diskette. Whatever you call it, this can be the best defensive weapon in your arsenal.

Most of the time the enemy you are defending against is yourself. This diskette will get you out of some very sticky spots that you wouldn't get into if you were paying attention. But sometimes this diskette will be needed to defend against data loss from an equipment failure, and occasionally from an outside attack (for example, by a computer virus).

Why Have a Safety Boot Diskette?

There is a problem waiting in your future. If you use a PC long enough, you will experience it, in one form or another. That's the bad news.

The good news is that there's a solution to that problem, which you can create now, before you have The Problem. The Problem comes in many forms; the solution has just one form: a Safety Boot Diskette.

The Problem

Do you boot your computer from a hard disk? Most of us do. If so, you are in for a rude surprise someday. You'll turn on your computer, and it will tell you it cannot boot.

The language your PC will use may vary. Four typical messages are:

- Bad or missing Command Interpreter

- Error loading operating system

- Sector not found reading drive C

- Bad partition table

And there are several more. Each one indicates something subtly different. Then again, they all mean the same thing: You cannot boot your computer from the hard drive, at least not right now.

Some Possible Forms the Problem May Take

There are many ways a PC can become incapable of booting from its hard disk. Here are a few:

- The CMOS setup information could indicate a different type of hard disk is installed than the one you actually have. (That could be the result of some random data glitch, or it could mean the backup battery for that CMOS setup RAM is dying or has died.)

- The partition table on the hard disk could be damaged. (Just one bit flipped the wrong way is enough!)

- One of the two essential, hidden, system files could have become damaged.

- The CONFIG.SYS file could be messed up, or it could call for some inappropriate device driver program to be loaded.

  Not all of the ways that your CONFIG.SYS or AUTOEXEC.BAT files can get messed up will produce the full symptoms of The Problem. Some will merely mean that some program you wanted was not loaded or some action you intended was not done. But all too often, especially when you are playing around with memory-management software, these goofs will lead directly to a PC that refuses to boot from its hard disk.

- The command interpreter could be damaged, or it could be from a different version of DOS than the two hidden files.

- The AUTOEXEC.BAT file could be messed up, or it could run some inappropriate program.

- You might have a computer virus.

- Your hard disk may have died (mechanically or electrically). This could mean something flipped a bit in one of the sector headers, or your disk head positioning mechanism could have drifted out of alignment. Both of these are usually repairable failures, meaning you can get back all of your data and the only tools you will need are some software programs.

- Your hard disk may have died (mechanically or electrically). It stops turning, or it is no longer able to pick up signals and process them correctly. This is the one failure of all those listed here that actually requires a disk repair or replacement.

It is often impossible to know, with just the single message your PC will present, which of the many possible problems you have. And it is impossible to solve that problem until you can boot your PC.

The Connection Between Memory Management and The Problem

Why, you may be wondering, is this whole discussion included in a book on memory management? That's simple. When you start experimenting with memory management, you will be altering your CONFIG.SYS and AUTOEXEC.BAT files. That gives you plenty of opportunities to cause The Problem. So creating a Safety Boot Diskette is a very important first step to take before you start playing around with memory managers. And once you are taking the trouble to create a Safety Boot Diskette, why not make it good enough to help you deal with The Problem in all its guises? You never know when one of them will pop up.

The Solution

If you have made a Safety Boot Diskette according to the prescription below, you will know exactly what to do. Insert that diskette in your A: drive and restart your computer. This time it will boot.

Furthermore, you will have ready at hand the tools you need to do some simple diagnostic tests. Most likely you can find out what is wrong almost immediately. With a little luck and some perseverance, you will be able to fix the problem. (Well, sometimes you may have to call for help. But when you do, if you have used your Safety Boot Diskette and followed the advice in Chapters 32 and 33, at least you will be able to give your helper a head start on fixing things.)

Now you know why having a Safety Boot Diskette is essential. Next you need to know how to make one for your PC.

A DOS Disk Is Not Enough

Maybe you thought you could solve the problem by grabbing an original DOS diskette and putting it in the A drive. Maybe you could get your PC to boot that way. Probably so. However, even if you do get it to boot, you will not have on that diskette all the things you need to treat whatever ails your PC.

If the hidden system files or the command interpreter on the hard disk were messed up, you could replace them with new copies from the DOS disk. That's what the SYS command is for. But how can you be sure that is the solution? If you guessed wrong, you could wipe out some important evidence of what went wrong and still not be able to boot your PC from the hard disk.

Even worse, if the DOS diskette you grabbed had a different version of DOS on it from the one on your hard drive, you could be creating new problems instead of solving the old ones. No, just a simple DOS diskette won't do. You need a good deal more than that.

Nine Essential Qualities
Your Safety Boot Diskette Must Have

To help you deal effectively with The Problem in all its forms, your Safety Boot Diskette needs to possess nine qualities. They are:

- It must be bootable. Furthermore, it must have the same version of DOS on it as is on your hard disk.

- It must be write-protected. This means its contents cannot be altered by whatever is wrong with your hard disk.

- It must have a copy of your PC's CMOS setup data stored in a special data file, and it must have a program capable of putting that information back into the CMOS setup RAM. (It is very nice if it also has the program you need to create that special data file. Later in this chapter, you'll learn where to get such a program.)

- If you normally use some device driver(s) to access your hard drive, your Safety Boot Diskette must have those drivers and a CONFIG.SYS file that loads them.

- If you normally log onto a network, your Safety Boot Diskette could have the appropriate drivers and other programs to log you into the network. Better not make that too automatic, though, for you may need to solve your local problems before you connect your PC to the network.

- It is prudent to have an AUTOEXEC.BAT file on your Safety Boot Diskette, even if you don't need it to load any programs. (The details of what it might contain are described a bit later in this chapter.)

- It should have a good virus-scanning utility program, and perhaps another program to repair viral damage.

- Your Safety Boot Diskette will be much more useful if it also has a number of utility programs on it. These will include a simple text editor, a file viewer, and some DOS external commands, at a minimum. Disk diagnosis and repair utilities are wonderful additions also.

- To help you recover from all versions of The Problem, your Safety Boot Diskette needs also to have a copy of the CONFIG.SYS and AUTOEXEC.BAT files you were using on the hard disk. (If you often change these files on your hard disk, you may need several sets of them on your Safety Boot Diskette.) If you use a menu program, the data file for that program should be included.

In fact, to meet all of those specifications fully, you might end up with a set of diskettes that collectively serve the role of your Safety Boot Diskette. Just identify one of them as the principal Safety Boot Diskette. That one will have at least the first four qualities listed above. The other qualities may be better served by files on supplemental diskettes.

Each PC Is Unique

Your PC is unlike anyone else's. Not only might you have a different collection of hardware pieces, even more likely your software setup will differ from that on every other PC in at least some respects. This is part of what it means to have a "personal computer."

Some PCs Aren't That Unique

An exception to this is if your PC is, in fact, one of a matched set of PCs. But be careful. They must be matched in every respect. If your PC is just like a bunch of others, then your Safety Boot Diskette will be an exact copy of that for each of the other PCs in that bunch. That could happen. It is pretty rare, though. And since it is so easy to make your own Safety Boot Diskette (one you are sure is fitted precisely to your machine) why not do it?

You Still Need One Safety Boot Diskette per PC

When The Problem visits, you don't want to have to hunt for your Safety Boot Diskette. Make one per PC and keep it right next to the PC it is protecting.

Keep Your Safety Boot Diskette Up-to-Date

Your PC changes from time to time. Each time it does, your Safety Boot Diskette needs to be updated as well. Some changes are more significant than others, so you may not make a new Safety Boot Diskette every time you alter your AUTOEXEC.BAT file. But think carefully before you decide not to do so. What if The Problem were to strike right now? Would you be adequately prepared? If not, take a few moments to make that new Safety Boot Diskette.

When and How to Make Your Safety Boot Diskette

The right answer to "When?" is easy: Do it now, before you are visited by The Problem. You say, "It's already too late for that." Oh, my! You'd better solve your current problem first, and then make your Safety Boot Diskette.

Assuming you have no immediate problem, take a look at the steps you must take to make your own personalized Safety Boot Diskette.

1. Use Drive A

The most important quality of your Safety Boot Diskette is that you can, in fact, boot from it. Most PCs can boot only from the first floppy drive (called drive A) or the first fixed disk (called drive C).

Put a diskette in your PC's drive A. Use the highest capacity diskette that drive was meant to handle. There are two reasons for this advice: It will let you put the maximum possible number of files on your Safety Boot Diskette, and it turns out that most diskette drives are more reliable when writing and reading disks at their highest capacity.

Most importantly, do not use drive B to create your Safety Boot Diskette, especially if it is a different kind of drive than your PC's drive A (for example, if A is a 1.2MB, 5 1/4" drive and B is a 1.44MB, 3 1/2" drive). Doing that will create a disk that you cannot use to boot your PC.

2. Format the Diskette and Make It Bootable

The easiest way to format your diskette is to use this DOS command:

```
FORMAT A: /S /V
```

You must be logged to whatever drive has your DOS system files on it (normally your PC's drive C, though it can be something else in certain cases). If you get the message Insert a system disk in drive A:, you probably were logged to the wrong drive.

Put a volume label on this diskette (by using the /V option with FORMAT command); any label will do as long as it is not all blanks. This is principally to help you identify this diskette if its paper label should come off.

You may be tempted to use a diskette you had formatted previously. Be careful. Part of what makes a disk bootable is its *boot sector*. That is a program that resides in the very first sector of the disk. It does not show up in any DIR listing. The boot sector program is put in place by the FORMAT, SELECT, or SYS programs.

If you formatted the diskette with a different version of DOS than is on your hard disk, you will have to re-create the appropriate boot sector, or it won't work with the hidden, system files from your hard disk. So don't just copy the system files and the command interpreter to an already formatted diskette. Do it the easy, sure way: Log to C: and type

```
FORMAT A: /S /V
```

3. Create Some Subdirectories

Many people think subdirectories are useful only on hard disks. Not so. On floppies they have the same virtues they have on hard disks.

First, subdirectories allow you to have two or more different files with the same name, as long as you keep them in different directories. On your Safety Boot Diskette, for example, that might be the AUTOEXEC.BAT file it uses when you boot from it (which must be in the root directory) and the copy you have on this diskette of the AUTOEXEC.BAT file on your PC's C drive (which you might have in a directory called \C-BACKUP).

Second, subdirectories help you keep your files organized. Keep all the files having to do with the CMOS setup RAM in one directory, keep all the antivirus programs in another, and so forth.

Third (though this advantage is seldom compelling for a Safety Boot Diskette), there is a limit to how many files you can put in the root directory, and no limit in a subdirectory.

Exactly which subdirectories you put on your Safety Boot Diskette is a matter of personal taste. Figure 5.1 shows one possible Safety Boot Diskette with the files that would go in each directory for a particular PC hardware and software configuration. (Remember: While this directory structure could be used by almost anyone, the particular files to put in each directory will have to be decided by careful examination of the PC for which the Safety Boot Diskette is being prepared.)

Here are some details on the system for which the example Safety Boot Diskette in Figure 5.1 was prepared, and on the files on that diskette. The Safety Boot Diskette detailed in Figure 5.1 has been customized for a laptop computer with a 10MB hard disk, using *Stacker,* version 2.0, to make it seem to have about 20MB of file capacity. The laptop system uses *MS-DOS,* version 3.30, so that is the system used to create the Safety Boot Diskette.

The laptop sometimes runs task-switching programs, so it is prudent to load SHARE. That fact is reflected both in the contents of A:\DOS and in the A:\CONFIG.SYS file (see Figure 5.2). The copy of the virus-scanning and cleanup software was the very latest available in mid-1992 when the figure was prepared. (DOS 6 includes a similar virus-scanning program, but the one shown here will work with any version of DOS.) The copy of PC Tools is very old, dating back to 1987. Sometimes it makes a lot of sense to use old utility programs if they will do what you need to have done and if, as is often the case, they are substantially smaller than the current version of the same program.

```
        Directory of A:\                    Directory of A:\UTILS

IO         SYS    22398          LIST      COM      8977
MSDOS      SYS    30128          PARK      COM       505
CONFIG     SYS      179          SST       EXE     44008
COMMAND    COM    25308          FC        EXE     45350
AUTOEXEC   BAT      175          FCDOC     EXE     46512
                                 VORCOMP   EXE     20448
                                 VORCOMP   DOC     36268
                                 NOTE      EXE     40832
      Directory of A:\DOS        PCTOOLS   EXE    167846
                                 PKUNZIP   EXE     23528
ANSI       SYS     1647          PKZIP     EXE     34296
ATTRIB     EXE    10656          SCHECK    EXE     29090
CHKDSK     COM     9819          SCREATE   COM       928
DEBUG      COM    15866          SDEFRAG   EXE     55485
DISKCOMP   COM     5848          STACKER   COM     40667
DISKCOPY   COM     6264
FDISK      COM    48983
FORMAT     COM    11671               Directory of A:\CMOS
HDFORM     EXE    21106
MODE       COM    15440          CMOSPUT   COM       155
SHARE      EXE     8608          CMOSGET   COM        78
SUBST      EXE    10552          CMOS      DAT        64
SYS        COM     4725
XCOPY      EXE    11216
                                      Directory of A:\VIRSTUF

    Directory of A:\C-BACKUP     VIRUSCAN  EXE     61149
                                 VSCAN85   DOC     33375
AUTOEXEC   BAT      435          CLEAN     EXE     83241
CONFIG     SYS      119          CLEAN85   DOC     15047
C-TREE     ZIP    23985
```

Figure 5.1. Files and directories on a Safety Boot Diskette.

The program HDFORM.EXE in the A:\DOS directory is a low-level formatting program that came with the computer. All the files in A:\UTILS listed before PCTOOLS.EXE and the programs PKUNZIP and PKZIP are shareware programs. See the hypertext database on the diskette that came with this book for more information on each of them, plus information about how you can get copies of them.

```
                Contents of A:\CONFIG.SYS
BUFFERS = 30
FILES = 30
BREAK = ON
LASTDRIVE = M
DEVICE = A:\UTILS\STACKER.COM
C:\STACVOL.DSK
DEVICE = A:\DOS\ANSI.SYS
SHELL = A:\COMMAND.COM /P /E:256

                Contents of A:\AUTOEXEC.BAT
@echo off
PATH A:\DOS;A:\UTILS
verify ON
PROMPT *** SAFETY BOOT DISK ***  $P $G
A:\DOS\SHARE /F:4096
echo.
echo ***** SAFETY BOOT DISK - MS-DOS ver. 3.30 *****
echo.
```

Figure 5.2. The CONFIG.SYS and AUTOEXEC.BAT files for the Safety Boot Diskette of Figure 5.1.

4. Save a Copy of Your CMOS Configuration Information

If your PC is in classes 3 through 6 (an AT or more advanced model), it has a battery backed-up CMOS RAM chip that holds some crucial configuration information. Be sure to put programs on your Safety Boot Diskette to allow you to store (and later restore) the contents of that CMOS setup RAM. The A:\CMOS directory in Figure 5.1 shows one such set of programs. They were published by *PC Magazine* in 1987 and are now freely available on many bulletin board systems. (See Chapter 20 for an important cautionary note about these programs.) The CMOS.DAT file is, of course, specific to the PC you are protecting with this Safety Boot Diskette.

There are many alternative programs to capture and restore the contents of the CMOS configuration RAM. One more is CMOS.EXE, which is a part of the WILSON.ZIP shareware utility package.

Most programs to save and restore the CMOS configuration information only save the first 64 bytes. That is all the data contained in the CMOS in IBM's original *AT*. Many modern clone PCs and some of IBM's *PS/2*s store some extended CMOS data in addition.

One of the very few programs that knows how to save that extended information is the MicroHouse International utility program, MH-SAVE; its companion program, MH-RESTR, can restore that extended CMOS information. You can get copies of these programs from the MicroHouse International electronic bulletin board system. (See the MemInfo hypertext database on the diskette included in this book.)

5. Create a CONFIG.SYS File
Especially Designed for Your Safety Boot Diskette

There are several reasons why you will want to have a CONFIG.SYS file on your Safety Boot Diskette (in the root directory). The most important one is to be sure you can access the files on your hard disk. Second is to be sure any programs you run find the same numbers of file handlers and buffers available as they had when you booted off drive C. (File handlers and buffers are discussed in Chapter 20.) A third reason is to be sure you load the same command interpreter you are used to using.

Study the following sections to discover just which things you must include in the CONFIG.SYS file you will put in the root directory of your Safety Boot Diskette. Then create it. Remember to use a text editor (if you use a word processor, be sure to save the file as "text" or "pure ASCII"). Use the DOS TYPE command after you are through to be sure that file has only the things you meant to put in it.

Guaranteeing Access to Your Hard Disk
(and Loading Other Device Drivers)

Examine the CONFIG.SYS file in the root directory of your PC's drive C. That is the one that takes effect when you boot from the hard drive. Look for any lines beginning with DEVICE=. Those are the lines that load device drivers.

Some of those device drivers may be essential to accessing your hard drive partition(s). There are two common cases where this will be so. The first is if your hard disk was partitioned using a non-DOS disk partitioning program. The second is if you are using a disk data compression program. In each of these cases you must identify the device driver program file, copy that file to a subdirectory on your Safety Boot Diskette, and add a line to your Safety Boot Diskette's CONFIG.SYS file to load that driver.

The non-DOS disk partitioning programs are ones such as *Disk Manager*, from On Track (for which the device driver file is called DMDRVR.BIN), or *SpeedStor* (SSTOR.SYS), from Storage Dimensions.

The most popular of the disk data compression device drivers are *Stacker*, from Stac Electronics; *SuperStor*, from AddStor; and *Expanz!*, from InfoChip Systems. Any of these device drivers that you do find may be located in a subdirectory on your hard disk. That means they will be loaded by a line in the CONFIG.SYS file in C:\ that looks something like these samples:

```
DEVICE = C:\DM\DMDRVR.BIN
```

```
DEVICE = C:\STACKER\STACKER.COM C:\STACVOL.DSK
```

When you find those lines, you will have to copy them to the CONFIG.SYS file you are creating for your Safety Boot Diskette, but then you will have to edit those lines. Assuming you copy the drivers to the A:\UTILS directory, these two samples would look like this:

```
DEVICE = A:\UTILS\DMDRVR.BIN
```

```
DEVICE = A:\UTILS\STACKER.COM C:\STACVOL.DSK
```

Notice that in the second line only the location of STACKER.COM had to be changed. It still is given the name of the compressed data file C:\STACVOL.DSK on the hard disk, since that is the data it is supposed to uncompress when you seek access to C:.

Another crucial device driver is SHARE. If you have a disk larger than 32MB or you ever do any task switching (let alone multitasking) this device driver is vital to the safety of your data. That is true even with DOS 5 or 6. If these conditions describe your PC, then you may wish to INSTALL the SHARE program in your CONFIG.SYS file (if you use DOS 5 or later), or else you can simply run SHARE from your AUTOEXEC.BAT file. Remember to do this on both drive C: and your Safety Boot Diskette.

Apply the KISS Principle
to Your Safety Boot Diskette's CONFIG.SYS File

"Keep It Simple, Sam" (or Suzy, or whatever other *S*-word you prefer here). There are some device drivers you definitely won't want to include in the CONFIG.SYS file you create for your Safety Boot Diskette. These include any memory-management programs. They may include network drivers. Keeping them out of your system helps simplify things. And when you are troubleshooting, keeping things as simple as possible is an absolute necessity.

Then there may be some device drivers that are totally optional. ANSI.SYS is one. It allows you to create a more interesting DOS prompt and helps some programs display color, but it isn't usually essential.

Set Up a Compatible Environment

Other lines in your C:\CONFIG.SYS file may specify a number of FILES, BUFFERS, FCBS, and STACKS. Duplicate each of them in your A:\CONFIG.SYS file (for the Safety Boot Diskette). That way all the programs you run will see the same operating system environment you have been used to. The one thing you really want to avoid is having some program fail for lack of enough FILES when all your attention is focused on why your hard disk won't boot. That could cost you hours before you realize what has gone wrong.

If you have a SHELL statement in C:\CONFIG.SYS, that, too, will need to be duplicated in A:\CONFIG.SYS. The SHELL statement specifies which command interpreter to load. The normal DOS one is COMMAND.COM. The SHELL statement also can be used to give some optional parameters to whatever command interpreter it specifies.

One reason to use a SHELL statement is to set up a larger (master) DOS environment space than the default 160 bytes. That is done with the /E:*nnn* option after COMMAND.COM. Another reason is to load a different command interpreter. The most popular of these are 4DOS and Norton's NDOS.

Once again, to keep you from thinking about too many things at once, especially when you're under a lot of stress, KISS!—put the same SHELL entry in A:\CONFIG.SYS as in C:\CONFIG.SYS. Edit it to use the command interpreter that you copied to your Safety Boot Diskette from drive C. (If you use a command interpreter other than COMMAND.COM, be sure you've copied that command interpreter to your Safety Boot Diskette.)

A Reason to Complicate Your Safety Boot Diskette

There is one reason why you might make the CONFIG.SYS file on your Safety Boot Diskette a bit more complex than it really has to be. If you are preparing it for a PC whose user is much less sophisticated than you are, you might want to include a network driver or a driver to allow access to an optical or Bernoulli disk. Do this if you can also create on that floppy enough of that user's normal working environment that he or she could actually work just from the floppy, while waiting for you or some other more knowledgeable person to come fix whatever is wrong with his or her PC's hard disk.

6. Create an AUTOEXEC.BAT File
Especially Designed for Your Safety Boot Diskette

For many of the same reasons that you want a CONFIG.SYS file on your Safety Boot Diskette, you also will want to have an AUTOEXEC.BAT file there. Some necessary device drivers load as TSR programs from the AUTOEXEC.BAT file. This is also where you set your DOS PROMPT and PATH values and put other information into the DOS environment. And it may be where you load SHARE.

Again, examine the contents of C:\AUTOEXEC.BAT. (Only an AUTOEXEC.BAT file in that location will be referenced when you boot from the hard disk.) Copy and adapt lines from it as appropriate to A:\AUTOEXEC.BAT on your Safety Boot Diskette.

Define your usual DOS prompt, or a special one to remind you that you are using your Safety Boot Diskette. Set up a suitable PATH. Remember that you should not expect to be able to access any of the directories on your hard disk, so don't put any of them in the DOS path, at least not before any directories you wish to include from drive A.

One more tip. You can add lines to A:\AUTOEXEC.BAT to explain to whoever uses this diskette what it is and why it contains what it does. This could be very useful. You are going to expend some effort designing it, and even if it is for only your own use, you may not remember just why you did things the way you did. Help yourself (or anyone else who may use this Safety Boot Diskette); include some explanations.

Both the AUTOEXEC.BAT file and the CONFIG.SYS file you create for your Safety Boot Diskette must be specifically customized to what your PC demands. Figure 5.2 shows what they might look like for one PC, but your files may differ from these, possibly by a lot.

7. Build in Anti-Virus Tools

Figure 5.1 shows some files in a subdirectory called VIRSTUF. That is short for Virus Stuff, a directory filled with computer virus detection and removal programs (and perhaps some text files explaining their use). Since computer viruses can cause hard disk boot failure, and since they often show very few other symptoms of their existence (at least until they do something horrendous to your PC!), it is always wise to check a PC in trouble for possible viral contamination. The best way to do this is to boot off of a known, virus-free diskette (which your Safety Boot Diskette will be) and then immediately run a virus-checking program on the PC's memory and hard disk.

One good program you might want to use is MacAfee's SCAN (and its associated CLEAN). These programs are usually revised on a monthly basis. That is one reason you might want to keep them on a separate diskette. On the other hand, you could do worse than to have some fairly recent version of SCAN on your Safety Boot Diskette also.

The subject of computer viruses is too far afield from our main purpose to devote much more space to it here. The point is, if you create and keep a Safety Boot Diskette with anti-virus software, you will at least be able to detect and recover from a computer virus attack with a minimum of grief. (This is especially true if you also follow the advice about backups later in this chapter.)

8. Add Utilities to Taste

When you think about what you will be doing with your Safety Boot Diskette and the circumstances in which you'll be using it, no doubt several important utility programs will spring to mind that you will want to put on it. Some are DOS external commands. A good set of those might include FORMAT, FDISK, DEBUG, DISKCOPY, and COMP or FC. If you have DOS 5 or 6, UNFORMAT, UNDELETE, and MIRROR might also be worth including (MIRROR only comes with DOS 5; if you have DOS 6, you might include Microsoft's diagnostic program, MSD in place of MIRROR.) The DOS 6 UNDELETE program does most of what MIRROR did in DOS 5.

> **Warning**   Watch out! It is okay to put MIRROR on your Safety Boot Diskette, but don't call it from the AUTOEXEC.BAT file on that diskette. Using MIRROR or any similar program could make a difficult problem into an unsolvable one. The purpose of MIRROR is to save a copy of the FAT, the boot record, and the directory structure. But if your hard disk is in trouble, those data areas may be what is messed up. Perhaps the backup copies of them (created the last time MIRROR ran, the last time you were able to boot from the hard disk) are still good. If you now run MIRROR again, you could possibly overwrite the only good copy of that information with garbage.

A file viewer, such as the Vern Buerg LIST program, and a small ASCII file editor for modifying CONFIG.SYS and AUTOEXEC.BAT files (even EDLIN if you wish, or NOTE, TED, QEDIT, or PC-WRITE) are also prime candidates for inclusion here. (You might be tempted to use the DOS 5 EDIT program. Don't. To do that you would have to include QBASIC.EXE, and it's just too big to be worth the space on your Safety Boot Diskette.)

Write-Protect That Diskette!

Be sure to write-protect the Safety Boot Diskette when you have completed it. This is essential, and gives you near absolute protection against having that diskette infected by a computer virus anytime in the future. (It also makes it much tougher for you to accidentally do something bad to it while you are in a state of shock and panic over the apparent failure of your hard disk.)

Test the Safety Boot Diskette

Be a cynic. Don't take anything on faith that you could test instead. This advice goes double when you are building a safety net. As soon as you have finished creating your Safety Boot Diskette and have write-protected it, test it. If you can actually boot from the Safety Boot Diskette and then access your hard disk (and any other devices you may have enabled, such as a network connection), then you can be sure it will work when you need it. If you only assume it will work, Murphy will bite you when you can least afford it.

To be absolutely certain the Safety Boot Diskette will work when you need it, try this experiment now: turn off your PC, open it up, and unplug the power connector from your hard drive. Then try booting from your Safety Boot Diskette. Without power, the hard disk won't work. This simulates the worst conditions you will ever face. This is a good way to be sure you did not accidentally leave some reference to a crucial file or directory on drive C in a place that keeps your Safety Boot Diskette from working.

A Final Precaution

Make a DISKCOPY of the Safety Boot Diskette, write-protect the copy, and put this copy away somewhere safe, far from the PC it is protecting. Floppy disks can fail, especially if you happen to pass them near a strong magnet or get them too hot. Backing up this diskette is fully as important as backing up your hard disk. The Safety Boot Diskette along with your hard disk backups can get you up and running in a minimum of time when (not if) your hard disk fails.

When and How to Use Your Safety Boot Diskette

The whole point of having a Safety Boot Diskette is to be able to boot from it whenever you cannot boot from your hard drive. This may happen whenever you install some new memory-management software, as that often requires several obscure steps. Until you figure them out, you may render your disk nonbootable. (Some memory managers offer you a way around this, but having a tested Safety Boot Diskette is a great comfort for those times.)

You also will want to use your Safety Boot Diskette anytime you suspect you might have a computer viral infection, or if your hard disk simply won't boot correctly for any other reason. This is not a book on hard disk repair. If the problem seems to be a hardware one, or even a data messup unrelated to your new memory-management software, you will have to consult a book that discusses those sorts of repairs. One such book is John M. Goodman's *Hard Disk Secrets* (IDG Books, Worldwide, 1993).

Prudent People Always Have Good Backups!

I know, you have heard this song a million times. So you must know the lyrics by heart by now. But do you do it? And do you make backups that are good enough?

Before you experiment with a new memory-management technique or strategy, do yourself a big favor and make sure your hard disk backups are in perfect order. No telling when you will make some mistake and render your disk unreadable. It happens. But it doesn't hurt nearly so much if you have good backups and know how to use them.

> There are many good backup programs you could use. You even can do backups in most cases by using just the DOS command COPY or XCOPY (though that will not work for very large files, nor will it be as easy to use as some of the more sophisticated backup programs). Prior to DOS version 6, the BACKUP utility that was included with DOS was barely usable. The DOS 6 MSBACKUP program (a licensed version of the Norton Backup) is a very easy to use and capable program, and it comes for free with DOS in both a Windows and a DOS-only version.
>
> Which program you use is not nearly as important as how you use it and—most important of all—how well you verify that it did its job. Simply relying on a program's internal verification strategy is not good enough. See the section "The Saddest Truth About Backups" later in this chapter for a better approach.

This section sets out briefly some things you may want to consider when evaluating any backup strategy. To treat this subject fully could take another whole book, so only the barest outlines are included here.

What Is a "Good" Backup?

A good backup is one that serves fully the purposes for which you do backups. But what are those purposes? There can be several. A couple are set forth here.

An important point not to forget: a good backup strategy is one that is easy to do, so that it will get done. It need not be nearly so easy to use those backups for recovery from disaster or to recover an archived file, since those things are done relatively infrequently.

Here are some purposes for which you would make a backup:

- *Recovery from disaster.* Almost every computer user understands that you make backups so you can replace your hard disk when it crashes and then restore the backed-up files to that new disk. What they may fail to consider is how often it is prudent to make backups. And they may not appreciate the desirability of making more than one set, keeping them forever, and of keeping a set of those backups at an off-site location.

- *Archival record.* Once you bother to keep permanent copies of all your valuable files, they can be useful even if your hard disk hasn't (yet) died. They provide an archival record of your work. When the file you need has been purged from the hard disk, your backup set may be the easiest place to find a copy.

Amazingly enough, there are some people who do not understand backups at all (even though they make them regularly). A friend of mine was asked how much he would charge to fly from Southern California to Connecticut and recover data off a crashed hard drive. He talked himself out of a lucrative job when he asked them if they had any backups. It turned out they had made a full backup just hours before the crash. But they had no idea why they had made it, or what to do with it!

Different Kinds of Backups

There are three distinct types of backups. You may need to use all three. They are:

- The *full backup.* This is what most people do, and the only kind they do. It involves making a full copy of all your hard disk's files to tape or some other medium. It cannot be done, practically, more than a few times a week, which is one of its chief drawbacks; often people recycle most of the backup tapes or disks in a few weeks, which is another great drawback.

- The *incremental backup.* This involves backing up only those files that were changed since the last time you did an incremental backup. It is practical to do incremental backups much more frequently than the full backups, and it can be practical to keep both occasional full backups and all incremental ones virtually forever. This combination is highly effective.

This works very well if all you have are relatively small files and you only work on a few of them each day. Back up everything only once a year, if you like, but back up all new or changed files every hour. That gives great protection at very little cost in time or backup media.

- The *differential backup.* This involves backing up the files that have changed since the last full backup. This typically is used where the files that change are large and have only small changes in them.

If you have a 3MB database and each day you change a few thousand bytes in that file, it would be tough to justify spending money on enough backup media to hold a copy of every day's version. The traditional solution to this has been to keep overwriting the backup copy from yesterday with one from today. This means you keep only the latest copy (and the last one you got in a full backup). That works, but it is not as safe a strategy as it could be.

There is now a better way to deal with large, slowly changing files. It involves using a special utility program, such as *Deltafile* or *RTPatch*.

> *Deltafile*, from Hyperkinetix, and *RTPatch*, from PocketSoft, are programs that can let you treat even large, slowly changing files as if they were many small files. This program compares today's version of your large database with yesterday's, and it generates a small program that can convert yesterday's file into a copy of today's. Using this effectively means you must keep around both the current and the most recent past version of that database (so you have something to compare with), but if that is feasible in your situation, it can make creating very safe backup sets both quick and cheap.

The Importance of Being Recent Enough

Disks never crash when you find it convenient. A crash almost always seems to come just 15 minutes before your weekly full backup. If you have not also been doing incremental backups, you will have lost a whole week's work. One good guideline is this: whenever the pain of doing a backup is less than the pain you would experience if you had to re-create all the work you did since the last backup, it is time to do another one. To make this work well, keep the backup pain minimal by using incremental and differential backups most of the time, and full ones only occasionally.

The Importance of Having More Than One Copy, Preferably in More Than One Location

All information storage media fail. Sometimes a failure is a matter of the medium wearing out; sometimes it is caused by an external disturbance. Whatever the reason, the result is the same. Your data gets lost.

If the copy that failed was your last copy, you have lost your data forever. This sad fact alone argues for keeping multiple copies. Another argument is that sometimes damage or loss strikes many things in the same vicinity. Fire and thieves are two examples. When you lose both your hard disk and the backup copy you kept handy beside the PC, having a spare copy of the data elsewhere is your only hope.

It is important not to reuse backup media. Here are some reasons why:

- *For archival uses.* Clearly, if you are depending on backups as your archival copy, you should never erase it as long as that information has any possible value. In many business contexts that means keeping backup sets for many years. Naturally this puts a premium on a backup strategy like those detailed above which minimize the cost and volume of the media required to do this.

- *To protect against viral file damage.* When computer viruses strike, they commonly infect files for a long time before they are detected. They do their damage only after they have spread widely. This means that, in addition to your hard disk files, all your recent backups are likely to be infected.

  Some viruses can be removed; many cannot. Sometimes your only hope is to find a backup old enough to predate the infection.

- *To protect against human error.* For every computer virus that has damaged a file there must be 10,000 people who have done as much damage through a simple blunder. Not all of these instances of damage are detected right away, either. Again, if the damage cannot be repaired easily, a backup that predates it is the best hope for recovery.

For example, suppose you manage somehow to mangle a database file at some record out in the middle of the file. You may not notice this fact as long as you access records before the damaged one. But you may find it is impossible to read any record after the damaged one. Depending on what is in the file and how you do your business, that problem could come to light immediately (when you have a recent, good copy of the file readily available), or it might take months.

In the latter case, you might have to reconstruct the whole file from a year-old copy plus all the incremental backups of its changes. That could be quite painful to do, but perhaps less so than losing the end of the file altogether.

One Way You Should Not Use Your Backups

Sometimes a person will back up his or her work files at one office, take those backups to another office, and then restore them to another PC in order to continue working on them there. That could be okay, but it also could lead to inadvertent loss of data.

Let us call the PC from which the files came *A* and the second one *B*. Suppose that an associate of that worker comes along and does some more work on those same files on PC *A*; now suppose the first worker finishes working on those files on PC *B*, backs up those files, and brings the back-ups to PC *A*. If he or she restores those files, they will overwrite the changes made by the second worker. Indeed, even if the two workers realize what they have done before any data is lost, they still have a serious problem. How can they merge the changes each made in separate copies of the files? There is no general, easy answer to that one.

When Backups Are Not As Helpful As You Might Expect

If you back up files on one PC using one version of a backup program, you may not be able to restore on another PC if the second machine has an older copy of the restore program. In DOS this problem occurs when the backup is done with version 3.3 or later and the restore is attempted with version 3.2 or earlier. The reason is that the form of storage of the backup information on the backup media changed between those versions. The newer RESTORE command understands both formats, so it can restore files backed up with the earlier version, but not vice versa. If you use a commercial backup program it is wise to check with the vendor about any similar incompatibilities their program may have.

Some Ways Backups Actually Can Hurt You

If you use some backup programs (including all versions of the DOS BACKUP and RESTORE commands up to version 3.2), beware: You can accidentally restore old versions of the DOS hidden system files and COMMAND.COM on top of newer ones. This will downgrade your DOS version.

Furthermore, if through a backup and restore cycle you end up with a mismatched set of DOS external commands (not all from the same version of DOS), the ones that don't match the version of the hidden system files and COMMAND.COM usually will not function. Worse than that, if your COMMAND.COM is of a version different from the hidden, system files, you cannot boot your computer from that disk at all.

The Saddest Truth About Backups

Many people who know it is important to make backups do so quite religiously. Unfortunately, not many of them do any kind of *testing* on a regular basis to ensure that their strategy for backing up and restoring will work when they need it.

Then comes the day of truth, and their hard disk fails. They replace it and attempt to restore their files, only to discover that their backups are worthless.

This can happen if the media they are using are flawed. Or it can happen if those media are stored inappropriately. Doing a verify read-after-write (as many tape backup programs do) is valuable, but it is not sufficient to protect you against this disaster-in-waiting.

Don't let this happen to you. *Test your process.*

For example, back up a subtree from your hard disk and restore it to a different disk. Then compare every file in both subtrees byte-for-byte. Only if they match exactly are you safe.

(If you only have one hard disk, create a subdirectory on it called C:\TEST. Now use the DOS command SUBST D: C:\TEST. Restore files backed up from C: to D:. Then compare them with the originals. The shareware program *VORCOMP* is especially nice for doing these comparisons.)

Make a point of repeating these tests from time to time. It takes a little effort, but safe is oh-so-much nicer than sorry.

This Was Meant to Scare You

This chapter was meant to scare you; it also was meant to offer you hope. The dangers described here can be avoided or their damage mitigated in a few, relatively easy steps. The trick is to take those steps now, before disaster strikes.

It would be lovely if you never needed this information—almost as good as if you have acted on it before your hour of need. Remember, "A word to the wise is sufficient."

HOW IT
ALL WORKS

II

If you've read all the previous material in this book, you are well prepared to learn about memory management. If you skipped the previous part (because, no doubt, you already know those things), welcome back. Now it's time to start the main story of this book—all about PC memory, what it is, how and when to upgrade it, and how to manage it.

This could be a very confusing story, but it doesn't have to be. The key is for you to learn all the special terms that are used and exactly what they mean in this context. Even experts often get some of these terms confused. So begin at the beginning, with basic concepts and definitions. With that foundation well in place, you then can go on to more complex topics.

Of course you want to know more than just some general ideas. So in Part II, you also will learn just how these ideas have been applied in a number of important, commercial memory-management products. And now, on with the story.

6

MEMORY FUNDAMENTALS

This chapter gives you the background necessary for any discussion of PC memory management. That includes the most basic issues, like the nature of memory; some fairly advanced ones, like the concept of demand-paged virtual memory; and a lot in-between.

In this chapter you will learn why you need memory in a PC, how it is used, some of the diverse forms it takes, and much more. You also will learn, in a general way, when adding memory to your PC can help you and when it cannot.

PC Architecture, an Overview

To put the discussion of PC memory into an appropriate context, I will first describe the overall architecture of any computer. Once you understand what the essential parts of a computer are and how they communicate, you can focus on the details of just the memory part. You also will need to know how information is represented. That's covered in this chapter as well.

The Five Essential Parts of Any Computer

Every computer, from the largest mainframe to the smallest laptop, has five essential, functional aspects:

- Input
- Output
- Storage
- Processing
- Control

If any one of these parts were left out, what you would have left would not be a computer.

Figure 6.1 shows these five essential parts. The next several pages describe each of them and explain why it is necessary to a computer's operation. This section also gives examples of how each part is implemented in a typical PC.

Input

Computers are machines built for the purpose of processing information. If they are to do that, there must be some mechanism for getting the information to be processed into those machines. The parts of a computer that do this task are called its *input devices.*

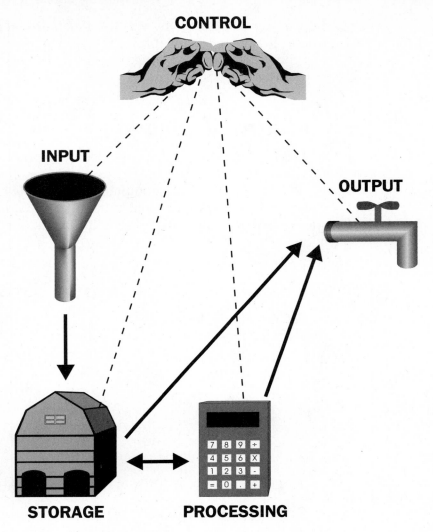

CONTROL

INPUT

OUTPUT

STORAGE   **PROCESSING**

Figure 6.1.   The five essential parts of any computer.

On your PC, the input device you likely use the most is the keyboard. You also input information whenever you load a program or data file using the diskette drive. Some PCs have tape drives; these, too, can be used to load information (both programs and data files) into the computer.

While those are the most common ways to put information into a PC, they are far from the only ones. If you have a mouse, you send messages to the computer each time you move it or click one of its buttons. A trackball, light pen, or graphic pad stylus are some alternative pointing devices that serve as input devices.

If you have a modem attached to a phone line, your PC can receive information through it from other computers at great distances. A scanner allows you to enter graphical information. (An optical character recognition program allows you to convert some of that graphical data into character form, but this is not an example of input. This is an example of processing information after it is inside the computer.)

Game aficionados may notice an omission: What about a joystick? Yes, this is another means of information input to the PC. If you wish to view it in that way, a joystick could be called a multichannel analog-to-digital-conversion input device. And in fact, game-port adapters have been used for serious data acquisition in certain applications.

> Game-port adapters may have as many as four channels of analog input and four digital ones. If the board allows you to attach two joysticks, each with two buttons, you have this full range of input possibilities. The motion of each joystick is converted into two numbers, one for its tilt left or right, and the other for its tilt forward or back. Each button-press is separately entered into the computer as a digital signal.

This brings up a whole other group of PC input devices. Scientists have developed many ways to use PCs to automate their experiments, and engineers have applied PCs to the control of diverse industrial processes. For all of those applications, some means of data capture is needed. So people have developed custom plug-in boards for PCs that do just that. Those, too, are input devices.

Output

Computers would be useless if they only processed information. You need to learn the results of their processing. PCs display their results in many different ways. The mechanisms they use to do so are called *output devices.*

The most common one is the screen, or monitor. Here words and pictures display both the information the computer has received (when it echoes characters as they are typed, or moves a cursor in response to a mouse motion) and the results of processing that information. The screen as an output device has many advantages, among them speed and color at reasonable cost. It also has one outstanding limitation: The images generally disappear after a short time.

Printers, the second most common form of output device, overcome the screen's transiency (and usually offer more resolution), but not without other limitations. Most people use both a screen and a printer. (Some people use more than one of each.)

Diskette drives and tape drives can be, and often are, used as input devices. They are used equally as output devices. When you save a document, spreadsheet, or other data file and then copy that file to a diskette and give it to someone else, you are using your diskette drive as an output device. Software publishers use diskettes as the output medium for their "publications." When you receive one of those disks, it is output for the publisher, but you use it as input to your PC.

Likewise, a modem works two ways. Information flows in from the telephone line, but other information flows out to the remote computer.

Many of the physical pieces in your PC have a dual function like this. Sometimes they can be viewed as serving in more than two capacities, as you shall see in just a moment.

Storage

If all the information you poured into a computer immediately fell through to output, no processing could be done. It is absolutely essential that the information hang around at least a little while. That is done in a part of the computer called *storage.*

Customarily, the information-storage places in a computer are divided into two parts. One is *storage;* the other is *memory.* There are two important distinctions between these parts: How quickly the processing part of the computer can access the information each contains, and how long that information stays around. (Chapter 2 also discusses this difference. If you want more details than are given here, you may want to review that section.)

Memory is the fast-access portion of the information-holding parts of the computer. This is where information must be placed to be processed, for only here is it available quickly enough not to slow down the processing part of the computer. In a PC, this is composed of RAM and ROM chips or modules. This is the memory that I will focus on in the rest of this book.

Two drawbacks of the memory part of storage (RAM and ROM) are that either its data disappears when power goes away (RAM) or it cannot be altered (ROM). Neither is suitable as a place to keep for a long time any information that is to be processed or that has just been processed. For that, you use *storage*. In a PC, storage is mostly disk drives (hard, floppy, optical, and so on) and tape drives. (Again, see Chapter 2 for more on this.)

Processing

Input, output, and storage offer a means to get information into the computer, keep it around awhile, and then get it out again. The fourth functional section, *processing,* is what alters the form of information, changing raw data into more useful forms.

In a PC, that section is mostly found in one *very large scale integrated circuit (VLSI)* chip called the *Central Processing Unit,* or *CPU.* PCs are designed around either a chip made by Intel in its 80x86 family of chips or some clone of one of them.

There are many microprocessor chips made that are not in the Intel 80x86 family, nor clones of those chips. Motorola makes some. Rockwell makes some. Intel even makes some of the non-80x86-clone microprocessors. But as I said in Chapter 1, I am only considering as a PC a computer that does use an Intel 80x86 chip or a clone of one of them as its CPU.

In fact, one of the most common ways to say what kind of IBM-compatible PC you have is to name the model of Intel CPU chip it uses. Thus, you often hear people saying, "I have a 286 computer," or "I just upgraded to a 486."

In Chapter 13, you will meet all the members of Intel's 80x86 family, and learn about a number of other processor chips as well. Here is just a brief list of the Intel names for the most popular CPU chips used in PCs:

- 8088 (XT)
- 80286 (AT)
- 386 (386)
- 486 (486)
- Pentium

The name in parentheses after the part number is the common name for a PC that uses that chip. The names XT and AT come from the models of IBM *PC* that used those chips. The numbers used as common names are just shortened versions of the full Intel model number.

To further confuse matters, Intel has created several versions of both their 386 and 486 chips, bearing suffixes such as DX, SX, and SL. The meanings of these suffixes differ between the 386 and 486. Again, the details are all in Chapter 13.

Not all the circuitry on the CPU chip does processing. That is done only in the portion referred to as the *Arithmetic Logic Unit*, or *ALU*. Also on the CPU chip are a modest amount of memory (registers and, in some models, some cache memory) and a bus controller portion that handles the flow of information on and off the chip. Another very important part of the CPU chip is the control circuitry, discussed in the next section.

Some PCs have one or more additional processor chips of a very different sort. One popular kind is a *math coprocessor.* Intel has introduced a math coprocessor for each model of CPU chip in the 80x86 family (except for the 486DX and Pentium, which include the math coprocessor on the CPU chip). Some manufacturers have cloned those chips. One manufacturer, Weitek, offers a totally different kind of math coprocessor chip for PCs, again in a family of designs, one for each member of the Intel 80x86 family of CPU chips. The discussion in Chapter 13 gives more details on this topic also.

Another popular coprocessor chip is a *video processor* (sometimes known as a *video, graphics,* or *Windows accelerator*). This, and several other coprocessor chip options, are briefly described in Chapter 27.

Control

Control is the last of the five essential parts of a computer. What would you have if this section were missing? Just a fancy calculator. A calculator accepts information input, stores it, processes it (adds, subtracts, multiplies, and divides numbers), and then displays the answer. The essential difference between a calculator and a computer is that the calculator performs the steps you tell it to, but it only performs each one as you tell it to (by pressing its keys). A computer can, in effect, press its own keys. (As an alternative image, notice that in Figure 6.1 *Control* is shown as a puppetmaster pulling strings that manipulate each of the other parts.)

When you say a computer is running a program, it is simply reading the program to learn which processing steps to perform and then performing them. Computers can run programs because they have all the parts a calculator has and one more. That added section is its control section.

There are also machines called *programmable calculators*. These are essentially very small computers. They have all the normal calculator parts along with the ability to store and execute small programs. They differ from the full general-purpose computers mainly by being more limited in capacity. Also, some of them cannot compute changes to their own programs, as a PC can.

The control section is located in another part of the CPU chip. Its job is to read instructions (program steps), and then decode and execute them. Consider just what that means in a little more detail.

A computer program is stored in memory as a sequence of numbers. Each number, or small group of numbers, represents one step in the processing to be done. Those groups are the computer's *instructions.* The computer's control portion directs the rest of the CPU to read those numbers one at a time. The control portion of the CPU watches this process until it sees that all the numbers in one group (a single, full instruction) have been read. Next, it determines what action that group of numbers says the computer should perform. (This step is called decoding the instruction.) It then directs the other parts of the computer to do that. And finally, it directs the reading of the next instruction.

Some of the Intel 80x86 CPU chips can do more than one of these steps at a time. This ability is a limited form of parallel processing called *pipelining*.

Most PCs have some of the control aspect built into one or more other places besides the CPU. Almost every model has a *Direct Memory Access (DMA)* controller chip. A DMA chip is used to speed the transfer of large amounts of information to and from the disk drives. It also may be used by scanners and other devices to move blocks of information. Some PCs also have a graphics coprocessor chip that can accept and execute some instructions in order to speed up the drawing of screen images. Some bus controllers have another full microcomputer on them. One example of this is a *Small Computer System Interface (SCSI)* host adapter used to run disk and tape drives and certain other peripherals. (The acronym *SCSI* has the unfortunate pronunciation "scuzzy.")

Each of these other processors can receive and execute instructions. The main CPU can hand off a portion of its work to each of them. In this way it spreads around the overall control function.

Which Parts Can Talk Directly to Each Other?

Just having the five critical parts that make up a computer is not enough to make a computer work. The parts must be appropriately interconnected. What does that mean, and how is it done?

One aspect of appropriate connection is that information must somehow get from the input part of the computer into its memory, from there to the processing section and back again, and finally to the output. So the connections have to go to those places. Another aspect is that the circuits at both ends of a link must operate at the same speed, or at least they must somehow be made to synchronize their operations.

The links between the parts of the computer have the general name *bus*. This can mean just a connection from one place to one other, or it can be a more general structure, linking together a number of different parts of the computer.

A bus is a group of wires. It can take many forms. One popular form is a collection of copper wires, enclosed in plastic insulation and molded together (called a *ribbon cable*). Another form is as a number of conductive traces etched on a printed circuit board. But a bus is more than just a group of wires connecting different parts of the computer. The bus also includes circuits (called *buffers*) to strengthen the signals, and it may include circuits (called *latches*) to keep fleeting signals around awhile for the benefit of slower circuits that must receive those signals.

Here is a list of the buses found in most PCs:

- CPU internal buses

- CPU-to-memory bus

- CPU-to-I/O bus

- Disk interface

- SCSI bus

- PCMCIA PC card interface

- Local bus

- Video output interface

- Parallel port

- Serial port

The rest of this section gives a brief description of each of these buses. Several of them are described in greater detail in Chapter 14.

Of all the buses outside the CPU chip, the CPU-to-memory and CPU-to-I/O buses have the greatest impact on memory management. These are the buses I'll focus on in most of the rest of this book.

Buses on the CPU Chip

The parts of the CPU chip are interconnected by several buses internal to the chip. These carry information from its input pins to the internal registers, to the instruction decoding section, to the ALU, and back to the registers and the output pins.

> Another way to describe the different buses inside the CPU is in terms of the kinds of signals they carry. One carries data and instructions, another the addresses in memory where those data and instructions are kept, and yet another the control signals by which the control section commands the rest of the CPU circuits to do their jobs.

CPU to Memory and CPU to Input/Output Devices

The information flowing on and off the CPU chip is mostly going to or from the main memory (RAM and ROM). Often that is all located on the same circuit board as the CPU chip, but in some cases, at least a portion of the memory will be on another printed circuit card. The connection between the CPU and main memory is called, not surprisingly, the *CPU-to-memory bus*, or just the *memory bus* for short.

The rest of the information going to and from the CPU chip is information for a wide variety of more distant parts of the PC. The connection to these more remote parts is called the *Input/Output bus* (or I/O bus for short). For a brief discussion of one exception to this generalization, see the upcoming section titled "Local Bus."x

Some PCs use the same bus circuits (buffers, latches, and wires) for both the memory and the I/O buses; others keep the two buses separate. There can be advantages to doing it each way. Obviously, sharing the circuits saves the manufacturer money. But often the memory and the CPU both can operate much faster than the other parts of the PC. In those cases, it can make sense to have one fast bus for the private, CPU-to-memory conversations and another, slower bus for the CPU-to-I/O conversations.

Other Buses in Your PC

In addition to the buses internal to the CPU chip, the bus on the motherboard going from CPU to memory, and the bus connecting the CPU to various I/O devices, there often are other buses in a PC. Descriptions of some of the most important ones follow.

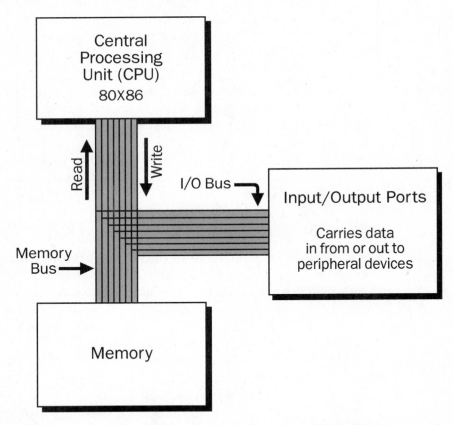

Figure 6.2. A bus connects the CPU with memory, and I/O data enters and leaves the CPU on a bus. Typically, this is one bus divided into two parts serving two different kinds of destination: memory and I/O ports. It is possible to put memory on the I/O bus, but that often degrades its performance, since typically the bus-to-I/O runs more slowly than that to memory.

Disk Interface

The disk controllers (for both floppy and hard disk drives) often are on a circuit board mounted separately from the drives they control. The cables connecting the controller to the drives are each a kind of bus.

> PCs use several different kinds of hard disks. Both MFM (Modified Frequency Modulation) and RLL (Run-Length Limited) drives use the ST506/412 disk interface. ESDI (Enhanced Small Device Interface) is another kind of hard disk interface or bus. A variant form of hard disk interface that has become very common is the *Integrated Drive Electronics AT Attachment*, commonly called *IDE/ATA*. Those, and the floppy disk interface, are the most popular variations on this PC disk interface bus.

SCSI Bus

Another popular bus used in many PCs goes by the name *Small Computer System Interface.* A *SCSI* host adapter may be used to talk not only to a hard disk drive, but also to an optical disk, tape drive, and other devices. In fact, up to seven of those devices can be connected to a single SCSI controller at once. The interconnection of all these devices forms the SCSI bus.

PCMCIA PC Card Interface

An important new bus has recently been defined for use in PCs. It is called the *PC card* interface. Originally proposed by the **J**apanese **E**lectronics **I**ndustry **D**evelopment **A**ssociation (JEIDA), it is now officially supported by the **P**ersonal **C**omputer **M**emory **C**ard **I**nternational **A**ssociation (PCMCIA), a combination standard-setting organization and trade association. Certain aspects of this new standard are included in standards issued by the **J**oint **E**lectrical **D**evice **E**ngineering **C**ouncil (JEDEC).

This new PC card interface allows a standard way to connect a computer to a wide variety of credit-card-sized plug-in cards. Some of these cards provide additional memory (RAM) for a PC. Others have memory (battery backed-up RAM or flash RAM) but are configured to look like a disk drive. Still others have read-only memory (ROM) with built-in programs. A feature of the ROM cards is that their programs can be executed directly from their location on the PC card instead of having to be copied first into the computer's system RAM. And finally, some PC cards carry hard disks or I/O devices (and, perhaps, some memory).

This new standard gives a very flexible means of enhancing any PC. One especially delightful feature of all PCMCIA cards is that you can insert or remove them without having to power down the PC—something that is at the least imprudent with most of the other PC buses. (Now used mainly in palmtop computers, they will be used eventually in a wide variety of PCs.)

> Plug-in cards are useful not only with computers. Some programmable musical instruments, games, and even microwave ovens have been built with sockets for them. The PC card standard was designed to allow the devices that accept PC cards to discriminate between those meant for use in their sort of device and those that are meant for use in totally different gadgets.

Local Bus

People used to think that the only messages that had to move ultra quickly to or from the CPU were those going to main memory. So every other part of the PC was attached to the CPU via the I/O bus. Now we find that our video cards are limited by the speed of that I/O bus.

In an effort to break this bottleneck, system designers have lately begun to offer something called a "local bus." That is a 32-bit bus, like the CPU-to-memory bus, but going to one or more slots where an option card can be plugged in an option card. The only option cards that will be built to attach to such a "local bus" will be those requiring the very highest rates of data flow, which include high-resolution video cards and network interface cards, and some very high-performance disk controllers.

Initially, each PC manufacturer that offered a "local bus" implemented it in a unique fashion. This meant that only special cards created by that manufacturer could be plugged into those bus slots.

Now we have two industry standards for the local bus. The first one to be completed sufficiently that manufacturers could start making products for it was the VESA local bus, or the "VL bus" as it is called for short. The other standard, called PCI for Peripheral Interconnect Interface, is one developed primarily by Intel.

There are technical advantages to each of these two standards, and it may be years before either of them manages to displace the other one from the marketplace. In the interim, you will have to be careful when choosing a new local-bus plug-in card to be sure it will fit into the kind of local bus slots, if any, that your PC offers.

Video Interface

The output of the video display adapter connects to the monitor on another, well-standardized interface, or bus. This one comes in two distinct forms. The original PC used a 9-pin TTL (**T**ransistor-**T**ransistor-**L**ogic) digital interface for both color and monochrome video. When EGA (**En**hanced **G**raphics **A**dapter) cards were introduced, they used essentially the same interface. With the introduction of the MCGA (**M**ulti**C**olor **G**raphics **A**rray) and VGA (**V**ideo **G**raphics **A**rray) video standards, a new video interface was needed. It is a 15-pin mixed analog and digital signal interface. (All these terms are described in detail in Chapter 8.)

Parallel Port

A PC's parallel output port (often used to connect to a printer) uses another standardized interface: the *IBM-to-Centronics printer cable* (or *bus*).

> The Centronics company introduced the first parallel printer interface on some of their printers. If you wanted to attach one of those printers to a computer, you had to get a special cable for that computer. All those cables had the same connector at the printer end, but they varied a great deal at the computer end.
>
> The original IBM *PC* was no different. It used a custom cable to connect to any Centronics-compatible printer. Now that the PC is so ubiquitous, many people think that the special IBM-to-Centronics cable is simply a "parallel printer cable." It is not. It is just one of many variations on that theme.
>
> Thus, the only place the interface to the printer becomes standard is at the printer end of these special cables. IBM's use of a 25-pin DB connector for the computer end is special to the PC world. We sometimes call that connector and the hardware that attaches to it an IBM *PC* parallel port. That could be thought of as one interface standard. Then the other end of an IBM-to-Centronics printer cable attached to that port becomes the Centronics-compatible printer port, another industry standard interface point.

Serial Port

The *serial ports* (also called *asynchronous communications ports*) on a PC conform to yet another standard. This one is called RS-232. Actually that standard has many alternative forms, including what is called EIA (**E**lectronic **I**ndustry **A**ssociation) voltage interface and TTY (**tele**type) current loop. Early PCs supported both these forms, but most modern ones only support the EIA voltage form. Also there are two standard physical connectors used in PCs for theses ports. The older, 25-pin connector is the one specified in the RS-232 document. IBM introduced a smaller, 9-pin version of this interface with its PC/AT. Many PC makers now use that variation of the serial standard for their PC's serial ports.

Many makers of very tiny computers (palmtops and laptops) use other variations. The connectors are usually much smaller and often have fewer wires. HP uses a five-wire version. Some go to as few as three wires. Still, these are all considered merely variations on RS-232. The signals on whatever wires they have resemble those on certain key wires of the full 25-wire version.

The most important point is that with an appropriate cable, suitable programs running at each end, and just a little luck, you can establish a serial communication link between any two computers that have an "RS-232" serial port.

Summary: What Is a Bus and What Are the Principal Buses in a PC?

To summarize, any means of interconnecting different parts of a computer is a bus, although that name is often reserved for interfaces that have been standardized, either by conventional practice or by a formal standards-setting body. In a PC, there are two main buses running from the CPU to other parts, one to memory and one to most everything else. The former is the *memory bus*; the latter is the *I/O bus*. In addition to these two, there are other interconnections, for example, from a disk controller to the disk drives.

Three Groups of Signals on the Bus

The two principal buses in a PC (memory and I/O) carry three different kinds of information:

- Data
- Address
- Control

Each kind of information is carried on a different group of wires in the bus.

Data

The first kind of information is the actual data to be transferred. (This may include instructions for processing as well as the data to be processed.)

The earliest PCs used only eight data wires in both the bus between the CPU and main memory and the CPU to I/O bus. The *IBM PC/AT* was the first to have 16 data wires in both the memory and the I/O buses. The latest (386DX and 486) PCs with EISA or MCA buses use 32 wires for data in both cases. The new Pentium PCs will have 64 data bus wires. There also are other cases between these extremes.

Chapter 14 goes into more detail on all this. (Don't worry if you don't understand some of the jargon you just read. It, too, will be explained later in this book.)

An important issue for any bus is how rapidly it can convey data from a source to a destination. PCs are binary machines. This means, among other things, that all data is carried as bits (ones or zeros), and each of those are represented at any one instant by a high or low voltage on one of the data wires.

The number of bits of data that can be carried from one place to another in a certain interval of time depends on two factors. One is the number of data wires. The other is the maximum rate at which bits may be sent down each of those wires.

The first factor, the number of data wires, controls how many bits can flow at once, in parallel. This is called the *data bus width*. The second factor, the maximum rate at which bits can flow on each wire, is called the *maximum bus cycle rate*. The product of these two numbers is called the *data bandwidth* of the bus.

Address

The second kind of information carried on a bus is the address to which the data is being written or from which it is being read. In the earliest PCs, 20 wires were used for this purpose. The latest (386DX, 486, and Pentium) PCs use up to 32 wires for this task.

As important as the speed with which a bus can convey data is the number of locations (addresses) to which it can distribute that information. This is determined by the number of wires in the bus devoted to conveying address information. The number 2 raised to the power of the number of address lines is the size of the address space that this bus can serve. Chapter 8 gives more details on address spaces, and Chapter 14 covers the impact of address bus width on PC performance.

Control

The final category of information carried on a bus is its control signals. These signals convey what is to be done and when.

For example, there is one wire that says whether information is flowing toward the CPU (called a *read operation*) or away from it (called a *write operation*). Another wire indicates whether the information is destined for a memory location or an I/O port. Some other wires say, "Do it. Now!" These are called *strobe signals.* And there are miscellaneous other control signals.

All of the operations in a PC are synchronous. That means that they all occur on the beat of a system clock. One wire in the bus carries that clock signal.

Although a strobe signal was just described as saying, "Do it. Now!," it actually says in effect, "Do it the very next chance you get (when the clock signal says it is time to do that sort of thing)."

The earliest PCs had only one system clock. Modern PCs have many clocks. This allows them to clock data in and out of memory at one, very fast rate and to clock information on the I/O bus at another, more modest rate.

Other control signals in the memory and I/O buses include wires called *Interrupt Request lines* and other wires on which the CPU acknowledges receipt of those requests, wires on which the DMA chip or other alternate bus controllers can request control of the bus, ones by which they can receive that control, and so forth.

The earliest PCs used 62 wires in their I/O bus. Some of the latest EISA and MCA machines have about three times as many. Fortunately, you do not have to know what each of these wires does in order to manage your PC's memory effectively. If you want to know more about them, though, you will find the details in Chapter 14.

Sending Messages to More Remote Places

In the last section you learned that the bus includes a wire to specify whether data is being transferred between the CPU and a memory address or an I/O port. This is a critical distinction, and one you need to understand.

Broadly speaking, the world outside the CPU, as seen from the CPU, consists of two parts: Memory and Everything Else. Everything Else is called **Input/Output** (I/O). The name Input/Output is used because memory is located mostly in the same box with the CPU chip, and many (though not all) of the other things are outside that box.

Another aspect of the Memory/Everything Else distinction is related to the distinction between a memory location and an I/O port. Each is a place that can receive one byte (eight bits) of information. What each does with the bytes it receives is what distinguishes them. Memory locations are almost always memory-like in their behavior. Most parts that get information at I/O locations are port-like in their behavior.

How Memory Locations Act

The key quality of a memory-like location is that it holds one byte of information at a time, and you can read that byte any time you wish. Some memory locations are read-only. (These are locations in ROM chips.) That means that while you can read what is stored there, you cannot alter it. Other memory locations are read-write. (These are locations in RAM chips or modules.) You can write any byte you wish to one of these locations, and you also can read that byte back at any later time. If you cannot do this, the location is not memorylike in its qualities.

> The third possibility—a write-only memory location—is literally a joke. You probably have a huge number of them in your PC; these are memory addresses which you have no memory chips at all. Therefore, while you can attempt to write information to those locations, there is nothing there to remember what you write, so you will never be able to read that information back again. Now, if someone offers to sell you a lot of write-only memory (WOM) chips, I trust you will know exactly how much to pay for them. (Nothing!) See, however, the upcoming discussion of "Memory-Mapped I/O Registers" and "Read-Back Versus Write-Only Registers." A write-only register is not a joke.

Further, the purpose of memory is to store (remember) a byte of information until it is needed again. You can think of a PC's main memory as being like a big bulletin board covered with small notes, each carrying a brief message, and each of those messages visible to the CPU at any time.

An Input/Output port is different. It differs both in its behavior (at least sometimes) and in its purpose.

How I/O Ports Differ from Memory Locations

There are two purposes for Input/Output ports. One is to receive information coming into the CPU (Input), and the other is to carry information out from the CPU (Output). In order to do this job, they must be able to carry a stream of bytes in or out. They also must be able to accept commands indicating just how they are to perform their task.

For example, if you wish to write a file to the disk, you first must send some bytes of information to the disk controller to tell it what it is going to do. (This includes where on the disk the file is going, among other things.) Then you have to send all the bytes of the file, which it will in turn deposit one at a time on the disk drive.

Thus, the two essential qualities of an input or output port are that it receives or sends streams of bytes, and that sometimes those bytes are commands for action by some piece of hardware. In a sense, I/O ports are like pipes. The bytes you stuff in one end pop out the other end, where they are consumed or acted upon by some recipient.

This is in marked contrast to a memory location, where if you write several bytes (before you read any of them), only the last one you write matters, and that one only because you can read it back again. All the others are simply overwritten and forgotten. None of those intervening bytes went anywhere or caused anything to happen.

Read-Back Versus Write-Only Registers

Some I/O locations are called *read-back registers*. That means that once you write a byte to that location, you can read it back again if you wish. That sounds a lot like a memory location. But it is more than just a place a byte can be stored. That byte's value indicates to the hardware containing the port some action it is to do.

An example of this is the set of registers on a VGA graphics card that holds palette information. You can reprogram the relationship between color numbers stored in video memory and the actual colors that appear on-screen by writing information to these addresses.

You also can read back whatever was most recently written to the palette registers. (As it happens, in this case you do so by reading a different set of addresses.) Thus, a program can first read the palette, saving it in some RAM locations. Next it can write a new palette, thus changing totally the appearance of the screen image. Finally, it can restore the original palette by copying back out to the palette registers whatever numbers it first read.

Other I/O locations are write-only registers. That is, whatever information you write to them is acted on and then disappears. You cannot read back what you wrote.

The EGA graphics card palette registers behave this way. So anytime a program alters an EGA card's palette, it has no way to restore the original values unless it can independently determine what those original values were.

Sometimes this is impossible. Programmers who wish to make this possible can do so. There is a standard, prescribed way to set up pointers to a data area in RAM where copies that have been most recently written to the EGA registers are kept. If those pointers have been set up, and if every program that writes new information to the EGA registers updates that EGA saved data table as well, it or any other program can know what the current values in those registers are.

Read-back registers are more difficult and more expensive for chip makers to construct than write-only registers. On the other hand, the read-back registers offer the programmer more flexibility in the use of that chip. This is why the EGA card used the write-only variety, and the VGA card (which was designed several years later) used read-back registers.

Still other I/O locations serve two, possibly completely unrelated, purposes at once. Bytes going out to these locations are absorbed and acted upon, or are passed along to some destination. Bytes read in from this port come from somewhere else.

An example of this third kind of port is the interface chip used in a serial communications port. The same address can be used for data going out to a remote computer or for other, totally different, data coming in from that computer. Getting dual use of the same I/O address in this way can be useful, as long as you know you won't have to read back the information you sent to the port.

When communicating between two computers, you normally want to read what you are writing, so you want your computer to display everything you type on your screen. There are two ways to accomplish this.

One easy way is to have your local computer send all your keystrokes both to the output port and to your screen. This is called *half-duplex communication* because characters are only traveling one way (at a time) on the cable between the two computers.

A better way is to read from the other computer a copy of what it received from you. That way you will know not only that you launched those bytes toward that computer, but that they actually got there. This is called *full-duplex communication* because as your PC is sending characters to the remote computer, it is sending echoes of them back to your PC.

At the port hardware level in full-duplex communication, the incoming and outgoing streams of bytes are completely independent. Only the echoing action of the distant computer makes the two streams contain the same characters (most of the time).

The Usual Rule: Memory Locations for Memory; I/O Locations (Ports) for I/O

The usual design uses memory address locations for main memory. That is where the CPU stores information for its immediate use. Likewise, the I/O port locations are used to send information to or from more remote portions of the computer. This is not always the case, however.

These more remote portions need not necessarily be physically farther away from the CPU, though often they are. They are, in any case, logically more remote. That is, they are not likely to be accessed as frequently, nor do they need to be accessed as quickly.

These more remote portions of the PC include the disk controllers (and through them the disk drives), the parallel and serial communications ports (and through them printers, mice, and modems), the keyboard controller (and through it the keyboard), and the control aspects of video cards (where the video mode or palette may be changed).

All of these are locations that are read or written to relatively infrequently and where speed is often not a great issue. They also have that pipelike quality of carrying streams of information on to some other consumer of that information. The CPU rarely, if ever, needs to see that exact same information again.

You might think that storing a file is like putting information into memory. Of course, files are stored precisely so they can be read later on. But that may not occur until after you have turned the computer off and back on again another day. Further, they are normally read once, rather slowly, into RAM. Then their information is accessed over and over again by the CPU very quickly, directly from RAM. So disk file storage is not at all the same thing as reading back information from a memory location or a read-back register.

In addition to the main RAM and the system ROM on the motherboard, other portions of the PC that are accessible as memory at memory addresses include the video image buffer (RAM) and various *option ROMs* located on plug-in cards. These are regions that hold programs or data and must be written to or read from the CPU very rapidly and relatively frequently.

Data in video RAM, for example, is often written and read back for further processing by the CPU. Programs in ROM must be available for instant use when needed. One simple example is an EGA or VGA card, where the techniques the computer must use to put information on-screen are expressed in programs permanently loaded into a ROM on the EGA or VGA card. These programs are used every time a program sends characters to the screen via a BIOS call (which is the easiest and most common way of doing that task).

Memory-Mapped I/O and Port-Accessible Memory

Occasionally, for some very good reasons, some RAM will be placed where it can be read or written at an I/O port address or throughout a range of I/O addresses. This is called port-accessible memory. Conversely, sometimes the designer of a PC or some component that goes into a PC will choose to place what is, functionally, an I/O port at a memory address. This is called memory-mapped I/O. A few examples follow.

Port-Accessible Memory Locations

- The CMOS chip in an AT, 386, 486, or *Pentium*-based PC that remembers the system configuration, the date, and the time (and possibly some passwords and a small amount of other information) is clearly memory. Information is written there and later is read back. It does nothing by simply being there; it is only useful when it is read back.

  Even though this is clearly memorylike information storage, the IBM *PC/AT*'s designers chose to make these RAM locations accessible at some I/O port addresses, a practice that has been followed by all PC clone makers ever since.

- Some motherboard system logic chip sets use a similar strategy to record configuration information they will use at power-up to create EMS memory, or do other special functions.

- EISA and MCA computers also store extended configuration information in memory locations that are accessible through I/O port addresses. This extended configuration information is used to help prevent or resolve resource conflicts between different plug-in (option) cards.

- Some SCSI host adapters have a data buffer located in I/O port space. The buffer is a memorylike region where information is temporarily stored on its way to or from the disk drives or other SCSI devices attached to the host adapter.

  These manufacturers made their host adapter buffers accessible by programmed I/O to avoid some problems that otherwise could arise when a memory manager rearranges the relationship between memory addresses and memory locations (called *remapping* memory).

Memory-Mapped I/O Registers

- Some early Western Digital motherboard system logic chip sets used the reverse approach. They took some I/O registers that must be programmed to set up the system logic and made them accessible only by writing to certain memory addresses.

- A number of Local Area Network (LAN) network interface cards (NICs) also use memory-mapped I/O for speed.

This last is an especially unfortunate use, from the point of view of memory management. Semiautomatic memory-management programs often search for memory addresses at which there is physical RAM, or that are otherwise being used by some hardware. They do this by writing information to those locations and then attempting to read it back.

If such a memory-management program finds read-back registers, it may not be able to tell them from actual RAM. But if it then attempts to load a program into those regions, that information may be broadcast over the LAN. (And, just seconds later, it may be replaced with some incoming message. No telling what will happen when your PC tries to execute what it thinks is a program at that location and it turns out to be some incoming E-mail message!)

In other cases, while the NIC will put RAM at some locations as a buffer for messages, it might not do so until it needs to use that buffer. The memory-management program may conclude that these are unused addresses and try to use them for some other purpose. That leads to a network that won't work.

In the most horrible case, if the memory-management program "walks over" control registers in its search for physical RAM, the LAN NIC could be commanded to do some very strange things to your PC and possibly to others as well. This could easily lock up the network or worse.

Another Use of I/O Mapping for Something Other Than Input or Output

- Communication between the CPU and a math coprocessor is not exactly like CPU-to-memory communication, nor is it exactly like normal I/O. It probably more closely resembles the former, yet Intel put the link between the CPU and the math coprocessor at some reserved addresses in the I/O address space (see Chapter 8 for details).

Bits, Bytes, Symbols, Characters, Sets, and Codes

You've now read several times that computers are information-processing machines. You've also read that they are much like calculators that can press their own buttons. That is, they work mostly by adding and subtracting, and doing other similarly elementary arithmetic and logical operations (the logical operations include comparing two numbers to see which is larger). You may wonder: Is information processing just a sort of arithmetic? If this seems unclear or confusing, perhaps you don't understand what information is. Let's clear that up right now.

What Is Information?

Information can be thought of as the answers to some questions. If you can formulate what you want to know as the answers to a series of simple enough questions, you can easily compute just how much information it will take to tell you what you want to know.

A single question that is answerable with a simple *yes* or *no* requires the minimum amount of information for its answer. That minimum amount of information is called a *bit*. The bit could mean a *yes* or a *no*, and it could be represented by a one or a zero or, in computer hardware, by a low or a high voltage somewhere.

All more complex collections of information can be represented as collections of bits. Those bits are often grouped for convenience. Most commonly in PCs they are grouped eight at a time, and the resulting eight-bit groups are *bytes*. The importance of this choice and some alternatives that have been used will be discussed shortly.

You also can speak of these bit collections as if they were numbers. That means that you can process the information represented by those bits by performing appropriate mathematical operations on those numbers. (So, yes, from this perspective, information processing is nothing more than a lot of arithmetic and logical operations.)

How Big Is a Fact?

How many bits do you need to store a fact? That depends on how many possible facts you wish to discriminate.

Consider one famous example: Paul Revere needed to receive a short but important message. He chose to have his associate hang some lighted lamps in a church tower. Longfellow immortalized the message as, "One if by land and two if by sea." This was a simple, special-purpose code. Computers work in much the same way, only they use a somewhat more complex and general-purpose code.

Actually, Paul's code was a little more complex than the phrase suggests. There were three possibilities, and the lamp code had to be able to communicate at each moment one of these three statements:

- "The British are not yet coming." (Zero lamps)
- "The British are coming by land." (One lamp)
- "The British are coming by sea." (Two lamps)

Paul chose to use one more lamp for each possibility after the first. This is like counting on your fingers. This works well if the number of possibilities is small. It would have been impossible for Paul to use that strategy if he had needed to distinguish among 100 facts, let alone the thousands or millions that computers handle.

The way to get around that bottleneck is to use what mathematicians call *place-value numbering*. The common decimal numbering system is one example. The binary numbering system is another (binary numbering is used in the construction of computers). The next example will help make this concept clear.

The Size of a Number

Suppose someone calls you on the telephone and asks you how old you are (to the nearest year). You could tell them, or you could make them guess. If you do the latter, and if you say you will only answer "yes" or "no" in response to various questions, here is the questioner's best strategy. (This assumes that over the phone the questioner is unable to get any idea of how old you are, but since you are a human, it is reasonable to guess that you are less than 128 years old.)

The first question is, "Are you at least 64 years old?" If the answer is *yes,* then the second question is, "Are you at least 96 years old?" If the answer to the first question was *no,* the second question would be, "Are you at least 32 years old?" The successive questions will further narrow the range until by the seventh question you will have revealed your age, accurate to the year. (See Figure 6.3 for the numbers to choose for each question.)

As the questioner gets the answers to each of the seven questions, he or she simply records them, writing a one for every *yes* and zero for every *no.* The resulting 7-bit binary number is the person's age. (This procedure works since the first question is the most significant one. That is, it determines the most about the person's age. And if you do as most people do and write down the answer bits from left to right, you will come out with a binary number stated in the usual way, with the **M**ost **S**ignificant **B**it (MSB) on the left end of the number.)

Here is what that process might look like. Assume you are 35 years old. Here are the answers you would give: "Are you at least 64 years old?" (no), 32 (yes), 48 (no), 40 (no), 36 (no), 34 (yes), 35 (yes). Your age (in binary) would be written 0100011.

This is an example of a place-value number. The first place is worth 64. The next is worth 32, then 16, and so on all the way to the last place, which is worth 1. By the worth of a place, I mean simply that you must multiply the value in that place (in binary this is always a zero or a one) by the worth of that place and add all the products to get the value of the number. In the example, add no 64s, one 32, no 16s, no 8s, no 4s, one 2, and a final 1. The result of this addition (32 + 2 + 1) is, of course, 35.

When you answer seven yes-or-no questions, you are giving the questioner seven bits of information. Thus, it takes seven bits to specify the age of a human being (assuming that age is less than 128). That is how large that fact is.

That is a fine way to specify a number. But most of the uses of computers involve storing facts that aren't numbers. How large are they?

The Size of a Nonnumeric Fact

To decide this you have first to decide how you will represent nonnumeric information. Consider another example. One very common use for a computer is word processing. A word processing document isn't filled mostly with numbers. It is filled with words, and they are made up of letters separated by spaces and punctuation symbols.

One way to represent such a document is as a string of symbols (letter, numbers, punctuation symbols, special symbols to represent the end of a line, tabs, and other similar ideas). How much information is there in such a document?

If you write down all the possible symbols that could occur in the document, you will see how many different ones there were (disregarding how often each one occurred). Then you could give each of those unique symbols a numeric label. At that point it is easy to see how many simple questions, like those used to fix your age, it would take to pick each symbol out of that character set.

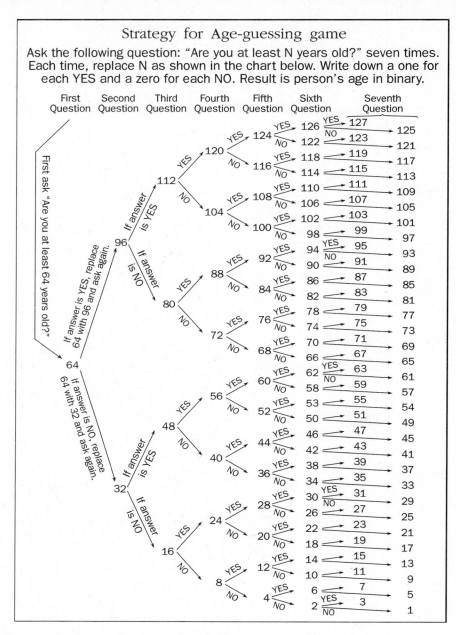

Figure 6.3. Optimal strategy for the age-guessing game.

Suppose you had a document with 43 different symbols occurring in it. This means you have a *character set* with 43 members. You could label those symbols with the numbers from 0 to 42. Figure 6.4 shows how many bits you will need to point to one member of that character set. In this case the answer is six bits, since 43 is less than 64. (With six bits you could pick out each member of a set with 64 members. You can pick out the members of a group with only 43 members by thinking of them as the first 43 members of that set of 64. You could not get away with using a five-bit number as a pointer, since that would only let you discriminate among members of a set of 32 items.)

This provides a way to represent symbols as numbers, and in the process it provides a measure of just how big those symbols are in terms of their information content. Each symbol holds as many bits of information as the size of the pointers needed to pick them out of the character set to which they belong.

This also provides a way to transform the original document (a string of symbols) into a string of pointers (numbers). In the example, each pointer would be six bits long. In that case the whole document would be six bits times the number of pointers (which is the same as the number of symbols—this is the total number of symbols in the document, not just the number of unique symbols). This is a form you can store in a computer. This is a form much like that actually used by typical word processors.

Information Storage, Memory Cells, and Disk Locations

PCs store information as binary numbers. Each memory location (byte) has eight parts, or memory cells. Each cell is able to hold a single one or a zero. The same is true of disk storage locations.

Thus the size of a fact (such as the document in the example) is quite directly related to the space it occupies in a PC's memory or as a file on a disk. The number of bits equals the number of memory cells needed. You may end up using more than that number of cells, but you can't get away with any fewer. (For example, you might choose to use up a whole byte to store each pointer number, even though the pointers were only six or seven bits long.)

How Big Is A Fact?

Number of possibilities this fact can distinguish	Number of bits needed to hold this fact
2	1
4	2
8	3
16	4
32	5
64	6
128	7
256	8
⋮	⋮
65,536	16
⋮	⋮
1,048,576	20

Figure 6.4.   How big is a fact? The answer depends on how many members there are in the largest group from which you can choose a unique member by using only this fact.

It is possible to get away with fewer locations and yet store the same total amount of information. The trick is to store more than one bit per location. That can be done if the memory cell can be put into more than two states. A computer built using that approach would not be called a binary computer.

Some people have built computers using various number bases besides two (which is what a binary computer uses). A ternary computer could store Paul Revere's answer in just one memory cell. It could store the age (in years) of a human being in five cells. But technologically it is so much simpler to build binary computers that they are the only ones being used commonly today.

Putting more information into fewer memory cells by using a number base other than binary is only one way to reduce the number of memory cells you need. It is not, in fact, normally used. One way that is used is to remove redundancy. This very different approach is explained in the following section.

You now know one way to encode a document into a computer file. This method gives one size for a document, the one required for that particular way of representing it. Is that file size the amount of information in that document? Not necessarily. If every symbol were independent of every other, it would be, but that's not often the case.

Document Size, Redundancy, and Information Content

Real documents often contain *redundancy*. That is, knowing some of the document allows you to predict the missing parts with an accuracy that is better than chance. (Try reading a paragraph in which all the vowels have been left out. You can do surprisingly well.) This means that you need to encode only some fraction of the symbols in the document to know all of what it contains. And that means the true information content of the document may be significantly less than the raw size (number of symbols times bits per symbol).

For convenience, most word processors store every symbol you enter into your documents. They make no attempt to reduce the document size to the bare minimum. This saves time, but it wastes disk storage space.

Sometimes you want to minimize the size of your files. You may send some of them over a phone line, and you wish to minimize the time and cost. Or you may find yourself running out of space on your hard disk.

Various strategies are available to take advantage of redundancy. One is an *archiving* program. Such a program can take several files, squeeze out nearly all the redundancy in each one, and then combine them into a single file with many fewer bytes than the original collection of files. ARC, PKZIP, and LHA (formerly called LHARC) are some very popular programs for this purpose.

Another approach is a software or hardware data-compression disk interface product (also called an "on-the-fly file compressor"). These products squeeze out the redundancy in files as they are stored to your disk or tape drives, and then they expand them back to their original, redundant form as the files are read from the tape or disk.

One of the leaders in this field is Stac. Their compression products are used by many tape drive manufacturers. Their latest product, *Stacker*, is a device driver that creates the illusion that you have a much larger disk drive than the actual physical size of your disk. (Typical compression ratios run about 2:1, with some files compressing to as little as a tenth their full size, and others compressing hardly at all.)

Stacker does its magic entirely transparently. (Once it is installed, you won't know it is doing anything; you will simply experience having an apparently larger, and often somewhat faster, hard drive.) Another product that does something very similar is *SuperStor,* by AddStor. A version of this product is bundled with *DR DOS* 6.

With version 6 of *MS-DOS*, Microsoft introduced their version of this idea in a utility program they called DoubleSpace. The main difference between DoubleSpace and the earlier on-the-fly file compression programs is that *MS-DOS 6* loads the file compression engine

(DBLSPACE.BIN) before it begins processing the CONFIG.SYS file. This avoids the confusions that caused the most grief among new users of Stacker or SuperStor.

Using these products gives you the appearance of more disk space, but at a cost. You will have to give up some of your precious 640KB of RAM to this function. For more on this, see Chapters 20 and 21.

Things can get even more subtle. The information content of a file may depend on who is looking at it.

If you have never seen a given document before, it will contain much that is news to you. That means it will contain a lot of information. You could not guess all of its content without using very many yes-or-no questions. Essentially, you need to see every symbol in the document, or nearly every one, and so the information content of the document is close to the number of symbols it contains times the size of the pointers needed to show you which symbol each one is in some agreed-upon character set.

Someone who knew ahead of time that this document was one of a certain small group of documents might find that it contained very little information. All that person needs in order to know all of what it contains is to figure out which one of the given sets of documents this one is. That will take a rather small number of questions (at least the number indicated in Figure 6.4 for the size of the group of known documents). For that person the document could be adequately replaced with just one pointer number. The size of that number is all the information that document contains *for that person.*

To see how powerful this approach could be, imagine that you worked in an office that created custom documents out of a limited number of standard parts (pieces of boilerplate text) along with a customer-specific header. You could replace each custom document just with that header followed by a short list of small numbers, one number per standard part you were including. The numbers could be small because each one only needs to store which of the limited number of standard parts it represents.

This shortened representation of the document is adequate for you to re-create the full document. That means you only need to store this small file on your hard disk to allow you to print out the full document anytime you wish.

To put numbers to this, suppose your office used only 256 standard document parts. Each one could be any length. Suppose they averaged 10,000 bytes. Your custom documents could each simply consist of the customer-specific header followed by a string of bytes, one per standard part to be included. This would allow you to compress your documents for storage on average by a ratio of 10,000:1.

Of course, since your customers don't have your collection of standard parts, you will have to assemble the full document for them before you can ship it.

Is such an approach actually practical? Yes. Something much like this is often used in law offices, by architectural specifiers, and in the writing of computer programs, for example.

Common Bit Groupings

Early teletypewriters used five or six bits per symbol. They were severely restricted, therefore, in the number of distinct symbols a message could contain (to 32 or 64 possibilities). For most of the past century the standard has been to use seven bits. That allows 128 symbols, which is enough for all the lowercase and uppercase letters in the English alphabet, all 10 digits, and a generous assortment of punctuation symbols. This standard even leaves 32 of the 128 possibilities for *control characters*. These latter values encode the carriage return (start typing at the left margin once again), the line feed (move the paper up a line), tab, backspace, vertical tab, and so on. The control characters also include symbols to indicate the end of a message and the famous code number 7, to ring the bell on the teletypewriter. Presumably, this last one was needed to get the attention of the person to whom the message was being sent.

Starting with the IBM 360 series of mainframe computers in the early 1960s, the most common grouping became eight bits, which has been named the *byte*. Many other mainframe and minicomputer makers used other size groupings, but all modern PCs have used the byte exclusively as the smallest chunk of information commonly passed around inside the machine, or between one PC and another. The more powerful PCs can also handle groups of two, four, or even eight bytes at a time.

There is a name for these larger groupings of bits. That name is *word*. Unfortunately, unlike a byte, a word is an ill-defined amount of information.

This is not unlike English. All letters, numbers, and punctuation symbols take up roughly the same amount of room. But a word can be as little as a single letter, or an almost unlimited number of letters. (Consider the words *I* and *a* and then remember the famous 34-letter word *Supercalifragilisticexpialidocious;* there are also a good many less artificial words that are nearly as long.) Things are not quite that bad in the world of computers, but still a computer word is far from a clearly defined constant.

One notion of a computer word is that it contains as many bits as the computer can process internally all at once. This rule makes the size of a word dependent on which computer you are talking about.

Another popular idea is that one word is the size of the data bus width. Again that would give us a size that depended on the particular model of PC.

By the first of these definitions, the earliest PCs had 16-bit words, but more modern ones have 32-bit words, and the Pentium would be said to have a 64-bit word. By the second definition the earliest PCs had 8-bit words, and again the most modern ones have 32-bit or 64-bit words.

Either of these definitions can lead to confusion. The good news is that all the different models of PC are more alike than different, so it helps you keep your sanity to choose one definition for word size and stick to it.

Fortunately, most people use 16-bits as the size of a PC's word, independent of which model of PC they are discussing. However, that definition is not universally used. So be careful when reading technical descriptions of PC hardware. A *word* may be something different from what you expect.

Some mainframe computers have had very odd word sizes, indeed. Sizes like 12, 36, and 72 bits have been used. Notice that none of these is an integral power of two. Fortunately, engineering common sense has come to the fore in the design of PCs. All of them use only 16-bit words or some other integral-power-of-two times a byte.

Where Are Facts Kept in Your PC?

Now you know that facts can be represented by collections of bits. The most common size collection used in a PC is a byte (eight bits). Where are these bytes kept? In memory and storage. Of these, the only facts that the CPU can readily get at are those kept in memory.

How does the CPU know where a particular byte can be found? It uses that byte's address. Every directly accessible memory location in the PC has an address. When information is sent in or out of the PC, it goes via a port, and that, too, must have an address. Not surprisingly, the addresses of memory cells are called *memory addresses* and the Input/Output addresses are called *I/O port addresses.*

Two is a very important number here. There are two address spaces (memory and I/O), and so one bit of information can discriminate between them. One wire in the bus (carrying that one bit of information) indicates which kind of address you are currently accessing.

Also, various integer powers of two are important. With a given number of address wires (say n), you can specify one of 2^n address locations. Sixteen wires provide 65,536 possible addresses. Twenty wires provide 1,048,576 addresses. With one byte kept in each of those one million plus locations you have exactly one megabyte of memory. (See Appendix A for more on this.)

In fact, the reason bytes are used is again based on the importance of powers of two. It takes just three bits to specify one of eight possibilities. So with eight bits in a byte, you can point to a particular one of the bits in the byte very efficiently using just three address bits.

You will meet these special sizes (8, 256, 65,536, 1,048,576 and the others in Figure 6.4) again in future chapters. In every case, the number is special, because it is equal to two raised to some integer (whole number) power.

Symbols and Codes

Codes are a way to convey information. If you know the code, you can read the information. I've already discussed Paul Revere's code. His was created for just one occasion. Codes created for general purposes are more useful.

Morse code is a well-known example. Its original purpose was to send messages consisting of letters, numbers, and some punctuation symbols from one place to another, using a single wire (and its electrical return path) and some rather crude signaling devices.

What actually is sent from one place to another is a succession of long and short pulses each separated from its neighbors by either a long or a short interval. The code indicates what a given pattern of *dits* and *dahs* means. The short intervals separate the dits and dahs of one letter (or other symbol). The longer intervals separate the symbols from one another. If you know the code, it is easy enough to reconstruct the signal. But you have to know the code.

In order not to be confused by all this talk of bits, bytes, symbols, characters sets, and codes, you must keep clearly in mind that the symbols you want to represent are *not* what gets stored in your PC. Only a coded version of them can be put there. If you actually look at the contents of your PC's memory, you will see only a lot of numbers.

Morse code is not very useful in PCs. This is because Morse code uses a variable length string of dits and dahs to represent the symbols. PCs have fixed size places to store information (bytes), so they work best if they use a code that also has a fixed size per symbol.

You will encounter three common codes in the technical documentation on PCs:

- Hexadecimal
- ASCII
- EBCDIC

The first code is used to make it easier to write binary numbers. The next is the most common coding used when documents are stored on a PC. The last of these three is an alternate coding scheme sometimes used for document storage. (This last one will not be used anywhere in this book outside this chapter, though it is referred to in some PC documentation and used by some PC programs.)

Hexadecimal Numbers

The first of these three schemes is *hexadecimal numbering.* It is a base-16 method of counting. Since Arabic numerals use only 10 digits, they have been augmented with the first six capital letters to get the 16 symbols needed to represent hexadecimal numbers (see Figure 6.5).

The advantages of using hexadecimal are twofold: First, it is an economical way to write large binary numbers. Second, the translation between hexadecimal and binary is so trivial that anyone can learn to do it flawlessly.

Any binary number can be written as a string of bits. A four-byte number is a string of 32 bits. That takes a lot of space and time to write, and it is very hard to read accurately. Group those bits into fours. Now replace each of the groups of four bits with the equivalent hexadecimal numeral according to the following chart. What you get is an eight-numeral hexadecimal number. Much easier to write and read accurately!

Converting numbers from hexadecimal to binary is equally simple. Just replace each hexadecimal numeral by its equivalent string of four bits.

For example, the binary number

`01101011001101011000110010100001`

can be grouped into fours of bits as:

`0110 1011 0011 0101 1000 1100 1010 0001 .`

This can, in turn, be written as a hexadecimal number. Look up each group of four bits in Figure 6.5 and replace with its hex equivalent. You'll get

`6B358CA1`

Now test your work. Using Figure 6.5, convert the final hexadecimal number back into the original binary one.

You will encounter many hexadecimal numbers in documents describing memory and memory management in PCs. That's because the important addresses are simpler when expressed in hexadecimal form.

You can recognize a hexadecimal number in two ways. If it contains some normal decimal digits (*0, 1, . . . , 9*) and some capital letters (*A* through *F*), it is almost certainly a hexadecimal number. Sometimes authors will add the letter *h* or *H* after the number. The usual convention is to use a lowercase *h*, and that is what is done in this book. Another convention is to make the hexadecimal number start with one of the familiar decimal digits by tacking a zero onto the front of the number if necessary. Thus the hexadecimal number A would be written *0Ah*. Notice that the hexadecimal number *5* and the decimal number *5* are the same. It isn't necessary to put the *h* after a hexadecimal number less than 10 (decimal).

Unfortunately, not all authors play by these rules. In some cases, you simply have to go by the context and guess.

Decimal	Binary	Hexadecimal
0	0 0 0 0	0
1	0 0 0 1	1
2	0 0 1 0	2
3	0 0 1 1	3
4	0 1 0 0	4
5	0 1 0 1	5
6	0 1 1 0	6
7	0 1 1 1	7
8	1 0 0 0	8
9	1 0 0 1	9
10	1 0 1 0	A
11	1 0 1 1	B
12	1 1 0 0	C
13	1 1 0 1	D
14	1 1 1 0	E
15	1 1 1 1	F

Figure 6.5.   The first 16 numbers in three number bases.

Engineers love hexadecimal as a way to represent addresses in a PC. For them, the important point is not that the special numbers are written so simply. It is that the binary number into which you can convert the hexadecimal number actually represents the arrangement of low and high voltages on the wires in the PC.

ASCII

The next common code you will encounter in PCs is called the *American Standard Code for Information Interchange,* abbreviated *ASCII.* This is the code that was developed first for teletypewriters, and it now is the almost universally accepted code for storing information in a PC. If you look into memory (or on a PC disk) where one of your documents is stored, you will need to translate the numbers you find there according to this code to see what the document says (see Figure 6.6).

Of course, since it is so commonly used, many utility programs exist to help you. Vern Buerg has written a program called LIST, which does this superbly well. It often is licensed by software companies and included with their products to help their customers read the on-line documentation, or READ.ME files.

ASCII only uses seven bits per symbol. When you store an ASCII document in a PC, typically the most significant bit is simply set to zero and ignored. That means there can be only 128 characters (symbols) in the ASCII character set. One quarter of these (for values 0 to 31) are reserved, according to the ASCII definition, for control characters. The rest are printable. Those symbols and the ASCII control code mnemonics are shown in Figure 6.6.

The IBM *PC* introduced some extensions to the standard ASCII code. Not only did they choose a set of symbols to print for code values from 128 to 255, they also decided on symbols for the first 32 values. The PC interprets those latter values as control characters in some contexts; in others it shows the IBM-defined graphics symbols instead of performing a control function. Figure 6.6 shows both the standard mnemonics for the ASCII control characters and IBM's Graphics symbol definitions for them. Figure 6.7 shows the IBM Graphics symbols for the extended-ASCII codes (values 128 to 255).

Here are the standard meanings of the ASCII control codes:

NUL	=	null
SOH	=	start of heading
STX	=	start of text
ETX	=	end of text
EOT	=	end of transmission
ENQ	=	enquiry
ACK	=	acknowledge
BEL	=	bell
BS	=	backspace
HT	=	horizontal tab
LF	=	line feed
VT	=	vertical tab
FF	=	form feed
CR	=	carriage return
SO	=	shift out
SI	=	shift in
DLE	=	data link escape
DC1-DC4	=	device control 1-4
NAK	=	negative acknowledge
SYN	=	synchronous idle
ETB	=	end of transmission block
CAN	=	cancel
EM	=	end of medium
SUB	=	substitute
ESC	=	escape
FS	=	file separator
GS	=	group separator
RS	=	record separator
US	=	unit separator

There is one more ASCII control code:

DEL	=	delete

with a code value of 127. These definitions are codified in an American National Standards Institute document, ANSI X3.4-1986.

Control Codes   ASCII   Printable Characters

Hex	Dec	00 / 0	10 / 16	20 / 32	30 / 48	40 / 64	50 / 80	60 / 96	70 / 112
0	0	NUL	DLE ▶		0	@	P	`	p
1	1	SOH ☺	DC1 ◀	!	1	A	Q	a	q
2	2	STX ☻	DC2 ↕	"	2	B	R	b	r
3	3	ETX ♥	DC3 ‼	#	3	C	S	c	s
4	4	EOT ♦	DC4 ¶	$	4	D	T	d	t
5	5	ENQ ♣	NAK §	%	5	E	U	e	u
6	6	ACK ♠	SYN ▬	&	6	F	V	f	v
7	7	BEL •	ETB ↨	'	7	G	W	g	w
8	8	BS ◘	CAN ↑	(	8	H	X	h	x
9	9	HT ○	EM ↓	)	9	I	Y	i	y
A	10	LF ◙	SUB →	*	:	J	Z	j	z
B	11	VT ♂	ESC ←	+	;	K	[	k	{
C	12	FF ♀	FS ∟	,	<	L	\	l	¦
D	13	CR ♪	GS ↔	-	=	M	]	m	}
E	14	SO ♫	RS ▲	.	>	N	^	n	~
F	15	SI ☼	US ▼	/	?	O	_	o	⌂

Figure 6.6.   The ASCII character set, including the standard mnemonics and the IBM Graphics symbols for the 32 ASCII control characters. Add the decimal or hexadecimal number at the left of a row to the corresponding number at the top of a column to get the ASCII code value for the symbol shown where that row and column intersect.

IBM Graphics Extensions to ASCII character set

Hex	Dec	80 / 128	90 / 144	A0 / 160	B0 / 176	C0 / 192	D0 / 208	E0 / 224	F0 / 240
0	0	Ç	É	á	░	└	╨	α	≡
1	1	ü	æ	í	▒	┴	╤	ß	±
2	2	é	Æ	ó	▓	┬	╥	Γ	≥
3	3	â	ô	ú	│	├	╙	π	≤
4	4	ä	ö	ñ	┤	─	╘	Σ	⌠
5	5	à	ò	Ñ	╡	┼	╒	σ	⌡
6	6	å	û	ª	╢	╞	╓	µ	÷
7	7	ç	ù	º	╖	╟	╫	τ	≈
8	8	ê	ÿ	¿	╕	╚	╪	Φ	°
9	9	ë	Ö	⌐	╣	╔	┘	Θ	∙
A	10	è	Ü	¬	║	╩	┌	Ω	·
B	11	ï	¢	½	╗	╦	█	δ	√
C	12	î	£	¼	╝	╠	▄	∞	ⁿ
D	13	ì	¥	¡	╜	═	▌	φ	²
E	14	Ä	₧	«	╛	╬	▐	ε	■
F	15	Å	ƒ	»	┐	╧	▀	∩	

Figure 6.7.   IBM's graphics extensions to the ASCII character set.

Even before IBM's *PC* and the many clones to it, there were other small computers. *Apple II* was one popular brand. Many different brands of small computers running the CP/M operating software also were popular. These computers all stored information in bytes.

Since they stored bytes of information, they were able to use a code (or character set) with twice as many elements as ASCII. Each manufacturer of those small computers was free to decide independently how to use those extra possibilities.

Some word processors, most notably *WordStar,* use that 8th bit to indicate the end of every word. Viewing programs like LIST have an option to mask off that bit, thus treating it as a zero no matter what its actual value may be. That makes viewing *WordStar* files much easier.

Epson made more printers for this market than anyone. They almost succeeded in creating a *de facto* standard for the second half of an *extended ASCII code* (mostly some graphics characters). But before it was quite accepted, IBM introduced their *PC,* and it came with a very different extended ASCII code (a different set of graphics characters, along with Greek letters and math symbols).

Epson got the contract to make printers for those early *IBM PCs.* These differed from their Epson brand printers mainly in two ways:

1. They had the IBM logo and part number printed on the case.

2. They used a different ROM chip internally to store the character shapes to print for each number with a value over 127.

Other printer manufacturers also developed versions of an extended-ASCII character set. Hewlett-Packard has at least three of them. Often the printer manufacturers offer emulations of the Epson set and the IBM set (plus, perhaps, their own set). This explains why you often see something quite different on-screen when you view a document and on paper when you print that same document. Only if your printer uses the IBM Graphics character set definitions does it look the same.

Not everything stored in your PC uses ASCII coding. In particular, programs are stored in what you might regard as the CPU's native language, which is all numbers. So LIST will not help you make much sense of them.

EBCDIC

Further, some manufacturers developed their own codes. One notable example is IBM. When they introduced the use of bytes in their 360 series of mainframe computers, they also introduced a new character encoding. Instead of taking the ASCII code and adding to it as they did later on with the PC, they created a whole new code. They called it the *Extended Binary Coded Decimal Interchange Code,* or *EBCDIC* for short.

This would be only a historical curiosity except that IBM still uses that code on some of their larger computers, they used it on their stand-alone *DisplayWriter* word processors, and they use it in their *DisplayWrite* word processing program for the PC. EBCDIC has become an alternative standard for document interchange, represented in the standard called *Document Content Architecture, Revisable Format Text,* or *DCA/RFT.* Figure 6.8 shows the EBCDIC character set. Notice that it lacks some of the symbols in IBM's extended ASCII for PCs. More important, the symbols it shares with ASCII are assigned to very different numbers.

Viewing an EBCDIC-encoded document requires a special viewer. There are some general-purpose utilities on the market that can do this trick. (The *Norton Utilities* is one.) Otherwise, you must either use the program that created the document or convert it to a format suitable for some other program to read and use.

The Several Kinds of Memory and Storage in PCs

Now you know that memory and storage make up one of the five essential parts of your PC. You also know something of how information is stored in memory. The next topic is the diverse kinds of memory and storage that you can have. Some of these are commonplace. Others are fairly uncommon, but you may want to add them to your PC. Still others are simply different ways to use the memory or storage you already have.

Random-Access Memory

Random-Access Memory (or RAM) is the most common type of memory in any PC. This is the workhorse memory. In most PCs, it is built using what are called *Dynamic RAM* chips, or *DRAMs.* These are the least expensive memory chips and modules to build, and they can hold more memory per chip or module than any other kind. They are not the fastest possible memory chips, though, so a small amount of more expensive, faster *Static RAM* (or *SRAM*) will sometimes be used as a memory cache. Also used are ROM chips of various types, but the term *RAM* doesn't normally include them. You will learn all about the differences and similarities in all these kinds of RAM in Chapter 16.

The most important part of memory for PCs running DOS is that with addresses from 0 to 640KB. (In hexadecimal, that is from 00000h to 0A0000h. You can see here how much more rounded and natural the hexadecimal addresses appear.) This is the region called, variously, *conventional memory, system memory,* or *lower memory.*

ATs and 386-, 486-, and Pentium-based computers can have *extended memory.* This is RAM at addresses beyond one megabyte. These PCs are able to address at least 15MB of extended memory, and in some models a great deal more. They are able to access this memory only when operating in a special mode (called *protected mode*). This makes extended memory much less useful to DOS, though with the help of a modern memory manager (including those shipped with DOS, versions 5 or 6), it can sometimes be used by DOS programs.

All PCs can also have RAM in other places. Every PC uses some for a video image buffer. That is commonly found on a plug-in video card, although in some PCs that circuitry is built onto the motherboard.

With the addition of a special *expanded memory card* any PC can have still more RAM that is made available only to programs through the intervention of an expanded memory manager program. The 386-, 486-, and Pentium-based PCs can make some of their extended memory appear to be expanded memory. They do this by using a different kind of memory-management program and do not need the special hardware expanded memory card.

Even this does not exhaust all the possibilities. Caching disk controllers and print buffers are two common examples of yet more places RAM may be found.

Control Codes EBCDIC   Printable Characters

		00	10	20	30	40	50	60	70	Hex	Alternate Code Assignments
Hex	Dec	0	16	32	48	64	80	96	112	Dec	
0	0	NUL	DLE	DS		SP	&	‾			Alternate Code Assignments
1	1	SOH	DC1	SOS		RSP		/			
2	2	STX	DC2	FS	SYN						
3	3	ETX	DC3	WUS	IR						
4	4	SEL	ENP	INP	PP						ENP or RES
5	5	HT	NL	LF	TRN						INP or BYP
6	6		BS	ETB	NBS						
7	7	DEL	POC	ESC	EOT						
8	8	GE	CAN		SBS						
9	9	SPS	EM		IT						
A	10	RPT	UBS	SM	RFF	¢	!	¦	:		SM or SW
B	11	VT	CU1	FMT	CU3	.	$	,	#		
C	12	FF	IFS	ENQ	DC4	<	*	%	@		
D	13	CR	IGS	ACK	NAK	(	)	_	'		
E	14	SO	IRS			+	;	>	=		ITB or IUS
F	15	SI	ITB	BEL	SUB	|	¬	?	"		

Upper half of EBCDIC character set

		00	10	20	30	40	50	60	70	Hex
Hex	Dec	0	16	32	48	64	80	96	112	Dec
0	0					{	}	\	0	
1	1	a	j	~		A	J	NSP	1	
2	2	b	k	s		B	K	S	2	
3	3	c	l	t		C	L	T	3	
4	4	d	m	u		D	M	U	4	
5	5	e	n	v		E	N	V	5	
6	6	f	o	w		F	O	W	6	
7	7	g	p	x		G	P	X	7	
8	8	h	q	y		H	Q	Y	8	
9	9	i	r	z		I	R	Z	9	
A	10					SHY				
B	11									
C	12									
D	13									
E	14									
F	15								EO	

Figure 6.8.   The EBCDIC character set.

Uses for RAM

RAM is used to store information that changes. This includes both programs and the data being processed by those programs. No program can run unless it is in RAM.

Some programs are built into a portion of the RAM that is read-only. They are discussed in the next section.

Other programs are stored on a disk. They must be copied from the disk into RAM before they can be run. Similarly, any data that is to be processed must first be copied into RAM so the CPU can get at it.

ROM Is a Kind of RAM

Read-only memory (ROM) is a generic name for a number of similar types of memory chips. They share an ability to retain information for very long times (years) without needing any electrical power.

They are, in fact, a subspecies of RAM, for they provide easy, quick, random access to the data they carry. But the most important fact about them is the nonvolatility of their contents.

Some kinds of ROM are not, strictly speaking, ROMs at all. These are the so-called *programmable read-only memory* chips, or *PROMs*. The many different kinds of PROMS are detailed in Chapter 16. The essential thing they add to the idea of a ROM is the possibility of changing their contents, although usually with some greater effort or time delay than is required simply to read from them.

Uses for ROM

ROM is used to store information that does not change, or at least that does not change often. This could be a collection of programs that will be used to activate the hardware parts of the PC, and perhaps some tables of fixed data.

The programs that are ROM-based are either those that get used so often they must always be loaded and ready to go, or those that must be run before it is possible to load any program from a disk drive.

Every PC must contain some ROM. Almost always it has a great deal more RAM.

One very important ROM (or group of ROM chips) is found on the motherboard of every PC. This is the one which contains the **P**ower **O**n **S**elf **T**est (POST) program. Without this ROM, the PC could not start itself when turned on. This ROM also contains program code to find and load an operating system (called *booting* the computer), and a large collection of miniprograms to activate the standard collection of hardware for that brand (and model) of PC.

Other ROMs may be found on plug-in cards. They contain special programs to activate the special hardware on that plug-in card. These are called *option ROMs.*

Some PCs even have DOS in a ROM. This is popular mostly in laptop computers and diskless workstations on a network, but it's starting to spread to stand-alone desktop machines. The advantage of putting DOS into a ROM is that it is always loaded, and the PC can start computing much more rapidly. This advantage is lost, however, once you move to an upgraded version of DOS. You must then boot off a floppy disk, just as if DOS weren't in ROM. (Or, of course, you could open up the system unit, pull out the DOS ROM chip, and replace it with a new version of that chip. This is too much hardware work for most people.) With the emergence of Flash RAM, which allows easy changing of the contents of a (pseudo) ROM, putting DOS into ROM may become practical for many more PCs in the near future.

A new kind of plug-in card for PCs, called the *PC card*, has been defined and is being promoted by the PC Memory Card International Association. These PCMCIA-conforming PC cards can carry RAM (including flash RAM), ROM, or a mixture of the two, and even I/O devices. In future PCs, especially the tiny palmtops, PC cards will be used for each of the purposes just described and many more.

Disk Storage

ROM keeps its contents essentially forever. That is fine for things that almost never change. The contents of RAM can be changed in a snap, but once power fails it loses all the information it contained. Neither of these is a good place to keep programs you run from time to time, or the data you are processing (documents, spreadsheets, databases, or whatever).

That is where rotating magnetic disks come to the fore. They are relatively slow, involve moving parts that wear out, are fragile, and have a number of other drawbacks, but on balance their strong points outweigh their drawbacks for most PC owners. Except for magnetic tape (which has other disadvantages), magnetic disks offer the least expense per megabyte to store information.

Hard disks store working copies of programs and data. (These disk drives have platters called *fixed*, though they actually spin very rapidly; they are called fixed because they cannot easily be removed from the PC.) Floppy disks store archival copies of programs and data. This is the usual means for loading new programs onto a hard disk and the usual way to take processed data off so it can be sent elsewhere. Some people do not have a hard drive on their PC, and they use floppy disks for all of these purposes.

An upcoming competitor to both tape and floppy disks is a class of removable superdisks. These include both hard disks that can easily be removed from the PC, complete with their mechanical read/write mechanism, and disk cartridges that can come out of the disk drive much as a floppy does, but which offer the speed and capacity of a fixed disk with the flexible use of a floppy disk. The total storage capacity you can have is limited only by your budget for media (diskettes or cartridges), although the total amount on-line at any one time is limited by the drive capacity. *Bernoulli* and *SyQuest* are just a couple of popular trade names in this category.

Optical disks offer an alternative to magnetic storage. These disks can hold huge amounts of information. They are read to and written from using a laser, sometimes with a magnetic assist. They are, however, much slower than hard disks, and so far, most of them are much more expensive per megabyte stored. Still, their capacity and features are sometimes just right for a given application; then they are worth their cost.

The optical disk drives that can be used only to read prerecorded disks (called CD-ROMs) are becoming quite affordable, and they are an essential part of any *multimedia-ready* **PC** *(MPC)*. The next more expensive variety of optical drive is much like a *one-time programmable* **ROM** (a *PROM*) in that it can write to any location on the disk just once, but then can be used to read from that or any other location any number of times. Such a drive is called a *Write Once, Read Mostly (WORM)* drive. The most expensive type of optical disk drive can both read and write to its own special kind of disk, and also can read WORM disks.

A hybrid of magnetic and optical disk storage technology that is just coming on the market is the opto-magnetic floppy disk drive, tradenamed the *floptical*. This device uses a conventional magnetic read/write head and combines it with the optical positioning mechanism from an inexpensive audio CD player. The combination allows you to record several tens of megabytes on a specially prepared 3-1/2" diskette.

When RAM Looks Like Disk Storage— Virtual Disks

DOS was designed to use disks. In fact, the letters stand for *Disk Operating System*. It presumes that information is going to be brought into RAM from a disk, processed, and then returned to a disk afterwards.

Sometimes you want to create a temporary file, just to hold some processed information awhile. Later on, the final data will be sent to a permanent file elsewhere. Ordinarily, DOS sends any file you create to a disk drive. For a temporary file, though, you might prefer to put that temporary information someplace in RAM. DOS doesn't know how to do that. But clever people have written programs that use a region of RAM to store information, yet present themselves to DOS as just another disk drive (and a super-fast one at that). This is called a *RAM disk*, or *virtual disk drive*.

Another use for a RAM disk is to store programs you run often. They can be copied to the virtual disk once, then loaded from there, and run many times during the day. That can save substantial amounts of time.

When ATs were new, there was no way DOS could use its extended memory directly, so running a special program to convert that extended memory into a virtual disk (also called a RAM disk) was about the only good thing one could do with it. IBM first shipped VDISK.SYS with *PC DOS* 3.0. Shortly afterwards, Microsoft shipped RAMDRIVE.SYS with *MS-DOS* 3.0. These are installable device drivers and once loaded they make DOS think it has one or more additional drives whose only distinguishing features are being extremely fast and forgetting *everything* whenever power fails or you have to reboot your computer. (The former is a very attractive feature. But never forget the latter one, or someday you *will* regret it.)

Now that there are enhancements to DOS, including memory-management programs that can let regular DOS programs take advantage of extended memory (at least on 386-, 486-, and *Pentium*-based computers), there may be better things to use your RAM for than simulating a disk drive. Still, if you have enough RAM in your PC, a RAM disk is a fine way to use some of it. This discussion of virtual disks is continued in Chapters 20 and 30, with some additional suggestions, cautions, and recommendations.

Another variation on this theme is the *solid-state disk drive.* This is simply a box with a huge amount of RAM in it with some special-purpose hardware to make it appear to be a disk drive. It may also include a battery backed-up power supply so it will have much of the nonvolatility of a real disk drive. Alternatively, it may use flash RAM to gain the same advantage. This sort of disk simulator is extremely fast, and using one has no impact on your use of the memory already in your PC. The disadvantage is simply the high cost of these units (at least so far).

A special kind of solid-state disk is a PC card (conforming to the PC Memory Card International Association's standard) with either battery backed-up RAM or flash RAM and configured to look like a disk drive. The primary advantage of this form of solid-state disk is that it can be used in very small computers, especially in the palmtop models that are too small to contain either a floppy or a hard disk. This may be the form of PC card that will become most popular in the next several years.

When Disk Storage Looks Like RAM— Virtual Memory

There are now so many uses for RAM that often it seems there cannot possibly be enough of it to go around. *RAM cram* is the name of this game. "How can I fit everything I need or want into RAM at once?" The notion of squandering some of your RAM on a virtual disk never enters the picture.

In these cases, the solution is sometimes the exact opposite of a RAM disk. Instead of running a program to make some RAM appear to be a disk, you can run a program to make some of your disk storage area appear to be extra RAM.

The benefit is simple: Disk storage space costs much less per megabyte than RAM. If you can use it in the place of RAM you can run programs too large to fit all at once in your actual, physical RAM. The down side is equally clear: disks are a whole lot slower than RAM chips (hundreds, even thousands of times slower). But if you have more time than money, or if you only rarely need that extra RAM, waiting awhile instead of paying a lot may not be so bad.

The CPU works only with the information in actual physical RAM. The trick these virtual-RAM programs play is to constantly swap information out of physical RAM onto disk and swap in new information, always keeping just ahead of what the CPU wants.

To a certain extent this can be done in any PC. The more advanced models (386-, 486-, and *Pentium*-based PCs) can assist in the process. They have a built-in means to map regions of logical memory to actual physical memory or storage. The mechanism is called *demand-paged virtual memory*.

In effect the CPU can alert the memory-management program when it is going to need information swapped, so that the program doesn't have to interfere in the ongoing processing as much. This increases efficiency. See Chapter 11 for more details.

Tape and Other External Storage

Magnetic tape is the oldest mass-storage medium used in personal computers. Before mere individuals could afford even floppy disk drives, audiotape recorders were used as the principal means of storing programs and data. They did not work very quickly. (You could easily spend many minutes waiting for a small program to load.) Still, they worked. And they did not cost much.

The original IBM *PC* came with an optional tape drive. It was better than the audiotape drives used with earlier personal computers, but not by much. Once floppy disk drives became affordable, the cassette tape drive as a PC's principal mass storage was history.

A somewhat different kind of tape drive is still much with us today. The streaming tape drive is probably the most popular means of creating backup copies of information on hard disks. Until optical disks and the removable superdisks (and their drives) get much cheaper, tape will probably continue to hold the bulk of this market.

Tape has a couple of advantages over floppy disks: It costs significantly less per megabyte, and it usually has a larger total capacity. Tape has one outstanding disadvantage: It is a serial access medium. To get to a specific piece of information on a tape means moving the tape past the read head all the way from wherever it is to the place the information you want is. Sometimes you can read only when the tape is moving in one direction; in that case, you must rewind it to the beginning before each search.

Yet another technology is also bidding to serve in this market for long-term, yet not absolutely read-only information storage. That is Flash RAM (also called Flash ROM) PC cards. These are memory cards that contain chips specially built to be nearly as fast at reading and writing data as DRAM, yet as stable at keeping that information as PROM. The only real disadvantage this technology has at the moment is its very high price per megabyte. Already it is finding favor for use in some laptop and palmtop computers, where its very small size, low weight, and invulnerability to shock render its high cost bearable.

Human Memory and Computer Memory, a Comparison

Comparing computer memory with human memory is more than simply interesting. There are significant parallels, and knowing them may help you remember the difference between *RAM memory* and *storage.*

Short-Term Versus Long-Term Information Holding

Your brain is constantly recording experiences in what psychologists call your *short-term memory.* Later on, if the events are important enough, they get copied to your *long-term memory.*

These two different kinds of memory serve very different purposes. The short-term memory is what you use to know what you are doing. It is how you keep track of where you are in the process, for example, of tying your shoes. Once you have tied them, you normally let yourself forget the details of what you did.

Long-term memory is how you know who you are. Only by remembering things from day to day can you have any notion of being a person who exists in time. Some individuals who have lost the ability to add information to their long-term memory are still able to do things (their short-term memory works), but they are utterly unable to remember the people they meet or the things they do.

This dichotomy nicely parallels the difference between the electronic (RAM) memory in your PC and the storage space it has on disk drives. The former is a scratch-pad keeping track of what the PC is doing at the moment, and remembering the results briefly. The latter is where all the long-term storage of information in a PC takes place.

Immediate Versus Remote Access

Another perspective is to think of the accessibility of information. You need to know many things to function well in life. But many more things may be useful to you from time to time. You make no effort to remember them; you are satisfied to be able to look them up when you need them.

The deciding factor is how often or how quickly you need the information. If you will be using it frequently or if you must be able to access the information very quickly, you'd best remember it. If you only occasionally need it, you can afford to leave it in a book somewhere and look it up on those rare occasions when you want it.

Temporary Versus Permanent Information Retention

Your brain is built to forget whatever is in its short-term memory after just a few minutes or hours. It retains information in long-term memory for years. That is much like computer memory (RAM), which "forgets" everything when power goes off, and disk storage, which "remembers" whatever it is told to store, essentially forever.

Of course, you do forget many things even after they have been put into your long-term storage. Or at least you lose the ability to access them easily. That is like moving information off your PC's hard disk onto some archival disk or tape. Unless you have superb catalogs of those archives, you may have similar difficulty finding information once it has been moved there.

Naturally these analogies are not exact parallels. Still, they may help you understand and remember the important distinction between computer memory (short-term, quick, and in readily available information-holding places) and computer information storage (long-term, slower, and in more remote holding places).

A Common Frustration (Why Adding Memory Is Not Always the Answer)

If you have ever gotten an `Out of memory` error message when you know you have more than enough RAM in your PC, you have known frustration. (like the person in Figure 6.9) Perhaps you had too little RAM when you first saw the message, and then you specifically bought more RAM in order to make the message go away. It didn't. This is really frustrating. Why does it happen?

Programs have to be in RAM (or ROM) to run. The CPU cannot read the instructions that form the program except from a location in RAM or ROM. By a quirk in the design of DOS, ordinary DOS programs normally must be loaded somewhere in the first megabyte (1,024KB) of memory. This is a leftover from the fact that DOS was designed to run on a PC, and the original PCs could not have more than one megabyte of memory.

Actually, things are worse than that. IBM reserved three-eighths of that first megabyte for special uses. Users' programs are supposed to stay out of that region. That leaves only the lower five-eighths (640KB) for your programs.

When you load up your PC with a lot of resident software, such as a network driver and a pop-up calculator, you may simply not have enough room for certain large programs to operate. Adding RAM to bring your PC up to the maximum that DOS can address (640KB) is almost always a good idea. But adding more RAM beyond that simply creates space that DOS cannot see or use. So you don't solve your problem that way.

Fortunately, there are some ways around this problem. Explaining them is a major part of what this book is about. The specific details are in Chapters 12, 15, and beyond. The intervening chapters give you the background to understand those evasive maneuvers.

Figure 6.9.   An all-too-common frustration.

Another Common Frustration (Why Big Disks Are Not Always the Answer)

Some people have a different problem. They know their computer needs more RAM to operate. But they wonder why a PC can't simply borrow memory from the disk drives. After all, they reason, the big computers at the office are able to run lots of people's programs at the same time and they *never* seem to run out of memory. Why can they do this and your PC cannot?

Mainframe computers commonly have a feature called *demand-paged virtual memory*. That means that when they run out of RAM, they simply move some of the information that is in the RAM off to a disk somewhere, and then reuse that RAM for some other purpose. When the program that had been using that RAM needs it back again, the process is reversed.

This works well, as long as you don't mind the delays introduced by all this information swapping. If the computer and the disk drives are fast enough, you might not even notice, especially if you are accustomed to sharing that large computer with a variable number of other users. Who's to say whether it's slow today simply because so many people are using it or because part of the time your job is being swapped to disk?

Mainframe computers have special hardware to make these swaps easy, fast, and (nearly) painless. Most PCs do not. Even on those that do, DOS doesn't know about this possibility, so it never uses that special hardware. It just doesn't try to do any swapping to disk. (Starting with version 5, DOS includes a task-switching program, but this is just an add-on to an operating system that really doesn't know about swapping. The task swapper can only swap whole programs, unlike a full demand-paged virtual memory system that can swap memory in small chunks called pages.)

You can augment DOS with a suitable memory-management program, and then you, too, can have and use virtual memory. You won't run out of RAM nearly as easily (though there are still some limitations on what DOS can do, even with the best of help). On the other hand, your formerly speedy PC may seem like it is swimming in cold molasses. Still, if before you could not run some important program at all, and now you can, that may be solution enough.

There are some alternative operating systems and operating environments that provide virtual memory as a standard feature. The former include *UNIX* and *Pick*. The latter include *Windows* and *GeoWorks Ensemble*. Some DOS programs have built-in virtual memory managers. The Borland products with VROOMM technology are in this category. Chapter 11 covers the principles behind these different kinds of virtual memory. Some of the implementations mentioned here are more flexible than others. Only a few deserve the name *demand-paged virtual memory*. Chapter 21 describes some of the available products to help you achieve virtual memory on your PC.

So What Is the Answer?

If you can't always solve your PC memory problems simply by buying and installing a lot of extra RAM in your PC, nor can you solve them with a larger hard disk, what is the solution, really? There are two steps to take. First, though, reconsider your real goal.

The Goal You Seek

Your real goal is, or probably ought to be, to make your PC do more for you in less time with less overall effort on your part. If you don't agree with this goal, of course, a lot of what you read here may not help you.

Your Goal Can Be Achieved in Two Steps

Here are the two principal steps to achieving optimal performance in your PC.

Step 1: Have Enough Memory and Storage

Be sure you have enough short-term and long-term information storage in your PC. That is, be sure you have installed enough RAM and have enough free disk space.

The first 640KB is special to DOS. If you don't already have that much RAM, you will need to upgrade your PC until you do. Any additional memory you install can be helpful, but you will have to take some special steps to take advantage of it.

Step 2: Use What You Have Wisely

Be sure you use what you have wisely. This means you must practice good memory management. First, unclog your RAM and your disk. Next, organize your use of each of them.

Many books have been written on how to organize and use your disk space wisely. This book focuses on how you can do the same sorts of things with your RAM. For that purpose, you do need to have some free space on your disk. Some of that will be used by memory-management programs; some will be used for temporary storage of information (in swap files, etc.). Just how much you need depends on which memory-management strategies you implement. Some tips are given in the detailed discussions of those programs in Chapters 20 and 21.

Now for a quick list of ways to unclog and organize your use of RAM:

1. *Reduce the Size of Each Program You Put into RAM*

- Reduce the size of DOS in RAM (by a careful choice of DOS version and the options you invoke).

- Use smaller rather than larger device drivers.

- Use the smallest TSRs that will do what you need.

- Consider changing application programs to ones that need less RAM.

2. *Be Sure You Don't Have Any Unneeded Programs in RAM*

- You always need DOS (unless you are willing to take the leap to another operating system—see the discussion in Chapter 12 before you try this).

- You may well be able to do without some of your device drivers. ANSI.SYS is often loaded when it really is not needed.

- That pop-up program that lets you answer your office mate's trivia questions is wonderful, but if you are experiencing RAM cram, get it out of there! Many less obvious cases also demand the same solution.

- DOS shell programs, program launchers, and task-swapping program managers can help a lot. But they also take up RAM, in some cases a lot of RAM. Consider carefully whether to use these aids, and if so, how to minimize their memory requirements.

- You may not need to use the particular application program you crave. If it just won't fit, you may not be able to use it. Functionally similar but less RAM-hungry alternatives almost always exist.

Here is one example: The AUTOMENU program launcher is wonderful, but it can be a bit of a RAM hog. There are two distinctly different ways of launching programs using AUTOMENU. One leaves AUTOMENU in memory while the program it has launched is running; the other does not. The first way has some advantages, but being miserly with RAM is not one of them. Read the documentation thoroughly and then choose your course carefully.

3. Move Whatever You Can Out of the First 640KB to Some Other Location

- In some PCs that will have to mean swapping things to disk.

- In others you can move the programs to upper memory or to expanded memory and still keep them where they can be accessed more or less instantly.

A Recap

In this chapter, you learned the five essential parts of any computer, and that memory is one of them. You now know the difference between memory and storage and why you need both. You have been introduced to the concept of a memory bus and an I/O bus (and briefly to some other buses), and you have learned about the three classes of signal that are sent over the memory and I/O buses.

This chapter also covered the important difference between memorylike and portlike places to put bytes of information. Speaking of bytes, this chapter explained what a byte is and how much information it can hold. It also drew distinctions between a number, a symbol, and a character set. Codes are used to store characters as numbers. Symbols must be described as numbered members of a character set before a computer can store references to them. And all of that led up to the notion of how large a fact is.

Next came an overview of the many different kinds of information-holding places in PCs, how certain of them can sometimes be made to substitute for others, and when and why you might wish to do this. The chapter closed with a proposed goal and a listing of steps to achieve that goal. The rest of this book is largely devoted to fleshing out those recommendations.

With this information in hand, you are now ready to learn some important details about how your computer reads and runs programs. That is the focus of the next chapter.

7

HOW PCS WORK

Knowing what a computer is doing can help you understand what you have to do (and why) in order to help it work the way you want. This chapter covers some fundamental topics, both in simple terms for the novice and in depth for the more technically minded.

You may have thought that knowing how your computer does things—really deep-down understanding of what the tiniest steps are that it takes to accomplish your aims—was something you had no need for or interest in knowing. Surprise! It really can be very helpful. Best of all, at the level you need to understand it in order to make the knowledge useful, it is relatively easy to learn.

Sometimes only a knowledge of at least the essence of what is going on will enable you to understand what steps to take in order to get your computer to do what you need. In this chapter you will learn about the crucial concept of the *computer interrupt,* and how it makes things much easier for programs in your PC and, at times, more complicated for you.

Before you can make much sense of that topic, though, you must understand (if only in a fairly general way) some of the details of how your computer runs programs and processes data. Then you can learn, if you wish, about Application Program Interfaces. If the thought of doing so intimidates or bores you, feel free to skip to the last subsection and get only the summary. That you *will* need; the rest of the material on APIs is optional.

A Digression on Computer Languages

Computers don't understand English. For that matter they don't *understand* anything. (Computers don't think, either, but that is a different story.) Computers do use language. Each kind of computer uses its own, unique language.

Why This Matters and to Whom

Why should you care about computer languages? You might be curious, and if so this is a fascinating topic. Or perhaps you already know a fair amount about computer programming; for you, this chapter will be a lot of review, but it also may put some ideas into a new and useful context. But what if you are neither particularly curious nor already a programmer? Why should you care about the language your computer uses?

You need to know at least that computers do use a language and that it is definitely not the same as any language you speak. Knowing that, and just a bit of what kind of language it is, you can better understand some of the limitations computers have. You also will be able to make more sense of the documentation you will get with various pieces of memory add-on hardware and memory-management programs. That, really, is why this section is in this book.

What Language Do Computers Speak?

Computers read, store, process, and output numbers (or at least they act as if they do). People say that computers have binary numbers stored in their memory cells. Actually, all that is in the memory cells are patterns of high and low voltages. Still, it is very convenient to interpret those patterns as numbers. So for the purposes of this (and almost any other) book on computers, I will say that those patterns of high and low voltages are really patterns of ones and zeros, or *binary numbers.*

When you type on the keyboard, you think of yourself as pressing keys to enter letters. That is not what actually happens. You press a key. A small, subsidiary computer in the keyboard notices this fact and it sends one (or more than one) number to the main PC system unit. That number represents the key you just pressed, but only because of an agreement between the keyboard computer and the keyboard controller in the PC on what code is being used to represent the keys.

Another way to say this is that the keyboard computer and the PC system unit's keyboard controller have a private language (their shared code for the keys). As it happens, in PCs there are two different codes for keys. The *IBM PC* and *IBM PC/XT* use one code. The *IBM PC/AT* and all later IBM models use a second code, or dialect, of that private language.

The clone PC makers and a number of other manufacturers have created keyboards able to work with PCs and XTs (and their clones), other keyboards able to work with ATs, 386, 486, and Pentium-based computers (and their clones), and yet other keyboards able to "speak" both key-code dialects. Unless your keyboard speaks the dialect your PC's keyboard controller is expecting to hear, no useful communication between them can occur.

The keyboard computer constantly scans the keys, one at a time, to see which ones are being held down. It sends a unique number the first time it notices one of the keys is being held down. It sends a different number when it notices that key has been released.

The first number is the key's scan code. This is a number that ranges from 0 up to one less than the number of keys on the keyboard. It is encoded into a byte and shipped off to the PC system unit's keyboard controller chip. The code sent for the release of a key is just 128 more than the scan code sent for that key being pressed. In binary, this means the first bit of the byte sent is zero if the key was pressed and one if the key was just released. (This means no PC keyboard can have more than 128 keys, or at least it would be unable to distinguish some pairs of those keys if it did.)

If you hold the key down awhile (more than about half a second, usually,) the keyboard computer will notice that fact, and it will send additional copies of the key-pressed scan code for that key. This is how the keyboard's typematic action works. The exact time before copies of the scan code start being sent and the rate at which they are sent depend in part on which keyboard you have. Many PC keyboards allow you to program that delay and repeat rate.

Similarly, every other way of putting information into the computer gets converted to a byte or a stream of bytes (8-bit binary numbers). That is what the computer "sees."

Some of the information you put into your computer is not data to be processed; it is instructions for how to process data. Those instructions are called a *computer program.*

Now you know. The language of any digital computer (like a PC) is strictly numeric. All the verbs, adjectives, and nouns in computer language are just different numbers or groups of numbers.

Groups of Binary Numbers as Instructions

English is composed of words organized into sentences. In a similar fashion, you can group the numbers in a computer language into meaningful units, called *instructions*, each specifying a single action.

In English, some sentences are as short as a single word; others contain many words. The language of PCs has a range of length to its instructions, from a single byte to a dozen or more bytes.

Some other computer languages do not have this range of "sentence" length. See the discussion of RISC versus CISC processors in Chapter 13.

Programs and Data Differ Only in Context

Partly because both the language of a computer and the data it processes are just special arrangements of numbers, computers can process their own programs. From one point of view, a given set of numbers may be a program to be executed. (*Executing a program* is jargon for reading the program and acting upon it. This also is called *running the program*.) In another context those same numbers could be considered data to be processed according to the directions of some other program.

This is how a computer can be used to help create computer programs. Running one program (the language interpreter or compiler) causes the PC to accept, as its input, some data that will be converted into another program. The difference between an interpreter and a compiler is simply whether the new program fragments are themselves executed right away (an *interpreter*), or are saved for later execution (a *compiler*).

Further, there are layers of programs in your PC. The lowest-level program loads the next higher-level program into RAM as if it were merely a bunch of data it was to process. Then it processes that data in a special way—it suspends itself and makes the PC run the data (the second program). When that program completes its actions, the lower-level program regains control of the PC.

As the higher-level program runs, it may load yet higher-level programs, relinquish control to them temporarily, and so on. Often there are literally dozens of programs all loaded into your RAM at once. One of them is active at any given moment. All the rest are in some suspended state, but may come into play anytime they are needed. (This idea is explored in more depth in Chapter 10.)

Computer Language Dialects

Not only are there several codes or dialects for computer keyboards, there are also a number of different computer languages (at the microprocessor level). The principal language of any computer is set by the CPU (central processing unit) chip it uses.

The reason that any PC can run almost any PC program is that the fundamental language used by all the microprocessor chips in the Intel 80x86 family is the same. The more advanced models of that family have a richer version of their common language, and for that reason some programs that use those richer language constructs can only be run on the higher models of PC incorporating those more advanced CPU chips. Still, most of the language is common to all the PC family. And simple PC programs work just fine on all PCs.

Remember, in this book, the term PC refers only to computers that use one of the Intel 80x86 microprocessors, or a clone of one, as their CPU chip. Other families of personal computer (for example, Apple's *Macintosh* family, the *Amiga* family by Commodore, or the computers made by Atari) are not PCs, in this sense of the word, precisely because they don't have an Intel-compatible CPU.

How People Make Sense of Computerspeak

If you have ever looked at an actual computer program, doubtless you were baffled by what you saw, at least at first. All you saw was a lot of apparently meaningless numbers or symbols. How, then, is it possible for people to create or read computer programs? Do you really have to learn to "speak Computer"?

Fortunately, the answer is no. In the early days of computers, it was necessary to program them in *machine code*, which meant that programmers had to write the actual numbers their computers were to read and execute. Now, however, there are computer programs that can read what are called *higher-level languages* and convert them into machine code.

Assembly Language

The higher-level computer languages can be arranged into a hierarchy. The lowest level of them is *assembly language*. This is primarily a means of directly expressing machine code in more readable form (substituting short strings of letters, called *mnemonics,* for each machine-code verb, for example). To a small extent, assembly language also enlists the computational power of the computer to help the programmer express ideas without having to worry too much about exactly what data or instructions goes where in memory, and other similarly picky details.

Still the assembly-language programmer must have a pretty clear idea of how memory will be used, and in exchange, the programmer can control very precisely the instructions that will be in the final program.

Higher-Level Languages

Other higher-level languages (called interpreters and compilers, with names such as Ada, BASIC, C, COBOL, Forth, FORTRAN, Lisp, Pascal, and so on) remove the programmer further from the details of crafting the machine code. These languages place a greater emphasis on expressing the logical structure of the program. That has both an up side and a down side. It makes writing complex programs much easier, but it prevents the programmer from seeing and thus from controlling the exact behavior of the computer at the lowest levels. This can make it possible to create programs quickly, but it hinders making those programs as efficient as possible.

Commercial programs often contain sections created in a very high-level language (for those parts where expressing a logical design is most crucial) and others crafted in assembly language (where it is of paramount importance to have total control over how the computer is going to do its work). Choosing the right mix is a matter of programmer preference and, to a certain degree, an art.

Here is another way of looking at the matter of computer languages. When programmers create a program, they can do so at one of several different levels of interaction with the computer. At one extreme, they are forced to work totally on the computer's terms, by writing in actual machine code. At an opposite extreme, they may be able to work in a fashion much closer to how they naturally would think about the problem their program is being built to solve. In that case the computer is doing the bulk of the work of translation from thought to computer code.

Just how that translation work shall be done is not a simple or obvious notion. Many competing programming languages and environments have been developed; each one touted as the best and easiest to use. Most of them have survived, because they actually are best for some people and some programming projects but not for others.

This notion of a *computer-human interface* has been explored in great depth, and it has been extended far beyond just how programmers interact with computers to include how other users of computers do also. This leads us to the notion of computers that are *user-friendly*, or said another way, to computer-human interfaces that are *intuitive*.

Intuitive User Interfaces

The term *intuitive user interface* is a very popular and often misunderstood one. Roughly speaking, it means making the computer act the way you would expect it to act.

Expectations are learned. Only after you have some experiences, can you have any expectations. Any interface could be intuitive if it was all you had ever experienced.

Everyone does something besides using computers. Indeed, all computer users did something before they first began using computers. And the expectations with which anyone approaches a computer are built on the sum of all his or her other experiences.

The designers of computer programs want you to use their products productively. To do that, you must learn what the product can do and how to make it do those things. The more that this does not require you to do tasks in different ways than you are used to doing them, the more intuitive the program will seem.

This has two aspects. The more one computer program is like all others you have used before, the more easily and quickly you will learn how to operate it. Second, the more the conventions used by this program's authors mimic other conventions you are used to in the larger world, the more obvious it will seem.

Sometimes this is pretty blatant; other times it is very subtle. In western culture, green means *go* or *okay*, and red means *stop* or *danger*. These are not computer ideas or standards; they come from everyday life. So if a computer program uses red for *okay*, it is bucking the user's other life experiences and that program will be perceived as relatively difficult to learn and use.

The more subtle cases arise when there is a less firm standard in real life, or when the idea to be expressed is not so clearly encoded into a simple construct such as a screen color or a single keystroke. Making a program easy to use means, on the one hand, making it easy to learn, and on the other, taking the least possible number of keystrokes to accomplish certain tasks. Those two goals are often in conflict.

Modern programs frequently have two ways to accomplish the more common tasks. One way is easy to learn; the other takes fewer keystrokes. For example there may be drop-down menus from which actions may be selected, and there may be shortcut keys to perform many of those tasks without first accessing a menu.

A simple and rather important problem that program designers must deal with is how, if the user doesn't know how to operate the program, he or she can get the program to explain how it can be used. There is no obvious parallel in everyday life that program designers could lean on, so many rather arbitrary ways have been used. The best-selling word processor of all time, *WordPerfect*, uses the F3 key to pop up help screens. Almost no other programs except those made specifically to work with *WordPerfect* use this choice.

IBM and Microsoft have promoted the use of the F1 key for getting help. This is neither less nor more arbitrary than F3. (You don't, in normal speech, use either one. See Figure 7.1.)

If these two companies have their way, however, using the F1 key for help will become universal (along with many other conventions IBM has defined as *Common User Access* methods, also called the *CUA standard*). If that happens, and to a large extent it already has, then these methods will seem to most PC users to be "intuitive."

The essential idea is consistency. If all the programs you use work the same way, once you have learned one of them, the rest will seem to be more or less intuitive to you.

What does all this have to do with memory management? If you wish to use a memory-management program, you may find it important to choose one that uses whatever it is you regard as an intuitive interface design. *WordPerfect* users often prefer to use *WordPerfect Office* as their shell program and task switcher, whereas users of Microsoft *Word* (in either its DOS or *Windows* version) may prefer to use *Windows* for their shell program and task switcher. This consideration can be as important as any technical issues of efficiency in memory use or range of programs that can be handled by the task switcher program.

The Problem of Dialects

Often people wonder whether they can use the same programs on a *Macintosh* and a PC. Or they may need to exchange documents or other data files created on one kind of personal computer with a user of another kind.

Since the different kinds of personal computers use very different machine code languages, it is generally impossible to share programs between them. The sharing of data files is much more feasible, though it still presents some problems.

Figure 7.1. Not the usual way people speak (but they often do press F1 on their PCs to get help).

It is sometimes possible to run a program meant for a PC on a *Macintosh* or other "foreign" computer. This is done by first running a program on the foreign computer that makes it emulate a PC. (For the *Macintosh,* one such program is called *SoftPC.*) If you then can get your

185

PC program loaded into the foreign computer, it can be run by the emulator program.

This sometimes works quite well, but it always involves a great sacrifice in speed. The reason is that the foreign computer first runs the emulator program, and that program reads and translates each one of the instructions in the PC program into equivalent ones in the foreign computer's language. That's a lot of work. It consumes much of the foreign computer's computational power to do this work, leaving relatively little of that power for actually doing the work of the PC computer program.

Program Porting

A computer program written to run on one kind of computer cannot be executed directly by a different computer. That is because different computers use different machine languages. That does not, of course, mean that programmers cannot make a version of the same program for each computer.

When programmers make such a new version, they essentially must go back to the original program logic and recode it in the new language. If a programmer uses a suitable high-level language to express the original program logic, it may be possible to create the new program nearly automatically.

More often, though, the new computer has different ways of doing some things, and those differences require some subtle rethinking of the way the program is designed. Most of the new code generation may be automatic, but very likely some of it will not be.

A good example is moving a *Windows* application to the *Macintosh* computer. There is a very strong set of conventions about how any program on a *Macintosh* shall work. These user-interface design guidelines are at some point going to conflict with the equivalent design recommendations for *Windows* programs.

At those points, it is necessary for the person creating the new version of the program to rethink how that program should operate. And the code to express those new ideas will essentially have to be written from scratch (or taken from a library of useful code routines for the target computer, in this case the *Macintosh*).

Creating a new version of an existing computer program for a different computer than the one it was originally written to run on is called *porting* the program. *Port,* in this context, comes from the notion of portability. (The program is being trans*port*ed from one computer to another.) Sometimes you'll hear of a *port* of a program, meaning the version of a program for a specific computer, or you may hear the expression *to port a program,* meaning to make a version for another computer.

Notice that these words refer to a concept that is **totally** different from the word *port* as in the *Input/Output ports* through which a PC receives information from, or sends information to, the outside world. (Both uses of the word *port* come from the same root meaning of port; they simply are quite unrelated concepts in PCs.)

Data File Porting

Different kinds of computers speak different machine languages; this is why there is a problem moving programs between those machines. What about moving data files?

The short answer is that you usually can, but it often takes quite a bit of effort. You may, in effect, have to do a translation of the data file that almost is like the translation needed to move programs between two different kinds of computer.

The details of this are a bit of a digression from our central topic of memory management. If you are interested in learning more about it, read on. If not, skip to the next section.

If you write a document in English, that language doesn't change as you move from a *Macintosh* to a PC, so you might think there would be absolutely no problem moving the document. Sometimes this is so, and sometimes it very definitely is not. To say a word processing document is in English is hardly sufficient to describe it. Each word processing program adds formatting information to the document files it creates, and each does so in its own unique way.

The best case is if you can use the same program (in different versions, of course) on the two computers. Then their data files may be relatively easily moved between the computers.

For example, you might use Microsoft's *Word for Windows* on a PC and *Word* on a Macintosh. Or perhaps your choice is *WordPerfect* on both machines. Microsoft *Excel* or Lotus *1-2-3* are spreadsheet programs available on both machines. Whichever pair of "matched programs" you choose, you can take a document or spreadsheet saved by the program on one machine and read and work on it in the corre-sponding program on the other machine. (Moving the files may require a step of translation called importing or exporting. Importing means asking your program to read a file in a format other than its own "native file format." Exporting means asking it to save the file in the format appropriate to some other version of that or another program.)

Even when moving data files from one version of *WordPerfect*, for example, to another, there are some rather subtle, yet important, issues of incompatibility to be faced. As software developers improve their products, the latest version available for one of the two machines will almost always have some features not shared by its sister program for the other machine. Which computer's version is ahead in this features "race" may well switch with each new version that is released. The point is, if you should choose to use a feature supported in the program on your computer, but not supported (yet) on the other computer, then when you transfer your data file it will not be interpreted on the target computer exactly as you had planned.

Far worse is trying to move documents created in a word processor on one machine to a computer for which there is no ported version of that word processor. The file format used by any available word processor on the target computer may be utterly incompatible with the original file. There are a number of programs that attempt to translate data files between any pair of a large number of file formats, but all such programs can only render approximately accurate translations. Without some such special translation program, the data files will turn out to be nearly total nonsense when viewed on the foreign computer.

Moving database files, spreadsheet files, and graphics files presents similar problems. There is no universal solution.

The nearest things to a universal file-porting solution so far are ASCII, CGM (**C**omputer **G**raphics **M**etafile), and EPS (**E**ncapsulated **P**ost**S**cript). Most word processors, database managers, and spreadsheet programs allow you to export the contents of one of their files to a pure ASCII form. (That means a file containing only ASCII characters.) Many graphics programs allow you to export and import CGM and/or EPS files.

- For word processors, this typically means you throw away all the formatting information. All you get in the exported file are the words. (Well, you do get end-of-line information, paragraph divisions, and maybe some line centering, but all the font, margin, and other fancy formatting information will be lost.)

- For a database or spreadsheet program, you may get either a fixed-length field export file or a *comma-delimited ASCII* export file. These can often be imported to a database program or spreadsheet program on the foreign computer with little problem. Notice, however, that all your spreadsheet macros will be lost. Similarly you may lose the linkages and the indices from a database file.

- Graphics files are best transported between different graphics programs, either on the same or different computers, using one of the fairly well standardized, interchange formats. CGM is one, and EPS is another.

These are hardly foolproof ways to move graphics files, though. Most graphics programs have limitations on how well they can create or read either CGM or EPS files. If you don't have a *PostScript* printer, EPS files may not do you any good, and CGM files often are unable to encode some of the subtleties of graphics data files.

So far this discussion has focused on the file format problems you may encounter. There are other, deeper issues as well.

The trap that first trips up most people when they attempt to transfer information from one computer to another is the simple-to-state but often hard-to-perform task of moving the file contents. The problem arises because you cannot normally copy the files to a disk on one machine and then read them on the other machine. Most computers have incompatible ways of storing data on a disk. Several solutions exist. Some *Macintosh* computers can read and write PC disks. Or you can get a special plug-in card (Central Point Software sells one) to put in your PC that will allow it to read and write *Macintosh* disks.

Another way to handle file transfer is over a phone line, assuming both computers have modems. This works well, and often it is the easiest way, even when the computers are right next to one another.

Another subtle problem is the matter of how a given (so-called) universal format of file is stored on each machine. Even something as simple as a pure ASCII file can present problems. *UNIX* stores ASCII files with every line ending indicated by a line feed character (see Figure 6.6). PCs use both a carriage return and a line feed character. To make sense of an ASCII file moved between a PC and a *UNIX* computer, the line endings must all be adjusted.

"Big-Endian" Versus "Little-Endian" Data Storage

You know that data is stored as numbers. If the numbers are bytes (8-bit binary numbers), each one gets stored in one memory location. But a single byte is not big enough to hold all the interesting numbers our computers must work with. A byte can only hold 256 possible values. To express the length of a Boeing 747 to the nearest centimeter, or your company's income (let alone the national debt) to the nearest penny, much more storage is needed.

Such large numbers can be written as a string of decimal digits, or they can be converted into an equivalent binary (or hexadecimal) number. Both strategies are used, but most of the time PCs convert all numbers to be stored into binary form.

The binary numbers that result will have more than eight bits. So they must be stored in more than one byte. (The exact number of bytes used to store the number varies with the program you are using. Most often two or four bytes are used, but if you must store the national debt to the penny, you'd better be using a program that can use at least eight bytes for that number.) The issue of endian-ness deals with how such a multiple byte binary number gets stored.

This is much like the issue, for a multiple-digit decimal number, of whether to write the most significant digit at the left or at the right. It is customary, in our culture, to write multiple-digit decimal numbers with the most significant digit at the left. So the number 4321 means four thousand, three hundred, twenty-one. If we used the opposite convention, it would mean one thousand, two hundred, thirty-four.

Intel chose to use the *little-endian* way to store multibyte binary numbers (see Figure 7.2). When pointing to a number in memory, the pointer always gives the lowest memory address at which any of that number is stored. In Intel's convention, this is always the least significant byte of the number.

Big and Little Endians

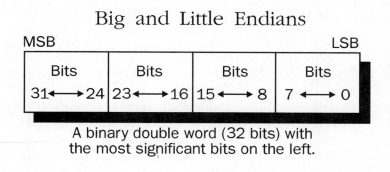

A binary double word (32 bits) with the most significant bits on the left.

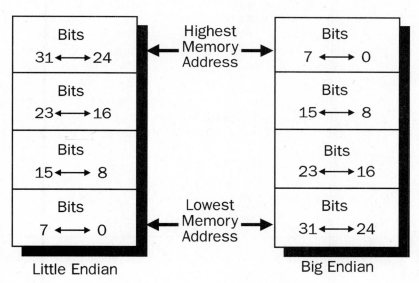

Little Endian   Big Endian

Figure 7.2. Big- and little-endian data formats.

Even in PCs (using Intel CPUs), some data is stored in big-endian order; ASCII data and binary coded decimal (BCD) numbers are, in particular. The pointers to these data are still pointing to the lowest address occupied by the data, but that is the start of the string or the most significant digit of the BCD number.

Big-endian order is used for all number storage in personal computers built around the Motorola 68000 family of CPU chips. Those include the *Macintosh*, *Amiga*, and Atari lines.

Endian-ness will affect you mainly when you are doing memory management and you snoop around in your PC's memory to try to make sense of what you see. Every number stored there (with the exception of BCD numbers, which are quite rare) will be stored in little-endian order.

Depending on the design of the utility program you use to snoop in memory, the little-endian order may look perfectly fine, or it may appear to be backwards. The DOS program DEBUG displays the contents of a region of memory in exactly the wrong way! Unfortunately, it was the first program to show memory contents in a PC, and so now most other utility programs that display memory contents use the same strategy. (Remember the discussion about how to make a program seem intuitive? The authors of the newer programs sought to accomplish this by emulating DEBUG.) All of these programs show the bytes of memory data arrayed from left to right in ascending order of memory address. This makes all the numbers appear to be in byte-reversed order. Since each byte is displayed using two hexadecimal numerals, the order seems even more messed up.

For example, the number whose hexadecimal representation is 1234h will be stored in memory with the byte 34h coming just before the byte 12h. Thus, in a DEBUG-type display, this would appear this way: . . . 34 12 . . . .

Important Tip   Notice which way your favorite memory utilities display the contents of memory, and remember the little-endian! That way you can interpret the displays you see appropriately.

Interrupts

The concept of an interrupt and the related concept of an exception are fundamental to the design of the Intel 80x86 processors. These are very powerful ideas, borrowed from mainframe computers. Having hardware and software interrupt support allows programmers to write more powerful programs much more easily.

Who Cares About Interrupts?

Clearly, anything that makes programming easier matters to programmers. What may not be quite so clear is that it also matters to you as a PC user. The most important significance to PC users is that PC programs cost much less and are available much sooner than they would be if interrupts were not available. But that's not all.

If you intend to do any memory management in your PC, you will have to understand, in principle at least, how interrupts operate. That's why this section of the book is here—it is a very important one for you to study.

In particular, you must be aware of the many possibilities for interrupt conflict and know how to discover and then resolve them. You also cannot understand what a *TSR* or *device driver* program is all about without at least a general understanding of how interrupts work. And it turns out that managing the TSRs and device drivers loaded in your PC is a critical part of the job of managing memory usage.

Before you can understand how a PC responds to each interruption in its normal activities, you have to have a fairly good picture of what those normal activities are like. So this next section explains how a PC processes instructions (executes programs) in more detail. Along the way you will be introduced to the concepts of flow of control, branching, looping, calling of subprograms, and software interrupts. In the following section, you will learn about two more ways the normal activities of the PC can get disrupted: hardware interrupts and exceptions.

Computers Run Themselves, Until People Meddle

In the last chapter, you learned that a computer program is a set of instructions that tells the computer what to do. Think of it as a script that the CPU reads and follows. First, the CPU reads one instruction. Next it figures out what that instruction means (this is called *decoding* the instruction). Then, the CPU does whatever it decided that instruction was telling it to do (this is called *executing* the instruction). Finally, the CPU goes on and reads the next instruction.

That may seem straightforward, but if you look at the details carefully, things get a bit more complicated. To appreciate what interrupts are and why they are valuable, you need to know a little more about some of those complexities.

The Normal Flow of Control

Most of the time, the next instruction is the one that is located in memory right after the one the CPU just finished executing. This is like reading a book. Normally you move from word to word, paragraph to paragraph, and page to page right through the book. In a computer program, we call this the *normal flow of control*.

From time to time this orderly process must be modified. There are several reasons that this is so, and there are a number of ways it may happen.

Unconditional Jumps

Programs often include tables of information that are needed for the computations they are to do. Sometimes the program's instructions run up against one of these tables. If the program is to go on any further, it must jump over the table. All computers provide some instruction for just this purpose. It is called an *unconditional jump*.

Using these unconditional jump instructions makes a program more like an article in a magazine than like a book. Frequently, when you read a magazine article, you find a place where it says something like "Continued on page 84." That lets the editors put an advertisement in the middle of the article, and still lets you find where to go to finish reading the article.

Unconditional jump instructions are valuable. Even more useful are their conditional kin.

Branching

The real power of a computer is not its ability to follow a sequence of instructions to be executed. Its real power comes from the fact that it can alter which instructions it will execute in the midst of executing them, based on the results of some earlier calculations it did.

For example, the computer may subtract two numbers and then do different things depending on whether the result is positive or negative. The place in a program where it makes such a choice is called a *branch*.

You may have answered a survey which used branching. For example, after question number 5 it might say, "If your answer to #5 was NO, jump to question #12." If you answered YES to number 5, you are supposed to continue with question #6.

A jump instruction that tells the CPU to jump if it obtained a certain result in a preceding step is called a *conditional jump*. Jump instructions (both conditional and unconditional), although very important, are relatively rare, constituting only about five percent of the total instructions in a typical program. (This fact will turn out to be important in the context of interleaved memory access. See the discussion in Chapter 16.)

Looping

Frequently, programs must repeat an action many times. There are two ways to accomplish this. One is to repeat the instructions for that action the right number of times. That works very well if the number of times the action is to be repeated is fixed and not too large. This approach doesn't work if the number of repetitions is either not known in advance or is very large.

What does work in those cases is to put the instructions for that action into the program just once, but enclose them in some others that cause that section to be repeated just the right number of times.

Such a section of a program is called a *loop*. The CPU reads and executes each instruction in the loop. Then, depending on whether or not it has done them enough times, it either jumps back to the start of the loop and executes them again, or it moves on the next instruction after the loop.

Making whether the CPU jumps back to the start of the loop depend on some condition clearly calls for the use of a *conditional jump instruction*. Sometimes the condition is based on counting the number of times the CPU has gone through the loop. Other times the decision is based on comparing the results of that action with some goal.

Recipes often say, "Season to taste." This is shorthand for the following instruction loop:

1. Add a little seasoning, less than you think is necessary.

2. Taste the result.

3. If you still think you need more seasoning, go back to step 1.

Any program can be broken down into regions in which the flow of control is normal (one instruction at a time in sequence), other places that have branch instructions, and yet other regions that are loops. This is enough to write programs that will do anything the computer is capable of doing. Figure 7.3 shows graphically the relationship between the normal flow of control, an unconditional jump, a branch, and a loop.

There are two special uses of what amounts to a branch instruction that are important enough to have been given special names. One is a *CALL instruction*; the other is a *software interrupt*.

Calls

The actions of even the most complex computer programs can be broken down into a large number of simple subactions. (Some examples are reading from the keyboard, writing to the screen, and printing.) Writing one of those programs is made much simpler if the programmer first identifies the simple subactions and writes a simple program to do each one. Then the main program can be made by stringing together all the subaction programs (which programmers refer to as modules) in the right order.

You might need a main program with a few instructions of its own (not part of any of the subactions), but between those instructions the program could include very many modules, possibly repeating each one several or many times. This idea is shown in Figure 7.4(a). A program created this way is said to use its modules as "in-line" code.

You could make a large program that way, but it would be unnecessarily large. A much more efficient way to create the main program is to have just one copy of each small program module and have the main program *call* for each one as it needs it. This idea is shown in Figure 7.4(b). This method of program instruction is referred to as using "subprograms" or "subroutines."

When the computer encounters a CALL instruction, it first records where it is in the program it is currently executing. Then it branches to the subprogram it is told to CALL and starts executing the instructions it finds there. When the CPU runs into an instruction called a RETURN, it jumps (unconditionally) back to the next instruction, after the original CALL instruction. (The difference between a RETURN and a JUMP is that a jump instruction includes the location you want the CPU to jump to. A RETURN instruction assumes that the CPU remembers where it came from the last time it executed a CALL instruction.)

> The place the CPU puts its "placemarker" and any other numbers it must remember about what it was doing (mostly contents of its internal registers) is called *the return stack*. Stacks are discussed more in Chapters 13 and 20.

If you have only a few repetitions of some very small modules, the additional CALL and RETURN instructions can actually make the second form of the program longer (see Figure 7.4). The more common situation occurs when each of the modules is many instructions long and is called many times. In that case the program with the CALLs and RETURNs is much shorter than the in-line version.

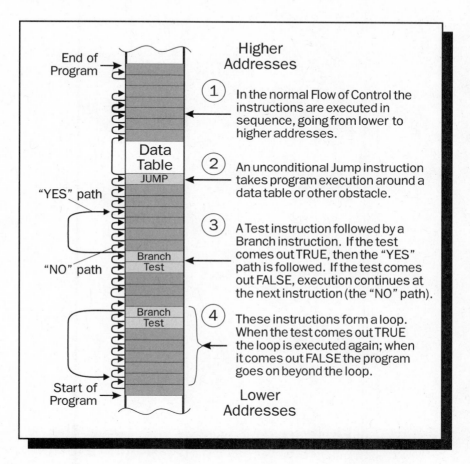

Figure 7.3. The basic elements of any computer program: regions with the normal flow of control, unconditional jumps, conditional jumps (branch instructions), and loops. Each box represents one instruction. The arrows on the left show the order in which the instructions are executed.

Using CALL instructions lets a programmer break up a big program into modules. As long as it is clear what each module is to do, a different programmer can write each of the various modules and still another programmer can write the main program. This modularity is what makes it possible for today's large programs to be written at all.

197

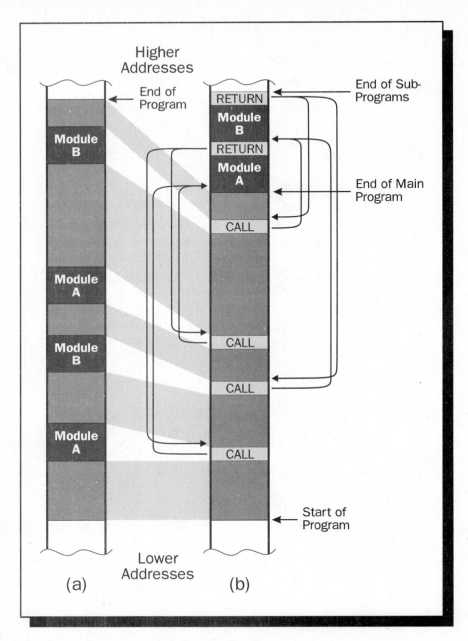

Figure 7.4. A complex action consists of many simple actions. (a) Stringing together the pieces (in-line code). (b) Reusing the pieces (subroutines or subprograms).

A limitation of using CALLs is that you must have all the subprogram modules in hand before the main program can be finished. This is because whoever creates the main program must know exactly where each of the modules is going to be in memory so the CALL instructions can point to them correctly.

> Ordinarily, the programmer puts a symbol that stands for the location of a module into the program's CALL instruction. A special-purpose computer program called a compiler, or a linker, then combines all the modules and the main program, putting in the actual module addresses once it figures out what they are.
>
> This works very well as long as the compiler or linker has all the modules available at the time it creates the final application program. That final program then will include all of the modules it calls within itself.

There is a way to invoke program modules without having them all in hand. This method is called the *software interrupt*. It allows an even higher degree of independence between the author of the application program and the authors of the various subprograms that the main program will be using.

What's more, software interrupts allow you, the PC's user, to change easily how a software program works long after it has been written by its authors. This is an extremely powerful feature of PCs.

Software Interrupts

A software interrupt is like a CALL instruction except that the programmer who writes it into a program need not have any idea where the subprogram that is going to respond to the interrupt will be located. Even the compiler and linker that finish the job of making the program don't need to know. Instead, what they must know is simply a standardized way of indicating which subprogram to use and how to communicate to that subprogram what it is supposed to do.

Like a CALL, a software interrupt is a way a program has of calling for help from some agency outside itself. When the CPU encounters a software interrupt instruction, it will stop executing the current program and go off searching for an appropriate other program to run. When that other program finishes its task the CPU will resume running the original program right where it left off.

In an Intel 80x86 processor, the way the CPU finds the subprogram to execute when it encounters a software interrupt is very flexible. Each software interrupt carries a number from 0 to 255. Whenever the CPU executes one of those instructions, it looks in a special table at the low end of memory to find out what the address is for the subprogram that will do whatever should be done next. This table must have an entry for any numbered interrupt that will occur. It need not have entries for numbers that will never occur.

The wonderful flexibility of this scheme lies in the fact that this table of numbers is in RAM. Its contents can easily and quickly be changed. So anytime you want to alter which subprogram will respond to a certain interrupt, all you have to do is load some program which will, once it knows where in memory it has been loaded, put its own address into that table in place of the one that was there originally.

The very next time that particular kind of software interrupt is encountered in any program that is being executed, your new subprogram will get called to service that interrupt.

The numbers in the table are called *interrupt vectors*, and the table is called the *interrupt vector table*. The subprograms that get called are referred to as *interrupt service routines* (sometimes abbreviated ISRs).

The new interrupt service routine is said to have *hooked* an interrupt when it places its own address in the vector table. If it is not prepared to perform all the services that a call to that interrupt might require, it simply stores within itself the address of the previously specified interrupt service routine. If it receives a call for service which it cannot handle, it simply passes that request on to the old ISR.

Some Reasons Interrupts Are Used and Some Problems They Can Lead To

You may now have some notion of the power of software interrupts. There are at least four key aspects of that power.

- First is the fact that a programmer writing an application program can assume that certain services will be provided on demand. Different programmers write the interrupt service routines that will provide those services.

  Not only are these two jobs done by different programmers, they are very likely working at different companies. The programmers at Lotus or WordPerfect write application programs which depend on the services that are provided by ISRs written by the programmers at Microsoft, IBM, and Digital Research.

- A second aspect of the power of interrupts is the way they save memory. Interrupt service routines do things that other programs need not just once, but many times. By having just one copy of an interrupt service routine in memory and making it available to all the different programs that may also be loaded in memory, a great deal of memory is saved over having each program include the instructions to do those tasks within itself.

- Third, and closely related to the first aspect, the application program that decides what needs to be done and the interrupt service routines that actually command the hardware are written by different people. They are combined inside one PC only when you run the application program on a particular PC.

    This means that the application programmer can focus on organizing the tasks to be performed, without worrying about how they are to be done. The ISR programmer, on the other hand, is altogether concerned with how to make this particular PC's hardware perform each task. That allows the creation of very general application programs and very hardware-specific interrupt service routines; together they make for powerful programs that run very well on a wide variety of PCs.

- The fourth important aspect of the power of interrupts is the ease with which they allow a PC user to alter how an application program does its job. Sometimes you put some new hardware into your PC; other times you load a new TSR or device driver program. This is another way of viewing the third advantage just mentioned.

    For example, almost every program puts information on-screen. There is a well-defined way to ask an interrupt service routine (the ISR for interrupt number 10h) to do this for you. The motherboard BIOS ROM contains a default ISR for this purpose. In all early PCs, that ISR knew only how to put information on a monochrome screen or a color graphics screen. It was unable to cope with an EGA or VGA display system.

    But when you install an EGA or VGA card in your PC, it comes with a BIOS ROM on that card. As soon as you boot up, your PC will notice that new BIOS and run a program in it. That program changes the number in the 17th slot in the interrupt vector table. (It uses the 17th slot because interrupt 10h is the 17th interrupt. Remember that 10h is the same as 16 decimal, and that interrupt numbers start with zero.)

From then on, if any program wants to put information on-screen in the usual way (by software interrupt number 10h), an ISR in the BIOS ROM on the video card will do the job (and, of course, it has been designed to do that just for the particular video card it lives on).

Interrupt service routines are generally a very good thing. But they cause some problems, in particular for memory management. I have stressed so far how much smaller and easier to write an application program can be since it can assume the existence of suitable interrupt service routines. On the other hand, those routines must be in your PC's memory to do their jobs. So they do take up some memory in addition to the size of your application program.

DOS itself is almost entirely a collection of interrupt service routines. The BIOS ROM on the motherboard contains more ISRs.

These ISRs not only take up memory, but sometimes you have no say over which portion of memory they take up. The ISRs that are located in a ROM, in particular, tend to be plopped down in a certain spot in your PC's memory, and that is where they stay. This can be quite a nuisance when you try to shoehorn in all the other programs you can. Chapter 21 explains this problem in some detail and shows several ways for working around it.

Responding to Outside Events—Hardware Interrupts

So far you have learned how your PC executes a program and may, as that program dictates, go off and execute some other programs. All of this is under the control of a master script—the main application program running at the time.

What about events that occur outside the PC? How does the PC become aware of them and how can it deal with them appropriately? For example, how does it know when you press a key on the keyboard and how does it decide what to do about that event?

There are two basic strategies for paying attention to the outside world: *polling* and *hardware interrupts.* The former strategy works on any computer, but it is inefficient and awkward. The latter requires special hardware support built into the CPU and other chips on the PC motherboard. It costs more to make a computer with interrupt support, but the added expense is well worth it.

When you learn how hardware interrupts are implemented in a PC, you will see their very close connection with software interrupts. But first you need to know how polling and hardware interrupts differ.

Polling

Polling simply means that the computer checks at regular intervals to see if something outside itself has occurred that needs its attention. A simple analogy may make the method and its limitations clear.

Consider Paul, a shopkeeper in a small store. If there are no customers in the store, Paul goes into his office and works on the books. But whenever a customer comes in, Paul must interrupt his book work and wait on the customer.

Paul polls. That is the strategy he must use if there is no bell or other way for customers to let him know when they come in. Every few moments Paul stops what he is doing and puts down a marker so he doesn't lose his place. He then goes out into the store to see if there are any customers that want help. If there are, he'll help them. If there are not, he'll return to his office and resume what he was doing before.

Interrupts

Irene runs a similar shop. But Irene relies on interrupts. She has a doorbell in her shop. Every time a customer walks in the door, it rings, alerting her to the customer's presence. So Irene works at her books steadily, without stopping to check the store, until the bell rings. Then she stops, puts down a marker to keep her place, and helps the customer. After she finishes with the customer, she returns to her books just as Paul does.

Clearly Irene's solution costs a bit; she had to buy and install the doorbell. Equally clearly, Irene can get more work done on her books, since she's not constantly stopping her book work to go check on the store.

Intel's 80x86 processor chips all have the necessary extra hardware built into them to support hardware interrupts. That is to say they have "doorbells" as a standard feature, plus the ability to react appropriately when one of those doorbells is rung.

There are 8 such doorbells in a PC or XT and 15 in all PCs based on later members of the 80x86 family of CPU chips. These "doorbells" are called *interrupt request lines* or *IRQ levels*. Different kinds of external events produce the effect of ringing different doorbells. Special hardware on the PC motherboard (one or two *interrupt controller chips*) translates the ringing of each doorbell into a particular number interrupt. The CPU responds to these interrupts in exactly the same way as it would to a software interrupt with the same number. The effective software interrupt number is set by the interrupt controller. (There are different rules for XTs and ATs. See Figure 7.6 and the discussion in Chapter 15 in the section "Resolving Resource Allocation Problems.")

In addition to these normal "doorbells," there is one that is more like a fire alarm. That is what is formally called the *nonmaskable interrupt*, or *NMI*. It is used to signal to the processor some critical problem requiring really urgent attention.

Figure 7.5 is a whimsical representation of one of these hardware interrupts. The keyboard sends a signal to the 8748 interrupt controller chip, which then sends a signal to the CPU.

Exceptions

There is one more way that the normal flow of control may be disrupted. The CPU has some special circuits within itself to detect problems that may arise there. For example, if you ask it to divide a number by zero, it will have a problem. (The answer would be infinity, and unfortunately, it would take nearly infinitely long for the CPU to figure that out. So it has a special circuit that watches to see if the divisor is zero and, if so, stops things before it tries to do the division.) When one of these difficulties springs up, the CPU interrupts itself by a mechanism called an *exception*.

There are three classes of exception: *faults*, *traps*, and *aborts*. The distinction between these three lies in when the CPU notices the difficulty and how hard it is for it to recover from that situation. Between the software interrupts, maskable and nonmaskable hardware interrupts, and three kinds of exceptions, there are six ways the CPU can get distracted from what it is doing and made to do something else (at least temporarily). Figure 7.6 lists all these ways.

Figure 7.5. A message from the keyboard—one of the most common hardware interrupts.

A Mini Review

So far in this section you have learned how your PC runs a program. Normally it reads and executes the instructions one after another, in the order that they are placed in memory. Every once in a while, though, it will find an instruction that causes it to alter the normal flow of control. This is a jump or branch instruction (or a CALL, RETURN, or software interrupt).

Class	Type	Cause	Interrupt Number
Exception	Fault	An error in an instruction is caught before it is executed.	Between 0 and 31
	Trap	An error in an instruction is caught after it is executed.	Between 0 and 31
	Abort	An error in an instruction is detected, but the offending instruction can't be identified	8
Software Interrupt		A trap caused by a special kind of program instruction designed for this purpose.	Between 0 and 255
Hardware Interrupt	Non-maskable (NMI)	External hardware device signals the CPU on its NMI pin.	2
	Maskable (INTR)	External hardware device(s) signal an event through an Interrupt Controller which signals the CPU on its INTR pin.	See note below.

NOTE: PCs and XTs have one Interrupt Controller and normally generate interrupts in the range from 8 to 15. ATs, 386s, 486s, and Pentium PCs have two Interrupt Controllers. They generate interrupts in the range 8 to 15 and also in the range 112 to 119.

Figure 7.6. The kinds of interrupt.

And to compound the problem of only a few IRQ lines even further, most devices cannot be set to more than two or three of the 15 possible IRQ levels. Some devices can use only one particular IRQ level. Adding several of these devices to your PC can present difficult and sometimes insurmountable problems.

Application Program Interfaces (APIs)

Here is another section you may think you don't need. Actually, you probably don't need to understand this whole topic. It is relevant to how programs interact with one another inside your PC. Indirectly, then, it impinges on memory management. On the other hand, if you aren't curious about this topic, feel free to skip ahead to the subsection entitled "How Can All This Hurt Us?"

Programs in PCs come in layers. (This idea will be explored in much more detail in Chapter 10.) The deepest layers are the BIOS and the operating system. The highest level is the application program you are currently running. There may be many layers in between. Messages are constantly flowing back and forth between the different programs in these different levels. The way they know how to communicate with one another is via their APIs.

For the rest of this chapter, I will lump together the BIOS, the operating system (for example, DOS), and any operating environment that may be running on top of the operating system (for example, *Windows*) and simply call that the operating environment.

What Is an API?

An Application Program Interface is a well-defined protocol for one program (the application) to send messages to and receive them from another program (normally a part of the operating environment). Another way to say this is that an API is a set of rules telling the programmer of an application how to ask for services of various sorts from the programs that will be running before, during, and after that application. It also specifies the form of any answering messages the operating environment may give back to the application program.

Why Is It Useful?

Since the API is an abstraction that defines only how to communicate with the underlying operating environment, it allows different programmers to develop both the pieces of the operating environment and the application programs at the same time. Furthermore, the programmers working on the operating environment pieces can improve their product in any way that does not change the API without any fear that these changes will adversely affect the operation of any application program that adheres to the API. And they don't have to tell the world just what those changes are.

As an example, each time DOS has been upgraded, many of the changes were totally invisible to almost all programs. Only specialized utility programs whose job it is to delve deeply inside the operating environment had to be modified to conform to the new ways things were being done "under the hood." Most programs designed to work with DOS, version 2, work just as well (or better) with DOS 6 and every version in between.

In What Ways Is an API Too Limiting?

Sometimes an application programmer wants to do something that simply is not possible, or at least is too slow or awkward to accomplish using the documented API connections to the operating environment. Frequently, it is possible to do whatever the programmer wants, but only by taking advantage of some features in the operating environment that are generally known (to good programmers) but are not formally a part of the API.

This is a lot like the tension between using only calls to BIOS interrupt service routines and going directly to the hardware. Here the higher-level, "approved" method is the API, and the lower-level, more dangerous method is using *undocumented features* of the operating environment.

Undocumented features can be very useful. In fact, many of them are so useful and so generally well known in the industry that they have become *de facto* supplements to the formal APIs. When that happens, the manufacturer of that portion of the operating environment cannot change those aspects of it without unduly upsetting the industry. (But any undocumented feature that has not achieved this level of prominence can and very likely will be changed anytime the manufacturer wants to do so.)

How Can All This Hurt You?

Some application programs, and even more utility programs, depend critically on various undocumented features of the operating environment. These programs may have to be changed anytime any piece of the operating environment is upgraded, even if all of the formal API is unchanged.

Memory-management software is some of the most ambitious software ever written. Its job is to squeeze out performance and space in your PC that no one ever knew was there. To do this, it interacts with every level of the operating environment in a most intimate fashion. It absolutely must make use of many undocumented features.

Since the programmers who write these memory managers often work for different companies than those making the parts of the operating environment, they may not be told just how those parts have been changed. Often creating the new versions of memory managers requires a lot of detective work by their creators. Sometimes they don't get things quite right the very first time out.

The result of all this is that if you are going to use a memory manager, you must be careful to work with the latest version. Or at least you must use a version known to work with the version of the operating environment you are using.

If you start using *Windows* 3.x, or if you upgrade to DOS version 5 or 6, you must upgrade your memory-management software to match. Failure to do so is an almost certain recipe for trouble.

If the only memory-management software you are using supplies simple EMS services, it may be possible to get away without an upgrade. Any more ambitious memory-management software, though (for example, those providing XMS, VCPI, or DPMI services), will need to be upgraded to a version compatible with the new operating environment you are using. (Just what EMS services are is discussed in Chapter 8. The memory-management standards XMS, VCPI, and DPMI are described in Chapter 12.)

If you are an early adopter of a new operating environment, don't be surprised if the first time you get a newly upgraded version of your memory-management program or other favorite utility program, it turns out not to work as it should. Remember, it's a tough job for programmers to figure out what those "other guys" did to the various parts of the operating environment, and thus how to make the necessary changes in their own product. Keep in close touch with the suppliers of your memory-management and other utility software. They may go through several minor upgrades after each major one before they get things just right.

A Recap

This chapter has been all about how PCs run programs, and how programs are able to work with one another. It began with the notion of a computer language and how it can be represented in numbers, and that there are many different computer languages.

People interact with computers through some sort of *interface*. Many of them exist. Some are easier to learn to use than others. They are often called *intuitive* or *user-friendly*. You learned a little about what that really means, including the difference between low-level and high-level computer languages.

Sometimes you need to move information from one kind of computer to another. In this chapter, you saw some of the difficulties that can entail, and got some hints about how it might be done successfully.

A very important topic for understanding how your PC runs programs and how those programs communicate with one another is that of *interrupts.* You learned here what they are and how they can be useful. You also got some warnings about the trouble you can get into if you do not pay close attention to interrupt conflicts.

Finally, you learned about an arcane-sounding topic: Application Program Interfaces. The issue here is mostly a matter of diplomacy—how the various manufacturers of software products that must work together can share enough information to make their programs work, without sharing so much that they either give away their competitive advantages or lock themselves into doing things in just one way forever.

You need to be aware of this political maneuvering, for it affects you. At least, if you make any effort to keep up with the latest in software technology, you are very likely to get bitten from time to time by some of the side effects.

In the next two chapters, I will get down to the heart of our material. You will learn about all the different kinds of memory in a PC. You may want to take a short break now, and then forge ahead.

8

MEMORY MAPS AND THE DIFFERENT KINDS OF MEMORY

Memory in PCs can be categorized and arranged in various conceptual ways. The most important notion is that of a memory map. The division of PC memory into system, expanded, extended, upper, and high memory is both crucial and often a source of great confusion. This chapter will help clarify all of these ideas.

Memory in your PC is made up of a number of small integrated circuit chips. They are mounted into packages and plugged in or soldered down somewhere within the box that is your PC.

Of course, those memory chips or modules take up some locations in physical space. But for the most part you, and certainly your programs, do not care if that space is the front-left corner of the motherboard, the front end of a plug-in card, or a bit of both. (The only time you do care is when you need to find them, either to fix or replace a loose or bad chip or to upgrade your memory. These issues are covered in Chapter 17.)

What matters to your programs (and to you in your role as your PC's memory manager) is where your PC's memory is in a different kind of space. This is the *logical space* called *memory-address space*.

The story told in this chapter is about that space (and a bit about some other logical spaces in a PC) and how it is divided up. The concepts and jargon covered here are among the most frustrating to many first-time would-be memory managers. Fortunately, if you take your time and study the material, you can become a wizard with the words about PC memory and you can learn to read a memory map with the best of them.

Memory Maps

A memory map is a diagram showing where your PC keeps information. Those maps also show places that are not used for that purpose, but possibly could be. Geographical maps are sometimes divided into regions to show which parts of the landscape are in which countries; likewise, memory maps may be divided into regions according to the uses made of those regions.

Each of the locations within your PC where information can be stored has an address of some sort. Without that address, the circuits in the PC have no way to indicate where any particular chunk of information is to go.

Most of those addresses are simply numbers that the CPU can generate on the address lines of its memory bus. Memory maps that show these addresses show just one long line of locations, numbered from zero to some maximum number.

Which Way Is Up?

In this culture, people read from left to right and from the top of the page toward the bottom. So you might think it would be natural to lay out a memory map in the same way, with the first (lowest) addresses at the left or at the top. Many people do this. They claim it is the "natural" way to make a memory map.

Other people take a different point of view. They note that it has become common to speak of the "bottom of memory" (referring to the lowest address, which is zero) and the "top of memory" (referring to the address with the maximum value). To them it makes more sense to put the top on top and the bottom on the bottom.

This argument is further bolstered by noticing that normally the programs that are layered in your PC are loaded in sequence from the bottom of memory, up. You rarely see anyone try to stack things in a room starting at the ceiling and working down, so of course, they argue, all memory maps should have their lowest address at the bottom of the page.

Is there one right answer to this question? Not likely. It is an issue more of style, or perhaps even a quasi-religious one. In this book (except for the right side of Figure 8.1 and some screen images captured from certain memory mapping programs, i.e., Figures 10.9, 10.13, and 19.1), all memory maps will be drawn with address zero (the bottom of memory) at the bottom of the page. I will refer to this as the "normal" way to draw those maps.

But watch out. When you read manuals for memory products you must be careful to figure out which way that author draws memory maps. Remember, both ways are perfectly okay. Still, once you have looked at a lot of memory maps, the way you aren't used to will seem pretty weird to you.

How Do Memory Maps Happen?

The CPU stores and retrieves bytes of information across its memory or I/O bus. Whether it is referencing a memory location or an I/O port, the steps are much the same. (You'll learn about the differences in the next section.) The CPU indicates which memory location or I/O port it wishes to reference by putting an address on the address lines. (This means putting high or low voltages on each of some number of wires, and then saying to the external circuitry, "Notice this address and take the action I have requested.")

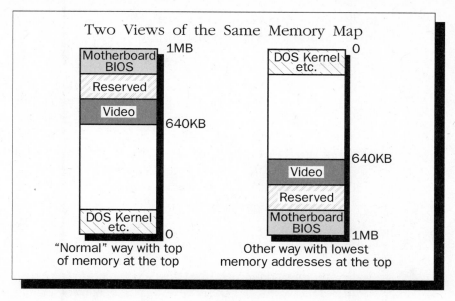

Figure 8.1. A typical memory map for a class 1 PC, looked at two ways.

The range of possible memory addresses, and thus the extent of that CPU's memory address space, is set by the number of address wires the CPU can control. On many PCs (but not every model) all of these address wires are connected to both the CPU-to-memory bus and the CPU-to-I/O bus. That means that you can add memory either on the motherboard (where it is connected to the CPU-to-memory bus) or on a card plugged into a slot connected to the I/O bus.

Since a PC is a binary machine, if you had just one address wire, you could specify only one of two address locations: one by a high voltage and the other by a low voltage. If you had two address wires, the first one would allow you to point to two places. The second wire would double that number. (For each of the two states of the second wire, you would have two possibilities for the first wire's state.) Each time you add another wire the number of possible address values doubles.

You have seen this idea before. In Chapter 6, the same relationship was developed, in the section "How Big Is a Fact?" The only difference is that there it was used to describe how many facts one could discriminate among by a number with a certain number of bits.

Since which memory location a particular byte of information is stored in is a fact, and since the address bus essentially represents binary numbers (with high voltages meaning one-bits and low voltages meaning zero-bits), the chart in Figure 6.4 can be read as the number of memory address locations the CPU can distinguish with a given number of address wires.

Later on you'll learn that this simple picture is not complete. Sometimes you can have a larger effective memory map than the number of address lines would indicate. When this happens, you have *virtual memory*. Conversely, sometimes you are limited to only a small fraction of the possible memory address locations because the CPU is operating in some mode that doesn't support using all the address wires. You also may be limited to only a portion of the memory address space when the bus doesn't include all the address wires that are on the CPU chip.

What matters most when the bus limits the size of memory address space is the number of wires in the CPU-to-memory bus. This is the path over which the CPU moves information in and out of memory located either on the motherboard or on a memory card plugged into a proprietary bus slot designed for such a card.

It is possible to put memory cards into a slot on the I/O bus. If you do so, the number of address lines in that bus will limit the range of memory addresses at which memory on such a card can be accessed. (Sometimes a more worrisome concern is that memory on such a card may not be accessible at the same speed as memory on the motherboard or a proprietary memory card put in a special memory-card-only slot.)

Memory Is Not the Only Kind of Space in a PC

In Chapter 6, you also learned that in addition to putting an address on the bus, the CPU either raises or lowers the voltage on a certain control line to indicate whether the address lines are indicating a place in memory space or one in I/O space. The locations in I/O space go by the name *ports*.

The picture given so far is a slight simplification. There are two issues to be concerned with: One is what control signals come out on pins of the CPU chip; the other is what control signals are available in the external bus (either memory or I/O). The details in both cases depend somewhat on which processor and which system bus (ISA, EISA, or MCA) you are talking about.

The 8088 CPU chip has three *status* pins; the 80286 has a *COD/INTA#* (Code or Interrupt Acknowledge) pin, an *M/IO#* pin (Memory or I/O Select), and two *bus cycle status* pins; and the 386, 486, and Pentium CPU chips have an *M/IO#* pin, a *D/C#* pin (Data or Control—renamed Data or Code for the Pentium), and a *W/R#* pin (Write or Read). Various combinations of voltages on these pins indicate each of the possible kinds of bus cycle.

That is what the CPU puts out. To make life easier for the designers of boards that plug into the I/O slots, the bus has signal lines that are more directly associated with each activity to be performed. Thus, in the ISA bus, there are four separate lines called *IOR#* (I/O Read), *IOW#* (I/O Write), *MEMR#* (Memory Read), and *MEMW#* (Memory Write). One of the many tasks of the motherboard system logic is to analyze the CPU output pins and assert the correct one of these four bus signals.

Since the only obvious difference between addressing a memory location and addressing an I/O port is the state of the *Memory or I/O select line* (indicated *M/IO#* for short), you might think that there are exactly as many ports as memory locations. This is not so. The reason is that while you could imagine putting the same number of combinations of high and low voltages on the address wires no matter what the state of the M/IO# line, only some of those combinations are treated by the CPU as valid port addresses. Intel has chosen to limit the port address space to the first 65,536 (64KB) locations.

If the data bus is wider than 8 bits, it can carry more than one byte of information at a time. For example, a 286-based PC is able to send two bytes to or from memory or I/O at once. In I/O space, this means that it can send to two adjacent (byte-wide) ports at once. If you view ports as being intrinsically 16-bits wide instead of byte-wide, you can have at most 32KB of those 16-bit-wide ports. Likewise, the 386DX, 486, and Pentium processors can access I/O space as at most 16KB 32-bit ports.

Actually, there are a few other valid locations in I/O address space, but they are not used for input or output ports. Intel has reserved a few locations in this space for communication between the CPU and a coprocessor chip. (You will learn more about this curious choice later in this chapter.)

> There are two other logical address spaces of great importance in your PC, though they are not accessed in quite the same manner. One of these spaces is the collection of **D**irect **M**emory **A**ccess (DMA) channels. The other is the collection of **I**nterrupt **R**e**q**uest (IRQ) lines. You learned about IRQs in Chapter 7. DMA is a strategy to allow moving blocks of information without requiring the CPU to read and write each byte. All PCs except the *PC Jr* have hardware on the motherboard to support doing several (at least four and at most seven) such transfers simultaneously.
>
> Access to locations in these spaces is controlled by the motherboard system logic. That aspect of the system logic may be located in some individual chips, called a *DMA controller* or an *Interrupt controller,* or their functionality may be included in the few large integrated circuits (called the *chip set*) conventionally used in the manufacture of current PCs. PCs in classes 1 and 2 have one Interrupt controller and all but the *PC Jr* have one DMA controller. All other PCs have two of each.

Segments and Offsets

The way that memory is accessed by an Intel 80x86 processor has been a source of much controversy. Some programmers vehemently argue that Intel's way of doing this is wonderful. Others say, with equal vehemence, that it is terrible. Nonprogrammers often call it mysterious.

The jargon for Intel's method is *addressing.* So what is a segment? What is an offset? And why should you care?

All members of Intels's 80x86 family of microprocessors can access a total of 1,048,576 (1M) memory address locations when they operate in what is called *real mode.* (The more advanced chips in that family can access more locations when they operate in *protected mode*; see Chapter 11 for details.) A glance at Figure 6.4 shows that to discriminate between 1,048,576 locations, you have to use a 20-bit number, hence these CPUs need to use 20 address lines.

All these chips "wake up" in real mode, which is designed to make them all look like very fast versions of the original 8086 and 8088. To understand segment:offset addressing, you need only to understand how the 8086 looks at memory.

The 8086 stores and uses information internally two bytes at a time. It has registers in which it can store 16-bit numbers, but none that can store 20-bit numbers. (A register is just a tiny bit of memory built into the CPU where a number can be held temporarily.) This means that it has to use two registers together to specify an address.

How do you get a 20-bit number from two 16-bit numbers? Many ways are possible, but the important one for us is the one Intel chose. Their choice was dictated at least in part by a desire to make the (then new) 8086 microprocessor somewhat backward-compatible with their previous best-selling chip, the 8080. That chip could store or process only one byte of information at a time, but more importantly, it had only 16 address lines.

Segment and Offset Registers

Intel's choice was to specify one set of registers in the CPU as segment registers. Another set of registers holds offsets. A special part of the CPU, called the bus interface unit in the 8086, is responsible for combining a segment value and an offset to generate a 20-bit address. That 20-bit address is called the linear address, and it is what is actually put on the 8086's address bus. How Intel chose to combine segments and offsets is shown in Figure 8.2.

Remember that in hexadecimal notation a 16-bit number can be written using four hexadecimal symbols. So each segment or offset number is precisely four hexadecimal digits long. The specific rule for combining a segment value and an offset is simply this: Put a zero at the end of the segment number and add it to the offset to get the linear address. (Tacking a zero on the end of a hexadecimal number is the equivalent of multiplying it by 16, just as tacking a zero on the end of a decimal number is the same as multiplying it by 10.)

What enrages some programmers and is greatly appreciated by others (and often confuses lay folk unbearably) is the fact that this strategy allows many different combinations of a segment value and an offset to point to the same location. Figure 8.2 shows a couple of examples; Figure 8.3 shows several more.

This scheme helped make the 8086 more compatible with programs written for the earlier 8080. If you just set the segment value and forget it, and then treat the offset as if it is the address, you get something that looks a lot like the 64KB memory address space of the 8080.

This made it easy to adapt programs that worked on the 8080 to run on the 8086. Choosing not to alter the segment register value once the program started running did limit those programs to being no larger than 64KB, so it clearly was not the way to write important new applications, but it did give an easy path for people who had created programs for the 8080 to move them over to the new IBM *PC* quickly.

Real Mode Address Calculations
Segment and Offset Values Are Written

Segment : Offset

(As is usual, these are given as hexadecimal numbers.) This is then converted to a linear address by use of the following formula:

Segment × 16 + Offset = Linear Address

Examples:

```
    0040:0012                0000:0412
     0040                      0000
   + 0012          or        + 0412
     00412                     00412

    1234:5678                179B:0008
     1234                      179B
   + 5678          or        + 0008
     179B8                     179B8
```

Figure 8.2.   Linear address calculation in real mode.

A **segment value** indicates the beginning of a region (also known as a segment) of memory. The **offset** indicates a distance into that segment.

Although there are only about one million total addresses in the memory address space of an 8086 CPU, it has 65,536 different segment possibilities, with 65,536 addresses in each one, giving over four billion **segment:offset** combinations.

Figure 8.3 shows this graphically. It also shows that a few segment values point to segments that appear to have fewer than the usual 64KB possible offsets. These are the segments that come up near the top of the memory map. This phenomenon is an important one that goes by the name of *address wrapping.*

Did you realize that adding a five-digit number to a four-digit number could produce a six-digit answer? Think of adding the decimal numbers 98765 and 5555. The result is 104320. Similarly when you add a segment value (which is now, with its added zero on the end, a 20-bit number) and a 16-bit offset you can come up with a number that can only be expressed fully if you are able to use more than 20 bits.

Since the 8086 has only 20 address wires coming out to the bus, it simply cannot put such a number on its bus. What happens when you add a large segment value to a large offset value? The 8086 does the arithmetic and then effectively throws away the 21st bit (the carry).

If the segment value is close to the maximum possible value, the segment begins up near the top of the memory address space. A range of offset values near their maximum (which would normally indicate locations near the top of the segment) result in linear addresses near the bottom of memory address space.

All class 1 and 2 PCs must do this. They have only 20 address wires coming out of the CPU, so they cannot possibly avoid address wrapping. All PCs in classes 3 through 6, on the other hand, have more than 20 address wires. They *could* keep the carry bit when combining the segment and offset numbers.

Those PCs could avoid address wrapping, but if they did, they would not be totally compatible with PCs in classes 1 and 2. When the AT was being developed, IBM realized that they had better make it compatible with the PC and XT. So they added some special circuitry on the motherboard that notices whenever the CPU is operating in real mode and at those times simply forces the A20 address line to the zero state. (The address lines are numbered starting at A0. Thus the 21st line is called A20.)

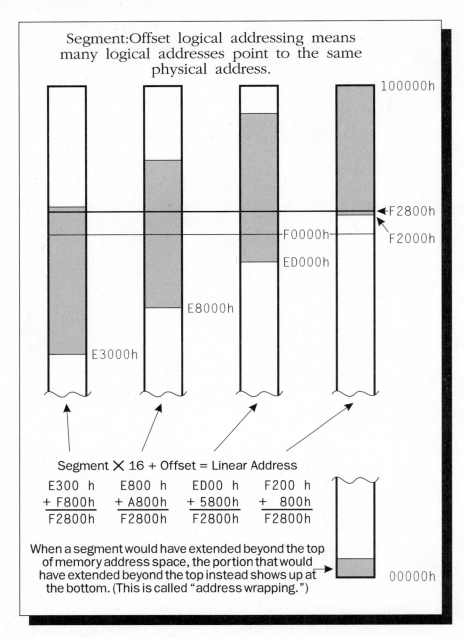

Figure 8.3. This figure shows the phenomenon of address wrapping and how multiple segment:offset values can point to the same linear address.

This was not an idle choice on IBM's part. There actually were (and still are) programs in wide use that assume address wrapping will occur. They access important data stored near the bottom of memory by pointing "off the scale" above the top of memory by just the right amount.

Perhaps the most important villain in this regard is the program developed by Microsoft to decompress compressed executable files. Any program that has been compressed by their EXEPACK program will have this special decompression program as a part of it. To work right, this program needs to have address wrapping enabled. (Well, there is another way to deal with this, that apparently was used in *MS-DOS* 5 and 6, but that doesn't really change this discussion. That special trick is discussed in the section "The High Memory Area" later in this chapter.)

Compatibility was such a highly desirable feature that when IBM's A20 line kludge was first pointed out, almost everyone thought IBM had done the right thing. All the clone makers followed suit. Even the latest 486 or Pentium-based screamer has address-wrap-forcing circuitry included in its motherboard system logic, and the 486 and Pentium chip designs include a way to force it to do address wrapping whenever it is accessing a memory location, even in its internal cache memory.

Kludge An inelegant but successful solution to a problem in computer hardware or software.

With this information as background, you won't be surprised to learn that the industry was amazed and delighted when just a few years later some engineers at Quarterdeck Office Systems (and shortly afterwards some others at Microsoft) discovered a marvelous way to get more real-mode memory.

They noticed that if they merely turned off the circuitry that turned off the A20 line, programs could access nearly 64KB more memory in real mode. This was only possible on PCs in classes 3 through 6, but by this time compatibility with the older class 1 or 2 PCs was less an issue than finding a way out of the ever-worsening RAM cram crunch.

This new discovery was called the *High Memory Area.* It is discussed in more detail later in this chapter.

Why Should You Care?

Anyone who is going to program a PC had better understand exactly how it addresses memory. But should you care if all you are going to do is use your PC? You betcha! At least if you aspire to managing your PC's memory effectively.

All the things you will read about memory and memory management will, at times, give a memory address in the form XXXX:XXXX (where the Xs represent hexadecimal numerals). That is a memory location in **segment:offset** form. The colon is the giveaway. Furthermore, some diagnostic programs you may use will require you to enter memory addresses in this form.

Anytime you see a number pair separated by a colon in a book or article about PCs it will be a memory address in **segment:offset** form. That means those numbers separated by the colon are expressed in hexadecimal. So the usual trailing *h* is not necessary. (One caveat: If the operating mode of the CPU is some version of protected mode, the number before the colon is actually a *selector.* It is still written in hexadecimal though, so the rest of this paragraph applies.)

Oh, another bit of good news: Because I/O port addresses are restricted to 64K, there's no need to use any of this **segment:offset** complexity for them. All port addresses can be written as just a single, simple 16-bit word.

Banks, Pages, and Paragraphs

The atom of information is the bit. PCs normally handle information in bytes (8 bits) or words (usually defined as two bytes), or sometimes in double words (32-bits). Some other useful terms for describing quantities of memory are *banks, pages,* and *paragraphs.*

What Is a Bank?

Information in PCs is kept in *banks.* These are not money banks. What are they? Actually there are two different definitions of a *bank of memory.*

> **Logical Banks** A *logical bank of memory* is a 64KB region of memory addresses starting at a multiple of 64KB. The first bank, called *bank 0,* extends from address 00000h to 0FFFFh. The eleventh bank, called *bank A,* extends from address A0000h to AFFFFh. (*Important note:* A logical bank refers to a range of memory addresses, without regard to whether or not you have any actual memory at those addresses.)

> **Physical Banks** A *physical bank of memory* is all the memory locations supplied by those chips that are accessed together when reading from one memory location.
>
> For example, many class 1 PCs use 256-kilobit DRAM chips. These chips each hold 1 bit of information for each of 256K different memory locations. They may be arranged into rows of nine 256-kilobit RAM chips each, in which case each row makes up one physical bank of memory, each able to hold 256 kilobytes of information (with parity). (Parity is a means of protecting you from almost any error that may occur in information stored in RAM. Chapter 16 explains it in more detail.)

Here are a couple more examples: In class 3 PCs, which access memory 16 bits at a time, a physical bank of memory must have 18 bits (including the parity bits), so if it is composed of 256-kilobit chips with each chip holding one bit in each of 256K locations, a physical bank will contain 512K bytes of RAM (with parity). Some 386- and 486-based PCs use 4-megabyte, byte-wide SIMMs (modules with 4MB locations, each storing one byte plus a parity bit). Because these PCs access their memory 32 bits at a time, a physical bank for them includes four of these SIMMs and provides 16 megabytes of RAM. Since the Pentium processor accesses memory across a 64-bit data bus, its physical memory banks are exactly twice the size of those in a 486. There are many other possible arrangements. Figure 9.3 illustrates physical memory banks for each class of PC. See Chapters 16 and 17 for more examples.

You will have noticed that a logical bank and a physical bank could refer to the same amount of memory, but they definitely need not do so. What is true for almost all PCs (for some very good design and engineering reasons), is that each physical bank contains a number of logical banks, and that number will be an integer power of two. (This is to say, a physical bank will contain 1 or 2 or 4 or 8 . . . or 256 logical banks.) You should also notice that while the definition of a physical bank of memory involves actual physical memory chips, the definition of a logical bank of memory refers only to a range of memory addresses.

A Bank Is Not a Segment

A logical bank is the same size as a real-mode segment, but it is definitely not the same thing. Remember, a logical bank must start at a memory address that is a multiple of 64KB. A segment can start at a memory address that is any multiple of 16 bytes.

In Chapter 11, you will learn that in protected mode the size of a segment may vary a great deal, so it's not even the same size as a logical bank or a physical bank (and a segment still may start at many more addresses than either kind of bank).

What Is a Page?

This is a tough one. There are many meanings given to *page* in relation to PCs and memory.

> **Page**   A page is any region of memory that can be manipulated in one operation.

This is rather vague, but it turns out to include many of the following meanings. Later chapters will expand on several of these definitions, so don't be concerned if some of them don't make much sense to you now. You may simply need to learn the meaning of some more jargon terms. Rest assured; these definitions are coming later in this book (or refer to the hypertext Memory Information System on the diskette that accompanies this book if you want a brief definition).

1. The regions of memory mapped by a 386, 486 CPU's memory-management unit. These are almost always 4KB in size. (The

Pentium normally uses 4KB pages, but it can have pages that are 1MB or 2MB in size.)

2. The regions of memory mapped by add-on memory-management hardware (for example, an *All Charge* card). These may have any of several sizes, though 4KB and 16KB are the most common values.

3. The quantity of information moved from one range of memory addresses to another, or to or from the disk, by Windows as an inseparable chunk. Normally this also is 4KB in size. There are just two exceptions. One is if you add a line to your SYSTEM.INI file in the [386Enh] section specifying Paging=No (which turns off swapping to disk altogether). The other is if Windows has created a very small temporary swap file—less than 512KB—which it may do if you have very little free disk space. In either case Windows is only able to move information in 64KB chunks, which is less efficient and can lead to Out of memory error messages that could otherwise be avoided.

4. The regions of memory on a PC card conforming to the PCMCIA specification that get switched into or out of the CPU's address space as a unit. These are always 16KB in size.

5. An *EMS* (*expanded*) *memory page* is normally a block of 16KB of RAM that is switched in and out of the CPU's memory address space as a unit. Under LIM version 4.0 of the expanded memory specification, the page size could be something other than 16KB, but to maintain compatibility with earlier versions of EMS in most implementations it is still kept at 16KB.

6. A *video page* (one meaning) is that region of video RAM used to hold one screen's worth of image data. A CGA, EGA, or VGA display card can hold a number of pages of text information (typically 2KB per page) simultaneously and can switch between them very rapidly.

7. A *video page* (another definition) is one of the regions of video display image buffer RAM that is switched into or out of the CPU's memory-address space as a unit. This definition refers to the way that video RAM on an EGA or VGA display card can be accessed through a window in the CPU's memory-address space that is smaller than the total memory on the video card.

8. A page in a *page-mode memory chip* is a collection of addresses on the chip for which the row address does not change. For example, a page-mode 256-kilobit RAM chip, organized as 256K locations that can each hold one bit, is actually organized as a square array of bit cells with 512 rows and 512 columns. In a physical bank of these memory chips (containing, for example, nine chips) a page for these purposes holds 512 bytes with parity. The significance of this page definition is that with these chips, successive memory accesses that stay within a single page can be much faster than ones that are on different pages.

9. While it is not a memory-page definition, do not forget that discussions about PCs also will often include reference to a page meaning a sheet of paper. This mostly will come up in a PC memory-management discussion when talking about memory in a printer, as in how much printer memory is required to print a full-page (paper page) graphical image.

What Is a Paragraph? Ah, this one is easy. There is only one meaning to the term *paragraph* in the context of PC memory. A paragraph is a 16-byte region of memory address space starting at a multiple of 16 bytes. A couple of examples would be the region of memory addresses from 01110h to 0111Fh, or from 91230h to 9123Fh. In hexadecimal, the start of a paragraph is always a number ending in zero. Segments start on paragraph boundaries.

The Different Kinds (Uses) of Memory

Bytes, words, paragraphs, pages, banks, and *segments* all refer to regions of memory or memory address space. These terms refer to the size and location of those regions. Some other important terms for referring to memory refer more to how that memory is used. They are the following:

- Real-mode memory
- Protected-mode memory
- System memory (also known as conventional or lower memory)
- Expanded memory

- Video (RAM)
- Video (ROM)
- Option ROM or RAM
- Upper memory
- Extended memory
- High memory

In this section, you'll learn what each of these terms means. You will learn not to misuse them, but still to recognize what those who do misuse them really mean. Also, you will learn some unfortunate terms some people use, like *expansion memory,* and what they mean.

Further, you'll learn a bit about how different regions of memory are used to serve very different purposes. All this information is essential if you are to understand the documentation that comes with memory-management software and hardware or the magazine articles published on this subject.

Real-Mode Memory

Real-mode memory is all the memory-address locations that can be accessed by the CPU when it is operating in real mode. (Chapter 11 will explain all the modes the 80x86 processor chips can use, which ones use each of them, and how they differ.)

Normally you think of real-mode memory as the region of memory addresses from zero to 1MB (which is the same as 1,024KB, or 1,048,576 bytes). PCs in classes 3 through 6 can also access the high memory area (HMA) as another chunk of real-mode memory, thus extending the range of real-mode addresses almost to 1,088KB. (See the section "The High Memory Area" for more on this.)

IBM made some fairly arbitrary decisions about how the first megabyte of memory address space should be used (see Figure 8.4). They decreed that the first five-eighths of it would be for RAM to be shared by the operating system and any programs you might wish to run. These are *logical pages 0* through *9.* They reserved the A and B pages for video RAM. Pages C and D were initially set aside for future use, with no description of what those uses might be. (Those pages are now used for many purposes, including added RAM and ROM.) The E and F pages were reserved for the system ROM.

233

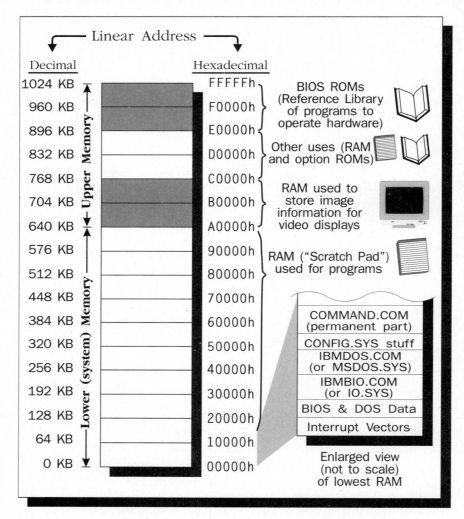

Figure 8.4. The uses IBM decreed for the PC's memory-address space.

When the IBM *PC* was first introduced, these decisions did not seem very oppressive. In fact, mainframe computers often reserve half of their memory address space for use by things other than the running programs.

So to get five-eighths of all available RAM for programs, an amount that was 10 times larger than all the memory available on most common personal computers just preceding the IBM *PC*, seemed really wonderful. (Remember, this was in the days of PCs and XTs, before there was any memory possible beyond 1MB.)

A few years later people had a very different perspective on IBM's decisions about the uses of the first megabyte. Those decisions were, after all, the source of the infamous "640KB barrier." And that is something many people were, by then, a great deal less than happy about.

Protected-Mode Memory

Protected-mode memory is all the memory address locations that can be accessed by the CPU when it is operating in protected mode. Only PCs in classes 3 through 6 can operate in protected mode, so they are the only ones that can have protected-mode memory. (Don't worry if this seems like gobbledegook. In Chapter 11, all this will be explained.)

Because DOS was designed as an operating system for a class 1 PC which could only run in real mode, it is unable to access any memory in protected mode. Thus, when the IBM *PC/AT* was first introduced, protected-mode memory was very nearly useless. Now, with the help of various memory-management techniques, it is some of the most valuable memory in your PC. You will learn more about this in later chapters.

Intel's Special Addresses

There are some very good reasons behind some of the seemingly arbitrary decisions IBM made about how to use real-mode memory. Some of them have to do with how Intel designed the 8086 (and all later members of the 80x86 family).

In particular, the decisions to put RAM at the bottom of the memory address space and ROM at the top were essentially dictated by Intel's design. The sizes of those regions were not dictated; it's just that there had better be some RAM (at least 1KB) at the lowest memory locations and some ROM (at least 16 bytes) at the highest.

This is because of the special uses Intel made of certain addresses in those regions (see Figure 8.5). The first 1,024 bytes are where the interrupt vector table must be located. (Review Chapter 7 if you are not clear what this is.) A location just 16 bytes below the top of memory address space (FFFF0h) is where the CPU looks for its first instruction when it is powered on and each time it is reset. (Intel refers to the 16 bytes from there to the end of memory space as being reserved for the initial instructions. You don't have to use all of them, but there isn't much else you can do with that space.) These locations are fixed by the hardware design of the CPU.

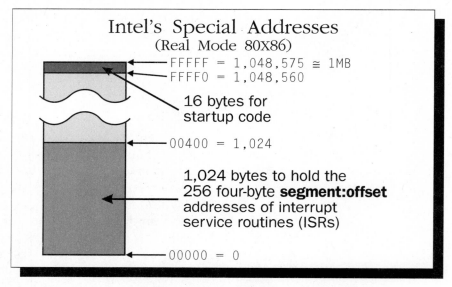

Figure 8.5. The only memory addresses that Intel made special.

Every time an interrupt occurs, the CPU will look at a location within the first 1KB of memory address space for the address of the interrupt service routine (ISR) it is to invoke. In order to take advantage of the flexibility inherent in this indirect approach to ISRs, you must have RAM in those first 1,024 memory locations. That allows any program to change at any time which ISR will respond to a given interrupt. IBM only had to put a small amount of RAM at the bottom of the address space, but for simplicity it put all of the RAM for general use starting at location zero and progressing upward.

If one does not have ROM at the top of the memory address space, when the PC is first powered on or its CPU is reset, it will have no idea what to do. The CPU will fetch a nonsense instruction from whatever is at location FFFF0h, which will be either RAM or WOM(!). That would be no good at all. (WOM was defined in Chapter 6 as **W**rite **O**nly **M**emory, which is to say, as no memory at all.)

So IBM set aside the top 128KB for system ROMs. That includes the start-up program code needed to get the PC going and a lot more.

> The system ROM BIOS includes as part of its start-up code a proce-dure (a group of instructions) to put numbers into at least the first part of the interrupt vector table. Those numbers are the addresses of some default interrupt service routines that also are located within the system BIOS ROM. In this way, the start-up program can guar-antee that something sensible will be done whenever an interrupt occurs, even if the rest of the operating system has not yet been loaded.
>
> The top of memory address space is at 1MB in real mode. What about the 80286, 386, 486, and *Pentium* processors? First of all, you must remember that they wake up in real mode. The start-up code loca-tion, therefore, is in real-mode memory-address space. But if you want to pick nits (or simply read the Intel data sheets on those processors), you should know that in protected mode the top 64KB of real-mode memory's contents are also accessible at the top 64KB of the protected-mode memory address space. (That top value will be either 16MB or 4GB, depending on which processor chip you are talking about.)
>
> The Intel data sheets give these addresses for the initial program in-struction locations: For the 80286 and 80386SX it is from FFFFF0h to FFFFFFh (just below 16MB). For the 386DX, the 486 (either DX or SX), and the Pentium it is from FFFFFFF0h to FFFFFFFFh (just below 4GB).

In addition to reserving these few (1,024 + 16) bytes of memory ad-dress space for special purposes, Intel also decreed some things about I/O address space. First, you will recall that this space is limited in all mem-bers of the 80x86 family to the first 65,536 (64KB) possible addresses. (An-other way of saying this is that when I/O operations are involved the CPU ignores all but the lowest 16 address lines.) This is referred to as the valid address range for *programmed I/O*. ("Programmed I/O" is a fancy way to refer to reading or writing information to I/O ports.)

The other special addresses in what would otherwise be I/O address space are those reserved for interprocessor communication. Mostly this means communication between the CPU chip and a math coprocessor.

In the 8088, 8086, and 80286 this communication occurs at I/O ad-dresses 00F8h to 00FFh. That's smack dab in the middle of the real I/O space, so those "port" addresses simply cannot be used for normal pro-grammed I/O. The 386 and 486 chips have moved that communication channel to just below the halfway point in the range of apparently pos-sible (but invalid) I/O addresses. On the 386SX the channel is at locations 8000F8h to 8000FFh (approximately 8MB), and for the 386DX or 486 it is at locations 800000F8h to 800000FFh (approximately 2GB).

System (a.k.a. Conventional or Lower) Memory

System memory refers to the region of memory address space from zero to 640KB, or it may be used to refer to whatever memory your PC has that can be accessed within that range of addresses. Other names sometimes given to these things are *conventional memory* and *lower memory. System memory* indicates that this region is used for the operating system. *Lower memory* is in opposition to *upper memory* (which is explained a little later in this section).

Some authors use a slightly different definition. They say system memory is all the memory below your video display image buffer. If you have an EGA or VGA display, that's the same thing, for those adapters use memory addresses starting just above 640KB for their image buffer in graphics mode.

If, on the other hand, you have a Monochrome or CGA adapter, you could, by this definition, have 64KB or even 96KB more system memory address space. Whether you have any accessible memory in that space is a totally different question.

Most motherboards will not supply system RAM above the 640KB line. But if you have a provision for backfilling RAM from an EMS board, certain kinds of shadow RAM, or are able to remap extended memory, you may be able to extend your system memory itself (and not just the address space) up to either 704KB or 736KB. These possibi-lities are all considered in depth later in this book.

If you have only 512KB of memory in your PC, it will all be in this range, so it will all be system memory. If you have 1MB of memory, it may be divided in any of several ways. One of them is to make 512KB system memory and the balance extended memory. With either of these possibili-ties, you will have less system memory than you have system memory address space.

System memory is a special region of your PC's memory address space. It turns out to be your most precious memory resource. This is true for several reasons, which are discussed in detail in later chapters.

Expanded Memory

Expanded memory is a wonderful way to "cheat." It allows even a lowly PC or XT, which can only address 1M of memory locations, to use up to 8MB or even 32MB of extra RAM. The strategy behind this is called bank-switched memory.

The steps by which this idea developed make an interesting story. Here are the highlights, organized under these topics:

- Early Paged Memory Cards

- Lotus-Intel Expanded Memory, Version 3.0

- Lotus-Intel-Microsoft EMS, Version 3.2

- The AQA Enhanced Expanded Memory Specification (EEMS)

- Extensions to LIM EMS, Version 3.2, and EEMS

- LIM EMS, Version 4.0

Although people initially thought that 640KB of RAM was a very generous allocation, that time of satisfaction has long since passed. Now the more common perception is that 640KB is a dreadfully small amount, scarcely enough to do anything useful.

Soon after the introduction of the IBM *PC*, some people tried to find ways to use more than 640KB of RAM. This was not a new problem. Earlier personal computers had far less memory address space to work with. Even large mainframes sometimes have less memory than their users wish they had.

Early Paged Memory Cards

A solution that had been used with mainframe computers, and some of the CP/M microcomputers that preceded the PC, was called paged memory. As you might imagine, somebody faced with the paucity of memory in his PC recalled that solution. Out of such thoughts came the first paged memory cards for PCs. One early company to do this was Tall Tree with a line of products they called their *J-RAM* boards.

An IBM *XT*, the most common PC at that time, could have at most 640KB of RAM devoted to programs and data. By adding a *J-RAM* board, the programs running in the XT could gain access to an additional 2MB of RAM. This additional RAM could be used only for data storage, but that still made a substantial enhancement to the XT's capabilities. (You could even put in several *J-RAM* boards, and thereby get even more RAM, up to a maximum of 8MB.)

Here is how the *J-RAM* board did its magic: The 2MB of RAM on the board was divided into many small pieces. One piece at a time was electronically attached, temporarily, to the CPU's bus at an otherwise unused region in the PC's memory address space. Later that piece would be detached, and another piece would be attached at the same range of addresses. This allowed access to the whole 2MB, albeit in a piecemeal fashion. Here, at last, was a wonderful way to use that empty C, or D, or E page.

This system worked just fine. It did require the PC's user to do two things. One was to insert the *J-RAM* board into an empty slot in the PC. The other was to run a special device driver program that knew how to manage this new hardware. (Like most such programs, this one was loaded by a line in the CONFIG.SYS file, and once loaded the program remained in the PC's memory until the machine was rebooted.)

The small pieces of RAM that are switched in are called *pages,* and the whole scheme is called *paged memory.* Here is how it works, in a bit more detail:

- First, an application program asks the paged memory manager (the device driver) for some memory. That manager program chooses one particular page from the pool of memory on the paged memory board and attaches it to the CPU's memory bus. As long as it's there, this RAM can be used by the CPU just like any other RAM. The CPU can store information there, and later it can retrieve that information.

- When the application program wishes to store more information than fits on that page, it has the CPU ask the paged memory manager program to remove that page from the CPU's bus and replace it with a different page. As long as the new page is attached to the bus it can be accessed just like the rest of RAM. The page that was removed from the bus is no longer accessible by the CPU.

- When the application again wants access to the information stored on that first page, all it has to do is have the CPU ask the paged memory manager to please remove the current page and replace it with the original one.

Switching pages in this fashion can be done very rapidly. It works almost as quickly as if the PC had all of the paged memory available all of the time.

The only programs that could use Tall Tree's *J-RAM* board were those that knew how it was built. And all those programs came from just one company. You guessed it, they came from Tall Tree Systems.

Tall Tree was not the only company making and selling paged memory boards for PCs. All of these products shared one outstanding drawback: Each board could do only what the programs its maker supplied could get it to do. You could not combine the functionality from two different manufacturers. These were strictly proprietary solutions to the problem.

Lotus-Intel Expanded Memory, Version 3.0

If there was one main reason for all the outcry over the 640KB barrier it was the smashing success of Lotus *1-2-3*. That was the killer application that, more than any other single reason, put PCs on businesspeople's desks. Indeed, this one application induced businesses to buy more PCs than all the other computers (mainframes, minicomputers, and the like) ever sold. With *1-2-3* and a PC, a businessperson had unheard-of power to do financial projections and analyses. It also tempted them to build ever larger spreadsheets. Running out of RAM was inevitable.

VisiCalc was the first superstar program for a personal computer. It put Apple on the map, way back in the early days of the *Apple II*. To make the program run acceptably fast, and because even a smallish spreadsheet could be useful, its authors opted to keep all of the spreadsheet data in RAM.

In the same era (the late 1970s, well before the emergence of the first IBM *PC*), personal computer users discovered two other wonderful uses for those little machines: word processing and database management. To this day these three categories are the three largest markets for personal computer software for businesses.

What was different about word processors and database programs from the start was that everyone realized that they would not be useful unless they could work with rather large documents and databases. That, and the tiny amounts of RAM (by modern standards) available in the first personal computers, forced their programmers to keep both word processor and database program data files on disk.

These programs brought into RAM a copy of only the small part of the data file that they needed to work with at that moment. When they needed another part they had to copy to disk the part they had just finished working on, then copy in the new part.

Naturally, this approach made these programs run more slowly than they would have if they could have kept the whole document or database in RAM, but the marvel was that they could do such useful work at all. This design decision means that programs in these categories can work with almost arbitrarily large data files and still not run out of RAM.

When Lotus introduced *1-2-3*, they knew they had to win over loyal *VisiCalc* users. They believed that they might do this by offering those people substantial new power, but they certainly weren't going to do so if their program ran a lot more slowly. And the IBM *PC*, while a good computer, was not that much faster than its immediate predecessors. So Lotus had little choice. They followed *VisiCalc*'s example and designed their program to keep all of its spreadsheet data in RAM also.

The screams of spreadsheet users who hated getting Out of memory messages had their impact. Lotus teamed up with Intel (who also had a strong vested interest in seeing the PC succeed) and established the first industry standard for paged memory systems. They called it the *Lotus-Intel Expanded Memory Specification (LI-EMS), version 3.0.*

Who ever heard of calling the first version of something "version 3.0"? Apparently the authors of the LI EMS document felt that their new standard would seem more up-to-date and be more acceptable in the marketplace if it carried the same version number as the latest release of *PC DOS*.

The LI-EMS document described a standardized way to build both a paged-memory board and a device-driver program to manage that board. It gave manufacturers some latitude in how they were to implement the standard, but the authors of the specification were careful to be sure that anyone who bought a board built to that standard would find that it would work with their copy of *1-2-3* and any other program that chose to support the LI-EMS method of accessing paged memory.

Once you got through loading DOS and *1-2-3* into a 640KB XT, there was only about a couple hundred kilobytes left over for the spreadsheet you were working on. So it might have seemed that adding a 2MB expanded memory card would allow you to build spreadsheets almost 10 times as large before getting an Out of memory message.

This turns out not to be the case (as many users of *1-2-3* who ran out and bought EMS cards soon found out). While *1-2-3* (releases 1.x and 2.x) does use EMS to store part of the current spreadsheet, it doesn't use it the same way it uses system memory. Spreadsheet data consists of two categories of information: items of data and pointers to those data items. Only the data items can be put into EMS memory. That means you will still run out of memory as soon as you fill up system memory with your spreadsheet's pointers.

The good news is that there are now many other ways to use EMS memory besides storing spreadsheet overflow. So your investment in the new EMS hardware wasn't wasted.

The moral to this story is to check carefully before you leap into anything. Many programs can use EMS memory, but like *1-2-3* they may not use it exactly as they do system memory. Sometimes you must have enough system RAM to let the program work without any EMS memory; then it will use whatever EMS it can find to let it do its work more quickly.

The LI-EMS 3.0 specification described both a software *Application Program Interface* (*API*) (a standardized way in which application programs could access paged memory by sending requests to the expanded memory manager device driver) and a hardware implementation prescription. Armed with this document any competent software and hardware developer could create yet another fully compatible EMS board and its driver software.

This standard called for the use of an *expanded memory page frame*, a region in the CPU's memory address space above the video RAM and below the system ROM. This page frame was to be 64KB in size and would be divided into four 16KB pages. The expanded memory manager (EMM) device driver program would receive requests from application programs and dole out the available RAM on the EMS board to them. It would, on request, switch whichever four pages were most recently requested into the four positions in the EMS page frame (see Figure 8.6).

You can add one or more EMS boards in a PC, but normally all of them will have to be made by the same manufacturer. That is so you can load just one EMM driver, and it will know how to control all of the boards. Using this feature it is possible to add up to 8MB of EMS memory in a single PC.

LI-EMS was a hit. Several major software manufacturers, WordPerfect among them, decided to support this new standard. A number of hardware companies built and sold EMS boards that complied with the standard. A healthy marketplace for EMS boards and EMS-using applications developed.

You may wonder about WordPerfect supporting EMS. All word processors are able to operate with their data files (documents) on disk, and only a small piece of those documents in RAM. But they can do more and work faster if they have access to more RAM. That is why *WordPerfect* and many other programs optionally support EMS memory.

If you have EMS memory and the EMM driver is loaded, these programs will ask the EMM to assign them some pages of EMS memory. If they get some (all the EMS pages might already have been assigned to some other programs), they will use those pages to perform whatever tasks they normally perform more rapidly, or to enable additional functionality that could not be supported without that added memory.

Lotus-Intel-Microsoft EMS, Version 3.2

Occasionally in the history of technology, a significant advance is made in a process or standard by an act of omission. The next chapter in the history of expanded memory is one example.

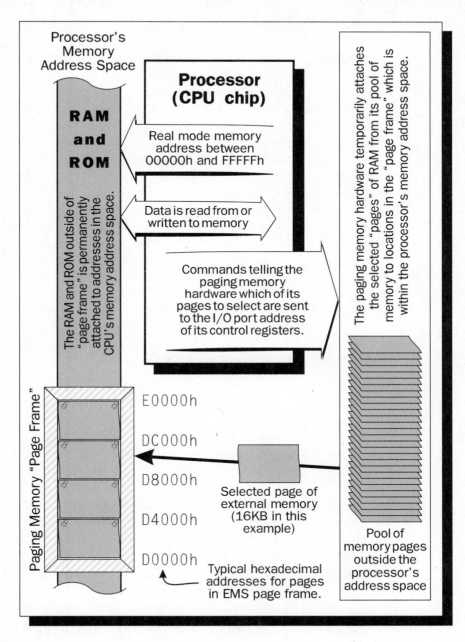

Figure 8.6.   The principle of paged memory.

By being so prescriptive, the LI-EMS 3.0 document put unnecessary restrictions on what EMS board makers could do. Essentially the LI-EMS, version 3.0, specified not only how an application program should ask for and use EMS services, it also specified how the EMM driver program should command the hardware. Since every EMS board manufacturer supplies a customized EMM driver program with the board, there is no reason an industry specification should have anything to say about how those two pieces talk to one another.

Microsoft joined the Lotus-Intel team and together they brought out a revision to the standard, called *LIM-EMS,* version 3.2 (see Figure 8.7).

The major innovation in this version was to completely drop all mention of how the hardware was to be built and how the EMM should communicate with it. Also, the API calls that related to a hardware detail were dropped. In fact, that is all that was changed in this version. This advance (and it was significant) was done purely by subtraction!

The overall result was to free up the marketplace, allowing more manufacturers to do more innovative things with EMS boards. And that helped everyone.

Enhanced Expanded Memory

Some people just can't leave well enough alone. (Thank goodness!) Engineers at AST (makers of EMS boards), Quarterdeck Office Systems (makers of *DESQview* multiwindowing, multitasking software), and Ashton-Tate (makers of the *Framework* integrated software package) decided they could come up with a significant improvement over LIM-EMS, version 3.2. They called it the *Enhanced Expanded Memory Specification* (or *EEMS*).

An add-in memory board that conformed to the EEMS standard, along with its matching driver software, could do everything a LIM 3.2 EMS board could do and more. The *more* came in several areas.

The most important new idea was that you were no longer limited to attaching just four pages of 16KB of RAM at a time to the CPU's memory bus; instead, you could attach pretty much as many of them as there was room for. There was almost no restriction on where those pages might be placed.

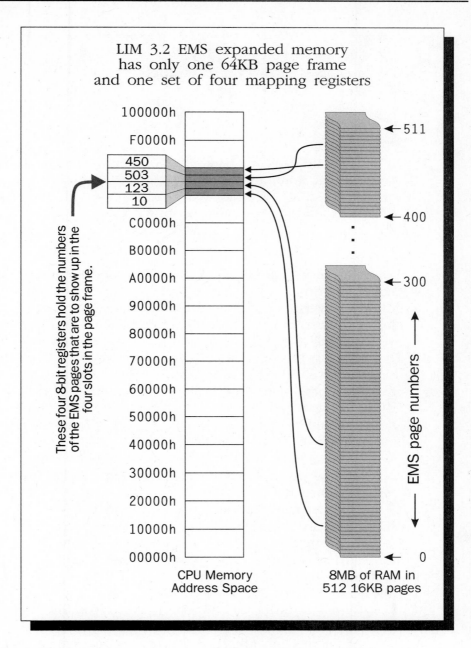

Figure 8.7. Key features of Lotus-Intel-Microsoft EMS, version 3.2.

You can have only one set of RAM chips attached at any one range of addresses. But in early PCs in particular, there were a lot of empty addresses. Chapter 14 begins with a further discussion of this point. See also the discussion in Chapter 15 in the section "Adding Memory on the Motherboard—When You Shouldn't."

For example, if you had only 256KB of RAM on the motherboard of your PC, you might find yourself putting as many as twelve 16KB pages of EMS RAM into the space above video RAM and another 24 pages below the video and above your existing RAM.

Using EEMS—Some New Possibilities

The EMS pages that are mapped above the video memory present some novel opportunities and challenges. First, you can have more of them than LIM-EMS, version 3.2, allowed. Second, with EEMS you are permitted to load programs there and run them from that location. This goes a bit beyond what DOS expected to deal with, at least prior to version 5, in as much as any program loaded into the region above the video memory is outside the region where DOS expects to load programs. A program will run from that location just fine, but getting there may take some doing.

The pages that are switched in below the video RAM look just like added system memory. Filling in the empty portion of the system memory space in this manner is called *backfilling*.

Some earlier EMS boards had also offered backfilling as an option, but not the way EEMS boards did. With those earlier boards you could use a portion of the 2MB on the EMS board to augment the motherboard's RAM, filling out system memory to a full 640KB of RAM. But the chips on the EMS board that were used for that task were fixed once and forever (or at least until you took out the board and reset some DIP switches). Only the rest of the memory chips could participate in the EMS mapping scheme, and they would only be switched in and out of the page frame, which was always somewhere above the video memory.

EEMS backfilling is different. It allows you to put switchable, expanded memory pages into regions of system memory.

Again, remember that this can only be done if you don't already have 640KB of system memory on the motherboard. If you map EMS memory pages into system memory, DOS can load programs there and they can run perfectly normally. What is new is that you can switch those memory pages, complete with the programs they contain, away into the pool of unaddressable memory, and replace them with some new pages. While the first set of pages are switched out, the programs they contain are in stasis, not doing anything. But now you can put some other programs into the new EMS pages presently attached to the CPU's memory bus.

Efficient Multitasking

You could let those new programs run briefly, switch them into limbo, and return the old programs, which could then be allowed to run again. If you switch often enough and fast enough, you get the illusion that both programs are running at once.

Of course they aren't. You're simply time-sharing the computational power of the CPU, but the illusion is very strong, and very nice. Your PC appears to run a bit slower, perhaps (and often not all that much slower), but you can make it do more than one thing at a time (or so it seems).

This is precisely what *DESQview* does and that is why Quarterdeck Office Systems joined in the effort to create the EEMS standard. An EEMS board and a PC with minimal RAM at fixed addresses provides the optimum environment for using *DESQview*. (Well, PCs in classes 5 and 6 don't need the EEMS board; they can get the same effect with their own internal mapping hardware.)

Having several sets of programs and switching between those sets is called *context switching.* It can be done without all this fancy hardware. For example, you might interrupt the running of one set of programs, copy them off to disk, load into RAM a new set, and then let those new programs run. That would be a context switch. This is what *DESQview* has to do if you do not have EEMS hardware (or some later improvement on that idea). The only real problem with this approach is speed. The context switches can easily take several seconds each. That precludes doing them many times per second, which is what you must do to maintain the illusion of simultaneous operation.

The power of an EEMS board is that it can do context switching so quickly and easily. You don't need to copy programs once they have been loaded into RAM the first time. You just have to reset which pages of expanded memory show up where in the CPU's memory-address space.

Other EEMS Features

Other added features of EEMS boards is that they provide multiple sets of registers, each of which can keep track of one set of page mappings. And those boards usually have a provision for activating one of those sets of mapping registers extremely rapidly. Even the description of which pages go where doesn't have to be copied when you do a context switch. You just have to tell the EEMS board which set of mapping registers to use.

A final innovation in EEMS was the notion that the page frame could be larger than 64KB. That is why you might have as many as twelve 16KB EMS pages mapped into the space above video.

Having all of these extra pages of EMS RAM that can appear at the same time and in all those different places in the CPU's memory address space means it is possible to do more and better memory management.

Naturally the makers of EEMS hardware and software attempted to make it fully backward compatible. That is, they tried to ensure that all application programs that know how to use EMS memory will find no difficulty dealing with an EEMS board. Unfortunately, that is only mostly true. Occasionally you must tell the EEMS EMM program to suppress some of its more advanced features if you wish to run it with certain older programs that aren't able to accept EMS pages mapped into more than one 64KB EMS page frame.

Extensions to LIM-EMS, Version 3.2, and EEMS

The designers of EEMS weren't the only folks who couldn't leave well enough alone. Many companies introduced EMS boards that incorporated one or another features that went beyond anything mentioned in either the LIM-EMS or the EEMS documents.

One nice example of this was nonvolatile EMS memory. A popular use for EMS memory is as a RAM disk. With suitable software you can make as much as you like of the EMS memory you have added look to DOS exactly like a super-fast disk drive.

That is all wonderful until you have to reboot your computer because some program got stuck (or "hung"—anything that so confuses things that you can't go on). You will lose all the information stored on the RAM disk in an instant. That is such a problem that many people decided they could use RAM disks only to store programs, not data files. That's unfortunate, for sometimes the best way to speed up your PC is to put some of its data files on a RAM disk. But you have to be aware that you may lose them if you must reboot.

That was an opportunity just waiting for a clever company to exploit. With the addition of a battery and a little extra circuitry, ABM created an EMS board that was just a normal LIM-EMS 3.2 board except that when power went off the battery would keep the mapped EMS pages from forgetting whatever they had stored in them.

This meant you could create a RAM disk in EMS memory and not lose a thing when you rebooted. With an external motorcycle battery attached to the board you could even unplug the computer and take it on a trip, plug it in when you arrived, and still find all your files on the RAM disk, intact! This board was such a nice idea they named it the *X2C* board. (Prounounce this name quickly and you will understand why it was so appropriate.)

Other manufacturers added yet other features to either the basic LIM-EMS 3.2 standard or on top of EEMS, giving us the opportunity to buy boards with some very nice features. It also meant going back toward a marketplace of incompatible, proprietary boards.

LIM-EMS Version 4.0

The obvious solution was to update the LIM-EMS standard, including in it the best of these new, added ideas. That's exactly what *LIM-EMS,* version 4.0, is. Its key features are shown in Figure 8.8.

It is a consensus standard. It incorporates support for EMS extensions by a variety of vendors including AST, ABM, IBM, Intel, Microsoft, and Quadtel.

It made the EEMS functionality a part of the standard, but it implemented those extensions in a different way. Alone among the makers of LIM-EMS 4.0 memory cards, AST supported both the old, EEMS way of doing those things and the new, LIM-EMS 4.0 way of doing them.

Here's a list of several other important ways that LIM 4.0 EMS differs from LIM 3.2 EMS:

- **Maximum total EMS memory increased**

  The maximum amount of EMS memory that can be addressed was increased, this time to 32MB.

- **Reduced granularity supported**

  One new feature that could have had a lot of impact had it been widely adopted was the notion of reduced granularity of memory. This idea came from an IBM expanded memory card they called the *XMA.* It means that the size of the EMS memory pages that get mapped in can be less than 16KB. Unfortunately this was not implemented in many EMS cards and so almost no software was designed to take advantage of it.

- **Alternate register sets**

  Providing a large number of alternate register sets allows a program like *Windows* or *DESQview* to switch between an unlimited number of programs, all without reloading any of the mapping register sets; the switching is accomplished by selecting a different set.

- **Page aliasing introduced**

  The new standard provided for the possibility that a single page of EMS memory (the actual chips) could be made to appear in two places in the CPU's memory address space at the same time. The program that asks for those mappings will be given a different name (actually, a *handle number*) by which to refer to that memory in each of those places. That is called *page aliasing*. Again, this was a nice idea, but only rarely used. *Javelin* was one of the few programs to take advantage of it, and that program, after a very promising introduction, sank quietly into obscurity.

- **Support for DMA to or from EMS memory**

  The new standard allowed for special DMA support. This feature permits using the Direct Memory Access controller on the PC's motherboard to send information to or from a region of EMS memory, just as with normal RAM in the system memory space. Only AST built boards that incorporated this feature, and again it was a good idea that did not seem to find many takers among the authors of application programs.

  You will have noticed that many features in the new specification are optional. The makers of EMS boards are free to include them or not. If they do include them, the specification says how those features shall be accessed, and there is a standard way for a program to find out if those features are supported in a given PC. But without a requirement that all makers of EMS boards include them, most of these fancy features simply had little impact on the industry.

  An unfortunate limitation of the LIM-EMS 4.0 standard is that any LIM 4.0 EMM driver must poll all the different EMS boards in a given PC (assuming you have more than one installed), and then offer to application programs only those features that *every* EMS board in that PC supports. There simply is no provision in the specification for having the driver support a different set of features in the regions of EMS memory that come from any one of the EMS boards in a system.

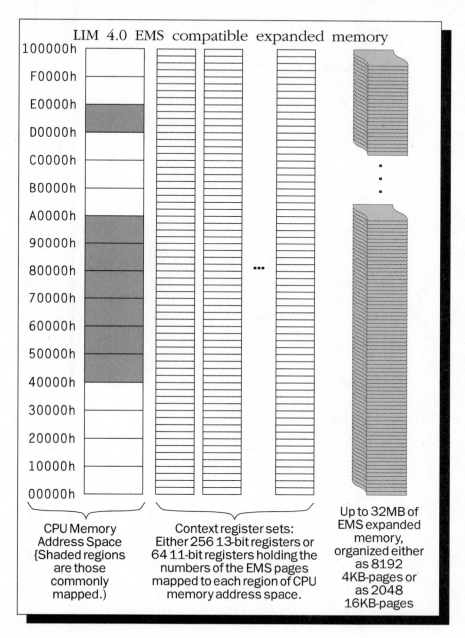

Figure 8.8. Key features of Lotus-Intel-Microsoft EMS, version 4.0.

An Important Warning About EMS Memory Boards

When LIM EMS, version 4.0, was announced, it was obviously a wonderful idea. Everyone wanted one of those great new EMS boards. Soon thereafter, many manufacturers, including Intel, announced that they were shipping version 4.0 EMS boards. This was misleading, at best.

It turned out what they meant was merely that they had upgraded their driver software (the expanded memory manager, or EMM) to support all the new features of the API. Anytime an application program would ask for one of the new features, the EMM would recognize the request and know whether or not its EMS board supported that feature. If it did not, the EMM would politely tell the application program, "Sorry, that feature is not available."

Only when they had time to redo the hardware design of their EMS boards and then manufacture new boards incorporating those new features would true EMS 4.0 boards become available. That took quite a while. In the meantime, almost every manufacturer of the earlier LIM-EMS 3.2 boards was offering their customers free or inexpensive "upgrades" to "LIM-EMS 4.0 compatibility." Once again, this merely meant they were shipping copies of their new EMM program.

If the EMS hardware could not do something before, it sure couldn't do it afterwards. More than a few folks got an unpleasant surprise from that one.

Even today, if you buy an EMS board, be sure to check out just which aspects of the LIM-EMS 4.0 feature set it supports. For example, many of the newer designs include support for the so-called large page frame. That means they can map EMS memory pages into the entire region from C0000h to DFFFFh. (A few of them can map EMS memory into the E page as well. It is too bad that more do not, as that is often an available space.)

But some of the biggest names in the field (Intel among them) are still shipping EMS boards that lack this feature. It didn't matter too much before DOS 5 raised people's consciousness about taking advantage of upper memory. Now it is well past just a nuisance to find out that you have paid good money for a board you thought would allow you to put up to 192KB of RAM into upper memory, only to find out it can't put any more than 64KB of RAM there.

Video Memory (RAM)

Video RAM is the memory in which your PC stores the information that results in the images that are displayed on your screen. Another name for this memory is the video-image-buffer memory. Every PC has some of this memory; how much depends greatly on the video standard used.

The relevance of video RAM to memory management is quite simple. Video RAM takes up certain addresses in the CPU's memory address space. While it is doing so, those addresses cannot be used for anything else.

Thus you had better know how much video RAM you have and what portion of the CPU's memory address space it uses. The total amount of video RAM on your video display adapter is whatever it is, but the size and location of the region of the CPU's memory address space it occupies may vary widely, depending on which video mode you are running. Therefore, in addition to knowing how much total video RAM is on your video card or system motherboard, you need to understand what video modes you use and how that affects memory-address space usage.

This is a complex subject. And an important one. There are subtleties lurking here that can, and often do, trip the unwary or uninformed. This section covers the whole subject quite comprehensively in the following subsections:

- Video RAM is Both Like and Different from System RAM
- The Video Display Adapter as Translator
- How the Monitor Creates Images
- Controlling the Monitor
- The Information Content of a Screen Image
- How Graphical Images Are Stored in Video RAM
- Text Mode Images
- Storing Text Mode Images and Rasterizing Them
- Screen Pages
- How to Fit 16 Gallons into a One-Gallon Bucket
- A Summary of What You Have Learned About Video RAM So Far
- The Several PC Video Standards

Furthermore, if you seek to understand what limits the performance (speed) of your PC, understanding exactly how video memory and the associated video display circuitry works is important. Some of that information is in this section; you can find more in Chapter 16 in the discussion of the difference between DRAM and VRAM.

Video RAM Is Both
Like and Different from System RAM

Video RAM appears to the CPU on its memory bus, just like the system RAM. It is not like that memory, though, in one important respect. This RAM is connected to both the CPU memory bus and to a special video display circuit that sends signals to the monitor.

The CPU puts information into this RAM, using its CPU-to-memory bus. The special display circuitry reads that information out of the video RAM over a separate data path and uses it to create the screen image. In fact, it re-creates that image about 60 or 70 times each second.

In some systems, the video RAM is located on a special video display plug-in card. That card also has all the special circuitry needed to send images to the monitor. In other PCs the video circuitry, including its RAM, is located on the system motherboard. In this latter case it will usually be well away from the main system RAM. That, and the fact that video memory is usually provided by banks of eight chips (instead of nine) or "by eight" SIMMs (instead of "by nine" SIMMs), normally make it pretty easy to tell which physical RAM chips make up the system RAM and which provide the video RAM.

The Video Display Adapter as Translator

How does the video display circuitry generate screen images? Essentially, the job of this circuitry is to translate from the information stored in the video image buffer memory to the signals the monitor uses to create what you see. To understand how it can do that job, you need to understand both how screen-image information is stored in the buffer and how the monitor makes an image appear on-screen.

There are two fundamentally different ways that screen image information is stored in the video image buffer memory. These are:

- **Bit-mapped graphics:** This is a direct representation of what you see on the screen, described in terms of the color and brightness of each dot on the screen.

- **Text (or alphanumeric) screen image:** This is a much more abstract representation in which the screen is described as an assemblage of characters (normally 80 per row for 25 rows).

It is much easier to understand how bit-mapped graphics work. After you understand that, you can then learn the additional details you need to understand *text mode.*

First, though, take a look at how the monitor makes images appear on-screen. That dictates what signals it must receive from the computer and that, in turn, heavily influences how information is stored in the buffer memory, especially for a bit-mapped graphic image.

How the Monitor Creates Images

The strategy used by a PC's monitor to make images appear on-screen is much like that used by television. It is called *raster scanning.* The monitor paints the screen with a tightly focused beam of electrons. Everywhere the beam hits the screen, a phosphor coating is activated and glows. If the beam intensity is high, the phosphor will glow brightly. If the beam intensity is very low, the phosphor will hardly glow at all. The glow of each spot of phosphor dies away smoothly during approximately the next several hundredths of a second.

Early image tubes for computers often used a radically different strategy than the one we use today. That other strategy was called *vector imaging.* Figure 8.9 (a) shows how a triangle might be drawn on the screen surface using this technique.

In a raster scan the electron beam is scanned across the screen from left to right to draw one line of the image. Next it snaps back to the left side, moves down a bit, and then draws the next line. This continues until the entire screen has been painted. Figure 8.9 (b) (c) shows this pattern of sweeping, and it shows how modulating the beam from on to off at appropriate times can be used to draw an image (in this case, a triangle) on-screen.

That description is almost right. Actually, though, to keep the monitor design as simple as possible, the moving down is done continuously. The only effect of this is to make each of the horizontal lines in the image slope down to the right by just a tiny amount.

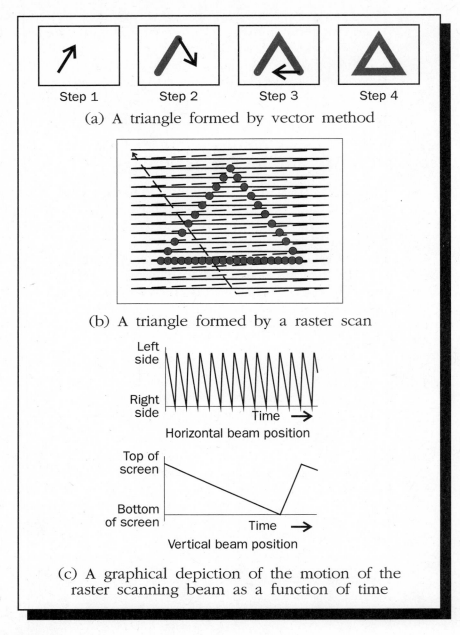

Step 1   Step 2   Step 3   Step 4

(a) A triangle formed by vector method

(b) A triangle formed by a raster scan

Left side

Right side

Time →

Horizontal beam position

Top of screen

Bottom of screen

Time →

Vertical beam position

(c) A graphical depiction of the motion of the raster scanning beam as a function of time

Figure 8.9. Vector- vs. raster-scanned images.

Even if the monitor is not connected to the computer, the electron beam will scan across the screen for line after line, steadily moving down the screen, and at the bottom snap up to start the process over again. This pattern of motion is what is called the *raster*.

Controlling the Monitor

In the absence of any signals from the computer every point on the raster will be equally bright. (On a TTL monitor this often is full-brightness white. Analog monitors typically show an all-black screen image when they are disconnected from the computer.)

The video display adapter circuitry must do two things simultaneously in order to properly control the monitor. First, it must control when the monitor starts each new image, and when it starts each line of that image. Next, it must supply information on how strongly the beam should illuminate each place on the screen as it passes over it.

Line Control

Synchronizing signals are generated by the video display circuitry to ensure that just as the computer is generating signals representing the color or brightness of a spot in the image, the electron beam in the monitor will be tracing the place on the screen where that spot is to appear. The signal to start a new screen image is called vertical (V) sync or vertical drive. The signal to start the next line is called horizontal (H) sync or horizontal drive.

Since all these signals have to do is convey when the monitor is to do certain things, it is adequate to use one wire for each sync signal, and on those wires the voltage is at every moment either high or low. The transition from one state to the other is the signal to the monitor to take those corresponding actions. Such a binary signal can easily be generated by digital logic circuits. The family of logic chips that is used in PCs goes by the name *TTL*, standing for *Transistor Transistor Logic*.

Illumination Control

The other kind of control the video display adapter must exert is to set the instantaneous brightness of the scanning beam. It must do this anew each time the beam scans through the raster pattern. From the computer's perspective, the screen image is composed of many lines, each containing many dots, spots, or picture elements. (IBM calls the picture elements *pels*; almost everyone else calls them *pixels*.)

There are two completely different ways to send this brightness information to the monitor. If there are very few brightness levels to convey, the simplest method is to use one or two wires (or that number of wires per color if the image is to be in color) and restrict the signals on each wire to the two levels, high and low. This is what is used by MDA, CGA, and EGA display adapters.

The circuits that generate and receive these binary signals are, once again, constructed using TTL designs. The monitors that use this strategy are called *TTL monitors.*

The alternative way to send the controlling signals is much more suited to subtlety in the resulting images. Here only one wire is used for each of the three primary colors (red, green, and blue). The H and V sync signals are still on separate wires and are digital signals, but the color signals are all analog ones. That means that their voltage level is allowed to be anything from zero to one volt.

Zero represents darkness and one volt is full brightness. Any voltage in between means the electron beam should have a similar intensity between its lowest and highest values. Thus the voltage on the wire varies in a manner that is analogous to the variations in beam intensity. Hence the name *analog monitor.*

There are a couple of subtle additional details you may wish to understand. The first has to do with how often the screen image is redrawn. The second is exactly how color is added to the image.

Sync Frequencies and Flicker   To make the image appear solid and steady, it must be redrawn with the appropriate frequency. The phosphor glow lingers a little, but it cannot do so long, or you would see ghosting and smearing anytime the image being drawn on-screen changed.

This means that the electron beam must revisit each part of the screen frequently enough to reactivate each phosphor dot before you notice that it has faded away. It turns out that most people will accept an image as steady if it is redrawn at least 60, or perhaps 70 times per second. If the image is redrawn less often than that, it will visibly flicker, an effect that most users find annoying at least, and that gives severe headaches to many.

Television gets away with redrawing its images only 30 times per second. How can it do this? By cheating. The television image consists of 525 lines. Only half of them are drawn each time the electron beam moves down the screen. The rest are drawn the next time it does so. This "interleaving" of two half-images (the odd-numbered lines and the even-numbered ones) helps fool our eyes. If the two images are not a lot different, most people cannot see any flicker at all.

That's fine for TV. Most of the images it displays don't have much contrast between what is on one line and what is on the immediately adjacent ones above and below. Unfortunately, this is often not true for computer-generated images.

It is not at all uncommon for two horizontal scan lines on a computer-generated image to be literally as different as black and white. The interlace strategy fails miserably in dealing with this sort of image. This is why it is so important to get a video display system that is capable of noninterlaced operation even at the highest resolutions you plan to use.

Creating Color Images   Color images are drawn just like the monochrome ones, except in triplicate. Three electron beams fly across the screen together. The beams paint the screen through a mask with holes in it. This "shadow mask" allows each beam to illuminate a small fraction of the screen area (a region composed of a lot of regularly spaced dots, one for every hole in the shadow mask).

Since the beams come from slightly different places, as they pass through the shadow mask they end up hitting the screen at locations that are near, but not quite on top of one another. The screen is covered with phosphor dots that glow in the three colors (red, green, and blue) when activated. When things are adjusted correctly, each beam only hits phosphor dots that glow in a single color. One beam activates only red-glowing dots, another green-glowing dots, and the third one only blue-glowing dots. The signals from the computer in this case must consist of the usual H and V sync signals plus three streams of brightness information, one each for the red, green, and blue subimages.

The Information Content of a Screen Image

The amount of information needed from the computer to control the monitor beam(s) for an entire screen image depends on two things. One is the resolution of the image. The other is its color richness. Let's look at each of those points in turn.

Resolution

The resolution of an image, from the computer's perspective, is set by the number of dots per line in the image (its horizontal resolution) and the number of those lines in the full image (its vertical resolution). Table 8.1 shows the resolutions of some common display adapter modes.

Table 8.1. Some common display adapter modes and their resolutions.

Adapter and Mode	Horizontal	Vertical
Monochrome Graphics (MGA)	720	350
Color Graphics (CGA) *Medium Resolution*	320	200
Color Graphics (CGA) *High Resolution*	640	200
VGA Text	720	400
VGA Graphics	640	480
Super VGA Graphics	800	600
Super VGA Graphics	1024	768
Super VGA Graphics	1280	1024

The computer's perspective on resolution is the only one that matters for memory management. The perspective of a person looking at the monitor is different, and obviously matters, but only as an aesthetic or practical matter, not as a matter of memory management inside the PC.

When you look at the screen, what you see depends not only on how many pixels the computer generated for that image, it also depends on some qualities of the monitor. In particular, the size of the electron beam(s), the spacing of the color dots or lines in the phosphor layer, and the speed with which a beam can be turned on and off will set an upper limit to the effective resolution of the images it can display. The first of these monitor-related limitations is called the spot size; the second is described by something called the monitor's *dot pitch*; the third limitation is related to the monitor's *video bandwidth*.

Dot pitch is the shortest distance between pixels of the same color on adjacent lines of the monitor screen. The closer the pixels, the sharper the detail. A typical distance for high quality monitors is .26 mm.

Video Bandwidth refers to the highest signal frequency a monitor can display. The higher the bandwidth, the sharper the image will be.

Color Richness

If the dots that make up an image are supposed to be only black or white, just one bit of information needs to be sent to the monitor to inform it what to do. If that spot could have any of some large number of colors, a more information-rich signal must be sent.

Naturally, the computer must store enough information to generate those signals. This means that for a single-intensity monochrome image, it must store one bit per pixel.

If every pixel on-screen may be any one of 16 shades of grey, or one of 16 colors (and if the color or grey value of each pixel is independent of that for all the others), the computer must store four bits per pixel.

Human eyes and minds are capable of perceiving a huge number of colors. So-called photorealistic images usually require a system that can specify the color of each pixel from a palette (a range of color possibilities) with over 16 million different colors. This requires storing 24 bits (three bytes) for each pixel in the image.

You often hear of the number of *bit-planes* in the video image buffer. Imagine a rectangular array of memory cells, one per pixel in the screen image we are storing. Each of these cells can hold just one bit of information. That array is enough to represent a monochrome image of uniform brightness.

Now consider several of these arrays layered on top of one another. With that you can represent a screen image with multiple bits stored for each pixel (see Figure 8.10). In the examples cited above, the monochrome image would have a 1-bit-plane image buffer, the first color image would require a 4-bit-plane image buffer, and the photorealistic image would require an image buffer with 24 bit-planes.

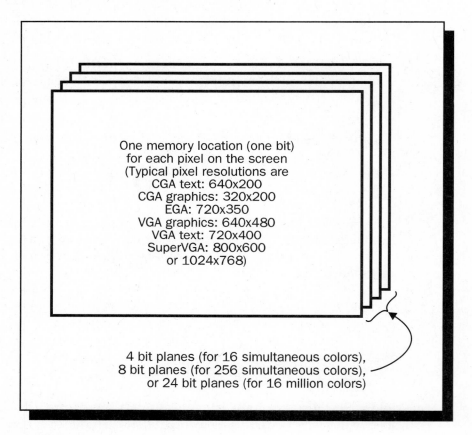

One memory location (one bit)
for each pixel on the screen
(Typical pixel resolutions are
CGA text: 640x200
CGA graphics: 320x200
EGA: 720x350
VGA graphics: 640x480
VGA text: 720x400
SuperVGA: 800x600
or 1024x768)

4 bit planes (for 16 simultaneous colors),
8 bit planes (for 256 simultaneous colors),
or 24 bit planes (for 16 million colors)

Figure 8.10.   Video image buffer bit planes.

A high-resolution image with a lot of color richness implies a very big video image buffer memory. For example, if you wanted to have full photorealism (24 bit-planes) and 1,024x768 pixels, you would need 2.25MB of video image buffer memory. That's a lot of RAM.

Even if you settled for a more modest resolution (say the VGA graphics image standard of 640x480 pixels), and a more modest palette (again using the VGA standard, choose 262,144 colors, which is 18-bit color), you would need to have almost 700,000 bytes of RAM. Not nearly as much as the previous example, to be sure, but still more than most folks want to pay for.

Palette Tables

There is an easy way out. Most images don't have to have more than some rather modest number of *different* colors in them. Certainly this is true for typical business graphics images. But it is nice to be able to choose just which colors those will be from a much larger set.

Real IBM VGA cards don't have 700KB of RAM. But they do allow one to choose the screen colors from a palette of 262,144 colors, and they do display 640-480 pixel images. How can they accomplish this? They do it by allowing only 16 simultaneous colors in any given screen image. That means they can get away with a 4-bit plane video image buffer. That, in turn, implies only a 153,600-byte video image buffer.

> The actual video image buffer memory is 256KB. This is done both for convenience and to provide some RAM that can be used for the palette lookup table, to be described in a moment.

To get the wide-ranging choice of what those 16 colors shall be, a VGA card goes through one extra step of translation.

The numbers stored in the video image buffer are just that: numbers. What you want on-screen are colored dots. A VGA card uses a (programmable) palette lookup table to change each of those 4-bit numbers into three corresponding 6-bit numbers. Each of those numbers are then converted (in a chip called a *digital-to-analog converter,* or *DAC*) into one of 64 voltage levels. Those voltages are the signals sent to control the instantaneous intensity of the monitor's three electron guns (see Figure 8.11).

How Graphic Images Are Stored in Video RAM

Now you know what signals the monitor requires and something about how the video display adapter generates those signals. That pretty well controls what information the computer must store in its video image buffer memory.

A bit-mapped graphic image is stored with some number of bits per pixel in successive locations in video memory. The video display adapter scans through the buffer memory in memory-address order. It reads the numbers stored there, converts them into colors using the palette lookup table and DAC, and then sends those signals on to the monitor. Simple enough, isn't it? Once you have understood all these concepts and jargon, that is.

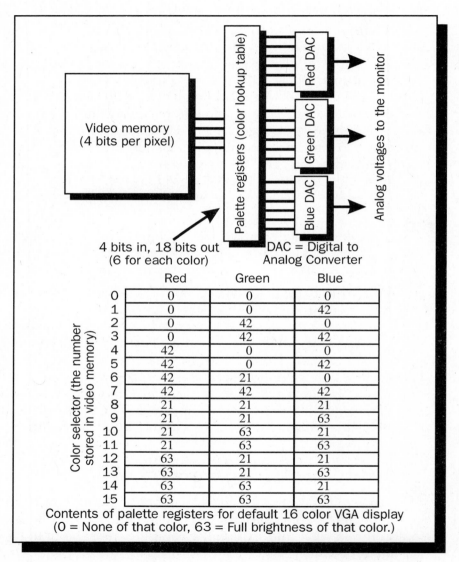

	Red	Green	Blue
0	0	0	0
1	0	0	42
2	0	42	0
3	0	42	42
4	42	0	0
5	42	0	42
6	42	21	0
7	42	42	42
8	21	21	21
9	21	21	63
10	21	63	21
11	21	63	63
12	63	21	21
13	63	21	63
14	63	63	21
15	63	63	63

Contents of palette registers for default 16 color VGA display
(0 = None of that color, 63 = Full brightness of that color.)

Figure 8.11. How a VGA card in 16-color mode converts the pixel color numbers into actual colors (amounts of red, green, and blue).

Usually all the bits for one pixel are stored together. Some adapters, though, store all the red information for the entire image, then all the green, then all the blue. For our present purposes that distinction is unimportant.

Character-based (text) images are both simpler and more complex. Let's see now what the differences are, and in particular how that impacts the required video RAM.

Text-Mode Images

The foregoing discussion presumed that the computer keeps track of the brightness or color of each individual pixel on-screen separately. This is done in *bit-mapped graphics* mode. But it isn't the only way to specify a screen image.

A much more economical way, in terms of video RAM needs, is to divide the screen into character cells. The most common division is 25 rows with 80 character cells per row. Then the computer can merely keep track of which character (from some stored set of characters) goes in each cell, along with what colors that character and its background are to be. This way of storing a screen image is called text (or alphanumeric) mode.

To see just how little video RAM you can get away with, consider IBM's original Monochrome Display Adapter (MDA) (one of the two video options for the original IBM *PC*). It operates only in text mode. With its 25 rows of 80 characters each, it has to keep track only of the contents of those 2,000 character cells. Each cell can have one of only 256 possible characters displayed in it. That means just one byte of character information has to be stored for each cell.

In addition, the MDA stores another byte for each cell. It doesn't really need all that extra storage, but another 2,000 bytes of RAM are so cheap that the MDA's designers opted to use that much. This was done primarily to make the method for writing information into the screen image buffer more like that used for the other video adapter introduced at the same time, IBM's Color Graphics Adapter.

Two of the bits in that *attribute byte* are used to indicate whether the associated character is to be displayed in high intensity and whether it is to blink. The remaining six bits are used to signal two more bits of information: whether the character is to be displayed with an underline, and whether it is to be displayed in reverse video (dark character on light background).

Even with the inefficiency of effectively using only four of the eight bits of each attribute byte, the MDA manages to store an entire screen image in less than 4KB.

The Color Graphics adapter (and all the higher models, like EGA and VGA, when they are operated in text mode) stores screen images in exactly the same manner as the MDA. The only difference is that those other video cards use each of the 256 possible values for the attribute byte in determining how the character should be displayed. Ordinarily, one bit will determine intensity and one turns blinking on or off, just as with the MDA. The remaining six bits are interpreted as two three-bit numbers to set one of eight possible foreground colors and a similar choice for background color.

Storing Text Mode Images and Rasterizing Them

Since a text-mode screen image requires only 4KB of information, putting the needed information into the video image buffer memory is a simple task—much simpler for the CPU than when it must construct a VGA graphics image, for which it must move into that buffer almost one-sixth of a megabyte of information.

On the other hand, the job of the video display adapter becomes much tougher. No longer can it simply read each number stored in the video buffer, convert it to the appropriate output signals, and then send that pixel's information to the monitor for immediate display. Let's see just what it has to do instead.

The information for the image to be displayed is stored as a succession of bytes: first an ASCII code for the character in a cell, and then an attribute byte for that character. While the characters are arrayed in the same general order as the raster pattern on-screen (left to right across each row of characters, with each row's data stored right after that for the row above), there is no direct mapping of bits in video memory to pixels on-screen.

Each character in a text-mode image occupies several pixels on each of several successive lines. The exact number of pixels per line and lines is called the character cell size, and it depends on the adapter you are using and the particular one of its text modes in which it is operating. An 80x25 character image on a CGA display uses a character cell that spans 8 pixels on each of 8 successive scan lines. On a VGA screen, the 80x25 text mode character cell is 9 pixels wide by 16 pixels high.

To generate the image, the video display circuitry has to do all the following steps:

1. As the first scan line starts at the top-left corner of the screen, the display circuitry reads the first character's ASCII code and attribute byte.

2. It then looks up in a font table the sequence of on and off bits that represent the dots to be drawn for the top scan line of this character.

3. It converts those in light of the character's attribute byte into the appropriate stream of signals for the monitor and sends them out. Then it moves on to the next character.

4. For each character on the line, it must repeat steps 2 and 3.

When that scan line is complete, it comes back to the same row of characters as many times as there are scan lines in a character cell. Each time it looks up a different set of bits in the font table, corresponding to a different vertical position within the character being drawn. Only when it has finished all the scan lines for the first row of characters can it move on to the second line. There it will repeat all the same steps for all the scan lines for the second row of characters. And it must repeat all that for every other row as it moves down the screen.

> This is much the same as the method used to generate dots on a page in a dot-matrix printer. The general name for this process is *rasterizing an image.* (Some printers and some video cards come with a special coprocessor whose sole function is to do rasterizing and thus relieve the main system's CPU of that task. These processors are called, naturally enough, *Raster Image Processors,* or *RIPs* for short.)

Screen Pages

Since text-mode screen images require so much less video-buffer-memory than do bit-mapped graphic ones, any video adapter that is capable of storing a graphic screen image could store multiple text mode images simultaneously. For example, the original MDA had only 4KB of buffer memory. The CGA had 16KB. That meant that in text mode a CGA adapter could store up to four screen images.

That can be very handy. It allows a program to write to one page while another one is being displayed. Then, when it is ready, the program can make the newly prepared screen pop into view. Another way to think about this is to visualize the CGA card's 16KB buffer as holding 102 lines of text image information. All of that buffer is attached to the CPU's memory bus all of the time. But when the CGA card is operating in text mode, only a 25-line region of the buffer memory is attached to the monitor.

EGA, MCGA, and VGA cards can all do this trick as well. Alternatively, one of those cards could hold a single super-size image and pan and scroll an imaginary window around that super-size image with the window's contents showing up on the actual screen.

Another use for this extra video memory is for virtual screens. Multitasking software like *DESQview* can let each of several programs have a region of memory address space it thinks is the "real" video image buffer. Those programs can write directly to those buffers, but what they write there will not show up on-screen. *DESQview* will then copy to the "real" image buffer (that is the active portion of that buffer) only those parts of each virtual screen image that belong in the corresponding program's window on-screen.

Next you will learn about how the opposite approach can also be useful. Even when the whole buffer memory is attached to the monitor, it need not all be attached to the CPU's memory bus. At least not all at once.

How to Fit 16 Gallons into a 1-Gallon Bucket

If you have been paying close attention, you may have noticed something mysterious. IBM reserved 128KB of the CPU's memory address space for video image buffers. (That is the A and B pages; or in another form that is all the addresses from A0000h to BFFFFh.) But a VGA card typically carries 256KB of video image buffer. How can they shoehorn all of that RAM into just the A and B pages?

The newest Super VGA cards and XGA cards present the same problem in a heightened form. They carry a full megabyte of RAM, or sometimes even 2MB. If all of that were to appear in the CPU's memory address space at once (in real mode), there would be no room for anything else!

The answer is that the video image buffer memory is treated just like expanded memory; it is paged into the CPU's memory address space a piece at a time. In fact, for most of their operating modes, the video display adapters with lots of RAM map into the CPU's memory address space no more than 64KB at a time. Super VGA cards do use the whole 128KB range in certain modes.

There are some interesting differences between paged video memory and EMS memory. First, the bytes written to paged video memory are not merely parked there. They influence what shows up on-screen. That makes those locations a sort of hybrid between what we earlier called a memory-like location and a port-like one. (This distinction applies to all video-image-buffer memory, not merely paged video memory.)

Second, this memory is normally only used to store image information. However, a portion of it could be used for program storage, and sometimes is, if it is not needed to store image information. (PC DOS 6 includes some special utility programs to help you do this.)

Third, the separate pages of video buffer memory may hold only bit-plane slices of the image information. This means that the bits of the byte(s) describing an individual pixel may be scattered across many pages.

This paged video memory technique makes it harder for programs to update the video image buffer, but not too much harder. And it allows us to enjoy those wonderful high-resolution, large-color depth images. That's well worth the extra bother these cards represent to a programmer.

All of this discussion assumes that the CPU is operating in real mode. Since DOS is strictly a real-mode operating system, this is usually the case. But there now are a number of operating environments that run on top of DOS that use protected mode (*Windows 3.x* and *GeoWorks Ensemble,* for example), along with a number of DOS-extended applications that also run in protected mode (for example Lotus *1-2-3,* release 3.x). These programs could access the video image buffer memory in a different way.

Specifically, if the CPU is operating in protected mode, it has access to all of at least 16MB and maybe as much as 4GB of memory address space. Why not simply put the video image buffer memory somewhere way up in that space, well out of the way of everything else? That way the whole image buffer could be accessible to the CPU at all times.

The XGA adapter and a few Super VGA cards can do just that. So far, though, there is little in the way of software support for this feature. When that software support is available this should allow those video systems to operate much more rapidly. It also will make writing programs for them much simpler.

A Summary of What You
Have Learned About Video RAM So Far

You now know, in a general way, how a common PC video display adapter functions. You have some idea of just how much memory it must have for a given resolution and color depth. And you found out how a palette lookup table can be used to get more variety in the colors on screen images without having to increase color depth and thus the amount of video RAM.

Table 8.2 shows some common video adapters and modes, with the number of pixels resolution (horizontal and vertical), number of simultaneous colors on screen, and amount of memory required on the graphics adapter.

Table 8.2. Adapter modes and video memory.

Adapter and Mode	Horizontal	Vertical	Colors	RAM
MDA (text only)	720	350	1	4KB
MGA (graphics)	720	350	1	64KB
Color Graphics (CGA) *Medium Resolution*	320	200	4	16KB
Color Graphics (CGA) *High Resolution*	640	200	1	16KB
EGA Text	720	348	16	64KB–256KB
EGA Graphics	720	348	16	64KB–256KB
VGA Text	720	400	16	256KB
VGA Graphics	640	480	16	256KB
VGA Graphics	320	200	256	256KB
Super VGA Graphics	800	600	16	256KB
Super VGA Graphics	800	600	256	512KB
Super VGA Graphics	1024	768	16	512KB
XGA and Super VGA Graphics	1024	768	256	1024KB
XGA and Super VGA Graphics	1280	1024	256	2048KB

Finally, you have learned how video cards with a lot of image buffer RAM can make do with only a smallish window into the CPU's memory address space. That is a lot of information about video display adapters. What you still have to learn is what different types of video adapters are available and how each one, in each of its normal operating modes, impacts the CPU's memory-address space.

The Several PC Video Standards

Over time many alternative video display adapters have been introduced. Some were niche market products. Others received wide acceptance. The following is a list of only the most popular of these video display options.

- In the beginning there was the *Monochrome Display Adapter* and the *Color Graphics Adapter,* and that was all. The *MDA* worked only in text mode. The *CGA* could work in two text modes (40 and 80 column) or two graphics modes (medium and high resolution).

- Hercules made its name responding to folks who wanted MDA-quality text and CGA-like graphics, even though they were only in one color. Their *Hercules Graphics Card (HGC)* has become a third standard, now commonly called a *Monochrome Graphics Adapter* (*MGA*).

- IBM's response, a few years later, was the *Enhanced Graphics Adapter (EGA)*. It combined the same text quality as the MDA with even better color than the CGA, and it could do all those good colors in its full bit-mapped graphics modes that had higher resolution than CGA.

- Various vendors improved on the EGA with a slew of *Super EGA* boards. Unfortunately they were mutually incompatible, except for their emulations of the good old MGA, CGA, and standard EGA modes. None of these clone enhancements was good enough to become another industry standard.

- Next came IBM's *Video Graphics Array* (*VGA*) and its little sibling, the *MultiColor Graphics Array* (*MCGA*). These further upped the ante in terms of both color depth and resolution.

- Again the competitive vendors brought out enhanced versions of the VGA. This time, though, they banded together to form the *Video Electronics Standards Association (VESA)*. This is a standards-setting body. They decided on a minimum set of features all Super

VGA cards should have, and they encouraged the writing of video drivers for most popular software that could activate those now-standardized features on anyone's Super VGA card.

- Most recently, IBM introduced the *XGA*. The march toward ever higher resolution and greater color depth continues. Unfortunately, in their initial implementation of the XGA, IBM chose to use interlaced output in the highest resolution modes. They are pushing to make XGA a new industry standard. Perhaps other video card makers will introduce a fully noninterlaced version of XGA.

That's the laundry list of popular video options. One thing they all have is backward compatibility. That is, you can run programs that expect to see one of the earlier, less capable display adapters in a PC with one of the newer ones, and it will work just fine.

This means that whatever region of the CPU's memory address space one adapter takes up, all later adapters must take up the same space, at least when they are emulating that earlier adapter.

But each new card also introduced new features. Some of the time this meant they had to use more of the CPU's memory address space. Figure 8.12 gives a summary of the regions of that space, which each of the popular video cards uses for its video image buffer in all of the most popular video modes.

Some comments might make this figure clearer. The MDA card has only 4KB of RAM on it. How, then, can it manage to take up a full 32KB of the CPU's memory address space?

The MDA was designed a long time ago (long, that is, in computer-industry terms). To keep its cost reasonable they used only 4KB of RAM, and to further cut corners, they simply didn't bother to decode all of the memory bus address lines. Lines A12, A13, and A14 were simply ignored. That means that the same 4KB of memory shows up in eight different places. You can use any of those eight address ranges, but almost all programs use only the one that starts at B0000h.

Lines A19, A18, A17, A16, and A15 suffice to indicate which 32KB region of the first megabyte of memory is being addressed. When they carry the values 10110, respectively, the region from B0000h to B7FFFh is selected. If that is true, then lines A0 through A11 point to which of the 4,096 bytes of memory on the MDA card is being addressed (addresses B0000h to B0FFFh). The states of A12 through A14 are only needed if one wishes to distinguish between those 4KB and some other 4KB region between B0000h and B7FFFh.

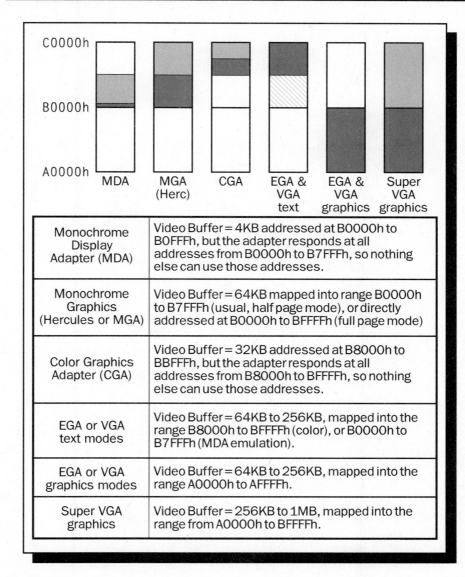

Monochrome Display Adapter (MDA)	Video Buffer = 4KB addressed at B0000h to B0FFFh, but the adapter responds at all addresses from B0000h to B7FFFh, so nothing else can use those addresses.
Monochrome Graphics (Hercules or MGA)	Video Buffer = 64KB mapped into range B0000h to B7FFFh (usual, half page mode), or directly addressed at B0000h to BFFFFh (full page mode)
Color Graphics Adapter (CGA)	Video Buffer = 32KB addressed at B8000h to BBFFFh, but the adapter responds at all addresses from B8000h to BFFFFh, so nothing else can use those addresses.
EGA or VGA text modes	Video Buffer = 64KB to 256KB, mapped into the range B8000h to BFFFFh (color), or B0000h to B7FFFh (MDA emulation).
EGA or VGA graphics modes	Video Buffer = 64KB to 256KB, mapped into the range A0000h to AFFFFh.
Super VGA graphics	Video Buffer = 256KB to 1MB, mapped into the range from A0000h to BFFFFh.

Figure 8.12. How the popular PC video adapters use memory-address space in various modes of operation.

Similarly, the CGA card carries only 16KB of RAM, but its footprint is also 32KB. In this case, only one address line was ignored (A14).

In contrast to the MDA and CGA, an MGA card does decode all the address lines. It carries a full 64KB of RAM. Originally this was the *HGC* (*Hercules Graphics Card*) from Hercules, but now its functionality is available from many vendors, so it is more generically called the Monochrome Graphics Adapter. With that much RAM it can do higher resolution graphics than a CGA card and the good text of a monochrome card, but all in monochrome.

The MGA has two modes of operation in terms of memory footprint. In one, it uses the entire B page (addresses B0000h to BFFFFh). That mode, called *full page,* allows the CPU to put information into any location in its video image buffer directly. The other mode, called *half page,* disables the upper half of the video image buffer memory on the card. The MGC has the half-page mode to allow an MGC card to coexist with a CGA card (as an MDA can).

All the rest of the popular video display adapters can make themselves appear to the CPU exactly like the MDA, MGA, or CGA boards, depending on which video mode you select. That means they use either the lower or the upper half of the B page for image data in text mode. (Most commonly these cards will "wake up" in CGA or EGA text-emulation mode, and thus will use only the region from B8000h to BFFFFh.)

In every one of their native (graphics) video modes the EGA, MCGA, and VGA put their video image buffer into the CPU's memory address space starting at address A0000h. The same is true of all the super EGA, Super VGA clone video cards, and the XGA in its default state. (Remember, the XGA and some Super VGA cards can alternatively put their video-image buffer in extended memory, starting at any multiple of 1MB.)

In almost all cases these adapters restrict their footprint to the A page, thus allowing them to coexist with an MDA or MGA card (whose image buffer starts at the beginning of the B page). One exception is that some Super VGA cards, in certain super-modes (beyond normal VGA resolution or color depth or both) will use the full A and B pages. This maximizes the speed with which the CPU can update the screen in those modes. The significance of this is that you must not count on having the B0000h to B7FFFh region available for other uses if you are going to use any of those modes.

Another exceptional case is that some of the clone VGA cards in text mode will use a portion of the lower half of the B page to store font information in addition to storing the image data (characters and attributes) in the upper half of the B page. Again, this precludes using those cards in that fashion and having an MDA or MGA installed in the system.

Video Memory (ROM)

Every PC video display adapter has at least one ROM. Some have two. Every adapter uses a ROM to store font information so that it knows what character shapes to display when it is in text mode. Any display adapter that goes beyond the standards supported by the motherboard BIOS ROM will have an option ROM with additional BIOS routines in it. (That includes the EGA and VGA cards in most ISA bus machines, and the XGA in Micro Channel machines.)

The Font ROM

The *font ROM* can be accessed only by the video display adapter circuitry. It does not appear anywhere in the CPU's memory-address space. That would make it seem quite irrelevant to managing the rest of a PC's memory. For the most part that is true.

The exception is that some video displays, especially those with 16-bit or 32-bit data paths to the CPU memory bus, will copy the font data into an otherwise unused region of the image buffer for faster access. That still would not matter except that sometimes that region shows up on the CPU's memory address bus in the lower half of the B page. This is done to enable programs to change the current font anytime they want.

Video Option ROM

The other kind of video ROM is a very important one to understand when doing PC memory management. The motherboard BIOS ROM in early PCs contained routines to put images on-screen (the INT 10h family of sub-programs). These programs only knew how to do their jobs on either an MDA or a CGA display. To provide similar functionality for EGA and VGA displays, IBM included on those cards what they called an *option ROM*.

At boot time, an option ROM will install some program or programs within itself as the interrupt service routine(s) handling one or more interrupts. (The details of how this is done are explained in Chapter 10.) This is a handy way to augment the motherboard BIOS ROM, especially for devices you want to be able to use before the operating system has loaded from disk. Since the video system is needed to display progress and error messages during the boot process, it is especially important that it be fully supported from the outset.

The option ROM on EGA and early VGA cards was just 24KB. It was mapped into the CPU's memory address space from address C0000h to C5FFFh. Later VGA models needed more room for BIOS code, so the ROM was increased in size.

There was a small problem IBM had to deal with. They had previously marketed a video board called the *Professional Graphics Adapter*, or *PGA*. It had a small option ROM that was mapped starting at C6800h. To allow that adapter to coexist with a VGA, IBM split the VGA's ROM, addressing the lower part from C0000h to C5FFFh and the upper part starting at CA000h.

There are very few PGA adapters out there. And now there are a lot of SCSI host adapters and other option cards that prefer to put their option ROMs in the range from C8000h to CFFFFh. So now almost all VGA board makers have retreated back inside the lower half of the C page for their option ROM. Since they need all 32KB for their interrupt service routines, this means they are incompatible with PGA cards. But at this point, who cares?

The Bottom Line for Memory Management

The most important point to notice in all this is that (except for PCs that have only a monochrome and/or CGA display adapter and IBM PS/2 or close clones), almost every PC on the market has a video ROM that starts at C0000h (and it usually extends to C7FFFh). This is important because it means those addresses are taken up in addition to the ones used for the video-image buffer. When you set out to make good use of your PC's upper memory, you must allow for those preexisting uses of that space.

IBM's *PS/2* models are exceptions because they have full support for the VGA (or MCGA in the low-end models) circuitry in their regular motherboard BIOS ROM. So do a few clone PCs, though not many. Of course that merely shifts the problem around. The same code routines are somewhere, and you have to find out where and avoid trying to use those memory addresses twice.

A Curious Problem with
Some 16-Bit Video Cards (the MEMCS16 Line)

Some video cards can plug into any slot in any PC, XT, AT, or other ISA bus machine. These are called *8-bit video cards.* Others are 16-bit video cards and have the second card-edge tongue to engage the extra slot connector in some of the I/O slots of an AT (or higher model PC). (See Figure 14.4.) Those slots carry data 16 bits at a time and so are called *16-bit slots.* The slots without that extra connector can transfer data only 8 bits at a time; naturally they are called *8-bit slots.*

Growing in popularity are 32-bit slots called local busses. It takes a lot of information to describe every color and shade of every pixel on a monitor. For that reason, 8- and 16-bit slots cause terrible bottlenecks in the flow of information. Local busses, however, transfer data significantly faster. The speed is limited only by the system's clock speed. Recent video boards boast a throughput of more than 50 million pixels per second— 25 times the rate of standard VGA boards.

Some of the 16-bit video cards will work as if they were 8-bit video cards whenever they sense that they are plugged into an 8-bit slot. Others require that you put them in a 16-bit slot. Many of the 8- or 16-bit cards can be told to act as if they were 8-bit cards no matter what slot you plug them into.

Why should you care about all this? Well, first of all, a 16-bit data transfer goes twice as fast as an 8-bit one. So all else being equal, a 16-bit video card working in a 16-bit mode will have its screen images updated a lot faster than an 8-bit card. That is good.

But there is a dark side to this, and it is not well understood by most people in the industry. As a consequence, your new video card may work just fine, but some other card might stop working as soon as you plug in your new video card. Worse, when you try to find out what's going on you rapidly become quite confused. Even if you seek outside help, whoever you turn to might also be confused. Of course, now that you're reading this section you won't have to worry about that if you remember what you are reading.

The culprit is one of the design features of the AT, a feature that has been copied to all the clones, including 386 and 486 machines. This feature was, fortunately, altered in the design of the *PS/2* Micro Channel machines (models 50 and higher), in all EISA bus machines (though you only benefit from the change there if you use an EISA video card).

In an AT or other 16-bit ISA machine, each time the CPU addresses an option (plug-in) card, that card (whether it is a video card or not) is supposed to respond by telling the CPU whether or not it supports 16-bit data transfers. If it does, the CPU will read or write information two bytes at a time. If it does not, the CPU will transfer those two bytes one after another on the lower eight of the 16 data wires. (Actually the motherboard system logic listens for the cards' answers and tells the CPU what to do.)

This works just great if every option card knows when it is being addressed and only "speaks up" then. But that is impossible if you follow IBM's rules exactly.

There are 24 address lines in an AT's ISA bus (numbered SA0 to SA23). When the CPU puts information on those lines it takes just a little bit of time for the voltages to show up in the I/O slot connectors. The reason for this small delay is that during that time the motherboard system logic is latching that data. That is, the system logic takes just an instant to notice the voltages on the address lines coming out of the CPU and then set the voltages on the corresponding lines in the bus. (Latching also implies that the system logic can sustain those bus voltages even after the CPU stops putting out its address voltages, which is sometimes necessary.)

To give option cards a chance to figure out if a given data transfer operation involves them, some of the address lines are duplicated in an unlatched form. These lines deliver the address of the upcoming data transfer about 100 nanoseconds before the latched lines. These unlatched address lines are called LA17 through LA19.

IBM specifies that an option card shall look only at these unlatched lines to make up its mind whether or not it should tell the CPU it can support 16-bit data transfers. The reason for using only those lines is so the card can send back its response (on a line called MEMCS16) in time to influence the CPU for that upcoming data transfer.

The difficulty is that with only three unlatched address lines, every card in a 128KB region will think that any access to any place in that region could be an access to that card. Consider what happens if you have a 16-bit video card with a ROM at C0000h and an 8-bit disk controller card with a ROM at C8000h (or, for that matter, anywhere in the C or D pages). Such disk controller cards are far from rare, by the way.

When the CPU wants to send a message to the disk controller it will confuse the video card into thinking the message might be for it. So, if it follows the rules, the video card will assert MEMCS16 (put a signal on that line) to inform the CPU that it does, indeed, support 16-bit video transfers. Unfortunately the message was not meant for it. And the disk controller card does not support 16-bit transfers.

If the CPU was sending out two bytes, only the first one will be received. The disk controller, listening only on the lower eight data wires, will miss the second byte the CPU sent on the upper eight wires. Likewise, if the disk controller is supposed to send two bytes to the CPU it will only send one at first, planning to send the second one on a later data transfer. But the CPU will assume that whatever is on the upper eight data wires is that second byte. Either way is a potential disaster.

This is not a problem for Micro Channel or EISA machines (with EISA video cards) because those new, improved I/O busses include many more unlatched address lines. But it sure is a problem for ISA machines.

The solution (as is often the case in this somewhat chaotic industry, it seems) is for the video-card manufacturer to cheat. If they design their cards well enough, they can just barely get away with this cheat.

Once their card notices that the LA17 through LA19 lines suggest an upcoming data transfer might be intended for it, the card monitors the SA15 and SA16 lines very intently. As soon as those lines have had just barely enough time to get to their proper state, the video card reads that state and makes a more accurate determination of where this next data transfer is supposed to go.

If the data transfer is actually intended for that card, then and only then will the card assert MEMCS16. If it can do so within about 12 nanoseconds after the SA lines go to their final voltage, the motherboard system logic will hear the response. Or at least it will do so in about 80 percent of the systems on the market. If the video card takes as much as 18 nanoseconds, though, it will almost surely have gotten its message out too late.

While many 16-bit video cards use just this "cheat," some do not. If yours doesn't, be prepared for a lot of trouble.

> You have two easy ways out of this problem. One is to set the necessary jumper or switch on the card to disable all its 16-bit operations. The other is to get a disk controller that also can handle data transfers 16-bits at a time.

Option Card Memory, ROM and RAM

Other option cards besides video often have ROM or RAM on them. Again, the ROMs are usually filled with new BIOS routines to activate whatever hardware is on that card.

RAM is less often on a plug-in card, but it may be. For example, a network card might have a buffer there or a disk controller might have a cache. If the card simply uses that RAM for its internal purposes it is not an issue for PC memory management. If, however, it puts that RAM on the CPU's memory address bus, it is definitely an issue.

A disk controller's cache RAM is a good example of what you don't need to worry about. The CPU never knows it is exchanging information with some RAM instead of directly to or from the disk drive.

A network card's buffer RAM may or may not be a problem. Several cases occur. If the buffer is used only by some on-board coprocessor to assemble and disassemble message packets going in and out to the network, it's not an issue. If the RAM is attached to the CPU's memory bus so the CPU fills it with the message information to go out or reads incoming messages from it, it definitely is a part of your memory-management puzzle.

The worst case is when that RAM is not always attached to the bus. You cannot find it by looking, but suddenly it will appear. If in the meantime you have put some other RAM in that region of memory address space, watch out—a crash may be coming right up!

Upper Memory

There are at least two common definitions of *upper memory*. One says it is the memory address space (the collection of memory locations) from A0000h to FFFFFh (640KB to 1MB). By this definition, everything in the first megabyte that is not lower (system) memory is upper memory.

The other common use for the term *upper memory* is to refer only to RAM that is accessible in the range from 640KB to 1,024KB (1MB) and which is not already committed to some special purpose (such as a video-display card's image buffer).

How the Term Upper Memory Is Used in This Book

> In this book I will use the term upper memory to refer to the space (the first definition above). Any region of RAM that appears in this space and that is made available for use by programs under the control of some upper memory manager is an *upper memory block*. Any other RAM in that region is simply some upper memory RAM.

Other Names for Upper Memory

The name *upper memory* for this region was coined by Microsoft relatively recently. It is fast becoming an industry standard. To help reduce confusion I recommend that you, too, use this term exclusively to refer to this range of memory addresses.

Before Microsoft started calling it upper memory, other people needed to call it something. And they did—many different things. There are a plethora of names for upper memory. For example, IBM and Hewlett-Packard call it *reserved memory*, while Quarterdeck Office Systems calls it *high memory*. Larson and some others use the term *controller memory*. (That last name may have been limited to referring to the region between video and the motherboard system ROM BIOS.)

All of those terms are still being used, so you need to recognize them and understand what they mean. The only difficult one is *high memory*. This is difficult because around the same time Microsoft told us all to call this region *upper memory* it started using the term *high memory* for another, totally different region.

Quarterdeck's literature is unfortunately quite inconsistent on this point. They use the term *high memory* quite freely to mean *upper memory*, then when they need to talk about what is the new high memory they simply also call that *high memory*. One is reminded of *Through the Looking Glass* and Humpty Dumpty's insistence that words simply mean whatever he wants them to mean (at the moment). Most confusing.

Uses of Upper Memory

When they introduced the first PC, IBM reserved this region for uses other than RAM for holding programs. The first third was to be used by video cards for their image buffer memory. The last third was reserved for system ROMs. The middle third was just plain reserved (see Figure 8.4).

Because of this design announcement by IBM, almost no PC maker puts any of their general-purpose RAM in that region. Video RAM gets put there, but almost no other RAM. Still, with many PCs, if you know how, you can induce them to put RAM there, which you then can use however you wish.

When PCs were new, almost all of upper memory was unused. As much as 320KB of that 384KB might have had nothing in it.

Since that time a vast number of people have found really good reasons to use a portion of upper memory. Now it is getting almost as clogged as lower memory. Video display adapters now use all of the first 128KB, instead of just one-quarter of it as they did in the beginning.

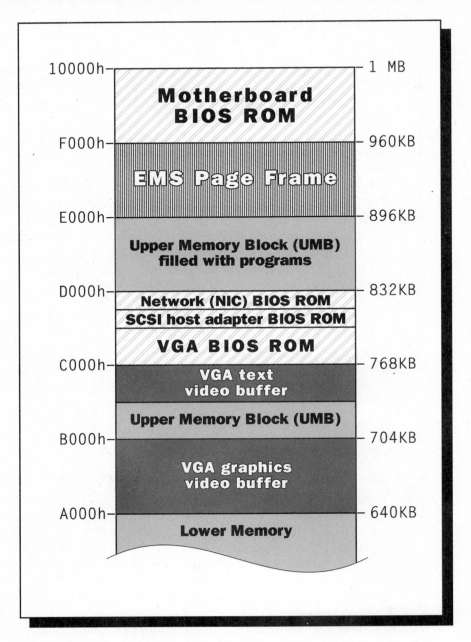

Figure 8.13. Upper memory and some typical uses for it.

System BIOS ROMs in some systems have grown all the way to 128KB. Those two developments shoot two-thirds of upper memory. Also, every option that requires an option ROM needs some of this real estate. And if you want EMS you'll have to find a contiguous 64KB of upper memory space that is empty, so you can put the EMS page frame there. Figure 8.13 shows a fairly typical view of upper memory in a modern PC.

But still, in many PCs, there are substantial portions of upper memory with nothing in them. Furthermore, with the latest innovations in memory-management techniques (for example, Quarterdeck's Stealth technology) it is possible to make much of what is in upper memory effectively disappear.

The Value of Upper Memory

The reason for all this crowding is the same as the reason that lower memory is so valuable. Between them, they comprise the first megabyte of the CPU's memory address space. And in real mode, that is the whole of the memory address space. (Well, almost. Read on a couple of sections for the singular exception.)

Extended Memory

Extended memory is the region of the CPU's memory address space above 1MB, or it is the RAM that is accessible at those addresses. This was something new with the introduction of the IBM *PC/AT*. No PC with an 8088 or 8086 CPU chip can have any of this stuff.

How come? Simple. The 80286 (used as the CPU of the AT) has more address lines than the 8088. Specifically it has 24 address lines, giving it a total memory address space size of 16MB.

But there's a catch. You can't get at any address beyond 1MB on an AT unless you go into something called *protected mode*. (The modes of the various Intel processors are described in detail in Chapter 11. All the members of Intel's 80x86 family are introduced in Chapter 13.)

Other Names for Extended Memory

The name *extended memory* comes from the notion that it is where you are if you extend the CPU's memory address space beyond its original 1MB limit. Makes a lot of sense. Unfortunately, that's not the only name by which you will hear it called. Here are a couple of the more confusing ones.

- Some people call it *linear memory.* (Don't confuse this with a *linear address,* please. The CPU computes a linear address from a **segment:offset** address, or in protected mode from the equivalent form, which is a **selector:offset** address. It does this for access to all regions of its memory-address space: lower, upper, high, and extended. And it does so in all its operating modes.)

- Perhaps the worst name for this memory region was coined by IBM. They called it *expansion memory.* Just try to keep that one and *expanded* memory straight in your mind! (They're totally independent ideas.)

Using Upper Memory:
The Problem and Some Early Solutions

DOS is a real-mode program. (After all, it was written for the original IBM *PC,* which uses an 8088 CPU chip and that has only that one operating mode.) So DOS knows nothing of extended memory, nor can it help programs use that space.

When IBM introduced the AT with its new extended memory, they had to think of something useful to do with that extra space. If they could, they could sell more memory chips.

What they came up with was VDISK. It is a fairly nice program that creates a virtual disk (now called generically a *RAM disk*) out of something else. If you have extended memory, it can use that. If you have expanded memory (and have loaded your expanded memory manager), it can use that. If you have neither, it can use some of your system memory.

You create a VDISK virtual disk by loading VDISK as a device driver in your CONFIG.SYS file. You give it some parameters to tell it what kind of memory to use and how much, and some other details.

You are not limited to creating just one virtual disk. You can have as many as you want. If you are taking the memory for them from system memory, VDISK will ask DOS for the memory it needs. DOS will check to be sure that there is that much memory available, and if so will allocate it to VDISK. If you are taking EMS memory, your EMM driver will do a similar thing.

But if VDISK is going to use extended memory, it is on its own. So IBM built into VDISK just enough smarts about extended memory to notice if another copy of itself had been loaded there first. VDISK does this by putting a small block of information laying claim to a certain amount of that memory at the beginning of each region of extended memory it is going to use.

VDISK uses extended memory from the bottom up. Each time you load another copy (by using another DEVICE= line in your CONFIG.SYS file), it walks over each previous instance of VDISK, finds the first unclaimed bit of extended memory, and there it sinks its claim flag.

(This is how the original versions of VDISK worked. It has been updated substantially starting with *PC DOS* version 4, and is now a much better neighbor to other users of extended memory.)

IBM introduced VDISK with *PC DOS*, version 3.0. When Microsoft shipped their version 3.0 of DOS, called *MS-DOS* 3.0, a few months later, they included a different RAM disk program. The Microsoft program was called RAMDRIVE. Like VDISK, RAMDRIVE can create a RAM disk out of system, EMS, or extended memory. It differs, though, in how it uses extended memory.

It knows about VDISK, so first it looks to see if VDISK has laid claim to any extended memory. Then it checks with the BIOS (through Interrupt 15h) to see what the address is of the top of extended memory. If there is enough space between the top of the VDISK-claimed regions and the top of extended memory, RAMDRIVE takes what it wants.

How it takes memory is what distinguishes it from VDISK. The differences are these: RAMDRIVE takes its memory from the top, and it hides what it has done from all programs that come along later by hooking INT 15h.

That means that whenever another program (which could be another copy of RAMDRIVE, or it could be almost anything else) asks the BIOS where the top of memory is, RAMDRIVE will get the request. It will ask the BIOS, and then after subtracting the portion it is using, return the corrected answer to the program that originally made the request.

Neither of these methods of allocating extended memory is really very good for anything other than permanent users like a RAM disk. Eventually someone came up with a better way to manage it, analogous to the way that DOS manages lower memory. It happened, but to understand that event fully you first must learn about yet another kind of memory space in your PC.

The High Memory Area

This is a special extra region of real-mode memory. It exists only on PCs in classes 3 through 6. PCs whose CPU is an 8088 or 8086 simply cannot have any of this memory space because they don't have enough address lines.

The high area extends from linear address 0FFFF0h to 10FFEFh. Notice that these are addresses with six hexadecimal symbols in them. That means there are 24 bits in these numbers. In the first of these addresses the leading symbol is a zero, so you could drop it. That would bring that number down to only 20 bits. But the ending address definitely has 21 significant bits in it.

At the start of this chapter, I made the point that IBM designed the AT especially to prevent it from accessing any addresses outside the first megabyte when it was in real mode. To do this they had to put in some special circuitry that would force the A20 line to stay in the low state. That meant that any attempt to move up past the 1MB limit would be converted into an access to a location in very low memory.

But for PCs in classes 3 to 6, if you simply turn off the special circuit that forces address wrapping to occur, the real-mode linear address (which is 16 times the segment value plus the offset) will be greater than 1M (which is 1,024K or 1,048,576) for sufficiently large segment values and offsets.

The address range for the high memory area (HMA), expressed in **segment:offset** form, is FFFF:0000 to FFFF:FFFF. Thus the segment value is the maximum possible, and the offset goes over its full range. In decimal notation the HMA runs from address 1,048,560 to 1,114,096. Such a small distance past 1MB, and yet it has proven to be so valuable.

> Some authors say the HMA starts at exactly the 1MB point. In that case, the starting address is FFFF:0010, or 1,048,576. This makes the size of the HMA exactly 16 bytes less than 64KB.

Address wrapping was included in the IBM *PC/AT*'s design for some very good reasons. But now there are better reasons for turning it off, at least at times. To insure that all your old programs which might have been written to assume that address wrapping would occur, it is generally prudent to leave the address-wrapping circuitry turned on except when a program particularly wants access to the HMA.

Getting Access to the HMA

You will also recall that the CPU was not involved in this address-wrapping game. It just computes the linear address in the normal manner. The motherboard system logic had to be built to enforce the rule, "Make A20 = 0 when the processor is in real mode." That means that you must ask that bit of logic circuitry not to do that if you want to get into the HMA.

How that can be done differs from machine to machine. Fortunately, although there are a lot of PC makers, there are relatively few system logic makers. That means that there are only a modest number of ways that the A20 line can be controlled.

This arcane knowledge was used by some program designers to allow their programs access to the High Memory Area. But the same problem arose as with VDISK's way of using extended memory. There was no central arbiter of who got to use that region of RAM. Now we have what are called XMS memory managers, and they are charged with that central responsibility. So the only people who must know how to access the A20 hardware controls are the people writing those memory managers.

High Memory Is and Is Not the Same as Extended Memory

This region looks like it is the first 64KB of extended memory. Indeed the linear addresses are the same and so are the chips you get to by going to those addresses. But in another sense, high memory is not the same as extended memory; it is accessed while the CPU is in real mode, and extended memory accesses require the CPU to be in protected mode (see Figure 8.14).

Managing the Formerly Unmanageable Spaces

Microsoft wrote another memory-management standard (called the *Extended Memory Specification*, or *XMS*) and a program to implement that standard. This standard gives an API for access to and use of the HMA. The Microsoft program to implement the XMS standard is HIMEM.SYS and Microsoft has given away copies of it with several versions of *Windows*, with *MS-DOS* 5 and 6, and to anyone who asked for a copy. IBM also included it with *PC DOS* 5 and 6. *DR DOS* 5 and 6 included that functionality in EMM286.SYS and HIDOS.SYS. (You should load only one or the other, but not both of these drivers).

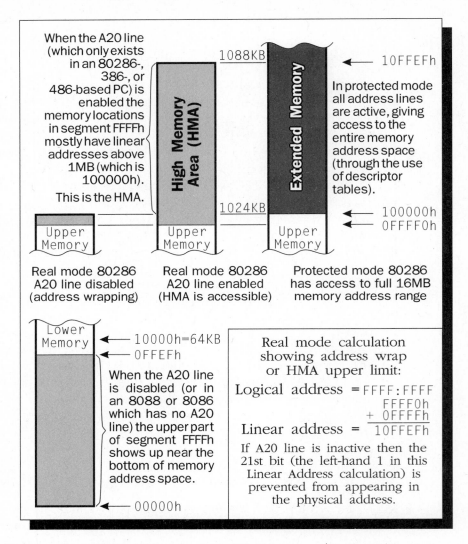

Figure 8.14. The High Memory Area (HMA), what and where it is. Notice that the HMA uses the same addresses and the same memory chips as the first 64KB of extended memory, but those two regions are accessed in totally different ways.

Actually HIMEM.SYS was not the first commercial use of the HMA. Quarterdeck Office Systems started using it with their QEXT.SYS program, an adjunct program to *DESQview.*

DOS manages lower memory. Upper memory did not, at first, need any managing because the only inhabitants of that region were the motherboard BIOS ROM and various option cards, each of which knew how to take care of itself.

Extended memory was not particularly well managed in the early days. And when the HMA became available, Microsoft realized it had to do something to help prevent chaos.

Furthermore, there is a clear potential for real trouble in the HMA. Notice that the memory chips that supply RAM to the HMA are exactly the same ones that supply the first 64KB of extended memory. The only difference is how you go about generating the same linear addresses and which processor mode you are in at the time.

Unless a unified method were developed for allocating both extended and high memory, programs would constantly be overwriting each other. While they were at it, Microsoft decided it was time to devise a method for managing any stray and available RAM in upper memory also.

Thus they built the XMS standard to do for upper, high, and extended memory roughly the same things that the EMS standard does for expanded memory. It gives programs a standardized way to request blocks of memory and to get access to those blocks. The manager program (in Microsoft's case for XMS that is HIMEM.SYS) mediates all requests and makes sure only one program gets to have access to any given block of memory.

Using the HMA

The XMS specification says that if a program asks for the HMA it will get all of it or none of it. It can't get any of the HMA if that memory is already in use as extended memory (called an *XMS block* (or an EMB for *extended memory block*) if it is allocated by the XMS memory manager). It also can't get the block if another program has previously asked the XMS manager for and been given access to the HMA.

There is an undocumented exception to the rule that only one program at a time can use the HMA. If DOS is resident in the HMA (which will be the case if you are using DOS 5 or 6 and have a line DOS=HIGH in your CONFIG.SYS file), then it will support an undocumented interrupt call that allows programs to find out if there is any leftover space in the HMA, and to get that space if there is any.

The only program to use that feature to date has been Microsoft's mouse driver, MOUSE.COM, and then only in versions 8.0 and 8.1 of that program. Apparently, this technique caused some problems with certain clone PCs, so Microsoft quit using it.

Another partially documented exception applies to DR DOS 6. It manages the HMA by the use of a memory control block chain, just as it manages lower memory. Normally programs don't get loaded into the HMA any time after DR DOS first uses it, but they could.

Finally, you can tell the XMS manager not to give away the HMA to any program that wants less than a specified amount of it. This last provision is an attempt to keep from wasting the HMA on a program that will only benefit from a small part of it and then later deny access to a program that could have used more of it.

Even when a program owns the HMA, it must ask the XMS manager to open and close the A20 gate by deactivating and reactivating the address wrap circuitry. This is done so that knowledge of how to do that operation can be built into the XMS manager, and no application program has to find out how to do it.

The XMS document suggests that programmers keep the A20 gate closed and locked almost all the time. It says that good programming practice would be to open the gate, reach in and get or put whatever information you need to transfer, and then immediately close the gate again. Doing this does take a little bit of extra time, but they point out that it adds safety, since if in the meantime some other program came along (perhaps getting control of the PC via some interrupt), it could come to grief if it expected to find address wrapping enabled and it was not.

An Interesting Observation

Microsoft wrote that rule. And Microsoft broke it. *MS-DOS* 5 and 6 leave the A20 gate open almost all the time. Why would they do this? And how can they get away with it? (IBM's *PC DOS* 5 and 6 do this also.)

Why did they do this? Perhaps to get just that little extra bit of speed. And maybe it was not such a little bit, when you consider that *MS-DOS* 5 and 6 keep the disk buffers and a significant part of the DOS kernel program code in the HMA.

How can they get away with it? They're not talking for the record on this point. It appears that they must have decided simply to copy those things in the lowest 64KB of memory that they thought programs might try to get at by address wrapping to locations in the HMA exactly 1MB above their normal locations. Then whether address wrapping is on or off those programs will get whatever it is they are after.

This technique, if it is what they are using, has two obvious drawbacks. One is that it uses some portion of what is already a pretty small, but valuable region, simply to duplicate information that is stored elsewhere. That is space inefficient. They'd better be saving a lot of time to make that trade-off worthwhile. The other disadvantage is that it seems unlikely that they could have anticipated all the information that every possible program would try to access by address wrapping. And a failure to do so totally could lead to some unpredictable events.

Why might Microsoft have thought they could be sure this would work? Well, in terms of what the EXEPACK program decompressor wants, they wrote that one so they know exactly what it needs. Early versions of *AutoCAD* used address wrapping. Maybe it looks for the same things as the EXEPACK decompressor. Or maybe Microsoft is counting on all *AutoCAD* users having already upgraded to a more recent version.

Still, there almost certainly are some other programs out in the world that depend on address wrapping for some purpose Microsoft did not imagine. Running one of them on a PC that is being managed by *MS-DOS* or *PC DOS* 5 or 6 could lead to some hard-to-find problems.

A Recap

In this chapter you learned about a number of important concepts, including many that are among the most confusing to a large number of PC users. The first important concept is that of a *logical space*. This is something quite different from physical space. In a PC, there are several important logical spaces. The most important of these is the CPU's memory address space. The I/O port-address space is next. Also described briefly were the DMA and IRQ spaces.

The simple rule for converting a real-mode **segment:offset** address into the equivalent linear address was next. This led to a discussion of address wrapping and the mysterious extra space called the High Memory Area that you can get at in PCs of classes 3 to 6 if you turn off address wrapping.

This chapter also defined a lot of jargon. You learned about many terms for both various quantities of memory (such as *bank, paragraph, page,* and *segment*) and you learned about the five principal kinds of memory in a PC (classified by their accessibility or use), namely *system, upper, high,* and *extended memory* that are all accessed at fixed regions of the CPU's memory address space, and *expanded memory*, which exists outside that memory address space except as pieces of it are brought into that space temporarily.

System (also called *lower* or *conventional*) *memory* and *upper memory* are the most precious kinds of memory in a PC. That is because DOS can run programs contained in those regions. The High Memory Area is also important, but of limited usefulness both because it is small and because of the restrictions Microsoft imposed on how it can be used.

Expanded memory can supplement the real-mode memory spaces, allowing programs to store and retrieve many megabytes of information without leaving real mode or incurring the delays inherent in accessing a disk drive.

Extended memory was the last kind of memory to be effectively put to use. Mostly this is because DOS itself only understands real mode, so it cannot get at nor can it manage extended memory. Now, however, with DOS extended programs, and with protected mode operating environments running on top of DOS, extended memory is becoming as useful as lower and upper memory (and for Windows users, much more useful).

A key point in the discussion of upper memory is that just having the upper memory space does not mean you have any RAM there. Chapter 9 tells you some of the techniques by which you can put some there. That chapter also introduces you to a number of other ways that memory and storage can be used interchangeably.

9

MUTABLE MEMORY

This chapter discusses how you can sometimes use different kinds of memory and storage interchangeably. However, before it does that, it explains what the motherboard system logic is and how its workings can affect memory management.

You have learned how memory and storage differ. Now you will learn how you can use one form of information-holding mechanism (RAM or disk storage) as if it were the other kind. Of even more use to many will be learning how you can sometimes convert one kind of memory into another kind of memory (for example, extended into expanded).

Doing these things is often the easiest or cheapest way to get what you want from what you already have. But there are drawbacks to most schemes that you must clearly understand if you are to avoid some bitter disappointments.

Before learning how to convert memory, it may help you to know how the memory portion of your PC is built. Along the way, you will learn how different parts of your PC's RAM get interpreted as lower, upper, high, or extended memory. This is just one of the things done by your PC's motherboard system logic.

Motherboard System Logic

The motherboard of your PC holds many different essential parts. In most PC models, this includes:

- The central processor (the 80x86 CPU chip)
- A socket for a math coprocessor
- Main RAM
- I/O slots
- The keyboard controller
- Direct Memory Access (DMA) controller
- Interrupt controller
- Real-time clock and setup data storage
- System clock
- The main ROM BIOS chips

  Some designs add to the preceding one or more of the following:

- Serial port controller
- Parallel port controller
- Floppy disk controller

- Mouse port
- Video display adapter
- Network adapter

The earliest PCs were built at a time when it was not possible to cram this much functionality on one circuit card. That meant that many of these functions, in particular those on the second list, had to be provided on plug-in option cards.

As the art of electronic circuit fabrication advanced, it became possible to put more and more on the motherboard. This was clearly advantageous in some situations, and disadvantageous in others. Makers of portable and laptop computers, in particular, found it desirable to put as many functions on the motherboard as possible. Even in desktop computers, doing that gives one advantage: It makes the whole system less expensive.

But there are also some disadvantages to putting as many functions as possible on the motherboard. It locks users into buying just the combination of functions put there by the manufacturer. The power of user choice is diminished. Also it makes upgrading the PC harder.

So we now have two competing trends. One is toward ever more integration of "standard" features into PC motherboards. The other is toward the modular PC in which one can alter major aspects of that PC by the simple expedient of exchanging one or more modules.

In particular, the CPU and math coprocessor socket, and sometimes main RAM, may be put on plug-in cards that go into one or more special slot(s), not just one of the regular I/O slots. This is done to make it easier to upgrade the processor and the speed or amount of main memory. The special slots are needed because the CPU has to be able to communicate with the RAM, and perhaps with some other parts of the PC at higher speed and perhaps over a wider data path, than the I/O bus allows. Wherever these functional parts may be located, they must somehow communicate with one another. That is where the "system logic" comes in. In the original IBM *PC*, this was approximately one hundred tiny integrated circuit chips. Each one did some elemental logic task, and could be bought out of a catalog of standard small-scale integrated circuit (SSI) and medium-scale integrated circuit (MSI) chips. More modern designs have replaced almost all of these standard parts with just one or a few custom designed very large-scale integrated circuit (VLSI) chips.

Whether the functional parts are all on the motherboard or not, usually the system logic is. Because of this, it is often called the *motherboard system logic*, a name which will be used many times in this book.

Whether the system logic is a large number of standard chips or a few specially designed ones, this collection of parts forms the "glue" that makes all the pieces of your PC work together. This notion leads to one of the other names you will sometimes see for it, *glue logic*. (This odd-sounding name is the standard jargon used by electronic circuit designers.)

Finally, since you usually see this functionality embodied in one or a few VLSI chips, and these chips are normally sold as a matched set by their maker, the motherboard system logic is also often called the PC's *chip set.*

Why You Need Motherboard System Logic

Most of the ICs (integrated circuit chips) in your PC need help communicating with each other and with the various peripheral parts of the PC. The system logic provides that needed help.

For example, one IC may need to send a signal to many other chips, but the sending chip may not be able to supply enough power to serve all the receiving chips. The system logic can "buffer" that signal. This means it will amplify the signal to make it strong enough to be able to drive all the receiving chips. This is especially important for the signals destined for the I/O slots, but it also applies to the signals driving the main RAM chips.

The information that comes out of a chip may need to be held temporarily for use somewhat later. That can be done with a "latch" circuit in the system logic. This approach is also useful for stretching a signal that occurs as a very brief pulse into a longer persisting one. This ensures that the circuits that need to see that signal will have time to do so accurately.

Sometimes one wire on a chip is used to supply or receive different information at different times (called *multiplexing*). Often this is done to keep the number of wires coming out of the chip to a minimum. You will learn how this is used inside your PC's memory chips in just a moment.

A pin on a chip that is multiplexed will very likely need to be switched by the external circuitry between two different sources of information at different times. Again, this is a job for the system logic.

One of the most important jobs the motherboard system logic does (and the reason this section is in this chapter) is decoding memory addresses. Decoding memory addresses means that it selects which groups of memory chips shall respond to the signals from the CPU.

In the following section, you will get to look at that last part of what the system logic does in a little more detail. Once you understand how it works, you will also have at least a general notion of what else the system logic does.

Memory-Address Decoding

The CPU has a number of address lines (20, 24, or 32 wires, depending on which member of the Intel 80x86 processor family your PC uses), some data lines (8, 16, or 32 wires), and some control lines. If you had one monster memory chip that had the same number of address lines and data lines as the CPU, plus suitable control lines and all the RAM you wanted, you could simply connect the two chips together and that would be that, so far as your PC's RAM was concerned.

Things are almost never that simple in a PC. But they are not so complicated that you can't understand them with a little effort.

Common Memory Chip Designs

The most commonly used memory chips hold just one bit of information for each of some large number of addresses. When the IBM *PC* was first designed, affordable memory chips (DRAMs) could hold at most 16K bits. Soon afterwards, 64K-bit and then 256K-bit chips came on the market. Now 1MB and 4MB chips are common and the 16M-bit chips are almost here. Figure 9.1 displays some common memory chip configurations.

Consider for a moment a 64K-bit chip. There have been various models made, but consider for the moment one popular design, the 4164. I'll use this chip as the example design repeatedly throughout the discussion in this section. The memory in this chip is organized as 64K locations, each holding one bit. Thus, this is a "64K by 1" chip.

Some other memory chip designs have four or eight data bit input pins. Naturally, if they store four or eight bits at a given memory address, and yet still have only 64K bits of total storage, they must have only 16K or 8K locations, respectively. (And so they are called "16K by 4" or "8K by 8" chips.) These chip designs are used in certain systems, but the most commonly used designs in PCs store only one bit per address location. Nibble-wide chips (x4 organization) are used in video memory and on some SIMMs. Byte-wide memory chips are almost always ROMs or PROMs.

A lot of modern PCs use DRAM memory modules. These are small circuit boards carrying several integrated circuit DRAM memory chips. While the module may supply 9 (see Figure 9.2) or even as many as 72 bits, the chips are mostly either single bit wide chips or, at most, nibble (4 bit) wide chips.

Not only is information inside a RAM chip said to be "organized" in a particular way, the total collection of RAM chips is also organized. The organization of the collection is into what are called "banks" of memory. A bank is defined as the collection of RAM chips that supplies all the bits of data accessed by the CPU when there is one memory address supplied to the address bus. Figure 9.3 displays memory bank configurations for the different classes of PC. This means that there are as many bits at each memory address in a bank as there are data wires coming out of the CPU. Figure 9.3 does not include the special case of Pentium-based PCs. Unlike all other Class 6 PCs, these computers have a 64-bit wide data bus, and thus their banks of memory will have twice as many chips as is shown for Class 6 PCs in Figure 9.3.

Thus a bank of memory for a class 1 or 2 PC will have only 8 bits (really 9 bits including parity) per location, while that for a class 6 PC will have 32 bits of data (36 bits including the one parity bit for each of the four bytes of data). Class 6 PCs that use a Pentium CPU chip have banks that are 64 bits wide—twice the width of any other Class 6 PC. Parity is a means of helping catch errors before they can do you any harm. See Chapter 16 for a further discussion of parity.

You must have full banks of memory in your PC. A partial bank just won't work. But even a full bank is often not enough. Many PCs have several banks of RAM as well as one or more banks of ROM.

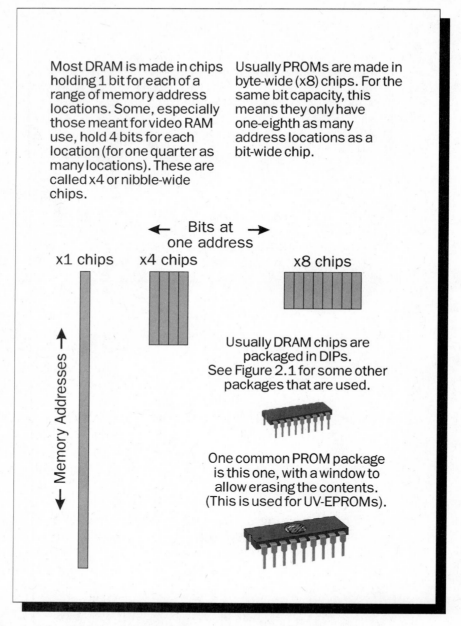

Most DRAM is made in chips holding 1 bit for each of a range of memory address locations. Some, especially those meant for video RAM use, hold 4 bits for each location (for one quarter as many locations). These are called x4 or nibble-wide chips.

Usually PROMs are made in byte-wide (x8) chips. For the same bit capacity, this means they only have one-eighth as many address locations as a bit-wide chip.

Bits at one address

x1 chips   x4 chips   x8 chips

Memory Addresses

Usually DRAM chips are packaged in DIPs. See Figure 2.1 for some other packages that are used.

One common PROM package is this one, with a window to allow erasing the contents. (This is used for UV-EPROMs).

Figure 9.1.   RAM and ROM chips may be "organized" in different ways.

Since PCs almost always use RAM in banks that are multiples of 9 bits (some number of bytes with a parity bit for each byte), a popular form of RAM now sold is the Single Inline Memory Module (SIMM). Here is a SIMM that has nine SOJ chips. If each chip holds 1M bit this will be a 1M-byte (x9) SIMM.

Other SIMM designs hold 8 bits per memory location, or 18, or 36 bits. The x8 modules are used for video (and in Macintosh computers). The others are used to provide full banks of RAM with parity for 16-bit or 32-bit computers.

Figure 9.2.   Sometimes RAM comes in modules called SIMMs.

Memory chips are designed to accommodate this fact. By having some connections that can be used to selectively put the chip to sleep or wake it up, you can connect many banks of chips to the CPU and arrange to have only the appropriate bank of them active at any one time.

Here are the details on how this is done. Memory chips have four kinds of connections to the outside world. (These are the pins or legs that come out of the integrated circuit and plug into a socket, or are soldered to a circuit board.)

Data Pins: This is where the information to be stored goes in, and where it comes out again when it is being read.

Address Pins: These lines are used to point to the memory cell inside the chip that actually holds the data.

Control Pins: The signals on these pins are used to activate portions of the internal circuitry, steer signals, and otherwise control everything that goes on in the chip.

Power Pins: Every memory chip needs electrical power to operate.

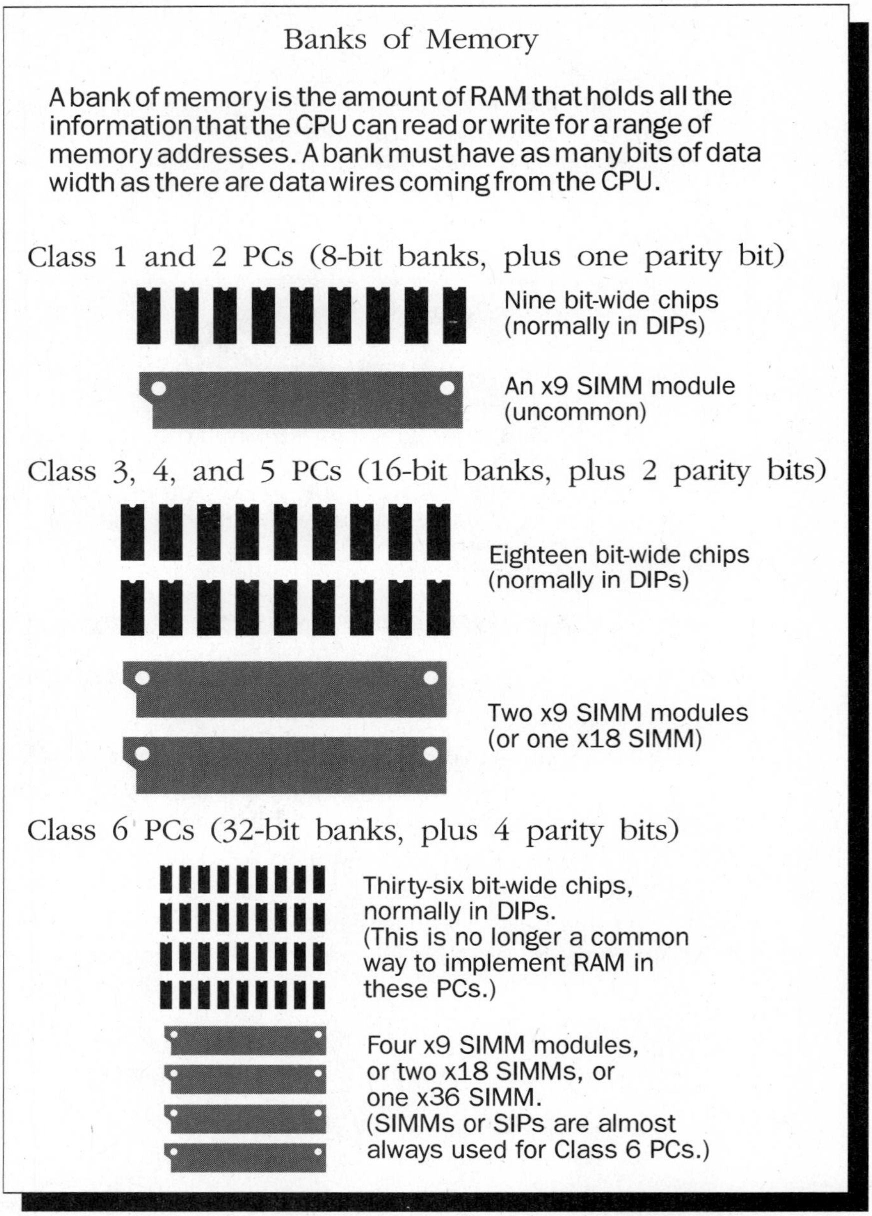

Banks of Memory

A bank of memory is the amount of RAM that holds all the information that the CPU can read or write for a range of memory addresses. A bank must have as many bits of data width as there are data wires coming from the CPU.

Class 1 and 2 PCs (8-bit banks, plus one parity bit)

Nine bit-wide chips
(normally in DIPs)

An x9 SIMM module
(uncommon)

Class 3, 4, and 5 PCs (16-bit banks, plus 2 parity bits)

Eighteen bit-wide chips
(normally in DIPs)

Two x9 SIMM modules
(or one x18 SIMM)

Class 6 PCs (32-bit banks, plus 4 parity bits)

Thirty-six bit-wide chips,
normally in DIPs.
(This is no longer a common
way to implement RAM in
these PCs.)

Four x9 SIMM modules,
or two x18 SIMMs, or
one x36 SIMM.
(SIMMs or SIPs are almost
always used for Class 6 PCs.)

Figure 9.3. Banks of memory in different classes of PC.

Since the memory chip you are studying (the 4164), like most DRAM chips, only stores one bit of data for any given location, it only needs to have one pin for data going into the chip. As it happens, there are actually two data pins. One handles data coming in (write operations) and the other data going out (read operations).

One more pin is used to tell the chip whether it is supposed to store a bit of information found by looking at the **D**ata **I**n (DI) pin, or supply a bit of information on the **D**ata **O**ut (DO) pin. This third pin is called the **R**ead or **W**rite pin (R/W).

On circuit diagrams and in books about PCs, you may see these line designations written with a line over them, with a trailing # sign, or with a trailing tilde. Any of these designations (or conventions) indicate that the line is "active low." That means that it performs its indicated function when the voltage on that line is near zero volts (less than about 0.8 volts), and it does not do so when that voltage is substantially above zero (around 2 volts is typical in the latter case).

Any line whose label does not carry the special mark (overline, pound sign, or tilde) indicates a signal that is "active high." This means that it is in its active state when the voltage is high (more than 1.6 volts) and that it is inactive when the voltage on that line is low (less than 0.8 volts).

You will often read or hear of a line being "asserted." That simply means to put a voltage on that line corresponding to its active state (near zero for lines that are active low, or near 2 volts for lines that are active high). Putting the opposite voltage on a line de-asserts that signal.

Thus the **D**ata **I**n line and **D**ata **O**ut lines, which are written *DI* and *DO*, are active high. When they are at a high voltage (about 2 volts), they indicate a binary one. When they are near zero volts, they indicate a binary zero.

The R/W# line can be viewed two ways. As a read line it is active high. As a write line it is active low. Thus when the voltage on this line is high, the chip is giving data to the CPU (which is reading it). When the voltage on this line is low, the chip is taking data from the CPU (which is writing to it).

Sometimes this line is simply labelled *W#*. That is okay, because if the chip isn't in write mode, it will be in read mode. (That is, when *W#* is de-asserted, *R* is being asserted.)

Since there are 2^{16} locations within a "64K by 1" chip at which a bit of information may be stored, you need to give the chip a 16-bit address to specify which location you want to access. You might have thought that the manufacturers would, therefore, put in 16 more pins for address information. That, it turned out, was too expensive, so it is not how DRAM chips are normally built.

Some faster memory chips need to have all their address lines available to the outside world constantly so that the address being given to them can be changed as quickly as possible. For them, the expense of the larger packages is justified.

Not only are the chips cheaper to make when they are put into smaller packages, using smaller chips also saves money for the PC manufacturers, since these chips take up less room on the circuit boards. So for both of these reasons, the manufacturers of these 64K-bit chips decided to divide the 16 address lines they needed inside their chips into two groups of eight each. Then they built multiplexing circuitry into these chips so only one of these sets would be attached to the external address pins at a time. That let them get away with only eight address pins.

This approach did mean that they needed some way for the external circuitry to indicate to a chip whether the address on the address pins was meant for the first group of internal address lines (called the *row address lines*) or the second group (called the *column address lines*). This was done in these memory chips by supplying them with two more pins, one called the **R**ow *Address Strobe* (RAS) and one called the *Column Address Strobe* (CAS).

Here are some variations on pin names you may encounter: *Data In* may simply be written with *Data Out* as (Q). The Read/Write line is sometimes called **W**rite **E**nable (WE). The RAS line is sometimes called the Refresh line (RE). (Chapter 16 includes a discussion of what "refreshing a DRAM" means and why it is needed.)

The idea is that the external circuitry (in the case of a PC, the system logic) is to put eight of the address bits on the address pins, assert the RAS pin, and then put another eight bits on the address pins and assert the CAS pin. When all four of these steps have been done, the memory chip knows which cell it is to access.

Finally, you need to supply some power to the chip. It doesn't work at all unless you do. All modern memory chips are built to use as few power wires as possible, which is two (one for plus five volts and one for zero volts, also called *ground*).

Add them up and this is what you get:

- Two pins for data
- One pin for R/W#
- Eight pins for addressing
- Two pins for RAS and CAS
- Two pins for power

You end up with 15 pins. The usual IC package at the time these chips were designed was a dual in-line package, or DIP (see Figure 9.1). These packages always have an even number of pins. The package commonly in use at the time had either 14 or 16 pins. So the 64K-bit memory chips were put in 16-pin packages with one pin left not connected to anything inside the chip.

The manufacturers of ICs are always improving their products. For memory chip makers, that usually means they are managing to stuff more bits inside a single chip. Soon after the 64K-bit chips were introduced, the next generation, the 256K-bit chips, arrived. These new chips need 18 bits of address information.

The manufacturers of these new chips were able to package them in the same 16-pin packages as the earlier models. They only needed to use the one remaining pin as an extra address pin. This was true, even though they now needed two more bits of address information, since that 16th pin was used twice; once for a row address bit and once for a column address bit.

Still newer generations have needed to use larger packages to get enough pins. The current 1M-bit, 4M-bit, and the upcoming 16M-bit and 64M-bit chips all fit very nicely into 20-pin packages, with some of the 1M-bit and 4M-bit ones being put in 18-pin packages.

Memory-Address Decoding

Now you can see how a memory chip can store a large number of bits in an equally large number of different address locations. But there is more to the story. The addresses covered by any one physical bank of chips are almost never the full address range of the CPU.

In the case of 64K-bit chips in a bank holding 64K bytes of information, you have only accounted for 16 of the address wires coming from the CPU. You know that for the microprocessors used in PCs, there are at least 20 address wires (and maybe as many as 32). How do you use the rest of them?

The "extra" address wires in the bus are used to decide in which bank of memory chips a given memory address can be found. If the address is somewhere within the range of addresses assigned to a certain physical bank of chips, the external circuitry must somehow enable these chips to do their work. Otherwise, it must disable them. As it happens, that job is also done using the CAS pin (in a proper time relationship to the assertion of the RAS pin). In this role (especially on ROMs and EPROMs), the CAS pin is sometimes called by different names: chip enable (CE), chip select (CS), or output enable (OE) are some common choices.

Notice that this means the system logic must combine anywhere from 4 to 16 address lines into one control line. This is the bank-selecting function, which is the part of memory-address decoding done by the motherboard system logic. Once the correct bank of chips has been selected, the rest of the decoding of the address to point to the actual locations of each of the bits is done inside the chips in that bank.

A Practical Example

Take a look at a practical example of the complete RAM layout for a PC. This is not the memory organization used in the original IBM *PC*, nor the original IBM *PC/XT* (neither of them could hold this much memory on the motherboard), but it was used in the later XT models, and it has been used in many clone PCs.

This memory organization is designed to supply exactly 640KB of RAM. You cannot supply that amount in one bank of chips, but it can be done quite nicely with four banks. Figure 9.4 shows one possible way such a memory system might be built.

This diagram is simplified quite a lot. It does not show, for example, the R/W# line or the RAS and CAS lines, nor are the separate Data In and Data Out pins shown for the memory chips. Also, the details of how the address line multiplexor and the bank-select logic work are left out. It does show, however, the essential features of address decoding as they are commonly done in PCs.

The banks of memory chips are arranged in this figure very much as they are in late model IBM *PC/XTs* and in many clone PCs. Banks 0 and 1 use nine 256K-bit (256Kx1) chips per bank, so each bank holds 256KB with parity. Banks 2 and 3 use nine 64K-bit (64Kx1) chips per bank, so each bank holds 64KB with parity.

The address-line multiplexor is an arrangement of electronic circuits that works like nine two-position switches, all working together. The first nine even-numbered address lines (A0, A2, A4, . . . , A16) go to one side of those nine switches. The first nine odd-numbered address lines (A1, A3, A5, . . . , A17) go to the other side of those same switches. When the multiplexor is in the **Row** position, the odd-numbered address lines get presented to the memory chips. When it is in the **Column** position, the even-numbered ones are connected to the memory chips.

The top four address lines (A16 through A19) go to the bank select logic circuit. There is a subtle point here. Notice that lines A16 and A17 go both to opposite sides of one of the nine switches in the multiplexor and to the bank select logic. Also follow the lines carefully and you will see that the output of that ninth multiplexor switch goes to the memory chips in Banks 0 and 1, but not to the chips in Banks 2 and 3. (This matches with the fact that the 256K bit memory chips have nine address pins while the 64K bit chips have only eight.)

Here is how the system works.

- The CPU puts a 20-bit address on the bus. (That means it raises some address lines to about 2 volts, to indicate binary ones, and holds others near zero volts, to indicate binary zeros.)

- If it is going to write a byte of data to memory, it also puts that byte on the data lines. If it is going to read a byte from memory, it must do nothing with the data lines yet; later on, it will read the data byte from them, after the memory chips have put it there.

- The bank-select logic looks at the high four address lines.

  If the top two lines (A18 and A19) both have a low voltage on them (indicating that the most significant two bits in the address are zeros), then the memory address must be in the bottom quarter of the first megabyte of memory (between 0 and 256KB). That means the address is in Bank 0. So the bank select logic activates the CE (chip enable) line for Bank 0, and keeps all the other three CE lines in their inactive state.

If the top line (A19) was zero (which means the address is in the bottom half of the first megabyte) and the next to top line (A18) was a one (so the address is in the top half of that bottom half of the megabyte), that would signal a location in the second quarter (between 256KB and 512KB). And, in that case, Bank 1 is activated.

If both the top address lines are ones, it means the address is in the top quarter of the megabyte (between 768KB and 1,024KB). In that case, none of the banks is activated. That is an address in upper memory.

The most complex case is when A19 and A18 are 1 and 0, respectively. That means an address in the range 512KB to 768KB. Not only is half of this range beyond 640KB, but if the address is in the other half, you must decide whether it goes to Bank 2 or Bank 3. This means the logic must look at both A17 and A16. See if you can convince yourself that Figure 9.4 gives the correct conditions for activating Banks 2 and 3.

Once the bank select logic has activated the correct bank of memory chips (and deactivated the other banks) and the multiplexor switches are set to the **Row** position, the system logic will assert the RAS line for all the memory chips. (Only the active ones, those in the selected bank, will respond.) That makes the active memory chips "latch" (remember) the row address.

Next the system logic switches the multiplexor to the **Column** position and then asserts CAS. This gives the active memory chips the rest of the address. Each chip in the active bank now knows which bit within it is being addressed. Depending on the state of the R/W# line, it will either read a bit from one of the data lines and store it in the indicated cell, or it will read a bit from the indicated cell and put it on a data line.

That explains how the eight data bits get into memory from the CPU or from memory back to the CPU. What about the ninth column of chips (on the right in Figure 9.4)? They are the parity chips.

When data is being written from the CPU to memory, the data byte goes both to the memory chips and to the Parity Generator/Comparator chip (near the top-right corner of Figure 9.4). The Parity Generator/Comparator chip generates one bit of parity information appropriate to the byte to be stored in memory. (PCs use odd parity, which means that between the eight data bits and the one parity bit there must be an odd number of binary ones.) It presents that bit on the ninth data line, from which it gets stored into the parity chip just as the other eight bits get stored into the other eight chips of that bank.

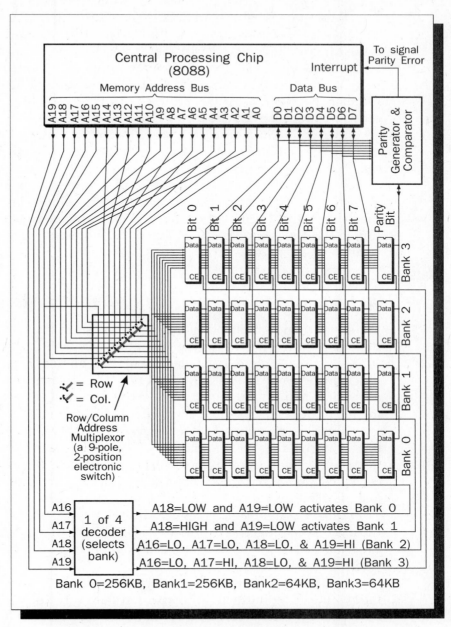

Figure 9.4. An example of memory-address decoding (see text for details).

When data is being read from memory, the first eight bits go directly to the CPU, and they also go to the Parity Generator/Comparator. The ninth bit goes just to the Parity Generator/Comparator. Those nine bits are examined in that chip and if an odd number of them are binary ones, then parity is good and the comparator chip does nothing. But if an even number of bits are zeros, the parity is bad. In that case the comparator chip sends an interrupt signal to the CPU to let it know that something is amiss.

Everything in Figure 9.4, except the actual banks of memory chips and the 8088 CPU chip, is a part of the motherboard system logic, as are many of the other parts that are not shown (such as the buffers for the data and address lines, the RAS and CAS signal generators, and so on).

All of this hardware (to do bank-select decoding, and to then direct the proper signals into the memory chips and handle the RAS and CAS timing signals) is just a portion of what the motherboard system logic has to do.

The Role of System Logic in Memory Management

The system logic is built in a fashion that allows it to do at least all the things that are required for the normal operation of your PC. If you want to do some aggressive memory management, you might like to have the system logic do some things it does not normally do. Sometimes it can.

For example, you might like to have it *not* decode some of the lower memory addresses, even if you have RAM chips there.

The reason you might like to have it do this is that then you could plug a hardware expanded memory card into a slot in the I/O bus. Since the memory address, data, and control lines all go to those slots, this board could respond as if it were a bank of memory at the addresses which you just disabled for the motherboard RAM. But since the plug-in card is an EMS card, it will be able to switch different pages of EMS memory into those address ranges at different times. This, and a suitable controlling program such as *DESQview*, makes it possible for you to do very effective multitasking even with a mere PC.

Just turning off address decoding for a range of lower memory is a fairly tame thing for the motherboard system logic to do. Mind you, it is beyond the normal operation, but not by much.

A much more dramatic extension of its normal operation is when the system logic is able to decode upper memory addresses and use them to activate additional RAM beyond that needed to fill lower memory. (This assumes, of course, that your motherboard has more than 640KB of RAM on it.)

One use for this upper memory RAM would be as a place to put programs. Another would be to create the effect of an expanded memory card. A third use, called shadow RAM, is when the system logic copies the information from a ROM into some RAM, disables the ROM and enables the RAM (now write-protected) for the same address range. The RAM will work just like the ROM, only it often can do so much faster. (Chapter 21 describes the first of these possibilities. Chapter 8 describes expanded memory and the LIM EMS standards. Chapter 20 gives more details on shadow RAM.)

Or, in some really wonderful PCs, the system logic can flexibly decode any range of addresses and for each one activate any of the banks of motherboard RAM, choosing which one to activate based on the contents of some programmable bank-select registers. That allows a full emulation of the LIM 4.0 EMS standard for expanded memory.

Not all system logic chip sets are able to do any of these things. If yours is, then either by selecting some options in your PC setup program or by running a suitable memory manager, you may be able to take advantage of those possibilities.

This suggestion for converting some ordinary motherboard RAM into EMS memory is getting us into the area of mutable (changeable) memory. Now I shall describe all the possibilities in a more systematic fashion.

Creating Expanded Memory from Other Kinds of Memory or Storage

In the last chapter, you learned about the many different kinds of memory that you can have in a PC. In particular, you learned that you could store programs and data in lower, upper, expanded, and extended memory (and sometimes in the High Memory Area). That is, you could do these things if you had these kinds of memory.

All PCs come with at least some lower memory, and many of them also have some high and extended memory. They usually don't come with expanded or upper memory. But what if expanded or upper memory is what you need? You could, of course, go buy an EMS memory card. But sometimes you can do just as well or better in a different way.

Why Would You Want to Do This?

Until quite recently, most software authors who wanted their programs to have access to more than 640KB of memory turned to expanded memory. There are two reasons for this:

- To make their programs usable by anyone, no matter which class of PC they had.

- To be able to stay in real mode. (Access to extended memory requires going into protected mode and back again, which is slow on 80286-based PCs.)

That is starting to change, but still there are a host of applications out there that want expanded memory.

If you have extended memory and can convert some of it to expanded, that surely will be cheaper than buying an EMS memory card. It may also allow you to reconfigure between EMS and extended as your needs change, possibly even within a work session. That is often not possible with a hardware EMS memory card. Perhaps most important is the possibility that the resulting EMS memory will actually work more quickly than actual hardware EMS.

Why Might You Not Be Able to Do This?

On the other hand, there are some reasons why converting extended into expanded memory is definitely not always the way to go. Sometimes it will be slower than a hardware EMS card. (If you save enough money, though, that might not be a compelling counter-argument.)

Sometimes there is nothing quite like the real thing. If your PC is in class 5 or 6, you might be using a program (called a LIMulator) to turn some of your extended memory into simulated expanded memory. For a lot of EMS-using programs, that works beautifully. But if you decide to run the Borland *Turbo Debugger,* you will have to unload your LIMulator before you can. Further, if the program you wish to debug needs EMS memory, you will have to get a hardware EMS board and use that. (Well, there may be an out: If your system logic can create EMS memory from some of your motherboard memory—through the setup program, and not by using a LIMulator software driver—that might be a "real" enough source of EMS for the *Turbo Debugger*—maybe.)

How to Do It

How can you make some other form of memory, or some disk space, act like EMS memory? There are several ways. Here is a description of each one with a brief discussion of what the advantages and disadvantages of each are. The options presented are these:

- Making extended memory function as expanded memory.

- Making disk storage function as expanded memory.

Making Extended Memory Function as Expanded Memory

How can you make extended memory function as expanded? You know by now that only PCs in class 3 or above can have extended memory, so unless you have one of them, this opportunity doesn't exist for you.

> Curiously enough, that might not be true for you. It is true that you can't have real extended memory in a class 1 or class 2 PC. But sometimes the manufacturers of these PCs use the term "extended memory" to refer to any RAM beyond 640KB that may be on their motherboard. In these cases, very likely, the system logic will be able to use that extra memory for shadow RAM or EMS, and possibly for both.

Assuming you have the sort of PC for which it is possible to convert some of its RAM into EMS memory, how might you do it? There are two basic techniques.

Using the Motherboard System Logic Chip Set and BIOS

The first is to induce your motherboard system logic to do the job. Only some system logic designs are able to do this. Whether or not yours can may also depend on which brand and version of BIOS you have. Also, be aware that even if you can do it, you may have to give up something else that you might want more.

There are three special things a system logic chip set and BIOS might do for you:

- Fill some upper memory addresses with RAM for general program use.

- Make EMS memory.

- Shadow some ROMs.

A few system logic chip sets and motherboard BIOS combinations can do all three. More of them can do only one or two of these things.

Using a LIMulator

The second method of converting extended memory into expanded is to use a special program called a LIMulator (**LIM** EMS em**ulator**). This trick works both with RAM on the PC's motherboard, and with RAM on a card plugged into a slot on the I/O bus. (The system logic trick described above will not work with that latter sort of RAM.)

Things get just a bit more complicated when you consider this approach. The reason is that there are two quite different techniques used by LIMulators to provide EMS memory. (Some LIMulator programs are able to use either technique, depending on what hardware capabilities you have; others only know how to use one or the other. For example, the DOS 5 or 6 program EMM386.EXE only understands method 1, which is why its use is limited to PCs in Classes 5 and 6.)

Method 1: The first technique only applies to PCs in classes 5 or 6 (those using a 386, 486, or *Pentium* CPU chip). It uses the special memory mapping capabilities of these CPU chips to move 4KB chunks of extended memory around in memory address space, as if they were EMS pages.

Method 2: The second technique involves copying information from some location in extended memory into one of four 16KB pages in a 64KB EMS page frame, located in lower memory (below 640KB). This can be used on PCs in class 3 or 4, though it is not desirable to use if you have a feasible alternative. (And class 4 PCs, by definition, have a hardware alternative.)

The first technique can be very fast (in a 386, 486, or Pentium-based machine). It is almost certainly faster in these machines than a hardware EMS board. The reason for this is the fact that most of these PCs can access their mother-board RAM (and any RAM on a proprietary plug-in card) much more rapidly than they can any memory on a card plugged into an I/O slot.

The second technique is not nearly as fast as the first. But it works, and it is cheap. Sometimes these are good enough reasons to use it. However, if you have a class 3 PC and can afford to upgrade it to class 4 (by adding a LIM EMS, version 4.0 board), do so.

Another significant difference between the two techniques is the smaller chunks of memory that the first one uses. That provides significant added flexibility, which is an advantage quite independent of the issue of speed.

Finally, the first technique can be used to put some simulated EMS memory into the lower memory address space, even when there already are some RAM chips there. This is because the memory mapping can be used to move these chips out of the way. This is very helpful if you wish to do multitasking or task swapping.

Making Disk Storage Function as Expanded Memory

Some of the same LIMulators that can convert extended memory into expanded have the alternative of making some of your disk storage appear to be expanded memory. This is a very cheap source of a lot of EMS memory, but it also makes for *extremely* slow (simulated) memory.

Another limitation to disk-storage-as-simulated-EMS memory is that this approach cannot support page aliasing, although as was noted in Chapter 8, that particular feature of LIM EMS 4.0 has hardly ever been used by commercial programs.

Comparing the Different Ways
to Get Expanded Memory

In addition to making expanded memory out of extended or other motherboard RAM, or simulating it with disk space, you can, of course, use a real hardware EMS board. Considering all these options and all the different classes of PCs to which each applies creates seven cases to consider. Here is a list, roughly in descending order of performance.

- **EMS strategy 1:** A class 6 PC (386DX-, 486-, or *Pentium*-based) using LIMulator software with only lower and extended memory physically installed.

- **EMS strategy 2:** A class 5 PC (386SX-based) using LIMulator software with only lower and extended memory physically installed.

- **EMS strategy 3:** A class 4 or 5 PC (286- or 386SX-based) using EMS memory converted from motherboard RAM by the system logic.

- **EMS strategy 4:** A class 2 PC (8088- or 8086-based) using EMS memory converted from motherboard RAM. (This is only worth doing if the motherboard has more than 640KB of RAM.)

- **EMS strategy 5:** Any class of PC (1 - 6) using a hardware EMS board.

- **EMS strategy 6:** A class 3 PC (286-based) with only lower and extended memory and LIMulator software.

- **EMS strategy 7:** A class 1 PC (8088- or 8086-based) with LIMulator software (which must, in this case, be using disk space to simulate EMS memory).

Strategies 3 and 4 require the presence of a motherboard system logic chip set with special capabilities. That was uncommon several years ago, but is very common in PCs built today, other than class 6 PCs, which have a better way to produce EMS memory anyway.

Strategies 6 and 7 place the EMS page frame in lower memory. That means you have 64KB less in which to run your applications. This fact alone may make these strategies unacceptable to many people.

Speed Comparisons

Strategy 1 is about twice as fast as strategy 2 because of the wider data bus in the DX machines (32-bit versus 16-bit).

Strategies 2 and 3 may be comparable in speed. Which one is faster depends on the details of the implementations of each method.

Strategy 4 will be about half as fast as Strategy 3, again, because of the difference in data bus width (16-bit versus 8-bit this time).

Strategy 5 will most likely be significantly slower than any of the preceding because the plug-in card is attached to the I/O bus, which cannot be allowed to run as fast as normal CPU-to-memory direct accesses. The exception is any slow PC, usually in class 1 or 2, with a CPU clock speed less than 10MHz.

Strategy 6 has two strikes against it. One is that this strategy requires switching the CPU from real to protected mode and back again frequently, and an 80286-based system is slow returning from protected to real mode. (See Chapter 11 for details.) But much more important is the fact that any data you put in the pseudo-EMS page in the lower memory page frame must actually be copied from that location to a holding place in extended memory before a new pseudo-page can be swapped in. (And the "swapping in" is also a copying operation instead of a simple context switch.) In fact, the only redeeming feature of this approach is that it works when you have no alternative way to get the job done.

Strategy 7 is the slowest of all. The only way the LIMulator can work is to create an EMS page frame in conventional memory, and copy data between there and a place on the disk. Because disks are tens of thousands times slower than electronic memory, this is enormously slower than any other approach. Still, it does work, and it is inexpensive. Sometimes that is all one really needs.

Recommendations

If you have a class 5 or 6 PC (386-, 486-, or *Pentium*-based), get and use a LIMulator designed for this class of machines. If you have DOS 5 or 6 you already have one such a program: EMM386. This approach is the least expensive way to go and also gives the highest performance. (What a nice combination that is!)

Don't use a hardware EMS board. Nor should you use a LIMulator software package that may have come with such a board. It will most likely work, sort of, but its performance is likely to be terrible compared with a LIMulator designed for these classes of PC.

If you have a class 2 or 4 PC, one with motherboard system logic capable of converting motherboard memory to EMS memory, use that feature first. Only add a hardware EMS board if you need more EMS memory than you can create from the motherboard memory when the motherboard is fully populated with memory chips or modules.

Important Clarification   If you have a motherboard which can provide up to 1MB of EMS memory and you decide you need to have 3MB, don't think you can simply buy and install a hardware EMS board that provides 2MB of EMS memory. If you do, you will find you have a choice of having the 1MB of motherboard system logic create EMS memory *or* the 2MB of EMS memory from the new plug-in board, but not both.

The reason for this is that you have to load an expanded memory manager (EMM) program to manage any EMS memory. Every such program only knows how to manage a particular source of that memory. If you load the EMM that came with your motherboard, you will get the 1MB of EMS memory. If you load the EMM that comes with the new hardware EMS board, you will get its 2MB of EMS memory. You cannot load both, and neither of these EMMs can make use of the other's EMS memory.

What you can do is buy two of the *same brand* of EMS board. Plug both in (setting the jumpers as directed in the documentation). Then load the EMM that comes with them and you will be able to use all the memory on both boards as EMS memory. Getting the same *brand* of board is crucial, though.

If you have a class 3 PC, you could simply use a LIMulator. However, if you do, you will not get the speed you could from a hardware EMS board. Furthermore, you will have to give up 64KB of lower memory to provide the EMS page frame.

On the other hand, the LIMulator is likely to be a good deal less expensive than getting a hardware EMS board. But if you need to add more memory than you presently have, you may well want to buy a memory add-on card that gives hardware EMS instead of one that can only give extended memory. If that board supports version 4.0 of the LIM EMS standard, your PC will now be in class 4.

There is one case in which this last suggestion may not be appropriate. If you often change from one set of programs for which you need a lot of expanded memory, but not much extended, to one in which the opposite is true, the LIMulator usually offers greater convenience in making that switch.

Some EMS boards can be reconfigured into extended memory boards by software. Others require you to open the case, remove them, and change some jumpers or DIP switch settings. (See Figure 9.5.) Especially in comparison to the latter method, altering how a LIMulator is configured is much simpler. Easiest of all are the LIMulator programs which, on a class 5 or 6 PC, can provide EMS or extended (XMS) memory from a common pool. This is discussed further in "Keeping Your Memory Options Open" later in this chapter.

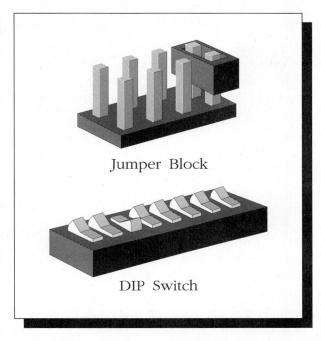

Jumper Block

DIP Switch

Figure 9.5. Jumper blocks with removable shorting jumpers and DIP switches are used to configure many add-on memory boards.

The name *DIP switch* comes from the fact that these switches are plugged into the same sort of socket as a ***Dual-Inline-Package*** integrated circuit chip, also called a *DIP IC*. (No, a DIP switch has nothing to do with measuring your PC's oil level!)

If you have a class 1 PC, you have only two options: Getting a hardware EMS board, or using the lowest performance solution, a LIMulator converting some disk storage into simulated EMS memory. Here, the tradeoff between cost and performance is even more marked than with class 3 PCs.

Creating Extended Memory from Other Kinds of Memory or Storage

The previous section showed you when and how to change some extended memory into expanded. There are times when you want to go in exactly the opposite direction.

Converting Expanded Memory to Extended

As was just mentioned, a hardware EMS board can only have its memory reassigned as extended by altering its setup. This can sometimes be done by software (a setup program), but more often you must change some DIP switch or jumper settings on the board. Likewise, if you had used your PC's motherboard system logic to convert some or all of your extended memory into expanded, you must go through the same sort of gyrations to get it back to extended.

Extended to Expanded But Using It as Extended Anyway (VCPI)

There is one way to convert extended memory to expanded and still be able to use it as extended when you need to. That is when you use a LIMulator that generates VCPI compatible EMS memory. (VCPI stands for *Virtual Control Program Interface*. This and several other memory management strategies are described near the end of Chapter 12.) The key feature of VCPI compatible EMS memory is that it can be obtained, upon request, by a DOS-extended program that otherwise could only use extended or XMS memory.

Why would you want to convert your extended memory into expanded, only to have a program use it as if it were extended? That sounds rather weird.

One good reason is so you can have that memory available to each program you run, either for use as expanded or as extended memory. This approach works just fine for any program that wants to see expanded memory. It only works for programs that want to see extended memory if they have been written specially to understand and use the VCPI services of your LIMulator. In that case, you can make almost all your extended memory available as expanded memory for these applications that need it that way, and still have all that memory available to large "DOS-extended" applications that must use extended memory.

Here are some of the advantages of this approach:

- The speed of the resulting extended memory is roughly that of the original real extended memory.

- With VCPI compatible EMS memory, any VCPI-aware DOS-extended application can get all the memory it needs easily.

- You get to use that memory as expanded until it is needed for use as extended memory.

- You don't have to decide ahead of time how much extended memory you will need if you can simulate it on the fly upon demand.

Why You Might Not Want to Use VCPI Conversion of Your Memory

Naturally, if you know ahead of time that you will **only** be using your extended memory as extended memory, then loading a VCPI compatible LIMulator and having your DOS-extended programs use VCPI calls for accessing the memory as if it were extended, which involves a lot of needless overhead. Don't go to all that effort unless you need to have the memory available both as expanded and as extended.

Keeping Your Memory Options Open

There is one other way to finesse the issue of how much extended memory to convert to expanded. Use a 386-class LIMulator that takes all your extended memory and creates from it one pool of available RAM. Then it gives that RAM either as EMS or as XMS memory to any programs that ask for it, giving each one whatever it wants.

> *QEMM386* was the first 386-class LIMulator to offer this feature. Now four of the leading 386-class LIMulators (*QEMM*, *386MAX*, *QMAPS*, and *Netroom*) offer it.
>
> This seems like a really wonderful idea. It works with any program that wants either EMS or XMS memory. (Unlike the VCPI approach,

it is not limited to providing XMS memory to VCPI-aware DOS-extended applications.) So why don't all the 386-class LIMulators do this?

One possible reason is that there is at least a theoretical way you could get into trouble using this approach. If any program were to query the memory manager to see how much EMS memory was available, then query it again to see how much XMS memory was available, it would get the same answer in both cases. If it then tried to allocate all of that memory of both kinds, it would not succeed. (If your PC had 8MB of total RAM, it could appear to have nearly 7MB of EMS and 7MB of XMS, but clearly you could not give any program 14MB of RAM to work with.) The requesting program should handle any such failure gracefully, but some memory manager makers don't want to take the chance that some program would not.

So far, this is only a theoretical problem; no programs on the commercial market seem to trip over it. (On the other hand, it is one you should anticipate and guard against if you ever write a program that could get confused in this way.)

Converting Disk Storage to (Virtual) Extended Memory

Converting disk storage space to simulated EMS memory is generally a terrible idea, since it functions so terribly slowly. Converting it to extended memory also has that drawback, but there are more situations in which this is exactly the right thing to do. For example, this is one of the meanings of virtual memory, and it is the one meant when speaking of demand-paged virtual memory. This strategy is used by *Pick, VROOMM, Windows,* and *GeoWorks* (among others).

Advantages of Storage to Extended Memory Conversion

The advantage of using some of your disk storage as if it were extended memory can be said briefly: Disk storage is cheap, so you can have almost unlimited amounts of it, at least compared to what you can afford of RAM. Who has heard of a PC with as much as 40MB of RAM? But PCs with 40MB of disk space, even those with more than 40MB of unused disk space, are quite common.

Some Problems with Storage to Extended Memory Conversion

Even if you were willing to accept the slower operation implied by swapping information to disk (which is the detailed means by which demand-paged virtual memory works), you can't always have an unlimited amount of that virtual memory. For example, *Windows* 3.x in enhanced mode allows you to have a maximum of three times as much virtual memory as actual, physical RAM.

Furthermore, using disk storage as simulated RAM involves much thrashing of information to and from the disk. This can lead to a couple of other problems.

The first of these problems is disk fragmentation. You may know that as DOS creates and extends files on the disk, they often end up being scattered across the disk in many fragments. When that happens, DOS can't retrieve that information nearly as rapidly as if it all were located in one contiguous region. That is why Microsoft suggests that *Windows* 3.x users install a permanent swap file, and that they do so only after defragmenting their hard drive. (You only need to defragment the logical volume (the drive letter) that you are going to use for that swap file, although you will gain added benefits if you defragment all your logical volumes.)

A second potential problem is a bit more subtle. It is disk cache vitiation. What is that, you say?

A disk cache is a region of RAM in which you keep an image of the information most recently written to or read from the disk (see Chapter 14 for more details on this). The idea is that each time you ask DOS to get some information from the disk, if it finds the information you want in the cache memory, DOS can simply return to your program immediately and save the time otherwise used for actually reading the disk. Likewise, if you ask DOS to write something to the disk, if from the cache record it determines that what you want has already been done, again it can save time and simply tell you the requested task has been done.

That normally works quite well. But, if you have a very large swap file and if that is on a disk that is being cached by either a software or hardware cache, you can totally ruin the whole process. This is because the swap file information is constantly being written and rewritten. If the swap file is larger than the disk cache, very soon the only things in the cache will be a record of what is in various areas of the swap region. Then, when you next ask DOS for some data that would otherwise still be in the cache, it will have to go read the disk to get it again.

If you are using a software cache, you can avoid this problem simply by not caching the particular logical volume on which you put the swap file. You can still cache all the other logical volumes (other drives), and get the benefits of the cache there.

If you are using a hardware disk cache, your only out is to make sure your swap file is substantially smaller than the cache. Then one portion of the cache memory, equal in size to the swap region, will be constantly thrashed but the remainder is still available to cache normal disk accesses.

A Recap

In this chapter you learned some very deep, nitty-gritty details of how memory chips are built and how they work. You also learned how the motherboard system logic does address decoding. This is the way in which it is able to activate only the appropriate RAM chips for each access to memory by the CPU. An entirely similar address decoding is also done by the system logic for all accesses to the motherboard BIOS ROM. (And similar processes go on within each option card plugged into the I/O bus to activate any RAM or ROM on that card.)

In this way the system logic determines which RAM chips are going to be in lower memory space, and which will be in extended memory (for PCs in classes 3 to 6). Sometimes you can alter how the system logic addresses the motherboard RAM. That can make it possible, in suitable PCs, to produce upper memory blocks into which programs can be loaded, to simulate LIM EMS-compatible expanded memory, or to "shadow" slow ROMs with faster RAM chips.

It even is possible to have more than 640KB of RAM on a class 1 or 2 PC and have the system logic make use of that extra memory. In those PCs for which this is a possibility, you may be able to get the same kinds of benefit from that RAM as you could with the higher-class PCs.

This chapter discussed some of the reasons why you might want to convert extended memory into simulated EMS memory, and some reasons why you might wish to do the reverse. It also described ways that you can use disk storage as either EMS or extended memory, and explained that often this is the least expensive way to get the additional memory your programs need.

This ends our exploration of the kinds of memory your PC can have. Now it is time to look at the ways those different regions of memory get used. Specifically, in the next chapter you will learn all about how lower memory gets used.

A major user of lower (and upper) memory space is the operating system (DOS) and the BIOS. Chapter 10 is also where you will learn what those things are and how your other programs use them.

10

HOW MEMORY IN A PC GETS USED

Now that you know what kinds of memory you have, how does each of them get used? In particular, this chapter focuses on the uses of lower memory, but some attention is also given to the other memory spaces. This chapter also explains the BIOS and DOS and the layering of programs in a PC.

Now you have learned all about the different kinds of memory you have in your PC. (Well, most of them at least.) In this chapter, you will learn about a few more and how the principal kinds of memory get used.

In particular, you will learn what a BIOS is and what an operating system such as DOS really does for you. You will also find out that your PC is filled with a virtual parfait of programs. Knowing about the layers can help you understand both what is going on, and how to make what you want to happen occur more easily.

What Is a BIOS?

The term *BIOS* has already been used many times in this book (the uses have included "BIOS ROM," "motherboard BIOS," and "option BIOS"). You may well be wondering just exactly what a BIOS is and why your PC seems to have so many of them.

What Does the Acronym Mean?

First you need to know what the letters mean. BIOS is an acronym for *Basic Input Output System.* This means that the BIOS is a collection of programs that helps other programs perform various input or output actions (things like receiving keystrokes from the keyboard, placing messages on the screen, beeping the speaker, printing your work, and saving information to the disk).

Frequently, *but not always,* you see the term BIOS associated with ROM. That is because many pieces, *but not all,* of the BIOS code in a PC are housed in a **R**ead-**O**nly **M**emory (ROM) chip (see Figure 10.1). The BIOS on the motherboard is one example. Another example is the ROM on an option card. Usually, this is an extension to the motherboard BIOS. There are also some BIOS pieces that are not in a ROM. This is explained in the section "Disk-Based BIOS Additions" later in this chapter. And some ROMs (the font BIOS on a graphics card, for example) contain something other than BIOS code.

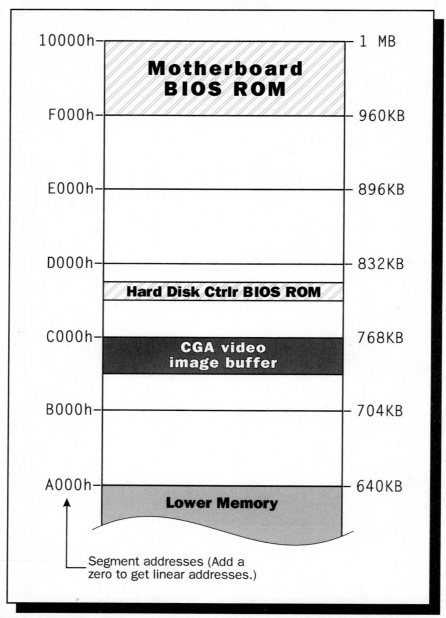

Figure 10.1. Where some BIOS ROMs are located in memory space in a typical XT clone.

Purpose and Nature of Any BIOS

Strictly speaking, the term BIOS should only refer to the program pieces that get called upon to assist other programs in performing various input or output functions. In common usage, the term is sometimes stretched to include a few other things. Also you should understand that not every kind of help a program may need with an input or output function will be performed by a part of what is called the BIOS. So, in a sense, the term BIOS is both broader and less broad in its coverage than you might at first think.

One example of the way the term BIOS is used to cover more than you might have thought is what is referred to as the *motherboard BIOS ROM*. This is a ROM whose contents include a lot of program code pieces that clearly are BIOS in nature. But it also includes the **P**ower **O**n **S**elf **T**est program (the POST) and the *bootstrap loader*, among other things.

> The POST is the first program to execute when you power on your PC. Its job is to inventory and test the major pieces that make up your PC. The bootstrap loader is the next program that executes. Its job is to try to find and load an operating system. (Later in this chapter you will learn more about each of these programs.)

Another example of something that is located in what is called a BIOS ROM but which is not really BIOS code is the initialization portion of the BIOS ROMs on option cards. Any option card that has some hardware functionality on it which cannot be activated by the routines in the *motherboard BIOS ROM* must be activated by some addition to that BIOS. In many (but not all) cases, this is provided by that card's manufacturer in the form of an *option BIOS ROM*. This ROM must contain at least one more thing: a small initialization program that gets called by the POST and whose purpose is to bond this new BIOS code seamlessly into the total BIOS function of the PC.

Those are some ways that the term BIOS is used to cover more than simply the most basic input-output program pieces. What about the ways in which the term is overly narrow? Most programs that put information on a disk drive need a lot of help doing so. Some of that help comes from program pieces that are a part of the BIOS, but some of that help comes from another section of the operating system. That other part is sometimes called the *Basic Disk Operating System* or *BDOS*. More frequently in *MS-DOS* or *PC DOS* discussions, it will be called simply the DOS part. You will learn more about what this is and the ways in which it helps application programs later in this chapter.

First, let's return to the BIOS and a more detailed look at what is in the motherboard BIOS ROM.

The Motherboard BIOS ROM

Every PC needs a motherboard BIOS ROM. That ROM contains the essential start-up programs (the POST and boot programs) without which the PC would never get started. In order for this start-up function to work, the motherboard BIOS ROM must be located in the CPU's memory address space just below the 1MB line. Remember, one of Intel's special addresses is FFFF:0000 (or FFFF0h as a linear address). That is where the very first instruction to be executed on power up or after a reset must be located.

Also, the motherboard BIOS ROM always contains the default set of *interrupt service routines.* Interrupt service routines (ISRs) are the mini-programs that are used by other programs to get the hardware to do something. The default set of interrupt service routines are simply the ISRs that are installed during the POST. Other programs may alter the pointers in the interrupt vector table to make their program serve as a given ISR instead of the default one.

The particular collection of hardware devices supported by the motherboard BIOS ROM varies from manufacturer to manufacturer. Normally it is whatever hardware is commonly included in PC configurations built by that manufacturer.

Another thing that a motherboard BIOS sometimes contains is a *setup program.* This is a program that allows you to record on a battery-backed-up CMOS RAM chip the specific details of your machine's configuration. (PCs in classes 1 and 2 normally do not have such a chip, nor a setup program. All other PCs have the CMOS configuration RAM, but not all of them have a setup program in ROM. Some PCs, in particular almost all the models of IBM *PC* and *PS/2,* require you to run their setup program from a diskette.)

Some PCs are able to program special features of their motherboard system logic chip set through some options accessed within the setup program. These may include such things as turning shadow RAM on or off, creating EMS memory out of some RAM on the motherboard, or adjusting the number of wait states for main RAM, just to name a few common options.

Some authors include the IBM BASIC ROM in what they call the BIOS. That ROM will be described in the section "Cassette BASIC" later in this chapter.

BIOS ROM Code Is Optional

A very important point was made a few paragraphs ago. The motherboard BIOS includes some default interrupt service routines. But nothing says you have to use them. Any program is free to replace some or all of them with ISRs of its own.

There are generally three reasons that this might be done. The first reason is, if you know that your hardware is different from the standard hardware, you may need to replace the ISR that deals with that category of hardware with one that is able to operate your PC's hardware. That is the main thing that an option BIOS ROM does. It also can be done by loading a device driver or TSR program.

The second reason for replacing the default ISRs in the motherboard BIOS is that you may have a program that does some task normally done by a program in the motherboard BIOS, but does it better. For example, the routines in the BIOS to support writing information to the screen are very general and not very fast. Many people have written improved versions. Replacing the motherboard BIOS ROM video ISR may be the most common instance of replacing a default ISR for this sort of reason.

The third reason for ignoring the motherboard BIOS ROM interrupt service routines has to do with a very different issue: protected mode. Normally all the miniprograms in the motherboard BIOS are written to run in real mode. That is the mode in which the PC starts up, and the PC stays in this mode as long as it is totally under the control of DOS. (Real mode, and how it differs from protected mode, is explained in Chapter 11.)

Some programs take the PC out of real mode. They must use different interrupt service routines (ones written to run in protected mode) or else every time an interrupt happens, they must stop whatever is going on, go back into real mode to service the interrupt, and then return to protected mode. Many DOS-based operating environments and DOS-extended programs will do just that. Some use alternative interrupt service routines that are written to run in protected mode. These will be included as a part of the DOS-extended application program.

As shown in Figure 10.2, IBM's *PS/2* computers have both a real mode part to their motherboard BIOS (the compatibility BIOS or CBIOS) and a protected mode part (the advanced BIOS or ABIOS). This was done to provide optimal support for *OS/2*, which runs in protected mode most of the time.

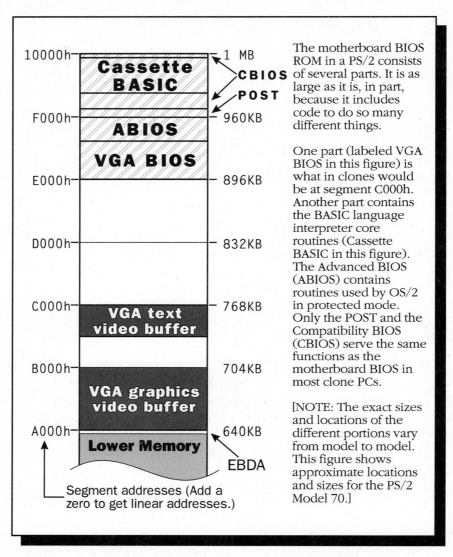

The motherboard BIOS ROM in a PS/2 consists of several parts. It is as large as it is, in part, because it includes code to do so many different things.

One part (labeled VGA BIOS in this figure) is what in clones would be at segment C000h. Another part contains the BASIC language interpreter core routines (Cassette BASIC in this figure). The Advanced BIOS (ABIOS) contains routines used by OS/2 in protected mode. Only the POST and the Compatibility BIOS (CBIOS) serve the same functions as the motherboard BIOS in most clone PCs.

[NOTE: The exact sizes and locations of the different portions vary from model to model. This figure shows approximate locations and sizes for the PS/2 Model 70.]

Figure 10.2. Where some BIOS ROMs are located in memory address space in a PS/2, model 70.

Other operating systems, like *UNIX*, are written to run exclusively in protected mode. When they load, the first thing they do is go into protected mode, and they never come back. That means they must ignore all of the real mode BIOS ISR programs. Thus, all of their ISRs are loaded into RAM.

Option BIOS ROMs (What and Where They Are)

So far, you've learned that option BIOS ROMs are mini-BIOS program collections in ROM chips mounted on certain option cards. That is their physical location and general nature. They include both the ISR programs needed to activate that option card's hardware and the initialization program to attach those ISRs into the larger BIOS seamlessly. An important fact about these ROMs is that they are always located somewhere in the CPU's memory address space.

Where in memory address space are they? IBM reserved the C and D pages (linear addresses from C0000h to DFFFFh) for this purpose. And usually, that is where they are placed.

In particular, any EGA or VGA card (or other video card that wishes to support those standards) must set its option ROM so it starts at C0000h. That is because all modern PCs look there for an option ROM before they do most of the POST. They must, since otherwise the POST could not put any messages on the screen.

Originally, there were no uses for the C and D pages. Now there are altogether too many! That space is getting very crowded in many PCs. You might want to move some option ROMs to some place outside those pages. Unfortunately, that won't work. The *option ROM scan* part of the POST only looks for option BIOS ROMs in the C and D page.

> There is one exception to this rule. Some PCs support putting one special ROM at E0000h. That ROM will get activated at the end of the option ROM scan just as if it were a normal option BIOS ROM. The name for such an E-page option ROM is the *user ROM*. This possibility has only rarely been used commercially.

Cassette BASIC

Only IBM-brand PCs (and *PS/2s*) have Cassette BASIC in ROM. (Because of its location, it sometimes is called ROM BASIC.) It has an interesting history.

When the IBM *PC* first came out, diskette drives were very expensive (and hard drives were not even an option) so IBM expected most of its customers to buy the PC without any disk drives.

A PC is not much good without some way of storing programs and data so that they don't disappear the next time you turn off the PC. So IBM included an optional means of connecting the PC to an external audio cassette tape player. That device more resembled an inexpensive audio tape deck than it did a modern, digital streaming-tape drive. The tape unit was slow and cumbersome to use, but at least it was affordable and worked (if you were patient enough).

The bootstrap loader program in the motherboard BIOS ROM on these PCs was built to look for a diskette drive and, if it finds one with a formatted disk in it, to attempt to load DOS from that disk. It was not built to do anything with a cassette tape drive. (This was probably because it would have been so painfully slow to load an operating system off one of these tape units.)

That presented a small problem. How could the system get going? The solution was to put a version of the BASIC language in ROM and use it as the operating system if no disk-based operating system could be found.

Anytime the boot program can't find and load DOS (in a true-blue IBM *PC* or *PS/2*), it will run the version of BASIC that is in ROM (see Figures 10.2 and 10.7). This version of BASIC expects to load and save all of its files from a cassette tape drive. But there hasn't been one of these sold, even as an option, for any PC made after the first couple of models. There isn't even a place to plug in such a cassette tape drive in any PC made by anyone since the introduction of the IBM *PC/XT*. So why is Cassette BASIC still put into a ROM on the motherboard of every IBM-brand PC and *PS/2*?

The ROM version of BASIC only incorporates the most commonly used commands, but it does have those. When IBM created its version of DOS (called *PC DOS*), it included a more powerful version of BASIC on its DOS disks. (Actually two of them, the somewhat powerful BASIC.COM and a more advanced version, BASICA.COM.)

If those disk-based versions of BASIC had been complete programs, then once one of them was loaded into RAM, there would have been two places in the CPU's memory address space with program code to execute the most primitive BASIC operations (one as a part of the Cassette BASIC ROM and the other in the copy of the program from the disk in RAM). That duplication seemed wasteful (and it would have been). So IBM made the BASIC programs on its *PC DOS* disks use the primitive BASIC routines in the Cassette BASIC ROM. That also made the disk-based BASIC programs smaller, saving space on the diskettes and allowing them to load BASIC into memory more rapidly.

Having once made that decision, IBM was pretty well stuck. Since each later model of PC or *PS/2* was supposed to be able to run any program (and that included DOS and BASIC) written for an earlier model PC, they had to continue to supply those primitive BASIC routines in ROM.

Clone makers were not limited in this way because they had no stake in *PC DOS BASIC.* (They also chose not to buy the rights to IBM's copyrighted BASIC ROM.) Instead, these manufacturers were able to use Microsoft's *MS-DOS,* which included a program called GWBASIC. That program contains all of the BASIC language (including the lowest level parts) on the disk.

Some (but not all) PC clone manufacturers renamed GWBASIC to BASIC or BASICA, or they wrote a small program called BASIC.COM or BASICA.COM to load and run GWBASIC.EXE. That allowed the users of these PCs to run BASIC (or BASICA) and get the same effect as running BASIC or BASICA under *PC DOS.*

This is why BASIC from any version of *PC DOS* will not run on a PC clone. It demands a true-blue PC with Cassette BASIC in ROM.

There are two further details to this story about BASIC and DOS. The first is that Digital Research does not provide any form of BASIC language interpreter or compiler with *DR DOS.* The second fact is that starting with version 5, Microsoft has dropped GWBASIC from *MS-DOS.* Instead, Microsoft now includes QBASIC.EXE. This is the editing environment and interpreter portions of their standalone product, *QuickBasic.* (You still must buy the full *QuickBasic* product if you want to get the compiler.) IBM, for version 5 of *PC DOS,* chose to keep BASIC and BASICA, but also incorporated QBASIC.

In DOS version 6, Microsoft has continued to supply QBASIC in lieu of GWBASIC. IBM, on the other hand, is dropping all support for BASIC with their *PC DOS*, version 6.

An important thing to know about QBASIC is that Microsoft and IBM also use the editor portion of this program to provide a full screen editor for DOS. So when you type the new DOS external command EDIT, you actually get the editing environment of QBASIC. The importance of this is that you must not delete the monster QBASIC.EXE and QBASIC.HLP files (over a third of a megabyte) unless you are willing to give up the functionality of the EDIT command. (And it explains why EDIT.COM is so very tiny (413 bytes), as it only has to launch QBASIC.)

In MS-DOS version 6, QBASIC got another job. In addition to providing the editor for EDIT, it also supplies the viewer for HELP. The on-line help facility is one of the great improvements in MS-DOS 6, which makes it even more imperative that you keep QBASIC.EXE on your hard disk.

IBM's *PC DOS*, version 6, includes a different editor, E, developed by IBM. This was necessary as they had decided not to continue supplying QBASIC. And, of course, that means their on-line help facility must use an IBM-developed engine as well.

Disk-Based BIOS Additions

Your PC has more than one BIOS. It has the BIOS in a ROM on the motherboard. It may have one or more option BIOS ROMs on option cards. And if it is running DOS, it has one more BIOS—the one that is contained in a hidden system file on every bootable DOS disk.

If you simply use the DOS DIR command (with no command-line parameters), you will never see this BIOS. But if you use a disk-snooping tool that shows files with the hidden and system attributes turned on, you will see two such files in the root directory of any bootable DOS disk.

If the disk carries a version of *PC DOS* or *DR DOS*, the hidden system files will be called IBMBIO.COM and IBMDOS.COM. If it is a copy of *MS-DOS*, those file names will most likely be called IO.SYS and MSDOS.SYS. (Some clone makers renamed those files in their proprietary versions of *MS-DOS* to either the IBM names or to something like TBIO.SYS and TDOS.SYS.)

The first of these two files (IBMBIO.COM or IO.SYS) is an extension to the BIOS routines in the various ROMs your PC may have. The second file (IBMDOS.COM or MSDOS.SYS) is DOS itself.

You may have still more pieces of BIOS that get loaded from disk. For example, do you have a mouse? You probably load either MOUSE.SYS (or a device driver with a similar name) from a DEVICE= line in your CONFIG.SYS file, or MOUSE.COM (or some similarly named TSR program) on a line in your AUTOEXEC.BAT file. Either way, the program that executes loads some code into RAM and attaches it into the operating system as an extension to the BIOS, in this case, to enable your programs to use the mouse. Almost any device driver or TSR program may be thought of as an extension to the BIOS.

Some Advantages Disk-Based BIOS Extensions Deliver

There are several important reasons why *PC DOS* and *MS-DOS* are designed to accept BIOS extensions from a disk-based program. Having part of the BIOS in ROM (some of it *must* be) and the rest on the DOS disk frees you as a PC user. You are not locked into whatever BIOS was manufactured into the ROM on the motherboard. You can update the disk-based part of your PC's BIOS simply by booting the machine from a newer version of DOS. (Of course in the process, you also will be upgrading your DOS version. That will be discussed later in this chapter.)

You can also augment the BIOS by loading device drivers or TSR programs that may have come on a diskette with some new hardware option you acquired.

Another advantage of loading part of your BIOS from disk is that you can boot your PC from a diskette that carries an operating system other than DOS. That disk's BIOS will very likely substitute itself for most or all of the existing BIOS. Examples of this are *OS/2* and *UNIX*.

Why You Might Want All of DOS and the BIOS in ROM

On the other hand, there can be some important reasons for not requiring, or even allowing, the loading of any of the BIOS from a disk. Indeed, some PCs don't even have disk drives; clearly they must find DOS some other way than by loading it from a disk.

Diskless work stations must somehow get DOS started and running before they can connect across the network to a machine with a disk drive. They must have everything they need to do this in ROM; all of their BIOS and DOS, plus their network drivers (which are extensions to the BIOS used to control the network interface card, and special software used to communicate across the network).

PCs in highly sensitive areas may need to be protected from any alteration in their operating system. By putting all of the operating system into ROM (and not having an accessible diskette drive from which a device driver or other modification to the BIOS or DOS might be loaded), one can make the PC about as secure as such things get.

Another reason for putting a complete copy of the BIOS and DOS in ROM is to allow very fast start-up of a PC. ROMs, and the information they contain, are typically attached quite permanently to some range of addresses in the CPU's memory-address space. This means that all of the programs a ROM contains are right there, ready for the CPU to execute. No loading is needed.

If all of the BIOS and DOS (and perhaps a menu program) are in ROM, the PC will be ready to use as soon as it is turned on, with no booting time at all. (Well, there will be some time needed, if only for the POST to check the hardware.) IBM's *PS/1* computers are built just this way. (They do provide for the option of booting from the hard disk or a diskette, but they can be set to boot strictly from ROM if you wish.)

Benefits of a Fully ROM-Based DOS and BIOS

Since ROMs mostly live in upper memory, putting all of the BIOS and all of the DOS program code into ROM would free up some lower memory. (Some small amount of RAM will still be needed for data tables.) This could increase the maximum program size that you could run. It also could allow you to load more device drivers and TSRs (for example, a network program) as well as some large applications.

On the other hand, if you have a class 5 or 6 PC, you can accomplish much the same thing by using a memory-management program (like *386MAX, QEMM, Memory Commander, Netroom,* or *QMAPS* or, with a bit more effort, the memory-management tools that are included with version 5 and 6 of *PC DOS, MS-DOS,* and *DR DOS*) and loading various parts of DOS and those extra device drivers and TSRs, into upper memory.

One fairly far-out possibility is that if all of DOS and the BIOS were put into ROM, the BIOS designer would know exactly what parts were needed and which parts would never be used again once the initial boot process was finished. Then the BIOS could be built to page out those sections of ROM once they were no longer needed.

Interesting as this idea may sound, so far no PC manufacturer has opted to do it. The main drawback may be that you could not then readily upgrade your DOS version (even by booting from a diskette) without losing this advantage. Indeed, if the BIOS designer had been too aggressive about what portions to page out if you upgraded to a newer version of the BIOS, you might end up attempting to invoke some portion of the now-missing motherboard BIOS ROM. Then your PC would crash.

Hardware ROM Upgrades

Disk-based BIOS extensions and option BIOS ROMs can be quite useful in setting up your system, but in the end, there are some problems that can better be solved by an upgrade of the actual motherboard BIOS ROM. BIOS upgrades can be purchased from the original manufacturer of your PC or from various third-party vendors (see the MemInfo hypertext database on the disk that is included with this book).

One important BIOS upgrade is a new version of the BIOS **H**ard **D**isk **P**arameter **T**ables (HDPT). Normally your BIOS ROM contains a number of different HDPT copies, one each for a variety of hard disk types. The values entered into the CMOS configuration RAM for drive type are used to pick which of the several BIOS HDPT entries will be used to describe the hard disk drives you have installed in your PC.

A chronic problem in the industry has been with PCs whose BIOS tables did not include any entry that matched the actual drives that were installed. Various ways have been invented to work around this, one of the best of which is the autoconfiguring hard disk controller. But to solve the problem at its root, you must upgrade your motherboard's BIOS so its tables include entries for the disk you actually have.

Upgrading your motherboard's BIOS ROM can also add support for any hardware options not contemplated at the time the original BIOS was written. One common example is enabling an older PC to use a high-density diskette drive.

Here are some more possibilities: Owners of PCs in classes 1 and 2 could add hard disk support in the motherboard BIOS ROM. That would free up the C page where normally those PCs have an option ROM for the hard disk controller card. Mouse drivers could also be added, eliminating the need to load them from the CONFIG.SYS or AUTOEXEC.BAT files.

Conventional Methods of BIOS Upgrade

Motherboard BIOS upgrades can be done with almost any PC, but it is such a nuisance that very few people do it. You have to order a custom BIOS made for you, and then when you get it, you have to open your PC, remove the motherboard BIOS chips, and replace them with the new chips.

The actual process of replacing a BIOS ROM is not very different from that of replacing some RAM chips. Anyone can learn how to do it safely. But there is some risk involved.(If you are going to do this, please review the precautions in Chapter 17.) And if you add to that risk the effort of finding a supplier and ordering from them a custom ROM, you will understand why this is not done very often.

BIOS Upgrade Using Flash EPROM

A recent innovation is the use of Flash EPROM (also known as Flash RAM or Flash ROM) to hold the motherboard BIOS. It promises some wonderful new possibilities, one of the most exciting of which is the greater ease of doing a motherboard BIOS upgrade. The only disadvantage of using Flash memory for the motherboard BIOS is that it costs a little more than a more conventional ROM.

If the manufacturer of your PC used Flash RAM for the motherboard BIOS instead of the usual ROM, then upgrading that BIOS can be as easy as running a program. The manufacturer could send you BIOS upgrades (offering new features or improved compatibility with your hardware) on a diskette or over a phone line. Some system manufacturers offer regular upgrades on an electronic bulletin board system (BBS). They may also be able to create a custom BIOS upgrade just for you.

Unlike the somewhat risky "under the hood" work involved in conventional BIOS upgrades, Flash RAM BIOS upgrades are virtually foolproof. If you have a new file with which to reprogram a Flash RAM BIOS, if anything goes wrong, you can recover simply by restoring the original program. The likelihood of doing some physical damage to any part of your PC is almost nonexistent.

Many hardware options that are simply not common enough to deserve space in everyone's ROM could have support in yours. And, if the manufacturers of those hardware options came out with upgraded device drivers, they could be incorporated into your motherboard BIOS ROM simply by loading a new version of the code.

This is not yet a common practice, but surely it will become much more so in the near future. At least we can hope it will.

What Is a DOS?

We have used the term DOS many times in this book. Do you know what it means? In this section you will not only learn what the letters stand for, but you will also find out the purpose and nature of DOS and what its different parts do. The section ends with a discussion of the various versions and brands of DOS.

What Does the Acronym Mean?

DOS stands for *Disk Operating System. PC DOS* stands for IBM's *Personal Computer Disk Operating System. MS-DOS* stands for *Microsoft's Disk Operating System. DR DOS* stands for *Digital Research's Disk Operating System*, a near-clone of *MS-DOS*. Those are the words, now what do they really mean?

The Purpose and Nature of Any O/S

First, it should be clear that DOS is an example of a more general beast, called an operating system (O/S). What is that? The following description applies generally to any O/S, but the details given here are specific to DOS.

An *operating system* is a program designed to manage and schedule the resources in a computer. It is in charge of everything, but its only purpose is to serve the computer user and the programs that he or she runs.

The operating system's management duties are mainly confined to allocation and scheduling. The operating system specifies which programs get to use what resources when, thereby preventing usage conflicts. For example, just think what a mess you would have if two programs in your PC both decided to use the printer at the same time. The output would be some sort of hash of the two separate programs' outputs. Nothing you would care to look at, no doubt. An operating system can prevent this kind of mess.

Typically, the operating system (usually DOS) manages the following resources in a PC:

- **Memory:** The operating system manages only the portions of RAM that might be used by different programs at different times. Therefore, it does not normally manage any of the ROM. DOS, unfortunately, can only recognize certain types of RAM in your PC, and it can't manage any memory that it doesn't recognize.

- **Storage:** For DOS this means mostly disk drives, although other possibilities exist. For example, some older mainframe computers used fast tape drives as their principal storage medium. An operating system written for such a computer was sometimes called TOS, for **T**ape **O**perating **S**ystem.

    The managerial task DOS performs with respect to storage is to assign different regions of the disk for use by different files. It also hides from programs the details of where on the disk it found those regions unless they ask for those details. DOS's SHARE program, first introduced with DOS 3.1, allows DOS to mediate requests by multiple processes for the same file. SHARE was introduced to support networks (and thus multiprocessing) but also opened the door to better support by DOS for multitasking.

- **Video:** Since DOS was written with the thought that only one program would be running in the machine at any one time, it does not attempt to manage the video resource.

DOS doesn't manage the video resource, but it does offer support for programs that wish to use that resource, principally through INT 21h. Any program whose output may be "redirected" (by using > or >> on the command line) is one that uses these services.

Various operating environments that work on top of DOS (for example, *DESQview* and *Windows*) allow multiple programs to run "at once" (meaning in closely interleaved slices of time, called *multitasking*). These operating environments must manage the video resource to keep each program's output confined to the particular portions of the screen that it "owns" at that moment.

- **Keyboard and other input/output devices:** Again, since DOS was not designed with multiple programs running together in mind, it mostly does not attempt to manage the various I/O devices.

Brief History of PC DOS, MS-DOS, and DR DOS

DOS was not born in a vacuum; it came into being in a particular time and environment. Many influences affected how DOS was built and how it has grown since then. Consider just a few of them.

When the IBM *PC* was being designed, there were two dominant standards in personal computing. One was the *Apple II* computer, which mainly dominated educational computing, especially in elementary schools. The other was a diverse collection of computers, made by many different manufacturers, but all known as *CP/M computers.* Most small businesses that used a computer had a *CP/M* computer.

The *Apple II* used a Synertek microprocessor, the 6502. All the *CP/M* machines used either an Intel 8080 or a clone of that made by Zilog called a Z80. The Apple machines ran Apple BASIC as their operating system, or later on, they used a disk operating system called Apple DOS. The *CP/M* machines were so called because each of them ran some variation of an operating system created by Digital Research and called *Control Program for Microcomputers,* or *CP/M.*

Microsoft was a fairly small company whose only important product was MBASIC. This was a version of the BASIC language which they had adapted and sold to virtually every manufacturer of personal computers. Any new personal computer was considered incomplete if it did not offer BASIC, probably from Microsoft.

The story of how Microsoft got to create *PC DOS* has been told many times. It now has reached the status of a legend. Like most legends, it probably is a mixture of three components: Elements that are factual, elements that are false, and elements that while not strictly factual, are yet "true" in the sense that they capture some essential truth about the story.

IBM planned to make a small computer with which to test the market. They thought it would sell mostly as a home computer or to the hobbyist's market, but they expected some penetration into the small-business market as well. They chose, therefore, not to commit too many resources to the development of their initial offering. Also, they wanted it to be brought to market in what was, for IBM, an unusually short time.

Most of the pieces of the original IBM *PC* were bought "off the shelf" from some vendor. Some of the parts were taken from other IBM products. (The keyboard, which seemed to many a strange departure from tradition, had previously been developed for a small scientific computer by another division of IBM.) They hoped to do much the same with the fundamental software they needed to offer with the computer.

Since IBM was more interested in the small-business market than in education, they decided to build a computer that was an improvement on the *CP/M* family of computers. For the central processor, they picked the Intel chip that was a direct successor to the 8080, the 8088. The features of this chip suggested they should be able to adapt both *CP/M* and many programs meant to run on *CP/M* machines to this new architecture relatively easily.

Naturally enough, IBM went to Digital Research to see if they could prepare the operating system for their new computer. (This was a first for IBM; formerly all their operating system software had been developed in their own laboratories.)

Here is where the story gets really interesting. According to the legend, when the IBM representatives showed up in Monterey, California, at the home of Digital Research, the company president, Gary Kildall, was out flying his plane. The man he had left in charge told the IBM folks, "No, I am sorry, we don't have an operating system for a computer based on Intel's 8088." After a short discussion, the IBM team left Digital Research.

They also knew they needed to have a version of BASIC for this new computer, so they continued on in their travels to Redmond, Washington, home of Microsoft. There they spoke to its founder and president, Bill Gates. First they struck their deal regarding BASIC. Microsoft would provide IBM with a version customized to run on their new computer, just as they had done for virtually all the manufacturers of new personal computers for many years.

> Then the IBM representative said to Bill, "Oh by the way, we also need an operating system for this new computer. We'd like something sort of like *CP/M*. Would you care to produce that for us also?" Now, Bill Gates did not have an operating system for the Intel 8088 any more than Digital Research did. But his response was quite different from theirs. "No problem," he said.

Microsoft got a contract to produce *PC DOS*, which was to include a version of its product MBASIC. The contract specified that Microsoft could sell versions of that same operating system to others, but not under the name *PC DOS*. Bill Gates discovered a small company nearby, Seattle Computer Products, which had an operating system that worked on the Intel 8088. It was fairly crude, but it was close enough that he bought the rights to it. On that base, *PC DOS* version 1.0 was built.

Over the next decade, DOS underwent many changes. Some were made by IBM in its *PC DOS* versions. Others were developed by Microsoft, either for IBM or for its own use in *MS-DOS*. Many innovations were introduced, chiefly borrowed from the minicomputer operating system, *UNIX*. Prior to version 5.0, *MS-DOS* was only available officially for sale to manufacturers of clone PCs. Retail sales by Microsoft started with version 5.0 in mid-1991.

The hierarchical directory structure that was introduced to DOS with version 2.0 is almost directly an import from *UNIX*. Another, more subtle sign of the *UNIX* heritage is buried deep inside DOS.

The directory separator character for DOS is the backslash (\), while for *UNIX* it is the forward slash (/). An undocumented DOS interrupt (INT 21h, Function 3701h) will change the character used to precede command switches (normally / in DOS and - in *UNIX*) to whatever you like. Another undocumented DOS interrupt (INT 2Fh, Function 1204h) will convert forward slashes into backslashes (so the DOS path parsing routines will work correctly). If you wish to make your DOS machine look more *UNIX*-like, these two interrupts will enable you to do so, but only for DOS versions 2.x and 3.x.

Eventually, Digital Research did develop a couple of operating systems for the Intel 80x86 family of microprocessors. The first was an extension of *CP/M* called *CP/M-86*. The next was a clone of *MS-DOS* called *DR DOS*. For a while, *DR DOS* was sold mainly to manufacturers who wanted to install it in their machines totally in ROM. Starting with version 5.0, Digital Research entered the retail market for DOS for PCs (late in 1990). *DR DOS* 6 is the version currently shipping. It is a very close clone of *MS-DOS,* but it is not identical to *MS-DOS,* nor even 100 percent compatible with it. *DR DOS* has been more than a year and one full version number ahead of *MS-DOS* (and *PC DOS*) ever since the introduction of *DR DOS* 5. As you might expect, many features in *MS-DOS* 5 are essentially copies of features *DR DOS* introduced with its version 5. MS-DOS 6 and PC DOS 6 essentially catch up to DR DOS 6 in terms of memory management, but move ahead of it in terms of on-the-fly file compression and some other features.

The Parts of PC DOS, MS-DOS, or DR DOS

We have spoken of DOS as if it were just one thing. But actually, it has several parts. First we'll look at the different pieces you will find on a DOS diskette. A little later in the chapter, I'll describe some of the internal parts of DOS and how it changes as it moves from the disk into memory.

Some people consider DOS on a bootable diskette to have five different parts: the boot sector, the two hidden system files, the command interpreter, and the external commands. The following descriptions explain each of these:

- The first part of DOS is the *boot sector.* It is the very first sector on the disk, and it contains both a program and a data table. The data table is used to tell the BIOS about the logical dimensions of the disk (numbers of heads, sectors, tracks, and so on), and the boot sector program is used to load the rest of the operating system.

- The second part is the first of the two essential, hidden files. Usually it is named IBMBIO.COM (for *PC DOS* and DR DOS) or IO.SYS (for MS-DOS). This contains mostly additions to or replacements for the motherboard BIOS or option BIOS ROM programs and some more data tables. The other important part it contains is called the SYSINIT module. (More on this shortly.)

- The third part of DOS is the second of the two hidden files. Usually it is named IBMDOS.COM or MSDOS.SYS. This is referred to as the memory file and device manager. (Some people would consider this the only part that is really DOS; the other parts they would consider as simply other aspects of the overall operating system.)

This is the part that does most of the work of memory management. It also allows you and your application programs to refer to your information on the external storage media by file name, without worrying about where that data is physically located on the disk or how big the file is.

- The fourth part is the command interpreter. The one that ships with *PC DOS, MS-DOS,* and *DR DOS* is called COMMAND.COM.

If you consider DOS the program that manages resources for the benefit of other programs, then the command interpreter is not a part of DOS at all. The two hidden files build in RAM what is called the *kernel* of DOS, and it is the only part of DOS that most programs need. But in another sense, the command interpreter is an absolutely crucial part of DOS, because it lets the user communicate with DOS and thereby select and start the programs you choose to run.

The command interpreter is what presents the DOS prompt, "watches" what you type on the keyboard, tries to figure out what you want to have happen, and then tries to "make it so." Without such a program, you would have no way to tell your computer what you wanted it to do!

Another name for the command interpreter is the *shell.* This name is borrowed from *UNIX,* in which there are often several shell programs available and each user gets to select a favorite one, perhaps a different one for each session or even each process.

The SHELL statement in the DOS CONFIG.SYS file owes its name to this *UNIX* usage. Don't confuse this meaning of shell with programs (often called DOS shells) that wrap themselves around the command interpreter to keep the PC's user from ever seeing the "horrible" raw DOS prompt. (Those programs include the DOSSHELL program that is included with DOS, starting in version 4, ViewMAX in *DR DOS,* the *PC Tools* Shell, *Xtree,* and the *Norton Commander.*)

- The last part of DOS you will find on a DOS diskette is the collection of programs called the "DOS external commands." These are simply various utility programs that get shipped with DOS. They are thought of as a part of DOS because they are bundled with the real parts of DOS.

Those are the pieces of DOS you will find on a DOS diskette. I will describe the internal components that make up some of these parts near the end of this chapter.

The Two Dimensions of DOS Versions

"DOS" is not a single product, as you have seen so far. Originally, Microsoft and IBM together created *PC DOS*, version 1.0, but since then, it has been developed along two different dimensions: the manufacturer and the version number.

The Manufacturer Dimension

DOS is no longer just an IBM product. The three main sources of DOS for PCs are IBM, Microsoft, and Novell. To complicate matters further, Microsoft sold its *MS-DOS* to various manufacturers of PC compatibles, who were encouraged to customize it so that it would work optimally with their particular collection of hardware parts. Thus, an important fact to know about any copy of DOS is whose version it is. Knowing it is IBM's *PC DOS* or Tandy's (or Epson's, or Toshiba's, . . .) *MS-DOS* or Novell's *DR DOS* implies some significant features and limitations as compared to any other manufacturer's version of DOS.

Up until version 5, IBM and Microsoft worked from the same original set of source code, and they tried very hard to make *MS-DOS* and *PC DOS* essentially the same product. Digital Research made *DR DOS* but did not have the advantage of getting to see Microsoft's and IBM's original source code, but they made *DR DOS* as close a clone as they could.

Starting with IBM's *PC DOS* version 5.02 (a very quietly released upgrade shipped in the fall of 1992), IBM has decided that it must part company with Microsoft. The agreement that lets the two companies share source code ends with the development of DOS version 6 in any case. So we may expect to see more and more divergence between *MS* and *PC DOS* from version 6 onward.

Since Novell purchased Digital Research they have made clear their intent to significantly increase the market share for what was *DR DOS* and will now be called Novell DOS. They will, as one might expect, stress support for networked PCs, but they will also make their DOS a viable option for any PC of any class.

These developments mean that the later the version number, the more important the manufacturer dimension of difference will be. If you buy the Microsoft *MS-DOS*, version 6, upgrade kit, you are essentially getting the "vanilla" version, as it is sold to the PC clone manufacturers before any customization has been done.

The Version Number Dimension

Next, you have the version number, or "generation," dimension. IBM has offered DOS in about 8 to 10 different versions. (The exact number of versions is not easy to determine. Sometimes IBM has introduced a modification that others would call a new version, but they don't announce that they have done so and they don't change the official version number. One such change was when IBM fixed the worst bugs in version 4.0. Microsoft did the same in its *MS-DOS* version 4.0, and renamed it 4.01 in the process. IBM continued to sell its corrected version simply as version 4.0.)

Microsoft has introduced at least that many versions of *MS-DOS*. Furthermore, the various clone makers have sometimes added yet another version on top of that (for example, Compaq and its version 3.31).

Choosing the Right DOS

How do you know which DOS to use? Does it even matter? Yes, it does. Here are some tips on how to choose the right version for you.

First is the matter of manufacturer customizations. Some "clones" are more like the IBM design than others. When important differences exist in the hardware, often the manufacturer will make some compensating change to its version of DOS. In those cases, you really should use the manufacturer-specific version of DOS for your machine. Neither the vanilla *MS-DOS* nor *PC DOS* will do, let alone *DR DOS (Novell DOS)*.

For example, if you have a Zenith portable with a built-in modem, you will never succeed in making any phone calls with it unless you run Zenith's custom version of DOS. Likewise, if your PC has some fancy power management features, most likely they won't work without the proper manufacturer's custom version of DOS. For best operation, buy your DOS upgrades (for example, to version 6) directly from your PC's manufacturer (for example, Zenith Data Systems).

But whether you must stick to your brand of DOS or not, you still have the question of which version (number) to choose. That raises a whole new flock of questions.

In general, each new version added some important functionality. Mostly these changes reflected the addition to the "standard PC" of some new hardware option. If you need to support 3 ½" disks, for example, you should use at least version 3.x. If you need to use a very large hard disk partition, you should upgrade at least to DOS 4 (and given what was wrong with that version, you would do much better to upgrade to DOS 5 or 6 (*MS, PC,* or *DR DOS*).

The most important upgrade, from the point of view of memory management, is the one from DOS 4 to DOS 5 (*MS-DOS, PC DOS,* or *DR DOS*). The further improvements in *DOS* 6 are significant, but not nearly so much as those in going from version 4 to version 5.

Where were those key differences made in DOS? They were not so much changes to the kernel (the core programs that do the management of resources) as they were in the incorporation of some new add-on pieces, and adding new functionality to a few old ones. The DOS Shell and the MEM program were drastically improved. And the capability to load DOS itself into the high memory area (HMA) and programs into upper memory were brand-new.

Some of these changes showed up in *MS-DOS* 4 (for example, the DOS Shell) but were so limited that they appear virtually new with *MS-DOS* 5. (And, of course, most people who are upgrading to DOS 5 are doing so from version 3.3 or earlier; DOS 4 deservedly was never very popular.)

Many of the changes took place in the SYSINIT portion of DOS (that part which first builds the kernel in low memory). And you have the new programs HIMEM.SYS and EMM386.EXE, plus various additions to the features of COMMAND.COM and MEM.EXE.

The main changes to MS and PC DOS 6 over their version 5 are not in the kernel code. Rather the bulk of the changes a user will notice are in the new utilities that have been bundled with DOS.

If you were not already a user of Stacker or SuperStor (or if you have had difficulty coping with those programs' need for synchronized pairs of startup files), then DoubleSpace will probably delight you. If you did not already use some third-party memory optimization utility, then MemMaker will make memory management much easier to do. And so on for each of the other utilities bundled with DOS 6.

In every case, Microsoft sought to make their version of these utility programs very safe and very compatible, and they sacrificed power in the bargain. If you already have and use some third-party utility programs, you most likely will find that you will want to continue using them, as they probably do the same things as the ones included with DOS 6 and do them somewhat better.

The one advantage the DOS 6 utilities have that no third-party utility manufacturer can offer is, of course, that they come with DOS at no additional charge. This matters not only now, but also will matter the next time you upgrade DOS versions. Remember, each time you upgrade DOS, it is often crucial that you upgrade the low-level utility programs you use with DOS. (It is okay to continue to use Stacker 2 or 3 with DOS 6, and you can get away with using a memory manager built for DOS 5, but you must upgrade your PC Tools or Norton Utilities if you are to avoid some serious version incompatibilities with the potential for damaging your data.)

Other Kinds of DOS

Mostly you speak of *MS-DOS* and *PC DOS* as one thing, albeit with some version and manufacturer variations. *DR DOS,* versions 5 and 6 (the retail product), is almost just another one of those variations. There are some other kinds of DOS that are much more different.

Probably the most important are the ROM-only implementations of DOS. These are used in the *PS/1* and some palmtop and laptop computers. Eventually, as Flash RAM becomes more popular, ROM-only DOS may become the norm even on desktop machines. Having it in Flash will probably be crucial, though, to make it easy enough to upgrade it when that is necessary or desirable.

Third-Party Replacements for COMMAND.COM

In the beginning, there was *PC DOS* and it came with COMMAND.COM as its command interpreter. Even *MS-DOS* and *DR DOS* use the same program (or at least one very much like the IBM Command Interpreter COMMAND.COM and with the same name). So do you really have any choice about this aspect of DOS?

Yes you do—now. For several years, there were no alternatives available; then a couple of small companies came out with substitute shell programs. The one that has had the most impact was *4DOS* from J.P. Software in Massachusetts. This was distributed as shareware initially and now is available both as shareware and as a retail product.

What is different about *4DOS?* Many things. It greatly reduces the amount of lower memory it uses by putting more of itself somewhere else (for example, in upper memory, in extended memory, or in EMS memory).

This feature alone makes it potentially very valuable for memory management in tightly packed systems.

You will learn later in this chapter how COMMAND.COM puts only a portion of itself near the bottom of lower memory. A larger portion is put near the top of lower memory where it is able to be overwritten by any program that may need that space. After such a program completes execution, the permanent part of COMMAND.COM will refresh the upper, transient portion from the COMMAND.COM file on the disk.

By swapping part of itself to EMS or XMS memory, *4DOS* is able to do something similar (open up more of lower memory for programs to use) and do so even more effectively. Furthermore, it is able to use those other parts without the delays inherent in reading a file from the disk.

Other features of *4DOS* include substantially enhancing the processing of batch files and allowing the user to link data files to the applications that created them (almost like the *resource fork* of a *Macintosh* file). Two other features that have been in *4DOS* for years, aliases for commands and an editable buffer of recently issued commands, became a part of *MS-DOS* starting with version 5.

4DOS is a very feature-rich program. In fact, it is so impressive that Peter Norton bought the rights to it and now includes it as NDOS within the *Norton Utilities,* version 6 or later.

Some Memory Spaces That DOS Cannot Find

A major part of the job DOS does for you is managing RAM. That means keeping track of what RAM is available for use, assigning it to programs that request it, accepting it back again when they are through, and putting it back in the pool where it can again be allocated later on. This keeps the usage of memory orderly, and while it can't prevent one program from walking all over some other one, at least it helps keep the honest and polite programs from doing so.

Quite appropriately for a personal computer, the PC allows you, the person whose computer it is, to do anything anytime you want. Your programs are also given this license.

There is nothing in the design of the PC (as long as it is running in real mode) to limit what any program can do with the resources of the PC. So in that situation, all an operating system can do is, in essence, advise programs where they may or may not tread and then hope that the programs behave themselves.

Of course, DOS cannot even do this much to manage any RAM of which it is unaware. And there are many places in your PC where you may have RAM that DOS does not know about. One hint: If the CPU cannot directly read or write to a patch of RAM, DOS is unlikely to be aware of its existence.

If you know about the hidden RAM in your PC, you can see to it that it is used to full advantage and, usually, you can keep it from being abused. Where are those hidden pockets of RAM?

Inactive EMS Memory

If you have any expanded memory on a plug-in memory card or created by the motherboard system logic from some motherboard memory, and if you have not loaded the appropriate expanded memory manager (EMM) device driver program, no program, DOS included, will be able to access that memory.

The EMM will manage the expanded memory once it is loaded and thus ensure that it is used as effectively and safely as possible. You just have to remember to load the right EMM program for the kind of expanded memory you have.

On Video Cards

We have talked at some length in Chapter 8 about video RAM. It is a batch of RAM that DOS does not notice. The original PC design plan was for all programs wanting to put information on the screen to go through the BIOS to get it done. If they all actually did this, there would be less trouble in the management of this RAM.

Unfortunately, for reasons already explained in Chapter 7, in the section "Direct Hardware Manipulation Versus BIOS Cells" (mostly the issue of speed), programmers often do not want to depend on the BIOS. They would rather have their programs put information into or read information out of the video RAM buffer directly. Mostly this is okay, but sometimes it does present problems, especially with programs that move the effective address of the video image buffer RAM to some location other than the standard ones.

It is not common to store programs (or indeed *anything* except image information and maybe font data) in the RAM on a video card. But if some of that RAM is not being otherwise used, you can load a program or a data table there and treat it simply as more of your RAM. (Be careful, though, that the part you want doesn't get paged out of view by the video driver, especially if you have an EGA or VGA display adapter with lots of RAM on it.)

On Hard Disk Controller Cards

Lots of hard disk controller cards have a little bit of RAM on them. They use it as a track buffer (to store information going to or from the disk a track's worth at a time). Some controllers have much more RAM, organized as a full-fledged disk cache.

Whichever of these types of RAM you have on your PC's hard disk controller, you need not be concerned that DOS cannot see it. You can't use it for anything but the one task it was meant to perform. In a sense, it is outside of the view of the CPU and therefore outside the view of DOS.

Data disappears from the CPU's view onto the controller card. Eventually it comes back. If it lingers briefly in a cache or track buffer, that is of no concern to you or to DOS. (Well, there can be one very important concern. See the discussion of the dangers of deferred write disk caches in Chapter 14.)

There is another use for RAM on some hard disk controller cards, and it is a concern for memory management. Specifically this will happen on certain *autoconfiguring hard disk controllers*. These controllers have a small patch of RAM that is mapped within the range of their option BIOS ROM. They put there the data for the **H**ard **D**isk **P**arameter **T**able (HDPT) copied from the disk drive. This patch of RAM can be a serious impediment to good upper memory management. In Chapter 21, you will learn the details of this problem and one good solution to it.

On Network Cards

Network cards sometimes carry RAM also. They use it mostly as a buffer area in which to compose messages to be delivered elsewhere across the network and to receive messages and disassemble them.

This memory may or may not be outside the purview of DOS and the CPU. If the network card receives information from the PC through some I/O ports (via programmed I/O), then assembles that information into messages in a buffer it maintains outside the CPU's memory address space, that RAM is as invisible as the buffer RAM on a hard disk controller card. And it is equally of no concern to you.

Some network cards place their RAM at some region within the CPU's memory address space. Then their network software will have the CPU or the DMA controller read or write information directly from or to that RAM. If this describes a card in your PC, you should be concerned with exactly where in the CPU's memory address space this RAM is.

DOS won't know about the network card's RAM and can't do anything with it. And what is worse, DOS or some other program could try to use those same memory addresses for some other purpose. Mostly, this will occur somewhere in upper memory. If you try to fill in the empty parts of upper memory with EMM386.EXE, or some third-party memory manager, you will have to be very careful not to place it where the network card wants to put its RAM buffer.

Most third-party memory managers attempt to locate all the users of upper memory before putting any RAM there. But if the network card only puts its RAM buffer on the CPU's memory address bus when it wishes to transfer data in or out of the PC (as is the case with some network cards), then those memory manager programs will be totally unable to see that RAM and may well set up a conflicting use for those same addresses. Finding this sort of conflict is not easy (to say the least).

The one advantage you have now is this: You know enough to ask the right questions. ("Does my network card use DMA or direct writes and reads by the CPU to its RAM buffer? Or, does it use only programmed I/O?" "If the former, when does that RAM buffer appear in memory address space?" "All the time, or only some of the time?" "Where exactly is that RAM located in memory-address space?") Look for answers to these questions in the documents that came with your network card, or ask your network administrator or the network-card manufacturer.

On Slave PC Boards

Some PCs have little PCs inside them. (Sort of like the nested Russian dolls! Almost.) These slave PCs are plug-in cards with another microprocessor on them. Often, they also carry significant amounts of RAM. One version of this sort of product, CPU upgrade boards, replace the main CPU and add additional memory at the same time.

Mostly that RAM is there to support the microprocessor on that board. That RAM is on a local memory address bus that only the processor on the card can access. If that is the case in your PC, then this, too, is RAM outside the purview of the CPU and thus not of direct interest to you.

Occasionally, though, the slave processor will share its memory with the CPU. In that case, just how and where it does so is of critical importance in figuring out how to manage your PC's memory. DOS may or may not be prepared to help you; it depends on the details of how that RAM gets shared. Check the documentation that came with the slave PC boards, or check with their manufacturer.

On a Solid-State Disk

Solid-state disks, by definition, are full of RAM chips. Also by definition, they look exactly like a disk drive. DOS will not see this as RAM. It will, instead, believe this to be a magnetic disk drive.

DOS will manage that RAM for you. But it will do so in the same way that it manages space on a disk drive, which is exactly the right thing for it to do.

In a Print Spooler or Other Peripheral Device

Another place you might have a substantial amount of RAM is in your printer or in a print spooler. This is quite similar to the RAM on a hard disk controller. It helps speed up the operation of your PC, and in most cases, you don't even have to think about it. Just enjoy the extra speed it gives you. On the other hand, that RAM is only available to do that one job, so it does not help you if you are short of extended or expanded memory, for example. Knowing how much you have will help you keep from wasting memory inside your PC with a redundant print spooling program.

The Layers of Programs in Your PC's RAM

Your PC is loaded with layers. The CPU's memory address space is filled with RAM and ROM (and may have some holes with nothing in them).

The RAM portions are usually broken up into many smaller units, each used for a different purpose. In this section, you will get a peek at each of those parts, and you will learn how they get there.

But first, it may be helpful to define some terms. At various points in this book (and no doubt elsewhere, as well) you have seen the terms device driver, ISR, TSR, utility program, and application program. You very likely have all of these in your PC's RAM each time you use it. Did you know that? Are you clear on what each of them is? If not, then this next discussion may be just what you need.

The Relationship Between Various Kinds of Programs

The system programs in your PC include the BIOS and DOS. The BIOS is a collection of miniprograms to activate the hardware parts of your PC. When you add some new piece to your PC, you can augment the BIOS in any one of three ways. One is by an option BIOS ROM on a plug-in card. The second is by loading a device driver program (using a DEVICE= line in your CONFIG.SYS file). The third way is by loading a suitable Terminate and Stay Resident (TSR) program (which will turn out to be one or more ISR programs). Which way you will do it is usually determined by what the hardware manufacturer gives you.

Whichever way you do this, you are putting into the CPU's memory address space either a device driver or an interrupt service routine (or more than one). An option ROM is simply built into some range of addresses. A device driver or ISR program gets loaded into RAM from the disk. In either case, the program must initialize itself in order to inform DOS and the BIOS of its existence and of which tasks it is prepared to handle.

Device Drivers

The device drivers that come with the DOS (in the BIOS file that is loaded from disk), and the extra ones you load through your CONFIG.SYS file, are all linked together into a *device chain*. When DOS needs some information sent to or read in from a device, it sends a message down the device chain. The first device driver that is capable of doing what DOS is requesting and that intercepts that message will do that task.

Interrupt Service Routines (ISRs)

Interrupt service routines are similar to device drivers, but they get called into action in a slightly different way. The default ISRs are located in the motherboard BIOS ROM. The start-up program that is also in that BIOS puts the addresses of these default routines into the appropriate places in the interrupt vector table.

You can load alternative ISR programs for any interrupt. Normally this is done by executing a TSR program containing the replacement ISR. During its initialization, the TSR puts its ISR's address into the interrupt vector table.

Terminate and Stay Resident Programs (TSRs)

The name says what these programs do. They execute, and when they are through, they don't give back the RAM they were using, or at least not all of it.

The reason for running a program that won't give back its RAM is to have that program stay around for use at some later time. In order to get control of the PC when that time arrives, the TSR must "hook" one or more interrupts. When one of the events corresponding to a hooked interrupt occurs, the TSR will gain control of the PC and do whatever it was designed to do. You will learn about the operation of ISRs and TSRs in more detail shortly.

Utility Programs

Strictly speaking, a *utility program* is any program with some utility (that is, it does something useful). Mostly, the name is given to small programs that you run from time to time to do some helpful task, rather than the main job you want your PC to perform. For example, the DOS FORMAT program prepares diskettes for data storage. It is a utility program. Your word processor puts data on those diskettes. The word processor is an application program.

In addition to the DOS external commands (which are utility programs shipped with DOS), most PC users own a number of other utility programs. Some help them manage files on their disk drives (directory programs, file viewers, and so forth). Some do simple, subsidiary tasks like printing envelopes or defragmenting a disk drive.

Application Programs

An *application program* is a program that does one of the things that you bought your PC to do. It could be a word processor, a database program, a spreadsheet program, a graphics program, or a communications program. In contrast, utility programs help you accomplish those ends, but they are not the main program to do any of them.

The most important thing to realize about device drivers, ISRs, TSRs, utility programs, and application programs is that you can have all of them in your PC at once. (Unless you are running a task-switching or multitasking program, you will most likely have either an application program or a utility program active, with all the others standing by, ready to do something helpful whenever necessary.)

What the Layers Contain

Consider memory from the bottom up, looking at each layer in turn. Figure 10.3 shows the layers of a typical class 1 PC. Figure 10.4 shows the layers in a typical class 4 PC. (Both these PCs are shown running *MS-DOS* 5 with a similar number of FILES, BUFFERS, and other CONFIG.SYS commands. Both have loaded the same size TSRs and application program. The class 4 PC has loaded DOS and the DOS disk buffers in the HMA. You can see how much more room that leaves in lower memory.) The other classes of PCs have similar memory maps.

See Figure 10.9 and Figure 10.13, later in this chapter, for another way of showing a memory map for a PC. Note that those figures show maps that are, by the definition given at the start of Chapter 8, upside down! The very bottom of memory is used for the interrupt vector table. That extends from address 00000h to 003FFh. These 1024 bytes (1KB) provide just enough room for 256 four-byte **segment:offset** addresses, each one pointing to an interrupt service routine for that class of interrupts.

You learned in Chapter 7 how interrupt service routines function. The sequence of events is summarized graphically in Figure 10.5.

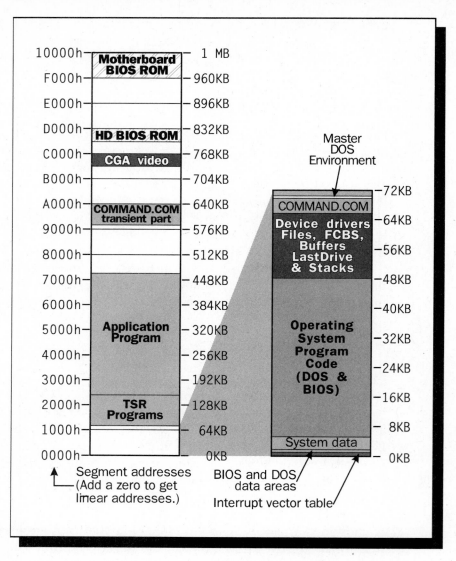

Figure 10.3. A typical memory map for a class 1 PC (an XT with CGA video).

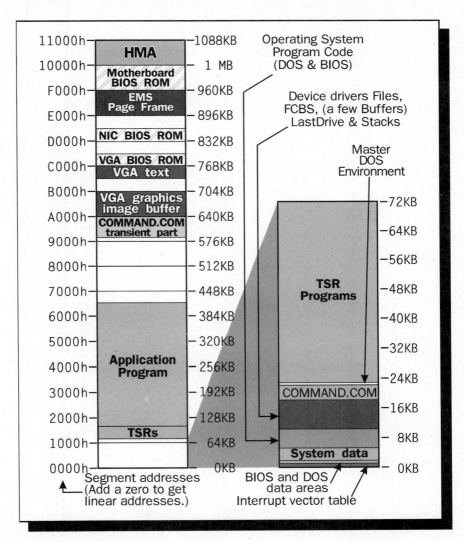

Figure 10.4. A typical memory map for a class 4 PC (an AT with VGA video, hardware EMS, and a network interface card).

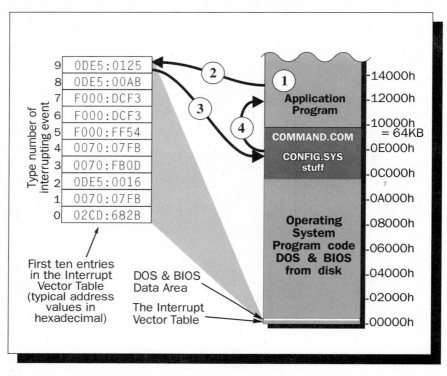

Figure 10.5. How an interrupt service routine (ISR) works.

The processing of an interrupt follows these four stages (indicated by the circled numbers in Figure 10.5):

First stage: You have an application program that is executing. An interrupt occurs. The CPU stops what it is doing, stores a marker so it can pick up later where it left off, and then goes to see what kind of interrupt this one is.

Second stage: Figure 10.5 was constructed to show an interrupt from the keyboard controller. That is an event of type 9. So the CPU looks in the tenth slot in the interrupt vector table (Interrupt zero corresponds to the first slot) to find the address of the appropriate interrupt service routine.

Third stage: The CPU now jumps to the indicated address (the entry point of the ISR). That means it begins executing whatever instructions it finds there. The ISR program does whatever it was written to do.

Fourth stage: When the ISR finishes, it executes a Return From Interrupt (IRET) instruction. That causes the CPU to resume the application program processing.

The next layer in the map is 768 bytes of data. The first 256 bytes are known as the BIOS data area. The rest are the DOS data area. This is where your PC keeps track of what pieces it has and the state of various tasks it is performing.

For example, the BIOS data table starts off with the I/O port addresses of your serial and parallel ports. At linear address 00410h are two bytes called the *equipment word*. It can be interpreted a bit at a time to show how many diskette drives you have, whether or not you have a math coprocessor, and other information about your machine's configuration. A byte indicating the current video mode (for example, monochrome, color, or 40- or 80-column text or graphics) is stored at 00449h.

Some modern PCs, in particular many *PS/2* models, need more than 768 bytes for this kind of information. They supplement this region with a layer called the *Extended BIOS Data Area* (EBDA). Figure 10.2 shows how this typically is placed at the top of lower RAM. The EBDA can be any multiple of 1KB in size, though usually it is just 1KB. A pointer to the EBDA is stored in the BIOS data area at 00414h.

The next layer in RAM contains the system files. This is the bulk of the instruction code from IO.SYS (or IBMBIO.COM) and MSDOS.SYS (or IBMDOS.COM). This includes all the default device drivers and all the interrupt service routines that collectively constitute DOS. (The part of the code in those files that doesn't end up here is that used to initialize the PC and build this arrangement of layers up to this point.)

After this comes a layer for the device drivers loaded through lines in the CONFIG.SYS file. That is followed by some system tables—one, for example, keeps track of open files, and another remembers the current directory on each logical drive. Also, this region of RAM is usually where the DOS disk buffers are located.

Next is the permanent part of the command interpreter. When COMMAND.COM (or *4DOS,* NDOS, or some other alternative command interpreter) is loaded into memory, initially it splits itself into two parts. One part is loaded here and another part is put up near the top of RAM (just under the EBDA, if there is one of those).

The permanent part of the command interpreter is followed by any TSR programs you may have loaded, and then whatever is the current application.

TSRs are interrupt service routines you load by running some program. Often they are loaded by lines in the AUTOEXEC.BAT file, though they can be loaded simply at the DOS prompt.

When a TSR is loaded, it "hooks" one or more interrupts. That allows it to be called before the normal interrupt service routine. If it can handle the interrupt, it will do so and return (with the IRET instruction). If it is unable to handle the interrupt (and if it was a "well-written TSR"), it will call the original ISR to allow it to handle the interrupt. This sequence of events is shown in Figure 10.6.

Steps 1 and 2, shown in Figure 10.6 (steps are circled), are just as they were in Figure 10.5. Since the CPU finds a new address in the interrupt vector table, it will jump at step 3 to the TSR instead of to the original ISR program. In step 4, the TSR does its thing. This will include determining if the TSR can handle the interrupt (in which case it does so), or if it cannot.

Steps 5 and 6 only occur if the TSR is unable to service the interrupt. These are where it calls the original ISR (using an address the TSR copied out of the interrupt vector table before it put its own address in there) and that routine returns (via an IRET) back to the TSR. Then the TSR returns, this time back to the original application program (step 7).

If the application program you are currently running needs all of the rest of the RAM, it can have it (up to the start of the EBDA, if there is one). Even if it doesn't need all that memory, it still might claim it (unless it's a "good program" that gives back to DOS all the memory it does not need). Any returned memory becomes free space, followed by the transient part of the command interpreter.

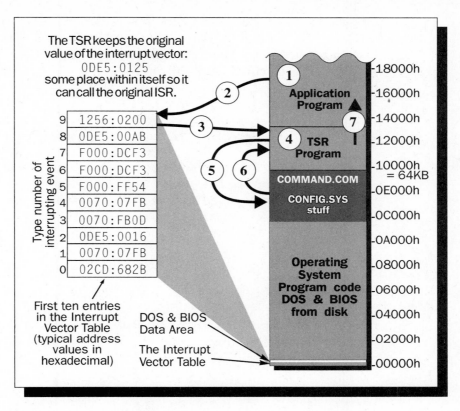

Figure 10.6. Terminate and Stay Resident (TSR) programs hook interrupts to replace or augment other ISRs.

That finishes the layers that make up lower memory. Upper memory is also filled in layers. The first one is for the video-image-buffer RAM. Chapter 8 described in some detail what this layer might contain. In any PC whose video is not supported by the motherboard BIOS, this region is followed by a video BIOS ROM. If you have other option ROMs, they will likely be placed somewhere in this area as well.

There could be some free RAM in upper memory, though there normally is not unless you do something very special to put it there. If you have expanded memory and are using an EMS page frame, it normally falls among these layers. At the top of the first megabyte of address space is the motherboard BIOS ROM.

Figure 10.4 shows one more layer on top of all the ones described earlier. It is the High Memory Area (HMA). If you use version 5 or 6 of

DOS and tell it to load itself high, then a portion of the system code will be moved up to the HMA. Most of the system file table and the disk buffers can be put there also. Alternatively, you can tell DOS not to use the HMA, and instead direct some other program to use it, possibly using more of it this way than DOS would have.

How the Layers Get There: The Boot Process

A pretty complex structure has just been described. How does it happen? To understand, you need to know all the steps your PC goes through when you turn it on. This is called the *boot process.* Figure 10.7 shows the steps of the boot process graphically. Here are some additional details.

The POST

The boot process begins by the execution of the Power On Self Test (POST) program. That program's first task is to be sure that it has not been corrupted. So it computes a simple checksum of all of its bytes and compares that value to what it knows it ought to be. If it passes that test, the POST assumes it is not damaged.

DIP Switches and CMOS RAM
Provide Configuration Information

Then the POST surveys the other parts of the machine. In a class 1 or 2 PC, it looks at the DIP switch(es) on the motherboard to see what options are indicated. IBM *PCs* have two switch blocks. IBM *PC/XTs,* and most clone PCs in classes 1 and 2, have only one. Here, one can choose which video controller (monochrome or color) and, for the color monitor, which mode (40- or 80-column text) the PC shall use initially. Here, too, you can indicate how many floppy diskette drives you have, whether or not a math coprocessor is installed, and how much RAM you have.

The RAM indications are different in different models. IBM *PCs* use the switch positions 3 and 4, on the first switch block, to specify how much RAM is on the motherboard. Switch positions 1 through 5, on the second switch block, indicate total lower (system) memory.

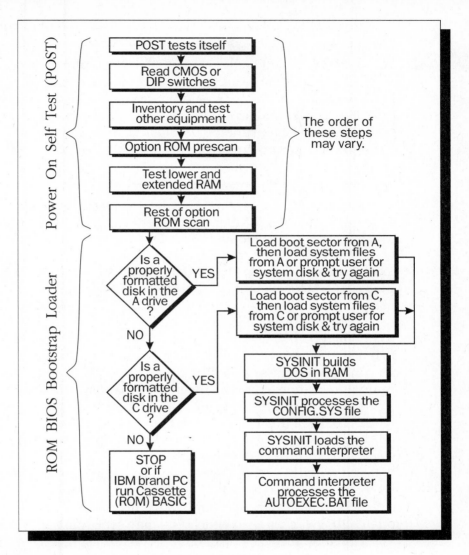

Figure 10.7. The steps in the boot process.

Warning If you set these switches to indicate a total amount of system memory higher than you actually have, then DOS will attempt to load the transient part of COMMAND.COM into nonexistent memory, just under what you have declared is the top of system memory. Do this, and your PC will not function properly.

Useful Tip If you set these switches to say you have less system memory than you really do, the PC will accept your word for what you have and ignore all the rest of the system RAM you may have on the motherboard or any plug-in card. If you also have a hardware EMS board, setting the motherboard DIP switches this way can be very useful when running *DESQview,* or a similar task switching program. That combination will allow you to do a much more effective job of task switching or multitasking.

An IBM *PC/XT* uses the switches on its single switch block a little differently than the IBM *PC.* Positions 3 and 4 are used to indicate how much RAM is on the motherboard. The XT finds out how much total system RAM you have by scanning its memory address space, 32KB at a time, looking to see what it can find. (It does this as it is testing the RAM during the POST.) Most clone PCs in classes 1 or 2 use the XT strategy, though many of them ignore the DIP switch settings for positions 3 and 4.

PCs in class 3 or higher don't have configuration DIP switch(es) on the motherboard. They have instead a battery-backed-up CMOS RAM chip to hold the same sort of information. That chip also keeps track of the date and time of day (the so-called "real time clock"). It may also hold advanced setup information to control the motherboard system logic.

Often, though, there is at least one switch or jumper on the motherboard of these PCs. This is to indicate whether the PC is to put its initial messages on a monochrome video adapter (write them to a buffer starting at address B0000h) or a color adapter (with a buffer starting at B8000h). The IBM *PC/AT* has one more jumper, to indicate the top of motherboard system RAM.

Clone PCs in classes 3 and above may have some jumpers or (less often) DIP switches with which you may set a number of other options. These include the size of ROM chip you are using for the motherboard BIOS ROM, the number of wait states you want for accesses to the motherboard RAM, the size of RAM chips installed there, and so forth.

Further Tests of the PC's Parts

After reading the CMOS or motherboard configuration DIP switch(es), the POST tests and initializes the keyboard. Then it attempts to find any serial and parallel ports you may have. It does this by searching at a standardized list of I/O port addresses. At each address, the POST sends out a set of byte values and attempts to read them back. If there is a properly functioning port of the correct type at that address, the returned values will be as expected. In that case, the address where a serial or parallel port was found is put into the BIOS data area, and after all addresses have been searched, the equipment word in the BIOS data area is updated to reflect the total number of each that the POST found.

The POST on most PCs only looks for the first two serial ports. Called *COM1* and *COM2*, they are conventionally located at 3F8h and 2F8h. (Actually, each uses eight successive port addresses. The usual number quoted for that port's address is what is known as its *base address,* the lowest of the eight addresses it uses. Thus, COM1 uses all the ports from 3F8h to 3FFh.)

The search order for parallel ports is first 3BCh, next 378h, and last 278h. The first location in this list where a parallel port is found becomes LPT1. The next becomes LPT2, and if all three have parallel ports, the last one is LPT3. So if you have only one parallel port, even if it is at address 278h, it will be referred to as LPT1.

The Option ROM Prescan

When IBM introduced the Enhanced Graphics Adapter (EGA) video card, it altered how every PC's BIOS had to operate. Previous to that, the POST would next test RAM. But before it can do that on a PC that might have an EGA or VGA card, it must look to see what kind of video display is installed so it will know how to put progress and error messages on the screen.

This is accomplished by an option ROM prescan. This means it looks for an option ROM for a video display. This is always located starting at address C0000h.

The test for any option BIOS ROM is done by following these steps: Begin by looking at the first two bytes. If they are 55h and AAh in that order, then you have a candidate. Read the third byte. Consider it a binary number (between 0 and 255 decimal). Multiply that by 512. That is the indicated length of this ROM in bytes. Now add up the binary value of that many bytes. As you add each new byte to the running sum, throw away the carry bit, if any. When you finish, you should end up with exactly zero if this is actually a valid option ROM.

If the option ROM candidate passes all these tests, the POST program assumes it is valid, and it then transfers control to the start-up program in that ROM. That program normally changes some values in the interrupt vector table and puts a message on the screen announcing its presence (and gives some copyright information). Once that initialization program completes its work, it transfers control back to the POST program.

> In more technical language, you can say the POST executes a far CALL instruction pointing to the fourth byte from the start of the ROM (offset 03h), and at the end of its initialization work, the option ROM's start-up program must execute a far RETurn instruction.

After the video ROM is found and initialized, if there is one, the POST is free to continue with its checking of the PC's parts. Next, it tests RAM (unless you are warm booting).

Cold Versus Warm, a Difference in Boots

There are two kinds of boot. The first is when you power on the PC initially. This is called a *cold boot*. The second is when you press the Ctrl-Alt-Del key combination (the "three-fingered salute"). This is called a *warm boot*. The main difference is that a warm boot skips the RAM test.

> **Tip**   If your PC gets really confused, you may have to reboot it in order to get it back on track. If you merely press Ctrl-Alt-Del, you may not have done enough. That will start loading all the programs in your PC all over again, but it will not first zero out the contents of RAM. Doing a cold boot will.
>
> There are potentially two different kinds of cold boot also. If you turn off power to the PC and wait a few moments (and you should *always* wait at *least* 20 seconds), then turn it back on again, you may be quite sure that everything in the PC is back to where it was.
>
> If, on the other hand, you just press a reset button, even though you see the RAM test being performed and therefore know that all of your lower and extended memory is being wiped clean, you cannot be sure that something isn't lingering in expanded memory, a port somewhere, or some RAM that DOS does not have access to.
>
> It is generally easier on the hardware to do a reset from the reset button than to have power turned off and back on again. So only do the latter when you really want to be sure you have reset everything in the PC to a normal start-up state.

The RAM Test

True-blue IBM *PCs* and *PS/2s* test every byte of their lower and extended RAM. Many clone PCs do this also. But beware, there are a few clone PCs out there that only seem to test RAM. They may or may not even check to see if you *have* any RAM! Also, some clone PCs allow you to jump past the RAM test if you wish. That is generally okay, as long as you have recently allowed the test to run to its completion without seeing any error messages.

In the process of testing RAM, the PC also learns how much it has. (The sole exception to this is an IBM *PC* with the DIP switches set to say it has less RAM than in fact is installed in the machine. It simply will stop checking at the indicated amount of RAM and never discover that it could have found more.)

> When it comes to finding problems with memory chips, the POST test is always the first one to use. It is right there, ready to go whenever you power up the PC or do a "cold boot." It is not, however, as complete a test as some diagnostic programs provide. So, if you have to smoke out a really stubborn, intermittent RAM problem, you may need to turn to a more powerful helper.

The Rest of the Option ROM Scan

Now the POST has assured itself that your PC is in good health (or at least it has reported any problems it found to you). A true-blue PC will beep once briefly at this point to tell you it is healthy. If it found a problem, it will give you a pattern of beeps to indicate what group of problems it has discovered. Some clone BIOSes use the IBM sound message convention; others will beep once as they start and twice briefly if they finish without finding a problem (and some other pattern of beeps to signal a problem).

Next, the POST looks for any more option BIOS ROMs it can find. It begins at the next multiple of 2KB after the last ROM it found. (That will be the video ROM if there was one.) At each place it looks, it follows the steps detailed earlier in "The Option ROM Prescan" section. Each time it finds a valid option ROM, it transfers control to the start-up program within that ROM. After it regains control, the POST goes on looking for additional option ROMs. It normally ends its search at DF800h (just 2KB below the end of the D page).

If you have a *PS/2*, DF800H is the last location at which you could have an option ROM, because all of the E and F pages are taken up by the motherboard BIOS ROM. If you have a PC with a smaller BIOS ROM, there may be room for one additional option ROM.

In such PCs, the option ROM scan may continue for one more step. The difference in this step from the others in the option ROM scan is that when it looks at location E0000h, the POST program doesn't look for a length value in the third byte. Instead, it simply assumes the ROM will be 64KB long (if it is there at all). A ROM in this location is sometimes called the *user ROM*.

Finally, the POST has finished its work. Now it is time to try to find an operating system. The POST transfers control to another program in the motherboard BIOS, the bootstrap loader.

Most PCs can boot either from a diskette in the first diskette drive or from the first hard disk. They cannot boot from any other drive. A few clone PC makers have incorporated some options in their BIOS bootstrap loaders, but normally these are the only two possible boot drives.

The BIOS addresses devices by a physical address. Its address for the first floppy diskette drive is 00h. Its address for the first hard drive is 80h. Other floppy drives are given addresses 01h, 02h, and so on. The second hard disk is given address 81h.

DOS names drives with letters. A will be the first floppy diskette drive. C will be the first hard disk, unless you don't have any hard disks, in which case C will be the third floppy diskette drive. If you have three or more floppy diskette drives, and one or more hard drives, DOS will have to give some letter higher than those given to any of the hard drive logical volumes to the third and subsequent floppy diskette drives.

The bootstrap loader first looks at the A drive. If it sees a disk there with a valid boot sector, it will load the contents of that sector into memory. This should be a boot program and the data to make up a table called a *BIOS parameter block* describing the disk it came from.

The BIOS bootstrap loader checks the sector it loaded to see if it appears to be a valid boot sector. If so, control of the PC is given to that boot sector program. It will look on the drive it came from for a copy of the operating system. If it finds the operating system files, they are loaded into memory and executed. But what if they are not?

> The boot sector is put on the disk in the process of formatting the disk. The boot sector will only look for a copy of the operating system that created it. A disk formatted with *PC DOS,* for example, cannot boot if the hidden system files on it came from *MS-DOS.* If you have this situation, you will get the message Non-system disk, replace and strike any key.
>
> This is a rare problem as either the FORMAT or SYS commands will put on a disk both a fresh copy of the two hidden system files, and a fresh copy of the boot sector that is to load those files. So the only way to get them out of sync would be if you used some utility program to change the hidden files. A much more common problem is copying onto a disk a copy of COMMAND.COM that is from a different version (either a different manufacturer or, more commonly, of a different generation) of DOS. That also won't work. In this case the message is Invalid COMMAND.COM and the system will simply halt until you reset it.

If the boot sector cannot find the proper system files to load, it will prompt you to put in a bootable disk and strike any key. (Incidentally, some computer viruses copy the boot sector to some other place on the disk, and then replace the original boot sector with their own code. When the bootstrap loader loads what it thinks is a valid boot sector into memory, it really is running the virus program. After establishing itself in memory, the virus program can then run the real boot sector. Such a "boot sector infector" virus can take control of your machine even if the diskette it was on was not bootable. By the time you see the message prompting you to put in a bootable disk, the infection has already occurred.)

What if the bootstrap loader did not find a valid boot sector program on the A drive? (That could be because the drive door is open, there is no disk in the drive, or the disk that is in the drive is not properly formatted.) In that case, it moves on to the C drive.

Booting from the hard disk has one additional step. The boot sector that is found at the start of the hard disk is called the *Master Boot Record* (MBR) or the *Partition Table.* That sector contains a program and a data table, similar to those in a diskette's boot sector, but with a small, important difference.

The MBR program looks at its data table (the partition table) to find out which one, if any, of up to four partitions on your hard disk is bootable. If it sees that one of them is, it will look in the first sector of that partition table for a boot sector just like the one on a floppy diskette. Once that sector is loaded into memory, the process continues very much as if the PC were booting from the A drive.

There is one more case to consider. Suppose that the bootstrap loader did not find a boot sector on either the A or the C drives. In that case, and only if yours is an IBM-brand PC, it will start running Cassette BASIC. You can't do anything useful when it does, but that is what will happen. (You will see a copyright message, including a version number for BASIC, that starts with the letter C.) All clone PCs simply stop at this point, some of them putting up annoying multiple messages with beeps; others simply doing nothing.

Initializing DOS in RAM

The boot sector program loads the two hidden system files (IO.SYS and MSDOS.SYS, or if you are booting *PC DOS* or *DR DOS*, IBMBIO.COM and IBMDOS.COM) into RAM and then transfers control to IO.SYS (or IBMBIO.COM). (Some implementations of DOS only have the boot sector program load the first of these two files [IO.SYS or IBMBIO.COM]; in this case, that program loads the other one [MSDOS.SYS or IBMDOS.COM].)

The file IO.SYS consists of three parts. One is the collection of BIOS extensions (device drivers and interrupt service routines) that are to be loaded. They supplement (or in some cases replace) those in the motherboard BIOS ROM.

Next is some initialization code that helps bond all these pieces into the operating system seamlessly. This section also may be responsible for doing some initialization of certain hardware parts of your PC. (Just what gets done here depends on the particular manufacturer-specific version of DOS you are using.)

The third section is called the *SYSINIT* module. Its job is to complete the construction of DOS in the RAM in your PC. It does this by first relocating itself near the top of RAM, then moving the MSDOS.SYS file image down in memory to overlay both the initialization section and the SYSINIT sections of the original IO.SYS memory image, and then it transfers control to the MSDOS.SYS program.

After both IO.SYS and MSDOS.SYS (or IBMBIO.COM and IBMDOS.COM) have finished their initialization steps, DOS is in RAM fully fleshed out and ready to go.

But the boot process is not over yet. The command processor must still be loaded, as well as any customizations you have requested in CONFIG.SYS and AUTOEXEC.BAT. In the following sections, these final steps will be described.

DOS Seizes Control of Memory

Incidentally, it is at this point that DOS takes control of your PC's memory. It declares its "ownership" of all system (lower) RAM starting just above its own layer and extending to the end of that system RAM.

Normally that end point is at 640KB. It can, however, be either higher or lower. If you have less than 640KB of RAM, naturally the end point will be lower. Also, if you have an Extended BIOS Data Area, the end point of the RAM that DOS owns will be reduced by the size of the EBDA.

On the other hand, if you have a video adapter that doesn't use the A page (hexadecimal addresses A0000h to AFFFFh) for its image buffer, and *if you have added some RAM starting directly above 640KB*, the end of the DOS-managed memory area will extend to the end of that added RAM. This could be as high as 736KB (in which case CHKDSK would report 753,664 bytes total memory).

And, if you have specified (by a DOS=UMB line in your CONFIG.SYS file) that you want DOS to manage upper memory also, the region DOS claims ownership over will extend to the end of the last block of RAM in upper memory (but this fact will not be reflected in the numbers CHKDSK reports). You can see the result of this by running MEM /C.

Whatever the extent of the region of memory-address space over which DOS claims ownership, it is one contiguous region. And from this point on, no program is permitted to use any of it (legally) without seeking permission from DOS. (Any UMBs DOS will be managing fall into one or more other regions which DOS cleverly attaches to lower memory, briefly, whenever it needs to load a program into upper memory. This strategy is described more fully at the very end of this chapter.)

CONFIG.SYS Time

Next comes the reading of the CONFIG.SYS file and acting on its contents. SYSINIT does this job. The only place SYSINIT will look for the CONFIG.SYS file is in the root directory of the drive from which you are booting.

SYSINIT reads the whole CONFIG.SYS file before acting on any of it. Starting with version 5, *MS-DOS* reads the file twice. The first time through, it only notices whether or not there is a directive DOS=HIGH (or DOS=HIGH,UMB). If there is, it will load a portion of the system code and, perhaps, the disk buffers into the High Memory Area (HMA) once that space is available (after an XMS manager is loaded). The second pass through the CONFIG.SYS file, SYSINIT reads all the lines again and this time acts on them as it did in earlier versions of DOS. Exactly what it does and in what order is described in detail in Chapter 20.

Then it goes on to process the remaining lines in the CONFIG.SYS file. The details of what you can put in a CONFIG.SYS file, and in particular the memory management implications of doing so, are discussed in Chapter 20.

As it loads device drivers and sets up the FILES and BUFFERS areas you requested in your CONFIG.SYS file, SYSINIT is adding yet another layer to those already in RAM. When it finishes this job, it is ready to load the command interpreter. The command interpreter is COMMAND.COM (in the root directory of the boot disk) unless some other file and/or location has been specified in a SHELL= statement in the CONFIG.SYS file.

The command interpreter comes into RAM and initializes itself. In that process, it moves a portion of itself to the top of RAM, overwriting the SYSINIT program. That is fine, since that program has now finished its work.

Once it is properly initialized, the command interpreter will look (again only in the root directory of the boot disk) for an AUTOEXEC.BAT file. If it finds one, it will reserve a small bit of RAM to keep track of that file. As it reads that file, usually a line at a time, it does whatever that command specifies.

This is where most TSR programs get loaded. Here, too, you may run some shell or menu program or start your first application program of the day. In any case, this is the last step in the boot process.

DOS Memory Control Blocks

DOS manages your memory. It does this by dividing that space into *memory arenas*. Each memory arena has, right at the front of the region (the lowest memory address), a single paragraph (16 bytes) called a *memory control block* (MCB) or *memory arena header*.

There is some program that "owns" each memory control block. At the outset, there is only one block, and it is owned by DOS (and its status is "free"). As programs request memory, and later as they give some or all of it back again, the one block gets broken up into many blocks. Always, though, each block has an owner.

Each block has a size which is always an integral number of paragraphs (that is, its size in bytes is a multiple of 16). The memory control block (memory arena header) contains both an indication of the block's owner and of its size. The ownership is indicated by a number called the *process ID*; it is equal numerically to the segment address that points to the beginning of the program that owns that block. (The phrase *segment address* simply means the linear address divided by 16. If you write the address in the **segment:offset** form and use a zero for the offset, this is the segment value you would use.) A memory control block's lowest address is always an exact multiple of 16; that is, each MCB starts on a paragraph boundary.

Technically, the process ID is the segment address of the start of that program's **P**rogram **S**egment **P**refix (PSP). But since that immediately precedes the instructions that make up the program, and they are both in the same memory control block, you can roughly say the start of the PSP is the start of the program.

Only blocks belonging to DOS can be considered "free," for it will only allocate blocks from the pool it "owns." On the other hand, some blocks that belong to DOS are used to hold pieces of the operating system, and they must not be freely reallocated to others. So, DOS must maintain **at least** two labels for blocks it owns—one for free blocks and one for blocks that are in use.

The Memory Control Block Chain

The blocks form a chain. If you know where the chain starts, you can "walk the chain" and find all the other blocks. At each arena header, you read the size of that arena and then step up in RAM that many paragraphs plus one to find the next arena header.

The MEM program that comes with *MS-DOS* 5 (and subtantially enhanced in version 6) is one such program. If you invoke it with the /D switch, it will show you each MCB in the chain. Unfortunately, the sizes are presented only in hexadecimal, and instead of showing the process IDs, it tries to show you the corresponding program name. (That is nice, but it keeps you from seeing quite all of what is going on.)

There are some subtleties here. First, you need to know that the sign of ownership (the process ID) is not always the segment address of the owning program. In particular, blocks that are free or those that are filled with operating system pieces get special process IDs. 0000h means free memory. 0008h means system stuff.

Some third-party memory managers have extended this notion with some other special process ID values (such as 0001h, FFFAh, FFFDh, and FFFFh). They generally do not tell you what those values mean to them, but whatever they are, they certainly are not segment addresses of programs owning those blocks.

Here is a second subtlety: Normal memory control blocks are of type M or Z, with Z only being used for the last block in the chain. But sometimes a memory control block will be subdivided by other memory control blocks. This only happens when the surrounding block belongs to the operating system (or to one of those third-party memory managers).

In that case, there will be a *device subchain* of memory control blocks within the main MCB chain. (It carries this name even though not all the blocks are for device drivers.) The last block of that subchain stops exactly where the surrounding block stops. So if you are able to step onto the start of the chain, you can continue walking the MCB subblocks and climb out onto the main MCB block chain with no interruption.

A third subtlety arises when you use *MS-DOS* to load programs into upper memory. In this case, DOS will create a memory control block (MCB) chain extending through upper memory. Each of the upper memory MCBs it creates will belong to a fictitious owner whose name is `"UMB      "` (the letters U, M, and B followed by five spaces) and whose process ID is the next paragraph after the MCB. Within each of these blocks, it will place either system code or programs it is loading high. Look at the listing in Figure 19.1 for an example of this.

Figure 10.8 shows the structure of a memory control block. Figure 10.9 shows the contents of a typical memory control block chain. In Figure 10.9, the columns after the first one give the items of information found in each memory control block in the order they are listed in Figure 10.8. For your convenience, they have been translated from little-endian hexadecimal to the more familiar way of writing hexadecimal numbers (the length is also given in decimal).

In this case, a special chain-walking program was used to display the information on each block in an easy-to-read form. (This figure includes a device block subchain.) IMPORTANT: Since this figure was generated by a program that walked the chain and wrote each line of output as it went, the lower memory addresses are at the top. This is exactly the *opposite* of the way memory maps are drawn in this book, but it is the way the output is presented by most MCB chain walking programs.

The program used to generate Figure 10.9 is called MCBS, and it is included on the diskette that comes with this book. In addition to the format differences between its output and that of the DOS MEM program, MCBS has one other important ability. It can be used to display memory control block chains that DOS either doesn't know about or tries to hide.

If you simply invoke it by its name, with no command-line parameters, it will show you just the M and Z blocks in lower memory. If you add a command-line parameter D (don't precede this or any other parameter for this program by a slash or hyphen), then MCBS will add a display of the device subblocks in lower memory.

You have two choices for how to see a chain of memory control blocks in upper memory. If you know where the chain begins, use the syntax:

```
MCBS U ssss
```

where ssss is the segment address of the first MCB in the chain. (If you know about two such chains you can put both of their addresses after the U.) If you don't know where the upper memory MCB chains are, you can attempt to find them by issuing the command:

```
MCBS A
```

which tells MCBS to run in its "automatic mode." In this mode, it will show you all the chains it can find. This will be more than DOS displays, but it still may not be all the chains that exist.

Feel free to try the MCBS U ssss format with any value for ssss that you suspect might start a chain. If you guess right, you will see the chain. If not, no harm will be done.

How DOS Creates and Manages the MCB Chain

What exactly is the process by which DOS creates and manages the MCB chain? If you understand that, then you understand how DOS manages your RAM.

Programs ask DOS for RAM. They can indicate at the outset how much they want, or they can say in effect, "Give me all you can." DOS looks through the MCB chain for blocks that it owns (free space) to see if it can find one that is large enough to satisfy the request. If DOS can't find a single block of memory large enough to satisfy the request, it simply tells the requesting program that it is out of luck. (DOS never tries to piece together several smaller blocks in order to get the requested amount of memory in total.)

COM programs are the apparently greedy ones. Which is curious, since they are also the ones that cannot use more than about 64KB of RAM. The reason they seem greedy is simply that they lack the EXE header, and that is where EXE programs store, among other things, a record of how much RAM they are going to need. The minimum size MCB that DOS will give a COM program is one that is just slightly larger than the program's file size. DOS gives all of the first block it finds that is at least this large to the COM program.

There are three strategies DOS can use when satisfying a request for memory. One is called *first fit*, the second is *last fit*, and the final one is *best fit*. Normally it uses first fit. And always when you ask DOS to load and execute a program, it will use the first fit strategy.

If you want to make DOS use one of its other two strategies for finding a block of memory for your program to use, you can do so (via

INT 21h, Function 58h). Unfortunately, loading programs using either alternative memory allocation strategy requires rather heroic efforts of undocumented DOS programming.

Structure of a Memory Control Block

Byte Position	Contents
0	Block Type [*]
1 and 2	Process ID [**]
3 and 4	Size / 16
5 to 7	reserved
8 to 15	Owner name [***]

[*]   Z for end of chain, M for all others except in device subchain where:

D = Device driver (from Device= Line CONFIG.SYS)
E = Device driver appendage
I = Installable file system (not currently used)
F = Storage area (if FILES > 5 in CONFIG.SYS)
X = File Control Blocks (FCBS) storage area
B = Buffers (from BUFFERS= line in CONFIG.SYS)
L = Drive information table
        (from LASTDRIVE= Line in CONFIG.SYS)
S = Code and data area for DOS stacks
        (from STACKS= Line in CONFIG.SYS)

[**]   The Process ID is 0000 for free space, 0008 for blocks owned by the operating system, and it is the segment value of the Program Segment Prefix of the owning program for all other MCBs.

[***]   Only in those MCBs whose Process ID is one greater than the segment value of that MCB (and thus is a block controlling the PSP of its owner) and only for DOS versions 4 or later, this area may contain the name of the owning program, either null terminated or padded with spaces.

Figure 10.8.   Structure of a memory control block (memory arena header).

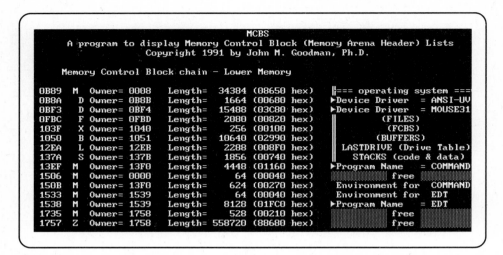

```
                              MCBS
        A program to display Memory Control Block (Memory Arena Header) Lists
                   Copyright 1991 by John M. Goodman, Ph.D.

        Memory Control Block chain - Lower Memory

   0B89  M  Owner= 0008  Length=  34384 (08650 hex)   === operating system ===
   0B8A  D  Owner= 0B8B  Length=   1664 (00680 hex)   ▶Device Driver   = ANSI-UV
   0BF3  D  Owner= 0BF4  Length=  15488 (03C80 hex)   ▶Device Driver   = MOUSE31
   0FBC  F  Owner= 0FBD  Length=   2080 (00820 hex)        (FILES)
   103F  X  Owner= 1040  Length=    256 (00100 hex)        (FCBS)
   1050  B  Owner= 1051  Length=  10640 (02990 hex)        (BUFFERS)
   12EA  L  Owner= 12EB  Length=   2288 (008F0 hex)     LASTDRIVE (Drive Table)
   137A  S  Owner= 137B  Length=   1856 (00740 hex)      STACKS (code & data)
   13EF  M  Owner= 13F0  Length=   4448 (01160 hex)   ▶Program Name    = COMMAND
   1506  M  Owner= 0000  Length=     64 (00040 hex)              free
   150B  M  Owner= 13F0  Length=    624 (00270 hex)   Environment for   COMMAND
   1533  M  Owner= 1539  Length=     64 (00040 hex)   Environment for   EDT
   1538  M  Owner= 1539  Length=   8128 (01FC0 hex)   ▶Program Name    = EDT
   1735  M  Owner= 1758  Length=    528 (00210 hex)              free
   1757  Z  Owner= 1758  Length= 558720 (88680 hex)              free
```

Figure 10.9. A typical memory control block chain. The first column gives the segment address for each memory control block (in hexadecimal). (Notice that lower memory addresses are at the top of this figure, unlike almost every other figure in this book.)

Normally, the first block in the chain that is large enough is what DOS uses. If it finds a block that is larger than the requesting program wants, DOS simply allocates the amount the program asked for from the beginning of the block. It cuts off the excess and makes a new block out of it.

To manipulate the MCB chain, all DOS has to do is alter the contents of the memory control blocks. For example, if it is allocating a portion of the last block (which is the most common allocation event), DOS shortens the last block (writes a new, smaller length value into the fourth and fifth bytes), changes its type from Z to M, and writes the new owner's process ID in the second and third bytes.

Doing these things has given the program what it wants, but if that were all DOS did, the MCB chain would no longer be valid. The chain must be extended until it reaches the end of RAM once more. And the last block in the chain must have a type indicator of Z. This is easy for DOS to accomplish. It just writes a new MCB record right after the end of the program's new memory block.

Similarly, if a program gives back to DOS some (but not all) of the RAM it owns, DOS simply lowers the length value in the MCB at the start of that block, and creates a new MCB at the start of the now free RAM with a process ID of 0000h and a length of whatever amount of RAM the program returned.

Look carefully at Figure 10.9. Did you spot the oddity? This display was generated by an MCB chain walking program. It must have been in RAM at the time this snapshot was taken, so where are the MCBs for it and its environment?

The chain walking program was written in *QuickBasic* version 4.5, and it was compiled with debug code and for stand-alone operation. Apparently in that one way of preparing an executable file in *QuickBasic*, the resulting file releases all of its allocated memory *before* it begins doing anything else! This is most unusual behavior.

Notice that the size of the environment block for COMMAND.COM is 624 bytes. That is the size that was requested in the SHELL statement on this PC. But notice that the environment for EDT (an electronic dictionary and thesaurus program) is only 64 bytes. That is because EDT went resident before any commands in AUTOEXEC.BAT had put things into the environment. This strategy is discussed in Chapter 20.

On the other hand, the 528-byte block of free memory at segment address 1735h used to be the environment for the chain walking program (which was, itself, loaded at 1758h). That environment block was large because by the time this program was run, the AUTOEXEC.BAT file had finished, and one of its last acts was to fill up the DOS environment fairly full (as you will see later in Figure 10.11).

Now you have learned about how DOS manages memory. Take a look next at some of the ways in which the memory blocks that DOS creates get used.

DOS Environment Blocks

When DOS launches any program, it allocates memory for that program. It also does two other things. One, it allocates another block of memory for what is called the *environment* for that program. Two, it builds a Program Segment Prefix (PSP) in the first 256 bytes of the program's main memory block. Then it puts the program into that block, starting right after the PSP, and lets it execute.

> There is somewhat more to be done for EXE files. They have some relocation information in their header that DOS must process. This fact is not relevant to the present discussion.

What is this "environment block"? It is nothing more or less than a sort of bulletin board, a place that DOS and other programs can put messages and from which they can read the messages put there previously.

The information in an environment block consists of many definitions or aliases. Figure 10.10 shows the structure of a DOS environment block. Each NAME being defined is forced to uppercase by DOS, but the definitions are not. Also, any spaces before or after the equal signs are significant, so don't put them in unless you really mean to include them as a part of the name of the object being defined (on the left of the equal sign) or as a part of its definition (on the right of the equal sign).

DOS Environment Structure

NAME1 = definition 1
00h
NAME2 = definition 2
00h
NAME3 = definition 3
00h
...
NAMEn = definition n
00h
00h
two-byte number of strings to follow (normally 1) [*]
full pathname of program owning this environment
00h

As usual in Intel processor based computers, this number is given with the least significant byte first (e.g., 1 = 0100h).

Figure 10.10. The structure of a DOS environment block.

The Master DOS Environment

The first program loaded by DOS is the command interpreter. If you don't use an AUTOEXEC.BAT file when you first see the DOS prompt, your PC will have a very simple chain of MCBs in memory. The last block before the free space will be the environment for the command processor. This is called the *Master DOS environment.*

If you then type SET commands at the DOS prompt, you can add definitions to that environment to your heart's content. (You may continue until you put 32KB of definitions into it, actually. That is a lot of typing!)

If, however, you use an AUTOEXEC.BAT file, the small block of memory that DOS allocates for the command processor to use while processing that file, it will limit the maximum amount of space you can have in your Master DOS environment.

If you do nothing special, that maximum size will be 160 bytes. Often that is not enough. If you are using DOS version 3.1 or greater, you can rather easily get around this problem. Place in your CONFIG.SYS file a line reading:

```
SHELL=C:\COMMAND.COM /P /E:624
```

to create a Master DOS environment with a size of 624 bytes. (This line assumes you have COMMAND.COM in the root directory. A better idea is to keep it in your DOS directory. How that changes this line is explained on the following page. If you are using DOS version 3.1, replace that last number with the number of paragraphs you want, so in this case it would read /E:39.) The /P in the SHELL statement tells COMMAND.COM that this is going to be the permanent command processor. That makes it process the AUTOEXEC.BAT file, or prompt you for the time and date, and it prevents it from going away if you should type EXIT.

Anytime you are at the DOS prompt, you can type COMMAND and press Enter. If you do so, you will load another copy of COMMAND.COM. Such a copy of COMMAND.COM is called a *secondary command processor,* and the things it does or controls are called a *child process.* (You can do a similar thing with any of the alternative command processors like NDOS.) If you later type EXIT at a DOS prompt and press Enter, that secondary command interpreter tells the primary one that it is through working. All the memory it was using is returned to the DOS pool of allocatable memory.

If you should use a SHELL statement that invokes COMMAND.COM and forget to add the /P switch, you are in effect declaring the original command interpreter to be a secondary processor. So when you type EXIT and press Enter, it will make itself go away. You will then be left with no command interpreter to give you a DOS prompt and to accept your commands. The only way out from there is to reboot your PC.

The details of what happens in this case depend on the version of DOS you use. *MS-DOS* 5 and 6 will put up the message Missing command interpreter just before it stops. *PC DOS* 3.3 at that point puts a rectangular character on the screen and seems to hang. In either of these two cases you can boot normally and run programs, etc. Nothing will seem amiss until that fateful moment when you forget and type EXIT when you shouldn't have.

In contrast to that behavior, some other versions of DOS will not even allow you to boot your PC if you specify a SHELL statement without the /P switch after COMMAND.COM. In that case, if your error was in the CONFIG.SYS file of your hard disk, you will have to boot from your Safety Boot Diskette (or some other bootable DOS diskette).

MS-DOS 6 includes a nice safety feature: If your CONFIG.SYS file includes and error that would prevent you from booting, simply tap the F5 or hold down either Shift key during the message "Starting MS-DOS" and it will completely skip processing the CONFIG.SYS and AUTOEXEC.BAT files. This will not totally replace a safety boot diskette, but it makes the use of one necessary a lot less frequently.

Naturally, if you are using an alternative command processor, you will have to consult the documentation that came with it to determine how to accomplish this same result. Also, if your copy of COMMAND.COM is not in the root directory of C:, you will need to put in the correct path. If you do use a path with COMMAND.COM, you should reiterate it after the name of the command processor. That is, the line in your CONFIG.SYS file might read like this:

```
SHELL=C:\DOS\COMMAND.COM C:\DOS /P /E:624
```

This SHELL statement will increase only the size of the Master DOS environment. It will not directly affect the size of any child process environments, which you will learn about in the following section.

Child Process Environments

When one program loads and starts another one, the first program is referred to as the parent and the second one as the child. Actually, every program running in your PC is a child of something. Even the primary command interpreter is a child of SYSINIT (which is now no longer around).

Each child process gets an environment block. It is filled initially with a copy of whatever was in the parent's environment block. Under COMMAND.COM, the size of the child environment will be just a little larger than necessary to hold the present definitions. If you use NDOS, the child environment size can easily be controlled; it defaults to 128 bytes more than necessary to hold the current definitions.

If the child process changes or adds definitions to the environment, it normally does so only to its copy. When it finishes and returns all its memory to DOS, that child environment is freed up and the definitions it holds are lost. Since they were not copied back to the parent environment, the parent cannot see them.

> If you need to modify the contents of the Master DOS environment, you can do so. There are various programs to help you do this. One such program is ENVEDT.EXE by Jim Kyle.

CALL Versus COMMAND /C

One batch file can run another batch file. If it just names the second batch file, that second batch file will run, but when the second file finishes, the first one will not pick up where it left off and run to its end.

One way around this (and the only way until recently) was to put the name of the second batch file as a command line parameter to a new copy of the command interpreter. This is done by a line such as this in your first batch file:

```
COMMAND /C SecondBatchFileName
```

What does this do? It runs a copy of COMMAND.COM just as if it were any other program. But since it is a shell program (in the *UNIX* sense of the term), it can read, interpret, and execute the second batch file. When that batch file finishes, the /C option tells COMMAND.COM to "turn itself in" (relinquish its memory), at which point your original batch file resumes.

There is a second way to accomplish much the same thing using modern versions of DOS (starting with 3.3). You can put in a line in your first batch file that reads:

```
CALL SecondBatchFileName
```

This acts almost exactly the same as the first way. But there are a couple of important differences.

First, this way does not load a second copy of COMMAND.COM. Since it does not do that, you have more RAM to run your second batch file and any programs it may execute. Second, the second batch file does not get its own child environment. That point can be quite important. Here's why.

Many batch files are written to communicate with other batch files via environmental variables. If you run the second batch file from within the first one using the CALL keyword, anything the second batch file puts in the environment will be available to the first batch file when it regains control of the PC. If, on the other hand, you use COMMAND /C to run the second batch file, it will get its own child environment, in which any new definitions it creates will be stored. When it ends and the first batch file resumes, the child environment will have been discarded. So, the first batch file will not be able to see any of the definitions the second one created.

A Typical DOS Environment's Contents

Now that you know what DOS environment blocks are, and when they get created, perhaps you'd like to look inside one and see what it contains. You can do this on your own PC simply by typing SET and pressing Enter. Figure 10.11 shows you the results of doing that on a PC with a fairly full environment. Study Figure 10.11 as you read the following pages. You will find examples there of at least some of the ideas discussed.

How DOS Uses the DOS Environment

DOS uses the environment for only three things. They are the COMSPEC, the PATH, and the PROMPT.

The *COMSPEC* is a string which points to the disk file copy of the command interpreter that was loaded when you booted. (NOTE: This string must not have any command line parameters on it, unlike the SHELL= statement in the CONFIG.SYS file.) DOS uses this pointer to load a fresh copy of COMMAND.COM anytime its transient part (up high in RAM) gets overwritten by a program.

The PATH is a list of subdirectories to be searched whenever COMMAND.COM is looking for a program you have asked it to run. For example, a simple PATH entry might read:

```
PATH=C:\DOS;C:\BAT;C:\UTILS
```

which would tell COMMAND.COM to look for programs whose names were entered as a command *without an explicit path* in the following places: First it will look in the current directory, then on the C drive in the \DOS directory, followed by the C drive, \BAT directory, and finally on the C drive in the \UTILS directory. If it did not find the named file in any of those places (with an extension of COM, EXE, or BAT), then it will give you the famous message Bad command or filename.

```
       An example of DOS environment contents

  COMSPEC=C:\DOS\COMMAND.COM
  PCWRITE=D:\PCW
  PROCOMM=G:\COMM\P\
  PCPLUS=G:\COMM\PCPLUS
  LIB=D:\BAC
  PCO=C:\PCO\PCO.CFG
  G-SPELL=C:\UT\SPELL
  CATDISK=/F?
  NU=C:\UT\NOR
  G4=D:\G4\
  TEMP=D:\TEMP
  TMP=D:\TEMP
  PROMPT=$d at $t$h$h$h  Directory = $p $g
  PATH=C:\DOS;D:\WIN;C:\UTILS;C:\SETUP
  PLACEHOLDER=A string to hold space for future use.
```

Figure 10.11.   An example of the contents of a DOS environment.

The PATH definition has a semicolon between each subdirectory and the next. It does not have to end with a semicolon. It cannot be more than 126 characters long, including the characters PATH=. You cannot get a longer PATH by putting two PATH statements in your AUTOEXEC.BAT file; instead the second definition will simply replace the first.

If you don't have an explicit definition for the PATH, all versions of DOS prior to 6 will simply enter the line PATH= with nothing after it into its Master environment; in DOS 6, the default path is equal to C:\DOS.

If you don't put a definition for the PROMPT into the Master environment, COMMAND.COM will use its default value, which is equivalent to ng, but it will not put that definition into the environment. If you don't define a PROMPT string, DOS 6 will put PROMPT=PG into the environment. See the section "Some Ways You Can Use the DOS Environment" to learn a little more about the PROMPT command.

How Other Programs Use the DOS Environment

Any program or batch file is entitled to look in the environment to see what definitions are there, or to change them or add to them. It is easy for any program (or batch file) to find its own environment, but DOS tries to make it tough to find the Master environment.

Many modern PC programs look for a special variable name in the environment. If they find it, they assume that whatever it is defined as is a message to them. For example, the programs in the *Norton Utilities* look for a variable NU= and whatever it is equal to is supposed to be the path to the rest of the *Norton Utilities* programs. (Look back at Figure 10.11. It contains definitions like this for eight different programs. The key words are PCWRITE, PROCOMM, PCPLUS, PCO, G-SPELL, CATDISK, NU, and G4. All these except CATDISK are path definitions for the corresponding programs. The keyword, CATDISK, has a different sort of definition. This one tells it one aspect of how to do its job. The variables LIB, TMP, and TEMP are ones that a number of programs use. LIB points to a directory in which some libraries are kept. TMP and TEMP point to a suitable place for programs to create temporary files.)

Batch Files, Replaceable Parameters, and the Environment

Batch files can make great use of the environment. They can put things into the environment using SET commands, and they can read values stored there by using "replaceable parameters."

For example, one batch file might set the value of a variable called WHERESAY, and another one might read it. Depending on the value assigned to WHERESAY, the second batch file will either print a message on the screen or on the printer.

The first batch file would have a line something like this:

```
SET WHERESAY=To Screen
```

or one that said:

```
SET WHERESAY=To Printer
```

This line, in either form, sets up a definition of the variable WHERESAY in the DOS environment.
The second batch file could read, in part, as follows:

```
If %WHERESAY%.==To Screen. GOTO ONSCREEN
If %WHERESAY%.==To Printer. GOTO PRINTIT
GOTO DONE
:ONSCREEN
ECHO You asked for a message on the screen.
GOTO DONE
:PRINTIT
ECHO You wanted this on the printer? > PRN
:DONE
```

Some Ways You Can Use the DOS Environment

Perhaps the most common use made of an environment variable set by the PC user is a redefinition of the DOS prompt. The simple A> or C> prompt tells one so little.

Even just putting a definition that reads PROMPT=PG into the environment helps a lot. Then you get a prompt something like C:\UTILS>, which is much more informative. (This particular prompt definition has become so popular that now Microsoft has made MS-DOS 6 put it in the environment by default.)

A more valuable use of the PROMPT is to let you know when you have "shelled out to DOS" from a program. Many programs have an option to "shell to DOS." That means the programs will temporarily suspend their operation and load for you an additional copy of COMMAND.COM. This lets you do simple DOS commands, after which you can return to your work exactly where you left off.

PC-Write is one such program. Its main program file is called ED.EXE. If you invoke that program from a batch file that has the following three lines, you will never again forget when you are shelled out to DOS:

```
PROMPT=Type EXIT to return to PC-Write. $P$G
ED %1 %2 %3 %4 %5
PROMPT $P$G
```

Perhaps the most annoying thing about the DOS environment is that it is so easy to run out of environment space. No matter how large you make your Master environment, the child environments are normally just barely large enough to hold the current definitions. If you then try to define something new (as in the example batch file just shown), you may well be confronted with the message Out of environment space. What can you do to avoid this?

If you are using NDOS or *4DOS*, there is a very easy solution. But if you are running pure *MS-DOS* or *PC DOS*, you will have to do a bit of work.

One reason NDOS and *4DOS* are nice is that they always give you 128 extra bytes to play with. If you are explicitly invoking a secondary copy of NDOS or *4DOS*, you can specify any larger size you want.

If you are using unmodified DOS, one possible way to deal with this is to define a dummy variable in your AUTOEXEC.BAT file just to hold some space in the environment. Then when DOS makes a copy of the current definitions in the environment for a child process, that space filling definition will be there. If the first thing the child process does is redefine that variable as nothing, then it can have all the space it wants (depending only on the size of that placeholder variable). Look at the last line of Figure 10.11 for an example of this approach.

When you shell out of most DOS programs, you get another full working copy of COMMAND.COM. The first program simply runs COMMAND.COM, and that gives you the DOS prompt. On the other hand, some programs' shell-to-DOS options just let you run a single DOS command (which you must type while you are still within your application program), and then they return to the application program.

If you really need more environment space, you can get it at the cost of some of your free RAM by simply running another copy of COMMAND.COM, but this time adding the command line parameter /E:nnn, where *nnn* is the size of the environment you want to get. This could be your one DOS command that the application program allows you to run. You will end up with a new DOS prompt, and a new, large allocation of environment space (partially filled by your earlier definitions). Now you can do most anything. Typing EXIT will get you back to your application.

Putting Things into the Environment (and Getting Them Out)

There are three DOS commands for putting definitions into the environment. The principal one is SET. If you type SET all by itself (and press Enter), you will see what definitions are currently in effect. If you redirect that output to a file (by typing SET>filename), not only will you capture those definitions for later perusal, a simple DIR listing will show you the size of that file, and thus the number of characters in your environment that you have used.

The PATH and PROMPT commands also put things into the environment. The only way to take something out is to redefine it as nothing. So typing SET ABC=DEF sets the value of ABC to DEF, but typing SET ABC= with nothing (not even a space) after the equal sign removes the definition of ABC from the environment.

Use Batch Files and Environmental Variables to Help Prevent Disasters

Most disastrous losses of data on a PC are the direct result of someone's careless act. Well-designed batch files and environmental variables can help minimize the potential for these disasters.

For example, the DOS manual is very clear in its statement that CHKDSK /F should *never* be run in a DOS window inside of *Windows*. They aren't just kidding. You can really mess up your disk if you make this mistake. In *any* multitasking or task-switching situation, one task may open a file and put data there; then before it has a chance to close that file, CHKDSK /F may come along and "clean up" what it sees as a lost chain or other problem. Result? Lost data!

Some task-switching or multitasking environments attempt to protect you from this sort of disaster. For example, *Windows* and the *MS-DOS* DOSSHELL both will refuse to run CHKDSK /F at a DOS command line. They protect you against that specific program doing damage. But they are not necessarily going to catch all such problems. Furthermore, *DESQview* will not protect you even from CHKDSK, and other task switchers may or may not.

If you create batch files like the ones suggested here for every task switcher and multitasker you use and for every utility program you identify as potentially dangerous, you will simply add another layer of protection to whatever the task-switcher or multitasker you are running may provide. That can never hurt you, and it just might save you from enormous grief.

Creating the following two batch files can protect you against this error quite nicely. (You may want to "pretty up" both of these with ECHO OFF statements. It might be helpful if you also added some REM statements to remind you of why you created these.)

Batch file number one (to run any task-swapper or multitasker): ("Task Swapper" in the second line represents a variable for which you would substitute the command you use to initiate your task-swapping environment, for example, WIN for Windows.)

```
SET TASKSHARING=ACTIVE
Task Swapper %1 %2 %3
SET TASKSHARING=INACTIVE
```

Batch file number two (to run CHKDSK): (This batch file assumes that you will invoke it with a drive as the first parameter and with /F as an optional second parameter. Fixing it up to cover all possible cases is left to the reader as an exercise, as is the creation of similar batch files to invoke other potentially dangerous utility programs.)

```
IF %2.==. GOTO NOPARMS
IF %2.==/F. GOTO DANGER
...
:DANGER
IF %TASKSHARING%==ACTIVE GOTO OOPS
IF %TASKSHARING%==INACTIVE DO CHKDSK %1 /F
GOTO DONE
:NOPARMS
CHKDSK %1
GOTO DONE
...
:OOPS
ECHO Watch it! You almost scrambled your FAT.
ECHO Lucky for you I saved the day.
:DONE
```

There are many other things you might build similar batch files to protect against. For example, it is not a good idea to run *GeoWorks* from within *Windows,* nor the reverse. Invoke each of them from a suitable batch file, and you will never make either of these mistakes.

By having each environment-launching application put some suitable message into the DOS environment, other programs will be able to see which environment is running and can then decline to run if it is not safe.

A Warning About Environment Definition Strings

Since each line in the environment is put there by a DOS command, the limitation DOS puts on the length of a command line (128 characters) applies also to each definition in the environment. Some people have tried various arcane ways to evade that limit. Their efforts were, at best, ill-advised.

The string most people want to lengthen is the PATH. But even if you get it longer in the environment, that is not going to help DOS use it. Indeed, impolite application programs regularly add their directory to the start of the PATH as they are installing themselves. If the result is a PATH over 128 characters in length (or really the maximum is a few characters less than that), DOS will simply ignore some of the characters at the end of the PATH.

If such an addition cuts off a vital directory on the end of the path statement, you could be unable to run some programs you depend upon and not know why. Worse, consider the following scenario. (This *is* artificial, but it makes a point.) Suppose you have two directories, one called BAD containing some dangerous programs and another called BADFIXES, with programs *having the same names* meant to undo the damage caused by the first set of programs. You put BADFIXES on your PATH, somewhere near the end. After some program installs itself and adds its directory onto the front end of the PATH, your total PATH becomes just five characters too long. The excess length gets ignored by DOS. Therefore, DOS now finds BAD instead of BADFIXES and may cause damage when you meant to be undoing it!

Even worse, some programs read environment definition strings into themselves. They have an internal buffer just 128 characters long. And they know environment definitions end in a zero byte. So they read the string into the buffer, continuing up to the zero byte. If the string is too long, it will run out of the end of the buffer and overwrite part of the program. Almost anything could happen after that, and most of the scenarios aren't very pretty.

Giving Up Your Environment to Save Memory

Programs, especially TSR programs, often give back their environment block to DOS. This is a fine thing for them to do if they know they won't need the information stored there. (It is definitely not a case of compromising their virtue!) If no new definitions are entered into the environment after this TSR gives that environment back and before the next one is run, then DOS will simply reuse that same memory block for the environment for the next program.

Program Memory Blocks

When DOS loads a program, it creates one memory block for the program and one for its environment. You now know quite a lot about the environment block. What is there you need to know about the program block?

The first thing in the program block is a data structure called the *Program Segment Prefix* (PSP). This is a region exactly 16 paragraphs (256 bytes) long. It is used by DOS to hold a number of facts associated with this program's operation (see Figure 10.12).

Some TSR programs give up their PSP and relocate themselves at the very start of their program block. They do this to save just that little extra bit of memory so you can run bigger programs after they have been loaded.

Are there any reasons you should be sorry that they do this? Not if they do it right. You will find that if a TSR gives up both its PSP and its environment, you will be unable to see its name in most chain-walking memory usage display programs. That is because these are the two places that the program's name is normally kept. Some programs (MCBS is one) can find the name of a memory control block's owner by inspecting the memory control block headers. (This only works with DOS version 4 or later.)

The programmer of such a TSR must be very careful how the giving up of the PSP is done. Doing this means losing the default disk data transfer area (DTA), the local Job File Table (JFT), and some other, often useful, data structures. Still, the memory savings are very tempting and with care, this can be done successfully.

Data Memory Blocks

In addition to the memory blocks set up by the loader whenever a program is run, any program may ask DOS for some more memory. If the program was given "all you've got" at the outset, the program will first have to give back whatever it can spare so DOS will have some memory from which to allocate the additional blocks the program wishes to create.

Any program may, at any time, ask DOS to increase or decrease its memory allocation. (It never hurts to ask, but you shouldn't count on always getting what you ask for, and neither should a program.) If it can, DOS will comply with all such requests.

Structure of a Program Segment Prefix (PSP)

Byte Positions	Contents
00 and 01	Program exit point (INT20h)
02 and 03	Memory size in paragraphs
04	--unused--(filled with zero)
05 to 09	CP/M entry point (far jump to 000C0h)
0Ah to 0Dh	Terminate address (old INT22h)
0Eh to 11h	Break address (old INT23h)
12h to 15h	Critical error handler (old INT24h)
16h to 17h	Parent's PSP segment
18h to 2Bh	DOS 2+ open file table (20 bytes)
2Ch to 2Dh	DOS 2+ environment segment
2Eh to 31h	Process's SS:SP on last call to INT21h
32h and 33h	DOS 3+ maximum number open files
34h to 37h	DOS 3+ open file table address
38h to 3Bh	DOS 3+ pointer to previous PSP
3Ch to 4Fh	--unused--(filled with zeros)
50h to 52h	DOS function dispatcher (CDh 21h CBh)
53h to 5Bh	--unused--(filled with zeros)
5Ch to 6Bh	FCB #1
6Ch to 7Fh	FCB #2
80h	Command tail length (N)
81h	Command tail (N bytes plus 0Dh)

Figure 10.12. The Program Segment Prefix.

Extending the MCB Chain

A very important part of modern memory management is to make use of any and all empty regions in upper memory. To do this, several steps must be taken. Often, different programs will be called into play to do each one.

- The first step is to provide RAM in those regions of upper-memory address space. (This assumes you have previously identified just where those regions are.)

- Second is asserting control over that memory. The modern way to do this is with an XMS memory manager. The DOS program that does this task is HIMEM.SYS. (This program is included with both MS-DOS and PC DOS versions 5 and later, as well as with Windows, version 3.x. Be sure to use the latest one you have, no matter where you got it.)

- Third, if you want DOS to manage this upper memory, the MCB chain must be extended across these RAM regions. Alternatively, if you are going to use a third-party memory manager, it may simply construct additional MCB chains in upper memory and use them itself.

- Finally, some program (DOS or a third-party memory manager) must do the work of allocating and deallocating portions of that upper memory RAM as programs need it and relinquish it. Any such managed blocks of upper memory space RAM are called *Upper Memory Blocks,* or UMBs.

Adding Upper RAM

There are many different ways to get RAM to appear in upper-memory space. If you have a PC in class 5 or 6, you can do this by asking the CPU's remapping function to put some of your extended memory into upper memory instead. That requires running a program. The DOS program for this purpose is EMM386.EXE. (This program is included with both MS-DOS and PC DOS versions 5 and later, as well as with Windows, version 3.x. Be sure to use the latest one you have, no matter where you got it.)

If you have a PC in class 2 or 4, you can't use the simple strategy available for class 5 or 6 PC users. You may be able to do the same sorts of things, however, but in a different way. There are two alternatives: Using your PC's system logic to make the upper RAM appear, or using a LIM EMS 4.0 board to do that.

Just how you would ask your PC's system logic to access upper RAM varies by the system. Some of them are understood well enough by programs like *UMBPro* and *QRAM.* Others are not so easily dealt with.

What if you have a LIM EMS hardware memory board? Any LIM EMS board plus its EMM and *QRAM* or *UMBPro* can give you 64KB of upper RAM if you are willing to give up having an EMS page frame. If none of your applications needs EMS memory, and sometimes even if one does, you can do this. What if you want UMBs and an EMS page frame? Not all EMS boards can do this trick. For sure, it will have to be a board built to the 4.0 version of EMS, but even then, none of these boards implement all the features of EMS. You will have to be sure yours has the features you need.

Then you will have to run the EMM driver that came with the board, followed by some program that knows how to ask the EMM to provide RAM where you have identified that it can safely go. *QRAM* from Quarterdeck Office Systems is one such program. Qualitas' *386MAX*, while mostly meant for class 5 and 6 PCs, also has a component (formerly sold as a separate program called *Move'Em*) meant for use on PCs in class 2 or 4 that does the same sort of things as *QRAM* and *UMBPro* from Quadtel.

Once you have some upper RAM, you must have some program take it under its wing and manage it for you. That will be an XMS memory manager. *QRAM* and *UMBPro* are two that often work well. You can only use HIMEM.SYS if you used EMM386.EXE to provide the upper RAM. If you use *386MAX* or *QEMM* on a PC in class 5 or 6, either will provide the upper RAM and manage it.

If you want DOS to manage upper memory, you usually will first give it to your XMS memory manager. Then DOS will ask for it and get it, after which it can build its MCB chain across those regions.

Bridging Over Non-RAM Regions

Memory control blocks are supposed to be regions of RAM. The MCB chain is supposed to be continuous from the top of the system files in lower memory to the top of DOS-managed RAM, wherever that may be. How does DOS deal with regions of ROM or other regions it simply must keep its hands off of?

It creates dummy MCB records just before each such space. They are marked as belonging to the system and having system stuff in them. That keeps DOS from allocating them to any other program. In Figure 10.13, you can see such a block at segment address 9FFFh. In this particular system, that block spans all of the video buffer areas (the A and B pages), the video option ROM, and an SCSI host adapter ROM.

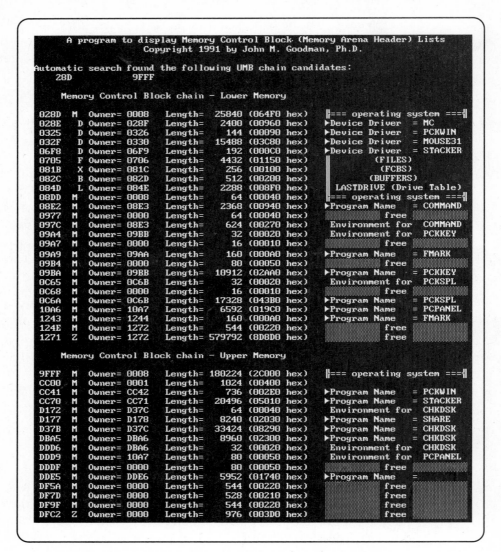

```
        A program to display Memory Control Block (Memory Arena Header) Lists
                    Copyright 1991 by John M. Goodman, Ph.D.

Automatic search found the following UMB chain candidates:
    28D           9FFF

        Memory Control Block chain - Lower Memory

    028D  M  Owner= 0008   Length=   25840 (064F0 hex)  ‖=== operating system ===‖
    028E  D  Owner= 028F   Length=    2400 (00960 hex)  ▶Device Driver  = MC
    0325  D  Owner= 0326   Length=     144 (00090 hex)  ▶Device Driver  = PCKWIN
    032F  D  Owner= 0330   Length=   15488 (03C80 hex)  ▶Device Driver  = MOUSE31
    06F8  D  Owner= 06F9   Length=     192 (000C0 hex)  ▶Device Driver  = STACKER
    0705  F  Owner= 0706   Length=    4432 (01150 hex)       (FILES)
    081B  X  Owner= 081C   Length=     256 (00100 hex)       (FCBS)
    082C  B  Owner= 082D   Length=     512 (00200 hex)       (BUFFERS)
    084D  L  Owner= 084E   Length=    2288 (008F0 hex)   LASTDRIVE (Drive Table)
    08DD  M  Owner= 0008   Length=      64 (00040 hex)  ‖=== operating system ===‖
    08E2  M  Owner= 08E3   Length=    2368 (00940 hex)  ▶Program Name   = COMMAND
    0977  M  Owner= 0000   Length=      64 (00040 hex)          free
    097C  M  Owner= 08E3   Length=     624 (00270 hex)   Environment for  COMMAND
    09A4  M  Owner= 09BB   Length=      32 (00020 hex)   Environment for  PCKKEY
    09A7  M  Owner= 0000   Length=      16 (00010 hex)          free
    09A9  M  Owner= 09AA   Length=     160 (000A0 hex)  ▶Program Name   = FMARK
    09B4  M  Owner= 0000   Length=      80 (00050 hex)          free
    09BA  M  Owner= 09BB   Length=   10912 (02AA0 hex)  ▶Program Name   = PCKKEY
    0C65  M  Owner= 0C6B   Length=      32 (00020 hex)   Environment for  PCKSPL
    0C68  M  Owner= 0000   Length=      16 (00010 hex)          free
    0C6A  M  Owner= 0C6B   Length=   17328 (043B0 hex)  ▶Program Name   = PCKSPL
    10A6  M  Owner= 10A7   Length=    6592 (019C0 hex)  ▶Program Name   = PCPANEL
    1243  M  Owner= 1244   Length=     160 (000A0 hex)  ▶Program Name   = FMARK
    124E  M  Owner= 1272   Length=     544 (00220 hex)          free
    1271  Z  Owner= 1272   Length=  579792 (8D8D0 hex)          free

        Memory Control Block chain - Upper Memory

    9FFF  M  Owner= 0008   Length=  180224 (2C000 hex)  ‖=== operating system ===‖
    CC00  M  Owner= 0001   Length=    1024 (00400 hex)
    CC41  M  Owner= CC42   Length=     736 (002E0 hex)  ▶Program Name   = PCKWIN
    CC70  M  Owner= CC71   Length=   20496 (05010 hex)  ▶Program Name   = STACKER
    D172  M  Owner= D37C   Length=      64 (00040 hex)   Environment for  CHKDSK
    D177  M  Owner= D178   Length=    8240 (02030 hex)  ▶Program Name   = SHARE
    D37B  M  Owner= D37C   Length=   33424 (08290 hex)  ▶Program Name   = CHKDSK
    DBA5  M  Owner= DBA6   Length=    8960 (02300 hex)  ▶Program Name   = CHKDSK
    DDD6  M  Owner= DBA6   Length=      32 (00020 hex)   Environment for  CHKDSK
    DDD9  M  Owner= 10A7   Length=      80 (00050 hex)   Environment for  PCPANEL
    DDDF  M  Owner= 0000   Length=      80 (00050 hex)          free
    DDE5  M  Owner= DDE6   Length=    5952 (01740 hex)  ▶Program Name   =
    DF5A  M  Owner= 0000   Length=     544 (00220 hex)          free
    DF7D  M  Owner= 0000   Length=     528 (00210 hex)          free
    DF9F  M  Owner= 0000   Length=     544 (00220 hex)          free
    DFC2  Z  Owner= 0000   Length=     976 (003D0 hex)          free
```

Figure 10.13. An MCB chain extending into upper memory.

This allows for an unbroken chain of MCBs from the bottom of memory (just on top of DOS) to very far up into upper memory, just below the motherboard BIOS ROM. Note also that the chain appears to end at segment 1271h. That MCB is of type Z, which normally signals the end of the chain. And indeed, at the moment this snapshot was taken, the chain did end there. The upper memory chain was simply another valid MCB chain. But with the system block at 9FFFh, the whole chain becomes one if you merely change the MCB at 1271h from a Z-type to an M-type.

Loading Programs into UMBs

When you ask DOS to load a program high, it does so in four steps:

1. It changes the Z block at the end of the chain in lower memory into an M block.

2. It marks that block's owner field to indicate that it is not free memory.

3. It loads the program in the normal manner.

4. Last, it restores the original Z block in lower memory, thus disconnecting the lower and upper MCB chains and resetting that Z block to show its status as free memory.

Notice what this sequence of steps does: By connecting the lower and upper memory MCB chains, DOS first makes available for allocation all the free RAM in upper memory space. By marking the free space in lower memory as "in use," it forces itself to jump over that region and seek the first large enough block in upper memory. Once the program has memory allocated for it and is loaded into that space, DOS restores the MCB chain in lower memory to its former state. (If DOS cannot find a large enough block in upper memory to load the program, it will undo all these steps and start over, loading the program into lower memory.)

Notice what this process does not do: DOS 5 has no way to force itself to load a program into any particular region of upper memory. Often the free RAM in upper memory space will be in several disconnected pieces. DOS can only be forced to put programs where you want them if you arrange the loading of the programs in a certain order. That order may be incompatible with having them function properly. Third-party memory managers (such as *386MAX, QEMM, QMAPS, Netroom,* and *Memory Commander*) can load programs into specific ones of these blocks independent of their load order. Now, with version 6, MS and PC DOS can do this also.

How can those third-party memory managers or DOS 6 manipulate things so that they can put a given TSR or device driver into a particular UMB? They do it by the same method that DOS 5 uses for loading programs high, but with one additional step. If they want to force DOS to skip over one or more UMB(s), these memory managers simply mark all the free memory in the UMB(s) to be skipped as "in use" until after DOS has finished allocating memory for the program they want loaded higher up from the next UMB beyond the skipped one(s).

A Recap

In this chapter, you learned about the many layers of programs you have in your PCs and how they get there. You found out what a BIOS is and why you need it, as well as what the parts of DOS are and what it is good for. In particular, you learned that DOS has primary responsibility for managing the uses made of your RAM. (Of all the RAM it knows about, that is.) You also learned about some of the places your PC may have RAM that DOS does not know about. Finally, you learned about memory control blocks, the DOS environment, and how the MCB chain is used to control the use of RAM. And you saw, briefly, how DOS can be induced to extend its protective hand across upper memory as well as lower.

Now you know most of what you need to know about real mode memory. There will be a few more tidbits on that area coming up to be sure, but at this point, it is time to reveal the mysteries of protected mode. That is complex stuff, but vital to understanding modern memory management.

FANCIER MEMORY MAPS (PROTECTED-MODE COMPLEXITIES)

Protected mode is different and special. In this chapter, you will learn all about the varieties it comes in. Also, you will learn about virtual memory and many different ways to fill in empty upper memory spaces.

This chapter covers a lot of potentially very confusing material. First, you will be introduced to what is called *protected mode*. Then you'll find out that really there are three different kinds of protected mode, each with its own special quirks you need to know about.

Out of this discussion will come the curious fact that your computer may have several different memory address spaces, some of radically different sizes than others. You will learn how to distinguish a logical address from a linear or physical one. And you will learn what virtual memory is, in each of its several meanings.

This leads quite naturally into a discussion of why you might like to fill in the holes in your PC's upper memory space, and how you can do that. This is covered first in general, and then some specific suggestions are given.

Sounds like a lot of ground to cover, and it is. But it isn't difficult to learn all this if you take it one step at a time. First, you need to know more about segments and offsets.

More on Segments, Offsets, and Modes

You understand segments and offsets, right? And how to combine them to get a linear address? Well, that is true, but not the whole story. You know what a segment is for an Intel 80x86 processor operating in what is called "real mode." And you know how to combine it with an offset when the processor is operating in real mode. But what if the processor isn't operating in real mode? What then?

All but the first couple of members of the 80x86 family have one or more other modes in which they can operate, and those other modes are collectively called *protected mode*. In protected mode, the rules change. Even the name for the number stored in a segment register changes from a segment value to a *selector*. With LDTs, a GDT, an IDT, TSSs, and IOPLs, there is a host of new possibilities in these new modes. Just learning all the alphabet soup is a challenge.

This can be one of the most confusing areas in memory and memory management to understand. The good news is that if you are not going to be writing full protected-mode programs, you need only a fairly general knowledge of what is going on, and that's something you can acquire without too much effort. Here is an easy place to start.

On the other hand, if you should wish to write protected-mode programs, you will need not only a thorough knowledge of the technical ins and outs of the 80x86 processors, but you will also need to have a good overall perspective on what they are doing. This chapter may help you acquire that perspective.

Real Mode

Real mode is called that because it is the operating mode that all members of the 80x86 family of microprocessors start in every time they are powered up, or when they are reset. Since it is the only mode for the 8088, and DOS was designed to manage an 8088-based PC, DOS is a real-mode (only) program.

There is a pin on the processor chip called *RESET.* Whenever the voltage on this line is raised to about two volts, the processor stops whatever it is doing. After that voltage gets low (to anything well under one volt), and after a short delay while the processor does some necessary internal housekeeping, it will go out to address FFFF:0000 and retrieve its first instruction.

The RESET pin is used when the PC is turned on to keep the processor from starting prematurely. It is activated by the Reset button on those PCs that have one. It also will be activated any time the power supply detects that one or more of its outputs have gone out of their specified voltage range. This last is done by a wire from the power supply called the *power good* line.

A logical memory address in real mode consists of a 16-bit segment number and a 16-bit offset (written **segment:offset**), which get combined to form a 20-bit linear address. The combining rule is: Multiply the segment value by 16 and add the offset value. The result is the linear address, which in this mode is also the physical address.

There is no distinction between a linear address and a physical address in real mode. There is a significant difference between the two in a subset of the 386-style of protected mode, and it is explained in the section "Protected Mode—386-Style" later in this chapter.

The maximum physical address in a PC in either Class 1 or Class 2 (those based on the 8088 or 8086) is 1,024K (1M), which is 1,048,576. Expressed in hexadecimal, the possible addresses run from 00000h to FFFFFh. This limit is set by the fact that these chips have only 20 address pins on the processor, so they have no way to put out anything larger than a 20-bit address value.

The maximum physical address in real mode for PCs in classes 3 through 6 is just slightly higher. For them, the maximum physical address is about 1,088K (which is 1.0625M). Actually, the limit is 16 less than that, or 1,114,096. Expressed in hexadecimal, the addresses run from 000000h to 10FFEFh (refer to Chapter 8, Figure 8.14, for an illustration of this). The CPU chips in these PCs have enough address pins to generate much larger addresses, but they are not able to do so in real mode.

This much you saw earlier in this book. Now for the complex stuff.

Protected Mode and Who Uses It

With the introduction of the 80286 microprocessor, Intel complicated the lives of PC programmers. They did so by adding to that processor a capability called *protected mode*, and they did it for some very good reasons.

The designers of the 80286 realized that this processor was going to be powerful enough to do some serious multitasking. That meant that, at least potentially, some users of PCs based on this chip would be running more than one program at the same time.

Whenever two or more programs are running at once, the potential for disaster is never far away. If both of the programs need to get keyboard input, which one gets the keystrokes? How does the user know to which program keystrokes will be sent? If both programs want to put a message on the screen, do they both get to do that? Anywhere they want, at any time? That could lead to some pretty messy and hard-to-understand screens. Likewise, output to the printer can't be a random mixture of lines or characters from each program. Even intermixing alternate pages from two different programs would be pretty confusing.

It was, therefore, to provide a means of protecting any simultaneously executing programs from one another. So the Intel chip designers included in the 80286 chip's design a number of hardware features to support such interprogram protections.

On the other hand, they also felt that backward compatibility was an absolute must. So they designed the 80286 chip to wake up in real mode, and in that mode it acts just like a faster 8086.

411

In fact, the way that the protected-mode features are implemented in the 80x86 processors requires that some work be done in real mode before it is even possible to put these processors into protected mode. So, designed as they are, they must wake up in real mode.

Intel could not compel their customers to offer operating system support for multitasking, but should one of them wish to do so, at least the necessary hardware features would be there. Or at least most of them would be, as it finally turned out.

DESQview had provided multitasking capability even on the earlier class 1 or 2 PCs, but it could not guarantee that the programs being multitasked would not step on each other's toes. It could (and did) do some virtualizing of the screen and keyboard (explained later), thus providing a means of keeping those programs from interfering with each other in the use of those resources, but it simply couldn't do anything about possible "illegal" memory references.

The idea of interprogram protection was another one that PC designers imported from the mainframe world. There, the operating system can do anything at any time. Mere user programs are strictly limited as to what they can do. Whenever one of the user programs needs to do something potentially dangerous (like input or output), it cannot do it and must, instead, issue a call to the supervisor program (the operating system), asking it to do the I/O task on the user program's behalf.

Likewise, a user program is restricted regarding the areas of memory it can access. This is to keep, for example, the game program you are developing from overwriting a part of my accounts receivable program that could be running on the same computer at the same time. Without such protections, it would be unsafe to let you develop your game on the same computer I was using to process the company's accounts receivable.

Who Uses Protected Mode?

So who uses protected mode? Not DOS. Nor any normal DOS program. They only know about the hardware of the 8086, and so they cannot activate the special hardware features of the higher level processors. They can't even get into protected mode, much less use it. (But see the discussion later about Virtual 86 mode, and how that lets real-mode programs have the benefits of hardware protections.)

Any program that was written explicitly to use protected mode can do so (provided it is run on a PC of class 3 or greater). When IBM shipped the first IBM *PC/ATs,* they shipped them with *PC DOS* 3.0 and that included the program VDISK. This was the first protected-mode PC utility program. The first protected-mode PC application programs came along many months later. What was planned to be the first protected-mode PC operating system, *OS/2,* took even longer. It is only now, many years later, reaching maturity.

Several alternative operating systems or operating environments that use the 80x86 processors in their protected modes have been developed or imported from mini or mainframe computers. *Xenix* and *UNIX* are operating system examples. *Pick* is somewhere between an operating system and an operating environment. *Windows* and *GeoWorks* are operating environments.

Each of these uses the protected-mode features of modern PCs extensively (when they are running on PCs which have them, of course). All but the last of these examples are programs that were being delivered to users before even the earliest version of *OS/2* was completed.

Anyone using a PC running DOS, for the first year or two at least, was most likely not using protected mode for anything other than maybe a virtual disk (RAM disk) and a disk cache. Quite a few people are still at that stage.

DOS Extenders

Recently, *DOS extenders* have come into vogue with programmers. These are programs that have been developed to make it easy (more or less) for a programmer writing a DOS program to get access to extended memory. They amount to a shell of protected-mode code that gets wrapped around the original real mode application. The result is a program that runs apparently like any other DOS program, but is able to access any amount of extended memory it may need. For the most part, the instructions in the program don't even have to be rewritten; the compiler and linker do all the necessary things to make the program work properly in its new larger "playground." (Compilers and linkers are described in Chapter 7 in the section "Programs and Data Differ Only in Context.")

Users of PCs don't use DOS extenders; only programmers do. Users can run DOS-extended programs on their PCs and then get the benefits of that technology. Now that DOS-extended programs are becoming quite common, more and more people are getting those benefits while running what otherwise appears to be an ordinary DOS program.

Most recently, with the development of good multitasking programs that run in protected mode on top of DOS, it is possible for regular old DOS applications to run in protected mode within one of the operating environments. For example, this includes running any DOS application in a DOS window of Microsoft *Windows* or *OS/2*.

Protected Mode—286-Style

First, you need to know that 286-protected mode is an operating mode that is available to the 80286 and to *all* later chips in the 80x86 family. Therefore, *everything* in this section applies to all PCs in classes 3 through 6.

The whole idea of protected mode is to protect programs. The most important things to protect against are invalid memory accesses and inappropriate I/O. How does the 80286 address these issues?

First, the idea of segments is greatly extended. No longer is a segment just any 64KB region of memory that lies within the first 1,088KB and starts at an address which is an integral multiple of 16. Now a segment is a variable length region of memory that may start anywhere in the full 16MB memory address space and have any length from a single byte up to 64KB. Each segment also carries some additional information called *access rights*. These bits are used to limit who can access this segment for what purposes and when a program that is in this segment may do any I/O operations.

Segments Versus Selectors

The way the 80286 is able to provide these protections hinges around a new way of computing linear addresses. In real mode, you just add 16 times the segment value to the offset to get the linear address. In protected mode, the conversion is done very differently.

In protected mode, there is still the notion of a logical address. (It is sometimes called the *virtual address,* for reasons that will become clear shortly.) The logical address is the address as it is seen by the programs running in the PC. They put a value in a segment register and generate an offset, and then expect that the processor will know what place in memory is being indicated.

You will even see protected-mode logical (virtual) addresses written in the usual **segment:offset** form. What is new and different is how the part before the colon (the segment number) gets used.

Protected-mode address calculation uses something programmers call *indirection.* The number in the segment register is used to point to a number that is then added to the offset to get the linear address. The number that gets added to the offset (the one pointed to) is known as the *base address.* The number in the segment register is now called a *selector,* because it selects which segment is to be used, but its value is not a part of that segment's address in any direct sense.

The selectors and the offsets are each limited to 16 bits, the same as in real mode. But the base pointer that is pointed to by the selector is 24 bits long. That allows linear addresses up to 24 bits long as well. This is how it is possible to specify a segment anywhere in the 16MB memory address range of the CPU with only a 16-bit number in the segment register.

The selector points to more than just a base address. It points to a line in a table, one column of which contains the base addresses (three bytes each) for all the segments that can be selected. Another column in this table gives the size of each of those segments (two bytes each). The final column contains access rights for those segments (one byte each). Each line of this table is called a *segment descriptor,* and the collection of all of them is called a *descriptor table* (see Figure 11.1).

Descriptors are actually eight bytes long. The last two bytes are simply reserved in 286-protected mode. They are used in the higher processors' 386-protected mode operation.

This process for going from a selector value to a descriptor and the base pointer value it contains, and then adding the offset to get the linear address, can only work if there is a descriptor table already prepared. Preparing those tables is the main task that must be done in real mode before it is safe to put the processor into protected mode.

Global and Local Descriptor Tables

Remember, the point of protected mode is to be able to have programs that cannot hurt one another. Using descriptor tables does this nicely. Every line in such a table describes a segment (that is only as large as it needs to be) to which the program has some sort of access. It might be able to read information from that segment, write to it, execute instructions that are in it, or some combination of these things. What exactly it can do with any given segment is spelled out by the associated access rights byte.

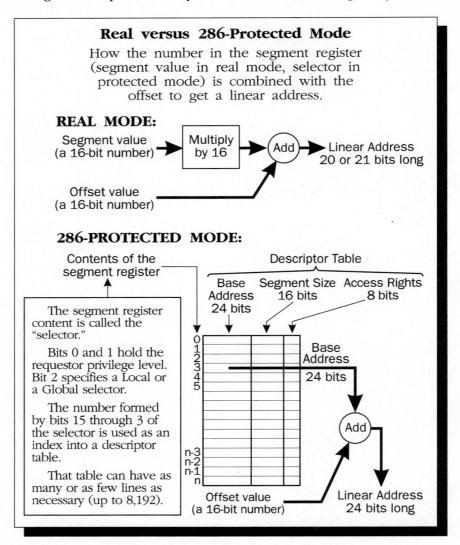

Figure 11.1. From logical (selector:offset) address to linear address in real and 286-protected mode.

Every single time a program attempts to access any memory location, that access is checked for validity first. To be valid, an access must be to a location within a segment to which that program has the appropriate access rights.

So, any portion of the CPU's memory address space that is not within one of the segments described in a program's descriptor table effectively does not exist for that program. Give each program its own descriptor table and you surely can keep them apart.

In fact, this solution overdoes things a bit. There is some information you really want to let every program have access to, and even some programs you'd like to have every program be able to run. You could put them into segments and put descriptors for those segments into every program's descriptor table, but the easier way is to have two descriptor tables each program can reference. One is private (the *Local Descriptor Table*) and the other is public (the *Global Descriptor Table*).

> Another problem with using only one descriptor table has to do with how you find those tables. There needs to be a master table that is somehow accessible to all programs which can help the CPU find the next descriptor table it needs to use. That is one kind of information the Global Descriptor Table contains.

Every task can access one **L**ocal **D**escriptor **T**able (LDT) and the **G**lobal **D**escriptor **T**able (GDT). One bit in each selector specifies which of the two tables to look in for the selected segment.

The CPU has an internal register that points to the GDT (called, naturally enough, the *GDT Register,* or GDTR). It has another one that points to the current LDT (the LDTR).

Task Switching Using Descriptor Tables

Intel's plan was that each time the processor is about to start running a new program, an LDT for that program shall be built. Then its address is loaded into the LDTR and the processor is told to begin processing instructions from the new program.

Later, when switching from that program to some other, the processor needs merely to save the values in all its registers in the *Task State Segment* (TSS), and reload them from a previously saved set for the new program to be run. (The Task State Segment is described in a descriptor table and pointed to by a selector.) The register that says which instruction to load next will point to the next instruction to be run in the new program, and the LDTR will point to the then relevant LDT.

What gets stored in the GDTR is both a pointer to the GDT and an indication of its size. That keeps the processor from retrieving data that may be stored beyond the end of the GDT and acting upon them as if they were a valid part of the GDT.

Similarly, what gets stored in the LDTR is a selector to the GDT, which describes the segment in memory containing that LDT. That segment descriptor specifies how large the LDT is, as well as where it is.

The result of all this hardware is that there is no longer just one linear address space for the CPU. There is one global address space, as specified by all the selectors in the GDT (plus the IDT, to be described in a moment), and one local address space per program, as specified by all the selectors in that program's LDT. Each of these address spaces is a subset of the whole CPU's linear address space (also called its *virtual address space*). These issues will come up again in the discussion of virtual memory later in this chapter.

Protections

Do you think that all this discussion of selectors, descriptors, and descriptor tables is confusing? Things get considerably more complicated when you realize what Intel has done to implement protections. These are rules that limit what a program can do and they apply, in a sense, over and above the access right restrictions built into each segment descriptor.

There are four levels of privilege in Intel 80x86 processors. Intel calls them *Rings*. Programs running at Ring 0 have total access to everything. Programs at each lower level (Rings 1 through 3) have weaker access rights. When the processor is operating in real mode, in effect, every program runs in Ring 0. But once the processor is put into protected mode, that changes. In protected mode, in order to get the benefit of the hardware protection features, very few programs are allowed to run in Ring 0.

Intel intended Ring 0 to be used only for the most trusted inner part of an operating system. Ring 1 was to be used for the operating system service routines. Ring 2 was meant to be used for various extensions to the operating system, and Ring 3 for user (application) programs.

Most authors of operating systems, DOS-extenders, and operating environments to date have not implemented this full model. Mostly, they use only two levels. Typically, a user program (an application or a general utility program) will run at Ring 3. And the operating system (all parts, not just the most trusted inner core) will run at Ring 0.

Segment Level Protections

Each time your program seeks to access a segment, it does so by using a selector. The two least significant bits of the selector define something called the *Requestor Privilege Level* (RPL).

The selector loaded into the Code Segment Register (which specifies which segment contains the currently executing program) has control, through the value of its two least significant bits, of the **C**urrent **P**rivilege **L**evel (CPL).

Every segment descriptor contains another pair of bits (part of the access rights byte) that specify what is called the *Descriptor Privilege Level* (DPL). On each access to a segment, in addition to checking the segment's inherent read, write, or execute access bits, the processor examines the DPL and compares it to the CPL. The program cannot get at the segment, even if it is specified as one that could be accessed for the desired action (reading, writing, or executing), unless the CPL specifies at least as high a level of privilege as the DPL.

The details of how the RPL, CPL, and DPL interact, and how the CPL gets modified by the RPL, are fairly involved. There also is a way that the CPL controls the I/O access rights of a program.

Each task is given a **T**ask **S**tate **S**egment, or TSS, in which it stores all the registers and some other information necessary to restart the task. One pair of bits in one control register is called the IOPL, or *I/O Permission Level.* In 386-protected mode, the IOPL is supplanted by an I/O Permission Bit Map, which is appended to the TSS. The IOPL applies a generic protection against I/O by unprivileged tasks. The I/O Permission Bit Map specifies port by port which ones are accessible to this task.

Fortunately, understanding all of the details is not essential to grasping what Intel was after. You can rest assured that much thought went into devising and implementing those details, so that operating systems and application programs could be written to work together gracefully.

Just because the hardware design of the processor was well thought-out does not mean that writing a good protected-mode operating system is simple. It certainly is not. *OS/2* was planned as the operating system to replace DOS when the AT was introduced (and was supposed to replace all the PCs and XTs). As you may know, neither happened.

DOS lives, and so do many PCs, XTs, and clones of them. And *OS/2* very nearly died. IBM did manage to rescue it and finally, with version 2.0, it looks like it will be a viable operating system for PCs. But it took them eight years to get there—a clear indication of just how difficult it can be to write a good protected mode operating system.

Interprocess Transfers of Control

Programs often call other programs to do some subtask for them. Sometimes these are subprograms written by the same programmers who wrote the main application. Often, however, the called programs are service utility routines in the operating system or some extension to it. In this latter case, the called program and the calling program may well have different privilege levels.

There are two different means by which the processor can allow programs to get the help of more privileged subprograms. One is called the *conforming segment approach*. The other is by the use of a *call gate*.

Conforming segments mean segments containing programs that belong to the operating system, and thus have a high privilege level, but which are known not to contain any instructions that could do potentially dangerous things, such as any I/O operations. These segments are flagged as conforming to let the processor know it is okay for a lower privilege program to invoke this higher privileged one.

Call gates are the means by which a user program can ask the operating system to do some I/O on its behalf (or any similar task that truly requires higher privilege than the calling program has). They are special selectors in the GDT which the processor recognizes and uses to transfer control up the privilege hierarchy.

The mechanisms described so far do pretty well at handling the normal flow of a program and any jumps or calls it may do. What is left to handle are interrupts or exceptions of any kind. (And there are now more kinds of exceptions possible since the processor is constantly checking to see that programs not be allowed to do illegal things like accessing some location in memory outside the segments to which they have access rights.)

Interrupt Descriptor Table

What happens when an interrupt or exception occurs? In real mode, the processor knows just where to look for the address of an appropriate interrupt service routine (ISR). It multiplies the type number for that interrupt by four and goes to that address (within the first 1KB since there are at most 256 types of interrupt) and retrieves the ISR address.

This won't work when the processor is operating in protected mode. The ISRs pointed to by the numbers in the interrupt vector table in low memory are all real mode programs. So the processor must now have some alternative way of finding ISRs that can operate properly in protected mode.

The mechanism used is quite analogous to the GDT. Recall that the GDT translates selector values into actual segment addresses, and through the segment size and access rights portion of the segment descriptor, gives the processor knowledge of what it is allowed to do in that segment.

Another descriptor table that can be accessed by the CPU at any time solves the problem. And setting it up is one more thing that must be done in real mode before the processor can be safely put into protected mode. This other required descriptor table is called the *Interrupt Descriptor Table* (IDT). It consists of up to 256 descriptors, one per interrupt type. The CPU has an **IDT R**egister (IDTR), which stores where in memory address space the IDT is located and how large it is.

Programs running in protected mode on DOS machines (using DOS-extenders or protected-mode operating environments on top of DOS) usually use a mixed bag of interrupt service routines. Some of the entries in the IDT point to real, full-fledged protected-mode interrupt routines. Others point to what amounts to front-end programs that actually end up using an underlying real-mode interrupt routine.

In contrast to this, full protected-mode operating systems like *UNIX* or *OS/2* use protected-mode interrupt service routines exclusively. That means that they cannot take advantage of any of the default (real mode) ISRs built into the BIOS (except that on *PS/2*s, the ABIOS has some protected mode ISRs for *OS/2* support). On the other hand, they can gain greatly from never having to switch the processor to real mode.

Such front-end interrupt handling programs will save some state-of-the-machine information, then switch to real mode and call the real-mode interrupt routine. After that ISR returns, the front-end program switches the CPU back to protected mode, delivers the result, and the application program goes on about its business.

A good way to think about this process is as if the CPU were two different processors. One works in real mode only; the other works in protected mode only. And the front-end interrupt programs mainly serve to communicate a request for a subtask to be performed and its results between the two.

Mostly, an application program neither knows nor cares which way a given interrupt gets handled. Both ways work. The advantage of the front-end to an existing routine is that less work need be done to create it. The basic ISR already exists. The front-end program just handles getting the CPU into a state that can use that ISR and back again, and moving any needed input and output information in the process.

The disadvantage to this approach is simple: There is more overhead, but even worse, it forces the 80286 to do what it does least well, namely, move from protected mode to real mode.

How to Get into Protected Mode and Back Again

Here is the dirty secret of the 80286. This section explains why Bill Gates called the 80286 a "brain damaged" microprocessor.

When the processor wakes up, it is in real mode. Once some real-mode program has set up a GDT, IDT, and at least one LDT, the processor can be put into protected mode. That last step is done by a single, simple instruction. All that is very straightforward.

The designers of the 80286 knew how much more powerful protected mode was than real mode. They imagined, therefore, that anyone who had a program that could put the processor into protected mode would never want to return. (Sort of a variation on "How you gonna keep 'em down on the farm, after they've seen Paree?")

So while they provided an easy mechanism for putting the processor into protected mode, there is no comparably easy method to get it back. They just did not anticipate the need.

As long as you use DOS, and as long as your protected mode programs specify the mixed bag of protected-mode and front-end-to-real-mode-ISR programs in their IDTs that were discussed earlier, there will be a need to switch both to and from protected mode frequently. When the 386 came out, it included a solution to this problem in the form of a new instruction. But how was it handled before then?

It was done by one of the greater kludges of modern times. Essentially, you must take advantage of the fact that the processor wakes up in real mode. So, if you are in protected mode and you want to go back to real mode, you just reset the processor.

> Resetting the processor returns it to its initial, power-on conditions. You may think of resetting only in terms of pressing Ctrl-Alt-Del. That does cause a processor reset (usually), but it is not the only way such a reset can be caused.

This is a fairly drastic way to do things. It has been likened to shutting off the engine of a car in order to shift gears. It certainly is less graceful than just executing one instruction.

How do you go about getting the processor to reset itself? It turns out that there are at least two ways to do this. One way was obvious to PC designers from the start, but it is not a very nice way. The other was always possible, but since it involves using an undocumented feature of the processor, it took quite a while before people discovered it.

"Knock Me Out, Buddy . . . Oh, That Felt Good!"

There is a hardware line into the processor called *RESET*. If you can force that to the high state, that will do the job. But how can that be done?

The answer lies in the fact that a PC contains more than one processor. It is less like a one-man band than it is like a small chamber orchestra. There is a main, or lead, processor. That is what is called the CPU (central processing unit). But there are also other helper processors doing smaller tasks under the general direction of the CPU.

One of these helper processors is the *keyboard controller*. Its job is to listen to the keyboard for messages indicating keystrokes. When it hears one, it will tug on the CPU's interrupt line, and then when the CPU is ready, tell it what keystroke the keyboard controller just received.

In many PCs, the keyboard controller is an Intel 8742 chip. That chip is actually a small computer all by itself. It has both a processor and some memory—enough to hold all the programs it needs to do its assigned job. That collection of programs is called the *keyboard BIOS*.

One of the IBM engineers realized that this subcomputer could be given a special extra job to do. If you sent it the right message from the

CPU (and provided it with the right external wiring), it could turn around and tug (briefly) on the CPU's reset line (see Figure 11.2). In effect, it could "knock out the CPU." Then when the CPU woke up again, it would be back in real mode.

Figure 11.2. Using the keyboard controller to reset the 80286 central processing unit (CPU).

The IBM *PS/2* computers and some modern PC clones have one bit of a special output port (92h) tied directly to the CPU RESET line. They can reset themselves with a single I/O-Output instruction.

To use this as a way of accessing a real-mode interrupt in the middle of a protected-mode program, or to return from a protected-mode subprogram to a calling real-mode program, you have to do something a bit more than just reset the processor. You certainly don't want to have your PC do a memory check and then initialize everything and run your AUTOEXEC.BAT file. That wouldn't do at all!

Different Kinds of Boots (Again)

This is not the only situation in which it is nice not to have the PC go quite all the way back to "square one." When you press Ctrl-Alt-Del (the "three fingered salute") to restart your computer, you don't really want to repeat the full POST.

In the last chapter, you learned that the PC has a way of skipping the memory test when you do what is called a "warm boot" (Ctrl-Alt-Del) as opposed to a "cold boot" (power off and on, or push a reset button) when it does the full POST. What you did not learn there was how it manages that trick.

There is actually one more step to the start-up process that was not described in Chapter 10. The first thing it does, even before checking on the integrity of the POST program, is find out if it is going to have to do the POST process and/or the boot process.

Every time any class 3 or higher PC is shut down or reset, a byte gets set in the configuration CMOS memory. That byte is called the *CMOS shutdown byte*. Every time those PCs begin to run the POST program (which is to say, every time they are turned on or reset), they first check that shutdown byte to see what was going on last.

There are many values that get stored in that location, each meaning something different. A value of zero means either a warm or a cold boot. Another special value means that this is a return from protected mode after a block move command (INT 15h). A different one means a return from protected mode after which the PC is to jump to a location specified in a designated location in the BIOS data area. Eight more values are used for various purposes by the POST program.

If the shutdown byte was a zero, the POST knows it is supposed to do a boot. To determine which kind of boot (cold or warm), it looks next at location 0472h. If it finds the number 1234h in that location, it will do a warm boot. Otherwise, it will do a cold boot. (The only differences between the two is whether or not the keyboard gets reset and whether or not RAM is tested.)

The IBM *PS/2* computers also check location 0472h for a different special value: 4321h. Finding that tells the POST to do something other than a normal boot. The IBM *PC/Convertible* used some other special values in this location to mean other special things it was to do.

Figure 11.3 shows in flow chart form the essence of how the POST determines what it is to do. These steps all come very near the start of the POST, before all but the first step shown in Figure 10.7.

The Mysterious "Triple Fault"

Many books and articles written in recent years that describe the way an 80286 is induced to return from protected mode to real mode refer to something called the *triple fault*. But they don't explain what that is. It seems to one who is first studying the field almost as if there is a conspiracy of silence on this point.

The Intel literature does describe something they call a *double fault*. That is, when a fault (remember, that is one kind of exception) happens and while the interrupt service routine is responding to that fault, another fault happens. Any double fault causes its own special kind of exception (an abort, causing an interrupt of type 8).

Normally, the designers of any complex microelectronic circuitry try to anticipate every possible contingency and plan what shall happen then. Or, at least, they attempt to document what does happen, even though it may be an unplanned consequence of other parts of the design.

Microprocessors are so very complex, though, that it is not always practical to document every possible occurrence. Apparently, Intel felt that a triple fault was such an unlikely thing to have happen that they did not bother to document what would happen if it did occur. So people had to have the experience and discover what would happen for themselves.

If a fault occurs while processing a double fault (hence, a "triple fault"), the processor simply throws up its hands and does a reset. That may or may not have been a built-in feature; it turns out to be the best way that exists for bringing an 80286 out of protected mode and back to real mode. So now people routinely cause that "extremely unlikely event"— they triple-fault quite intentionally whenever they wish to have an 80286 go back to real mode.

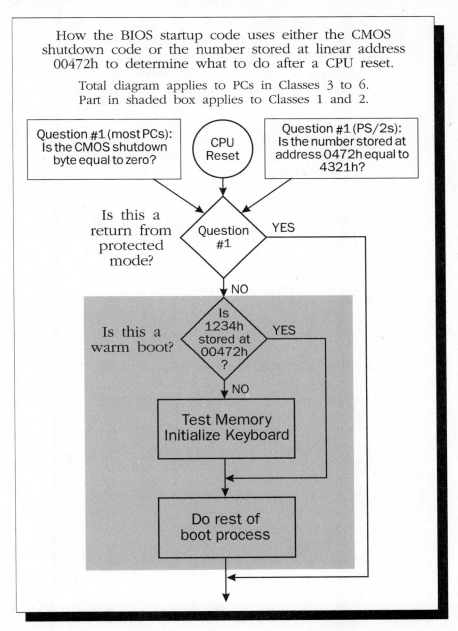

Figure 11.3. How the BIOS knows which kind of start-up to do after a CPU reset.

The advantage to using the triple fault over the keyboard controller reset is that it can be done more quickly. Even so, this process is none too quick. Remember that after a reset, the processor must do some internal housekeeping, during which time it is not processing any instructions in your program. This can take nearly a millisecond. Not long by human standards, but almost an eternity by the standards used in describing speedy computer operations.

Remember, the resets that are used to return from protected mode are essentially unnoticeable to the PC's user. The only way you might notice that they are happening (and learn just how slow they are) is if you were in the middle of a time-sensitive operation like telecommunications. If one of these resets happens then and if you are communicating at a very high bit-per-second rate (for example, 9,600 bps), you may find that you have missed some of the incoming characters.

Protected Mode—386-Style

The introduction of the 80386 (now most often called just the 386) was widely hailed as a major technological breakthrough. Some said simply, "Thank goodness, they finally got it right!"

The 386 solved the most terrible problem of the 80286; the 386 has a way to return from protected mode to real mode using only normal instructions. No longer was it necessary either to use the keyboard controller to "knock out" the CPU, or to triple-fault it into a reset. But that was not all. The 386 included two other very significant improvements over the 286, both of which affected its implementation of protected mode.

Just because a 386 can be returned from protected mode to real mode without using the triple fault or reset procedures doesn't mean that all programs will use the "better" alternative. Many programs treat all PCs in Classes 3 and higher as if they were the same. To do this they must assume that they need to use the triple fault to reset the processor each time they wish to return from protected mode to real mode. Only programs that have been specially written to take advantage of the 386 will use the instruction it supports to make these mode transitions.

The first major improvement in the 386 is that at last you have a full 32-bit computer. Memory addresses and data are each given 32 pins on the package, and they move internally as 32-bit quantities.

The 386 holds 32-bit numbers in almost all its registers. The only registers that appear to be shorter are the segment registers (which hold 16-bit selector values). Actually, they are much wider than they appear. Each segment register holds 104 bits, though only the 16-bit selector portion is "visible" to a programmer.

The other major innovation in the 386 is the introduction of paging as yet another level of translation between the logical (**segment:offset**) addressing scheme used by programs, and the actual physical address used by the electronics that connect to the memory chips. This is especially significant for memory management.

With the 386, a generation of microprocessors had reached maturity. The rather small differences between the 386 and the 486 make this point very strongly. The 486, with over four times the complexity of the 386 chip, adds nothing substantial to the machine architecture.

The real contribution of the 486 is that it brings onto the chip many support parts that had previously been implemented with additional IC chips on the motherboard. In particular, it incorporates the 80387 math coprocessor and 8KB of memory caching.

The *Pentium* is the next member of the 80x86 family, and it carries the development forward another notch. The *Pentium* is about three times as complex as a 486, yet it still is totally compatible with the earlier members of the 80x86 family, and it still operates in the same modes as the 386. (Chapter 13 describes the differences of the *Pentium* from the other members of the family in more detail.)

The 386 is fully backward compatible with the earlier members of the 80x86 family. That means that it supports all the older processors' instructions and operating modes, so it has both a real mode and a 286-protected mode of operation. But it also has two brand-new modes: 386-protected mode and virtual-8086 mode.

How does 386-protected mode differ from 286-protected mode? And is there yet another 486- or *Pentium*-protected mode? To answer the last question first, no, the 486 and the *Pentium* do not add any new modes of operation. They support all the earlier chips' modes, so they too can run in any of these modes: Real, 286-protected, 386-protected, and virtual-8086.

The main differences between 386-protected mode and the earlier 286-protected mode are what follows fairly naturally from the fact that the 386 uses 32-bit data and addresses, whereas the 286 used only 24 bits for address and 16 bits for data.

Larger Segments in a Larger Total Memory Address Space

In particular, while logical addresses are still expressed by a segment register value and an offset, the offset register holds 32 bits, so the offsets can range up to a maximum of 4GB (if the segment is that large). The segment register value (the selector) is still only 16 bits long, but the base address, like the offset, can now be a full 32 bits long.

To make room for the larger base address, the segment descriptors in both the GDT and LDT must be longer. The full eight bytes are now brought into play (see Figure 11.4). The interrupt descriptors in the IDT are similarly enhanced.

By adding two bytes to the descriptors (or really by using the two bytes that previously were marked as "reserved"), there is room for more than just another byte added to the base address. The number specifying segment size is increased from 16 to 20 bits. The actual segment size is further modified by interpreting this number in the light of a "granularity bit."

The upshot is that in the 386, a segment can begin at any linear address in the entire 4GB memory address range of the processor, and it can have any size up to 1MB (to the byte). Or, when the granularity bit is set to one, the segment size is multiplied by 4K, and then segments can be any multiple of 4KB up to 4GB.

When programmers say that the 386 finally gives them a "flat memory space," they are referring to setting the granularity bit to one and the segment size to its maximum value. Then, with the base address set to zero, the full 4GB memory address range is accessible in a single segment. You only need to point the offset to whichever byte you wish to access.

On the other hand, if you set the granularity bit to one and the segment size to zero, it really means a segment size of 4096 (valid offsets from 000h to FFFh). This makes segments the same size as the pages that are mapped by the paging unit.

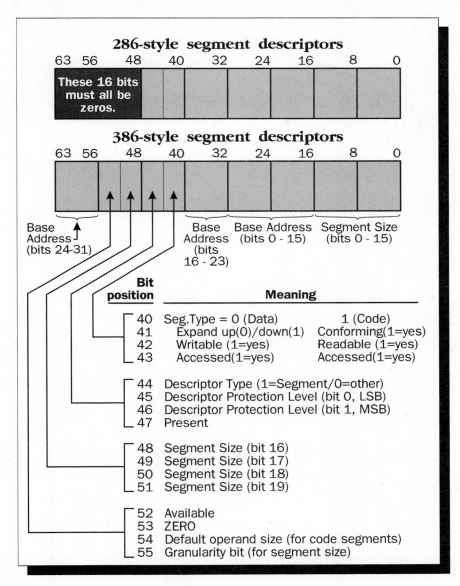

Figure 11.4. Segment descriptor structures.

The 386SX

Intel now offers the 386 in several forms. The next one to be offered after the original 386 was called the 386SX. (At that time, the original one was renamed 386DX.)

It would appear that the *SX* stands for *Single word eXternal bus*, and the *DX* for *Double word eXternal bus*. Intel did not say. And now, they have very much muddied the waters by having the suffixes *DX* and *SX* mean something totally different for the 486.

The 386SX is significant mainly because it has a 16-bit external bus, and so is very much like the 80286, but it is the full 386 internally. That means that a 386SX can run all the same software as any 386DX, albeit somewhat more slowly. Intel priced the 386SX low enough that it would, they hoped, drive the 80286 completely out of the market. (At the time they had a monopoly on 386 production, but not on 80286 chips.)

While the difference between a 386SX and a 386DX that is talked about the most is the fact that its data bus is restricted to 16 bits, that may not be the most significant difference. The width of the data bus only affects the speed with which it can do its work.

The other key difference is the number of address lines. This limits the size of its physical memory map. This means that you can not run every program that works on a 386DX on a 386SX, and in particular, none that require more than 16MB of total RAM. Virtual memory can mitigate this limitation; still the vastly slower speed of access to virtual memory makes this a real barrier for some uses.

From the perspective of memory management, the important point is that the 386SX is a true 386. And that means that all the good memory-management tricks that apply to any 386 will work with a 386SX.

Paging

The paging features in the 386 are very powerful. This is hardware support for full demand-paged virtual memory. (Just what that is and how it can work is discussed a bit later in the section on virtual memory. Here, only the mechanism is described, leaving the discussion of how it can be utilized for later.)

The conversion of a logical address (in **segment:offset** form) generated by the program into a linear address proceeds as before (see Figure 11.1). What is new in 386-protected mode is the option of turning on paging.

> The offset part of a logical address may be built up of many parts. Even the 8086 offers a rich assortment of addressing modes in which immediate arguments can be combined with register values or values stored in memory. The discussion in this chapter is all about how that offset, once generated, is combined with the segment register value to get a real physical address that can be put on the CPU's address bus pins.

Paging serves as an additional translation step. The logical address is generated by the segmentation unit (a subpart of the CPU). Then, if paging is enabled, that address is further translated by the paging unit (another subpart of the CPU). The steps the paging unit takes are shown in Figure 11.5.

There are several significant things to notice about 386-paging. One is that the size of a page is always 4KB. The size of a segment could be anything from 1 byte to 4GB, but a page, in this sense, is always the same size.

Another is that pages have privilege levels. There is a whole other layer of protections invoked once you start using paging. They supplement the protections available at the segment level.

Paging allows any region of physical memory to appear at any place you may desire in the CPU's linear memory address space. In particular, you can move some of the RAM from what is normally lower (system) memory out to the far reaches of extended memory, and vice versa. That allows you to do all the tricks of LIM EMS 4.0, swapping without either (a) having to buy an add-in hardware EMS board or (b) having to remove motherboard memory chips and/or disable motherboard memory address decoding. All you need is some software to tell the paging unit what to do. This software is called, in this case, a *386-LIMulator program.*

Also, you can make memory appear in otherwise empty places in upper memory space. You can even make things that are there disappear, if you like, by mapping them out. Then you can refill those linear addresses with RAM from some other place in physical memory. (This last trick is the basis of the technology Qualitas uses in their *BlueMAX* product, which they call "BIOS compression," and it is the basis of the technology Quarterdeck introduced with *QEMM,* version 6.0, which they called "Stealth.")

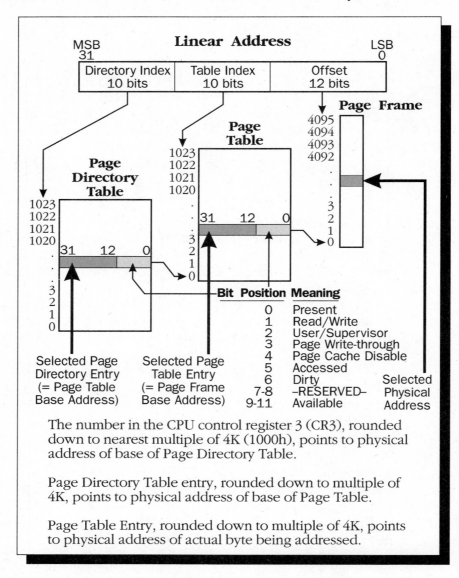

Figure 11.5. 386 (and 486) paging: From linear address to physical address. The "dirty" bit is not used in connection with Page Directory Table entries. Both the "Page Write-through" and "Page Cache Disable" bits are only used on the 80486.

The Translation Lookaside Buffer (TLB)

There is a lot of calculation and table lookup going on to get from a segmented logical address to a linear one, and then to a physical one. And it has to be done for every single memory reference. That could be an intolerable drag on the computer's performance, except that Intel built in a couple of features to help out.

First, the segment descriptor (which includes the base address) is pulled in from the descriptor table by the CPU each time a new selector is loaded into a segment register. That descriptor is cached, out of sight but very much close at hand, in the invisible 88 bits of the segment register. This means that the CPU does not need to be continually rereading the descriptor table (in memory) to do its logical-to-linear address conversions.

Second, the **T**ranslation **L**ookaside **B**uffer (TLB) is a cache for page table entries. The most recently referenced pages have their entries kept here. That allows the paging unit to do linear-to-physical address conversions without constant references to memory. Between them, these two features make it possible to do memory references just as fast (or faster) with a 386, as with any earlier 80x86 processor.

Virtual-8086 (V86) Mode

The other new operating mode introduced with the 386 is called *virtual-8086* (V86) mode. As its name suggests, it allows one to make the 386 emulate the 8086.

"But doesn't it do that already? I thought that was what it meant to wake up in real mode." Yes, that is true. But virtual-8086 mode adds something very important on top of that idea. It allows the 386 to *emulate the 8086 while running in protected mode.*

This does two things for you. One is that you can run real mode programs (including all your old, familiar DOS programs) and get all the protections inherent in protected mode. The other is that you can have multiple V86 sessions running in the 386 simultaneously. (Of course, only one program is really running at any given instant; however, if the programs take turns quickly enough, it will seem as if all are running simultaneously. This is what is meant by multitasking.)

The Operating Monitor Program

Before you can go into V86 mode, the CPU must be put into protected mode. So you first run some program that will set up the proper descriptor tables and do the other necessary things, then switch the CPU into protected mode. This program normally will also stay around monitoring the activities of each V86 session and providing any needed services, while arbitrating any requests for access to I/O. This program is sometimes called the *virtual machine control program*, or the *monitor* for short.

Next, the monitor will set up segments and descriptor tables, and load programs into those segments. You might choose to load *DOS, plus your usual TSRs, plus a real mode DOS application program.* This will be one V86 task.

Each V86 machine can get up to 1,088KB of memory (simulated lower plus upper memory and HMA) all to itself. Each one can be loaded with a different real mode operating system (*e.g.*, a different version of DOS).

At this point, the monitor is ready to start the V86 task. It does this by transferring control to the V86 task, and in the process, setting a CPU control bit to the virtual mode state.

Normally, to make the real mode programs that are running in that V86 task believe that they are running in a real 8086 computer (or a 80286, since they can have an HMA), the paging unit is told to map all the memory that task is using to the first 1,088KB of linear memory space. That remapping is repeated for each V86 task just before each task is allowed to run for a while.

Privilege Considerations

The monitor runs, typically, with Ring 0 privilege. It can do anything. Each V86 task runs at Ring 3. It cannot do much of anything other than compute. Any I/O it wishes to do must be with the indulgence of the monitor program.

Every time there is an interrupt, the monitor can, if it wishes, regain control of the PC. Then it will either process that interrupt or "reflect" it back to be handled by the copy of DOS and the BIOS that is loaded in the virtual machine.

This works fine if the only Ring 0 program is this monitor. But it can be a source of difficulty if you try to run any other Ring 0 program from within one of the V86 sessions. The problem can arise whenever the DOS program you choose to run in your virtual 8086 machine is actually a DOS-extended program.

One case where this comes up is if you run a LIMulator. That puts the 386 into protected mode and then runs your DOS applications in V86 mode. If you now try to run Lotus *1-2-3*, Release 3.0, the machine will come to an abrupt halt. You will have caused a **G**eneral **P**rotection **F**ault (GPF).

This happens for any DOS-extended program unless the LIMulator was built to offer VCPI (**V**irtual **C**ontrol **P**rogram **I**nterface) services, and the DOS-extender to take advantage of them. All this will be explained in more detail in Chapter 12.

Paging and Multiple Virtual Machines

The scenario described with a protected-mode monitor program launching, supervising, and supporting a real-mode program running as a V86 task can be repeated. The monitor can create as many V86 sessions as you have room for in your memory. (In fact, with the use of the virtual memory techniques discussed in the next section, you can create any number of V86 sessions. However, the performance of the programs in each of them would be degraded after a while to the point that you would not want to go on adding more V86 sessions.)

When you have more than one V86 session with an active program, it is important that you provide a means for sharing the CPU's computing power among these sessions. The basic mechanism used is the interrupt. Remember that, ordinarily, whenever an interrupt occurs, the monitor gains control of the PC.

At that time, if it wishes, it may suspend the V86 task that has been running and run another. Or, after doing whatever is appropriate for that interrupt, the monitor may let the current V86 task proceed.

If the monitor takes control in this fashion through the timer interrupt, it can implement "preemptive multitasking." That means it stops each program after some set time, and moves on to the next program.

Virtualizing Devices

The notion of protected mode was developed to allow more than one program to operate in the computer at once. But most programs use the keyboard and the screen. How can you prevent them from interfering with one another?

It gets particularly tough if the applications are the usual sort of not-very-well-behaved programs you have in the DOS world. Many of these programs use direct hardware access instead of calling on the BIOS when they wish to put things on the screen or read from the keyboard.

If only they stuck to the BIOS calls, then you could easily hook these calls and keep the different programs from interfering with one another. That is what *DESQview* does on a PC in classes 1 through 4. Once you get to classes 5 and 6 and have access to V86 mode, things become much easier.

Now you can "virtualize" I/O ports and regions of memory. Each program running in a V86 task thinks it has its own video image buffer, but actually all of them are somewhere safely away from the real video card's RAM buffer. Then the monitor program can copy portions of the video image created by each individual program into the real video buffer to let a portion of that program's output show up in a window on the screen.

Similar things can be done for every port and every critical region in memory. The basic 386-mode protections support this very nicely.

> One improvement of the 386-protected mode over the 286-protected mode is in the way it handles permission to do output. The 286 only grants or denies permission to a program for all ports at once. The 386 stores with each task (in its Task State Segment, or TSS) a map of all the individual I/O ports showing which ones that task (program) is allowed to access.

Advantages and Disadvantages of Protected Mode

Consider the pros and cons of using protected mode. There are certainly some strong advantages, but there are also some disadvantages you may not want to lose sight of.

Advantages of Protected Mode

Using protected mode makes it possible to build really robust multitasking systems—that is, systems that can protect one program against the misadventures of other programs with which it is sharing the PC.

This can be done even on an 80286-based PC. But it is much easier and can be done much better on the higher level PCs (based on a 386, 486, or Pentium CPU) by running the multiple programs in multiple Virtual 8086 sessions.

Protected mode also has a benefit, even if you run only one program at a time. Its protections will help "smoke out" many subtle bugs that otherwise would go unnoticed. In that sense, it protects programs against themselves (which is another way of saying "against programmer errors").

Disadvantages of Protected Mode

Using protected mode requires some setup. You can't just be there, as you can with real mode. This is not so bad if you only have to do it once, and then can stay in protected mode for the rest of the day.

But the protected-mode programs that are common on PCs today are not like that. The protected-mode operating environments and the DOS-extended programs all return to real mode many times a second to use some real-mode interrupt service routines. This costs something in terms of performance. There is significant overhead in going back and forth all the time. This is especially bad if you are using a PC whose CPU is an 80286 or if you are running a program that doesn't take advantage of the specialness of a 386 or better processor.

Finally, you are going to restrict yourself to running only reasonably well-behaved DOS application programs. And you will be unable to use some of your favorite utility programs until you have exited from any protected-mode operating environment (for example, *Windows*) or have rebooted your machine with a real-mode operating system (DOS) without any protected-mode enhancements.

Why It Is Hard for DOS to Take Advantage of These Modes

So far, you have learned some of the wonderful aspects of protected mode (in all its various forms). And you have seen how a properly designed protected-mode operating system can deliver all that wonder to you. But you probably run DOS on your computer, and you wonder if you can get all these benefits without giving up DOS.

Well, it is hard for DOS to take advantage of protected mode and all its glories. The basic reason is that DOS itself is a real-mode program. It was designed before there was any such thing as protected mode. The latest versions of DOS have been redesigned and can now do more; but at its heart, DOS is meant to work in real mode with no more than 1MB of address space and, of that, no more than 640KB of RAM for general program use.

DOS runs in real mode. DOS manages memory with a knowledge of only the first megabyte of memory address space. And DOS depends heavily on a BIOS which is nothing but a collection of other real-mode programs. (If you have a *PS/2*, your BIOS may have a section, the ABIOS, with some protected-mode ISRs, but that is the exception, and it only helps an operating system that knows about it, like *OS/2*.)

We use DOS because of what it does for us. It provides a very flexible work environment and gives support to our DOS programs. They depend on DOS for disk access and other services. So these programs will have many of the same problems DOS does running in anything other than real mode.

It might seem from these comments that it would be impossible for DOS programs to take advantage of the protected or virtual modes of the 80x86 processors. That is not quite so, as much of the rest of this book will demonstrate.

How Do Memory Maps Happen? (Revisited)

In Chapter 8, you learned about memory maps. Now it is time to revisit that subject. Your new knowledge of protected mode will illuminate some corners of that subject you might otherwise miss.

When an Address Is Not an Address

Near the beginning of Chapter 8, you learned how the number of address lines in the memory bus determines the maximum number of possible memory locations. That sets the size of the physical memory map.

That section closed with the thought that sometimes you might have either fewer or more possible memory locations than this would seem to indicate. Now you may be beginning to see why this might be so.

It is useful to think of a PC as having three interrelated memory address spaces. They are called the *logical,* the *linear,* and the *physical* memory address spaces. You have met each of them earlier in this chapter. This section is just a quick review.

Logical (Virtual) Memory Address Space

All computer programs refer to memory locations. Those programs written to run on an Intel 80x86 must make those references in what is called the logical or virtual memory fashion. That is done by specifying two numbers. One of them is stored in a segment register; the other is called the offset and may be composed of some combinations of numbers stored in registers and memory locations.

The segment number is always limited to 16 bits. But in protected mode, it is called a selector, and its size only limits the number of possible segments it can specify, not how big they can be nor where they can be.

The offset number is limited to 16 bits in the earlier versions of the 80x86 processors (and in the later ones when they are emulating the earlier ones). Starting with the 80386, the maximum size of the offset number is increased to 32 bits.

Linear Memory Address Space

Linear memory address space is what the CPU generates from a segment value and an offset. It is a range of numbers in a single dimension, even though it is formed from two independent numbers.

In real mode, the rule for getting from a logical address to a linear one is "multiply the segment value by 16 and add the offset." One side effect of this rule is that there are many different logical addresses (segment and offset combinations) that yield the same linear address.

PCs in classes 1 and 2 have only 20 address lines, so they cannot issue a request for access to any more than 1M locations. Since each of those holds one byte, these PCs have a 1MB (1,024KB, or 1,048,576 bytes) total linear memory map size.

PCs in classes 3 through 6 have more address lines. This allows them to have slightly larger real mode memory maps, up to 1,088KB (less 16 bytes), which is 1,114,096 bytes.

In protected mode, the selector (the number in the segment register) points to an entry in a table of segment descriptors. These descriptors say where and how big the segments are. The base address of the segment gets added to the offset to get the linear address.

In 286-protected mode, the base address is 24 bits long. That means the linear address space is 16MB (16,777,216 bytes) in total size. In 386-protected mode, the base address can be 32 bits long, the same as the total number of address lines on the chip. That means that the maximum linear address it can create and use is 32 bits large, for a 4GB (4,294,967,296 bytes) total linear memory address space.

Physical Memory Address Space

Physical memory is the stuff you can touch—the chips. The things that cost you real bucks.

The CPU exchanges information via its bus with the actual memory chips. The addresses the CPU puts on the address lines in the bus form the physical address.

The physical address space size is limited first and foremost by the number of address lines in the bus. But it can have other limits also.

The CPU generates a physical address and then drives those bits on the address pins as voltages. It does this by converting a linear address to a physical one. In all but the 386, 486, and Pentium members of the 80x86 family, the linear and physical addresses are the same. In these latest members of the family, they can be either the same or different.

Only if the 386, 486 or Pentium has its internal paging unit enabled, will there be a difference between linear and physical addresses. And just how it does its job can affect the total size of the logical memory address space as well.

When that unit is enabled, the relationship between the three spaces can be quite complex. The maximum size of the logical (or virtual) memory space can be many times as large as the linear or physical spaces.

How Virtual Memory Can Get So Large

The comment was made just a moment ago that, in real mode, there are many different **segment:offset** combinations for each real-mode address. But because the segment numbers are arithmetically combined with the offsets, all of the logical addresses are somewhere within the 1,024KB or 1,088KB of the linear and physical address spaces. So the size of the logical space is effectively the same as the other two.

That changes dramatically when you enter protected mode. Now the segment numbers (which are now called selector values) have nothing directly to do with a place in memory space. So, in effect, each different value for the selector specifies a whole new memory address space. You will not necessarily be able to get to the same data by any two different segment values, no matter what offsets you choose.

That means that you have a much expanded virtual (or logical) memory address space any time you run the CPU in protected mode. Just *how* large will depend on how big the various descriptor tables are and the segment sizes specified in those tables.

At maximum in 286-protected mode, a program can have access to 8,192 segments in the GDT and a like number in the LDT. Each one can point to a segment with 64KB of memory locations in it. This gives a total virtual memory size of 1GB (1,024MB).

Similarly, in 386-protected mode, you can have the same 16,384 segment descriptors (half in the GDT and half in your LDT), but now a segment can be as large as 4GB. That allows us access to a total logical memory address space of 64 terabytes (65,536GB or 67,108,864MB)—a truly awesome amount.

> Actually, the number of possible segments in the GDT is one less than in the LDT. This is because the GDT has a special use for a selector value of zero. That is done to support the notion of a null pointer, which is implemented via the null (zero) selector value.

The Meaning of Virtual Memory Space in Excess of the Size of Physical Memory

But what does it mean to have these large virtual address spaces? How can they exist if the address lines can't point to them?

The answer to that is both subtle and important. It may take some careful thought, so don't hesitate to read this section more than once.

A key fact: Each page in the page table carries a bit called the *Present bit*. This is used to indicate whether or not the data for this page is actually in physical RAM at this moment. Similarly, each segment descriptor carries its Present bit to show whether or not the data for that segment is in linear memory (and hence in some physical memory).

Not all the data indicated by the Page Table or Descriptor Tables needs to be present at once. In fact, nowhere near all the possible segments or pages can be present at once.

What happens when a page or segment is not present? If the CPU is about to execute an instruction that would send it to that location, it will notice right away that the location it wants is not present, and it will stop itself from trying to access it.

This observation by the CPU triggers an exception. And the exception handler can be written to take care of it in a way that lets us use, potentially, the whole of your much larger virtual memory address space. The exception generated when a page is not present is called a *page fault*.

The other key fact you need to know is that the segment descriptor structure shown in Figure 11.4 and the Page Table entry structure shown in Figure 11.5 only fully apply if the Present bit is set to one. If the Present bit is a zero for either of these structures, the CPU will simply ignore most of the rest of the bits. (Only bits 40 through 47 in a nonpresent segment descriptor have any meaning to the CPU. Only the very first bit of a nonpresent page table entry does.)

Now imagine that you wish to store some huge quantity of information into virtual memory. You can fill up all of the physical RAM you have. Then you can copy some of that information off to some other place (for example, a disk drive), mark those segments or pages as "not present," and record in the segment descriptor or page table entry where you put the data.

Next, you can remap those physical RAM locations to other logical addresses. That merely means you are going to set up a segment descriptor that points to the same base address but has a different selector value (is on a different line of one of the descriptor tables).

These pages you mark as present, and again you load them with data. Keep up this process until you have filled up all the possible segments you can define with data. Almost all of it will have been copied off to disk, but so far as your descriptor table entries are concerned (and your page table entries, as well), you will still have access to all of it.

Indeed, if the CPU tries to get at one of the segments that is not present, the page fault interrupt service routine (or the corresponding routine for a not-present segment) will simply read the disk location information from the page table entry or segment descriptor in question, copy the data back from disk into physical RAM, and set the base address in the page table entry or segment descriptor to point to it.

Of course, if there is not enough free RAM at the time, the exception handler must first do the reverse process, storing some data from RAM to disk to make room for the data it will be bringing in. This is the process for creating and using "demand-paged virtual memory."

Another Use for Paging and Virtual Memory

Frequently, the issue is not storing more data than you have RAM. Instead, it is how to get the data you store where you want it to appear in memory address space, and perhaps later on having other data in these same locations. You could copy the information around from one set of RAM chips to another, but it is easier and faster simply to remap those physical locations to whichever virtual ones you want them to appear to have. This is called *remapping*.

I/O Address Space Is Much Simpler

Input/Output Port address space is much simpler. There is only one kind and size of this space. It is 64KB (65,536 bytes) in total size for all members of the Intel 80x86 family and there is no distinction between a logical, linear, or physical view of this space.

The What and Why of Virtual Memory

Now you know the mechanics of virtual memory. (Here the term is used in the sense of memory that is being remapped or swapped, so its correspondence to physical memory changes from time to time.) When and why is it used?

What Virtual Memory Is, Generally

Virtual memory is a great way to make computer programs think they have almost unlimited amounts of memory to use. Just think of it: never again a Not enough memory message!

It also can be used to access more actual RAM than the linear or physical memory address space allows. Expanded memory on a class 1 or 2 PC is a very good example of this.

And should you find you want more RAM than even all the expanded memory chips you own, you can extend your virtual memory onto a disk drive. Expanded memory emulators often do this.

Context switching is easy with virtual memory. You just change some descriptors in a descriptor table and voilà! The contents of linear memory have instantly changed. This is often used in multitasking systems.

A Special Kind of Virtual Memory

The use of page faults to implement demand-paged virtual memory is an extremely powerful application of these ideas. It is used commonly in mainframe computers. With the advent of the 386, you have the option of using it in PCs as well.

So far, DOS doesn't know about this possibility. Some DOS programs do, though, including *Pick;* the Borland products incorporating their VROOMM technology, such as *Paradox; Clipper,* version 5; and *Windows,* version 3.1.

It is similar to how EMS pages of memory get swapped into the CPU's view when needed. It differs in that the application programs do not have to do anything special. Unlike EMS-using programs which must call for the pages they wish the CPU to access, a program running in a demand-paged virtual-memory system simply assumes all the pages are always present, even though that can't possibly be true. The hardware and the system software (the exception handler) take care of making that lie appear to be true.

Some Reasons for Using Virtual Memory in a PC

Here, in list form, are several good reasons for using virtual memory in a PC:

- Data stored in a virtual memory location is accessible as easily, if not quite as quickly, as if it were in real RAM.

- Virtual memory provides the best mechanism for task switching and multitasking.

- Extended memory can be remapped to fill in holes in upper memory.

- You can swap slow RAM out and replace it with faster RAM (assuming you have some of each).

- ROMs can be *shadowed.* This means you copy data from ROM to some faster RAM, and then map the ROMs out and the RAM in (and make that RAM read-only at the same time).

- You can cause unneeded ROMs to disappear (or any ROM until it is needed, if you can figure out when that will be).

- You can create multiple virtual PCs, each with its own linear memory address space extending from 0 to 1MB (or even 1,088KB), and operating in a simulated real mode. (This requires both the use of virtual memory techniques and V86 mode.)

The How of Virtual Memory

This will be a brief review of what the different members of the 80x86 family can do in the way of virtual memory tricks. The details of how each is done have already been covered.

The Virtual Memory Possibilities of the 286 Chip

The 80286 can directly address up to 16MB of physical memory. It has some memory-management possibilities (with the segment descriptor tables), but it lacks full support for demand-paged virtual memory (no page-fault mechanism or page tables). It has a virtual memory address space of 1GB.

Normally, if you use this virtual-address space, you will be paging information in from disk. Notice, however, that you could be using some very large array of RAM, too large to address with only the 24 address lines of the CPU. In that case, you will be able to have up to 1GB of RAM effectively attached to the CPU whenever it needed it.

Using in excess of 16MB of RAM with an 80286-based PC has been totally infeasible until recently, purely on economic grounds. (And it is arguable whether it is feasible even now.) More to the point, the 386DX and 486 are readily available (and soon the Pentium will be also) and they have a full 4GB of physical memory address space. So anyone who needs that much RAM should just move up to one of the newer processors.

The Virtual Memory Possibilities of the 386 Chip

The 386SX has the same physical memory limitation as the 80286 (16MB), since it has the same number of address pins on the CPU chip package. It has a much larger virtual address space (though not quite as large as that of the 386DX) since its internal workings are built exactly like those chips (but it still has only the 24 address pins)—the virtual address space for the 386SX is approximately 256GB.

The 386DX and 486 can directly address 4GB of real, physical memory address locations. Their virtual memory address space is the super-impressive 64TB. (That is 64 terabytes!)

All of these chips have full hardware support for demand-paged virtual memory, which makes them excellently suited to multitasking or to running super large applications that need more memory than is actually available. They also excel in systems where one wishes to remap memory, which turns out now to be almost any PC at all.

The way they do this is with the page table mechanism. This does not work by itself, of course. One needs some system-level software to activate these features.

DOS 5 and 6 have some limited capabilities along this line. Various third-party memory managers have even more.

Virtual Memory Using Special Motherboard System Logic

Before there were 386 chips, people wanted to do some of these more advanced things with their PCs. Since the paging mechanism in a 386 is interposed between the segmentation unit that computes linear addresses and the address pins on the chip's package, you can see that one could create an external paging unit for an 80286 that would do much the same job.

Some makers of motherboard system logic built in some of that support in their chip set. Mostly, they support the remapping features, ROM shadowing, and maybe the creation of EMS memory out of extended memory. Since they cannot easily implement page faults, they cannot easily support a full demand-paged virtual memory system.

Special software is usually needed to activate these special features. If all you want is some ROM shadowing or EMS memory, you may be able to get that by some entries in your setup (configuration) CMOS. Even then, you will need to load an EMM (expanded memory manager) program for the EMS.

A number of third-party memory manager makers have either included support for the more common of these special system logic chip sets, or they have created special versions of their programs that run on these special systems. *QMAPS* and *UMBPro* take the first approach. They each work with a wide variety of systems. Some examples of the second method are Quarterdeck's *QEMM* for 386 systems, *QRAM 50/60* for *IBM PS/2*, models 50 and 60, and their *QRAM* for 286 systems with a chip set made by Chips and Technologies.

Many other chip set makers have incorporated similar features, but since their market share is smaller, not all the third-party memory manager makers support these other chip sets.

Some clone PCs will come with a customized version of DOS that knows about their special chip set features, and thus can support their use. This is just one more reason why it is usually preferable to use the same brand of DOS as your computer, if one exists. (Not every clone maker chose to customize DOS for their brand of PC.)

Virtual Memory Using Third-Party Add-On Memory-Management Units

Yet another approach to making an AT clone (a PC built around an 80286 chip) work like a 386 is that taken by All Computer with their *All Charge Card* or RYBS with its *HiCard* line. These devices can add paging hardware to any 80286-based PC. They don't work exactly the same way that a 386 does, so you must use the special activating software that comes with these units to get them to show their stuff.

Filling in the Gaps Below 1MB— What This Means and How It Can Be Done

At this point, you are very likely keenly aware that your PC may have some room in its upper memory space—some holes between its RAM and ROM where you haven't got anything, but which could be most useful if only you could fill in the gaps with RAM.

The Goal and the Principle of the Solution

IBM "reserved" the top three-eighths of the memory address space in the original *IBM PC.* They only knew at the time a few things to use that space for, but they wanted it available when they thought of more wonderful uses for it later on.

In many (perhaps most) PCs, nowhere near all of upper memory space is filled. These are memory address locations the processor can address (even in real mode), but until there is something at these locations, there is no way they can be used.

Then there are some areas that have ROMs in them, but it turns out that those ROMs are seldom if ever used. One example is the IBM BASIC ROM in "true-blue" IBM-brand PCs and *PS/2s,* which was discussed in Chapter 10. Unless you want to run the Basic interpreter (BASIC.COM or BASICA.COM), you won't ever need that ROM. But it is filling up a portion of your memory address space anyway.

Another example is the ROM in many clones that holds the setup routine. Some of them allow you to pop up their setup screen at any time. They need that ROM around always to support that feature. Others only allow you to access the ROM at a certain point in the boot process. On those PCs, it would be wonderful if you could simply "disappear" that ROM once the system was up and running (until the next time you reboot it).

So the goal is to identify and remove from the upper memory address space any "junk ROMs" that may happen to be there, and to fill in all of the space that is open with RAM for programs to use. The rest of this chapter goes over quickly the options you have for doing this.

By the way, you may also have some open space in your lower memory address space. If your PC has less than the full 640KB of system RAM, then you will want to fill in that hole as well.

Concept of Memory Granularity

You have met this concept once now, in connection with the segment descriptors in a PC running in 386-protected mode. There, a single bit in each descriptor told whether to view the segment size number in that descriptor as being a number of bytes or a number of 4KB pages.

The notion of memory granularity comes up in several places. Think of memory as a substance. What are the smallest pieces into which you can break it? The smallest manipulable pieces are what you think of as the grains of that substance.

In the case of LIM EMS memory (version 3.2, at least), the grain size was 16KB. The 386 uses a 4KB page size when remapping memory. That is the granularity of that scheme. PCMCIA cards also use 4KB pages of RAM or ROM.

Why use chunks like that? Why not allow arbitrarily small pieces of RAM to be moved around? The answer is that if you allowed each byte to be moved around, you would need to maintain a table of which physical memory was at what logical or linear address, and that table would itself be considerably larger than your total usable RAM!

With the 386 paging scheme, in contrast, 8KB suffices (4KB each for a Page Directory Table and one Page Table) to map 1,024 4KB page frames. So only 8KB is used to map up to 4MB. That is easily an acceptable amount of overhead.

Fragmentation of the Available Space

Upper memory is not a vast wasteland. It is more like a somewhat crowded closet. If there are empty spaces, they may well be scattered among the full ones.

This is not the optimal situation for loading programs into upper memory. Ideally, you would like to have one large space there, unbroken by any obstacles. Then you could load the maximum size and number of programs into that space, once you had filled it with RAM.

You can see something of the problem by looking back at Figures 8.12 and 8.13 in Chapter 8, and at Figure 10.4 in Chapter 10. If you have EGA video, an EMS board, a network card, and a hard disk that requires a special BIOS ROM, you could easily have not one, but as many as five empty regions of upper memory space. Even this is not the worst possible case. You will learn more about this problem and about some ways of dealing with it in Chapter 21.

Filling in the Gaps Below 1MB—Specific Approaches

So now you know that you want to fill in any gaps in the memory spaces below 1MB with additional RAM. How might you do that? There are many ways it can be done. The following sections just summarize them. Details on the more plausible ones can be found in several later chapters of this book.

Hard Wired Memory Boards

IBM published the design of each model of their PC line so that other manufacturers could make add-on cards that would work in IBM personal computers. This "open architecture" was critical to the early success of the PC. It was also largely responsible for the explosion of clone computers that eventually drove IBM to drop the PC line and create the *PS/2* line.

They also published the specifications for their *PS/2* models, but this time they were careful to keep a bit more control over who could clone them and how. Still, IBM encourages others to make add-on cards for the *PS/2* models as well.

Since the design of each model of the IBM *PC* and *PS/2* has been published, it would be possible to design and build a custom board that would plug into the I/O bus and supply RAM to fill in all the holes in your lower and upper memory spaces.

This can work if the PC has all the address, data, and control lines you need on the I/O bus, and if it does not decode these same addresses for use on the motherboard (or if you can get it to stop doing so, perhaps by setting some switches or jumpers). In fact, these conditions are met in most PCs.

In the original models of the IBM *PC* and the IBM *PC/XT*, it was not possible to put 640KB of RAM on the motherboard. You had to add one or more additional memory cards to get up to the full complement of lower memory. This is why they had to provide all the memory access signals on the I/O bus.

The final XT models from IBM, and all clones since that time, have provided the full 640KB of RAM on the motherboard. Some of them are so designed that you cannot turn off the memory address decoding circuits for lower memory on the motherboard.

Most of IBM's AT models, AT clones, and 386SX-based PCs require add-in memory cards to bring them up to a full 16MB RAM complement. On the other hand, 386DX and 486 computers normally provide some alternative way to add memory. The issue for them is that the ISA bus only provides 24 address lines and 16 data lines and only runs at a maximum of 10MHz clock speed. That limits you to 16MB maximum RAM and to slower access than if you can connect RAM to the CPU's full memory bus with its 32 bits of both address and data.

You could build a memory card, but doing so is quite a complex undertaking not suitable for most PC users. It is much easier (and often cheaper) simply to buy some commercially available board that includes the capabilities you want, and to set it to do whatever it is you want it to do.

The EEMS and LIM EMS 4.0 Method

One such readily available add-in memory card is a LIM 4.0 EMS or an EEMS card. (You can use a LIM 3.2 EMS card, but that is likely to be more limited in what it can do and thus limiting to you. At least get the LIM 4.0 software driver for the card if you choose to use an older LIM 3.2-style card or if you use an EEMS card.)

Normally, these cards allow you to add memory to lower memory space (if you don't already have 640KB there)—this is called *backfilling* system memory. They also allow you to add memory as expanded memory, which may include filling in all the available regions of upper memory, or it may be able to fill in only some of them. And finally, these cards can supply some or all of their memory as extended if that is what you need.

The issue around filling in gaps in upper memory gets to be fairly subtle, and it is not always easy to tell what a given memory card is capable of doing. All EMS cards can create at least a single 64KB region of RAM in upper memory (assuming you have at least one hole that large in which to put it). Some can create a single region of RAM of any size you want, so long as it is confined to the C and D pages. They call this a "large page frame." (A few can go into the E page as well.)

Some EMS cards can fill in multiple regions in these pages. Some can also fill in any unused regions of the A or B pages, and a few can even reach into the F page. Be careful when selecting an EMS card, for these cards vary a lot in their capabilities. (And most manufacturers *don't* tell you up front what limitations their cards have.)

Motherboard System Logic Method

If your PC has motherboard system logic with memory-management capabilities (for example, the Chips and Technology *NEAT* chipset) you may be able to get upper memory RAM without having to add any hardware. There are two ways to get at these capabilities.

Some systems let you create shadow RAM and/or EMS memory through entries in their setup program. Another way is to use special memory-management software, for example, Quarterdeck's *QRAM*, Qualitas' *Move'Em* (which now is included in *386MAX*), or Quadtel's *UMBPro*. These third-party programs can sometimes offer you options your setup program cannot.

Hardware Add-On Memory Managers

If yours is a PC in classes 1 through 4 (an XT or AT clone), you can fill in upper memory by using an add-on memory-management card. The *All Charge Card* gives this power to an AT. The *All Card* does similar things for an XT. V Communications offers the *MegaMizer,* and RYBS has a line of *HiCards.* These are just a few of the devices on the market to meet this need. You can learn more about them in Chapter 27.

How DOS Alone Can Do This Job

Recently it became possible to fill in gaps in upper memory using only the features provided with DOS—but not just any DOS and not for every PC.

You must be using DOS version 5 or 6, and you must have a class 5 or 6 PC. That means your CPU is a 386, 486, or Pentium. You also must have plenty of RAM installed, as a combination of lower and extended memory.

Then, if you load the device drivers HIMEM.SYS and EMM386.EXE (or EMM386.SYS in place of both of these if you are using *DR DOS*), you can have them convert some of that extended memory into both high and upper memory. However, these drivers don't do the job automatically. You have to use the memory display tools DOS provides (or some third-party ones), and then manually edit your CONFIG.SYS and AUTOEXEC.BAT files to achieve your goals. *MS-DOS 6* and *PC DOS 6* include programs to help automate this work: *MS-DOS 5, PC DOS 5,* and *DR DOS,* both versions 5 and 6, have no such helper program.

This may be the safest way to go. Certainly, the DOS tools are able to work with a wide variety of clone PCs. But this may not be the best way, and it certainly is not going to be the easiest way to fill in upper memory.

How Third-Party Memory Managers Can Fill Gaps in Memory

In any PC with suitable hardware support for memory mapping (and enough RAM), a suitable software program can be used to fill in all the gaps you want to fill. It will even be possible to shadow ROMs, move ROMs (or their shadow images) to new addresses, and of course, create EMS memory. Some products allow you to make most of your ROMs disappear (or seem to do so), and others let you move the video image buffer up out of the way of large DOS programs. The possibilities are mind-boggling.

It is important to note both that software alone cannot do this and that the software you will need may well depend on which hardware you are trying to activate (and which of the aforementioned mind-boggling set of possibilities you are trying to get). If your PC is one in class 5 or 6, then it is built around a 386, 486, or *Pentium* processor chip and that CPU is all the hardware you will need (aside from RAM—the more the better!). If you have a PC in one of the other classes, then you need one of the special motherboard system logic chipsets, a hardware EMS board, or an add-on memory-management device, in addition to the special software.

Chapters 20 and 21 detail some of those mind-boggling possibilities and explain how to achieve them. Part III of this book will help point you to the right sections of Part IV for you to read. And Part IV is all about the gadgets and programs that will help you best approach memory-management nirvana.

A Recap

This has been another long chapter and, more than most, it contains explanations of some very confusing concepts. You might need to stop now and take a few deep breaths, sit back, and think carefully about all that you have learned here.

First, you were introduced to the notion of *protected-mode* operation as an option for the more advanced members of the Intel 80x86 chip family. This was contrasted with their more usual *real mode* of operation. All members of the family wake up in real mode, but starting with the 80286, they can all do more. The 286 only has one version of protected mode. The 386 and 486 have three of them (286- and 386-protected mode, and virtual- 8086 mode).

You learned that using these new modes dramatically expands the available physical-memory-address space. They expand the virtual-memory-address space even more. And you have now learned to distinguish the logical-memory space (which is the same as the virtual-memory space) from both the linear- and the physical-memory spaces.

Only in a 386, 486, or *Pentium*, and only when paging is enabled, are there any differences between linear and physical memory. But when you are using one of these processors and have turned paging on, you get access to a host of new possibilities, including demand-paged virtual memory—potentially a way of letting all your programs think they each have all the memory they could ever use.

You also learned that I/O address space is much simpler. It doesn't change between real and protected mode, although in the latter mode you do have the possibility of limiting which programs can use which I/O devices.

Virtualizing devices and locking programs into segments with restricted access rights to those and other segments, as well as to I/O, provide the basis for secure, robust multitasking operating systems. The features of the 286 chip support much of this, but it becomes a full-fledged reality once you move up to the 386, 486, or *Pentium*.

The last portion of this chapter is mostly concerned with why and how you might fill in some gaps that IBM left in your PC's memory map, in particular, those that occur in the upper memory region. You will need to learn more details about the solutions described, but this brief overview may have helped focus your attention on some achievable goals, and given you at least some strong hints about how to achieve them.

The next chapter is largely history. It tells how we got into the mess called the "infamous DOS 640KB barrier" and recounts the various ways people have devised to get around that limit. Along the way, it explains some of today's hottest jargon: terms like XMS, VCPI, and DPMI (and several more).

12

THE INFAMOUS
DOS 640KB BARRIER

This chapter is largely history. It tells how we got into the mess we call the "infamous DOS 640KB barrier" and recounts the various plans people have devised to get around that limit. Along the way some of today's hottest jargon is explained: terms like XMS, VCPI, and DPMI (and several more).

Perhaps the one most-hated feature of DOS-based PCs is what we call the "DOS 640KB barrier." This single difficulty has made PCs infamous. To some of its critics, seeing with all the benefit of hindsight, IBM was just plain "dumb" to have reserved a region of the CPU's memory address space for video RAM and ROM, BIOS ROMs, and other operating-system uses right smack-dab in the middle of what otherwise would be a perfectly good vast expanse of program RAM. Other people dismiss this criticism, but only because they dismiss DOS itself. "DOS is so stupid that it can't see beyond the first megabyte anyway, so what's the big deal fussing over its 640KB barrier. The whole DOS and PC mess is hopelessly crippled and might as well be discarded," they say.

All these people, although blessed with a certain amount of hindsight, lack historical perspective. This chapter attempts to remedy some of that.

DOS shows no signs of dying. It is still the dominant PC operating system and seems likely to continue in that role for quite a few more years. That is why most applications are being developed to run under DOS (or under *Windows*, which in its present form depends on DOS).

This means that, no matter what you think of it, we're all stuck with DOS for quite some time to come. Because of this, we need to figure out ways to work with it and get around its limitations the best we can. This chapter reviews some of the steps that already have been taken to do just that.

First, though, some history.

The Infamous DOS 640KB Barrier

When IBM introduced the IBM *PC* in 1981, it came with *PC DOS* version 1.0. This hardware and software defined a new computer standard in the small computer marketplace. One feature of the PC that set it far apart from its predecessors (mainly the *Apple II* and all the *CP/M* machines) was its relatively vast memory address space. It could address up to 1MB of memory. This was 16 times more than any other small computer. (The history leading up to the PC, including the role and nature of the *Apple II* and *CP/M* machines, is covered in Chapter 10 and discussed further in Chapter 13.)

IBM defined some uses for various regions of that memory space. As we saw in Figure 8.4, the upper 384KB was dedicated to video display image buffers, ROMs, and various other special system uses. Only the first 640KB was intended for RAM for general use, and even a small portion of that first 640KB is used up by the operating system.

This was a reasonable decision on IBM's part. They were, in part, responding to the design decisions that Intel made in creating the 8088 microprocessor chip. And they were actually being uncommonly generous toward applications programmers. Their previous standard, on mainframe computers, was to take half of the processor's memory address space for the system and let the applications have the other half.

The reason that RAM is at the bottom of memory address space (addresses near zero) and ROM and other system uses are at the top (addresses just below 1MB) is that Intel's design requires you to put RAM in at least the first KB (if you wish to take advantage of the flexibility and power of its interrupt-handling design features) and ROM in the last several addresses before the 1MB top of memory address space. This point was made previously in Chapter 8 in the section "Intel's Special Addresses" and is diagrammed in Figure 8.5.

DOS was designed to run the first IBM *PC*, and its limitations are largely what you should expect of an operating system with that as its design goal. All of application memory (which is the only portion of the memory address space that DOS needs to manage) was to be in one vast expanse of RAM. (Just the thing people want today and fault DOS and the PC design for not providing. Our definition of what "vast" means has changed, that's all.)

What Is the Problem?

So what is the problem? Simply stated, computer users want more. They want more speed, more RAM, more disk space, and most of all, more capable applications. Actually, most computer users don't think about the means for getting "more"; they only want their computers to do what they want their computers to do.

Programmers love rising to a challenge. They are always pressing the hardware limitations of the computers for which they create programs. In the case of the PC, Lotus *1-2-3* was the first application which really pushed the PC's limits. And by pressing those limits, it empowered its users as never before.

As a result, people ran out of memory. At first, they simply ran out of RAM. That was back when RAM was too expensive for most PC users to buy the full 640KB. The solution then was very simple (albeit costly): buy more RAM chips and install them.

Later, that approach ran into a brick wall: the DOS 640KB barrier. There was nowhere to add more RAM to a PC once that limit had been reached.

Initially, the PC would not even accept that much RAM. The first version of the motherboard BIOS ROM interpreted the DIP switch settings for the amount of RAM installed differently than all later versions. Those earliest PCs could only access up to 544KB of system RAM.

Today, most PC users run into this problem one way or another. Running out of memory is far from unusual. So the problem is, how can you shoehorn into your PC all the programs you need (or want) to run without getting that dreaded "out of memory" message?

How Did We Get Here?

It is doubtful that the PC's designers ever thought their design would prove to be as popular as it did. Nor could they anticipate how cheap RAM would become.

Remember, the first model of the PC came with as little as 16KB of RAM, or as much as 64KB of RAM. At first, the possibility of extending that to 640KB was just that—a theoretical possibility. And it wasn't a possibility that most people took very seriously. RAM simply cost too much. Only a fool or a prince would want to buy more than 640KB, or so it seemed to many of us at the time. "Surely," we said, "it will take forever to exhaust the possibilities of that much space."

Why Did It Become a Problem?

Well, we learned. "Forever," at least in this business, seems to be only about two or three years! By then, people were clamoring for more memory space in their PCs.

Not only was *1-2-3* a big hit (and a very big program, by earlier personal computer standards at any rate), but RAM prices fell in response to the demand for PCs that resulted from the popularity of *1-2-3*, and as the makers of RAM chips learned how to make their products more cost-effectively.

Installable Device Drivers—Wonderful and Yet . . .

One of the greatest things about *DOS* is its flexibility. Much of that has been built into the design from a very early stage.

The provision in the design of DOS for installable device drivers is a mechanism that allows application programmers to include subprograms with their applications to offer support for more and better peripheral devices. (See Chapter 10 for a detailed description of how device drivers and TSR programs work.) For example, a word processor may come with several hundred printer drivers. You choose the ones you need and install them on your disk. Your program can then load them as needed and use them to communicate with your printers.

Thus, you may have a mouse driver, an external disk driver, and who-knows-what other device drivers loaded via your CONFIG.SYS file, and then your application program may load a *Btrieve* data file manager, a printer driver, and more. All of these pieces give us great benefits, but they also use up RAM.

TSR Programs—Also Wonderful and Yet . . .

The invention of the **T**erminate and **S**tay **R**esident program (TSR) did not help matters either. At first, Microsoft and IBM declared that DOS could only do one thing at a time. It was, they said, a single-tasking operating system. But then someone noticed that Microsoft had snuck something interesting into DOS. The PRINT external DOS command was actually a program that ran "in the background," passing characters to the printer as fast as it could take them while letting you go on computing "in the foreground" with your application program.

It was not clear how that could be done in a "single-tasking operating" system, and Microsoft was not talking. But Philippe Kahn at Borland reverse-engineered PRINT.COM and figured out how to do it. (Others did also, but Mr. Kahn's *SideKick* was the first commercially successful TSR program.) Once PRINT and *SideKick* had shown the way, huge numbers of useful TSR programs were developed. And every one of them competed with all the others and with application programs for that precious 640KB of RAM.

How Networks Add to the Problem

Then came networking. People found out just how wonderful computing could be and how much more productive they could be if their PCs were connected to other PCs and to a larger computer called a *file server*, where huge data files could be kept and made accessible to all. Once they made this discovery, almost every company wanted to install a **Local Area Net-work** (LAN).

But connecting PCs to a network (and making it work reliably) is a complex operation. Your PC must have some special hardware to do this, and it also needs to run some special software to extend DOS so it can see the files stored on the server (and perhaps some other network resources as well). At least this is possible, thanks to another DOS design feature for flexibility called the *installable file system.* But, once again, taking advantage of this feature means adding a new layer of software, and that means using up even more of your precious RAM. Ouch!

Not all networks follow the "client-server" model with its central file server and individual workstations; some are called "peer-to-peer" networks with each computer able to play the role of either workstation or server—or even play both roles at once. To do each of these roles means running some special software, so a fully implemented peer-to-peer network can put even greater demands on the RAM in each machine than is the case for client-server networks.

In the end we just have too many good uses for our PC's limited RAM. And we want to use it for all of them at once. That sure seems to be a problem. In fact it is. That's why the DOS 640KB barrier is *the* problem with PCs to many PC users.

Several Ways Around the DOS 640KB Barrier

There are several possible approaches to solving this problem. Let's look at them and see what is good and bad about each one.

Change to a Different Kind of Computer— Not Practical for Most of Us

If you are like most PC users, you or your company has a lot invested in your DOS-based PC. Someone paid for the hardware and software, and someone has invested a lot in your training. Simply tossing all that investment is not something anyone does lightly. Furthermore, don't forget that your data represents the greatest value you have. Therefore, if you convert to a different kind of computer, you will have to find a way to convert or otherwise make all those old data files accessible.

Since DOS-based PCs dominate the marketplace, programs developed for them do too. If you switch to a different kind of computer system, you will have to choose all new applications and you may not have the same range of choice. Also, they may be more expensive than the programs you are accustomed to buying.

Some Plausible Alternative Hardware Platforms

But what if you want to switch? What reasonable alternatives exist? Here's a brief survey of your principal options.

Apple's Macintosh Line

Probably the most popular alternative small-business computer is the *Macintosh* from Apple Computers. Graphics artists, in particular, love their Macs.

Programmers, especially those who feel burdened by the DOS 640KB barrier, also love Macs. This is because, as is further discussed in Chapter 13, all models of the *Macintosh* share a very expansive memory model. If you need more RAM in a Mac, just add some more. All very simple.

You even can get some of the same applications in a version that runs on a Mac and in a PC version. Microsoft *Word, WordPerfect,* and Lotus *1-2-3* are just a few. But remember, these are all programs that were initially developed for DOS-based PCs and many folks believe that they are still better on PCs than on any other platform.

> Of course, there are some applications that started on *Macintosh* computers and have come over to the PC. Microsoft *Excel* is one. Aldus *PageMaker* is another. These either work exactly the same on both PCs and Macs or they work better on a Mac.
>
> Some ports of popular DOS programs to *OS/2* may have some advantages, but mostly the ports are one or more versions behind the original PC implementation in terms of features.

If you are able to find *Macintosh* versions of the same application programs you used on the PC, you could access your old data files, but only if you can get them onto a disk that the Mac can read, or if your new Mac and your old PC are on a common network. Either of these things can be done, but they are not always as easy as you might like. If your data files were created by a PC application for which you don't have a corresponding Mac application, you'll be faced with data file conversion—and that is almost never a fun process. (See the section on data file porting in Chapter 7 for a further discussion of this issue.)

Commodore's Amiga Series

If your needs tend toward multimedia, converting to an Amiga may make a lot of sense. Otherwise, it probably does not. The problems most PC users would face converting to an Amiga are like those converting to a Mac, if not worse. (If you do make the conversion, the benefits you'll gain are also a lot like those you'd get with a Mac.)

An Amiga does offer one delightful possibility, however. When used with the Commodore Bridge card, it emulates a PC and runs DOS-based software better than any other non-DOS small computer.

All the computer alternatives in this section can support some sort of PC emulation, either through emulation software such as *Soft PC* or through a hardware emulator. (See Chapter 1 if you are unclear about what an emulator is.)

The software emulators work, at least for reasonably well-behaved DOS programs. But oh, are they slow! You can spend lots of bucks getting the fastest one of these alternative computers and find that when it is emulating a PC, it makes a slow IBM *PC/AT* look pretty zippy.

For the most part, hardware emulators are pretty good, but they are also somewhat slow. The problem is that they depend on the "foreign host computer" to do a lot of things like disk access or other I/O. The overhead in communicating those needs to the other computer and retrieving the results can make the best of the "PC on a card" solutions slow down markedly.

All except the Commodore *Bridge* card, that is. When you use that, you get an actual PC. The Amiga "specialness" shuts off and lets the *Bridge* card do its thing, which happens to be acting very much like a PC/AT. It even lets you plug in a standard ISA option card, if you wish.

But using an Amiga in this way won't get you around the DOS 640KB barrier. If anything, it will make that limitation even more annoying.

Sun or Other "Workstations"

Workstations are really nothing more than small minicomputers, or terminals to such computers. They tend to have very high-resolution graphics and lots of computing power. Most of them run some version of *UNIX* as their operating system.

Converting to a workstation is a viable possibility for at least some PC "power users." The conversion is not without its costs, however. Even if you run a program like *VP/ix* or *Merge 86* that lets you run your DOS applications as a process under *UNIX*, you will have to master the basics of *UNIX*. And if you are the sole master of your PC, you will end up becoming what in *UNIX* parlance is termed a *system administrator*. The name was not chosen lightly. There is a lot of work to be done to set up and maintain any *UNIX* system.

Further, if you primarily run DOS applications on top of *UNIX*, you will be layering your potential problems. When it all works well things are fine, but if you have a problem, you will have more places to look before you can pin it down and expunge it.

Some of the more powerful PCs are reaching up into the performance territory previously only available on a RISC-based, *UNIX* workstation. So if your reason for converting is more to get access to that computing power, rather than simply to leave DOS behind, perhaps you will want to check out the latest PC offerings before abandoning DOS.

Change Operating Systems— Only Slightly More Practical

You could stick with PC hardware and change to an operating system that would let you leave the DOS 640KB barrier totally behind. This would require new software, but your hardware investment would be preserved.

As you think about switching, however, remember that you will have a substantial learning curve to climb in mastering your new operating system. You have already made a big investment in learning to use a DOS-based PC. This invested time is not a trivial thing to discard.

Alternative PC Operating Systems

You will have several choices if you change operating systems. What are they, and which ones might be realistic for you?

OS/2

OS/2 is the operating system that was supposed to completely replace DOS, at least on class 3 or higher PCs. That was the original idea when the IBM

PC/AT was introduced. *OS/2* has no 640KB barrier. It runs in protected mode all the time and can freely use all the RAM you can add to your PC. (Some early versions of *OS/2* can use only a bit less than 16MB.)

Until 1992, *OS/2* was not a very good option for most people. With the delivery (at last) of *OS/2*, version 2.0, things look considerably brighter for that beleaguered operating system. The appearance of OS/2, version 2.1 in mid-1993 essentially completes the suite of features originally promised for version 2.0.

Still, since there are fewer *OS/2* applications available than DOS applications, you will largely have to depend on how well IBM delivers their promise of *OS/2* offering you "a better DOS than DOS" (by which IBM means that your regular, old DOS applications will run better and faster using *OS/2* as the operating system than when you boot using DOS) and "a better *Windows* than *Windows*." The industry's judgment on that claim is yet to be rendered. Also realize that *OS/2* version 2.x can only run on PCs in class 5 or 6.

As more true *OS/2* applications become available, converting to it may become an increasingly attractive option. But if you want to know what you can do now, you are probably better off learning what you can do to enhance DOS and work around the 640KB barrier, rather than trying to switch to a new, still wet-behind-the-ears operating system.

UNIX

You could switch to *UNIX* without changing hardware. It even is possible to continue using your DOS applications and no longer be troubled by the 640KB DOS limitation.

You had better have a fast 386- or 486-based PC, though, with plenty of RAM and lots of disk space. The *UNIX* operating-system files alone will take up over 20 megabytes on your disk, and you will not enjoy using the system if you don't have many megabytes of RAM. (When a *UNIX* machine runs low on RAM, it uses disk space as virtual memory. You won't run out of RAM, but you may run out of time or patience.)

If you have only a 286-based PC, *Xenix* is a possible option, but on that platform in particular it will not really deliver the full benefits of *UNIX*. If your PC is less capable than that, you must upgrade your hardware before switching to any form of *UNIX* makes sense.

See also the comments about *UNIX* in the discussion of workstations earlier in this chapter. They apply if you put *UNIX* on your PC just as much as if you change to a workstation running *UNIX*.

Pick

Pick Systems have developed an innovative way of treating computers. They create a "virtual Pick machine" on any of several supported platforms. Then applications can be developed to run on that virtual machine. In effect, they turn any computer they are prepared to handle into an emulator for a fictitious computer: the native Pick machine.

Pick is usually bundled with an application, so for most people (other than application developers) it is not an option as a general operating system. You may be using *Pick* right now, on top of DOS, and not even know it. Only by asking your applications' developers can you find out.

Windows NT

What about the new kid on the block from Microsoft, Windows NT? Actually, this is so new it is not yet real. Unless you particularly enjoy working on the "bleeding edge," you had best wait awhile before even thinking about migrating to Windows NT.

NeXTSTEP 486

There is another new kid on the block, this time from NeXT. After finding that he couldn't sell enough NeXT machines to make NeXT the success he had planned, Steve Jobs turned his company's direction from hardware-based to a pure software company. His next (and perhaps last) great hope for becoming a major player in that market is the NeXTSTEP operating system. Seeing Jobs demonstrate it is thrilling. The important question is, will actually using it be just as nice? And so far, we simply don't know.

One Way to Make an Operating System Change a Bit More Palatable

The discussions about *OS/2* and *UNIX* mentioned that you might be able to continue to use your DOS applications if you move to one of those operating systems. *OS/2* offers its compatibility mode in which it can run DOS applications. Some flavors of *UNIX* have add-on system software available (for an additional cost) to do something similar. (*VP/ix* is one, and *Soft PC* is another.) Using one of these could make the transition from a DOS-based PC considerably easier.

There are limits though. Not every DOS application can run in the DOS-emulation environments available for *OS/2* or *UNIX*. And don't forget that if you are in day-to-day charge of your PC (that is what a *personal* computer is all about for most of us), then you will have to master the new operating system anyway. Your principal gain from using these DOS emulation capabilities is the ability to continue to use your old application programs and the data files they create.

There are some distinct advantages to going to either *OS/2* or *UNIX* that should not be overlooked. Foremost among them, you may be able to gain a more robust multitasking environment.

But while the added complexity may be tolerable in some situations (and the more robust multitasking may even be crucial), for many users, the required investment in system software and supervisor training and in ongoing system maintenance simply is inappropriate.

Learn Useful Workarounds—the Easiest Approach

This is what the rest of this book is about! Most PC users will be better served (at least for the next several years) by mastering these techniques than by switching to either a new hardware system or a new operating system.

Augmenting the Hardware—Sometimes Wonderful

The DOS 640KB barrier will not seem so bad if you can get around it successfully. Sometimes the way to do that is to add some new hardware to your PC. An EMS board, for example, can allow many applications the room they need to work. And with suitable software support you may be able to push most of your TSRs off into EMS as well.

Many people have found happiness in an add-in EMS memory card, but don't leap too quickly. It may not be what you need. Or you may be able to get the same effect, at a much lower cost, with just a software program (and perhaps some additional *extended* memory).

This is especially true if yours is a PC in class 5 or 6, and it may even be true if you have a less powerful one. Also, remember that if you can afford to wait a bit for your PC to do its work, you may prefer to use a pure software solution and save yourself a lot of money. That is why *Above Disk* has been a successful product for many years, to mention only one example.

How Not to Waste Your Money

If you are going to spend money on some hardware augmentation of your PC, you'd like to know you are getting your money's worth. There are both general issues to remember and details to consider on each product you might buy. Here are some of the general issues.

When Not to Spend the Minimum You Can Get Away With

If the deal seems too good to be true, it probably isn't true. Also, if you need after-sale support, you may find it cheaper to get this as a privilege of buying your hardware and software from a full-service vendor than having to buy the support separately after buying the hardware and software from a discount dealer.

Don't Buy for the Far Future

Change happens in the PC world at an amazingly fast rate. This is particularly true of PC hardware. Mostly, we see a trend that is quite opposite to that for other consumer goods: PC hardware costs are constantly dropping and their capabilities constantly rising. So what you can barely afford this year may be an impulse purchase in another year or two. That means that you are best off purchasing now what you know or suspect you will need to use within the next six months. Let the needs of the far future be accommodated at the lower prices that will be available then.

For more on how to acquire what you need, and doing so sensibly and safely, see Appendix B.

Augmenting Specific Programs—DOS Extenders

Most of the techniques for getting around the DOS 640KB barrier mentioned up to this point are system-wide changes. Generally, they will enable you to do more. But sometimes the problem you are faced with is much more specific. You may, perhaps, have only one major application that keeps running out of room.

In recent years a technique has been developed to deal with this. It is not a strategy for the end-user of a product—rather it is a strategy for the program's developer to use. This is the world of DOS extenders.

What Is a DOS Extender?

A *DOS extender* is a program library that the developer of a DOS application can use when developing that application. In essence, the DOS extender wraps a program around an otherwise normal DOS application. The wraparound program runs first. It takes control over the PC, putting it into protected mode. Then it runs the enclosed, ordinary DOS application.

> The DOS (real-mode) application will have probably been modified a very little bit. When it is recompiled with the DOS-extender program library, it becomes a protected-mode program.

When the application program (which is now running in protected mode) wants some operating-system services, the DOS extender intercepts those requests. The extender then switches the PC to real mode and sends the requests on to DOS. Also, the DOS extender provides some direct memory-management services, to allow the DOS application to get the use of extended memory for its data storage requirements.

> The DOS extender may run the application in a virtual-8086 session, or it may simply let it run as if it were a protected-mode program. The latter approach is more common (so far). The most important difference between these two approaches is that in the first case the DOS application will be running at Ring 3 privilege level and in the latter case it will be running at Ring 0 along with the DOS extender.
>
> This matters mostly when you try to make two or more DOS-extended applications share one PC. If both are running at Ring 0 and each thinks it is in charge, a serious conflict arises. But if they are already running their underlying application at Ring 3, they can both be made to cooperate with yet another program, a DPMI server. (For more on what that means, see the next section.)

(If terms like *protected-mode, virtual-86(V86) mode,* and *Ring 0* or *Ring 3* confuse you, turn back to Chapter 11 and soon they'll become old friends.)

Andrew Schulman, in *Extending DOS,* puts it this way: "Real mode *MS-DOS* thinks it is talking to a normal program, and the protected mode program thinks that *MS-DOS* knows how to handle its requests. The DOS extender sits in the middle, lying out of both sides of its mouth."

There are two variations on this theme. One is the 286-DOS extender and the other is the 386-DOS extender. The former converts "normal" DOS programs into protected-mode ones that can run on any PC in classes 3 or higher. The latter takes advantage of the specialness of the 386 (which is shared by the 486 and Pentium), creating programs that are limited to running on class 5 or 6 PCs.

Many important DOS applications have been DOS-extended in recent years. Some of the most famous of the 286-DOS-extended applications are Lotus *1-2-3,* Release 3.x; *AutoCad,* Release 10 or later; *Informix SQL* and *Informix 4GL*; and the *TOPS* networking system. *Interleaf Publisher, Mathematica, Paradox/386, Foxbase+/386,* and *AutoCad 386* are a few of the programs that have been 386-DOS-extended.

What Do You Need to Use a DOS-Extended Application?

You need a PC with extended memory, preferably lots of it. DOS-extended applications can use as much of it as you have.

Having expanded memory will not do. If you have a class 5 or 6 PC and have converted your extended memory into simulated expanded memory (using a LIMulator), your DOS-extended application may be able to use it, but only if the LIMulator provides VCPI services. (See the next section to learn about VCPI services. See Chapter 9 to review what a LIMulator is.)

Augment the Operating System— the Most Valuable Way Out

Many people realized that if DOS is the problem, which it is, then changing DOS is the answer. But is it possible to change DOS without giving up DOS? The answer to this is a qualified yes.

DOS does many things for us. The only one that is relevant in the context of the 640KB barrier is its management of RAM usage. DOS thinks of the PC as having only one RAM area, and that extends from just on top of DOS itself up to the top of what programmers call the *Transient Program Area*, or *TPA*. Normally that is at linear address 9FFFh, which is the top of the first 640KB.

Normally, the TPA is blocked from growing any larger than 640KB by the video image buffer RAM. In some special situations you can extend the TPA by 64KB or even 96KB.

One of these special situations is if you use only a CGA video card. Because the CGA video image buffer starts at address B8000h, you could add up to 96KB to the TPA. This also applies if you use an EGA or VGA display, but are willing to forego using them in anything but their color text modes. Another case is if you use a monochrome text (MDA) or monochrome graphics (Hercules or MGA) card. In this case you could extend the TPA by 64KB. (**PLEASE NOTE**: This case is *not the same* as a VGA card driving a monochrome high-resolution graphics display.) See the discussion in Chapter 8 in the section "The Several PC Video Standards" and look at Figure 8.12.

One effective way of adding RAM to the TPA, therefore, may be to add extra RAM on a card and arrange to have it addressed in the A page (640KB to 704KB) or A and lower half of the B page (640KB to 736KB). But you can't do this if you use EGA or VGA graphics at all.

Another effective way is to move the top of the TPA dynamically; some memory managers do just that. Or move it semi-permanently; that is done in systems that support the RSIS standard. We'll soon discuss this further.

So the solution to our limited DOS memory can be found in several steps. First, you have to find more memory for DOS to manage. That may mean any of several different things. Second, you have to induce DOS to manage that memory. That could mean tricking DOS, or it could mean adding some other memory manager on top of DOS. Both ways can work.

There are several different approaches that have been tried, each with more or less success. Here is a quick rundown on the major ones.

Attempts at a General Solution

If a solution is to be a general one—that is, if it is to apply to any DOS-based PC—it must take the form of a new standard. Then all developers of hardware and software will know how to develop their products in a way that is compatible with that standard.

Naturally, some products will not be adapted to these standards. Not everyone has the same needs, so it makes sense for manufacturers to tailor some of their products to the needs of only some PC users.

Standards

Standards come in two forms. The first are the *de facto* standards. These are simply the way things are done in some industry segment. The second are *formal* standards. Those are set by some official standard-setting organization, usually after long deliberation by all interested parties.

The DOS-extending, memory-management standards come in both flavors. Most of the important *de facto* standards have been converted from de facto to formal standards fairly rapidly. Importance, in this context, means anything that has achieved a significant market impact.

Let's see what some of the more prominent standards are and how they relate to one another. These are not all the new standards for extending DOS, just the standards that relate to memory management and the extension of DOS in order to allow the use of more than 640KB of total RAM.

You are about to enter a veritable zoo, filled with strange creatures called by exotic names such as EMS and its EMM, XMS, VCPI, DPMI, and RSIS. It may help you to keep track of where you are in the zoo if you refer to Figure 12.1.

EMS

The best known and oldest of these standards is the *Expanded Memory Specification,* or *EMS*. Chapter 8 contains a lengthy description of this standard and its evolution over time. The first version of EMS, version 3.0, came out in 1985. And the latest variation, EMS version 4.0, was introduced in 1987.

Briefly stated, EMS is a standardized way of accessing paged memory. Paged memory is some RAM which is not located anywhere in the CPU's memory address space, but can be brought into that space, a page at a time, whenever it is needed.

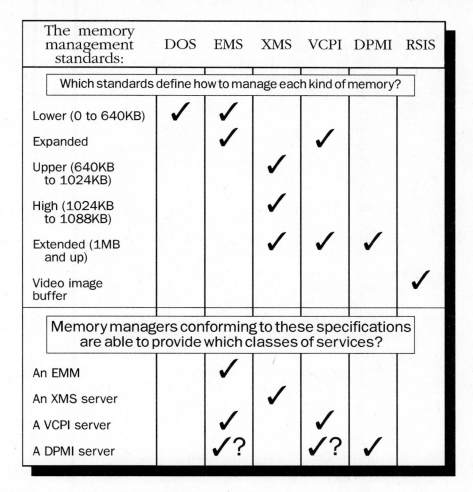

The memory management standards:	DOS	EMS	XMS	VCPI	DPMI	RSIS
Which standards define how to manage each kind of memory?						
Lower (0 to 640KB)	✔	✔				
Expanded		✔		✔		
Upper (640KB to 1024KB)			✔			
High (1024KB to 1088KB)			✔			
Extended (1MB and up)			✔	✔	✔	
Video image buffer						✔
Memory managers conforming to these specifications are able to provide which classes of services?						
An EMM		✔				
An XMS server			✔			
A VCPI server		✔		✔		
A DPMI server		✔?		✔?	✔	

Figure 12.1. The relationships between the major memory-management standards. ✔ means YES; ✔? means SOMETIMES YES.

Because EMS memory can be added to any PC, and because the EMS standard has been around so long, a very large number of application and utility programs have been adapted so they are able to use EMS memory. That means that creating an EMS memory capability in your PC can be one of the more powerful ways of increasing its effective amount of RAM.

There are two distinctly different ways to supply EMS memory in your PC. One is *hardware EMS*, and the other is *emulated EMS*.

Hardware EMS means an actual memory card with special hardware to supply EMS compatible memory. (It normally comes with an **E**xpanded

Memory Manager (EMM) driver program that knows how to operate that particular brand of EMS hardware.) An alternative way to get hardware EMS memory is through the setup routine in PCs with a suitable motherboard system logic chip set.

The second way to get EMS memory is through emulation. Again, there are two variations on that approach. In 386-, 486-, or Pentium-based PCs, you can use a LIMulator program to convert some of your extended memory into expanded. In any PC, you can use a LIMulator to convert some disk space into virtual expanded memory.

XMS

The Microsoft *Extended Memory Specification*, or *XMS*, was also discussed in Chapter 8. This is an attempt to do for the allocation of upper, high, and extended memory the same sorts of things that EMS does for paged memory. This standard was first introduced in 1988.

The upper memory that an XMS memory manager can manage is RAM located in the upper memory space (from 640KB to 1,024KB). High memory is the region from 1,024KB to 16 bytes below 1,088KB. Extended memory is all memory from 1,024KB up. Any PC could have upper memory, though very few do without some help by either added hardware or software. To have either high or extended memory, you must have a PC in classes 3 through 6, which is to say, the CPU must be an 80286, 386, 486, or Pentium.

A very important point to remember is that the first 64KB of *extended memory* is the *same physical RAM* as the *high memory area*, or *HMA*. You can only have those physical memory chip bit-storage cells in use for one purpose at a time. So if you use this region as high memory, it won't be available as extended memory, and vice versa.

A memory manager written to conform to the XMS standard will see to enforcing this for you, provided that all your application programs use that XMS manager's services to gain access to the HMA.

There are several ways to access extended memory. Using the XMS manager's services is only one. Many programs know how to find your PC's extended memory and they just help themselves to it. These programs come in two distinct groups. Programs in the first group, which are patterned after VDISK.SYS, stake their claims to extended memory starting from the bottom up. Those in the other group, which are patterned after RAMDRIVE.SYS, take extended memory from the top down. (See Chapter 8 for a detailed discussion of these two strategies.) And now we have modern programs that ask the XMS manager for an allocation of extended memory.

When any XMS manager is loaded into memory, it checks to see if you have any extended memory that is not already in use. It is written to detect either kind of program that directly uses extended memory. Top-down users present no real problem. The XMS manager simply uses whatever extended memory that those programs did not already take. Bottom-up users of extended memory are another matter. If an XMS manager detects one of these, it will go ahead and load itself into RAM, but it will thenceforward decline to give any XMS services in high or extended memory to any requesting programs.

Once an XMS manager loads and successfully acquires control over your extended memory, it will convert that memory (usually all of it) into what is called XMS memory. And it will permit the first program that wants to have access to the HMA to get it.

Any program that seeks to use extended memory directly after an XMS manager has taken control will find that there is no extended memory available. You can accommodate any program that uses the top-down method for getting extended memory by directing the XMS manager when it loads to leave however much extended memory that program will need as unclaimed extended memory.

The HMA is not created right away. Indeed, if no program asks for access to the HMA, it may never actually exist. It is mere potential until it is used. If it is not used, then the corresponding region of extended memory may be used as XMS memory by any program that may need it. But *only* if it is not previously used as the HMA.

Since it requires the presence of extended memory, XMS applies to fewer PCs than EMS. But it has some advantages in those PCs that can support it. On the other hand, it is less of an exclusive standard than EMS.

One advantage of using XMS is that it uses extended memory. Almost all class 3 or higher PCs come with at least some extended memory. (If you have a 1MB PC, either 512KB or 640KB of that 1MB is available as system memory, which you may know as lower or conventional memory. The rest is used for shadow RAM and/or extended memory. Often you can choose in the setup program which way it will be used.) Usually for

PCs in these classes you can easily add more extended memory. In contrast, getting hardware EMS memory requires you to add a special type of add-in memory card, an EMS card.

> Remember, you can make some extended memory appear to be EMS memory, but that is not the same as actually adding EMS memory; rather, you are simply making your extended memory masquerade as EMS memory. Likewise, you can make some disk space appear as if it were some EMS memory. This pseudo-RAM is so slow that it almost is of no use. (Unless that is all you can get and you really need it, in which case it is the whole use!)

XMS is a less exclusive standard than EMS because there are other ways besides using an XMS memory manager that any program can get access to upper or extended memory; but expanded (EMS) memory absolutely cannot be used (or even seen) without the help of an *EMM (Expanded Memory Manager)*. High memory is special; you generally must use an XMS memory manager to get at the HMA, although some programs contain the special knowledge needed to manipulate the A20 gate and thus get at the HMA without outside help. (Chapter 8 covers all these points quite carefully. If you are confused by this discussion, please reread that chapter before you go on.)

VCPI

In 1988, the same year that XMS was introduced, another standard emerged: the *Virtual Control Program Interface*, or *VCPI*. It is much more limited in its scope than either EMS or XMS.

VCPI essentially only addresses one problem—running a DOS-extended program on a PC that is also emulating EMS memory out of some extended memory. That, in turn, means that this standard is only relevant to users with PCs in classes 5 and 6—those with 386, 486, or *Pentium* CPUs.

Why is there a problem? The EMS emulator (LIMulator) program must run in protected mode in order to get at the PC's extended memory. The DOS extender also runs in protected mode. Usually each of them thinks it is "king of the hill." That is, each believes itself to be the only protected-mode program running in the PC.

When the LIMulator is first loaded, it takes control of the PC. It runs at Ring 0, and it runs all other programs in a V86 emulated PC. They run at Ring 3. That is one feature of V86 mode.

If you now try to run a DOS-extended program, it will attempt to take control of the PC. That means it will set up its own GDT, IDT, LDT, TSS, and Page Directory Table and at least one Page Table. Then it tries to load the addresses of those tables in the relevant CPU registers. That is where the trouble happens. The CPU won't allow the DOS-extended program to do this because it sees a Ring 3 program attempting to assert what are only Ring 0 privileges. (If any of this is confusing to you, then you need to study Chapter 11 some more.)

Something had to be done. Too many people wanted the possibility of running a DOS-extended application and having EMS memory also.

The VCPI standard addresses this problem in a rather simple way. A *VCPI server* (which is the program to implement VCPI, just as an EMM implements EMS or an XMS memory manager implements XMS) provides all the services of an EMM plus some new ones.

The essence of the solution is this: The VCPI server hands off control of the PC to the DOS-extended application whenever it runs, yet it can retake control when it needs to do so. Specifically, the VCPI server is the EMS emulator, so if the application wants some EMS-appearing memory, it will end up calling the VCPI server to supply it. Further, the VCPI server must be called by the DOS-extended application whenever it wants some extended memory.

An interesting minor point: The VCPI server allocates EMS memory in the usual 16KB pages. On the other hand, it allocates extended memory in 4KB pages. The physical address of the actual memory chips supplying either kind of memory will be aligned on 4KB boundaries, since it must be supplied by the paging apparatus of the CPU.

The only reason the VCPI server provides a mechanism for directly allocating 4KB extended memory pages is to enhance the performance of the DOS-extended application. That application is constantly switching between V86 and protected mode, and it can work more efficiently if it is able to allocate memory in either mode.

For this scheme to work, the VCPI server and the DOS-extended application must cooperate very closely. Not all EMS emulators are VCPI compatible, and not all DOS-extended applications are VCPI-aware. Both are required for this solution to work.

A VCPI-aware DOS-extended application must have two modes in which it can operate. (These modes do not have anything to do with the protected modes of the CPU; rather, they have to do with how the application manages memory.) In one mode, which it uses if there is no resident VCPI server, the application must manage all of extended memory for itself. In the other mode, it must defer to the VCPI server's management of extended memory, and therefore, it must request all the memory it needs from that server.

The VCPI specification very clearly states that a VCPI server shall provide EMS services. In fact, the officially approved way for a DOS-extended application to find out if there is a VCPI server active is for the application to look first for an EMM and ask it for some EMS memory. If that succeeds, then the DOS-extended application is supposed to do all its memory allocations via the VCPI server.

There is an interesting problem lurking here. Some people want to put RAM into upper memory, but don't want any EMS services. They may use EMM386.EXE (in conjunction with HIMEM.SYS) to do this. They often do so by invoking EMM386 with the command-line parameter NOEMS. That would seem to be just fine, so long as you had no use for EMS services.

The problem arises if you then try to run a DOS-extended application. If that application follows the rules, it will try to allocate some EMS memory first. When it finds that it can't do that, the DOS-extended application will simply refuse to run at all.

In 1992 the VCPI standard was updated, at least informally, to permit running DOS-extended applications in the presence of a VCPI server that has no page frame. The fix comes in two forms, one to the VCPI server and the other to the DOS-extended applications.

The first fix is that you can now shut off the VCPI-compatible 386-LIMulator's EMS page frame without shutting off its EMS services. That requires use of the FRAME=NONE command-line parameter to EMM386.EXE (and a similar parameter to most any of the other popular 386-LIMulators). This option for EMM386.EXE was not documented until MS-DOS, version 6, but it worked just fine with earlier versions of that program period.

The other fix is that most recently updated DOS-extended applications know enough to try to get VCPI services, even if they are unable to get any EMS services.

Some people want to have emulated EMS memory for the purpose of mapping it into lower memory. That way they can make *DESQview* work most effectively. But they also do not want to give up 64KB of upper memory space to an EMS page frame. This is another time you will find you need the FRAME=NONE parameter for EMM386.

The VCPI strategy was, it must be stressed, intended only to help one DOS-extended application coexist with the VCPI server. Or at least only one at a time. It is not a solution that works well in a multitasking environment if you have several DOS-extended applications all vying for control of the PC.

Also remember that VCPI is of no significance to any PC in classes 1 to 4. They can only have EMS memory by using a real, hardware EMS board (or by emulating EMS from disk memory or from Shadow RAM on the motherboard), so the conflict with DOS-extended applications simply doesn't arise with these PCs.

DPMI

The DOS Protected Mode Interface (DPMI) standard is the most recent innovation in DOS memory-management extensions. It is supposed to solve all the remaining problems. (At least those that are in evidence at this time.)

The major differences between a VCPI server and a DPMI server are: (1) A VCPI server is only usable on a 386-, 486-, or *Pentium*-based PC. A DPMI server can be used on 80286-based PCs as well. (2) A VCPI server hands off control to its client DOS-extended applications. A DPMI server maintains full control at all times.

The VCPI server runs at Ring 0 privilege level. Usually the VCPI server allows its clients to take over from it in which case they also run at Ring 0 level. A DPMI server, on the other hand, runs its clients at a lower privilege level. This makes it possible for the DPMI server always to regain control and mediate any critical resource accesses by any of its clients.

A very important point about both the DPMI and the VCPI specifications is that they were only intended to be of use to two small groups of people: those who write DPMI or VCPI servers and those who write the DOS extenders used to create DOS-extended applications. Everyone else is merely a passive beneficiary of the effect of those specifications on those two target groups.

The first commercially available DPMI server was *Windows,* version 3.0. At the time of its release, the DPMI specification was still in committee and only version 0.8 of the specification had been published.

The committee has now finished its first complete round of work. Version 1.0 of the DPMI specification has finally been released. But it is still far too early to know the true impact this standard will have on the marketplace.

If the claims of its proponents are to be believed, soon we will have all DPMI-aware (and VCPI-aware) DOS applications and DPMI (and VCPI) service-providing memory managers. Then we will have no more conflicts between programs vying for the same resources. That is what they say.

So far (up through version 6), the DOS memory managers, HIMEM and EMM386, do not provide DPMI services. Most of the third-party memory managers do, at least in their latest versions.

RSIS

There is one more standard of some importance that relates to memory management and how to get around the DOS 640KB barrier. This is called the *Relocatable Screen Interface Specification,* or *RSIS.*

RSIS is not as popular as EMS and XMS, nor even as well known as VCPI and DPMI. Yet RSIS has been around longer, and possibly is used more commonly, than all but the most popular of those better known memory-management standards.

The first of the two problems that RSIS is meant to help solve is that DOS wants to see a single, large region of RAM. It then knows how to allocate memory from that pool for utility programs, device drivers, and applications. The video image buffer gets in the way of extending that reach of RAM. If you could move the video image buffer up somewhat, then you could have more RAM for DOS applications. Another way to say that is you would have a larger TPA.

The second problem that needs a solution, and for which RSIS can be the solution, is dealing with multiple programs vying for the screen resource. In a multitasking or even a task swapping environment, each program would like to think it owns the entire screen all the time. Clearly that cannot be allowed, or the screen image would be an incomprehensible mixture of the outputs of all the different programs.

The solution to this problem is for the multitasker to allocate a region of the screen (typically a rectangle called a *window*) to each program it is running. Only the output that the program generates which would normally fall within its window is allowed to get through to the real screen. In some cases one window may overlay a part of another window. Then only the top window's program gets to write to the part of the screen that the two windows have in common.

If only all programs sent all their output to the screen through calls to the BIOS video interrupt (INT 10h), then a solution would be quite easy to implement. In that case, the multitasker could simply hook that interrupt and mediate all attempts to read or write to the video image buffer.

To support programs that want to store information in the video buffer and later read that information, the multitasker cannot simply refuse to write to parts of the screen that a given program does not own. Instead, the multitasker sets up virtual screens. These are regions of RAM somewhere, which could be located in extended or expanded memory if the multitasker is able to access those regions. The programs running under the multitasker are fooled into thinking that the virtual screen is the real one. Then the multitasker watches each of those buffers and periodically updates the real screen so it properly reflects the contents of all the virtual screens.

This works very well if the programs being multitasked use nothing but BIOS calls to access the buffers. If they attempt to write directly to the image buffers (as is very common in programs seeking high performance), then the multitasker will have no way of knowing that this is happening. At least that is true in real mode.

This is why *DESQview* classifies all programs by whether or not they write directly to the screen. Those that do get the whole screen or they are stopped from running. (A portion of their output may show in a window, but the underlying program is suspended.) Those that use only BIOS calls can run and have only the appropriate parts of their output show on the screen. The same is true for *Windows*, version 3.0, in real or standard mode.

Going into Virtual 86 mode can provide a solution even for the not-so-well-behaved programs. Each client program running under a multitasker can be given its own megabyte of memory (including the screen buffer, which is then only a virtual one). Whatever it writes to its virtual screen buffer can be transferred appropriately to the real screen buffer by the multitasking program. This is what *Windows* 3.x does in 386-enhanced mode.

So far, it would seem we had no need for a special, new standard. But it can be helpful if there is a standard way for a program to find out where the virtual screen buffer (which it is supposed to use) is located. Any program that knows the location of its virtual screen image buffer, and that "promises" to write only to that virtual screen, need not have all its attempts to write to screen memory intercepted and redirected by the multitasker. That speeds things up quite a bit.

Starting with IBM's ill-fated *Top View* multitasker, and continuing now in *DESQview* and V Communications' *Memory Commander,* the RSIS specification has given programs a standard methodology for screen image buffer access. Only the programs that know enough to ask for the help of an RSIS supervisory program get that help. All others must be handled in the ways just described.

At this time not very many programs are RSIS-aware. If you have one and install it under *DESQview*, you can declare that it will not write directly to the screen, even though it may do so. That will allow you to run it in a window even on an XT.

Vermont Views is a software product that many programmers use to create the screen output portion of their products. Any program that uses *Vermont Views* will be RSIS-aware.

V Communications has made a point of RSIS. They want as many programs as possible to be RSIS-aware. Their interest is because of the very special way they handle memory management in their *Memory Commander* and *MegaMizer* products. (The former is a memory manager only meant for use on a 386, 486, or Pentium-based PC. The latter is a similar product meant for 8088-, 8086-, or 80286-based PCs.)

What makes *Memory Commander* so special is that normally it tries to move the video image buffer up in memory space as far as it can. Then it fills in the space below that relocated image buffer with RAM, thus expanding the TPA. After *Memory Commander* does its magic, DOS may find it has as much as 900KB in which to load applications. But this can only work with RSIS-aware applications or those that use only BIOS routines to access the video image buffer. You can read more about *Memory Commander* in Chapter 21.

Pitfalls on That Path

All of these attempts to extend DOS by some add-on standards are subject to some common difficulties. These include the usual problems that plague any attempt to do something new, compounded by some things that are unique to this situation.

Perhaps the toughest problem facing the developers of any program that attempts to enhance DOS is doing what amounts to operating-system software development without being allowed to see the present operating-system software source code. Microsoft, not surprisingly, has not shared that source code with those outside the company. They tell outside developers general information, and occasionally they will share some pieces of recommended source code for some fragment of what needs to be developed. But this is far from telling the inner secrets of how DOS really was built.

So problems can be expected to occur. And when they do, the troubleshooting task is greatly hindered by the mysteries that cling to the operating system with which the new program is expected to work.

Another difficulty faced even by Microsoft's programmers is that commercial marketplace considerations often force the release of "finished" programs well before the specification upon which those programs were to be designed have been finished. That very clearly was the case with DPMI and *Windows* 3.0.

This doesn't mean that *Windows 3.0* implements DPMI incorrectly. Microsoft simply could not possibly have supported the full DPMI standard with *Windows* 3.0, as that standard hadn't been fully decided upon by the committee at the time they were finishing the writing of *Windows* 3.0.

Another substantial source of difficulty has been that DOS enhancers have to cope with all manner of programs written before those enhancements existed. Often people needed to use some resource in PCs long before the systematic "right" way to do so was developed. Now programs using some ad hoc solution are expected to work alongside those using the "right" approach. Making operating-system enhancements that are tolerant of historical happenstance greatly increases the effort needed to develop those enhancements.

Finally, all new software has bugs. Anything with a version number ending in point-zero can be expected to be especially richly endowed with them. When the software is not an application, nor even a utility program, but something you run underneath everything else you use (except for DOS itself), then its bugs may manifest themselves in quite bizarre ways. It will not necessarily be evident where to look for the difficulty.

But, if you are a bit adventurous, you can gain great benefits from putting the latest and greatest DOS enhancers to work on your PC. Just be very sure your backups are in very good shape, please! (See Chapter 5 for some cautions about backups; you will be much happier if you read them now, before you begin your grand adventure.)

A Recap

This chapter has been mostly about the past. But it is the past as prologue to the present and future. Seeing how we got where we are illuminates the possibilities for future progress, not to mention making much clearer why you must do some things in the seemingly odd ways that are currently necessary.

After defining the DOS 640KB barrier and explaining why it is a problem, this chapter reviewed the principal options you have for surmounting or evading this barrier, or at least for reducing its impact on your daily work.

It ended with a review of the various memory-management standards that have been developed to guide the creation of DOS enhancers that will work compatibly with one another. These include EMS, XMS, VCPI, and DPMI, which are often listed as the primary DOS memory enhancement standards. It also included RSIS, a relatively old but not well-known standard with the potential for helping programs gain greater performance in many multitasking environments.

The next chapter contains more history: the history of the integrated circuits we depend on so much, and in particular those we use as the processors in our PCs.

BRIEF HISTORY OF SOME CHIPS

This is the story of the processor chips that define the kind of PC you have. It also covers some earlier chips and some chips that are used in building the non-PC kinds of personal computer.

This chapter is all about chips. (Sorry, no fish with these chips; they're just computer chips.)

Without integrated circuit chips, we wouldn't have any personal computers. Exactly which ones you have in your PC make it the sort of PC it is. (Clothes may "make the man," but chips make the computer in a far deeper sense.)

In this chapter you will learn something of the history behind the processor chips that define PCs. This introduction will emphasize the internal and external address and data bus widths for each processor chip.

You will also meet the coprocessor chips most used in PCs, and "second sourced chips" and some competing chip families are also explained. The chapter concludes with a discussion of RISC versus CISC processors.

Prehistory of Intel 80x86 Family

Before Intel made microcomputers, they made other kinds of integrated circuits. One of their major markets was for calculator chips. Each of these was designed for a single customer, until an Intel engineer had the insight that all the different Intel calculator chips had more in common than they had differences. He then proposed making a universal calculator chip, to be customized for each new customer by some programming, which could be stored in a ROM chip.

That was the critical step that started us on the path to today's computer on a chip. There has been a dramatic growth in the complexity and power of the microprocessors produced since then, both by Intel and by their competitors, but they all are just more extreme examples of this basic concept.

The Intel 80x86 family of microprocessors are the defining chips for PCs. Before introducing all of the members of that family (and some of their siblings and cousins), let's look at their principal forebears.

Earlier Intel Processors

In 1971 Intel introduced the 4004. This was their first real microcomputer on a chip. Intel sold it primarily for use in industrial control applications (as a so-called "embedded controller"), such as traffic-light controllers and microwave ovens.

The 4004 was a four-bit processor. That is, it stored, internally manipulated, and moved to or from memory only four-bit quantities (nibbles of data). Unlike our more modern processors, the 4004 had a separate data space (all of 5,120 *bits*, organized as 1,280 nibbles) and program-instruction space (4KB, organized as 4K 8-bit words), plus 16 I/O ports.

The 4004 was packaged in a 16-pin DIP (see Figure 2.1). Four of those pins were used to transfer information in or out of the chip. (Instructions were read in from program memory on these pins, and data flowed on these pins on its way in from, or out to, either the data memory or the I/O ports.) All the rest of the pins were used for power, clock, and various control signals.

Some fairly involved external circuitry was required to decide when to read various pieces of the address being referenced, and when to supply the referenced data (when the chip was reading data) or receive it (when the chip was writing data).

A follow-on design to the 4004 was the 4040. This also was a four-bit parallel CPU chip. Again it had separate data and program (instruction) memory-address spaces. The data space was the same size (5,120 bits), but the program space was doubled to (wow, think of it!) 8KB. More significantly, the 4040 added support for external interrupts.

Both the 4004 and the 4040 had a fixed number of internal index registers. This meant they were limited to running programs that had no subroutines nested more than seven levels deep.

In 1972, just a year after introducing the 4004, Intel brought out the 8008. And two years after that, they introduced the 8080. These were the first byte-wide microprocessors.

Besides being able to transfer information in whole bytes, these microprocessors were more modern in their memory architecture. These processors had only a single memory address space for both data and instructions. In the 8008, it was 16KB (that's 16K bytes) in size, while the 8080 could address up to 64KB. Any part of this space could be used to store data or program instructions. Both processors supported external interrupts.

The 8008 was packaged in an 18-pin DIP. Eight of the pins were used to transfer a byte of data in or out, or half of an address. What those eight pins were being used for at any given time was indicated by the state of the machine, and that was signaled as a binary number on three other pins.

The 8080 was quite revolutionary. First, it was packaged in a 40-pin DIP, the largest package used for an IC up to that time. This allowed Intel to dedicate 8 pins to a data bus (for information going either in or out) and 16 other pins to an address bus (output only). The remaining 16 pins were used for power, clock, and various control signals. For the first time, it wasn't necessary to share any of the pins for two or more different functions. This greatly simplified the design of the support circuitry for this processor.

The 8080 also introduced the notion of a stack maintained in external memory. Now programmers were free to nest subroutines as deeply as they wished. This also enabled relatively easy context switching (for example, when processing an interrupt). (By storing the state of all the CPU's internal registers on the stack, you could easily reload them later to restore the machine to exactly the state it had been in when it was interrupted.)

Other features of the 8080 included 512 I/O ports and the ability to "tri-state" its output lines. That latter feature means that the CPU could effectively disable all its output lines on command. When it did so, another processor connected to the same bus could take over. This was the first support for what we now call "multiple bus masters."

The 8080 was the heart of the first highly successful small computers for business applications. The operating system for those computers was created by Digital Research, and called *Control Program for Microcomputers*, abbreviated *CP/M*.

Many different manufacturers made *CP/M* machines. Each one customized theirs in some way, and the result was that while all had much in common, they were in many ways fundamentally incompatible. In particular, it was impossible to interchange data files easily between different brands of *CP/M* machines, since each one used its own proprietary disk format.

Intel also introduced an improved version of the 8080, called the 8085. Mostly this was improved by bringing onto the chip some of the support chips that were commonly used with an 8080. This chip's main market turned out to be embedded controllers, rather than general-purpose computers.

Some Cousins

Intel was not the only manufacturer of microprocessors. MOS Technologies, Mostek, Motorola, Rockwell, Standard Microsystems Corporation, Synertek, and Texas Instruments were some of the microprocessor manufacturers in this country. Some of them used their own designs; others licensed designs from some of their competitors. Arguably the most successful of the other microprocessor makers in the late 1970s was Zilog.

Zilog created the Z80, which was a super version of the Intel 8080. Zilog built its name and fortune making these "more of an 8080 than an 8080" processor chips. Most *CP/M* machines made after the Z80's introduction used that chip instead of the Intel 8080.

> The Z80 has a number of additional instructions beyond those found in the 8080. *CP/M* was only written to expect an 8080, so in many *CP/M* computers that used the Z80, that part of its specialness was wasted. Later on, some people modified *CP/M* to take advantage of at least some Z80-specific instructions. In a way, this is analogous to what happened with the 80286. When it was first introduced to the PC marketplace (in the IBM *PC/AT*), it was only used as a faster 8086. Only later did much software appear that took advantage of what is special about the 80286.

Zilog tried to follow up that success with a next-generation microprocessor, the Z8. But IBM chose Intel's 8088 (their next-generation microprocessor) for use in IBM's new personal computer. Intel soon made up for the market share they had lost to Zilog and then some.

A Competitor

While the *CP/M* computers were sweeping into offices, *Apple II* computers were taking schools by storm. Apple chose the MOS Technologies 6502 as the heart of their computer. This chip was "second sourced" by Rockwell and Synertek.

> A common misunderstanding is to think that all Apple computers used Motorola microprocessors. The 6502 was designed for MOS Technologies by a former Motorola employee and the 6502 is essentially an enhanced version of the Motorola 6800, but Motorola chips were not used by Apple until their *Lisa* computer. Apple does use Motorola processors, in particular those in the 68000 family, for all its *Macintosh* computers.
>
> At that time it was standard practice in the electronics industry for any manufacturer of integrated circuits to grant licenses to other IC manufacturers to make identical chips. The reason was that most

system designers refused to use a chip that could only be bought from one source.

This practice of producing chips designed by competitors was called "second sourcing" the design. It was almost required to make any new IC design a success.

A part of the system designers' concern was over monopolistic pricing. A more serious concern was that something might happen to the manufacturer's production line processes and they would suddenly be unable to supply chips to their customers in adequate numbers. Having a second source with a totally independent manufacturing line was good protection against this hazard.

A recent occurrence points out just how real this hazard can be. When Mount Saint Helens blew its top in 1981, most of Intel's production facilities experienced a dramatic drop in the "yields"—that is, in the percentage of chips they made that worked. This is one reason that Intel now has production facilities in Ireland as well as in Oregon, near their headquarters.

The designs that came from Motorola and Intel at comparable dates are quite comparable in other ways as well. Intel's 80486 and Motorola's 68040, for example, have about the same complexity and very similar capabilities. They are, however, totally incompatible with each other. That is why the *Macintosh* and a PC cannot both run the same programs.

There is one very significant difference in the evolution of these two families of microprocessor. Intel started with what we now view as a rather small memory-address space (1MB) and gradually grew it up to its present (4GB) size. Motorola, in its 680x0 series, always had a 4GB memory-address space. IBM put the ROMs in the PC as high in memory space as they could. It really wasn't their fault that later on Intel "raised the roof," and thus left IBM's ROMs in the middle of what otherwise might have been a lovely, open expanse of RAM. Designers using the 680x0 family of chips have never had this unfortunate experience, which is why so many Mac programmers are so smugly sure that their computers are superior to PCs.

The Intel 80x86 Family Members

Now it is time to meet the members in the Intel 80x86 family. These are the CPU chips whose use is one of the defining characteristics of what we are calling a PC. Figure 13.1 shows all the members of this family and some of their salient features.

CPU Model	Number of Data bus lines	Number of bits in Physical Address	Physical Memory Address Space
8086	16	20	1MB
8088	8	20	1MB
80286	16	24	16MB
386DX	32	32	4GB
386SX	16	24	16MB
386SL	16	24	16MB
486DX	32	32	4GB
486SX	32	32	4GB
Pentium	64	32	4GB

Figure 13.1. The Intel 80x86 family members.

The 8086

The first member of the family was the 8086. Introduced in 1978, it was their first 16-bit microprocessor. That meant it had 16 data bus lines. It also expanded the memory-address space with 20 address lines.

Because they still were using a 40-pin package, this expanded number of lines required some shared use of certain pins. Their choice was to have 16 pins serve alternately for data and the least significant 16 bits of the address. The four pins used for the most significant bits of the address were also shared, in that case with some status signals.

The 8088

The 8086 was a radical step up in capability and complexity. Too much so for some of Intel's customers. Therefore, the very next year Intel introduced a variant form of the 8086, called the 8088. This was just like the 8086 internally, but it had only an eight-bit data bus externally.

This simple change made this chip much more attractive to system designers. At some cost in terms of speed, they could greatly simplify the design of their computer systems (and lower their cost). Only half the number of buffer and latch chips were needed for the narrower data bus, for example.

This is the chip that IBM chose to be the CPU in their first personal computer, the *IBM PC*. The tremendous success of that computer in the marketplace made the 8088 the single most important microprocessor chip in history.

The 80186 and 80188

In a development similar to the introduction of the 8085 as an 8080 with support chip functionality included, Intel introduced in 1982 the 80186 and 80188. They also included a small number of additional instructions (the same ones added to the real mode instruction set in the 80286). At first, it appeared that one of these was destined to become the CPU in the next generation of PCs.

IBM tried. At least according to rumor, they initially designed the 80188 into their *PC Jr*. Then, before that machine was ready for market, they found a serious problem.

The only substantial advantage of using the 80188 over the 8088 is simply that much of what was external support circuitry for an 8088 is incorporated on the chip in an 80188. That includes the interrupt controller and DMA controller. But because of a conflict between the way Intel implemented the on-board interrupt controller and the way DOS uses interrupts (in violation of Intel's "reservation" of the first 16 interrupts for its own use), it was not feasible to use the on-board interrupt controller in the 80188 for a DOS-based PC. At that point, the advantages of the 80188 were insufficient to justify its extra cost. IBM went back to the 8088 for the *PC Jr* and, if the rumor is to be believed, had a "fire sale" on 80188s.

The 80286

The 80286, also introduced in 1982, improved on the 8086 in a different way. Like the 8086, it was a full 16-bit machine, both internally and externally. It now had an expanded memory-bus width (24 bits), and it offered a new, "protected" mode of operation. In that mode, it could address up to 16MB of memory.

Best of all, it was fully backward compatible and it could run DOS just fine. Intel knew what the market needed and wanted, and they delivered it. IBM adopted this chip for the CPU of their next generation of PC, called the IBM *PC/AT*.

The 80386 (Now the 386DX)

In 1985 Intel brought out their next member of the family. Dubbed the 80386 (now shortened to simply 386), this chip was a vast improvement over anything that had gone before. With nearly 10 times the number of transistors, and able to run with a clock speed over three times that of the original 8086, this was a very powerful computer.

Better yet, it was again fully backward compatible. Intel was keenly aware that the PC was a huge success, and that DOS ruled. Most ATs were simply being used as if they were very fast XTs. (Well, some folks did use

VDISK or RAMDRIVE to make a virtual disk out of their extended memory, but that was about all the use that most people made of the protected mode and larger address-space capabilities of the 80286.) So the 386 was made to wake up in real mode and look and work simply like a super-fast 8086.

The 80386 was Intel's first full 32-bit microprocessor. It had a 32-bit data bus and a 32-bit address bus. That meant it could address up to 4GB of real, physical memory. It offered two new operating modes, in addition to the real mode and 286-protected mode offered by the 80286. To many programmers, an even more significant feature was that it could be changed from protected mode back into real mode by a simple instruction, rather than requiring the arcane and slow methods used with the 80286. The 386 also included support for demand-paged virtual memory and other paging memory schemes. (See Chapter 11 if any of this jargon confuses you.)

This chip became another smash hit for Intel. But to help it along even more, they created a couple of alternate versions of the 80386.

The 80386SX

In 1987 the 80386SX hit the market. This was simply an 80386 with the external data bus reduced from 32 bits to 16 bits. That single change meant that it could be put into a system whose motherboard was essentially the same as that used with an 80286. The cost of an 80386SX system should, therefore, be almost identical to that of the earlier generation 80286-based PCs. To be sure this was so, Intel priced the 80386SX almost as low as the 80286, while keeping the price on what it now called the 80386DX (the original 80386 design) considerably higher.

The 386SX has a different package and pinout than the 80286, so it can't simply be plugged into the CPU socket of a PC motherboard designed for the 80286; some changes do have to be made in the motherboard design. Also the BIOS must be different, since it needs to support the greater capabilities of the 386SX. Those are the main differences between the motherboards of an 80286-based PC and one built around the 386SX.

This great similarity has been exploited by some vendors who offer simple upgrades for 80286-based PCs using a 386SX CPU chip. You can find more on this in Chapter 27.

These prices were clearly dictated more by marketing factors and policies than by manufacturing cost. The two chips are virtually identical in design, and cost essentially the same amount to make. Intel launched a vigorous advertising campaign to kill the 286, in favor of the 386SX. Some cynics pointed out that Intel had been forced to make second-source arrangements for the 80286 chip, but had so far resisted doing so for the 386. So by killing off the 286, they apparently were also trying to kill off their biggest competitors, while protecting their high profit margins on the 386DX.

For whatever reasons, the 386SX proved to be another wonderful success story for Intel. It has become the minimum acceptable level of CPU for most new business purchases of PCs. Key to its success is the fact that it can run virtually all the software created for the 386DX or 486, albeit somewhat slower. (The only exceptions are applications that require addressing more than 16MB of physical RAM.)

The 80386SL

Intel calls its 386SL a Microprocessor SuperSet. It consists of two chips, the 386SL CPU chip and the 82360SL I/O chip.

The combination of these two chips makes up everything needed to produce a working PC except for the RAM and ROM. The I/O chip includes everything that normally would be a part of the motherboard system logic chip set. Further, it supports various strategies for minimizing power consumption.

One very interesting innovation is Intel's System Management Mode. This is a new operating mode for the CPU in which it can be used to program how the chip set will operate the rest of the time. That allows a complete separation between the CPU as executor of PC compatible programs and in its role as system management aid.

The intended market for this chip set is the makers of laptop and portable computers. The 386SL has been adopted by quite a few portable computer makers already, and it appears to be the start of a new wave in CPU chips. This trend is further enhanced by the inclusion of the POWER.EXE program in DOS 6. That program can be used to control the power-saving features of any PC with suitable hardware—and 386SL-based PCs are typically members of that group.

Soon we may also see power-management features included in desktop PCs. As more and more PCs are being left on constantly, and as more people become concerned about the environment (not to mention their electric bills), the thought of having a PC that will shut down many of its most power-hungry parts whenever they are not being used is very attractive.

The 80486 (Now the 486DX)

In 1989 Intel introduced the first member of its 80x86 family with more than a million transistors on the chip. This 80486 (or now more often simply called the 486) is very much compatible with the 386. In fact, it almost doesn't innovate at all. It does move onto the chip a large amount of the support logic required to build a 386 system, and it incorporates a math coprocessor equivalent to the 80387. It also includes a memory cache. This permits a PC system designer to use a faster clock speed without having to get faster memory chips for main RAM.

The 486 has taken off with the same fast-rising sales curve as the 386. It seems likely to be another super-success story for Intel. Again, though, Intel was not content to sit still. It tried another variation on this chip also.

The 80486SX

The 486SX has been called a "bastard chip." It has been roundly denounced by the computer press as a fraud. The first generation of these chips were simply 486 chips whose floating point unit (math coprocessor) had failed the quality assurance test. Later 486SX chips were made with the FPU intentionally disabled.

The name is clearly an attempt to capitalize on the success of the 386SX. With the 386, one could rationalize the names DX (for **D**ouble Word **E**xternal bus) and SX (for **S**ingle Word **E**xternal bus). With the 486, no such easy meaning is apparent, nor has Intel suggested one. The pricing of the 486SX is a clear admission of the high profit margin built into the DX version; this is the same as was the case with the 386DX and SX.

The 80487SX

Where it becomes really painful is when you decide to upgrade a 486SX system by adding a math coprocessor. Instead of being able to buy just an FPU unit in a chip, you must use the 80487SX. And this turns out to be a full 80486DX with an extra pin. The extra pin simply shuts down the 80486SX. And, not surprisingly, the 80487SX costs about the same amount as the 486DX.

In an attempt to make this seem like an intelligent design, Intel has recently been advertising that someday there will be other alternative chips to go into the 80487 sockets on an 80486SX motherboard. What, exactly, those other chips would do was not clearly specified at first.

The Overdrive and DX/2 chips

Intel finally began delivering new chips to go in the extra socket on a 486SX motherboard—ones that were more than just a way to get full 486DX performance. They dubbed these chips OverDrive chips.

At almost the same time, Intel released the 486DX/2 chip. Both the DX/2 and the OverDrive do the same thing. They only differ in the marketing channel used to bring them to end users. Manufacturers buy the DX/2 chips and make them the only CPU on the motherboard. An end user with a 486SX system can buy an OverDrive chip and put it in the extra socket on their PC's motherboard and thereby essentially convert it into a DX/2 PC.

Both the DX/2 and OverDrive chips differ from the usual 486 by running most of the internal parts twice as fast as the input/output portion and twice as fast as the clock signal supplied to the chip. Thus, when you connect a 50MHz DX/2 or OverDrive chip to a 25MHz motherboard, you will get almost double the computing speed, but no increase in the speed with which information flows on or off the CPU chip.

Since most of the time a 486 chip is "talking to itself," this is a very effective ploy. Nothing has to be changed in the motherboard design or construction to nearly double the PC's effective speed. (The BIOS in some early 486SX-based PCs might have to be upgraded.)

The Pentium

Early in 1993, Intel announced the next member of the 80x86 family. Called the Pentium (a made-up word that clearly would be eligible for trademark protection—as the original designation, 586, would not be), this chip is another major advance in the art of integrated circuit processor manufacturing.

Other Members to Come

Intel has repeatedly assured the industry that whatever new goodies they manage to pack onto each new generation of processor chip, they will continue to make members of the 80x86 family that are fully 386 compatible. (And that means fully compatible with programs written for any member of the family, right back to the original 8086 and 8088.)

Intel has described, in admittedly somewhat vague terms, the processor they expect to announce in the year 2000. Called the Micro 2000 (at least as a code name while it is being developed), this chip will have at least 100 million transistors on it. It will incorporate, they say, four processors, each as powerful as the 486, plus two digital signal processors (perhaps for speech and handwriting recognition), and lots of RAM and ROM. There will probably be other important new features. One feature will surely be a significant portion of the chip (about 10 percent, according to one estimate) devoted simply to testing the rest of the chip.

Moore's Law

How, you may be wondering, can Intel predict so confidently what they will be doing most of a decade from now? It is because of a strange and wonderful observation that one of Intel's founders and former chief executive officers made.

Back in the late 1960s, Gordon Moore looked carefully at the history of the chips that Intel and others in the industry had been able to manufacture. He noticed a regularity. He announced it and it became known as "Moore's Law." He had no real explanation for it; he just noticed that it seemed to hold true.

Moore's Law can be stated in several ways. One commonly quoted form says that every two years, roughly, the maximum complexity that can be made in a production integrated circuit will double.

This increase in complexity comes from several sources. One is that the minimum size of the features that can be crafted into the surface of ICs keeps going down. Another is that the maximum size of the wafers that can be handled keeps going up. A third contributor is the more or less steady flow of "breakthroughs" in IC fabrication technology. Another way of stating Moore's Law is that the minimum feature size in production integrated circuits will decline by a factor of about 10 every decade. Figure 13.2 shows what an amazingly good job Moore's Law does of describing the steadily increasing complexity of Intel's microprocessors. Yet no one claims to know why it should be true!

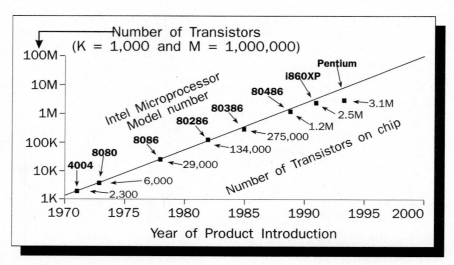

Figure 13.2. Moore's Law.

Some Siblings

Most of this chapter contains the story of the microprocessor CPU chips. But some mention of the most important coprocessor chips may also be useful.

Intel Coprocessors

For each member of the 80x86 family, there is a matching math coprocessor. (The one exception is the 486, which incorporates the equivalent of an 80387 in it.)

Thus, the 8086 and 8088 have the 8087. The 80286 has the 80287. A later version of the 80287 is called the 80287XL. It is significantly different from the 80287. In fact, in some ways it more resembles the 80387, except that it is a 16-bit chip.

Interestingly, when the 80386(DX) first came out, the 80387 was not ready. So they built the 80386DX to be able to use either the 80387DX or, until it was ready, the 80287 (or 80287XL at that time).

The 386SX has its 80387SX. And according to Intel, the 486SX has the 487SX, but, as noted earlier, this pair of chips is hardly comparable to the other pairs in this family grouping.

Clone Coprocessors

There were official second-source manufacturers for the 8088, 8086, and 80286. Intel did not set up any similar agreements for the x87 math coprocessors. But that has not stopped a number of companies from developing what they claim are replacement chips for the Intel x87 math chips. ITT, Cyrix, and MathCo all have a line of math chips they say are not only able to work just like the x87 series of Intel chips, they say these clone chips will work faster, or produce more accurate results, or run cooler, or all three! Intel has contested those claims, but most independent tests seem to bear out the clone makers' claims.

"And Now for Something Completely Different"

(...with apologies to Monty Python.) There is one manufacturer, Weitek, who doesn't claim to manufacture clones of the x87 chips. Weitek says quite frankly that their math chips are very different from Intel's. They also say their chips are a lot better as floating point computation coprocessors.

For the earlier models of Intel 80x86 CPU chips, Weitek made a chip set (the 1167 chip set). Later, they were able to put all the needed circuitry on a single chip, so we have the Weitek 3167 for use with a 386 CPU. And there is a 4167 for use with a 486 CPU.

Many programmers agree with Weitek. And Intel and most PC makers have cooperated with Weitek. So you will find two coprocessor sockets in many of the higher performance PCs. (Or in a 486DX system, one such socket.) This is to allow you to have an Intel (or clone) coprocessor and a Weitek one.

Some programs know about the Intel processor and can take advantage of it if you have one installed. Some know about the Weitek chips. If you use both kinds of programs, you may wish to have both kinds of math chips in your PC.

Money Saving Tip If none of your programs use either form of math chip, you will only waste your money and some electricity if you install either. So check out your programs or check with their manufacturers first, before you spend money for a math chip of any kind (or before choosing a 486DX-based PC over a 486SX-based one).

More Cousins

The concept of a second source was explained previously. Intel was essentially forced by standard industry practice to set up second-source arrangements for the 8086 and 8088. Several companies signed such agreements. Harris probably made the most non-Intel 8088 and 8086 chips. They used a CMOS design that consumed far less power than the Intel design—a feature that made those chips very popular, especially with portable and laptop computer makers.

NEC introduced its V series of chips, with the announcement that the V20 was a pin-compatible replacement for an Intel 8088, but that it had an enhanced instruction set that included all the instructions of the 8080. That meant it could easily run *CP/M* programs without modification, using an emulator program that takes advantage of the 8080 instructions included in the V20 chip. Their V30 was a similar clone with enhancements of the 8086.

The NEC V series chips also run a few percentage faster than the equivalent Intel chip. NEC had a modest success with these chips. Intel was miffed. They sued NEC for copyright infringement. NEC countersued. Eventually, the suits were settled without either party winning decisively.

The rulings in those suits were most interesting. The judge ruled that yes, NEC had used some of Intel's microcode in a way that would not have been legal if only Intel had a valid copyright. But since Intel had manufactured and sold some 8088 chips without the copyright notice etched into the silicon, their claimed copyright was null and void.

AMD was a licensed second-source producer for the 80286. AMD claimed that their contract with Intel also allows them to make legal copies of the 386. Intel vigorously disagreed. The matter went to court in several related law suits.

AMD prevailed and now makes a 40MHz 386 clone chip. In part because it is rated to run faster than the fastest Intel 386, this chip has been quite successful. AMD promises more models in the near future.

AMD announced plans to make 486 clones as well. Again, Intel tried to stop them. And yet again, the courts ruled in AMD's favor. Chips and Technology, who made their name making clone BIOSes, now has introduced a line of CPU chips. They include a 386 clone and some super-386 chips which offer a number of very interesting new features, some quite similar to Intel's System Management Mode in the 386SL. Still, since those chips are not quite exact clones in their behavior, the marketplace may or may not accept them.

It appears that we can look forward to a continuing stream of clone and enhanced clone chips following a short time after the introduction of each new Intel chip—at least for any of Intel's chips that are wildly successful in the marketplace. That is good news for consumers, since competition has always helped lower prices.

RISC Versus CISC Chips

To close this discussion of CPU chips, it may be worth spending a moment on RISC and CISC chips. These terms have been in the press a lot lately. What does each one mean, and why might it matter to you?

RISC stands for **R**educed **I**nstruction **S**et **C**omputer. CISC stands for **C**omplex **I**nstruction **S**et **C**omputer. The essential difference is this: A RISC chip understands relatively few instructions. But it can execute each one very quickly. Programs for a RISC machine must be more complex. But they may end up running faster than those for a comparable CISC machine. Or then again, maybe they won't. (Benchmark measurements of performance have been inconclusive on this point.)

All the Intel 80x86 chips are pretty much CISC chips. So are the Motorola 680x0 (68010, 68020, ... ,68040) chips used in the *Macintosh* and *NeXT* computers. Some workstation computers, from IBM and a variety of other vendors, use RISC chips.

Does it matter to you? Probably not. The trend in the industry is to make more and more interoperability. That means that whatever new CPU chips are developed and whatever new systems are built using them, if DOS programs are the rule, then those new computers will be built to run DOS programs. If *Windows* is the order of the day, then they all will run *Windows.* And so on.

The new computers may have to emulate a PC in order to run DOS programs. But do you care if it does that? Not if it does it well enough.

MEMORY—PUTTING IT ALL TOGETHER, AND A SELF-TEST

Now you know the fundamentals of what memory is and how PCs work. This chapter will help you cement that knowledge. It will also help you clear up any confusion that might stand in the way of understanding memory management.

The preceding eight chapters presented many facts about PC memory. Are you confident that you absorbed it all? Perhaps a review of the key concepts will help you.

There are also a few more key concepts you need to learn about. For example, you need to know what a cache is, and the distinction between a memory cache and a disk cache. You'll find that information in this chapter as well.

The chapter ends with a short self-test to help you find out how much you really know about PC memory. Make sure your knowledge is complete before you plunge into the next stage: learning about how to add memory to your PC, what PC memory management means, and how to do it.

Common Confusions Clarified and Key Concepts Reviewed

Certain ideas are very confusing to many people. It is important for you not to be misled by any of these common confusions. So to help you avoid or correct any misimpressions, here is a quick review.

A Place Is Not a Thing

A place is not a thing! Memory-address *space* is different from *memory*. Please keep this distinction firmly in mind. For example, think of a library. A building full of bookshelves has the potential to become a library, but until it is filled with books it cannot serve a library's purpose.

You can't put books on a shelf you don't have, and neither can you use memory chips you can't address. Having the memory-address space is a crucial first step. However, just as having shelves is no guarantee that they will be full of books, having memory-address space is no guarantee that you will have memory chips there. Figure 14.1 is here to help visual thinkers get clear about this crucial distinction and keep it firmly in mind.

You can have memory without memory addresses. For example, you can have some RAM for which there are no addresses in the CPU's memory address space. A printer's buffer memory is one instance of this. A hardware EMS board's RAM is another example of this. Pages of expanded memory are given temporary addresses in the CPU's memory-address space whenever the CPU is supposed to access them. Without these addresses, it simply cannot see them.

Figure 14.1. A place is not a thing! Memory addresses are necessary in order to access memory, but having addresses doesn't mean you have memory at those locations, any more than having a bookcase means you have books.

Actually, all memory chips that can be used must have an address of some kind. In the case of the printer buffer RAM, there is a processor within the printer whose address space contains the RAM chips. Without at least that sort of address, no information could be moved into or out of the chips.

How Big Is a Memory-Address Space

There are four levels at which the size of memory-address space can be limited. The very lowest physical level is that you must have sockets in which to put memory chips or modules before you can access them electronically. Next, you must have a way to convey information to or from those chips or modules. That means you can be limited in the amount of memory you can access by the design of the memory bus. Third, the CPU must have enough address pins to drive all the address lines in the memory bus. And finally, the CPU may be limited (for example, by its present operating mode) as to the number of different combinations of bits it can present on its address pins. Now, we'll take a closer look at how the CPU and the memory bus can limit the size of memory-address space.

How the CPU Limits the Range of Possible Memory Addresses

The memory space that matters when you are dealing in actual physical memory chips is the *physical-address space.* That space is defined by the range of numbers presented to the address lines of these chips.

The number of address pins on the CPU chip provides one limit to that range. All PCs fall into one of three categories based on this criterion.

Figure 14.2 shows these categories and which models of CPU chip fall in each group. It also shows the maximum size for the logical (or virtual) memory-address spaces. Whether or not a program can access the full range of the logical memory-address space depends upon the operating mode of the CPU chip, and the particular content of the GDT and LDT if the processor is running in one of the protected modes. (If you are not familiar with GDTs and LDTs, refer to Chapter 11.)

Category	Processor Type	Maximum Physical Memory	Maximum Virtual Memory
XT	8088 or 8086	1MB	1MB
AT	80286 or 386SX	16MB	1GB or 64TB
386	386DX or 486	4GB	64TB

Figure 14.2. Three PC categories according to the maximum size of their memory address spaces.

How the Bus Limits the Range of Possible Memory Addresses

The CPU is connected to the rest of your PC across a *bus*. This is a group of wires that carries three kinds of information. *Address information* flows out from the CPU to the memory chips being addressed. *Data* flows either out (during a "write" operation) or in (during a "read" operation). *Control signals* flow one way or the other, depending on their function, as shown in Figure 14.3.

In many PCs, the bus is split into a memory bus and an I/O bus. Typically, all the necessary control signals are supplied in both places so memory can be added on the I/O bus as well as on the memory bus. However, sometimes not all of the address lines will show up in the I/O bus, so the effective size of the memory address space on the I/O bus may be smaller than on the memory bus.

The Common PC Buses

The first PC had 20 address pins on its CPU, and the I/O bus in that machine had wires for each of them. In that machine, the bus did not limit the size of memory-address space. This was also true of all later models of the IBM *PC*, IBM *PC/XT*, and all the clones of those machines (that is, all PCs in classes 1 and 2).

Following are the common PC buses that will be discussed in the next few sections. Each of these buses has a different way in which it limits access to memory-address space.

- Industry Standard Architecture (ISA)

- Micro Channel Architecture (MCA)

- Extended Industry Standard Architecture (EISA)

- Personal Computer Memory Card International Association (PCMCIA) PC Card Interface

- Local Bus

- Proprietary Bus

Group	Names of pins	Direction → From CPU ← To CPU	Meaning
Data	D0 to D15	↔	Data lines
Address	SA0 to SA19	→	Address lines (latched)
	LA17 to LA23	→	Address lines (latchable)
Control	ALE	→	Address latch enable
	M/IO#	→	Memory or Input/Output
	R/W#	→	Read or Write
	MEMCS16#	←	16-bit data transfer is OK
	MEMR#	→	Memory Read
	MEMW#	→	Memory Write
	IOR#	→	I/O Read
	IOW#	→	I/O Write
	IRQ n	←	INT request (3-7,9-12,14-15)
	DMA n	→	DMA request (0-3, 5-7)
	DMA ACK n	←	DMA acknowledge (0-3,5-7)
	RESET	→	Reset all cards
	OSC	→	System clock (Oscillator)

Figure 14.3. The principal wires in the ISA bus showing which are in each group and what they mean (not all the control signals are shown here).

ISA

In the IBM *PC/AT,* the CPU chip has 24 address pins. The bus also was expanded, but only in certain I/O slots. This I/O bus became the standard for all the PC clones as well. It is called the *Industry Standard Architecture* bus, or ISA.

Figure 14.4 shows the full ISA slot connector, with its 16 data lines and 24 address lines. (Actually, counting both latched and unlatched address lines, there are more than 24 wires devoted to address information.)

PCs in classes 3 and 4 have this full bus in some slots. The rest of their slots and all the I/O slots in a class 1 or 2 PC have only the portion marked "8-bit section."

When the first 386DX-based PCs arrived on the market, they used the same bus as the IBM *PC/AT*, and this limited the size of the memory-address space that could be addressed across the bus. Another limitation of these buses was that to assure compatibility with all the plug-in cards made for earlier PCs, the maximum speed of signals in the I/O bus was limited to 8MHz (or, in some clones, 10MHz). This was significantly slower than the CPU in many of the newer PCs, not just those using 386 CPU chips, although the speed mismatch was worst for them.

MCA

When IBM introduced their new *PS/2* line of small computers, some models (50 and above) used a new bus called the *Micro Channel Architecture* (MCA) bus. This bus had physically incompatible slot connectors, allowing IBM to make a clean break with its past PC family of machines.

The MCA comes with several variations. One of the most important is the size of the bus data path, which can be either 16 or 32 bits. The address width also varies, with some versions carrying 24 address lines and others 32 lines. This bus is faster than the ISA bus, but it still can be slower than the fastest CPU chips, thus limiting the speed of access to memory across the bus.

Figure 14.5 shows the MCA slot connector as seen looking down on the motherboard. The two long pieces (top left and top right) actually form one long connector, joined where each is labeled "**KEY**." (The missing contact numbers, 46 and 47, represent the width of the notch for the key.) Some models of *PS/2* have an extension to one of their MCA slot connectors. The extension can take either one of two forms. One is called the *video* extension and the other is the *Matched Memory* extension. Whichever extension a slot may have, it will be added at the end of the slot connector toward the rear of the system unit, thus next to pins A01 and B01.

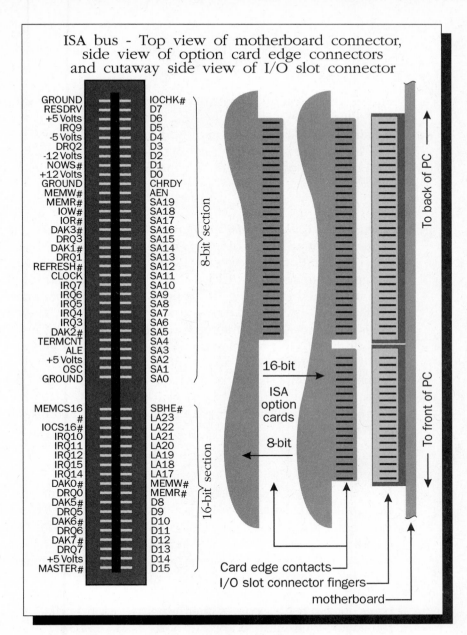

Figure 14.4. The Industry Standard Architecture (ISA) PC bus.

EISA

The clone makers banded together to create a response to the MCA. They devised the *Extended Industry Standard Architecture* (EISA) bus, a superset of the ISA bus. Like the full 32-bit version of the MCA, the EISA bus includes lines for a full 32 bits of data and a full 32 bits of addresses.

Figure 14.6 shows how the EISA slot connector can accommodate either a special EISA plug-in option card or a traditional ISA one. Figure 14.7 lists all the pins, distinguishing those that only an EISA card can connect to from those that both ISA and EISA cards engage.

PCMCIA PC Card

The *Personal Computer Memory Card International Association* (PCMCIA) has issued a standard describing how memory cards shall be built for PCs (and other applications). These credit-card-sized objects connect to the PC by plugging into a special PCMCIA PC card socket. That socket amounts to another important PC bus. It supports up to 26 bits of address and 16 bits of data. Since it has 26 address lines (two more than the ISA bus), it enables access to 64MB of memory-address space (2^2=4 times the ISA limit). (In addition to this 64MB memory address space, a PC card can have an "attribute memory" and an I/O port address space, each of which is potentially the same size as the main or "common memory" address space.) Figure 14.8 shows the general appearance of a PCMCIA PC Card and indicates the numbering for its connectors. Figure 14.9 lists the function of each pin.

Local Bus

In Chapter 6, you learned that a recent innovation in PC buses is something called the *Local Bus.* This is a bus from the CPU to one or more slots for special plug-in cards. What distinguishes this bus is that it carries all the same wires as, and works at the same speed as, the main CPU-to-memory bus. Thus, it imposes no limits on the address space beyond those imposed by the CPU.

Initially available only in a proprietary form from each PC manufacturer, local bus now comes in either of two standardized forms. The first to become well-defined and supported is the *VESA local bus*, or *VL-bus*. An alternate local bus standard is the Peripheral Component Interface, or PCI bus.

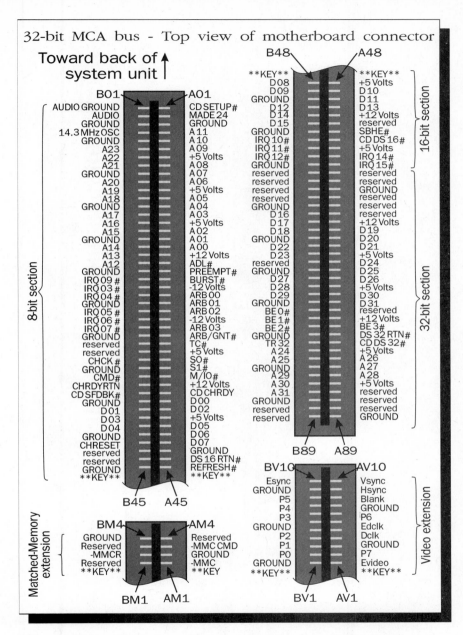

Figure 14.5. The Micro Channel Architecture (MCA) PC bus.

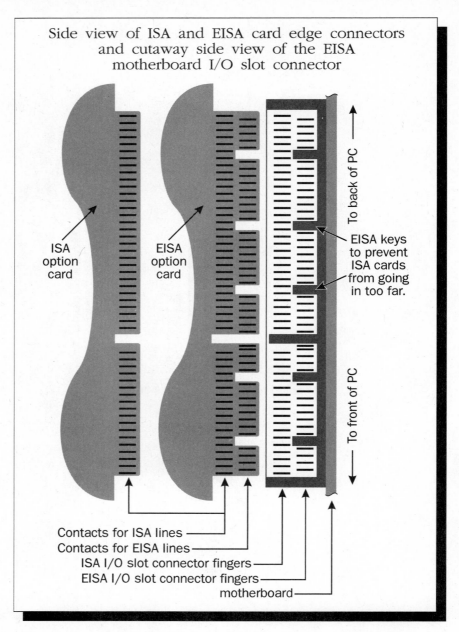

Figure 14.6. The Extended Industry Standard Architecture (EISA) PC bus connector with ISA and EISA cards.

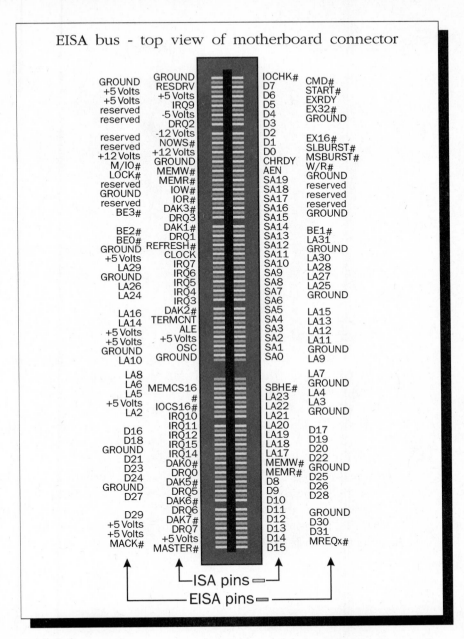

Figure 14.7. The EISA bus connector showing the ISA and EISA lines in the connector.

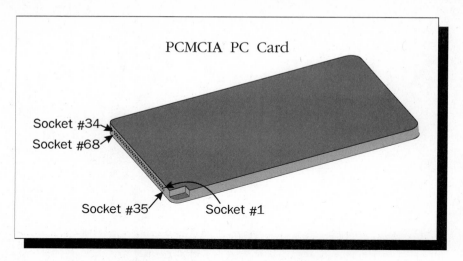

Figure 14.8. PCMCIA PC card showing how pins are numbered.

Proprietary Buses

Anytime the CPU is faster or has more address or data lines than the I/O bus (or the local bus, if the motherboard has one), it makes sense to have a *proprietary memory bus* as well. This is a place where additional memory can be added and where it will be accessible to the CPU at the full speed of main RAM, and over the whole of the CPU's memory-address space.

Not all PCs that could benefit from such a bus have one, but many do. The problem with such buses is that they are proprietary. No two manufacturers of PC clones make them in quite the same way. That means that the owners of these clone PCs are stuck buying memory cards from the manufacturer of the PC (or in a few cases, from third-party vendors), usually at a premium price. The Local Bus is an attempt to overcome this objection while maintaining all the advantages of those proprietary buses.

PCMCIA PC Card
Memory Card Pin Definitions

Pin No.	Signal Name	Function	Pin No.	Signal Name	Function
1	GND	Ground	35	GND	Ground
2	D3	Data bit 3	36	CD1	Card Detect
3	D4	Data bit 4	37	D11	Data bit 11
4	D5	Data bit 5	38	D12	Data bit 12
5	D6	Data bit 6	39	D13	Data bit 13
6	D7	Data bit 7	40	D14	Data bit 14
7	CE1#	Card Enable	41	D15	Data bit 15
8	A10	Address bit 10	42	CE2	Card Enable
9	OE#	Output Enable	43	RFSH	Refresh
10	A11	Address bit 11	44	RFU	reserved
11	A9	Address bit 9	45	RFU	reserved
12	A8	Address bit 8	46	A17	Address bit 17
13	A13	Address bit 13	47	A18	Address bit 18
14	A14	Address bit 14	48	A19	Address bit 19
15	WE/PGM#	Write Enable	49	A20	Address bit 20
16	RDY/BSY	Ready/Busy	50	A21	Address bit 21
17	Vcc	Power	51	Vcc	Power
18	Vpp1	Prog. Voltage1	52	Vpp2	Prog. Voltage2
19	A16	Address bit 16	53	A22	Address bit 22
20	A15	Address bit 15	54	A23	Address bit 23
21	A12	Address bit 12	55	A24	Address bit 24
22	A7	Address bit 7	56	A25	Address bit 25
23	A6	Address bit 6	57	RFU	reserved
24	A5	Address bit 5	58	RESET	Card Reset
25	A4	Address bit 4	59	WAIT	Extend bus cycle
26	A3	Address bit 3	60	RFU	reserved
27	A2	Address bit 2	61	REG	Register Select
28	A1	Address bit 1	62	BVD2	Batt.Volt.Detect2
29	A0	Address bit 0	63	BVD1	Batt.Volt.Detect1
30	D0	Data bit 0	64	D8	Data bit 8
31	D1	Data bit 1	65	D9	Data bit 9
32	D2	Data bit 2	66	D10	Data bit 10
33	WP	Write Protect	67	CD2	Card Detect
34	GND	Ground	68	GND	Ground

Figure 14.9. PCMCIA PC card Memory Card pin designations.

RAM and ROM Are
Very Different from Disk Storage

RAM stands for *Random-Access Memory* and usually is used to refer to memory locations that can have information written to them as well as read from them. ROM, which means *Read-Only Memory,* is a special kind of RAM, but it is not normally what is meant when RAM is mentioned. Both of these are electronic information storage places and work very fast. RAM (other than ROM) loses its contents once power is removed from the chips. (ROMs don't forget, but neither can they remember anything new, just whatever information was originally manufactured into them.)

Disk storage is usually magnetic in nature and involves moving parts. It allows for read-write storage that is persistent (when power is off). Disk storage is thousands of times slower than electronic memory chips.

Because of these differing characteristics, RAM, ROM, and disk storage are used for three different purposes in PCs. RAM is scratch-pad memory, a place for the CPU to put programs and data while it is working with them. ROM holds programs or data that are unchanging and must always be available in an instant. Disk storage is where most programs and data that are used in RAM get stored long-term.

Typically, your PC will have a few megabytes of RAM, a small fraction of a megabyte of ROM, and many megabytes of disk storage space. Figure 14.10 shows a whimsical representation of the difference between memory (RAM) and disk storage to help you keep the distinction clear in your mind.

Not All Memory Is Created Equal

Portions of your CPU's memory-address space have RAM in them. Other portions have ROM. Still other portions may be empty.

Not all regions of memory within your PC are of equal value to you. In particular, the first megabyte of the CPU's memory-address space is special. It is all that DOS knows about.

Figure 14.10. A scratch pad is like memory (RAM), as compared with a warehouse, which is like disk storage.

The Five Kinds of RAM in a PC Where Programs May Reside

There are five kinds of RAM in a PC where programs may reside. Each has its own special characteristics. They are:

- Lower, system, or conventional memory
- Upper memory
- High memory
- Extended memory
- Expanded memory

Of the first megabyte, the first 640KB (which is called *lower, system, or conventional* memory) is extra special. That is where programs normally go in RAM managed by DOS.

Upper memory, the region from 640KB to 1MB, was reserved by IBM for video-image-buffer RAM, various ROMs, and other uses. Often at least some of that space is empty. When that is the case, if you can make some RAM appear there, it can be used for additional programs. Doing that requires the assistance of some extra hardware or special memory management software. Which you need depends on which class of PC you have.

High memory is real mode memory between 1,024KB and 1,088KB (less 16 bytes). You won't have this unless you have a class 3 or higher PC and more than 640KB of RAM installed. If you meet those conditions, and if you run a special program that can disable memory address wrapping in accordance with the XMS standard, then the High Memory Area (HMA) becomes available for program use.

Extended memory is all the RAM you have which is accessible at physical memory locations in the CPU's memory-address space above 1MB. The first 64KB of extended memory are the same set of memory locations as the HMA. The difference is that the HMA is accessible in real mode, while extended memory is only accessible in protected mode.

The CPU can directly access all of the lower, upper, high, and extended memory, provided it is operating in the correct mode (and in the case of high memory, provided address wrapping is disabled). DOS manages the uses of lower memory. The XMS standard describes how to manage upper, high, and extended memory. A memory manager written to conform to XMS also has knowledge of how to enable and disable address wrapping. Using that and DOS allows access and management of all the RAM in your PC that can be used for programs, with one exception.

The one exception is *expanded (EMS) memory*. This is memory that is not in the CPU's memory-address space, but which may be brought into that space a page (16KB) at a time, as needed. EMS memory, in this sense, is only available to you if you have a special EMS memory card installed and have loaded an expanded memory manager (EMM) device driver. It is sometimes possible to create what appears to be EMS memory from some extended memory by use of special features of your PC's system logic, or by running a LIMulator program. Some LIMulator programs can also use some disk storage space to create the illusion of EMS memory. (See Chapter 9 for more details on this.)

Other RAM

PCs sometimes have other RAM that is not of the previous five kinds. Examples include RAM buffers on a network interface card, a hard disk controller, or buffers in a printer or other peripheral device. Those RAM locations can only be used by the devices they are on, not by your CPU. That is memory that will not directly be a part of the story this book tells about memory management in your PC.

Speed Issues for Memory

Not all memory is equally quick. Sometimes the issue is the basic speed with which the memory chips themselves can respond. How fast the CPU can get information to or from those chips is also important.

Video buffer memory is often inaccessible to the CPU most of the time, because it is being used by the video output circuitry. That makes its apparent speed much lower than the rest of RAM, as shown in Figure 14.11. ROMs also are often slower than main RAM, although that does not show in Figure 14.11. The reason is that in this PC, the ROMs have been "shadowed" by using some of the main RAM, and thus appear to be just as fast as main RAM. (See Chapter 20 for a full discussion of shadow RAM.)

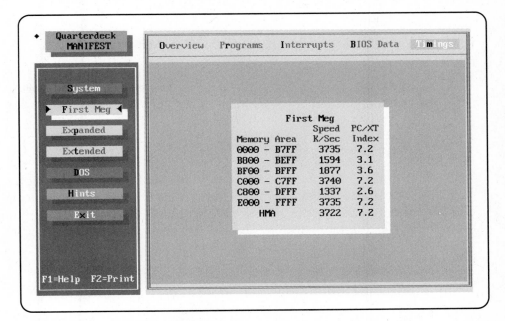

Figure 14.11. RAM and ROM speeds may vary.

Memory on the motherboard typically is connected to the CPU via a memory bus that runs as fast as the CPU (or half as fast in the case of DX 2 processsors—in any case much faster than the I/O bus for fast PCs). Memory installed on a card in the I/O bus may not be accessible nearly as quickly. The maximum clock speed on the bus provides one speed limit. The number of data lines provides another.

Accessing extended memory on an 80286-based PC presents special problems. If your program is running in real mode, such accesses require that you switch into protected mode and back again. The latter switch is particularly slow.

From even this brief discussion of the different kinds of RAM in a PC, you may have realized that the speed with which you can access RAM can limit your PC's performance. So can the speed of access to disk storage. Luckily, there are steps you can take that greatly mitigate those limits. What those steps are, and how you can take them, is the subject of the next section. It is all about caching, what it is, how it works, how memory and disk caches differ, and why you probably want to have both in your PC if you can.

A Memory Cache Is Not a Disk Cache

Both memory caching and disk caching can be very useful. It is important that you know what they are, and even more so that you be very clear about how they differ.

What Is a Cache?

In general, a *cache* is a temporary holding place for information on its way to or from somewhere else. If the process of transferring information in or out of its source can go much more quickly than transferring it in or out of its destination, parking it briefly in a cache can make a lot of sense.

Memory Cache

A *memory cache* is a small amount of very fast RAM that, effectively, sits between the CPU and the main system RAM. If the RAM in the memory cache and the CPU are equally fast, and both are much faster than the main system RAM, and if the information that gets stored in the memory cache is well-managed, then this structure can let the CPU keep working at full speed much more of the time than would otherwise be the case.

Any PC could have a memory cache, but it is only useful in PCs in which the CPU is much faster than the RAM chips in main memory. As it happens, that is the case for almost any PC in which the clock speed is 20MHz or higher.

Every 486- or Pentium-based PC has a memory cache built into the CPU chip. Many of them also have a *secondary memory cache* on the motherboard. (That means the CPU communicates with the on-chip primary cache, which communicates with the secondary cache, which communicates with main system RAM.) Many of the faster 386 systems also have a memory cache built onto their motherboards.

How a Memory Cache Can Help

Whenever the CPU seeks to read from a memory address, if the information it desires has been copied to the cache, it will be supplied to the CPU almost instantly. If, instead, the information must be brought from main memory, it may take much longer. The CPU will be idle while it is waiting for that information to arrive. So repeated reading of the same information can be greatly speeded by a cache.

Repeated writing of the same information to the same memory location can also be speeded up in much the same way. The term "cache hit" describes anytime information in the cache allows the CPU to skip a memory access cycle. The rest of the times are called "cache misses." The percentage of hits is called the cache hit rate, and it is a measure of the effectiveness of the cache. (Sometimes the ratio of hits to misses is quoted instead.) Since the degree of redundancy in the information being read or written depends on the program that is running, any cache's effectiveness will vary. Cache hit ratios can be as high as 90 percent in favorable circumstances, and the hit percentage rarely falls below 50 percent. So a cache will typically speed average accesses by a factor of two to ten. (This assumes that the CPU and cache are both much faster than main RAM.)

Disk Cache

A disk cache is similar in concept. It is located between main memory and your disk drives. Electronic memory is always tremendously faster than any rotating mechanical system like a magnetic disk drive. So a disk cache is always a useful addition to a PC. Figure 14.12 shows schematically how a disk cache and a memory cache differ.

Later in this chapter, in the section "How to Get a Disk Cache in Your PC," you'll learn the steps you must take to get these benefits. First, though, you need to decide what sort of cache you want. To decide that, you need to understand what the possibilities are and the advantages and disadvantages of each.

Various Cache Strategies— Choosing What Information to Cache

The general notion of a cache is simple enough. However, how you decide what information to store in the cache and how you make sure it stays up-to-date are much more difficult issues.

There are several strategies used in creating and controlling an information cache. They differ in their complexity and performance. The cheapest to build, unfortunately, are also the least effective. (Oh well, that is probably what you expected.) Here is a brief description of several common cache strategies.

While in many of these descriptions there may be an emphasis on how that kind of cache applies to disk caching, almost all the arguments also apply to memory caching. The reason for emphasizing disk caching in a book about PC memory is that one of the best uses for memory is as a disk cache under control of a disk cache program. Memory caching can't be added to a PC; you have to get a new motherboard to get memory caching if your PC doesn't already have that feature. (On the other hand, if you do have a memory cache, you may be able to increase its size. Some, but by no means all, memory cache circuits include some empty RAM sockets for just that purpose.)

A Simple Buffer

The simplest version of caching is a *simple buffer*. For disk caching this is a single region of memory in which the most recently read information from the disk is kept. This speeds things up because you only stop to read the disk each time you need a new buffer-full of information. And the time it takes to read that buffer of information is about the same as reading just one byte from the disk.

Another disk buffer is used to assemble a package of information which then is sent to the disk all at once. DOS provides disk buffers for just these purposes. The usual size of a disk buffer is 512 bytes, the same size as a sector of disk storage space.

Caching Reads, but Not Writes

The next improvement is to have the buffer region used to hold recently read information divided up into many parts. Each one contains the results of one read from the disk. Each time your program wishes to read some information from the disk, DOS will first check the several different regions of the read cache to see if the information is already on hand. If it is, the disk read delay can be avoided. If it is not, then you must wait for the disk read and, when the data arrives, one of the regions in the read cache will have its contents overwritten with the new data.

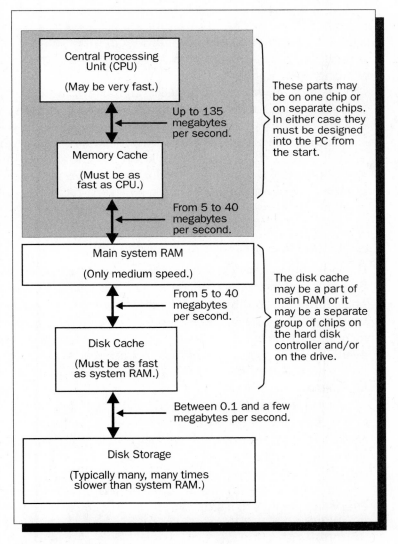

Figure 14.12. Memory caching versus disk caching.

529

The reason this strategy can be so effective is that repeated reading of the same information is very common in most computer programs. Instructions often are organized into loops and the CPU must reread each of those instructions every time it goes through that loop. Likewise, some lookup tables get referenced over and over again.

A Read-Ahead Cache

The next improvement is to tell the circuitry that controls the cache to anticipate what information may be needed and try to have it ready and waiting in the cache.

The usual way this is done is that whenever one sector on a disk must be read, several additional ones also get read. Usually, the extra sectors are the rest of the sectors on that same disk track, as those are the ones most quickly available. This reading ahead may be able to proceed in parallel with the CPU's regular work if the cache filling is not controlled by the CPU but by the cache controller circuitry (as is the case when the cache is on a disk controller, or when a software cache uses DMA data transfers).

A Write-Through Read and Write Cache

It is possible in many systems to further increase performance by caching writes as well as reads. This is called a *Read and Write Cache.* This provides an additional speedup that is smaller than the one obtained from simply read caching, since repeated writes of the same information to the same locations are rarer than repeated reading of the same information. But still, doing both helps more than just caching reads.

There are two strategies that can be used. The more conservative one is called a *write-through cache.* When a write-through cache is used, the first time some information is to be written to a given location, it is written there and a copy of it is stored in the cache. The next time that the same information is to be written to the same location, the fact that it already exists in the cache (called a *cache hit*) shows that it need not be written again to the destination.

Each time the information to be written is not found in the cache, everything comes to a stop (briefly) while the information gets written to the destination and the cache.

There is a subtle danger in any write caching system. Unfortunately, it is not always dealt with properly. For instance, you could try to write some information to a ROM or even to a memory address location without any memory (which could be called a location in a WOM! See the definition in Chapter 6). If you do this and the cache controller is not aware of the nature of the destination, it may keep a copy of what you tried to write in the cache.

If you try to read from that location a short time later, your program will find the information you tried to write still in the cache. It will be returned to your program as if that were what was actually at that location. Of course, it is not. Much later, after that region of the cache has been reused, an attempt to read that location will return whatever is in the ROM (or something unpredictable if it was in WOM).

The only way this can be dealt with effectively is to tell the cache controller in advance that those locations must not be cached for writing. It is both acceptable, and in the case of slow ROMs, very desirable to cache reads from those locations. The design of the 386, 486, and Pentium includes a mechanism for marking pages of physical memory as not cacheable, but not all PCs use that feature as they should.

A Write-Deferred Read and Write Cache

A more dramatic speedup of your system can be achieved if you use a read and write cache that implements something called *deferred writes*. This means that whenever information is to be written to some location, it is merely written to the cache. Then the cache controller has the job of determining if it also needs to be written to the ultimate destination, and if so, it will do so as soon as it can, but in the meantime, the computer will be going about its other business. Thus, it will appear as if every write takes essentially no time at all! That is the ultimate in cache speedup of writes.

This strategy can be used both for memory caches and for disk caches. Since you never wait for writes to take place, the speedup can be enormous. But there is a dark side to this that you must be aware of.

If for some reason your PC gets "hung" or you lose power, then any information that had been written to the cache, but not yet copied to its ultimate location, is lost. That is not a problem with a memory cache, as all the information in main memory also gets lost. But it can be a serious problem with a disk cache.

If you are using a hardware disk cache (with the cache RAM on the disk controller) there is a distinction between the situation in which the CPU gets "hung" and when you lose power. In the former case, the disk controller will continue to write information to the disk drive. But in the latter case, of course, it will not.

Many programs carefully structure their disk writes to be sure that each entire transaction gets written to disk in its entirety or not at all. These protective schemes can be totally frustrated by a write-deferred cache, as the program will think that anything written to the cache is on the disk, but it only gets to the disk whenever the cache controller gets around to putting it there.

If you are going to use a write-deferred disk cache, at least be aware that you may corrupt your files whenever you reboot or lose power. Critical disk systems (for example, those on a network file server) must not use this approach unless they also use an *Uninterruptible Power Supply (UPS)*. Preferably, the UPS should have some power failure detection hardware to signal when input power is lost, and suitable software running on the server to monitor that signal and shut down the network gracefully.

Cache Strategies— How to Find Information in the Cache

Up to this point, the description of the various cache strategies has focused on which information should be kept in the cache. How the cache controller finds information that is in the cache was glossed over.

Practically by definition, the cache memory is always smaller in size than the slower target information storage region it is used to support. So you can't keep a copy of everything that might show up during a read or a write in the cache. Eventually, you'll run out of room. Therefore, some strategy is needed to choose which items to keep where and how to find them again as they are needed.

There are three major strategies that can be used:

- A fully associative cache

- A set associative cache

- A direct mapped cache

The better memory caches in PCs use a version of the set-associative strategy, as a compromise between cost and performance. Most commonly these are either *two-way* or *four-way set associative* caches. The cheaper PCs with cache use only a *direct mapped* cache. Most disk cache vendors will not tell you what strategy they use.

A cache sits between two places that information may reside. It helps to think of one as an **information repository** (the slow side) and the other as an **information consumer and creator** (the fast side).

The cache itself stores a collection of data items and some part or all of the addresses associated with each one. The job of the cache controller is to keep each data item in the cache up-to-date (or else to mark it as "invalid"). Keeping it up-to-date means making sure that the same data are, in fact, contained at each cache location and whatever place it is supposed to be representing in the information repository.

Each time the information consumer sends some information to the repository (a write operation), what arrives at the cache is a data item (some bytes of information to be stored) and an associated repository address. Each time the consumer wishes to read from the repository, it will send to the cache just the repository address. The cache will respond with the data. It gets that data item either from within itself (a cache hit) or from the repository. This is diagrammed in Figure 14.13.

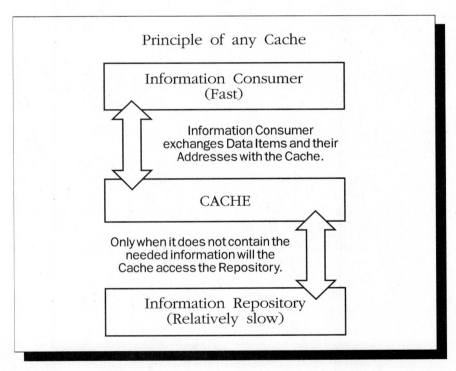

Figure 14.13. A cache mediates between a fast information consumer and a slower information repository.

Fully Associative Cache

Now consider the strategy for a *fully associative read and write cache*. This is the most effective of the three cache strategies, but it also is the most difficult (and expensive) to implement.

Each time the information consumer sends an address with a request to *read* from that address to the cache, the cache controller scans through its entire collection of cached items to see if one of them has the requested address. If so, it supplies that item to the consumer and the transaction is complete. If not, the cache controller will go to the repository, retrieve the requested information, and pass it on to the consumer. The cache will also overwrite the oldest item in its collection with the data item just retrieved from the repository and its associated address, as shown in Figure 14.14. Notice that each data item stored in the cache has its full address stored with it. (This figure was drawn for a cache that stores two-byte data items that may come from anywhere in a repository with 16MB total capacity. That means it has 8M two-byte locations, hence the 23-bit address.)

When the information consumer wants to *write* information to the repository, it sends both the data item and its associated address to the cache. The controller now scans its whole collection, looking for a matching address. There are three possible results. One is that it will find matching data and a matching address. Two, it may find a matching address but no matching data. Finally, it may fail to find a matching address.

In the first case, the cache controller knows the repository already holds the desired data at that address, so it just informs the consumer that the transaction is complete. In the second case, it must send the data and address on to the repository for storage. It will also update the data it has stored for that address in the cache. In the third case, it will send the data item and address to the repository for storage. It will also overwrite the oldest data item and address it has stored with the ones just sent to the repository.

The only difference between a fully associative *write-through* read and write cache and a fully associative *write-deferred* read and write cache is whether the information consumer is forced to wait until the cache is finished writing to the repository, or whether the information consumer is allowed to continue with its work in parallel with the writing to the repository.

This is the most effective and the most expensive kind of cache. A small part of the expense is that it takes more RAM to store the full address of each data item along with the item. The greater part of the expense comes from the need to search every address stored in the cache each time. That implies doing a whole lot of comparisons. To make it able to do all of these comparisons quickly enough requires many separate comparison circuits, and that is expensive.

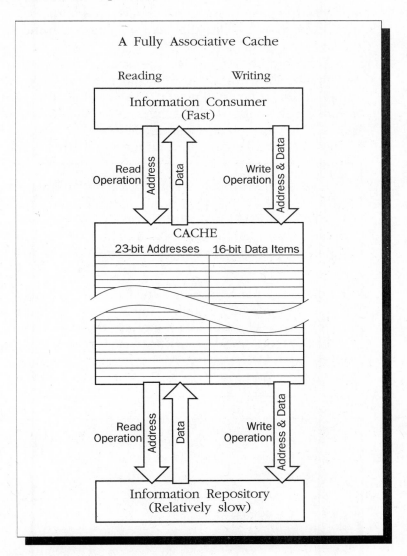

Figure 14.14. A fully associative cache.

A Direct Mapping Cache

The opposite extreme would be a ***direct mapped read and write cache***. This is how it works.

Each time an address arrives at the cache (whether it has a data item along with it or not), the address is broken into two parts. The least significant portion is called the *index*. The most significant portion is called the *tag* (see Figure 14.15).

For example, suppose you are sending 16-bit data items to a repository in a 16MB memory-address space. This can be addressed as 8M of 16-bit words, so you will need to have a 23-bit address to specify each location. Further, suppose the cache is able to store 64KB of data items (which is 32K 16-bit items) and their associated addresses. In this case, each 23-bit address is broken into a 15-bit index and an 8-bit tag.

It may seem odd, but normally this is how the size of cache memory is quoted. Only the RAM needed to store the data items gets mentioned. The RAM needed to store the tags is not counted. In the present example, the tags take up almost half as much RAM as the data. In a more practical design, the fraction of RAM used for the tag is much less.

If you have a memory cache which can be expanded it is because the RAM chips already installed that are devoted to storing tags can do so for more cache locations than there those for which RAM chips are installed. You can add more fast RAM chips up to the point at which all the tag RAM is utilized. At that point you will have run out of cache expansion room.

One way to make the tags take up much less of the total cache RAM is to use larger data items. The 486 uses 16-byte data items instead of the 2-byte ones used in the example just described.

Using longer data items will, of course, mean that there will be fewer of them in the cache (assuming you have a fixed amount of cache RAM). But larger data items also mean you don't need to address as many places in main memory. The result is that the number of bits in the index decreases by the same amount as the number of bits in the total address. So the number of tag bits per data item stays the same.

Using the same example but with 16-byte data items, the 64KB cache (data) memory would hold only 4K data items. So the index need only be 12 bits long, and you can access memory in 16-byte groups so you only need 20 bits of address. Once again the tags will be 8 bits long. However, you now are storing only one eighth as much tag information as data instead of half as much, as was the case before.

The cache stores data items and their tags. It doesn't hold the entire address from each data item. When the cache is searched, only one item gets looked at—the one pointed to by the index.

So in effect, a direct mapped cache can be thought of as a large number of tiny, independent caches. Each tiny cache stores only one data item (and its tag). Each address in the repository corresponds to just one of the tiny caches. If the tag is n-bits long, there will be 2^n places in the repository corresponding to each location in the cache. In our example, each of the 32K cache locations is associated with its own, unique set of 256 locations in the repository. Within each of these tiny caches, the same strategies apply as do for the fully associative cache.

A cache with room to store only one data item would seem completely ineffective, but it is not. If that one item gets read and reread many times before another item in the set of items associated with that particular tiny cache gets read, then the cache has a chance to do you a lot of good. Since each of the tiny caches serves a limited set of locations, and since they are all well spaced away from one another, in many circumstances this sort of cache works quite well.

A direct mapped cache is much simpler and less expensive to build than a fully associative one. First, you are not storing the entire location for each data item in the cache, only its value and its tag's value. But of much more importance, you do not have to look at every item in the cache each time. You only look at one location; the one pointed to by the index.

A Set Associative Cache

There is a middle ground between the fully associative cache and the direct mapped cache. It is called the *set-associative cache.* Consider the most common of those used in PCs, a **4-way set associative read and write cache.**

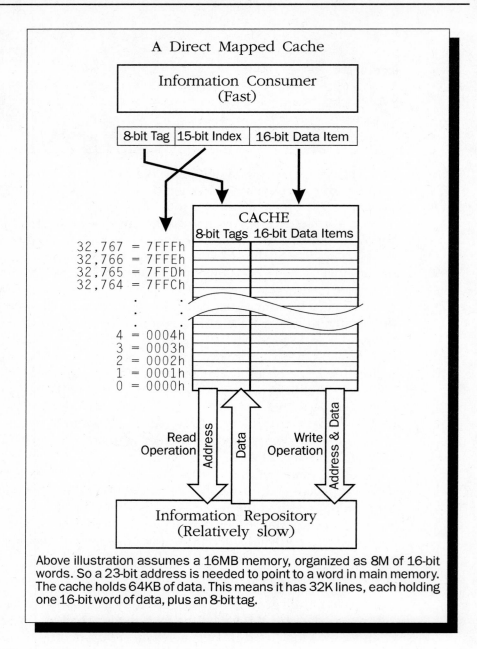

Figure 14.15. A direct mapped cache.

As in the case of the direct mapped cache, the addresses arriving at the cache are divided into a tag and an index. The difference is that now you will store not just one data item and its tag for a given index, but four items and their tags. That means that you must divide the cache memory into four equal parts. So for a given amount of fast RAM, you can only store data items for one quarter as many index values.

For the example case, that means you divide the 23-bit address into a 10-bit tag and a 13-bit index. The 64K data item cache can now be thought of as 8K tiny caches, each fully associative and each holding just four data items (with their associated tags). Figure 14.16 shows how this cache differs from the other two.

Figure 14.17 further clarifies how, in either the direct-mapped or set-associative cache designs, the information repository gets broken up into numerous smaller collections of data, each one cached independently. In that figure, you see the 8M addresses in the example repository listed both in decimal and hexidecimal. The hex numbers have been broken into two parts to show explicitly what the tag and index values are for each location. Since programs normally access memory or disk storage in a restricted region, most accesses will be to locations with the same or nearby tag values, but the accesses will be widely spread across the range of index values. If all the accesses are within one tag value region, the direct mapped or set associative cache will work exactly as efficiently as the fully associative design, and yet it will require much less hardware complexity in its construction.

The only subtlety not discussed so far concerns the set associative cache and how to decide which member of a four-member set to discard when you must overwrite one with some new information. Probably, the best method would be to discard the data item in the set that hasn't been accessed for the longest amount of time. However, doing that accurately requires storing more information and doing more comparisons than the benefits justify. So an approximation of the data item that hasn't been accessed in the longest amount of time is used instead.

Building such a set-associative cache takes a bit more effort than building the simple direct mapped cache, but it will perform much better—enough so that it frequently justifies the extra cost. This is the sort of cache that is built into the 486 for data, and into both the 386 and 486 for the Translation Lookaside Buffers. (See Chapter 11 for a definition of the Translation Lookaside Buffers.)

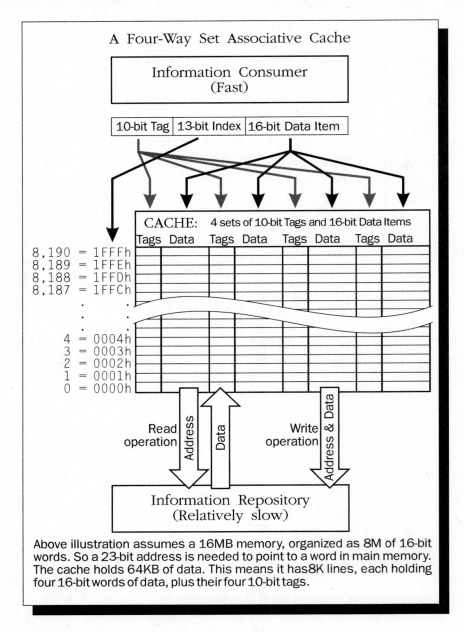

Figure 14.16.   A four-way set associative cache.

How the Index values distribute the information repository data items among the lines of cache memory

This illustration assumes a 16MB information repository (e.g., main RAM), organized as 8M of 16-bit words. A 23-bit address is needed to point to each word in this repository. The cache holds 64KB of data organized as 8K lines, each line holding four 16-bit words plus their tags. This means the index values are 13-bits long (to be able to address the 8K lines in the cache) and the tags are 10-bits long (the rest of the 23-bit addresses of the data items).

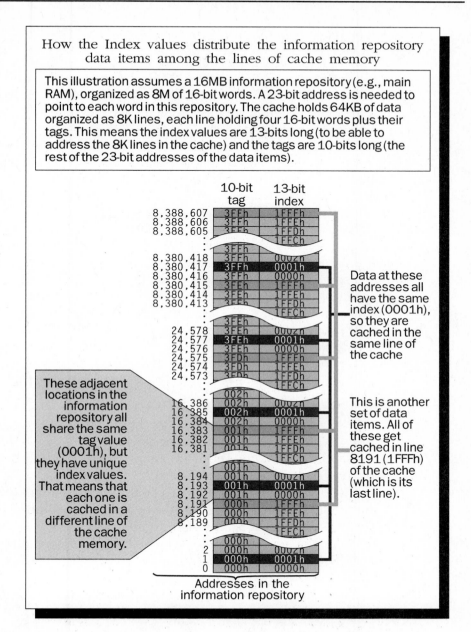

Figure 14.17. How an information repository gets allocated to cache lines in a direct mapped or set associative cache.

How to Get a Disk Cache in Your PC

There are two ways to get a disk cache in a PC. One is to install a caching disk controller card. (This is called a *hardware disk cache*.) The other way is to install a disk cache program. (This is called a *software disk cache*.) The first way costs a whole lot more than the second and, surprisingly, it may not be that much more effective.

The software disk cache works by taking over some of your RAM for its purposes. If you have a lot of extended or expanded memory that you are not now using, that could be the very best way to put it to use. (If you are using DOS 5 or 6, the MEM/C command will show how much memory you have and how much is free.)

Frequently, and especially on a single-user system, a good software disk cache will even out-perform a hardware one. Furthermore, the memory used by the disk cache can, if you have a suitable disk cache program, serve double duty as a printer buffer or get loaned temporarily to programs that need a little extra RAM. Those are certainly things you cannot do with the RAM on a caching disk controller card.

If you want the ultimate in disk caching, you will want to use both a software and a hardware disk cache. But realize that you are going to pay much more for only slightly faster disk access.

Some Software Disk Cache Options

The simplest form of disk caching is provided by the DOS disk buffers. In your CONFIG.SYS file, you can specify how many 512-byte buffers you want DOS to maintain. These are simple buffers giving you the lowest performance caching, but they are better than nothing.

If you don't have any other cache installed, you will want to have a line in your CONFIG.SYS file that reads BUFFERS=30, although the number may be other than 30. A larger number will let DOS do a better job of caching information. But it does so at substantial cost in terms of RAM usage. (Each time you increase this BUFFERS= line by one, you use up approximately 1/2KB.)

If you are using DOS 5 or 6, you may not be affected as much by such a line, but only if you also have a line in your CONFIG.SYS file that reads DOS=HIGH. This line directs DOS to load as much of itself into the High Memory Area as it can. It will also load the DOS buffers there if they will fit. Usually, about 35 disk buffers will fit in the HMA (along with the portion of DOS that goes there). Use MEM/D to see exactly how much lower memory is being used for BUFFERS. If it shows only 512 bytes are used by BUFFERS (this will be shown as 000200h by MEM in DOS 5), then you know your buffers are in the HMA.

To add a software disk cache to your system, you must first get the program and install it on your hard disk. Then, if the install program did not already do so, you'll have to add a line to either your CONFIG.SYS or AUTOEXEC.BAT file to activate the cache each time you boot your PC. Check the documentation for the cache you'll be using to find out which file you must modify and precisely how.

> **Warning**   Never, ever have two or more software disk cache programs active at once. You can lose data if you do.

Even if you are using a software disk cache program, you will still need at least a few DOS buffers. Consult the documentation that came with your disk cache program for a recommended value.

> **Be Aware of This**   A few programs expect to find a large number of DOS buffers and will complain or misbehave if they don't find them, even though you have a more effective cache program installed.

The next step up in software disk cache programs is probably Microsoft's *SMARTDrive.* That program is included with every copy of *Windows, MS-DOS* or *PC DOS*, version 5 or 6, While the DOS 5 version of this program was a dog compared to the industry leaders, such as *Super PC-Kwik,* the DOS 6 version of SMARTdrive is a very respectable disk cache program. In any event, it is much better than just using the DOS buffers.

There are many commercial disk cache programs that are wonderful. Chapter 30 lists several.

You can control how a software disk cache program will work, at least to a degree, by the way you set it up. The line you add to your CONFIG.SYS or AUTOEXEC.BAT file can invoke the program and also give it some instructions about how you want it to do its job. (Chapter 20 details the various kinds of line you can have those files.)

Typically those instructions consist of some combination of numbers, often referred to as *command line parameters*, and what are called *command line switches*. A switch is a forward slash character (/) followed by one or more numbers or letters or other symbols. Just which parameters and switches are valid for any particular program are spelled out in its documentation.

Super PC-Kwik is the most popular commercial software disk cache. Its file name is SUPERPCK.EXE and it gets installed by a line in your AUTOEXEC.BAT file. By default, it will take all of your expanded memory for the cache. You can limit how much it takes, or direct it to use extended memory, or even tell it to use lower memory. (This latter choice is usually not a good idea if you have any expanded or extended memory available.)

Besides those basic choices, *Super PC-Kwik* offers over three dozen documented options (and a number of undocumented ones). Some are toggles; they can only be turned on or off. Others accept a numeric value to specify how much of some feature you want. Taken together, all these choices permit literally more than a million million (10^{12}) possible ways to set up the program. Of course, you can ignore all of them and then the program will use its default values. Finding the very best way to configure this program for your needs can take some experimentation and careful consideration of the suggestions in the manual that comes with that program.

A Warning About Disk Caches and Large Swap Files

In Chapter 9, in the section describing how a virtual memory system may use some of your disk space as if it were memory, you learned about a subtle interaction between a large swap file and a disk cache. Now that you are focused on disk caches, it may be a good time to go back and re-read that section.

How to Get a Memory Cache in Your PC

There is really only one way to get a memory cache in a PC. You must buy a PC that includes that feature. It must be included at the time the motherboard is designed. Some PCs come with provisions for a cache, but you will only get one if you buy and install the extra RAM chips and a cache controller chip.

The Problem of Cache Coherence

In describing the details of how a cache works, the point was made that the main job of the cache controller is to be sure the contents of the cache at all times accurately reflects the contents of the corresponding locations in the slower information repository. If every change in the repository's information comes through the cache, this is not a hard task.

What can make maintaining this "cache coherency" or "cache synchronization" tough is when information comes from other sources to the repository and doesn't go through the cache. In your PC, you have two such potential sources for changes in memory contents that don't go through the memory cache.

Every model of PC except the IBM *PC Jr* has a *DMA chip*. This **Direct Memory Access** controller is a subsidiary processor whose sole function is to move blocks of information from one region of memory to another, from a region of memory to a port, or from a port to a region of memory. It does that job as directed by the CPU, but it does the job independently of the CPU. Naturally, this can change information that is stored in memory without each change flowing through the memory cache.

The second source of independent changes to the contents of memory is any *alternate bus master.* Early PCs have only one master processor, and that is the CPU. Later models, especially those with MCA or EISA buses, have incorporated support for multiple bus masters. This means you can have several "central" processing units, each equally capable of being in charge. They must negotiate among themselves to decide which one is going to be in charge of the bus at any moment, but that priority can change over time.

This means that memory contents can be changed, as it were, "behind the back" of the cache controller. The only effective way to deal with this is to give the cache controller the ability to "snoop the bus." That means it watches every bus access. If the address at which a write is about to take place corresponds to a data item in the cache, the controller will mark that item in its cache storage as "invalid."

There are several variations on this approach, but they only differ in how the valid/invalid information is stored or manipulated. All memory caches must have some such mechanism, or it is unsafe to use in an environment like a PC, where multiple information consumers (for example, the CPU, DMA controller, and alternate bus masters) could be altering the contents of the cached repositories of information (in particular, the PC's main RAM).

Unlike the case of main RAM, in most PCs the disk drive is an information repository with only one "door." That is, all accesses to the disk can normally be forced to go through a disk cache, whether it is in hardware or software. Thus, unless you have a very unusual system with shared access to a disk drive from two PCs over a SCSI or other network, you are not likely to run into this problem with a disk cache.

A Self-Test on Memory and PC Fundamentals

This and the previous eight chapters presented many ideas, some of them possibly quite confusing to you. To be sure you are clear about the ones that will be most essential, read over the following list of topics and questions.

If you find that you are unsure about your knowledge of any of them, perhaps you should go back and reread some sections before you plunge ahead. Or, at least be alert to the possibility that you may need to do so as you go further into the book and find something there that confuses you.

Also, to reward you for reading this test, even if you turn out to know all the topics perfectly, there is a small amount of new information thrown in.

1. What is the difference between input/output ports and memory locations? (Review in the section titled "Sending Messages to More Remote Places" in Chapter 6.)

2. Memory versus disk storage; what are the fundamental differences and how can they be blurred by virtual memory and virtual disks? (Review in the section titled "The Several Kinds of Memory and Storage in Our PCs" in Chapter 6.)

3. There are five kinds of PC memory: **C**onventional, **U**pper, **H**igh, **E**xtended, and exp**A**nded. Are you clear on the differences and similarities of each pair of these five kinds of memory? Check yourself on this carefully; it may be the most important thing covered in these nine chapters. (Review in the section titled "The Different Kinds (Uses) of Memory" in Chapter 8.)

Note the one capitalized letter in each memory name (**C**, **U**, **H**, **E**, and **A**). These are often, but not always, used in program documentation and for command line switches to indicate a reference to the corresponding kind of memory.

4. What are memory pages? Can you describe how the term differs when applied to video memory, EMS memory, and Virtual-8086-mode paging of memory? What are the different sizes of the different kinds of pages? (Review in the sections titled "Banks,

Pages, and Paragraphs," "Expanded Memory," and "Video Memory" in Chapter 8 and in the sections titled "Protected Mode 386-Style" and "Virtual-8086 (V86) Mode" in Chapter 11.)

5. What is a BIOS and what is a DOS? (Review in the sections titled "What Is a BIOS?" and "What Is a DOS?" in Chapter 10.)

6. Can you describe the major layers of programs in your PC? Don't forget to include those in ROM as well as those in RAM. (Review in the section titled "The Layers of Programs in Your PC's RAM" in Chapter 10.)

7. Do you know the principal features of protected mode? All of the Intel 80x86 processors wake up in real mode. Only some can go into protected mode. Do you know which ones? (Review in the section titled "Protected Mode and Who Uses It" in Chapter 11.)

8. Do you understand segments and offsets in real mode? How about selectors versus segments in protected mode? (Review in the section titled "Segments and Offsets" in Chapter 8 and in the section titled "More on Segments, Offsets, and Modes" in Chapter 11.)

9. Are you clear on the difference between virtual mode, a virtual disk, and virtual memory? These are three very different ideas that use the same word, so confusion is common. (Review in the sections titled "When RAM Looks Like Disk Storage—Virtual Disks" and "When Disk Storage Looks like RAM—Virtual Memory" in Chapter 6 and in the section titled "How Virtual Memory Can Get So Large" in Chapter 11.)

10. Do you know the difference between logical, linear, and physical memory? Can you say how each member of the Intel 80x86 family, in each of its modes, converts logical to linear to physical memory addresses? (Review in the section titled "How Do Memory Maps Happen (Revisited)" in Chapter 11.)

11. Can you explain a cache, a cache hit, the difference between a memory cache and a disk cache? What is the cache synchronization problem? (Review in the section titled "A Memory Cache Is Not a Disk Cache" in Chapter 14.)

If you feel comfortable with these ideas, congratulations! Now you are ready to move on to the next stage, which is adding memory to your PC.

ADDING MEMORY—
WHEN AND WHERE
TO DO IT

You can't manage what you don't have. Often, the first step to effective memory management is to add memory to your PC. In this chapter, you will learn when to do it, where it can be put, and about all the different kinds of memory chips or modules you can use.

Many people think they have a PC memory problem, and some of them do. However, sometimes the people who really do have a PC memory problem can solve it by giving their PC more RAM to work with.

In this chapter, you will learn how to determine whether or not you need to add memory to your PC system. The chapter will also tell you where to put that memory to make sure it does what you expect and need it to do.

When to Add Memory

Do you need more memory in your PC? How can you tell? It may be that you need more disk storage space. Or, maybe you need a faster PC. Other times what is holding you back has nothing to do with the PC hardware you are using. For example, you may be using an out-of-date program that simply doesn't know how to make effective use of the memory resources your PC already has.

The questions that start the preceding paragraph are real ones. They are important ones, too. So how do you know if you need more memory in your PC? There are some symptoms that make it pretty obvious. Others need careful interpretation. Here are half a dozen common symptoms that suggest a need for more memory, followed by a discussion of each of them and some tips and pointers that may help you answer those important questions.

- You get an Insufficient memory message anytime you try to load certain large (and important to you) application programs.

- You get an Insufficient memory message, but only if you are also logged into your company's Local Area Network (LAN).

- You are using virtual memory (perhaps by running *Windows*, *AboveDISC+*, or *Turbo EMS*) and your disk light seems to stay on most of the time.

- You need more video resolution and/or you want more colors on the screen at once.

- You need to print full page graphics on your laser printer and it is unable to do so.

- You frequently find yourself waiting for the printer to finish what it is doing so you can regain control of your PC and go on with your work.

When You Can't Run an Important Program

One strong clue that you may need more memory in your PC is when you find yourself unable to load and run an important application program. If you get a message that says something like Insufficient memory, it can mean one of three things:

- You don't have enough RAM in your PC.

- You may have enough RAM, but some other programs have already laid claim to too much of it.

  or

- You have plenty of free RAM, but the program you want to run doesn't know how to use the kinds of free RAM you have.

So, before you rush out and buy RAM, check out your system a little more. The first place to look is at the documentation that came with the application you want to run. (Now that's novel; read the directions?! Yes, please.)

What Kind of RAM Are You Short of?

All programs want conventional, lower RAM. They'd be delighted to have enough of that. (This is why *Memory Commander's* trick of pushing video out of the way and backfilling lower memory all the way out to 900+ KB can be so wonderful—when you can use it. See Chapter 21 for details on what it does, how, and when it can or cannot be used.)

But often there just isn't enough free lower memory to go around. This is when you find out how your application program differs from the others.

For example, Lotus *1-2-3,* Release 2.x, will use expanded memory (EMS) if you have it, to supplement your supply of lower memory. So will the Gem version of *Ventura Publisher,* in certain situations. Lotus *1-2-3,* Release 3.x, on the other hand, wants to see some lower memory and lots of extended memory (XMS)—so does *Windows* 3.x. You have to know what your program needs before you can go about supplying that need.

Borland's *Turbo Debugger* wants to see real, honest-to-goodness hardware EMS memory. Most users of expanded memory are happy as clams with simulated expanded memory, but not if they want to run the *Turbo Debugger.* Programs do differ, so check out yours.

Can You Move Things Around to Free Up What You Need?

Once you know what kind of RAM is in too short supply at the moment, consider the possibility that you may have some "RAM-sitters" tying up a bunch of it. One solution may be to move them to somewhere where they will be less in the way. A "RAM-sitter" is any program that, once it has been run, leaves a portion of itself in RAM, reducing the amount available for any program loaded after it. Any **T**erminate and **S**tay **R**esident (TSR) program is one of these. So are device drivers. You might even include the DOS disk buffers (or any other item you set in your CONFIG.SYS file that uses RAM) in this category. Here is a short list of possibilities to consider.

- If you only have difficulties when you are logged into a network, remember that network drivers typically take up a lot of RAM. Some of them must have lower memory; nothing else will do. Others can happily be moved into upper memory (if you have RAM in that region available for use by programs).

- In addition to loading various device drivers, TSRs, DOS data structures such as FILES and BUFFERS, and network drivers into upper memory, you may find yourself able to make many or all of them appear to disappear until they are needed. The Netswap feature of *Netroom* can do exactly that. So can a few other TSR managers.

- Or you may be able to open up some free space in upper memory by using *QEMM* 6 or *386MAX* 6, which can make some of the ROMs in that region appear to disappear so that more RAM can be added there. Once that is done, you will be able to load more of the things now clogging lower memory into upper memory space.

Where do those programs or ROMs go when they are made to "disappear"? There are two different strategies. One is to move them up into extended memory and somehow run them from there. The other strategy is to move them out to a page of expanded memory and only page it into the CPU's memory address space when the CPU needs to access that program or ROM. Chapter 21 explains both strategies further.

- If you can get away with running your memory-hog application in a PC that has been stripped clean of all its "RAM-sitters" (device drivers, excess DOS buffers, TSR programs, and so forth), but you want to use these things the rest of the time, perhaps one of the batch file techniques or boot managers discussed in Chapter 20 will save the day.

These are just some of the strategies to consider. You will learn more about each of them in Chapters 20 and 21.

But Sometimes There Is Nothing Quite Like a Little More RAM

If the preceding suggestions did not help you find a way to make that important application run gracefully alongside the other things you need to use, perhaps it is time to consider adding more RAM. This is particularly true if you know your programs are using either extended or expanded memory, and they still are coming up short because you don't have enough of that sort of memory.

Or, of course, it applies if you don't already have the full complement of lower memory (640KB). Every PC user today really must have that much RAM as a bare minimum.

One very good way to get the effect of more RAM without having to actually buy real RAM is to make some of your disk space stand-in for the RAM you are missing. This is one meaning of the term virtual memory.

The most prominent drawback to this approach is speed. Disks don't have much. At least not compared to electronic memory chips. But if you have a program that needs expanded memory beyond what you may already have, consider using a LIMulator that can create EMS memory out of disk space (for example, *AboveDISC+* or *Turbo EMS*).

Another way to use virtual memory is to run *Windows* 3.x in enhanced mode. If you do this, be sure you have enough free space on your hard disk drive for the *Windows* swap file. You can guarantee this and make the swap file perform somewhat better by installing a permanent swap file. Still, for many people and situations, the default temporary file works just fine. However, be warned that the amount of space you have left on your disk can affect how much free RAM you will seem to have.

When Virtual Memory Access Is Painfully Slow

Maybe you already are using virtual memory. And maybe you are going slowly crazy waiting for your PC to do things. If you notice that the drive access light on your hard drive doesn't flicker but comes on and stays on, then your work is being seriously impeded by the limited speed of your hard disk.

The problem could be caused by your programs accessing regular files on the disk almost constantly. But more often it is a sign of virtual memory run amok.

You really need to know if you are using virtual memory. Only then can you be sure of what is going on and how to make things better. Check the programs you are running to see which ones (like *Windows* 3.x when it is running in enhanced mode) do use virtual memory. If none of the programs you are running knows how to use virtual memory, then that can't be the source of your difficulties.

If you are waiting for disk swapping altogether too much, sometimes adding more real RAM can make life easier.

Some programs swap information to disk constantly no matter how much RAM you have. They use overlays or other strategies designed to cope with limited amounts of RAM being available, and their design is so single-minded about this that they won't stop even when it is most inappropriate. *CorelDRAW!* is one of those programs.

One way to deal with such a program is to get lots of RAM and make a huge RAM disk (for *CorelDRAW!*, a couple of megabytes is a bare minimum amount and even 10MB is none too large!). Now direct your programs to that disk as the one they should use for swap files, temporary files, and overlays.

This may mean that you have to set up a pointer in some configuration file for the application program. You may need to use the DOS SET command to create aliases for TEMP and TMP, and possibly also for some special environmental variable name that your application looks for. And you may need to copy some or all of your application's files (both program and data files in some cases) to the RAM disk. Just remember to copy back all the data files as soon as you exit from the application so you don't lose them when you next turn off or reboot your computer. (Using the SET command and creating and managing RAM disks are covered more fully in Chapters 20 and 30.)

Getting More Functionality

Finally, you may wish to add more RAM, and not really have any alternative way of accomplishing your goals because you want to add new functionality to your PC. This could be in any of several areas, with video and printers being the most common.

Your PC's video card uses RAM to store screen image information. The more RAM it has, the more detailed an image it can store. Not all video cards can accept additional RAM, but many modern ones can. Then, you may be able to get screen images with greater resolution (for example, going from 640 by 480 pixels to 800 by 600, or on to 1024 by 768, or even 1280 by 1024). You may also be able to get more different colors simultaneously in those images.

If your video card can't accept more RAM, you may wish to buy more RAM already mounted on a new video card that can make use of it. That is a delightful way to add RAM to your PC (all packaged and ready to go).

Several studies have shown that people who use high-resolution screens (especially those displaying black text on a white or light-colored background) are often able to type more, in less time and with fewer errors, than those using one of the more old-fashioned video displays with ill-formed bright characters on a dark background.

This fact may encourage you to spend more money on a video upgrade than you otherwise might. That can be a very sound decision. Some studies have even shown that companies that do this get their investment back in as little as a few months.

Printers use RAM, especially laser printers. Your printer may have come with less than 1MB of RAM, but it may be able to accept several times that amount. Typically, the benefits of putting RAM in a printer fall into three areas:

- The larger amount of RAM allows the printer to store up a more detailed picture of the page it is about to print. That means you can have more and larger graphic images mixed with the text on your pages.

- Some printers use downloadable fonts. Often, the amount of RAM they have severely limits the number of fonts you can put on a page.

Note: The "Ransom Note School of Typography," a derogatory reference to any use of a huge number of fonts on a single page, is often very bad design. So limited printer memory may actually force you to produce better-looking pages. But if you know how to use fonts well, being able to download everything you need at the outset can save a lot of time when printing complicated documents.

- A large RAM buffer in a printer can be used to store up one or more long print jobs. Once all the information is in the printer, you can go back to using your PC for other things. The more sophisticated printer buffers will also allow you to reprint single pages or page ranges from your documents, any number of times and other tricky things. But without enough RAM to hold the whole document, or several of them, you can't possibly take advantage of these sophisticated features.

Where to Put More Memory

"Enough!" you say. You are convinced that you want to add more RAM to your PC. Now you need to know where and how to do it. Consider first where you need to add RAM. What choices do you have and what are the considerations you need to think about as you choose?

That is the subject of the rest of this chapter. Chapter 16 will help you understand the wide assortment of RAM you can buy. Chapter 17 will tell you how to install it safely.

On the Motherboard—When You Should

The first place to consider putting more RAM in your PC is on its motherboard. Almost all PCs put most of the system RAM there, and often there are empty sockets just waiting for more RAM chips or modules.

You may be able to add memory on a plug-in card, but often this isn't a desirable place to put it. Following are a couple of reasons why adding RAM on your PC's motherboard may be preferable.

Suppose your goal is to increase your PC's lower memory (if it has less than 640KB) or its extended memory. Some PCs simply won't recognize any memory added into a plug-in slot until all the sockets on the motherboard have been filled. This is no longer very common, but it does sometimes happen.

Also, memory that is added on the motherboard often works faster than those same RAM chips installed on a plug-in card. If you have a class 5 or 6 PC, this can be true for two reasons. (Chapter 3 describes six classes of PC, for the purposes of memory upgrades and memory management. Please read that chapter if you are not sure which class of PC you have.)

Why Motherboard Memory Is Best for Fast PCs

Your CPU probably runs at a clock speed well above the rated maximum for the I/O bus. Most PCs won't attempt to run the I/O bus any faster than 8MHz or 10MHz. They limit themselves in this way for some very good reasons. The fastest AT IBM ever built ran at 8MHz. So most manufacturers of plug-in cards designed them to work that fast, and they simply won't work if pushed much beyond that speed.

The CPU-to-memory bus on the motherboard, on the other hand, usually runs at the full CPU clock speed (which for class 5 and 6 PCs is not very likely to be slower than 12MHz and could be as fast as 50MHz). So data flows in and out of memory anywhere from 1.5 to 6 times as fast as it would across the I/O bus, just because of the differing clock speeds.

Furthermore, if your PC has an ISA bus (and most of them do), that limits data transfers to 16 bits at a time. The CPU-to-memory bus on class 6 PCs transfers data 32 bits at a time (or 64 bits at a time for a Pentium-based PC). That makes the speed advantage of motherboard memory over I/O bus installed RAM in those PCs a factor of between 3 and 12 (or 24).

If your motherboard supports interleaved memory access (and if you install one of the "magic" amounts of RAM on the motherboard), those figures could easily double yet again. See Chapter 16 for a discussion of what interleaved memory access is and how to determine the magic amounts of RAM for your PC if it includes support for this feature.

Motherboard Memory May Be More Flexible

Another situation in which it would be better to add memory to the motherboard is when the system logic on that motherboard can use any such memory more flexibly than if it were added on a plug-in card.

Usually, only motherboard memory can be used to provide shadow RAM. Also, your PC's system logic may be able to make some of the motherboard memory appear in otherwise empty regions of upper memory for use as an upper memory block. And often, it can make some of the motherboard memory appear to be true hardware EMS memory.

On the Motherboard—When You Shouldn't

Sometimes the motherboard is precisely the worst place to add RAM. Be sure to find out if your PC is in this group before you make a mistake.

There are only two situations in which you should not add RAM to the motherboard, even though there may be empty RAM sockets available for you to use. One case is when you have a PC or XT with a hardware EMS board and you want to be able to do effective multitasking (using, for example, *DESQview*). The other case is if you have a class 3 or 4 PC and wish to have EMS memory.

The PC or XT Case

Consider first the situation for PC and XT owners who have (or plan to get) a hardware EMS board. If that board supports LIM EMS version 4.0 (or EEMS), then the owners could use it to map RAM into almost any region of physical memory space. But that can only be done if there is an empty space in which that EMS memory can show up.

Only one group of RAM chips can use a given set of memory addresses at once. Use, in this sense, means to decode those addresses and turn on buffers and latches attached to the memory or I/O bus. (It need not necessarily mean actually having RAM chips at those addresses!)

If you can depopulate the motherboard of your PC or XT and stop it from decoding memory addresses where those RAM chips used to be, then you can backfill that space with pages of LIM 4.0 EMS memory. In turn, that will enable you to run *DESQview* and, under its control, run several large programs (seemingly) at the same time, even on a lowly PC or XT.

The various models of the IBM *PC* have two groups of eight switches on the motherboard. Each group is mounted in a plastic block with two rows of leads, just like an integrated circuit that is mounted in a **D**ual **I**nline **P**ackage (DIP). Thus, these groups are called DIP switches. By the settings of one group of switches, you tell the PC how much memory you have on the motherboard. With the other group you indicate how much total memory you have in the system, as shown in Figure 15.1. This strategy means that you don't even have to remove the motherboard memory chips to get the full benefit of a hardware LIM 4.0 EMS card. Just set the switches to direct the PC to ignore all but the first bank of memory on the motherboard.

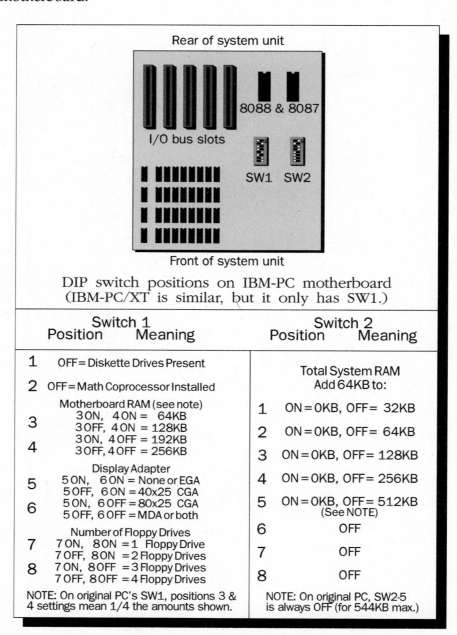

Rear of system unit

8088 & 8087

I/O bus slots

SW1   SW2

Front of system unit

DIP switch positions on IBM-PC motherboard (IBM-PC/XT is similar, but it only has SW1.)

Switch 1 Position	Meaning	Switch 2 Position	Meaning
1	OFF = Diskette Drives Present		Total System RAM Add 64KB to:
2	OFF = Math Coprocessor Installed		
3	Motherboard RAM (see note) 3 ON, 4 ON = 64KB 3 OFF, 4 ON = 128KB	1	ON = 0KB, OFF = 32KB
4	3 ON, 4 OFF = 192KB 3 OFF, 4 OFF = 256KB	2	ON = 0KB, OFF = 64KB
		3	ON = 0KB, OFF = 128KB
5	Display Adapter 5 ON, 6 ON = None or EGA 5 OFF, 6 ON = 40x25 CGA	4	ON = 0KB, OFF = 256KB
6	5 ON, 6 OFF = 80x25 CGA 5 OFF, 6 OFF = MDA or both	5	ON = 0KB, OFF = 512KB (See NOTE)
		6	OFF
7	Number of Floppy Drives 7 ON, 8 ON = 1 Floppy Drive 7 OFF, 8 ON = 2 Floppy Drives	7	OFF
8	7 ON, 8 OFF = 3 Floppy Drives 7 OFF, 8 OFF = 4 Floppy Drives	8	OFF
NOTE: On original PC's SW1, positions 3 & 4 settings mean 1/4 the amounts shown.		NOTE: On original PC, SW2-5 is always OFF (for 544KB max.)	

Figure 15.1. The DIP switches on an IBM *PC*.

You can still have the use of 640KB of lower memory (and really even more than that with task swapping or multitasking). You'll just be using pages of EMS memory in place of fixed address RAM on the motherboard (or any other kind of memory expansion option card).

With an IBM *PC/XT,* you will have to physically remove the RAM chips you don't want it to see. Those machines look at each region of lower memory, working up from the bottom, to see if RAM is installed there. As soon as it finds a hole, it quits looking. (That is what it is doing, in addition to testing the RAM chips' integrity, while it's scrolling numbers on the screen before starting the boot process.) The good news is that it turns off memory address decoding for any addresses in or beyond that first hole (to the end of lower memory, at least).

Not all XT clones are this considerate. Most of them in recent years have been made with the full complement of 640KB of system RAM on the motherboard. (Some had even more RAM. They typically use the rest for shadow RAM or as EMS memory if you so instructed their setup program.)

In a PC like this, you are simply not going to be able to do effective multitasking, precisely because you cannot effectively empty lower memory space. So you have nowhere to put the EMS pages you would like to be loading with all the different programs you want to multitask. You can still do a sort of multitasking. But it will be of a vastly inferior sort, since it will involve much copying of information and, because of this, will work very slowly.

The AT Case

What if you have an AT? (This discussion applies whether you have an IBM *PC/AT* or a clone PC in its class. The question is simply, does your PC have an 80286 CPU chip?)

You could get EMS memory by buying and installing an EMS memory option card. You may be able to get some by instructing your PC's motherboard system logic to convert some of the RAM on that motherboard into EMS memory. Finally, you certainly can get emulated EMS memory (created out of your PC's extended memory) by using a suitable LIMulator program, such as *LIMSIM.* (Chapter 29 lists several other LIMulators.)

The last of the three is the sure thing, and it costs very little money. But it also has a problem. You may be tempted to install lots of extended memory in your AT and run the LIMulator. If you do this, you may be disappointed at the sluggish performance of the resulting simulated EMS memory. The issue here is that the LIMulator must be constantly switching the CPU into and out of protected mode. And that takes, relatively speaking, a very long time. (You don't even need a lot of extended memory—if you have enough patience. *AboveDISC+* and *Turbo EMS* can make simulated EMS memory out of disk space.)

So your best bet would be to get a hardware EMS card (being very sure it conforms to the LIM 4.0 EMS standard, and in particular, provides the features you want), and then fill it up with RAM.

> **Don't overlook this** If you use simulated EMS memory on an AT (or any class 3 PC), whether that memory is converted from extended memory or disk space, the EMS page frame will be in lower memory. You get a lot of new EMS memory, but you have to give up 64KB of your very precious first 640KB, plus whatever room the LIMulator program uses.

There are two possible exceptions to this advice. One is that you may sometimes need EMS and XMS (or extended) memory. You can get both from the motherboard memory. Although you may be able to set up your new EMS card to give you a mixture of the two kinds of memory, usually you cannot go back and forth in your allocation of RAM to these two purposes nearly as easily as you can for memory on the motherboard.

The other exception comes into play if you have a motherboard system logic chip set that supports the creation of fast EMS memory out of motherboard memory. Note the word "fast." This is, of course, a relative term. You are concerned with how fast the EMS memory created by the chip set works, compared to the speed of the simulated EMS memory a LIMulator program can provide.

On a Plug-In Memory Option Card

If you are going to add RAM, but not on the motherboard, where else can you add it? You have several choices. The most obvious one is to put it on an option card that plugs into the I/O bus.

There are three different kinds of memory option cards you can use: a proprietary memory option card, an I/O bus memory option card, and a PCMCIA PC memory option card. They differ significantly, so looking at each one in turn may be helpful.

A Proprietary Memory Option Card

Earlier, you learned that a 386DX or 486 CPU chip has 32 data pins. This lets it communicate with its main memory 32 bits at a time. The ISA bus, on the other hand, only includes 16 data wires. So no memory option card that plugs in there can transfer information as many bytes at a time as the CPU can accept. Also, the ISA bus imposes a severe limitation on the rate at which those data transfers can take place.

Therefore, many PCs in classes 5 and 6 offer one or more proprietary memory option card slots on the motherboard. You usually have to buy the memory option cards from the manufacturer of the motherboard. If you put RAM on this sort of card, it will work every bit as fast as if it were on the motherboard. Normally you would first fill up the motherboard sockets, and then get one of these add-in memory option cards and use it until you have all the RAM you want. (Or, until you run out of money for RAM.)

The only disadvantages of these cards are that they are often expensive, and if the RAM is soldered onto them (rare, but it happens), those chips cannot be used later on in some other way. If you can live with those disadvantages, this is a great way to add all-purpose RAM to your PC.

The Usual I/O Bus Memory Option Card

Most people who add RAM that isn't on the motherboard do it using a memory option card that plugs into the I/O bus. Although there are some limitations to this approach, which have already been described, it can work quite well. In many PCs, it is every bit as good as adding memory to the motherboard.

Furthermore, you can add more memory this way than if you use only the motherboard and sockets. There will be some limit as to the amount the motherboard can accept. Once all its sockets have been filled with the largest capacity RAM chips or modules, then you have no other option but to use a memory option card of some kind.

Not all memory option cards are created equal, so watch out. Be sure you get one that does what you want and need.

Conventional Memory Backfilling Cards

The most limited memory option cards can only augment (backfill) your lower memory up to a maximum of 640KB (that is, the combined total of what is on your motherboard and what is on the memory option card cannot exceed 640KB). These memory option cards used to be both popular and very useful.

Now, with most PCs carrying more than 640KB of RAM on the motherboard, the old memory option cards are pretty well obsolete. (This is not to say you may not find one in a store; if you do, pass over it quickly and see what else is available.) If you need to add lower memory, normally a better way is by using an EMS memory card or an upper memory card.

Cards Supplying Only Extended Memory

Some people need only more extended memory. They don't want and can't use expanded memory. For them, the perfect memory option card is one that supplies just what they need. There are several such cards on the market. But be quite sure that you won't later want EMS memory before you choose one of these.

Cards That Supply Only Expanded (EMS) Memory

The opposite case is also possible. In fact, if you have a PC in class 1, you can't have extended memory anyway. So you probably want just a simple EMS memory option card. If yours is a PC in class 3, however, you would be wise not to limit your options in this way.

A related issue is the width of the edge card connectors on the memory option card. If it has just one tongue, it is what is called an 8-bit card. That means it only connects to the portion of the ISA bus that is common between PCs and ATs. (See Figure 14.4.) That also means it only has 20 address lines available to it. Such a card cannot supply extended memory no matter what PC it is plugged into.

Upper Memory Option Cards

The normal plan for PCs doesn't put general-purpose RAM into upper memory. So most makers of memory option cards don't provide for the possibility of putting any of their RAM there, except in the form of an EMS page frame.

Now that it has become highly desirable and quite convenient to load programs into RAM in upper memory, using DOS 5, for example, people want RAM wherever they can put it in upper memory space. So now we are beginning to see upper memory option cards.

One such card is the *MegaMizer* from V Communications. It comes with memory-management software to help you load programs high. It also can be used to expand the TPA (**T**ransient **P**rogram **A**rea) from the normal maximum of 640KB to as much as 736KB in certain systems. This card is discussed further in Chapters 23, 24, and 27.

More Flexible Memory Option Cards

The best memory add-in cards can supply any mixture of three kinds of memory; they can backfill as needed, and then use the rest of their memory as either EMS or extended memory.

The differences start here. How can you tell the board what allocation you want between EMS (expanded memory) and extended memory? Some require you to open up the PC and set switches or move jumpers each time you wish to change the allocation. Others can do this using software alone.

Can you change the allocation between the two forms of memory on the fly? Often if that is what you wish, the best way to do it is to tell the memory option card to supply only extended memory. Then you may be able to make as much of that extended memory as you need appear to be EMS memory, but only for as long as you need it in the form of expanded memory.

Usually, you have to reboot the PC to make any change you have specified to the allocation between EMS and extended memory take effect. There is a way to get a more dynamic sharing, but it only works if you have a class 5 or 6 PC. This is to set the card to supply only extended memory, and then use a LIMulator that supports the VCPI standard to convert almost all your extended memory into (simulated) EMS memory. Then programs that know how to ask for it can get all they want in either form.

Precautions to Observe When Using More Than One Memory Option Card

If you want more memory than will fit on one memory option card, be careful. You may have to use only a single brand of memory option card. Many companies make EMS cards, including Aculogic, AST, Boca, and Intel, to name just a few. Each one designs their cards a little differently. So each card requires its own brand of expanded memory manager (EMM) to operate its paging hardware. You can only load one of these EMM programs at a time. So if you have two or more different vendors' EMS cards, you most likely will be unable to use more than one of them for EMS memory.

On the other hand, you probably can use all but one brand of memory option card for extended memory. Then you can use the remaining card for whatever mixture of EMS and extended memory you wish. The EMM you load should be the one that came with the last card. The only card it will be talking to is the one it understands, which is why only that card will be able to provide any usable EMS memory.

Resolving Resource Allocation Problems

Whenever you use more than one memory option card, you must face the issue of possible resource conflicts. Resolving these conflicts is often the toughest part of adding RAM to a PC.

An EMS card must have exclusive use of an I/O port (or a small group of ports) through which its EMM driver can communicate with it. It may also need to have exclusive use of an *IRQ* (*Interrupt Request Level*). Read the documentation that comes with the card carefully. Each card will come from the factory with some default setup. You may have to change it especially if you put multiple cards of the same kind in your PC.

Some modern designs of EMS cards will do all the work for you. The older ones still force you to figure out what must be done and how to do it.

An EMS card is also set up to put its EMS page frame at a particular address. Normally that is a contiguous region, at least 64KB in size, somewhere in upper memory space. It must not be in use for any other purpose.

If you are going to load programs into upper memory, remember to keep that space as unfragmented as possible. Chapter 21 explains how upper memory fragmentation severely limits the usefulness of upper memory.

There are also resource allocation issues when installing extended memory option cards. Here, the issue is which range of physical addresses shall be decoded for the chips on a given card. That can be set up, again, either by a hardware mechanism (DIP switches and/or jumpers) or through software. What you must avoid is having any two places in your PC responding to the same physical memory addresses at the same time.

Well, two cards can "listen" with no problems. That means, the CPU can write to both of them at the same time. The problems come when the CPU wants the chips at an address to "speak." If two chips speak up at once, the potential for confusion is just as bad as at any cocktail party. You could even force the memory option cards to damage one another!

A PCMCIA PC Memory Option Card

The newest way to add substantial quantities of RAM to a PC is on a PCMCIA compatible PC card. These are cards about the size of a stack of three or four credit cards, and they have a 68-pin connector on one end. (See Chapters 6 and 14 for more details on this card.)

These cards can be used for many purposes, but foremost among these is as a source of RAM. The specification allows putting up to 64MB on a single card. You can also get Flash RAM cards configured to look like a disk drive.

So far, the memory capacity of these cards is nowhere near the 64MB limit, but within a couple of years, cards with these capacities will be available. Even now, for palmtop and laptop computers, these cards are a very attractive way to install memory. One of the delightful aspects of the design of these cards is that you can interchange them as freely as floppy disks. No need to shut down or reboot your PC each time.

In an Expansion Chassis

What if you want to put in a memory option card, but all your PC's slots are filled? In that case, you have three choices:

- Remove something from a slot to make room for the new memory option card. (It should be something you won't miss too badly.)

- Replace a couple of cards with one that does the job of both. With the progress in printed circuit cards and IC chip fabrication, more functionality can be put on a single plug-in card than was ever possible in the past.

  or

- Use an expansion chassis.

An expansion chassis is merely a box with a power supply and a motherboard that sports a bunch of I/O bus connectors. It has just enough circuitry to support that bus. It must then be connected back to the main system box, usually by a fat cable that goes between two special option cards. One option card plugs into the system unit's I/O bus, and the other plugs into a bus slot in the expansion chassis.

This works, but it costs an awful lot. So if you can use either the first or second choice (both of which will free up at least one slot in your system unit), doing so will save you money.

On a Video Card

A video card is another very popular place to add RAM to a PC. Earlier in this chapter, the reasons why you might like to do this were discussed. Naturally, your video card must have some empty sockets or you won't be able to add RAM to it. Your alternative then is to replace that video card, either with one that has some empty sockets or with one that already has more RAM mounted on it.

On Other Kinds of Option Cards

A number of different kinds of option cards have a provision for adding RAM to them. A coprocessor or slave processor card are among the most common.

If you put a 286 or 386 upgrade card into a PC or an XT (for example, an Orchid *Tiny Turbo 286* or an Intel *Inboard 386/PC*), it must have most of the system memory on that same card. This is because it will need to communicate with its system memory over a bus having more address wires than exist in the XT version of the ISA bus. Otherwise, it would suffer from the same limited memory address space as the XT.

Often, there is not enough room on the upgrade card for all the memory you might like to have. So there may be a provision for a daughterboard RAM card that plugs onto the plug-in upgrade card. Aside from the limitations on total RAM you can install, adding RAM to a coprocessor or slave processor board is much like adding motherboard memory to your main PC.

In a Peripheral Device

The most common RAM-containing peripheral device for a PC is a printer or print spooler. You may be able to add quite a lot of RAM here. It can be a very effective place to put RAM, though there are some reasons why you may wish to keep that RAM in the PC system unit instead.

The only other peripheral that can use a lot of RAM is a solid state disk. This is essentially a box with a lot of RAM and a battery backup system, or a box with a lot of Flash RAM (a special kind of EEPROM; see Chapters 2 and 16 for more details) and an interface that presents that information's storing capacity in the guise of a very fast disk drive. If you are lucky enough to have a solid state disk drive, and still have some money left over for more RAM (or Flash RAM—a.k.a. Flash ROM or Flash EPROM), by all means, add all you can. This will be your fastest, nicest disk drive, and disk space is like closet space —you can *never* have too much!

Now back to printers. Here are three different ways to use added RAM for your printer, each having pros and cons.

Print Spooler

A print spooler, at its most basic, is a bunch of memory in which you can accumulate information on its way to a printer. The memory can take in information rapidly, much more rapidly than the printer can print it. Then the spooler can dole that information out as the printer is prepared to use it.

Print spoolers are very good things. When you have finished one task and are ready to print out your work, it is often very nice to get the job on its way in a few seconds and then get back to work on your next task.

Dedicated print spoolers outside the PC have both benefits and liabilities, as compared to implementing a print spooler through software within your PC.

On the plus side, external print spoolers don't get messed up if you "hang" your PC. You can reboot, even change operating systems if you like, and the external print spooler and printer keep chugging along. If yours is an unstable system, or if you frequently find yourself rebooting, perhaps as you log on and off of your company's LAN, then having a large amount of RAM in an external print spooler can add greatly to your productivity.

On the other hand, any RAM you put in an external print spooler is not going to do you any other good. In contrast to that, if you use a print spooler created in RAM by a device driver or TSR program, it does not commit that RAM to that purpose forever.

One print spooling program, the *PC-Kwik Print Spooler,* which PC-Kwik Corp. sells in their *Power Pak* product, takes this one step further. PC-Kwik Corp. notes that most of the time you want to have a large amount of RAM serving as a disk cache. And most of the time you don't need any for the print spooler, since you aren't printing then. But when you do need memory for the print spooler, you really need it. If you are forced to wait while your printer works, then having instant access to your disk drive (if only you weren't waiting for the printer) will do you no good. So their *Super PC-Kwik* disk cache program is designed to be able to share its pool of memory with their *PC-Kwik Print Spooler.*

569

Dot-Matrix Printers

Most dot-matrix printers have some RAM in them. It is used to buffer at least a line or two of incoming text. Sometimes you can add RAM to the printer and thereby increase its input buffer. This is one place where a tiny investment in RAM can pay great dividends in increased convenience and overall productivity. Just a few dozen KB can give you very significant benefits.

Laser Printers

Laser printers are, from one point of view, merely high-resolution dot-matrix printers. However, they can be much more than that. Although most of them can print simple text, they all can do much more.

Printers that support *PostScript* fonts, for example, are often more powerful computers in their own right than the PC to which they get connected. Even a simple *LaserJet* has a lot of computing power built into it, so it can properly interpret PCL (**P**rinter **C**ontrol **L**anguage) information being sent to it.

A computer needs to have memory. It needs it for both program and data storage. Many of the programs your printer needs are permanently loaded into some ROM chips. But to a degree, modern laser printers can also be reprogrammed and that means they need a good deal of RAM.

Further, if you will be printing pages with graphic images or multiple fonts on them, you may need to have a lot more memory in your PC. The original Hewlett-Packard *LaserJet* could only print a 3-inch-square graphic image per page with its default amount of memory. Several additional megabytes are necessary to support printing full-page graphic images.

You may be able to avoid adding memory to your LaserJet and still print large graphic images successfully. The trick is to use a print spooling program that compresses the image data, such as LaserTools, or PCACHE. As long as the graphics you want to print have a lot of regions of a single color (either black or white), the compressed version of many of those graphics will fit within even the default amount of memory. Print spoolers in general are discussed further in Chapter 30.

You will find the address and phone numbers of the LaserTools company in the MemInfo hypertext database on the diskette that accompanies this book.

Adding Memory to Your Printer— Where Do You Put It?

Each print spooler and printer is different. Look at yours and at the manual that came with it. You may need to contact the manufacturer for a more technical manual or some detailed directions.

Most laser printers can accept RAM only on special memory option cards. The manufacturer will be delighted to sell you those cards, usually with RAM installed. And if the model of printer is sufficiently popular, there may be third-party sources for compatible RAM cards. Extra fonts may sometimes be added in the form of a ROM card.

A Recap

This chapter opened with a discussion of how you can tell if you will benefit from adding RAM to your PC. And then in case you decided to add RAM, the chapter examined the question of where that RAM might most profitably be added.

Now you know how and where to add RAM. In the next chapter, you will face the often daunting question of which kind of RAM to add. That is followed by chapters on how to add RAM safely and how much to add.

16

ADDING MEMORY— THE DIFFERENT KINDS

The world of memory chips and modules is filled with jargon. You need to know some critical facts about memory chips and modules so you can ask the right questions and be sure you buy parts that will work in your PC.

Folks who make and sell memory chips and memory modules often seem to live in a different universe. Their talk is heavily larded with technical arcana that you feel sure you really shouldn't have to understand. Why are those people like that?

If these sound like your thoughts, the sad fact is: you've overlooked something. Those people talk about all those technical arcana precisely because you *do* need to know those facts about the memory parts you are about to buy. If you overlook even one of them you easily could select something that won't work in your PC, or worse, that may seem to work but then will prove unreliable in the long run.

In this chapter, you will learn the right questions to ask in order to be sure you select memory parts that will fit in the sockets you have or are about to buy, that will work with your PC correctly, and that will be reliable for the long term.

Memory Chip Jargon and Facts

There are many aspects to memory parts that matter. Knowing how many bytes you need is only the first level of information required. You must know what kind of memory chips you seek, in a functional sense. Each of those functional kinds of memory also comes packaged in an amazing variety of forms. You must get the right ones on this count also.

There are even more subtle issues than these. For example, don't overlook the issue of memory chip speed. There are several ways to measure this, so you need to know not only what speed rating you need, but which kind of speed rating that is. Your system may further confuse matters by using the memory parts in a way that allows it to use slower chips than you might have imagined, and still get the PC to run at its full, rated clock speed.

Let's look at each of these issues in turn. You will be delighted to discover that yes, you can learn all this and it does make sense once you find out what people mean by all that jargon.

Kinds of Memory Chips

In Chapter 2 you were introduced to several kinds of memory used in PCs. You also learned about some of the popular packages in which electronic memory is sold. You may wish to review that chapter now, before reading the further details set out here.

All electronic memory made today is built as an integrated circuit. This means that each part you buy consists of some huge number of individual transistors, diodes, and capacitors interconnected in a very complex fashion chosen to give that part the functionality you require.

There are many different ways to combine these very low level electronic devices to get the various kinds of memory functionality. Other ways of interconnecting them can make logic gates, and assemblies of those gates are used in the creation of microprocessors.

Focusing on the memory devices, you may need to get SRAM, DRAM, VDRAM, PROM, EPROM, EEPROM, or Flash RAM, depending on your application. In Chapter 2 you learned a little bit about these parts and how they are used. Here you will learn the basic technique used to create these chips. This information should make the properties of these chips seem a little less mysterious.

Once you understand the pieces a little better, you will be ready to learn about how they get combined into a functional memory subsystem for your PC.

SRAM

Static **RAM** (SRAM) was the first kind of electronic memory chip created. It still is the fastest design. For that reason, SRAM chips are used in creating memory caches. It is not the least expensive design (per bit), so it is not commonly used in large memory arrays.

The basic circuit that makes up a memory cell capable of holding one bit in a Static RAM chip is formed from several transistors (at least four). This circuit has two parts. In one, called a *flip-flop circuit*, there are two transistors constantly reinforcing each other's present behavior. This circuit is also known as a bi-stable circuit because it has two stable states in which it can exist. As long as power is applied it will stay in the one it happens to be in, unless you intervene quite forcefully to change its state.

Transistors are a little like valves. They can be on (carrying a flow of electricity) or off (blocking that flow). It is possible for them to be only partly on, but in digital circuits they are almost always fully on or fully off.

Digital computers are composed almost exclusively of digital circuits. The few places in your PC where analog circuits get used include the video display's final output to the monitor (if you have a VGA or better display adapter) and a sound board or a game port, if you have either of those. Some analog circuits are also used in your disk drives. All your PC's memory circuits are fully digital in nature.

In the flip-flop circuit, the transistor that is on forces the other one to be off, and the second one that is off forces the first one to stay on. Here is another kind of flip-flop that you may find easier to understand:

Imagine a circuit with a photodetector and a relay. Suppose it is built to switch a lamp on or off, depending on whether or not light is falling on the photodetector. If you arrange the circuit so that whenever light is falling on the photodetector the lamp will be turned on, you will have created a flip-flop circuit. When the lamp's light falls on the photodetector, the circuit turns the lamp on, thus keeping its light falling on the photodetector. Call that a one-bit. If the lamp is off, and there is no other light around, the circuit will keep the lamp turned off. Call that a zero-bit.

The first part of each memory cell mimics this behavior, and thus will hold itself in either one of two states. One of these states is used to indicate a binary one; the other state indicates a binary zero. If this part were all that was in the cell, it would never change its state (as long as power was on).

The second part of each bit cell in an SRAM chip is the part that is used to store a one-bit or a zero-bit into that cell; that is, this second part has the job of changing the state of the first part whenever information is written to this cell. The way this part works can again be indicated by reference to the photodetector-relay circuit just described.

Suppose the lamp is off, the photodetector is in darkness, and so the relay is off. If you shine a light on the photodetector, even briefly, the relay will come on, the lamp will come on, its light will shine on the photodetector and that will keep the relay and lamp on. This is how you can force the circuit to store a one-bit.

Suppose now you hold something over the photodetector to block light from falling on it (again, you need only do this briefly). When you do this, the relay will turn off and the lamp will go dark. Now, even when you take your shade away from the photodetector, the lamp will remain off. This is how you can force the circuit to store a zero-bit.

There is another way the lamp and photodetector combination could be wired. You could arrange to have light falling on the detector turn the light off and, conversely, the absence of light would turn the lamp on. This is called an *oscillator*. The lamp will constantly be turning itself off and on at a rate that is set by some properties of the lamp and photodetector. Just such an oscillator circuit (but made out of transistors) is the source of the various "clock" signals in our PCs.

SRAM chips consist of thousands or millions of such cells. They use electric signals, instead of lamps and photodetectors, but their operation is basically the same. Each cell holds exactly one bit.

Other circuits on the SRAM chip are responsible for reading and "decoding" the information presented on the address lines to select the correct memory cell or cells to activate. Yet other circuits carry the data in or out of the chip.

Many SRAM chips are made to store multiple bits per address. For example, a byte-wide chip will store eight bits for each possible combination of high and low voltages (ones and zeros) on its address lines. If such a chip has 64K memory cells (bits), it will have 8K locations. We refer to such a chip as an "8K-by-8" memory chip.

DRAM

DRAM stands for **Dynamic RAM**. These are electronic memory chips that also hold vast numbers of bits in memory cells. We use more of these chips than any other kind in our PCs. They are used for main memory, for video image buffers, in print spoolers, and elsewhere. These are your everyday, workhorse memory chips.

They differ from SRAM in one key way. Instead of a full flip-flop circuit created out of at least four transistors, they use a single transistor plus a capacitor to store each bit. This construction detail has two implications of profound significance.

The first is that it takes less room on the silicon wafer to build each memory cell. That means that these chips can be made much denser than SRAM chips. In turn, that means you can buy several million bits in a chip, instead of just a few thousand. The price of a memory chip depends mostly on how much silicon it uses, so on a price per bit basis, DRAM chips are always much cheaper than SRAM.

> The number of certain types of chips that are made and sold also affects their price. Since DRAMs are cheaper, many more of them are made and sold, making them even cheaper.

The high density and low cost of DRAM make them wonderful. The other implication of how they are built provides the one serious limitation of DRAM. Since each bit is stored only as a charge on a capacitor, they are not nearly as stable as SRAM. (The transistor in each cell is there to let you read out the state of charge on the capacitor without unduly discharging it.)

Left to itself for only a small fraction of a second, a DRAM chip will "forget" all the information that was stored in it. That would make it useless were it not for another interesting and nonobvious fact about DRAM.

Every time you read the data out of a DRAM, you end up (in the act of reading it) reinforcing those data values. That means that if a bit cell is storing a zero (has a low voltage on its capacitor), reading it will force that capacitor's voltage even lower. Or if it was initially charged up to a relatively high voltage, reading that bit will force the charge even higher.

> This is not unlike your own memory. If you are asked to remember a number, you may forget it after awhile. But if you are frequently asked to repeat that number, you will find that you can remember it very easily.

Asking a DRAM to state what data it is holding, in order to force it to hold the data more securely, is called *refreshing* the DRAM. The highest priority activity in any PC is refreshing its DRAM's contents.

DRAMs are built with their memory cells arranged in a large rectangular or square array. Thus a 256-kilobit DRAM chip (that means it stores 218 bits) has its 262,144 memory cells arranged into 512 rows of 512 cells each. Normally, each new generation of memory chips has the size of a cell reduced by a factor of two in each direction. That leads directly to a doubling of the number of rows and the number of cells per row. This is why the next generation after the 256-kilobit chip was the 1-megabit chip, then the 4-megabit chip, and now the 16-megabit chip.

Here is a piece of really good news: You can refresh all of the contents of a DRAM chip by reading any one location in every row. You don't need to read every single location. That is good news because it means we can devote much less of our PC's time to the essential job of refreshing DRAM, and more of it to the interesting job of computing.

Because these are the least expensive chips (on a per bit basis) and the densest (most bits per chip), they are the most commonly used in PCs. Your main RAM is composed almost certainly of DRAMs.

> Some very fast PCs have been built using SRAM chips or a variant kind of DRAM memory chip called *pseudo-static RAM*. SRAM chips are very fast and both kinds need no external refresh circuitry. (Pseudo-static RAM is merely DRAM with automatic refresh circuitry built onto the chip.) Both kinds cost more than DRAM, and so are not often used for main RAM.

There is some overhead associated with the job of refreshing DRAM. Not only does it take up a fraction of your PC's time, it also requires some special circuits built just for this purpose.

This is not a very big deal when you are talking about refreshing millions of bits. (Remember, even the original PC, if it had at least 128KB of RAM as was quite common, had over a million bits in that RAM. Modern PCs with multiple megabytes of RAM have tens of millions of bits to refresh.)

On the other hand, if you only have a small amount of memory to refresh, the overhead cost for the refresh circuitry can significantly increase the price per bit. This is another reason why SRAM is used in fast memory cache circuits. Supposing you could find fast enough DRAM chips, their cost plus that of the refresh circuitry could easily exceed the cost of the same bit capacity in SRAM, even though the DRAM chips themselves are much cheaper than SRAM.

VRAM

Most video display cards use DRAM for their video-image-buffer memory. A few of the higher performance ones use something called VRAM instead. What is that? Why is it special? And why doesn't everyone use it?

Video **RAM** (VRAM) is a special kind of DRAM. What is special about it is that each VRAM chip contains two sets of circuits devoted to carrying information in from the outside world and storing it in the cells or carrying it out from those cells to the outside world. Normal DRAMs only have half this circuitry. We say that VRAM is *dual-ported memory.*

The memory chips in the video image buffer are among the very hardest working chips in your PC. The display adapter is constantly reading and rereading them as it constantly rewrites the image on the screen.

In fact, those memory chips are so busy with that task that they almost don't have any time to let the CPU put information into them. Of course they cannot be *quite* that busy or you never could create any images to view. But it is almost that bad.

If you run a memory speed benchmark program, you will see different speeds listed for different regions of your memory-address space (see Figure 14.11). Regions that contain ROM often show a slower speed than those containing RAM. EMS memory is a bit slower than main RAM. But the very slowest of all are the memory locations in the video image buffer.

That doesn't mean that the RAM chips on your video display adapter are slowpokes. To the contrary, they are probably just as fast as any in your PC. But they are *very* busy, so they respond to the CPU relatively slowly.

VRAM was invented to help out in just this situation. The two ports in a VRAM means that, at least potentially, the CPU can be using one port (one set of circuits in the chip to steer data between the pins and the memory cells) to load data into the video image buffer, or to read from that buffer, if necessary. And at the very same time, the display circuitry can be reading out the information stored in the buffer so it will know what to paint on the screen.

The two ports are not the same. One is a parallel port. The other is a serial port. Let's see just what that means.

Most VRAM is "organized" as nibble-wide or byte-wide memory. This is in contrast to most DRAMs which are bit-wide devices. That is, on a VRAM you will have four or eight pins through which you can put in four or eight bits of data, and some number of address pins to say where in the chip to store the data. A DRAM usually has just one pin for input and one for output. For equal numbers of memory cells you get something like a 256K-by-1 DRAM or a 32K-by-8 VRAM.

The parallel port of a VRAM allows the CPU to load in bytes of information at once (or nibbles, anyway). The serial port allows the display circuitry to "clock out" data bits one at a time.

Remember that the memory cells are arranged in a rectangular array. In the case of a 32K-by-8 VRAM there would be perhaps 128 rows, each having 256 bit cells, and there would be eight of these arrays.

When the CPU supplies an address to the parallel port, an access takes place at a certain row and column position in each of these arrays at once, one bit going into or out of each array. This organization is much like that of the bit planes described in Chapter 8 (and diagrammed in Figure 8.10).

Along one edge of each array there is a single row of bit cells. These are extras, in addition to the advertised memory capacity of the chip. When an access is made through the serial port, the specified address causes one row of each array to have its cell's contents copied "sideways" into the extra row for that array.

Now those bits can be read out to the serial port one at a time. This is done by shifting them along the row until they get to the end. Think of the cells as a "bucket brigade" passing their contents along from one to the next to the next. A special "clock" input to the chip sets the rate at which this shifting takes place.

It also is possible to load information into the chip through the serial port, but that is not normally done in a video application. Also, the serial port output sometimes has as many data pins as the parallel port. In that case, the data is being clocked out of the extra row a corresponding number of bits at a time. This is done for use in systems where the rate at which pixels must be drawn exceeds the maximum clock speed (usually 33MHz) that can be used on the VRAM chips.

VRAM sounds wonderful. You'd think it would completely solve the problem that was described above—of the CPU having difficulty getting opportunities to access video buffers made up of DRAM. But it doesn't really do so in practice. The reasons for this are pretty abstruse, but suffice it to say that while a VRAM video card's RAM will appear to be somewhat faster than that on a DRAM video card, the difference is often not very dramatic.

Here are two reasons that using VRAM in a video image buffer may not speed up your PC as much as you might imagine it would. First, many programs assume the video image buffer is made out of DRAM chips. They impose some pauses in the flow of information from the CPU to prevent the occurrence on-screen of "snow" or other irregularities. (They may wait until a vertical or horizontal retrace time to pump in a burst of data, for example.) This helps DRAM video cards perform very well, but it slows down VRAM cards unnecessarily.

You can avoid this problem, at least with some application programs, by getting a special VRAM-aware video driver program (usually from the maker of the VRAM video card). But for applications for which no such driver exists, the VRAM card cannot run any faster than its cheaper DRAM kin.

A second reason for the relative ineffectiveness of VRAM is that it works best for bit-mapped video images, but many applications put the video card into a text mode.

When you are working in a text mode, the job of the video display circuit is radically different from what it does with bit-mapped images. (See Chapter 8 for details.) In text mode, it reads from the serial port just some codes corresponding to the characters it must display. Then it must look in some font memory (commonly another part of the same VRAM array on the video card) to see how to create those characters on the screen. The character codes are stored in the order the characters appear on the screen, but the font information is altogether somewhere else. That constant need to refer to both the codes and the font data requires many references to the video contents via both the serial and parallel ports. That interrupts the CPU's access to this memory almost as much as if it were composed of DRAM chips.

So, since VRAM chips are more complex and thus cost more to make, most video card makers don't choose to put VRAM on their cards. With specially designed coprocessor boards that have been optimized for the use of VRAM, the speedup can be more dramatic. Those are much more expensive than typical video cards, and so they are not yet very popular.

ROM

For the most part, the ROMs in your PC are there to stay. Different ROM chips on various cards may be made using different technologies. The manufacturer of that card chooses whatever seems best from its point of view. You have no role in that decision.

You might upgrade your motherboard BIOS ROM, by replacing it with another, similar chip containing new information. But that is about all the changing of the ROM chips in your PC that you are likely to do. Still, they are memory in your PC, so for the sake of completeness, here is a description of the various kinds of ROM manufacturers use.

The most common and cheapest ROM circuits to manufacture are *mask-programmable ROMs.* Simply stated, an **I**ntegrated **C**ircuit (IC) manufacturer's customer can specify that when the IC ROM chip is built, it shall have a certain pattern of ones and zeros built into it. The data is added to the design in a late stage using a *mask* to specify where the ones go (and the rest of the locations get zeros).

Mask-programmable ROMs are cheap, but only if you make enough of them holding the same information. This is a fine way for a maker of PCs to distribute the BIOS programs. But it only works if they make and sell enough PCs in a year to justify the initial setup cost for the ROMs.

PROM

Programmable **R**ead-**O**nly **M**emory (PROM) is an oxymoron. Either it is read-only, in which case you cannot change its contents (program it), or it is not. In the case of what we call PROM, it is not.

PROMs store information for years. Unlike SRAM, DRAM, and VRAM, you don't have to keep supplying power for a PROM to retain its data.

How can it do this? The original, and still most common way these chips are built produces what is called a *One-Time-Programmable **ROM**,* or *OTP ROM.* These chips are sometimes called *fusible-link ROMs.* At each memory cell location they have a thin wire shorting out two points in the circuit. That makes the locations all report that they are storing one bits. Applying a special programming signal and address signals to the chip can cause it to overload a particular one of those thin wires. It blows out, just like a fuse. From then on, that location will report that it is holding a zero bit. (The usual jargon for programming a particular pattern of 1s and 0s into an OTP-ROM is "burning the PROM.")

Clearly no one can change any of the zeros back into ones, but it is possible to go on changing other ones into zeros. This is what is meant by these chips being OTP (per bit location).

These are fairly inexpensive chips to build. As long as the user of the chips gets the program put into them right the very first time, they are a cost effective way to distribute programs. Should you buy a replacement BIOS chip, for example, it may come in an OTP ROM.

EPROM

EPROMs are even more of an oxymoron. These are **E**rasable **P**rogrammable **ROM** chips. Like a PROM, they come from the factory, holding ones in every location. An engineer who has purchased these chips can force them to change individual bits to zeros wherever he or she wishes. That is what it means to program the chip. Then, if the engineer finds out that change was a mistake, or simply if she changes her mind, she can erase the chip (turning all the zeros back into ones). These are a popular choice for ROM in prototype circuits in a laboratory. They also are often used in products expected to sell in only modest numbers.

Most of these chips have a quartz window in the top of the package. They are erased by shining a very bright **u**ltraviolet (UV) light through that window. Since sunlight could erase them in a few hours and a room's fluorescent lights could erase them in a matter of days, they normally will have an opaque label stuck over their window once they have been programmed.

To reprogram one of these chips you would have to remove it from the circuit, remove the protective label, and then put the chip under a bright UV light source for a fraction of an hour. After that you put it in a special programmer and reprogram it. Finally, you can return it to the circuit.

These chips are also often referred to as UV-EPROMs. They are used by many manufacturers for products with short life cycles. Once the chip has served its purpose in one product it can be erased and reused. (Once again, you as an "end user" of PC products do not have a choice about the type of ROM used in a part you buy. You just get whatever the maker of that part chose.)

EEPROM

EEPROM! Oh no, here we go again. What does this extra E add? It means electrically, as in **E**lectrically **E**rasable **P**rogrammable **ROM**.

These chips are just like EPROMs except that erasure can be done while the chip is still mounted in its socket, buried deep inside your PC. (That is, it can be if the socket can supply the correct voltages.)

EEPROMs can be used for all the same purposes as any other ROM, plus they can be used to store information you want to change more often than that in a UV-EPROM.

Flash RAM

Flash RAM is the newest of this genre. It really is a variant form of an EEPROM. The main difference is that Flash RAM is optimized for repeated reprogramming. That makes it possible to use this as a replacement for disk drives in certain applications. Some other common names for Flash memory include Flash ROM and Flash EPROM, or simply Flash memory.

> There is more than one kind of memory chip construction that gets casually referred to as Flash memory. You really don't care which technique was used, as long as the properties of the chip are what you need.

It is still electronic memory, and thus it is fast and shock-insensitive. In both those ways, it is much superior to a disk drive. But it is also much more expensive (per bit). So disk drives are used still, except in those special circumstances where the good features of Flash make its use preferable.

For small amounts of information storage, Flash may be the most cost-effective way to go, at least if that information must be easily changed from time to time. So it is finding a use in some PCs for holding the BIOS ROM information.

Reliability and Parity Bits

Electronic memory chips are quite reliable. But they do occasionally make a mistake. They may get some of their bits flipped by a random power-line glitch, or a cosmic ray, etc. These things do not occur very often, but they definitely occur.

IBM believes very strongly that your data is of supreme importance. Rightly so. To protect you from mistakes your computer might make, they included some error detection circuitry in the memory subsystem. We call that the parity circuit.

The makers of most clone PCs agree with IBM in this regard. Furthermore, starting with the Pentium, Intel has begun incorporating parity checking into a number of aspects of the CPU's operation. (Those are integrity checks that are in addition to any that the PC may incorporate in its memory subsystem.)

Parity

Most PC memory systems store nine bits for each byte of information to be held. Eight bits holds the data byte in question. The ninth bit holds what is called the *parity information.*

Parity means the even-ness or odd-ness of some collection of bits. By storing a parity bit, it is possible to make any byte plus its parity bit have an odd number of ones in it. That is called using *odd parity*, and it is what is done in your PC.

Whenever a byte is stored in RAM, its parity is computed and stored along with it. When that byte is read, the parity bit is also read. The parity of the byte is recomputed and compared with the parity bit as read. If they differ, you have a "parity error."

IBM's choice for what to do when this happens is simple: A message appears on-screen (either PARITY CHECK 1 or PARITY CHECK 2), and the computer stops. Some clone makers are a little more helpful. Their machines put up a message that says at what address the parity error occurred, then the computer stops.

Parity checking can catch most errors before they can hurt you. What it cannot do is fix those errors. There is no way the parity circuit can tell which bit got flipped.

Parity errors come in two kinds: temporary and permanent. They are sometimes referred to as "soft" and "hard." If you get a parity error, the first thing to try is simply restarting your PC and seeing if it ever happens again. If not, you had a soft error and you can just ignore it.

If you get persistent parity errors, especially if they occur when you are accessing the same regions of RAM, you may have one or more defective RAM chips. (If yours is one of the helpful clones that tells you where you were accessing in memory before the parity error occurred, you will know when this is happening. If yours is an IBM PC or one like it that simply gives you the unhelpful PARITY CHECK 1 or PARITY CHECK 2 message, you can only guess by knowing which program you were running at the time.) Chapter 31 gives some suggestions for how to deal with this situation.

ECC

An even more powerful strategy is the use of ECC (**E**rror **C**orrecting **C**odes). This is commonly done on hard disk drives, and sometimes it is done for main memory in large computers. Without it our hard disks would give us faulty information or simply be unable to return our data to us at least once every few hours. This would be unacceptable to most PC users.

ECC is implemented by storing a few more bits for each group of bits to be protected. Just one parity bit suffices to catch most (but not all) errors. A fairly modest number of additional bits, suitably used, will allow one not only to detect errors, but also (with some assumptions about how errors happen) allow you to infer where they occurred and put things right again automatically.

So far, ECC is not used in PC memory systems, although manufacturers have begun to discuss doing so. As the number of bytes of RAM used in PCs goes up and up, eventually it will be both modest in cost and almost invaluable in its protections, so ECC will be used in PC memory; it's only a matter of when.

Chip Sizes

The size of a memory chip does not normally refer to its physical dimensions. Rather, it describes the chip's capacity for holding data.

Common usage is to describe a chip by either its total capacity (as in a 256KB chip) or by its organization (as in a 32K-by-8 chip). The latter way tells you more. And you need to know that extra information, as your memory circuits must have memory chips whose bit cells are correctly "organized" for them to be able to use the chips.

> **Warning**   Memory chip makers are dreadfully inconsistent in how they use B in the size designation of memory parts. It could stand for **bit** or for **byte** (8 bits). Look for words that say explicitly what is meant, or you will be left guessing from context or other clues.

Chip Packages

Memory chips get packaged in a variety of ways. If you were a manufacturer, you could even buy them in bulk without any packages around them. But to protect them enough for normal people to handle them without damaging them, they must be protected by some sort of package.

Chapter 2 included a list of some common package names and drawings of a few of them. What is important is that you find out what package you need to fit the sockets you have, then buy the memory you need mounted in that fashion.

The most common discrete chip packages are DIPs, SIPs, and ZIPs. The most common modules are SIMMs, SIPs, and SIPPs. The chips used in those modules are usually put in SOJ or Miniflat packages.

Memory Modules

Memory modules are nothing more or less than a bunch of memory chips stuck on a small circuit board and sold as a unit. The notion is that you normally use groups of chips together, so selling you such a prepackaged group is a convenience.

That is true, but it also means you invest more in each part. Since the parts are inherently nonrepairable, it also means you throw away more value if any one chip fails.

On the other hand, memory modules can be quite reliable and they are getting cheaper every day. You will find that PCs and PC boards will be using SIMMs or other memory modules more and more instead of discrete chips.

Reading the Chip or Module Labels

Figure 16.1 shows a typical memory chip's labeling text. This example uses NEC's notation, but all the manufacturers use similar styles. The figure also shows you what the various parts of the label mean.

The most important things to decode off a memory module's label are its part number and its speed code. From the part number, you can find out everything else about it (by asking someone who has access to the appropriate memory chip manual). The speed rating is normally shown by a number set off from the rest of the part number by a hyphen. It gives the access time in tens of nanoseconds (usually).

Get the Right Size Modules

Buying memory modules presents a special opportunity to make mistakes. Normally you will buy a SIMM by its capacity in bytes (for example, a 1MB SIMM). That refers to the total amount of data it can store. But the same data capacity can come in two different forms. You and your PC memory circuitry care deeply which one you buy.

SIMMs for the PC market are mostly organized as by-9 modules. That means they include a parity bit for every byte of data they store. That is what you want for your main RAM.

Some SIMMs are by-8 designs. That is what *Macintosh* computers use. Also, some video cards for PCs will use them. But they won't work in a PC for main memory.

There are rare exceptions (of course). A few PCs can have their parity checking circuits turned off. In them you could get away with by-8 SIMMs. But you would be taking unnecessary chances on data corruption, so don't do it.

A video card can get away without parity checking (and most of them do) simply because you rarely read information from the screen image buffer, and you probably wouldn't notice if a few pixels were to show you wrong information. That is the idea, anyway. So don't be surprised when you don't find any parity chips on a video card.

Also, be aware that this means you can't count on a SIMM that says "for use in a video card" being a VRAM module. More likely, it will be an ordinary, single-ported DRAM, but it will be organized as a by-8 module.

Rated Chip Speed

Memory chips have two speed ratings. One is called the chip's *access time*. The other is its *cycle time*.

Access time, as you might guess, means how soon after you ask the chip for some data you can expect to find the data presented at the Data Out pin(s). Asking for the information in this context means putting an address on the address lines and doing the proper things with the RAS and CAS lines. (See the discussion in Chapter 9 for more details.) The access time is also the time after you present the chip with some data that you must keep the data on the Data In pin(s) in order to be sure the chip "got it."

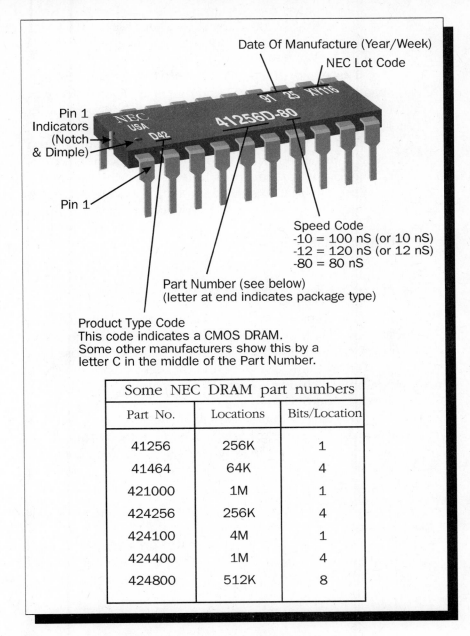

Figure 16.1. How to read a typical memory chip's label.

Cycle time means how soon after reading from one location in this chip you can read from another. That is often three or four times longer than the access time.

The access time is usually what is spoken of when you quote "the speed" of a memory chip. And that is what you mostly care about. That is what the number after the dash in the part number designates (see Figure 16.1 in particular the callout for the Speed Code).

You also care about the cycle time, especially if your program is just reading through memory, location after location. But as it happens, the ratio of cycle time to access time is about the same for all chips. What's even nicer is that it is close to being the same as the ratio between the minimum time between memory accesses and the time between system clock pulses in most PCs. This means if the access time for a given memory chip is suitable for use in your PC, the cycle time probably will be also.

Chip Speed Significance

Memory chips are built to go as fast as possible. Then they are tested to see how fast they can go, really. Those that can go extremely fast get labeled and sold as premium, super-fast chips. Those that go a bit slower get labeled as such, and are sold for slightly less money. This process keeps on until the chip fails even the slowest acceptable speed test. Those chips are discarded.

This means that if you buy a 100nS rated chip (one with a —10 near the end of its part number), it will, for sure, work that fast. It will *not*, almost for sure, work in only 80nS. If it had been able to do that, it would have been labeled that way (with a —8 near the end of its part number).

> **Warning** You *must* buy chips specified to work at least as fast as your system will ask them to work. It doesn't hurt anything but your pocketbook to buy chips rated to work even faster. Buying chips that are not rated to work as fast as your system requires will almost certainly make them useless to you and a danger to your system's operation.

Please realize that simply buying faster memory chips and installing them will by itself *not* speed up your PC. It will just make those memory chips loaf along at a speed below their maximum capability.

Sometimes you can benefit yourself by installing faster RAM chips. If you replace all the slow RAM chips with faster ones and *if* you then can set the motherboard or memory option card carrying those chips to use a lower number of wait states, then you will speed up your PC.

Also, in some PCs, you can replace the slow RAM chips with faster ones, and then speed up the system clock and have everything run faster. The problem with this is that *everything* is what runs faster, not just the RAM chips. You replaced the slow RAM chips, but can the other chips on that circuit board keep up with the new, faster clock speed? Sometimes they can, and sometimes not. If you feel adventurous, perhaps you can experiment. Most PC users decline to participate in such risky activities.

Knowing How Fast Your Memory Chips Must Be

The best way to find out how speedy your new memory chips (or modules) must be, is to read the documentation that came with your PC, its motherboard, or the memory card on which you will be installing the chips (or modules). Yes, read the manual.

The second best way is to look at what you already have. If you are merely increasing the amount of RAM by adding chips or modules to what is already installed, you probably will want to get ones that match (or can go faster than) the ones you already have.

The issue used to be quite simple. You just took the CPU clock speed in MHz (megahertz, or millions of cycles per second) and divided it into 1000. The result is the period of time between successive clock cycles in nanoseconds. That is also called the *clock period*. Then, if your memory chips had a rated access time less than about one clock period, you could feel pretty safe. You'd be skating on thin ice if you bought memory chips that ran much slower than this. (For example, if you had a 10MHz XT clone, you'd need memory chips rated at 100 nanoseconds or less.)

Things are not nearly so simple any more. Memory cache, wait states, page-mode chips, and interleaved access, in particular, all help let you get away with chips that run far slower than the simple calculation would suggest. A good thing, too. For our CPU chips have gotten faster and faster very quickly, and affordable fast memory chips have not kept pace.

What a memory cache is and how it works are explained in Chapter 14. With a memory cache, the CPU runs at full speed, almost always. When it needs information from memory, it can get it from the cache instead. The relatively less frequent accesses from the cache to main memory can each be much slower and still keep the cache adequately supplied with information.

Wait states are explained in Chapter 17. That leaves page mode and interleaved access to explain. Here is what they mean.

Page-Mode Chips

Usually you must present to a DRAM chip the address of the location you wish to access in two parts. One is called the *row address.* The other is the *column address.* The process goes like this: Give a row address, assert RAS, give a column address, assert CAS, read the data. (For a write, the sequence is to first present the data, then present the row address, assert RAS, present the column address, and then assert CAS. Only then may you change the data presented.) See Chapter 9 for additional discussion of this point. (See also Figure 9.1.)

A page-mode chip is one which allows you to access all the locations in one row without having to reassert the row address. The first access to a row is done in the usual fashion. The next several may be done simply by supplying the new column address and reasserting CAS.

That saves some time. But it is only useful if you need to access several different addresses in one row before going to another row. If the memory system design is done right, that will happen a fair number of times. This can be useful enough to make the extra work involved in the design and fabrication worth doing.

If your system supports page-mode access, be sure that the RAM chips you buy do also. Most modern DRAMs do, but not all of them. Ask your supplier.

Interleaved Memory Access

Interleaved memory access is another technique to help the CPU run faster without requiring the memory chips to go equally faster. This technique is uncommon on any PC with a system clock speed less than about 20MHz, but it is quite common for faster systems.

As with page-mode access, this technique depends for its effectiveness upon the frequent occurrence of a regular pattern of accesses to memory. Most programs are read from memory, one byte after another, in a strict sequence. Only about 5 percent of the time does the program have a jump instruction that forces an alteration in that flow. (See the discussion in Chapter 7.)

If your PC supports interleaved memory accesses, and if you have one of the "magic" amounts of RAM, this approach will almost double the effective speed of your RAM chips.

Here is how it works: The RAM in any PC must be organized into banks. Each bank holds as many bits per location as the number of data wires in the memory bus. So for an 8088- or 8086-based PC, the bank width is one byte. For a PC whose CPU is an 80286 or a 386SX, the bank width is two bytes (16 bits). The bank width for PCs whose CPU is a 386DX or 486 will be 32 bits. A *Pentium*-based PC will have a 64 bit-wide bank of memory.

For a PC to make use of an interleaved memory access strategy, *it must have an even number of banks of RAM*. If it does, then it can alternate memory addresses between the even bank(s) and the odd bank(s). Now, when memory is accessed in order of location in memory address space, it will be accessed alternately from an even bank and from an odd bank.

The number 5 percent cited earlier in this section refers to JUMP instructions. For interleaved access you also must be concerned with data references that are mixed in with the instructions. They can mess up the strict alternation of even and odd memory address accessing and thus diminish the effectiveness of the interleaved access strategy.

Suppose the clock speed is such that 50nS chips would be needed without interleaved access. Such chips are available, but they are very costly. If interleaved access is used, the chips could be mere 100nS chips (relatively cheap ones) and things will still work okay.

They would work okay 95 percent of the time, that is. What about that other 5 percent of the time (or more, allowing for data accesses)? What happens then?

If something special were not done, as soon as a JUMP instruction or data reference took the program from an even address directly to another even address, or from an odd one to another odd one, the CPU would read invalid data and, most likely, your PC would crash.

Fortunately the necessary fix is pretty easy. Any motherboard that supports interleaved memory access will have some special, extra circuitry built in. This special circuitry watches the addresses presented to memory. Whenever an odd address follows an odd address or an even one follows an even one, the circuitry forces a wait state (or, if you already were using one wait state per memory access, it forces an extra one or two).

This means that the rate of memory accesses will falter, briefly, as it must for data integrity to be assured. But the average rate will still be much higher than would have been possible otherwise.

Calculating the Magic Amounts
of RAM for Your Interleaved PC

Suppose your PC is one that can support this interleaved memory access approach. It can only do so if you install a "magic" arrangement of RAM chips or modules. Here is how you can figure out just what those magic arrangements will be.

Remember, the goal is to have an even number of banks of RAM. Let's look at some examples. First, suppose you have a fast 386SX. Its bank width is 16 bits. That means that if you use "by-1" memory chips (that is, 256K-by-1) you will have to have 18 of them per bank (including one parity bit per byte). If a chip holds 256 kilobits, this means a bank will hold 512KB, that is 512 kilo*bytes* (of data with parity). So the magic numbers for this system, when it is using 256-kilobit chips, would be any multiple of 1MB.

Now look at what happens if you choose to use 1-megabit chips. A bank will now hold 2MB. In this case, the magic amounts of RAM are multiples of 4MB (megabytes).

Turning to a larger bus system, consider a 486 with its 32 bit-wide memory accesses. A bank for a 486 will contain 36 bit-wide chips. Or it may use SIMMs, in which case it will use four byte-wide SIMMs (or two 18-bit wide SIMMs or one 36-bit wide SIMM) per bank.

If you use 1-megabit chips (or 1 megabyte SIMMs) in such a system, the magic amounts of memory are going to be multiples of 8MB. From these examples you should be able to compute the magic numbers for your system.

PCs designed around the new *Pentium* chip will need a multiple of 2MB (using 256K-by-1 memory chips) or a multiple of 16MB (using 1 megabit chips)—exactly double the amounts of memory needed for a 486—in order to achieve "magic" status. This is because the *Pentium's* data bus is 64 bits wide—which is twice as wide as the data bus in a 486.

What if you don't want to put in a magic amount? There are two possibilities. One is that your PC was built to insist on interleaved access and thus to insist on even numbers of banks being filled. In that case, it just won't work with any other values. The other, more common case is that the PC's system logic will notice how much memory is installed, and it will only turn on interleaved memory access if it finds a magic amount. In that case, if you choose some other amount of total RAM, you'll be forcing your PC to use a less efficient and thus, on average, a slower way to access its memory.

Double and Triple Speed CPUs

Recently a new way to speed up your CPU has become popular; one that doesn't involve speeding up everything else on the motherboard. That is by using a speed doubling (or speed tripling) CPU. So far, Intel only makes this technology in versions of its 486 chip called either Overdrive or DX/2 chips.

The DX/2, 50MHz chip, for example, is meant for use in a normal 25MHz 486DX motherboard. This chip uses an internal clock that runs at exactly twice the speed of the external clock. That means that you get almost twice the computing speed without having to use any faster RAM chips (or anything else) on your motherboard.

Both IBM and Intel have indicated that they will soon be introducing clock tripler chips, with internal clock speeds up to 99MHz. This will enable users to nearly triple the computational speed of their PCs without any increase in required speed for the RAM chips.

The only way this technology can work effectively is by using memory caching extensively and by having the math coprocessor on the CPU chip. Since both the primary memory cache and the math coprocessor are included on the chip with 486s and not with the earlier members of the x86 family, Intel decided it would not be effective to use clock doubling on any of the earlier designs.

The field of memory chip and memory-system design is a very active one. Improvements are made frequently. Still, for the most part, we have seen only modest increases in the speed of memory chips over the past decade—certainly less dramatic ones than the improvements in processor speed over that same time period.

That may be about to change. A new company, Rambus, Inc., has launched a new approach to the problem. They are promoting a new bus for interconnecting high speed devices. Their plan uses a rather simple modification to the standard DRAM chips, in the form of a special interface that the manufacturer of those ICs could build into the chip. Such a new design would be called an *RDRAM*. Rambus is not going to make these chips. Instead they are licensing the technology to the established IC makers. (So far Fujitsu, Hitachi, NEC, and Toshiba have signed on to make *RDRAM* devices.)

Once there are *RDRAM* chips available, they can be interconnected via a new bus called the *RAMBUS*. This is a short (maximum length about 10cm) 28-wire bus (including all necessary signal and power lines). It carries data nine bits at a time. By using a burst mode method of access (give an address and a number of bytes you want, then blast all of those bytes, with their parity bits, in succession over nine parallel wires), it can support transfers at speeds up to 500MB/S (that is 500 mega**bytes** per second—more than ten times faster than the fastest buses now in use in PCs).

If you are a designer of PC systems or high speed subsystems, you will want to contact Rambus at the address given in the MemInfo hypertext database on the diskette that accompanies this book for more details. Anyone else will want to watch for products incorporating this exciting, new approach. It could be an even better solution to the data transfer bottleneck than the Local Bus that is just now coming into use.

A Recap

Choosing memory chips or modules can be tricky because you need to know arcane details about them. For example, you need to know not merely how much data they will hold (their total capacity), you also need to know how that capacity is organized. And you need to make sure you get your memory chips or modules in the right packages.

Further, you need to be aware of speed issues. They get complicated by other things, including how many wait states your memory system inserts (which may be something you can change), whether or not your system supports interleaved memory accesses, whether or not it can take advantage of page-mode chips, and whether or not you have a memory cache installed.

The information presented here will, at least, alert you to the issues. It may also have sufficed to inform you about what they mean. Still, the bottom line on choosing new memory chips is often this: Get more of what you already have, or read the documentation on whatever part has the sockets into which you will be plugging the chips or modules.

There is one aspect of this that has not yet been explained. That is what a wait state is and why you may need to use one or more of them. That, and how to safely install your new RAM, are the subjects of the next chapter.

ADDING MEMORY
SAFELY AND EFFECTIVELY

Anyone can add memory to his or her PC. This chapter lists some precautions that will minimize the chance of damaging your new or existing memory, the rest of your PC, or yourself. This chapter also explains wait states and reviews how to choose the right chips or modules for your PC.

So you've decided you need more RAM in your PC. You've read Chapter 16. You've gone to your memory supplier, asked the right questions, and you have some freshly purchased RAM. Now you want to know how to install it safely, right?

Wait just a moment. Are you sure you got the kind of memory you need? You *did* read Chapter 16, didn't you? If not, you'd better do so now. (You may be able to return whatever you bought if you bought the wrong kind. And it generally works better to try returning things *before* you use them.)

This chapter opens with a review of memory chip speed issues. It explains wait states. It concludes with a repeat of the bottom-line advice about how to choose memory chips.

Most of the chapter is about how to handle memory chips, option cards, and memory modules safely. Indeed, you'll learn how to do any kind of work inside your PC safely.

Memory Chip Speed Issues Revisited

Many people are a bit confused about memory and speed in their PCs. A quick review of this area may help you avoid doing something you will later regret.

The speed at which your PC computes is set by an internal metronome called the *system clock*. The speed at which it transfers data to other parts is set by a different clock—in many PCs, the I/O bus clock. And there may be still other clocks to control your hard disk, your video system, modem, and so on.

If you have a 12MHz AT, your system clock runs at 12MHz. If yours is a fast 486/33MHz machine, the system clock runs at 33MHz. One megahertz (MHz) equals one million cycles per second. So that fast 486 sees 33 million cycles of its system clock go by every second.

Of all the clocks in your PC, the one that matters most for memory purposes is the system clock. But it is far from all that matters.

Some of the time, the CPU chip is doing work within itself. At various moments, it will need to get some information from memory or to put some there. When it does, it may be limited in how fast it can get back to its internal work by the speed with which the memory system responds.

There are two primary and one other case in which the system clock speed is not the relevant one for memory access. The primary cases are when you have a memory cache or when you are using a clock-doubling (or tripling) CPU chip. The other case is when the memory in question has been installed on the I/O bus. These issues are discussed in Chapter 16.

Assume for the moment that your CPU is directly connected to the memory parts of your PC. (That means that you don't have a memory cache installed.) In that case, the speed of the memory system absolutely and directly affects the speed with which the CPU can get through any instructions it executes which refer to memory. This includes loading those instructions.

A Trick Question

But how does the speed of that memory subsystem depend on the speed of the memory chips in it? Here is where most people make their first mistake. The correct answer is: It doesn't! That is, *provided the memory chips are fast enough,* just how quickly they can do their work has *no* impact on the speed with which the CPU can get back to work on other things.

The CPU doesn't know how soon the memory chips are ready. Nor does the system logic. There is no way for those parts to observe that about the memory chips.

So the designers of the system have to make some assumptions. They express those assumptions mainly through something called *wait states*.

Wait States

What is a wait state? Why do you need them? How did the number of them that you have get set? Can you change that setting? Should you? These are some of the questions you may have right about now. Answering them is the next order of business.

The system clock controls how fast the CPU performs each step in its operation. If nothing stops it, when it goes to read or write to the memory chips, it does so just as fast as it can.

In the early days of PCs, system clock speeds were fairly modest—about 5MHz. Even the fastest AT had a system clock that went at only 8MHz. Now vendors are bragging about their latest and greatest PCs, trumpeting its speed as 66MHz.

The system clock speed in available PCs has risen by a factor of more than ten over the past decade. In that same time period the speed of affordable DRAM has perhaps tripled at best.

This means that now, more than ever, CPU chips are ready and raring to go long before the DRAM chips are. If a system designer knows by how much the CPU speed and system clock exceed the speed of the DRAM chips, it is quite easy to build in a compensating feature. This is a mechanism that tells the CPU, in effect, "Hold your horses, the memory chips will be ready for you in just a moment." This extra pause to allow for slightly sluggish memory chips is enforced each time the CPU accesses memory.

Figure 17.1 represents the process that goes on between the CPU and the memory subsystem both for reading and writing. It shows one wait state (the shaded portion of the diagram).

Actual PCs may have anywhere from zero wait states (meaning the memory is *assumed* to be capable of keeping up with the CPU) to five or six wait states (when the memory chips are *assumed* to be very much slower than the CPU).

Notice the word *assumed*. That's right. The system designers have to make assumptions.

In one situation, the system logic can detect when the memory chips are ready and when they are not, and thus it can dynamically adjust the wait states to compensate appropriately. The memory chips in question are on the video display adapter. That adapter often must tell the rest of the system to wait for it to finish reading out some information to the monitor before it will allow a memory access by the CPU or DMA chips.

So the number of wait states inserted into a memory access depends on exactly when the request for memory access comes in the cycle of the video adapter's other, more important task of supplying the screen driver with image data.

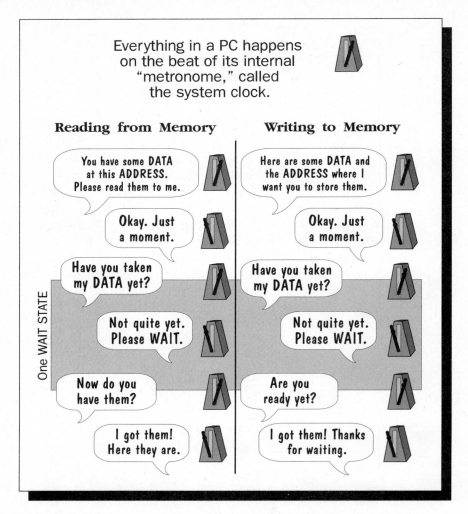

Figure 17.1. Wait states help memory keep up with a too-fast CPU.

Since designers don't know which chips you will buy and install, they often make quite conservative assumptions. In other systems, the assumptions are subject to change. That is, you can alter the number of wait states the system logic will insert in each memory cycle.

How you do this, or even whether you can do this, depends on what the system designers did. You may have some jumpers that can be changed on the motherboard. Look for information about this in your system or motherboard documentation. Or you may have some options you can select in an "Advanced Options" screen of your system's configuration setup program.

You could set the number of wait states to as low a value as your system allows. If that worked with your RAM chips, the system would work as fast as it possibly could. But it might not work, and then your data could get damaged.

You could choose the slowest setting (the maximum number of wait states), but then you may be wasting the potential for speed that your memory chips actually have. The right procedure is to first choose the speed of memory chips you will install, and then set the wait states to the correct corresponding value.

How to Choose Memory Chip Speed

First, look at what you already have. If your PC is working now, you may assume that its memory chips aren't too slow. So getting more just like them should work okay.

> Sometimes a PC is *not* working correctly, and the reason may be that someone set it up with the wrong memory chips or the wrong number of wait states. If your PC is not working correctly now, don't assume it has the right memory chips. Check it out. This is probably best done by looking in the manual for that PC or its motherboard.

A very good idea is to read the manual. Which one? Well, if you have purchased a complete PC system you probably have only one set of manuals. They describe everything about the system. Look in them for a section on memory or on the motherboard.

If you bought pieces and put the PC together yourself, you are the system's manufacturer. In this case, the manual you want is one that should have come with your motherboard. This also applies if your PC was built for you by a dealer.

Frequently you will have a choice. You can spend more money, buy faster memory chips, set the wait state number lower, and get maximum system performance. Alternatively you may be able to buy less expensive, slower memory chips, set the wait state number higher, and settle for the less-than-stellar performance your PC will now be forced to deliver. Still it may be plenty fast enough for your needs.

But without the motherboard or system manual (or advice from the manufacturer of the motherboard or the system), it's tough to figure out how to choose the chips or how to set the number of wait states. The presence of a memory cache and either page mode or interleaved memory access further compounds the difficulty of figuring out what memory chip speed and wait state number will be optimum.

Fractional Wait States

You may have bought a system that was advertised as having "only 1.3 wait states." But when you go to set the number of wait states you find your choices are just things like *0*, *1*, or *2*. What does this 1.3 wait-state number mean? How could you possibly make the PC wait a fraction of a cycle?

The simple answer to that last question is that you can't. Every individual memory access has zero, one, two, or some other integral number of wait states inserted.

But if you have interleaved access, page-mode chips, or some other special memory-access strategy, the number of wait states may well depend on the exact sequence of memory accesses. So it is quite possible that the *average* number of wait states would be a non-integer like 1.3.

I'd better also point out that the number you get depends on the test you perform. The exact sequence of instructions controls how memory is accessed. To paraphrase the EPA, "Your average number of wait states may vary."

How about Memory Chips Installed on an Option Card?

If you install memory chips on a proprietary memory card, chances are it will work just like memory on the motherboard (provided you plug it into a special memory card socket). So the same issues apply, as do their resolutions.

But if you put memory chips on a standard option card plugged into the I/O bus, all of a sudden the relevant clock changes. Now you don't care about the system clock. You care about the I/O bus clock. (Slow PCs use only one clock, but then they'll work with just about any chips you can buy and they don't need wait states.)

Brand Idiosyncrasies

Finally, there is the issue of brand idiosyncrasies. Unfortunately, not all chips are created equal, even when their manufacturers say they are.

You will often find in the manual of a motherboard or memory card a list of approved suppliers or part numbers for memory chips. Buy from that list. They mean it.

Here's what happens. The manufacturer of the motherboard or memory card buys some chips, builds a prototype, and goes into production. Then, apparently, they test their product with lots of chips. And they prepare a three-column list. Column A is for chips that work. Column B is for chips that don't work. Column C says simply, "If you choose a chip not listed here, you're on your own."

How to Add Memory Safely

Memory chips are static-sensitive devices. That means you can zap them without half trying. But if you learn some simple precautions, you can avoid damaging them (if you at least halfway try to follow those precautions!).

Precautions to Avoid Zapping Memory Chips (or Anything Else in Your PC)

Here is how memory chips get zapped. You can easily build up a static charge on your body of several hundreds or even thousands of volts. Memory ICs (integrated circuits) are meant to run at a mere 5 volts, give or take half a volt. Any voltage noticeably larger than this can do them harm.

Voltage itself does not damage anything. The currents it causes to flow do the damage. Two things keep the currents from flowing: Resistance, and the lack of any voltage *difference* to urge them on. One thing diverts the currents safely: metal or other conductive shielding.

1. Electrically Isolate Your PC before Opening It Up

This leads to the first and most basic advice to protect you and your PC: Electrically isolate your PC from ground and from its peripherals before you open the case. As long as the case is closed the components inside are pretty safe. Once you open the case they become vulnerable.

There are two advantages in this approach over what some people suggest (that is, being sure your PC is grounded). First, if you ground the PC, you will provide it with a firmly defined voltage; if yours is different, that difference can and will make some currents flow somewhere, the first chance they get.

Second, if you use your PC's power cable to ground it, you also are supplying AC voltage to the power supply, right up to the switch in that box. It shouldn't get out of there, but if it does (for example, if the unit has some electrical leakage in it, or if you bump the switch by accident), your personal safety could be at stake, not merely that of your memory chips. It really ruins your day to be electrocuted!

How do you ensure that your PC is electrically isolated? Disconnect it! Unplug the power cable. Unplug the cables to your monitor, printer, modem, and all other external parts. Once you have done that, you know you are safe.

2. Equalize Your Voltage to That of Your PC

By making your voltage the same as your PC's before you reach inside it, you will keep static electricity from flowing from you to the chips you touch. That is the basis of electrostatic safety.

> **A Basic Rule for Safety**   *Every* time you are about to reach inside your PC, touch a bare metal part of the case first.

Follow this advice and you won't go wrong. But how do you do it? There are two ways. Each is right for some people. Neither is perfect for everyone.

The first method is to attach yourself to your PC via a grounding strap. You can get a strap that hooks around your wrist and fastens with Velcro. A wire extends from that strap, ending in a clip you can attach to your PC. Be sure to attach it to a metal part of the case. Paint insulates.

The second method is both simpler and, for some people, much harder. It requires you to develop a good habit, and then follow that habit *each and every time* you approach your open PC. Make the first part of the PC you touch the power supply or some bare metal part of the chassis (see Figure 17.2).

What is hard about this method is that it depends upon forcing yourself to acquire this habit. You may find that the ground-strap approach removes the need to think so much. But it also tethers you, and of course, you must be in the habit of using the strap.

Proper Handling of Option Cards

Option cards are vulnerable once you remove them from your PC (if they are already installed) or from the shipping package (if you just bought one). Keep them where they are safe until you need to work on them, and then return them to safety as soon as you can.

Hold PC option cards by the edge—not in the middle—and never by the tongue that sticks out and has little gold strips on it (see Figure 17.3). That tongue is the part of the card that sticks down into the I/O slot connector. Keep those gold fingers clean and the card will work longer. (But don't rub them too hard in an effort to clean them, or you could rub off the thin layer of gold.)

Figure 17.2. Always ground yourself to the frame before reaching inside a PC.

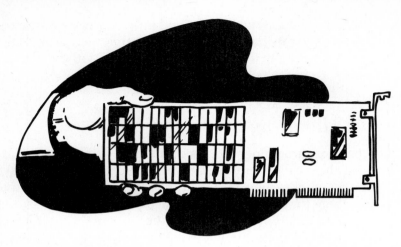

Figure 17.3. Hold option cards by the edges, not by the gold card edge connector.

When you remove an option card from the system unit or its protective packaging, where can you safely put it down? The absolute worst place is in a box of foam packing material. That's very likely to be deadly.

The best place is on a slightly conductive surface. An insulating surface is okay (like a wooden or plastic tabletop), but a slight conductor helps drain off static charges slowly and without doing harm. The antistatic bag those boards are shipped in is a convenient slightly conductive material. But don't worry if you don't have one handy; just carefully place the card on a plain wood table.

Be aware that some option cards carry batteries on them. Be careful not to set those cards down on a metal surface. You could short out the battery.

Don't lay option cards on your bed, nor on a vinyl-covered couch. Rubbing on the plastic fibers in the bed covering or the couch upholstery can deliver static electric charges to the board, and possibly damage it.

Be careful when you go to insert the card in your PC. Line up the tongue with the slot connector. Be sure you are putting the card in an appropriate slot. If it has two tongues, make sure the motherboard has two connectors for them to go into. When you are sure the card is lined up correctly, press down on it gently but firmly until it is seated as far as it goes. Don't get carried away. Excess force could break either the card or the connector.

Removing cards is much the same, but in reverse. A lot of force may be required. First, though, be sure you have taken out or loosened any retaining screws. Otherwise you may break something trying to force the card out.

Try to pull up equally on both ends of the card. You may rock it gently, if necessary, in a motion that rotates the card in its own plane. Don't bend the card side to side.

Adding Memory Cards

Remember that there are three common bus widths in the world of PCs. (This refers to the number of data wires, not the number of address wires.) They are 8-bit, 16-bit, and 32-bit. The standard ISA bus only has 8- or 16-bit slots. The former use a single connector; the latter have two connectors, one behind the other. The only 32-bit bus slots are in EISA or MCA machines (or on a local bus or for a proprietary memory card).

Some PCs with a local bus option will have the normal ISA or EISA slot connectors plus a local bus connector for up to three of the slot positions. A *Pentium*-based PC may have at least some 64-bit slots.

Be sure your memory card is inserted into a slot with the right bus width. The only exception to this is for some video cards. These are 16-bit cards that can automatically detect if they are inserted in an 8-bit slot. If they see that, they will turn off their 16-bit I/O circuitry and use only the 8-bit portion.

Also reread the section in Chapter 8 about the curious problem with 16-bit video cards in some PCs. You may find another 8-bit ROM or other video card will malfunction if the 16-bit card is not built in a special way. If you do see such a symptom, just set the switch or jumper on the 16-bit video card to force it to use only 8-bit data transfers on the bus; or, if it is one of the 16-bit video cards that can sense an 8-bit slot and adapt itself, move it to an 8-bit slot.

Proper Handling of Chips

Isolated chips (and modules like SIMMs) are the most vulnerable parts you will handle. The first rule is to hold the conductive container they come in before you pick up the chip itself. Indeed, keep chips in their protective containers until the last possible moment (see Figure 17.4). Then promptly put them into sockets and, preferably, put that circuit card into the system unit soon.

Plastic bags that look smoky and a bit reflective are usually conductive, and will help drain away static charges and shield against electrostatic currents. So to a degree are the pink plastic bags. (Frequently, one of those bags has a label that tells you it is an antistatic bag.) Clear plastic bags are not good protection. They could even be a source of danger. Rubbing nonconductive plastic is one of the easiest ways to build up a static charge and hurt something.

Black, conductive foam blocks are often used to hold integrated circuits safely. When the pins of the IC are stuck in that kind of foam the IC is well protected. Long, conductive plastic tubes are another popular and safe way to pack ICs for handling and shipment.

Styrofoam (the white, hard foam plastic used in coffee cups and as "peanuts" for packing) is totally different. Push an IC in a piece of this, and you may as well throw it away.

How to Remove Older, Smaller Memory Chips (DIPs)

Memory chips used to come in only one form: a small rectangular block of plastic or ceramic with leads coming out of two opposite sides and bending down to form two parallel rows of legs. These are called *Dual Inline Packages*, or *DIPs* for short (see Figure 16.1).

Many tool kits sold for use with PCs include something called a *chip puller*. It is meant for removing DIPs from their sockets. (Careful: Some DIPS are soldered to the circuit card. Only try removing those that are in sockets.)

Chip pullers are not very useful. The easiest and safest way to get a DIP-packaged IC out of a socket is to pry up *gently* on each end alternately with a small, flat-bladed screwdriver. Continue to work it up a little at a time until it is completely free of the socket. (Figure 17.5 shows both tools.)

The problem with using a commercial chip puller is that while you're supposed to grab the chip from under both ends and just pull it out of the socket, all too often your grip will slip at just the wrong moment. Then the chip may get wrenched out of the socket at one end while it is still deeply inserted at the other end. This badly bends its leads. Do that a few times and those leads will snap off, destroying the usefulness of that IC.

Figure 17.4. Keep chips in their protective containers as long as possible.

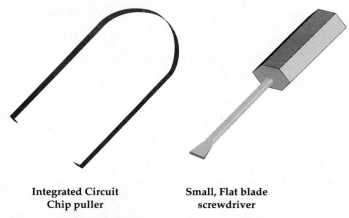

Integrated Circuit   Small, Flat blade
Chip puller   screwdriver

Figure 17.5.   A commercial chip puller and a more convenient, safer tool to use.

How to Install Your New Chips

Inserting an IC into a socket is not very difficult, but you must be careful. Check first that the pins are straight and parallel to each other. Be sure pin 1 is going into hole 1. (Figure 16.1 shows two common ways chip makers mark pin 1. Often sockets will be marked with a notch at the end with hole 1. Also usually all the chips on a single circuit board will have their #1 ends pointing in the same direction.) Gently push the pins back in line if any of them are splayed out or bent inward too far.

If you install a chip backwards, you won't do any damage to it—until you supply power. You will then instantly destroy it. Well, they sometimes manage to survive, but do you need to test that point?

Look very carefully when inserting a chip into a socket. Check to be sure each lead goes into its hole. Watch out for leads that slip out and down between two sockets, or ones that fold under the chip, or ones that get stuck part way into a hole and then collapse like an accordion.

Push down a little way and recheck everything. Then push down firmly, but not too firmly, please. You actually can break the plastic body of an IC if you push too hard.

Installing and Removing Memory Modules (SIMMs, SIPs, SIPPs, and ZIPs)

Memory modules are like miniature option cards. They go into their sockets similar to the way option cards go into slot connectors. Each SIMM is notched near pin 1 (see Figure 2.1). You also may be able to tell how to orient it from a picture in your PC's system manual or by looking at any other SIMMs already installed (and that you know work).

One important difference is in how they get retained once they have been put all the way in. Option cards may have a hold-down screw or a clamping screw. Memory modules more likely will be held in place by one or two little fingers on the sides of the socket that snap over the edges of the module's circuit card or into the holes in that card.

Some SIMM sockets require you to put the SIMM in at a slight tilt. Then you rotate it gently to an upright position, at which point it will snap into place. Other socket designs simply have you slide the SIMM into place in one straight motion, just like plugging an option card into a slot.

Check carefully for the little fingers that may be holding a SIMM in its socket before you remove it. You can break the socket or the SIMM if you are too rough. You may find it helpful to have a small screwdriver or straightened-out paper clip to push those fingers out of the way when you want to remove a SIMM.

The other packages present very similar issues when installing them or removing them. The best advice for all these situations is the good old one:

> Haste makes waste (so take it easy).

How CPU Type and Motherboard Design Affect How Much Memory You Can (or Must) Add at One Time

Review the information in Chapter 16 on the size of a bank of memory. You must add RAM in full banks. And if you want to gain the effect of memory interleaving, you will need to add RAM in the larger, "magic" amounts described in that chapter.

Where to Put the Chips

With some PCs it is easy to tell where the memory chips need to go. Other designs make it much tougher. The classic bank of memory is a set of 9, 18, or 36 sockets, each able to hold a single *by-one* DRAM chip. In that case, every chip in the bank must be identical.

Often, if the bank consists of 18 or 36 sockets, they will be arranged in two or four rows of 9 sockets each. The sockets in each row hold the bits of one byte of data plus the parity bit. There are four common arrangements for the bits in one of those rows. Reading left to right, with the notched ends of the chips pointing up, they are: P LSB . . . MSB, P MSB . . . LSB, LSB . . . MSB P, and MSB . . . LSB P (where P stands for the parity chip, and LSB and MSB stand for the least- and most-significant bits).

Another popular layout is to use two nibble-wide chips (thus getting eight bits) and a single *by-one* chip for parity. You might, for example, use a pair of 44256 chips (those contain 256K bits, organized as 64K by 4) and one 4164 (which contains 64K bits organized as 64K by 1).

Which arrangement your PC uses is not necessarily something you must know right away. If one of the memory chips proves to be bad (or badly installed), however, and if you have a memory diagnostic program that points you to the chip to change, you must know how your PC's chips are arranged in order to interpret that information correctly.

Sometimes a bank will be constructed to take either one of two different sizes of memory chip. In one case, that means two kinds of chips that come in the exact same package, but with different bit capacities. If that is the kind of bank of sockets you have, be sure you use the same capacity chip in each socket of that bank. In another case, the board may be built to take either of two physically different memory chips.

Variations on these different layout strategies can be combined on a single motherboard. Figure 15.1 shows the "traditional" layout for the IBM PC, PC/XT, and most XT clones. Figure 20.1 shows the *IBM PC/AT* layout. Figure 17.6 shows a very complicated (and unusual) layout. Don't expect to understand this last layout without a good deal of study.

Checking Your Work
Before Powering Up the PC

Once you have installed your new memory chips or modules, no doubt you will be eager to try them out. Don't be too eager. Double-check your work and you may save a lot of money. Remember the advice I gave you earlier.

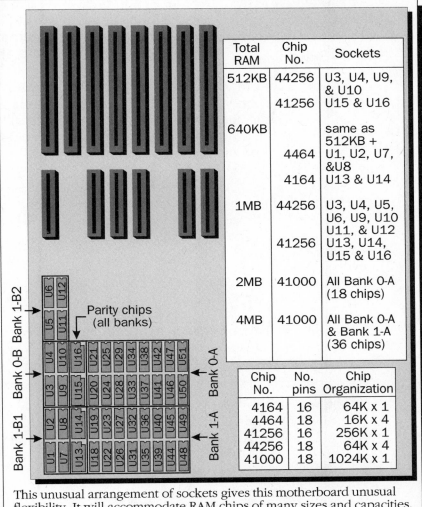

Total RAM	Chip No.	Sockets
512KB	44256	U3, U4, U9, & U10
	41256	U15 & U16
640KB		same as 512KB +
	4464	U1, U2, U7, &U8
	4164	U13 & U14
1MB	44256	U3, U4, U5, U6, U9, U10 U11, & U12
	41256	U13, U14, U15 & U16
2MB	41000	All Bank 0-A (18 chips)
4MB	41000	All Bank 0-A & Bank 1-A (36 chips)

Chip No.	No. pins	Chip Organization
4164	16	64K x 1
4464	18	16K x 4
41256	16	256K x 1
44256	18	64K x 4
41000	18	1024K x 1

Parity chips (all banks)

Bank 1-B2
Bank 1-B1
Bank 0-B
Bank 0-A
Bank 1-A

This unusual arrangement of sockets gives this motherboard unusual flexibility. It will accommodate RAM chips of many sizes and capacities, to give total RAM from 512KB to 4MB. Parity chips for Banks 0-A and 1-A are at the left end of each row. Parity chips for Banks 0-B are to its right. Parity for Banks 1-B1 and 1-B2 are to right of Bank 1-B1. U13, U14, U15, and U16 are special, dual sockets able to accept either 16-pin or 18-pin RAM chips. All the rest are 18-pin sockets.

Figure 17.6. Several different ways that banks of memory chips (DIPs) may be organized.

One way to tell if the chips are in backwards is to compare them to the other chips on the board. All ICs sport one of two distinguishing marks to show where pin 1 is located. They may have a dot (or shallow round hole) near pin 1. A DIP may have a notch in the end nearest to pin 1. (See Figure 16.1.)

Normally all the chips in a bank, if not all the chips on the entire board, will face in one of two directions, with those directions at right angles to each other. So the notched ends might, for example, all point either east or north. If you saw one of your new chips had been put in with the notch either to the south or west, you'd know that something probably was wrong.

And double-check for pins that have missed the socket, or those that are bent under the package or accordioned instead of going down into the socket. Almost all errors of this kind can be seen if you look very carefully. This is a good time to get out the old magnifying glass (or strong reading glasses) and a bright light.

Some Precautions for After You Close Up the Box

Ah, at last you have decided that everything looks pretty good under the hood, so you are ready to close up the box. This, too, is a time when simple precautions can pay large dividends in terms of your system's safety.

You may choose to test the system first with the main system unit open so you don't waste time fastening all the screws and then have to undo them again if you forget something. But it also carries a certain degree of danger. Remember that the system unit protects its contents pretty well.

If you do choose to try out your system before you close the box, please be very careful to avoid dropping anything inside. Also resist the temptation to reach inside and wiggle cables or press on chips with the unit turned on. You are more likely to harm than help yourself by those maneuvers.

Finally, remember to turn off power (and, preferably, disconnect the power cable) before you button up the case. It is extremely easy to drop a screw and short something out. This isn't a problem while the PC is turned off. It can be fatal to the PC while it is turned on.

Set up your system so it offers maximum protection against chip-zapping static discharges. Block line surges. Arrange things to minimize the entry of electromagnetic noise. Those sound like wonderful bits of advice, but how do you follow them?

Power-Line Surge Protection

First, use a three-wire cord to plug your PC into a grounded electrical outlet. Plug all the parts of your PC into the same outlet or circuit if you can. If you must use multiple circuits, try to get ones all on the same "phase" of the power line. (Consult an electrician if you are unsure what that means or how to tell which circuits connect to which phases.)

Use a good surge protector. You can get inexpensive power strips or "power centers" (a strip with many switches) that include good surge protection. Some even have telephone-style RJ-11 jacks to allow looping your phone line through the surge protector. That can save your fax machine, fax card, or modem from expensive damage.

A good surge protector has at least three surge-clamping elements. Most of the inexpensive ones use *MOVs* (*Metal-Oxide Varistors*), which are little, round, flat objects that look rather like a mint patty with two wire legs. You want three of these so you can have one connected between the *hot* line (the narrower of the two flat blades on a three-wire plug) and the electrical *neutral* wire (the wider flat blade), and the other two connected between each of those two wires and the *ground* (the round or U-shaped blade). (These plug-blade descriptions are for the standard U.S. grounded outlet. The principle applies in other countries, but the connector may vary in its design.)

Protect the Phone Line Too

Surge protection for your phone line is similar. Again three MOVs would be best. The two active phone wires (*tip* and *ring*) and ground are connected just as described for the two power leads and ground in the previous paragraph.

Stop Ground Loops

Another important issue is preventing any ground loops. These can happen when you plug in two pieces of your computer system and then connect them with a data cable. If both units use three-wire cords (as they should), they each will be grounding their case or chassis. That is good. When you then connect the two boxes with a data cable, you can short those cases together via that cable also.

Isn't that just more of a good thing? No. Definitely not.

Any loop of wire through which a changing magnetic field passes will have enormous currents flowing through it. They will be enough to set up possibly significant voltage differences between the different parts of your system. These are not chip-zapping sorts of voltage, but more likely noise sources that may confuse the circuits of your computer.

The solution is to ground both boxes as usual. Then cut the wire that connects the two cases together over the data cable. Just cut it in one place, at one end of the cable. You don't need to (nor should you) interrupt the *signal ground*; just the *case ground* (also called the *protective ground*) connection. If you use shielded cables (always a good idea), connect the shield to the protective ground pin at one end of the cable only.

Keep Out the Zaps

One place a closed PC system is particularly vulnerable to static discharge is through the attached keyboard. If you have a keyboard with a metal case this may not be much of a problem. Otherwise it can be. (Of all the common makers of keyboards, only IBM uses metal cases.)

There are several commercial products available to help you protect your PC from static electric shocks. One is a slightly conductive plastic pad you put under the keyboard. Another is a small stick-on strip that goes on the space bar. Each has a wire you connect to the PC system unit's case. These products work, but if you can't find one, or if you wish to save a little money, you can easily make your own.

Put a grounded sheet of metal under the keyboard, extending to where a typist would rest his or her hands. Or put a grounding strip on the space bar. Connect either one to the case of your PC system unit (see Figure 17.7). To avoid a shock when you touch the metal plate, connect it to your PC's case through a large resistance (about 10M ohm is a good choice). Whichever way you do it, these techniques will catch most of the static charges you bring to the PC before they can do any damage.

Figure 17.7. Two keyboard grounding strategies—a plate under the keyboard and a grounding strip on the space bar.

Activating Your PC's New Memory

Finally, you have your PC all back together and it works. But it doesn't seem to notice that you added all that RAM. What is wrong?

Maybe nothing. Think about where you added the memory and see if you have to do something to inform your PC about the existence of this new RAM. If you have a PC or an XT you may have to set some DIP switches to inform it about the new memory it has to work with. In an AT, 386, 486, or *Pentium*-based machine you must change an entry in the configuration setup screen. Those comments only apply when you are adding lower or extended memory. Expanded memory is totally different. As long as you have a compatible brand of EMM driver program loaded it should see and use all the hardware EMS memory you have.

Some add-in memory cards also need some jumpers set correctly. Getting all these things right can take a bit of doing, which is why it may not be a bad idea to do your initial testing before you close up the box.

If you've checked all these things and your PC still doesn't recognize your new RAM, you have a more serious problem. Turn to Chapter 32 for some advice that may help you track down and fix whatever is wrong.

Finally, a plea for common sense. Your own personal memory will not be perfect. So take notes on what you had before and what you have done to change it. You will find yourself referring to those notes many times as you have to go through reconfiguring programs (as well as your hardware) to recognize and optimally use your new RAM. Then enjoy your newfound freedom from Out of memory messages.

Now you know everything you need to know about adding memory to your PC. Everything, that is, except how much to add. That's the subject of the next chapter.

18

ADDING MEMORY— THE RIGHT AMOUNT

Adding too much memory only wastes money (and electricity). Adding too little doesn't get the job done. How do you know how much to add? This chapter covers that and also how much to assign to each type of use.

In Chapter 15 you learned that you needed to add memory to your PC, and you learned where to put it. In Chapter 16 you learned which kind of memory to buy. In Chapter 17 you learned how to install it safely. But wait. There is one thing you must consider before going down this path too far. How much new memory does your PC need?

If you add too little RAM, you will be right back where you started, faced with those awful Out of memory messages. If you add too much RAM, at least you won't have that problem. Instead, you will have wasted money on memory chips (and will continue to waste money on electricity to power them).

Truth be told, the cost of that added electrical power is tiny, and even the cost of RAM chips is rather modest and steadily getting smaller. So it is better to err on the side of too much added memory.

The purpose of this chapter is to help you find out what the minimum amount of memory is that you will want to add. Anything over that will almost certainly be even better. Naturally, your goal should not be to get just the exact amount of RAM for now. You will need to anticipate to some degree your future needs. Also, it is not possible to add memory in arbitrary amounts. There are definite RAM increments you have to use.

Further, it often doesn't make sense to add memory even in the smallest increments. You may find that for performance reasons you will choose to add much more memory than the minimum you could have gotten away with. One reason for this is the existence of certain "magic" amounts of RAM in at least some PCs which improve performance (see Chapter 16). Also by putting any "excess" RAM to good use, it is often possible to greatly increase a PC's apparent speed.

In this chapter you will learn some rules of thumb and other considerations that will help you choose the right amount of memory to add to your PC. You will also learn some of the good ways to put to use any excess RAM you may end up with. (You will learn more about the latter topic in Chapters 20 and 30.)

What Is the "Right Amount" of Memory to Add?

What is the "right amount" of memory to add? It depends. In particular, it depends on what software you will be running. Without that information, there is no way to determine a correct or optimum amount of RAM.

Let Software Drive Hardware Decisions

> The cardinal rule for selecting any PC hardware is this: **Choose the software first.** Then buy whatever hardware you need to run it.

You need to know more than just a raw number of bytes of memory your program requires. You need to know what kinds of memory it can and will use. Some programs need extended memory; others cannot even find that kind. Some programs want all the expanded memory you can offer them; others ignore it completely.

For example, Lotus *1-2-3* in its 2.x Releases uses only conventional and expanded memory. They can run in a PC that has only 640KB of lower memory and nothing else, but if you have expanded memory, *1-2-3* will use it too, to allow you to build larger spreadsheets.

Microsoft *Windows,* version 3.x, is able to use lower, upper, high, and extended memory. When it is running in 386 enhanced mode it creates its own simulated expanded memory for any DOS programs you run under *Windows,* but *Windows* itself always ignores any real expanded memory you may have. (The exception is *Windows,* version 3.0, in real mode.)

Lotus *1-2-3,* Release 3.x, has very peculiar "tastes." It will work only if you have just the right mix of memory resources. You must have 640KB of lower memory plus at least 384KB of other memory it can use. Watch out, though. It is quite fussy about that extra memory.

You can have 386KB, or more, of real ex*ten*ded memory and *no* expanded memory. That is fine. Or you can have 384KB, or more, of VCPI-compatible simulated ex*pan*ded (EMS) memory (and any amount of ex*ten*ded memory). That will work. But you *must not have just a little* available ex*pan*ded memory, even though you may have lots of available ex*ten*ded memory. Once *1-2-3* sees any ex*pan*ded memory it simply ignores all of your ex*ten*ded memory. And then if the amount of ex*pan*ded memory you have available is not what it needs, *1-2-3* will refuse to load.

Whatever type and amount of memory your programs need, that is what you must provide. As you learned in Chapter 9, it is often possible to make one kind of memory appear to be another. When dealing with a finicky program with specific needs, this capability becomes very useful. You may well find yourself reconfiguring your PC many times in order to run application programs with differing memory needs. This reconfiguring is an aspect of memory management that you will learn more about in the next several chapters.

Some Useful Rules of Thumb

Sometimes you can read right on the box (or in the manual) just how much memory (and of what kinds) a given application needs. Sometimes the manufacturers have been less helpful. Here are some useful "rules of thumb" with which you can estimate the RAM requirements of your programs, based on their type.

Conventional DOS Applications

These programs use lower memory. You may get away with less than 640KB total lower memory, although with RAM so cheap these days, it doesn't make much sense not to have filled your PC with at least its full quota of lower memory. (This includes backfilling the lower memory space to its capacity with LIM 4.0 EMS memory. Often, on a PC in classes 1 to 4, if a suitable EMS board is available you may wish to have less than 640KB of actual physical lower memory installed in order to facilitate multitasking.)

Since DOS itself doesn't know how to access any more than the first 640KB of RAM, you don't need anything more than that for simple DOS programs. If you have any extra RAM, either extended or expanded, you can put it to good use as a disk cache or a RAM disk (or both).

If you have upper memory available, some DOS applications can make use of it as well. Mostly, though, that memory will be used as a place to stash TSRs and device drivers to get them out of the way, thus leaving more lower memory for the main DOS application program to use.

EMS-Memory-Using DOS Applications

Some DOS applications also can take advantage of expanded memory. Today most of them do this by using the services of a LIM EMS-compatible expanded memory manager (EMM). Older programs expect to find LIM 3.2-compatible EMS memory. Newer ones often expect more services than were described in that standard; they are looking for a LIM 4.0 level of EMS memory.

There are several possible sources for expanded memory. Also, there may be different ways of creating expanded memory from those sources that will give the resulting EMS memory some significantly different properties.

One way to get EMS memory is by using a hardware memory option card that is wired to provide EMS memory. Another way is to convert some of your extended memory into simulated expanded memory. A third way is for the motherboard system logic to convert some of the RAM on the motherboard into expanded memory. The first and third ways give you real, hardware EMS memory. Expanded memory obtained by the second method is only simulated EMS memory. Still, for most (but not all) programs, those differences don't matter.

What matters more is which version of EMS is supported by the EMM driver program and which of the features of the EMS standard are supported by the underlying hardware or software source of the expanded memory to be managed by that EMM. You can get EMM drivers that conform only to the older LIM 3.2 standard, or ones that have been upgraded to LIM 4.0 compatibility. Independent of this distinction, the hardware that is providing the EMS memory may have limitations as to which features of the specification it can support. (This is discussed more fully in Chapter 8.)

For example, even though you may be using a LIM 4.0-compatible EMM driver, if your hardware cannot page EMS memory into lower memory space, then any program that asks the EMM to do paging of that sort will not be able to get what it is asking for. The EMM will understand the request, but since it knows the hardware can't do that, it will simply politely decline to perform that requested service.

If the driver only had LIM 3.2 capabilities, it would not even recognize such a request by a program. If you are running programs that expect LIM 4.0 EMS memory, you must upgrade your EMM, even if you don't change the hardware, so the driver can properly respond to all program requests for EMS services—even if the response it gives is a refusal to do what has been requested.

A caution: If you are going to convert some of your motherboard RAM into expanded memory, either by using a special feature of your PC's motherboard system logic or by running a LIMulator program (on a PC in class 5 or 6), you must be careful not to convert too much of it. You need to leave at least 64KB of extended memory so you can have an HMA. You may need to leave even more extended memory as extended memory if you have applications that will only accept memory in that form.

Once you have provided EMS memory, and after you have loaded all the EMS-aware programs that you plan to use, you can run the DOS MEM command to see how much of the EMS memory is not being used. (That assumes you have DOS 5 or 6. If you don't, there are various alternative utility programs that will show you what memory you have in all its different forms. See Chapter 28 for some suggestions.)

If you have any EMS memory left over, you can put it to good use. Perhaps the best uses are as a disk cache and for a RAM disk. Chapters 20 and 30 describe these and some other possibilities.

DOS-Extended Applications

DOS-extended applications expect to be run on a PC in class 3 or higher. They use both lower and extended memory. They normally expect to find and use a lot of extended memory which they will allocate to themselves directly.

If the DOS extender used to create the application was VCPI-aware, and if the DOS-extended program is running on a class 5 or 6 PC, then the application will also be able to use any simulated expanded memory provided by a VCPI-compatible LIMulator program.

Exactly how these programs use extended memory and expanded memory varies a great deal. Again, that old-standby example, Lotus *1-2-3*, Release 3.0, will take extended memory in chunks as it needs it. Release 3.1 will grab all available extended memory when it starts, just in case it is going to use it later on.

The *1-2-3* strategy for using memory is tricky to understand. Just to load the program, it needs all of the lower 640KB (less whatever DOS and a few TSRs may be taking) plus 384KB of extended memory. It can substitute for that extended memory some VCPI-compatible, simulated expanded memory.

The reason it can do this is that the VCPI standard allows VCPI-aware applications (like Releases 3.x of *1-2-3*) to ask for and receive blocks of memory two ways: either as EMS (expanded) memory or directly as extended memory. The VCPI server doesn't exactly convert the simulated expanded memory back to extended, but the effect is much as if it did.

After getting just enough memory to load, *1-2-3* can use additional memory to support larger spreadsheets. If you have some expanded memory available, it will use that. If you have only extended memory available, it will use that. If you have both, it will use only the expanded memory.

If all you have is expanded (and lower) memory and if that expanded memory was provided by a hardware memory option card (or from motherboard RAM converted by the system logic), then *1-2-3* will refuse to load. It cannot use that memory in place of its required minimum 384KB of extended memory. It is only when the expanded memory is provided by a LIMulator that it can be used to provide the minimum memory needed by *1-2-3* to load.

The real catch to watch out for is this: If you use a LIMulator to convert only a portion of your extended memory to simulate expanded memory, that portion better be the right size. After that memory gets used by any TSRs and device drivers that load before *1-2-3*, the remaining amount of EMS memory must not be anything in the range from 0 to 384KB. Anything outside that range is fine.

The reason this is a concern has to do with the default operation of some LIMulators. *Super PC-Kwik*, for example, will, by default, take all of your extended memory (except for the 64KB needed for the HMA) and convert it to simulated expanded memory. The DOS 5 memory manager, EMM386.EXE, on the other hand, converts only 256KB unless you direct it to do otherwise. (In contrast, the EMM386.EXE program that comes with DOS 6 will do the same thing as *Super PC-Kwik* in this regard.) So running *Super PC-Kwik* with no special instructions will work just fine with *1-2-3*, as will using the DOS 6 version of EMM386.EXE, but using the DOS 5 EMM386.EXE will not.

Finally, you need to know that *1-2-3*, Release 3.x, will run just a little bit faster if it gets its memory as extended, directly, instead of using VCPI-compatible, simulated expanded memory. So if *1-2-3*, Release 3.x is your primary application and you don't have any other compelling need for expanded memory, run whatever LIMulator you use with a FRAME=NONE parameter (or equivalent; consult the documentation for the program you will be using). Not only will you speed up *1-2-3* a little, you also will gain more room in upper memory space for TSRs and device drivers.

Windows and Windows Applications

Version 3.0 of *Windows* requires close to 1MB of RAM (lower plus extended or XMS memory) to run in anything but real mode. Version 3.1 (and Windows for Workgroups) simply won't run at all with anything less (as it does not have a real mode option). And that is just to run *Windows*—if you want to run any substantial *Windows* applications, you need even more RAM.

> *Windows NT* needs even more RAM than this—lots more. However, since *Windows NT* (like OS/2) supports full virtual memory, it can run programs with ridiculously small amounts of RAM (which for *NT* is still measured in megabytes!). You simply wouldn't want to wait as long as would be required to do anything useful in a RAM-limited configuration.

Windows 3.0 in enhanced mode on a PC in class 5 or 6 can sometimes convert any available simulated EMS memory to extended memory for its own use. It can only do this if the memory was provided by a VCPI-compatible LIMulator that uses a shared memory pool strategy—it can't do anything with EMS from an expanded memory board.

> *Windows* 3.1 supports a new specification called the *Windows Global EMS Import Specification* by which it is able to take simulated EMS memory from any LIMulator. *Windows* 3.1 also supplies its own XMS services, taking over that function from any previously loaded XMM (XMS memory manager).

This first 1MB of RAM takes care of getting *Windows* to run. Now what about the additional memory to run programs under *Windows*?

A good rule of thumb here is that you will need at least 1MB for *Windows* plus 1MB for each major application you wish to run at once. (Count any major applications that you will have open on the desktop or reduced to an icon at any one time.) You can run many small *Windows* utility applications (often called *applets*) without using much additional RAM. Applets are things like the calculator and clock programs that are included with *Windows*.

If you plan to run *Windows* as your operating environment, and if you are running it in enhanced mode (thus on a 386-, 486-, or Pentium-based

PC), you can also run DOS-based applications in a window simultaneously with your *Windows* applications. You can figure on needing about 1MB of additional RAM for each such DOS application you will have active at the same time as your *Windows* applications.

If you are running *Windows* in standard mode (on any class of PC from 3 on up), it will suspend all other programs whenever you launch a DOS application. The DOS application will then run using the whole screen. In this case, if you don't have enough RAM for everything, the suspended *Windows* applications will be swapped to disk. Naturally, if you have enough RAM to keep that from being necessary, you will save some time each time you start or stop the DOS application.

Whether you need any real EMS memory for DOS applications running in a *Windows* window depends on which mode *Windows* is running in (in enhanced mode it can provide simulated EMS memory for a DOS application) and the needs of the applications.

Remember, if you run short of physical RAM while you are running *Windows* in enhanced mode, it will use virtual memory (simulating the effect of more RAM by swapping things to the disk). That works, but it sure is slow. In standard mode, *Windows* will swap things to the disk to make better use of what RAM you have, but it cannot quite make programs believe they have more RAM than is really there.

On the other hand, if you have more RAM than *Windows* and the applications you are running under *Windows* require, the excess can be put to good use as a RAM disk or disk cache.

DESQview and Programs Running Under It

DESQview (often referred to as *DV*) was written to run on all classes of PC. Therefore, it can run with only 640KB of lower memory. But it will be very limited in what programs can be run in a *DV* window without more memory than that.

DV will also use any expanded memory you can provide. If possible, on PCs in classes less than 5, reduce your lower memory as far as you can (be sure to turn off address decoding as well as, or instead of, simply removing RAM chips). See Chapter 15 for the details of how to do this in different PCs in these classes.

Then supply as much LIM 4.0 EMS memory as possible. This must be supplied by a hardware EMS board that supports mapping EMS memory below 640KB. In this environment *DESQview* can really shine.

On a class 5 or 6 PC you can use LIMulator-created, simulated EMS memory. Furthermore, these PCs can map away the physical lower memory and replace it with the simulated EMS memory. So a PC in those classes should be provided with all possible extended memory.

The minimum you will need is just whatever the RAM requirements are for each program you plan to run at once, plus most of the lower 640KB for DOS and *DESQview*. If any of the programs you will be running under *DV* need XMS memory services, you will have to load the DVXMS.DVR device driver program along with *DESQview*. This will be done automatically provided you let the *DV* installation program put that file on your hard disk.

See Chapter 21 for more details on using *DESQview* and managing memory for it. This includes information on how to use *DV* with *Windows* to best effect.

GeoWorks

GeoWorks is an operating environment and it typically is sold with a collection of GeoWorks-aware applications. The operating environment manages all available memory on behalf of all GeoWorks-aware applications. It first uses your lower memory, then any available upper memory, expanded memory, and extended memory in that order. Finally, it will provide virtual memory by using space on your disk. So, for its purposes, you can provide almost any form of memory you like.

GeoWorks can function with as little as 512KB of RAM and some disk space. It will not work very quickly, though. As with *Windows*, you will get the best performance if you provide about 1MB for the program and another megabyte for each large application you wish to run at once.

Starting with version 1.2 of the *GeoWorks Ensemble*, it is possible to run *GeoWorks* as a task under the DOS 5 or 6 DOSSHELL program or the *DR DOS* 6 TaskMAX task-switching programs. When you switch away from *GeoWorks* to another application, of course, the memory needs of that other application must be met in addition to whatever *GeoWorks* is using.

OS/2

Originally *OS/2* was jointly developed by Microsoft and IBM as the successor operating system to DOS. It was intended mostly for use on high-end PCs. So its RAM needs were not tightly controlled.

For versions 1.x of *OS/2*, you will need to have at least 4MB of RAM just to get the operating environment up and running well. Each major application will require another 1MB or more. All of this RAM must be lower or extended memory.

Starting with version 2.0, the *OS/2* RAM needs have been trimmed somewhat. You can run it (rather slowly) with only 3MB of RAM. Still, the more RAM you can give it, the better. Also, it can run most *DOS* and *Windows* applications in an *OS/2* window. Each of those windows works best if given another megabyte or so. (The *Windows* applications will only run in standard mode under *OS/2* version 2.0; version 2.1 can run *Windows* applications in enhanced mode as well.)

UNIX or an Alternative Operating System

If you choose to run *UNIX* or any other operating system on your PC, you will have to provide it with the kinds and amount of RAM it requires. Mostly, these systems want to find the full 640KB of lower RAM plus as much extended memory as they can get.

These systems use the motherboard BIOS ROM only for the boot process. Then, they switch into a fully protected mode of operation with their own RAM-based BIOS. Normally, on a PC in class 5 or 6 (and mostly these operating systems don't work very well on anything less), they will use the memory-mapping features to completely remove the motherboard BIOS ROM from the CPU's logical-upper-memory space and fill in all of the logical-address space from the bottom up with RAM to the limit of what you have provided. In this way they completely avoid the 640KB barrier.

Give any of these systems as much RAM as you can. Don't hold any of it back. Remember to make all of that RAM extended (or lower) memory. If there is more than you must have to run the operating system and your application programs, you can always put it to good use: Create disk caches or RAM disks using utility programs meant to operate in those environments.

Some Recommendations

The foregoing were general rules of thumb and some specific instances as examples. They may have helped you, at least if your specific needs were discussed as one of the examples. But you may still have some confusion about the general issues. Let's review some points.

Should I Add Extended or Expanded Memory?

The real question is not just between two options: extended versus expanded memory. It is a choice among four options: Hardware EMS memory, simulated EMS (using the services of a LIMulator), plain extended memory, and XMS managed extended memory.

When Only Extended Memory Will Do

Some programs, especially older ones, expect to find extended memory—real, available extended memory. They will be unable to run if an XMS memory manager has grabbed all of your extended memory first.

The original VDISK.SYS was one such program. It took what it needed from the bottom of extended memory. LaserTools' *Print Cache* is another. Either of these programs can be told to use expanded memory instead, but doing that may conflict with your other memory-management plans. You can meet the needs of this class of programs simply by reserving some of your extended memory when you load your XMS memory manager. (Just how this is done depends on the particular XMS memory manager you are planning to use. Chapter 21 will give some examples and you can find others in the documentation that came with your XMS memory manager.)

There is one subtlety here. When it first loads, an XMS memory manager will notice if the first 64KB of extended memory is free. If it is, that region could become the HMA. But it does not actually become the HMA until some program asks the XMS manager for access to it. If you have only reserved a modest amount of your extended memory and some program comes along and claims it, you may preclude any later program getting access to the HMA. That will not be a problem if you plan to load DOS in the HMA, as it will always get there first. This could be a problem if you were intending to let *DESQview* or *Windows* use the HMA. Or it could be a problem because your pure-extended-memory using programs will find 64KB less available extended memory than the amount you reserved when you loaded your XMS memory manager.

When XMS Memory Is Fine

Most modern programs that want extended memory actually want XMS-managed memory. *Windows* 3.x is one example. So are many DOS-extended applications. In this case, you will want to allow your XMS driver access to most or all of your extended memory.

When Only Expanded Memory Will Do

Expanded memory is an option for all PCs, while only PCs in classes 3 and above can have extended memory. Because of this, many programs were written to take advantage of expanded memory and to ignore any extended memory.

This was especially true several years ago, when most PCs were those in classes 1 and 2. Now that there are many higher performance PCs, it is getting to be less true. Still, Microsoft's DOS version of *Word*, to name one very popular example, will use only lower and expanded memory and no extended memory.

Usually, EMS-using DOS applications will settle for simulated EMS memory. But not all will. Borland's *Turbo Debugger* is one example of a program that insists on "real" EMS memory.

When Any Kind Is Okay

Many DOS-extended programs don't really care which of two or three of the four kinds of memory you have. They will happily use extended or XMS-managed, extended memory, or VCPI-compatible, simulated expanded memory. But, if you have both simulated EMS and some unmanaged (not XMS) extended memory, these programs may see only one or the other.

If you have both hardware EMS memory and extended memory (which is only a good idea on 80286-based PCs) you may have to dedicate each kind to one use. For example, you may commit all of your extended memory to serve as a disk cache and/or RAM disk, and then let programs use the EMS memory for data storage or task swapping. Alternatively, if your applications are mostly DOS-extended ones, you could use up your EMS memory for the disk cache and/or RAM disk and let the applications have your extended memory.

When You Need Both Extended (or XMS) and Expanded Memory

If you run *Windows* in standard mode and some EMS-using DOS applications under *Windows*, you will have to have provided both XMS memory (for *Windows*) and EMS memory. That means you have to load two memory managers, or you must use a combination manager like *QEMM* or *386MAX*. (The latter solution is only possible in class 5 or 6 PCs.)

Likewise, if you wish to run first an XMS-using application and then an EMS-using one without reconfiguring your memory in the interim, you may have to provide both kinds of memory at the outset. Perhaps the best solution in this case is a memory manager that can provide both these kinds of memory and switch the allocation dynamically. But that is not an option unless you have a PC in class 5 or 6.

Using Extra Memory Flexibly

If you don't mind buying and installing lots of RAM—way more than you think you ever will need—you could set up some large amount as XMS memory, another large amount as EMS memory, reserve some as extended memory, and create a large disk cache and a large RAM disk. That would be memory nirvana.

Not very many people are in that pleasant situation. For most of us, it is necessary to make some decisions about how the RAM we have will be used.

Look at all your applications. See if you can get away with only one of the four kinds of memory (hardware or simulated EMS memory, and XMS managed or bare extended memory). Then provide that one for all uses (except the small amount of extended memory needed to enable the HMA). If you cannot make your life that simple, though, you'll just have to bite the bullet and evaluate what each program needs and add up your requirements based on which programs you plan to run in any one session.

If yours is a PC in class 3 or above, remember to leave at least 64KB of extended memory for the HMA.

For Those with Higher-End PCs

People who have 386-, 486-, and *Pentium*-based PCs (in classes 5 and 6) are lucky. They can use a LIMulator to create EMS memory out of their extended memory. By choosing a suitable LIMulator program, it is possible to make that allocation dynamically adjustable. Essentially, these LIMulators give the same answer to any program that asks either "How much EMS memory is available?" or "How much XMS memory is available?" The LIMulator just reports the total available memory in either form. When it is asked to supply that memory as either EMS or XMS, it will do as the program requests.

EMM386.EXE and HIMEM.SYS are the EMS and XMS memory managers provided with DOS. The version of EMM386.EXE that came with DOS 5 was completely *inflexible* in its strategy for allocating RAM between the extended and simulated-expanded forms. This is one good reason for supplementing DOS 5, at least, with a third-party memory manager. (The version of EMM386.EXE that comes with DOS 6 supports a fully flexible memory pool, able to be accessed by programs as either EMS or XMS memory on demand. Along with that change went a change from the DOS 5 default of only converting 256KB of extended memory into EMS to the new DOS 6 default of converting all of XMS memory into the flexibly handled memory pool.)

Some people have been confused by a sparsely explained option for the DOS 5 version of EMM386.EXE. That is the option to run the program at the DOS prompt with a command line switch of ON, OFF, or AUTO. (The DOS 6 version offers the same option, and it still is only briefly explained in the official DOS documentation.)

The meaning of these three settings is not at all the same as having the ability to supply memory from a common pool as either EMS or XMS memory. Instead, it refers to turning on or off the ability to convert memory from XMS to EMS altogether.

Normally the program defaults to the ON state. In that state it converts a fixed amount of memory from XMS to EMS (in DOS version 5) or all of XMS to EMS (in DOS 6, unless you specify a smaller amount). If you turn it OFF it will cease doing this conversion. As you might expect, once some program has asked for some EMS memory and been given it (and also once some memory has been mapped into upper memory space for use as a UMB), EMM386 will refuse to turn off. It must do that in order not to pull the rug out from under the program(s) to which it has given EMS or UMB memory.

The AUTO setting refers to another aspect of how EMM386 and all similar LIMulator programs work. There is no need for them to convert any XMS memory until some program wishes to use some. Also, they cannot be providing EMS services during the time that a program like 386-enhanced mode *Windows* (which does its own EMS memory simulation) is active. In AUTO mode EMM386 simply waits until a program requests memory before it sets up the tables necessary to support that conversion, and then converts only what it must.

In either the ON or AUTO modes, EMM386.EXE also accepts the command from *Windows* to go to sleep whenever *Windows* wishes to take over EMS services, and then to wake up once again when *Windows* is through, or wake up temporarily whenever a client program that received EMS memory from EMM386 originally needs to alter its allocation. Being asleep, in this sense, does not mean that EMM386.EXE discontinues supplying EMS or UMB memory it previously supplied; it merely means it is not open to receiving requests for additional EMS or UMB memory.

The Middle Ground

If you have an 80286-based PC, on the other hand, your best bet is to add memory on a hardware option card that can supply either LIM 4.0 EMS memory or extended memory. Normally the allocation between these two forms is fixed by switches or jumpers, or perhaps in a more recent design, by running a setup program. Either way, it is a fixed allocation (until you rerun that setup program or open the case and flip some switches or move some jumpers).

Installing a hardware option card works fine, but does not offer as much on-the-fly flexibility as the class 5 and 6 memory managers. This means you will have to choose carefully how much to make available in each form.

The Low End

Another easy case is that of a PC based on the 8088 or 8086 CPU chip. Those PCs cannot have an HMA, nor can they have any extended memory. So the only thing you can do for them is add a hardware EMS board.

When you add a hardware EMS board to one of these PCs, be sure you get one that gives you maximum flexibility in mapping EMS pages. If you map the pages carefully, you may be able to make use of upper memory even in a mere (class 2) PC or XT.

RAM Disks and Disk Caches

In all classes of PC, a disk cache is a very good thing to have. If you have a hardware disk cache (a caching disk controller), the benefits of a software cache may not be as noticeable, but in almost all other PCs it will speed performance greatly. Even those with the hardware disk cache will be speeded up somewhat more.

A RAM disk is another story. It can help you, but only if you are prepared to do some work to make it useful. No DOS program expects to find a RAM disk, nor could it recognize one if it looked. You will find more advice on this point in Chapter 20.

Adding Memory—Closing Comments

In this and the previous three chapters, you have learned whether or not you need to add more RAM to your PC, what kinds to add, how much to add, where to add it, and how to do so safely.

This completes another phase in our discussion of the principles of PC memory and what you can do with it. At this point you know what a PC's memory is, how your PC uses it, and, finally, whether and how to add more memory to your PC.

What is left for you to learn is how to manage that memory. This will take us several more chapters, for there are a number of aspects to that question. When you finish, you will have all the general principles you need to understand most any PC memory question.

19

MEMORY MANAGEMENT— THE TASK

Now that your PC has all the memory you need, this chapter will tell you just what it means to manage that memory.

643

Up to this point in the book you have been learning all about what PCs are, what types of memory they contain, and how much of each kind you need. You also learned how to get that memory, where to put it, and how to do so safely. Now you need to learn how to actually *use* it well.

This chapter and the next two focus on managing your PC's memory. By the time you finish them, you will understand basic memory management principles and you'll be prepared to apply them in your PC. This chapter explains what memory management consists of. The next couple of chapters deal with accomplishing the task.

Managing Your Memory Resources—the Physical Task

Having RAM is one thing—*using* it is quite another. Using it well and not keeping it from being used in yet other useful ways takes even more doing.

The RAM we are concerned with in this chapter is only the RAM used for programs. It does not include RAM that is in a memory cache, a hardware disk cache, or a printer buffer, as those kinds of memory are dedicated to fixed purposes.

These other kinds of memory also need to be managed, but that is generally accomplished by built-in hardware. For example, the memory cache is normally used under the control of a specialized device called a *cache controller*. The cache controller decides which sections of main RAM get imaged in what parts of the cache, and it also watches to be sure the cache is always an up-to-date copy of the RAM it is imaging. Memory in a hardware disk cache (on a caching disk controller) is controlled in a similar fashion. The control of RAM in a printer buffer is different in detail, but it is similar in that it is done by a dedicated controller in the buffer.

Since you, the PC's user, do not have any control over how these functions are performed, you have no role in the management of that memory. On the other hand, knowing what options for management of those kinds of RAM exist may help you choose which of those products to buy. (For example, you learned in Chapter 14 that a direct mapped cache is not as effective as an associative one, but that the latter is usually going to be more costly.)

The first level of memory management is a physical task. This is mostly a matter of being sure all your RAM will be addressable by the CPU. It also is concerned with preventing or resolving memory-address conflicts. The second task, logical memory management, deals with how that RAM gets parcelled out for different programs to use.

You Have to Have Space for Memory Before You Can Have Memory

Before you can manage memory, you have to *have* memory. Further, that memory must be accessible to the PC's CPU. Sometimes we use memory that is not constantly CPU-accessible—for example EMS memory—but still each portion of it must be CPU-accessible every single time that portion is going to be used.

In order to make a particular group of RAM chips or modules accessible to the CPU, two conditions must be met. The first is that the CPU must have some otherwise unused memory address space in which that RAM can be made to appear. The second is that you have a means to decode those addresses and supply them to the RAM chips or modules in question.

Another way to state the second condition is you have to have sockets whose pins are driven by the appropriate memory-address decoding circuits and data buffers, etc. If your PC's motherboard doesn't have suitable sockets and associated system logic, you will have to buy a plug-in board that does. (See Chapter 9 for more details on what address decoding is and what other steps the system logic must perform.)

You Have to Have Memory in Those Spaces Before You Can Use It

Just having sockets, suitable system logic, and some empty memory address space is not enough. You also must have RAM chips in those sockets. (See the section titled "A Place Is Not a Thing" in Chapter 14.)

Several of the preceding chapters have discussed how to accomplish this first, physical level of memory management—that is, how to provide memory for the CPU to use.

Managing Your Memory Resources—the Logical Task

Just having RAM that the CPU can address is not enough to make it really useful. At least, not anymore—in the earliest small computers, long before the days of the PC, it *was* enough. In those relatively primitive computers, only one program at a time was ever loaded in the computer. That program had to know all about the hardware it was to use, and it had to do everything it needed to do in order to make that hardware do its bidding.

Now we have a much richer environment in our PCs. In addition to the basic hardware parts, we are likely to have several different programs loaded into ROM or RAM, any of which may take control of the PC for an interval at almost any time. In such a situation it is vital that there be some central authority charged with parcelling out the machine's resources. This is the only way to ensure that no program "steps on the toes" of another program, so to speak.

Allocation and Conflict Resolution

This central authority must allocate resources, and must prevent or resolve any conflicting requests for those resources. Normally we vest this power in our PC's operating system. If, however, that operating system does not know about all the resources we happen to have in a particular PC, then we must augment that operating system with additional programs that have the requisite knowledge of those other parts. In a PC running some version of DOS we add those pieces in one of three forms—device drivers, TSR programs, or complete operating environments. (Chapter 10 describes each of these except operating environments. They were introduced in Chapters 1 and 7 and are discussed further in Chapter 21.)

De-Allocation and Re-Allocation

The simplest form of resource allocation is simply to assign a resource to a program. Once. Forever. (Or at least until you reboot the computer and everything starts all over again.) This certainly works. It does have severe limitations, though. Once a resource is claimed by one program, it cannot be used by any other.

Imagine if your PC's printer were to be taken by one program and you could not use it to print from any other program until you rebooted the computer. That would be awkward at best. Even worse would be if the screen or keyboard were captured by the first program you ran and never released for use by any other.

The same is true of the less visible resources in your PC, such as regions of RAM. These, too, may be needed by several programs successively. But if they have been taken by one program and kept "permanently," they will be unavailable to any later program that may need them.

Thus we come to the notion of allocating and de-allocating memory. When a program needs some RAM, it must be able to get it. This is called *allocating* memory to the program. No other program is then permitted to use the same region of memory as long as it is allocated to this one program.

Once that program has finished using that region of RAM, it should be able to relinquish it for reuse by other programs. This is called *de-allocating* the memory, or returning it to the pool of allocatable memory.

For this to work, there must be a record of which regions of RAM have been given to what programs. Such a central record could be made available to all comers, and then maintained by all the programs, "on an honor system," but it is far better to have one program responsible for maintaining that record on behalf of all other programs.

We give this task to our PC's operating system—in other words, to DOS. But this only works for those resources DOS is prepared to manage.

What DOS Does for You

As mentioned in previous chapters (6 and 10), DOS means **D**isk **O**perating **S**ystem. Its primary jobs are allocating the disk resource and the RAM in lower memory space. The former job it does through a *file system.* The latter job it does by use of a *memory control block chain.*

> The file system used by DOS comes in one of two types: FAT-12 and FAT-16. These are tables of 12-bit and 16-bit numbers, respectively, which indicate which *clusters* on the disk (also called *allocation units*) have been assigned to a file. Closely related to this is the directory and subdirectory structure, which records which files own each chain of clusters. (Clusters, FATs, and DOS's file allocation strategies are discussed in many books on hard disks. It would take us too far afield to describe them here.)

Manage the First 640KB
(or Up to the End of Conventional Memory)

DOS manages lower memory for us. Chapter 10 explained in some detail the DOS memory control block strategy by which it allocates lower memory. The essential point for our present discussion is that no program is authorized to use any lower RAM except by having that RAM allocated to it by DOS. That means that DOS will build one or more memory control blocks for the program to indicate that those regions of RAM are now "owned" by that program.

DOS will let you know if it can't allocate the needed blocks. If a program asks for more memory than is available, DOS will tell the program it cannot be loaded. The loader program (the one trying to load the program) will usually then tell the PC user that this program cannot run because there is not enough memory to load it.

The amount of memory a program wants or needs is determined in part by the program's type. Programs that have been built in the .COM file format simply take all available lower memory. (More precisely, they take over the largest remaining block of lower memory.) If they have been well written, they will promptly give back to DOS all of the memory in that block in excess of the minimum RAM they need to run.

In contrast, programs built in the .EXE file format inform DOS what size pieces of RAM they need. DOS then allocates several memory control blocks to satisfy those needs.

Sometimes programs, once begun, will want to use more memory than they originally said they needed. They must ask DOS for additional RAM allocations. If DOS has enough free memory it will supply it. If not, it will refuse.

This central control scheme helps keep one program from running roughshod over the RAM being used by other programs. It does not require the programs to be particularly "lawful" and that turns out to be a very good thing. Otherwise, in our rough-and-tumble PC world, many program authors would choose to flaunt the rules in order to get whatever resources their programs needed, no matter what the cost to other programs.

Whenever a program is through with a block of memory, it can give that memory back to DOS for later reuse. And when a program ends, it either tells DOS to "terminate it" and take back all its memory or to "terminate it and leave it resident," which means to leave it with its RAM allocation intact. This latter ploy is what makes a TSR (**T**erminate and **S**tay

Resident) program. If that program has hooked one or more interrupts or inserted itself into the device chain before terminating, it will be able to gain control of the PC at appropriate future moments. (Chapters 7 and 10 explain how TSRs work, and in particular, what it means to hook an interrupt.)

> This memory control block strategy gives a means of recording who has the right to use each portion of RAM. Unfortunately, as long as the processor is running in real mode, there is nothing to *compel* a program to stay within its assigned regions of memory. So one must still depend, to a degree, upon the lawfulness of the programs run in one's PC. Otherwise, there is no telling what may happen.

If you extend the RAM in your PC above 640KB, for example by backfilling to 704KB with a LIM 4.0 EMS card or a product like the *MegaMizer*, then DOS will extend its memory management to include that additional 64KB of RAM. (You can do this if you don't have an EGA or VGA graphics card, or if you are sure never to use them in one of their graphics modes. Another way to get program RAM in this region is by using *Memory Commander* and its video image buffer relocation strategy. See Chapter 21 for more on this.)

What DOS Didn't Do (Till Version 5)

DOS is limited in its view of your PC. Since it was originally written for a plain 8088-based PC and since IBM had reserved all the memory address space above 640KB for other uses than program RAM, DOS was built to assume that there was never going to be any more RAM than that.

It creates one chain of memory control blocks, starting just above its own low memory program code and extending as far as it found contiguous RAM. That is where it stops.

This is true for all versions of DOS up to 5.0. Now, with the newer DOS versions (*MS-DOS* 5 and 6 and *DR DOS* 5 and 6) it is possible to do more. Even with the earlier versions of DOS, it was possible to trick it into doing more, with the help of third-party memory managers.

Manage Upper, High, Expanded, or Extended Memory

Since the earlier versions of DOS did not have any idea that there might be RAM available for programs to use in upper memory, and it did not even know that the HMA or extended or expanded memory could exist, DOS includes no provision for managing these RAM regions. It is unable to allocate them for programs to use.

People got around this limitation in several ways. If you could make some RAM appear in upper memory, then you could put programs in that RAM. The first trick for any program that wished to use upper RAM was to find the RAM and take it over for its use. A harder trick, essentially an impossibility, was to be sure no other program would find the same RAM and also use it.

The Third-Party Memory Manager Method for Managing Upper Memory

Once again we see the need for some central authority to allocate and de-allocate memory. Third-party memory managers were created to solve just this problem. Interestingly, they do not actually do the memory allocation and de-allocation. They simply make it possible for DOS to do that job, even though DOS thinks it is only dealing in lower memory allocations.

Some of these manager programs only work with RAM in upper memory that has somehow been put there previously. (That might have been done using a special setup option to make the system logic convert some shadow RAM into upper memory, for example.) Others attempt to create upper RAM in any holes in upper memory. Some of those use extended memory (if they are running on a class 5 or 6 PC); others use the system logic to convert shadow RAM (on a class 2 or 4 PC); still others use RAM on a hardware LIM 4.0 EMS-compatible expanded memory card (usually for class 2 and 4 PCs).

These third-party memory managers do their sneaky trick to fool DOS into allocating upper memory by first creating one or more memory control block (MCB) chains in the upper memory RAM. (One chain suffices if there is only one contiguous region of upper memory address space filled with RAM that is available for programs to use. If there is more than one such region, each region may get its own separate chain, or they may all be linked into one chain.) The blocks of memory indicated by these upper memory control blocks we call *Upper Memory Blocks*, or *UMBs*.

At the outset, each region of upper RAM will have a separate MCB chain consisting of only one block (of type Z), asserting ownership over the whole region. Later on, they get subdivided into multiblock chains as programs take pieces out of each region. This strategy closely resembles the way DOS builds MCB chains in lower memory (see Chapter 10).

Now, when any program is to be "loaded high" (meaning, it is to be loaded into a UMB), the memory manager does so by fooling DOS into doing the job.

The way it does this foolery is quite simple. It modifies the lower MCB chain. The only MCB header that must be modified is the very last one in lower memory. Normally that block is of type Z (signaling the end of the chain), is of whatever size covers the remaining free RAM in lower memory, and is marked as being free memory (owning Program ID=0).

After it is altered, that last lower memory block no longer indicates that it is the final block (its type is changed from a Z to an M). It indicates that its size is whatever is necessary to point to the start of the appropriate upper memory control block chain as the next block, and it is shown as having an owner other than DOS, so the memory it is controlling is not free. At this point the lower memory chain of MCBs is linked to the upper memory chain (or one of the upper memory chains). Any program that "walks the chain" will go directly from lower memory into upper memory and to the end of that upper memory chain.

Next, the third-party memory manager asks DOS to load the program. Since the DOS memory control block chain now extends into upper memory, and since the first large enough available block of memory is in the upper memory block, DOS puts the program there.

After DOS has loaded the program, the third-party memory manager restores the last memory control block in lower memory to its original form. In this way it keeps the DOS memory control block chain looking just as it always did, except for the brief interval while DOS is loading programs into upper memory.

An important point to notice here: If there are several noncontiguous blocks of RAM in upper memory, each one can have its own chain of memory control blocks. The third-party memory manager can, in setting up the altered last lower memory control block, extend the DOS chain into whichever upper memory region it might wish. In this way, it can easily control where in upper memory each program that is loaded high will go.

This flexibility turns out to be quite important. Often you cannot fit into upper memory the maximum number of programs, especially if the available RAM is fragmented, without choosing carefully which programs go into each region and in which order they are loaded. Up until version 6, DOS is not able to be this flexible—a point already made in Chapter 10.

What Third-Party Memory Managers Did About the HMA and Extended Memory

Even before DOS was modified to be aware of the HMA, a few programs, most notably *DESQview* from Quarterdeck Office Systems and Microsoft's *Windows/286*, were able to make use of it. They would load a portion of themselves into that region if it was not already taken by some other program.

DESQview normally needs to use the services of *QEMM-386* (on 386-based PCs), *QEMM-50/60* (on IBM *PS/2* Models 50 or 60), or *QEXT* (on 80286-based PCs). Prior to version 5, these programs only could assist *DESQview* in loading some of itself into the HMA. Version 5 and later versions also provide full XMS-compatible memory management of upper, high, and extended memory for the benefit of any program.

Windows/286 used HIMEM.SYS to manage those memory regions, and thus to allow it access to the HMA for a portion of its code. Both *DESQview* and *Windows/286* can use either HIMEM.SYS or any other third-party memory manager that provides XMS-compatible services (for example, *386MAX*).

What DOS 6 Does

DOS 5 and 6 include the ability to manage upper memory. Those versions of DOS also include the ability to load any one program into the HMA, and it can provide XMS-compatible services for access to upper and extended memory.

The *MS-DOS* provided programs HIMEM.SYS (the XMS-compatible memory manager) and EMM386.EXE (a LIMulator for use only on class 5 or 6 PCs) are the means by which *MS-DOS* or *PC DOS* do what they can do in these areas. HIMEM.SYS and EMM386.EXE provide the basics of upper, high, and extended memory management. (DOS 6 includes some enhancements to EMM386.EXE and the new MemMaker program, discussed in Chapter 21. This puts the DOS memory management tools into the same league as the third-party alternatives, but with their latest up-dates, those programs continue to be somewhat better at their special tasks than the DOS tools.)

In *DR DOS*, versions 5 and 6, you would use just one of the programs: EMM386.SYS, HIDOS.SYS, or EMMXMA.SYS. Which one you use depends on the class of PC you have. EMM386.SYS is for class 5 and 6 PCs. HIDOS.SYS is for class 3 and 4 PCs. EMMXMA.SYS is only for use on *PS/2* machines with expanded memory cards compatible with IBM's XMA standard.

The details of how DOS grabs control of and allocates UMBs differs significantly from the methods originally used by the various third-party memory managers. Now, almost all those third-party memory managers have gone over to a strategy that closely resembles that of *MS-DOS* 5 and 6, though there are still some slight differences. They have changed their methods so that they can support the DOS LOADHIGH (or LH) and the DEVICEHIGH commands, as well as their own, proprietary equiva-lents. (The LOADHIGH and DEVICEHIGH commands are discussed in Chapter 20. The steps DOS takes to load a program high are detailed in Chapter 10.)

When you load *MS-DOS* 6 it first builds the memory control block chain in lower memory, just the same way all earlier versions of DOS did. Then it looks at your CONFIG.SYS file. If you have a line there that reads `DEVICE=C:\DOS\HIMEM.SYS`, then the HIMEM.SYS XMS-compatible memory manager gets loaded. Provided the HMA is not already in use (and no program has taken part of the first 64KB of extended memory), you now have an accessible HMA for any later program to use.

If CONFIG.SYS has a line reading `DEVICE=C:\DOS\EMM386.EXE` (which must come after the line loading HIMEM.SYS), and if yours is a PC in class 5 or 6, that program will load. You can specify how it will do its job by several parameters on the DEVICE= line. You must put these parameters after the file path and name (for example, `DEVICE=C:\DOS\EMM386.EXE`). Separate the parameters from the filename and each other by spaces.

If you specify either the RAM or NOEMS parameters on the EM386.EXE command line in CONFIG.SYS, EMM386 will attempt to fill any holes it finds in upper memory. (If you specify RAM, or if you don't use either of these key words, it also will attempt to create EMS memory and put an EMS page frame into upper memory, which naturally reduces by 64KB the amount of upper memory that will be available for filling in with UMBs.)

EMM386 creates upper memory RAM and simulated EMS memory by calling upon HIMEM.SYS to give it a suitable amount of extended memory. (The version of EMM386.EXE that comes with DOS 5 asks for 256KB of XMS memory by default; the DOS 6 version takes all of available XMS memory by default. Either version can be instructed to take a different amount if you wish.)

Provided HIMEM.SYS can supply the requested XMS memory, EMM386 will be able to do its job. Any UMBs that it creates will now be managed by HIMEM.SYS.

If your CONFIG.SYS file has a line that reads DOS=UMB (or DOS=HIGH,UMB), you are directing DOS to take control of all your UMBs. It does so by asking HIMEM.SYS to allocate to it all of the available UMBs it has under its control. If you don't specify DOS=UMB, then HIMEM.SYS will retain control of the UMBs and any other program that knows the XMS protocol can request a portion of upper memory and receive it.

If a program that wants upper memory asks HIMEM.SYS for it (according to the XMS protocol), and if you did specify DOS=UMB, then the program will be told by HIMEM.SYS that there is no RAM available. Any such program should know enough to also ask DOS for upper memory, and perhaps it can get what it needs that way.

If you let DOS manage upper memory, once it has taken control of all of the UMBs that HIMEM.SYS had, it will allocate from that pool just as it does from lower memory. In order to do this, DOS builds a memory control block at segment address 9FFFh. That means it must reduce by one paragraph the size of the preceding block, which is the last lower memory control block, and thus is usually a free block and is of type Z.

If your PC has an **Extended BIOS Data Area** (EBDA), it is usually located in the last one or two KB of lower memory. When the BIOS creates the EBDA, it alters the number stored in low RAM that tells DOS how much lower memory you have. In that case the block that is here described as being at segment address 9FFFh will instead be located one paragraph below the bottom of the EBDA.

This new memory control block lies at the very top of lower memory, just below the video image buffer area. It will be constructed to show a size that is large enough to include all of the video image buffers, plus any option ROMs that may lie just past those buffers. It will point to another memory control block near or at the beginning of the first UMB.

DOS may have three or more separate memory control block chains. Each one ends with a control block of type Z, with all the other blocks being of type M (except for any subblocks created to hold items loaded into memory while processing the CONFIG.SYS file).

One chain is the usual lower memory control block chain. Another is a master chain for asserting DOS' ownership of upper memory. That chain has blocks whose owner names are all "UMB   " (the letters UMB followed by five spaces). Finally, there is the chain built from segment address 9FFFh, extending through each of the blocks of upper memory owned by DOS. It subdivides those blocks as DOS "loads programs high."

A portion of the first UMB owned by DOS may be taken by DOS to hold some data for EMM386. That is usually the only use made of the upper memory chains first created by DOS.

Any program can easily find the DOS-created upper memory allocation chain. It need merely look at linear address 9FFF0h (segment address 9FFFh), or the paragraph just below the EBDA. If there is a memory control block there, the program can walk that MCB chain in the usual manner. Finding the other chains DOS created in upper memory is harder, but also less important, as they are not used for program loading.

The DOS memory control block chain strategy differs from most third-party memory managers in two ways. Those other programs often don't start the chain at 9FFFh. That means that finding the start of their chain is not easy for programs other than the memory manager that created the chain. In addition, they typically do not have nested chains, as DOS does.

Figure 19.1 shows the memory control block chains created by MS-DOS 6 in a particular 486-based PC. Just as in Figures 10.9 and 10.13, the first column gives the segment address of each memory control block. The second column gives the type of each block. The third column shows the PID of the owning program. The program names were taken from the memory control blocks (rather than from the environments as is done by most MCB display programs).

```
                                     MCBS
          A program to display Memory Control Block (Memory Arena Header) Lists
                          Copyright 1991 by John M. Goodman, Ph.D.

          Memory Control Block chain - Lower Memory

028D  M  Owner= 0008    Length=    38608 (096D0 hex)   ▐=== operating system ===▌
028E  D  Owner= 028F    Length=     1072 (00430 hex)   ▶Device Driver   = HIMEM
02D2  D  Owner= 02D3    Length=     4240 (01090 hex)   ▶Device Driver   = EMM386
03DC  D  Owner= 03DD    Length=      736 (002E0 hex)   ▶Device Driver   = PCKWIN
040B  D  Owner= 040C    Length=     2704 (00A90 hex)   ▶Device Driver   = PCKRAMD
04B5  D  Owner= 04B6    Length=     1664 (00680 hex)   ▶Device Driver   = ANSI-UV
051E  D  Owner= 051F    Length=    20544 (05040 hex)   ▶Device Driver   = STACKER
0A23  F  Owner= 0A24    Length=     4432 (01150 hex)         (FILES)
0B39  X  Owner= 0B3A    Length=      256 (00100 hex)         (FCBS)
0B4A  B  Owner= 0B4B    Length=      512 (00200 hex)         (BUFFERS)
0B6B  L  Owner= 0B6C    Length=     2288 (008F0 hex)      LASTDRIVE (Drive Table)
0BFB  M  Owner= 0008    Length=       64 (00040 hex)   ▐=== operating system ===▌
0C00  M  Owner= 1304    Length=       32 (00020 hex)      Environment for  PCKSPL
0C03  M  Owner= 0000    Length=       48 (00030 hex)   ▒▒▒▒▒▒▒▒ free ▒▒▒▒▒▒▒▒
0C07  M  Owner= 0C08    Length=    16960 (04240 hex)   ▶Program Name    = MOUSE
102C  M  Owner= 102D    Length=     2368 (00940 hex)   ▶Program Name    = COMMAND
10C1  M  Owner= 0000    Length=       64 (00040 hex)   ▒▒▒▒▒▒▒▒ free ▒▒▒▒▒▒▒▒
10C6  M  Owner= 102D    Length=      624 (00270 hex)      Environment for  COMMAND
10EE  M  Owner= 10EF    Length=     8240 (02030 hex)   ▶Program Name    = SHARE
12F2  M  Owner= 12F3    Length=      160 (000A0 hex)   ▶Program Name    = FMARK
12FD  M  Owner= 0000    Length=       80 (00050 hex)   ▒▒▒▒▒▒▒▒ free ▒▒▒▒▒▒▒▒
1303  M  Owner= 1304    Length=    17328 (043B0 hex)   ▶Program Name    = PCKSPL
173F  M  Owner= 1740    Length=     6592 (019C0 hex)   ▶Program Name    = PCPANEL
18DC  M  Owner= 18DD    Length=      160 (000A0 hex)   ▶Program Name    = FMARK
18E7  Z  Owner= 190C    Length=   553328 (87170 hex)   ▒▒▒▒▒▒▒▒ free ▒▒▒▒▒▒▒▒

          Memory Control Block chain - Upper Memory

CC00  M  Owner= CC01    Length=     3600 (00E10 hex)   ▶Program Name    = UMB
CCE2  Z  Owner= CCE3    Length=    78288 (131D0 hex)   ▶Program Name    = UMB

          Memory Control Block chain - Upper Memory

9FFF  M  Owner= 0008    Length=   183856 (2CE30 hex)   ▐=== operating system ===▌
CCE3  M  Owner= CCE4    Length=    45520 (0B1D0 hex)   ▶Program Name    = SUPERPC
D801  M  Owner= CCE4    Length=       32 (00020 hex)      Environment for  SUPERPC
D804  M  Owner= D805    Length=     8960 (02300 hex)   ▶Program Name    = PCKSCRN
DA35  M  Owner= D805    Length=       32 (00020 hex)      Environment for  PCKSCRN
DA38  M  Owner= DA39    Length=    10912 (02AA0 hex)   ▶Program Name    = PCKKEY
DCE3  M  Owner= DA39    Length=       32 (00020 hex)      Environment for  PCKKEY
DCE6  M  Owner= 1740    Length=       80 (00050 hex)      Environment for  PCPANEL
DCEC  Z  Owner= 0000    Length=    12592 (03130 hex)   ▒▒▒▒▒▒▒▒ free ▒▒▒▒▒▒▒▒
```

Figure 19.1. The several memory control block chains created by *MS-DOS* 6 in a particular 486-based PC with a lot of TSR programs.

This figure was created by use of the program MCBS, a copy of which you will find on the diskette that accompanies this book. To see all possible MCB chains, MCBS was used with the command line parameter A. (No slash or hyphen should precede the A.) Since the resulting display was too large to fit on the screen all at once, the program's output was captured in two steps and the resulting images were edited to produce this figure.

In this case, the A and B pages were skipped over totally (by telling the UMB-providing program to exclude that region), on the assumption that they might be used by the video card for image buffers. The region from C0000h to CC000h is filled with option ROMs. The motherboard BIOS ROM starts at F0000h. The E page is used for the EMS page frame. That leaves a single open area in upper memory from CC000h to DFFFFh (80KB). That is initially all one large UMB. Later it is divided into two parts, the first part holding EMM386 data. Finally, the remaining free upper memory is suballocated by the chain that starts at 9FFF0h.

A Recap

Allocating memory can only be done when there is some memory available to be allocated. The operating system and (for memory it cannot see) add-ons to the operating system are charged with parcelling out memory to programs upon request. They also receive those memory regions back again when the programs are finished with it. This process is called allocating and de-allocating memory.

By having only one program responsible for this activity in each region of memory, programs are prevented from asserting ownership over memory regions that have already been given to another program. (Of course, in real mode, there is nothing to keep any program from writing to any memory address, whether that address has been allocated to it or not, except restraint and good judgment on the part of its programmer.)

Now that you understand the task of memory management, and even some of the details of how DOS allocates memory, you are ready to study the strategies and tactics of good memory management.

MEMORY MANAGEMENT— STRATEGIES AND TACTICS

Just knowing what has to be done is not enough. You also need to know some effective means to that end. This chapter covers ways you can manage your PC's memory manually.

Now you know how to get all the memory you need in your PC. And you understand the task of memory management in a general sense. This chapter will teach you how to apply that general understanding in a number of very specific ways. From it you will learn how to manage the memory in your PC manually.

In the next chapter, you will learn how to use various tools to help make the job easier. Some of these tools even offer to do the whole job for you. You will do a better job if you not only use their help, but also apply the knowledge you will gain from this chapter and the next one.

Managing Your Memory Manually

Managing your memory manually means doing those things you can do to set up an efficient memory environment in your PC. This includes choosing the right settings for various switches and setup parameters, creating useful CONFIG.SYS and AUTOEXEC.BAT files (possibly many sets of them), and loading just the right mix of helper programs.

DIP Switch Settings

The first level of setup for any PC is done with the case (and power) off. This involves setting various DIP switches or jumpers. Doing this in an IBM *PC* or IBM *PC/XT* will tell the computer some things about your configuration, and also about your choices for how it will work—likewise for the XT clones.

There are fewer of these switches or jumpers to set in ATs and more advanced models of PC. Still, there will be at least one, and maybe a few you can use. You need to know about them and what they can do for you.

What the Various Switch Positions Mean

This discussion covers first what DIP switches may be found on various models of PCs, and what they each represent. Then it describes when those switch settings take effect, and when you may wish to lie to your PC as you set them.

The DIP Switches in an IBM PC

In Chapter 15, Figure 15.1, you saw what the switches on the motherboard of an IBM *PC* look like. That figure also states briefly what each one does. Now you will learn more details about those switches.

The first switch block (called *SW1*) allows you to tell the PC about various general configuration items (such as how many floppy disk drives you have and which video mode you want the PC to use when it starts). This switch also indicates how much RAM is on the motherboard. The second switch (*SW2*) is only used to signal the total (lower) memory in the PC.

There are two models of the IBM *PC*. The first, sometimes called the PC1, has 16KB of RAM soldered onto the motherboard in one bank, with three banks of sockets in which an additional 48KB of RAM can be placed. If you want more than 64KB total RAM in a PC1, you have to add a plug-in memory option card.

In this version of the PC with its original BIOS chips, the maximum lower RAM you can have is only 544KB. This limit comes from the fact that the BIOS was written to test and use only as much memory as is indicated on SW2. The original BIOS for this model doesn't use all the switches on SW2. It reads only the first four switch positions on that switch block.

Each position on SW2 indicates one bit of a binary number. If the switch is off, the corresponding bit is a one. For SW2, position one is the least significant bit (LSB). Add two to this binary number and multiply the sum by 32KB to get the total lower memory specified by SW2.

The maximum number you can specify in four bits is 1111 binary, or 15 decimal. Adding two and multiplying by 32KB gives the PC1's maximum lower memory of 544KB.

```
Binary Number           1 1 1 1
Convert to Decimal    8+4+2+1=15
Add 2                   15+2=17
Multiply by 32              ×32
                      _____
Result                    544KB
```

The next (and final) model of IBM *PC* is often called the PC2. Its motherboard is able to take up to four banks of 64K-bit RAM chips, for a maximum total memory of 256KB. Its BIOS is enhanced to allow reading five bits from SW2 and addressing up to 640KB of lower memory. (Naturally, you must add a plug-in card with at least 384KB of RAM on it to get this much memory.)

In Chapter 15, Figure 15.1 shows such a motherboard with SW2 set for 640KB of lower memory. Test yourself. See if you can verify that fact from the image of the motherboard and the chart below it. The interpretation of the SW2 switch bits is different for the PC1 and the PC2, in line with the different RAM capacities of those motherboards.

> Figure 15.1 shows SW1 set to indicate no math coprocessor, all four banks of RAM on the motherboard filled, a CGA display set for 80 column mode, and one (physical) floppy drive. DOS will use that one physical drive as two logical drives, A and B. Again, see if you can verify this interpretation of the switch settings.

The DIP Switches in an XT

The IBM *PC/XT* was very much like the earlier PCs. In its original form, the XT had exactly the same RAM layout on the motherboard as the PC 2. Later models used two banks of 256K-bit chips, plus two banks of 64K-bit chips, to accommodate the full 640KB of addressable lower memory on the motherboard. (Figure 9.4 shows this "classic" XT memory chip arrangement.)

This latter XT model is the PC that was cloned so enthusiastically by so many different manufacturers. As you might imagine, not all those clones are alike. The memory layout, in particular, varies a great deal.

The earliest clones of the IBM *PC (PC2)* and *PC/XT* copied IBM's design for RAM exactly. Some later-model clones used the later IBM design to get 640KB of RAM in four banks.

Other clones used two banks of 256K-bit chips (each organized as 256K locations by one bit per location), plus four 256K-bit chips whose organization was 64K locations by four bits per location (64K-by-four chips), and two 64K-bit chips (64K-by-one). That allowed them to create two banks of 256KB each, using nine of the 256K-by-one chips in each bank, just as IBM had done. The remaining six chips form two banks of 64KB per bank, using two nibble-wide chips and one bit-wide chip per bank. You may encounter some other variation in RAM layout. As always, you should read the documentation that came with your system or its motherboard for details.

There is only one switch block on an XT's motherboard. Its eight positions signal the same information as SW1 on a PC2. The memory indicated by positions 3 and 4 is supposed to be the motherboard memory, but in many clones, those switch positions are not used in any way.

The DIP Switches in an AT

The IBM *PC/AT* has one single-position DIP switch. It is used to indicate just one bit of configuration information: which monitor the BIOS is supposed to start out using (monochrome or color).

It also has some jumpers that can be set. One is of particular interest in connection with memory management. The RAM on the motherboard of an AT is arranged in banks of 18 chips each. (Each bank is actually two rows of nine sockets.) That lets each bank supply the necessary 16 data bits plus two bits of parity.

The original IBM *PC/AT* used some very strange 128K-bit memory chips. Each of them was actually two 64K-bit chips soldered together, piggy-back style. Using them, the minimum amount of installable RAM was 256KB. Since there is only one other bank of RAM sockets, and they are identical to the first bank, the maximum amount of motherboard memory using those chips is 512KB.

If you want to add a hardware EMS board and get the most from a program like *DESQview,* you should have as little lower memory on the motherboard as possible. That is where the AT's special jumper comes in. Figure 20.1 shows the arrangement of the major parts on an *IBM PC/AT* motherboard, and it shows all of the AT's switches, jumpers, and connectors for completeness. Only J18 is of significance for memory management for most users. (If you are going to upgrade the motherboard BIOS ROM, then the 8-pin jumper block near the rear of the board may have to be turned around in its socket by 180 degrees.)

Jumper block J18 is the AT's special memory limit jumper. Putting a shorting bar across its first two pins enables the second bank of RAM chips. This is the default position for an AT with 512KB of RAM. Putting the shorting bar across pins 2 and 3 disables that bank (turns off its address decoder), leaving only the first bank active. Thus, to cut the motherboard RAM to its minimum, and thereby let *DESQview* work at peak effectiveness, you want to put the shorting bar across pins 2 and 3.

If the RAM chips are 256K-bit chips, as is now common, the first bank (Bank 0) will hold 512KB of information. That is the minimum amount of RAM you can put on most AT's motherboards. Clone ATs always use at least 256K-bit chips and so have 512KB as their minimum amount of lower memory, unless they implement something equivalent to the J18 jumper on IBM's AT motherboards.

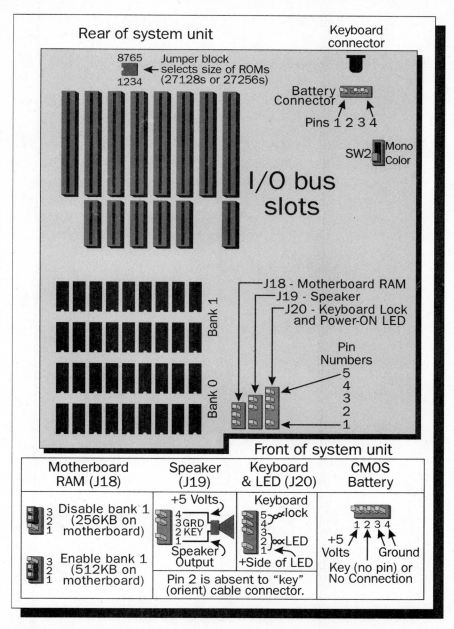

Figure 20.1. The IBM *PC/AT* motherboard layout, showing the special memory limit jumper, J18, and all the other switches, jumpers, and I/O slot and ribbon cable connectors.

DIP Switches and Jumpers in Other PCs

Some other PC designs have additional jumpers to allow you to set the number of wait states for main RAM and for other purposes. Check the documentation for the system or the motherboard to see what your PC has.

When Do the DIP Switch Settings Take Effect?

Just changing the position of one of the DIP switches will not affect anything. The BIOS and motherboard system logic must notice that you have done so.

The POST includes a step in which it does exactly that. Each time you reboot your PC, it notices any changes you may have made to the DIP switch or jumper settings. If you do the safe thing and disconnect your PC from power before opening up the case, when you first turn it on, it will notice the changed switch settings. The only time it will not do so is if you are being daring and making changes while the PC is turned on and running.

When to Lie to Your PC

It is a very good idea to be truthful with your PC. There are a few times, though, when you can benefit from not telling it the whole truth.

One such case is if yours is an IBM *PC* and you would like to have it not recognize all of the RAM on the motherboard. You might want to do this if you are planning to map in EMS pages to backfill memory up to 640KB. In that case, set SW2 to indicate the actual amount of real, fixed, and lower memory you want it to see. You can later add memory up to the 640KB limit by backfilling from a hardware EMS card.

Another case, strangely enough, concerns the setting for the math coprocessor. Any well-written program that wishes to take advantage of a math coprocessor will test for its existence directly. So the position of the switch on SW1 in position 2 is actually of no significance for its indicated purpose. But its position can matter. Not often, but sometimes. For example, one early design of paging memory board, the *JRAM* card from Tall Tree Systems, did not work correctly unless SW1 was set to precisely the wrong setting.

Unless you have a good reason, like the one just mentioned, don't lie to your PC. It isn't nice, and maybe your PC won't work as well as it could otherwise.

CMOS Setup Issues

How can an AT get away with almost no switches? It does so by having another way to store configuration information. All newer PCs, from the IBM *PC/AT* on, come with a built-in storage place for changeable configuration information.

We call this place the *Setup CMOS or the CMOS configuration RAM.* CMOS stands for **C**omplementary **M**etal-**O**xide **S**emiconductor and describes the process by which these chips are made. RAM chips made using this technology take an extremely small amount of electrical power to keep them remembering whatever you tell them.

The Setup CMOS chip also houses the "real time clock" circuit. That is an oscillator that is used to keep track of the passage of time, even when your PC is turned off. A battery powers this oscillator and it keeps the CMOS RAM from forgetting its contents.

The Setup CMOS must store, at a minimum, the amount of lower and extended memory you have, which type of display adapter you are going to use, and how many floppy and hard disks are installed in your PC (and which type each is). All of this information fits comfortably into less than 64 bytes.

CMOS Save/Restore Programs   The IBM-compatible CMOS information fits within 64 bytes. Many modern clones store additional information in their configuration CMOS. (This additional information may include such things as whether to use shadow RAM, whether to make EMS memory from motherboard memory, the number of wait states to use when accessing main memory, the ratio of the I/O bus clock to the system clock, etc.). The integrity of the stored information is assured through the use of two or three different checksums. One checksum protects the date and time information. Another checks the IBM-compatible configuration data. If the PC has additional data stored in the CMOS, it will be protected by a third checksum. Each time you boot, the POST checks to be sure the CMOS data are valid. If it finds an error, you'll be alerted by an on-screen message.

The importance of these details is this: Not all programs that save the CMOS data to a file know enough to look and see how much there is. So they might only save the first 64 bytes, even if your PC stores more information than that. If you attempt to restore your configuration from such a saved file, you will not get any checksum errors and yet you may not have restored the extended portion of the CMOS. If your CMOS setup shows more options than the minimum described above, be sure to double-check all of those additional fields anytime you restore the CMOS data from a file (for example, on your Safety Boot Diskette).

See discussion in Chapter 5, the section "When and How to Make Your Safety Boot Diskette," for a pair of programs that can save and restore the extended portion of the CMOS data.

The information for the Setup CMOS is entered through a setup program. The original IBM *PC/AT* uses a program you run from a special diskette. IBM still uses this method for their *PS/2* line. You boot from the "reference diskette" and choose the View or Change Configuration options from a menu.

Most clone PCs use a different strategy. They have the setup program built into the motherboard BIOS ROM. You invoke that program by pressing some special "hot key" combination. You may have to do this at a special time during the POST and boot process, or you may be able to jump to that program at any time. Figure 20.2 shows an example of such a setup program, in this case for an AT clone with a motherboard BIOS by Award Software.

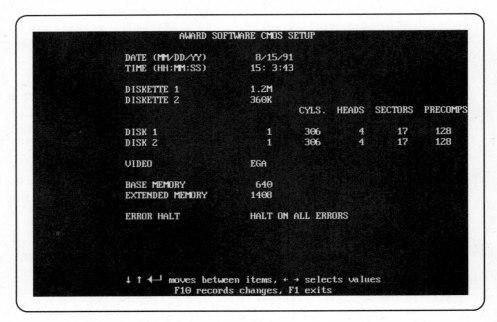

Figure 20.2.   A typical clone AT setup program.

The advantages to having the setup program built into your PC's motherboard BIOS are clear: You never have to worry about finding (or losing) the right diskette, and you can run that program in an instant, anytime.

The disadvantages are also clear, especially if yours is one of the PCs that can jump to the setup program any time. To do this, they must keep that ROM constantly in the CPU's memory address space. That takes up room you might rather use for some other program. Also, if you are in the middle of some application program, and you suddenly accidentally invoke the setup program, you will very likely lose some of your work in the application that you were running at the time. This is because usually you cannot leave the setup program without rebooting the PC (so it will notice whatever changes you may have made).

> If you use a memory manager that can remap the addresses of existing ROM and RAM chips, you may be able to make the SETUP portion of the BIOS ROM disappear from the CPU's view and replace it with upper memory RAM. This can be done with any 386-specific memory manager, and with a 286-specific one if the PC's hardware has been augmented with a memory mapping unit (for example, the *All Charge Card*).

Memory Options in the Setup CMOS

At the very minimum, you will have to tell your PC how much lower and extended memory it has. If you have 2MB of RAM on the motherboard, you can allocate as much of this as you wish (up to 640KB) to lower memory, with most or all of the rest becoming extended memory. If you fail to account for all of your RAM between these two numbers (and an allowance for shadow RAM if your PC supports that feature) you will simply waste any leftover RAM. Also, the next time you boot your PC, it will notice the extra RAM and warn you that you have chosen an invalid set of numbers for the configuration.

Normally, you will set lower memory to 640KB. There is only one case where you may not want to do so. This is if you have a PC in class 4. That means the CPU is an 80286 and you have either a LIM 4.0 EMS hardware expanded memory card, or your PC has special system logic capable of creating LIM 4.0 EMS-compatible expanded memory. For a PC in this class, you may well wish to set up less than 640KB of lower memory RAM (of the usual sort), and then backfill the rest of lower memory space from your EMS memory to enhance the performance of a task switcher or multitasker. Doing this is not possible with the ROM BIOS on some class 4 PCs. Those machines insist on having agreement between the amount of RAM they see and the amount that is listed in the Setup CMOS. You'll have to experiment to find out whether or not your PC will permit you to tell it you have less lower memory than is actually installed.

Shadow RAM

Some PCs support "shadow RAM." That means they can use some of the motherboard RAM to make faster-working copies of the motherboard BIOS ROM, the video ROM (for VGA or EGA), and perhaps of some other ROMs. That is generally a good thing to do.

ROM Shadow Warning   There is one situation in which shadowing a ROM is definitely not a wonderful thing. That is anytime the BIOS contains code that was written assuming that it would be executed at a certain speed. Putting that code into faster RAM invites problems.

This mostly happens in older PCs. One place it may show up is with an older EGA or VGA card that has been put into a fast PC. The program code in the option BIOS ROM on those cards may make the assumption that the clock speed will be no more than 10MHz. But if that ROM gets shadowed in fast motherboard RAM, it may attempt to execute that code at full CPU clock speed (perhaps as high as 33MHz or even 66MHz). Then the video display will not work right.

Another place this kind of problem may show up is in any attempt to access the floppy diskette drives. That will most likely happen if you have a special floppy disk controller card with an option BIOS ROM on it. The reason you might have such a card is to support more or different types of floppy disk drives than your PC would otherwise be able to support. The reasons you may have problems shadowing this ROM are just the same as for the video option ROM. If you have problems of that sort, try turning off ROM shadowing and see if they go away.

Shadow RAM can be implemented in many different ways. In all of them, the essential idea is that while it is booting up, you have your PC copy the contents of some slow ROM chip or chips into some faster RAM, then cause the ROM(s) to be deactivated and replaced with that RAM, which now is usually also write-protected. By this process, the RAM is able to emulate the ROM, and do so at a higher speed. Figure 20.3 shows one way this can be done. (In the column showing the state of line C, the value X means that the state of that line doesn't matter whenever the B line is LO.) The most significant issue for memory management is to determine what your PC will do with any RAM that you could have used for shadow RAM but didn't. There are three possibilities.

1. The first is that a certain amount of RAM (at least 128KB, and possibly as much as 384KB) is reserved for use as shadow RAM, whether you use it for that or not. In this case, you definitely want to tell the setup program to use all the RAM it can for shadowing ROMs. You have nothing to lose if you do this, and it will almost always help speed up your PC. Whatever RAM was set aside for shadowing, but is not used for that purpose, just goes to waste.

2. The second possibility is that if you don't use *any* of that RAM for shadowing ROMs, all of it can be added to the rest of your extended memory (or perhaps added to any expanded memory you may have directed the system logic to create). In some PCs, that will be done automatically. In others, it requires that you select that option on a setup screen.

   In this case, you may not want to use any of your motherboard RAM for ROM shadowing. If you were to use any of it, you would only be able to use a small portion of the RAM set aside for shadowing, as normally the ROMs in your PC's upper memory space take up only a small fraction of all of the upper memory space. But if you choose not to use any of it for shadowing, then all of it can be added to your extended memory.

   In a class 5 or 6 PC, this is an easy choice to make. In those PCs, the ROMs can be shadowed by any 386 memory-management without wasting any of the RAM that is not used for shadowing.

3. Finally, your PC may allow you to use some of its motherboard RAM for shadowing ROMs and automatically add any leftover RAM to the pool of extended memory. This also presents an easy choice. Let the RAM be used to shadow whatever ROMs you have, and let the rest become additional extended (or expanded) memory. You lose nothing significant, and you will gain some speed without having to run a special memory-management program.

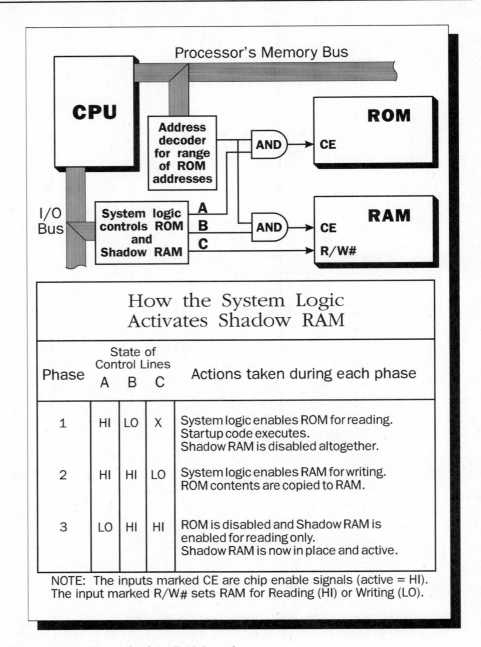

Figure 20.3. How shadow RAM works.

Some people have been stung by shadow RAM. They bought Lotus *1-2-3*, Release 3.x. The box says that one needs 1MB of RAM to run that program. So they bought a PC with 1MB of RAM on the motherboard. Boy were they surprised when they tried to load *1-2-3* and got the message `Insufficient memory`.

What is going on? Lotus *1-2-3*, Release 3.x, wants to have 1MB of RAM for DOS plus *1-2-3*'s own use. That includes 640KB of lower memory and 384 of extended memory. If your PC used its 1MB of RAM as 640KB of lower memory, and then took some or all of the remaining 384KB for shadow RAM, there simply is not enough left over as extended memory to meet *1-2-3*'s needs.

Additional Setup CMOS Options

Some PCs have an extended CMOS with lots more information in it. These PCs can often be customized even more finely than usual. Figure 20.4 and 20.5 show two screens of setup for one such PC, using a Phoenix BIOS. There is little surprising about the first screen, but the second screen goes into great detail with many options not seen in simpler PC's setup programs.

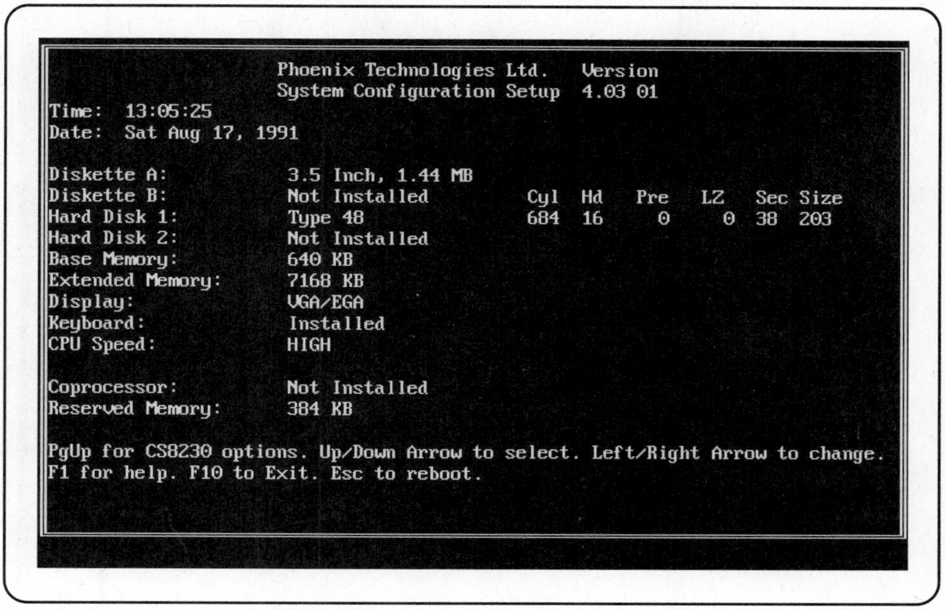

```
                    Phoenix Technologies Ltd.    Version
                    System Configuration Setup   4.03 01
Time:   13:05:25
Date:   Sat Aug 17, 1991

Diskette A:            3.5 Inch, 1.44 MB
Diskette B:            Not Installed         Cyl  Hd   Pre   LZ   Sec Size
Hard Disk 1:           Type 48               684  16    0     0   38  203
Hard Disk 2:           Not Installed
Base Memory:           640 KB
Extended Memory:       7168 KB
Display:               VGA/EGA
Keyboard:              Installed
CPU Speed:             HIGH

Coprocessor:           Not Installed
Reserved Memory:       384 KB

PgUp for CS8230 options. Up/Down Arrow to select. Left/Right Arrow to change.
F1 for help. F10 to Exit. Esc to reboot.
```

Figure 20.4. Extended CMOS setup program, main screen.

Notice that this particular BIOS allows you to choose to shadow ROMs or not in 16KB pages (except for the BIOS ROM, which is assumed to be 64KB in size, filling the F page). Sometimes the BIOS will have many fewer choices (see Figure 20.6). Even the thirteen independently shadowable segments indicated in Figure 20.5 may not be enough, for example, if you have two adjacent ROMs and wish to shadow only one of them. Option ROMs must start on multiples of 2KB, but you could easily have two that overlap the same 16KB page. (The solution in this case, for a PC in class 5 or 6, is to disable all ROM shadowing and let a memory management program, such as QEMM or 386MAX, do the ROM shadowing for you. Those programs allow you to specify regions to shadow in 4KB increments.)

This particular BIOS (Figures 20.4 and 20.5) does not allow setting up any EMS memory. That is not surprising, as it is a BIOS for a 386-based PC. In that class of machine, the commonly preferred way to create EMS memory is through use of a LIMulator program.

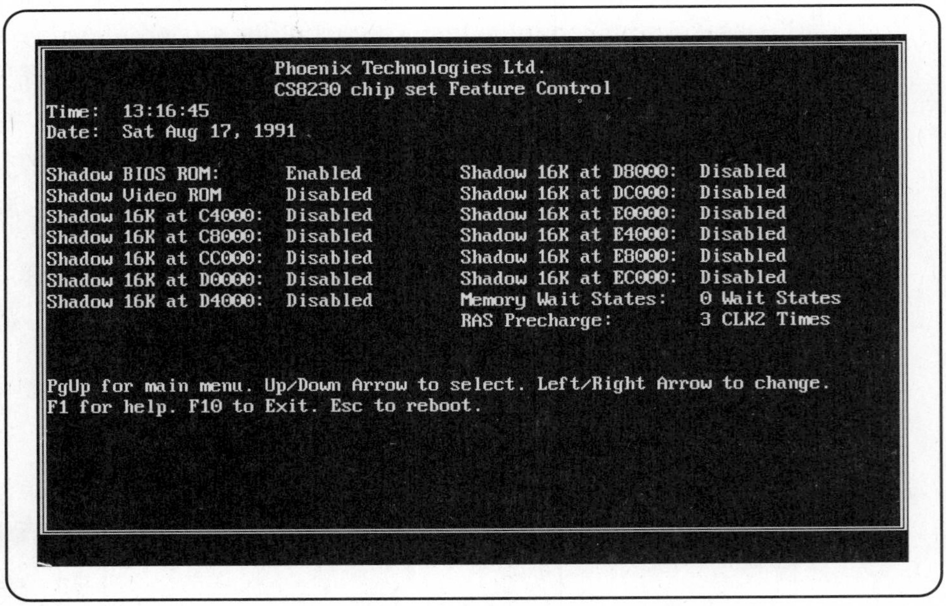

```
                    Phoenix Technologies Ltd.
                    CS8230 chip set Feature Control
Time:    13:16:45
Date:    Sat Aug 17, 1991

Shadow BIOS ROM:        Enabled      Shadow 16K at D8000:   Disabled
Shadow Video ROM        Disabled     Shadow 16K at DC000:   Disabled
Shadow 16K at C4000:    Disabled     Shadow 16K at E0000:   Disabled
Shadow 16K at C8000:    Disabled     Shadow 16K at E4000:   Disabled
Shadow 16K at CC000:    Disabled     Shadow 16K at E8000:   Disabled
Shadow 16K at D0000:    Disabled     Shadow 16K at EC000:   Disabled
Shadow 16K at D4000:    Disabled     Memory Wait States:    0 Wait States
                                     RAS Precharge:         3 CLK2 Times



PgUp for main menu. Up/Down Arrow to select. Left/Right Arrow to change.
F1 for help. F10 to Exit. Esc to reboot.
```

Figure 20.5.   Extended CMOS setup program, advanced options screen.

Figure 20.6 shows yet another variation on this theme. This is a Quadtel BIOS for a class 4 PC. (Quadtel is now a part of Phoenix Technologies Ltd.) This BIOS has a number of interesting new options. It allows setting the serial and parallel port addresses for I/O port hardware on the motherboard, choosing the number of wait states independently for two regions of motherboard RAM, and it can be used to set up a memory cache. In another version it would also be able to create EMS memory out of motherboard RAM.

Customizing Your PC Via CONFIG.SYS

Once you have your PC configuration information entered, either as settings of DIP switches and jumpers or through the setup program into the Setup CMOS, you are ready to boot your machine. Here is your next opportunity to customize it. Using this opportunity carefully can further help you manage memory.

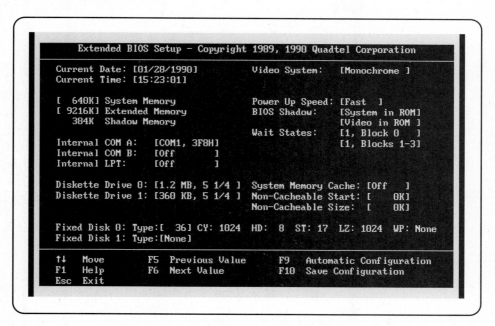

```
         Extended BIOS Setup - Copyright 1989, 1990 Quadtel Corporation

   Current Date: [01/28/1990]        Video System:     [Monochrome ]
   Current Time: [15:23:01]

   [  640K] System Memory           Power Up Speed: [Fast  ]
   [ 9216K] Extended Memory          BIOS Shadow:     [System in ROM]
      384K  Shadow Memory                             [Video in ROM ]
                                     Wait States:     [1, Block 0   ]
   Internal COM A:    [COM1, 3F8H]                    [1, Blocks 1-3]
   Internal COM B:    [Off       ]
   Internal LPT:      [Off       ]

   Diskette Drive 0: [1.2 MB, 5 1/4 ]  System Memory Cache: [Off    ]
   Diskette Drive 1: [360 KB, 5 1/4 ]  Non-Cacheable Start: [    0K]
                                        Non-Cacheable Size:  [    0K]

   Fixed Disk 0: Type:[  36] CY: 1024  HD:  8  ST: 17  LZ: 1024  WP: None
   Fixed Disk 1: Type:[None]

   ↑↓   Move        F5   Previous Value     F9   Automatic Configuration
   F1   Help        F6   Next Value         F10  Save Configuration
   Esc  Exit
```

Figure 20.6.   Setup screen for a Phoenix (Quadtel) BIOS on an AT clone PC.

Warning   First things first! Have a Safety Boot Diskette close at hand. You probably will need it while you are working on customizing your PC's CONFIG.SYS and AUTOEXEC.BAT files.

If you don't already have a Safety Boot Diskette, go back to Chapter 5 and create one. Do it now.

In Chapter 10, you learned about the steps in the boot process. There you saw that the CONFIG.SYS and AUTOEXEC.BAT files are used to create a custom working environment each time the PC boots.

The Nature of the CONFIG.SYS File

Both of these special files are plain, ASCII text files. That means that you can use the DOS TYPE command to display their contents. They are not like a word processing document, which has both text and formatting information.

Be very careful to use a simple ASCII text editor when you edit these files. If you do use a word processor, use it in the mode that will create a "pure text file" without any formatting codes. Almost any word processor can be made to do this, but you have to know how.

Where the CONFIG.SYS File Must Be to Take Effect

The only place either a CONFIG.SYS file or an AUTOEXEC.BAT file can be placed, and be effective during boot, is in the root directory of the disk from which the DOS system files were loaded. You may keep copies anywhere else you like, but they will not be read by DOS at start-up.

Later in this chapter, you will learn the virtues of keeping copies of these essential files in a directory other than the root directory. But those are just copies, for reference and to copy back to the root directory. They cannot be the working copies.

What Goes in a CONFIG.SYS File

There are several kinds of statements that you can put in your CONFIG.SYS file. Almost all of them have some impact on the use of memory in your PC. Figure 20.7 shows a sample CONFIG.SYS file. The following sections detail the memory impact of each type of statement that a CONFIG.SYS file may contain (including several that do not appear in Figure 20.7).

MS-DOS and *PC DOS*, version 6, allow you to create very fancy CONFIG.SYS files with menus and conditional execution of specified lines. This, and the "Clean Boot" and "Interactive Boot" options provided by DOS 6, make troubleshooting your CONFIG.SYS file much easier. But none of the new features in any way changes the memory use impact of the various types of lines you may include in a CONFIG.SYS file.

Remarks (REM)

Starting with version 5 of DOS, it became possible to add remarks to your CONFIG.SYS file. This can be a great help. DOS will simply ignore any line that begins with the three letters REM followed by a space. (*DR DOS* will display such a line, but otherwise ignore it.)

In addition to using this to add comments describing why some other lines have been included or what their parameters mean, you can use this to temporarily disable lines you don't want to take effect. Leaving them in the CONFIG.SYS file, "remarked out" (by putting REM followed by a space at the start of the line), makes it much easier to reactivate them some time in the future.

The only impact on your PC's use of memory that a REM in your CONFIG.SYS file will have is to free up whatever RAM would have been taken by the line that got REM'd out. (The exception to that is if you REM out DOS = HIGH, you could end up with *less* free lower memory.)

```
DOS          = HIGH,UMB
DEVICE       = c:\dos\HIMEM.SYS
DEVICE       = c:\dos\EMM386.EXE RAM 2048 FRAME=E000 I=CC00-DFFF
DEVICEHIGH   = c:\uv\ANSI-UV.SYS
DEVICEHIGH   = c:\setup\STACKER.COM /NB /EMS @ @
FILES        =    80
FCBS         =     1
BUFFERS      =    40
LASTDRIVE    =     Z
STACKS       =   0,0
BREAK        =    ON
INSTALL      = c:\dos\SHARE.EXE /f:4096
INSTALL      = c:\mouse\ballpnt\MOUSE.COM
SHELL        = c:\dos\COMMAND.COM c:\dos /p /e:624
```

Figure 20.7. A sample CONFIG.SYS file.

DOS = HIGH (HIDOS in DR DOS)

This command is only valid in DOS 5 or later. This causes DOS to load as much of itself as it can into the HMA. In *DR DOS*, it also causes some of

DOS to be loaded into upper memory, if any Upper Memory Blocks (UMBs) are available.

This command has no effect unless you also load an XMS-compatible memory manager. That could be done by a DEVICE statement that specified HIMEM.SYS, or by loading any of several third-party memory managers.

This command always reduces the amount of lower memory that DOS takes up (assuming you have a PC in class 3 or higher with at least 64KB of extended memory, so you can have an HMA, and that you are loading an XMS memory manager). However, it may let DOS use the HMA when some other program could use that space more efficiently. The only way to be sure if this command will save you some lower memory after all your programs have loaded is to experiment with it.

DOS = UMB

This command is only valid in DOS 5 or later. This tells DOS that it is to manage any upper memory RAM that is available for programs to use. It does this by asking the previously loaded XMS driver for all the upper memory under its control. Once that memory has been allocated to DOS, it can then be reallocated by DOS as needed by programs.

The DOS = UMB command may be combined with the DOS = HIGH command as DOS = HIGH,UMB. This command has no effect if you do not also use a DEVICE statement to load an XMS-compatible memory manager and have some upper memory blocks. This could mean loading both HIMEM.SYS and EMM386.EXE, or it could be accomplished by loading any of several third-party memory managers.

Since this only affects how memory is managed, it need not have any impact on your PC's memory usage. On the other hand, if DOS is unable to load some assortment of programs into upper memory, and a third-party memory manager can, then you may be better off not using DOS = UMB and relying on that other memory manager to do the job instead.

FILES Statement

This statement affects PC memory usage to a small extent. However, choosing the right value for it can have a large impact on your PC's ability to do what you need or want it to do.

The FILES statement sets the limit for how many files may "open" (readily accessible or in use) at any one time. It does this by specifying how many entries to allow for in the system file table. This sets the maximum number of file "handles" that may be in use at once. Legal values are from

8 to 255. Each new entry takes up about 40 to 60 bytes of RAM (depending on the version of DOS, with more recent versions taking up larger amounts).

The default value for FILES is 8. That is almost always too small a value. Many programs recommend setting FILES = 20 in your CONFIG.SYS file. That is a good minimum value to use.

> When DOS loads a program, it creates a 20-entry job file table in the Program Segment Prefix (PSP). Unless the program knows how to extend this table (which can be done easily enough, but often is not), 20 file handles is the maximum this single program can use. So except for special programs and situations where more than one program has files open at once, 20 files is the maximum you'll ever need.

If you are going to be running a multitasking or task switching environment on your PC, you may need a much larger value for FILES. The *Windows* documentation suggests at least 30. *GeoWorks* likes to see around 80. Since the impact of additional FILES entries is minimal, you probably ought to choose a fairly large value, more than the minimum you think you can get away with.

Some third-party memory managers (and *DR DOS*) can load the system file table into upper or high memory. Doing so can relieve you of even its modest use of lower memory.

FCBS Statement

The FCBS statement does a similar job for File Control Blocks. They are the older way of referencing a file on the disk. Valid numbers for this statement are 1 to 255. The default is 4. The additional number of bytes of RAM used when you increase the FCBS value by one is the same as when you increase the FILES value by one (40 to 60 bytes).

Since most modern programs use file handles instead of file control blocks, you may be able to get away with setting FCBS = 1. On the other hand, doing this might cause your PC to crash. *SideKick,* to name one popular program, uses the FCB strategy for disk access. It definitely needs to have more than one FCBS defined in your CONFIG.SYS.

BUFFERS Statement

You may find it worthwhile to focus some of your attention on the BUFFERS statement. This specifies how many disk buffers DOS is to set up. Since each buffer takes up almost 550 bytes of RAM (512 bytes for the sector of data plus some overhead), saving even a few of these can make up for a lot of excess file handles or file control blocks.

Everything that DOS reads from and writes to the disk has to reside in a disk buffer at least briefly. If there are enough buffers set up, DOS can leave all the most recently read or written sectors in those buffers. Then, if it should need the same information again, it can get it without having to go to the disk. This is the same benefit you get from a disk cache, although the DOS buffers do a less "intelligent" job and so they deliver less of a benefit.

In particular, DOS must look at the File Allocation Table (FAT) information, the root directory, and perhaps several subdirectories every time it seeks a new file. Keeping a copy of this information in RAM can greatly speed its work.

The default number of BUFFERS depends on the class of PC and the version of DOS you are using. In any case, it probably is too small. Typical values are 2 and 3, though in some situations the default value may be as high as 15. The legal maximum is 99 and the minimum is 1. Starting with version 4 of DOS, it became possible to specify both the total number of buffers and also a number of secondary cache buffers. Microsoft recommends you set BUFFERS = 20 to 50, with the size increasing as the size of your hard disk goes from about 40MB to around 120MB.

Granted, you will use some additional RAM if you specify a substantial number of BUFFERS in your CONFIG.SYS. But you will gain a great deal in the performance of your system.

There are two exceptional cases that push the optimal value for BUFFERS in opposite directions. One is if you use a disk cache (either a hardware caching disk controller or software disk cache program). The other is if you are loading DOS into the HMA.

If you use a disk cache, you will not need to have nearly as many DOS disk buffers. The disk cache will give you all the performance improvement you could hope for from even a very large number of DOS buffers, and usually a great deal more. That means you can reduce the number of BUFFERS you specify in your CONFIG.SYS file. Several cache programs suggest you set BUFFERS = 3 when you are using them. Check the documentation that came with whatever cache you are using to see what its manufacturer recommends.

Why does loading DOS into the HMA push things in the other direction? *MS-DOS* itself cannot use more than about 40 thousand bytes of that 64KB region. But whenever you do load DOS there (using the DOS=HIGH command), the DOS disk buffers go there also. This happens automatically. In that case, you can set BUFFERS as high as 40 or even 45 without exceeding the space in the HMA. (If you're not using *DR DOS*, watch out. If you set BUFFERS high enough that not all the buffers will fit in the HMA, then *all* of the BUFFERS will be put into lower memory. A mistake made in the BUFFERS command can make a difference of over 26,000 bytes in free lower RAM.) So long as you don't exceed the number that fits in the HMA, you lose nothing in terms of available lower or upper memory by increasing BUFFERS.

Finally, a warning about a rare problem. A few programs know they will require good buffering of disk accesses, and they will complain if you don't have BUFFERS = 20 or more in your CONFIG.SYS file. They complain even if you have a disk cache in place. A very few of them will even refuse to run unless you increase the number in your BUFFERS statement. A bit dumb on their part, but what are you going to do? (Answer: Use that many DOS buffers even if you otherwise would not need them.)

If you use DOS version 5 or later, go ahead and load the DOS kernel and disk buffers into the HMA, and set BUFFERS = 40 or so. That will give you a good solution even without a disk cache program. If you can, also run a good disk cache program (or use a caching disk controller). Then your disk access time will be kept to something near the absolute minimum.

> If you use the Microsoft mouse driver, version 8.0 or 8.1, and if you have DOS loaded in the HMA, you may need to set your BUFFERS to a lower value. The reason this might be so is that you can let that version of MOUSE.COM load itself into the HMA along with DOS. But it can only do so if you have left enough space in the HMA for it to fit. In order to do this you may not have the BUFFERS set to any value about 20. (Experiment with different numbers of BUFFERS and then check each time using the MEM /D command to see that your BUFFERS and your mouse driver both got loaded into the HMA.)

LASTDRIVE Statement

The LASTDRIVE statement tells DOS how many drives it needs to be prepared to handle. If you don't have such a statement, DOS will set itself up to handle just the number of drives you actually have, or perhaps one more than that number, or as a minimum, five drives.

If all you have are actual, physical drives, you don't need a LASTDRIVE statement, but it could turn out to be helpful. In particular, if you want to be able to create "substituted drives" (using the SUBST command) or to access network drives on certain kinds of networks, you will have to be sure the implicit or explicit value of LASTDRIVE is high enough. Legal values range from E to Z (for 5 to 26 drives).

> Watch out. Some network software wants to create drive letters be-yond the maximum that LASTDRIVE specifies. If you are connected to such a network, you will have to keep LASTDRIVE smaller than Z for that reason.

The impact of LASTDRIVE on RAM usage is minimal, but not non-existent. Each extra drive letter you allow for will take away from 81 to 88 bytes of lower memory. (The lower value is for DOS 2.x or 3.x; the higher one for DOS 4.0 and later versions.)

STACKS Statement

Every program needs at least one stack. That is a place in RAM where it can stash some numbers briefly. DOS also uses some stacks for its work. Application programs ordinarily create stacks for themselves. The STACKS statement allocates some "public" stacks.

Since programs cannot count on you having specified any public stacks (nor can they know how much of those stacks will already be filled if they do exist), good programming practice dictates that each applica-tion or utility program should provide itself with whatever stack space it is going to need. For this reason, the default value of STACKS is 0,0 on the IBM *PC*, IBM *PC/XT*, and IBM *PC-Portable*. Almost all other PCs use a default value of 9,128. Implementing the STACKS command takes some overhead, so setting STACKS = 9,128 (or allowing it to be set to that by default) will use up almost 2KB of lower RAM.

To eke out all possible free lower RAM, use the statement STACKS= 0,0. If you get a message that says something about Out of STACK space (after which your PC will probably be "hung" and you will have to reboot), try increasing the STACKS numbers. The first number is how many stacks you want DOS to create; the second number is the size of each in bytes. (If you use *Windows*, version 3.x, you should not set STACKS=0,0. *Windows* wants some stacks available for its use. Microsoft recommends STACKS=9,256, as-suming you are using DOS 3.3 or a later version—or STACKS=9,192 if you are using DOS 3.2.)

While you are experimenting with STACKS is definitely a time you should have your Safety Boot Diskette close at hand. Whenever your PC hangs and you must reboot, you may not be able to boot successfully from your hard disk until you change your CONFIG.SYS file. But if you don't have a floppy to boot from, how can you change the hard drive's CONFIG.SYS file? I hope you see the potential problem clearly enough that you'll be sure you are prepared (with your Safety Boot Diskette) before you begin these experiments.

> If you are using DOS 6, you have an attractive alternative in the Clean Boot and Interactive Boot features. These can allow you to boot your PC from the hard disk even when the CONFIG.SYS file is hopelessly messed up. (I still recommend strongly that you create a Safety Boot Diskette, as it will give you considerable protection from a wide range of possible problems besides a messed up CONFIG.SYS or AUTOEXEC.BAT file.)

DEVICE and DEVICEHIGH Statements

The DEVICE statements in your CONFIG.SYS file are used to load device driven programs. This is the primary way you augment DOS, enabling it to deal with new devices. These can be real, hardware devices or "merely" logical ones, created purely in software. DEVICEHIGH (HIDEVICE in *DR DOS*), available in DOS version 5 or 6, does the same thing. If UMBs are available and if they are being managed by DOS, it will attempt first to load the device driver into upper memory. If it cannot do so, it will act just like the DEVICE statement. Figure 20.7 shows several DEVICE or DEVICEHIGH statements. (To get DOS to manage the UMBS you must also have the DOS=UMB statement in your CONFIG.SYS file.)

Each of these statements causes DOS to load and run a device driver program. That program typically takes up more memory while it is loading and initializing than it does later on, but it hangs onto some memory until you turn your PC off or reboot it. Each device driver takes a different amount of memory. Checking the documentation for that program may give you some clues. Often, though, you will simply have to try booting your PC with and without that device driver to find out how much RAM it uses.

Many device drivers can operate perfectly fine in upper memory. If you have UMBs available, load whatever device drivers you can there. Doing this requires use of the DEVICEHIGH variation of the DEVICE statement or the use of a third-party memory manager. A few device drivers will not work in upper memory, so be prepared to use your Safety Boot Diskette (or the DOS 6 Interactive Boot procedure) to recover in case your PC gets stuck.

INSTALL Statements

The INSTALL statement (introduced with version 4 of DOS) allows you to run a TSR program from within the CONFIG.SYS file. Why would you want to do this? One reason is that when you load a TSR from your AUTOEXEC.BAT file or by typing its name at the DOS prompt, DOS will load the program and it will also create for its use a copy of the current DOS environment. You may view that as a waste of RAM. By using an INSTALL statement, you may completely avoid committing that extra RAM to this program. (The only time you won't avoid creating an environment is if you are using DOS 6 and have used some SET statements in your CONFIG.SYS file.)

Perhaps the main reason for wanting to use an INSTALL statement to load a program has nothing to do with RAM consumption. This is a way to get a **T**erminate and **S**tay **R**esident (TSR) program into memory before the command interpreter is loaded. This could be important if you wanted to be sure that this particular TSR's services were available absolutely as early as possible. SHARE is one candidate for this treatment, as it protects you against accidents that can happen in any situation where task switching might occur.

There are also some TSR programs that you definitely must *not* load via an INSTALL statement. These are TSRs that either look in the DOS environment for some message to tell them how to perform their function, or those that call upon the services of the command interpreter to, for example, run a batch file. Since there is usually no DOS environment, and there certainly is no command interpreter in memory at the time an INSTALL statement is executed, any such TSR would fail miserably.

How can you tell if you have any such TSR programs? Sometimes they will tell you about looking for an environmental variable (for example, *Xtree* and the *Norton Utilities* do this) or about launching a batch file (for example, *AUTOMENU* does this) somewhere in their documentation. In other cases you may only find out that they simply don't work when INSTALLed, but do when run from within your AUTOEXEC.BAT file.

Some TSR programs are able to release most or all of their environment space while they are initializing. These programs will not benefit as much from being INSTALLed instead of merely loaded through AUTOEXEC.BAT, as will those that keep their copy of the environment.

Even if a TSR keeps the whole of its environment, the amount of RAM that gets wasted thereby can be kept rather small by the simple expedient of putting all your SET statements late in your AUTOEXEC.BAT file. Doing this minimizes the need to use INSTALL instead of loading TSRs from a batch file.

The SHELL Statement

The SHELL statement allows you to specify a command interpreter other than COMMAND.COM. It also allows you to give various parameters to whatever command interpreter you load.

One way this may impact memory usage is through the difference in size of various alternative command interpreters. NDOS and *4DOS* take up much less lower memory than COMMAND.COM, as they keep more of themselves in other places (extended or expanded memory or on disk).

The SHELL statement will also influence memory usage if you add parameters that affect how much memory the command interpreter takes for itself or for the master DOS environment. Most notably, the /E switch (starting with DOS, version 3.2) allows you to specify a number of bytes for the master DOS environment. That number gets rounded up to the next multiple of 16 bytes. The default value is only 160 bytes; often that is far too little to contain all the definitions one might usefully put in the environment.

Other Things You Can Put in CONFIG.SYS

The COUNTRY, KEYB, and DISPLAY commands are similar to the DEVICE command in that they load programs (the filenames are COUNTRY.SYS, KEYB.COM, and DISPLAY.SYS). These are special device drivers used to customize your PC for international use. The NLSF program NLSFUNC.EXE can be INSTALLed to allow easy switching between different code pages or country codes. All of these programs take up RAM, either in lower or in upper memory.

You can also include a BREAK statement (= ON or OFF). This directs DOS to check for a pending Ctrl-Break keypress every time it is about to do a disk access, as well as when it is about to read from the keyboard, or write to the screen or printer. (NOTE: This setting is not permanent. It can be reversed by any program at any time, or by typing the BREAK command at the DOS prompt.) This is perhaps the only valid statement in a CONFIG.SYS file, other than REM, that has no impact on RAM usage. It merely causes DOS to set or reset a flag bit inside itself.

Starting with DOS 6 you also can put SET statements in your CONFIG.SYS file and you can set up menus. The SET statements definitely will affect memory usage, at least a little bit. In particular, using even one SET statement will force the creation of an environment space for each TSR that is loaded via an INSTALL statement.

The DOS 6 menuing commands don't have any impact on the use of memory, except if they cause different device drivers or TSRs to be loaded, or different values to be specified for FILES, FCBS, LASTDRIVE, STACKS, and BUFFERS for different ways of traversing the menus.

Does the Order of the Lines in CONFIG.SYS Matter?

Most versions of DOS read the CONFIG.SYS file just once, top to bottom. But the order in which the lines get acted upon depends on what they are, as well as the order in which they are read. Starting with DOS 5, an extra pass is made through the file. The first pass checks for the presence of a line saying DOS = HIGH or DOS = HIGH,UMB. This is necessary so DOS can load a portion of itself into the HMA before doing any of the other things the CONFIG.SYS file may dictate.

In Chapter 10, Figures 10.9 and 10.13 show the memory control block chain in the same PC with two very different CONFIG.SYS and AUTOEXEC.BAT files. In both cases, they show the device subchain of blocks within the first block, which is marked as belonging to the operating system. Studying the addresses in these figures also shows you the order in which the various components, created from lines in the CONFIG.SYS file, were loaded into RAM.

If you check, you will see that the size listed for the first memory control block (which is of type M) is exactly equal to the sum of the sizes for all the sub-blocks it contains, plus 16 bytes for each of those memory control sub-block headers. This is what it means to say that an M-type memory control block belonging to the operating system surrounds the device sub-blocks.

Some of the device drivers shown in Chapter 10, Figure 10.13, loaded themselves into upper memory. Had they been loaded with DEVICEHIGH statements, they would have shown up in device sub-blocks in upper memory. They would have also shown up within a surrounding memory control block that is owned by the operating system.

Here is a list of all the different items that get loaded into memory because of an entry in the CONFIG.SYS file. This list is given in the order that those items load.

- The DOS 6 on-the-fly file compression device driver, DBLSPACE.BIN, gets loaded absolutely first, before anything specified in CONFIG.SYS. But if you have a line in CONFIG.SYS indicating that you want it to be loaded high:

```
DEVICEHIGH = C:\DOS\DBLSPACESYS /MOVE
```

  it will end up in upper memory (if there is room). This also applies to the *Stacker* version 3.1, an alternative on-the-fly file compressioned device driver.

- *Device drivers* get loaded next (after DOS loads a portion of itself into the HMA, if it is going to do so). The device drivers get loaded in the order in which the DEVICE lines occur in the CONFIG.SYS file.

  That can be very significant, for one driver may need to use the services of a previously loaded one. In particular, you must load HIMEM.SYS before EMM386.EXE, which must come before any line specifying DEVICEHIGH. Similarly, if you plan on using expanded memory to fill in upper memory, the EMM program must be loaded before you ask it to create those UMBs.

  Another reason to be concerned about the load order is that if you are trying to fit some or all of your device drivers into upper memory blocks (UMBs), the order in which you load them may determine how many will fit. The reason for this is explained in the next chapter.

  If you are changing the order in which device drivers are loaded, you must give preference to the order in which they will work right over the order in which they fit best. In such a case, you may be able to get all your device drivers loaded into upper memory by using a third-party memory manager that allows you to specify which UMB to use for each device driver, independent of the order in which they are loaded.

- Next comes the *system file table,* whose size is set by the FILES command.

- The system file table is followed by the *FCBS table.*

- Then come the *DOS disk buffers.*

  Even if all the buffers are put in the HMA, a small space will be used in lower memory.

- The DOS disk buffers are followed by a region whose size is set by the LASTDRIVE command. This is called the *Current Directory Structure.*

- The last region (sub-block) within the operating system M-type memory control block is marked *STACKS.* This contains both some program code and the actual stacks themselves. If you specify STACKS = 0,0, this whole region is omitted.

  The order of the FILES, FCBS, BUFFERS, LASTDRIVE, and STACKS sub-blocks is independent of the order in which the corresponding statements occur in the CONFIG.SYS file. Further-more, they can come before or after the DEVICE, INSTALL, and SHELL statements and still have no effect on where those blocks end up in memory.

- Files loaded by INSTALL statements get M-type memory control blocks of their own, outside the one owned by the operating system which contains all the device sub-blocks. The INSTALLed files come right after the other items loaded through the CONFIG.SYS file, and before the command interpreter. (They will have environment blocks also if you are using DOS 6 and have any SET statements in your CONFIG.SYS file.)

- The SHELL statement causes the permanent command interpreter (usually COMMAND.COM) to be loaded into an M-type block of its own and a master DOS environment to be created in yet an-other M-block. (Each memory control block belongs to some program. The master DOS environment belongs to the permanent command interpreter.)

  You can put the SHELL statement anywhere in the CONFIG.SYS file. It informs DOS which command interpreter to load and what com-mand line parameters it will be given, but that action must be deferred until after the rest of the CONFIG.SYS file processing is complete.

The new ability in DOS 6 to put SET statements in the CONFIG.SYS file can create some unusual memory block allocations. The perma-nent command interpreter is given an environment block just below itself in memory when it is first loaded, just as is the case for any other program loaded thereafter. The command interpreter then creates a new environment block for itself, just above itself in memory and transfers the definitions from the original block to this new one. The new one is of the size specified by the /E:nnn command line parameter (if you are using COMMAND.COM). The original environment block given to the command interpreter is not used thereafter, but normally it is not returned to DOS for reuse by another program.

Setting Up Expanded Memory Boards and Drivers

Expanded memory is another area for manual memory management. If you have a hardware EMS expanded memory board, it probably needs to be set up before you can use it. Even a LIMulator may need to be given some instructions before it will work properly.

The programs that get loaded into memory through the CONFIG.SYS file combine with some of the pieces of DOS and the BIOS into several complex structures. Each of these structures has a quality of order to it which affects how the resulting operating environment will do its work. One such structure is called the *device chain*. Another ordered structure is formed around each interrupt that gets hooked.

The order in which the device drivers go into the device chain determines which one will handle any given request by DOS for device services. DOS issues the request and then passes it down the chain until it encounters a device driver that knows how to satisfy the request. That device driver grabs the request and does the work.

The DOS default devices form the original chain. Mostly, character devices get added onto the front of the chain. That makes it easy to substitute a new character device driver that will totally replace the original DOS default one. That is what happens when you load ANSI.SYS. It replaces the original CON (console) device.

The block devices are supposed to be added to the end of the chain. That is okay for ones that support new block devices, such as a CD-ROM or a tape drive. But that strategy doesn't allow block devices to replace the DOS default disk driver. Programs that can do this, such as third-party disk partitioning device drivers or on-the-fly data compression device drivers, must do some very special undocumented tricks to get into the chain ahead of the DOS disk device.

Both device drivers and TSR programs can hook interrupts. The order in which they do this is almost solely determined by the order in which they get loaded. This may differ radically from the order in which their program code is placed in memory, especially if some of them are loaded into upper memory. (Some device drivers won't hook certain interrupts until the first time they are called. For example, an XMS memory manager usually only hooks INT 15h when it is first asked to provide some service. Also, certain TSR programs constantly re-hook certain interrupts. *SideKick* is infamous for re-hooking INT 9 every time INT 8 happens—18.3 times per second. In both these cases the order in which various programs are hooked to a given interrupt may not be simply the order in which they were loaded.) Functionally, the only significant ordering is that of the interrupt hooking.

Hardware EMS Board Setup

Most hardware memory add-in boards have some DIP switches and/or jumpers, or they can be configured through a setup program. Either way, the things you need to tell any such board include:

- How much RAM is installed on the board.
- How much of that RAM is to be used for backfilling lower memory.
- How much of that RAM is to be used as extended memory.
- How much of that RAM is to be used as expanded memory.
- The I/O port address at which the EMS mapping registers can be commanded.
- Where in upper memory to place the EMS page frame.

If you are backfilling lower memory, you may need to specify the address at which backfilling should begin. Similarly, for extended memory you may have to tell the board where the present supply of extended memory ends.

The details of how all these things are set vary greatly from model to model and maker to maker of hardware expanded/extended memory boards. Check the documentation that came with yours to find out what you must do and how to do it.

Remember that you cannot use any expanded memory provided by this board unless you load the expanded memory manager (EMM) device driver that came with the board. Also, if you changed the board's port address, you may have to tell the EMM program what port to use. All the rest of the features of the board that you configured during its setup should work with no further effort on your part.

LIMulator Setup

If yours is a class 5 or 6 PC (with a 386 , 486, or *Pentium* CPU), you will be best served by having a LIMulator supply simulated EMS memory (and also backfill lower memory and the holes in upper memory). Your PC's CPU chip provides all the memory-management hardware you need.

The first choice you must make is where to put the EMS page frame. Most LIMulator programs will take a stab at finding a good place. Many of them choose quite badly in a lot of situations.

The good news is that if you have a reasonably good utility program to display memory usage, you can pick a good location yourself without much effort. You have an advantage over any mere program; you know what hardware pieces are installed in your PC. You have made it your business (haven't you?) to find out what resources each uses, including the regions of upper memory each may use. Armed with this knowledge, you can resolve ambiguous issues much more easily than a program that only knows what it seems to see in memory-address space.

If you feel unsure about what your PC's hardware is, and which regions of upper memory each piece uses, you will have to do some research. Chapter 3 has some suggestions that may help you. The programs listed in Chapter 28 can also aid you in your research. It is vital that you know as much as you can about your PC and the needs of each of its parts. This is the only way that you can make the informed judgments that are necessary for good memory management.

Before you choose a place for an EMS page frame, stop a moment and consider. Do you really need any EMS memory? If you do, must you have an EMS page frame? Often it is quite helpful to have one, as many programs can take advantage of it. But if you don't allocate 64KB of upper memory as an EMS page frame, you can use it instead to load more TSRs and device drivers into upper memory, or you can let *Windows* use it. If yours is a "fully packed PC" (one with lots of option ROMs, device drivers, and TSRs using lower and upper memory), then either of those might be a better use of upper memory than an EMS page frame.

Watch out for this one. If you use any DOS-extended applications that are VCPI compatible (for example, *AutoCAD386* or Lotus *1-2-3*, Release 3.x) and you are running a memory manager that could provide VCPI services (most of them), you must allow the memory manager to create EMS memory. When you shut off EMS, you shut off VCPI as well. However, you may not need to have an EMS page frame. Check with the publisher of your DOS-extended applications to be sure. (This caution may not apply if your DOS-extended applications were updated very recently. Check with their publishers to be sure.)

If you only need EMS, but not a page frame, you can direct most memory managers to give you that. For example, with EMM386.EXE, you use the parameter FRAME=NONE. (This is not documented in the DOS 5 manual, but it works. In DOS 6 it is documented, albeit very tersely.)

Assuming you do want an EMS page frame, what are the issues you should consider in placing it? The default location is often the D page. That is, the memory address range from D0000h to DFFFFh. In many systems, that turns out to be a very bad choice.

Look at a map of your PC's upper memory. Are there several holes in between your video image buffer(s), video option ROM, network interface card ROM, SCSI host adapter and other option ROMs, and the motherboard BIOS ROM? If the map is pocked with holes, you first need to consider moving any of the things that break up that space that can be moved.

Almost always, the video option BIOS code will be either in the motherboard BIOS ROM (as in a *PS/2*) or in a ROM at C0000h. That means it normally is either as high as it can go, or as low as it can go. (Well, some 386 memory managers offer to move the ROM to an unused region of the B page, if you have such a region. That is as low as it can possibly go.)

As usual, there are some exceptions. A very few PCs put the video BIOS ROM at E0000h. In those PCs, the option ROM prescan knows to look there instead of at segment C000h.

Network **I**nterface **C**ards (NIC), SCSI host adapters, and other options may plant their ROMs in upper memory in a much more arbitrary manner. Usually, they can be told to move their ROMs to a different address range. That may be done by moving some jumpers, or it may require you to run a special program.

Your goal at this stage is to make as much room as you can in one big piece. Upper memory can be used much more effectively when it is not fragmented.

Once you have done as well as you can in this regard, you are ready to place the EMS page frame. Your upper memory space will now consist of regions that are in use alternating with regions of free space. If you ended up with two or more regions of free upper memory space, and if one of them happens to be 64KB or just a little over, use that one for the page frame. The other hole(s) can then be filled with UMBs. (If your LIMulator does not fill in all those holes automatically, tell it to do so with an "Include" statement. The syntax varies with the manager, but all of them have a provision for doing this.)

If you did manage to get a single large hole in upper memory, the best place for the EMS page frame is usually the *top* end of that hole. The reason for this lies in a special feature of several of the third-party memory managers that allows them, temporarily, to borrow the page frame and thus increase the amount of available upper memory while loading TSRs into UMBs. This trick and why it can be so very valuable is described in more detail in the next chapter.

This feature is called "FlexFrame" by Qualitas *(386MAX* and *BlueMax)*, "Squeeze" by Quarterdeck Office Systems *(QEMM)*, and "LoadExtend" by Quadtel *(QMAPS)*. Whatever the name, the idea is the same.

When you can use this strategy, it will often allow you to load at least one (or more) extra TSR into upper memory. If the page frame is anywhere but directly above the UMBs, this strategy won't work.

A memory manager may think it can make a TSR fit into a UMB if only it will temporarily loan the EMS page frame to extend that UMB during the TSR's initialization phase. Then, when it tries to do this, surprise! The TSR doesn't get as small as expected and the memory manager cannot take back the page frame RAM safely. In this case, a well-written memory manager will simply shut off EMS services, or at least those requiring the use of the page frame. *QMAPS* and its optimization program, SMARTMOV, are even clever enough that if this ever happens, on the very next boot SMARTMOV will alter the directives to *QMAPS* so that it won't try loading that TSR high.

The LIMulator provided with DOS and *Windows*, EMM386.EXE, normally plants the EMS page frame at D0000h unless you explicitly direct it to put it elsewhere. Most third-party 386 memory managers will put it at the top of the open space in upper memory as their default. One exception is *QEMM*, which often chooses the lowest possible address in upper memory for the page frame. That is unfortunate, as it prevents their "Squeeze" technique from working unless you manually move the page frame.

Using EMS Memory
Created by Your PC's System Logic

If yours is a PC whose motherboard system logic can create some EMS-compatible expanded memory out of RAM on the motherboard, and if you wish to take advantage of that option, there are several setup steps you must go through. In the configuration setup for your PC, there may be a choice to make about how much RAM to convert to EMS memory, and possibly one about where to place the EMS page frame. Once you have specified these things, the requested expanded memory will be created. A few PCs will also ask you to choose an I/O port address for the EMS hardware. Still others ask you for none of this information. In the latter case, the expanded memory manager (EMM) that is shipped with the system will make all the choices for you, or you can direct it to make them as you wish through command line parameters when you load that device driver through your CONFIG.SYS file.

As with a plug-in hardware EMS board's expanded memory, this EMS memory is not immediately available to programs that may want to use it. The point of the LIM-EMS standard is that all programs that wish to use expanded memory need to ask the EMM driver for access to that memory. So again, you must load the EMM driver, and it *must* be the one that is provided by the manufacturer of the motherboard or the system logic chip set, before any programs can get to use expanded memory.

The only exception to this is if you load a third-party memory manager that knows about various brands of system logic chip sets. In this case, it may be able to find the expanded memory you created and make it available for programs to use. In effect, that memory manager will become your EMM in addition to being your XMS manager. *QMAPS* and *UMBPro*, both from Quadtel, are examples of programs with this capability. *QRAM* and *QRAM50/60* from Quarterdeck Office Systems can also do this, but only with a few models of system logic.

Customizing Your PC Via AUTOEXEC.BAT

The final step in booting your PC is processing the AUTOEXEC.BAT file. That represents, therefore, the final chance to customize your PC for a given work session automatically. Here are the details of what that file is and how you can use it to help you manage your PC's memory.

Please remember that to be effective this file must be in the root directory of the disk from which you are booting. Also, it must be a pure ASCII text file. These are the same two conditions that must be met by a CONFIG.SYS file if it is to be effective.

Generally, any command that you can type at the DOS prompt can be placed in the AUTOEXEC.BAT file. You can also put in REM statements (these are remarks which won't show on-screen as the file is processed, but which may help you remember why you did various things) and ECHO statements (these do show on the screen). In addition to documenting various aspects of your AUTOEXEC.BAT file, the REM or ECHO command can be used to keep one or more lines from being executed temporarily.

DOS also provides a fairly simple-minded batch file programming language. This allows you to create an AUTOEXEC.BAT file that contains loops and branches, uses definitions from the DOS environment, and, through the ERRORLEVEL set by one program, controls which actions are taken later in the batch file. Figure 20.8 shows a sample AUTOEXEC.BAT file.

Some of the things that are commonly done in an AUTOEXEC.BAT file do not have any lasting impact on PC memory usage. For example, if you simply execute a program to change the NumLock state on your keyboard, or to update your DOS clock from a real time clock on a plug-in card, the programs that perform these tasks will occupy some RAM while they are executing but when each of those programs finishes, it will give back all the RAM it was using to DOS.

Other things you may do in your AUTOEXEC.BAT file do have a lasting impact on how memory is used in your PC. Here is where most people load the TSR programs they want to have ready at the touch of a hot key. Here, also, is where most definitions get entered into the DOS environment. Likewise, you may wish to use the AUTOEXEC.BAT file to set up your DOSKEY aliases.

When you load a TSR, it takes up some RAM. How much it uses to load versus how much it finally ends up reserving for itself can be an important issue, especially if you plan to load the TSR into upper memory. This point is discussed in detail in the section on "loading programs high" in Chapter 21.

```
@echo off
echo            ********              Invoking programs
rem    Turn off NumLock and set DOS clock from real-time clock
c:\utils\LOCK N 0
c:\utils\CLOCK
rem    Load popup utility program into upper memory
LOADHIGH c:\utils\@LAST
echo.
echo            ********         Put things into DOS environment
echo.
set COMSPEC=C:\DOS\COMMAND.COM
set PCWRITE=C:\PCW
set NU=C:\NORTON
rem         Following two assignments will be modified if RAM disk exists.
set TEMP=D:\TEMP
set TMP=D:\TEMP
PATH C:\DOS;C:\BATCH;C:\UTILS
PROMPT $p $g
rem         Test for RAMDisk; point TMP, TEMP, and PATH there if it exists.
md E:\TEMP > nul
if not exist E:\TEMP\NUL goto noramd
   set TMP=E:\TEMP
   set TEMP=E:\TEMP
   PATH=E:\;%PATH%
:noramd
```

Figure 20.8. A sample AUTOEXEC.BAT file.

The order in which you load TSRs often affects how they work. It can even make the difference between their working or making your PC hang instead. Some other ways to help manage intransigent and competitive TSRs are discussed in the section on task-swapping program managers, also in Chapter 21.

In this section, you will learn a couple of simple tricks that can help you minimize the amount of RAM that gets used up during the processing of your AUTOEXEC.BAT file. These techniques may not save you vast amounts of RAM, but if just a KB or two makes the difference between loading that large application and not being able to do so, your efforts to tweak your AUTOEXEC.BAT file will have been amply rewarded.

DOS Environment Size

First is the matter of DOS environment size. In an earlier section of this chapter, you learned that you could load TSRs from within the CONFIG.SYS file. This is done by using the INSTALL command (for DOS version 4 or later). When you do this, the TSR will be placed in RAM with no extra memory committed to a copy of the DOS environment (usually—

DOS 6 users may find their INSTALLed TSRs do get an environment if they use any SET commands in CONFIG.SYS). Not having an environment is fine for many programs, but it is not for others.

Each time the command interpreter loads a program, it creates a copy of the DOS environment for that program. That copy contains only the environment definitions currently in effect, and the size of this "child process" environment is only a little more than it must be to hold those definitions. You may have set up a large "master DOS environment." (You do this by using the /E:nnn parameter to COMMAND.COM in a SHELL statement in the CONFIG.SYS file.) That becomes the environment for the permanent copy of the command interpreter. (For more details about the DOS environment and child processes, see Chapter 10.)

The good news is that no matter how large that master environment, the copies given to TSR programs need not be nearly as large. That can save a lot of RAM. A few of the more modern TSRs know how to give back almost all of their environment space. For them, keeping the initial size of the environment small is unimportant. Many other TSRs don't know that trick. For them, keeping down the environment size they get will definitely save RAM, possibly a substantial amount of it.

The way you can control the size of the environment space given to TSRs is simply by moving the commands that cause definitions to show up in the environment to the latest possible place in your AUTOEXEC.BAT file. These commands are PATH, PROMPT, and SET.

If you specify the explicit path to each program you run in the AUTOEXEC.BAT file, you do not need to define the DOS PATH until after all TSRs have been loaded. Similarly, the prompt doesn't show on your screen until the AUTOEXEC.BAT file completes. So don't define either the PATH or the PROMPT until just before that time. Whenever possible, put all SET statements near the end.

If you load five TSRs (which is a rather common thing to do in an AUTOEXEC.BAT file), and if your environment ends up holding 400 bytes of definitions (also not uncommon), this technique will allow you to save about 2KB of RAM.

But watch out for programs that expect to use some definition in the environment to tell them where their other files are, or how to do some task. If you can give each such program the information it requires by using command line parameters, do so. Otherwise, you will have to SET that definition into the environment just before running that program.

The other way to minimize the RAM "wasted" on copies of your DOS environment is to keep all the definitions there as short as possible. Often, the longest single definition is the PATH statement.

You can shorten that line drastically, if you are willing to give up a bit of space on your disk drive. Here is one way.

The PATH Statement

Many people make their PATH statement long, including many different directories where they may have executable files. That certainly makes it easy to run those programs from wherever on the disk you may happen to be. An alternative is to create a directory for batch files. In that directory, create a batch file to run each program you may wish to invoke from any place on the disk.

The advantages to the latter approach are clear: Your PATH statement could read simply:

```
PATH=C:\BATCH;C:\DOS;C:\UTILS
```

This reduces—nearly to a minimum—the amount of RAM you will use up in copies of the DOS environment (or all those that get created after you have issued this PATH definition). Further, if you mistype a command, DOS only has to check in those three places before it can let you know you have typed a Bad command or file name.

It is prudent to include the DOS directory on the PATH so you don't have to create a batch file for each DOS external command. Similarly, including a UTILS directory lets you put all your miscellaneous utility programs there without having to create a batch file for each one. Do specify the full path to each of these directories, including the drive name (as was done in the example above), so it will work no matter which is the current drive.

The disadvantages are, perhaps, a bit harder to see. One is that you must remember to include in each batch file the replaceable parameters %1 %2 %3... after the program name. That allows you to invoke the program with command line parameters by calling the batch file with those parameters on its command line. This will only work if there are no more than nine things you might want to specify on the command line.

To make this clearer, consider the DOS version of Microsoft's *Word* version 5.5. You can invoke this program to edit a particular file, run a specified macro, turn off the blinking graphics cursor, and specify about half a dozen other things about how it will work, all with command line parameters. If you use the parameter /L, you are telling *Word* to reopen the last document you were editing.

The following batch file could be used to start *Word* from any directory. If you don't specify a file name, it opens the last document you were working on, at the place you left off. Otherwise, it opens the document you specify with whatever other command line switches you may wish to use.

```
@echo off
echo.
echo            WORD.BAT  —  Invoking Microsoft Word
echo.
if %1.==. goto lastdoc
echo                     To edit  %1
echo.
d:\word55\WORD %1 %2 %3 %4 %5
goto done
:lastdoc
echo                  Loading last document edited.
echo.
d:\word55\WORD /L
:done
```

The other disadvantage to this technique (this is where it becomes a matter of trading disk space for RAM) is that each batch file will take up an entire "allocation unit" (also called a cluster) on your disk. With most modern versions of DOS and for modest size partitions, this is 2KB. It can be much larger. If you create one hundred batch files to run one hundred different programs, that disk space usage can add up to something significant. However, most people won't need that many batch files and can afford to commit the disk space needed for those they do create.

If you are tight on disk space and have found enough other ways to save RAM, or if you simply don't want to create all those batch files, go ahead and let your PATH be very long. Remember, though, to keep it under 128 characters. Using the SUBST command can help you in that regard. It helps because you can replace several long directory paths by fictitious drive letters. However, you must have a large enough value for LASTDRIVE for this to work.

Making Good Use of a RAM Disk

One of the joys of saving RAM is putting what you have saved to good use. A RAM disk is one of the things you can do with your "spare RAM." However, a RAM disk is only as wonderful as the uses you make of it. DOS will not do anything with it automatically.

What things it makes most sense to do with a RAM disk depend on the class of PC you have, how much RAM you have, and which programs you will be running. Whether or not you have a hard disk also matters.

Users of Wimpy PCs
Can Win Big with a Small RAM Disk

If you don't have a hard disk, a RAM disk can save you from ever again seeing the message Insert a system disk and strike any key. This message comes from the permanent part of COMMAND.COM (the part near the bottom of lower memory) whenever you exit from a program that has overwritten the transient part of COMMAND.COM (the part that resides near the top of lower memory). At that point COMMAND.COM must go to disk for a fresh copy of itself.

The place COMMAND.COM goes is specified in the DOS environment as the definition of the term COMSPEC. Each time you boot DOS will set this definition for you to point to the drive from which you booted. You can display the current definition by typing SET and pressing Enter.

If you booted from a floppy in the A drive, you will see the definition COMSPEC=A:\COMMAND.COM. Anytime you take out your DOS diskette and run one of the many programs that trashes the transient part of COMMAND.COM, you will get that annoying prompt to put back your DOS diskette.

The solution is to create a small RAM disk, copy COMMAND.COM to it, and then repoint the COMSPEC to that copy. This can be so much of a convenience that you may choose to dedicate even a portion of your precious 640KB of lower memory to this task, if you have no other place to make a RAM disk. That is quite a common situation with older laptop computers, for example.

So Can Users of Monster PCs

At the opposite extreme, if you have some super powerful PC with multi-megabytes of extended or expanded RAM, you could create a huge RAM disk, put all the files of your most common applications there, and then point your PATH to that location. That will let those applications run super fast.

How to Make a RAM Disk and Make a Small PC Whiz

To create a RAM disk, you must run a RAM-disk-making program. That could be either a device driver or a TSR. DOS comes with either VDISK.SYS or RAMDRIVE.SYS, both of which work just fine. And there are many fine commercial or shareware alternatives available, some of which are listed in Chapter 30.

In the first case (a PC with no hard disk), you must consider carefully what RAM resources you have. You certainly don't want to commit more than a minimum amount of your lower memory to this job.

If you have expanded memory available, you can use a RAM disk program that loads most of its code and all of its data into expanded memory. If you also have UMBs available, you can put the rest of the program there. These steps will let you minimize the impact on the space you'll have left in which programs can run.

If you have only lower memory available, use VDISK.SYS, RAMDRIVE.SYS, or perhaps a shareware program such as *VARIRAM*, and be sure to make the RAM disk size just barely large enough to hold COMMAND.COM (and perhaps a few other essential DOS external commands and often-used programs). Put the statement to make the RAM disk in your CONFIG.SYS file or your AUTOEXEC.BAT file, following the instructions that came with it. Then put the following lines in your AUTOEXEC.BAT file (these lines assume your RAM disk ends up being your C drive):

```
COPY A:\COMMAND.COM C:\ > NUL...
 [copy those essential DOS external and other often-used
  programs to C:\]
SET COMSPEC=C:\COMMAND.COM
PATH=C:\;A:\
```

RAM Disk Tips for Power Users

In the second case (a "power PC"), put your huge RAM disk anywhere **but** in lower or upper memory. If you don't have unlimited amounts of RAM, it is a good idea to invoke each of your major applications with a batch file that copies its main program and all necessary overlay and support files to the RAM disk. (Check each program's documentation to see which are the absolutely necessary files and copy only those.)

You could create your data files on the RAM disk, too. That would make everything run absolutely as fast as possible. But remember, RAM disks forget everything if you lose power or must reboot your computer. It would be safer to spend a little bit more time while you work, by keeping the data files on your hard disk, than having to spend huge amounts of time repeating your work if the system should happen to hang in the middle of the program's execution. If you do choose to work with data files on the RAM disk, interrupt your work frequently to copy those data files to the hard disk or a diskette.

At the end of the batch file that loaded the RAM disk and started your application program, copy the data files (if any) back to the hard disk. Also copy any configuration files for the application that may help it remember what you were doing and any preferences you may have configured for it. (For example, *Word* uses MW.INI to remember what file you were editing and many preferences you may have altered.) Finally, your batch file should erase all those files from the RAM disk, making it ready for the next batch file to load the next major application you choose to run.

If you are going to put many files on your RAM disk, be sure to put them in a subdirectory. The root directory, unlike a subdirectory, can only hold a limited number of files. You can specify the number of root directory entries when you create the RAM disk, but that is not necessary if you just remember to use subdirectories.

With a large RAM disk, you can also copy a lot of utility programs that you commonly use to another subdirectory on the RAM disk, and make that the first directory on your PATH. Test to see that the directory in question exists before doing the copying and certainly before setting the PATH to point there. The batch file command IF EXIST comes in handy for this. (Even an empty directory will have the fictitious file NUL in it.)

One last tip: Sometimes the volatile nature of a RAM disk can work in your favor. If you use SET commands to point the variables TEMP and TMP to yet another subdirectory on the RAM disk, many applications will put their temporary files there. When you reboot, any leftover temporary files will automatically get deleted (which is just what you want to happen). A warning though—be sure your RAM disk is big enough. The makers of *CorelDRAW!* used to recommend this trick, but they recently stopped doing so. Their reason? Too many users were running into trouble when they ran out of RAM disk space. For *CorelDRAW!*, they now say, don't try this unless you have around 5 to 10 *megabytes* of free space on your RAM disk.

Using RECORDER to Optimize RAM Disk Usage

Speeding up your PC by putting files on a RAM disk is generally a pretty good idea. Knowing which files to put there may not be easy, though. Several years ago, *PC Magazine* published a program called RECORDER. It is a TSR that watches all disk accesses. After it has had time to accumulate a record of those accesses, you can direct it to write them all to an output file.

Examining that record will help you discover which files are most often accessed. Armed with this information, you will be able to make informed decisions about what to include on the RAM disk, and what can safely be left on the hard disk. You can get a copy of RECORDER from many local bulletin boards or from the Ziff-Davis forum on CompuServe. (GO ZIFFNET, and then download the file from the "Software and Utility Library.")

How to Make a RAM Disk Bigger Without Using More RAM

The limit on how large a RAM disk you can make is set by how much total RAM you have and how much of that you can spare. There is one technique that will let you almost double the apparent size of a RAM disk without taking any extra RAM to do it.

There are now several on-the-fly file compression programs that compress data as it is written to a disk and expand it again as it is read back. Some of them can do this trick for a RAM disk as well as for a hard disk or floppy disk. *Stacker,* starting with version 2, is one of those. Install *Stacker* and have it "stack" the RAM disk. Poof! Your RAM disk suddenly looks nearly twice as large as it once was.

Although Microsoft doesn't point this out, the DOS 6 program DoubleSpace can be used to compress a RAM disk. Don't use it that way! While it will work, each time you do this you will find that you have used up one more drive letter. Soon your RAM disk will be Z and the next time you reboot you won't be able to create the RAM disk at all.

Understanding how this happens involves learning all about the special hidden, system control file DoubleSpace uses, called DBLSPACE.INI. The details have not been documented by Microsoft. You can find a discussion of them in the book *DOS 6.0 Power Tools* by John M. Goodman and John Socha (Bantam, 1993). Alternatively, you can simply heed this warning and not try DoubleSpacing your RAM disks.

Doubling the size of a disk is the *Stacker* default. In some cases, you can get a RAM disk that is ten times as large as before. How much increase you can get depends on the degree of redundancy in the files you will be storing there. For example, many graphic image data files can be compressed a great deal. On the other hand, executable files rarely compress to less than two-thirds their original size. So if they are all you will be storing on your RAM disk, your gain in apparent size will be less than 50 percent.

Don't rely on the *Stacker* utility SCHECK to tell you at the outset how large your new RAM disk will be. It can give only an estimate and an upper limit. So you should experiment. After you find out the typical compression ratio you get with your files (using Stacker's SDIR and SCHECK programs), you may need to give some special commands to *Stacker* to create a RAM disk with an appropriate maximum compression ratio.

There is one way that this approach will cost you extra RAM, and that cost comes in the most painful place. You must load the *Stacker* device driver into either lower or upper memory. If you have LIM 4.0 EMS expanded memory, you can direct *Stacker* to put part of itself out in EMS memory. Also, be sure to turn off *Stacker*'s internal cache if you are using any third-party caching program. See Chapter 30 for additional information on this technique, on *Stacker,* and on its competitors.

How to Manage Your PC's "Mind" Without Losing Your Own

Anyone who plays around with optimizing a PC's configuration runs into the problem of keeping track of what he or she is doing, and of what the programs installed on the PC are doing. It is very easy to get quite confused. Here are some pointers that may help you.

The Problem of Arrogant Installation Programs

Many installation programs want to alter your PC's critical CONFIG.SYS and AUTOEXEC.BAT files and possibly the WIN.INI and SYSTEM.INI files in your Windows directory. They may need to do so in order to make your PC's configuration adequate to run their program.

The polite ones tell you what they want to do and give you the option of permitting, editing, or altogether prohibiting those changes. Many less polite installation programs just go ahead and make the changes they think are needed, often without even notifying you of what they are doing. Those are the arrogant programs. They are the villains of this piece.

It is hard enough for a human being to assess what a given PC's configuration is and, knowing the needs of the program, to alter that configuration appropriately. No installation program (nor any author of an installation program) is smart enough to be able to do this job automatically in all cases without many times making mistakes. Generally, the more knowledgeable the program's authors, the more humble they are on this point and therefore, the more likely they are to offer you a chance to get involved in the process.

There is an easy way to protect yourself against the arrogant programs. Make a subdirectory off the root of your hard disk, and copy all the files in the root directory to that subdirectory. (One name you might use for that directory is C:\ROOTBACK.)

At the very least, copy your CONFIG.SYS and AUTOEXEC.BAT files to that safe holding area. They are the ones frequently altered by arrogant installation programs. Some installation programs even copy some version of COMMAND.COM to the root directory. If that version is different from the one already on your hard drive, you may suddenly be unable to boot from the hard drive. Having that backup copy in a subdirectory (and a Safety Boot Diskette) is nice protection against this and several other kinds of trouble.

You may need to provide similar protection for your *Windows* WIN.INI and SYSTEM.INI files as well. This also applies to any other major applications that use special configuration files that inform them of how you want them to work. More and more, installation programs are *Windows*-aware and will attempt to alter your *Windows* environment, as well as the DOS one.

As soon as you have completed the installation of a new program, look to see how the AUTOEXEC.BAT and CONFIG.SYS files in the root directory compare with your safety backup copies. The differences tell you very clearly what the installation program did. (A good file comparison program for this, and many other purposes, is *FC* or *FCDOC* by Mike Albert. These shareware programs almost never get confused by the differences in files, and they can show you those differences even in very large files in a clear manner.)

Remember to keep your backup copies of these critical files current. The comparison is meaningless if the safety copies of those files were not identical to the root directory files just before you began the new program installation.

The Value of Alternate "Personalities" for Your PC

You may find it useful to have several alternate sets of CONFIG.SYS and AUTOEXEC.BAT files. Each pair will customize your PC differently, providing it with a unique "personality" for a given work session.

This may be necessary if you wish to run a very RAM hungry application, such as *Ventura Publisher* for GEM, and at other times want to have a number of TSR programs loaded or be connected to a network. It may simply be impossible to do all that at once.

Another situation that could be helped by this approach is if you sometimes want to run DOS applications that want a lot of expanded memory, but not much or any extended memory, such as Lotus *1-2-3*, Release 2.x, and at other times want to run programs that want all the extended memory you can give them, such as *Windows*, version 3.x.

Yet another candidate for this approach is when you only rarely want to use some peripheral, such as a full-page scanner, and that peripheral takes a rather large device driver. You must load the device driver through your CONFIG.SYS file, but you might not want to do so except when you want to make use of the scanner.

In all these cases, you could create custom configuration file pairs for each situation. Then copy the relevant pair to the root directory (renaming them in the process from whatever special names you used to store them to the standard names CONFIG.SYS and AUTOEXEC.BAT) and reboot your computer. In Chapter 35 you will find some examples of this approach.

DOS 6 Menus in CONFIG.SYS

If you are using DOS 6 you can accomplish the same thing in a different way. DOS 6 allows you to build menus within the CONFIG.SYS file.

A DOS 6 menu consists of menu blocks and configuration blocks. Each block is named. The top-level menu block carries the reserved name "menu"; all the rest may be named anything you like.

As with the INI files that come with Windows and many other modern programs, the block names are enclosed in square brackets and the left square bracket must be in the first character position on the line.

Menu blocks can contain four kinds of lines: SUBMENUs, MENUITEMs, a MENUDEFAULT command, and a MENUCOLOR command. The lines that start SUBMENU= name other menu blocks. The lines that start MENUITEM= name configuration blocks. The MENUDEFAULT line specifies which of the submenus or menuitems will be activated if the user enters no choice, and, optionally, it specifies how long the user has to make a choice. Not surprisingly, the MENUCOLOR command sets the foreground and background colors in which the menu will be presented.

As you navigate the menu structure, you are choosing which blocks of commands and directives within the CONFIG.SYS file will get executed. The various blocks are named, and the last named menu block's name is put into the DOS environment as the definition of the special environment variable CONFIG. (DOS 6 also puts another definition into the environment, namely PROMPT=PG.)

In your AUTOEXEC.BAT file you can test the value of the environment variable CONFIG and branch to a suitable block of commands. This allows you to control from the CONFIG.SYS menus the sections of both the CONFIG.SYS file and the AUTOEXEC.BAT file that will be executed.

Chapter 35 shows several examples of DOS 6 menus. These include some that use alternative paths through both the CONFIG.SYS and AUTOEXEC.BAT files.

Subdirectories to the Rescue (Generally)

If you haven't discovered how subdirectories can simplify your life, please do so now. They are wonderful. You can have files with the same name in two different subdirectories and DOS will know that they are different files. If you organize all your files into subdirectories according to some rational scheme that makes sense to you, then you will have much less difficulty finding the files you want when you want them.

If you put each of your application programs and all its related programs into one directory or *branch* of your directory tree (a branch is a subdirectory and all the subdirectories below it), that will help keep it separate from all other programs. Nearly every program seems to come with a README.1ST file or a READ.ME file. Only by separating programs can you be sure that a new one does not overwrite an older one, and that each one is clearly associated with the program it describes.

A good idea is to put the data files for that application in one or more subdirectories under the main application directory. In any case, if you have a large physical hard drive subdivided into several smaller logical drives (a very good idea), try to put the data files into subdirectories on the same logical disk drive as the application program that created them. This keeps accesses to the disk in the same general region on the disk, and that speeds up those accesses.

Subdirectories to the Rescue (Some Specific Recommendations)

Here is a useful variation on the idea mentioned earlier. In addition to a C:\ROOTBACK directory containing a copy of everything in your root directory, you may wish to create a subdirectory called C:\CONFIGUR. In it you could keep all your variations on CONFIG.SYS, AUTOEXEC.BAT, and any menu definition files. This subdirectory would be, in a sense, a repository for alternate PC personalities.

For example, suppose you use AUTOMENU. It refers to a data file called AUTOMENU.MDF (Menu Definition File). A complete personality for your machine is contained in three files: CONFIG.SYS, AUTOEXEC.BAT, and AUTOMENU.MDF.

You might choose to create one set of these files for everyday normal use. Call them your NRM set. Another set would be a set for troubleshooting problems. This set would create a very minimal environment, but still you might want the menu file to help you access various utility programs. Call that set your TRB set. Maybe you only occasionally use *Windows*. For those occasions you might like a set you could call the WIN set.

You might name the files in your NRM set CONFIG.NRM, AUTOEXEC.NRM, AUTOMENU.NRM. As the names suggest, these are the NRM versions of CONFIG.SYS, AUTOEXEC.BAT, and AUTOMENU.MDF. Make similar files for the other sets and give them the extensions TRB and WIN. Keep all these files in your C:\CONFIGUR directory.

Changing personalities now is just a matter of copying the appropriate set of files to the root directory (and renaming each file as you do so to the proper extension—SYS, BAT, or MDF), and then rebooting your PC. That is easy enough to do manually, but it can be made even easier.

Using Batch Files to Ease Matters

You don't need to put the C:\CONFIGUR directory on your DOS PATH. It would be best if you didn't do so, as none of the files in it are executable anyway.

Put a series of batch files in some other directory that is on the PATH. You will use these batch files to automate the task of changing your PC's personality. For example, you might have one called SET-NORM.BAT.It would read:

```
@echo off
echo                 SET-NORM.BAT
echo         Setting up Normal work environment
REM   Be sure you are on the right disk drive
C:
REM   Be sure you are in the right directory
CD \CONFIGUR
COPY CONFIG.NRM \CONFIG.SYS > NUL
COPY AUTOEXEC.NRM \AUTOEXEC.BAT > NUL
COPY AUTOMENU.NRM \AUTOMENU.MDF > NUL
REBOOT
```

You could make similar files called SET-TRB.BAT and SET-WIN.BAT. Alternatively, you could create one master batch file called SET-ENV.BAT. It could read like this:

```
@echo off
echo                 SET-ENV.BAT
echo         Resetting your PC's personality.
echo.
REM Test first for no command line argument
IF %1.==. GOTO ShowSyntax
IF %1==NRM GOTO NRM
IF %1==TRB GOTO TRB
IF %1==WIN GOTO WIN
:ShowSyntax
echo     At the DOS prompt type
echo             SET-ENV name
echo     where name is the personality you want.
```

```
GOTO done
:NRM
CALL SET-NRM.BAT
:TRB
CALL SET-TRB.BAT
:WIN
CALL SET-WIN.BAT
:done
```

Of course, if you are using AUTOMENU, you could have these choices as menu entries. Or, you could include the contents of the smaller batch files in the one large file (instead of using CALL statements), both to save disk space and to make a file that will work even with earlier versions of DOS. With the help of a batch file language extender (such as that included with the *Norton Utilities*) you could make a menu within the batch file.

These batch files assume you have a program, REBOOT.COM, that simply does the equivalent of Ctrl-Alt-Del. Now you do! It is on the diskette included with this book.

Using Boot-Time Configuration Managers

Yet another way to accomplish these same goals is to use a boot-time configuration manager. Two good ones are BOOT.SYS by Hans Salvisberg, and CONED (CONfiguration EDitor) by Ira T. Ashkenes. Both are shareware programs. (DOS 6 users may find these programs offer helpful features in addition to those supported by the menuing features of DOS 6.)

V Communications, the makers of the *Memory Commander* memory manager, recently introduced a boot-time configuration manager called *Boot Commander*. They claim that it is one of relatively few boot-time configuration managers to deal properly with the fact that in DOS 5 and 6 the CONFIG.SYS file is scanned twice. As you may remember, the first scan is used to determine if DOS is to load a portion of itself into the HMA. The second scan does everything else.

If you use the DOS=HIGH directive in some of your configurations, but don't use it in others, any boot-time manager that assumes it can do its job merely by intercepting the process before the first DEVICE is loaded will be unsuccessful in dealing with all your configurations. But *Boot Commander* can. So can any boot-time configuration manager that reboots your computer after you have chosen your configuration, as will the batch files described above.

All of these do the same essential job. They each allow you to set up a variety of personalities expressed in CONFIG.SYS and AUTOEXEC.BAT file alternatives. Some put each alternative in a separate file; others create one monster file with all the options in it. Then, at boot time, you are given an option of which of these alternate versions you wish to use. CONED, for example, now supports a choice from among over 6,000 separate personalities. These programs may be found on many bulletin boards and on CompuServe.

Some Tips on Maximizing Your Free RAM

If you are experiencing RAM cram, you may be able to get relief without adding memory. Just use what you have more efficiently. Here are some tips on what you might do.

Minimize DOS's Use of RAM

What version of DOS are you using? That makes a major difference in how much RAM DOS takes for itself. Each successive version of DOS from 1.0 through 4.0 used more RAM than the one that came before it, with 4.0 representing the largest jump in RAM requirements. In exchange for paying this price in RAM, you got more features with each new version.

That "obvious and natural" trend was broken by DOS 5. With that version, you get more features and yet it takes up a smaller amount of RAM than the prior version. This is certainly true if you compare it to DOS 4. It is even true if you compare it to DOS 3.3, if you count just lower RAM usage. (This is only true if you have some extended memory and allow DOS to load part of itself in the HMA. On a class 1 or 2 PC, DOS 5 needs just a little more lower memory than DOS 3.3, but a lot less than DOS 4.) DOS 6 requires the same amount of RAM as DOS 5 (provided you use the same features). Of course, if you choose to load some of the extra new utility programs that come with DOS 6, they will take up extra RAM.

Beyond the matter of which version of DOS you have, there are a number of ways you can control how much RAM DOS uses. Careful attention to these might be just what you need to deal with an annoying case of RAM cram.

In version 4, DOS offered the user a three-way installation choice (through the SELECT program). The choices were to put all of DOS in RAM that you could; this gives you the greatest possible performance. Another choice was to put the minimal DOS in RAM for maximum free RAM space. The final choice was some compromise between the first two. The SELECT program and the DOS manual were not at all clear on what these choices actually did. Many users had no idea what to choose and simply picked one at random.

Happily, with DOS 5 this feature has gone away. It is gone, but not regretted. Now you can control what you put in RAM with a clear knowledge of what you are doing at each step.

One of the biggest ways DOS uses RAM that you can minimize is in its disk buffers. See the discussion of the BUFFERS command earlier in this chapter for ways to do this. Specifying STACKS = 0,0 and FCBS = 1 in your CONFIG.SYS file also can help some. Neither of them helps nearly as much as reducing the number of BUFFERS, and sometimes eliminating STACKS or FCBS is not a good idea. These points are also discussed in more depth earlier in this chapter.

Finally, you can replace COMMAND.COM with an alternative command interpreter. NDOS and 4DOS take up dramatically less room in lower memory.

Avoid Unnecessary Device Drivers and TSRs

Most of us augment DOS by the addition of various device drivers and TSR programs. These could be programs that come with DOS, such as ANSI.SYS, HIMEM.SYS, EMM386.EXE, and DOSKEY. Or, they could be third-party programs such as *Super PC-Kwik*, a mouse driver, or a CD-ROM device driver.

Each of these programs provides DOS with important new functionality. It also uses up some RAM. The discussion of this point earlier in the chapter focused on how to move these drivers out of the way. First, be sure you need them.

Besides saving RAM, eliminating superfluous device drivers and TSRs can make your system more stable. Each one you add gives you more functionality, but it makes your system less "plain." That makes it just that much harder for the next program you load to be sure it knows how to deal with your system safely.

Do not eliminate device drivers that you really need. If you do, you may find yourself unable to access your hard drive or some partitions on that drive. This will be the case if you are using a third-party disk partitioning program or an on-the-fly file compression program. See the section "When Memory Managers Can Be Dangerous" in Chapter 31 for more details on the virtues of these programs and some pitfalls they bring with them.

How to Get Rid of
Third-Party Disk Partitioning Software

If you decide you want to get rid of a third-party disk partitioning program, how can you do it? The bad news is you will have to completely back up your disk and then redo the partitioning and high-level format (also called the logical format). The former task you do with the FDISK program; the latter one you do with FORMAT.

The good news is that this is a wonderful time to upgrade your version of DOS and perhaps also to do a complete "spring housecleaning" and reorganization of your files. That can lead to greater operating efficiency in the future.

But first, be *very* careful. Have a working Safety Boot Diskette close by your machine. (See Chapter 5 for what this is.) Be sure your backups are valid and complete. Complete means you have backed up *all partitions*, even though you may be thinking of changing only some. ***You could lose all your data in all your partitions the instant you run FDISK.*** (The worst aspect of many versions of DOS FDISK is that even if you merely confirm an existing partitioning of your disk, it will wipe out the first 16 cylinders, or thereabouts, in any DOS partition.) A valid backup means one from which you can restore programs and data files without any errors. Test this point. Don't make assumptions, especially on something that could affect the safety of your data.

Now might be a very good time to reread the discussion of how to make and test backups in Chapter 5. Only when you are sure your backups are valid and complete is it safe to proceed.

Get DOS version 3.3 or later. This is necessary if you are going to get full use of a disk with greater than 32MB total capacity and avoid using any third-party partitioning software. It also is necessary if you are going to use on-the-fly file compression software with a disk over about 16MB total capacity.

> This also might be a very good time to redo the low-level format. That allows you to choose the optimum interleave for your system, in case your disk is not already set for it. *SpinRite,* or the Calibrate program in the *Norton Utilities*, can help you decide what that optimum number is. Run one of these programs before you begin. Then do the low-level format for the whole disk. (Why would you do this? After all, *SpinRite* and Calibrate claim to be able to nondestructively redo the low-level format on your disks. The reason you may wish to do an old-fashioned, full low-level format is that those programs cannot touch the regions of the disk that lie outside the DOS partition.) Finally, run FDISK, FORMAT, and restore your files.

Once you have tested your backups and have a safety boot disk in hand, go ahead and run FDISK. Create whatever partitions you wish to have. If the disk is large, it is a very good idea to break it up into several logical drives. The arguments for doing so are similar to those for using subdirectories within a drive.

FORMAT each partition (with the new version of DOS if you are upgrading). Restore your files with the old or a new directory structure.

Don't Use FASTOPEN

The idea behind FASTOPEN is a good one. Too bad its implementation has so many problems. Every time you access a file on the disk, DOS has to know precisely where on the disk that information can be found. The notion of FASTOPEN is that you can speed that process by keeping a copy of the navigational information DOS uses in RAM. As long as the copy in RAM is absolutely a faithful copy of what is on the disk, this is a good idea. Unfortunately, all too often, keeping the RAM copy up to date is too difficult for FASTOPEN to do.

Microsoft and IBM have not yet admitted publicly that there might be any problems with FASTOPEN. The automatic installation procedures for several versions of both *PC DOS* and *MS-DOS* will put a call to FASTOPEN into your CONFIG.SYS file for you. Get it out of there!

The anecdotal evidence is just too strong. FASTOPEN corrupts files on your disk. Not always, but sometimes. And that is too often. The GeoWorks company, among others, has published this advice for their users.

Use ANSI.SYS Judiciously

The ANSI.SYS device driver allows DOS to handle the keyboard and screen in a much more flexible manner than it can without that driver. The augmented features also bring it into compliance with the ANSI standard for how terminals shall behave.

Having those added capabilities can be nice. It makes it easy to have colorful prompts, put a clock display on screen, redefine your function keys, and so forth. But there is a cost. ANSI.SYS, like all device drivers, takes up some RAM. You can get alternative versions of this program, and some of these give you more yet take less of your RAM.

> Three examples are ANSI-UV.SYS, which is bundled with *Ultravision* from Personics, DVANSI.SYS that is included with *DESQview* from Quarterdeck Office Systems, and MCROANSI.SYS, a freeware program available on many bulletin boards. These alternatives reduce the RAM needs and they work faster, plus DVANSI and MCROANSI are "DESQview aware."
>
> MCROANSI is even faster and smaller than DVANSI, and it eliminates the keyboard redefinition features of ANSI.SYS. That latter aspect may sound like a defect, but it also is a protection against "ANSI Trojan Horse batch files" and other nasty and malicious programs that may attempt to redefine those keys for you, sometimes with horrible results.

You may think you need ANSI.SYS (or an equivalent device driver) when you really don't. For example, many communications programs (such as *Procomm Plus*) have the same capability built in. That only works while you are on-line, but if that is the main time you wanted those capabilities, you don't need to waste RAM on ANSI.SYS.

When You Should Use SHARE.EXE

The DOS external command SHARE first appeared in DOS version 3.1. Its stated purpose was to protect files from corruption when multiple users on a network might try to access them simultaneously.

> The problem is this: Process #1 opens a file and reads some data. Process #2 reads the same file. Process #1 changes the data and writes those changes back to the file. Process #2 does likewise. The changes the second process made will be in the file as it finally exists on the disk, but since Process #2 never saw the changes made by Process #1, those changes will be overwritten and lost.
>
> The only way to solve this problem is to prevent all but one process at a time from opening any file with "permission to write." (It is perfectly fine for any number of processes to open the same file as long as only one is able to change its contents.)

With version 4.0 of DOS, SHARE got a new job. The older, file-control block (FCB) method of accessing files is too limited to work correctly on a disk volume that is larger than 32MB. This version of DOS was the first (from Microsoft or IBM) to support such large volumes. If you load SHARE with DOS 4, you not only are protected against file damage by multiple programs accessing files at once, you also are protected against file corruption from any program that uses FCBs for file access.

The problem is that an FCB cannot contain large enough numbers to point to where files reside on anything larger than a 32MB disk. If an FCB-using program tries to access a file that happens to lie beyond that limit, it will instead step on top of some other file near the beginning of the disk. The problem is much like that of address wrapping in an 8088.

You may think you don't have any "old-style" programs. Perhaps you don't. But be aware: Many popular old standards still use FCBs. *SideKick* is one.

If you have upgraded to DOS 5, you no longer need SHARE to protect you from FCB-using programs. In this and later versions of DOS, SHARE is used only to protect files from multiple, simultaneous accesses.

Thus, if you use DOS 5 or 6, and if you are not running on a network, you may think you don't need to load SHARE. Think again. If you run any task-switching or multitasking software, you may have multiple processes (programs) on your own machine accessing the same files at the same time. The potential for file corruption is every bit as bad in this case as it is on a network.

You might think this was valid for multitasking but not for task switching. After all, in task switching, only one program is running at any time. True enough, but if one task opens a file and then is suspended before it closes that file, any other program might open the same file and corrupt it if SHARE was not loaded.

So use SHARE any time you may be running any multitasking or task-switching software, or if you have a large disk and are using version 4 of DOS. This means that all users of *Windows, DESQview, GeoWorks Pro, Software Carousel, WordPerfect Office,* or any similar program need to run SHARE. It also includes anyone who ever "drops to DOS" from within an application and may attempt to access the same files that application is using.

Of course, if none of those situations matches yours, don't waste RAM on SHARE. Just be *very* sure your situation doesn't fit.

Trim the RAM Usage of the Device Drivers and TSRs You Do Use

Check the manual or documentation on each device driver and TSR you load. You may not have noticed some command line options that could limit how much memory they take up. Sometimes you can run a setup program and choose some limitations to the features of the program in order to trim its RAM size. *SideKick*, for example, lets you choose the maximum size of a file that can be edited by its Notepad and even eliminate other of its features altogether.

Trim the Use of RAM by Your Application Programs

The same thing applies to your application programs. Many times, a program that won't load because you don't have enough free RAM can be induced to load a more limited version of itself with some command line switches, or by reconfiguring the program through its setup utility.

Check with the manufacturer's technical support department. Look on local bulletin boards or on CompuServe. Ask for tips at your local user group.

Networks and RAM Cram

Many PC users were blissfully free from "RAM cram" until their PC was put onto a network. All of a sudden many of their favorite applications wouldn't run.

This is because any network takes some additions to DOS in order to work. The network drivers must augment the notion DOS has of the disks it is managing to include those available across the network. They may also be responsible for formatting information packets in special ways and otherwise managing the interface between DOS applications, DOS, and the network.

All that program code (and some essential data tables and buffers) takes RAM. Usually, quite a lot of RAM. Losing more than 100KB to your network software is not at all unusual.

What can you do about this? Several things:

- Be sure you have eliminated all the other unnecessary uses of lower and upper memory.

- Try to pick a network that uses a minimal amount of RAM. (Of course, if you are not responsible for the choice of network, that is not an option for you.)

- Try to move the network drivers out of the way. In Chapter 21, you will learn more details on how that can sometimes be done.

Networks and **N**etwork **I**nterface **C**ards (NICs) also present a couple of other problems related to RAM. They, more than any other part you add to your PC, are likely to use memory-mapped I/O. And they sometimes have RAM for a buffer which they connect to the CPU's memory address space only when the network driver needs to access it. Both of these behaviors can cause serious problems for modern memory managers. See the discussion in Chapter 6 for more on these points.

What if you use *Windows* and have upgraded to *Windows for Workgroups*? Does that help you in any important way with memory management? The new *Windows for Workgroups* is essentially just *Windows*, version 3.1, plus a peer-to-peer network (similar to Artisoft's *LANtastic* or Novell's *NetWare Lite*), plus Microsoft *Mail* (the latter is an e-mail program).

Windows for Workgroups uses exactly the same amount of memory as *Windows*, and it also loads network drivers that take up similar amounts of memory to those loaded for one of the alternative networks. You can buy *Windows for Workgroups* in a bundle pack that includes the needed network interface cards. The NIC problems with this system are also just the same as with NICs you get from some other source for this or any other network.

Putting What You Have to Good Use

The Goal Is Not Free RAM

Remember, the goal is *not* to have a lot of free RAM. The goal is to have as much as you need.

Any "Waste RAM" Can Be Put to Good Use

Any excess RAM, beyond that which you need to load your applications, can usually be put to good use. You can load helpful TSR programs that let you do more in less time. You can add a disk cache, print spooler, or RAM disk. All of these are excellent ways to use any spare extended or expanded memory.

Be Careful Not to Destabilize Your System

On the other hand, if you only have a little leftover memory, don't sweat it. Having just that little bit of extra RAM may make the difference between a system that barely works most of the time, and one that actually works, and works well, all of the time. System stability is a great virtue.

A Recap

In this chapter, you learned all about the many strategies and tactics that can help you manage your PC's memory. You found out some of the ways you may need to configure the hardware (with DIP switches, jumpers, or by running one or more setup programs), plus how to customize your PC's operation through entries in its CONFIG.SYS and AUTOEXEC.BAT files.

You now know what Shadow RAM is, and how it can be helpful. You also found out that while it sometimes is a feature you could use, you might not always want to use it just because you can. You know how to use a RAM disk effectively. And you have some ideas for making it easy to change your PC's personality from time to time, as the tasks you want it to do change in their requirements.

The chapter ended with a review of ways to clear out your RAM, and a reminder that you need not be overzealous in that effort. Once you find you have more RAM than you actually need, you can always find good uses for it. Some were suggested here. More details on that subject may be found in Chapter 30.

The next chapter will continue the subject of memory management, this time with an emphasis on programs you can use to assist you, or in some cases, programs that claim to do it all for you automatically.

MEMORY MANAGEMENT— AUTOMATIC SOLUTIONS

You can do memory management all by yourself, but it sure helps to have good tools. Some will do almost the whole job, all by themselves. This chapter introduces you to the topic of "automatic" memory management.

Automatic memory management—it has a nice ring to it. You see the advertisements about the wonderful programs you can buy that will do everything you need . . . and more! They practically promise to brew your coffee while optimizing your computer.

The semiautomatic and automatic memory managers are wonderful programs, but don't be fooled. Although you can leave them to run completely automatically, even the best memory managers will do a better job for you if you get involved in the process.

Unfortunately, some of the companies seem to believe their own hype. Their programs make it relatively difficult for you to get involved. Fortunately with all of these programs, you can get appropriately involved if you learn how. It may not always be easy, but it is always worth doing.

Some Programs That Manage Memory for Themselves

Before talking about the modern miracle programs, first consider the relatively simple memory-management strategies that more mundane programs use every day. You have some programs in your PC that daily are doing some pretty wonderful memory management for themselves, without any intervention on your part.

Traditional Coping Strategies

Every program uses RAM for two purposes. One is for the program's instructions (which is also called its "code"). The other is for the data it is to work on.

Small programs, which work on small amounts of data, can fit everything into RAM at once. They are given what they need by DOS when they are loaded. Once they have it, they use it until they are finished. Then they give it all back. These programs don't need to do much memory management at all.

However, other programs either have too much code or too much data (or both) to fit into RAM all at once. They must use some strategy to deal with this. Two common strategies are code overlays and data segmentation.

Program Code Overlays

Many large programs load only a portion of themselves into RAM at once. A full-featured word processor, to name just one example, often has so many things it can do that the computer instructions to describe them all take up more room than all of the RAM in your PC—certainly more than all of the lower memory (the region from 0 to 640KB). When you first load such a word processor, only a small core part of it gets loaded. That part then manages the work of all the other parts.

When you are editing a document, the core program loads an editing module. When you stop editing to check the spelling of words in your document, or to use the thesaurus to help you find just the right word, the core program loads a special module to do that task. In order not to take up more RAM, it loads that new module into the same CPU memory address locations as the editing module. Naturally, that wipes out the editing module's code in RAM, but since that was only a copy of that portion of the program, and it was taken from a disk file originally, it can be readily replaced in RAM when you are ready to return to editing.

After you decide you have finished your document, you may choose to print it. That might need yet another module, and again the core program can load that module's code over whichever other module has most recently been in RAM (see Figure 21.1).

The round-edged portion at the top of Figure 21.1 represents your disk drive. All of the word processing program is kept there. It might be in several different files, or all of the modules may be put together into one file. Some programs use a combination of these two approaches.

The tall columns in the lower part of Figure 21.1 represent a portion of the CPU's memory-address space. That is where the program and its data must be when the program is actually running. Each column shows what is where in RAM at one phase of operation of the word processor. The data part at the top always occupies the same region, as does the portion containing the core code. The region in between is occupied successively by one or another module, each containing the code needed to do a particular job.

This is just one example, and a somewhat over-simplified one at that. Still, it captures the essence of program overlay as a means of coping with a program that is too large to fit into RAM.

The number of modules, or overlays, into which a given program gets broken depends on the programmer's notion of what are the definable separate tasks it has to do, and on how constricted the space is in which the program must fit. Normally, the number of overlays is kept as small as is feasible, in order to minimize the number of times during a work session that the program must return to the disk drive to retrieve another overlay.

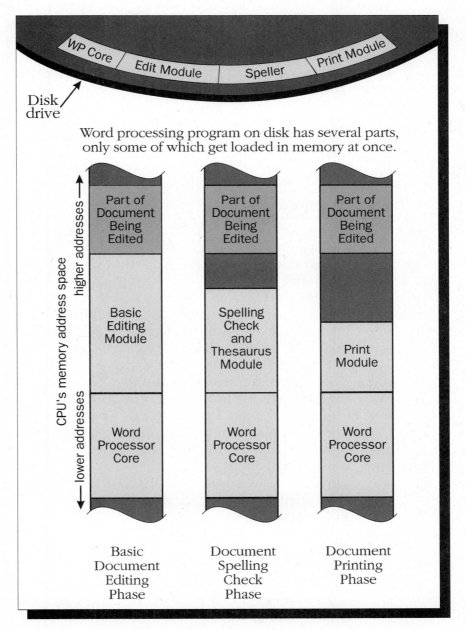

Figure 21.1. Using overlays for program code lets large programs fit into modest amounts of RAM.

Often it is easier to write the program all in one massive piece, but when that piece becomes too large to fit comfortably in RAM, the programmer must decide on a strategy for breaking it up into smaller parts.

Notice that not all the modules are the same size. That means that memory is not being used to total efficiency all the time. On the other hand, there is no delay in fetching code from the disk, except when you change from one major task within the program to another. Normally, people don't switch from editing to spell-checking or to printing all that often. So this inefficiency of RAM usage is tolerated in order to let the program run more smoothly. This is especially important for programs that are running on PCs with disk drives that aren't very fast (especially those with only a floppy disk drive, as is common in older laptops).

Data Segmentation

Word processors face another common problem as well. They often are used to working on very large documents. And for safety's sake, it is prudent to have more than one copy of that document in the computer while you are working on it.

Normally, there are at least three copies of all the contents of your document in the computer while you are writing or editing it. One is the most recently saved version. Another is the prior version. The third, or working copy, is the one actually being edited (see Figure 21.2).

The word processor first loads its code into memory, or at least the core part of the code and probably the main edit module. Then when you tell it what document you want to edit, it will read a portion of that file into a data space in RAM. (If space is really tight, the first overlay might be just the file management code that loads and saves document files. If space allows, this will be integrated into the edit module, as it gets used quite often during editing.)

If not all of the document can fit in that RAM space, the program simply reads in what does fit. Then it helps you edit that portion. When you move on to a part of the document that is not yet in RAM, the word processor must first write out to the disk the part you have just been working on. That goes into a temporary file (#1). The next part of the document is then read into RAM.

You edit that portion and move on. The word processor appends that portion to the temporary file (#1), and loads the next section it is to work on. This may continue for many cycles of load, edit, and write.

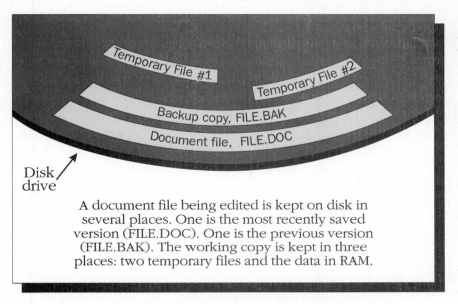

Figure 21.2. Data segmentation is a way to cope with data files larger than available RAM.

What if you decide to go backwards in the document and edit something you had written earlier? This is where the second temporary file comes in. The portion before what you are now editing will be contained in temporary file #1. The portion that comes after what you are now working on will be in temporary file #2.

As you move back and forth through the document, a chunk gets written to one temporary file, and then a similar sized chunk gets removed from the other temporary file and put in RAM. This process continues until you decide to save the document.

At that point, the editor will combine all three parts (the contents of temporary file #1, what is in RAM, and the contents of temporary file #2) into one file, probably temporary file #1. Next, it erases the NAME.BAK file and renames the NAME.DOC file to have a BAK extension. Finally, it renames the temporary file NAME.DOC. This becomes your most recently saved version. (Of course, your file is probably called something more interesting than just NAME.)

If you then go on and edit the file further, the process will start all over from the beginning. This is by no means the only strategy a word processor might use. But it resembles, at least roughly, the strategies that actually are used.

There is an important difference between the program overlay strategy and the data segmentation one. The first strategy used modules of code and each did some particular task. The second used arbitrary chunks of the document—as much as would fit in the available data space in RAM.

A More General Solution—
Real-Mode Virtual Memory Managers

Program code overlays and data segmentation are different specific strategies. They differ because they were devised as the best possible solution to two different cases in which a program must deal with having too little RAM to do its job. Other, more general strategies have been devised. They don't pretend to be "tuned" to the needs of any one program or situation, yet they perform very well in a wide variety of cases.

Borland's VROOMM Strategy

A number of programs from Borland now feature something they call *VROOMM,* or *Virtual Runtime Object Oriented Memory Management*. These programs include their database program, *Paradox,* and their spreadsheet, *Quattro Pro.* This is essentially an attempt at a strategy that has the best features of both program overlays and data segmentation.

Instead of breaking up a program into a few, large modules, each of which does a complex group of related tasks (which is what program overlay strategies typically do), VROOMM involves breaking up each program into many very small, and highly specific, subtasks. Each one is coded into a module of its own. This strategy means that the core of the program has many more modules to manage, but each one is much smaller.

Since they are so much smaller, the time to load each one of these modules from the disk is almost insignificant. So there is no appreciable interruption in the user's work flow as new modules get brought into memory. Also, since they all are so small, they fill the space in memory much more efficiently.

For example, imagine filling a room with large, bulky pieces of furniture. There would inevitably be at least several substantial spaces between pieces. Now, contrast that with filling the room full of peas, or indeed with any large number of relatively small objects. The chances of getting them all to fit without much in the way of wasted space is much higher.

The program's core portion monitors what pieces are needed and loads them if they are not already in memory. When the memory space for these objects is full, it will overwrite those objects that it sees have been least recently or least frequently used.

A side benefit of this approach is that Borland has been able to build a vast library of useful modules. They can now create new programs, of a very different nature from those that have gone before, much more quickly by using these building blocks rather than traditional techniques.

Program-Level Virtual-Memory Management

Some other companies have gone even further in the amount of memory management built into their programs. Nantucket's *Clipper,* version 5, is one example. This is a database program compiler and it includes a full, real-mode, virtual memory manager.

This means that any program created using *Clipper,* as well as all the data that is manipulated by that program, will be viewed by the program as consisting of a large number of small, fixed size pages. Since the pages are of a fixed size, some number of them will exactly fill the space allocated by DOS for the program and its data.

The *Clipper* virtual-memory manager monitors which pages are needed and makes sure they are always in RAM when necessary. When the pool of RAM fills up, the VMM either swaps pages to expanded memory or a disk file; discards the pages (if they are program code, and thus can be reloaded from their original source on the disk); or writes them to disk (if they are data pages, and thus might have changed from the form they had on the disk previously).

Clipper's VMM distinguishes several subregions of RAM that it manages, and it uses slightly different rules for each one. But overall, the idea of pages being read into RAM and swapped, discarded, or written back to the disk applies to all of them.

These are only two examples of commercial programs for the PC that use some sort of real-mode virtual memory scheme. Any program that must deal with large amounts of data, and which may have a large amount of overlay code, could benefit from a similar approach. Creating the basic support for this approach takes a lot of work but once it is set up, all programs created to use it gain substantial benefits in terms of performance.

The only reason that this approach may not be seen a great deal more in the near future is if protected-mode memory-management solutions become more attractive. Since the latter approach only works for programs running on PCs in class 3 or higher, protected-mode memory management is not an option for authors creating applications that must also run on class 1 or class 2 PCs. (See Chapter 3 for a definition of the six classes of PC for purposes of memory management.)

Protected-Mode DOS-Extended Programs

In Chapter 12, you learned about DOS extenders. These are programs used by a program developer to allow what is otherwise a normal, real-mode DOS program to use all of the lower and extended memory in a class 3 or higher PC.

The DOS extender itself is a protected-mode program that gets wrapped around the application being extended. It takes over control of the PC, and then loads and manages the application program. The extender intercepts all the application's requests for operating-system services. Some it will satisfy by itself, and others it will pass on to DOS. Before it passes a request on to DOS, though, it must switch the PC from protected mode to real mode, and after DOS finishes the extender must switch the PC back again.

DOS extenders are not something you use to run an application you already have. They are tools used by program developers to enhance their programs before you get a copy.

Many large, modern PC application programs are being built using a DOS extender. *Lotus 1-2-3*, Release 3.x, *Paradox*, version 3.5 (which also uses VROOMM), and *Oracle* are just a few.

Getting Help— Semiautomatic Memory Management

So far in this chapter, you have been learning about what one program can do, essentially all on its own, to manage memory for its own use. Now consider the larger question of how one program can be used to help manage memory for the benefit of several other programs.

Many approaches have been tried to achieve this end. First, you'll look at some programs that shuffle other programs in and out of memory as a means of letting each one have more space when it is active. Next, you'll examine the degree to which support for this sort of activity has been built into recent DOS versions. Finally, you'll look at some more general memory managers that intervene between the CPU and its memory, or use the memory-mapping abilities of the 386 and 486 to rearrange memory.

Making More Room by Moving Things Around (Launchers and Swappers)

There are three main approaches to memory management by moving programs in and out of memory: Sequential loading of programs, using a TSR manager, and using a task swapper.

Another approach that somewhat resembles program shuffling is loading programs into out-of-the-way places. Most particularly, loading programs into upper memory or the HMA.

Sequential Program Loading

Normally DOS reuses RAM by the simple expedient of sequential loading of programs. That is, when one program completes its work, the RAM it was using is made available for the next program to use. Not all of RAM can be reused this way, because some of it contains pieces of the operating system that must be kept around to support each of the successively loaded application programs.

Further, some programs don't just do their job all at once. Pop-up utilities and programs meant to run "in the background" do their work a little at a time, or in batches, in between times that other programs are working. Naturally, to do this, these utility programs must remain in RAM or be returned to RAM whenever they are going to do some more work.

DOS Shell Programs as Program Launchers

One kind of program that many people enjoy using is called a *DOS shell program*. At one level, this is simply a program that puts a new face on the command interpreter (COMMAND.COM, NDOS, or whatever one you have loaded). *XtreeGold* is an example of this genre (see Chapter 1, Figure 1.7).

You may be confused by the use of the term shell in this way. Earlier in this book, you read the term shell used in a rather different way. That other meaning was borrowed from *UNIX*. In that sense, the term shell is used to mean the command interpreter itself. Thus, you have the SHELL statement in the CONFIG.SYS files to specify which command interpreter you want DOS to use.

But you can also use the term shell, and this is the sense in which it is being used now, to refer to any program that works on top of the command interpreter, and which presents a different user interface to the user. Commands entered there get translated appropriately by the shell program, and then get passed down to the command interpreter, which acts on the translated equivalents as if they were typed at the DOS prompt.

These programs keep the user from having to confront the infamous DOS prompt, and they make file management operations much easier. But they can be used in another way.

You can either "shell to DOS" from one of these programs (that is, get to a DOS command prompt, or something that functions as if it were a DOS command prompt), or you can use the shell program directly to launch an application.

In the former case, you will use the shell to go to a particular directory, and then "step outside" the shell to work directly with the command interpreter. In the latter case, you set up a menu of programs you'd like to be able to launch, and then whenever you want, you simply pick an item off that menu. The shell program finds the correct file, and tells the command interpreter to load it and let it run.

This is a crude form of memory management, but it is one step above just letting the command interpreter successively load applications. The only way in which it is a step above is that it makes telling the command interpreter what to do a bit easier.

The important thing to realize here is that a program, once launched by the shell program, runs exactly as if it had been loaded at the DOS prompt. You cannot normally interrupt it and launch a different program. The only way memory is managed in this scenario is that as each program completes its work, it will release all the RAM it was using, and only then do you get back to the shell program where you may pick another program to be run.

Don't get "locked out." The shell program depends upon each program it runs ending and returning all its memory to DOS before control returns to the shell program. If you should be imprudent and run a TSR program from this sort of shell program, you'll find that you can't get back to the shell program afterwards. That is precisely because the TSR has not given up its RAM even though it is through working for now. It is almost as if you "stepped outside" the shell, the door shut, and then you realized you had left your keys inside! At this point, you can try forcing the TSR to unload itself. If you don't succeed, the only other solution is to reboot.

Swapping Programs (TSR Managers and More General Task Swappers)

Some programs go a step beyond the shell programs. They can load and run many different programs. To do this, they simply regard the available RAM for program execution as a stage and themselves as the stage manager. They tell the programs they are managing when to get on stage and work, when to get off, and where to go when they are off-stage. One popular example of the class of program is WordPerfect *Office*.

There are a number of advantages to using such a task manager. If you have a large amount of expanded or extended memory (in particular, if that memory is managed, and thus is available either as EMS or XMS memory), you can put regular DOS programs into almost all of it. These programs cannot run when they are out in the EMS memory pool or up in extended memory, but from these places, they can be brought into lower memory much more quickly than they can be loaded from disk.

This lets you load up your PC with lots more programs at once—many more than will fit into lower memory. Furthermore, these programs can be interrupted in the middle of their work, swapped out to their holding area, and later on returned to lower memory to pick up where they left off. You don't have to save your work and close your application before you can go to another one. This gives you the illusion that all the programs are running at once.

Of course, this also creates a certain vulnerability. If you mess up badly in one program and cause your PC to "hang," you can lose data you had not yet saved from the other applications you were running at the same time.

The task swapper gives the illusion that all of these programs are running at once, but only if they are the kind of programs that wait for you to decide what to do next. Any program that is waiting for your input is idle and may as well not be in lower memory at all (so long as it can return there when you are ready to talk to it). But this is not the same as multi-tasking (which you will learn more about shortly).

Many programs allow you to "shell to DOS" so you can do some other task and then return to the original program. If you run these programs from a task swapping program manager, it is better to use that manager to switch to a DOS prompt rather than to shell to DOS from within the program. You will generally get to and from the DOS prompt more rapidly, and you will get more free RAM to use while you are there.

TSR Managers

One very useful subcategory of task swappers are **T**erminate and **S**tay **R**esident (TSR) program managers. Normally, a TSR program expects to take up some of your PC's lower memory (or possibly its upper memory) on a semipermanent basis. The program will sit there waiting patiently for your signal, and then it will spring into action.

If you load a lot of TSRs simultaneously, you may end up with almost no available RAM for your application programs. Network drivers are TSR programs. As a category, they are among the most RAM-hungry of all TSRs. So PCs connected to networks have the problem of RAM cram more than most.

Network programs also exemplify a type of TSR that differs in one significant way from conventional pop-up TSR programs. The latter are utilities, such as *SideKick,* that you invoke with a hot key. When you do so, they take over your PC for a while. You use them to do something, and then you let them "go back to sleep" until you want to use them again.

In contrast, a network program is activated by one of two kinds of events. One is a request by your program for access to a remote resource. The other is an incoming message from the network. These events happen quite frequently, but each one requires only a brief bit of action on the part of the TSR. Since these TSRs only take over the PC very briefly, and since they typically produce no screen output while they do so, you may not even be aware that they are there.

Print spoolers are another kind of TSR that shares this general invisibility. They respond to events generated by programs in your PC or by your printer, and mostly do their work invisibly "in the background."

One group of TSR managers only knows how to manage pop-up programs. Others can help with managing the more difficult, "invisible" TSRs.

How a TSR Manager Works

Here is how the simpler TSR managers work: The manager is itself a TSR. It is loaded first. It gets a large amount of RAM from DOS initially. Into this area it loads all the TSRs it is to manage, one at a time.

As each TSR gets loaded, it does some initialization steps, just as it would normally. The TSR manager notices the effects of all these steps. (For example, it must notice any interrupts the TSR hooks—see Chapter 10 for the details of what a TSR does when it initializes itself.) Once the TSR is fully loaded and ready to work, which it indicates by its traditional "Terminate and Stay Resident" call to the operating system, the TSR manager whisks it away to a temporary storage place. The manager also restores the state of the PC to exactly what it was before the TSR loaded.

When you set up this kind of TSR manager, you must tell it what TSRs it will be managing and what hot keys each one expects to respond to. Sometimes you can even tell it that a particular TSR will be looking for one hot key, but you choose to use a different one for it instead. That might be because two of your TSRs are expecting to react to the same hot key. In that case, you must choose a different one that you will use for each so the TSR manager will know which one you meant to invoke.

Now, after loading, initializing, and then putting aside all the TSRs to be handled, the manager settles down to monitoring all keyboard input. In this way it is just like any other pop-up program. What is different is the number of hot keys it may be looking for and what it does with each one.

Whenever the manager sees a hot key you have indicated, it must wake up one of the TSRs. To do this it loads back into RAM the image of that TSR as it existed in memory just after it finished its initialization. The manager also resets the interrupt vector table entries, and any other changes that TSR made to the working environment. So the TSR gets to see the PC just as it would have if it had never been taken from its place in lower memory.

Now, the TSR manager passes on to the TSR the keystroke it is expecting to see. The TSR pops up as usual. To your eye, it was always there and ready to go. When you finish with it, the TSR "goes back to sleep" just as it normally would.

The TSR manager leaves that TSR in RAM until the next time it sees one of the special hot key keystrokes. If that hot key is meant for the TSR now in RAM, the manager will simply pass the keystroke to it (possibly translating it in the process from what you typed to what the TSR expects to see, if you had defined such a difference). If, however, the new hot key is meant for another TSR, then the manager must remove the present TSR and replace it with the one you have called for.

Notice that it is not enough for the TSR manager to overwrite one TSR with another. Often, a pop-up program will have a data area within itself where it keeps information temporarily. An example is the *SideKick* Notepad, which is a small editor. You can write something there (or cut it from an application's screen display and paste it there). Then, you can put away the Notepad temporarily. Later on you will be able to pop the Notepad back up and use that information.

For this to work, the TSR manager must copy the current RAM-image of the TSR to the holding area before copying in the next TSR. Or, if memory paging is supported for the region of RAM in question, and if the TSR manager knows how to activate that paging, it may simply page out the one TSR and page in the next one. (See Chapter 8 for a general discussion of memory paging schemes, and Chapter 11 for a description of protected-mode paging in class 5 or 6 PCs.)

The more powerful TSR managers, the ones that are able to task swap even the invisible TSR programs, work in much the same manner. The essential difference is that they watch not only for keystrokes, but also for those internal events that may call for waking up one of the invisible TSRs.

Where the Swapped TSRs Go

The TSR that is being swapped out of lower (or upper) memory must be put somewhere. Preferably, it will be put in a place from which it can be returned very quickly.

The best choice, usually, is expanded memory, especially if it is LIM 4.0 EMS compatible expanded memory, and if your PC has empty memory address space in lower memory where the EMM (expanded memory manager) can put EMS pages. That makes it possible for the TSR manager to load the TSR onto an EMS page, and when it is ready to swap the TSR out or back in again, it can do so simply by telling the EMM to swap the relevant pages of memory. That can be done extremely rapidly.

If you have a PC in class 5 or 6, you can create simulated EMS memory using a LIMulator program. Since that memory is typically even faster than hardware EMS boards, it is an even better place to put these swapped program images.

The next best choice is extended memory. Usually this involves actually copying the bytes of information that make up the TSR's image in RAM from lower to extended memory or back. That takes more time than simply swapping EMS pages, but it is still a whole lot faster than doing the same thing to a swap file on a disk drive.

The swap space of last resort is a file on a disk drive. This works just fine if the TSRs are not swapped too often. But it can't work fast enough for some uses. Especially for the invisible TSRs that may need to spring into action many times per second. Thus, if this is the only swap resource you have, you will effectively be limited to swapping only pop-up TSRs, and they will pop up noticeably slower than if they had not been swapped out.

Advantages of a TSR Manager

This sounds like it adds a lot of complexity to your PC's normal functioning. It does, but it also brings with it two great advantages.

First, the amount of RAM taken up by the TSR manager, after all the TSRs it is managing have been loaded, will be reduced to just the size of the largest single TSR it has loaded, plus a small amount for the manager's code. Since one manager can load and manage a dozen or more TSRs, this can save you several hundreds of KB of RAM.

The second advantage is more subtle. TSR programs have been infamous for their tendency to "fight" with one another. You often must load them in a very special order, and sometimes even that is not enough to let them get along amicably. By making each TSR see your PC as if it were the only one loaded, a TSR manager program can make many of these conflicts vanish.

A Disadvantage (or Limitation) of Most TSR Managers

You must be aware of one very important pitfall lurking in all TSR managers. Any program that is not in the CPU's memory address space is not running. For most TSRs, that is not an issue. But it sure is for some.

If you have a TSR that is busily doing communications over a phone line, swapping it out of lower memory will suspend it. That means all the characters that arrive from the phone line while it is swapped out will be lost. Similarly, you must not swap out a network driver, or you will lose your network connection.

Sometimes there are ways around this disadvantage. First, you must be using a TSR manager that will monitor events such as an incoming character or network messages, and then swap back the relevant TSR to handle that event. Second, the TSR manager must be using a swap space that is accessible very quickly. That rules out using a disk swap file. Even extended memory may not be fast enough.

Among the TSR managers and more general task swappers, one stands out in this context. It is *Netroom* from Helix Software with its special feature, NETSWAP. This puts the network driver in the EMS page frame, and whenever another TSR would like to use that space, *Netroom* swaps out the driver and swaps in the EMS memory the TSR wants. What is special is that the portion of *Netroom* that stays in memory guarantees that the network connection will remain active.

Another possible way around this is to have a small, permanent TSR (one that is never swapped out) whose only job is to keep a network or host session connection alive. SoftLogic Solutions, the makers of *Software Carousel*, a general purpose task swapping program, offer a companion product, *OLE* ("Open Link Extender"), with just this function. Helix Software also offers *Connecting Room*, which does a similar job for terminal emulation software, and *Headroom*, a general purpose task swapper.

OLE has nothing to do with the Microsoft defined inter-program communication protocol called OLE (*Object Linking and Embedding*). Microsoft's OLE has nothing to do with network communication.

General Program Swappers

General purpose task swappers (or task-swapping program managers, to give them their full description) are very much like a TSR manager. The principal difference is that they are used to manage and swap among a number of programs that are not normally resident programs.

There are two kinds of general purpose task-swapping program managers. One kind you set up just as you would a TSR manager, building a menu of applications it will manage. The other kind lets you create and modify that list on the fly.

WordPerfect *Office*, *Software Carousel*, and *Headroom* are some of the more popular of this first kind of task-swapping program manager. The DOSSHELL program (for *PC DOS* or *MS-DOS*) and TaskMAX (for *DR DOS*) are the most prominent examples of the latter kind.

The first kind is set up just like a TSR manager. You go through a setup process and build a menu of applications you can run. When you start one of them, it is loaded into RAM and allowed to run. It thinks it is the only application program loaded in the PC, and it has all the lower RAM above the task-switching program manager's own code to use.

Whenever you want to swap to another task, you hit a hot key and either return to the menu, where you can pick which program to run next, or you can swap directly to another program if it is already loaded. Typically, there will be a limit to the number of applications such a manager can manage. If you fill it up, you must go back to the setup procedure and replace one or more entries on the menu with your new choices.

The second kind of task swapping program manager loads and then shows you a list of all your files. You can choose from that list the programs you wish to run and they get added to your menu of active tasks. Or, you may define groups of programs that you may wish to choose from, thus forming a hierarchical (outline style) menu of programs you can run.

At any time, you can delete an entry from your active task list and replace it with another. There is much less separation between using this sort of task swapper and setting it up for use, than with those in the first group.

One disadvantage of the DOSSHELL program is that it only knows how to swap to a disk file. You can get around this limitation to a degree by setting the TEMP variable to point to a RAM disk that you have created in either expanded or extended memory. The added overhead of the RAM disk driver will add (slightly) to the time it takes the task swapper to go from one task to another.

TaskMAX, the *DR DOS* version of DOSSHELL, can swap directly to expanded or extended memory, or to disk. In fact, it will use those resources in the order listed, moving on to the next one when one is exhausted. This is something you cannot readily emulate with the DOSSHELL program nor, for that matter, with many third-party task swapping program managers.

"Loading Programs High"

Another way of getting a program out of the way, besides swapping it out of the active region of memory, is to put it off in a portion of that region that is at least somewhat out of the way. Upper memory and the High Memory Area (HMA) are usually what is meant by an out-of-the-way place.

This has one advantage and an associated disadvantage. The advantage is that these programs, while out of the way (out of lower memory), are still in the CPU's memory-address space. Therefore, they can be accessed instantly without even the overhead of swapping an EMS page into the memory-address space. The disadvantage is that they are not really gone from that space, and so you soon will find that even all the nominally out-of-the-way corners of that space get filled up.

Loading Programs in the HMA

Before you can load anything into the HMA, you have to have one. The HMA is a region of the CPU's real-mode memory-address space on all 80x86 CPUs starting with the 80286. Therefore, it is a possibility for any PC in class 3 or above, but only if that PC has more than 640KB of RAM. Often, because some of the motherboard RAM is held back by the system for use as shadow RAM or possibly for use as hardware EMS memory, you will find you must have something more than 1MB before you get any RAM in the HMA.

That may all be old hat by now. What may not have been obvious to you is that you really don't have an HMA to play with until you have also loaded an XMS manager. (Such a manager is called an XMM.) You need an XMM because it knows how to control the A20 gate that allows or prevents access to the HMA. HIMEM.SYS is the XMM you get for free with DOS versions 5 and 6, or any recent version of *Windows*. Alternatively, you can get one as a built-in feature of most any other memory manager these days (such as *UMBPro, 386MAX, Memory Commander, Netroom,* or *QEMM*).

Before there was an XMS standard, some programs, most notably QEXT.SYS (a component of *DESQview*), QEMM, and *Window/286*, knew how to manipulate the A20 gate and thus could, and did, use the HMA. DOS-extended programs prepared using Rational System's DOS/16M product also have this knowledge built-in. But to use the HMA for anything other than one of these (and a few other) special programs, you must first load an XMM program.

One of the rules in the XMS specification is that only one program is allowed to use the HMA at a time. Normally, the first program that asks the XMM for access gets it; all others will then be denied. (See the note at the end of Chapter 8 for a description of some undocumented or poorly documented exceptions to this rule.)

You can invoke the XMM with a command line parameter to limit access to the HMA to programs that "promise" to use more than some minimum amount of it. That helps keep it for the best user. (For example, your CONFIG.SYS file might contain the line

```
DEVICE = C:\DOS\HIMEM.SYS /HMAMIN=40
```

This loads HIMEM.SYS and forces it to restrict the use of the HMA to a program that will use at least 40KB of it.)

Quite a few programs want to use the HMA. You need to decide which one to allow in there. Microsoft and IBM both will assure you that always the right answer for anyone using DOS 5 or 6 is to let it use the HMA. Quarterdeck Office Systems demurs. They insist that their programs QEXT.SYS (a component of *DESQview* useful on 80286-based computers) and *QEMM* (for 386- or 486-based ones) will make more effective use of it. What is the right answer?

By now you may have figured out that on this, as on most questions in this field, there is no one "right for everyone" answer to that question. It depends. You need to look at what you will be doing with your PC in order to choose wisely.

If you are going to run *DESQview*, by all means use *QEMM* (if yours is a class 5 or 6 PC) or *QRAM* (for PCs in classes 3 and 4) as your memory manager and let them use the HMA. Since Quarterdeck wrote all these programs, they understand one another better and will work together more gracefully than any other combination.

If you are going to run *Windows*, by a similar argument, you might think you should follow all of Microsoft's recommendations and use HIMEM.SYS and EMM386.EXE as your memory-management team, and let DOS use the HMA (with a DOS=HIGH statement in your CONFIG.SYS file).

Microsoft really tries to make this decision a "no-brainer." They virtually insist on installing their HIMEM.SYS, SMARTDRV.SYS, and (if you have a PC in classes 5 or 6, their EMM386.EXE) whenever *MS-DOS* 5 or 6, or *Windows* 3.x is installed. Exercise your right of choice. You may like an alternate way to use and manage your memory a whole lot more.

That certainly will work. But it is not nearly as obvious a choice. You could use *386MAX, QEMM, Memory Commander,* or *QMAPS* on class 5 and 6 PCs, or *MAX, QRAM,* or *UMBPRO* on class 3 or 4 PCs, and any one of them will probably do a better job of helping you manage your PC's memory and use the HMA more efficiently than the straight DOS tools would.

There is not much point in talking about *Windows* and class 1 or 2 PCs in the same breath. *Windows* 3.0 will run on them in real mode only, and then just barely. *Windows* 3.1 won't run in real mode on any PC.

In fact, if you do use one of these third-party memory managers, you will get some benefits that you cannot get with the Microsoft programs. Most prominent among them, the other memory managers take up less of your lower memory, and many of them are able to supply EMS and XMS memory out of a common pool (thus saving you from having to choose an allocation between these two uses at the outset). The latter advantage to using a non-DOS memory manager went away with DOS 6, as now EMM386.EXE also supplies EMS and XMS memory from a common pool.

One very nice thing about the Microsoft programs for managing memory (HIMEM and EMM386) is their very high level of compatibility. That is Microsoft's highest objective. They have decided to let others seek the highest levels of performance and they strive, instead, to make their products work on the widest possible range of PCs.

If you are planning to set BUFFERS=30 or more in your CONFIG.SYS, then adding DOS=HIGH to let DOS use the HMA probably makes a lot of sense. If, on the other hand, you have a good disk cache program and so plan on only setting BUFFERS=3, you will have a harder choice. Because then, DOS will only be using about two-thirds of the HMA at most, and it will deny all other programs access to the rest of it.

Some network drivers also offer to use the HMA. If they can make good use of it, that may be the best way to use your HMA. If, on the other hand, you plan to use *Netroom,* that may let you use the HMA for DOS or something else, and still not have to give up any lower or upper memory for the network driver.

The best answer in this situation may be simply to try several alternatives and see which ones give you the most memory for your programs. That includes letting *Windows* take the HMA, if you are going to run it, and seeing how much free memory you get in a DOS window. Also, notice matters of convenience. You may prefer a memory manager that requires less from you in the way of hand tweaking before it gives you what you want and need.

A Curious Fact About the HMA and Extended Memory

A curious fact about the HMA and extended memory is that the first 64KB of RAM above 1MB will either be your HMA or it will be extended memory. It cannot be accessible as both. That is necessary for data integrity. (Otherwise, one program could be using the HMA while another altered those same bytes thinking it was that other program's extended memory data buffer.)

Which is it? It is not the HMA until an XMM says it is. But once it is declared to be the HMA, that is what that region of RAM is forever (or until you reboot).

For example, if VDISK.SYS (the *PC DOS* RAM disk utility) has already claimed that region for use as part of a RAM disk, HIMEM.SYS will not allow you to use that region as the HMA. And once VDISK has taken it, that memory will belong to it until you reboot.

VDISK is a bit of a strange duck. Most other programs use extended memory differently. They allocate it from the top down. And they may deallocate it when they are through with it.

If you attempt to access the HMA while some other programs have appropriated to themselves that portion of extended memory, the XMM will notice this and refuse you access. (That could happen because a top-down extended memory user has taken virtually all your extended memory, or because VDISK, nearly the only bottom-up user of extended memory, has taken any of it, starting right at 1,024KB.)

Once you are able to use the XMM to access the HMA, not only will that region be locked as the HMA, but usually *all* of extended memory that is not already in use gets grabbed by the XMM. From then on, that memory is only available as EMBs (extended memory blocks), and they can only be obtained by asking the XMM for them.

Programs that only know how to allocate extended memory by the top-down (INT 15h) strategy will find themselves locked out of it once any program takes up residence in the HMA. And, until they are upgraded to comply with the XMS standard method of asking for extended memory, there is no way around this problem, unless your XMM can be directed to leave some extended memory unmanaged and available as extended memory. (Almost all of them can; you simply need to learn how to do this. With HIMEM.SYS you would use a command line in your CONFIG.SYS file that looks somethimg like this:

```
DEVICE=C:\DOS\HIMEM.SYS  /INT15=256
```

This example reserves 256KB for use by programs that allocate memory from the top down, using the INT15h strategy.)

Loading Programs Into Upper Memory

"Loading high" is the term used to describe loading a program into an *upper memory* space. This is the region of the CPU's memory address space from 640KB to 1,024KB (1MB). That is confusing, since high memory (the region from 1,024KB to 1,088KB) is not the same place as upper memory, but "loading high" is the term that has become standard nonetheless.

Usually there is a lot more space in the upper memory area that is not being used than there is in the HMA. If yours is a PC in class 1 or 3, though, you probably don't have any RAM in these locations, so you can't make use of that space. (And, if yours is a class 1 PC, you also don't have an HMA.)

Luckier PC owners (with PCs in classes 2, 4, 5, and 6) will find that they do, or more likely that they can, have RAM in those otherwise empty spaces. Any such upper memory RAM that is available for programs to use (as opposed to RAM that is committed for use as a video-image buffer or a network-interface-card buffer) is precisely the sort of out-of-the-way place you would like to use to store some TSRs and device drivers.

The RAM is not quite all you must have to make this possible. You must have some central mechanism for allocating that memory to programs. That means that you need to have loaded as a part of your (device driver augmented) operating system some memory manager that can dole out that RAM. (See Chapter 10 for a discussion of how device drivers are used to augment the operating system as it is assembled in layers in your RAM.)

The memory manager for upper memory is again the XMM. If you have some upper RAM and your XMM knows about it, you can get access to it in the form of UMBs (upper memory blocks). You do this by asking the XMM for them.

Alternatively, if you are running DOS 5 or 6, you can direct DOS to grab all the UMBs it can and then you can let it do the allocating of that RAM to programs as they need it. If you include the line MS-DOS=UMB or DOS=HIGH, UMB in your CONFIG.SYS file, then after each time it runs a new program, DOS will ask the XMM if it has any available UMBs. If the XMM says it does, DOS will take control of them immediately.

From then on if any program asks the XMM for a UMB, it will be told there are none available. But, if that same program asks DOS, it may find that it can get what it needs that way.

Some TSRs are able to load themselves into UMBs. This is getting to be more and more common. Actually, it is a wonderful capability. It allows those programs to fit themselves into far tighter spaces in upper memory than any separate memory manager could do. On the other hand, it provides a much tougher job for the optimization routines that come with memory managers, such as *QEMM* and *386MAX*.

When any such program wishes to load itself into upper memory, it will get that memory by first asking the XMM for a UMB. Failing that, if DOS 5 or later is running, the program will ask DOS for a memory block in upper memory. If it can't have that, then it will have to settle for being loaded low.

Actually, the program gets loaded low first. While it is there and doing its initialization, one step it goes through is to see if there is enough upper memory to load its final resident image high. If it finds that memory, it can use it. Otherwise, it will just finish off the initialization process and go resident in low memory where it is.

Sometimes these utility programs will totally fool a memory manager and its optimization program. This can happen in the following way: If the program finds that it can load its resident portion into a UMB, it will do so. Then it will end normally (*not* go "TSR"). It only issues the usual TSR call to DOS if it needs to remain in lower memory. Usually when a program terminates "normally," DOS takes back all of its memory. But if the UMB the program used to load its resident portion came from the XMM, DOS won't know about it. That is how it is possible for these programs to appear to terminate normally and yet have the effect of a TSR.

Why should it be more challenging to load a TSR into upper memory than into lower memory? That is the topic for the next section. Once you understand this topic, you also will know why you would prefer to let TSRs that can load themselves high do so. And you will understand why the issue of load order is so much more critical with any programs that get loaded high than it is for those that get loaded low.

The Four Sizes of a TSR

When a program loads in lower memory, DOS gives it whatever RAM it wants, up to all the unused portion of lower memory. Any TSR program will use what it needs to do whatever initialization it must do, and then it will give back to DOS all of the lower memory that it doesn't have to keep. Mostly, TSRs are optimized to use as little RAM as possible after they are through initializing. Up to that point, they are free to use enormous amounts of RAM if they wish. When you are loading TSRs into lower memory, you usually have several hundred kilobytes of lower memory it can use. Thus, the amount of RAM the TSR wants for its initialization is not very important.

Upper memory comes in a very different sort of package. Often in upper memory space, there will be not just one, but several disconnected regions of memory address space without anything in them. If you have a LIM 4.0 EMS board or a suitable LIMulator, you can cause some of the expanded memory (or extended memory in the case of a 386-based LIMulator) to show up as RAM in those holes in upper memory space. (Chapters 8 and 11 explained these possibilities in some detail.)

That means you may have not just one upper memory region, but several. And each of them will be only modest in size. Fitting TSRs into those smallish regions can get tricky.

This is where the four sizes of a TSR come in. (For the purposes of this discussion, device drivers are essentially the same as TSRs. The problem of their fit is exactly the same.)

A TSR starts out as a file on the disk. It has some size. This is called its *file size*. Then it gets loaded into RAM. It takes up some amount of space at that time. That is called its *load size*.

If the file is a COM file or a SYS file, its load size is usually the same as its file size. If it is an EXE file, though, it could take up much more room when loaded than it did on the disk. That depends on what the relocation information stored in its EXE header specifies. Further, some programs have been compressed. They take up less room on the disk than they do when loaded, even if they are COM files.

While it is initializing, the TSR may request more memory from DOS. That could make it have a maximum size that is still larger than its load size. The maximum size it gets during the initialization phase is called its *initialization size*. And finally, after it finishes its initialization and returns all the excess memory to DOS, the TSR assumes its final size. This is called the *resident size*.

A lot of TSRs don't have sizes that differ all that much from one of these four conditions to another. Others have dramatically different sizes.

Here is one example: ANSI-UV.SYS's file size is 1,997 bytes and its resident size is 1,664 bytes. Not very different at all. But that is only one simple case. Now consider these other examples.

Version 8.01 of the *Microsoft Mouse* driver, MOUSE.COM, occupies 46,704 bytes on the disk (its file size). After it finally goes resident, its size is only 16,960. So its resident size is only a third of its file size. Most likely, its maximum size is near the file size, but it could be even larger.

If you ask OPTIMIZE (the optimization utility that comes with *QEMM*) about the sizes of the *Super PC-Kwik* disk cache program, SUPERPCK.EXE, it will tell you that the initialization size is some indeterminate amount, perhaps as large as 500KB. While the file size is 73,062, its resident size (for a particular set of command line parameters and disks to cache) when it loads itself into upper memory is only 52,720.

STACKER.COM, version 2, has a file size of 40,667 bytes. Its load size is, presumably, about the same. After going resident, its size depends on how many drives it is managing, on whether or not it has placed some of itself into EMS memory, and whether or not it is supplying a cache. In one case, with three drives and no cache, Stacker took up 65,536 bytes of expanded memory and 20,544 of upper memory. Figuring out what Stacker will need is complex at best.

If the largest UMB that is available is large enough for a program's load size, DOS thinks the program will fit there. This is also true of some third-party memory managers. Other third-party memory managers attempt to assess the real maximum of all these sizes to see if a given TSR will fit into a given UMB.

If the TSR actually grows larger than the UMB, your PC will very likely crash. That is one problem that must be faced when attempting to load TSRs or device drivers into upper memory.

Another problem related to the various sizes of TSRs comes when you consider loading more than one of them into a single UMB. They may fit one way, but be unable to fit if loaded in a different order. (This problem is totally unrelated to the problems of TSRs that "fight" if they aren't loaded in the right order. Also realize that you will never be faced with this problem if you are using a TSR manager, and thus are only loading one TSR at a time. That is, you won't face this problem with TSRs. You still may have to contend with it if you try to load several device drivers into the same UMB.)

Here is an example. Consider loading MOUSE.COM and PCPANEL into one UMB. The file sizes of certain versions of these programs are 46,704 and 25,714 bytes, and their resident sizes are 16,960 and 6,672 bytes respectively. Suppose for the moment that their initialization and load sizes are no larger than their file sizes.

You must have a UMB at least as large as the larger of these programs, and it must be larger than the total of their resident sizes, or you cannot load them both. That means you need a UMB that has a little more than 46,704 bytes of space in it.

Suppose you have one with 48KB of free RAM (49,152 bytes). If you load MOUSE.COM first, it will end up taking away from that 48KB its 16,960 resident size. That leaves you with 32,192 bytes; more than enough to load PCPANEL. After both of them have loaded, you will have 25,520 bytes left over.

But if you were to load PCPANEL first, after it went resident, you would only have 42,480 bytes free. Not enough even to load MOUSE.COM.

Some memory managers employ a clever trick to get around this sort of problem. If the EMS page frame happens to be just above the UMB into which they are going to load a TSR, one of these special memory managers can temporarily "borrow" the EMS page frame to extend the RAM beyond the end of the UMB. (This means the memory manager must do two things. One is change the size field of the MCB at the start of the UMB to include the EMS page frame's RAM. The other thing it must do is make a note to itself that the page frame region is not available for normal EMS uses until this TSR loading is finished.) Then the memory manager can let the TSR load into the UMB and the page frame. So long as the TSR shrinks itself down as anticipated, this works just fine. Once the TSR has gone resident, the memory manager can return the EMS page frame to its original function.

That may not work, though, if the TSR fails to shrink as much as the memory manager anticipated. That doesn't happen too often, but it does sometimes. Then the EMS page frame memory is trapped as a UMB. It no longer can be used for swapping EMS pages. This is why some of the makers of memory managers offer this feature, while others believe it is too risky to include.

Now can you see why a TSR that loads itself has an advantage? It knows just what it is doing. Usually it will initialize itself in lower memory, and then copy its resident portion into the UMB. That way, it only needs exactly as much free space in the UMB as it will finally occupy.

When OPTIMIZE reports an indeterminate size for *Super PC-Kwik*, it is because when that program loads, it typically takes all of available lower memory and uses it during initialization. ("If the table is that large, why shouldn't I spread out my paperwork all over it? I'm going to clean up after myself when I am done.") So OPTIMIZE has no idea what size space this program will need to initialize itself, and thus it cannot load that program high. Not all programs are quite this extreme, but the general truth remains: Any program that can load itself high can probably do so more efficiently than any memory manager could.

Getting Obstacles Out of the Way

In many PCs, upper memory is a jumble of different things. All the spaces in between some other use are initially empty. But if you can put RAM there, you can use them as UMBs (after you load an XMM). Since the obstacles are located wherever they happen to fall, you may well find your upper memory RAM is broken up into many different, not contiguous spaces. Figure 21.3 shows both an XT and a 386-based PC's upper memory spaces. These may seem like extreme cases, but actually they are quite typical.

In the column on the left of Figure 21.3, you see that this XT has a monochrome display adapter, a hard disk, a hardware EMS board, and a network interface card (NIC). The motherboard BIOS ROM is only 48KB in size, but with all those other things in upper memory, the remaining space is broken up into five parts.

The column on the right of Figure 21.3 shows the situation for a higher-powered PC. This one has a larger motherboard BIOS ROM (64KB), which allows it to control a hard disk without needing an additional option ROM. On the other hand, it has a VGA card. That requires an option ROM, and it also takes up three times as much space for its video image buffers. For this PC, the empty space is broken into four parts.

Of the 384KB of upper memory space, the XT is using only 176KB, leaving 208KB free. This is wonderful. You could load a lot of TSRs and device drivers up there. But not as many as you might think. This is not all one big space, it is five smaller ones. Many TSRs (including several popular network drivers) would not fit even in the largest of these. And very few DOS programs can be loaded in two fragments into two different UMBs and still be able to run. (One of the improvements in DOS 6 is that LOADHIGH now allows you to specify two or more different regions of upper memory into which to load a program that can use portions of each of several regions. That feature was added in order to help people deal with situations such as that diagramed in Figure 21.3.)

The story on the 386 is not that much different. Here the PC is using 256KB of upper memory, but that still leaves a healthy 128KB that could be used for programs. But notice the sizes of the four blocks into which this space is broken. None is large enough for a large network driver; most are not large enough for many common TSRs or device drivers.

> The primary objective in configuring your computer for optimum upper memory use is to move the obstacles to one end or the other of upper memory space.

Get all the emptiness together, and then fill it with RAM. One large open expanse of RAM can be used much more effectively than many small pieces, even though the small pieces have as much total space.

Barriers to Extending System Memory

Actually, following that advice is not always quite the best thing to do. An alternative is to take whatever upper memory space is below your video image buffer and attach it to lower memory. (You still want to bring all the rest of the empty space together if you can.)

If you have a PC that is only equipped with a monochrome or CGA video card, or if you are willing to commit yourself to using your EGA or VGA only in text mode or CGA graphics emulation, then you can push the ceiling on lower memory upwards. If you can add RAM to the empty space in the A page (and, for all but the monochrome system, the lower half of the B page), you can have 704KB or even 736KB of system memory. That is a lot nicer than just 640KB.

But sometimes there is a barrier. Some PCs need more space for BIOS and DOS data than fits in the 768 bytes allowed for that purpose in low memory. They put the extra information in an "extended BIOS data area" (EBDA, or sometimes written as XBDA) and usually they put that at the very top of lower memory. On machines with 640KB of lower RAM, that will show up as a reduction in the apparent total memory to 639KB. IBM's Micro channel *PS/2*s do this, as well as a few clone PCs. (See Figure 10.2.)

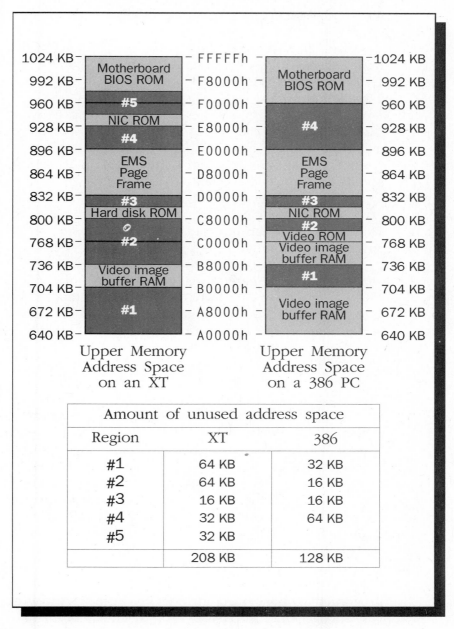

Figure 21.3. Upper memory fragmentation. The numbered regions are the memory areas available for use.

Thus, you can extend system memory on almost any PC in classes 2, 4, 5 and 6 by mapping RAM into the A (and maybe the lower half of the B) page. This only works while you are in text mode (or CGA graphics), and it only works if you don't have an EBDA or other data table at the top of lower memory that gets in your way.

Some memory managers offer a feature that lets them relocate the EBDA, if they find one, to a location near the bottom of lower memory. That allows them to extend the open area of RAM up to the bottom of your video image buffer.

What if you forget and change into graphics mode on your EGA or VGA card? You can hope your memory manager will intercept that command and stop it from working. At worst, the video mode will change and whatever program you loaded into the A page will be blown away. Memory managers that offer to let you use the A page for program RAM are not uniformly good about protecting you, so be careful here.

Read the documentation carefully to see what protections are claimed. Then do some experiments to see if you believe them, before you trust anything important to these regions.

There is one other approach to extending system memory that is worth mentioning here. *Memory Commander* supports a standard now called *RSIS*. This is a protocol that provides a standard way for an RSIS-aware program to ask the memory manager where the video image buffer is. Then the program can safely write directly to that buffer, rather than having to use the slower BIOS calls.

This allows *Memory Commander* (which only runs on PCs in classes 5 and 6) to move the video-image buffer and tell all RSIS-aware applications to use it. It also traps all BIOS write-to-screen requests and redirects them to that buffer in its new location. If you are running only programs that are either RSIS-aware or use only BIOS calls to write to the screen, *Memory Commander* can sweep all of the obstacles in your upper memory space together and put them at the extreme top of upper memory. Then it will fill in all the rest of upper memory and add it to your lower memory.

In the case of the XT in Figure 21.3, that would increase the effective size of lower memory from 640KB to 848KB. In some cases, with fewer upper memory obstacles, the expansion can go well beyond 900KB. Since *Memory Commander* changes its strategies on the fly, based on what the program you are running at that moment requires, it can apply this technique to only those programs for which it works. Whenever you run a program that Memory Commander knows may try to write directly to the video image buffer at its real address, or any program that it doesn't know about, it will put the video image buffer back where it belongs before it lets the program begin executing.

Moving an Option ROM

Generally, option ROMs must be placed in the CPU's memory address space somewhere in the C or D pages (linear addresses from C0000h to DFFFFh). Just where each one goes depends on who made it and how. For many of them, the location of the option ROM can be set to one of several choices by moving some jumpers, setting DIP switches, or running a software setup program.

Some option ROMs have standard places to go. The video option ROM for a VGA or EGA card almost always starts at C0000h, though its size may vary. Hard disk controllers for XTs usually start at C8000h. These are about the only two that have really accepted standard positions.

Frequently, network-interface cards will default to starting at address D0000h, but they typically provide for moving that ROM elsewhere. ESDI and SCSI host adapters may default to C8000h, but they also have other locations that are possible.

Still, you probably will only have a limited number of choices. Setting all of them to get out of each other's way and avoid the EMS page frame (if you must have one) is quite a challenge in many PCs.

Oh, and look out for this: If you move the address of some option card's BIOS ROM, you may have to tell some software you are running that uses that card where you have moved the ROM. If the ROM puts its own address into the interrupt table at bootup, that may not be necessary; otherwise it most likely will be. (As usual, the best advice is to read carefully all the documentation that came with each option card.)

A Special Problem (and Special Opportunity) with Certain Hard Disk Controllers

Hard disks come in many different sizes. The BIOS must know what the sizes are for each hard disk to which it must talk. It needs to know many different numbers about it, not merely the total MB capacity.

The table of necessary numbers is called the *Hard Disk Parameter Table* (HDPT). The original XT controller set the numbers with jumpers on the controller card. With this you had very few jumpers and correspondingly few choices of hard drives.

The AT incorporated a table of HDPT tables in the motherboard BIOS ROM. When you set a "drive type" in the setup routine, the number you specify is used as an index into this table of tables. The table you point to within the larger table becomes the HDPT for that drive.

On a moment to moment basis, the BIOS does not consult the CMOS for your drive type. Instead, once it has learned what drive types your PC has, it stores numbers in the interrupt vector table at the locations for INT 41h and INT 46h. Those numbers point to the appropriate HDPTs for your first and second hard drives.

Even this solution is too limiting. There are too many drives in the market to have all of them accounted for by one of the entries in your BIOS ROM. Several ways of dealing with this problem have been developed over the years.

The simplest solution conceptually, but not always the easiest or least expensive, is to buy a custom BIOS with a drive table entry for each drive type you plan to use. That takes ordering the special BIOS chips, waiting for them to come, and then installing them. There are faster ways, and ones that may seem safer or easier to you. Also, if later on you change to yet another unsupported drive, you will have to order an even newer BIOS ROM.

If you have a motherboard BIOS that supports a "user defined drive type" (typically number 47 or 48), then it will allow you to enter the critical numbers describing your drive into some table that it will keep safely until you change those numbers. Most often, the numbers are recorded in the CMOS, and at boot time they will be copied to some unused locations in the interrupt vector table, building the appropriate HDPTs in that low memory region. Then the INT 41h and INT 46h vectors are pointed to those HDPTs so the BIOS can find them. (Less commonly, the BIOS will contain some non-volatile RAM and will put those numbers there.)

Another solution is to use an *autoconfiguring hard disk controller*. This is a hard disk controller that stores the drive's dimensions on the drive itself. At boot time, it reads them and copies them into RAM, and then points the 41h and INT 46h vectors appropriately.

Finally, the least satisfactory solution for a number of reasons is to use a third-party disk partitioning software program. This lets the BIOS initially read the drive size from the motherboard BIOS HDPT copy. But when the driver loads, it alters the interrupt vectors to point to tables it builds in RAM. As you will learn in Chapter 31, this has lead to some very serious problems with *Windows,* as well as with other programs.

Many people have opted for the use of an autoconfiguring hard disk controller. Typically, such a board has an option ROM on it. That ROM will often show up at C8000h (this is where the hard disk ROM would be in an XT, but it shows up there for these boards even in PCs that belong to the higher classes). You can alter that location if you need to (you will have only a few alternate locations, though). Actually, there is something you can do that is even better in most cases.

It turns out that for compatibility reasons, the makers of these controller cards usually make them act exactly like a standard hard disk controller of the type used in ATs. That is, they act that way once they have gotten past their special startup procedure.

During that startup procedure, they will read the drive dimensions and put them in RAM somewhere. After that has been done, the option ROM code is not used at all until you reboot. (Controllers that use this approach include ones for each of the popular PC hard drive types—MFM, RLL, ESDI, and SCSI. If your hard disk controller is described as being both autoconfiguring and "register compatible" with the AT standard, it very likely is one that uses this strategy.)

Here is a real opportunity! That ROM takes up perhaps 16KB of space in your upper memory. Instead of merely moving it up or down, how about making it vanish altogether? In a PC in class 5 or 6, that is easy to do. Just tell your memory manager to include that region when it is mapping in RAM. (Strictly speaking, you tell the UMB provider, which is a part of your memory-management "team" of programs—EMM386.EXE in the case of *MS-DOS* or *PC DOS*.)

That works sometimes. Other times it fails horribly. To see why, you have to know one more detail.

When the autoconfiguring hard disk controller reads the disk dimensions off the drive, it puts them somewhere in RAM. Where can it do that?

Two choices have been popular. One is in some RAM that is on the controller card. In that case, the only safe range of memory addresses, within which this RAM can be put, lies in the region claimed by the option ROM. That is the only part of memory-address space the controller can be quite sure it is eligible to use, and that no one else is going to be using.

The other choice that is commonly used is to put the numbers that make up the new HDPTs into a region of the interrupt vector table that the disk controller manufacturer hopes won't be used for anything else.

Neither choice is wonderful. In the first case, it will keep us from overlaying the region occupied by the ROM with UMB RAM. Doing that would hide the HDPT from the BIOS. (Only 16 or 32 bytes of the 16KB are used for the HDPTs, but without knowing which 16 bytes, the whole region must be preserved. Even if you find the table(s), you can at best recover 12KB of the 16KB.) In the latter case, all too often the manufacturer did not pick a place in the interrupt vector table that really isn't other-wise used. So when you load whatever else uses that spot, suddenly your hard disk seems to change size radically. That can lead quickly to data corruption on the drive.

Adaptec, for its very popular 2372 series of disk controllers, chose to put the new HDPT numbers in the interrupt vector table starting at the location for INT 60h and extending through the location for INT 67h. Microsoft originally called these user interrupts, so it would seem to be a reasonable choice. Too bad it was not.

The problem is, lots of "users" of PCs have decided on different uses for those interrupts. Perhaps the most common user of one of these interrupts is any EMM program. So if you have real or simulated EMS-compatible expanded memory, you will be using INT 67h for that purpose.

Not surprisingly, you can't simultaneously use that location for two purposes. If you only have one physical hard disk, only the locations for INT 60h through INT 63h get used. But if you have two physical hard disks and you have an EMS card, you are in trouble. As soon as your EMM loads, your second hard disk appears to have some really weird and probably invalid dimensions, like 1 head and 500 sectors per track.

There is a quick solution to both these bad choices. It is a program called MOVEHDD.SYS. Clyde Washburn, of Washburn and Company, wrote this little gem and contributed it to us all, free. You can download a copy from CompuServe.

This is a device driver of minimum possible resident size. Remember, the numbers in the interrupt vector table's 66th and 71st 4-byte "slots" would normally point to ISRs for interrupts of type 41h and 46h, respectively; instead they point to the HDPTs for the first and second hard disk. MOVEHDD. SYS uses these pointers to find the HDPTs. If it finds them either in the interrupt vector table or in the C or D pages it copies those tables to locations inside itself and repoints the INT 41h and INT 46h vectors to those new locations. Now you can load other programs that use the affected locations in the interrupt vector table, or you can overlay that region of upper memory with some RAM for UMBs. Why, MOVEHDD even is nice enough to zero out the portion of the interrupt vector table that was used for HDPT information after it has done its copying. (Doing that helps prevent some very subtle compatibility problems you otherwise might have.)

Making Setup ROMs Disappear

You sometimes can reclaim even more of upper memory by causing another ROM that doesn't get used after boot time to vanish. Many PCs now have their setup program (to enter numbers into the CMOS configuration RAM) located in a ROM on the motherboard. Most of them leave that ROM attached to the CPU's memory-address bus at all times.

If yours is a PC in class 5 or 6, you can remap memory to make that ROM disappear and replace it with RAM. What you give up is the ability to enter the setup program just any time. You will have to reboot and then jump there before your memory manager gets a chance to again map the setup ROM away.

Actually, that is not so much a sacrifice as it is a prudent security precaution. If you don't do this, you may someday lose some data because you inadvertently hit the hot key that takes you to the setup program and the only way out may be to reboot your computer.

Moving the EMS Page Frame

There is one more common obstacle in upper memory that you may need to move. That is the EMS page frame.

The original EMS specification only contemplated putting the EMS page frame in some 64KB region (starting at a multiple of 16KB) in the C or D pages. That was because in its original documentation IBM said that the A and B pages were for video-image buffers, and the E and F pages were for BIOS ROMs.

Any LIM 4.0 EMS provider should be able to put the page frame anywhere in the first megabyte. But most of the implementations are more limited. This is especially true of hardware EMS boards. They commonly cannot put the frame below C0000h, nor have it extend above DFFFFh. You might want to put the EMS page frame in the E page, if your PC doesn't have any ROM there, as most of them don't. But unless your hardware board is pretty special, you just can't do it.

So normally, the only way to get the obstacles out of the way and put all the empty space (and later on the upper memory RAM) together is to move the EMS page frame down against the video-image buffer, or at least down against the VGA or EGA ROM.

LIMulators (especially those designed for use on class 5 or 6 PCs) are generally more flexible. They can put the EMS page frame just about anywhere that is not already spoken for. They even put it below A0000h sometimes. (That can be a problem for EMS software that was not written to allow for that possibility.)

If your LIMulator allows the possibility of borrowing the EMS page frame while loading TSRs, it will do so *only if you put the page frame just above the UMB space.* This can almost always be done, but you must be alert. *QEMM,* for example, is especially prone to put the EMS page frame down at C0000h or C8000h, or sometimes even at 90000h instead.

Some Versions of DOS That Are Extra Helpful

When it comes to managing your PC's memory manually, some versions of DOS are a whole lot better than others. Here is a quick review of what the best versions now on the market offer or fail to offer, along with some comments on some of the drawbacks that you will get along with their helpfulness in memory management, should you chose to use them.

DR DOS 6

What *DR DOS* lacks in total compatibility with *MS-DOS,* it more than makes up for with its superior memory-management features, in the esti-mation of many people. This version of DOS not only can load its kernel code into the HMA if you like, it can load it into an upper memory block. (So you could then use the HMA for some other program.)

Like *MS-DOS,* it can load the disk buffers into the HMA. If you try to load more than will fit, it puts the excess (only) out in upper memory (if you like), or in lower memory if it must. It can put all of the *DR DOS* data structures either in high or upper memory. This means it is often able to give you over 620KB of free space out of the lower 640KB of RAM.

It also has a HIINSTALL statement for the CONFIG.SYS file, in ad-dition to HIDEVICE and HILOAD, which are like *MS-DOS's* DEVICEHIGH and LOADHIGH, respectively. And it offers direct control over whether the upper and lower memory-control-block chains are linked with the MEMMAX command.

The *DR DOS* TaskMAX program allows switching from one program to another, as does the *MS-DOS* DOSSHELL program. The major dif-ference is that TaskMAX is more flexible about where the swapped out programs get parked. (Another difference is that TaskMAX is a separate program from ViewMAX, the *DR DOS* equivalent to DOSSHELL. That means you can use TaskMAX with a third-party shell program or simply at the DOS prompt.)

The *DR DOS* MEM command gives more information than that in *MS-DOS,* and it does so more clearly. This even includes showing the memory-control-block chain within the HMA.

Before you rush out to buy *DR DOS,* you should know that its installation program does some rather strange things. For example, there is a file on the installation disks called README. The install program will attempt to erase from your disk all files whose names match the names of its files, no matter what directory they may be in. Oops! Watch out for that one.

The *DR DOS* installation program has the three level optimization choices that *MS-DOS* had in its SELECT command in version 4 and has now dropped. As with the *MS-DOS* program, the *DR DOS* one does not adequately explain what your choices will do to the way it will install DOS.

You cannot boot *DR DOS* 6 from a removable disk (like a *Bernoulli* or SyQuest cartridge) unless you do some fairly non-standard things, nor can you boot it from some SCSI drives. Only a floppy or an extremely compatible hard disk will do.

And these are just the tip of a pile of minor nuisances and incompatibilities you will have to get used to if you switch to *DR DOS.* Many people have done just that and are very happy with their choice. Even more have not made the switch. The opportunity presented by *DR DOS* lets you decide just how much you wish to stay near the center of things, and how much you are willing to move out onto the fringe for some very real benefits (at some equally real cost).

Now that Novell owns Digital Research, *Novell DOS*—which is what they will call the next version of *DR DOS*—will have additional features to attract customers, especially in the area of network support. Still, it won't be a product of Microsoft or IBM, and so it won't be 100% compatible with *MS-DOS* or *PC DOS.*

Here is an interesting quirk that is explained in the *DR DOS* manual, but not as clearly as you might wish: In the installation process, you are allowed to specify how much upper memory you want to have created and some other things about it. Then a simple question is posed: Would you like compatibility with *Windows* in standard mode? If you answer YES, then all your answers about upper memory are discarded. This is because *DR DOS* achieves *Windows* standard mode compatibility by refusing to put any RAM into upper memory.

MS-DOS and PC DOS 5

DR DOS showed us the way to integrate memory management into the operating system (when their version 5 came out). Microsoft was quick to follow. *MS-DOS* 5 (and *PC DOS* 5, which is very nearly the same thing) includes almost all the goodies that were in *DR DOS* 5, plus a few of its own. For example, while *DR DOS* pretends to be IBM's *PC DOS* version 3.3 to any program that asks it, *MS-DOS* allows you to set up a table of answers to give to various programs. Thus, those that can stand the truth are told version 5. All others you list in the SETVER command are told what they want to hear.

But looking just in terms of memory management, *MS-DOS* 5 is clearly not up to doing what *DR DOS* can do, especially *DR DOS* 6. While *MS-DOS* can load TSR programs and device drivers into upper memory, and put the DOS kernel into the HMA along with the DOS disk buffers, it cannot INSTALL programs into upper memory. Further, if you can't fit all the disk buffers in the HMA along with DOS, then *all* of them come out and the only other place they can go is lower memory.

However, you may be quite sure that *MS-DOS* 5 (or *PC DOS* 5) is *way* ahead of any earlier version of *MS-DOS* (or *PC DOS*). Almost everyone will gain some significant benefits from moving up to at least version 5. And you will do even better (with both *DR DOS* and *MS-DOS*) by adding to DOS one of the better third-party memory managers.

One of the reasons you will help yourself if you add another memory manager on top of DOS is that you can then deal effectively with what is otherwise a rather annoying conflict for DOS. The order in which programs are loaded has two significances, and they often are at odds. The first has to do with fitting them into RAM efficiently. The second has to do with making them work correctly. I want to explain first why the load order might be important for efficient use of RAM. Then I'll explain why that must take a back seat to some other considerations.

When you ask *MS-DOS* to load TSRs and device drivers into upper memory, you have very little control over the places they end up. If you are trying to shoehorn in as many TSRs as you can, with *DR DOS* 5 or 6,

MS-DOS 5, or *PC DOS* 5, you will have to use the order in which you load them as your primary means of control. Loading them in descending order of size generally gets more of them into a given amount of upper memory space. (*MS-DOS* and *PC DOS* 6 solve this problem. See next section for details.)

That may be what you would like to do from the point of view of fitting them into upper memory. But that is not always possible or desirable from the point of view of making them work correctly, nor is it even possible in all cases.

First of all, DOS will load all device drivers before any TSRs. Even if you put INSTALL statements before or among your DEVICE statements in your CONFIG.SYS file, all the device drivers will be loaded first, then the TSRs specified in INSTALL statements.

Even within one of those categories, you are not always free to load them in any order you might wish. For example, until you load an XMM program (for example, HIMEM.SYS) and then a UMB provider (for example, EMM386.EXE), you can't load any device drivers into upper memory at all. And some device drivers will depend on the prior existence of a particular other device driver in order for them to work correctly.

Typically, you can do a limited amount of reordering of DEVICE statements and later on of INSTALL statements. But the amount is strictly limited. So you can't really use the largest to smallest plan suggested earlier.

The same thing applies to TSRs loaded through AUTOEXEC.BAT. Your primary concern has to be with whether or not they will work and do what you want. Fitting them into upper memory must defer to that.

If all your upper memory program RAM is in a single block, you will not do too badly by being unable to follow the largest to smallest load order. But if your PC's upper memory looks anything like those in Figure 21.3, then you will have a tough time getting efficient use of it with only the tools DOS provides.

Many of the third-party memory managers allow you to specify explicitly in which regions of upper memory each device driver or TSR will be loaded. You indicate that to the memory manager directly, usually by a command line parameter, instead of relying on the position of that TSR among all that are being loaded. This allows you to fit TSRs into a collection of variously sized UMBs more efficiently, and still not give up the full and proper function that comes with loading them in the exact right order for that reason.

You might wish you could load some TSRs before certain device drivers. That cannot be done using just DOS. But there is a way you may be able to do it. In the book *Undocumented DOS*, Jim Kyle describes a clever program, DEVLOD, that can load certain device drivers from the AUTOEXEC.BAT file. That might allow you to reorder your TSRs and device drivers in the manner you desire. But it may not, because DEVLOD has some pretty severe limits as to the kinds of driver it can safely be used to load.

Another way to load device drivers from the DOS prompt is by using the program *Dynamic Memory Control* (or DMC for short). See the discussion in Chapter 34 for the details of this method.

MS-DOS 6

MS-DOS 6 and *PC DOS* 6 have in many ways closed most, but not all, of the gap with *DR DOS* 6. In other ways they have moved beyond it.

In terms of memory management, the basic tools remain HIMEM.SYS and EMM386.EXE with the LOADHIGH and DEVICEHIGH commands. However, significant improvements were made to EMM386.EXE that gives it in some ways even better capabilities than the *DR DOS* 6 equivalent.

One way Microsoft has improved EMM386.EXE, DEVICEHIGH, and LOADHIGH is that now you can specify for each program as it is loaded both which region of upper memory you want to have it go into and what size that region must have free before you will permit that program to load there. There even is a provision for specifying more than one region of upper memory that a given program is to have allocated to it, along with the amount of RAM to be allocated in each of those regions. These features allow for much better optimization of upper memory use, and for greater robustness of the resulting system.

One way in which Microsoft has failed to advance as far as *DR DOS* 6 is in the use of the HMA and the loading of DOS data structures into both the HMA and UMBs. IBM's *PC DOS* 6 does a bit better than *MS-DOS* 6 in that it will load SETVER in the HMA along with the DOS kernel and the DOS disk buffers. However, both Microsoft's and IBM's DOS is not able to put only a portion of the DOS disk buffers into the HMA, and if they won't all fit, these versions of DOS cannot put the buffers into upper memory.

Another way in which these new versions of DOS fail to catch up to *DR DOS* 6 is that no change has been made to the way that DOSSHELL manages its swap file. Unlike the *DR DOS* 6 TaskMax program, DOSSHELL still can only swap to a single disk drive (which could be a RAM disk for speed) and it will fail as soon as you run out of space on that drive.

The other most significant advances in *MS-DOS* and *PC DOS* 6 in terms of memory management are their inclusion of a memory optimization program and substantial improvements to the MEM command. The memory display command MEM is not yet quite as comprehensive as the corresponding command in *DR DOS*, but it is much better than it was previously.

The *MS-DOS* 6 memory optimization utility, MemMaker, will not do anything that a very skilled and well-versed power user could not do manually by editing the CONFIG.SYS and AUTOEXEC.BAT files. It will, however, help any user get to that point more quickly and easily. The next section details what this program does and how it works.

(There are many other new features and utility programs in *MS-DOS* 6 and *PC DOS* 6. None of them is relevant, however, to memory management. If you want to read all about them, you may consult the book *DOS 6.0 Power Tools* by John M. Goodman and John Socha.)

Semiautomatic Memory Managers/Optimizers—How They Work

At the start of this chapter you heard how wonderful a memory manager can be—how some of them claim to do everything for you automatically. Now you will learn just what these programs really can do and how they do it.

Automatic memory optimization is much the same whether it is being done by the new *MS-DOS* 6 MemMaker or by the venerable MAXIMZE from Qualitas or OPTIMIZE from Quarterdeck. In all cases the program that does the optimization simply automates the process you otherwise would have to go through manually. Since these programs are operating inside the PC while the various TSR and device driver resident programs are being loaded, they get to see some things that are tough to learn as a PC user doing the steps manually. On the other hand, these programs are merely programs, and as such, they are not nearly as clever as even an only moderately experienced human being.

Some people have become confused about the distinction between the different parts of a memory manager/optimizer. There are four essential functions any such program must provide. It may provide them in a single program (single disk file), or in several different files.

The first function is providing XMS services. The XMM program does this. The DOS XMM is HIMEM.SYS. This program grabs control of extended memory, creates XMS memory from it, creates and manages the HMA, and manages UMBs.

The second function is the provision of upper memory spaces (UMBs) for programs to use. It also may include providing EMS services and an EMS page frame, plus mapping EMS memory into a portion of lower memory space. This function on a Class 5 or 6 PC is usually performed by a LIMulator program. The DOS program for this purpose is EMM386.EXE.

On PCs in Classes 2 and 4 upper memory can be created from either motherboard shadow RAM or hardware EMS memory. This is sometimes done by one program and sometimes by two, working in concert. *QRAM* and *386MAX*, for example, are able in some PCs to do both jobs, while in other machines they must cooperate with an expanded memory manager (EMM) provided by the maker of the hardware EMS board that is installed in that computer.

Most of the third-party solutions combine these first two functions into a single program. Thus *QEMM*, *386MAX*, *Memory Commander*, and *Netroom*, for example, all provide both XMS and EMS services (and VCPI and in some cases DPMI services as well), plus they map memory into upper memory space to create UMBs.

The third function involved in the automatic or semi-automatic management and optimization of PC memory is that of loading device drivers and TSR programs into upper memory blocks (and, in some cases, into the HMA). This is done in DOS by the internal commands (supported by COMMAND.COM) DEVICEHIGH and LOADHIGH.

Before DOS 5 put these functions into the operating system, the third party memory management programs all did this third job in a unique, proprietary way. That meant that they each had to provide special programs to load device drivers or TSR programs into upper memory blocks. Shortly after MS-DOS 5 was introduced, all the makers of third-party memory management and optimization programs adapted their products so they would use exactly the Microsoft strategy for loading programs into UMBs.

Those manufacturers often still include their own high-loading programs, but those programs are only needed these days if you are using an earlier version of DOS on your PC. (Even if you are using DOS 5 or 6, if you are also using a third-party memory management program like *QEMM*, you can still use those special high-loading utility programs, like LOADHI, if you like; there are, however, few if any good reasons to do so.)

The fourth function of all of these programs is to edit your CONFIG.SYS and AUTOEXEC.BAT files. They do this in order to make those startup files contain the proper sets of commands to put just the optimum mix of TSRs and device drivers into upper memory (and also to create the HMA and move DOS into it, etc.)

This fourth function is almost always done by a separate program from those that perform the other functions. In *MS-DOS* 6 that program is MemMaker. In *QEMM* it is OPTIMIZE. The *386MAX* version is called MAXIMIZE. Quadtel calls theirs SMARTMOV (which works with *QMAPS* or *UMBPro*).

It is important that you realize that this is a separate program and that it does not become resident. That means that it can be a very large program and yet using it will not use up any of your valuable memory (except for the time this program is doing its job).

The optimizer typically does its job in three phases: System evaluation; Resident program sizing; and Calculations and final adjustments. Here are the details of what happens in each phase.

System Evaluation

During system evaluation, the optimization program tries to find out what you have in your system in the way of hardware, and also see what you are planning to do with it. This means that it will notice the amount of lower and extended memory you have. It may notice any EMS memory you have. It will also notice if you have *Windows* installed, and remember the directory in which it found *Windows*. The optimization program also reads your AUTOEXEC.BAT and CONFIG.SYS files very carefully.

The program may present you with a lot of information during this phase and ask you a lot of questions about how you want it to do its job. Or it may give you only a little bit of feedback on what it is doing and ask you few if any questions. The DOS program MemMaker allows you to choose which approach it will use. The verbose and interactive mode is called "Custom Setup." The laconic mode is called "Express Setup."

The kinds of questions you typically get asked include confirming where your *Windows* directory is, telling the optimizer which, if any, of the resident programs you wish not to have loaded high, even if it could, and whether or not you plan to run *Windows*. The significance of this last question for most of the optimizers is that if you are going to run *Windows* they will reserve a small amount of upper memory space (usually 24KB) for *Windows* to use for its translation buffers. As you read earlier in this chapter, *DR DOS* 6 has a much more drastic response—at least if you tell it you plan to run *Windows* in Standard mode. In that case it ceases trying to use upper memory altogether.

A few (unfortunately few) of the memory optimization programs try to follow any CALL statements you have in your AUTOEXEC.BAT file and see what, if any, memory management implications those CALLed batch files may have.

Resident Program Sizing

In the next phase of optimization the optimizer must learn just how much upper memory would be required to load each of your device drivers and TSR programs into upper memory. It does this by loading them into lower memory and noticing how much RAM they use at various stages of the process.

The optimization program does this step by first saving your CONFIG.SYS and AUTOEXEC.BAT files in their original form (so they can restore your system to its starting condition, just in case what they do to improve things actually ends up making matters worse). Then it edits those files, inserting special commands to tell DOS to have it load each of the programs called for in those files.

Next the optimizer will reboot your PC. That is done so that DOS will be forced to reload all your device drivers and TSR programs, this time using the services of the optimizer program. (In the case of DOS 6, an auxilary program called SIZER is used to do the actual loading. You cannot use this program directly; it is only usable by MemMaker.)

As it loads the programs, the optimization program (or its auxilary loader program) records for each device driver or TSR program the amount of RAM it uses to load; the maximium amount it uses during initialization; and the final amount it uses when it "goes resident" and returns control to the loading program.

Calculations and Final Adjustments

Now, armed with all this information on what you want your PC to do and how you wish to have the optimizer do its job, the program gets down to its real work. It calculates how much lower memory would be saved for all possible ways it can arrange the device drivers and TSR programs you have told it that it may move in all the available regions of upper memory. If you only have one region of upper memory into which programs may be loaded, and if all the device drivers and TSR programs you are loading will fit there, there is only one case to consider. In many more common situations there may be multiple regions and many programs to be loaded. Often not all the programs can fit in upper memory at once, and some of them cannot fit at all into certain of the upper memory regions currently available. In these cases the optimizer may have to consider thousands or even millions of possible arrangements before deciding which one is optimum.

Having the optimizer do this exhaustive search through all possible arrangements can be an effective way to use the power of your PC. Or it may be a waste of time. If you understand the principles of memory management that have been presented up to this point in this book, you may know almost for sure which things should go into upper memory and which should not. If you have some such insight, be sure to tell the optimizer not to bother trying to load certain programs high. Even reducing the number of programs it must consider by one or two can dramatically reduce the time it will need to do its exhaustive examination of all possible program arrangements in RAM.

Finally, when the optimizer thinks it has found the best arrangement, it will edit your CONFIG.SYS and AUTOEXEC.BAT files one last time. This time it puts in the necessary DEVICEHIGH and LOADHIGH commands (or their proprietary equivalents) to put just the right programs into the right regions of upper memory. And one last time it reboots your PC.

All of the memory optimization programs then "brag" about what a wonderful job they have done. Indeed, sometimes they have something very nice to brag about. Other times they may proudly tell you that they have found a new optimized arrangement of your resident programs and report that you now have so-and-so-many **fewer** KB of free lower memory. If that happens, it merely means that you were smarter than the program, and that you will want to have it return the configuration of your PC to what it was before the optimizer began its work.

The Problem of Memory Optimization and Menus

DOS 6 includes another new feature that can interact with the new MemMaker (or any "automatic memory optimization" program) in a problematic way. This other new feature is the support for menus in

CONFIG.SYS. (The issue discussed in this section could also apply to a pre-DOS 6 PC with a menu in its AUTOEXEC.BAT file.)

If you have a menu, that implies that the user can make choices at boot time. These choices typically influence which device drivers and which TSR programs get loaded into RAM.

The problem is that once you have more than a single set of resident programs that could get loaded by the startup programs (CONFIG.SYS and AUTOEXEC.BAT), then there almost certainly will be more than one optimum arrangement of those programs. In general, each new collection of resident programs demands an independently determined optimum arrangement in memory, if you are to get the most free lower memory for application programs in each case.

MemMaker was not built to allow for this. (Neither were any of the third-party memory optimization programs.) MemMaker acts as if you have a simple set of startup files with only one, fixed set of resident software to be loaded.

There are a couple of things you can do to get full benefit from MemMaker when you have menus in either of your startup files. The first thing is to be sure and answer all of the menu choices exactly the same way each time the memory optimizer reboots your PC. This guarantees that you always load the same set of resident software. Once the optimizer is finished, it will have determined the best arrangement for those programs in RAM.

The other thing you can do is build your menus so that all of the resident software is loaded by a unique set of menu lines for each independent path you could take through the menu tree. In terms of the DOS 6 menu commands, that means that you must not put any commands or directives in a [COMMON] menu block, except for commands that do not affect memory usage at all. (See Chapter 20 for an introduction to the DOS 6 CONFIG.SYS menu support, and for a discussion of the memory usage implications of each command or directive that can be included in a CONFIG.SYS or AUTOEXEC.BAT file.)

By having DOS execute a fully independent set of commands that affect memory usage for every possible path through the menu structure, you make it possible for MemMaker to be used once for each of those paths, and thus optimize the memory usage for each configuration. Only by avoiding having any of the commands that get edited by MemMaker shared by two or more configurations can you be sure to have the optimization of one configuration not mess up the optimization of some other configuration.

Chapter 35 shows some examples of startup files, including some with menus in CONFIG.SYS. Study them to see how to make your options all fully independent of one another.

Third-Party Semiautomatic Memory Managers

Up to this point, you have read about the DOS memory managers (HIMEM.SYS, usable on any PC in classes 3 through 6, and EMM386.EXE, usable only on PCs in classes 5 and 6), and you have seen several brief mentions of a few third-party memory managers (mainly *QEMM* and *386MAX*). However, you have many more choices than these statements might suggest.

Here is a list of at least most of your options. It is followed by a short discussion of some special considerations, and what is special about certain products. Perhaps that will help you focus on the products most likely to help you with what you need. The products in each of these groups are listed here in no particular order.

> You can look up the manufacturer for any of the listed products and find out how to reach them in the MemInfo hypertext database on the diskette that accompanies this book.

Semiautomatic Memory Managers
Specifically for PCs in Classes 5 and 6

QEMM, 386MAX, BlueMAX, Memory Commander, QMAPS, All386, HI386, and *LIMSIM* (all are software products).

Semiautomatic Memory Managers for PCs in Classes 3 and 4

Software only: *QRAM, MOVE'EM* (now included in *386MAX*), *UMBPro,* and *LIMSIM.*

Hardware and software products: *All Charge card* and *HiCard2+.*

Semiautomatic Memory Managers for PCs in Classes 1 and 3

MegaMizer and *Ready RAM* (hardware and software).

Semiautomatic Memory Managers Useful on Any Class of PC

UMBPro; AboveDISC+; Turbo EMS; and *Hijaak,* version 2 (with RPM) (all are software products).

Windows 3 Compatibility

Since *Windows* has sold so many copies, compatibility with it is a major issue. And, with its three different operating modes, *Windows* 3.0 can run on almost any PC, so every memory manager must contend with this issue. *Windows* 3.1 only runs in standard and enhanced mode. That means that it is not an issue for owners of PCs in classes 1 and 2, and for memory managers that focus on that market (except as some of them aim to upgrade such a PC to a higher class, and thus enable it to run *Windows* 3.x more effectively).

Enhanced Mode Issues

When you run *Windows* 3.x in enhanced mode, it takes over your PC. It becomes the highest-privilege program running. That means that if you first run some memory manager that puts your PC into protected mode, it better be willing to give up control to *Windows* or else you cannot run *Windows* in enhanced mode.

If the memory manager offers VCPI compatibility, then it will defer to any VCPI-aware DOS-extended program. Any such memory manager sees *Windows* in enhanced mode as just another one of these VCPI-aware DOS-extended programs. *Windows* goes well beyond most DOS-extended programs in that it can also be a DPMI or VCPI server, but that is only an issue for programs that run under *Windows.*

All 386 memory managers are LIMulators as well. If you told them to set up EMS services and perhaps then allocated some of that expanded memory to various programs, all of that information must be passed to *Windows* when it starts up. From then on until you exit *Windows,* it will handle all those things for you. The memory manager, in essence, is told to "go to sleep" for the duration.

Microsoft and the vendors of third-party memory managers have agreed upon a standard data structure that must be passed to *Windows* so it can properly handle everything it must. Then it is safe for the memory manager to go to sleep.

If you use *QEMM, QMAPS, 386MAX,* or *Memory Commander,* you will be able to run *Windows* 3.x in enhanced mode. But to do so, you must be running one of the very latest versions of those programs. The issues of *Windows* enhanced mode compatibility are fairly straightforward, but it took the industry quite a few months to work them all out. Of course, you can use the Microsoft memory managers. They worked with *Windows* from the start (as you would expect).

Standard Mode Issues

Windows running in standard mode presents some interesting extra difficulties, especially in version 3.0. Most manufacturers of third-party 386 memory managers chose not to deal with them, and instead told their customers either to run *Windows* 3.0 in enhanced or real mode. With version 3.1, supposedly the kinks in *Windows* standard mode have been removed, or at least changed enough so that it will be easier for memory managers to cooperate with it. Still, you may have to upgrade to the latest version of your memory manager before it will work with *Windows* 3.1 in standard mode.

Whenever *Windows* is about to start, it sends out a "broadcast message" to let other programs already running in your PC know what it intends to do. If a memory manager that has put the PC into protected mode (and this includes EMM386.EXE) sees that *Windows*, version 3.0, is about to start in standard mode, that memory manager sends a signal to *Windows* telling it not to load. Only the most recent versions of the protected-mode memory managers do anything differently for *Windows* 3.1 (specifically, allow it to load in standard mode). That's why you may need an upgrade. The reason it is alright to let *Windows* 3.1 load in standard mode on top of these memory managers is that only in that version, *Windows* standard mode is now VCPI-aware.

One exception is Quarterdeck Office Systems. They decided that it was important to make *QEMM* compatible with *Windows* 3.0 in standard mode. They achieved this goal, but not without jumping through some hoops. They load *Windows* by running a special loader program and after it puts *Windows* into RAM, and before it lets *Windows* run, it patches the code in RAM to assure compatibility with *QEMM*. This is a very specific kludge. It works, but it will not work except with *Windows*, version 3.0.

Another memory manager that claims compatibility with *Windows* 3.0 standard mode is *AboveDISC+*.

Some Special Tricks That Memory Managers Play

Some of the commercial memory-management products can do some extra, and rather fancy tricks. Here is a brief description of some of them, and which products can do each one.

Compressing the BIOS

This is the "blue plate special" at Qualitas. If your PC is really an IBM brand *PS/2*, they know more about its BIOS than IBM does.

> This is literally true. The folks at Qualitas have made such a study of this subject that IBM admits, at least informally, that Qualitas probably has a more complete list of what is where in which PS/2 models than any single person at IBM does.
>
> As of this writing, there are 16 models of *PS/2s* currently being sold. They are the 25, 25 286, 30 286, 35SX, 35LS, 40SX, L40SX, 55SX, 55LS, 57SX, P70 386, 70 386, P75 486, 80 386, 90 XP 486, and 95 XP 486. In addition, there were a number of models sold previously that now have been discontinued (for example, the original models 30, 50, and 60). Qualitas estimates that there are more than 60 different variations on the BIOS for IBM *PS/2* machines.

Since Qualitas knows so much about each of the different *PS/2* BIOS variations, it was able to develop *BlueMAX*, a variation on *386MAX*, which comes with some extra capabilities. The special thing that *BlueMAX* can do is recover more RAM for you by overwriting the BIOS regions that are not needed once you have finished booting under *PC DOS*. These regions include a section called the ABIOS (Advanced BIOS, which is only included for *OS/2* support), the portion that does the POST, and Qualitas has chosen to include the portion that has the core of the BASIC language interpreter. They reason that very few people these days really need to run BASIC or BASICA and so that address space would be put to better use as a part of a UMB. (See Figure 10.2 for a rough picture of the pieces of the BIOS ROM code in a *PS/2*, Model 70.)

BlueMAX not only maps RAM on top of those portions of the motherboard BIOS ROM that you don't need, it also remaps the rest of the BIOS into one solid chunk (thus helping consolidate the obstacles in upper memory). This is what they mean by "compressing the BIOS." In this way, *BlueMAX* can offer you about 70KB to 80KB of extra UMBs. No other memory manager can do this trick.

Naturally, since this is built on remapping memory to cover up portions of the BIOS ROM, it assumes you are running on one of the *PS/2s* with a 386 or 486 processor. That excludes only the lowest three of the current models (25, 25 286, and 30 286). It also excludes the earlier models 30, 50, and 60.

If you really need to run BASIC programs, a better way than using BASIC or BASICA (or GWBASIC for clone PCs) is to use Microsoft's *QuickBASIC*. An interpreter-only version of this, called QBASIC.EXE, is included with *MS-DOS* 5 and 6 and *PC DOS* 5. The full compiler is sold by Microsoft as *QuickBASIC*.

Borrowing the EMS Page Frame

The clever trick of borrowing the EMS page frame was mentioned earlier in this chapter. It is a means of loading TSRs and device drivers into upper memory blocks that would otherwise be too small. If the resident sizes of a group of TSRs are smaller than the UMB, you would think at first blush they would all fit there. But, if the initialization sizes are noticeably larger, and especially if that applies to the last one of them to be loaded there, then often they will not all fit.

If the EMS page frame happens to lie just above that UMB, and if the memory manager can borrow it for the period of time needed to load those TSRs and device drivers, then it often can make available enough RAM to initialize all of the TSRs and device drivers you wished to load into that UMB. And, if they all shrink down to the resident size they were expected to assume, then the EMS page frame can be returned to its originally intended use.

A number of memory managers include special programs that try to figure out just what is the optimum arrangement of device drivers and TSRs in upper memory. They usually do this by loading all of them into lower memory and seeing what the final resident sizes are, as well as what the maximum initialization sizes were. Then they calculate a load placement (and sometimes a load sequence) that will work optimally. Some of them include the possibility of borrowing the EMS page frame; others do not.

As explained earlier, the makers of memory managers that do not support this option may fear that the TSRs, once they see the extra

UMB space, will not shrink down to as small a size, and thus will not release the EMS page frame area. Sometimes that does happen, but not very often. In any case, the memory managers that offer this feature include a way to turn it on or off on a program-by-program basis, so you can protect yourself from those exceptional cases.

Qualitas did this first with *386MAX*. They call it "FlexFrame." *QEMM* now offers it under the name "Squeeze." In *QMAPS*, it is called "LoadExtend." At this time, these are the only three memory managers that support this feature.

Instancing of TSRs

Most DOS programs were written on the assumption that only one copy of them would be running in RAM at a time. But, if you run a multitasker (like *Windows* or *DESQview*), you could run more than one copy of some programs simultaneously. There can be a problem if you do this.

The problem comes about this way. First you run a TSR program in a DOS window under *Windows*. Now you run another copy in another DOS window. Each is called an "instance" of that TSR. Ideally, you would like to put just one copy of the program's instructions in memory and simply refer to it multiple times. That works if the program doesn't store inside itself anything special about what it is doing. If it has any data, though, when you access it through the second window, you will see (and perhaps mess up) the data stored from the first window.

Some of the memory managers have built-in a provision to take care of this. They call it "instancing." If you know a program keeps data inside itself and you might be loading multiple copies of it, you can force the memory manager to keep separate copies in RAM to avoid the problem just described. At this time, only *AboveDISC+*, *386MAX* (and *BlueMAX*) from Qualitas, *Memory Commander* from V Communications, and *QMAPS* from Quadtel offer this feature.

Automatic Hiding of BIOS ROMs

Quarterdeck Office Systems took the PC world by storm when they announced in 1991 that they had figured out how to give *QEMM* users vastly more upper memory by what they called their new "Stealth" technology. This technology proposes to hide *all* your ROMs. It does not mean merely getting rid of ROM code that you are never going to use. It means getting rid, *temporarily*, of ROM code you really do need.

The key word is temporarily. As long as the memory manager can figure out when you need to access that ROM code, and only while you are doing so return it to the CPU's memory-address space, then you can use those addresses the rest of the time for a TSR or device driver. Amazing!

What is more amazing is that it actually can work. At least sometimes. But beware. It doesn't always work.

The idea behind this technology is pretty simple. Still, any implementation of it must elaborate on the basic idea quite a bit to give an acceptable degree of safety and stability.

A memory manager that proposes to do this hooks *all* your interrupts. It then notices whenever you call one of those interrupts, and where the interrupt service routine (ISR) code is that responds to that interrupt. That code must be there when you call it. (Or, it must be somewhere; the memory manager can rejigger the pointers to direct your call to the code at any location where it may have chosen to move that code.) But the ISR code doesn't have to be around the rest of the time.

Such a memory manager will map some RAM into that region of memory-address space (and map the ROM out) until you make that interrupt call. When you do, since the memory manager has hooked that interrupt (and all other interrupts), it gets control. Before it passes the interrupt service request on to the interrupt service routine, presto-chango, it maps the RAM out and the ROM back in.

That means that when the call gets to the place the interrupt service routine used to be, it actually is there. When the interrupt service routine finishes, the memory manager will again get control and, presto-chango again, put the RAM back. Now the ISR is no longer there, but the TSR is. This even works when a TSR sits in memory at the same location as the ISR it wishes to call!

In fact, the only time this approach cannot work is when a program knows where in memory some ISR is located and it directly CALLs that location instead of going through a software interrupt. Most commonly, this happens when one ISR in a ROM wishes to get some help from another ISR located elsewhere in the same ROM. The writers of both ISRs know where they will end up, so it might well seem simpler to point at the subprogram and ask it directly to help out, instead of going through the indirection of the interrupt vector table and the overhead of an interrupt call. Similar things are sometimes done by certain commercial programs.

So Quarterdeck included an optional extra kludge, just to deal with these other programs, insofar as it could. They call normal Stealth

"Stealth:M" (for memory). That means they just map the ROMs to oblivion and put RAM on top of them, until an interrupt forces them to bring the ROMs back again (briefly).

Their alternative strategy they call "Stealth:F" (for frame). This does not allow them to recover as much upper memory space for RAM, but it will work with programs that are, from their point of view, more ill-behaved.

In this variation, they put the EMS page frame on top of the ROM they suspect may get called without the caller going through the interrupt procedure. That ROM is left in plain view almost all the time. Whenever a program asks for access to expanded memory, that ROM briefly disappears, just long enough to allow the needed page(s) of EMS memory to show up in the page frame. Once they have been accessed for whatever purposes, they get put away again and the ROM is made to reappear, in case it should be called without notice.

This does help. More programs are tolerated by Stealth:F than by Stealth:M. But, still not all of them are. *GeoWorks* is one that definitely does not work with either version of Stealth. Doubtless, there are others.

Stealth may give you a whole lot more upper memory. Or, it may give you a whole lot of grief. The installation program for *QEMM*, version 6, attempts to discover if Stealth will or won't work on your machine. As is noted in the manual, the tests do not always come up with the right answer. Sometimes you are told you cannot use Stealth when you can; sometimes you'll be told it will work okay, and only discover later on that it bombs.

It is worth a try. If it works for you, then you will greatly enjoy the extra UMB space. But please make several lengthy tests before you commit anything of value to a system running Stealth.

Qualitas responded to *QEMM* version 6 with its own variation on the same theme. In *386MAX,* version 6, they included what they call "ROMsearch." The basics are the same. The main difference is in how they decide which areas it is safe to map out and which they had better not.

A Memory-Management Product That Isn't a Memory Manager

RYBS makes memory-management products. Some of them are hardware add-ons for PCs in classes 1 to 4. They offer a pure software memory manager for PCs in classes 5 and 6. And they offer one product that is meant to help you use any other memory manager.

AtLast is an optimizer you can use with the DOS 5 or 6 memory-management programs or with any other memory manager. It claims special ease of use and the ability to find a more nearly optimal way of loading things into upper memory. So if the DOS memory managers seem to do enough, but you'd like a little help getting them to do all they are capable of doing, this may be a product you'll want to look at.

Choosing a Memory Manager

With all this variety to choose from, how do you make a sensible choice? As always, the right answer is: "It depends!" To help you, here are some tips.

- If you are using an IBM *PS/2* with a 386 or 486 processor, *BlueMAX* will recover more upper memory space with greater safety than any other memory manager.

- If you wish to run *DESQview*, *QEMM* knows more about how to help you get the most from it than any other memory manager.

- *QEMM* and *AboveDISC+* are the only memory managers that let you run *Windows* 3.0 in standard mode. (Remember, this is not an issue if you use *Windows* or *Windows for Workgroups*, version 3.1.)

- *QMAPS* and *UMBPro* have the widest knowledge of different brands of motherboard system logic chip sets, so they are best at recovering shadow RAM.

- *Memory Commander* has the greatest ability to move the video image buffer around (and can even do so dynamically, on a per program basis), so it can let you run larger DOS programs than any of the rest.

- If fitting more things into upper memory is your chief concern, look carefully at the three memory managers that can borrow the EMS page frame to help out. They are *QMAPS, QEMM,* and *386MAX.* Remember to put your EMS page frame just above your UMB space or this will do you no good.

- *Netroom,* with its Netswap feature, lets you share the same upper memory region for your network driver and the EMS page frame; something none of the others are as good at.

Some Times When You Don't Want a 386 Class Memory Manager, Even Though You Have a 386, 486, or Pentium-based Computer

Most of this chapter has been devoted to describing what wonderful things you can do with a 386 memory manager (one that knows how to use the special hardware features of the 386 CPU chip). You need at least a 386-based PC to take advantage of these programs. If you have one, you may have become convinced that you'd never want to use anything less.

However, that is not always the case. Here are some reasons why you may prefer to use something simpler. (The comparison here is between something like *QMAPS*, the full 386 memory manager from Quadtel, and *UMBPro*, their junior-level offering.)

If you run *Windows* 3.x exclusively, and you either run it only in its enhanced mode or never run any DOS applications that need EMS memory, then you don't need to create an EMS page frame. That means a LIMulator is a feature you may get in your memory manager and never need to use.

You can turn off that feature, but you still will be loading all that code somewhere. Mostly it goes into extended memory, where you may not have been noticing it. It is taking up RAM, though, and that means you have that much less RAM for other uses.

Fancier memory managers also run slower than the simpler ones. And the simpler ones, by not trying to emulate EMM programs, will not be incompatible with DOS-extended programs that are not VCPI-aware. (See Chapter 12 for an explanation of VCPI and VCPI-aware programs.)

An Important Warning

Many memory managers are touted for their ability to return to you what they perceive as wasted space in the B page. You may want to take advantage of those abilities, but then again, it could be dangerous.

The Opportunity

When IBM defined the PC architecture, they specified that the A and B pages would be used for video. That meant for video-image buffers. They further said the lower half of the B page was for monochrome cards and the upper half for color. That was how things started out.

When IBM introduced the EGA card, and later VGA, they put the A page to use for graphics modes for those two adapters. They used the color part (upper half) of the B page for EGA and VGA text mode (which was usually in color). They did not touch the monochrome space (lower half of B page). That allowed some users to get the benefit of running a graphics program on an EGA or VGA monitor, while seeing a monochrome text-mode display of the command menu on a companion monochrome monitor.

If you only have one monitor, and if it is connected to an EGA or VGA card, then you will never be using the lower half of the B page for anything. That is 32KB of the CPU's memory address space that is going to waste.

An even bigger opportunity looms if you have only a monochrome card, or only a CGA card, or if you are only going to use your EGA or VGA display adapter for text mode output. Then the whole of the A page and half of the B page are up for grabs.

Isn't there some way you could put these spaces to some better use? There are, it turns out, several ways this can be done.

A popular one with many memory managers is to put RAM in those spaces. It creates a separate UMB with 32KB, 64KB, or 96KB, or it may create two separate UMBs, one with 64KB and one with 32KB. The separateness makes using them effectively more difficult, but it is much better than not having that much additional RAM.

AboveDISC+, from Above Software, includes ABOVE640 which does this. Quarterdeck includes with its memory managers VIDRAM, which also can do it. RYBS calls their program that does this VIDMEM.

Qualitas has introduced us to another way to use that space. In *386MAX*, version 6, they support relocating your video option ROM from C0000h to the monochrome adapter space. This assumes, of course, that you have either EGA or VGA and don't have an MDA or Hercules card in your system. Doing that releases as much as 32KB of the C page for program storage (once extended memory is mapped in there and it is managed by an XMM which, among other things, *386MAX* is).

Memory Commander takes, as usual, a different tack. It will move all the video-image buffers up as far in memory-address space as it can, in the process squeezing out all the holes. Then it fills RAM into the resulting large hole and connects it to lower memory. This gives you an enormous space for regular DOS programs.

The Problem

Not very many people use two monitors per PC. So when clone makers created clone video cards, one way they could distinguish their products was to incorporate new graphics modes. And to do so, many found the possibility of using more of the A and B pages irresistible. Naturally, for compatibility, they also supported modes of operation that are exactly like those used by IBM.

So while you may think you have those holes, and even worse, your memory manager may think so, actually you might not, or at least, you may not always have them. Also, since video cards often have enough memory on them to fill all of the A and B pages (and then some), certain programs that know a lot about how video cards work can map RAM into those holes for their use. Again, a hole you thought you had isn't really there (perhaps only part of the time).

Mostly, the programs that attempt to decide how you should use your upper memory (like OPTIMIZE from Quarterdeck or MAXIMIZE from Qualitas) run in text mode. That means that while they are running, your video card is acting quite sedately. It only gets flamboyant in its use of the A and B pages when you switch into some extravagant video graphics mode. So the optimization programs don't see and don't necessarily understand what extravagances your video card is capable of.

Most of the good memory managers will notice if you have EGA or VGA capability and will assume you probably are going to go into some graphics mode sometime. Therefore, they will keep their hands off of your A page.

Not seeing any problem with doing so, they may suggest you let them map RAM into the lower half of the B page or in certain cases, into the A page. Before you decide to let them do so, consider the following rules. If you cannot live with *all* of them, don't let your memory manager try to do you any favors by placing RAM or moving a ROM into the A or B pages.

- If in setting up your memory management, you chose some very aggressive option that assumed you would only be in text mode, don't ever try running any program that uses graphics mode. That includes such normally character-based programs as *1-2-3* for DOS when it shows you a graph.

- Don't switch your VGA to emulate a monochrome display adapter. This can happen if you run a program that expects to see a monochrome card and your video card is smart enough to "auto-switch."

- Don't use *SoftKicker* or *ExcelMore*. (They use the space they know exists in the lower half of the B page to let them give you their enhanced views.)

- Don't ever switch to any video mode higher in resolution or number of simultaneous on-screen colors than the standard IBM modes. That means no 800 by 600 resolution and no 640 by 480 with 256 simultaneous colors, let alone the modes that go all the way up to 1280 by 1024 with 256 colors. Lots of "super VGA" cards offer some of these extra, non-IBM modes, and they are very tempting. Often to achieve operation in one of these extra fancy modes, these video cards must use all of the A and B pages.

- Watch out for video cards that mention in their literature something about "caching fonts in RAM for faster text in graphics modes." This is a valuable technique, but it involves putting the font data in video RAM mapped to some space where the video image buffer is not. Guess where that might be? Just where your memory manager wanted to put that extra UMB.

Some Ways to Handle the Problem

Some of the memory managers have been built to help protect you. That protection may also limit you, possibly uncomfortably.

For example, if you run ABOVE640, it is a TSR that not only maps some RAM into the holes in your A or B pages, but also monitors all INT 10h calls. When one of your programs attempts to go into a graphics mode, it will block that call. That protects the contents of the RAM it mapped in, but it also prevents you from, for example, displaying a graph from within *1-2-3*. You can unload ABOVE640 by running RESET640, but only if you have not loaded any other TSRs after ABOVE640.

VIDRAM and VIDMEM have similar protections built in, with similar effects. The only memory manager that does things really differently, and still provides effective protection, is *Memory Commander*.

At the heart of *Memory Commander*'s specialness is the way it keeps track of what it will do. Most memory managers have you insert, either manually or with their help, various instructions to them into the lines of your CONFIG.SYS and AUTOEXEC.BAT files. *Memory Commander*, in contrast, inserts no such commands.

Instead, it maintains a special database of programs. For each one, it keeps track of what kind of program it is (a normal DOS program, a TSR program, a device driver, or a shell program). It also keeps track of appropriate information for each kind of program, such as which video modes it uses and other details. Figure 21.4 shows a typical screen display from the program that maintains that database. This screen shows what it records about a device driver or TSR program.

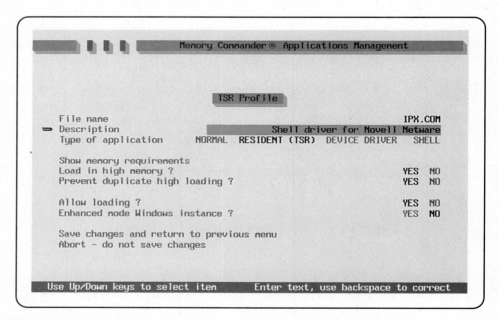

Figure 21.4. *Memory Commander's* database of programs.

Since *Memory Commander* knows so much about each program you might run, and since it watches as DOS loads every program and checks its database to see what is permissible for that program, it is uniquely able to choose when to map RAM where. This lets you run some very large text-based DOS applications at one time, and run a more modest sized, graphical DOS application a few moments later. *Memory Commander* simply moves the top of system memory up or down, as appropriate.

Naturally, *Memory Commander* cannot have every possible program in its database. It ships a substantial set and then allows you to edit that database to include programs you know about. You can even override the decisions V Communications made about programs listed in the database they sent you. That way, if you have a program that could be run in graphics mode, but you know you aren't going to use it that way, you can tell *Memory Commander* to let you have more DOS system memory for it. (And, if you later try to cheat, it will prevent you from doing so.)

With *PC DOS* 6, IBM has introduced yet another variation on this same theme. In this case they sought to let users of PCs in any class have some UMBs by taking advantage of unused video image buffer memory.

PC DOS 6 includes three special programs called UMBMONO.SYS, UMBHERC.SYS, and UMBCGA.SYS that are intended for use in systems with both a monochrome (MDA or MGA) and a color (CGA, EGA, or VGA) video adapter, but in which you are only using one of those adapters. You load one of these device drivers in order to allow you to use some of the memory on the unused video card for a UMB. (Which one you load depends on what kind of card your unused video card is.)

These device drivers include some pretty good "defense mechanisms" that attempt to keep you from getting into troubble. In particular, if a program uses the INT10h interrupt call to change video mode when one of these device drivers is loaded, the device driver will prevent that call from working. If some program tries to write directly to the nominally not-in-use video adapter, the UMBxxxx.SYS device drivers will at least attempt to make your machine crash or hang before you can do any damage to your data.

A Final Tip on Setting Up Memory Managers

When you are ready to experiment with a memory manager, there are several things you can do to make your life a great deal more pleasant. Also, there are some tips you can learn that will save you time.

First and most important: Have a tested Safety Boot Diskette close at hand, and be sure your hard disk backups are *valid* and *complete*. (If you have *any* doubt at all about what these things mean, please go back and reread Chapter 5, and the section "Some Tips on Maximizing Your Free RAM" in Chapter 20.)

The reason you will very likely need the Safety Boot Diskette is that when you are altering your CONFIG.SYS and AUTOEXEC.BAT files, as you will be doing at least a little with any memory manager, you are constantly putting your PC at risk. It may not be able to boot from the hard disk if these critical files get messed up. Being able to boot from a floppy is at those times a great comfort and convenience.

There may be an even easier way to cope with a not-quite-right set of CONFIG.SYS and AUTOEXEC.BAT files. Most of the modern memory managers offer you the option of aborting them at boot time. Most use the simple expedient of having you hold down the Alt key while you boot. (*LIMSIM* uses the Shift key, or in some earlier versions, Ctrl-Alt-Shift.) You must not do this too soon, or you will get a keyboard failure message from the POST (the Power On Self Test program that runs before DOS boots). However, you must not do this too late or your memory manager will already have begun its work. Once the memory manager begins, it is no longer looking for that special key press.

If you are running version 6 of *MS DOS* or *PC DOS*, you have another option. Those versions of DOS includes a special feature called "Clean Boot" and another one called "Interactive Boot." The first one, invoked by pressing the F5 function key or holding down either Shift key during the message "Starting MS-DOS," will cause DOS to completely ignore the CONFIG.SYS and AUTOEXEC.BAT files. The latter feature, invoked by pressing the F8 function key, forces it to offer you on a line-by-line basis the option of executing or ignoring the commands in your CONFIG.SYS file, and of executing or ignoring your AUTOEXEC.BAT file. (It only allows you to execute or ignore your whole AUTOEXEC.BAT file, but then you can interrupt that file in the middle, usually, by pressing Ctrl-Break at a suitable time.)

Whichever way you do it, by using your Safety Boot Diskette, by aborting your memory manager as it tries to load, or by using the DOS 6 "Clean Boot" or "Interactive Boot" features, you can get access to your hard disk once more to try yet another round of file editing and testing. Look forward to quite a few of these. It often takes that to get memory management just right.

Of course, the semiautomatic memory managers can try to help you and they will reduce the number of cycles you need to try. But they won't eliminate them altogether. At least not if you aren't content to settle with just whatever they happen to give you, and wish instead to try your hand at making things even better.

Automatic Memory Management

Now consider the really automatic memory managers. Mostly, these are operating environments. They do whatever they must to let you do some very special things. One of the tasks they must undertake is memory management, and they tend to do that in whatever way is their way. You have only a limited ability to intervene and modify how they will do their work, but you do have some leeway. If you use one of these environments, it will help if you learn what ways you can intervene and how to use each one.

The following is just a brief introduction to these environments and how they use memory. Many authors have devoted entire books to one or another of them.

The Magic of Time Sharing

First, though, you need to understand what is so special about what these environments can do for you. They all are capable of *time-shared multitasking,* sometimes called "time sharing" for short.

Literally, this means that they allow many programs each to use your PC, and to do so in a way that gives the illusion that they are all doing so at once. Wait a minute. Isn't that how task-swapping program managers were described? Almost.

Task-swapping program managers can give you the illusion that all your programs are running simultaneously, but only if you think most of them stopped because they were waiting for your input. If you know one or another of them has plenty of useful work to do, and if you expect that program to do its work while you are working with another one, you will be sadly disappointed in your task-swapping program manager.

On the other hand, that is exactly what you can expect from a time-shared multitasking environment. You load up a program, get it started on some task, switch away from it, and start up another, and so on, until you have a bunch of tasks working at the same time. Each one keeps on working even though you are no longer watching its screen. (Or, perhaps you can see just a bit of that screen in a window on your monitor.)

There Ain't No Such Thing As A Free Lunch (TANSTAAFL). This phrase expresses another truth about any multitasking scheme. The computing power of your PC is merely being spread among the several running programs. So each one runs slower than it would if it were the only one running in your PC. In fact, the sum of the speeds of all the programs is not quite as great as the speed any one of them would have if it were running alone. The difference is the computing power needed by the multitasking operating environment to control the whole shebang.

The convenience of being able to pull up one program after another, and then swap easily among them is seductive. When you add to that the ability to set one program to doing a long task, switch away from it to do other work, and sometime later switch back and find the task done, the combination becomes downright irresistible. At least for some folks.

Multitasking is not for everyone. But, if you aspire to working in that sort of a whirlwind manner, these operating environments may be just your cup of tea.

DoubleDOS

DoubleDOS has been around for many years. It is a two-task time-sharing executive. That means you can run exactly two DOS programs under *DoubleDOS*, and each one thinks it has the PC to itself.

The limitation to only two programs is one way that this environment is showing its age. When *MS-DOS 5* was released, it turned out that *DoubleDOS* was totally incompatible with that new version of DOS. This was a much more serious sign of its age.

The manufacturer of *DoubleDOS*, SoftLogic Systems, did not want to upgrade the product to work with DOS 5. Indeed, they had not been "marketing" *DoubleDOS* for several years prior to the introduction of DOS 5. However, customer demand forced them to upgrade this old workhorse in mid-1992, so now it can be used with the latest DOS versions safely.

It used to be quite popular with operators of bulletin board systems. They could run their BBS software in one partition, and while it was listening for a phone call, or even while a call was being handled, they were able to do some significant work in the other partition.

This system can function quite nicely with two programs of moderate size even on a class 1 PC. If you can fit both programs plus *DoubleDOS* and DOS in your lower memory (640KB), you can use this solution. The screen and the keyboard are either dedicated to one program or to the other. The only exception is the hotkey that takes you from one to the other.

This program has lost its luster and now is not selling many copies. However, there are a lot of copies out there, and they still do the same wonderful things they always did.

DESQview

An equally venerable program, but one that has matured along with the industry, is *DESQview*. This multitasking, multiwindowing operating-environment program is one of the two most popular ways to let several programs share one PC. (The other is Microsoft *Windows*.)

The programmers at Quarterdeck Office Systems have been responsible for many innovations. They introduced the concept of a windowing program for PCs. Years later, they discovered and made public the idea of using the HMA. And most recently, they brought us the Stealth technology in *QEMM*, version 6.

DESQview is the flagship product of that company. It is a real-mode DOS program that implements a text-based windowing system. And it is a multitasker. You can run up to 70 programs and between them use up to 255 windows on-screen, all at once. (Since each window is composed of text characters, there are a limited number of positions and sizes they can have. That means the maximum practical number of programs is far less than these theoretical limits.) Figure 21.5 shows what the *DESQview* screen looks like. In the upper right corner is the main menu. Elsewhere you see three open windows, each displaying the output of a different program.

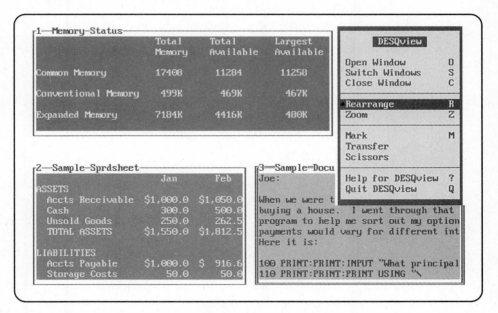

Figure 21.5. *DESQview* permits the user to run several programs at once.

Some people use *DESQview* as if it were simply a DOS shell and program launcher. Others take advantage of its task switching capabilities. But you are not using it to full advantage until you use it for multitasking.

By careful design, *DESQview* presents to most programs the standard appearance of DOS. In fact, you can run Microsoft *Windows* in a window under *DESQview*. (You can only do this if *Windows* is running in either Real or Standard mode. Quarterdeck says that the only real advantage of *Windows* 386-enhanced mode is its ability to run DOS programs in windows simultaneously. Since *DESQview* already does that anyway, they did not bother to make it possible to do that with *Windows* also.)

In addition to multitasking, *DESQview* offers the possibility of cutting information from one window, and pasting it into a different application running in another window. It also supports inter-program communications for those programs that know how to talk to the special DV API (Application Program Interface).

The DV API is a series of protocols for communicating requests to *DESQview.* These protocols are made available to programs running in a *DESQview* window in addition to all the standard ways a program has to ask DOS for services.

Powerful as it is, *DESQview* is not the most powerful multitasker available for PCs. In fact, it has a few rather severe limitations. (But, viewed from another perspective, each of these turns out to be a distinct advantage.)

DESQview runs in real mode. This means you can use it on any class of PC. It also means that it does not take advantage of any of the extra capabilities of a PC in class 3 or higher. It can be supplemented with one of the Quarterdeck memory managers (*QEXT* for PCs in classes 3 and 4, and *QEMM* for those in classes 5 and 6). Then it can take advantage of the extra memory those PCs can have, though it still does not use their protection features much.

Since *DESQview* runs in real mode, it cannot use any more than the 640KB of lower memory, any UMBs you have, and perhaps the HMA (depending on the class of PC), plus any expanded memory you offer it. Extended memory is strictly outside its view.

If you run *QEMM* on a 386- or 486-based PC, you will be able to map extended memory into the holes in upper memory. That will give *DESQview* the upper memory blocks it wants. You can also convert all the rest of extended memory into simulated expanded memory. That is wonderful. In this situation, *DESQview* really shines.

QEMM is a VCPI server (and, in its most recent versions, a DPMI server). That means that if you run *DESQview* on top of *QEMM*, you can then run a DOS-extended application in one of the *DV* windows. That program can access extended memory. But *DESQview* itself cannot.

You can do almost as well, surprisingly enough, on a lowly 8088-based PC. The key is to use it with a hardware EMS board that can page EMS memory into locations in lower memory address space. That means you must have an EEMS- or LIM 4.0 EMS-compatible memory card (and not just any of them—remember the discussion about EMS boards that promise LIM 4.0 compliance, but don't really do all the things the standard describes). You also must be able to turn off memory-address decoding on the motherboard in the region of lower memory you wish to fill with EMS memory pages.

How *DESQview* Uses Memory

How exactly does *DESQview* use the memory in your PC? There are two extremes. One applies if you are using a PC without upper or expanded memory; a class 1 PC, in other words. The other extreme applies when you are running it on a class 5 or 6 PC and using *QEMM* or another good 386 memory manager. *DESQview* running on PCs in classes in between use a variation of one of these schemes.

DESQview is strictly a real-mode program. It relies on some other memory manager(s) to do the necessary mapping of extended memory into upper memory space, to provide access to the HMA, and to convert extended memory into simulated LIM 4.0 EMS-compatible expanded memory.

The folks who made *DESQview* want you to choose either *QEXT* or *QEMM*, since they sell both of these programs, but you can also use almost any other memory manager. However, you might have to give up some minor portion of the features *DESQview* otherwise would bring you, since other people's memory managers don't understand how *DESQview* is built as well as the programmers of *QEMM* and *QEXT*. The most likely place you will notice the difference is when you run a program in a *DV* window and that program wants to write directly to the screen. The *DV-QEMM* combination is better able to virtualize video, and thus can let that program run in a window that is smaller than full-screen. *DV* with most other memory managers cannot.

On a Class 1 PC

If you only have a class 1 PC, *DESQview* just has the 640KB of lower memory to play with. In this situation, it gets loaded on top of DOS and any device drivers or TSRs you may have loaded before it. *DESQview*, in this situation, takes up about 150KB of lower memory.

DESQview uses whatever memory is left for the programs it loads for you. As you open a window, the first program gets loaded just below the video-image-buffer area. The next one gets loaded just below that. And so on until you run out of RAM—which won't be long unless your programs are very tiny.

When *DESQview* runs out of lower memory, it swaps programs to a file on the disk. This allows it to multitask, but since disk accesses are so slow, any attempt at multitasking is going to look more like moderately frequent task switching. That can be very annoying. So commonly, if you are using *DESQview* on a class 1 PC, you will set it up so that it will display just one program at a time in a full-screen window, with only that program needing to be in RAM. Then you are using *DESQview* solely as a task switcher.

On a PC in Classes 2 Through 4

When you add to the basic PC the ability to map expanded memory into lower and upper memory address space, you give *DESQview* the opportunity to display a lot more of its power. If you use only LIM 3.2 EMS-compatible expanded memory, you will get more capabilities than if you don't use any EMS memory, but you don't get much more.

If you have only LIM 3.2 EMS memory, *DESQview* will do just what it did on the class 1 PC, except that it will do the program swapping to EMS memory. Since the programs must be in lower memory to run, and LIM 3.2 EMS boards cannot map memory there, all program swaps will involve copying information up from lower memory to the EMS page frame and then switching the EMS pages out. The other pages get switched in and their contents get copied down to lower memory. This is a lot faster than swapping to disk, but it does take a noticeable amount of time, especially if your PC is not very fast and your programs are large.

If you have LIM 4.0 EMS memory, then *DESQview* can directly swap programs that are residing on one or more EMS pages into the lower memory address space. (That also assumes you can turn off the memory address decoders for that range of addresses on the motherboard.)

This configuration allows real multitasking. Those context switches can be made a great many times per second without using up an inordinate fraction of the PC's computing power. And that is the precondition for making it seem as if all the programs are running simultaneously.

On a PC in Class 5 or 6

DESQview on a 386-based PC running *QEMM* can do a lot more. Again, the bottom of lower memory is filled by DOS (including the interrupt vector table and the DOS and BIOS data areas). If your CONFIG.SYS or AUTOEXEC.BAT files specify any device drivers or TSRs, those will be loaded next. All this is just the usual way DOS boots on a PC.

When you type DV at the DOS prompt and press Enter, the command interpreter loads *DESQview* on top of whatever else is already in memory. If there are some available upper memory blocks or if the HMA is available, *DESQview* will load a portion of itself into one or both of these places. If you have enough upper and high RAM available, *DESQview* can move all but about 10KB of itself out of lower memory.

In Figure 21.6, you see this situation diagramed. The region marked DOS is all the stuff that gets loaded into lower memory before *DESQview*. The part labelled *DESQview* is just that small 10KB stub. The rest of *DESQview* is loaded into whatever UMBs are available, and the HMA if it is available.

The region marked Process #1 is where the first program you open under *DESQview* goes. Notice that it is shoved up against the under side of the video-image buffer. If you are running only text-mode programs, that can be as high as the 736KB mark.

The region marked Common Memory is a pool of memory that *DESQview* maintains for its use, and as a place through which the various programs it is managing may communicate with one another.

The region marked Shared System Memory is provided to allow programs to write to each other's windows and to do other, similar tasks. It may be very small or quite large, depending on how much of that sort of thing your programs do.

The region above the Shared System Memory and below Process #1 is just empty memory. *DESQview* is not using it for anything at this time. If Process #1 needed more conventional memory, that would be the most it could get.

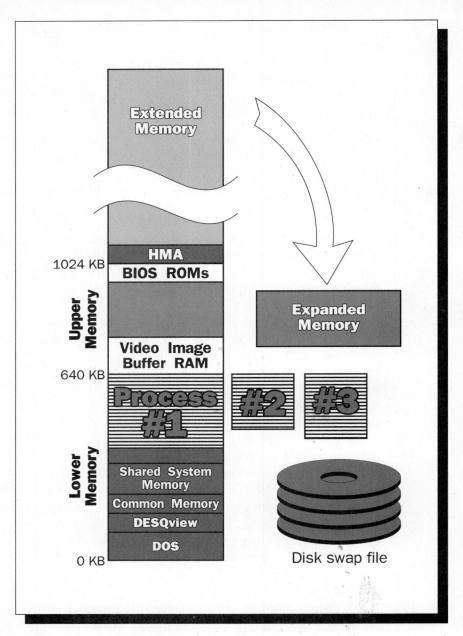

Figure 21.6. How *DESQview* uses memory.

When you want to load a second process, *DESQview* swaps out the first one. It loads the second one also starting just below the video-image buffer. It makes no attempt to cram both processes into lower memory together, even if they would fit. It doesn't need to do that because it is running on a class 5 or 6 PC, and so can do the memory paging needed to swap programs in and out again extremely rapidly.

Figure 21.6 also shows a third process. It, too, would get loaded with the same top address. Each of these programs stays out in the pool of expanded memory when it is not in lower memory. If *DESQview* runs out of room in expanded memory, it will open a swap file on the disk and put swapped out programs there.

Windows

Microsoft's *Windows* program is another multitasking, windowing operating environment that runs on top of DOS. It offers a graphical user interface, and it comes with a set of utility programs. It is also the best-selling piece of software ever (excepting only DOS itself).

Windows is now at version 3.1. Unlike the EMS standard, it did not start out at version 3.0. There have been commercial versions with numbers from 1.0 to 2.x. But, in the interests of brevity, versions 3.0 and 3.1 are the only versions discussed in this book. If you use *Windows* and are at all serious about memory management, you need to upgrade to at least version 3.0.

Starting with version 3.0, *Windows* is more than just one program. It is, in effect, a collection of programs in a box. When you launch the main program, it looks at your hardware and makes a decision about which other programs to load along with itself.

Usually this is described by saying that *Windows* operates in one of three modes. They are called "Real mode," "Standard, or 286 mode," and "386-enhanced mode." That is, *Windows* 3.0 runs in any of three modes. With version 3.1, Real mode has been dropped. (If *Windows* starts in a mode other than what you wanted, you may be able to force it to go into your choice of operating mode. Still you will have to have at least a minimally sufficient set of hardware to make this possible.)

Figures 21.7 through 21.10a were captured on the same PC with exactly the same programs loaded. Only the mode of *Windows* was changed between pictures. Notice the variation in how much free memory *Windows* reports from one mode to another. Figure 21.10b was captured on a different PC, but one with a similar amount of RAM and loaded programs.

The background graphic being used, called the "wallpaper" in *Windows* parlance, was too big a file to fit into lower memory. (It is CHESS.BMP, which is over 150KB.) So, in Real mode, *Windows* simply declined to load it, and used a simple patterned background instead.

Real mode *Windows* (see Figure 21.8) has fairly modest hardware prerequisites. Nominally speaking, that is. It can run on any PC with only 640KB of RAM. The problem is that saying it can *run* overstates things. It can *crawl* on that sort of PC.

Standard mode *Windows* 3.0 (see Figure 21.9) requires a little more hardware. Specifically, you must have at least 192KB of the lower 640KB free plus at least 256KB of extended memory. You may have more than that amount of total RAM, but if, after deducting what is reserved for shadow RAM and what has been used as expanded memory, you don't have at least 256KB of extended memory left, you won't be able to run *Windows* in Standard mode.

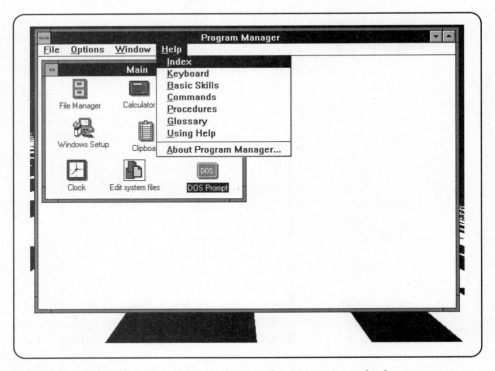

Figure 21.7. *Windows* 3.0: To see what mode you are in and what resources you have, choose "About Program Manager" from its Help menu.

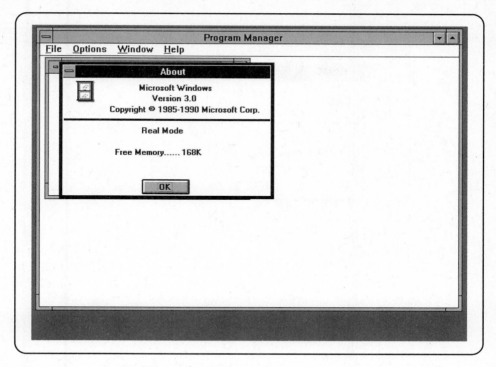

Figure 21.8. *Windows* 3.0: Real mode.

Naturally, this implies that you are running on at least a class 3 PC. They run faster than class 1 PCs (usually). On that level of hardware, *Windows* no longer crawls. Here it can walk. It still is an overstatement to say it runs.

If you want to run *Windows* applications as well as *Windows* itself, you will find that you need more than this minimum amount of RAM. The more the better. But it must all be extended. Expanded doesn't count.

Windows 3.0 in 386-enhanced mode (see Figure 21.10a) needs at least 2MB of extended memory (plus the 640KB of lower memory). Also, it needs (as you might have guessed from the name) a 386 or 486 CPU chip. That means you are going to be running it on a class 5 or 6 PC. Again, that is a minimum amount of RAM. You'd like to have all you can get. The more you have, the less *Windows* will have to swap to disk and the faster your PC will go.

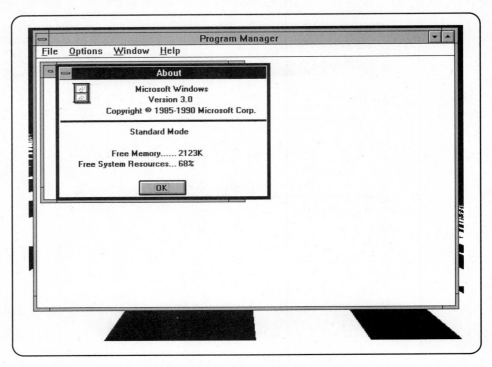

Figure 21.9. *Windows* 3.0: Standard (286) mode.

Now you are talking some real speed. If you have at least a 16MHz 386SX, you can run *Windows* with an acceptable level of performance. (Unless you are a very impatient person. Or, one who has had the misfortune to become accustomed to a screamingly fast PC and then have to move back to this level.) At last it can be said that *Windows* runs on this sort of PC without too much exaggeration.

For all modes, the optimal hardware is something even more powerful than this. At least 4 to 8MB of RAM, a really fast, large hard drive, and at least a 20 or 25MHz 386DX as the CPU would be about right. Anything beyond that is gravy.

This has all been about the various modes of *Windows* 3.0. Now the latest version is 3.1 (see Figure 21.10b). (The very latest version of *Windows*, at this writing, is *Windows for Workgroups*, which is from the point of view of memory management just *Windows* 3.1 plus peer-to-peer network software.) What is new and different with version 3.1?

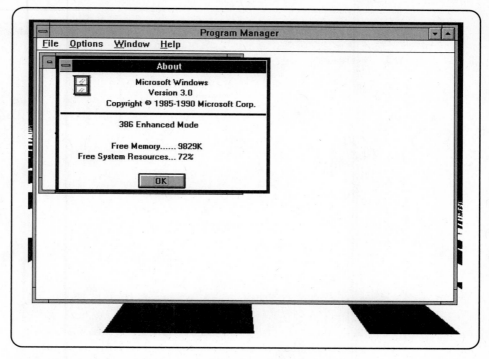

Figure 21.10a. *Windows* 3.0: 386-enhanced mode.

As I have pointed out several times now, *Windows* 3.1 no longer supports *Windows* Real mode on any PC. Another difference is that 3.1 runs faster and has less of a proclivity to crash, plus when it does, it has better ways of dealing with those crashes. (When one program you are running makes a mistake and does something that would have brought *Windows* 3.0 completely to its knees, you usually can simply terminate the offending program under *Windows* 3.1 and continue to work with the rest.)

Another significant difference is that *Windows* 3.1 supports a true WYSIWYG interface, but only if you stick exclusively to the new *TrueType* fonts. (For many people that is not much of a restriction, given the explosion in the number of available *TrueType* fonts and their rapidly descreasing price.)

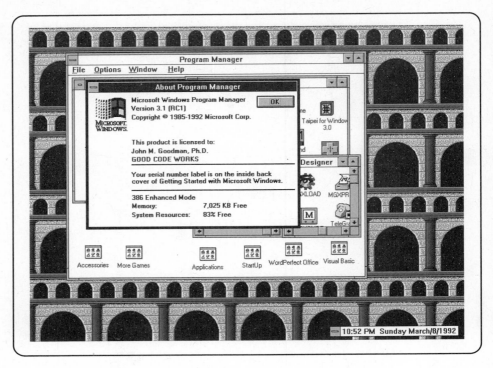

Figure 21.10b. *Windows* 3.1: 386-enhanced mode.

With the introduction of *Windows for Workgroups*, version 3.1, and the announcement of *Windows NT*, version 3.1, one gets the sense that Microsoft feels that they have arrived, with this version, at a plateau. We won't be seeing a version of *Windows* that offers anything significantly different from version 3.1 for several years. (*Windows NT* is really a different beast. It replaces DOS, rather than running on top of it, and it uses full 32-bit code throughout—which restricts it to operating on class 6 PCs. Indeed, with the amount of RAM and disk space NT requires, only owners of extremely powerful PCs can even contemplate running *Windows NT*.)

In the following discussion, any time you see the phrase "the latest wrinkle" or something equivalent, you may assume it refers to an aspect of version 3.1 of *Windows*.

Okay, so *Windows* is a **big** program. And it has a lot of stuff to do, which makes it pretty slow. What does it offer beyond what *DESQview* can?

First, it runs *Windows* applications. These are programs written specially to take advantage of the *Windows* API (*Application Program Interface*;

see Chapter 7). That lets the authors of these programs plan on using almost unlimited amounts of RAM. It also allows them to concentrate on making a program to do some computing task well, and leave the device drivers to control the plethora of printers, video cards, and other hardware for PCs up to the programmers at Microsoft (or those at the vendors who make those optional hardware gadgets). And *Windows* applications naturally multitask (**if** they have been written correctly—which **most** of them have).

> Because of these benefits to programmers, a number of really powerful applications have been written that will only run under *Windows* (or perhaps under *OS/2*, version 2). For many people, the existence of these applications is the sole reason they bought and use *Windows*.
>
> You can run *Windows* applications under *DESQview*. But you must first buy *Windows* also. Then you run *DESQview*, and in one of its windows run *Windows*, and inside that run your *Windows* application. That makes sense if you also want to run a number of DOS applications and if you like the *DESQview* task switching and multitasking features better than the equivalent ones in *Windows*. But, if you are going to run a *Windows* application most of the time, perhaps you only need to buy and use *Windows*.

Next, *Windows* can run DOS applications too. But only one at a time and only in full screen mode (during which time all *Windows* applications are suspended). That is true except if you are running *Windows* in 386-enhanced mode. In that mode, it can run multiple DOS applications, each in a window of its own and even multitask them with each other and with *Windows* applications. (Watch out, though, you are asking an awful lot of your PC at this point. So it will slow down, most likely quite noticeably, unless yours is a really powerful PC.)

Like *DESQview, Windows* also supports interprogram communications. It does so even more elaborately than *DESQview*.

One technique is called Cut and Paste. There is a feature called the Clipboard and you can use it to store temporarily text or graphical images you are moving from one program to another.

Another, more powerful technique is called *DDE*. This stands for *Dynamic Data Exchange*. It is a protocol that allows *Windows* programs to exchange data automatically, completely out of sight of the *Windows* user.

Your graphs might just update themselves when you change the data in your spreadsheet. To work this way, though, the applications must have been programmed to exchange all the appropriate messages. Also, you must have started each program you want to have communicating with one another, and perhaps have loaded the appropriate data file for each one.

The newest wrinkle on this plan is called *OLE*, or *Object Linking and Embedding*. This means that you may in the future be creating *Windows* documents for which you use several *Windows* application programs. One is your word processor, another is a graphics program. Yet another is a spreadsheet. However, you only see the document. When you double-click on a graph in the document, your graphics program will leap into action and load the graphic so you can alter it. When you double-click on some text, the word processor will pop up in a similar manner. Unlike DDE, you won't have to launch each of these applications before you begin working on your "compound document."

Wow! That sounds great. And it can be. But all those features come at a cost. The underlying program (*Windows*) has to know how to manipulate your PC's resources exquisitely well. That includes doing a massive job of memory management.

How Does *Windows* Use Memory?

Windows uses memory quite differently in the three different modes. Here is a quick once-over of how it does so.

Real Mode

Real mode *Windows* is quite simple (see Figure 21.11). It runs in lower memory. If you also load an expanded memory manager (EMM), you can run a DOS application (one at a time) under *Windows* and it will be able to use EMS memory. That can be important, for after you have gotten through loading DOS and *Windows* into lower memory, there is not a lot of room left for any DOS applications. Most large *Windows* applications will simply not load in this configuration.

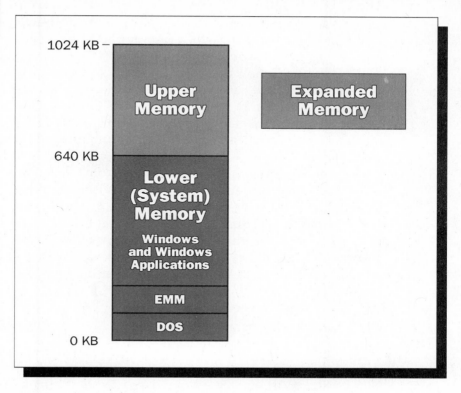

Figure 21.11.   How *Windows* 3.0 uses memory: Real mode.

Standard (286) Mode

Standard mode *Windows* was written to run on a class 3 PC. So it assumes that you may not have any upper memory RAM (no UMBs). It uses lower and extended memory for itself and all *Windows* applications. You may have loaded an EMM, in which case any DOS application you run under *Windows* will have access to that memory. *Windows* will not use it, nor will your *Windows* applications.

Once you get up to a machine that can run *Windows* in Standard mode, you have enough PC to do some serious work under *Windows*. In fact, this is the mode that runs *Windows* fastest, about 10 percent to 20 percent faster than 386-enhanced mode for the same hardware.

Still, if you want to run a DOS application, you will find that all your *Windows* applications (and most of *Windows* itself) get swapped out when you launch the DOS application program. That means those other programs are suspended.

Windows can multitask *Windows* applications, but at this level it still cannot time-share the PC with a DOS application and anything else. That only comes with 386-enhanced mode.

Figure 21.12 shows how *Windows* 3.0 uses memory when it and some *Windows* applications are running in Standard mode. The different shading levels indicate that while *Windows* and its applications are not using any upper or expanded memory, if the hardware can supply RAM of those kinds, any DOS applications you plan to run under *Windows* will be able to access it.

When you launch a DOS application from this mode of *Windows*, you get a memory map something like the one shown in Figure 21.13. Here you see that almost all of *Windows* and all its applications have been removed from the PC. Just a small stub called DOSX and a small program called the switcher remain. Their total size is about 45KB. This allows the DOS application to have almost as much lower memory to work in as it would have if you had exited from *Windows* before you started the application.

386-Enhanced Mode

Things get really interesting when you get to enhanced mode. Here *Windows* is using the full power of the 386 CPU. It runs DOS applications in V86 sessions (Virtual-8086 sessions; see Chapter 11 for explanation of this concept), virtualizes all the hardware, and thus can allow them to run simultaneously and in small windows.

Windows in this mode puts almost all of its own program code into extended memory, outside of all the V86 sessions. Each such session is reduced in size, though, by any TSRs you may have loaded before you started up *Windows*. This is one reason you are encouraged to run most of your TSRs in separate windows. The exceptions are things like disk cache programs that must be constantly in RAM, ready to work, and which need to be accessible to all programs.

Windows runs as a demand-paged virtual-memory operating environment. The word virtual here means that it offers the applications running under it not only the RAM that is free (lower, upper, and extended lumped together, with expanded ignored), but also some virtual memory (see Figure 21.14). Programs get to act as if they could use all of that space as if it were real, physical RAM in your PC.

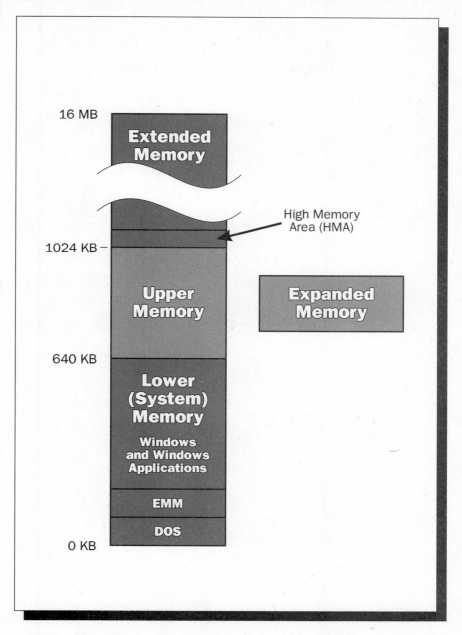

Figure 21.12. How *Windows* 3.x uses memory: standard (286) mode (running a Windows application).

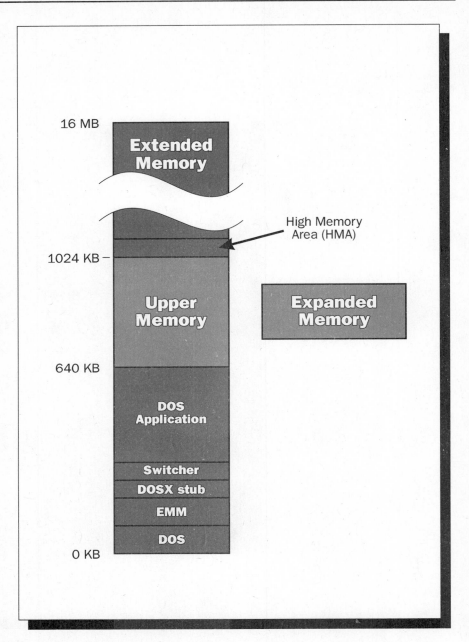

Figure 21.13. How *Windows* 3.x uses memory: standard (286) mode (running a DOS application).

Virtual memory simply means that *Windows* creates a swap file on the disk where it can stash chunks of programs or data that must be removed from memory to make room for other programs or data. It first tries to swap those items to extended memory, but when it runs out of that, then it swaps to the disk.

The amount of virtual memory you can have is limited by several things. First, you get to choose whether to install a permanent swap file or ask *Windows* to create and use temporary ones (and delete them afterwards). You want *Windows* to use a permanent swap file if either (1) you are going to be running *Windows* almost all the time, or (2) you can afford to commit that much space on your disk to this purpose permanently.

If you use a permanent swap file, your amount of virtual memory will be equal to the size of that file. You may make the swap file as large as you like, but at most, your virtual memory will grow to be three times as much as your actual, physical RAM.

If you choose to have *Windows* use a temporary swap file, these same comments apply. But now one extra one is added. The size of the temporary swap file will be limited by *Windows* to the smaller of two sizes. One is the size it must have to hold what it wants to swap out. The other is an amount it determines is reasonable for your system.

Normally, it wants to leave you (and itself) at least half a megabyte of free space on your disk drive. And it will never take more than half of the free space, no matter how large it is, nor will it ever take more than three times as many bytes of disk space as you have bytes of (lower plus upper plus extended) RAM. If *Windows* finds less than 1MB of free disk space (and no permanent swap file), it simply won't run.

When you install *Windows*, you must choose whether or not to create a permanent swap file. You also can create or delete the permanent swap file later on. Since that file must use a single contiguous region of your hard disk, you will probably want to defragment your disk before allowing *Windows* to create a permanent swap file. Also, be aware that you cannot put a permanent swap file on a logical volume created by an on-the-fly file compression program like *Stacker*, *DoubleSpace*, or *Superstor*, nor on a RAM disk. The temporary swap file can be fragmented and it can be placed on any disk, including a RAM disk (although Microsoft usually recommends against putting the swap file on a RAM disk).

This is the only mode in which *Windows* uses UMBs if they are available. It will build its "translation buffers" in a UMB. For non-networked PCs, those tables are at most 8KB; on networked PCs the maximum size is 24KB.

Generally, you will get the best results if you leave that much space in upper memory (in free RAM in a UMB). If you don't, then *Windows* will have to put those translation buffers into lower memory, thus reducing the amount of free RAM available in all DOS windows.

Like *QEMM, Windows* 3.x is a VCPI server. It is also a DPMI server (and so is QEMM for versions from 5.11 on). That means it can run several DOS-extended programs without any interference between them. But that only applies to DPMI-aware DOS-extended programs.

GeoWorks

GeoWorks is another multitasking, windowing operating environment that runs on top of DOS. Like *Windows,* and unlike *DESQview,* it has a graphical user interface. In fact, it is perhaps the nicest looking of the three.

It also offers a full WYSIWYG (**W**hat **Y**ou **S**ee **I**s **W**hat **Y**ou **G**et) interface that uses the same scalable font mechanism to write to both the screen and printer. *Windows*, in version 3.1, is able to do this also, but only for *TrueType* fonts. Many people who were using *Windows* before version 3.1 have rather extensive collections of fonts in other formats than *TrueType*. If they want to get the advantage of a full WYSIWYG interface, they must either use a third-party utility program that adds WYSIWYG to fonts that *Windows* cannot scale (such as Adobe *Type Manager* or Zenographics *SuperPrint*), or get one that can convert their old fonts to the new, *TrueType* format.

GeoWorks is available bundled with a single application program or with a full collection of applications (see Figure 21.15). The basic GUI can be used by any programmer who wishes to do so, or it will be once the GeoWorks company releases the software development kits it has long promised, but not yet delivered.

GeoWorks is lean, mean, and, relatively speaking, fast. It provides full preemptive multitasking for *GeoWorks*-aware applications. It can run, albeit a bit slowly, on class 1 PCs with as little as 512KB of RAM. (In such a PC it runs slowly, but still a good deal quicker than *Windows* can, and it can do more at the same time.)

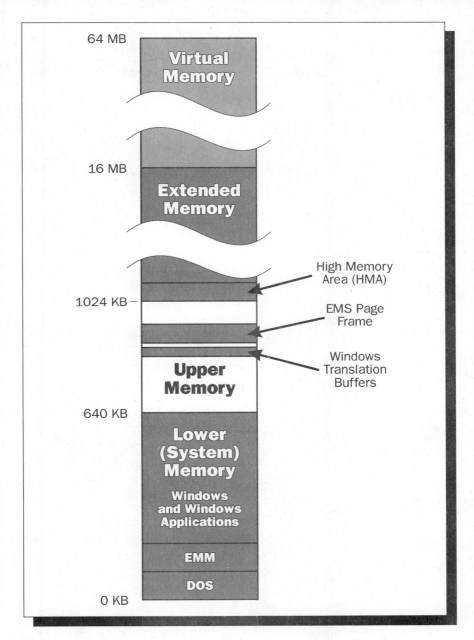

Figure 21.14. How *Windows* 3.x uses memory: 386-enhanced mode.

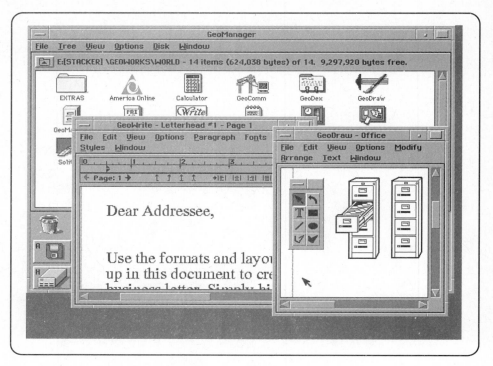

Figure 21.15. This is *GeoWorks* Ensemble.

Preemptive multitasking means that *GeoWorks* does not give more than a brief time slice to each program before it forces the PC to move on to the next program. *Windows* uses the same strategy for DOS applications, but for *Windows* applications, it uses a much softer approach.

Windows applications are supposed to be responsible, and to check with *Windows* several times per second to see if there is some other program that needs some of the CPU's time and attention. Unfortunately, a great many of them fall down in this regard. When *CorelDRAW!* is redrawing the screen or printing a document, for example, it will simply not allow you to switch away to another program.

Unsurprisingly, *GeoWorks* will run faster and do even more if you give it more RAM and let it run on a faster, more powerful PC. What is surprising is that it can do so much, even to the extent of providing good interprocess protections, on a mere class 1 PC.

GeoWorks has the most flexible and capable mechanism for using your PC's memory and storage. It will swap things to EMS memory until that runs out, then to XMS memory, and finally to disk storage.

In many ways, *GeoWorks* is wonderful. It does, however, have some drawbacks.

The one, outstanding drawback is the present lack of good *GeoWorks* applications. Outside of the very nice small applications that come bundled with the operating environment, there are no true *GeoWorks* applications on the market. That may change fairly soon, but until it does, this will be the greatest drawback to using *GeoWorks.*

It cannot run a DOS application. Well it can, but when it does, all the rest of *GeoWorks* and all *GeoWorks* applications shut down for the duration.

And, if you want to task switch between that DOS application and some *GeoWorks* ones, you will have to supplement *GeoWorks* with some other task switcher. (The DOS 5 or 6 task switchers, DOSSHELL or TaskMAX, work just fine.)

Managing the Managers

All three of the operating environments just discussed, *DESQview, Windows,* and *GeoWorks,* do a fine job of managing the resources in your PC. They make it possible for you to do many things that are simply impossible using only DOS. But they also are very general programs. Your needs are specific.

Why This Is Important

You deserve a personal computing work environment that works the way you want it to. It is, after all, your *personal* computer. To achieve this, you will have to do some work managing the managers you "hire" to work in your PC.

How to Do It

The specific details of how you can improve on the memory management of *DESQview, Windows,* and *GeoWorks* vary. That means you must look at each in turn. *DESQview* had first turn last time around. This time, I'll start by considering *Windows.*

Windows

There are four essential system files that govern how *Windows* does its work. In addition, there may be many smaller initialization files (extension INI) and configuration files (extension CFG) for different programs, plus the program information files (PIFs) that are used to launch non-*Windows* applications.

The four essential system files are your CONFIG.SYS and AUTOEXEC.BAT files, and two files that are specific to *Windows.* The latter files go by the names WIN.INI and SYSTEM.INI.

> Before you begin to edit any of these critical files, make sure you have a copy of them as they are now, just in case something goes wrong. One good way to do this is to use a program like Phil Katz's PKZIP program to create a single file holding all the INI, CFG, PIF, and GRP files in your *Windows* directory. Use the date as part of the name.
>
> By compressing these files (which is one of the things that PKZIP does) and combining them into one file (the other thing PKZIP is good for), you will have a small enough file that you can afford to leave it on your disk, and you know all the pieces of it will stay together. Also, make a backup of that file so you can UNZIP it on another machine if you have to, and so you don't lose your customizations of *Windows* if your hard disk crashes.

Editing these four files is such an important task that *Windows* provides you with a special editor for just that purpose. Unfortunately, Microsoft doesn't tell you about it. Go to the File menu in the Program Manager. Click on NEW, and accept the default of New Item. Now select Browse. Go to the SYSTEM subdirectory under your *Windows* directory. There you will find SYSEDIT.EXE. Load that, give it a descriptive title (e.g., SysEdit), and click on OK. You now have a new icon in one of your program groups (whichever one was highlighted when you first clicked on NEW).

When you double-click on this icon, you get the screen shown in Figure 21.16. You can bring any of the four files to the front by clicking on the visible portion of its window. Edit it as you would in Notepad. Then Save the changes using the options on the File menu.

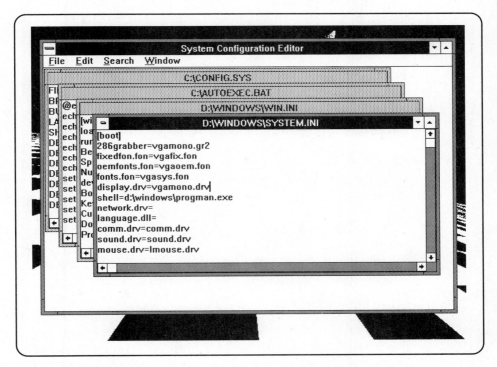

Figure 21.16. *Windows* 3.0: SysEdit allows editing of all four critical system files.

All the *Windows* INI files are plain, ASCII text files, just like CONFIG.SYS and AUTOEXEC.BAT. The INI files also all have a common structure, unlike CONFIG.SYS and AUTOEXEC.BAT. (This structure is the same as the menu files that one can use in a CONFIG.SYS file under DOS 6.)

Each INI file consists of one or more sections. A section is headed by a section label. That is a line that begins in the very first column with a left bracket, has a name for the section, and then a right bracket. For example, the first section in SYSTEM.INI is usually titled [boot].

Any line that begins with a semicolon in the first position is treated as a remark (it is ignored). All the other lines in that section have the form of a definition, much like the lines in the DOS environment. One difference is that in an INI file, usually capitalization does not matter.

Each definition can be thought of as a keyword being equated to a value. Often the values are simple TRUE/FALSE, YES/NO, or ON/OFF choices. Sometimes they will be expressed in letters or words, other times in numbers (either an amount, or with 1=TRUE, YES, or ON and 0=FALSE, NO, or OFF).

WIN.INI

Most of WIN.INI is concerned with controlling the appearance of *Windows* and how it works with various peripheral devices. So mostly, it is not important for memory management.

There is an exception to this. *Windows* applications are either able to create and use their own separate INI file, or they may add a section to WIN.INI and use that. When an application does insert its initialization information into your WIN.INI, you need to examine it to see if there are any memory-management implications. (And don't forget to examine all the other application-created INI files in your *Windows* directory, or in any directory on your PATH.)

For example, *Word for Windows* puts its INI information into WIN.INI. In its section, headed [Microsoft Word] you may find a line that starts EMMLimit= followed by a number. That specifies the maximum amount of memory that program is allowed to use when it starts up. If you cannot start WinWord because you haven't enough free memory, try lowering this value. The default value (what is used if this line is not present) is about 750. (This is an amount in KB, but don't include KB on that line. Just give the number.)

Microsoft *Excel* may put as many as 17 lines in its section of WIN.INI. Only EMMReserved and SwapSize have an obvious effect on memory. The default for each is 128 (which means 128KB). You may lower them if you are running low on free memory.

SYSTEM.INI

The SYSTEM.INI file is concerned with more fundamental issues. So many of its entries have some impact on memory usage. The principal ones to be concerned with are in the [386Enh] section. This only applies to you if you are going to be running *Windows* in enhanced mode. That is the only time *Windows* uses upper memory, and that is where the most frequent problems of memory management arise.

The relevant lines from that section may look something like this:

```
[386Enh]
DMABufferIn1MB=No
DMABufferSize=16
DualDisplay=No
EMMExclude=B000-C7FF
EMMInclude=C800-DFFF
EMMPageFrame=E000
EMMSize=655360
HighFloppyRead=Yes
IgnoreInstalledEMM=No
MapPhyAddress=
NoEMMDriver=False
ReservePageFrame=True
System Rom Break Point=True
```

Of these, the most critical ones are the first three that begin with the letters EMM. While that sounds like expanded memory, they really are referring to *upper memory **segment** addresses*.

These lines are just like the corresponding parameters you may have to give to any memory manager. Like all semiautomatic memory managers, *Windows* attempts to see which upper addresses are in use and which are free, and it decides on a place to put the EMS page frame. These three lines let you tell it which segments to include, which to exclude, and where you want the page frame. The fourth EMM line specifies the page frame size. Normally you'll use the default value unless you want the effect of FRAME=NONE, in which case set EMMSIZE=0.

In the sample shown above, the monochrome video buffer region is being excluded (along with the CGA or color text region and that for a video option ROM). The page frame is forced to start at E0000h, and the region from just after the video option ROM to the start of the page frame is being declared as open and available for UMBs.

Configuration (CFG) Files

Unlike INI files, CFG files are usually binary in nature. That means they must be created and maintained by the application they support. Don't try to edit them.

Program Information Files (PIFs)

Windows applications know how to tell *Windows* about all the resources they are going to need. DOS applications have no such ability. That is why the mechanism of PIF files was created.

A PIF file points to an application and contains all the things *Windows* wants to know about that application so it can run it most effectively. If you start a DOS application for which there is no corresponding PIF, *Windows* uses one called —DEFAULT.PIF.

Windows provides a special tool for editing PIF files. And nicely enough, it installs an icon for the PIF Editor in your Accessories or Main group.

The appearance of the PIF Editor screen depends on which mode of *Windows* you are currently running. Different things are relevant in standard and enhanced modes. Figure 21.17 shows what the PIF Editor screen looks like in standard (or real) mode. Figure 21.18a shows the main screen for enhanced mode, while Figure 21.18b shows the advanced options screen that is only available in that mode.

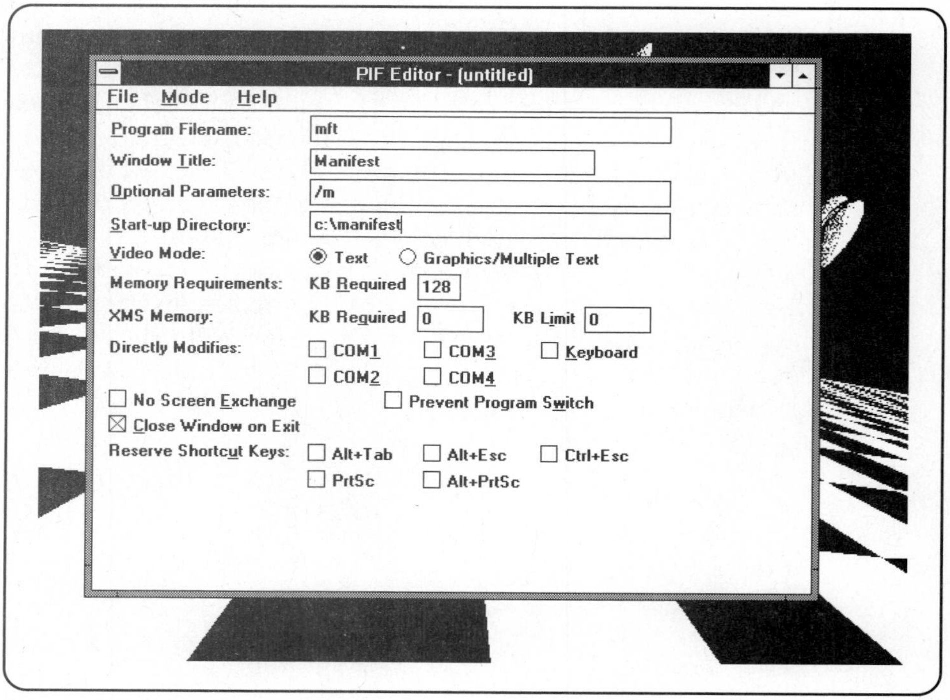

Figure 21.17. *Windows* 3.0: PIF Editor for 286 system.

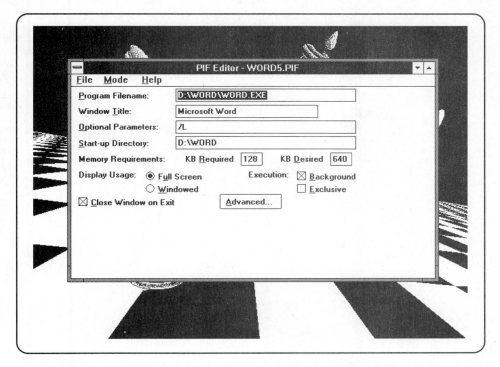

Figure 21.18a. *Windows* 3.0: PIF Editor for 386 system, standard options.

It is possible to change the mode of the PIF Editor without changing *Windows'* mode. It will start up in the same mode as *Windows*, but there is a menu item to set it to the other one if you like.

You may find it helpful to edit the PIFs for any DOS applications you run often. Don't forget to look at —DEFAULT.PIF also, as that one may get used even more often. To create a new PIF, simply copy —DEFAULT.PIF to a new name and edit it.

In the standard mode PIF screen, you get to specify how many KB of free *extended* memory (really XMS memory) must be available to load this application, and how much, at most, to let this application have. In the advanced screen, you can specify the same things (but you can use different numbers), and you can also specify the amount of simulated EMS memory the application may use. Plus, for all four memory allocations, you can specify if they should be locked. Specifying yes will keep the application in memory all the time. That helps it run faster, but it can profoundly degrade the rest of your system's operation.

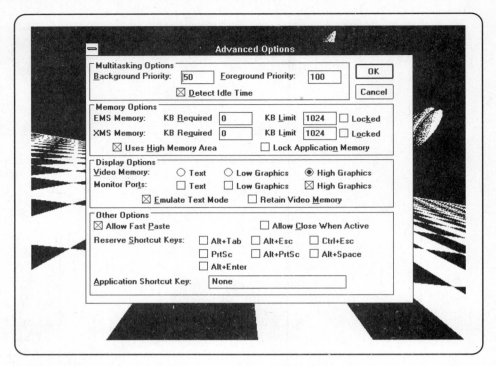

Figure 21.18b. *Windows* 3.0: PIF Editor for 386 system, advanced options.

The video-memory options allow you to specify how much simulated video-image-buffer memory to set aside for this application. The checkbox to Retain Video Memory tells *Windows* that even if the application is currently using only a text-mode display, keep all the specified memory for it to use later on. This is normally only needed if you are running out of memory and fear that some other application might grab what this one needs, and thus keep this one from going into graphics mode.

The three terms text mode, low graphics, and high graphics, can be translated roughly to 16KB, 32KB, and 128KB. The amounts may vary with the capabilities of your particular video display adapter.

DESQview

In *DESQview*, you must set up each application you are going to run. As you do so, you have the opportunity to set various parameters that tell *DESQview* how to run it. These include some that affect memory usage.

Before you start tweaking those values, it is a good idea to see how much memory you have available in your present setup. Go to the Open Window menu. Open the Memory Status window (the usual keystrokes for this are M followed by s, or you can use the "point and shoot" method to select it).

The Memory Status window will look similar to the window shown in Figure 21.5. Notice that the first line of numbers is given in bytes, while the other two lines are given in kilobytes.

The critical entries to focus on are the two lower numbers in the right-hand column. These give the maximum size program you can load into conventional memory, and the maximum size of any program you can load into expanded memory and page into lower memory.

> Actually, you will only be able to load a program that is a little bit smaller than these numbers indicate. You must allow approximately 10KB to 12KB per program for *DESQview's* overhead.

Knowing these numbers, you now are ready to add a new program to *DESQview's* menu, or to modify the parameters of one that is already there. From the *DV* main menu, select "Open Window." You'll get a screen like that in Figure 21.19. Now select "Add a Program." Figure 21.20 shows the Add a Program screen you get next.

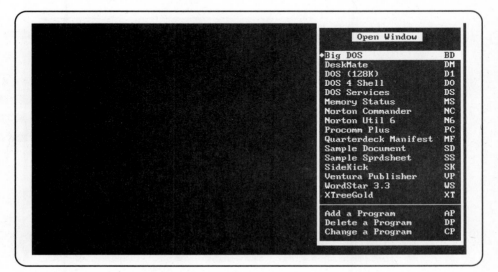

Figure 21.19.   The *DESQview* Open Window menu.

Once you've chosen a program to add (or you could have chosen one already on the Open Window menu that you wished to modify), you'll be shown the main "Change a Program" screen (see Figure 21.21). Figure 21.22 shows the additional screen you can go to if you need to set up some of the Advanced options for a program.

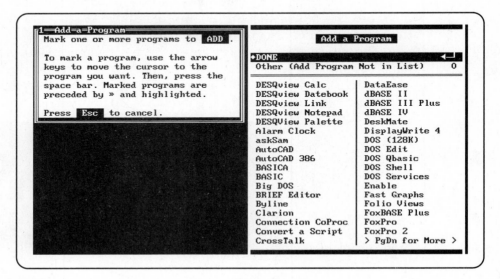

Figure 21.20. The *DESQview* Add a Program screen.

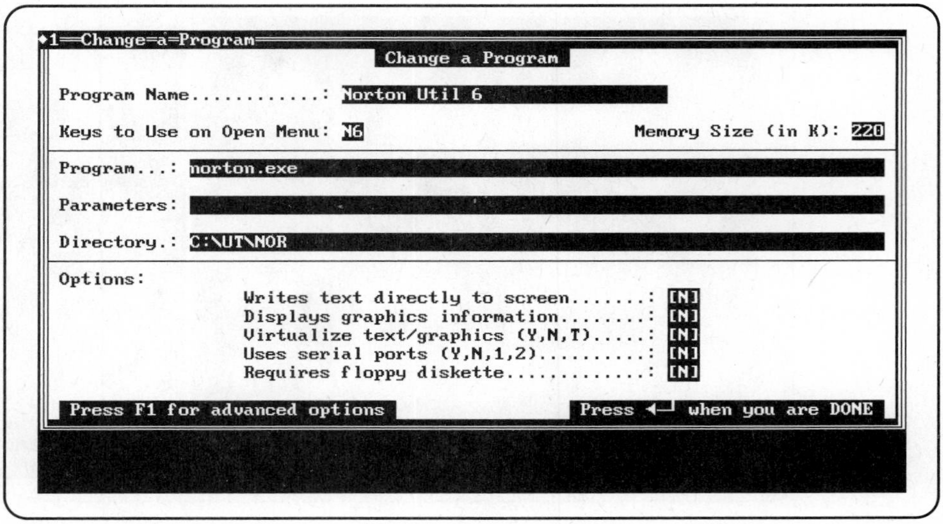

Figure 21.21. The *DESQview* Change a Program screen.

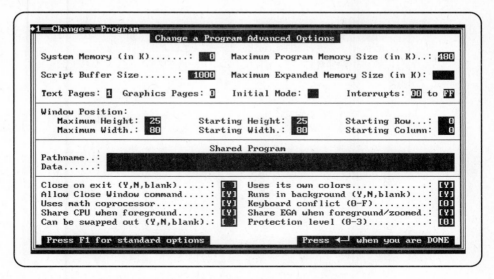

Figure 21.22. The *DESQview* Advanced Options screen.

You will recognize most of the numbers you will be filling in on these screens from the corresponding entries in the *Windows* PIF Editor. Both *DESQview* and *Windows* must face very similar issues in managing memory for multiple programs, so it is no surprise that their program setup screens ask for similar information.

In fact, *DESQview* uses files that very closely resemble the *Windows* PIF files. They are files with the extension DVP, and there will be one of them for each entry on the Open a Window menu. (DVP stands for *DESQview* **P**IF.)

GeoWorks

Now consider how *GeoWorks* manages memory and how you manage it. This case is a little bit different from the other two operating environments, inasmuch as *GeoWorks* is only going to be running the *GeoWorks* applications that were shipped with it. So it already knows all about the resources they require.

In Figure 21.23, you see the *GeoWorks* Preferences menu. This allows you to select one of twelve areas for customization. This is very similar to the *Windows* Control Panel.

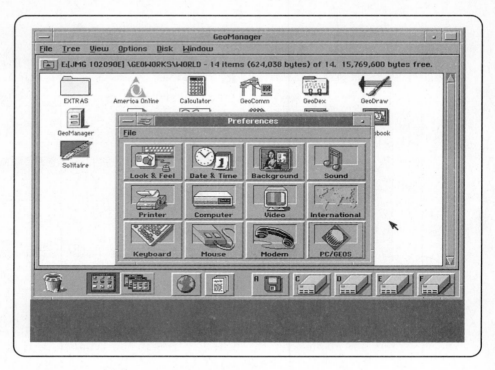

Figure 21.23. The *GeoWorks* Preferences menu.

The menu choices that most affect memory usage are the Computer and PC-Geos ones. Figure 21.24 shows you the Computer dialog box, and Figure 21.25 shows the PC-Geos dialog box.

Usually, the entries on these screens will be close to optimum. But, if you are having trouble with *GeoWorks,* you could try different values to see if they help. In particular, the number of handles may need to be increased. (That will be a surprise, no doubt, as it already seems like a very high number. Compared to the FILES setting in your CONFIG.SYS file, no doubt it is.)

If you are running SHARE—and you really ought to if you value your data—then you may need to increase its parameters also. There are two numbers you can give to SHARE. One is the maximum number of files to keep track of. The other is the maximum number to have locked at once. The default values for these are 2048 and 20. Good values to try are 4096 and 50.

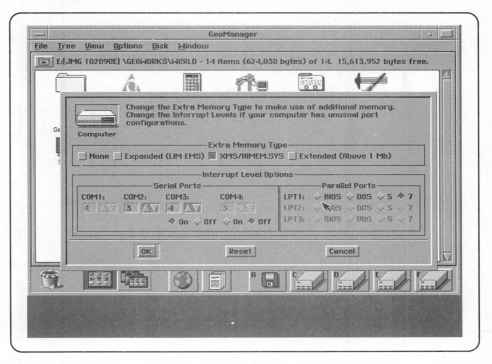

Figure 21.24. The *GeoWorks* Preferences/Computer dialog box.

That means that in your CONFIG.SYS or AUTOEXEC.BAT file, when you invoke SHARE, do so with the added information /F:4096 /L:50 put after the name SHARE. Remember to include the full name of SHARE, namely SHARE.EXE, if you are loading it with an INSTALL statement in your CONFIG.SYS file.

Be Sensible

This chapter is all about how memory management can be done for you, and how you can intervene to help improve the results. Before leaving this topic, there are some commonsense suggestions you'll want to consider.

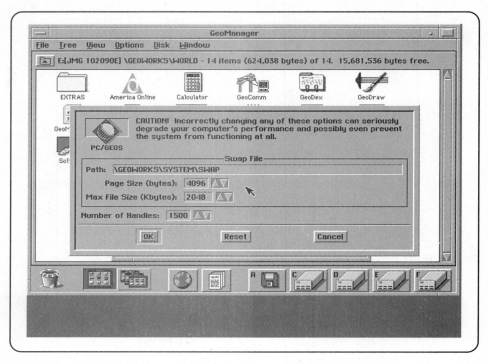

Figure 21.25. The *GeoWorks* Preferences/PC-Geos dialog box.

What Does It Mean to Optimize?

Literally, optimizing your PC means to get the very best conceivable setup for it. The *very* best. With all the best of intentions, that can be hard to do. And it may not be worth doing. In fact, it may be worth *not* doing it. Consider why that might be so.

Can a Program Do That for You?

There are many places you can change any PC's memory configuration, and if you load even half a dozen TSRs and device drivers into upper memory, and if you have two or three separate regions (UMBs) into which they may be loaded, the number of possibilities to consider rapidly approaches the astronomical.

Programs like OPTIMIZE (from Quarterdeck Office Systems) brag about how many cases they are examining. You surely don't want or need to look at each one yourself.

Actually, you are a lot smarter than even the best of these programs. They just compute all the possible arrangements for your TSRs and device drivers and try every one. You could look at most of those arrangements and throw them out at a glance as being highly implausible. So you would end up checking a lot fewer and, no doubt, coming out with just as good a result.

Also, while a program like OPTIMIZE (or MAXIMIZE from Qualitas, or SmartMove from Quadtel) can try a huge number of possibilities, it may not even try what actually would be the best arrangement. This can happen because any such program is bound to be working with limited information.

The issue of TSR size was discussed earlier in the chapter. You found out there that it is not always easy to know what size a TSR actually will be, either at its maximum or in its final, resident state. Testing it in low memory may give very misleading results.

Furthermore, some of the "optimization" programs attempt to find a better order for the DEVICE lines in your CONFIG.SYS file and for the TSR invocation lines in your AUTOEXEC.BAT file. They may not know about some interprogram dependencies that will make some of their proposed arrangements most imprudent, if not actually harmful.

Should You Try to Do It Yourself?

So what should you do? Must you forgo the benefits of those programs and do it all yourself? Not at all. The best advice, usually, is to let these programs take their best shot at optimizing your system.

Then you step in and tweak things. Do experiments. Try out different orders for things. Or, simply tell the optimizer not to touch certain programs and then let it try again.

But please be sensible. Remember, your goal is not actually to produce the very best fit for your TSRs. Your goal is, presumably, to do some computing. Time you spend on optimizing is time you are not spending on computing. So settle for some reasonable approximation to the optimum solution.

Why Cutting It Too Close Can Be Very Bad

In fact, if you did find the very best possible solution, meaning that one which leaves you with the very least free memory in upper memory space, and the very most in lower memory space, you may have just built yourself a very large problem.

Remember that if you want to use *Windows* in 386-enhanced mode, it would like to find from 8KB to 24KB of upper memory free for its translation buffers. Denying it that room will force it to put them in lower memory, and that will take away a corresponding amount from every DOS window you open.

If you want to run *DESQview,* a similar caution is in order. In fact, it must be redoubled. Remember that *DESQview* likes to load most of itself into upper and high memory so as to open up a maximum amount of room in lower memory. You simply will be unable to open windows for programs that need a lot of RAM unless you let *DESQview* do these things. So be sure to load as few device drivers and TSRs as possible before you run *DESQview.*

Once you decide that you want some empty UMB space, it often makes your upper memory-management game short and sweet. After you get some reasonably good arrangement that leaves you whatever amount of free space you have determined you want, then run your multitasker and load all the rest of your TSRs into windows in that operating environment. This is good advice whether you are using *DESQview* or *Windows.*

Very likely, there will be some TSRs that you will want to load "under" certain application programs so that those programs will have the direct benefit of those TSRs. For others of your TSRs, you will merely want to load each of them in a window of its own.

If, for example, you have been loading *SideKick* so you could pop up its calendar, put *SideKick* in a window by itself. Pop up that window when you want access to the calendar.

But, if you have been loading a keyboard macro program to enhance some other application, you will want to load that application into a *DESQview* or *Windows* window using a batch file that first loads (also into that same window) the keyboard macro program. That way those macros take effect for that application. And the macro program doesn't take space in any windows where its effect is not needed.

Finally, if you cut things too close, you may find out, to your regret, that you have managed to make your system quite unstable. If any of the programs you so cleverly tucked into some tight space should happen to need a bit more RAM sometime, it could easily cause your system to hang in the middle of some critical job you were doing. Or, it could make the system unbootable altogether. That is hardly what you want after all that work you put in to make things "just so." Therefore, ***don't*** make things all that extremely "just so."

You May Need Help

Even with the information from this book and other sources, getting the most from your system often takes a lot of experimentation. If you have limited time, you may find it helpful to ask others what they have found works for them.

You may also become confused at some point. That happens even to experts. Asking others for help at such a point can be very illuminating, often not only to you, but also to the person you ask. Chapter 33 has some suggestions for how you can seek out helpful people.

A Recap

My, that was a large chapter. It covered a lot of territory. The unifying theme was how you can partially or totally automate setting up memory management for your PC.

First, you learned about programs that manage memory, but just for themselves. These include programs that have been built with overlays or those that load only part of the data they are working on at a time. At the other extreme are programs that contain a full-blown, real-mode virtual-memory manager.

Turning to the subject of managing memory on behalf of a collection of programs, you learned about a number of ways that those programs can be pushed around, whisked "off stage," and otherwise kept out of each other's way. This included a discussion of TSR managers, which often have the side benefit of insulating contentious TSRs, shell programs, and task-switching program managers from one another. It also included a discussion of loading device drivers and TSR programs "high" (into upper memory).

That often gives you all you need. But if you crave yet more, you may want to use a full multitasking, windowing operating environment. You learned a lot of details about the three most popular of these programs for DOS machines, *DESQview, Windows,* and *GeoWorks.*

The chapter ended with some pleas for exercising a little common sense. It is easy to get carried away with memory-management tweaking. Of course, if your idea of fun is telling your friends how you got an extra 17 bytes of free RAM last week . . . .

This completes this discussion of the principles and common practices of PC memory management. After a short self-test and a concise review of the options available to owners of PCs in various classes, you will move on to a somewhat wider, but less deep survey of the memory-management product marketplace.

A REVIEW OF MEMORY-MANAGEMENT PRINCIPLES

This completes the story of how PC memory works and how it can be managed. In this chapter, you can check your understanding in preparation for the practical applications in the chapters that follow.

This is the end of Part II, the largest part of this book. In it is a discussion of all the basic principles you need to understand in order to manage memory well in your PC. In addition to general principles, there are quite a few examples to show how those principles are applied in practice. Naturally, not every commercial product that might be useful is discussed in this part.

Now, before going on to a quick review of the options you have for your kind of PC, and then on to an equally quick survey of almost all the products on the market for PC memory management, you may want to take the following self-test. This will help you be sure that you have learned all of the most essential points (and some of the less vital ones) in the preceding seven chapters.

The self-test at the end of Chapter 14 did the same thing for Chapters 6 through 14. Between that test and this one you will have checked your understanding of all of Part II.

Another Self-Test

As always, you are on your honor here. Don't be too easy on yourself. Imagine you had to describe the answer to each question to someone who is just learning about memory management. If you cannot do so confidently, perhaps you need to review the indicated sections one more time.

On the other hand, nobody said you had to understand everything. You may simply choose to accept that, for now, you are less than confident about one or more of the following points. Then, if you run across a place where you need to understand that point, you can go back and review it.

You can use this test to help you find the relevant portions of the book, or you can use the Index. And remember that the Glossary (Appendix C) is a good place to look up a brief explanation of many of the key terms in this field.

1. Why might the owner of an IBM PC *not* want to install 640KB of lower memory? What kind of memory would that person be likely to add instead? (Review in the section titled "On the Motherboard—When You Shouldn't" in Chapter 15.)

2. Explain why RAM that is added on the motherboard is often more quickly accessible than RAM added on a plug-in card. (Review in the section titled "On the Motherboard—When You Should" in Chapter 15.)

3. In what way is RAM in an external hardware print spooler more beneficial than the same amount of RAM on the motherboard used by a software print spooler? (Review in the section titled "In a Peripheral Device" in Chapter 15.)

4. To reverse the question, in what situations is it better to have that RAM in the system unit? (Hint: Consider the benefits of possible shared uses for that RAM.) (Review in the section titled "In a Peripheral Device" in Chapter 15.)

5. What kind of RAM chip uses four to six transistors per bit to store information—SRAM, DRAM, or VRAM? (Review in the section titled "Kinds of Memory Chips" in Chapter 16.)

6. What kind of RAM chip uses only one transistor and a capacitor per bit—SRAM, DRAM, or VRAM? (Review in the section titled "Kinds of Memory Chips" in Chapter 16.)

7. What does it mean to *refresh* a DRAM, and why must you do it frequently? (Review in the section titled "Kinds of Memory Chips" in Chapter 16.)

8. What is special about VRAM? Where is it most used? (Review in the section titled "Kinds of Memory Chips" in Chapter 16.)

9. Why is *PROM* an oxymoron? What is the key benefit of any kind of PROM? (Review in the section titled "Kinds of Memory Chips" in Chapter 16.)

10. What is special about Flash memory? (Review in the section titled "Kinds of Memory Chips" in Chapter 16.)

11. What is *odd parity*? How is it used to protect data in RAM? (Review in the section titled "Reliability and Parity Bits" in Chapter 16.)

12. How much information can be stored in a 64K-by-8 RAM chip? What is the significance of the *by-8* part of its description? (Review in the sections titled "Chip Sizes" and "Chip Packages" in Chapter 16.)

13. How do a DIP and a SIMM differ? (Review in Chapter 2 and in the section titled "Chip Packages" in Chapter 16.)

14. What is meant by the "organization" of a RAM chip? (Review in the section titled "Chip Packages" in Chapter 16.)

15. When do you want a by-9 SIMM and when a by-8 one? (Review in the section titled "Chip Packages" in Chapter 16.)

16. What is a RAM chip's *access time*? Its *cycle time*? Which one is indicated by the information stamped on the chip? (Review in the section titled "Rated Chip Speed" in Chapter 16.)

17. Can you speed up your PC by simply putting in faster RAM chips? (Review in the section titled "Rated Chip Speed" in Chapter 16 and in the section titled "Memory Chip Speed Issues Revisited" in Chapter 17.)

18. How can you figure out what the "magic" amounts of RAM (to enable interleaved memory access) would be for your PC? (Review in the section titled "Interleaved Memory Access" in Chapter 16.)

19. How do *wait states* help you? At what cost? Can you alter how many your PC uses? How? (Review in the section titled "Memory Chip Speed Issues Revisited" in Chapter 17.)

20. If you plan to open your PC and insert some new RAM chips or modules, there are two very important precautions you need to take. Describe what you should do before opening the case. Describe what you must do *every* time you are about to reach inside the case. (Review in the section titled "Precautions to Avoid Zapping Memory Chips (or Anything Else in Your PC)" in Chapter 17.)

21. How can you decide how much *expanded* and how much *extended* memory you need to have in your PC? (Review in the section titled "Should I Add Extended or Expanded Memory?" in Chapter 18.)

22. What are some programs that use unmanaged *extended* memory? (Review in the section titled "Should I Add Extended or Expanded Memory?" in Chapter 18.)

23. What are some programs that use only XMS managed *extended* memory? (Review in the section titled "Should I Add Extended or Expanded Memory?" in Chapter 18.)

24. What are some programs that use EMS-compatible *expanded* memory? (Review in the section titled "Should I Add Extended or Expanded Memory?" in Chapter 18.)

25. How can the same RAM be made to appear as either EMS or XMS memory? Which class of PC must you have in order to do this? (Review in the section titled "Using Extra Memory Flexibly" in Chapter 18.)

26. Can the DOS-provided memory managers (HIMEM.SYS and EMM386.EXE, for *MS-DOS*) provide EMS and XMS memory in that flexible manner? (Review in the section titled "Using Extra Memory Flexibly" in Chapter 18.)

27. What kinds of RAM are managed by PC memory-management programs and what kinds are not? (Hint: RAM that is outside the system unit is one kind that is not.) (Review in the section titled "Managing Your Memory Resources—the Physical Task" in Chapter 19.)

28. What does it mean to *allocate* RAM and to *deallocate* it? Why is this useful? (Review in the section titled "Managing Your Memory Resources—the Logical Task" in Chapter 19.)

29. What are the DIP switches on an IBM PC used to indicate? How is an IBM PC/XT different? How are some XT clone PCs different still? (Review in the section titled "On the Motherboard—When You Shouldn't" in Chapter 15 and the section titled "DIP Switch Settings" in Chapter 20.)

30. What is the J18 jumper used for on an IBM PC/AT? (Review in the section titled "DIP Switch Settings" in Chapter 20.)

31. What memory-management choices can be expressed through a typical class 3 through 6 PC's setup program and stored in its configuration CMOS memory? (Review in the section titled "CMOS Setup Issues" in Chapter 20.)

32. What are the nine most commonly used types of statements in a CONFIG.SYS file that have an impact on memory usage? How does each of them affect memory usage? (Review in the section titled "Customizing Your PC via CONFIG.SYS" in Chapter 20.)

33. Give two reasons why the order of DEVICE statements in a CONFIG.SYS file may be significant. (Review in the section titled "Customizing Your PC via CONFIG.SYS" in Chapter 20.)

34. What kinds of information are typically recorded in the setup of a hardware EMS board? (Review in the section titled "Setting Up Expanded Memory Boards and Drivers" in Chapter 20.)

35. What other step must you take before the EMS memory on that board will be available to your programs? (Review in the section titled "Setting Up Expanded Memory Boards and Drivers" in Chapter 20.)

36. How can you reduce the amount of RAM used for copies of the DOS environment? Describe at least two different techniques (without including any batch files other than AUTOEXEC.BAT). (Review in the section titled "Customizing Your PC via AUTOEXEC.BAT" in Chapter 20.)

37. How can other batch files help you achieve this goal? (Review in the section titled "Customizing Your PC via AUTOEXEC.BAT" in Chapter 20.)

38. If you install a disk cache, are its benefits automatically available? (Review in the section titled "A Memory Cache Is Not a Disk Cache" in Chapter 14.)

39. If you install a RAM disk, are its benefits automatically available? (Review in the section titled "Making Good Use of a RAM Disk" in Chapter 20.)

40. If your answer to either number 38 or 39 was *no*, describe what else must be done. (Review in the section titled "Making Good Use of a RAM Disk" in Chapter 20.)

41. Describe at least four strategies for increasing free lower memory in your PC. (Review in the section titled "Some Tips on Maximizing Your Free RAM" in Chapter 20.)

42. Describe the idea behind *program code overlays* and *data segmentation.* How are they similar? How are they different? (Review in the section titled "Traditional Coping Strategies" in Chapter 21.)

43. What does a TSR manager do? (Review in the section titled "Making More Room by Moving Things Around (Launchers and Swappers)" in Chapter 21.)

44. What does a task-switching program manager do? (Review in the section titled "Making More Room by Moving Things Around (Launchers and Swappers)" in Chapter 21.)

45. How can loading a program high be helpful? Where does this mean the program will be placed? (Review in the section titled "Making More Room by Moving Things Around (Launchers and Swappers)" in Chapter 21.)

46. Which of the techniques you described for questions 43, 44, and 45 are supported by which versions of DOS? (Review in the section titled "Some Versions of DOS That Are Extra Helpful" in Chapter 21.)

47. What are the four sizes of a TSR? When do they matter? (Review in the section titled "Some Versions of DOS That Are Extra Helpful" in Chapter 21.)

48. What is *instancing* of a TSR? When is it important? (Review in the section titled "Third-Party Semiautomatic Memory Managers" in Chapter 21.)

49. What is *time sharing?* (Review in the section titled "The Magic of Time Sharing" in Chapter 21.)

50. How are *DESQview* and *Windows* similar? How are they different? (Review in the sections titled "DESQview" and "Windows" in Chapter 21.)

51. Which of them (*DESQview* or *Windows*) does *GeoWorks Ensemble* most closely resemble, and how? (Review in the section titled "GeoWorks" in Chapter 21.)

52. Why might you need to "manage" an automatic memory manager? (Review in the section titled "Managing the Managers" in Chapter 21.)

53. Which four files control how *Windows*, version 3.x, operates? (Review in the section titled "Managing the Managers" in Chapter 21.)

54. Which other files hold configuration and customization information for programs running under *Windows'* control? (Review in the section titled "Managing the Managers" in Chapter 21.)

55. Which files serve the same roles for *DESQview*? (Review in the section titled "Managing the Managers" in Chapter 21.)

56. Is total PC memory optimization possible? How? (Review in the section titled "Be Sensible" in Chapter 21.)

57. Is total PC memory optimization desirable? Why, or why not? (Review in the section titled "Be Sensible" in Chapter 21.)

If you are able to answer these questions and those at the end of Chapter 14 confidently, you are nearing wizard-level mastery of PC memory management. Congratulations!

Armed with this knowledge, you are ready to tackle the formidable array of memory-management products on the marketplace, to understand what each one does, and to decide whether or not it will be valuable to you. Naturally, your answers will depend a lot on what kind of PC you have and what you wish to accomplish.

The next part of this book quickly reviews the options for owners of various classes of PCs. The following part surveys the marketplace. The last part gives additional information that will be helpful, especially when, even with your newfound expertise, you run into a problem.

AN OVERVIEW
OF YOUR
OPTIONS

This part of the book presumes you know the concepts and language of PC memory management.

If you find that you don't understand some of what you read here, you may find the quick definitions in the MemInfo hypertext database on the diskette that accompanies this book will be all the help you need. If not, you can use the Index or Table of Contents to help you find the other sections of this book where the items you don't yet understand are explained in detail.

This part has three chapters—one each for owners of PCs in classes 1 and 2, classes 3 and 4, and classes 5 and 6. This separation reflects the differing kinds of memory management that are appropriate to each class of PC.

Not all possible memory-management options and tricks are mentioned here. This part focuses on some of the most popular and cost-effective. If you are interested in exploring the outer reaches of your universe of possibilities, you will find more options mentioned in Part IV. You will find others in magazines or stores from time to time. Analyzing each of them will be easiest if you understand all the principles described in Parts I and II.

After reviewing the options presented here, go on to Part IV where you will find a brief discussion of many of the products you might get to help you augment or manage your PC's memory. Part V includes a number of examples to show you explicitly how to implement memory management without upgrading your hardware. Finally, the information in Part V will help you when things don't go quite as well as you had expected.

23

FOR OWNERS OF PCs IN CLASS 1 OR 2

These PCs have the most limited options for memory management. But they do have some. This chapter gives a brief listing of them.

The PCs in classes 1 and 2 are the low end of the PC spectrum. Featuring an 8088 or 8086 processor, they can address no more than a megabyte of memory locations. The options for managing their memory and those for upgrading them are limited but not nonexistent.

Although all class 1 and 2 PCs have some limitations in common, others are unique to a particular model. Perhaps most important is whether yours is a more-or-less standard form factor PC, or whether it is housed in a proprietary case.

The most upgradeable PCs are those that come in either an XT-style or a "baby" AT-style desktop case. If yours is an original IBM *PC* or if it is a laptop, or has some other unusual case design, your add-in and upgrade options will be much more restricted.

Memory Management for PCs in Class 1

Class 1 PCs can have no more than 640KB of lower memory. If yours does not have even that much, the most important option for you is to bring it up to its maximum capability in this regard.

Getting Up to the Starting Line, and Then Some

Don't, however, rush out and buy new memory chips or an add-in memory card simply to get a full 640KB of RAM. Get something that will do even more for you. In particular, you can get a multifunction card that will give you more RAM, including LIM 4.0 EMS-compatible expanded memory, and additional ports and, if you don't already have one, a real-time clock.

Managing the Memory You Have

Let's assume you have just the 640KB of lower memory to work with, and perhaps some LIM 3.2 EMS memory. What can you usefully do with it? The answer to this depends on one more thing. Do you have a hard disk?

Class 1 PCs Without a Hard Disk

If you don't have a hard disk (as, for example, many portable and lap-top computers in class 1 do not), you may find the most useful memory-management trick is to create a small RAM disk out of some of your lower memory. Then copy COMMAND.COM to that RAM disk and SET the COMSPEC variable to point to it. Do this in your AUTOEXEC.BAT file and it will allow you to run programs from any floppy and never be prompted to Insert a system disk and strike any key when ready. (See Chapter 20 for details.)

You might even want to create a small disk cache in conventional memory. The difficulty with this is that if you make it very large at all, you will run out of room to run your application programs.

If, in addition to your 640KB of lower memory, you have some LIM 3.2 EMS-compatible expanded memory, you could create your RAM disk and disk cache there. That would allow you to make both the RAM disk and the cache much larger than would be prudent when they are created in lower memory, as in EMS memory they no longer compete with your DOS applications for RAM.

With a larger RAM disk, in addition to storing COMMAND.COM, you can store any small utility programs you use often. Change the DOS PATH to point there first.

You also can use a set of batch files, each one of which moves one of your major applications into the RAM disk and runs it from there. This could make your PC work much faster.

A few class 1 PCs have DOS and their major applications in ROM. The suggestions about a RAM disk above don't apply to them, except the part about putting utility programs there.

> A tip for users of floppy-only PCs: Don't think that making backups is not an issue for you. Your diskettes can fail, just as a hard disk can. Make multiple copies of any file you value. Even better, keep one copy in another location, well away from your PC.

Class 1 PCs with a Hard Disk

If you do have a hard disk, your most useful upgrade option may be to run a program like *AboveDISC+*. This will allow you to create simulated EMS memory, which can let you run many programs that cannot run with only 640KB of RAM to play with, or it will let programs you can run create larger spreadsheets or otherwise use some additional features.

Of course, you must also have a fair amount of patience. Disk-based EMS simulators are anything but speedy.

Be sure you are not loading up your lower memory with any unnecessary TSR programs or device drivers. You might find that a TSR manager program is your next most useful upgrade option. (That is one that can keep all your TSRs as RAM-images on disk until they are needed, and then bring them into RAM one at a time.)

Adding Things

There are some interesting memory-related items you may wish to add to your PC. The most obvious is a LIM 4.0 EMS hardware memory add-in card. That will upgrade your class 1 PC to class 2. If it also can map memory throughout upper memory space, get *QRAM*, *UMBPro*, or *386MAX* and you will be able to load programs into upper memory as easily as your friends who have much more powerful PCs.

If you cannot find such an EMS card, or if you are sure you only want upper memory and will never want EMS memory, you could get a *MegaMizer* from V Communications. This includes both added (upper) memory and a memory-management program.

There are many other ways you could enhance your PC. But before you spend much money doing so, consider actually converting it into a substantially higher class of PC. Compare that with simply getting rid of your present PC and buying a new one. You may be surprised to find out how economically either of these can be done.

Significant Upgrades

There used to be a lot of advertisements for add-in processor upgrades targeted at your PC. Intel used to make an *Inboard 386/PC*, which took an *IBM PC* all the way up to a 16MHz, class 5 PC. A less ambitious option was the Orchid *Tiny Turbo 286* card. This raised such a PC to class 3. However, both of these and many similar products are no longer available. It simply is no longer cost effective to do that sort of upgrade.

A better choice is to replace the motherboard. You can now get 386SX motherboards for what XT motherboards used to cost just a year or two ago. Moving up to a 486 is not out of the question. If you do choose a motherboard upgrade, go as far as you can afford to go. The advantages of moving into at least class 5 are substantial.

You may need to replace your PC's case and power supply at the same time you replace the motherboard. Before you can install any AT-style plug-in cards you will have to be sure your case is the standard AT height (which is taller than XT height), or they may not fit. (By the time you decide you are ready to do this much upgrading, you may wish to consider other options. Be sure to read the last section in this chapter before you buy anything more for your PC.)

Memory Management for PCs in Class 2

A class 2 PC already has either LIM 4.0 EMS memory or upper memory created from shadow RAM. This is in addition to the lower 640KB of RAM it probably has. (For some purposes, it actually would be better if it did not have the full 640KB of lower memory installed. This is discussed shortly.)

Managing the Memory You Have

If your PC has a hardware LIM 4.0 EMS expanded memory card, you'll want to load the EMM program that came with the EMS memory board. That will give you EMS memory, but no upper memory blocks in which you could load programs. (If you are willing to give up the page frame, *UMBPro* will use that RAM for one 64KB UMB and help you load programs there.)

To do that you also will have to load a memory manager of some sort. *UMBPro*, *QRAM*, and *386MAX* are three good ones for this purpose.

If your PC creates EMS memory out of motherboard memory, you could load either the EMM that came with the motherboard, or use a program like *UMBPro*, *QRAM*, or *386MAX* that understands your motherboard's chip set. You may need to specify in your system setup that you want the motherboard chip set to create EMS memory, or one of the latter programs may be able to direct it to do so for you.

(*UMBPro* understands more brands of chip set, but if *QRAM* or *386MAX* understands yours, do you care? Just be sure to find out which chip set you have before you buy your memory manager.)

Naturally, you won't get as much from these programs on a class 2 PC as you would on one in class 3 or 4, as your class 2 PC cannot address any locations beyond 1,024KB (1MB), and so you can't have a High Memory Area (HMA). That means you won't be able to use DOS=HIGH in your CONFIG.SYS file, though you could use DOS=UMB.

The foregoing suggestions are all aimed at ways you might get some upper memory into which you could load TSRs and device drivers. That will let you run larger programs in your lower memory.

Alternatively, once you have created some upper memory (or even if you choose not to), you can make very effective use of the lower memory and the LIM 4.0 EMS memory you have by running *DESQview*. First, though, try to disable as much of your lower memory as you can. Here is a real case of "Less is more." (See Chapters 15 and 20 for details.)

Some class 2 PCs can make RAM available anywhere in upper memory. Most cannot. You can only create UMBs where you have RAM. If you have empty upper memory spaces that you are unable to fill with RAM, you may wish to consider adding a means to do so.

Adding Things

The *MegaMizer* card and software, for example, will let you create upper memory blocks (UMBs) anywhere you have empty upper memory space. This is useful only if your present means of creating EMS and upper memory is inadequate (but this is not at all an uncommon situation).

An even more common item to add to a class 2 PC is more RAM. You already have some way to support EMS memory, so add more of it. This means you can create a larger disk cache and/or RAM disk, and it makes *DESQview* run better. Aside from disabling lower memory, adding more EMS memory is the single most powerful way to add power to your PC.

Before you go much farther in upgrading your PC, consider your options for changing your PC altogether. Also look at the remarks at the very end of this chapter.

Significant Upgrades

All the remarks listed above for class 1 PCs apply here. You can jump to a much higher class of PC quite economically by a simple motherboard change. You may find, however, that you will then want to spend even more on upgrading your hard disk to one that works as fast as your new motherboard.

You will be able to move your video card, your floppy disk drives, and (if you don't feel compelled to upgrade it) your hard disk to the new configuration. That allows you to create a much more powerful PC with a minimal expenditure.

On the other hand, if you end up replacing or upgrading every part of your PC, you could most likely have bought a whole new system for less money. Think ahead a bit. If this looks like where you're headed, go there directly. That means you can sell your present PC or give it to someone else in your organization or family.

Class 1 and 2 PCs Are Not Obsolete

Some people look down on these PCs, just because there are now others in higher classes that can do so much more. Remember, these PCs still can do all the wonderful things they ever could before.

You might not imagine that anyone would want your old clunker. Think again. Many charitable organizations cannot afford a computer at all, yet they desperately need one. Consider giving your old machine to them. You may save more in taxes than you could have gotten in cash.

Even if everyone in this country who could use a PC already had one at least as good as yours, there are many would-be buyers in some other country that would absolutely love your PC, no matter what kind it is. Some brokers specialize in buying up old PCs here and shipping them abroad.

Whatever you have, you can upgrade it to a level where you will be satisfied with its performance, or you can sell or donate it to someone who would be delighted to use it. Which you choose will depend on your needs and your budget.

In any case, don't sell your present PC short. It is as powerful as many mainframe computers were in the 1960s!

24

FOR OWNERS OF
PCs IN CLASS 3 OR 4

These mid-range PCs have some very significant options for memory management. They also can be upgraded in several ways. Here's a rundown of some of those options.

These classes of PCs represent the middle of the spectrum. Until very recently they were the standard for most business computing. They have now been supplanted almost completely in the U.S. by the newer, more powerful PCs in classes 5 and 6, but they are still in wide use elsewhere in the world.

These older PCs are still quite powerful machines. And they do have some very interesting memory-management options.

When it comes to upgrading one of these PCs, as with those in classes 1 and 2, a very significant issue is the form factor of the PC. If yours is a desktop or tower unit, very likely upgrading it will be quite simple. If it is a laptop or portable, your options will be much more limited.

Memory Management for PCs in Class 3

A class 3 PC has an 80286 processor, some lower RAM, and perhaps some extended RAM. You might think that it would have 640KB of lower memory installed as a matter of course. That turns out not to be the case.

Some makers of these PCs chose to install 1MB of RAM, but then to split it as 512KB of lower memory and 512KB of extended memory. Others give the owner the option of setting a jumper or a configuration entry to specify that the memory should be used as 640KB of lower memory and 384KB of extended memory.

The original IBM PC/AT has the option of reducing its lower memory all the way to 256KB. This is done by moving the jumper J18 to the correct position. This is a very valuable possibility for memory management, but only if you also add a hardware EMS memory card. Some clones support something similar. (See Chapter 20.)

Getting Up to the Starting Line, and Then Some

If your PC doesn't have 640KB of lower memory and it doesn't have any EMS memory, you cannot run many larger PC programs. You need more RAM, for sure.

Don't just go out and buy some RAM chips. Most likely you won't have anywhere to plug them in, or if you do, they only will make more extended memory. You must solve your missing lower memory problem another way.

If you plan to run *Windows* as your main operating environment, all you want is the full 640KB of lower memory plus lots of extended memory.

Get a memory card that can backfill the lower memory you are missing, and then supply the rest of its contents as extended memory.

If you are likely to run many DOS programs (not under *Windows*), you may want to go at things a bit differently. You will benefit greatly from a hardware memory card that can supply LIM 4.0 EMS-compatible expanded memory, especially if you can disable most of your present lower memory.

This card may also be able to supply extended memory. It should be able to map the EMS memory into any region of lower memory where you have no other RAM chips, and into as much of upper memory as possible.

Salespeople may tell you that all you need is the ability to map EMS pages into lower memory from some lower limit up to 640KB, and to create one 64KB page frame in upper memory, usually in the C or D pages. That is definitely not optimal.

You'd like to be able to map EMS pages into all of lower memory (or at least from 256KB) up through the A page and half of the B page, plus anywhere in the C, D, and E pages. It would even be nice (though you will find it is very rare) to be able to map EMS pages into the first quarter or half of the F page, in case your PC does not have a ROM there.

Once you get your lower memory reduced and a hardware EMS card with lots of RAM, you can run *DESQview* effectively. Both of these conditions matter, so check carefully what is possible on your PC.

While you're at it, you might try to get a card that also offers some input-output ports, or some other feature you will value. Your PC already has a real-time clock, so don't pay extra for another one. (In fact, if you get one, be sure it can be disabled so it won't conflict with the one you already have.)

Memory cards come in two varieties: 8-bit and 16-bit. The difference is clear when you look at them. Get the two-tongued 16-bit kind. Memory on that type of card will work twice as fast as any you plug in on a single-tongued 8-bit card.

Managing the Memory You Have

Any PC in class 3 or above with at least a little bit of extended memory can have a High Memory Area (HMA). That is a very valuable bit of real-mode memory "real estate." Use it.

You must load an XMS-compatible extended memory manager (XMM). DOS includes HIMEM.SYS. That functionality is also included, along with much more, in products such as *UMBPro*, *QRAM*, and *386MAX* (and others mentioned in Part IV).

If you are using DOS 5 or later, you can load a significant portion of DOS itself into the HMA. Alternatively, you can put some of your memory manager or certain network drivers there. Whatever you do, choose the program that will use the HMA most nearly to the full. Only one program can get it, so don't waste any more than you must.

Class 3 PCs Without a Hard Disk

Many laptop and portable PCs fall into class 3. Some of them have hard disks; others do not. If yours is a class 3 PC without a hard disk, you will want to follow the suggestions given in Chapter 23 for owners of class 1 PCs without a hard disk. You may also want to investigate an alternative version of DOS (*DR DOS* 6, for example) or an alternate command interpreter (such as NDOS, which comes with *The Norton Utilities*, version 6 or later).

One significant difference is that you can create your RAM disk and disk cache out of extended memory. That frees you to make them large without having an adverse impact on your free lower memory. So make them large and use them creatively.

Just be careful that you don't put data files on a RAM disk and then lose them when you power down or reboot. If you do put data files there, save them early and often to a floppy diskette. (Chapter 20 gives some suggestions on how batch files can help you automate this process.)

Class 3 PCs with a Hard Disk

You may be planning to run programs that could use EMS memory. You could create some out of extended memory using a LIMulator program. This works, but not nearly as quickly in this class of PC as using a hardware EMS board, and you must put the page frame for simulated EMS memory in lower memory unlike that for hardware EMS memory. On the other hand, it also does not cost nearly as much as the hardware solution. Evaluate your needs. If you only rarely want EMS memory and are willing to put up with a slightly sluggish performance, use the LIMulator. Otherwise, get a hardware EMS card. (You could use a LIMulator that converted some disk space into EMS memory, but that would be even slower—a whole lot slower.)

All the usual suggestions (create RAM disks, use a disk cache, reduce TSRs, use task swappers or TSR managers, and so on) apply to this class of PC. Read over the suggestions in Chapter 23 to see which ones you could adopt.

Adding Things

Your greatest gift to a PC in this class is more RAM. Add it as extended memory, or if you plan to run DOS applications that use EMS memory, as expanded memory. (The latter is an especially good option if you can reduce the amount of lower memory and if you plan to use *DESQview*. Remember, though, that *Windows* and some DOS-extended applications can use only extended memory.)

Class 3 PCs can benefit a lot from LIM 4.0 EMS-compatible expanded memory add-in cards. This hardware EMS memory is, on these machines, much faster than extended memory that has been converted to simulated EMS memory by use of a LIMulator program.

Also important is that the memory card connect to the full AT bus. That means it must have the two tongues with gold fingers on them. That is a 16-bit memory card. You can use an 8-bit card if you happen to have one lying around, but it will be slower than using simulated EMS memory made from extended memory. (However, it will put the EMS page frame in upper memory, out of the way of your application programs.)

If you are careful in your choice of add-in memory card, you will not only be able to get EMS memory—you will also be able to map some other EMS pages into spaces in your PC's upper memory. That will allow you to have UMBs into which you can load various TSR programs and device drivers. To do this, you must load the appropriate XMS memory manager in addition to your EMS memory manager.

Before you get carried away adding things to your PC, check out the advice in Chapter 23. You may do better to sell or pass on your PC and get a new, complete system that is in a higher class instead.

Significant Upgrades

There are some special cases to consider when it comes to upgrading a class 3 PC. If yours is an *IBM PS/2*, Model 50 or 60, you may want to use an Intel *Snapin 386* processor upgrade. That unit has been optimized just for your PC, and it carries it up into class 5.

Some other class 3 PCs can accept a variety of processor upgrades. These generally make more sense than upgrading a class 1 or 2 PC, if only because you can use the memory you already have and access it across the same memory and I/O bus you used before without any penalty. For that reason, the processor upgrades that make the most sense are those that convert your 286-based PC to a 386SX (hence, to class 5). If you want class 6 performance, either get a whole new PC or upgrade your motherboard.

The other way to upgrade your PC's effective class is to add only memory-management hardware to it. The *All Charge Card* used to be one popular way to do this. It has fallen from favor lately. The principal reason is that the *All Charge Card* requires the use of special software to take advantage of its proprietary way of managing memory. Any upgrade that uses an actual 386SX CPU chip will allow you to use standard 386 memory-management techniques.

If yours is a desktop PC, its case is probably just right for holding a 386 or even a 486 motherboard. So you can upgrade to a real class 5 or class 6 PC easily. Prices are steadily coming down. So for many class 4 PC owners there is almost no choice, except how far up the scale to go and how much RAM to buy.

Memory Management for PCs in Class 4

These PCs are no different than class 3 PCs except that they already have fast EMS memory available. All the foregoing advice, therefore, applies. Also read the section in Chapter 23 on class 2 PCs, as your EMS memory may be like that discussed there.

Adding Things

As always, the nicest gift to any capable PC is more RAM. In class 4 PCs you want more and more extended memory and more and more hardware EMS memory. The right balance between these two kinds depends on the software you plan to use.

If your motherboard system logic is capable of converting extended memory into *fast* EMS memory, just add a lot of extended memory. The question is only whether that EMS memory is as fast as what you can add on a hardware EMS card.

If you want upper memory blocks so you can load programs high, you will have to get them either from EMS memory or from converted shadow RAM. Or you can buy a *MegaMizer* card or a *HIcard2+* and let it supply that memory. In any case, your XMS manager (the one that gave you an HMA) will also be the manager of your upper memory blocks.

Significant Upgrades

Look at the advice under this same heading earlier in this chapter. Most of what applies to class 3 PCs also applies to those in class 4.

One difference is that class 4 PCs often include a hardware EMS card. If yours does, you will pretty much have to give up your investment in that EMS card if you replace your 286-based motherboard with one using a 386 or 486 CPU chip.

This is because hardware EMS memory is not nearly as effective in a class 5 or class 6 PC as simulated EMS converted from extended memory. On the other hand, many hardware EMS cards can be rejumpered to provide extended memory instead. The only limitation is that if they are ISA cards they will at most have 16 data wires. That means that the memory on them can only be accessed at I/O bus speeds, rather than the faster direct connection of CPU-to-memory-on-the-motherboard. That applies both to memory on these boards when it is used as extended memory or as EMS memory. Therefore, even used as EMS memory these boards will be outclassed by simulated EMS memory made from extended memory in a class 6 PC (but not in a class 5 PC).

25

FOR OWNERS OF PCS IN CLASS 5 OR 6

These are the premium PCs. They have the most capabilities in terms of memory management. But without some help and direction, they won't do any more than a mere class 1 PC. Learn here what you need to do.

If you have a class 5 or 6 PC, you have a premium machine. It has more capacity for memory management than PCs in any other class. But if you just boot it up with DOS, your PC will simply act like a very fast class 1 PC.

The reason is that the basic DOS program doesn't know about the added capabilities of the 386, 486, and *Pentium* CPU chips. You have to augment DOS with some programs that do. (They could be some of the programs that come with DOS, or some that you get from a different manufacturer.)

Memory Management for PCs in Class 5 or 6

The same exact methods for managing memory work for both class 5 and class 6 PCs. The only differences between these two classes are how much total memory they can have and how many bytes at a time they can transfer in or out of that memory.

The first thing you need to do for these PCs is put them into protected mode. That is necessary for any access to memory past the first megabyte (or, more precisely, past the first 1088KB). Furthermore, this opens the door to effective memory management using the special protected-mode features such as paging and access protection.

This means you will want to load a memory manager through a DEVICE statement early in your CONFIG.SYS file. Which one you use depends on what memory manager you wish to use. If you use the DOS-provided tools you will have to have two DEVICE statements, one for HIMEM.SYS and one for EMM386.EXE. If you use one of the third-party 386 memory managers, you will have only one such line.

> You may, of course, use several other DEVICE lines in your CONFIG.SYS file. They serve one of three purposes. Some load device drivers for optional hardware such as an optical disk. Others create additional logical devices such as a software disk cache or a RAM disk. And, finally, you may use some DEVICE lines to load device drivers like ANSI.SYS or KEYB that modify how your PC's output appears on-screen or prints, or how your PC processes keyboard input.

Once you have augmented DOS with suitable memory-management software, you can direct your PC to fill in any holes in upper memory with

RAM. It can be made to replace unused ROMs with RAM or to move ROMs and even the video image buffer around to expand the area available for DOS programs. And you can create simulated EMS memory. All of these things are done by directives to the memory-management programs you load through your CONFIG.SYS file.

You can load programs (both TSRs and device drivers) and possibly some of the DOS data structures (BUFFERS, the system file table, the Current Directory Structure, and so on) into either upper or high memory. This is usually done with a combination of special directives (like DOS=HIGH) and special forms of the usual commands (for example, by using DEVICEHIGH in place of DEVICE in your CONFIG.SYS file or using LOADHIGH in front of TSR invocations in your AUTOEXEC.BAT file). Moving the system file table and Current Directory Structure to upper memory cannot be done with just the DOS memory management tools; you must use some third-party alternative or supplement. *QEMM* can do this, but you also can do it by using the DOSMAX program that you will find on the diskette that accompanies this book.

> The current version of DOSMAX was designed to work with *MS-DOS* and *PC DOS* versions up through 5. It causes some difficulties when it is used with *MS-DOS* 6. Specifically, DOSMAX does not allow *MS-DOS* 6 to pass environment variables that are defined during CONFIG.SYS processing to the master environment created by COMMAND.COM. That means that you will not be able to use SET statements in your CONFIG.SYS file nor can you branch on the CONFIG environment variable. If you want to do these things and get the benefits of DOSMAX, you will have to get an updated version of the program from its author once it is available.

Additionally, you can stash lots of TSRs in (simulated) expanded memory and make each one appear in the CPU's memory-address space only as it is needed by using a TSR manager. Or you could run a more general task-switching program. That would allow all of your applications to share the lower memory-address space in turn, each one loaded there as it became active, and remaining somewhere off in extended memory the rest of the time.

Finally, you might run a multitasking operating environment such as *DESQview* or *Windows*. That could allow you to run several regular DOS, DOS-extended, and *Windows* applications simultaneously.

Adding Things

As always, adding RAM is a gift to your PC that it will repay bountifully. For PCs in classes 5 and 6, you *always* want to add *extended* memory. That is because hardware EMS (expanded) memory would be slower and more limited in its use.

You want to add memory on the processor's memory bus (or on a local bus if your PC has one). This means that you will be adding it on the motherboard, on a proprietary memory card plugged into a special memory card slot, or on a memory card plugged into a local bus slot.

Avoid adding memory on cards plugged into the normal I/O slots, unless your PC has an EISA or MCA 32-bit I/O bus. Then be sure your memory add-in cards take advantage of the advanced features of that bus.

Significant Upgrades

If you have a class 5 PC (based on a 386SX) and you are not satisfied with its speed, or if you need more than 16MB of RAM, you will need to upgrade to a class 6 PC. That means you will have to replace the entire motherboard. Nothing less will do.

You can keep your hard and floppy disk drives and their controllers, your video card, and any other plug-in cards. Or you may end up replacing some of those functions with ones built onto the new motherboard.

If you can get a motherboard with one or more local bus slots and a video card and/or disk controller that transfer data at the full processor speed and data bus width, you will achieve dramatic increases in video and disk speeds.

What about upgrading a class 6 PC? Although this is the top class, it can be subdivided into several subclasses, and upgrades are possible by moving up from one subclass to another.

If yours is a 386DX-based PC, you can increase its processing speed by replacing the CPU chip (and the 387DX math coprocessor if you have one) by a RapidCAD chip set. This will speed all programs some and it will speed any programs that use the math coprocessor much more.

If yours is a 486SX-based PC, you probably have an extra, empty socket on the motherboard. This was originally intended as a place you could plug in a 487SX chip, but now it is called the OverDrive socket to indicate a much better use for it.

You learned in Chapter 13 that the 487SX is merely a 486DX with an extra pin, and it costs nearly as much as the 486DX chip. For the same price or only modestly more, depending on the speed of your 486SX, you can get an OverDrive chip that will not only add the math coprocessor, but also double the computational speed of the CPU chip.

OverDrive replacements are available for 486DX chips also. Plugging in one of these new CPU chips makes your 486DX into a DX/2 running at twice the original motherboard system clock speed.

The final upgrade possibility in terms of CPU chip is to move from a 486-based system to one that uses a *Pentium* chip for its CPU. Since the *Pentium* is designed for a 64-bit data bus, this can only be done fully by changing to a new, *Pentium*-specific motherboard. A less costly, partial upgrade is available. Some recent 486 systems include a special socket for a version of the *Pentium* that will work with only a 32-bit wide data bus. Intel has promised that version of the *Pentium* will be released in late 1993 or early in 1994.

Besides changing the CPU chip, the other most significant upgrade to a class 6 PC is changing to an advanced bus. That means changing the motherboard. You could upgrade the I/O bus to EISA or MCA, or you could add a local bus. Any of these, plus upgrading the cards that plug into that bus, or upgrading your disk to a faster one, could increase your PC's performance.

The significant thing to notice about all these upgrades is that they do not add anything to the memory-management possibilities (except that going from class 5 to class 6 breaks the 16MB RAM limit). You get more speed, but that is about it.

You have nowhere to go beyond the *Pentium* CPU chip at this time. Of course, that will change. You can expect more capable new processors to be introduced roughly every two to three years.

We've been promised that all future members of the Intel 80x86 family will support all the features of the 386, 486, and *Pentium* chips. What will they offer in addition? While there have been no promises in this regard, it seems likely that most of the improvements in future models will lie in bringing more support circuitry onto the chip and adding parallel processing, rather than in adding new modes of operation.

We'll see more speed, and higher levels of integration. That means smaller PCs and ones that will do what present PCs do, only faster. What it will not mean is any dramatically different memory-management strategies.

That's good news. It means that once you have assimilated all the principles and techniques described in this book, and once you have upgraded your system to a class 6 PC, you will be able to run any program or do any task that any PC can for many years to come. And you will understand the ways in which your PC does those things.

SPECIFIC PRODUCTS

This part of the book lists many, but not all of the PC upgrade and memory-management products you may wish to consider getting. You will get the greatest benefit from this section if you already understand the principles explained in Parts I and II.

Of course, you may be in a hurry to see how your favorite product is described, or to see what options you might have besides some you are already familiar with. In that case, by all means start here and check things out.

HOW TO USE THIS PART OF THE BOOK

There are limits to what even a book this size can contain. Check here to learn why some things are included and others are not.

Chapters 27 through 30 (and the MemInfo hypertext database on the included diskette) comprise the most product-specific parts of this book. They are all about products you can buy or get from a bulletin board to help you with memory upgrades and memory management.

Chapter 27 covers hardware products. Chapter 28 is on software tools that help you assess what you have and what you need. Chapter 29 covers memory-management software. This part of the book closes with Chapter 30, which describes some valuable software programs you may wish to add to your system once you have cleared out enough memory to hold them.

> The MemmInfo database lists many more manufacturers and products than are described in the printed text, but the descriptions are much more terse. The diskette is also somewhat more up-to-date than the text.

A Modest Disclaimer

The listings of products in this part of the book are meant to be close to comprehensive. Even so, it is not complete. Nothing printed on paper could be. New products are always coming out.

Furthermore, I don't know all of the products in the marketplace. I know about quite a few, and most of them are listed in this book. Some that are not in the book were omitted because they seemed not to offer anything extra or different from those that are listed. All the most popular products are here, and several you may have never heard of. A few may have been omitted because I was unaware of just how helpful they could be.

An Invitation to You, the Reader

That is where you come in. As a reader of this book, you are a certified IP, that is, an Interested Person. What do you know about memory upgrade and memory- management products that you would like to see mentioned in the next edition?

Please write me with your suggestions. Be sure to tell me if you would like to be given credit for those suggestions in print. Also, tell me what experiences you have had with the products you mention. I am interested in knowing both tales of marvelous achievements and tales of horrible frustration. The former indicate products we all will want to consider. The latter may point out products (or procedures) to avoid.

You may send your suggestions and your battle tales (or what a friend of mine calls "Tales from the Trenches") to me at the following address:

John M. Goodman, Ph.D.

P.O. Box 746

Westminster, CA 92684-0746

HARDWARE-BASED PRODUCTS

If you don't have the chips you need, you must add them. If you don't have sockets for those chips, you have to add a memory card. That is also one way to install memory-management capabilities. Other hardware upgrades include changing your processor chip or plugging in a coprocessor. This chapter covers all this and more.

Some hardware products help you add memory to your PC. Others help you use what you have more effectively. Some products add more than just memory. Such multifunction cards are a very good way to add those functions while committing only one of your valuable I/O slots.

The following sections discuss the hardware upgrade options you have for both increasing the amount of memory and making it more useful. In addition, they cover various other hardware options you may wish to use, or ones that, while having nothing to do with a memory upgrade or memory management, may confuse you into thinking that they do.

Memory Chips and Modules

The most obvious products associated with memory upgrades are memory chips and memory modules. In Chapters 2 and 16 you learned about the variety of memory chips and modules on the market and how to choose the right ones for your PC. Chapter 17 added some more information on speeds of memory chips that is important to keep in mind.

There is little point in discussing memory chips by brand. They are primarily a *commodity* product. This is supposed to mean that everyone who makes memory chips does it so similarly that you really won't care whose chips you buy. That is almost true. However, in some memory cards you will find that certain manufacturers' parts work better than others. Normally, the board manufacturer's literature will tell you which are the approved chips or modules and which are ones definitely to avoid. Any that are not mentioned are risky choices at best.

Aside from that caveat, though, you can buy memory chips as you might buy gasoline or flour. Shop by price. Memory prices fluctuate widely and quite rapidly. You will have to shop around to be sure you are getting what is, this week, a good deal.

Also buy from a reputable dealer or distributor. You want people who stand behind their products, and who will be around when you may need them several weeks or months from now.

Products to Add Memory

These are the products that hold the memory chips or modules you wish to add to your PC. Of course the motherboard is often the first place you will put those chips or modules, but when you run out of room there, consider these products. (You also may need one of these if the mother-board is strategically the wrong place for you to be adding RAM. See Chapter 15 for more on that point.)

Adding Lower or Upper Memory Only

When PCs were young, memory was expensive, and almost all PCs came with less than 640KB of RAM on the motherboard. A popular memory product in those days was a plug-in card designed to bring your PC's lower memory up to 640KB.

IBM made such a card, as did many other manufacturers. One popular brand was called *Top Hat*. It was a half-length card and carried 128KB of RAM, just enough to "top off" a standard IBM *PC/AT* that had originally come with only 512KB of RAM on the motherboard.

These products have gone out of vogue. Nearly all PCs come with, or are able to accept, at least 640KB of RAM on the motherboard (and often a great deal more). But a new niche market has developed. This is for a board that adds RAM in a PC's upper memory space.

One of the first of these was the *All Card* from All Computers. This card was designed specifically for use in class 1 PCs. It could be bought with an optional memory-management module, or just as a memory add-on card. This product is no longer marketed (though you may be able to buy one directly from All Computers). Their focus is now on their products for higher-class PCs: the *All Charge Card* (software plus hardware) and *All386* (software only).

One of the newest entrants into this field is the *MegaMizer* from V Communications. The market for this board is owners of any PC in classes 1 to 4. It can be used to add upper memory to those PCs and manage it much as you can in a class 5 or 6 PC by using their software-only product, *Memory Commander*. Also usable in the same way are some members of the RYBS *HIcard* series of products.

Extended Memory Boards

Once there was an IBM *PC/AT*, it created a market for plug-in memory option cards (also called memory boards) that could hold lots of memory chips. The motherboard could hold only 512KB (initially) and the AT could address up to 16MB.

IBM built some "memory expan**sion** option cards" to meet this need. (Note that *expansion* here doesn't have anything to do with expan**ded** memory!) Again, many other vendors introduced products for the same purpose.

Intel's *Above Board* and AST's *RAMpage* are a couple of the better known. Quadram has also been an established vendor in this marketplace for years. Acculogic is a fairly recent entrant with some interesting products (*RAMpAT* and *SIMMply-RAM* lines). And there are the inevitable, no-name clone boards. (All of the boards mentioned in this paragraph can also be used to provide EMS memory.)

How can you choose one of these boards wisely? For machines in Classes 1 through 4, the best advice is not to buy any board that can add only extended memory. Getting one that can be configured either to add extended or expanded memory gives more flexibility. For PCs in class 5 or 6, where simulated EMS memory is just as good (for most purposes) as hardware EMS and more flexible to use, the right choice often is a memory board that only adds extended memory. Many of the manufacturers of EMS memory boards also offer some models that are just straight extended memory boards.

That said, these too have mostly become commodity products. The one remaining distinction among them that may matter is that some have easier setup procedures than others. For example, the Acculogic boards don't require you to move any jumpers or set any DIP switches. Everything is controlled by software, and furthermore, their software is moderately good at figuring out how the board needs to be configured for your PC all on its own.

> **Warning**   There are some programs that are more sensitive about memory than others. They may not work with all EMS or extended memory boards. If that is so, their documentation typically will tell you which brands are okay and which to avoid.

EMS Board and EEMS Boards

Extended memory cards are useful only for PCs in classes 3 and above. Expanded memory cards can be used in any PC (though it is not normally a good idea to use them in PCs in classes 5 and 6). Back when most PCs were class 1 or 2 machines, the makers of memory add-in cards had a strong motivation to create expanded memory cards.

The earliest of the paging-memory cards predate the LIM-EMS specification. For example, Tall Tree sold *J-RAM* cards that provided paging memory by their own proprietary methods. Once the LIM-EMS standard came on the scene, all makers of paging memory cards jumped on the bandwagon.

LIM EMS-Compatible Designs

Intel provided the first Lotus-Intel-Microsoft-compatible expanded memory cards. Soon afterward, sales of their *Above Board* cards were being eclipsed by those of AST's *Six Pack*, *Rampage*, and *Rampage/AT* cards.

The first wave of EMS memory cards were all 8-bit designs. That means they have just one tongue to go into the XT subset of the ISA bus. They can only transfer data 8 bits at a time.

Later, AT-specific designs were introduced. These have two tongues to fit into both connectors of a full ISA slot. They can transfer data 16 bits at a time.

You want to use the kind that fits your PC. If you have a class 3 or 4 PC, you have the full ISA bus with two connectors per slot (at least for most of the I/O slots). For such a PC, you definitely want to use an AT-specific design.

Only those 16-bit designs are capable of providing either extended or expanded memory or any mixture of the two you may desire. That is because the address wires needed to refer to extended memory are only to be found in the second, smaller connector on an ISA slot. So any 8-bit card is limited to addresses below 1MB.

LI 3.0 EMS and LIM 3.2 EMS Boards

The first EMS-compatible expanded memory boards all adhered to either the LI 3.0 or LIM 3.2 versions of the EMS standard. That limited what they could do. In particular, they can only map EMS memory into one 64KB page frame, which must be located somewhere in upper memory, usually in the C or D pages.

EEMS Boards

AST, Ashton-Tate, Quadram, and Quarterdeck Office Systems collaborated on an improved EMS standard. They called it Enhanced EMS, or EEMS. Only EMS boards made by AST and Quadram complied with this new standard. If you have or can get one of these boards, it can be made to function as if it were a LIM 4.0 EMS-compatible expanded memory board. You can do this by simply getting a new EMM device driver for it. Remember, you must get your EMM driver from the manufacturer of the card.

LIM 4.0 EMS Boards

The most up-to-date version of the Expanded Memory Specification is 4.0. Now all makers of EMS hardware (and software emulators) brag about their compliance with this standard. Unfortunately they only have to do a very limited kind of complying to be able to make this claim.

The most important distinction is which regions of upper-memory-address space and of lower-memory-address space a given board can use for mapping of EMS pages. A secondary distinction is the number of sets of page map registers the board holds.

For maximum usefulness, you want a board that can map EMS pages into any location in lower memory (or at least any location above 256KB), without stopping at 640KB. And you want to be able to map almost all of upper-memory space as well.

Intel's *Above Board* cards, despite having been made by one of the co-sponsors of the EMS document, do not do this. (Intel helped design the specification but did not promise to implement all of its features.) These EMS cards can map lower memory just fine. But they are limited to 64KB (or in some models, up to 128KB) of upper-memory space into which they can map EMS pages. The more restricted models can create an EMS page frame, or they can create 64KB of UMB RAM, but not both. The most capable versions can map the full C and D pages, and so can provide an EMS page frame plus 64KB of UMB RAM.

The *RAMpAT* boards from Acculogic can do a little better, but they have their limits also. You cannot put the page frame for even these very capable boards in the E page. They were designed with that limitation, because when IBM first announced the PC's memory architecture, they said the E and F pages were reserved for use by motherboard BIOS ROMs.

But a great many PCs (both IBM brand and clones) don't use the E page at all. Many only use part of the F page. If you could put your EMS page frame all the way up against the bottom of the motherboard BIOS ROM, you would have the best possible chance of getting all the upper memory (UMB RAM) you could in one large block. Too bad these (and most other) EMS cards won't let you do that.

Some PCs allow you to use their motherboard system logic to map some shadow RAM into upper memory space and make it available as UMBs. You could combine that with a hardware EMS board, if you like, as a way of getting more total upper memory and much more EMS memory.

Remember, though, that you must only have one EMM and it must come from the maker of the hardware it is to control. This means that, practically, you will want to use an EMM to control the plug-in hardware EMS card and have the motherboard system logic provide only UMBs from the shadow RAM. That may not use all of the shadow RAM, but you will be able to get more total memory, as the plug-in card will very likely be able to hold megabytes of RAM instead of the typical 128KB to 384KB of usable shadow RAM.

If you do this, and if you have the EMS board put the EMS page frame in the D page, you may end up with two regions of UMBs—one above and one below the EMS page frame.

There is a way around this difficulty. But it has a problem also. Put the EMS page frame as low as you can. Typically that would be just above the video image buffer, or perhaps above the video ROM and a hard disk controller ROM. This works, and it gives you one open space for UMBs.

It forces you to give up something, though. Putting the page frame there makes it impossible for memory managers that know how to "borrow" the EMS page frame while loading TSRs or device drivers to perform this trick in your PC. This trick only works when the EMS page frame is *above* the UMB area.

Unfortunately, you won't find any clear text on the box, or even in the manual, for most EMS cards telling you which regions of upper memory space they can use. You will have to ask some searching questions. Don't depend on your friendly dealer to know the answers. Check with the factory. (It is best to get the answers in writing, so you can more easily hold the company to them if something doesn't seem right later on.)

The ideal solution is to find a board that will map EMS pages from at least the 5 page (just above the 256KB boundary) all the way up to the middle of the F page. You won't find that anywhere, but you want to get as close as you can.

The lower portion of upper memory (the A and B pages) are especially important if you plan to run only text mode or only CGA- or MGA-graphics-mode video displays. You can then expand the region available for DOS programs by at least 64KB and perhaps as much as 96KB.

The number of sets of page-mapping registers matters when you do multitasking, for example, by running *DESQview*. Having more helps make things go more quickly. But even a single set will do all right, as *DESQview* can emulate additional register sets in RAM.

Multifunction Boards

Many memory cards have other functionality built onto them as well. If you are getting an EMS card for a class 1 or 2 PC, look for a real-time clock, if nothing else. If you also get some serial, parallel, or game ports, so much the better.

If your PC already has a real-time clock (as a few class 1 or 2, and all class 3 through 6 PCs, do), then be sure *not* to get another one on your new memory card, or at least be sure you can disable it. You don't want the two clocks contending with one another.

Sometimes you can get a *floppy disk controller* (*FDC*) too. That would allow you to replace the original FDC card with your new memory card and that means you get all your new memory and other features without having to give up even one I/O slot. In many class 1 or 2 PCs, that can be crucial.

Perhaps you can't find that sort of multifunction card. If you are short on I/O slots, a different kind may be your salvation. Replace the two cards typically used in a class 1 or 2 PC to control the floppy and hard disks by a single combo disk controller card. Now put your new memory (only) card in the slot you just freed up.

Products to Help Manage Memory

Changing your processor moves your PC into a whole new class, and that opens up new possibilities for memory management. There are several ways you can upgrade the processor, ranging from a simple plug-in replacement for the CPU chip to changing the whole motherboard.

Be sure to evaluate some alternative strategies before picking one. Many of these products that once were cost-effective are no longer.

Add-On Memory Managers

These are cards that upgrade your processor's memory-management capabilities. They do this in one of two ways: adding upper RAM or adding memory paging.

Hardware Upper Memory Providers

The first strategy is to have RAM on the card which that card's circuitry can map into holes in upper memory. Loading an XMS-compatible memory manager (often supplied with the hardware) will then give you UMBs into which you can load programs.

> This is a very good approach for a PC in class 1 or 2. Those PCs don't have enough address lines to support more than 1MB of memory, and they have no RAM that can be made to appear anywhere in upper memory (aside from the video image buffers, that is).

Prior to DOS 5, you also needed some special utility programs that could load your other programs into those UMBs. These utility programs typically come with this sort of add-on hardware. The *HICard* series (from RYBS), and the *MegaMizer* (from V Communications) are examples of these products. Even if you are using DOS 5 or 6, you will need to use the special device driver that comes with the memory card to provide the UMBs. The DOS commands DEVICEHIGH and LOADHIGH can only be used to load programs into UMBs that have been created previously.

Memory-Mapping Hardware Add-Ons

PCs in classes 3 and 4 already have a lot of memory in them. The problem is getting more than 640KB of it below the 1MB line. That can be done easily in a class 5 or 6 PC by remapping extended memory into regions of upper memory. The products in this group do the same thing for a 286-based PC.

The most popular example of this genre for several years was the *All Charge Card*. This is a solution only for class 3 or 4 PCs (with 80286 CPU chips).

The *All Charge Card* is a small (roughly 2-inch by 4-inch) circuit board that is interposed between your CPU chip and its socket. It augments the capabilities of the chip to add something resembling the paging memory circuits on a 386 chip. However, it does not do that job in precisely the same way. (This is hardly surprising, when you consider that it was designed years before the 386 was first sold, and the designers of the two chips are a continent apart.)

That means that you must use the special memory-management software that comes with the *All Charge Card* instead of any third-party 386 memory managers like *386MAX* or *QEMM*. A few years ago that was not much of an issue. IBM liked this product so much that, for a while, it was shipping an *All Charge Card* bundled with every *PS/2*, Model 50 or 60, that it sold. (That ended when they phased out those models.) Now this product is dated, and only useful if you already have an 80286-based PC and can live with the constraints that using an *All Charge Card* will bring you.

The more modern way of dealing with this problem is to use a plug-in processor upgrade (see the next section).

Plug-In Coprocessor Boards and Modules

For several years, it has been possible to buy plug-in boards to upgrade your PC's processor. These are not mere processor upgrades, though. They are full plug-in cards. Often they will have a CPU chip of a higher level than the host PC into which they will be plugged, plus some substantial amount of RAM. Some also add a memory cache.

Coprocessor Cards and Slave PCs

Some of these are really an entire PC built on a plug-in card. They use the host PC only for input and output, including access to the disk drives. Others are actual upgrade devices. The latter ones usually have you pull out the CPU chip in your PC and plug in a cable from the upgrade unit.

If you wish to upgrade a PC in class 1 or 2 to anything higher, you will have to provide some way to address memory beyond the 1,024KB limit of class 1 or 2 PCs. Otherwise, having a higher level processor would do you little good. So these upgrades pretty much have to come on a board with RAM on it.

Boards of this sort that were designed several years ago had trouble fitting as much RAM as you might want on a single card along with the new processor (and math coprocessor socket) and the ancillary circuitry required to make it all work. Typically they offer a place to plug in a daughterboard with additional RAM.

The Intel *Inboard* series of products is a good example. They used to make and sell two of these products. One was the *Inboard 386/PC*. This was a board that upgraded a 4.77 MHz IBM *PC* (only the IBM *PC* brand or a Leading Edge *Model D* clone PC) to a 16MHz 386SX computer with up to 3MB of RAM. The other member of the Inboard family was the *Inboard 386* for use in any AT clone computer. Both of those products have now been discontinued.

Orchid, Microway, and Aox are other vendors who plied these waters. Even IBM's *PS/2* owners had some options. If they wanted to upgrade a Model 50 or 60, they could use the Aox *MicroMaster* (originally this product and the ISA-bus version called the *ATMaster* would upgrade a 286-based PC to a 386SX system; the current version will upgrade the PC all the way to a 486DX or SX). Mostly, though, users have moved beyond the plug-in processor upgrade board to the plug-in processor replacement.

Processor Replacement Modules

Intel's *SnapIn 386* is a good example of this new breed. This is a module that plugs into a *PS/2*, Model 50 or 60 (only that brand and those models), to upgrade those 80286-based PCs to 386SX. The Microway *FastCache*, *FastCache Plus*, and *FastCache-SX*, the Sota *Express/386*, the Kingston Technologies *SX/Now!*, the Cumulus *386SX*, and the Evergreen *386 SuperChip II* are other examples. Most of these other products are not as limited as the Intel offering. They can be used in almost any 80286-based PC to get full 386SX functionality.

Why These Modules Are Popular

There are some good reasons why these modules have become so popular. First is the fact that the 80286 and the 386SX both have an external bus that has 16 data wires and 24 address lines (plus a similar assortment of control lines). That means that the design of a PC based on either of them will be much the same. Second is the great popularity of *Windows* 3.x. This program, like many other protected-mode programs, is able to do much more if it is run on a PC with 386 memory paging and memory-protection features built-in.

By actually using a 386SX chip and some interface hardware, these products make it possible for an upgraded 286-based PC to appear to *Windows* exactly like any clone 386SX PC. This means that you can use all the memory-management software discussed elsewhere in this book that was designed for 386 or 486 computers. (Note: There may be some software limitations or incompatibilities, but generally a great deal fewer than with the plug-in coprocessor boards.)

Some Cautions

The above-mentioned advantages are powerful reasons for going with the module route. The only good reason for not doing so is that it implies investing some money in what is already an arguably obsolete technology. Yes, you get to move up to the 386-level of computing. Yes, you will be able to run all the great software. But notice, you may not have speeded up the PC as much as you have enhanced its memory-management abilities. So you may have a dog of a 386SX computer. This is especially true if you start with a slow AT clone (with a system clock speed of 12MHz or less).

Some of the add-in processor upgrade modules include a faster clock. But they must slow down whenever they access your main RAM. If they have a good memory cache on the module, this will not happen as often as it would otherwise, but it still will happen enough to limit the upgraded PC's speed noticeably.

The best reason not to use a module like this is the constantly falling price of motherboards. Now it is feasible, for almost the same amount of money, to get a whole new motherboard. You will pay a bit more once you fill it with new, faster RAM chips or modules, but then you will be getting a much faster computer without any compatibility headaches. (Well, almost none. Any clone has at least a few!)

Replacement Processor Chips

Lately it has become possible, at least in some PCs to simply replace the CPU chip with a new, more powerful CPU chip. These PCs have been designed specifically to allow for upgrading in this fashion.

There are three families of PCs for which this is currently possible. One is a subgroup of the 386DX-based PCs. Intel makes a two-chip set called *Rapid CAD* that can be plugged into the CPU and math coprocessor sockets in some 386-based PCs in place of the original CPU chip and math chip (if you had one). This combination will increase the speed with which the PC will run almost all software—and in some cases the increase will be very dramatic.

The second group of x86 family members that can be upgraded in this fashion are the 486s. Intel makes *OverDrive* clock-doubler chips to replace the 486SX and 486DX CPU chips. These chips run most software nearly twice as fast as the chips they replace. In many 486SX systems you don't even have to remove the old CPU; just plug in the OverDrive chip in a special socket provided for that purpose.

Finally, some 486-based PCs have a special, extra CPU socket that is able to accept a special version of Intel's *Pentium* chips. Intel hasn't yet released that version of the *Pentium*, but it promises to do so some time in 1993 or 1994.

> **Warning**   These "hot" new CPU chips will actually run a lot warmer than the chips they replace—so much so that they can easily overheat. One very good solution is to mount a small fan and heat sink directly on top of the CPU chip(s). The fan connects to the power supply just like a disk drive. (If you don't have any spare cables coming out of your power supply, you can get a Y-cable adapter to let you plug both the fan and a disk drive into a single one of the cables from the power supply.)

Some Coprocessors Are Different

Before leaving the subject of coprocessors, you may appreciate some explanations of coprocessors that have nothing to do with memory enhancement or management. Otherwise you might well be confused by some of the advertisements you read.

Math Coprocessors

Math coprocessor chips, also called *floating point units* or *numeric coprocessors,* (and thus *FPUs* or *NCPs*), are units that work in cooperation with the CPU to help speed programs that do a lot of specialized math operations. There are two fundamentally different kinds—those made by Intel or clones of them, and those made by Weitek. (Chapter 13 lists some of the other manufacturers of these chips.)

Why They Are Useful

The Intel 80x86 CPU chips are quite complex. They respond to any of a large set of instructions. Each new member of that family had at least a few, and often a whole lot of, new instructions in the set it could understand.

There are some operations that none of the 80x86 chips, up until the 486, could do easily. These include working with floating point numbers and evaluating trigonometric functions.

So Intel designed the 80x87 family of companion chips that only know how to do those special math operations. If you have a matched pair of 80x86 and 80x87 chips in your PC, and if your programs know how to ask for the 80x87 chip's help, the programs will run up to five times faster than they would without the math coprocessor's help.

Note that the program must know how to ask for this help. If it does not, the 80x87 chip will simply sit there, doing nothing. So check your applications to see which ones, if any, want the help of an Intel 80x87 chip. The 486DX incorporates the 387 chip's functionality, so there is no comparable 487 chip. (Intel's PCEO division can supply you with a list of over 2100 business application programs that know how to use their x87 math coprocessors.)

There is an Intel 487 chip, but it is a full 486DX with an extra pin. It is meant to work with the 486SX, which is just a crippled 486DX. (The math section of a 486SX is disabled at the factory.) The extra pin on the 487 chip is used to tell the 486SX to go to sleep whenever a 487 is around to take over.

The Weitek chips work in a similar fashion, but with some differences. They are even more effective in speeding up programs that know how to make good use of them and totally useless for all other programs!

What They Do in Address Space

The FPU chip has to watch every instruction that is passed to the CPU. When it sees the sort of instruction it is designed to handle, it takes that one. Like a baseball fielder, it must have some way to tell its teammate (the CPU) what it is doing: "I got it. This one's mine."

That interprocessor communication takes place at some reserved addresses in I/O port space (or in an extension of that space for most members of the x87 family). That means that these chips don't do anything in memory address space except watch for instructions being read by the CPU.

Why Adding One Is Not a Memory-Management Issue

Now you can see why installing a math coprocessor has no direct relevance to memory management or upgrades. But if you had not read this, would you have known that?

Video Coprocessors

Video coprocessors are another kind of CPU helper chip. These live on the video display adapter. Their job is to accept high-level instructions and do a lot of low-level work moving pixels around on the screen.

Once again, they do no one any good at all unless your programs know how to ask for their help. Most makers of video cards with coprocessors supply drivers for *Windows*, *AutoCAD*, and several other popular applications. If you use those applications, these coprocessors can draw images on your screen dramatically faster than the CPU alone.

> Actually, the main reason the CPU cannot do the job as quickly is that the bus limits the flow of information from the CPU to the video-image buffer. If your PC sports a high-speed, wide-data-bandwidth *local bus*, it may reduce your need for a video coprocessor.
>
> On the other hand, the inexorable trend for ever more colors and more resolution (which together mean vastly more bits of video-image data to be manipulated) can make the use of a video coprocessor ever more desirable despite the fastest of local bus technology. The truth of this is shown by the fact that most VL bus (VESA local bus) video cards currently on the market have been built with a special video accelerator on the card.

Video coprocessors do nothing with memory address space. They are another nonissue when considering memory management or upgrades.

Other Coprocessors

You may have read about several other kinds of processors that can be used in a PC. They all work with the main CPU, so in that sense they are coprocessors.

Some are called *Digital Signal Processors*. These are chips that can be used for video image processing (in which case they are a kind of video coprocessor), speech recognition or synthesis, and other tasks demanding great powers of mathematical manipulations of a certain kind.

Supposedly, there will be several of these (as well as several 486-class processors and a lot of RAM and ROM, and so on) built into the chip that Intel creates for the 80x86 family near the end of this decade (the chip Intel refers to as the *Micro 2000*). For now, these are special-purpose gadgets, most likely to be included in some high-end multimedia PCs, or in a *video accelerator card*.

The last beast comes in two varieties. One is a card that sits beside your VGA card and makes it go faster. The other is a new VGA card with the accelerator on it. Ergon Technologies' *XLR8-IT for Windows* (and a similar product for *AutoCad*) were early examples of the first approach. The Diamond *Stealth VRAM* board or the Portacom *Eclipse II* were early examples of the latter. In 1992 and 1993 this market segment virtually exploded with new products, then quickly collapsed as local bus video boards and motherboards became more common.

You can get a *SPARC* coprocessor board which will let you run *SUN OS* (a variant of *UNIX*) with DOS as a task in an X Window. This is another kind of slave PC which is optimized for this particular non-DOS operating system.

There are *transputer* boards and *neural network* cards. These are a totally different way to approach the writing programs and managing of memory (the transputer) and another totally different way to approach the writing of programs (neural networks). Again, look on these as slave computers within your PC. They will use your PC merely as a sophisticated terminal.

Motherboard Replacement Options

The most cost-effective way to upgrade your PC's processor is to replace the motherboard. This can bring with it an increase in the speed of the CPU to memory bus, and sometimes an upgrade of the I/O bus. The first of these may allow you to add more memory than could be addressed on your old motherboard. The second may allow you to take advantage of a more sophisticated and faster disk controller, video display adapter, and/or network interface card.

Moving up in the class

What are the principal options? Whatever Class of PC you have now (except for those in Class 6), you could move up to one in a higher class by the single step of replacing the motherboard.

If you start with an 8088 or 8086 CPU chip, you could move up to an 80286 design. That is certainly inexpensive but it is not, generally, a good idea. You are cutting yourself off from too much modern software, and 80286-based motherboards are becoming almost as hard to find as 8088-based ones.

Move up from your 8088-, 8086-, or 80286-based PC to at least a 386SX-based one. And if you can afford the extra increment, go on to the 386DX or beyond.

Better buses

You could upgrade your bus from ISA to 32-bit EISA or MCA. This will allow you to access arbitrarily large amounts of main RAM, instead of being stuck with a "mere" 16MB. And if you do, you will also be able to move up to some more sophisticated plug-in cards.

Another bus upgrade possibility is to add local bus. The cost to a manufacturer to add support for the VESA local bus (VL bus) is very small, so motherboards that sport up to three VL bus enhanced I/O slots should cost you almost nothing additional. However, the video or other option cards you may buy to plug into those VL bus slots and take advantage of the higher-speed operation they make possible do cost a good deal more than standard ISA video cards, at least currently.

As this is being written, the Intel-sponsored alternative local bus standard, PCI, is just beginning to move from concept to purchasable products. Originally conceived as a means for a motherboard maker to integrate high-speed peripheral devices on the motherboard, the PCI specification now includes local bus I/O slots as well.

Check to see what options you have that include PCI-accelerated peripheral components. Compare them with VL bus boards to see which will give you the best bang for your buck.

What to Change and What to Keep

If you move up in any of these ways, which parts of your old PC does it make sense to keep? If you are trying to move up at minimal cost, most of the rest of the parts will serve you for a while. The only upgrade that will frustrate any such attempt at frugality is one that takes you from an ISA bus to an MCA bus. That change will force you to get all new plug-in cards.

Remember, if you move up from an 8-bit (XT-style) ISA bus to the full AT-style, 16-bit version, and if you don't upgrade your video or hard disk controller cards, you will be stuck with a very low level of performance. That is true no matter how fast your new CPU's clock may be. Video and disk access are just too important to most users to slight in this way, and new, faster disk and video controller cards can often be purchased quite inexpensively.

Similarly, if you move from a 16-bit bus to a 32-bit bus, you may need to reconsider your disk subsystem design, or you will likely waste much of the new bus's potential. A bus-mastering 32-bit disk controller and a very fast disk drive will be a good match to that new bus.

If you add local bus support, you won't get any benefit from that feature until you also upgrade some of the peripheral devices to ones that take advantage of it. If you need faster screen painting, get a local bus video card (preferably one with a video accelerator on it). If you need faster disk access, get a hard disk controller that connects to the local bus (provided your hard drive can support the faster data transfer rates). Getting a hard disk controller with a lot of cache RAM on it may be very helpful in smoothing out the flow of data to and from the hard drive. Finally, if you seek faster access to a very high-bandwidth network (perhaps a fiber-optic based super-high-speed one), then get a local bus network interface card.

If you are contemplating changing your PC's motherboard, you also will want to look carefully at the adequacy of the case and power supply you now have. They are not very expensive pieces, so often it makes sense to upgrade them as well.

Look for a quiet power supply with a strong fan (or more than one) and a higher wattage rating than you have used before. Enough fans and adequate power are easy to get and inexpensive insurance against a number of potential future problems.

Look for a case that offers easy access to the pieces mounted inside. That will make your job as a motherboard installer much easier, and it will make any future upgrades that much more pleasant.

Reread the cautions in Chapter 17 on how to prevent shocking your new motherboard to death. You will have to put the RAM chips or modules in it, and then put it in the case. At those times, it is quite vulnerable to static discharge. But simple precautions usually suffice to prevent that sort of damage.

Other Hardware-Based Solutions

Don't forget, before committing to any upgrade strategy, to look at the option of simple, whole PC replacement. That's right; give up your present clunker and replace it with the lovely new screamer you have always wanted.

You can help yourself afford it if you sell what you now have. Or you may help your company justify the cost of your new toy—ah . . . er—*workstation* if you pass along the old PC to a coworker.

Alternatively, give it away to a deserving party. That could be a family member or a local charity. Many schools and other nonprofit agencies desperately need to computerize their operations, but cannot afford the equipment necessary to do so. While you are at it, why not help them learn how to use the new computer? That will make sure your donation is put to good use, and it will give you an opportunity to do some good for a cause you believe in.

SOFTWARE-BASED PRODUCTS–TOOLS

Having all the memory chips you need is far from enough. Your programs must be able to access them before they do you any good. Here you will learn about some tools that can help you assess how well you are doing that.

This chapter is all about tools. The tools in question are programs you can run on your PC to help you assess your needs in the first place, and then to decide how well you have met them when you are through. In between, they may help you find and resolve difficulties.

There is a lot of overlap in what these tools can do for you, which is good. You will often want to have a second opinion—to confirm a problem before you spend a lot of time, effort, or money trying to fix it.

Still, you don't need to get all of these tools. Pick a few good ones and get familiar with what they can do. Knowing your tools well is often more important than having more powerful tools.

ROM-Based Diagnostics

You may already have a powerful set of diagnostic tools at your fingertips and not even know it. Many modern PCs include an informational or diagnostic utility program in their motherboard BIOS ROM. Most often this feature is found in BIOSes made by American Megatrends, Inc. (AMI) or Quadtel (now Phoenix Technologies, LTD.)

When you boot the computer, you may find you have a choice of entering the setup program, the diagnostic program, or continuing with the boot process. Some PCs allow you to jump to that menu at any time during the work session. Others make that choice available only at boot.

Port 80 Cards

Another kind of diagnostic tool that you might wish to get is what is sometimes called a Port 80 card. At various points in your PC's boot process, the POST program puts out a byte to I/O port 80h. Each byte indicates that another phase of the POST has been completed successfully. Not all PCs use the same address for this diagnostic output. Some XTs use port 60h; Compaq uses port 84h in some of their computers; the *PS/2*, models 25 and 30 use port 90h; most *PS/2s* use port 280h; and many EISA machines use port 300h.

As long as your PC is working normally, you have no need for this kind of tool. If, however, in your attempts to add memory or otherwise upgrade your PC, you happen to create some irreconcilable conflict, your PC may refuse to start at all. (This also can happen when some piece of its hardware breaks or stops working.) In that case, a means of monitoring these progress messages may be most helpful.

Several companies make these cards. Most of them also include on the card a ROM-based diagnostic program—sort of a super-POST—and a means to activate that program instead of or in addition to your regular motherboard BIOS ROM's POST routines.

One model is called the *POSTCard*. It was designed by Award Software and is now manufactured and marketed by Unicore. Another is the *Pocket Post* card, created by Data Depot and marketed by Micro House International. The Pocket Post has unusual flexibility in the number of different ports it can be told to monitor to receive the diagnostic output bytes. Landmark sells the *KickStart I* and *KickStart II* (those are with and without added ROM diagnostics), and Paramount sells the *Blue Magic* card.

Informational and Diagnostic Programs

This section includes descriptions of just over a dozen utility programs that you can get on diskette. You surely don't need all of them, but among these you will certainly be able to find a couple that you will want to have.

Some are simply informational. That is, they show you what you have in your PC. Others are also diagnostic; they actually test the working of various parts.

> **Important Caution**   None of these programs gets all the answers right. So you really will need more than one before you can fully trust what they tell you.

You should be aware that some of the authors of these programs refer to theirs as a "diagnostic program" when all it really does is show you some information about the current configuration of your PC. A real diagnostic program will also do tests of the hardware to assure proper function. The following descriptions call a program diagnostic only if it does actual tests.

AMIDIAG

AMI builds diagnostics into their motherboard BIOS ROMs. They also have gone the next step and are selling the same configuration information and diagnostic program found in their BIOS ROMs as a diskette-based program, called *AMIDIAG*, for PC owners whose BIOS does not include that capability. This is a good program, but it does have a limitation. You can only run it from its own bootable diskette.

They do this to ensure that you won't have any resident software in your PC that might get in the way of their tests. This can help them test your hardware better. On the other hand, it does not allow them to show you your operating environment, nor do tests in that setting.

Since a substantial part of the working environment for your programs is crafted by the extensions to DOS that you load, and since some kinds of hardware cannot even be activated without loading a device driver, this is often a significant limitation to the power of this tool.

ASQ

Qualitas, developers of *386MAX*, bundle a program they call *ASQ* (Ask Qualitas) with their memory managers. The present version is 2.0. Qualitas also gives away *ASQ*, version 1.3. In either version, it is purely an informational utility. It also offers some tutorial screens to explain basic concepts of memory management. *ASQ* was written for Qualitas by another developer, and it does not have quite the same high level of excellence as *386MAX*.

CheckIt

Touchstone Software's *CheckIt* is one of the finest and easiest-to-use utility programs on the market. It tells you a lot about your system and does it in a user-friendly fashion. It is not, in version 3.0, totally accurate in mapping memory. A new version, CheckIt Pro, comes in separate modules to do informational reporting and actual diagnostic testing.

CheckIt is able to tell more about interrupts, and more accurately, than most informational utilities. It also can do a fair variety of diagnostic tests. Used with the optional floppy test diskettes and loopback plugs, *CheckIt* can be most of what you need to test and configure a PC.

Control Room

Control Room is an information utility, a tutorial program, and a means of setting up various aspects of your PC's operation. The authors intend that you run it as a TSR and then launch all your other applications from within it. This program used to be one of the most useful and easiest to use information-reporting utilities on the market. Since Ashton-Tate, the original publisher, was bought by Borland, the future of this program is unclear.

Discover

Helix Software, publishers of *Headroom*, *Netroom*, and *Connecting Room*, also offer *Discover*. This is their informational utility program. While capable enough, it has little to distinguish it from the rest of the programs in this genre. It does include a small text editor, mainly to support changing your CONFIG.SYS and AUTOEXEC.BAT files from within the program.

INFOPLUS

INFOPLUS is a program by Andrew Rossman, now released to the public domain. It offers 16 pages (some more than one screen long) of information on your PC. No tutorials, no diagnostics. Just lots of facts.

There is little interpretation of those facts, so you may find many of them confusing. But if you want a whole lot of numbers that describe your PC, this is one way to get them. And the cost is certainly right! Get INFOPLUS from your local bulletin board or CompuServe.

InfoSpotter and Remote Rx

Merrill and Bryan, creators of the *Turbo EMS* memory manager, also wrote *InfoSpotter*, *Remote Rx*, and Skylight. *InfoSpotter*, version 2.5, is one of the most comprehensive DOS character-based informational utility programs available. It can be run as a stand-alone program or as a TSR you can pop up any time you want to check on something. It also includes diagnostic routines to check certain aspects of your PC's hardware, though they are not as extensive as those in *CheckIt*. *Skylight*, version 2.0, is perhaps the best of the *Windows*-based hardware and software reporting programs.

One unusual feature of *InfoSpotter* is its support for Micro Channel machines. It can list and help you edit the Programmable Option Select (POS) features that are used for automatic configuration in those machines.

Remote Rx offers capabilities to those in *InfoSpotter* in a remote operation package. Using it, you can check the configuration and test much of the hardware of a PC from a remote location by connecting to it over a phone line and modem. You also can use this program to run application programs remotely, and it includes an editor to allow you to fix problems with the CONFIG.SYS, AUTOEXEC.BAT, or other small text files on the remote system. It also is network aware.

Manifest

Quarterdeck Office Systems bundles *Manifest* with *QEMM/386* and also sells it as a separate product. It has gotten a reputation as the industry's finest memory display utility. It probably does not display any more information than *InfoSpotter*, and in some areas less, but its presentation is one of the nicest and most readily understandable. It gives information on more than just the memory in your PC, although clearly that is its area of greatest strength.

Manifest also makes recommendations as to how you might improve the management of memory in your PC. (Most of its recommendations are sound, although of course it tends to stress buying and using *QEMM*.)

Norton Utilities and Norton Desktop for Windows

The *Norton Utilities*, currently at version 7, are justly famous as one of the industry's finest utility products. They include a System Information module that is quite comprehensive and a Disk Editor that is truly exceptional. The Norton Control Center offers functionality similar to the setup portion of *Control Room*.

If you wish to explore memory and your PC's configuration, you can use many utilities. If you wish to explore your PC's disk drives at the very deepest level, nothing quite matches the Norton Disk Editor for convenience and power. It has a read-only mode in which you can explore in total safety, as well as a read-write mode in which you can make changes to the disk contents on a very micro-scale. (Upgrade to version 7. The improvements in the Disk Editor alone are almost shockingly good; the testing modules added in version 7 move this collection of programs from a mere informational utility plus disk editor to a full-fledged diagnostic one as well—and the file recovery capability remains the best in the industry.) Also included in Norton Utilities is NDOS, a substitute for DOS' COMMAND.COM.

The *Norton Desktop for Windows (NDW)*, currently at version 2.2, carries much of the power of the *Norton Utilities* over to the *Windows* environment. The System Info module of *NDW* gives all the same information as the DOS version, and adds to it some *Windows*-specific information. Version 2 was a marked improvement in an already fine product, and a necessary upgrade if you plan to use *NDW* with *Windows* 3.1 or *DOS* 6.

PS/View

Smith, Brittain, Inc. publishes only one PC software product. It is *PS/View*. This is a unique program, of no use to most PC owners, but invaluable for some. If you have a PC with a Micro Channel (MCA) bus, especially if yours is some model in the IBM *PS/2* line, get a copy of *PS/View*. You will love it. *InfoSpotter* (version 2.5 or later) can do some of what *PS/View* can do, but *PS/View* is able to do quite a bit more.

The best news is that with this program you may almost never again need to use your *PS/2*'s reference diskette. (Keep it around, though, for those rare problem situations where you cannot access your hard disk.) *PS/View* will let you perform from the hard disk, without rebooting, most tasks you normally can do only after booting from the reference diskette. (*PS/View* was written primarily to support those machines, though it can be useful as well for any clone PC with an MCA bus.)

QA Plus

Diagsoft markets *QA Plus*. It is a program very similar to *CheckIt*. In fact, they both started with the same source code. Each has been rewritten, though, so they are no longer the same. *QA Plus* comes in a consumer version and as *QA Plus/FE* (for Field Engineer), the technician's version. Diagsoft also markets *QA Floppy* to test your floppy disk drives.

These are good programs, but their user interface is not as user-friendly as that in *CheckIt*. Also, *QA Plus* is rather intolerant of resident programs, and it may fail if your PC is running in protected mode. That means it shares some of the limitations of *AMIDIAG*, discussed above.

System Sleuth and Windows Sleuth

Dariana Technology Group publishes *System Sleuth* (the consumer version), *System Sleuth Pro* (an advanced model), and *Windows Sleuth*. These are primarily informational utility programs, but *System Sleuth Pro* includes another module called STEST to do diagnostic testing.

The DOS products are quite similar to *CheckIt* and *QA Plus*. *Windows Sleuth* was the first of a new genre, which now includes *Skylight* and the *Norton Desktop for Windows* SysInfo module—both mentioned above. Each of these programs has gone through several versions of improvements, but they are still a little rough around the edges.

Other Tools

These are by no means the only diagnostic and informational tools available for PCs. Some that have been left out of the foregoing list are ones intended for only very specialized uses or for only the most technically advanced users. Often they are more expensive, and they may come in one version for 8088- and 8086-based PCs and a different version for PCs whose CPU chip is an 80286 or higher model.

All too often, all you get for the added cost is added inconvenience. These other programs usually don't do any better job of testing, or tell you any information you cannot get by using a cheaper, consumer-oriented program that is easier to use and understand, such as those listed in this chapter.

SOFTWARE TOOLS—
MEMORY MANAGERS

These are the tools that you will use to manage the memory in your PC. They range from the very simple to the very complex.

This book is about memory management in PCs. This chapter lists the tools you will be using. Elsewhere in this book you have learned the principles behind these tools. That is important, because even the most automatic tool programs can use some help from time to time, and the more you understand what they are doing, the better prepared you will be to assist them in getting things just the way you want them.

Kirk Kokkonen's TSR Utilities

If you have any TSR programs you use, and if you enjoy a hands-on approach to managing your PC, you'll probably love this utility package. At least try it out—it's free.

> Kirk Kokkonen of TurboPower Software has created—and given to the world—a wonderful set of utilities. They are called the *TSR Utilities*. The latest version, 3.4, is included on the diskette that accompanies this book. The source codes for these utilities are available on CompuServe and many bulletin board systems. Typically, they will be in an archive file called TSRSRCXX.ZIP.

This utility set was substantially upgraded starting with Version 3.0, and now they are fully able to deal with the complexities of TSRs that get loaded into upper memory. Chapter 34 shows you some examples of how you may wish to put these utilities to work in your PC; the TSR.DOC file on the diskette includes even more.

What Is in the TSR Package?

These programs can be grouped—by their function—into four areas. The documentation files that come with the utilities describe all of them. These four areas are:

- Reporting programs
- Control programs
- Network-aware versions
- A programmer's aid

Seeing What You Have and Where It Is

MAPMEM, RAMFREE, and DEVICE are the reporting utilities in this package.

- *MAPMEM* shows the memory control block chain. With optional parameters, it can display both the chain in lower memory and any chains in upper memory. It can also give information about expanded and extended memory.

- *RAMFREE* tells you the space available for the next program that DOS will load (the same as what some versions of CHKDSK report as available memory).

- *DEVICE* shows the chain of device drivers in either of two formats. One display shows only those loaded through CONFIG.SYS and shows them in the order they were loaded. The other display shows all the device drivers in the chain, in the order in which they handle requests for service. This display is a bit more difficult to read, but it tells the real story about the priority with which the device drivers do their work.

MAPMEM tells you not only which programs "own" which regions of RAM, it also shows you which interrupts they have hooked. If you do not run WATCH (another program in this package) as your first TSR, then MAPMEM can only tell you about the interrupts that presently point to each TSR. If you run WATCH first, that program keeps a log of all the changes made to the interrupt vector table as each TSR becomes resident. By using that information, MAPMEM is able to show you all the interrupts hooked by each TSR, including those that were later taken over by another TSR.

WATCH gives MAPMEM more information to work with, but its use is optional. It is optional, that is, except if you wish to use DISABLE (about which you will learn more in a moment). DISABLE requires that you run WATCH before any TSR you later will be disabling.

Electronic Teflon

The major purpose of these utilities is to enable you to remove TSR programs from memory without rebooting your computer. You can remove a few recently written TSRs by simply giving them some special command or hot-key combination. Almost any TSR can be removed by use of these TSR utilities.

An unavoidable side effect of the way that TSRs link themselves into interrupts is that when you unload one, you must simultaneously unload all the TSRs loaded after it. However, with another of the utilities in this package, you can temporarily disable any individual TSR you wish, without affecting those loaded before or after it.

MARK, FMARK, DISABLE, and RELEASE are the heart of the TSR utility package. MARK is a small TSR that records the contents of the interrupt vector table and some other information about your system as it was at the moment that the copy of MARK was loaded.

If you are loading many TSRs into RAM at once, you may find it helpful to group them and to load a copy of MARK before each group. Then later on you can unload all of the TSRs loaded after a certain one of those MARKs without touching the ones loaded before it.

Each copy of MARK that you load will use about 1600 bytes of RAM. That can mount up. If you have ten TSR programs and you put a mark between each of them, there goes the better part of 20KB. You can ease the sting a little by loading the MARKs into upper memory, even if the TSRs they are "marking" are loaded into lower memory.

A better way to ease the sting is to switch to using FMARK. This program is just like MARK, except that it puts its stored information into a disk file. That lets FMARK itself use only about 150 bytes of your RAM. The disk file it creates will be between one and two KB, or about the size of the MARK that this FMARK replaces.

RELEASE is the program used to unload TSRs. If you have several copies of MARK loaded, you can direct RELEASE to unload any particular one of them you wish (and in the process unload all the TSRs that were loaded after that copy of MARK). Since these utilities allow you to "pull the rug out from under" TSR programs that otherwise would tenaciously hold onto their RAM allocations, I call the TSR utilities "electronic Teflon."

DISABLE is the program used to—you guessed it—disable a TSR temporarily. In order to do this, it needs to know more than just the information stored by a copy of MARK. The only way it can get the information it needs is if you have run WATCH before the TSR you now wish to disable.

Before it became common to load TSRs into upper memory, they always landed in lower RAM stacked up at ascending addresses in the same order that they had been loaded. Now, with DOS 5 or a later version, and with the other memory managers, it is possible to load some TSRs into upper memory and load others low. A consequence of this is that the simple ordering of yesteryear has been lost. One of the major ways in which the TSR utilities have been upgraded is to take account of this new complexity.

I commented that almost all TSRs could be unloaded by using the utilities in this set. Using MARK and RELEASE suffices for most. Some TSRs modify the operating environment in ways that MARK does not know about. They cannot be managed quite so simply. You can try using MARKNET and RELNET (which you will learn more about in a moment); sometimes that works. But some TSRs simply cannot be safely removed by any program.

Network-Aware Versions

If your PC is on a *Local Area Network* (LAN), it gets modified in more subtle ways by many TSR programs. Network drivers are particularly prone to alter some deeply buried details of DOS so they can do their job. MARK cannot record all of these changes, nor can RELEASE restore them. But MARKNET and RELNET can—at least in most cases. Specifically, this is one good way to manage the Novell NetWare TSR programs.

You also can use MARKNET and RELNET to handle the loading and unloading of "problem TSRs." These are the programs that have nothing to do with a network, but still make too many or too subtle changes in DOS to be properly managed by MARK and RELEASE. Like FMARK, MARKNET works by storing its data on the disk. Thus it only takes up a couple of hundred bytes of RAM. The disk file it creates is about twice as large as that created by FMARK; the exact sizes of these files depends on various aspects of the setup of your specific system.

Eating Memory

EATMEM is the final member of this package. It is meant mainly for programmers, but it could also be helpful as you are studying memory uses in your PC or as you seek to upgrade or improve the management of that memory.

EATMEM, as its name suggests, uses up RAM. You invoke it with one command line parameter: the number of kilobytes of RAM to "consume." EATMEM is a TSR with no function other than to hold space.

The main use of EATMEM is to diagnose problems arising from insufficient free memory. If you think you are experiencing symptoms due to insufficient memory, you can check out your guess in the following way.

Assume you see a problem when you run a certain program. Exit the program. Now, get rid of some TSRs or device drivers that you can do without, at least temporarily.

> If you have loaded suitable MARKS you may be able to do this with RELEASE. At worst, edit your CONFIG.SYS or AUTOEXEC.BAT files and reboot.

See if the problem you were attempting to diagnose goes away. If it did, perhaps the problem was caused by not having enough free memory. Then again, maybe it was due to interference by one or more of the TSRs and device drivers you removed.

To test that possibility, run EATMEM and specify a size equal to that used by all the TSRs and device drivers you removed. EATMEM will not interfere with any other program, but it will tie up a bunch of RAM.

If your problem comes back, you can safely conclude it was caused by too little memory. If the problem is still gone, you need to look more closely at the TSRs or device drivers you removed. One or more of them, in combination with the program you left in RAM, is causing your difficulties.

A subtle point: If you remove some TSRs or device drivers from upper memory, be sure to replace their RAM use with a copy of EATMEM that also is loaded high.

When These Programs Are
Not Enough, or Are Not Safe to Use

These are wonderful programs. They show you information about your system's use of memory and interrupts that are not nearly as easy to get by any other means. They also enable you to load and unload whole groups of TSRs with great facility. (The TSR.DOC file shows details on building the necessary batch files.)

But they are not always able to do their jobs correctly. Some TSRs do things they cannot undo. Problems usually arise when one TSR is directly linked to another one. If you release both you'll be okay, but not if you release just one of them. Even worse is when a TSR links to a device driver loaded through your CONFIG.SYS file. RELEASE simply doesn't know how to remove a device driver. Consequently, RELEASE must not be used to remove the linked TSR. You will find more details on these and other limitations in the file TSR.DOC.

One file that TSR.DOC warns you not to try to remove with RELEASE is FASTOPEN. But if you are following the advice in this book, you won't use FASTOPEN in the first place!

> You could use the *Dynamic Memory Control* (DMC) programs NOTE and FREENOTE in place of MARK and RELEASE. The DMC programs know how to do the same tricks for TSRs, and with their companion program LDEVICE, they can do the same for most device drivers. See Chapter 34 for details on how to use DMC. Realize, though, that their greater capability comes at a cost: DMC is a commercial program; the *TSR Utilities* are free.

Other TSR Managers

The Kirk Kokkonen *TSR Utilities* provide a good way to manage TSR programs. And they have the great virtue of being free. But they are not for everyone.

Some people want to run one program that will manage all the others, and do so relatively automatically. They want what I have called a TSR manager. This section describes a few of them.

Referee, PopDrop, and PopDrop Plus

PopDrop and *PopDrop Plus*, from Bloc Publishing, are simple TSR managers. *PopDrop* provides much the same functionality as the MARK, DISABLE, and RELEASE programs described above. *PopDrop Plus* adds two more features.

One is the ability to swap a pop-up TSR out to expanded memory and, when you press that TSR's hot-key, swap it back in (to the EMS page frame). This allows you to pop up that TSR over most any program. With just *PopDrop* (or *Referee*, or MARK and RELEASE) you could load and unload the TSR, but if it was not in memory, you could not bring it back there automatically. And in particular, you could not bring it there while you were in the middle of running another program.

The other added feature in *PopDrop Plus* is the ability to load programs into UMBs. Of course, if you are running DOS 5 or 6 you already have that capability built into DOS.

Headroom, Netroom, and Connecting Room

Headroom, from Helix Software, does all the things that *PopDrop Plus* and the other programs mentioned above can do, and it does a few more. For example, it can swap some device drivers to expanded memory. It can monitor an I/O port and—when it sees a certain bit pattern appear there—swap in an application program that knows how to deal with that situation. (This could be a communications program that needs to be activated if the phone rings, for example.)

Netroom, also from Helix Software, adds another wrinkle. It is optimized for the purpose of swapping out LAN drivers. These tend to be very large TSRs or device drivers, and they need to be able to return and do their work in a flash, whenever DOS or the network needs them.

Connecting Room is a similar product from Helix, but this product is optimized to manage a host session on your PC. Both *Netroom* and *Connecting Room* will keep your connection (to the LAN or to the host) alive while your network software or terminal emulation software TSR is swapped out.

Both of these programs return the swapped-out TSR when it is needed. *Netroom* does this by monitoring requests for network services. *Connecting Room* does it by watching for you to press the host session hot key. When the host wants you, *Connecting Room* will ring a bell; you have to press the hot key to get back into the session. Even if you take a moment to do so, any message coming from the host will be saved for you.

The Swap Utilities and Related Programs

Another kind of program manager that merits mention is exemplified by the *Swap Utilities* from Innovative Data Concepts. Each of these programs is meant to be used with one particular, large application program.

SwapIS and the Other Swap Utilities

InfoSelect is a free-form database program that can be run as a TSR program. (There is now a *Windows* version of *InfoSelect*; this discussion applies just to the original, DOS version.) If you do this, you'll find that it takes up about 103KB of your lower memory. The advantage of doing this is that you can pop up *InfoSelect* from within another application—either to record a random thought or to look up something you previously stored in its database.

All this works just fine as long as you only want to run smallish application programs. But it definitely precludes running any large ones while *InfoSelect* is resident.

SwapIS is the *Swap Utility* for *InfoSelect*. If you run *SwapIS*, it will first load itself, then *InfoSelect*, then swap *InfoSelect* out to expanded or extended memory, or to disk. You can then pop up *InfoSelect* any time you want, just by touching a hot key. The added benefit is that you will still have almost as much free lower memory as you had before.

> To get numerical, *SwapIS* leaves a 7.5KB stub in lower memory, and it uses almost 50KB of EMS memory for itself. The swapped image of *InfoSelect* takes up another 110KB of EMS memory. This means you have to give up 7.5KB of lower memory, and 160KB of EMS memory to use this approach, as opposed to giving up 103KB of lower memory and no EMS memory if you load *InfoSelect* directly.

SHROOM

Another program with a similar capability is SHROOM. This program, which is available as shareware in the file SHROOM.ZIP on CompuServe and other bulletin boards, will give one application (call it program A) the ability to swap itself out of lower memory and run any other application (call it program B) you wish. Program B will find that it has almost all of your lower memory space free in which to do its work. As soon as you exit from program B, you will find yourself back in the original application program A, right where you left off.

If program B (the one you swap away to) is COMMAND (or NDOS or *4DOS*), you will get a DOS prompt. At that point you can issue any normal DOS command and run any application program or batch file. When you are through, just type EXIT and press Enter. Poof! You're back in program A once more as if you had never left it.

One precaution you *must* observe with any swap program like these is not to load any TSRs while you are swapped out of the first application. If you do so, you will lock in some lower memory just above the swap program's stub and that will prevent the original application from returning to its place in lower memory.

Warning   Don't ever try to swap out any disk cache program. Also, don't swap out a LAN driver or a TSR that connects you to a mainframe host session, unless the swap program you are using has been optimized for that use.

DOS Shell Programs and Program Launchers

Task swappers and TSR managers are valuable, but sometimes you'd like to do something they cannot easily help you do. This brings us to the land of DOS-shell programs and program launchers.

A *program launcher* is any program that presents a menu of programs you might wish to run. When you pick an item off the menu, the corresponding program runs. When you exit that program you get back to the menu, ready to pick the next program to run.

A DOS-shell program is any program that hides the command interpreter's prompt and, generally, that makes it easier to do various simple DOS operations. Many of them could also be called file managers, as they are especially useful as tools to automate some of the common tasks of disk file maintenance.

Automenu

Automenu, from Magee Enterprises, is a program launcher. You build one or more menu definition files, then *Automenu* will present those menus to you. From each one, you can either pull up another menu or launch a program. *Automenu* has two ways to launch programs.

The first way it launches programs is to create a batch file to do it. Then *Automenu* exits, returning to DOS all the memory it was using, and as it goes, it asks COMMAND.COM to run the batch file it just created. The last step in that batch file reinvokes *Automenu*.

The second way is for *Automenu* to load and run the program directly, on top of itself. The first method gives the batch file and any program it runs the maximum possible amount of lower memory to work in. The second method gives much less, as *Automenu* is still in RAM, taking up some space. The advantage to the second method is speed, though in most systems the speed gain is minimal.

XTree, XTree Pro, and XTree Gold

Executive Systems' *XTree* is perhaps the most popular DOS shell program. It provides a very easy-to-learn means of seeing and manipulating the files on your disk. You can tag groups of files and move, copy, or delete them with just a few key strokes.

XTree Pro markedly enhances those capabilities. It is faster, and it allows you to have multiple disks "logged" at the same time. This means you can rapidly switch between them without having to wait each time for it to reread the disk directories. It also allows you to manipulate all the files on all the logged disks as a group. For example, tagging all files with the archive attribute turned on.

XTree Gold went much further. It is mouse-aware, and it added the ability to view many files in their native format, along with a file transfer utility, XTLink, in its latest version. Also, *XTree Gold* permits you to build a menu of applications you would like to run. You can use this program as your home base. Some people start *XTree Gold*—using a line in their AUTOEXEC.BAT file—and never leave it. From within it they choose which other programs to run and launch them, or they drop to a DOS command line to do simple DOS commands, or they use *XTree Gold*'s built-in disk maintenance tools to do those sorts of chores very simply and quickly.

If your PC is connected to a network, there is a network version of *XTree* that you may wish to use. Its main advantage is that it can directly manipulate access rights to files, directories, and groups.

PC Tools SHELL

The *PC Tools Utility* package is quite comprehensive. Some wit said, "The only file not in PC Tools is KITCHEN.SINK." It includes one, the SHELL program, that its aficionados love to use just as I have described using *XTree Gold.*

Magellan

Lotus's *Magellan* is the program that popularized the inclusion of file viewers within a DOS shell program. Its greatest strength is in helping you locate a file on your disk, either by its name or by a string of characters it contains. In addition, it can do all the other things any good DOS shell can do, and its file viewers are very fast.

Norton Commander

The Norton Commander is a bit different. It runs and displays a screen of information about two directories on one or two disk drives. Then it presents you with the real DOS prompt. At that point you can do anything you normally would at such a prompt. The Norton Commander's greatest strength is in its ability to manipulate files. It also includes a number of native format file viewers and an easy link to MCI Mail.

A Batch File, Enhanced

You can make a menu with a simple batch file. If the items are numbered 1 to 10, you could then have other batch files named 1.BAT through 10.BAT. Each of them would run some application, and end by returning to the same directory and rerunning the original MENU.BAT file.

You can carry this a whole lot further if you use an enhanced version of the DOS batch language. Many such programs are available. *STACKEY* and *BATUTIL* are just a couple that you may find on a local electronic bulletin board.

The *Norton Utilities* collection of programs includes a Batch Enhancer that lets you add exploding windows, sound effects, and colors to your batch files. Used creatively you can create a custom menu program in just a few minutes with most of the power of many commercial ones.

Builder, from Hyperkinetics, carries this idea a whole lot further. It adds over 200 new commands, and it allows you to create fancy batch files that are then compiled into executable programs.

Titus DOS

Titus DOS, from Titus Communications Corporation, is an unusual product. It creates a graphical environment, rather like *Windows* in appearance, from which one can launch DOS applications. You can even use *Windows* icon files to set the appearance of the buttons that launch the various applications.

But it is not in any sense a *Windows*-like environment. You can only run DOS applications, and then only one at a time.

There are many more DOS shells and program launchers available. Some are commercial programs, some are shareware, and some are free for the taking from bulletin boards. All of them offer features similar to those discussed for the products listed here. None are markedly better than these.

Task-Swapping Program Managers

The next step up from a DOS shell and program launcher is a task-swapping program manager. This is a program that can do for applications what the TSR managers do for TSR programs. It can let you run more than one application, and while you are in the middle of any one of them, enable you to switch to another one, or back to the menu to start up yet another program.

DOSSHELL and TaskMAX

MS-DOS and *PC DOS* have included their DOSSHELL program since version 4. The DOSSHELL that came with version 4 was not very good. The DOS 5 or 6 version is much better.

DOSSHELL does not automatically give you the ability to swap tasks. You must activate that by choosing Activate Task Swapper on the Options menu.

A basic limitation of this program is that it always swaps programs to a disk file, which makes it much slower than task swappers that can swap to EMS, XMS, or (plain) extended memory.

You can speed up the DOSSHELL by creating a large RAM disk and directing it to swap to that location (by setting the TEMP variable in the DOS environment). Please be sure that the RAM disk is large enough. Unpredictable things may happen if DOSSHELL runs out of space there.

DR DOS has a corresponding program, TaskMAX. In version 6, it is able to swap to expanded or extended memory as well as to disk. Unlike DOSSHELL (with the RAM drive trick described above), if it runs out of room in one place, it will automatically spill over to the next slower storage medium. Another difference between TaskMAX and DOSSHELL is that the latter combines a DOS-shell program and a task swapper, while TaskMAX is just a task swapper. TaskMAX can be run from within its companion DOS-shell program, ViewMAX, or directly from the DOS prompt.

As with all the programs discussed in this section, if you run a TSR from within the task swapper, you will be able to switch away from it and later on switch back. But while that TSR is swapped out, you will not be able to activate it with the usual hot key. Only a true TSR manager can accomplish that feat.

WordPerfect *Office*

The WordPerfect *Office* program is a task-swapping program manager. Like DOSSHELL or TaskMAX, it allows you to set up a number of tasks which you can activate one at a time and, once they are active, you can swap among them. The programs that have been activated, but which are swapped out, are not running. They are in a suspended state until you swap back to them. (This is true for all the programs discussed in this section.)

The most special feature of *Office* is its close integration with the other products of the WordPerfect Corporation, and its use of the same keystrokes. So if you use WordPerfect products already, *Office* is a natural choice in this category of software.

Software Carousel

SoftLogic's *Software Carousel* is one of the most popular task-swapping program managers. Its features are much like those of the other programs listed here. One special feature is its companion product *OLE* (Open Link Extender). This is a program you run before *Software Carousel* that will keep your mainframe communications sessions going even when you swap away the TSR that you normally use to communicate with the mainframe. (Thus it works much like the Helix program *Connecting Room.*)

Headroom

You have already met *Headroom* as a TSR manager. It also can be used to swap among application programs, so it fits here too. For swapping away from a host session, use the companion product from Helix, *Connecting Room.*

OmniView, B&F, and SwitchIt

Sunny Hill Software's *OmniView* is much like *Software Carousel*. *B&F* (Back and Forth), from Progressive Solutions, is a popular shareware task swapper. *SwitchIt*, from Better Technologies is yet another member of this class. Each has its own special features, its ardent champions, and its detractors. None is clearly superior to all the others in this class.

Multitasking Program Managers

This group of memory-management programs is covered at some length in Chapter 21. For completeness they are listed again here.

DoubleDOS is a two-task executive. That limitation is helping it disappear from the marketplace (although not as fast as its manufacturer might like—some people love it so much it just won't die!). *DESQview* is able to swap many tasks, putting them into stasis if it must, but letting them all keep running if that is possible given the memory resources it has to work with. Both *DoubleDOS* and *DESQview* are character-oriented programs, although they can run graphics mode programs in their windows.

Microsoft's *Windows* (and its network version, *Windows for Workgroups*) and *GeoWorks* are the most popular fully graphical multitasking operating environments for DOS. All of the programs in this section must run on top of DOS, but each of them hides DOS from the user almost totally, and each of them provides many services to the programs running under them. DOS is still used for all file access and disk management services, though that fact is often well hidden from the user.

Memory Allocators and UMB Providers

Memory management means several things. The TSR managers, DOS-shell programs, program launchers, and task swappers all control how programs use memory. Now we turn to a very different kind of memory-management tool—those programs that alter the very form of memory, as it is seen by programs, including those already discussed in this chapter.

These are the memory allocators that one adds on top of DOS to allow the allocation of memory that DOS is not aware of. They include managers of LIM-EMS-compatible expanded memory, and XMS, VCPI, and DPMI servers. Generally, you need at least one of these programs before you can use any of the others mentioned above to its full effectiveness.

A few of the programs mentioned earlier in this chapter will appropriate extended memory to themselves by the top-down technique. You must leave enough extended memory available in that form for them to use. That is the one exception to the general rule that these memory allocators are needed to run the program managers.

The following lists of programs may help you find what you need. You must check each one to be sure it provides the kinds of services you most want. Also be aware that just because a program provides something, it may not provide as much as you want. For example, the LIM 4.0 EMS standard allows for up to 32MB of expanded memory. *AboveDISC+* can provide at most only 4MB, while *Turbo EMS* can provide all the way up to 32MB.

Programs That Control Expanded Memory

Every manufacturer of a hardware EMS board will supply a matching EMM (expanded memory manager). This is a device driver program that knows how to operate that brand of EMS board. Normally you should use only the EMM that comes with the hardware. Don't try mixing hardware brands. If you must use several EMS boards of different brands in one PC, configure all but one brand of board to supply only extended memory.

PCs that have special motherboard logic chip sets can sometimes provide hardware EMS memory from motherboard RAM. Those machines will come with their own EMM, but you have more options in this case. You can use their EMM or you can run a program that provides EMS services and more, provided it understands that brand of motherboard chip set.

- *AboveDISC+* knows about memory managed by an *All Charge Card*, as well as the IBM XMA card, any EEMS memory card, or any PC that uses the Chips and Technologies *NeAT CHIPSet*.

- *QRAM 50/60* understands the chip set in *IBM PS/2* Models 50 and 60.

- *QRAM* understands various models of Chips and Technologies chip sets that provide shadow RAM.

- *High386*, from RYBS, understands certain models of Chips and Technologies chip sets that provide shadow RAM.

- *BlueMAX* understands all models of IBM *PS/2*.

- *386MAX* understands various models of Chips and Technologies chip sets that provide shadow RAM.

- *LIMSIM* understands the Chips and Technologies *Neat 286 CHIPSet* machines and any Intel architecture EMS boards.

- *QMAPS* and *UMBPro* understand many Chips and Technologies chips sets including their *NeAT, LeAP, LeAPSX, PEAK,* and *ScAT* sets, plus various chip set models from Headlands, Intel, Opti, Texas Instruments, VLSI Technology, UMC, and Western Digital.

If you don't know what kind of chip set your motherboard uses, you can use the CHIPSET utility that comes with QMAPS and UMBPro, the LOADHI report from QRAM, or the CHIPS program that comes with *386MAX* to see if yours will work with that program. Otherwise you will have to use the EMM that came with your motherboard.

Programs That Provide Only XMS Services (No EMS Services)

Microsoft's HIMEM.SYS and Quadtel's *UMBPro* provide XMS services. If you use HIMEM.SYS, you must also use EMM386.EXE to provide UMBs and then only on class 5 or 6 PCs. (If you provide UMBs by some means other than using EMM386, HIMEM.SYS cannot find them. It will continue to provide all XMS services related to extended memory and the HMA, it just won't attempt to manage upper memory.) *UMBPro* can create UMBs from shadow RAM. If you have previously loaded an EMM for a hardware LIM 4.0 EMS expanded memory board, *UMBPro* can also create UMBs from EMS memory (these options available for class 2 or 4 PCs), as well as being able to convert extended memory on a class 5 or 6 PC.

Programs That Can Create UMBs

Most any (LIM 4.0 EMS compatible) EMM can map memory into some empty spaces in upper memory. If you don't use that memory as a page frame, or if it can map more than you choose to use for the page frame, the rest can be used for upper memory blocks (UMBs).

All of the LIMulators can provide UMBs on a class 5 or 6 PC. That includes the DOS program EMM386.EXE. Some of the LIMulators can also do this on certain class 4 PCs. Generally, the list given in the section "Programs That Control Expanded Memory" also indicates the programs that can provide UMBs and for which class 4 PCs they can do this.

Other LIMulators not mentioned in the previous list include *All 386*, *Turbo EMS*, and *Memory Commander*. *Move'Em* was a memory manager that is now included as an aspect of *386MAX*.

MM.SYS (the one that comes with the *MegaMizer*, and then only with that card) can create UMBs. It also can provide UMB-related XMS services (and only those XMS services).

Programs That Support VCPI

The *Virtual Control Program Interface* (VCPI) is only an issue for LIMulators on class 5 or 6 PCs. All of the modern LIMulators support this specification, at least in their latest versions.

Programs That Support DPMI

The *DOS Protected Mode Interface* (DPMI) specification is much newer and only a few of the memory managers presently support it. These include *QEMM*, *BlueMax*, and *386MAX*. *Windows* 3.x is also a DPMI server.

30

SOFTWARE-BASED PRODUCTS—OTHER GOOD USES FOR RAM

Sometimes it really pays to waste things. This chapter tells you some good ways to squander your RAM resource (and why you really should!).

Using the suggestions you have read so far, you may be able to clear out all the junk from conventional memory. Don't go overboard; that is, don't let your enthusiasm for that task lead you to forget something you need.

Some Particularly Useful Ways to Squander RAM

After you have cleared out your PC's memory as much as is prudent, look to see what extra RAM you have—RAM that is not being used by any TSR or device driver and which your applications don't need. Often you won't have any leftover RAM, but if you do, here are some valuable ways you might put that RAM to good use.

RAM Disks

RAM disks (also called virtual disks) are one very good way to spend any leftover RAM. You learned all about this in Chapter 20. Here is a short list of some RAM disk programs you might wish to use:

- VDISK (included with *PC DOS*)

- RAMDRIVE (included with *MS-DOS*)

- The *Memory Commander* RAM disk (included with *Memory Commander*)

- Quadtel's RAM disk (included with *UMBPro* and *QMAPS*)

> SRDISK is a shareware RAM disk program with some interesting features that is included on the diskette that accompanies this book.

- ADJRAM41.ZIP, VARIRAM.ZIP, and XPANDISK.ZIP (all shareware)

- The RAM disk that comes in PC-Kwik's *Power Pak* and *WinMaster* packages.

Perhaps the most interesting of these is the *Memory Commander's* RAM disk, in that it takes up *no* lower or upper memory at all. All of the program code and the RAM disk data space is in extended (XMS) memory.

The shareware RAM disk programs listed above feature the ability to grow or shrink on the fly. This is especially valuable if you must put them in lower memory (for example, on a class 1 laptop).

The PC-Kwik RAM disk is able to borrow memory from the *Super PC-Kwik* disk cache, and to do so only while files are stored on the RAM disk.

Disk Cache Programs

Disk cache programs are another clearly valuable use of RAM. I hesitate to say of excess RAM, for until you have a disk cache loaded you have not finished loading what you need, in my view.

The DOS disk cache, unfortunately, has not always been the best one to use. It used to be much slower than most of the alternatives, and it has caused some serious problems (see Chapter 31). The latest versions, which came with Windows 3.1 and DOS 6, are markedly improved, making it about on a par with the best the industry has to offer. Still, if you want the very, very best, you will want to check out the others listed here.

What are the good ones? Here is another very short list:

- *Super PC-Kwik* (from Multisoft)

- *Hyperdisk* (shareware)

- *Memory Commander*'s disk cache (included with *Memory Commander*)

- Quadtel's disk cache (included with *UMBPro* and *QMAPS*)

- Norton Cache (included with *The Norton Utilities*)

The best thing about *Super PC-Kwik* is its ability to share its pool of memory with *Windows*, its own companion programs, and other applications, especially with the *PC-Kwik* print spooler. So get the Multisoft *Power Pak* if you want to use *Super PC-Kwik*.

The best thing about *Hyperdisk* is that it takes up less lower and upper memory than most any other cache, except, that is, for the one that comes with *Memory Commander*. Again, that one takes up *no* lower or upper memory.

Print Spoolers

You get no computing done when you are waiting for your printer. Print Spoolers are programs that can accept jobs for the printer, store them temporarily in memory or on disk, and then dole them out to the printer as it is ready. In the meantime, you get to go on computing.

DOS includes a disk-based, somewhat rudimentary print spooler called PRINT. It's okay, but there are better ones available. *Windows* includes its Print Manager. This program has some added features beyond those available with PRINT, but still it is far from the most convenient or fastest way to go.

Here is another short list of programs you may want to consider getting:

- The PC-Kwik print spooler (part of PC-Kwik Corp. *Power Pak*)
- *PrintCache* (from LaserTools)
- Quadtel's Print Tools (included with *UMBPro* and *QMAPS*)

A Few Other Important Device Drivers

This section lists a few other device drivers you may want to get and load. Some are almost mandatory in most modern PCs.

- ANSI.SYS (or NANSI.SYS, MCROANSI.SYS, ZANSI.SYS, DVANSI.SYS, etc.)
- SHARE
- MOUSE.SYS
- MOVEHDD
- *Stacker* (or *SuperStor*, or *Expanz!*)

See the discussion of ANSI.SYS and SHARE in Chapter 20. Load MOUSE.SYS when you want mouse support for all your programs. Load MOUSE.COM (listed in the next group of programs) from a batch file and use MARK and RELEASE to get it out of memory when you aren't using it if you are only going to use it occasionally. MOVEHDD is discussed in Chapter 21.

Stacker is discussed in Chapters 5, 6, 20, and 21. Especially interesting is the possibility of using it to double the effective size of a RAM disk (see Chapter 20). If you use DOS 6 you get DoubleSpace included with it. That program can do much, but not all, of what Stacker can, and naturally it has the attraction of coming with DOS at no extra cost.

A Few Interesting TSR Programs

And finally, here are some TSRs you may not have thought to load, but that you may wish to use:

- MOUSE.COM
- PC-Kwik Screen Accelerator (part of PC-Kwik Corp.'s *Power Pak*)
- PC-Kwik Keyboard Accelerator (part of PC-Kwik Corp.'s *Power Pak*)
- CED
- *PCPANEL* (from LaserTools)

CED augments COMMAND.COM in some ways that are similar to the innovations found in NDOS and *4DOS*. The main difference is that CED is just a TSR and not a replacement command interpreter.

You want *PCPANEL* only if you have a PostScript printer. *PCPANEL* is a program that intercepts all output bound for your printer. If the print job is a PostScript job, it is allowed to pass unaltered. If it is an HP PCL job, the printer's *LaserJet* emulation is turned on, or it wraps the job in appropriate PostScript code. And pure ASCII print jobs are similarly bundled with the PostScript code they need in order to be printed. (Many PostScript-capable printers that are advertised as having the ability to switch emulations automatically are actually just PostScript printers, or dual-emulation printers—usually PostScript and PCL—that don't actually autoswitch; they simply have a copy of *PCPANEL* bundled with them.)

DEALING WITH DIFFICULTIES

This part of the book may be the most important of all. Its subject is how you can help yourself out of any difficulties you may find yourself in as you attempt to put the things you learned elsewhere in this book into practice.

The first chapter covers a number of common problems. The second one gives a systematic approach to any problem. The third tells you how to find additional help when you need it. With this information, and a little patience, you most likely will be able to accomplish whatever you choose. Good luck and have fun.

31

A BESTIARY OF MEMORY-MANAGEMENT "GREMLINS"

Not every problem is here, but many are. Check and see if perhaps your quandary has been faced and fixed by others.

This is not a book on troubleshooting PC hardware. I am assuming, therefore, that malfunctioning hardware is not the source of your difficulties. Of course, misconfigured hardware may be. That we will deal with, at least somewhat. But the primary focus will be on getting your PC memory management right.

Some Common Puzzlements

Not everything that is puzzling actually means something is wrong. Often you simply don't see what is going on clearly. Or perhaps you lack some understanding that would make what you see perfectly reasonable.

Not All Things That Puzzle Are Problems

Here are some examples of things people often get confused by, but which really do not indicate something is amiss with their PC.

The Case of the Missing Memory—#1

You add some memory to your PC. You fire it up and run CHKDSK. That is how you have been accustomed to seeing what memory you have. You don't see any change in the numbers that CHKDSK reports.

What is going on? CHKDSK reports only statistics on the space on your disk drive and in lower memory. If you add expanded or extended memory, it will not show up there. You simply need to use some alternative memory-reporting program.

The Case of the Missing Memory—#2

You add some memory to your PC. Specifically, you add an expanded memory card. You fire up your PC and run *Manifest*. That is supposed to be the best memory-reporting utility around. But it fails to show your new memory at all. What happened?

You forgot to load the EMM (expanded memory manager) device driver program through a DEVICE statement in your CONFIG.SYS file. Or perhaps you tried doing so, but you incorrectly typed the line or left off the EMM program's extension.

Once you get the CONFIG.SYS file just right, you will see a message from the EMM when it loads. After that, *Manifest* will show your new memory and any EMS-aware program will be able to use it.

The Case of the Missing Memory—#3

You have 8MB of RAM in your PC, all on the motherboard. You know that means you have at least 7MB of extended memory. But MAPMEM says you haven't got any available extended memory. You are sure you haven't loaded that many programs. So what is going on?

You have loaded an XMS memory manager (could be HIMEM.SYS or could be some LIMulator like *QEMM* or *386MAX*) through a line in your CONFIG.SYS file. It has taken all of your extended memory for its use. All of it is now XMS memory. Or maybe a lot of that has been converted to simulated expanded memory if you used a LIMulator. Run MEM /C on another memory-reporting utility and look for available EMS or XMS memory.

The Case of Too Much Memory

You have 8MB of RAM in your PC. You know that means you have about 7MB of extended memory. You run a memory-reporting program and it tells you that you have almost 10MB of available XMS memory and a similar amount of available EMS memory. How can that be?

A variant form of this is that your memory-reporting program gives various amounts of XMS memory in use for this and that, then reports a total of XMS memory that is more or less than the total of the different uses it describes.

The answer here is that many memory-reporting programs do not get all their answers right. One way they can get fooled is if you have loaded a LIMulator that makes the memory under its control available as either XMS or EMS. The memory reporter may simply add the reported amounts of XMS and EMS memory when, in actuality, both numbers refer to the same RAM. Thus it will get a total that is twice what it should be.

Sometimes the Peculiar Is a Problem

Here's a puzzling situation that does indicate a problem. It can be understood easily enough. Solving it is tougher.

You run the integrated multi-application package *Framework*. It loads a lot of itself into extended memory and runs just fine. Later on you reboot, and this time you load HIMEM.SYS. Now *Framework* won't work. It says you haven't got any available extended memory. What happened?

Framework uses raw extended memory from the top down. When it is through, it returns that memory to the available pool of extended memory. HIMEM.SYS is an XMM (extended memory manager). It grabs all your extended memory and makes it into XMS memory. Once it has done that, all of the extended memory that was available is taken and now can only be accessed as XMS memory (or the first 64KB can be accessed as the HMA, but then not as XMS memory).

The only solution to this quandary is to use applications that understand the XMS way of accessing memory, or to forego loading an XMM (and thus forego using the HMA or running any program that requires access to extended memory by the XMS method). Or you can reboot a lot with different configurations each time. (This suggestion can be made more practical by using special batch files or boot managers. See the discussion of this in Chapter 20.)

Some Things to Watch Out For

There are some common problems connected to PC memory that you need to be aware of. And you need to know the signs to look for and how to interpret them when you see them. Here are several.

POST 201 Messages

If, during the boot process, you get a message on-screen that includes the number 201, you have a problem with some of the RAM in your PC. The 201 indicates an error detected by the POST program when it attempted to test and initialize the RAM. The other numbers on that line are clues as to where the memory failure occurred in the CPU's memory address space.

How do you interpret those other numbers? I usually don't. Instead, I look to see what the last number was that the POST put on-screen as it was clocking off the regions of RAM it had tested and found to be good. That tells me the problem is in the next bank of RAM.

Once you know where a RAM problem is, to the nearest bank, the solution is to change the chips or modules that make up that bank. Often they are cheap enough that you can throw away the bad bank. If that is not the case, you can do further tests, by simply swapping individual chips, to pin down exactly which one(s) are defective.

Watch out. You might find out that all the chips are good, but one or more were badly seated in their sockets. Test the putative bad ones at least once to be sure they are bad.

If you have an intermittent 201 error message, you probably have some marginal RAM. This is better tested by a third-party program such as *CheckIt* that can repeatedly test sections of RAM. First decide which bank is in question (by the procedure just described), then test it for 24 hours or so. That ought to smoke out any bad chips.

PARITY CHECK 1 (or 2) or I/O MEMORY ERROR

Any IBM-brand PC or *PS/2* checks memory on every read operation to be sure that each byte it reads is valid. It uses one extra bit for each byte, called the parity bit, to provide this assurance. If it reaches the conclusion that a byte was invalid, it puts one of two messages on-screen: PARITY CHECK 1 or PARITY CHECK 2. Then it halts the PC.

What do these messages mean? Why two of them? They indicate some glitch in memory. It could be a bad memory chip or simply a flipped bit caused by some minor power line spike or cosmic ray.

Whatever the cause, at least one byte in RAM was invalid when the CPU went to read it. Where? That is what the 1 or 2 in those messages is about. But it is only a very coarse hint. If the RAM failure occurred on the motherboard, the message ends in 1. If it occurred on a plug-in memory card the message ends in 2.

Some clone PCs are kinder to you. They also catch and report parity errors, and then halt the PC, but they report more fully. A typical message from one of them might read I/O MEMORY ERROR AT XXXXXh. The Xs here stand for some hexadecimal number indicating the memory address where the error was detected. (The lowercase h at the end of the sample message may not appear on your screen; still, the address displayed is almost certainly a hexadecimal number.)

If the cause was a flaky RAM chip, seeing the same address on each of several successive reboot attempts (or addresses close enough together to be in the same memory bank) will point out which bank of chips contains the flaky one. If the address wanders from occurrence to occurrence, it might indicate a marginal power supply or a low voltage condition on the power line.

What should you do if you see these messages? There are several cases to consider. If they happen rarely, you may choose simply to ignore them. Most likely your RAM is functioning okay, and the messages indicate some rare glitches from the power line or wherever.

If you are getting a lot of parity error messages, you have to decide if you believe the messages. You may have some bad memory chips or ones that can't quite run fast enough for your PC. Another possibility is that your PC's power supply might be putting out a marginally too low voltage. Either way, if the parity errors are real, you need to fix your hardware to make them cease. On the other hand, sometimes the parity-checking circuitry gives false error indications. If you have some independent way to assess the validity of the information that was being read at the time the message occurred, and if the messages are happening altogether too often to ignore, you can choose simply to turn off parity checking. You can do this in either one of two ways. Load a TSR that hooks the interrupt by which the parity error is reported and then does nothing with it. Or turn off the parity-checking hardware. (You may or may not be able to turn off the parity-checking hardware. Some motherboards offer this option in their configuration setup routine. Some memory option cards have a jumper or DIP switch for this purpose.)

You can get a program called PARCHK from various bulletin boards (in a file PARCHK.ZIP, most likely). Its documentation file is larger than the program and mostly explains why you only rarely will want to use it! PARCHK will work in any PC, but it has two disadvantages. One is that it globally turns off parity checking for all memory addresses. If you had merely turned off the parity-checking circuitry on one plug-in card, the remaining RAM would still be protected. The second disadvantage to the TSR is simply that it uses up some RAM. That is a minor problem, as the program is very small.

Stack Overflow Message

If you get a message STACK OVERFLOW, usually this means you have a stack somewhere in memory that has overflowed. If you have a line in your CONFIG.SYS file that reads STACKS = 0,0, try changing it to something like STACKS = 9,128 (the default value) or even STACKS = 16,256. The larger the numbers, the more memory you are using for these public stacks, but if it solves your problem, that may be a necessary expenditure of RAM.

There is at least one other way this message can occur. Larson Computing (the publishers of *LIMSIM*) says that if you are converting motherboard memory into hardware EMS memory on a PC that has a NeAT CHIPSet and you see a STACK OVERFLOW message, it could mean your memory chips are working just a tad too slowly.

You could replace those RAM chips with faster ones, add more wait states, turn off memory interleaving (which will cause more wait states to be inserted), or run your PC at a slower clock rate. If you know you have an 82C212 chip as a part of the chip set, replace it with an 82C212B.

When Windows Won't Run in 386 Enhanced Mode (but Will in Standard Mode)

You need to have a PC in class 5 or 6 to run *Windows* in enhanced mode. You also must have enough free memory. Sometimes you know you have met both of those conditions, but still you can't get *Windows* to run in enhanced mode.

Try putting a line in the SYSTEM.INI file in the [386Enh] section that reads:

```
EMMExclude=A000,FFFF
```

If that solves the problem, try reducing the range indicated in that statement (and restarting *Windows* each time) until the problem occurs again.

When the problem shows up again, the last region you made available to *Windows* (by not excluding it) is probably a region of upper memory space that *Windows* is trying to use, but which is not really available for use. Finally, when you have found all the places you must exclude, leave the EMMExclude statement in the SYSTEM.INI file with just those regions excluded (but leaving in as much else as you can so *Windows* can use any upper memory space it finds that truly is available).

Alternatively, you may solve this problem by denying the use of those upper memory regions to your LIMulator. All LIMulator programs provide some means of excluding regions similar to the EMMExclude statement shown above.

Windows Crashes During Logo Screen Display

When *Windows* first switches into graphics mode, it also puts the processor into protected mode and tries to grab all the upper memory it can. If it crashes at that moment, this often indicates that there is a network interface card or other device using some upper memory in a way that *Windows* cannot detect. The technique for solving this problem is the same as for the previous problem.

Intermittent Message: `Error Reading (Writing) Drive X:`

If you see a message that reads Error reading drive C or some such, it could indicate flaky hardware. More often though, it indicates that you have a disk controller that is using DMA (*Direct Memory Access*) to move data to or from the drive, you are running some protected-mode memory manager that remaps memory, and the controller is not "double-buffered." (Naturally, this can only occur on a class 5 or 6 PC, or on a PC with an *All Charge Card* or some other paging hardware option added to it.) The most common offending disk controllers are ones that control the SCSI drives.

The source of the difficulty is that the disk controller (or more precisely, the SCSI host adapter) *thinks* it knows where in memory address space its buffer is located. Then the CPU switches things around (under the direction of a 386 protected-mode memory manager, like *Windows* or *386MAX*). Thereafter, the disk controller finds nonsense where it expected its data. This could trash your files, or it could give the error cited.

The solution varies according to the protected-mode memory manager you are running. If it is *Windows*, add the following line to the `[386ENH]` section of the SYSTEM.INI file:

```
VirtualHDIRQ=Off
```

If you are running another memory manager, refer to the documentation that came with it. Look for references to double-buffering or VDS (*Virtual Device Specification*).

`Cannot Start System` (Asks for System Disk)

If you install *Windows* 3.0 and find you cannot start your PC, it may indicate that you are using some disk-partitioning software that is incompatible with SMARTdrive, the disk cache program that comes with *Windows*.

(This problem is supposed to have been solved in the latest version of SMARTdrive, 4.x, that comes with *Windows* 3.1 and MS-DOS 6.)

This happens with many disk-management programs. Programs like *Disk Manager*, *SpeedStor*, and *VFeature* can modify how DOS and the BIOS see your disk. They do this for good reasons.

One reason these programs may *have* to do this is that no PC can directly accommodate any disk with more than 1,023 cylinders. Also, no version of DOS prior to 3.3 could accept a disk with more than 32MB of total capacity. If you have such a large disk or early version of DOS, you may need to use a disk-management program to help you access all of your disk.

Another reason people use these disk-management device drivers is that their disks do not have the same dimensions as any of those listed in the table of *Hard Disk Parameter Tables* (HDPTs) in their motherboard BIOS ROM. This means that there isn't an ideal drive type number to enter in your configuration setup program. Anything you choose will misrepresent the dimensions (number of heads, cylinders, and sectors per track) of your hard drive. These disk-management device drivers can fool the BIOS into accepting the drive you have and still let you use most of it.

The problem with SMARTdrive arises because these device drivers must modify the BIOS picture of the drive as soon as they load. The apparent size of the disk at boot time is set by the drive type in the configuration CMOS, in conjunction with the HDPT copies in the motherboard BIOS ROM. Once a disk manager gets control, it can, and often does, change the HDPT in RAM.

SMARTdrive is too smart for its own (or your disk drive's) good. It uses the CMOS entry to find the HDPT in your motherboard BIOS ROM and it believes what it finds. This is not what it should do. It should follow the pointers for INT 41h and INT 46h in the interrupt vector table.

If you are lucky, the only result will be a failure to boot. If you are unlucky your hard disk contents may be trashed.

There are several solutions to this problem. The first is to be aware of the potential. If you know yours is a system that might be hurt, be very careful.

If you change to *Windows* version 3.00a or a later version, it will notice the possible problem and suppress the loading of SMARTdrive. If you choose to use another disk cache program, you must remove the reference to SMART-drive from your CONFIG.SYS file and make the problem go away. Or you could redo your disk subsystem so that you no longer need that disk-management device driver, which is probably the best solution.

Your choices are to upgrade your motherboard BIOS, get an autoconfiguring hard disk controller, or give up using all of your hard disk's capacity. The first solution works only if your disk really doesn't have more than 1,023 cylinders. The other two will always work, but the autoconfiguring controller is much nicer than giving up real estate on your disk drive.

Any change in how your hard drive is viewed means you will have to back up everything, make the change, reformat the disk and restore all your files. See the discussion in Chapter 20 in the section titled "Get Rid of Unnecessary Device Drivers and TSRs" for more on this.

Windows 3.0 UAEs

A *Windows* 3.0 UAE is equal to a GPF in any other program, including Windows 3.1. *UAE* stands for *Unrecoverable Application Error*. *GPF* stands for *General Protection Fault*. Both mean that some program tried to do something it was not supposed to do.

When *Windows* catches an application doing such a no-no, it stops everything and puts up the UAE message. (See Figure 31.1. This image was forced. Solitaire did not actually cause a UAE.)

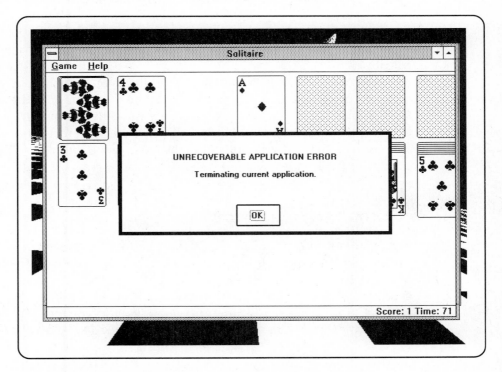

Figure 31.1. The dreaded *Windows 3* UAE dialog box.

Usually this means that some application program was mis-programmed, and *Windows* is merely pointing that out. Sometimes it indicates a problem with *Windows* itself. Either way it means a major nuisance. The only safe thing to do is click on OK (even though it assuredly is not), save your work in any open applications, and exit from *Windows*. Then reboot your computer just to be on the safe side.

Windows 3.1 is much improved in this regard. It can catch GPFs and then allow you to terminate just the one offending program, without having to exit *Windows* and reboot your computer.

When (and Why) Windows 3 Runs Out of System Resources

System resources is a name *Windows* uses to describe some small regions of memory that programmers call local heaps. For *Windows* 3.0 it consists of two 64KB regions, one used by the *Windows* program GDI.EXE and the other by USER.EXE; *Windows* 3.1 has increased the total heap to 192KB.

Every icon on your screen uses some of that resource. So does every object in *Excel*. Other programs also use up system resources. Once the amount of free memory in either heap is down to about 15 percent of its maximum value (around 19KB), *Windows* will refuse to open any new applications.

Figure 31.2 shows *Windows* 3.0 running in Standard mode with very little on the desktop. In Figure 31.3 the same PC is running the same version of *Windows* in the same mode. Only now there are many groups on the desktop. The system resources, which were 88 percent free in the first case, are down to only 11 percent in the latter case. (It took 230 files in nine groups to get this result.)

Packed File Corrupt Message

The Microsoft program *EXEPACK* makes EXE files smaller on disk. But it has a problem. Any program *EXEPACK* has been used on cannot be loaded in the 0 page (between 0 and 64KB). With earlier versions of DOS, this seldom was an issue, as DOS itself tended to fill up all of the 0 page. Now, with DOS 5 and aggressive memory-management techniques in common use, many applications are finding themselves loaded below the 64KB line.

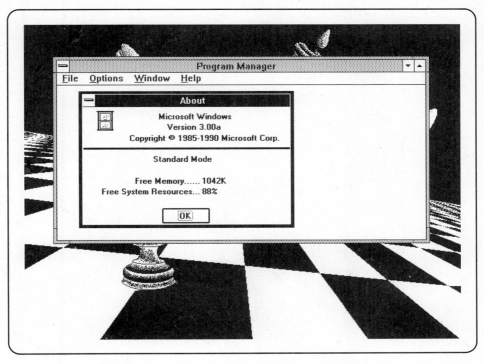

Figure 31.2. *Windows 3*.x can show you your available system resources, as well as the mode you are in and the amount of free memory you have.

DOS 5 provides a fix for this. It is called LOADFIX. All it does is use up some memory (much like EATMEM) so that the next program to load will end up starting above 64KB. That is not a very elegant solution, and it rather grates to have to throw away hard-won memory like that.

So if you see the `Packed file corrupt` message, first try running LOADFIX to see that this solves the problem. (That makes sure the packed file was not really corrupt.) Then edit your CONFIG.SYS file to load into lower memory some device driver that you had previously been loading into upper memory, or make a similar change to your AUTOEXEC.BAT file. Then reboot. Now you won't need LOADFIX. You will also have more free upper memory, which can usually be put to good use.

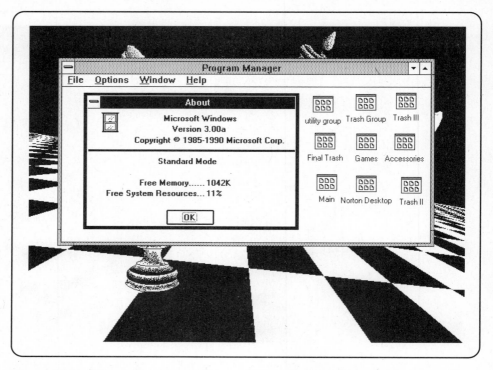

Figure 31.3. Too many icons and a too-big wallpaper file can seriously reduce your system resources, even though your free memory is nearly unchanged.

Memory Commander's Red Screen

Windows 3.0 puts up a UAE when it detects a GPF. *Memory Commander* does something a little different (and a little nicer). It shows you a screen looking something like Figure 31.4, except it is in bright white letters on a stark red background.

This is a little more realistic than the cheerful UAE...OK? message that *Windows* 3.0 gives you. The details shown here may not help you much, but you can try terminating the current process without rebooting—so you can maybe save some work—then reboot to get your system back to a stable state.

```
 ┌──── Memory Commander Diagnostic Center ────── V2.11  S/N M702331 ──┐
 │ A fatal error occured in your application COMMAND.                 │
 │ Error occured at: 1299:1503                                        │
 │ Fault due to:     General Protection fault                         │
 │ Memory mode:      A                                                │
 │                                                                    │
 │ DOS might have been corrupted, a reboot(R) is recommended. You can │
 │ terminate(T) the application and return to DOS or display(D) debug │
 │ information.                                                        │
 │                                                                    │
 │ Reboot(R), Terminate(T) or Display(D) ?                            │
 └────────────────────────────────────────────────────────────────────┘
```

Figure 31.4. *Memory Commander* tries to tell you what went wrong.

QEMM and some of the other protected mode memory managers in their most recent versions do something quite similar. And in every case, the proper response is the same. Stop the offending program, save any work you can, then reboot.

An interesting fact: You won't get the *Memory Commander* red screen when you are running *Windows 3.x*, even if you have *Memory Commander* loaded as your primary memory manager. Likewise with *QEMM* or any of the others; because when *Windows* starts up, it takes over from the other memory manager.

When Memory Managers Can Be Dangerous

This mostly is a couple of *Windows 3* horror stories. There may well be other examples with other memory managers. (Please send your examples to me so I can include them in the next edition.)

Windows 3 and SMARTdrive, Not Always What You Want

The *Windows* install process (like the MS-DOS 6 one) almost insists upon loading SMARTdrive. It may do this even when you already have some other disk cache program loaded. That is dangerous. Furthermore, if you have one of the disks and disk-management programs discussed earlier, SMARTdrive can be a danger even if there is no other cache loaded.

So be very careful when you install *Windows* or any other protectant mode software. Don't let it install SMARTdrive unless you are sure that will be safe to do so.

> **Tip** The Windows SETUP program will offer to reboot your PC when it is finished so that its changes to your startup files will take effect. Don't let it do that for you.
>
> Exit to DOS and inspect your CONFIG.SYS and AUTOEXEC.BAT files to see what has been changed. Remove or add "REM_" at the start of any line you suspect might cause a problem. Then you can reboot safely.

Windows 3.x and DeskLink

DeskLink (from Traveling Software) is a fine way to connect two PCs together and transfer files between them. It differs from its sister product, *LapLink*, in that *DeskLink* makes the drives of one machine appear to be drives on the other. That can be wonderful. But don't run *DeskLink* if *Windows* is active on either machine. Nor should you start *Windows* or any other protected mode software while *DeskLink* is active. If you do, you will almost certainly trash the hard disk contents on the PC running *Windows*.

Traveling Software has a newer application called *WinConnect*. It runs under *Windows* (only) and is perfectly safe.

The bad news is that many non-*Windows* compatible programs are old enough that their documentation doesn't alert you to the possible problems. You have to be alert and remember the horror stories you hear, or you may become the next person to have one to contribute.

A Hidden Benefit of Memory Managers

Protected-mode memory managers are not just one huge horror story. Thank goodness. Often they work with no problems at all. Then you can enjoy some pretty wonderful advantages.

But sometimes, even when programs cannot run smoothly with your new memory manager, that is not altogether a bad thing. What is happening, most of the time, is that the memory manager is helping to smoke out some bad programming bugs that had been in your applications all along. They merely did not show up before.

Over time, this means that all our PC applications will be getting more and more bug free, as their programmers are forced—by the protected-mode memory managers—to face the errors of their ways. In the end, that is good for all of us. (Even if that doesn't make it any nicer to be confronted with a General Protection Fault right now.)

Closing Comment

That closes out our bestiary of memory-management gremlins. Remember, send in your stories (preferably including both the horror experience or puzzlement and how you eventually dealt with it). You will be helping future generations of readers avoid whatever it was you stubbed your toes on. Thank you.

WHEN THINGS GO WRONG

This chapter is a straightforward guide to what to do when nothing is working as you expected. Don't panic, carry a towel, and spread out this chapter next to your PC as you work.

944

Wouldn't it be wonderful if everything worked out just as you wanted, all of the time? If things were going that well, you'd probably not be reading this chapter. Instead you'd be off enjoying your newly capacious PC with all the memory you could want and all of it properly managed.

That is, you say, not how things have been going for you lately? Okay. Here are some suggestions for finding the source of your problems as quickly as possible.

> Maybe you're one of those people who read the instructions before you leap in. Maybe that's why you're reading this chapter now, just in case you may need its help later on. How wonderful! Please do read it and try to remember what you learn here.
>
> In particular, remember to record how things are before you begin any substantial modification of your system. Be sure you can restore it to exactly the form it had when you began. And remember to have a *tested* Safety Boot Diskette nearby.

Checking for Easy Things

A large part of the time, difficulties turn out to have been caused by something incredibly simple. For example, your PC is just not working at all. Did you remember to plug the power cord back in? See what I mean? *Really* simple things!

You may think you're not dumb enough to do things like this. You are. I am. No one is immune to the occasional lapse of clear thinking or memory. So before you go looking for arcane problems, look for the very simple ones—as many as you can think of.

If your PC won't work at all, and you know the cord is securely plugged into the back of the system unit (and you did check to see that the power switch was turned on, didn't you?), make sure there is electricity available from the outlet where the cord is plugged in.

You may know that you pulled the plug out of the back of the PC's power supply and left it plugged into the wall. But did it actually stay there? Maybe the cord got knocked out of the wall socket. Or maybe you just happen to be in the middle of a power outage.

If you took your PC apart, test it before you put it back together; at least before you put it all the way back together. That will save time screwing in screws and unscrewing them, over and over. Also, don't slide your system unit back into some slim space where you have to shoehorn it in and pry it out. (Actually that is not just good advice for before you test it. Keep plenty of room around your PC for good ventilation at all times.)

If your IBM *PC* doesn't recognize the new RAM you added, remember to check the DIP switch settings. Likewise, if you alter the RAM configuration in any PC from class 3 up, you have to remember to change the settings in the configuration CMOS. In this case you will be reminded when you boot by a message that says the configuration information is in error and asks you to run the setup program.

Be sure you have inserted the option cards correctly. If one is tipped or not all the way into its slot, it could keep that card from working. It might also prevent other parts of your PC from working.

Did you catch any of the ribbon cables or drive power cables while you were working inside your PC? That happens, too. If one end of a ribbon cable comes just partway off its connector, some contacts won't be making a good connection. That can prevent something about your PC from working right.

The most frustrating aspect of this last kind of problem is that you may have been adding a new memory card, and it may be that now your disk drive is not working. What is the connection between the memory card and your disk drive? Maybe nothing more than the fact that they are close together, and you weren't looking carefully enough when you withdrew your hand one time. Putting on the cover can also pull on cables sometimes.

Even if a ribbon cable is firmly connected at both ends, it can fail to do its job if one or more of its wires gets cut or shorted to some inappropriate voltage. This can happen if the ribbon cable is pressed too hard against the sharp ends of leads that stick out of the back sides of most option cards.

If some RAM chips or modules are not working, look at them. Look carefully. Get a bright light out and put on your strongest reading glasses. Get your head almost down inside the case if you need to, or take the memory card out and hold it up near a bright light. Very often you can see exactly what is wrong if only you will look carefully, and patiently.

The remarks at the beginning of this chapter that read, "Don't panic," and "Carry a towel" are advice taken from *The Hitchhiker's Guide to the Galaxy*, by Douglas Adams. The towel may not help you much, but reminding yourself *not* to do "something, anything," just to be doing something (a sure sign of panic) is often very important. It is all too easy to make a little problem much worse if you do something hasty.

If you installed some new software and it isn't working right, you could end up being unable to boot your computer at all. That is why you have a Safety Boot Diskette. Also remember that often you can abort the loading of a new memory manager by pressing some special key at the right time, or if you are using DOS 6, you can use the Clean Boot or Interactive Boot procedure. (See the discussion of this in Chapter 21 under "A Final Tip on Setting Up Memory Managers.")

A Systematic Approach to Memory Problems

If you have tried all the simple things you can think of, and nothing seems to help, it is time to get more systematic. Here are some steps to follow, one at a time. This is almost sure to reveal where your problem lies.

Rule Out Coincidence

Consider the possibility that your problem happened coincidentally with your latest upgrade. Some part of your PC could simply have chosen that moment to die. Or you could have killed a part without being aware of it.

There is an easy way to check out this possibility. Undo everything you just did. Put the PC back *just as it was*.

That means removing any new memory chips or modules you installed, and putting back any you had taken out. It means putting your AUTOEXEC.BAT and CONFIG.SYS files back to exactly the form they had before you began your latest round of upgrades or other experimentation. (Naturally this leads to another bit of good advice: Before starting any upgrade or other modification of your system, be sure you have a valid backup of your current startup files. These include your CONFIG.SYS and AUTOEXEC.BAT files, but nowadays they also include your WIN.INI and SYSTEM.INI files if, like many of us, you are a Windows user.)

Now test to see if the problem has gone away. If not, and if you really did restore everything to the way it was, you probably have a coincidental or an *iatrogenic* problem. (*Iatrogenic* means *doctor-caused*. In this case, you're the doctor.)

If this is your problem you will have to do the sorts of troubleshooting that are called for whenever a PC fails. This book is not about those methods. Get one that is, or find someone who has experience fixing PCs to help you.

Sneak Up on the Problem

Assuming that the problem went away when you put things back as they were, you know something you did caused the problem. But just what did you do?

Most people, in their enthusiasm and eagerness, do too many things at once. If they all work, that approach is fine. But when something goes amiss, having done many things at once makes it that much harder to find out which one you did not do correctly, or which one caused a problem.

Redo all the steps of your upgrade or other modification to your PC. But this time, insofar as possible, do them one step at a time, and test your PC after each step.

This advice applies just as much to a software modification as it does to a hardware one. Change your CONFIG.SYS file and your AUTOEXEC.BAT file gradually from what you know works to what you want to have.

This is not always possible. Sometimes you must make several, related changes before you can do a valid test. In that case, if you encounter a problem, you may wish to "remark out" the ECHO OFF line you probably have at the start of your AUTOEXEC.BAT file. This won't stop all of the changes from taking effect, but at least it will give you some on-screen clues about where your PC is in the processing of the AUTOEXEC.BAT file when things start going wrong.

Diagnostic Software That May Help

Reread Chapter 28. The tools described there can help a lot at a time like this. Sometimes the test of your PC that matters is not whether it boots and you get the total memory you expected; instead you need to see *what* is located *where* in memory, or which interrupts are being used and for what. A diagnostic or informational utility program can be just what you need to learn those things quickly and easily.

If, after following all this advice, you still can't solve your problem, you need help. Often, all you need is to be able to describe what is frustrating you to someone who understands. As you do, *you* may think of new things to try.

But sometimes you actually need someone else to tell you what to do, or someone actually to do whatever is necessary. How do you find that sort of help? Read the next chapter for some suggestions.

GETTING HELP FROM OTHERS—SOME TIPS

Maybe the Computer Bug Busters don't have a branch in your city. Here you will find some practical advice for those times when it seems nothing works right.

You say you've decided you need help, but you don't know where to turn? This chapter gives you some tips that may solve that problem.

Who Ya Gonna Call?

You have a computer with some ailment in it, some signs of malaise. It has a bug. You wish you could simply call the Computer Bug Busters (see Figure 33.1), but they don't have a listing in your local phone book. Now what?

Your PC's "MVP" (Most Valuable Peripheral)

What you want is someone who will understand and sympathize with you. Someone who shares your concern. Someone who knows more than you do, but is willing to spend as much time as it takes to get your problem solved.

The person most likely to fit all those requirements is someone who has a system exactly like yours. Your problem is, therefore, in some very real sense that person's problem too. That makes that person want to solve your problem with you before it hits their system too.

I call a person who has a system with all the same hardware and software pieces as yours *your PC's most valuable peripheral* (MVP).

You aren't likely to find anyone just like that, though. The best chance you'd have is if you are at a large company and lots of people have systems very much like yours. Then you probably also have a company guru (perhaps called the PC Coordinator) to whom you can turn.

Lacking that, what can you do? There is often a very good answer a short distance away. And most likely you never knew it existed. Best of all, it is an extremely cost-effective source of help and new information.

The User Group Connection

A computer user group is a voluntary association of people who share a common interest in computers. These groups come in many varieties, with differing levels of specialization.

You may find a group that has as its focus all personal computers, no matter the kind or brand. Or you might be able to find one focused on PCs. If you are using your PC almost exclusively for one application—for example, electronic (desktop) publishing—you may be able to find a group that specializes in just that one field.

Figure 33.1. Who ya gonna call?

Once you have found this group, get involved. Almost certainly you won't find any one person in that group who fits the profile of your PC's

MVP exactly. But you may well find several people who, in the composite, are just that. Depending on the nature of your specific problem at the moment, you may end up calling one or another of this small group within a group.

To make this work, you have to be willing to contribute also. Remember, user groups work when the members give as well as take. Indeed, the more you give to the group and its members, the more you'll learn and benefit from it.

Vendors Actually Do Care (Most of the Time)

Often your problem is with something you bought. Whether it is hardware or software, somebody created it and offered it for sale. They want you to be happy with it.

Furthermore, they are the most likely people in the whole world to have heard of your problem before. Call the technical support line for whatever company makes and sells the gadget or program that is giving you grief.

Sometimes they can help you even when their product is not at fault. If you thought it was, so did someone else before you. And the tech support crew now knows what to suggest that you try.

Many companies express their concern by providing free telephone support (you may pay for the call, or in some cases there is a toll-free support line, but at no charge for their time). But if they don't offer a toll-free number, it may be well worth your dime to call them.

What to Do Before You Call

You've decided to call the manufacturer. Or perhaps you're going to call a friend. In either case you need to do your homework first. Here is a short list of the things you need to do before you pick up the phone. Otherwise, no one can help you effectively.

- Take good notes.

- Read the manual first!

- Collect all relevant information.

- Be at your computer when you call.

Good Telephone Manners Pay Off

Some people have "an attitude" when they call for help, especially when they are calling a manufacturer. That never helps them or the person they're calling.

Assume the other person actually wants to help you. They probably do. Also, do your best to help that person do his or her job as easily and well as possible—you both will win that way.

Helping Them Help You

Follow directions *exactly*. This is easier to say than to do, but please try. If you are told to do one thing and you actually do something else, the person helping you has a wrong picture of what is happening and why.

If you have some question about the instructions, either because you didn't quite hear or understand it, or because you think it is the wrong thing to try, please ask your question out loud. Only in that way can the other person know when they have to clarify their directions to you. Or they may agree with your argument and decide with you to have you try something else.

Don't get ahead of the person who is trying to help you. For example, you may be told to type some sequence of characters. Don't press the Enter key until you are told to. The person dictating may not yet have finished the command they had in mind for you to try. If you think of useful things to try, either tell the helper, or write down your ideas and later on go over them with the helper.

All of these suggestions are just common sense and courtesy. If you were helping someone else, you would want that person to follow them, wouldn't you?

Getting Help Without Talking to Anyone

You don't have to call anyone. You may be able to get the help you need in some other manner. Here are some possibilities to consider.

Find a book (like this one, perhaps) with suggestions for things to try. Sometimes you'll find something helpful at your local library. Other times you will need to browse the offerings at the local bookstores.

Call the manufacturer's BBS. Many manufacturers run electronic bulletin boards as a means of providing support to the users of their products. These are not only sources of information, they may be places from which you can download the latest version of some device driver that is not working for you.

One advantage these BBSs have is that they are commonly available to you 24 hours a day. That means you can call when you have your question. It also means you can choose to wait and call when long distance phone rates are at their lowest levels.

Some manufacturers have an automated facsimile information service. This means you can call them from a touch-tone phone, navigate some menu tree listing items they can send you, and then select one or more to have faxed to your facsimile machine. All this is automatic and immediate.

If you belong to CompuServe you know that they have a very large number of *forums.* Each of these is a bulletin board service within the larger information utility service.

Some forums are public ones, sponsored by CompuServe. Others are specific to one manufacturer. You can post questions any time and read answers to others' questions. Often your query will be answered within a few hours or at most a few days.

Manufacturers who sponsor a forum normally assign several employees to pay close attention to all the messages posted there. These people are able to provide authoritative answers to questions, and they will take suggestions to their upper management where those suggestions are taken quite seriously. These forums are also excellent places to download the latest device drivers or patches to programs, or to read about the known bugs and suggested workarounds. (A *patch,* in this context, means a small program that will modify your copy of an application or utility program, fixing something that was wrong about it in the process. A *workaround* is a procedure you can follow to accomplish your goal, even though the program you meant to use doesn't work quite right.)

There also are likely to be some free **b**ulletin **b**oard **s**ystems (BBSs) just a local phone call away. Most user groups run one or more, as do many individuals. Sometimes a library will operate a BBS as a service to its community. Exec-PC is one of the largest subscription BBS services (see Appendix E). That's another avenue you might try.

If you do call either CompuServe or a local or national BBS, remember to be polite, be clear, and be concise. No one wants to read angry ramblings. You'll get much more help if you compose your thoughts carefully before you call.

Most systems have some means by which you can upload a message you have composed off-line, before your call. That lets you check your typing, your spelling, your syntax, and—most of all—your facts.

Finally, remember to contribute. Just as with user groups, these electronic meeting places tend to be mostly voluntary associations. When you give, you will get more. And the process will work better for everyone. Share your experiences, both good and bad.

When to Get Upset, and How to Do It Effectively

There are a few manufacturers who really seem not to care about their customers. It is hard to see how they have stayed in business, but it does happen. (Maybe it's just the one technician you got. Try calling a second time and see if you can get someone more helpful.)

If you really have a lemon of a product and a company that doesn't seem to understand or want to accommodate you, what can you do about it? Get upset, of course.

The trick is to get upset *effectively*. That means that you don't want to simply vent your rage. You want results.

Go ahead and vent your rage somewhere if you must, but pick someplace that is safe and that won't hinder you from getting what you want. Normally this means that you won't want to vent your rage at someone working for the company you are mad at. That makes them defensive and makes it less likely you will get satisfaction.

Once you have vented as much rage as you must, calm down. Think carefully of how you might induce the company to do what you want them to do.

By the way, you must be very clear about what it is you want. You must do more with a recalcitrant company than just tell them what is wrong. You have to know quite precisely what you think they can do to make you feel okay about them and their products. Or at least to make you feel okay about your present interaction with them.

You might want a refund. Or a new copy of the software. Or someone to look at your PC and see what is wrong. Whatever it is you want, if you can't articulate it, you probably won't get it.

Now think about how to induce them to do what you want. Do you threaten to give them bad publicity? Perhaps, but that is best saved for a fairly last-ditch attempt. Do you tempt them with good publicity? That is better, but only if you can plausibly deliver on your offer. It is okay to let them know you are very much upset. That you are feeling frustrated, or even angry. Just be careful not take out your anger on the person you hope will help you. That rarely works.

A Tip for the Truly Desperate

Here are some final tips for the truly desperate. You have tried all the things suggested earlier. None of them did the trick. You still are upset and frustrated. So what more can you do?

Call the company president. If the company is a large one, you won't get to speak to the president. But if you are referred to someone else, they will know (or you can tell them) that you were "referred by the president." That often encourages them to be just a bit more helpful.

Actually, in many companies in our industry, you will get to speak to the president. Many PC-related companies are quite small and their presidents are very concerned with customer relations. And if your question is technical, you may be able to talk directly to the person in the company who wrote the program or designed the hardware device. In other words, to the real expert.

Put your story in writing. Give the background. Show that you have considered and tried all the obvious things. Make it easy for the people you are dealing with to take you and your troubles very seriously.

If all else fails, tell others your saga. Share it on a BBS. Write it as a letter to the editor. Or write an article for your local user group newsletter. Send a copy of what you write to the company president. That may produce enough of a shock to get things moving for you.

Some Final Words

And if all you try fails, go ahead and cry. Then let it go. Move on to the next thing. PCs are not all of your life, I hope. And no one thing you wanted your PC to do is worth getting overly upset about.

Remember, these little boxes are great sources of joy. They can do wonderful things, marvelous things. Put yours to work and your previous disappointments will melt away to the status of a dimly remembered bad experience. Chalk it up to experience.

This is the end of the story this book has to tell—for now. (There are two more sections to the book; they include some examples to help you get started doing memory management and some useful appendices. Also, please remember to check out the MemInfo hypertext database and the shareware programs that you will find on the diskette that comes with this book.) There will be, I hope, several more editions. I hope to hear from you with some anecdotes, tips, and war stories that will enrich those future editions. In the meantime, happy memory managing.

VI

EXAMPLES AND TIPS FOR OPTIMIZING YOUR PC

The previous parts of this book taught you all the principles you need to know to optimize memory usage in your PC. Armed with that knowledge, you can do that job just as well as any guru. That assumes, of course, that you absorbed all the information that was in those parts.

For many people that is not going to be the case. At least, they would find it easier to absorb those principles if they could study some examples of what they look like when they are put into practice. This part fills that need.

Chapter 34 shows you some tips and techniques that work in any PC and that are useful no matter what version of DOS you use or what other memory optimization techniques you employ. Chapter 35 shows some additional things you can do if you know you will be running only one program at a time.

Chapter 36 covers the techniques appropriate to a multitasking situation, with special emphasis on things to do when running Microsoft *Windows*. Chapter 37 shows examples of upper memory creation and how programs get loaded there. Chapter 38 shows how various memory optimizers achieve their results.

The part ends with a chapter showing examples of good uses for any "spare" RAM you may have. By studying all these examples, and then practicing on your own PC, you too can become a memory management guru.

34

TWEAKING AUTOEXEC.BAT AND CONFIG.SYS TO OPTIMIZE MEMORY

If you learn best by looking at the work of others, study the examples here to learn some ways to make the most of your PC, no matter what class or DOS version you have.

One of the best ways to learn how to do something is to see what it looks like when an expert does the same thing. This chapter shows some examples of DOS memory optimization using a variety of techniques that work on PCs in any class, running any version of DOS.

Your system is different—most likely it is different in at least some ways from every other PC on the planet—and so you cannot simply copy these examples and expect that doing so will optimize your system. Use these examples as simply that—examples that show you a style and some useful tricks. Then apply the ideas behind those examples to your own system. Once you have done that, check your work (using the tools described in Chapter 28).

By trying out various ideas and seeing which ones actually help, you will be learning the practical aspects of DOS memory management. It can be fun. It can even become addictive. So watch out, and remember the cautions in the section "Be Sensible" near the end of Chapter 21.

It can be wonderful to have your PC loaded up with device drivers and TSR programs, ranging from network drivers to pop-up calendars. At least it is wonderful if you can load them all in an order in which they don't end up "fighting" with one another. However, putting all those different programs in RAM simultaneously can leave you with precious little free RAM in which to run your main application programs.

Ordinarily, PCs load device drivers with DEVICE statements in the CONFIG.SYS file. They usually also load a number of TSR programs through lines in the AUTOEXEC.BAT file. This works, but it means you must alter those startup files and reboot any time you wish to remove a device driver or TSR program from memory.

Most of the tips in this chapter focus on how to keep from loading a device driver or TSR program until you actually need it, and then unloading it as soon as you have finished using it. You can do this without having to reboot your PC. The remaining comments are reminders of some global configuration settings that influence the amount of free RAM you have.

TSR Strategies

Do you run some programs that use a terminate-and-stay-resident (TSR) utility program, and others that don't? For example, you may use an editor that you like to use with the aid of a mouse, and a database or spreadsheet that doesn't understand mice at all.

In this case you can make more RAM available for the database or spreadsheet program if you don't load the mouse driver until you are about to run the editor, and if you then unload the mouse driver once you have finished using the editor. Here is a batch file that does this:

```
C:\UTIL\MARK
C:\DRIVERS\MOUSE.COM
D:\SUPERED\EDITS %1 %2 %3
C:\UTIL\RELEASE
```

This batch file assumes several things. First, it assumes you have put the MARK and RELEASE programs in C:\UTIL. Further, your TSR mouse driver (MOUSE.COM) is kept in C:\DRIVERS. Your mouse-aware editor is called EDITS.EXE and is put in D:\SUPERED. Finally, it assumes that EDITS can accept up to three command line parameters (e.g., the name of the file to be edited). Call this batch file ED.BAT and put it in a directory that is on your PATH. From then on, each time you run the ED batch file, you will load the mouse driver, run the editor, and then unload the mouse driver—all automatically and without further effort on your part.

The MARK program is itself a TSR and it uses about 1.5KB of RAM. When it is used in the manner just described, this is not normally a problem. If, however, you wish to run a very large application program, that 1.5KB could be just the difference between being able to run the program and not having it fit into memory. In that case you might use the alternative form of MARK called FMARK. This program is a TSR that does what MARK does, but uses only about one-tenth as much RAM.

The reason MARK needs to use some RAM is that it stores a copy of the contents of the interrupt vector table, plus some other data about the state of your PC as it was just before MARK loaded. Then when you use RELEASE, those data are used to restore the PC to exactly the state it was in just before MARK was loaded. In that act both MARK and any TSR programs that are loaded after MARK seem simply to disappear from memory. (They actually aren't removed from RAM, but since the RAM is marked as free and any alterations to the interrupt vector table or elsewhere in the PC have been reversed, the effect is the same as if the programs had been removed.)

FMARK gets away with only one-tenth as much RAM because it keeps the data needed for its removal in a file. See the TSR.DOC file for more details on this and for examples of how to use FMARK.

> MARK, FMARK, and RELEASE are three of the programs in the TSR Utilities package created by Kirk Kokkonen, a copy of which is on the diskette that accompanies this book. The TSR.DOC file describes many different ways to use these programs; this batch file shows only one.

You can create similar batch files to run any application that needs helper programs. The batch file will first load the helpers, then run the main application, and finally unload those helper programs when you are through. Be sure to use MARKNET and RELNET instead of the simpler MARK and RELEASE if your PC has network drivers loaded (even if you are not logged onto the network at the time you run these batch files).

The principal limitation to this technique is that you can only use it to control the loading and unloading of TSR programs. The MARK and RELEASE programs don't understand how to load and unload device drivers. On the other hand, you already have a copy of the TSR Utilities and they are free.

In the next section you will learn three ways to get around that difficulty. The first way is also free, if you can use it. The second will cost you the price of another book. The last involves buying a commercial memory management program.

> A very different problem, and one whose solution doesn't involve saving RAM, is how to temporarily turn off a TSR program. The DISABLE program—which is another one you will find in the TSR Utility package—can do this for you. See TSR.DOC for details.

Device Driver Strategies

Suppose you have a device driver that you wish to load only when you run certain programs, so that it's not using RAM the rest of the time. How can you achieve this effect without rebooting your PC? There are at least three ways.

Use a TSR Alternative

The simplest, but one that applies only to certain device drivers, is to use a TSR alternative. Perhaps the best known device driver for which this is an option is MOUSE.SYS. Almost all the brands of mouse come with both a MOUSE.SYS and a MOUSE.COM file. The former is a device driver, normally loaded through a DEVICE= or DEVICEHIGH= line in the CONFIG.SYS file. The latter is a TSR program, normally loaded through a line in a batch file (though it could be loaded with an INSTALL= statement in the CONFIG.SYS file).

Both MOUSE.SYS and MOUSE.COM do the same thing, and you only need to load one of them. If you have been in the habit of loading MOUSE.SYS, but you want to be able to have it in RAM only some of the time, you may wish to switch to using MOUSE.COM in the manner suggested in the preceding section.

Use DEVLOD

In the very fine book, *Undocumented DOS* (Andrew Schulman, Ed.) Jim Kyle describes a program he wrote called DEVLOD.COM. This program can be run at the DOS prompt and used to load a device driver. It doesn't work properly with all device drivers, but for a device driver that is compatible with DEVLOD, it allows you to avoid loading that device driver until you want to use it.

The problem with DEVLOD is that while it can let you load a device driver at the DOS prompt, it is not able to unload that device driver thereafter. Doing so properly is a trickier task than unloading a TSR program.

Use DMC

The program *Dynamic Memory Control* (or DMC, for short) is the only program on the market that can do the full job of dynamically loading and unloading device drivers, as needed. It can be used to do this in either of two ways.

In the first mode, DMC closely resembles the MARK and RELEASE programs. The corresponding programs in the DMC package are called NOTE and FREENOTE. The very considerable difference is that DMC includes a program called LDEVICE. Using these programs to load and unload a device driver might look like this:

```
D:\DMC\NOTE
D:\DMC\LDEVICE C:\DRIVERS\SCAN.EXE
E:\FAXAPP
D:\DMC\FREENOTE
```

where I have assumed that you wish to load a program called SCAN.EXE to support using a scanner, but that you only wish to load it just before you run an application program called FAXAPP (presumably to send fac-simile messages), and that you want to unload the scanner's device driver immediately after exiting the FAXAPP program.

Since it does more or less the same job as MARK, you won't be sur-prised to find out that NOTE occupies about 1.5KB of RAM. The DMC program provides an alternative way to load and unload TSRs or device drivers. Like the FMARK program, this approach stores the needed data about what the system looked like just before the TSR or device driver was loaded in a file on your hard disk. Unlike FMARK, the DMC approach reduces the use of extra RAM all the way to zero. That is, they can load and unload either TSR programs or device drivers without using any additional RAM!

The DMC method is to use a special conversion utility called RTSR (for Removable TSR creation program). Run RTSR on any of your device drivers or TSR programs and you will create new executable files that are removable versions of the originals.

Now, to load the converted device driver or TSR you simply invoke the new EXE program. To remove it you invoke it again, with an added /U command line parameter. Our previous example would look like this:

```
C:\DRIVERS\SCAN#
E:\FAXAPP
C:\DRIVERS\SCAN# /U
```

where SCAN#.EXE is the RTSR converted version of SCAN.EXE.

> The DMC package also provides a shell program to allow using al-most all of its features by picking items off a menu. With its ability to load and unload even very complex memory managers like EMM386.EXE and HIMEM.SYS, the DMC program is really quite a marvelous product. You can find information on how to reach Adlersparre & Associates, the makers of DMC, in the hypertext MemInfo database on the diskette that accompanies this book.

CONFIG.SYS Settings

Chapter 20 includes a lengthy discussion of all the kinds of lines that can go in a CONFIG.SYS file. Some of those lines load device drivers, install TSR programs, or specify which command interpreter you wish to have DOS load. Other lines set various flags or define the size of certain critical DOS data structures.

The discussion in Chapter 20 tells you what your options are for each of the lines that sets a flag or specifies a DOS data structure size. It also suggests why you may wish to choose one or another value for each one.

Review that discussion before you adopt any of the following suggestions to be sure you don't have some good reason for setting your CONFIG.SYS values differently. Having said that, here are some popular choices.

Setting the "Right" Number of FILES

If you run only one DOS program at a time (and don't do any task swapping), include this line in your CONFIG.SYS file:

```
FILES = 20
```

If you do much task swapping or run multiple programs in a multitasking environment, such as Windows or DESQview, then use this line:

```
FILES = 50
```

For GeoWorks this value should be at least 80. However, don't exceed 255.

Setting the "Right" Number of FCBS

Not very many PC users know which of the programs they run use the modern "file handle" method for accessing files, and which use the more old-fashioned "file control block" approach. The FILES setting only affects the former programs. The FCBS setting affects the latter.

If you know you aren't going to run any of the old-style programs that use file control blocks (FCBs), then add this line to your CONFIG.SYS file:

```
FCBS = 1
```

That will save you a small amount of memory. On the other hand, it may cause your system to crash if you should run one of the old-style programs. Most users don't put any FCBS setting in their CONFIG.SYS file, which is equivalent to putting in the line:

```
FCBS = 4
```

This value "wastes" only about 200 bytes, an amount most people regard as trivial. (If you are seriously concerned about such a tiny difference in the amount of free RAM you have, you probably are going at memory management in an inappropriate way. See the discussion at the end of Chapter 20, and consider adopting one of the other approaches described in this chapter.)

Setting the "Right" Number of BUFFERS

The BUFFERS setting can be an important one. This tells DOS how many disk buffers it should set up. Since each one takes up a little more than half a kilobyte, this setting can affect free RAM very significantly.

The default value for BUFFERS in the older versions of DOS was ridiculously low. Starting with DOS 5, the default value became more or less reasonable. Still, it is a good idea to give this setting some thought, and then include a line in your CONFIG.SYS file that sets the value explicitly.

If you are using a good disk cache program (Smartdrive or some third-party alternative), the proper line is usually:

```
BUFFERS = 3
```

On the other hand, if you are not using any disk caching program, and you are running a version of DOS prior to 5, then use:

```
BUFFERS = 20
```

Users of DOS 5 or DOS 6 can specify a second number, the number of secondary cache buffers. This defaults to 0 or 1, depending on the DOS version. If you don't have the line DOS=HIGH in your CONFIG.SYS file, then use:

```
BUFFERS = 30, 6
```

If you do have DOS=HIGH in your CONFIG.SYS file—which is only valid for DOS versions starting with 5—then the best value (even if you do have a disk cache program loaded) is likely to be:

```
BUFFERS = 40, 8
```

The reason that this is okay, and won't cost you 20KB or more of lower memory, is that when DOS=HIGH is specified, the DOS kernel and all but one of the DOS disk buffers are put in the HMA. Watch out, though. If you specify too large a value for BUFFERS (more than about 48, usually), then **all** of the buffers will drop down to lower memory. Check your work with the MEM command to be sure that only half a KB (200h) is allocated in lower memory from BUFFERS.

Setting the "Right" Number of STACKS

The default values for the STACKS setting is 9,128 in all but the oldest PCs (IBM *PC*, IBM *PC/XT*, or IBM *PC-Portable*) for which the default is 0,0. Many memory management optimization programs tell you to use the line:

```
STACKS = 0,0
```

This could be a very bad idea. If you get away with it, you will save more than a kilobyte of RAM for other uses. If you see the message "Stack Overflow" or "Exception 12" you know that you have not succeeded in getting away with this. In that case you can try leaving out the STACKS line altogether (thus using the default values). If you run *Windows*, Microsoft recommends strongly that you do include a STACKS line, and in particular, one that reads:

```
STACKS = 9,256
```

This uses over 2KB of RAM, but it makes your system appreciably more stable. That is a benefit that is well worth the small cost in RAM to most people.

Not Setting LASTDRIVE too Large (or too Small)

The correct value for LASTDRIVE depends on several things. Are you going to use the SUBST command? Is your PC on a network, and if so, which kind of network is it? Are you running DOS 6, and if so, have you used DoubleSpace (or a third-party replacement such as *Stacker*, version 3.1)?

If you know you won't be using the SUBST command at all, and your PC is not on a network, you may not need a LASTDRIVE statement. In that case, your effective last drive letter will be just large enough to include all of the drives you actually have (including any logical drives created by software that got loaded during startup), or it will be E, whichever is larger.

Unless you are critically short on RAM, you could play it safe by using a line that reads:

```
LASTDRIVE = M
```

or, as long as your PC is not connected to a network that requires you to leave it some drive letters for remote drives after the letter specified in your LASTDRIVE statement, then you could use:

```
LASTDRIVE = Z
```

At most this will use up an extra 2KB of RAM, which is a significant quantity, but often an affordable amount to dedicate to this use.

Other CONFIG.SYS Considerations

Don't load any unnecessary device drivers, or install any unnecessary TSR programs. (Consider the strategies mentioned in the first section of this chapter if you want to get the absolute most free RAM you can, and yet must use some device drivers or TSR programs from time to time.) Do load those that are essential to the proper operation of your PC.

Don't set the master environment size excessively high. At the DOS prompt, use the command

```
SET > XXXX.TMP
```

to create a file XXXX.TMP (or whatever other temporary file name you wish to use) that contains all of the current definitions in your DOS environment. Use the DIR command to see the size of this file. You need to have a master environment that is at least that large, but you probably don't need one that is much larger than that. Suppose the XXXX.TMP turns out to contain 342 bytes in definitions. Then a good value for the master environment might be 384 bytes, or perhaps, to give yourself a bit more room for new or temporary definitions, 432 bytes. (It must be a multiple of 16 bytes.) To set this latter value use the line:

```
SHELL = C:\DOS\COMMAND.COM C:\DOS /E:432 /P
```

assuming that you are using COMMAND.COM as your command interpreter, and that you keep it in your C:\DOS directory.

AUTOEXEC.BAT Tips

Most of the tips for how to set up your startup files to save RAM have to do with settings in the CONFIG.SYS file. Still, there are at least a couple of points worth making about the AUTOEXEC.BAT file.

Avoid Wasting RAM for Duplicate Environments

Executing the AUTOEXEC.BAT file is the last phase of your PC's boot process. This typically is the place you load most of your TSR programs. It also is the place you set up most of your environment definitions. These two steps can interact in a way that wastes a lot of RAM. Or, you can avoid doing that.

This is only an issue if you load some TSR programs that do not discard their DOS environment. (Every DOS program that gets loaded is given an environment space. Many, but by no means all, modern TSR utility programs are smart enough to relinquish their environment space, or at least to reduce it to a minimal size. This is discussed in more detail in Chapter 10.)

If you do load some TSRs that keep their environment spaces, be sure to put all your SET statements and your PATH and PROMPT definitions near the very end of your AUTOEXEC.BAT file. This could save you several kilobytes of RAM.

Balancing a Long PATH Against a Large Value for LASTDRIVE

Many authors suggest that you keep your PATH definition very short. This gives you certain benefits, but denies you others.

A short PATH can be searched more quickly by DOS. If your hard disk is fast, though, this will not be very noticeable. A very long PATH definition can include many subdirectories, allowing you to run programs easily from any one of those subdirectories no matter which directory on what disk is the current DOS default directory.

A middle ground approach is to include very many directories on the PATH, but to make the names of each of them as short as you can. This works, but it could mean you had a lot of one-letter name directories whose purposes were no longer obvious just from looking at the names. (A different way to shorten your PATH statement, by using batch files to launch applications, is described in Chapter 20.)

One argument for a short PATH definition is that it will allow you to make the master DOS environment smaller. That is true. There is one way to have lots of directories in your PATH definition, make all of them meaningful names, and still keep the PATH length within bounds. This can be done by using the SUBST command to replace long subdirectory names with pseudo drive letters. For example, the command

```
SUBST H: C:\APPS\WORD
```

allows you to replace the 12 characters `C:\APPS\WORD` with just three characters, `H:\`, in your PATH definition. On the other hand, remember that each extra drive letter you add to LASTDRIVE uses up between 80 and 90 bytes of RAM. You have to refer to that substituted drive a lot of times in your PATH definition to allow you to save enough in environment space to make up for what LASTDRIVE uses.

Therefore, I suggest that you only use SUBST to shorten a PATH definition that exceeds about 120 characters. I strongly suggest you keep your PATH definition to less than 120 characters, even though with DOS 6 you can use the SET command to define an arbitrarily long PATH in your CONFIG.SYS file. This is because any PATH definition that is longer than about 125 characters is an invitation to disaster. (Some programs will bomb when they attempt to read the PATH definition if it exceeds the normal maximum length of a DOS command, which is 126 characters.)

35

MANAGING WHAT GETS LOADED IN RAM

If you know you are only going to run one program at a time, you have some special opportunities for managing the programs that are in memory from moment-to-moment. This chapter shows examples of several of them.

In the preceding chapter, I discussed only strategies for controlling what gets loaded in RAM without rebooting your PC. This is often what you want, since rebooting may take quite awhile. More importantly, if you are running in a task swapping or multitasking environment, you will lose any unsaved data from all the other tasks running whenever you reboot your PC.

All of those tips are just as useful if you do end up rebooting your PC. In this chapter, you will learn some other approaches that demand rebooting your PC or that control what happens whenever you boot it. You can use them in conjunction with the tips in Chapter 34.

A Single Program Strategy

The GEM version of Ventura Publisher, Version 2.0, was a real memory hog. It very nearly could not be run on a PC running DOS 4. The only way it would fit into memory was if one reduced the FILES and BUFFERS to nearly a minimum, and had no TSR programs or device drivers loaded except for the required mouse driver.

The normal way to invoke the GEM version of Ventura Publisher was by running a batch file that had been created when Ventura Publisher was installed, called VP.BAT. Here is an alternative. This uses a modified version of that batch file, plus some other associated files. This set of files lets you have whatever loaded up version of CONFIG.SYS and AUTOEXEC.BAT you like, yet still run Ventura Publisher in the requisite clean fashion just by typing VP and pressing the Enter key.

First, here is the modified VP.BAT:

```
@echo off
echo.
echo        VP.BAT  --  Set up and run Ventura Publisher
echo.
echo        First we will save the old CONFIG.SYS and
echo        AUTOEXEC.BAT files, then copy new ones from
echo        C:\CONFIGUR directory and reboot.
echo.
c:
cd \

if not exist cf.old ECHO goto cf-okay
   *** Warning: CFS.OLD is about to be deleted. ****
   PAUSE
```

```
:cf-okay
if exist cf.old DEL cf.old
if exist cf.sav REN cf.sav cf.old
REN config.sys cf.sav
COPY c:\configur\cf-vp config.sys

if not exist ae.old goto ae-okay
  ECHO *** Warning: AE.OLD is about to be deleted. ****
  PAUSE
:ae-okay
if exist ae.old DEL ae.old
if exist ae.sav REN ae.sav ae.old
REN autoexec.bat ae.sav
COPY  c:\configur\ae-vp autoexec.bat

c:\setup\reboot
```

This batch file copies CF-VP and AE-VP to CONFIG.SYS and AUTOEXEC.BAT, respectively, and then reboots the computer. Here are the contents of the file CF-VP:

```
FILES     = 20
BUFFERS   = 16

BREAK     = ON
```

and AE-VP:

```
@echo off
echo  AE-VP  --   Special AUTOEXEC.BAT for Ventura Publ.
echo.
PATH C:\DOS;C:\UT\MAIN;C:\SETUP
PROMPT $P $G
c:\mouse\MOUSE
D:
CD \VENTURA
DRVRMRGR VP %1 /S=SDFAST86.VGA /M=32 /X=D: /A=10
echo.
c:\setup\GOBACK
```

The batch file GOBACK completes the action:

```
@echo off
echo.
echo    GOBACK.BAT -- Return from special configuration
echo.
c:
cd \
```

```
if not exist ae.sav goto oops
if not exist cf.sav goto oops

echo      Restoring AE.SAV to AUTOEXEC.BAT
echo          and CF.SAV to CONFIG.SYS.
del autoexec.bat
del config.sys
ren ae.sav autoexec.bat
ren cf.sav config.sys
if not exist ae.old goto finishup
if not exist cf.old goto finishup

echo      Renaming AE.OLD to AE.SAV
echo          and CF.OLD to CF.SAV
ren ae.old ae.sav
ren cf.old cf.sav

:finishup
c:\setup\reboot

:oops
echo      This batch file restores old AUTOEXEC.BAT
echo      and CONFIG.SYS files which must have been
echo      saved as AE.SAV and CF.SAV.  It also will
echo      rename AE.OLD and CF.OLD (if they exist)
echo      to the .SAV versions. It only does either
echo      task if *both* files in the pair exist.
echo.
echo      Apparently you don't have both AE.SAV and
echo      CF.SAV, so we can't do this job for you
echo      now.  Check your files and try again.
```

> The program REBOOT.COM, which is called by both VP.BAT and
> GOBACK.BAT, is a very short program (only 16 bytes!) that does the
> same thing as pressing the Ctrl-Alt-Del key-combination. A copy of
> this program is on the diskette that accompanies this book.

The essence of this approach is that when the VP batch file is run, it
loads a new pair of startup files (CONFIG.SYS and AUTOEXEC.BAT) and
reboots your computer. The new AUTOEXEC.BAT file runs the specified
application, Ventura Publisher, and then restores the original startup files.

At the very end, the GOBACK batch file rebooted the computer a final time to restore things to the way they had been before the VP batch file was first invoked.

The reason for dividing the work of restoration between AE-VP file (renamed as AUTOEXEC.BAT) and the GOBACK.BAT batch file is that the latter file must delete the AUTOEXEC.BAT file. If you try doing that from within that batch file, you will halt the process at that point with a message about a missing batch file!

Global Personality Choices by Use of Batch Files

The previous suggestion dealt with just one application. Sometimes what you want is an easy way to alter your PC's "personality" and then leave it configured in that new way indefinitely while you do a number of tasks.

A simple way to accomplish this end was given in Chapter 20, in the section "Using Batch Files to Ease Matters." Here are some more examples. The alternative personalities that are set by the batch files described here will show up again in the multiple-personality DOS 6 menu example given in a later section in this chapter.

The Example Configurations

These examples assume that you have a PC which has a CD-ROM drive, a Bernoulli removable high-capacity floppy disk drive, and a network connection. Sometimes you want to boot a very "clean" and minimal DOS setup. Other times you want to boot DOS with a fair number of device drivers and TSR programs, and with a particular set of values for FILES, FCBS, STACKS, BUFFERS, and LASTDRIVE. Still other times you want to add support for some combination of your three special peripheral devices (CD, Bernoulli, and network).

The first step is to create a special pair of startup files for each of the nine configurations. Here is a possible set of names for them:

Configuration	AUTOEXEC.BAT File	CONFIG.SYS File
Minimal	AE-MIN	CF-MIN
Normal	AE-NORM	CF-NORM
Normal & Network	AE-NORM.NET	CF-NORM.NET

Configuration	AUTOEXEC.BAT File	CONFIG.SYS File
CD-ROM	AE-CD	CF-CD
CD-ROM & Network	AE-CD.NET	CF-CD.NET
Bernoulli	AE-BERN	CF-BERN
Bernoulli & Network	AE-BERN.NET	CF-BERN.NET
CD & Bernoulli	AE-BOTH	CF-BOTH
CD, Bernoulli, & Network	AE-BOTH.NET	CF-BOTH.NET

After the startup files have been created, you will create a set of batch files—one for each pair of startup files—to copy the corresponding pair of startup files to the root directory, giving them the special names CONFIG.SYS and AUTOEXEC.BAT as they are copied. It is these batch files you invoke to alter your PC's personality.

The following files were built for a particular PC. The configuration (startup) files are kept in C:\CONFIGUR. The batch files also reference REBOOT.COM which is kept in a directory called C:\SETUP. The network is Windows for Workgroups. The "normal" configuration includes loading the DOS 5 or 6 memory management software (HIMEM.SYS and EMM386.EXE), plus SETVER.EXE, and RAMDRIVE.SYS device drivers, and installing SHARE.EXE.

The DOS version is assumed to be 6. If these files were to be used with DOS 3.3 through 5, you would merely need to delete the line that refers to DBLSPACE.SYS. To use them with an earlier version of DOS you also would have to remove the @ sign at the start of the first line of each of the AUTOEXEC.BAT files.

The "minimal" configuration includes setting a number of environment variables and loading UNDELETE.EXE (the DOS 6 undelete utility). The normal setup adds to this loading SETVER.EXE, SMARTDRV.EXE, and RAMDRIVE.SYS.

A few comments on the style used in these startup files may be in order—also a caution.

REMark lines are used in both the CONFIG.SYS and AUTOEXEC.BAT files. (REMark lines have always been acceptable in batch files. DOS 6 introduced their use in a CONFIG.SYS file as well.) I have used a lot of "white space" both within the lines and as blank lines between sections of these files. This is perfectly acceptable to DOS. (This is another valuable and little-known fact.) I encourage you to emulate this style in your own batch files, in order to make them easier to understand.

The lines of the CONFIG.SYS file have been put in a particular order. This was done so that when you read the file, you will be seeing the lines in the order in which DOS will process them. As is explained in Chapter 20, the line order usually doesn't matter to DOS, but it can affect your understanding of what happens when.

You might protest, "But I wrote these files, so I will surely remember what I meant by each line." If so, you simply have not had much experience in this regard. Within an amazingly short time, you will forget what you did and why.

Now for the caution: If you use any memory optimization program, expect to have it mess up your carefully chosen style conventions. Your remarks will survive the optimization process, but the line order may get changed, and almost certainly the "excess" white space within any line will be removed. If you really value the style suggestions I have made here, you may find yourself reediting your startup files many times, including after each time you reoptimize your system.

The Startup File Pairs

Here are the special startup file pairs. In each case there is an AUTOEXEC.BAT file and a CONFIG.SYS file. In each case these files have been renamed to AE-xxxx and CF-xxxx, where xxxx is an abbreviation for the particular configuration these files create. Naming this way allows them all to be kept in a single subdirectory on your hard disk.

The Minimal Configuration (MIN)

Here is AE-MIN:

```
@echo off
REM   This is the minimal AUTOEXEC.BAT configuration.
```

```
REM      Start DOS UNDELETE protection
LH c:\dos\UNDELETE.EXE /load
echo.


echo      Setting environment variables
PROMPT [DOS 6:MIN] $p $g
PATH C:\DOS;G:\WFWG;C:\UTIL;C:\SETUP
SET TMP=G:\WFWG\TEMP
SET TEMP=G:\WFWG\TEMP
SET NU=C:\UTIL
echo.
```

and CF-MIN:

```
REM   Here is a quite minimalist configuration.
STACKS  = 0,0
FILES   =  10
BUFFERS =   5
SHELL   = c:\dos\COMMAND.COM c:\dos\ /p
```

The "Normal" Configuration— Stand-Alone Case (NORM)

Here is AE-NORM:

```
@echo off
REM      This AUTOEXEC file loads usual configuration.


ECHO     Starting SMARTDRV, DOSKEY, and MOUSE.
LH c:\dos\SMARTDRV.EXE
LH c:\dos\DOSKEY.COM
LH c:\mouse\MOUSE.COM
echo.


REM      Start DOS UNDELETE protection
LH c:\dos\UNDELETE.EXE /load
echo.


echo     Setting environment variables now
PROMPT [DOS 6:NORM] $p $g
PATH C:\DOS;G:\WFWG;C:\UTIL;C:\SETUP
SET TMP=G:\WFWG\TEMP
SET TEMP=G:\WFWG\TEMP
SET NU=C:\UTIL
echo.
```

and CF-NORM:

```
REM    The "normal" CONFIG.SYS commands and directives
FILES      =     80
FCBS       =   16,0
BUFFERS    =   30,0
STACKS     = 9,256
LASTDRIVE  =      z
DOS        = high,umb
BREAK      = on
DEVICE     = c:\dos\HIMEM.SYS
DEVICE     = c:\dos\EMM386.EXE noems highscan
DEVICE     = c:\dos\SETVER.EXE
DEVICE     = c:\dos\SMARTDRV.EXE /double_buffer
DEVICEHIGH = c:\dos\DBLSPACE.SYS /move
DEVICE     = c:\dos\RAMDRIVE.SYS 1024 512 128 /e
INSTALL    = c:\dos\SHARE.EXE /f:4096
SHELL      = c:\dos\COMMAND.COM c:\dos\ /e:624 /p
```

Adding Bernoulli Support—Stand-Alone Case (BERN)

Here is AE-BERN:

```
@echo off
REM      This AUTOEXEC file loads Bernoulli support.

ECHO    Starting SMARTDRV, DOSKEY, and MOUSE.
LH c:\dos\SMARTDRV.EXE
LH c:\dos\DOSKEY.COM
LH c:\mouse\MOUSE.COM
echo.

REM     Start DOS UNDELETE protection
LH c:\dos\UNDELETE.EXE /load
echo.

echo     Setting environment variables
PROMPT [DOS 6:BERN] $p $g
PATH C:\DOS;G:\WFWG;C:\UTIL;C:\SETUP
SET TMP=G:\WFWG\TEMP
SET TEMP=G:\WFWG\TEMP
SET NU=C:\UTIL
```

```
SET OAD_DRIVER=C:\UT\OADDOS
SET OAD_UTILITY=C:\UT\OADDOS
echo.
```

and CF-BERN:

```
REM         Load support for Bernoulli
FILES     =     80
FCBS      =     16,0
BUFFERS   =     30,0
STACKS    =  9,256
LASTDRIVE =      z
DOS       = high,umb
BREAK     = on
DEVICE    = c:\dos\HIMEM.SYS
DEVICE    = c:\dos\EMM386.EXE noems highscan
DEVICE    = c:\dos\SETVER.EXE
DEVICE    = c:\dos\SMARTDRV.EXE /double_buffer
DEVICEHIGH = c:\dos\DBLSPACE.SYS /move
DEVICE    = c:\dos\RAMDRIVE.SYS 1024 512 128 /e
DEVICE    = c:\ut\oaddos\DOSCFG.EXE /l=001 /m1 /v
DEVICE    = c:\ut\oaddos\DOSOAD.SYS /l=001
INSTALL   = c:\dos\SHARE.EXE /f:4096
SHELL     = c:\dos\COMMAND.COM c:\dos\ /e:624 /p
```

Adding CD-ROM Support—Stand-Alone Case (CD)

Here is AE-CD:

```
@echo off
REM      This AUTOEXEC file loads CD-ROM support.

ECHO     Starting SMARTDRV, DOSKEY, and MOUSE.
LH c:\dos\SMARTDRV.EXE
LH c:\dos\DOSKEY.COM
LH c:\mouse\MOUSE.COM
echo.


ECHO     Loading CD-ROM support
c:\dos\MSCDEX.EXE /d:mscd001
echo.


REM      Start DOS UNDELETE protection
LH c:\dos\UNDELETE.EXE /load
echo.
```

```
echo       Setting environment variables
PROMPT [DOS 6:CD] $p $g
PATH C:\DOS;G:\WFWG;C:\UTIL;C:\SETUP
SET TMP=G:\WFWG\TEMP
SET TEMP=G:\WFWG\TEMP
SET NU=C:\UTIL
echo.
```

and CF-CD:

```
REM        Load support for CD-ROM.
FILES      =      80
FCBS       =      16,0
BUFFERS    =      30,0
STACKS     =      9,256
LASTDRIVE  =      z
DOS        =      high,umb
BREAK      =      on
DEVICE     =      c:\dos\HIMEM.SYS
DEVICE     =      c:\dos\EMM386.EXE noems highscan
DEVICE     =      c:\dos\SETVER.EXE
DEVICE     =      c:\dos\SMARTDRV.EXE /double_buffer
DEVICEHIGH =      c:\dos\DBLSPACE.SYS /move
DEVICE     =      c:\dos\RAMDRIVE.SYS 1024 512 128 /e
DEVICEHIGH =      c:\setup\drivers\MTMCDD.SYS /d:mscd001 /t:3 /i:5 /s:2
INSTALL    =      c:\dos\SHARE.EXE /f:4096
SHELL      =      c:\dos\COMMAND.COM c:\dos\ /e:624 /p
```

Adding Both Bernoulli and CD-ROM Support—Stand-Alone Case (BOTH)

Here is AE-BOTH:

```
@echo off
REM     This AUTOEXEC file loads support
REM     both for CD-ROM and for Bernoulli.

ECHO    Starting SMARTDRV, DOSKEY, and MOUSE.
LH c:\dos\SMARTDRV.EXE
LH c:\dos\DOSKEY.COM
LH c:\mouse\MOUSE.COM
echo.
```

```
ECHO      Loading CD-ROM support
c:\dos\MSCDEX.EXE /d:mscd001
echo.

REM       Start DOS UNDELETE protection
LH c:\dos\UNDELETE.EXE /load
echo.

echo      Setting environment variables
PROMPT [DOS 6:BOTH] $p $g
PATH C:\DOS;G:\WFWG;C:\UTIL;C:\SETUP
SET TMP=G:\WFWG\TEMP
SET TEMP=G:\WFWG\TEMP
SET NU=C:\UTIL
SET OAD_DRIVER=C:\UT\OADDOS
SET OAD_UTILITY=C:\UT\OADDOS
echo.
```

and CF-BOTH:

```
REM         Load support for Bernoulli and CD-ROM.
FILES       =    80
FCBS        =    16,0
BUFFERS     =    30,0
STACKS      =  9,256
LASTDRIVE   =      z
DOS         =  high,umb
BREAK       =  on
DEVICE      =  c:\dos\HIMEM.SYS
DEVICE      =  c:\dos\EMM386.EXE noems highscan
DEVICE      =  c:\dos\SETVER.EXE
DEVICE      =  c:\dos\SMARTDRV.EXE /double_buffer
DEVICEHIGH  =  c:\dos\DBLSPACE.SYS /move
DEVICE      =  c:\dos\RAMDRIVE.SYS 1024 512 128 /e
DEVICE      =  c:\ut\oaddos\DOSCFG.EXE /l=001 /m1 /v
DEVICE      =  c:\ut\oaddos\DOSOAD.SYS /l=001
DEVICEHIGH  =  c:\setup\drivers\MTMCDD.SYS /d:mscd001 /t:3 /i:5 /s:2
INSTALL     =  c:\dos\SHARE.EXE /f:4096
SHELL       =  c:\dos\COMMAND.COM c:\dos\ /e:624 /p
```

The "Normal" Configuration—
Networked Case (NORM-NET)

Here is AE-NORM.NET:

```
@echo off
REM     This AUTOEXEC file loads usual items and
REM     connects to the network.

ECHO    Starting SMARTDRV, DOSKEY, and MOUSE.
LH c:\dos\SMARTDRV.EXE
LH c:\dos\DOSKEY.COM
LH c:\mouse\MOUSE.COM
echo.

ECHO    Starting network connection
g:\wfwg\NET start
echo.

REM     Start DOS UNDELETE protection
LH c:\dos\UNDELETE.EXE /load
echo.

echo     Setting environment variables
PROMPT [DOS 6:NORM-NET] $p $g
PATH C:\DOS;G:\WFWG;C:\UTIL;C:\SETUP
SET TMP=G:\WFWG\TEMP
SET TEMP=G:\WFWG\TEMP
SET NU=C:\UTIL
echo.
```

and CF-NORM.NET:

```
REM     Usual CONFIG.SYS stuff plus network support
FILES      =     80
FCBS       =   16,0
BUFFERS    =   30,0
STACKS     = 9,256
LASTDRIVE  =      z
DOS        = high,umb
BREAK      = on
DEVICE     = c:\dos\HIMEM.SYS
DEVICE     = c:\dos\EMM386.EXE noems highscan
DEVICE     = c:\dos\SETVER.EXE
```

```
DEVICE      = c:\dos\SMARTDRV.EXE /double_buffer
DEVICEHIGH = c:\dos\DBLSPACE.SYS /move
DEVICE      = c:\dos\RAMDRIVE.SYS 1024 512 128 /e
DEVICE      = c:\workgrp6\PROTMAN.DOS /i:c:\workgrp6
DEVICEHIGH = c:\workgrp6\WORKGRP.SYS
DEVICEHIGH = c:\workgrp6\EXP16.DOS
INSTALL     = c:\dos\SHARE.EXE /f:4096
SHELL       = c:\dos\COMMAND.COM c:\dos\ /e:624 /p
```

Adding Bernoulli Support— Networked Case (BERN-NET)

Here is AE-BERN.NET:

```
@echo off
REM     This AUTOEXEC file loads Bernoulli
REM     support and connects to the network.

ECHO    Starting SMARTDRV, DOSKEY, and MOUSE.
LH c:\dos\SMARTDRV.EXE
LH c:\dos\DOSKEY.COM
LH c:\mouse\MOUSE.COM
echo.

ECHO    Starting network connection
g:\wfwg\NET start
echo.

REM     Start DOS UNDELETE protection
LH c:\dos\UNDELETE.EXE /load
echo.

echo    Setting environment variables
PROMPT [DOS 6:BERN-NET] $p $g
PATH C:\DOS;G:\WFWG;C:\UTIL;C:\SETUP
SET TMP=G:\WFWG\TEMP
SET TEMP=G:\WFWG\TEMP
SET NU=C:\UT\NOR
SET OAD_DRIVER=C:\UT\OADDOS
SET OAD_UTILITY=C:\UT\OADDOS
echo.
```

and CF-BERN.NET:

```
REM       Load support for Bernoulli and network
FILES     =    80
FCBS      =  16,0
BUFFERS   =  30,0
STACKS    = 9,256
LASTDRIVE =     z
DOS       = high,umb
BREAK     = on
DEVICE    = c:\dos\HIMEM.SYS
DEVICE    = c:\dos\EMM386.EXE noems highscan
DEVICE    = c:\dos\SETVER.EXE
DEVICE    = c:\dos\SMARTDRV.EXE /double_buffer
DEVICEHIGH = c:\dos\DBLSPACE.SYS /move
DEVICE    = c:\dos\RAMDRIVE.SYS 1024 512 128 /e
DEVICE    = c:\ut\oaddos\DOSCFG.EXE /l=001 /m1 /v
DEVICE    = c:\ut\oaddos\DOSOAD.SYS /l=001
DEVICE    = c:\workgrp6\PROTMAN.DOS /i:c:\workgrp6
DEVICEHIGH = c:\workgrp6\WORKGRP.SYS
DEVICEHIGH = c:\workgrp6\EXP16.DOS
INSTALL   = c:\dos\SHARE.EXE /f:4096
SHELL     = c:\dos\COMMAND.COM c:\dos\ /e:624 /p
```

Adding CD-ROM Support—
Networked Case (CD-NET)

Here is AE-CD.NET:

```
@echo off
REM     This AUTOEXEC file loads CD-ROM support and
REM     connects to the network.

ECHO    Starting SMARTDRV, DOSKEY, and MOUSE.
LH c:\dos\SMARTDRV.EXE
LH c:\dos\DOSKEY.COM
LH c:\mouse\MOUSE.COM
echo.

ECHO    Loading CD-ROM support
c:\dos\MSCDEX.EXE /d:mscd001
echo.
```

```
ECHO      Starting network connection
g:\wfwg\NET start
echo.

REM       Start DOS UNDELETE protection
LH c:\dos\UNDELETE.EXE /load
echo.

echo      Setting environment variables
PROMPT [DOS 6:CD-NET] $p $g
PATH C:\DOS;G:\WFWG;C:\UTIL;C:\SETUP
SET TMP=G:\WFWG\TEMP
SET TEMP=G:\WFWG\TEMP
SET NU=C:\UTIL
echo.
```

and CF-CD.NET:

```
REM        Load drivers for CD-ROM and network.
FILES       =     80
FCBS        =     16,0
BUFFERS     =     30,0
STACKS      =  9,256
LASTDRIVE   =      z
DOS         =  high,umb
BREAK       =  on
DEVICE      =  c:\dos\HIMEM.SYS
DEVICE      =  c:\dos\EMM386.EXE noems highscan
DEVICE      =  c:\dos\SETVER.EXE
DEVICE      =  c:\dos\SMARTDRV.EXE /double_buffer
DEVICEHIGH  =  c:\dos\DBLSPACE.SYS /move
DEVICE      =  c:\dos\RAMDRIVE.SYS 1024 512 128 /e
DEVICEHIGH  =  c:\setup\drivers\MTMCDD.SYS /d:mscd001 /t:3 /i:5 /s:2
DEVICE      =  c:\workgrp6\PROTMAN.DOS /i:c:\workgrp6
DEVICEHIGH  =  c:\workgrp6\WORKGRP.SYS
DEVICEHIGH  =  c:\workgrp6\EXP16.DOS
INSTALL     =  c:\dos\SHARE.EXE /f:4096
SHELL       =  c:\dos\COMMAND.COM c:\dos\ /e:624 /p
```

Adding Both Bernoulli and CD-ROM Support—Networked Case (BOTH-NET)

Here is AE-BOTH.NET:

```
@echo off
REM      This AUTOEXEC file loads both CD-ROM and
REM      Bernoulli support and connects to the network.

ECHO     Starting SMARTDRV, DOSKEY, and MOUSE.
LH c:\dos\SMARTDRV.EXE
LH c:\dos\DOSKEY.COM
LH c:\mouse\MOUSE.COM
echo.

ECHO     Loading CD-ROM support
c:\dos\MSCDEX.EXE /d:mscd001
echo.

ECHO     Starting network connection
g:\wfwg\NET start
echo.

REM      Start DOS UNDELETE protection
LH c:\dos\UNDELETE.EXE /load
echo.

echo     Setting environment variables
PROMPT [DOS 6:BOTH-NET] $p $g
PATH C:\DOS;G:\WFWG;C:\UTIL;C:\SETUP
SET TMP=G:\WFWG\TEMP
SET TEMP=G:\WFWG\TEMP
SET NU=C:\UTIL
SET OAD_DRIVER=C:\UT\OADDOS
SET OAD_UTILITY=C:\UT\OADDOS
echo.
```

and CF-BOTH.NET:

```
REM      Load support for Bernoulli, CD-ROM, & network.
FILES      =     80
FCBS       =     16,0
BUFFERS    =     30,0
STACKS     =     9,256
LASTDRIVE  =      z
```

```
DOS          = high,umb
BREAK        = on
DEVICE       = c:\dos\HIMEM.SYS
DEVICE       = c:\dos\EMM386.EXE noems highscan
DEVICE       = c:\dos\SETVER.EXE
DEVICE       = c:\dos\SMARTDRV.EXE /double_buffer
DEVICEHIGH = c:\dos\DBLSPACE.SYS /move
DEVICE       = c:\dos\RAMDRIVE.SYS 1024 512 128 /e
DEVICE       = c:\ut\oaddos\DOSCFG.EXE /l=001 /m1 /v
DEVICE       = c:\ut\oaddos\DOSOAD.SYS /l=001
DEVICEHIGH = c:\setup\drivers\MTMCDD.SYS /d:mscd001 /t:3 /i:5 /s:2
DEVICE       = c:\workgrp6\PROTMAN.DOS /i:c:\workgrp6
DEVICEHIGH = c:\workgrp6\WORKGRP.SYS
DEVICEHIGH = c:\workgrp6\EXP16.DOS
INSTALL      = c:\dos\SHARE.EXE /f:4096
SHELL        = c:\dos\COMMAND.COM c:\dos\ /e:624 /p
```

Notice that each AUTOEXEC.BAT file uses a slightly different DOS prompt definition. This was done so you can see at a glance which configuration you have most recently booted.

Batch Files to Set Up Each Personality

Here are the batch files that allow easy switching to each of these nine personalities, again starting with the one to set up the "minimal" personality. Remember to keep these batch files in a directory that is on the DOS PATH, and you will be able to run them from any directory on any drive.

```
@echo off
REM   MIN.BAT  --  Loads minimal configuration.
C:
CD \
COPY c:\configur\AE-MIN c:\AUTOEXEC.BAT
COPY c:\configur\CF-MIN c:\CONFIG.SYS
c:\setup\REBOOT.COM
```

Here is NORM.BAT:

```
@echo off
REM   NORM.BAT  --  Loads normal stuff.
C:
CD \
COPY c:\configur\AE-NORM c:\AUTOEXEC.BAT
COPY c:\configur\CF-NORM c:\CONFIG.SYS
c:\setup\REBOOT.COM
```

Here is BERN.BAT

```
@echo off
REM   BERN.BAT  --   Loads support for Bernoulli.
C:
CD \
COPY c:\configur\AE-BERN c:\AUTOEXEC.BAT
COPY c:\configur\CF-BERN c:\CONFIG.SYS
c:\setup\REBOOT.COM
```

Here is CD.BAT:

```
@echo off
REM   CD.BAT   --   Loads CD-ROM support.
C:
CD \
COPY c:\configur\AE-CD c:\AUTOEXEC.BAT
COPY c:\configur\CF-CD c:\CONFIG.SYS
c:\setup\REBOOT.COM
```

Here is BOTH.BAT

```
@echo off
REM   BOTH.BAT  --   Loads support for Bernoulli
REM                  and CD-ROM
C:
CD \
COPY c:\configur\AE-BOTH c:\AUTOEXEC.BAT
COPY c:\configur\CF-BOTH c:\CONFIG.SYS
c:\setup\REBOOT.COM
```

Here is NORM-NET.BAT

```
@echo off
REM   NORM-NET.BAT  --   Loads normal stuff and
REM                      network support.
C:
CD \
COPY c:\configur\AE-NORM.NET c:\AUTOEXEC.BAT
COPY c:\configur\CF-NORM.NET c:\CONFIG.SYS
c:\setup\REBOOT.COM
```

Here is BERN-NET.BAT

```
@echo off
REM   BERN-NET.BAT  --   Loads support for Bernoulli
REMM                     and network.
```

```
C:
CD \
COPY c:\configur\AE-BERN.NET c:\AUTOEXEC.BAT
COPY c:\configur\CF-BERN.NET c:\CONFIG.SYS
c:\setup\REBOOT.COM
```

Here is CD-NET.BAT

```
@echo off
REM   CD-NET.BAT  --  Loads CD-ROM and network support.
C:
CD \
COPY c:\configur\AE-CD.NET c:\AUTOEXEC.BAT
COPY c:\configur\CF-CD.NET c:\CONFIG.SYS
c:\setup\REBOOT.COM
```

Here is BOTH-NET.BAT

```
@echo off
REM   BOTH-NET.BAT  --  Loads support for Bernoulli,
REM                     CD-ROM, and network.
C:
CD \
COPY c:\configur\AE-BOTH-NET c:\AUTOEXEC.BAT
COPY c:\configur\CF-BOTH-NET c:\CONFIG.SYS
c:\setup\REBOOT.COM
```

This is a complex set of files covering an equally complex set of possibilities. You may have trouble remembering just which batch file does what. One solution is to have a menu batch file that lets you pick which one of these nine batch files to run from a list. An even simpler idea is to have a batch file called CFG-LIST.BAT that contains these lines:

```
@echo off
echo.
echo    Your configuration choices and the batch file
echo    to run in order to set up a given one of them:
echo.
echo        CONFIGURATION              BATCH FILE NAME
echo        -------------              ---------------
echo  Stand Alone:
echo        minimal                    MIN
echo        normal setup               NORM
echo        with Bernoulli             BERN
echo        with CD-ROM                CD
echo        with Bernoulli & CD-ROM    BOTH
```

```
echo   Networked:
echo        normal setup                NORM-NET
echo        with Bernoulli              BERN-NET
echo        with CD-ROM                 CD-NET
echo        with Bernoulli & CD-ROM     BOTH-NET
echo.
```

Switching between these same nine configurations can be done in another way, using DOS 6 menus. That is the subject of the next section.

DOS 6 Menus in CONFIG.SYS

DOS 6 has been heralded for many things, but one of the nicest has received relatively little press coverage. That is the feature introduced to DOS in this version which lets you construct multiple configuration menus in your startup files. Along with that very important feature comes a much less vital, but still very much welcome addition: Control of color in CONFIG.SYS.

The Structure of a DOS 6 Menu

A DOS 6 menu consists of many "blocks"—groups of lines that are either all processed, or else none of them are. Each block is given a label. The first block must be called [MENU]. (A block name must be enclosed in square brackets and it must start at the beginning of a line. The name may be in all capital letters, as is the case in the example shown here, or in all lowercase letters, or a mixture of the two.)

Each block is either a *menu block* or a *configuration block*. In the example below the blocks named [MENU], [NET], and [NO-NET] are menu blocks. All the rest are configuration blocks.

Menu blocks contain lines that specify choices the user can make when that block of lines is read. Some of the options may be to go to another submenu; others can specify that execution go directly to some configuration block. Menu blocks contain three other kinds of lines. One is used to set colors, another to specify a default choice, and a third to specify a timeout value.

A configuration block can contain any lines that could be put in an ordinary, non-menued CONFIG.SYS file. In addition, you can have one or more special line(s) that say to *include* all the lines of some other configuration block(s) as if they had been put in this block.

Finally, you can have one or more blocks with the special name [COMMON]. The lines in these configuration blocks will be executed no matter what choices the user makes in traversing the menu blocks.

No matter how complex such a menued CONFIG.SYS file gets, there will be one and only one configuration block that is executed because it was chosen from a menu. (Other blocks may be executed because they were named in an INCLUDE line in the configuration block that was chosen or in an INCLUDE line in one of the included blocks. Also, any [COMMON] blocks will be executed.) The name of the one chosen configuration block is called the name of the configuration the user chose, and that name is put in a special environment variable called CONFIG.

Example of DOS 6 Menued Startup Files

Here is an example DOS 6 multiple configuration CONFIG.SYS file. This file and its associated AUTOEXEC.BAT file (shown next) offer all the same options as the nine batch files and nine sets of startup files displayed in the preceding section of this chapter.

```
REM      Sample DOS 6 menu in CONFIG.SYS file.

REM      (Put here a reminder to yourself of which
REM      version of your configuration menu this is.)

[MENU]
REM      This is the opening set of menu choices.
REM      ----------------------------------
MENUITEM     = MIN, Minimalist configuration
SUBMENU      = NO-NET, Configurations not on network
SUBMENU      = NET, Configurations on the network
MENUCOLOR    = 14,1
MENUDEFAULT  = MAIN, 60

[MIN]
REM      Here is a quite minimalist configuration.
REM      -------------------------------------
STACKS   = 0,0
FILES    =  10
BUFFERS  =   5
SHELL    = c:\dos\COMMAND.COM c:\dos\ /p
```

```
[NO-NET]
REM      These menu choices have no network support.
REM      ----------------------------------------
MENUITEM      = BERN, Include Bernoulli support
MENUITEM      = CD, Include CD-ROM support
MENUITEM      = BOTH, Include Bernoulli & CD-ROM support
MENUITEM      = NORM, Normal non-networked configuration
MENUCOLOR     = 10,0
MENUDEFAULT   = CONFIG4, 60


[NET]
REM      These menu choices all load network drivers.
REM      ----------------------------------------
MENUITEM      = BERN-NET, Bernoulli & network support
MENUITEM      = CD-NET, CD-ROM & network support
MENUITEM      = BOTH-NET, Bernoulli, CD-ROM, & network
MENUITEM      = NORM-NET, Network plus normal setup
MENUCOLOR     = 10,0
MENUDEFAULT   = CONFIG8, 60


[BERN]
REM      Load support for Bernoulli removeable drives
REM      with 'normal' complement of DOS drivers.
REM      ----------------------------------------
INCLUDE USUAL
DEVICE      = c:\dos\SETVER.EXE
DEVICE      = c:\dos\SMARTDRV.EXE /double_buffer
DEVICEHIGH = c:\dos\DBLSPACE.SYS /move
DEVICE      = c:\dos\RAMDRIVE.SYS 1024 512 128 /e
DEVICE      = c:\ut\oaddos\DOSCFG.EXE /l=001 /m1 /v
DEVICE      = c:\ut\oaddos\DOSOAD.SYS /l=001


[CD]
REM      Load driver for CD-ROM support
REM      with 'normal' complement of DOS drivers.
REM      ----------------------------------------
INCLUDE USUAL
DEVICE      = c:\dos\SETVER.EXE
DEVICE      = c:\dos\SMARTDRV.EXE /double_buffer
DEVICEHIGH = c:\dos\DBLSPACE.SYS /move
DEVICE      = c:\dos\RAMDRIVE.SYS 1024 512 128 /e
DEVICEHIGH = c:\setup\drivers\MTMCDD.SYS /d:mscd001 /t:3 /i:5 /s:2
```

```
[BOTH]
REM     Load support for Bernoulli removeable drives &
REM     CD-ROM with 'normal' complement of DOS drivers.
REM     ----------------------------------------------
INCLUDE USUAL
DEVICE     = c:\dos\SETVER.EXE
DEVICE     = c:\dos\SMARTDRV.EXE /double_buffer
DEVICEHIGH = c:\dos\DBLSPACE.SYS /move
DEVICE     = c:\dos\RAMDRIVE.SYS 1024 512 128 /e
DEVICE     = c:\ut\oaddos\DOSCFG.EXE /l=001 /m1 /v
DEVICE     = c:\ut\oaddos\DOSOAD.SYS /l=001
DEVICEHIGH = c:\setup\drivers\MTMCDD.SYS /d:mscd001 /t:3 /i:5 /s:2

[NORM]
REM     Load 'normal' complement of DOS drivers.
REM     -----------------------------------------
INCLUDE USUAL
DEVICE     = c:\dos\SETVER.EXE
DEVICE     = c:\dos\SMARTDRV.EXE /double_buffer
DEVICEHIGH = c:\dos\DBLSPACE.SYS /move
DEVICE     = c:\dos\RAMDRIVE.SYS 1024 512 128 /e

[BERN-NET]
REM     Load support for Bernoulli removeable drives,
REM     the 'normal' complement of DOS drivers and
REM     network drivers for Windows for Workgroups.
REM     -----------------------------------------------
INCLUDE USUAL
DEVICE     = c:\dos\SETVER.EXE
DEVICE     = c:\dos\SMARTDRV.EXE /double_buffer
DEVICEHIGH = c:\dos\DBLSPACE.SYS /move
DEVICE     = c:\dos\RAMDRIVE.SYS 1024 512 128 /e
DEVICE     = c:\ut\oaddos\DOSCFG.EXE /l=001 /m1 /v
DEVICE     = c:\ut\oaddos\DOSOAD.SYS /l=001
DEVICE     = c:\workgrp6\PROTMAN.DOS /i:c:\workgrp6
DEVICEHIGH = c:\workgrp6\WORKGRP.SYS
DEVICEHIGH = c:\workgrp6\EXP16.DOS

[CD-NET]
REM     Load driver for CD-ROM support with the
REM     "normal" complement of DOS drivers and
REM     network drivers for Windows for Workgroups.
REM     -----------------------------------------
INCLUDE USUAL
```

```
DEVICE     = c:\dos\SETVER.EXE
DEVICE     = c:\dos\SMARTDRV.EXE /double_buffer
DEVICEHIGH = c:\dos\DBLSPACE.SYS /move
DEVICE     = c:\dos\RAMDRIVE.SYS 1024 512 128 /e
DEVICEHIGH = c:\setup\drivers\MTMCDD.SYS /d:mscd001 /t:3 /i:5 /s:2
DEVICE     = c:\workgrp6\PROTMAN.DOS /i:c:\workgrp6
DEVICEHIGH = c:\workgrp6\WORKGRP.SYS
DEVICEHIGH = c:\workgrp6\EXP16.DOS


[BOTH-NET]
REM     Load support for Bernoulli removeable drives,
REM     CD-ROM, "normal" complement of DOS drivers, and
REM     network drivers for Windows for Workgroups.
REM     -----------------------------------------------
INCLUDE USUAL
DEVICE     = c:\dos\SETVER.EXE
DEVICE     = c:\dos\SMARTDRV.EXE /double_buffer
DEVICEHIGH = c:\dos\DBLSPACE.SYS /move
DEVICE     = c:\dos\RAMDRIVE.SYS 1024 512 128 /e
DEVICE     = c:\ut\oaddos\DOSCFG.EXE /l=001 /m1 /v
DEVICE     = c:\ut\oaddos\DOSOAD.SYS /l=001
DEVICEHIGH = c:\setup\drivers\MTMCDD.SYS /d:mscd001 /t:3 /i:5 /s:2
DEVICE     = c:\workgrp6\PROTMAN.DOS /i:c:\workgrp6
DEVICEHIGH = c:\workgrp6\WORKGRP.SYS
DEVICEHIGH = c:\workgrp6\EXP16.DOS


[NORM-NET]
REM     Load "normal" complement of DOS drivers and
REM     network drivers for Windows for Workgroups.
REM     -----------------------------------------
INCLUDE USUAL
DEVICE     = c:\dos\SETVER.EXE
DEVICE     = c:\dos\SMARTDRV.EXE /double_buffer
DEVICEHIGH = c:\dos\DBLSPACE.SYS /move
DEVICE     = c:\dos\RAMDRIVE.SYS 1024 512 128 /e
DEVICE     = c:\workgrp6\PROTMAN.DOS /i:c:\workgrp6
DEVICEHIGH = c:\workgrp6\WORKGRP.SYS
DEVICEHIGH = c:\workgrp6\EXP16.DOS


[USUAL]
REM     This lines are not used by themselves, but are
REM     used with all the other configurations except
REM     the minimal one.
REM     -----------------------------------------------
```

```
FILES       = 80
FCBS        = 16,0
BUFFERS     = 30,0
STACKS      = 9,256
LASTDRIVE   = z
DOS         = high,umb
BREAK       = on
DEVICE      = c:\dos\HIMEM.SYS
DEVICE      = c:\dos\EMM386.EXE noems highscan
INSTALL     = c:\dos\SHARE.EXE /f:4096
SHELL       = c:\dos\COMMAND.COM c:\dos\ /e:624 /p

[COMMON]
REM    This block label is here to catch any statements
REM    that are added to the end of your CONFIG.SYS by
REM    an application installation program.

REM    At this point the possibilities for the
RREM   configuration environment variable (CONFIG) are:
REM    MIN, BERN, BERN-NET, CD, CD-NET, BOTH, BOTH-NET,
REM    NORM, and NORM-NET.
```

The following AUTOEXEC.BAT file completes the job of configuring the PC according to the choices made in the CONFIG.SYS menus. Notice that the CONFIG environment variable is automatically set by DOS to the name of the last menu item that was selected, which is the name of the configuration block the user chose to execute. The REMark lines at the end of CONFIG.SYS and the ones at the beginning of AUTOEXEC.BAT are there to make it easy for you to remember all the possibilities that these files support.

```
@echo off
REM     Example DOS 6 menu AUTOEXEC.BAT file.

REM     At this point the possibilities for the
REM     configuration environment variable (CONFIG)
REM     are: MIN, BERN, BERN-NET, CD, CD-NET, BOTH,
REM     BOTH-NET, NORM, and NORM-NET.

IF %CONFIG%.==MIN. goto FinishUp

LH c:\dos\SMARTDRV.EXE
LH c:\dos\DOSKEY.COM
LH c:\mouse\MOUSE.COM
```

1001

```
if %CONFIG%.==CD. c:\dos\MSCDEX.EXE /d:mscd001
if %CONFIG%.==CD-NET. c:\dos\MSCDEX.EXE /d:mscd001

if %CONFIG%.==BERN-NET g:\wfwg\NET start
if %CONFIG%.==CD-NET g:\wfwg\NET start
if %CONFIG%.==BOTH-NET g:\wfwg\NET start
if %CONFIG%.==NORM-NET g:\wfwg\NET start
echo.

:FinishUp
REM     Start DOS UNDELETE protection
LH c:\dos\UNDELETE.EXE /load
echo.

echo    Setting environment variables
PROMPT [DOS 6: %CONFIG%] $p $g
PATH C:\DOS;G:\WFWG;C:\UTIL;C:\SETUP
SET TMP=G:\WFWG\TEMP
SET TEMP=G:\WFWG\TEMP
SET NU=C:\UTIL
if %CONFIG%.==BERN. SET OAD_DRIVER=C:\UT\OADDOS
if %CONFIG%.==BERN. SET OAD_UTILITY=C:\UT\OADDOS
if %CONFIG%.==BERN-NET. SET OAD_DRIVER=C:\UT\OADDOS
if %CONFIG%.==BERN-NET. SET OAD_UTILITY=C:\UT\OADDOS
echo.

:OutAHere
```

These are very large start-up files, at least in comparison to what most people have been accustomed to using. Also unusual is the fact that the CONFIG.SYS file is considerably larger than the AUTOEXEC.BAT file.

You may have wondered why in the example startup files, more use was not made of the [USUAL] configuration block (and why essentially no use was made of the [COMMON] block). The [USUAL] block contains lines that are processed for eight of the nine configurations. You will find a number of other lines that occur in each of those eight configurations and that look precisely the same in each one. Why not simply move one copy of them to the [USUAL] block and then delete all the other occurrences of them?

Doing that would certainly make the CONFIG.SYS file quite a bit smaller. But it also would make true memory optimization impossible! The only lines that can be put in any configuration block that is shared by two or more configurations are those lines that do not get changed by a memory optimization program.

DOS 6 Menus and Memory Optimization

If you decide you want to use this menu approach to multiple configurations, be sure to read carefully the discussion in Chapter 21 in the section "The Problem of Memory Optimization and Menus." Once you put multiple paths of execution into your startup files, you must allow for that fact when you attempt to optimize your PC's use of memory.

That means that any configuration block that is shared among multiple configurations may include lines that set a number of FILES, FCBS, BUFFERS, or STACKS, a LASTDRIVE line. Directives such as BREAK, SWITCHES, and NUMLOCK are fine as well.

Also okay in a shared configuration block are DEVICE lines that load drivers that you know must always be loaded in lower memory, any INSTALL statements (since those also always load the specified program into lower memory), and a SHELL statement.

What must not appear in a shared configuration block are any DEVICEHIGH lines or indeed any DEVICE lines that your memory optimization program might end up changing to DEVICE lines.

While many lines in the separate configuration blocks may start out looking the same, they may end up being quite different. Here are a couple of typical lines that have been altered by MemMaker:

```
DEVICEHIGH /l:1,7280  = c:\workgrp6\WORKGRP.SYS
DEVICEHIGH /l:1,11168 = c:\workgrp6\EXP16.DOS
```

The /l:1 in each of these lines means that MemMaker has determined that these device drivers should be placed in the first UMB. The number after that gives the initialization size for this program. (See Chapter 21 for a discussion of how TSR programs and device drivers get loaded into upper memory, including a definition of the initialization size.)

For the startup files shown in the example in this section, there are nine paths through the menu structure. To optimize the usage of lower and upper memory, you must run MemMaker, or whatever optimization program you choose to use, nine times. Each time the optimization program will run through all the phases, including system evaluation, resident program sizing, and calculations and final adjustments.

Configuration Managers

Before there was DOS 6, many people were using multiple configurations. Only some of them were power batch file programmers able to create the sort of multiple startup file pairs and the batch files to load them that were discussed in the section "Global Personality Choices by Use of Batch Files" earlier in this chapter. The rest of them used a configuration manager program.

Some configuration managers simply automate the creation and management of multiple sets of startup files. One good example is CONED, by Ira T. Askenes.

Other configuration managers use an approach that is very much like that used in DOS 6. Two shareware examples of this are BOOTCON from Modular Software Systems, and BOOT.SYS by Hans Salvisberg.

You can look up information on these and other configuration managers in the MemInfo hypertext database on the diskette that accompanies this book.

TWEAKING MEMORY FOR WINDOWS AND DOS PROGRAMS UNDER WINDOWS

When more than one program is running at once, memory management gets more challenging. Here are some ways to cope.

- Which of the Previously Mentioned Strategies Apply *1007*
- Optimizing Memory for Microsoft *Windows 1007*

  If You Run Only *Windows* Programs *1009*

  If You Run DOS Programs Under *Windows 1016*
- *Windows* PIF Files and Memory Usage *1025*

1005

As soon as you decide to run more than one program at once in your PC, your memory management task becomes significantly harder. "At once" in this context doesn't just mean time-sliced multitasking—for example using Windows. It also includes times you wish to start one program, suspend it and run another, and then return to the first one—what has been called task swapping elsewhere in this book.

Which of the Previously Mentioned Strategies Apply

Everything you learned in Chapter 34 applies to any PC running any programs whatever. So, of course, those techniques are applicable to the multitasking situation.

The techniques discussed in Chapter 35 are only useful up until you start running the first of several programs you anticipate running together. That is because all of those techniques involve rebooting your PC, which will cause you to lose any unsaved data from all the programs that are running at the time.

You can use the "personality switching" tricks presented in that chapter to configure your PC optimally for an upcoming multitasking session. For example, you might wish to have a DOS 6 menu system set with one option being optimized for running *Windows* and Windows applications only, and a different one for running *Windows* with a mix of Windows and DOS applications. The information presented in this chapter will help you create those configurations.

While this chapter focuses on the memory management steps to take for *Windows* use, many of the ideas can easily be applied to other multitasking situations. So if you use DESQview, or perhaps just do some simple task swapping, you will want to study these examples for ideas you can try out on your PC.

Optimizing Memory for Microsoft Windows

In Chapter 21 you learned the generalities of how *Windows* uses memory. You learned there about the three modes in which *Windows* 3.0 can run (real, standard, and 386-enhanced), and that *Windows* 3.1 also runs in standard or 386-enhanced mode, but it cannot run in real mode. Only PCs in Classes 5 and 6 can run *Windows* 3.x in 386-enhanced mode. Even they will only do so if they have enough memory installed, or if you force them to do so by invoking WIN.COM with a /3 command-line switch.

You may wish to review Chapter 21 and Chapter 18 to see both how *Windows* uses memory and how much of it you need in order for *Windows* to work well. Now that RAM prices have come down, most people feel that you should have at least 4MB of RAM in any PC on which you will be running *Windows*. Larger amounts are even nicer, of course. (Still vendors persist in offering PCs that are supposedly Windows-ready—sometimes even with *Windows* preloaded on the hard disk—with as little as 1MB or 2MB of RAM on the motherboard. That lets them quote an unrealistically low price for those PCs, since you must increase their RAM complement before doing any serious Windows work.)

Windows can be run in standard mode on any PC in Class 3 or higher. Many people who have PCs in Class 5 or 6 still choose to run *Windows* in standard mode (by using the /s command-line switch for WIN.COM), because they have found that it runs just a little bit faster that way. They are willing to give up the added flexibility that comes with 386-enhanced mode in exchange for that ten or fifteen percent speed gain.

When *Windows* 3.x is running in 386-enhanced mode it is able to give each DOS application you launch a separate "virtual machine." You can exercise considerable control over the memory environment in those virtual machines. The following sections show examples of many of the things you can do in this situation.

Standard mode *Windows* presents fewer options for memory management, but there are a few, and getting them set right can be quite important. The following sections show you how to do that too.

Before you leap into Windows memory management, you have to consider carefully how you plan to use *Windows*. There are two major distinctions you must make. The first is whether or not you plan to run any DOS programs while you are in *Windows*. The second is whether you plan to run mostly or exclusively in standard mode.

More realistically, the first question could be restated as, "Do you plan to spend a significant amount of your time running DOS applications under *Windows*?" If you only plan to spend a few minutes of each working day doing so, many of the memory issues described here will not be of much importance to you. On the other hand, if you don't pay attention to, at least, the most significant issues, you may find that you cannot get your DOS application to run under *Windows* at all.

First, I shall discuss the case in which you won't be running any DOS applications, or at least not for any significant fraction of your workday.

Please read both this and the following section, though, as you may find some things of value to you in each one.

If You Run Only Windows Programs

Windows itself and all Windows application programs use only lower and extended memory (really XMS memory), and upper memory if you have any. *Windows* and Windows applications completely ignore any EMS memory you may have.

What does this mean for memory management? If you are using a PC in Class 5 or 6, you probably have been creating some EMS memory out of extended memory using a LIMulator program. Or maybe you only were loading the LIMulator to create upper memory blocks. Either way, you can free up a significant amount of extended memory for *Windows* to use simply by electing not to load any LIMulator program. If you are running DOS 5 or 6, that means that you **will load** HIMEM.SYS, but **will not load** EMM386.EXE. Doing this can free up more memory for *Windows* and its application programs to use than any other single step you could take. (To put some numbers on this: You'll avoid using about 100KB of extended memory for the program code, plus 384KB of extended memory that would be mapped as lower memory, plus 64KB for an EMS page frame, and around 8KB that EMM386 uses in lower and upper memory.)

On the other hand, you need to realize that if you don't load EMM386.EXE, you will thereby stop providing any UMBs into which you could load device drivers and TSR programs. That doesn't hurt *Windows* at all, but it could prevent you from running a large DOS application. This is true not only for a DOS application you attempt to run from within a DOS window in *Windows*. You also may find that you can't run your large DOS application from the DOS prompt before you have even loaded *Windows*. (The solution to this quandary is to have a ready-to-run alternate personality for your PC that does load EMM386.EXE and then moves programs to upper memory as needed.)

DOS Memory Management Steps to Take

These considerations, and others that are discussed in Chapter 21, lead to the suggestion that you include in your CONFIG.SYS file these lines:

```
DOS     = HIGH
DEVICE  = C:\DOS\HIMEM.SYS
FILES   = 30
```

```
BUFFERS = 20
STACKS  = 9,256
INSTALL = C:\DOS\SHARE.EXE
```

and that you **not** include a DEVICE line to load EMM386.EXE.

> If you have *MS DOS* or *PC DOS* 5 or 6 versions, and/or *Windows 3.1*, then you will have at least two versions of HIMEM.SYS and EMM386.EXE. Be sure to use the latest version, whether it came with DOS or with *Windows*. (Windows 3.0 came with Emm386.SYS, instead.) You could modify the lines of your CONFIG.SYS file to point to the Windows directory, or simply copy the latest versions of these files to the C:\DOS directory. The latter approach is probably better, in that you will automatically get the latest version when you upgrade your DOS version and when you next upgrade *Windows* (provided you again copy the versions of HIMEM.SYS and EMM386.EXE that come with that version of *Windows* to C:\DOS).

See the section "Disk Cache Issues" later in this chapter for another suggestion you may wish to use in your CONFIG.SYS or AUTOEXEC.BAT file.

This approach also means that you can skip all use of MemMaker, since you will have no UMBs into which you could load any device drivers or TSR programs. Skip using MemMaker (or whatever is your favorite memory optimization aid) for this configuration only. Do optimize upper memory use in any other configuration you use that does create UMBs.

Turning Off Windows EMS Services

When you run *Windows* in 386-enhanced mode, it normally creates its own supply of EMS memory for DOS applications. By adding to the [386Enh] section of your SYSTEM.INI file the following lines

```
EMMSize=0
NoEMMDriver=True
```

you tell *Windows* not to bother loading the program code for its LIMulator, and in this way you will save another significant chunk of extended memory for other uses.

Remember that you must use an ASCII text editor (such as EDIT in MS-DOS 5 or 6 or Notepad in *Windows*) whenever you alter any of the four key startup files, CONFIG.SYS, AUTOEXEC.BAT, WIN.INI, and SYSTEM.INI. Alternatively, you may use any editor that allows you to read and save files as pure ASCII text—so long as you are **very certain** that you will **always** remember to save these files in that special way!

One particularly convenient way to edit your startup files with an editor that is sure to save them in the right format is by using the SysEdit program provided with *Windows*. See Chapter 21, in the section "Managing the Managers," to learn how to add an icon for this program to your favorite program group.

Windows Virtual Memory

When you run *Windows* 3.x in 386-enhanced mode, it can use more RAM memory than you actually have. The way it does this is by using virtual memory. This means that, whenever it is running low on memory, *Windows* will swap some of the programs that are not active at the moment to a file on your hard disk.

It only does this if you let it. That is, you have to allow *Windows* to set up either a permanent or a temporary swap file. A permanent swap file works best, but it does mean committing a substantial chunk of hard disk space to that one purpose. However, if you often run Windows programs exclusively, that use is well justified.

Defragment your disk drive before you set up the permanent swap file. Even if you have a lot of free space on the drive, if it is not all in one contiguous block, *Windows* cannot use it for a permanent swap file.

Windows can use a swap file that is up to three times as large as the amount of RAM you have. It will not do this, however, unless doing so would still leave you with at least that much free space on your disk after the swap file is created. (Normally, *Windows* will insist on creating at least a 512KB swap file and on leaving at least 512KB of free space on the disk. That means that if you have less than 1MB of free space, it will utterly refuse to create a swap file.) So if you have 4MB of RAM, you'd have to have 24MB of free disk space before *Windows* would let you set up a maximum-size, 12MB permanent swap file.

If you don't have that much free space, or if you don't wish to commit 12MB of your free space to a *Windows* permanent swap file, you can still get virtual memory. Just tell *Windows* to create a temporary swap file. This will not work as quickly as the permanent swap file, but it will let you have the illusion that you have more RAM than you actually do. Just how much more you will get will depend on how much free disk space you have at the time.

The way to tell *Windows* what you want in the way of virtual memory is by running the Control Panel program. (The icon for this is created in the MAIN program group by the *Windows* SETUP program.) Double-click on the "386 Enhanced" icon, and when the dialog box opens, click on the "Virtual Memory..." button. The dialog box that appears next just tells you what you presently have in the way of virtual memory. If you wish to alter it you must select "Change>>".

Disk Cache Issues

A very good use of RAM in almost all PCs is as a disk cache. You load a disk cache program into lower or upper memory, and that program then uses some additional RAM for its cache storage. (Some disk cache programs can load some of their program code into expanded memory along with their cache data, but only if you have chosen to use expanded memory for the cache data. Since in the present scenario you won't have any expanded memory, you can't take advantage of that feature.)

The best place, usually, from which to take RAM for the disk cache data storage is extended memory (or XMS memory). But doing this cuts down on the memory that *Windows* has available for its own use. A partial solution is to have the cache program give back some of the RAM it normally would use for cache data storage and let *Windows* use that RAM for whatever it wishes.

If you use SmartDrive as your disk cache, you control this behavior with some command line switches on the line in your AUTOEXEC.BAT file that loads SMARTDRV.EXE. See Chapter 39 for the details.

RAM Disk Issues

Another very good use of RAM is for a RAM disk. The use of a RAM disk as a way to speed up *Windows* is discussed briefly in Chapter 15, in the section "When Virtual Memory Access Is Painfully Slow."

If you are running *Windows* 3.0, you should be aware that it cannot ever use more than 16MB of RAM. If you have more than that amount, put the excess to use as a combination of a disk cache (the portion that won't be loaned to *Windows*) and a RAM disk.

If you are running *Windows* 3.1, it can take advantage of all the memory you have. In that case you will want to limit the amount you commit to a RAM disk, so as to keep from starving *Windows*. But, as is noted in Chapter 15, sometimes a RAM disk can be used to speed up *Windows* more than by letting it have the RAM for its own uses. Also remember that you can sometimes benefit from compressing a RAM disk (using Stacker, or some similar product). See Chapter 20 for more on this.

Please don't try compressing a RAM disk by using the DOS 6 program DoubleSpace. It will work, sort of, but if you try to have DoubleSpace automatically compress a RAM disk each time you boot, you will find that you have a problem. DoubleSpace alters its (hidden) DBLSPACE.INI file every time you compress a new drive, and that means that the next time you boot, your RAM drive will show up at a different letter. That will mean that DoubleSpace will not be able to find it to compress.

If you manage, somehow, to get around this problem, you are likely to have an even worse one. Each time you boot, DoubleSpace will find the RAM disk one drive letter higher in the alphabet, until finally you will run out of legal drive designations!

Saving and Accessing
Special Windows Configurations

Ideally you would like to have *Windows* configured optimally for the way you are using it at the time. If sometimes you run DOS applications and other times you don't, you would like to have two different *Windows* configurations (as well as two different DOS configurations) for those two different situations.

You can do this, with just a little bit of effort. There are two steps to the process. First is creating and saving each of those configurations. Second is making sure *Windows* uses the correct one each time you start it.

The easiest way to do the first of these steps is this: Edit SYSTEM.INI to include the lines that make *Windows* work optimally for one usage pattern—say the one in which you will only be running Windows programs. Now copy SYSTEM.INI to a new file named SYSTEM.WIN. Reedit SYSTEM.INI for the situation when you will be running DOS applications (using the suggestions you will find a bit later in this chapter). This time copy SYSTEM.INI to SYSTEM.DOS. (You may, of course, use whatever names you may prefer.) Then arrange to have your AUTOEXEC.BAT file copy one of these saved versions to the real working copy that is named SYSTEM.INI.

If you use the many batch files approach to setting up your PC's personality (see Chapter 35), then put the lines that copy the SYSTEM.DOS or SYSTEM.WIN file to SYSTEM.INI in the batch files that copy the appropriate startup files to CONFIG.SYS and AUTOEXEC.BAT. If, on the other hand, you choose to use the DOS 6 menu approach, you can use the value of the CONFIG environment variable to control which of the saved versions of SYSTEM.INI gets copied to the active file.

System Resources

Chapter 31 pointed out that you can run out of system resources in *Windows* even if you have a lot of unused RAM. The system resources are a special region in RAM (or actually several 64KB special regions) that must each have some unused space in them, or *Windows* will grind to a halt.

Usually the best tip is to have only a few program groups, not too many program items within those groups, and to keep to a modest number the programs you run and the windows they open or other objects they create on the screen. Each of those actions uses up space in the system resources.

There is not a lot more you can do about this. But here is one way you can cut down on the complexity of your *Windows* screen. You won't save a lot of resource memory this way, but simplifying the screen can be quite beneficial, apart from the resources it saves, by helping you find the icons you want more easily. This idea is very similar to the one mentioned in the previous section, only now you will be creating and saving multiple sets of group files, and for each set, an associated PROGMAN.INI file.

Set up *Windows* one way, exit from *Windows* with the "Save Settings on Exit" option checked on the Options Menu in Program Manager. Copy PROGMAN.INI file to PROGMAN.P00. Also copy all the files with extension GRP to new files with the extension G00.

Now go back into *Windows*, delete groups, create new groups, and do whatever else you need to do to create another useful configuration. Again exit from *Windows* and copy the PROGMAN.INI and GRP files to new files with extensions P01 and G01, respectively. Repeat this process as many times as you wish.

The last step is to create a little batch file to restore all the files with one of those extensions to their active form. Here is what that batch file might look like:

```
@ECHO off
ECHO  SETCFG.BAT - Sets up a Windows configuration
ECHO.
IF %1%!==! GOTO ShowSyntax
IF NOT EXIST PROGMAN.P%1 GOTO BadNumber
COPY PROGMAN.P%1 PROGMAN.INI
COPY *.G%1 *.GRP
GOTO AllDone
:BadNumber
ECHO  You have specified an undefined configuration
GOTO AllDone
:ShowSyntax
ECHO       Use the command
ECHO          SETCFG nn
ECHO       to setup the Windows configuration
ECHO       number nn.
ECHO.
ECHO       Valid nn values are in the range 00 to 99.
ECHO       (Be sure to include the leading zero in nn
ECHO       if the value is less than ten.)
:AllDone
```

Naturally, you will want to modify the range in the fourth from the last line in the batch file to reflect the actual range of configurations you have created. (You might also add some ECHO lines that show the user which numbers correspond to which configurations. Give a title, or one-line description for each one. Even if you are the user, you will someday appreciate that little touch when you find you have forgotten exactly how configuration 17 differs from configuration 03.)

Other Tips

There are a host of other things you can do to *Windows* that have at least some impact on its use of memory. A few are mentioned in the next section on running DOS applications with *Windows*. As far as the rest of the things you could do, unfortunately, most of them won't have a large enough impact to make worrying about them worthwhile.

One that might be worth considering is shrinking your wallpaper. You can convert the BMP file you usually load into a smaller RLE file and thereby save on the use of both disk space and, when that wallpaper is loaded, RAM. *Windows* does not include any tool to do this. The shareware programs *Paint Shop* and *WinGIF*, among others, have this ability.

The program Memory Hogs, in the *Kamyan Utilities* group, can be used to display the amount of memory currently being used by any program or dynamic link library (DLL). Alternatively, you can have it show only the memory used by programs. Normally you will be concerned with all uses, so you'll probably want to leave the DLL display turned on. Since the amount of memory a given program or DLL uses can change dynamically (and quite dramatically), you will have to run the Memory Hogs program for quite a while to get a feeling for which things are using the most memory in your system. You can tell Memory Hogs to update its display periodically on its own, or you can update the display whenever you wish to see what memory is being used. (You also can use Memory Hogs to "compact memory" before you check the amount that is in use. This will tell *Windows* to clean up any fragmentation in the heap spaces. That is something it will do on its own, when it gets around to it. Having it do that before you reevaluate the memory usages may give you a more accurate picture of what memory is actually in use.)

Once again, even if you almost never run any DOS applications, I recommend you study the next section. You may learn something there that you will be able to use (or even that you will someday find you must use).

If You Run DOS Programs under Windows

If, like many *Windows* users, you sometimes run DOS applications in a DOS window, you will be faced with some very different issues in memory management than if you only run Windows programs. This section covers those issues, and gives you some pointers on how to respond to them.

Don't forget to read the preceding section as well as this one. Some of the tips you will find there may be helpful to you in this setting as well.

DOS Memory Management Steps to Take

Windows can only use lower and extended memory (and upper memory if you have any). DOS applications, on the other hand, can only use lower (and upper) and expanded memory. DOS-extended applications can use all of these kinds of memory.

If you are running *Windows* and plan to run a DOS application in a window inside of *Windows*, you need to be sure you supply enough of the right kinds of memory for all of the programs (both Windows and DOS applications) that you will be running.

For starters, if you are running DOS 5 or 6 (and I recommend you do so if you want to run DOS applications under *Windows*), your CONFIG.SYS file will need to include these lines:

```
DOS     = HIGH
DEVICE  = C:\DOS\HIMEM.SYS
DEVICE  = C:\DOS\EMM386.EXE {parameters}
FILES   = 30
BUFFERS = 20
STACKS  = 9,256
INSTALL = C:\DOS\SHARE.EXE
```

This is almost the same as the lines shown in the preceding section called "DOS memory management steps"; the only difference is that here there is a line to load EMM386.EXE. Heed the TIP in that previous section about using the latest version you have of both HIMEM.SYS and EMM386.EXE, whether they came with DOS or with *Windows*. The versions shipped with *Windows* also will work just fine with all your DOS applications.

Heed the CAUTION in the section "Turning off Windows EMS services" about being sure you use a suitable editor to modify your startup files.

Since, in this case, you are loading EMM386.EXE, you could be creating some upper memory blocks. You might prefer to load SHARE into one of them. In that case, remove the INSTALL line shown here and replace it with a LOADHIGH line in your AUTOEXEC.BAT file.

In addition to these lines, you may well want to have a SHELL statement to load your command interpreter and tell it how large a master environment you want. Don't go overboard on the environment size. Remember, you will be reducing the size of every DOS window by the size of that master environment. (See Chapter 10 for more on the environment.)

The FILES line in CONFIG.SYS controls the size of the system file table. That governs the maximum number of files that may be open at one time for all the programs that are running simultaneously. Microsoft's recommendation for *Windows* is to set FILES=30. Do so unless you also run some DOS applications outside of *Windows* that require a larger setting.

When you open a DOS window inside *Windows* (when *Windows* is running in enhanced mode), another file table comes into play. You get to set its size by adding a line to your SYSTEM.INI file in the [386Enh] section that reads:

```
PerVMFiles=15
```

or whatever value you choose. The default value is 10, which is fine for many programs, but not enough for others. Mostly database programs are the ones that really need a lot of file handles. For them you may wish to make this setting as large as 50. The maximum you can have is 255 minus the number you set in the FILES statement in CONFIG.SYS.

Some Key Questions

The command-line parameters for EMM386.EXE are just shown as {parameters} in the example CONFIG.SYS line above. What are your options for those parameters, and what impact will they have on your PC's memory usage?

The answers to these questions depend on several things. What version of DOS are you using? What version of *Windows*? How much RAM do you have? Do you have an EISA-bus PC with more than 16MB of RAM?

Do you plan on running DOS application programs that need EMS memory from within *Windows* when *Windows* is running in standard mode? (There are basically two reasons you might be running *Windows* in standard mode. One is that you want the extra speed that standard mode offers, the other is that you are using a PC in Class 3 or 4.)

Are you loading any TSR programs or device drivers that could be put into upper memory? Can any of them use EMS memory to reduce their consumption of lower and upper memory?

The fundamental goal in this scenario is to be sure that your DOS windows are large enough (have enough free memory) that you can run the application programs you want to run. Often, with modern RAM-hungry applications, that is not easy to insure.

Clearing Out Lower Memory Before Starting Windows

Each time *Windows* opens a DOS window, it is starting a "virtual machine" (using the Virtual 8086 mode of the CPU). Chapter 11 explains just what this means.

The most important point about virtual machines to remember for the present discussion is that each virtual machine that *Windows* creates will have a copy of DOS and all the device drivers and TSR programs that were loaded before you started *Windows*. This means that you want to keep the number and size of those programs to an utter minimum in order to make your DOS windows as large as possible. Here are some explicit suggestions for how you can do that.

If you are using DOS 5 or 6, you can load a significant part of DOS into the HMA. Do that and you will free up some additional lower memory for the DOS applications that run in a window inside *Windows*, as well as for any DOS applications you may run when *Windows* is not loaded.

Don't load any pop-up TSR programs. Instead, load them in a DOS window after *Windows* gets going. Then, instead of popping them up with their usual hotkeys, you can switch to the window that contains the pop-up program in its already popped up state. (This will, of course, use up some RAM and—what is worse—some of your system resources. So don't load every TSR you own in a window just in case you might want to use it someday!)

Consider using the techniques described in Chapter 34 for loading device drivers and TSR programs only when they are needed. Apply those techniques inside of a DOS window whenever you can. Thus, instead of running an application directly, you might run a batch file from Program Manager. (Doing that causes *Windows* to open a virtual machine and run the batch file in that machine.) The batch file can be constructed so that it loads whatever helper programs your DOS application requires and then runs the application.

There is one important distinction between this approach and that suggested in Chapter 34: Many times you will be able to get away without having the batch file unload those helper programs after you are through with them. Simply close the DOS window (type EXIT at the prompt or let the batch file complete executing), and all of those programs will vanish along with the virtual machine in which they were loaded.

This doesn't always work. If a device driver you loaded this way managed to change the state of the underlying copy of DOS that all of *Windows* and all of the DOS windows within *Windows* rely on, ripping out that driver precipitously could crash your machine. How can you know if that is going to happen for any particular device driver? Try some tests.

First save your work in all the other DOS windows or Windows applications you may have running. In fact, you should always do this before trying anything that is the least bit risky. (Some would say that just running *Windows* can be a bit risky—so they would recommend saving your work frequently in any case, which is good advice.) Then open a new DOS window by double-clicking on the MS-DOS icon. Next, try loading the device driver. You can load a device driver from the DOS prompt by using DEVLOD or DMC, as was described in Chapter 34. Now type EXIT and see what happens. Try doing a few more things to be sure you haven't killed off a part of DOS that is important, but that isn't going to show you its demise until you access the disk or do some other critical operation.

Don't get too carried away with this strategy. In particular, don't try loading a disk cache in a window inside of *Windows*. You need your disk cache program safely stashed in RAM all of the time, both before and after you run *Windows* and all the time in between. The same goes for network drivers, print spoolers, and other programs that provide system-wide services.

On the other hand, you can safely load a mouse driver from a batch file that launches a DOS application that is mouse-aware. *Windows* maintains its own mouse driver, so you don't need to have any mouse driver loaded before you run *Windows* unless you are going to run mouse-aware DOS applications outside *Windows* as well. Likewise, you could load a device driver to support a scanner just before running a program that needs it, then unload it once you exit that program. (This assumes that the program that uses the scanner is a DOS-based program. If it is a Windows-based program you will need to have the device driver loaded either through *Windows*—by a line in SYSTEM.INI—or in your CONFIG.SYS file before you start *Windows*.)

Here is another tip: If you run a DOS application that needs lots of memory to load, and that runs exclusively in text mode, you could run it from a batch file that first loads VIDRAM (a part of *QEMM 386* or *QRAM* from Quarterdeck), then runs the application. This could let you have as much as 704KB or even 736KB of RAM in that virtual machine. (A similar program from Above Software is called Above640. RYBS offers VIDMEM to do the same thing.) This technique and the dangers it poses are discussed in Chapter 21.

EMS and Windows Modes

Remember that *Windows* in 386-enhanced mode can supply EMS memory to DOS applications that run in DOS windows. In fact, those applications running in such a window can only get EMS memory by having *Windows* supply it.

To get *Windows* to supply EMS memory, you have to make sure it will run in enhanced mode. Sometimes it will refuse to do so even if you have a Class 5 or 6 PC and enough RAM. The reason it may refuse to go into enhanced mode is that you may have a hardware EMS board installed and its EMM driver loaded. *Windows* must be able to turn off that driver and take over providing EMS services, or it cannot go into enhanced mode.

This is a rare problem, simply because almost everyone using a PC in Class 5 or 6 creates EMS memory by using a LIMulator and not by using a hardware EMS board. If you think you have this problem, you can try adding the line

```
IgnoreInstalledEMM=True
```

to your SYSTEM.INI file in the [386Enh] section. This will force *Windows* to go into enhanced mode and to load its own LIMulator unless you have another line in that section that reads

```
NoEMMDriver=True
```

Be careful with these commands. You can force *Windows* to do what you want, but you may not like the results. In particular, if your previously loaded EMM is supplying some EMS memory to a program, and if that program later on tries to get that EMM to remap that assigned EMS memory, your system may crash (or worse).

You also can control how *Windows* supplies its EMS memory. If you loaded EMM386.EXE in your CONFIG.SYS file, you may have told it where to put the EMS page frame. You can, and should, reiterate this choice by another line in your SYSTEM.INI file in the [386Enh] section that reads:

```
EMMPageFrame=nnnn
```

where nnnn is the segment address where you want the page frame to start. Further, you can specify the size of the EMS page frame by the line

```
EMMSize=xxxx
```

where xxxx is the size in bytes. Normally this defaults to 65536, and that is normally what you want. Only use this to reduce the EMS page frame to a smaller amount if you must. (Most EMS-aware DOS programs assume the page frame will be 64KB in size. They may not work if it is any smaller amount.) Setting EMMSize=0 is the same as the FRAME=NONE option for EMM386. (That option is documented for DOS 6, but it also works with DOS 5.)

There are several other lines you could add to your SYSTEM.INI file to control how *Windows* provides and uses expanded memory. Mostly they are not needed, and you are best leaving them out. One line you might need in a few rather unusual cases is

```
AllEMSLocked=True
```

or

```
SysEMSLocked=True
```

which tells *Windows* to leave any EMS memory that is allocated in your real memory and not to swap it to the disk. The first version of this line is what you need if you have a disk cache program running that uses expanded memory from a LIMulator. (But that is a bad idea in any case unless the disk cache program cannot be configured to use XMS or extended memory instead.) The second version is what you would use if you have a DOS application running in a window that uses a large amount of EMS memory, and you wish to save the time that would otherwise be required to swap that information to disk each time the DOS application itself is swapped to disk.

Those are the things you will need to consider about EMS memory if you have a Class 5 or 6 PC and are running *Windows* in enhanced mode and a DOS application in a DOS window.

On the other hand, a DOS application that needs EMS memory and is running in a DOS window under standard mode *Windows* can only get its EMS memory from some source that is in place before *Windows* starts. That means that if you are using a Class 4 PC, or if you simply choose to run *Windows* on your Class 5 or 6 PC in standard mode, you will want to load the expanded memory manager before you run *Windows*.

Upper Memory Blocks (UMBs) and the Windows Translation Buffers

If DOS applications can get their EMS memory from *Windows* when it is running in enhanced mode, why would you want to load EMM386.EXE in your CONFIG.SYS file? Why not simply depend on *Windows* for that service?

The answer lies in the utility of UMBs. Even if you don't want any EMS memory for DOS applications outside of *Windows*, and you don't need to supply it for DOS applications running inside *Windows*, you need to load EMM386.EXE in order to have it create upper memory blocks.

And there are at least two reasons why you want upper memory blocks. First, if you have any device drivers or TSR programs loaded before you start *Windows* which could have been "loaded high" (into upper memory), you will get larger DOS windows by making sure they do load high. Second, *Windows* needs some RAM in either lower or upper memory for something called its "translation buffers." These take up at least 8KB, and for networked PCs as much as 24KB. If you don't have at least that much unused RAM in a UMB or totally empty upper memory space into which *Windows* can map some extended memory, it will have to put its translation buffers into lower memory and, in the process, subtract that much free space from every DOS window.

The proper line to use to invoke EMM386.EXE and ask it to provide EMS memory and upper memory blocks is

```
DEVICE=C:\DOS\EMM386.EXE RAM {other parameters}
```

whereas to get it to provide only upper memory blocks you need the line

```
DEVICE=C:\DOS\EMM386.EXE NOEMS {other parameters}
```

If you are running DOS 5, you can tell EMM386 not to create upper memory in certain regions of upper memory address space by using an X parameter. Use this to make sure that you have at least 24KB left for *Windows* to find and use for itself. If you are running DOS 6, you can use the WIN parameter for this purpose.

The {other parameters} in this command may include some that tell EMM386 which regions of upper memory space it may fill with RAM it has remapped from extended memory and which regions it must not use. (The discussion in Chapter 37 details how those parameters are used.) If you use them, it would be a good idea to have a similar set of instructions to *Windows*, so it will make its decision about where in upper memory it can place its translation buffers consistent with the choices you have forced on EMM386.

The lines you need to use are these:

```
EMMExclude=aaaa-bbbb
```

or

```
EMMInclude=aaaa-bbbb
```

where the numbers aaaa and bbbb are beginning and ending segment values. If you need to specify multiple ranges for either statement, put only one on each line and include as many copies of that statement as you need with each one specifying a different region. The EMMInclude statement has precedence over the EMMExclude line. So if the regions specified on the two lines overlap, the EMMInclude action will take place in the overlap region.

If you are running DOS 6 and use the WIN option to EMM386, then use EMMInclude and specify the same range of addresses as you used in the WIN parameter. Then use EMMExclude to block out access to all other addresses in upper memory space so *Windows* will leave them alone. For example, you might have put the line

```
DEVICE=C:\DOS\EMM386.EXE RAM WIN=D000-D5FF
```

in your CONFIG.SYS file. Then put these lines in SYSTEM.INI in the [386Enh] section:

```
EMMInclude=D000-D5FF
EMMExclude=A000-CFFF
EMMExclude=D600-FFFF
```

to make *Windows* look only in the region you have saved for its exclusive use.

Other Tips

Near the end of the section "If You Run Only Windows Programs" in the subsection "Other Tips" is a suggestion about how to avoid using up too much memory on your *Windows* wallpaper. That suggestion applies, of course, equally well when you run DOS applications in windows within *Windows*. In fact, you should read all of the section "If You Run Only Windows Programs" to see if any of the other tips you find there apply and will help you.

There is one more tip that is well worth remembering. If you find, someday, that *Windows* refuses to open a DOS window, and it claims the reason is that there is not enough memory left, you may be able to solve the problem very easily. Just empty the clipboard.

In *Windows* 3.0, the clipboard could not hold any item larger than 64KB. In *Windows* 3.1, that restriction is gone. Now you can easily have hundreds of KB tied up in whatever it is you last cut or copied to the clipboard. You can clear the clipboard in either of two ways. Open the clipboard viewer and from its Edit menu select Delete. The faster way is to copy to the clipboard a new item that is very small. (A single letter is enough.) Since the clipboard can only hold a single item at a time, that will cause it to discard whatever it was holding previously. If you had most recently copied a large bitmap to the clipboard, this simple step can free up a lot of memory. (One way you might have copied a large bit map to the clipboard without really intending to do so is by accidentally hitting the PrintScreen key. That copies a bitmapped picture of the entire screen to the clipboard.)

Windows PIF Files and Memory Usage

So far in this chapter you have learned how to set up your memory management for *Windows* and Windows applications. You also learned how to set up memory management for DOS applications you run from a DOS prompt in a DOS window. Now you can turn your attention to tweaking how individual DOS applications that are run directly from within *Windows* will use memory. Once you have that done, you will have finished optimizing your PC in this regard. Now your programs will run together as well as they can under *Windows*.

When *Windows* runs a Windows application, that application is able to tell *Windows* what resources it wants or needs. DOS applications don't tell *Windows* this information. To bridge this gap, Microsoft has created Program Information Files, also known by their extension as PIF files. Chapter 21 describes PIF files and shows you what the three screens of the PIF editor look like (Figures 21.17, 21.18a, and 21.18b).

You can run a DOS application under *Windows* in any of three ways. One is by opening a DOS window, then running the application at the DOS prompt, just as you used to do before you got *Windows*. Another is by creating an icon for a program group and then double-clicking on that icon. When you choose this approach you get to tell Program Manager the name of the program to associate with the icon. You can use the DOS application program's name, or you can use the name of an associated PIF file. Finally, you can run a program by double-clicking on its name or on its PIF file's name in File Manager.

In the second and third ways of starting a DOS application you have the option of using the application program directly or its associate PIF file. Only if you use the PIF file will its setting influence how *Windows* lets that DOS application use memory. If you don't use a PIF, *Windows* will use whatever settings it finds in the special PIF file called _DEFAULT.PIF. (Any filename that starts with an underscore is typically a special system file.)

Chapter 21 describes the general issues involved in editing a PIF file, but it doesn't give you any rules of thumb for choosing the numbers to put into the various boxes. In this section you will learn just such a set of useful "rules" that will serve you pretty well most of the time.

The PIF editor offers you two modes of operation, standard and enhanced. It starts in the mode that matches the mode in which *Windows* is currently running, but it permits you to change to the opposite mode so you can specify, in one session, all the settings for a PIF file for both modes of operation. Use this feature. You need to specify the settings for both modes in case you run that DOS program in each of the modes someday.

In the standard mode screen there are only three memory numbers you can set. One is called "Memory Requirements." Set that one to 128. (A higher setting is useless.) Set the XMS Memory KB required and KB desired to zero unless you are preparing a PIF for running a DOS-extended application.

In the enhanced mode primary screen, set both Memory Requirements boxes (requested and required) to -1. This will make *Windows* give your application as much memory as it can. Or, if you know the DOS application you will be running cannot use more than some small amount of RAM, set a number just a bit larger than that in both boxes to conserve memory for other programs.

Again, in the XMS Memory boxes, zeros are best unless you know your DOS application requires some XMS memory (as DOS-extended applications may). Entering -1 in these boxes gives all possible XMS memory to a DOS-extended application.

The EMS Memory boxes only appear on this screen. The KB Required box tells *Windows* how much EMS memory it must offer the DOS application, and the KB Requested box tells it not to offer more than the indicated amount. Set the number in both boxes to zero if your DOS application cannot use any EMS memory. Set both to the amount that application wants if you know it can take advantage of EMS memory. Don't set the KB Required to zero, even if the application could get along without any. If you did use zero for this setting, *Windows* wouldn't create any EMS memory for the program unless it asked for some, and the program might never do that since it could see that none was waiting for it before it asked.

If your DOS application runs in text mode only, check Video Mode Text in both standard and enhanced screens. If it uses multiple screen "pages" of text, check that box in the PIF editor's standard mode screen. If the DOS application uses EGA or VGA graphics, check Low Graphics or High Graphics on the enhanced mode screen.

The most reliable and quickest operating DOS windows are full-screen ones. So check full-screen unless you must have the DOS application appear in a window. You always can change from a full screen to a window (and back again) by pressing Alt-Enter.

Don't check Exclusive Execution unless you want to stop all *Windows* programs dead in their tracks whenever you switch this DOS application to the foreground. You often can leave Background Execution box unchecked as well, unless you want to let your DOS application continue working when you have switched the focus away from it. (A communications program that you want to continue downloading in the background is a perfect example of one for which you definitely want to check the Background execution box.) Nearly always you want to check Close Window on Exit. Don't check any of the Monitor Ports or Monitor Directly boxes (ordinarily)—asking *Windows* to watch over your program's shoulder as it does its work will substantially slow things down.

Good values to enter on the enhanced mode Advanced Options screen for the Foreground and Background priorities are 1000 and 100 respectively. That will let your DOS program have most of the CPU's time when it has the focus, yet let it, and the *Windows* programs, run a fair amount when they are in the background.

Don't lock any memory unless you know you must. Locking memory can speed up the program for which you are editing the PIF file, but it slows everything else down—often dramatically, since it tells *Windows* that the EMS and/or XMS memory allocated to this program must not be swapped to disk even if the program is no longer in the foreground and maybe even if it isn't using that memory at all.

For more information on these and the other PIF settings, and for many other tips about making *Windows* work better for you, I recommend Brian Livingston's fine book, *Windows 3.1 Secrets*.

EXAMPLES OF CREATING AND LOADING UPPER MEMORY

In this chapter you will find explicit examples of the steps you must take to create upper memory blocks (UMBs) and then fill them with programs.

Chapter 10 describes memory control blocks in lower and upper memory and briefly mentions how DOS can be made to load programs into upper memory. Chapter 11 described in general terms several ways that upper memory can be created. Chapter 20 discusses the statements that one can use in a CONFIG.SYS file, including the DEVICEHIGH lines that load device drivers into upper memory. Chapter 21 discusses loading programs into upper memory from the AUTOEXEC.BAT file.

Studying all those sections will help you understand what is possible. What you may not get from them is an understanding of exactly how to do those things—exactly what steps you must take to create upper memory blocks and then load programs into them. This chapter fills that need.

There are many memory managers on the market. Up until version 5, DOS had none, so if you wanted to do any memory management you had to buy some third-party product. Now, with versions 5 and 6 of DOS, you can either use the DOS memory managers, or you can still buy a third-party product. The utility makers have concentrated on making their products in some fashion better than the memory managers that come with DOS; still, many people are quite content with the results they get from using the DOS-provided tools.

The examples in this and the next chapter show how the DOS tools work. They also show how some of the most popular or unique of the third-party products work. For more on the differences between the different memory managers and when to choose which one, see Chapter 21, especially the section "Choosing a Memory Manager."

Creating Upper Memory

Creating upper memory can mean any of several things. One is causing some memory chips that are located on a hardware expanded memory board to appear in a region of the CPU's upper memory address space and leaving them there. Another is telling the motherboard system logic to convert some shadow RAM into an upper memory block. A third is mapping some extended memory into one or more regions of upper memory address space. Which one(s) you can use and precisely how you must go about it vary with the class of PC you have and, in some cases, with the brand of PC and of any add-in memory cards in that PC. Naturally, the exact syntax of the lines in your CONFIG.SYS file will also depend on which brand of memory manager you choose to use.

The first two examples are for PCs in Class 4. (They could have been for PCs in Class 2, but then there would be no extended memory to concern yourself with.) All the rest of the examples in this section are for PCs in Class 5 or 6. (See the inside front cover for a chart of the PC classes, and Chapter 3 for a detailed explanation of each class.)

Upper Memory from EMS

One way to create upper memory blocks is by using a hardware EMS memory board and an expanded memory manager (EMM). These tools are normally used to create and manage expanded memory—memory that is paged in and out of the CPU's memory address space (both lower and upper). They also can be used to park some memory in a region of upper memory space and not page it out. Once that memory is in place, it can be used by some other memory manager as a UMB.

Suppose, for example, that yours is a Class 4 PC (an AT or equivalent) with an Intel *Above Board* in it, and suppose that you wish to use *QRAM* to manage upper memory. You need to include these lines in your CONFIG.SYS file:

```
DEVICE=C:\INTEL\EMM.SYS
DEVICE=C:\QRAM\QRAM.SYS
```

The first line loads the Intel expanded memory manager program. That makes memory available in a region of upper memory space. The second line loads the Quarterdeck memory manager that will take charge of that UMB.

Both of these device drivers can also take some command-line parameters to tell them how to do their work. The command lines shown here are the simplest possible ones, and were created assuming that the drivers will work satisfactorily using only their default settings.

Quarterdeck suggests that you let its OPTIMIZE program set up its memory manager to work in the best possible way. You certainly can try that, and it is the easiest way to go. However, you may be able to do an even better job on your own. Most plausibly, this can be done by letting OPTIMIZE do its best job, then tweaking the results a bit further.

If you also want to have XMS services you will need to add the following line

```
DEVICE=C:\QRAM\QEXT.SYS
```

as QRAM.SYS only provides management services for upper memory (unlike the DOS program HIMEM.SYS, which manages both upper and extended memory). QEXT.SYS provides all other XMS services, including creation and management of the HMA.

To load DOS into the HMA use the following line:

```
DOS=HIGH
```

or if you wish to load programs into upper memory using the DOS (versions 5 and 6) commands DEVICEHIGH and LOADHIGH, you will have to change that line to read

```
DOS=HIGH,UMB
```

You need not use DEVICEHIGH and LOADHIGH, as QRAM comes with its own programs to do those jobs. If you are running DOS 5 or a later version, you may find the DOS tools to be preferable. (Of course, if you are still using a version of DOS prior to 5, you will have to use the Quarterdeck-provided tools for loading programs into upper memory.)

Upper Memory from Shadow RAM

What if the PC in question fell into Class 4 because it had motherboard shadow RAM instead of a LIM 4.0 hardware EMS memory board installed? For most PCs of that sort you can use the setup program in the motherboard's BIOS ROMs to tell the motherboard system logic to convert some of the shadow RAM into EMS memory. If you can convert more than 64KB, then you can have both an EMS page frame and a UMB.

If all you want to do is load programs into the upper memory that your PC's motherboard system logic has created out of shadow RAM, you need not have any lines in your CONFIG.SYS file that refer to EMS memory. On the other hand, if you wish to use some of that memory as EMS memory, you will need to load the EMM program that came with your motherboard. In either case, you could load UMBPro as your upper memory manager. (UMBPro was developed by Quadtel, which is now a part of Phoenix Technologies.) UMBPro is probably the best on the market at finding shadow RAM and using it as upper memory for program loading.

Thus you might have either just this line:

```
DEVICE=C:\QUADTEL\UMBPRO
```

or you might have both of these lines:

```
DEVICE=C:\DRIVERS\MM.SYS
DEVICE=C:\QUADTEL\UMBPRO
```

where I have assumed that the expanded memory manager that came with your motherboard is called MM.SYS, that you are keeping it in the C:\DRIVERS directory, and that you are keeping the UMBPRO programs in the C:\QUADTEL directory.

Although you can use command-line parameters to command UMBPro, it expects to find an INI file in the directory from which it was loaded. That file will contain all the things you might otherwise have specified on the command line.

As is true for its competitors, UMBPro comes with auxiliary programs to let you load TSR programs and device drivers into upper memory even if you are using a version of DOS prior to 5, and it also is able to make memory that DOS 5 or 6 can use. If you want to have DOS do the loading into upper memory (using the DEVICEHIGH and LOADHIGH commands), you must also have specified DOS=UMB (or DOS=HIGH,UMB) in your CONFIG.SYS file.

Upper Memory Using HIMEM and EMM386

If you are using DOS 5 or 6, you can use the DOS-provided memory management tools, HIMEM.SYS and EMM386.EXE. The first of these, HIMEM.SYS, is a manager of upper and extended memory, and a creator and manager of the HMA. The second program, EMM386.EXE, is a converter of XMS memory (extended memory as seen after HIMEM.SYS takes over management of it) into upper memory and expanded memory, and it serves as an expanded memory manager.

The lines you need in your CONFIG.SYS file (and they must be in this order) to use these tools are the following:

```
DEVICE=C:\DOS\HIMEM.SYS
DEVICE=C:\DOS\EMM386.EXE
```

As is usual with memory managers, you can add a number of command-line parameters to these commands.

Most people don't need to add anything to the HIMEM.SYS line. If HIMEM doesn't recognize the motherboard system logic chip set, and therefore doesn't know how to control the A20 line, you will have to add a /MACHINE:*xxxx* (where *xxxx* is replaced by the appropriate code or machine type number).

Another reason for adding a parameter to the HIMEM command is if you wish to reserve some of your extended memory for use by an older program that uses the INT15h ("white lie") strategy for acquiring extended memory. The parameter you need to add is /INT15=*nnn*, where *nnn* is replaced by the number of KB of extended memory you wish to reserve. If you don't use this parameter, HIMEM will convert all of extended memory into XMS memory, and no program can get at any of it without HIMEM's permission.

The default action of EMM386 depends on the DOS version. Under DOS 5 it will convert only 256KB of XMS memory into EMS memory, and it will not create any upper memory at all. Under DOS 6 it converts all of your XMS memory into EMS memory. (In both cases it also replaces 384KB of lower memory with simulated EMS pages, using XMS memory as the source.) The reason that the default amount of XMS memory to convert was changed is that under DOS 6, programs can get at the converted memory as EMS memory or they can still get at the same memory as XMS memory.

If you want upper memory blocks, you must add something on the EMM386 command line. There are two main possibilities. If you want upper memory and EMS, add the word RAM. If you want only upper memory, use the word NOEMS.

If you want upper memory blocks and VCPI services, but no EMS page frame, use the command line

```
DEVICE=C:\DOS\EMM386.EXE RAM FRAME=NONE
```

This will use up the same amount of extended memory as if you had allowed it to create an EMS page frame, since EMM386 must load its core program plus its LIMulator module into extended memory, and it must simulate 386KB of EMS memory to page into lower memory and map some extended memory into the upper memory space for UMBs. The difference (and this can be very important) is that with FRAME=NONE it will allow you to load up to 64KB more of device drivers and TSR programs into upper memory.

Since you are using the DOS memory managers, no doubt you will be using the DOS-provided tools for loading programs into upper memory. That means you have to tell DOS to take control of upper memory. To do that, add to your CONFIG.SYS file the line

```
DOS=UMB
```

or, if you want to have DOS load as much of itself as it can into the HMA,

```
DOS=HIGH,UMB
```

In addition to the RAM or NOEMS command-line parameters, the most common ones are parameters that specify where the page frame is to be located and ones that include or exclude regions of upper memory address space. The included regions are ones you are telling EMM386 to use for upper memory and/or the EMS page frame. The excluded regions are ones you are telling it to be sure to leave alone. Here is a typical EMM386 line with a number of parameters on it:

```
DEVICE=C:\DOS\EMM386.EXE RAM 3072 FRAME=D400 I=E400-F7FF X=A000-D1FF
```

The first parameter, RAM, says to create both upper memory and an EMS page frame. The next parameter, 3072, says to convert 3MB of extended memory into simulated EMS memory. (This form is appropriate to DOS 5. Just leave out this parameter on a PC running DOS 6.) The FRAME=D400 parameter says to put the EMS page frame with its lowest address at D4000h, and its highest address at E3FFFh. (You use the segment portion of the addresses only in these parameters.) The I=E400-F7FF parameter says to include the region from E4000h through F7FFFh. Without telling it to do so, it will ordinarily not include anything in the E page. The X=A000-D1FF parameter tells EMM386 not to use any upper memory space lower than address D2000h.

The DOS 6 version of this line (for the same PC, with the same hardware options installed) would look almost the same. Most likely it would read

```
DEVICE=C:\DOS\EMM386.EXE RAM FRAME=D400 I=E400-F7FF
 X=A000-D1FF WIN=CC00-D1FF
```

Here you can see that the space from CC000h through D1FFFh has been declared available and reserved for Windows to use. In the DOS 5 version it was merely excluded from use by EMM386 without noting why. In DOS 6 you can remind yourself why you excluded that region by using the WIN parameter.

In either case, it is a good idea to add to the [386Enh] section of your SYSTEM.INI file the lines

```
EMMExclude=A000-CBFF
EMMInclude=CC00-D1FF
EMMExclude=D200-FFFF
```

to inform Windows which portion of upper memory you want to have it use, and which to leave alone.

If you are not really confident of your ability to choose the right values for these command-line parameters, you can run a memory optimization program and let it figure them out. If you are using DOS 6, the program MemMaker is included with DOS. If you are running an earlier version you could use the *AtLast* program from RYBS to do the same job.

Please remember, though, that you are probably both smarter and better informed that either of these programs (or any other memory optimization program). So don't just accept what they tell you without thinking about it critically. Now that you have read this book you are well equipped to challenge some of the dumb things that any program of this genre will sometimes do.

Upper Memory Using QEMM

Quarterdeck's memory manager for Class 5 and 6 PCs is called QEMM386.SYS. This one program replaces both HIMEM.SYS and EMM386.EXE. (It also can be used with DOS versions prior to 5 for which there were no DOS memory management tools.) The line you need in your CONFIG.SYS file is simply

```
DEVICE=C:\QEMM\QEMM.SYS
```

or, as with EMM386.EXE, you can add parameters to indicate where you want the page frame and what regions of upper memory space to be sure to use or to be sure to avoid using. A more complex example might look like this:

```
DEVICE = c:\qemm\QEMM386.SYS RAM FRAME=E000
 INCLUDE=CC00-DFFF EXCLUDE=A000-CBFF
```

This looks like two lines on the page, but in the actual CONFIG.SYS file, all of this must be on a single line. *QEMM*, like *QRAM*, comes with OPTIMIZE. You can run that program and let it figure out all these command-line parameters (and more). Doing so will at least get you near to the best configuration; tweaking the results and testing your changes can often improve your memory management even further.

Upper Memory Using 386MAX

The other of the two most popular memory managers for Class 5 and 6 PCs prior to DOS 5, and still one of the two most popular other than the DOS tools, is *386MAX* from Qualitas. It is very similar to QEMM in many respects, but the normal way to invoke it is slightly different. Here is a typical CONFIG.SYS line that loads 386MAX:

```
DEVICE = C:\386MAX\386MAX.SYS PRO=C:\386MAX\386MAX.PRO
```

There is only one command-line parameter here. It is the full path and name of a profile file that contains all the information that otherwise would be specified on the command line.

Like its competitors, *386MAX* comes with a memory optimization utility program. Qualitas calls theirs MAXIMIZE. Run it and answer its questions. When you have finished, inspect the 386MAX.PRO file to see what MAXIMIZE did. This is where you apply your tweaks, if you wish to try your hand at further improving things.

Upper Memory Using Memory Commander

Chapter 21 contains a discussion of the most unusual of the available memory managers for Class 5 and 6 PCs. It is *Memory Commander*. The CONFIG.SYS line to load *Memory Commander* doesn't look all that different from the others:

```
DEVICE=C:\MC\MC.SYS
```

but what is novel is that you can also have other lines loading some other memory manager in your CONFIG.SYS file without any conflict. This is because, as long as the line loading *Memory Commander* comes first, it will simply suppress the loading of any other memory manager. (*Memory Commander* comes with a database of programs it knows about. That includes all the popular memory managers. If you are using one that it doesn't understand, you can add it to the *Memory Commander* database.)

When you boot your PC, if you hold down the Alt key at the right time, you can cause Memory Commander to avoid loading itself. In that case your other lines that load the alternate memory manger will come into play. This provides a very simple way to switch between two different memory managers.

The other novelty of Memory Commander is that it never needs any command-line parameters on the line that loads the MC.SYS device driver.

(Neither does it ever alter any of the lines in your CONFIG.SYS file or AUTOEXEC.BAT file, except to add a line at the end of AUTOEXEC.BAT that invokes its memory optimization program.)

Loading Things into Upper Memory

There are three ways in which you can cause some of your device driver or TSR programs to be loaded into upper memory. Which one you use depends on which memory manager you are using, and to some extent on which version of DOS is installed on your PC.

The Three Basic Strategies

The first technique, and for many years the only available way, is to use a third-party high-loader program. These come in two flavors: One for loading device drivers and the other for loading TSR programs.

The second technique is to maintain a database of programs and have the memory manager device driver responsible for watching as each program is loaded and intervening to load into upper memory those it has been told to load there. This technique was used originally only by *Memory Commander*. Now, several of the third-party memory managers can do this. (Figure 21.4 shows one entry in the *Memory Commander* database—in that case for the Novell NetWare IPX.COM program which is a TSR program.)

The third technique, which is possible only if you are using DOS 5 or 6, is to use the DOS commands DEVICEHIGH and LOADHIGH. These are simply DOS-provided versions of the original third-party device and TSR high-loader programs.

When DOS 5 first came out, the DEVICEHIGH and LOADHIGH commands only worked if you used the DOS-provided memory managers, HIMEM and EMM386. Soon, however, the other memory manager makers modified their products to permit using the DOS tools with them as well.

Examples of Proprietary High-Loaders

Here are a couple of examples of the CONFIG.SYS lines you might use to invoke a third-party device high-loader. The first example is for use with QEMM; the second for use with 386MAX.

```
DEVICE = C:\QEMM\LOADHI.SYS /R:1 C:\SETUP\STACKER.COM /NB /EMS @ @
DEVICE = C:\386MAX\386LOAD.SYS SIZE=3024 PRGREG=3
 FLEXFRAME PROG=C:\PCKWIK\PCKWIN.SYS
```

In the first line (the QEMM example), the program that actually does the loading of a device driver into upper memory is LOADHI.SYS. The program being loaded high is STACKER.COM. (What appears here as the second and third lines is in actuality only one line.)

> Incidentally, this line shows how to load STACKER, version 2.0, with 64KB of its program code being put into expanded memory, and with no disk caching internal to Stacker. Those two steps minimize the memory that is used by this device driver, yet give good performance—assuming that you have some other disk cache loaded, as you should in order to get the benefit of caching for all of your drives, instead of merely for those that are compressed Stacker drives.

The parameter /R:1 that comes between the device high-loader program and the program being loaded high tells the device high-loader to put the program into a particular region of upper memory. In this example, STACKER.COM is being loaded into the UMB with the lowest memory addresses.

The second line (the 386MAX example) adds a few new wrinkles. The device high-loader program in this case is 386LOAD.SYS. The program being loaded high is the PCKWIN.SYS *Windows* interface driver (used with the *Super PC-Kwik* disk cache, version 4.x). This line tells 386LOAD.SYS several things. First, it says that the program being loaded needs 3,024 bytes at most during its initialization. Second, it specifies that the program is to be loaded into the third UMB ("Program Region 3" in the Qualitas way of referring to it). Finally, it says that 386LOAD.SYS is to use its "Flexframe" technique of borrowing the EMS page frame during the loading of this device driver.

Here are examples of the lines used with the same two memory managers for loading TSR programs into upper memory. Again, the first example is for QEMM; the second for 386MAX.

```
C:\QEMM\LOADHI /TSR /R:1 C:\DOS\SHARE.EXE /F:4096
C:\386MAX\386LOAD SIZE=26416 PRGREG=2 FLEXFRAME PROG=E:\PCPANEL\PCPANEL
```

These lines are very much like the lines for loading device drivers into upper memory. The only significant difference is that the high-loader programs are now called LOADHI.COM and 386LOAD.COM. (The extension is COM instead of SYS; a difference that is commonly used to indicate a program to be run at the command prompt, as opposed to a device driver.)

LOADHIGH and DEVICEHIGH (DOS 5 and 6)

The DOS commands LOADHIGH and DEVICEHIGH differ from the third-party, proprietary high-loader programs in several important ways.

First, they are internal commands. (Actually LOADHIGH is an internal command, built into COMMAND.COM. The directives in CONFIG.SYS are processed by IO.SYS, and it is that module that contains the new DEVICEHIGH directive.) So instead of loading a special program that does the loading of the target program into upper memory, these directives simply tell DOS to do that job itself. In order for that to be possible, DOS must have control of upper memory. That requires that your CONFIG.SYS file have a line that reads either DOS=UMB or DOS=HIGH,UMB.

Second, in DOS 5, there was no way to indicate which region in upper memory to use. So if you had several UMBs of different sizes, you had to juggle the order in which you put the DEVICE or LOADHIGH lines in your CONFIG.SYS or AUTOEXEC.BAT file in an attempt to control the loading process. With DOS 6 that oversight has been remedied. *MS DOS* 6 and *PC DOS* 6 permit you to tell DEVICEHIGH or LOADHI to allocate to a single program specified amounts of memory in each of several regions of upper memory. That is a level of sophistication not yet matched by the third-party programs, or by *DR DOS* 6.

A third difference is that you can use the third-party TSR high-loader programs in an INSTALL statement, whereas there is so far no INSTALLHIGH command in DOS. If you want a TSR to be loaded into upper memory using only the DOS tools, you simply must use LOADHIGH (or LH) in your AUTOEXEC.BAT file instead of an INSTALL line in your CONFIG.SYS file.

The syntax for the DOS 5 versions of these commands was very simple. You simply substituted DEVICEHIGH for DEVICE and inserted LOADHIGH (or LH) in front of a line in AUTOEXEC.BAT that loaded a TSR program.

Thus the line

```
DEVICE = C:\UV\ANSI-UV.SYS
```

loads the Ultravision alternative version of the ANSI.SYS device driver into lower memory while

```
DEVICEHIGH = C:\UV\ANSI-UV.SYS
```

loads it into upper memory (in the UMB at the lowest address which has enough room). And the line

```
C:\DOS\SHARE  /F:4096
```

loads SHARE into lower memory, but

```
LH C:\DOS\SHARE  /F:4096
```

loads it into upper memory.

With DOS 6 new complexities have come into the game. Now you may (but don't have to) specify several more things to control how the DEVICEHIGH or LOADHIGH directives will be carried out.

Thus, the previous examples could be changed to something like these lines

```
DEVICEHIGH = /L:1,2000 C:\UV\ANSI-UV.SYS
LH /L:1,13984 C:\DOS\SHARE /F:4096
```

Here, the number after /L:1 specifies a region of upper memory, and the number following indicates how much memory from that region should be allocated for this program. The yet more complex versions of these directives, in which multiple UMBs are specified, are not commonly used.

The easiest way to get the appropriate sizes to put on these lines is to run MemMaker and see what lines it inserts into your CONFIG.SYS and AUTOEXEC.BAT files.

A Recap

This chapter described and showed examples giving the details of how to invoke memory management programs to create upper memory blocks (UMBs) and load device drivers and TSR programs into them. The next chapter completes the examples, showing you examples of setting up a variety of helper programs.

38

PUTTING THE REST OF YOUR RAM TO GOOD USE

Chapter 30 listed a number of programs that can make good use of any spare RAM you may have. Here are examples of how to use them.

Chapter 30 discusses a number of programs you might like to use if you find that you have some available "excess" RAM. What that chapter did not do, and what this one does, is show you the actual syntax of the commands that you must use to load those programs. Not every program that is mentioned in Chapter 30 is described here, but a representative sample is.

RAM Disks

In Chapter 20 the point was made that almost every PC user can benefit from creating a RAM disk. It won't do you any good at all, though, unless you also know how to use it. So, review the discussion in Chapter 20 first. Then, if you are convinced that you want to have a RAM disk in your PC, read this section to see some examples of how you might achieve that end.

When you create a RAM disk you allocate memory in two ways. First, there must be some region of RAM in which data will be stored. That is the RAM disk itself. Second, there must be some region of RAM to hold the device driver program that creates the RAM disk.

For all but the RAM disk that comes with *Memory Commander*, the program region must be somewhere in the first megabyte of the CPU's memory address space. (That is, it must be in either lower or upper memory.) Only *Memory Commander* knows how to put the program code for its RAM disk into extended memory along with most of the code for the memory manager and the RAM used for the RAM disk's data storage.

For all the other RAM disks you get to choose whether to load the program into lower or upper memory—assuming you have some upper memory in your PC—and whether to put the data area in lower memory, expanded memory, or extended memory. (Some RAM disk programs can put a portion of their program code in expanded memory, but they will still have to have some of it in lower or upper memory.)

The best place to put the data storage for PCs in Classes 2 and 4 is expanded memory. For PCs in Classes 3, 5, and 6 extended memory is the preferred option. (PCs in Class 1 have neither of these kinds of memory, so for them you must create the RAM disk in conventional memory.)

Creating a RAM Disk in Extended Memory

The simplest way to make a RAM disk is to use the RAM disk device driver that comes with DOS. For PC DOS in versions 3.0 through 5.0 and all versions of DR DOS that program is called VDISK.SYS. For MS-DOS, starting with version 3.0, and for PC DOS starting with version 5.02, the name is RAMDRIVE.SYS.

To create a RAM disk which will store its data in extended memory using RAMDRIVE.SYS, add a line like this one to your CONFIG.SYS file:

```
DEVICE = C:\DOS\RAMDRIVE.SYS 3072 512 192 /E
```

This example creates a 3MB RAM disk using extended memory for the data storage. The RAM disk has a sector size of 512 bytes (which is both the default value and usually the best choice), and it can hold up to 192 entries in its root directory.

You don't have to specify all three of these numbers, but if you specify two they will be interpreted as disk size and sector size, and if you specify only one it will be interpreted as the disk size.

You can even omit the numbers altogether, but then you will only get a 64KB RAM disk with 512 byte sectors and a maximum of 64 directory entries in the root directory. That is so small that it is nearly useless, so this is almost never done except on Class 1 PCs in which the tradeoff between lower memory for the RAM disk and lower memory for applications often forces one to keep any RAM disk created to something very near its minimum possible size.

Creating a RAM Disk in Expanded Memory

To create a RAM disk in expanded memory using RAMDRIVE.SYS you need a line in your CONFIG.SYS file similar to this one:

```
DEVICE = C:\DOS\RAMDRIVE.SYS 1536 /A
```

where, for variety, I have shown a line that creates a 1.5MB RAM disk that uses the default sector size and number of root directory entries. (The default sector size is almost always what you want, and as long as you remember to put almost all the files on your RAM disk into a subdirectory, the limit on number of directory entries will not cause any problems.)

Variable Size RAM Disks

Perhaps the most interesting RAM disks are those whose size is not fixed. These come in two variations. Some automatically vary their size so they can just exactly fit whatever files you have stored on them. Others require you to explicitly vary their size from the DOS command line.

PC-Kwik RAM Disk

One example of a RAM disk whose size varies automatically is the one that is a part of the PC-Kwik *Power Pak*, and that also is included with their *WinMaster* product. These products also include the *Super PC-Kwik* disk cache program. The PC-Kwik RAM disk uses a portion of the *Super PC-Kwik* disk cache memory for its data storage. (It also uses some lower or upper memory for its program, as do almost all RAM disk programs.)

What is special about this RAM disk is that it only takes memory from the disk cache for the RAM disk when you actually store some files on that RAM disk. If you wish, it can also relinquish RAM back to the disk cache when you delete files.

> If you are considering configuring the PC-Kwik RAM disk so it can vary its size, please consider your action carefully. Once the RAM is relinquished to the cache, the data it contained may be immediately overwritten with cache data. Because of this possibility, the designers of the *Power Pak* and *WinMaster* made their RAM disk program with a special feature. It will prevent you from trying to undelete any files you have deleted on a PC-Kwik RAM disk that is set up to relinquish all its unused space.

Creating a RAM disk with the PC-Kwik *Power Pak* is a two step process. You need a line in your CONFIG.SYS file to load the RAM disk device driver program something like this

```
DEVICE = C:\PCKWIK\PCKRAMD.SYS
```

and you need a line in your AUTOEXEC.BAT file to load the *Super PC-Kwik* disk cache so that the RAM disk will have some RAM to work with. (The details of that latter line are discussed in a later section of this chapter.) You can put another line just like the one shown here in your CONFIG.SYS file and you will get two RAM disks. The sizes and other parameters of those RAM disks are set by parameters in a special configuration file called PCKWIK.INI, usually located in the C:\PCKWIK directory.

> Until you have loaded the *Super PC-Kwik* disk cache program there is no memory allocated to that disk cache, and thus no memory available for the RAM disk to use. If you have anything in your AUTOEXEC.BAT file that tries to access your RAM disk before the

disk cache is loaded you will get an error message. You often can ignore it safely. Even better, use the error message to help you find and move the line(s) of your AUTOEXEC.BAT file that access the disk drive to some point later than the line that loads the disk cache.

This is not only a possible problem with the PC-Kwik RAM disk. It can occur with any RAM disk that is set up in two steps as that one is. The SRDISK program, discussed next, is another RAM disk that behaves the same way.

SRDISK

The shareware program SRDISK is included among those on the diskette that accompanies this book. This program is typical of the RAM disk programs that can be resized from the DOS command line.

As with the PC-Kwik RAM disk, it takes two steps to create an SRDISK RAM disk. The first is usually done through a line in your CONFIG.SYS file. The second through a line in your AUTOEXEC.BAT file. Alternatively, you can use the commercial program *Dynamic Memory Control* program (DMC) to load, and even to unload the RAM disk device driver from the command line. (DMC is described further in Chapter 34.) Here is a three line batch file that loads and sizes an SRDISK RAM disk:

```
D:\DMC\NOTE
D:\DMC\LDEVICE C:\MEMINFO\SRDISK\SRDXMS.SYS
C:\MEMINFO\SRDISK\SRDISK /F:1440
```

where I have assumed that DMC is in a directory on your D drive called \DMC, and that you installed the programs from the diskette that came with this book into the default directory, C:\MEMINFO (with the SRDISK programs in the SRDISK subdirectory under that directory).

The first line of this batch file loads a place marker program, NOTE, to facilitate later removing the RAM disk program from memory. The second line loads the RAM disk program. The third line tells the RAM disk how big it is supposed to be.

In this case the RAM disk that is created uses extended memory for its data storage. It will look exactly like a high density 3-1/2" floppy diskette drive, with a 1.44 MB maximum capacity, 18 512-byte sectors per "track," and two "sides"—except, of course, that it will work much faster.

If you later wish to change this RAM disk's size, you can do so with the SRDISK command. See the documentation file in the SRDISK directory for details.

If you wish to remove the RAM disk altogether, you can do that with this command:

```
D:\DMC\FREENOTE
```

which tells DMC to unload the NOTE it loaded and all resident programs (TSRs and device drivers) loaded after it.

Disk Cache

While almost any PC user can benefit from a RAM disk, **every PC user** will benefit from a disk cache. So, if you don't have one installed in your PC now, get one and install it.

Disk caches come in two types: hardware and software. A software disk cache is a program that runs in the main RAM in your PC and speeds up accesses to your disk drives. A hardware disk cache is a feature of some disk controllers. These controllers have both a large amount of RAM and some specialized cache controller hardware to manage that RAM.

In either case, the way that the disk cache works is by storing information in RAM temporarily on its way to or from a disk drive. This benefits you whenever you are able to retrieve information from the cache instead of having to wait while it is retrieved from the (much slower) disk drive. It further benefits you whenever the cache can receive information destined for the disk drive, then can let you get back to computing while it puts the information away. (See Chapter 14 for the details of how disk caches work.)

It is perfectly okay to have both software and hardware disk caching. Never load two software disk cache programs in your PC at the same time, though, or you may end up trashing the data on your disks. You might get away with duplicate software disk cache programs (and merely waste RAM and slow your machine down a bit), but all too often you will reap disaster instead.

SmartDrive

Up until at least version 4.0 of SmartDrive (which was bundled with Windows 3.1), you were best advised simply to avoid using that DOS-provided disk cache program. Now, with DOS 6 and version 4.1 of SmartDrive, it is nearly as good as the best cache programs on the market. The combination of its fine performance and acceptable level of configuration flexibility with its very low price (free!) is one that many people cannot resist.

How do you install SmartDrive? You may not have to! Recent versions of the *MS-DOS* and *Windows* SETUP programs install SmartDrive automatically.

If you already had another software disk cache program installed, you could end up losing data as soon as your PC reboots, which may be before you exit from the SETUP program. To play it safe, remove or "remark out"—at least temporarily—the lines in your startup files, CONFIG.SYS and AUTOEXEC.BAT, that refer to any other software disk cache program before you run the DOS or *Windows* SETUP program.

If you wish to install SmartDrive manually, you need to be aware of an important distinction. The SmartDrive program that came with Windows 3.0 and DOS versions 4 and 5 was a version 3.x and it was contained in a file with the name SMARTDRV.SYS. This is a device driver program and is installed through a line in your CONFIG.SYS file that looks something like this:

```
DEVICE = C:\DOS\SMARTDRV.SYS 2048 512
```

This line tells SmartDrive to create a disk cache with its data buffers in extended memory. (This program can only use extended memory for its data buffer area.) The buffer area is 2MB in size, most of the time, but that size can be reduced down to 512KB with the remaining RAM being loaned temporarily to *Windows* 3.x or any other program that knows the Windows protocol for requesting that memory.

You can add a /A parameter at the end of the command line if you wish to have the data buffers created in expanded memory. If you leave off the numbers you will get a cache whose initial size is 256KB and that can loan all of the cache memory to *Windows*.

The DOS 6 version of SmartDrive (like the one included with Windows 3.1) is a normal executable program, SMARTDRV.EXE. That means that you either load it from a line in your CONFIG.SYS file that reads

```
INSTALL = C:\DOS\SMARTDRV.EXE 2048 512
```

or a line in your AUTOEXEC.BAT file that reads

```
SMARTDRV 2048 512
```

where I am assuming that you have the C:\DOS directory on your path. These lines create the same sort of disk cache as the DOS 5 example (2MB initial size, 512KB minimum size, using extended memory for the cache buffer). DOS 6 allows you to add a number of additional parameters if you wish.

You can specify which drives to cache and which not to cache, and for each one whether to cache both reads and writes or only reads. (That is, store in the cache only information on its way from the disk—read caching only—or any information that is on its way either to or from the disk—which is called read/write caching, but is described by SmartDrive as write caching.)

For any drive whose letter you don't include on the command line, SmartDrive will decide whether and how to cache it based on what kind of drive it is. SmartDrive normally only does **read caching** for floppy disk drives and phantom drives created using the DOS utility program INTERLNK. It does both **read and write caching** for hard disk drives. It ignores CD-ROMs, network drives, and certain other drives.

SmartDrive attempts to avoid caching any logical volumes that have been created out of a compressed volume file by DoubleSpace, Stacker, or some equivalent on-the-fly file compression program. It will cache the "host volume" that contains the compressed volume file. That is exactly what you want to have your disk cache software do.

If you add a drive letter after the program name with a plus sign following it, you are telling SmartDrive to cache both reads and writes for that drive. The letter with a minus sign says not to cache that drive. The letter with nothing after it says to do read caching, but not do write caching for that drive.

Thus the following line

```
SMARTDRV C+ J- 2048 512
```

says to be sure and do both read and write caching for the C drive and to do no caching for the J drive; all other drives are cached according to what SmartDrive thinks best.

You can install SmartDrive with just the one line just presented. That is the right way to do it for many PCs. However, on many other PCs, using just that one line is a sure recipe for data loss.

If yours is a PC in Class 5 or 6, and if you run any program that puts the CPU into protected mode and activates the memory mapping features of the CPU, then you must do one more thing to make SmartDrive safe. *Windows* 3.x running in its 386 Enhanced mode is one such program. Almost any 386 memory manager (such as *QEMM, 386MAX, Netroom, QMAPS,* or *Memory Commander*) are other examples.

What you have to do is be sure that all data on its way to or from the disk stops briefly in a small region in lower memory. You can have your main disk cache in either expanded or extended memory. You can load the device driver program into upper memory. What you also must do is load a small piece of the program into lower memory so that it can create and maintain that crucial small lower memory data transfer area.

The step you need is a line in CONFIG.SYS that reads:

```
DEVICE = C:\DOS\SMARTDRV.EXE /DOUBLE_BUFFER
```

Don't try using DEVICEHIGH. It shouldn't work, and if it did manage somehow to load this piece of SmartDrive into upper memory, it would totally defeat the purpose for this line.

The reason this line is sometimes necessary is that some disk controllers "know" where in physical memory the disk buffer is located. They put information into it and take information out of it whenever they are ready. If you are running your CPU in 386-protected mode and are doing some memory remapping, the logical memory addresses and the physical ones will not be the same. The result is that the CPU puts information into a buffer at some logical address and the disk controller tries to retrieve it from the same address, but this time interprets it as a physical address.

There is no way to keep this from happening. The only thing you can do is be sure that the transfer area in RAM is located somewhere that never gets remapped. Loading SMARTDRV.EXE into lower memory somewhere well below the 256KB point and specifying the /DOUBLE_BUFFER command line parameter does exactly that.

The only disk controllers that you need to worry about are ones that do this sort of direct reading and writing to RAM. They are often referred to as "bus mastering disk controllers," but the more important point than how they take control of the I/O bus is the fact that they write and read directly to RAM addresses.

The safest disk controllers are those that send their data in and out via I/O ports. Since those port addresses never get remapped, the whole issue disappears. (The Always *IN-2000* is one of the fastest and most popular SCSI host adapters on the market, and it transfers its data exclusively through I/O ports.)

If you are unsure whether or not you need "double buffering," add the SMARTDRV.EXE /DOUBLE_BUFFER line to your CONFIG.SYS file. Also load your usual memory management software and be sure that it is providing some upper memory. Reboot your PC. Now at the DOS prompt enter the command

SMARTDRV

with no command line parameters after it.

SmartDrive will print on the screen a table showing you which drives it is caching and whether it is doing only read caching or both read and write caching for each one. In the last column, labelled "buffering," it will show whether or not it thinks you need to use double buffering to access this drive safely. If all of the entries in that last column are "no" then you may safely remove the SMARTDRV.EXE / DOUBLE_BUFFER line from your CONFIG.SYS file. If any of the entries is "yes" then you must use double buffering. If some of the entries are question marks, it means that SmartDrive can't tell if double buffering is needed or not. In that case you will have to consult with the maker of your disk controller to be sure.

While the portion of SmartDrive that manages the lower memory transfer buffer (the double buffer) must be loaded into lower memory, the main program code for the disk cache can be loaded into upper memory. In fact, SmartDrive normally loads itself there if you don't somehow prevent it from doing so.

If SmartDrive has loaded itself into upper memory and you are using double buffering, you may find that instead of making things run really quickly, they seem to be slowed down. This is not a common problem, but it can occur. If it does, the solution is simple.

Add the command line parameter /L to the line that loads the main SmartDrive program. Thus, in your AUTOEXEC.BAT file it might look like this:

```
SMARTDRV C+ J- 2048 512 /L
```

The /L parameter tells SmartDrive not to load itself into upper memory. You will have to be sure and tell your memory management software not to load it there as well.

Super PC-Kwik

The most popular of all the disk cache programs on the market, aside from SmartDrive, is *Super PC-Kwik*. (It is hard to know how many people use SmartDrive, since they don't have to go out and buy a copy. So the only feasible comparison is of the popularity of the various commercial disk cache programs.)

The PC Kwik Corporation (formerly Multisoft) includes *Super PC-Kwik* in their *Power Pak* and *WinMaster* products, as well as selling it by itself. Like SmartDrive, it is an executable program that you load through a line in a batch file or at the DOS prompt. (This is unlike many of the other disk cache programs on the market which are installable device drivers that normally are loaded through use of a DEVICE line in the CONFIG.SYS file.)

The line can be as simple as this:

```
SUPER
```

which will load the disk cache and set it up according to the parameters you have stored in a configuration file called PCKWIK.INI. Naturally, if you have the program in a directory that is not on the DOS path, you will have to add the drive and directory in front of the program name, so the line would read:

```
C:\PCKWIK\SUPER
```

for the program's default location.

Unlike SmartDrive, *Super PC-Kwik* doesn't have to be installed twice to get the protection of double buffering. Usually it can tell when that is necessary and do the safe thing. You can override its normal tests by a line in the configuration file that reads either `BusMaster=Yes` or `BusMaster=No`. Saying `Yes` forces Super PC-Kwik to do double buffering; saying `No` prevents it from doing that.

An Important Warning About Disk Caches and File Compression Programs   Software disk caches can be divided into two groups, depending on where they insert themselves between your programs and the disk controller. One group, which includes *Super PC-Kwik* and most of the early disk cache programs, operate at the "physical level"—where the disk locations are described in terms of heads, cylinders, and physical sector numbers. The other group, which includes SmartDrive, *Norton Cache*, and most of the other recently designed cache programs, operates at the "logical level"—where data locations are described in terms of the drive letter and logical sector number within that logical drive.

Do you care about this arcane difference? Yes, you certainly do. At least you do if you also use any program that lets you swap drive letters around. The *Stacker* and *SuperStor* on-the-fly file compression programs are two popular examples of programs that do this.

If you load any disk cache program that works at the logical level and then swap drive letters around you are going to confuse the poor disk cache program. And the next thing you know, the data on your disk drives will be irretrievably scrambled. This is not a problem if your disk cache program operates at the physical level.

If you choose to use SmartDrive or any other disk cache program that works at the logical level, be sure to do all drive letter swapping before you load the cache. That way you will not cause any data damage from disk cache program confusion. (Disk cache programs that work at the physical level do not see the logical letters for the drives and thus cannot become confused by any drive letter swapping. You may load them either before or after you swap drive letters.)

It is not always clear from a manufacturer's documentation at which level a given disk cache program works. You may have to ask the manufacturer explicitly. If you find any warnings about drive letter swapping, you can be certain that cache works at the logical level and then you need to be scrupulously careful to observe the warnings in this section. If you find something that says the disk cache program is only able to cache all the logical volumes on one physical disk partition or else cache none of them, you can be pretty sure you are dealing with a disk cache that works at the physical level. (Unfortunately, not all such programs tell you that they behave in this way.)

Print Spoolers

The third most popular use of "excess" RAM is for print spooling. If you often find yourself waiting for your printer to print something before you can return to work, then loading a print spooling program can help speed up your work sessions a lot.

There are three basic print spooling strategies. Two of them involve loading a program in your PC. The third is to put a printer buffer box between your printer and your PC.

The distinction between the two kinds of print spooling programs is where they keep the files to be printed. One kind keeps the files on the disk drive and reads just a little chunk of it into RAM before sending that chunk to the printer. The other kind keeps all of the files in RAM in their entirety until they get shipped out to the printer.

The DOS Program PRINT

The DOS program PRINT is a background file printing TSR program. You can load it from the DOS prompt or by a line in your AUTOEXEC.BAT file that reads:

```
C:\DOS\PRINT
```

or you can add a number of command line parameters to tell the PRINT program just how you want it to do its job, like this:

```
C:\DOS\PRINT /Q:20 /U:12 /M:5 /S:4 /B:1024 /D:LPT2
```

A "real" print spooling program actually intercepts the data on the way out of an application program that would ordinarily go to the printer port and stashes it somewhere until the printer is ready for it. PRINT doesn't do this. Instead, it is used to print information that is already stored in files on the disk. PRINT maintains a list of all the files it has been told to print and a pointer to where it is in the file at the top of the list. Each time the printer is ready for some more data, PRINT will read a chunk from the file it is currently processing, ship that chunk of data out to the printer, and update its pointer.

The only memory PRINT needs is for its program code and for the buffer that holds the chunk of data that is about to be sent to the printer. You can load PRINT (and its buffer) into upper memory if you like.

Spooling to Disk

A much better print spooling program is *PrintCache* from LaserTools. This program (PCACHE.COM) actually does intercept output that other programs think is going to the printer and save it away somewhere until your printer is ready to receive it.

PCACHE can be set up to use a region of your hard disk as its buffer, or to use a region of RAM. If you are short on RAM for other purposes, and if you can spare some disk space, set it up to use the disk. You might think that this would slow down the print spooling operation, but it doesn't do so noticeably. The reason is that your printer is much slower than the hard disk, so PCACHE always has plenty of time to retrieve each new chunk of data before the printer is ready for it.

PCACHE is loaded by a simple line in your AUTOEXEC.BAT file that reads something like this:

```
D:\PCACHE\PCACHE
```

or, if you prefer to load the program code into upper memory,

```
LOADHIGH D:\PCACHE\PCACHE
```

In either case the program uses the information it has stored in its PCACHE.CFG file to tell it where to buffer data and many other things about how to do its job.

The easiest way to install PCACHE and to configure it optimally is to use the INSTALL program that comes with it. Just remember that you will get the best use from your RAM if you don't buffer data there; you almost certainly have some better use for your RAM. (The only exception is if you have a huge amount of "excess" RAM and almost no free disk space.)

PrintCache has a number of other valuable features. For one, it has a Windows component that works much better than Print Manager, or that can work with Print Manager.

A unique capability of *PrintCache* is that it can be used with even the oldest HP *LaserJet* printers with the least RAM inside the printer and yet allow you to print nearly full-page graphic images. It does this by compressing the data before sending it to the printer in a fashion that the printer understands and can therefore decompress as it is printing. This feature may be the most valuable aspect of an otherwise quite valuable program if you happen to have an HP *LaserJet* with limited memory and a need to print large graphic images on it.

Spooling to RAM

Sometimes it does make sense to buffer print data in RAM. One example is provided by the PC Kwik *Power Pak* print spooling program.

The *Power Pak* includes the *Super PC-Kwik* disk cache program and four other utilities. One of those other utilities is a print spooler, PCKSPL.EXE. (The others are their RAM disk, keyboard accelerator, and screen accelerator.) The command to load PCKSPL in the latest version of the *Power Pak* or *WinMaster* is simply

```
C:\PCKWIK\PCKSPL
```

which assumes that you have set up the parameters that tell it how to do its job in the PCKWIK.INI file in the C:\PCKWIK directory.

What is novel about PCKSPL.EXE is that it doesn't use any RAM for a print spooling buffer, nor any disk space. It simply borrows some RAM from the *Super PC-Kwik* disk cache program when it needs some. As soon as the data have been sent to the printer, PCKSPL returns that RAM to the disk cache.

PC Kwik's argument is that you don't need any disk cache RAM if you are waiting for your printer. And once you are not sending data to your printer you don't need to have any RAM tied up as a print spooling buffer. This strategy works quite well.

As with all the other print spooling strategies, this does involve committing some lower or upper memory for the program's code, even though it doesn't take any extra memory or disk space for the print spooling data buffer.

Closing Comment

The best gift you can give your PC is more RAM. It won't do you any good, though, unless it gets used. Maybe you are already running programs that use every single byte of RAM to the max. If not, consider using some of the programs described in this section. You will use up RAM, but in return you will get a faster responding, more pleasant to use PC.

Maybe you have found an even better way to use your PC's RAM than any I have described anywhere in this book. If so, I want to hear from you. Please write to me at the address given in the Introduction (and repeated in Chapter 26). I have learned much from others and am happy to add to that knowledge your hard-won wisdom. Tell me, please, if you would like to be acknowledged in a future edition as the source of whatever tip you share with me.

This is a big book. Now that you have reached the end of it, you probably have gotten a fairly good overview of the possibilities inherent in PC memory managment. Please stop briefly and think about how you want to apply this new knowledge. Realize that you won't do a perfect job of optimizing your PC in any single step. Typically it will take much tweaking and fiddling, and will happen over an extended period of time. Welcome to the adventure!

A FEW WORDS ON UNITS

A brief discussion of how to talk about very large and very small numbers and an explanation of why a thousand may or may not be the same as a kilo of something.

In the computer field, as in many technical disciplines, it is necessary to talk about quantities that range from the very large to the very small. For example, your computer could easily have 4,194,304 bytes of RAM. The access time to those RAM chips might be a mere 0.000000080 seconds.

Writing such extreme numbers in this way is tedious, and they are hard to read. There must be a better way, and there is. In this chapter you will learn more about how very large and very small numbers can be indicated compactly. You also will learn about an interesting confusion that plagues the world of PCs: When a kilo is not a kilo.

Schemes for Indicating Size

Long ago, scientists faced the problem of writing numbers to represent very large and very small quantities. They devised a simple and effective strategy for dealing with them. This strategy is called *scientific notation*. You probably use a variation of it in daily speech without even knowing it.

Scientific Notation

The scientists' method for easily describing numbers of all sizes springs from the observation that when you have a quantity, your primary interest is the approximate size; the exact number is often of substantially less interest. In the first paragraph, for example, the number of bytes of RAM in many popular PCs is given as 4,194,304 bytes. It is almost as good to know that there are some millions of bytes, and for nearly every purpose it is sufficient to say there are about 4 million bytes.

You use this idea in common speech when you say about some man, "He earns in the low six figures, annually." That means his annual income is at least $100,000.00 and probably no more than $300,000.00. (These are the smallest and a middling size amount for which six decimal digits are needed to state the number of dollars.)

The way that scientists normally express numeric quantities in this style is to write the number in two parts. One part of the number tells which rough size category (the number of digits before the decimal place, or the number of zeroes after the decimal place before the first nonzero digit) that number falls into. The other part is an indication of where, in that size category, this particular numeric quantity falls.

The first part, the rough size of the number, is sometimes referred to as its "order of magnitude." It is written as an integral power of ten. The second part of the number, where it fits into that order of magnitude, is written as a number between one and ten. The whole number is then written (in what may seem a backwards order, putting the most important information last) as the number between one and ten times ten raised to the power of the entire number's order of magnitude.

Our two examples from the first paragraph in this chapter, therefore, could be written as 4.2×10^6 and 8.0×10^{-8}. The first numeric quantity is the number 4.2, then a multiplication sign, and finally 10 raised to the sixth power. The second one is 8.0 times 10 raised to the negative eighth power. Another name for scientific notation is *exponential notation*.

Engineering Notation

Not everyone is comfortable with reading and writing exponential numbers like this. Saying them gets even trickier. So engineers, practical souls that they are, have come up with a similar, yet simpler way of dealing with the very large and the very small. It is *engineering notation*.

Here the idea is to give the rough size category a name. To keep the number of names to a manageable number, only powers of one thousand are named. The indicator of position within each category is given as a number between 1.000 and 999.999.

Using this scheme, our two example numbers are 4.2 million bytes and 80 nanoseconds. The size category name may stand on its own, as *million* does here, or more commonly, it will be used as a prefix to a unit of some kind, as with *nano-* and *second*. Since we use these rough size indicator names to indicate multiplying a unit of measurement (for example, *byte* or *second*) by a power of one thousand, we can call those rough size categories *engineering unit multipliers*.

This book, and most documentation you will read in order to use and understand memory and memory-management software and hardware, uses engineering notation. Figure A.1 lists the commonly used engineering unit multipliers and shows how those same quantities would be written as powers of ten and as powers of a thousand. The last two columns give the engineering notation names by which we refer to those multipliers and the abbreviations for them which are used when writing out quantities.

All of the multiplier names start with lowercase letters. For all positive powers of a thousand (numbers larger than one), the abbreviation starts with an uppercase letter. All of the abbreviations for the names that stand for negative powers of a thousand start with lowercase letters (mostly these are Roman letters, but in the case of micro it is the lowercase Greek letter *mu*).

Multiplier	written as a power of 1000	written as a power of 10	Name	Abbre-viation
1 000 000 000 000	1000^{+4}	10^{+12}	tera	T
1 000 000 000	1000^{+3}	10^{+9}	giga	G
1 000 000	1000^{+2}	10^{+6}	mega	M
1 000	1000^{+1}	10^{+3}	kilo	K
0.001	1000^{-1}	10^{-3}	milli	m
0.000 001	1000^{-2}	10^{-6}	micro	μ
0.000 000 001	1000^{-3}	10^{-9}	nano	n
0.000 000 000 001	1000^{-4}	10^{-12}	pico	p

Figure A.1. Engineering notation names for the commonly used positive and negative powers of a thousand, with their standard abbreviations.

In everyday usage, the letter abbreviation for *kilo* is written with a lowercase *k*. This is an exception to the pattern. The exception for *kilo* is based on its antiquity in common speech. People spoke of (and wrote about) kilometers long before the engineering notation scheme was formalized.

You might argue that the correct way to denote a kilo of bytes ought to be kB. Certainly this is supported by some commonly cited authorities in such matters. Actually, the computer industry is more consistent with the philosophy of engineering notation than it is with common usage on this point. Normally, in computer documentation you will find *KB* written for kilobyte, a practice also used in this book.

Some Special Cases for Computers

The engineering notation scheme works well, most of the time. But you will find some places where a kilo is not a kilo (nor a mega a mega).

For example, if you have a 20MB hard drive (one capable of holding 20 megabytes of information) you may have been surprised the first time you ran the CHKDSK program and saw that you actually had over 21 million bytes total space on that drive. The reason for the discrepancy is that engineers are not only practical folk; they hate inefficiency. As you will see in a moment, by not letting *kilo* mean one and only one thing in all contexts, they were able to salvage both simplicity of speech and high efficiency in the use of the hardware in our computers.

Unfortunately, something had to be sacrificed. In this case, it was the simple idea that a word means what it means, no matter what. As reasonable as that sounds, in the computer field, at least, it definitely is not always true.

The Special Role of Powers of Two

PCs are binary machines. That is, everything internally is done using ones and zeros. This includes the addressing of memory locations. To point to one of a large number of memory locations, the computer puts some high and low voltages on a number of wires. (High, in this context, means about two volts. Low means less than half a volt.) High voltages stand for ones; low voltages stand for zeros.

The number of different addresses that can be pointed to in this fashion depends on the number of wires. If you have n wires, you can indicate any of $2n$ possible locations. For example, if you have six wires you can specify any one of 64 possible locations. When you raise two to the tenth power (2^{10}) you get 1,024. The near coincidence of 1,024 and 1,000 is the source of all our confusion about the meaning of kilo.

Powers of two are very special numbers in our PCs. The "natural" amounts of memory or storage that a designer will put in a PC are exactly those quantities that can readily be expressed electrically by all possible patterns of voltages on some number of wires; this is always two raised to the power of the number of wires. One such natural number of locations is two to the tenth power, or 1,024.

Great Confusion in the Name of Simplicity

Engineers working on computer design just naturally fell into the habit of referring to 1,024 locations as a kilo of them. Since those engineers were deciding how the computers would work, they could have decided to use only 1,000 of the 1,024 possibilities in order to support their desire to refer to that quantity as a kilo of locations. Doing so would have preserved the common meaning for the term *kilo*, but it would have meant giving up 2.4 percent of the possible addresses. And that would have offended those engineers' sense of efficiency.

Their solution to this conflict was a natural but often confusing one. They decided to use *kilo* to refer to 1,000 of something, *unless it is a number of memory address locations* (or quantities of memory or storage, generally) in which case *kilo* refers to 1,024.

In the same way, *mega,* which normally means *a million,* is actually a kilo times a kilo. This means that for memory or storage, and *only* in these cases, *mega* means 1,024 times 1,024, or 1,048,576.

As you might expect, the story does not end there. *Giga* means a thousand million. But really it is a kilo times a mega, so *giga* means exactly 1,000,000,000 if it refers to anything other than memory or storage; but it means 1,073,741,824 whenever it refers to an amount of memory or storage.

Notice that while there is only a little more than two percent discrepancy between 1,000 and 1,024, a more than seven percent discrepancy exists between a giga of bytes and a giga of anything else. The difference becomes more important as you begin dealing in larger quantities.

This is not just an academic matter. While it will be sometime before you can afford a gigabyte of memory in your PC, it already is possible to buy a hard disk with over a gigabyte of storage capacity.

This Is Only an Issue for Memory or Storage

There are other large quantities we have to talk about in describing PCs, most notably speeds. Your PC has a clock in it that runs at some millions of cycles per second. One million cycles per second is called one *megahertz;*

it is abbreviated MHz. This *mega* really does mean a million: exactly 1,000,000.

The same holds true for any other reference to positive powers of a thousand no matter what the context, as long as it does not refer to numbers of memory locations.

No Confusion When Speaking About Small Things

Since the special meaning of *kilo* for computers arose from the binary nature of addressing locations with multiple wires, it has no relevance to discussions of very small numbers. In talking about PCs, the quantities smaller than one with which we must deal are usually amounts of time.

Fractions of a second may be moderately small, as in the milliseconds it takes to access a hard drive, or a lot smaller, as in the microseconds it takes to execute an instruction or the nanoseconds it takes to access a memory location. In all of these cases the power of a thousand indicated by the prefix (negative one, two, and three, respectively) do mean exact (negative) powers of a thousand (0.001, 0.000001, and 0.000000001, for example).

A Recap

Discussions of PCs have many references to very large and very small quantities. The common scheme for making those references uses engineering notation. That means using a (positive or negative) power of one thousand multiplied by a number between one and one thousand. In both speech and writing we denote these powers of a thousand by special names such as *kilo* or *micro*.

This works well except for one glitch. A rose may be a rose by any other name, but a thousand and a kilo are only sometimes the same. If you are discussing numbers of locations for memory or storage, a kilo means 1,024 (and a *mega* and a *giga* mean the square and the cube of 1,024), whereas for all other references to large quantities, *kilo* and its kin mean exactly 1,000 and various powers of one thousand.

B

NOW THAT YOU KNOW WHAT YOU WANT, HOW DO YOU GET IT?

A guide to buying software and hardware at the right price and without unwarranted risk. Find out why using a credit card is an especially good way to make purchases.

As you read this book you may have decided that you need to add more memory or some memory-management software to your PC. This appendix will help you decide where to get them in a way that will not cost you more than is necessary, nor less than is prudent. It also will help you protect yourself from unscrupulous dealers.

When You'll Want to (or Have to) Buy from the Manufacturer

Some hardware and software products discussed in this book are made by only one company and sold directly from only that company to the end user (you). If that is the case for the product you have decided to buy, you really have no choice but to buy from the manufacturer.

Fortunately, this is not the case for most memory-management tools and options. These products are available from a wide variety of sources. In this appendix you will learn what those sources are and how you might choose between them.

Sometimes, even though you can buy something from other vendors, you still will choose to go directly to the manufacturer for it. Why might you do this? And why might you choose not to?

One situation in which you might want to buy directly from the manufacturer is when you want to upgrade some product you already own to a new version, and the manufacturer offers you, as a registered owner of their earlier product, a very attractive upgrade price. One reason you might not want to do this is that their price might not, upon careful checking with alternative sources, be nearly as attractive as you first thought.

Before you accept the upgrade offer, it's a good idea to check your local computer stores, especially the discount dealers, any consultant or value-added resellers you have used before, and perhaps some of the major mail-order companies. Sometimes one of these sources will have the product available for purchase by just anyone for less than the manufacturer is charging to upgrade registered owners of the previous version.

When You Don't Want to Buy from the Manufacturer

Mainly, people choose not to buy from the manufacturer for convenience, secondarily for cost savings. If your corner computer store stocks what you want and the price is right, it is much more convenient to buy it there than to mail a letter and a check to the manufacturer and wait several weeks to get the product. If you can save money at the same time, so much the better.

Further, if the computer store is a good, full-service one, you may get some additional benefits. You may get free installation, for example, or some training. You almost certainly will get more help from them when you have problems if you are their customer.

On the other hand, you may not need those benefits. In that case you might choose to turn to a computer dealer in your town who stresses discount pricing or to one of the many national mail-order firms. By doing so you may be able to save a lot of money over ordering from the manufacturer.

Choosing a Vendor: What Are Your Options?

Once you decide to buy from someone other than the manufacturer you have a wide variety of options. Here are several (with some comments on the benefits and drawbacks of each).

Full-Service Dealers

Full-service computer dealers are usually authorized by the manufacturers to vend their products. Often dealers must send their salespeople to training classes and promise to stock and sell certain minimum quantities of the manufacturer's goods.

These stores usually have extensive displays of products and may give free demonstrations. They also may have on-site service facilities to handle repairs of hardware, and they may offer training classes, either free or for a nominal charge. You also will likely be able to exchange defective merchandise on the spot—no mailing delays or charges to put up with.

All this costs money, so dealers are likely to charge close to full list price for what they sell. Why then would you want to buy from such a store? For the services offered, of course.

If you find a good full-service dealer, cherish that dealer. Pay whatever the dealer asks for those products and you will, in the long run, save money over buying the products at discount and then paying for the services elsewhere.

Unfortunately, some dealers only claim to offer full service. They charge high prices, but they fail to follow through after the sale. Some of their salespeople know more jargon than facts and are more motivated to make a sale than to solve your problems. Avoid those dealers.

One way to help avoid them and find the better dealers is to ask other people about their experiences. Chapter 33 suggests many places you might turn to for that help. User groups are particularly good for this.

Discount Dealers

There is another group of dealers whose main claim to fame is that they sell software and hardware at substantially less than the full list price. If you know what you want, such a discount store can be very valuable to you. You can buy things off the shelf, without a delay, and still get a price that is often not much higher than the very cheapest price from any source.

Realize that you won't get a lot of hand-holding or after-sale service from these dealers. Often their salespeople know very little technically about their products (though occasionally you may be pleasantly surprised), and there may even be no salespeople as such, just cashiers to accept your money.

Also, since these dealers do have a store to pay rent on and they do have inventory on hand, their prices may not be quite as good as you can get from, for example, a national mail-order firm.

Value-Added Resellers (VARs)

Some dealers specialize not just in selling hardware or software; they focus instead on selling solutions to problems. The accepted term for these vendors is *value-added reseller*.

That "added value" may consist only of knowing what pieces to buy and how to put them together, or it may consist of custom software written for their clients. In either case, these value-added resellers (*VARs*) tend to focus on particular markets. For example, one VAR may specialize in solutions for law offices, another in solutions for videotape rental stores, and so on.

Sometimes a VAR is called a *VAD* (for value-added dealer). Mostly those are the VARs who have a storefront location. Those who call themselves VARs are more likely to have an office or shop somewhere, but usually they will meet with a client at his or her place of business.

Having someone come in, analyze your business, and then sell you just what you need can be an easy and cost-effective way to improve your business. Be sure the VAR you pick has had experience in your particular specialty. And before you sign on the dotted line, check with some of the VAR's former clients to see how they liked the services they received.

Consultants

When you are not an expert, it may be best for you to buy someone else's expertise. Such an expert-for-hire is called a *consultant*.

A consultant can help you decide what you want. This book gives general advice. A good consultant will interview you at some length before making any recommendations in order to be sure that his or her recommendations match your needs and budget. Beware of consultants who fail to draw out some important aspect of how you do business or what you hope to accomplish.

You might use a consultant to review proposals by other vendors. You may have decided what to get, but then find you don't fully understand the competing claims of different vendors. A consultant can help you analyze those bids. This may not be worth doing if you are making only a modest purchase, but if you plan to spend several thousand dollars, this approach may easily save you 10 percent or 20 percent. That could pay the consultant's fee with a bit left over for you.

A consultant can also serve as your computer buying agent. The advantages here are that you don't have to waste time shopping, and the consultant knows what to look for and where to look. Finally, consultants can serve you by putting the parts together and making sure they work, and by training you or your staff to use the new system.

Sometimes a VAR will offer "free consulting services." That may be a good deal for you, or it can be a sucker deal. The problem is that if you aren't paying the consultant, the consultant isn't working for you, really. The VAR probably expects the consultant (whether that person is the VAR him/herself or an employee) to help you choose the best, most appropriate things to buy from among what that VAR sells. Pointing out how you might not have to buy anything is a particularly unlikely recommendation from one of these "consultants."

Since there are no licensing requirements for consultants, you really have to use recommendations and references to evaluate the quality of a consultant before you can trust him or her fully.

Mail Order

For many years it has been true that the least expensive way to buy new computer parts and programs was through mail order. Some giant companies buy vast quantities of goods at very attractive prices and stock them in some remote (low-rent) place. Advertising in national and local magazines, these companies will accept your orders either by mail or telephone and ship you the products.

It used to be that these were not good places for novices to buy. This is changing. Some, but not all, of these vendors now have quite competent sales and technical support staff who can help you analyze your needs and choose among their offerings just what you want. Many are members of the Direct Marketing Association; they are committed to a high standard of service.

In some ways there are no differences between ordering by phone (using a credit card) and by mail (either sending a check or using a credit card number). In other ways the differences are very important. If you order by phone, you will likely receive your shipment sooner. You have some legal protections if you order using a credit card, but you have others if you mail your order and a check.

If you order something through the U.S. Mail from a company in the United States, that transaction is covered by the "Mail-Order Rule" of the Federal Trade Commission. That rule provides certain assurances to the consumer. Most notably, the merchant must ship the product when promised or allow you to cancel your order.

Credit card purchases are special. For more details on your protections when you use a credit card, see the section on "Buying with 'Plastic'" later in this appendix.

> **Warning** If you order by phone and have the goods sent to you COD using a private courier or freight service, you lose all those legal protections. That is about the worst way to buy anything, from a consumer-protection point of view. Well, there is one worse way: *I hope you know never, ever to send cash!*

Swap Meets

One wit said, "The only problem with buying things at a swap meet is that the guarantee only lasts till the station wagon tailgate closes." He went on to say, "Your best protection is to shop early in the day, then rush home and test what you have bought right away." Of course, he's right!

In many parts of the country, swap meets are held more or less regularly, mostly on weekends. Some are general purpose. Others are focused on computer-related goods.

Generally these are just open-air markets. Merchants and private individuals sign up to sell things (and pay the swap meet operator some fee to do so), and customers can come and shop. The customers may or may not have to pay an entrance fee.

How does this differ from buying at a computer store? These vendors only have to pay a small fee to rent the space in which they sell their products for the few hours of the swap meet. Regular computer store owners have to pay rent and utilities all the time. This allows the swap meet vendors to operate with much less overhead costs and thus to sell things for less.

Notice that it *allows* them to sell for less. Nothing requires them to do so. Therefore, to protect yourself you must be aware of current prices for similar items in the retail stores, both full-service and discount, before you go to the swap meet.

You probably won't get an opportunity to try out the things you are considering. A good idea is to see if the vendor also has a storefront location where you can come during normal business hours if you have any problems with what you buy. Be sure also to find out what that vendor's return or replacement policy is for goods which are defective or simply unsatisfactory.

Swap meets can be a very good place to buy computer hardware and software. Just realize that this is true only if you know exactly what you need, what a good price for those items would be, and are prepared to support yourself after the purchase without necessarily getting any help from the vendor.

Electronic Bulletin Boards

Computer software is a strange sort of product. In essence, it is not anything tangible, just information. When you buy software in a store you usually also get a lot of things with it. These may include a book, and they almost certainly will include one or more floppy disks (or a CD-ROM disk).

You don't have to buy software that way. Since the essential product is just information, it can easily be sent to you over a telephone wire. You won't get a fancy box or a printed, bound book that way, but you can get quality software. This method is convenient and often very inexpensive as well.

Many of the finest programs on the market are distributed through a concept known as shareware. This means that the authors of these programs have copyrighted them, but instead of allowing only people who buy the program to have a copy, they let absolutely anyone who wants a copy have one. In fact, they just upload a copy of their program to one or a few BBS computers. (These are computers connected to phone lines. These computers run special software that allows them to answer the phone when your computer calls them.) Other people download that program and later on upload it elsewhere. In this way the program goes from BBS to BBS until it is widely distributed around the world.

You can call your local BBS and download a wide assortment of software from all over the world, all for the price of local phone call and perhaps a subscription fee to the operator of the BBS. (You also can, of course, call other BBSs farther away, which might be worth doing if they happen to have what you want, and your local BBS does not. In that case you would be doing other local BBS users a favor if you would subsequently upload your new software to your local BBS.)

The name *BBS* stands for *Bulletin Board System*. Other popular terms are *EBBS* (standing for *Electronic Bulletin Board System*) and *RBBS* (standing for *Remote Bulletin Board System*). In almost all cases these computers have programs and other files you can download and the ability to let people post messages for others to read. It is that latter feature, which resembles the bulletin boards at a local grocery store, that gave these systems their name.

Some BBSs are operated by local computer user groups, some by individuals, and some by manufacturers of computer software or hardware. There are also commercial systems that resemble BBSs. All of these systems can also play an important role in helping you get what you want at the best price, which is discussed in the section "Reviews and Recommendations" later in this appendix.

How does the shareware program's author benefit from this? There is normally a message included with the program file that tells you what your rights are to it. They usually include the right to try the program out for a limited time and the right to give copies of it to anyone you choose. They do not include the right to go on using the program unless you pay the author, directly, some specified amount of money. This is marketing on the honor system.

Often, when you send in your registration fee, you'll get something more than just the warm, good feeling that you've done the right thing. You may get a later version of the program, a printed manual, or access to technical support.

Many shareware authors belong to the Association of Shareware Professionals. This trade association holds its members to high standards of quality and ethics. They also provide ombudsman services to consumers who may feel they have been treated unfairly by an ASP member. Look for notice of ASP membership in shareware documentation. When you find it you can be sure you are dealing with a professional.

How can you get software this way? Here are five ways:

- If you know someone who has what you want, just ask them for a copy.

- You can equip your computer with a modem and a communications program, call a BBS that has what you want, and then download it.

- You can go to a user group meeting and buy some shareware on floppy disk from their library.

- You may find shareware for sale at your local computer store.

- You can send away to mail-order companies that specialize in putting shareware software on floppy disks and selling them to individuals.

Some computer magazines, especially those distributed regionally, publish lists of electronic bulletin board system phone numbers and information on local user groups (who may operate a BBS, either for their members only or for the general public). Most BBS file collections include electronically searchable lists of other BBS phone numbers. Some BBS operators charge a subscription fee; many more do not. Naturally, you can expect better access or a more diverse collection of files on a subscription BBS.

One of the better known subscription BBSs is Exec PC in Milwaukee. Some of the better known suppliers of mail-order shareware are Public Brand Software, Public Software Library, and Software Laboratories.

Information on how to reach each of these organizations can be found in the MemInfo hypertext database on the diskette that comes with this book. See also the section "Information Utilities" later in this appendix.

Please be aware that if you buy shareware on a floppy disk, you almost always are paying that vendor merely for the service of copying that software onto the floppy disk and giving it to you. You still must follow the author's requirements for registration before you own the right to continue using it beyond the trial period. (The rare exceptions will be clearly marked with "Fully paid-up registered copy," or some similar language.)

How can you know what software you could get this way? When you call a BBS you can get a full listing of the software it offers, or you can search for some particular titles or for all titles in a particular subject area. If you contact one of the mail-order shareware software companies, they will happily send you their catalog. Ask your friends, your local computer store, and your user group what shareware they have to offer.

Some Reassuring News and a Warning   Many people worry that if you have a modem, your computer may become infected with a computer virus. That could happen, but it could also happen in many other ways.

The only way your computer can catch a virus is if you run a program that is infected. Just downloading it from a BBS will not infect your computer. On the other hand, running any program you get from any source carries a small risk of infecting your computer.

Learn how to practice *"safe computing."* This includes acquiring software only from reputable sources (including many BBS systems), and it should include checking the software you get with a virus-scanning program before you first run it. (Do this even with shrink-wrapped, commercial software.)

Buying Used

Computer software, by its nature, never wears out. People get tired of what they have, though, and the industry moves on to newer, better things with amazing rapidity.

This means that what you seek may be what someone else is ready to dispose of. You may save yourself a lot of money if you can find a way to buy what you want used.

Of course, if you do, you won't get a manufacturer's guarantee. You won't get a store's support. You most likely won't have any recourse at all if what you bought either doesn't work or simply isn't what you wanted. If those warnings haven't deterred you, perhaps you are wondering where you can find used items for sale.

One good place to look is at the classified and display advertisements in the business and sports sections of your local newspaper. A national source of advertisements for used computer hardware and software is *Computer Shopper* magazine.

There is even a national marketplace in used computers maintained by the Boston Computer Exchange. They neither buy nor sell used computers, but they help would-be buyers and sellers get together. Their interest in doing so is that they are paid a commission on each sale they broker.

They also publish prices for used computers and this serves much the same role as the *Kelly Blue Book* for used cars. It is an excellent way to find out a reasonable price to pay for whatever you seek no matter what its source.

Private Parties

Finally there is the possibility that you can buy what you want from a private individual. Here the same caveats apply as in buying used, with the additional warning that if you buy from a friend you may jeopardize your friendship, and if from strangers you may know even less about them than you do about mail-order sellers of used goods.

Still, if your friend has what you want, it might just be the very best way for you to get it. Offices have been trickling down PCs for years. As they get the newest, hottest machines for their power users, they hand off the older ones to other workers. When upgrading a power user's machine, they may pass on the parts extracted or the software no longer needed to another user. You can do the same thing within your circle of friends.

You need to be aware of the legal restrictions on the use of commercial software. Normally you can sell or give all your copies of a program and its documentation to someone else and then they become its legal owner or licensee. You may have to notify the manufacturer to fully comply with your license agreement with them.

What clearly is not proper or legal is to sell or give away copies of your commercial software when you get rid of your old computer, yet keep copies yourself and go on using those programs. Equally bad is getting an upgrade to an application program and then selling or giving away the older version to someone else. Normally your (discounted) upgrade fee simply transfers your license to use the software from the older version to the upgrade. At that point no one is licensed to use the older version. Do these things in a business setting and you could get fired. Do it as a private party, and you will earn your "official black eye-patch" for software piracy. Just say no!

Protecting Yourself from Disappointment or Worse

Buying anything is a risk. If you get exactly what you ordered, it might turn out not to do what you want. Even if you do get what you want, it may not work correctly. How can you reduce your risk to an acceptable level?

Reviews and Recommendations

First, you can check some sources other than the manufacturers and dealers of the products you plan to purchase. Look for magazine reviews and ask other computer users for their recommendations.

Magazines

One magazine that has a very good reputation for its comparative product reviews is *PC Magazine*, published by Ziff-Davis. It also carries in-depth single-product reviews and columns by industry experts. A similar magazine, but one covering a wider range of computers (not just PCs as defined here), is *PC/Computing*, also from Ziff-Davis. Yet another such magazine with a similar scope, but directed more at technically inclined readers, is *Byte*, published by McGraw-Hill. Regular reading of any of these or similar magazines can help you keep abreast of the industry.

PC Coordinators and Local Gurus

If you work for a large company you very likely can find someone there who is more expert than you and who can give you recommendations on what to purchase and what to avoid. If you are buying for company use, you may be required to choose from a list of approved vendors' products, but even if you are not, it is a good idea to get what advice you can from your company's personal computer coordinator or other in-house "guru(s)."

User Groups

Naturally you will want to ask your friends for their experiences and advice. If you don't know anyone who has the sort of things you are contemplating buying, though, this may not be very helpful. In that case you might wish to seek out a local computer user group. These are voluntary associations of people who are interested in computers. Often they focus on a particular kind of computer (for example, an IBM PC- or compatibles-oriented group) or on a particular software product (for example, a *Paradox* user group).

In addition to helping you choose what to buy, a user group can also help you learn how to use whatever you buy more effectively. They often have **S**pecial **I**nterest **G**roups (SIGs) devoted to a variety of topics. These are subgroups that focus more narrowly than the main group.

Many user groups also operate electronic bulletin boards. This is a great way to ask questions and receive answers, usually within a few days or less. User group members can help you learn how to set up a modem, use communications software, and use their BBS. This help will also make it easier for you to use other, more remote BBSs and information utilities.

Information Utilities

CompuServe Information Systems (*CIS*) is the best known of the *information utilities*. There are many others. These are very large computer systems with the ability to support thousands of simultaneous callers. They serve as super-BBSs.

On most of these information utility services you will find subgroups on a wide variety of topics. Here you may post questions or read those posted by others along with answers others have posted to those questions. This can be a valuable resource for evaluating vendors and products as well as for learning how to use those products once you buy them.

Unlike most user group BBSs, the information utilities charge you by the minute for accessing their information. In this they are really no different from the electric, gas, water, and telephone companies.

Other information utilities besides *CompuServe* include *Genie*, *BIX* (*Byte Information Exchange*), *Prodigy*, and *America OnLine*.

Start Out Slowly

When you select a vendor a wise plan is to buy only a little bit from that source at first. This is especially true if the vendor is a mail-order firm located far away from you. If the first experience is wonderful, you have more reason to believe that your second and subsequent purchases will be similarly wonderful experiences.

Check an Old Phone Book

Some computer stores are here today and gone tomorrow. Such a store is not the ideal place to buy things. Sometimes problems don't surface for a while. When they do, you may well want to go back where you bought the troublesome item, discuss your problems, and get a solution.

It is not possible to predict the future, but a useful indicator of stability is a store that has been around for awhile. Check your local library for old phone books and see if the store you contemplate patronizing was listed two, three, or five years ago. If they were around then, most likely they will also be around a similar time into the future.

Buying with "Plastic"

Consumers in the United States have some special advantages when they buy from a merchant and use a credit card to pay for the purchase. Whether you order in person, by phone, or by mail order you often can charge your purchases, and if you do so you gain several benefits.

One benefit you get when using a credit card for your purchases is a level of assurance that the merchant is running an honest business. Normally a merchant cannot get a bank to permit it to accept credit cards for payment unless the bank believes the merchant is not defrauding the public. So simply seeing that the merchant has passed this hurdle is one level of protection.

Next, if you buy with a credit card and later are dissatisfied with your purchase, you can of course argue with the merchant. Ultimately, however, if you and the merchant simply cannot agree on how to handle the dispute you may have a wonderful option sometimes called the *right of recision*.

Your *right of recision* is a fancy way of saying that, in certain circumstances, you can simply tell your bank that you refuse to pay for some item you purchased and they will automatically credit your account for the price of the goods or services. Thereafter, the dispute is a matter between your bank and the merchant; you don't have to worry about it any further.

You have, in fact, not just one right of recision. You have two different, yet very similar rights. The first is a "stop payment" right. The second is a right to refuse to pay. Do they sound similar? They are, but they differ in subtle ways and knowing the details may be crucial to your ability to exercise either of them.

The first right you have is an absolute right to "stop payment" on a credit charge if you have tried in good faith to get satisfaction from the merchant and have failed to do so. There are special rules for this right that make it applicable to only some charges, but when it applies it is both powerful and convenient for you to use.

Typical limitations on this right are that you must have purchased the goods from a merchant either in your home state or within 100 miles of your home address and you must have paid more than $50.00. That means only some of your credit card purchases are covered by this form of your rights. On the other hand, you may invoke this right any time before you pay for the charge you dispute, no matter how long after the purchase or its billing that may be.

The other right is less limited, but also a bit trickier to exercise. This right applies to all your credit card purchases, regardless of how much they cost or where you made them.

You have the right not to pay for things that are not what they were represented to be. But to get the benefits of this right, you must write a letter to your credit card company within 60 days after they mail the bill with the questionable charge on it.

You can ask the bank that issued your credit card for more details on your rights, although you may not get a full and frank disclosure of your rights in this way. For one thing, the people you talk to may not be very well informed on the subtleties of these rights. For another, the bank's interests and yours are hardly the same. They want no trouble and to make money. Keeping you from making waves is in their interest. That may or may not include making you happy. Often it merely means, to them, that they should keep you in the dark about how to make waves.

Thus, to ask your bank for advice on how not to have to pay them money they say you owe is a bit like asking the IRS how to minimize your taxes. They do, in fact, have the most authoritative information, but they may not make it all that easy to get.

An easier source is a recent book by a California attorney, Howard Strong, called *Credit Card Secrets That You Will Surely Profit From*. This 200-page book has a very readable discussion of all the ins and outs of credit card buying and will explain these rights about as fully as you could wish. It costs $33.95 and is available from the Boswell Corporation, Box 7100, Beverly Hills, CA 90212-7100.

A Recap

A wise consumer must be an educated one. You have to be aware of what the marketplace offers in order not to be taken in by the first delightful-sounding advertisement. This appendix has reviewed some of the ways you might get that education and some of the places you might check to see what is being offered for sale and at what prices.

You have learned here that cheapest is not always best; sometimes a higher price carries with it added services or other value. How much you should be willing to pay for anything you buy will depend on what you need or want in the way of additional support after the sale.

The value of user groups, BBSs, and information utilities are other important topics that were covered, along with a caution about computer viruses. And finally you know now why using a credit card is often the very safest way to buy almost anything.

PROGRAMS ON THE COMPANION DISK

This chapter describes the contents of the diskette that accompanies this book.

The programs and data files on the diskette that accompanies this book have been chosen to help you learn more about memory in your PC, and to help you to do more effective memory management. A few of the programs are freeware; the rest are shareware.

Freeware means that these programs are copyrighted by their authors. You may not alter the programs, nor may you sell them. You may, however, give away copies freely, as long as you comply with any restrictions mentioned in the documentation. You also don't have to pay anything to have the right to use them.

Shareware programs are also copyrighted by their authors. In this case, though, the author has chosen to restrict your usage rights just a little bit more than for freeware. In particular, you are free to give copies to anyone, so long as you don't charge them, and you are free to try out the programs to see if they are useful to you. But, and this is important, you need to pay the author a registration fee if you choose to continue to use the program.

Shareware is "try before you buy" marketing for software. It works, but only because enough people have been honorable and have paid the designated registration fees for the shareware programs they use regularly. Please join the ranks of the honorable ones. By doing so you will serve not only the interests of the shareware authors, you will help out all of us who use PCs.

As long as shareware works, shareware authors will continue to create and update their products. And we, the users of those programs, get to have first-rate software with the option of trying it before we commit to buying it. Furthermore, since the distribution costs to the shareware authors are trivial to non-existent, the registration fees are typically a tiny fraction of the cost of equivalent shrink-wrapped commercial software.

The rest of this appendix describes briefly the features you will find in each of the programs included on this diskette. If you haven't already installed the companion disk to your hard drive, see the last page in the book for information on how to do this.

When you use the installation program we have provided, the MemInfo hypertext database is put in a directory called \MEMINFO on whatever drive you designate. Each of the other programs is put in a subdirectory under this directory. The directory name for each program is listed at the beginning of that section.

Many programs will include a file named README, README.1ST, or something similar. It's a good idea to read this file before using the program or reading the manual.

MemInfo Hypertext Database

Author: John M. Goodman, Ph.D.
P.O. Box 746
Westminster, CA 92684-0746
Filename of Manual: (none)
Directory: \MEMINFO

The MemInfo hypertext database rolls several functions into one, easy-to-use package. It is a glossary and a reference guide to both the products mentioned in this book and to their manufacturers.

The glossary contains definitions of over 800 terms about PCs and memory—ranging from the most basic to the very arcane. You can jump from one term to another in a flash. You can digress to learn about some term that is mentioned in a definition, then easily return to your original search. In addition to the indexed key words, you may jump to any word in any definition anywhere in the database.

The products guide has been arranged so that you can look up a product either by its name or by the category of product into which it falls. From the brief description of each product you can jump to information on how to contact its manufacturer. In the manufacturers screen you will also see listed other products from that manufacturer that are described elsewhere in the database and, of course, you can jump instantly to those descriptions.

The manufacturers guide is arranged alphabetically by company name. You can quickly find any company that is listed. In its information screen you will find out the company's address, phone numbers (typically including an 800 number, if any, a main voice line, a facsimile number—labeled FAX—and sometimes an electronic bulletin board number—labeled BBS), and a list of the memory-related products they offer. From that screen you can jump to the screen describing any of those products.

You start the database by typing the command MEMINFO and pressing the Enter key. Alternatively, if you wish to look up a specific term, add it after the word MEMINFO (with a space in between) and if the term is indexed in the database you will go directly to its description.

To learn more about how to use this database, press F1 any time you are in the program. Follow the on-screen prompts. The hypertext engine used is the *XTEXT* product from Flambeaux Software. (While they are not listed in the manufacturers database, information on how to contact them is included in the help screens.)

TSR Utilities (freeware)

Author: TurboPower Software
P.O. Box 49009
Colorado Springs, CO 80949
Directory: \MEMINFO\TSR
Filename of Manual: TSR.DOC

The TSR Utilities are a collection of programs useful for managing DOS memory, particularly for managing memory-resident programs. The most popular use of these utilities is for removing TSRs from memory without rebooting the PC. The TSR Utilities include 11 programs:

- MARK marks a position in memory above which TSRs can be released.

- RELEASE removes TSRs from memory.

- FMARK performs the same function as MARK but uses less memory by keeping its data in a disk file.

- MARKNET works like MARK, but saves a more complete picture of system status (for use with networks, primarily).

- RELNET removes TSRs marked with MARKNET.

- WATCH is a TSR itself whose job is to keep records of other TSRs.

- DISABLE disables or reactivates TSRs, leaving them in memory.

- RAMFREE shows how much RAM memory is available.

- MAPMEM shows what memory-resident programs are loaded.

- DEVICE shows what device drivers are loaded.

- EATMEM uses up memory for controlled program testing.

Memory Management Kit (shareware)

Author: Biologic
P.O. Box 147
Manassas, VA 22110
Directory: \MEMINFO\MEMKIT
Filename of Manual: READ.ME (each program has its own manual)
The Memory Management Kit is a complete, real-mode PC memory manager. It works in conjunction with *MS-DOS* to provide comprehensive memory management features that *MS-DOS* left out. The Memory Management Kit can:

- Load device drivers and TSRs into upper memory on 8088 and 80286 PCs (not just 80386 PCs).

- Utilize the shadow RAM capability of many chip sets to create upper memory (the file CHIPSET.DOC contains a complete listing of supported chip sets). This may eliminate the need to use the *MS-DOS* program, EMM386.EXE (or any other 80386 expanded memory manager), resulting in a speed increase of 10 to 40 percent!

- Optimize upper memory by automatically determining which order and in which memory regions your drivers and TSRs should be loaded.

- Create up to 736K of conventional memory.

- Create 64K or more of upper memory on a 80386 PC.

- Convert extended memory to expanded memory on a 80286 PC.

- Create up to 32 megabytes of expanded memory from disk space.

- Load TSRs into extended or expanded memory.

Listed below is a brief listing of the main features offered by each of those programs in the Memory Management Kit:

HRAM

- Creates upper memory on 8088 and 80286 PCs.
- Enhances the utilization of upper memory on 80386 PCs.
- Optimizes upper memory.

VRAM

- Converts extended memory to expanded memory.
- Creates up to 32 megabytes of simulated expanded memory from disk space.

MIN-MEM

- Loads pop-up TSRs into expanded or extended memory.
- Swaps TSRs to disk.

Windsock System Resources Monitor (freeware)

Author: Chris Hewitt
Directory: \MEMINFO\WINDSOCK
Filename of Manual: README.TXT

WINDSKRM is a full-featured resource and memory monitor for Windows. It features a resizeable display, a graph of usage history over time, and more. The WindSock Windows System Resource monitor provides both histogram and bar indicator displays of the percentage of the User, System, GDI, Menu and String heap resources currently in use.

The control menu allows the user to:

- Iconize the program and still see useful information.
- Cause WindSock to "float" on top of other windows.
- Set the alarm threshold values for each heap.
- Run a log file of resource usage.
- Adjust the monitor's sample rate.

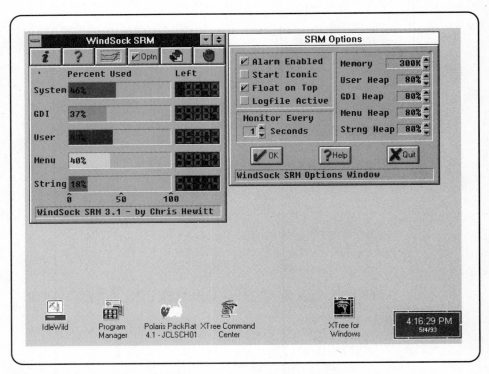

Figure C.1. *WindSock* display showing options screen.

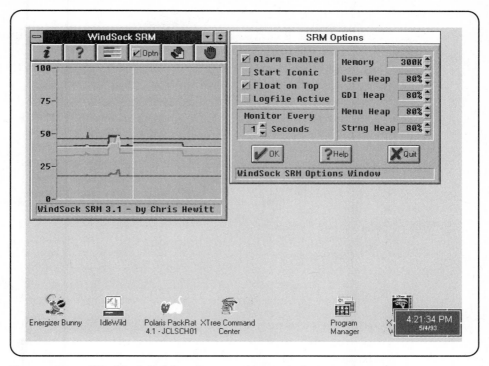

Figure C.2. *WindSock* display showing history of resource usage.

The Last Byte Memory Manager (shareware)

Author: Key Software Products
440 Ninth Avenue
Menlo Park, CA 94025
Directory: \MEMINFO\TLB
Filename of Manual: LASTBYTE.DOC

The Last Byte Memory Manager is a collection of software that can provide up to 384K of additional memory to your computer in the upper memory area between 640K and 1M. It does this by using a variety of techniques:

- Using shadow ram memory.

- Using existing read/write (RAM) memory.

- Mapping expanded memory (EMS) pages into the upper memory area.

1095

With The Last Byte Memory Manager, device drivers and memory resident programs can be moved up into upper memory, leaving more conventional memory available for your application programs. Depending on your hardware, you may also be able to extend the total conventional memory from 640Kto as much as 736K.

The Last Byte package also includes several advanced utility programs that can move the DOS environment, DOS FILES storage and DOS BUFFERS storage into upper memory. Other advanced utilities create ram disks, print spoolers, command line recall buffers, emulated expanded memory, and memory-resident program "markers" (to facilitate their removal from memory).

There are several advantages to using The Last Byte Memory Manager:

- It will work with any processor chip, even the 8088 used in the original IBM PC.

- It does not use protected mode. The Last Byte is totally compatible with any protected mode software, not just Microsoft Windows.

- It does not require any extended memory. Some memory managers depend on the processor's ability to remap physical memory from above 1MB into the upper memory area.

- On motherboards that use one of the supported memory controller chips, The Last Byte Memory Manager can use the unused shadow ram, unshadowed ROMs or adapter cards.

DOSMAX (shareware)

Author: Phillip Gardner
10461 Lever St.
Circle Pines, MN 55014
Directory: \MEMINFO\DOSMAX
Filename of Manual: DOSMAX.DOC

DOSMAX.EXE is a device driver which will maximize the use of low memory by moving MS-DOS 3.1 and above system data to upper memory blocks provided by your upper memory manager. The package also includes several programs that serve closely related purposes.

For users of DOS, version 5 or above, who are loading DOS high, DOSMAX can prevent DOS from loading into the HMA and move the DOS kernel to an upper memory block. This can improve performance by giving control of the HMA to programs which use it more efficiently than DOS does, while still keeping that portion of DOS out of lower memory. Some of the programs that can use the HMA to good effect include Microsoft *Windows* and Quarterdeck's *DESQview*.

DOSMAX can also move a portion of COMMAND.COM into an upper memory block. This feature recovers even more space in low memory.

Support is provided for:

- Allowing DOS to go to the HMA, but still moving the sub-segment data types to UMBs.

- Forcing DOS low and keeping the sub-segments moveable.

- Moving only the DOS SYSTEM code block into upper memory.

- Providing only WINDOWS high file support.

- Moving a portion of COMMAND.COM into high memory instead of the HMA.

- Moving the primary COMMAND.COM's environment (master environment).

- DOS Versions 3.1 - 3.31, DOS 4.x, and DOS 5.x (or better?).

DOSMAX automatically moves all the data that can be moved, provided you have enough free upper memory. It will automatically stop moving data when it determines that upper memory would be fragmented if the move was completed.

A command line mode is provided for moving the master environment, controlling *Windows* support, and checking and reporting on the status of the high memory area reserved for COMMAND.COM.

System Requirements include the following:

- 186 processor or better.

- Requires *MS-DOS* Version 3.10 or better.

DOSM86.EXE is included to support 8086/8088 processors.

QInfo (shareware)

Author: Greg Wilson
1252 Fordham Dr. #101
Glendale Heights, IL 60139
Directory: \MEMINFO\QINFO
Filename of Manual: QINFO.DOC

QInfo displays the amount of free memory (conventional, EMS, and XMS), available disk space and other useful information. Network drives are identified by "<NET>" beside the drive letter and substituted drives (created using the DOS command SUBST) are identified by "<SUBST>". Disk space is summarized and totaled with percentages color coded as follows:

WHITE - 50% or less full

YELLOW - Greater than 50% full

RED - Greater than 70% full

BLINKING RED - Greater than 90% full

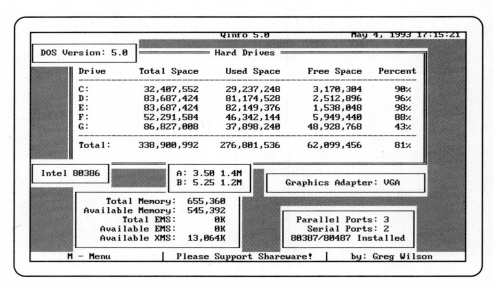

Figure C.3. QInfo shows drive statistics and other information.

While QInfo is displaying the above information, a menu can be displayed by pressing the "M" key. The options available from this menu are:

- Edit CONFIG.SYS

- Edit AUTOEXEC.BAT

- Edit other file

- Display Memory Map

- Display Environment

- Set Date/Time

- Display CPU Speed

SR Disk (shareware)

Author: Marko Kohtala
PL 115 SF-01451
Vantaa
FINLAND

Directory: \MEMINFO\SRDISK

SR Disk is a virtual disk device driver and controller capable of using over 32M of XMS (2.0) and/or EMS (4.0) memory. The disk can be disabled and its size can be changed without rebooting.

- Compatible with *MS-DOS* versions 3.0 to 5.x and *DR DOS* 5 to 6.

- Can use extended memory on 286 and up with HIMEM or other XMS 2.0 driver.

- Can use expanded memory conforming to LIM EMS version 4.0.

- Can be installed multiple times and the device drivers chained together to form larger disks using many different kinds of memories.

- Resizeable and can preserve disk contents if the new format has room enough.

- Removable—it can be disabled without rebooting.

- Supports 32-bit sector addressing introduced in DOS 4. Thus RAM disks larger than 32MB are possible. Disks of up to 63MB have been tested.

- Is highly configurable, including having adjustable sector size, cluster size, root directory entry count and number of FATs.

- Can create RAM disks whose formats match the standard DOS floppy disk formats.

- Can be used with DISKCOPY from DOS, version 3.2 up. You can copy to or from a SRDISK drive using DOS DISKCOPY.

- Can have its RAM disks write protected.

- Can, optionally, be used to set environment variables SRDISKn (n=1,2,...) to point to the installed SRDISK drives.

EMM286 (freeware)

Author: JJex Software
Directory: \MEMINFO\EMM286
Filename of Manual: EMM286.TXT

EMM286 is an Expanded Memory LIMulator for Class 3 or 4 systems. The program provides both an EMM driver and a command line user interface in one executable file.

The resident portion of the driver uses less than 4k of conventional memory, with defaults, plus a 64k EMS page frame. All functions of the LIM EMS 4.0 specification dated October 1987 are supported, with the following exceptions:

- Alternate/DMA Register Sets (Function 28)

- Data aliasing to multiple physical pages

- Backfilling memory below 1 megabyte

  (Software alone cannot provide any of these functions)

The program's features include:

- The ability to work with any application that is EMS aware.

- Optional driver switches allow the override of defaults.

- Command line switches allow the driver to be disabled, re-enabled or to display the current status of any installed EMM driver.

- Plain text status/error messages appear during installation and with command line functions.

You must remember that EMM286 requires an XMS driver, like HIMEM.SYS, for handling the transfers to/from extended memory.

MCBS (freeware)

Author: John M. Goodman, Ph.D.
Directory: \MEMINFO\MCBS
Filename of Manual: (none)

MCBS is a program which displays a list of Memory Control Blocks (Memory Arena Headers). The program shows the Memory Control Block chain(s) in both lower and upper memory. This is the program that was used in the preparation of many of the figures in this book.

You can run the program with a number of different command line parameters. Issuing the command MCBS ? will show you a list of almost all the options it supports.

- The L parameter displays only low memory chains and optionally takes a segment address at which the chain starts.

- The U parameter displays only high memory chains. At least one segment address is required, and up to two may be given.

- The B parameter displays both low and high memory chains with one address being required to specify the start of the upper memory chain to be displayed, or two addresses (one each in lower and upper memory) to specify the start of each chain.

- The D parameter displays low memory chains and shows device driver sub-blocks as well.

- The A parameter will cause the program to show as much information as it can find. In this mode (which is the only one not mentioned in the on-line help screen), MCBS attempts to find all the memory control block chains in lower and upper memory automatically.

You should be aware that finding the chains in upper memory by any automatic process is not always possible. So if you suspect that a chain starts at some address (for example, just after the end of an option card's BIOS ROM), use the D or U parameter and that address to test your guess.

ResGauge (freeware)

Author: Richard Franklin Albury
P.O. Box 19652
Raleigh, NC 27619
Directory: \MEMINFO\RESGAUGE
Filename of Manual: RESGAUGE.WRI

ResGauge is a simple, nonintrusive utility which monitors free system resources in *Windows* 3.1. ResGauge can easily be configured to alert you when free system resources drop too low, permitting you to save your work before problems occur.

ResGauge works like the Clock program in *Windows* 3.1. You can:

- Reduce the program to an icon and still see useful information

- Hide the title bar for a cleaner look

- Set the colors, size, etc...

- Cause ResGauge to "float" on top of other windows

The main menu has facilities for:

- Select which heap you want ResGauge to monitor (System, GDI or User)

- Remove the menu and title bars from the window

- Set the alarm threshold value

- Set the gauge color for the heap currently monitored

SeeMem (freeware)

Author: Tedrick Housh, Jr.
8511 West 85th Terrace
Overland Park, KS 66207
Directory: \MEMINFO\SEEMEM
Filename of Manual: SEEMEM.DOC

SEEMEM displays information about the current use of MS-DOS memory by the operating system, resident processes and data.

It is designed to make full use of the memory management features in *MS-DOS*, *PC DOS*, or *DR DOS*, version 5 or 6. It provides displays that resemble those of the DOS program MEM, but with the difference that SEEMEM can display upper memory use even when DOS is not managing that region.

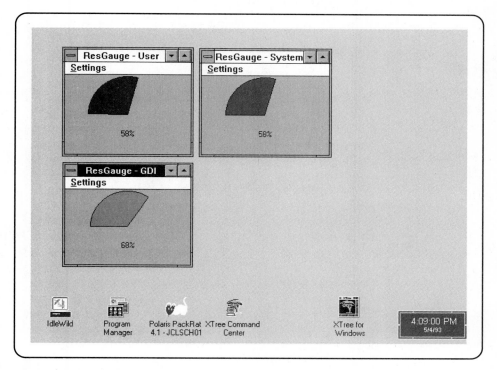

Figure C.4. *ResGauge* displays.

SEEMEM has three output displays. They are:

- A display of every memory control block (MCB) between:

  Segment 0 and the top of conventional memory (Segment 9FFFh on a 640k machine),

  The top of conventional memory and the start of the High Memory Area (HMA) if any,

  The top of Upper Memory (Segment 0FFFFh).

  For each MCB, SEEMEM displays these details:

  Its segment address (in hex)

  Its size (in both Kilobytes and bytes)

The segment of its "owner"

Its type (e.g. TSR or Environment)

Its name (if determinable)

- A display of EMS (Expanded Memory) if applicable:

The version number of the EMS device driver

The page frame segment

The total size of the installed EMS memory

The number of mapping register sets available

Whether or not you can have nonvolatile handles (which will survive a warm boot)

The number of DMA channels

The maximum number of EMS handles supported

The number of free handles

The number of free pages

The page size

The amount of free memory

The handle number for each handle in use

The number of EMS pages

The page size

The amount of EMS memory used

If available, the handle name

- A display of XMS information (if a driver is installed):

The XMS version and revision numbers

The XMM Control Vector in segment:offset form

The total amount of XMS free memory

The size of the largest free XMS block

Whether the A20 line is currently enabled

Whether HMA is implemented

Whether the HMA is available for use

Whether DOS is resident in the HMA (DOS=HIGH in CONFIG.SYS)

If so, how much of the HMA DOS has left and is, therefore, available for additional buffers, etc...

SEEMEM also displays:

- The location of DOS when it is located elsewhere (i.e. ROM or Conventional memory)

- Whether UMBs are implemented

- Whether UMBs are controlled by device driver or by DOS itself

- Whether UMBs are linked to conventional memory (DOS 5.00) or are independent

- Whether UMB's are implemented by DOS=UMB in CONFIG.SYS (DOS 5.00)

Reboot (freeware)

Author: (public domain)
Filename of Manual: (none)

This 16 byte program performs the same function as pressing the Ctrl-Alt-Del key combination. It allows the system to be rebooted from a batch file.

INDEX

A

M

Y-Z

figures

Add to Your Sams Library Today with the Best Books for Programming, Operating Systems, and New Technologies

The easiest way to order is to pick up the phone and call

1-800-428-5331

between 9:00 a.m. and 5:00 p.m. EST.
For faster service please have your credit card available.

ISBN	Quantity	Description of Item	Unit Cost	Total Cost
0-672-30318-3		Windows Sound FunPack (Book/Disk)	$19.95	
0-672-30309-4		Programming Sound for DOS and Windows (Book/Disk)	$39.95	
0-672-30240-3		OS/2 2.1 Unleashed (Book/Disk)	$34.95	
0-672-30288-8		DOS Secrets Unleashed (Book/Disk)	$39.95	
0-672-30298-5		Windows NT: The Next Generation	$22.95	
0-672-30269-1		Absolute Beginner's Guide to Programming	$19.95	
0-672-30326-4		Absolute Beginner's Guide to Networking	$19.95	
0-672-30341-8		Absolute Beginner's Guide to C	$16.95	
0-672-27366-7		Memory Management for All of Us	$29.95	
0-672-30190-3		Windows Resource and Memory Management (Book/Disk)	$29.95	
0-672-30249-7		Multimedia Madness! (Book/Disk/CD-ROM)	$44.95	
0-672-30248-9		FractalVision (Book/Disk)	$39.95	
0-672-30259-4		Do-It-Yourself Visual Basic for Windows, 2E	$24.95	
0-672-30229-2		Turbo C++ for Windows Programming for Beginners (Book/Disk)	$39.95	
0-672-30138-5		Secrets of the Visual Basic for Windows Masters (Book/Disk)	$39.95	
0-672-30145-8		Visual Basic for Windows Developer's Guide (Book/Disk)	$34.95	
0-672-30040-0		Teach Yourself C in 21 Days	$24.95	
0-672-30324-8		Teach Yourself QBasic in 21 Days	$24.95	
❏ 3 ½" Disk		Shipping and Handling: See information below.		
❏ 5 ¼" Disk		TOTAL		

Shipping and Handling: $4.00 for the first book, and $1.75 for each additional book. Floppy disk: add $1.75 for shipping and handling. If you need to have it NOW, we can ship product to you in 24 hours for an additional charge of approximately $18.00, and you will receive your item overnight or in two days. Overseas shipping and handling: add $2.00 per book and $8.00 for up to three disks. Prices subject to change. Call for availability and pricing information on latest editions.

11711 N. College Avenue, Suite 140, Carmel, Indiana 46032

1-800-428-5331 — Orders   1-800-835-3202 — FAX   1-800-858-7674 — Customer Service

Book ISBN 0-672-30306-X

What's on the Disk

The companion disk contains a collection of the best shareware and freeware memory management tools, including the following:

- *MemInfo*, John Goodman's hypertext database of memory management terms and resources
- TurboPower's *TSR Utilities*
- Biologic's *Memory Management Kit*
- Windsock *System Resources Monitor*
- Key Software's *The Last Byte* memory manager
- *DOSMax*
- *QInfo*
- *SR Disk*
- *EMM286*
- *MCBS*
- *Resgauge*
- *SeeMem*

Installing the Disk

The software included with this book is stored in a compressed form. You cannot use the software without first installing it to your hard drive.

> To install the files, you need at least 2.3M of free space on your hard drive.

1. From a DOS prompt, change to the drive that contains the installation disk. For example, if the disk is in drive A:, type A: and press Enter.

2. Type INSTALL drive (where drive is the drive letter of your hard drive) and press Enter. For example, if your hard drive is drive C:, type INSTALL C: and press Enter.

This installs all the files to a directory called \MEMINFO on your hard drive. Be sure to read the file README.TXT for more information.

Memory Management for All of Us Deluxe Edition Reference Card

Different Kinds of Memory

Conventional Memory
Conventional memory (also called lower or system memory) is the first 640KB of RAM on your system. DOS uses conventional memory to load all your software programs—as well as some basic DOS files.

Upper Memory
Upper memory is the area of RAM between 640KB and 1MB. DOS uses upper memory to store various BIOS routines, as well as video memory. Since DOS doesn't use all of the upper memory area, there are numerous upper memory blocks that can be used to load device drivers and other small programs.

High Memory
The high memory area is the first 64KB RAM of extended memory.

Extended Memory
Extended memory is any RAM above the 1MB mark.

Expanded Memory
Expanded memory is RAM linked through a special page frame in upper memory to some memory that is outside the first MB (and thus is inaccessible to real-mode programs).

Different kinds of memory.

Bits and Bytes

Unit	Size
byte	8 bits
kilobyte	1,024 bytes
megabyte	1,048,576 bytes
gigabyte	1,073,741,824 bytes

The Difference Between Memory and Disk Storage

	Memory	Disks
Usage	Temporary storage	Permanent storage
Speed	Fast	Slow
Amount of Storage Space	Small	Large
Storage Method	Electronic	Physical

DOS Memory Management Commands

CHKDSK	The CHKDSK command, typed at the DOS prompt, checks the status of a disk and displays information about your system's use of conventional memory.
DEVICE	The DEVICE command is used in the CONFIG.SYS file to load device drivers into lower memory.
DEVICEHIGH	The DEVICEHIGH command is identical to the DEVICE command—except that it loads the device driver into upper memory area.
DOS	The DOS command (valid for DOS Version 5 or later) is used in the CONFIG.SYS file to load DOS into the high memory area (HMA) and/or give DOS control of upper memory blocks (UMBs).
EMM386.EXE	The EMM386.EXE driver uses extended memory to simulate expanded memory and/or provide upper memory blocks. This driver must be loaded by a DEVICE command in your CONFIG.SYS file after HIMEM.SYS.
HIMEM.SYS	The HIMEM.SYS driver is an extended memory manager and provides access to your PC's high memory area. This driver must be loaded by a DEVICE command in your CONFIG.SYS file.

LOADHIGH	The LOADHIGH command can be used to load device drivers and programs into your system's upper memory area.
MEM	The MEM command, typed at the DOS prompt, displays details of your system's memory use.
MEMMAKER	MEMMAKER is a DOS 6 utility program that optimizes your system's use of memory. It automatically edits your CONFIG.SYS and AUTOEXEC.BAT files to move device drivers and programs to upper memory, in the most efficient manner.
RAMDRIVE.SYS	The RAMDRIVE.SYS driver is used to create a RAM disk using your system's memory. This driver must be loaded by a DEVICE command in your CONFIG.SYS file.
SMARTDRV.EXE	The SMARTDRV.EXE driver is used to create a disk cache using your system's memory. This driver must be loaded in your AUTOEXEC.BAT file; another portion of this program may need to be loaded in CONFIG.SYS as well.

How Much RAM Do You Need?

Total RAM	Applications
640KB	Basic DOS operations, basic word processing (small documents), and basic PC games (few graphics).
1MB	Normal word processing (medium-size documents), normal PC games (simple graphics), and basic spreadsheet (small files).
2MB	Basic Windows operations (no multitasking), advanced word processing (large documents), advanced PC games (extensive graphics), normal spreadsheet (medium files), basic database (small files), and basic presentation graphics (simple graphics).
4MB	Normal Windows operations (multitasking, simple DDE operations), advanced spreadsheet (very large files, complex calculations), advanced database (large files), advanced presentation graphics (complex graphics), basic desktop publishing (simple documents), and basic drawings (simple drawings).
8MB	Advanced Windows operations (advanced DDE and OLE operations), advanced desktop publishing (long, complex documents), and advanced drawings (complex, multilayered drawings).

DOS Memory Management Features

Feature	DOS 6	DOS 5	DOS 4	DOS 3.3 (and earlier versions)
MEM	Yes	Yes (limited)	Yes (limited)	No
MEMMAKER	Yes	No	No	No
SMARTDRV.EXE	Yes	No	No	No
SMARTDRV.SYS	No	Yes	No	No
EMM386.EXE	Yes	Yes	No	No
HIMEM.SYS	Yes	Yes	No	No
RAMDRIVE.SYS	Yes	Yes	No	No

The Difference Between RAM and ROM

	RAM	ROM
Read capability	Yes	Yes
Write capability	Yes	No
Volatile	Yes	No
Speed	Faster	Slower
Storage type	Temporary	Permanent
Ideal for storing:	Data that changes frequently	Data that doesn't change

Types of Memory Chips

DIP *Dual in-line package.* This chip is a flat rectangle with 16 metal legs, and kind of looks like a spider. DIPs plug into sockets on your motherboard.

SIMM *Single in-line memory module.* A SIMM is kind of like a miniature expansion card, a few inches long, that has several RAM chips presoldered to the card. A SIMM doesn't have legs; it has an edge connector instead, and slides into a SIMM socket on your motherboard.

SIP *Single in-line package.* A SIP is a long, multichip chip, kind of like a SIMM. The big difference between a SIMM and a SIP is that a SIP has a single row of legs instead of an edge connector.

ZIP *Zigzag in-line package.* A ZIP is a SIP with two rows of legs, on the same edge of the chip.

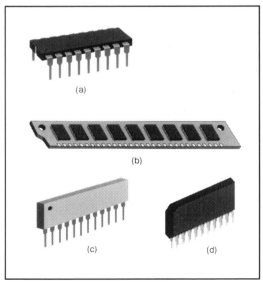

Examples of a DIP (a), a SIMM (b), a SIP (c), and a ZIP (d) chip.